Network Radio
Ratings, 1932–1953

DATE DUE

			PRINTED IN U.S.A.

Network Radio Ratings, 1932–1953

*A History of Prime Time Programs
through the Ratings of Nielsen,
Crossley and Hooper*

JIM RAMSBURG

McFarland & Company, Inc., Publishers
Jefferson, North Carolina, and London

Ratings data used to create the monthly and annual ratings averages and rankings in this publication are copyrighted information of the Nielsen Company and are licensed for use herein.

LIBRARY OF CONGRESS CATALOGUING-IN-PUBLICATION DATA

Ramsburg, Jim, 1935–
Network radio ratings, 1932–1953 : a history of prime time programs through the ratings of Nielsen, Crossley and Hooper / Jim Ramsburg.
p.   cm.
Includes bibliographical references and index.

ISBN 978-0-7864-4558-5
softcover : acid free paper ∞

1. Radio programs — United States — Rating.
I. Title.
HE8697.25.U6R35 2012   384.54′43097309041— dc23   2011051540

BRITISH LIBRARY CATALOGUING DATA ARE AVAILABLE

Front cover image © 2012 Pictures Now

Manufactured in the United States of America

McFarland & Company, Inc., Publishers
Box 611, Jefferson, North Carolina 28640
www.mcfarlandpub.com

To Miss Print of 1956

Table of Contents

Preface

A LONG ANSWER TO THREE SHORT QUESTIONS

This candid account of the scramble for billions of dollars during broadcasting's most fascinating period began with an altogether different idea.

I simply wanted to create an entertaining multi-media presentation profiling the most popular personalities and programs from Network Radio's Golden Age through film and audio clips, and relating my many stories about them. I've been a public speaker for most of my life and relish the opportunity to inform and entertain audiences.

But I wanted to get the essential facts absolutely straight about "Old Time Radio."

Historians seem to differ on the answers to three simple questions:

When exactly was Network Radio's Golden Age?

What were its most popular programs?

Who were Network Radio's greatest stars?

For one who spent his career in radio programming and broadcast advertising, finding the definitive answers seemed a simple matter. All I had to do was refer to the networks' audience popularity ratings.

Most conclusions about the era's program ratings and rankings have used data published 50 years ago in Summers' *Thirty Year History of Programs Carried By the National Radio Networks.* But the text contains the ratings from only *one week* of each year's *ten month* broadcast season from 1930 to 1960.

Such incomplete samplings are interesting, but hardly conclusive, so I set out to get the entire story.

Months of inquiries to networks, universities and museums for complete collections of annual Network Radio ratings turned up nothing. It was hard to believe. Audience research from Network Radio's Golden Age — surveys that cost the networks, their stations, advertisers and agencies millions of dollars — had apparently vanished into dumpsters!

Then I struck researcher's gold at the Wisconsin State Historical Society in Madison. The Society houses the archive collections of the National Broadcasting Company and the Nielsen Company — including the complete annual sets of "lost" Network Radio audience rating books dating back to 1932.

They are all there — except 1949. Then, with another stroke of luck, I located that one missing year of ratings at the library of the Ohio State University in Columbus. The collection of 24 C.E. Hooper semi-monthly rating books completed my annual tracking of over 150 prime time programs each year for what I've since determined to be the 21 years of Network Radio's Golden Age.

These complete sets of ratings — combined with industry data and incidental information from other reliable sources — provided the basic facts to chronicle Network Radio's domination of an era that only a remaining few of us witnessed as it happened. But as a surprising bonus, they also led to a wealth of new stories. These pages are filled with over 700 of them that document the ups and downs of the industry and Network Radio's most familiar names.

WHO CARES?

That's been a challenging question since first beginning this long project.

Who *really* cares about the monthly and annual ratings of programs — many long forgotten — or of the people involved — most all of whom are long dead?

Well, *they* did. *They* weren't just the stars of each program — *they* were also the seldom mentioned or anonymous others who supported each scripted and produced program with their creative and technical talents, and whose families' livelihoods were dependent on the popularity of their combined efforts.

It's in their memory that these complete scores of each season have been compiled and the resulting stories from each year of Network Radio's Golden Age have been written.

Believe me, it's been fun.

THANKS FOR THE MEMORIES — AND MUCH MORE

My sincere thanks are owed to the Nielsen Company, survivor of Network Radio's national rating services, for permission to use the copyrighted Crossley, Crossley/CAB, Clark-Hooper, C.E. Hooper and A.C. Nielsen weekly and bi-weekly ratings data employed for this text.

I take full responsibility for the resulting monthly and annual averages, rankings and conclusions drawn from those ratings. Reader comments are welcome at my Web site: www.jimramsburg.com.

Copying, computerizing and analyzing the hundreds of historic rating books was a massive job. But the truly heavy lifting was done by the Wisconsin Historical Society's service which delivered tubs of raw data to the Chalmer-Davee Library at the River Falls campus of the University of Wisconsin, just 50 miles from our summer home in Balsam Lake, Wisconsin.

My thanks go to Harry Miller at the Wisconsin Historical Society and to Alyson Jones and her staff in the Archives Department of the UWRF Chalmer-Davee Library for their cooperative support.

Four additional resources helped

1

substantiate the accuracy of this work.

For statistical data of radio households, station growth and broadcasting revenues, I relied on FCC figures from Sterling & Kittross' highly respected text, *Stay Tuned: A Concise History of American Broadcasting.*

That information combined with my ratings data enabled me to define Network Radio's Golden Age as the 21-year span between 1932 and 1953.

My second major resource is an exceptional Web site, *J.J.'s Newspaper Radio Logs* at www.jjonz.us/RadioLogs/, which contains the daily radio station schedules from *The New York Times, The Washington Post, The Chicago Tribune* and *The Los Angeles Times* from 1930 through 1960.

John Dunning's *On the Air: The Encyclopedia of Old Time Radio* and Jim Cox's many books specializing in Network Radio's different genres provided accurate and colorful details about many of the hundreds of programs and personalities whose successes and failures are recorded in this book.

Honorable mention for incidental material goes to the Internet archives of *Time* magazine, Frank Nye's biography of C.E. Hooper,

Hoop, the many Web sites dedicated to "Old Time Radio," plus the recorded program vendors who keep the genre alive, Radio Spirits, RadioArchives.com, RUSC.com and Brando Radio, among many.

All "Old Time Radio" fans should also be aware of Turner Classic Movies which occasionally airs films of the era based on radio's most popular programs and personalities. The cable network keeps Network Radio's Golden Age fresh in the hearts of millions.

My personal thanks are owed to many.

Steve Raymer and his staff of the Pavek Museum of Broadcasting in Minneapolis are a dedicated group who maintain the finest collection of historic radio and television studio, transmission and reception equipment available anywhere for public viewing. Its Web site provides interesting material for all broadcasting fans at www.museumofbroadcasting.org.

Broadcast technical consultant and radio historian Mark Durenberger has been of special encouragement and counsel, especially in my understanding the mechanics of radio which I've attempted to explain in simple chronological terms in Chapter Two.

I also owe deep thanks to a good neighbor, Bev MacNellis, who took time from her tireless civic activities in Estero, Florida, to lend her professional talents to the preparation of this work.

A treasured pal for nearly 50 years, former NBC vice-president Burt Sherwood has contributed memories of his early days in Chicago radio which climaxed in his managing the network's WMAQ.

And I can't forget Leo and Jo Jordan of Peoria who invited Patty and me into their home to review Leo's fascinating collection of memorabilia left to him by his uncle, Jim Jordan — known to millions as *Fibber McGee.*

Who's Patty, you ask?

She's simply the most beautiful and wonderful person I've ever known, my business partner and my wife of over 50 years.

To all of you: Thank you!

The multi-media presentation about Network Radio's Golden Age that inspired all this?

It went on the shelf— temporarily.

I gotta get back to it one of these days.

Meanwhile, I have some stories to share with you in print...

1

Facts Never Broadcast

A GAME OF NUMBERS

This is the history of Network Radio's Golden Age as it's never been told before — as a high stakes game of numbers when radio was the only game in town. Like any game it had its winners and losers.

The scores that determined the players' success or failure back then — and ever since then in all of radio, television and cable — are ratings. Ratings is a term coined by pioneer researcher Archibald Crossley in 1930 for the results of his radio audience surveys of sometimes questionable accuracy. Nevertheless, ratings have always determined the winners and losers in broadcasting's ongoing battle for audience popularity and advertising revenue.

When the biggest names of stage and movies began appearing regularly on Network Radio for big money in the autumn of 1932, they quickly learned that their survival in the medium depended on a strong showing in the ratings. It could be a real struggle.

Singing bandleader Rudy Vallee and comedians Eddie Cantor, Ed Wynn, Jack Pearl, *Amos & Andy* and Burns and Allen all had Top Ten rated shows in 1932–33, the first season of Network Radio's Golden Age. None were on the Top Ten list ten years later.

That can be said with definitive certainty because this story of the Golden Age is based on the complete Crossley, Crossley/CAB, Clark-Hooper, C.E. Hooper and A.C Nielsen full-season ratings from 1932 through 1953, never before

published outside the broadcasting and advertising industries. As simple statistics, those ratings mean little. But they provide a wealth of stories when put into the context of the nightly, monthly and annual competition among programs, performers, networks, advertisers and their agencies. What follows are hundreds of those stories — tales of success, failure, luck, stupidity and irony involving legendary performers and programs — plus some turkeys that should have never been hatched.

RADIO WAS SPELLED AM

FM and TV were just letters of the alphabet during most of Network Radio's Golden Age.

The four competing coast-to-coast chains of AM radio stations linked by telephone lines combined to dominate American entertainment and information as no concentrated communications force ever had — or ever will again.

Radio fan magazines treated network personalities like movie stars — which many were. They were pictured smiling behind boxy or bullet shaped microphones emblazoned with the logo of their network homes — homes that often changed for reasons seldom explained to the listening public. The magazines often neglected to mention the stars' sponsors and never identified the advertising agencies involved or the true mechanics of the business. Instead, it was all smiles. It was how the stars, their networks and sponsors all wanted their industry portrayed.

It was all a happy facade.

TUNING IN TO REALITY

In reality, broadcasting has always been a business — a unique business with a unique history — furthered in its technical development and public popularity by the 20th century's three greatest tragedies: two world wars and a global economic depression.

Network Radio in its Golden Age was commercial broadcasting at its highest level. It was a hard-nosed business based in technology, capitalized upon by industry, loosely controlled by government, exploited by marketers of consumer goods, ruled by dollars and dictated by ratings.

These pages contain thousands of nightly, monthly and annual rating averages resulting from the daily competition for audience popularity during the 21 years when America depended on radio as its primary source for constant entertainment and information. Competition could be fierce because millions of advertising dollars were at stake for all concerned every year. As a result, programs and talent were constantly shuffled among sponsors and networks to find a winning formula that produced higher ratings.

It could be foolhardy, too, when some of the most respected network and advertising executives made costly blunders that were the fodder of gossip, but only within the industry's walls.

The fan magazines never had such a good story.

2

Spinning the Webs

WE JOIN OUR PROGRAM ALREADY IN PROGRESS...

Long before the networks were established and the first ratings were published, radio already had a rich history full of colorful characters who contributed in one way or another to its Golden Age, beginning nearly a hundred years earlier with an American invention that converted electricity into a means of communications.

Participants in the process came from technology, industry, government, show business and marketing In many cases they never met or even knew of the others involved. Yet, their ideas and actions forged the links to what became known as chain broadcasting — Network Radio. Briefly told in non-technical terms and chronological order, here's how it all came together:

A BRUSH OF GENIUS

Our story begins in 1838 when noted American portrait artist Samuel Morse, 47, first demonstrated his communications invention, the *telegraph*—which some historians assert was stolen from others. Morse's simple interruption of direct current in differing durations — "dots" and "dashes" to represent each of the 26 letters of the alphabet and ten digits from one through zero — established electricity as a tool to communicate instantly over long distances — wherever its wires of conductivity could be strung.

Morse the artist became Morse the entrepreneur.

Six years later, May 24, 1844, he opened the first permanent telegraph line — a government financed wire between Washington, D.C., and Baltimore — with a four word transmission, *"What hath God wrought?"*

He wrought a lot.

The telegraph inspired others to learn what else could be done with electricity — the mysterious, unseen and potentially lethal force.

GREAT SCOTS!

Acceptance of Morse's telegraph spread throughout the world. Its use of electricity became the lifelong fascination of a bright youngster in Scotland, James Clerk Maxwell.

Later in life, as a 33-year-old physicist, Maxwell theorized in 1864 that still another invisible phenomenon might exist that could transmit electricity through the air — much like the wind carries sound waves — but far more powerful.

Maxwell claimed that these waves — he called them *electromagnetic waves*—could be strong enough to penetrate a brick wall if enough electrical force were generated behind them. Maxwell's theories became the technical foundation of broadcasting, although they remained unproved for the next 30 years.

Maxwell wasn't the only young Scot influenced by Samuel Morse's telegraph.

When Alexander Graham Bell was born in 1847, telegraph lines were already springing up along railroad tracks in his native Edinburgh. It eventually became Bell's obsession to go Morse one better and enable everyone to communicate over telegraph-like wires by *voice,* not a complicated code of dots and dashes. Bell emigrated with his concept to the United States in his early twenties.

By the age of 29, Bell had devised a means to convert human speech into electric impulses at one end of an electrically charged wire and then reverse the process at the other end. The *telephone* was born in 1876 — and along with it came the original technology for the microphone and chain broadcasting.

CORPS COME TO LIFE WITH RADIO

Bell patented the telephone and nine years later incorporated his holdings as American Telephone and Telegraph Co (AT&T). The company would eventually become a major supplier of broadcasting equipment, a pioneer in commercial radio and the linchpin of all radio networks.

Three years after Bell introduced the telephone, Thomas Alva Edison — age 32 and already famed as the inventor of the phonograph — took a 50-year-old idea, tinkered with it and came up with the electric light bulb in 1879.

Along with its obvious benefits, the light bulb — a sealed glass enclosure from which all air had been removed — became the prototype from which the vacuum tube emerged, a critical element to future radio transmission and reception. Ten years later Edison combined all of his holdings and founded General Electric Co (GE).

Most developments involving electricity during this period employed *direct current*. But shortly after Edison introduced the light bulb, industrialist George Westinghouse demonstrated the advantages of *alternating current*—developed by a 27-year-old Serbian immigrant, Nikola Tesla, in 1883. Although Westinghouse was primarily interested in AC for its use in electric transmission, alternating current would prove to be the necessary element for broadcasting speech and music.

Within a five year span, the three companies which 30 years later became radio's foremost equipment, station and network pioneers were established and incorporated: Westinghouse Electric (1884), Bell's AT&T (1885), and Edison's GE (1889). Of course, the very word *radio* was generally unknown at the time and Network Radio was still nearly 40 years in the future.

CURTAIN GOING UP

Far removed from the university and corporate laboratories that developed the technical side of radio — *about as far removed as one could get* — another corporation was founded in 1885 that would play an instrumental role of what Americans would eventually hear on Network Radio.

Benjamin Keith, 39, and Edward Albee, 28, opened The Bijou theater in New York City, the first American theater to present variety acts under the umbrella title, *Vaudeville*. The pair's Keith-Albee-Orpheum chain would eventually control hundreds of Vaudeville houses across America and provide stage experience for Network Radio's biggest stars. Eddie Cantor, Jack Benny, Burns and Allen, Bob Hope and Fred Allen were just a few of the thousands of young hopefuls who entered the grinding split-week, two to five shows a day Vaudeville circuits in their teens.

Vaudeville enjoyed 35 years of popularity, peaking in 1910 when over 2,000 theaters in cities and towns across America featured variety and amateur acts, both good and bad — often the latter.

THE AD VENTURES BEGIN

The late 1800s also saw the birth of yet another industry that would eventually play a key role in Network Radio.

Francis Ayer, 21, opened an advertising agency in 1868 and named it for his father who bankrolled the enterprise, N.W. Ayer. Thirty-year-old J. Walter Thompson bought Carlton Smith Advertising in 1877 and gave it his name. Chicago's Daniel Lord and Ambrose Thomas hung out their Lord & Thomas shingle in 1881 for the agency that eventually became Foote, Cone & Belding.

All three pioneering agencies originated when newspapers and magazines dominated media None could have known the influential roles they would play — or the fortunes they would make — when Network Radio was introduced in 1926. Agencies became the unseen

middle-men who knotted the ties between the radio audience's most popular programs and the advertisers who sponsored them,

Most advertising supported Network Radio programming was produced by agencies. The networks simply provided the studio facilities and fed the programs along leased telephone lines to their affiliated stations for broadcast. But the chains were quick to share in any bragging rights their programs' popularity achieved and allowed the public to assume that they were responsible for creating them.

By coincidence, about the time when advertising agencies first appeared, *medicine shows* began roaming the small towns of America's south and Midwest, giving local townsfolk — *the rubes* — free entertainment interspersed with sales pitches for tonics, pills and salves.

The essence of commercial broadcasting is in those medicine shows of the late 1800s.

MEANWHILE, BACK IN THE LAB…

Heinrich Hertz was a 30-year-old physics professor at the University of Heidelberg, long captivated by Maxwell's electromagnetic waves theories. In 1887 he set up a crude arc generator, shot sparks across his laboratory and proved that the waves did exist, traveling at the rate of 186,000 miles per hour — the speed of light.

Hertz's early contributions to broadcasting's fundamental process were honored in 1933 when his name replaced *cycles* as the international measurement term of electromagnetic waves — *kilohertz* for AM radio frequencies, (one thousand cycles per second), and *megahertz* for FM, (one million cycles per second). The United States adopted the term some thirty years later.

A YOUNG MAN'S GAME

Like computer sciences a century later, electronics was the field of young men full of curiosity and eager to make a name for themselves. None was younger than Guglielmo Marconi, a teenager inspired by reports of Hertz's experiments. Marconi had more than

just intelligence and a curious nature — he also had the support of his father, a wealthy Italian landowner.

Marconi built a spark generator, combined it with a telegraph key and transmitted the first *wireless* telegraphic signals aboard electromagnetic waves between hills on his family's estate near Bologna. The year was 1895 and Marconi was only 21.

Proving that the entrepreneurial spirit wasn't limited to America, Marconi went to England where he patented his transmitter and antenna system in 1897. Two years later he demonstrated his wireless process to the British Navy by transmitting telegraphic signals across the English Channel and between ships 75 miles apart. Wireless communication's value to naval safety was obvious.

Marconi's title as The Father of Radio has been long debated. One title, however, is indisputable: Marconi was the Father of The Radio *Business*. He was the first to make real money with the contraption.

In the fall of 1899 he sailed to the United States, founded the American Marconi Company in New York and made his first important sale to the U.S. Navy for wireless telegraphic communications between ships and shore. When the 19th century closed the young Italian was only 26 and already on his way to becoming the wealthiest member of an already wealthy family.

And with the formation of American Marconi, the fourth corporation responsible for the creation of American broadcasting was in place. Marconi joined AT&T, GE and Westinghouse at the starting gate and the race for patents was underway. It wouldn't end until America entered World War I, almost 18 years later.

FESSENDEN'S FIRSTS

Marconi made international headlines by attempting to transmit the letter "S" in Morse Code by wireless across the Atlantic in late 1901. But the real impact on broadcasting's future was a feat accomplished a year earlier by a 34-year-old Canadian, Reginald Fessenden.

Physics professor Fessenden,

working at the time with the U.S. Weather Bureau, experimented with parts taken from a Bell telephone and a low powered alternating current generator. He reasoned that alternating current would allow him to create a steady stream of *continuous* electromagnetic waves capable of carrying the actual sounds of voice and music — not just the noise of sparks generated by a telegraph key.

His work paid off on December 23, 1900. Across a one mile span at Cobb Island, Maryland, Reginald Fessenden's voice became the first ever heard in a wireless transmission saying the now familiar words, *"Hello! Test, one, two, three, four...."*

In effect, Fessenden became to Marconi what Bell had been to Morse. They both converted the coded communications tool of a few into a common utility for the masses. *Radio Telephony* was the first term adopted for wireless voice transmission, a mouthful that became simply, *Radio*.

But Fessenden realized if he was to be heard at any distance beyond a mile he would need a factory-produced alternating current generator — or *transmitter* —of far greater power than he could build in his laboratory. He turned to General Electric in Schenectady, New York.

Ironically, GE was the company founded by Thomas Edison, a bitter opponent of alternating current. Nevertheless, GE undertook Fessenden's project, took his money and assigned a newcomer on its staff to work with Fessenden — a 28-year-old Swedish immigrant, Ernst Alexanderson.

The Canadian and Swede made broadcasting history together.

IT CAME UPON A MIDNIGHT CLEAR

Fessenden and Alexanderson's achievement came on Christmas Eve, 1906, when they set up Alexanderson's massive alternating current generator with its 50,000 watts of power on the shore of the Atlantic Ocean at Brant Rock, Massachusetts. Fessenden took to the air and sent Christmas greetings to all who could hear him. Then he picked up his violin and became the first musician ever heard on radio.

And he was heard.

Amateur hobbyists scattered along the East Coast picked up his transmission as did wireless operators at sea, some of them working on banana boats owned by United Fruit, an early pioneer in shipboard wireless. Fessenden, himself, had designed United's system of wireless telegraphy to track its cargo fleet in the Caribbean. One can only imagine the delightful shock that Fessenden's Christmas gift of readings and music gave to those lonesome individuals accustomed to hearing nothing but Morse code and static from their earphones.

In effect, the *radio program* was born on December 24, 1906.

WHO'S ON FIRST?

Fessenden's first broadcast motivated entrepreneurs and educators to begin thinking about establishing *radio stations* to broadcast at regularly scheduled times to serve the public — or their own egos.

Among the first was Charles "Doc" Herrod, the operator of a vocational school in San Jose, California, who began broadcasting in 1909 to publicize his establishment. Doc Herrod became radio's first disc jockey, playing phonograph records while he pitched the benefits of learning electronics at his trade school. Herrod's backroom operation later became KQW/San Jose — today's KCBS/San Francisco.

In 1912, Scripps' *Detroit News* established experimental station 8MK which later became WWJ. Five years later, the University of Wisconsin began a series of daily weather reports in Morse code on 9XM in Madison, which evolved into WHA Radio. WHA switched to voiced reports in January 1919, which some historians contend were the first regularly scheduled series of spoken broadcasts.

While others dabbled with establishing radio stations between 1910 and 1920, engineering pioneers John Ambrose Fleming, Edwin Armstrong, Lee De Forest, Harold Arnold and others made significant contributions to broadcasting's transmission and reception. Scores of patents were issued to different individuals and corporations which led to confusion, larceny and law-

suits. Nevertheless, public curiosity and interest in radio were on a roll in America with no signs of slowing. Before long, wireless signals for industrial use and amateur amusement filled the air.

Then, on April 6, 1917, it all fell silent.

WORLD WAR I: TRUCE AND CONSEQUENCES

When the United States entered World War I, all broadcasting in the country was ordered off the air for the duration. The government commandeered the powerful shortwave transmitters that Marconi and others had established along the coastlines of the country for military communications and all wireless transmission within the United States was forbidden.

More important to radio's future, all patent rights were suspended. The suspension enabled manufacturers to develop radio equipment for the military that combined all the latest technical advancements without worry of patent infringement. It improved the state of the art considerably and gave manufacturers ideas about a future free of patent restrictions.

World War I ended on November 11, 1918. Beyond improving the technical aspects of radio, America's 20 month involvement in the war produced two other effects.

First, military service introduced thousands of doughboys to the basics of radio. They returned to civilian life eager to experiment as broadcasters, listeners or both. The wartime prohibition of amateur radio ended in 1920, and a reported 8,500 hobbyists brought radio into their homes, leaning over their homemade "breadboard" sets. Magazines directed to amateur radio appeared and sales of radio parts hit two million dollars — *(approximately $22.6 million in 2012)*.

Wartime communications had also convinced the American government of radio's strategic importance to the United States *and* to any potential foreign enemies. Taking precaution to its extreme, the Navy led a government effort to nationalize and seize control all radio facilities in the country.

General Electric forced the issue

to a head with its proposed sale of powerful Alexanderson transmitters to the U.S. based shortwave stations owned by American Marconi, a subsidiary of the Italian's British corporation. The foreign-owned American Marconi also held a number of U.S. patents. That also troubled the government. To settle the matter, government and industry met.

Franklin Roosevelt, the 37-year-old assistant secretary of the navy represented the government and General Electric President Owen Young made the case for private industry which owned key patents. They agreed that something had to be done to keep American broadcasting free of foreign interests. The question was how to do it.

Young came up with the answer.

LET'S PLAY MONOPOLY

Owen Young proposed to Roosevelt — who would become the trust-busting 32nd president — that the government endorse the *creation* of a monopoly, the Radio Corporation of America (RCA).

RCA — principally owned by GE, Westinghouse, AT&T and United Fruit — would pool its partners' 2,000 radio related patents and buy out American Marconi's patents and facilities. This would settle any potential patent disputes among its principals, expedite radio's technical development and bring all of Marconi's holdings in the United States under the ownership of an American corporation.

FDR bought the idea, championed it in Washington and RCA was born on October 17, 1919, less than a year after World War I ended. The new company was chaired by GE's Young.

David Sarnoff, Marconi's 28-year-old protégé and General Manager of American Marconi, was selected to be RCA's chief operating officer. Sarnoff's rags to riches story has been well documented — and often glamorized by an RCA publicity department eager to please the boss. Sarnoff, it was said, never let facts get in the way of a good story, especially his.

RCA took over Marconi's high-powered shortwave installations and began marketing the longwave (AM), radio equipment manufactured by GE and Westinghouse. But Sarnoff would have far greater ambitions for his company — including the creation of the first permanent radio network in 1926.

PITTSBURGH CALLING...

By coincidence, RCA shared its October 17, 1919, birthday with another radio pioneer's milestone event. On that night, Frank Conrad, a 45-year-old engineer at the Westinghouse factory in Pittsburgh, powered up 8XK, an experimental radio station housed in a tent-like structure on the roof of the building. Conrad gave himself the nightly time job of talking and playing records on the station. No one at the time suspected the great impact that his little station would have.

Within a year, the surprising popularity of Conrad's 8XK led Westinghouse to recognize the profit potential in manufacturing radio receivers and establishing major market AM radio stations. The Westinghouse group of stations began with KDKA/Pittsburgh in 1920 — the first AM station officially licensed by the U.S. Commerce Department — and expanded in quick order with WBZ/Springfield-Boston, KYW/Chicago and WJZ/Newark, all in 1921.

RADIO ROARS
INTO TWENTIES

AT&T also got into station ownership in 1920 by establishing WEAF/New York with a limited schedule of makeshift programming. Although AT&T's manufacturing arm, Western Electric, was successful on the equipment side of the communications industry, actual station operations were foreign to the telephone giant.

That situation wouldn't last long.

RCA joined the station ownership ranks *for one day*, July 2, 1921. As little more than a publicity stunt, WJY/Newark had but one program: a second hand account of the Heavyweight Championship bout between Jack Dempsey and Georges Carpentier. The station's transmitter blew out before the end of the fight.

GE was the last of RCA's major owners to enter broadcasting with its own station. WGY, located at the company's Schenectady factory, opened in 1922. Stations suddenly popped up everywhere across America — over 500 signed on by 1923. The links for a broadcasting chain were formed although the first permanent radio network was still three years away.

Meanwhile, stations were on their own to provide programs that would justify the $20 to $60, *($265 to $795)*, that listeners were asked to pay for their Westinghouse *Aeriola* or Crosley *Harko* radio sets. Early broadcasters were all faced with the same problem — how to fill those gaping hours of vacant airtime every day with something more than static.

The situation led to a number of programming firsts. The most notable at the time were KDKA's reports of the Harding-Cox presidential elections on November 2, 1920. The Westinghouse station in Pittsburgh may have taken its cue from Detroit's WWJ which claims the first live coverage of a news-making event, its city's municipal primary elections on September 1st of that year.

WWJ also claims the first series of *sponsored* programs — the weekly *Detroit Bank Concerts* in February 1922. Because commercial radio was yet to come into the open, any mention of the bank's sponsorship had to be the softest of soft sell. The same was true for Iowa Power & Light's daily sponsorship of two hours on WMT's schedule in Cedar Rapids, Iowa. The station charged the utility five dollars a day with half of the fee applied to the station's electric bill.

Station owners — from major corporations and big city newspapers to small town retailers — were all learning that it cost money to operate radio stations. Something had to be done to just to keep the things on the air.

VAUDEVILLE'S
NEXT TO CLOSING

By 1922, the singers, musicians and actors who stations could snag to perform in their studios began asking for money because Vaudeville employment for them was getting scarce.

Between 1920 and 1925 the number of Vaudeville houses in America plummeted from a thousand to a mere 25. The theaters weren't closing — they were switching to movies. Even the giant Keith-Albee-Orpheum circuit joined the movie revolution which ironically began at Vaudeville's peak in 1910 when films were introduced as occasional novelties between live stage acts or as purposely bad "chasers," to clear out theater audiences between shows.

Ten years later movies were chasing Vaudeville out of the theaters. By 1920, the weekly movie audience was reported at 35 million and growing.

Headliners like Will Rogers and Eddie Cantor deserted the Vaudeville circuits for Broadway revues and Hollywood stardom. Most of the Vaudeville's also-rans drifted back into obscurity while a lucky few, most notably Freeman Gosden and Charles Correll (*Amos & Andy*) and Jim and Marian Jordan (*Fibber McGee & Molly*), eventually earned fame and fortune beyond their wildest dreams in the new medium that still struggled to pay its bills in the early twenties.

SMOKING IN THE LOBBY

Worse yet for stations' bottom lines in 1922, the American Society of Composers, Authors and Publishers (ASCAP), was preparing to charge broadcasters for the music that performers played or sang on radio. ASCAP's demands threatened to increase station expenses considerably and shut down poorly financed operations altogether.

The ASCAP situation prompted worried station owners to organize as the National Association of Broadcasters (NAB), in April 1923. NAB eventually became one of the country's most powerful industry lobbying groups and ASCAP's strongest adversary for years to come.

FOR WHOM MA BELL TOLLS

No station owner was more aware of radio's fiscal problems than AT&T. WEAF — the first station to capitulate to ASCAP's demands by paying a one year license fee of $500 (*$6,700*) — was a both-ersome drain on the corporate balance sheet. But instead of shutting down the station and cutting its losses, AT&T surprised observers and opened a *second* New York station with a plan that would shape the future of broadcasting in America.

AT&T introduced WBAY — a *Toll Broadcasting* station.

Much like AT&T charged tolls for use of its local and long distance telephone lines, WBAY would sell blocks of its time to those who wanted to broadcast messages over its facilities. The first published "toll" was $40 to $50 (*$540–$675*), per quarter hour. Near-sighted purists complained that Ma Bell had become broadcasting's whore.

WBAY signed on the air on July 25, 1922 — but nobody could hear the station. Its signals, transmitted from mid–Manhattan, were so riddled with interference that AT&T closed the station after three weeks and shifted its toll broadcasting concept to WEAF.

And so, by default, WEAF went down in broadcasting history on August 28, 1922, as the first radio station to openly broadcast a paid announcement — a ten minute oratory extolling life in an apartment development in suburban Jackson Heights, Queens. To most everyone's surprise, the commercial drew results and the real estate developer came back for more commercials with toll money in hand.

Was WEAF *really* the first station to broadcast a commercial? Probably not.

For many of the country's financially strapped broadcasters, a little cash was just too tempting to resist in exchange for a few hundred friendly words on behalf of a local merchant. AT&T simply brought the practice into the open.

The telephone giant attempted briefly to collect license fees from other stations who seized on the idea of selling time for survival and potential profit. But that brazen maneuver didn't last long. Radio station time salesmen soon became as common as newspaper space salesmen, just not as successful — yet. Nevertheless, the need for attractive programming still remained for most stations.

Once again, Ma Bell came to their rescue.

GETTING HEAR FROM THERE

Network Radio began with a five minute experiment on January 4, 1923 — a saxophone solo played over a high quality AT&T long distance telephone wire linking New York's WEAF with WNAC in Boston. Six months later AT&T demonstrated the first *broadcast quality* lines with a network broadcast from the National Electric Light Association's convention in New York City via WEAF to GE's WGY and Westinghouse's KDKA and KYW.

But that kind of cooperation among RCA's partners didn't extend very far. AT&T prohibited GE and Westinghouse from using its telephone lines for their own networking experiments. The two electrical giants considered shortwave transmission to link stations and produced a highly publicized broadcast on November 23, 1923, that reached GE's KGO in Oakland from Westinghouse's Newark and Pittsburgh stations via a shortwave link in Hastings, Nebraska. But results were spotty.

David Sarnoff took note of all of this and decided that RCA should become more deeply involved in broadcasting and networking, too. His motivation was the same that made station owners of GE and Westinghouse — to sell radios.

RCA and Westinghouse had jointly introduced *The Radiola Grand* in 1923, the first console radio with a built-in speaker. Radio broadcasts could now be heard simultaneously by the entire family — not just one hobbyist wearing a pair of earphones. *The Radiola* carried a hefty price tag of $623 (*$4,275*). (For perspective, contemporary dollar amounts have been adjusted for inflation and 2012 equivalents appear in parenthesis.)

Sarnoff knew that no family would spend that kind of money on a radio unless there was something the family wanted to hear. If necessary, he'd try to provide it.

In need of an established station, possibly to anchor a network, RCA purchased WJZ from Westinghouse on May 14, 1923, and moved the

Newark facility into New York City. Because AT&T refused to lease its broadcast quality lines to any potential competitor, RCA turned to Western Union's inferior telegraph lines for its first networking attempts. The experiments were soon abandoned and Sarnoff began investigating some other way — *any way* — to circumvent AT&T's tight grip on quality telephone line transmission of chain broadcasts.

Sarnoff briefly floated an idea that a network could consist of a group of super-powered AM stations — *RCA owned super-powered AM stations, of course* — strategically placed in major cities from coast to coast. His concept called "Super Radiocasting" went nowhere. But did illustrate RCA's monopolistic ways and Sarnoff's chutzpah.

While its RCA partners continued to spin their wheels, AT&T continued its pioneer networking. It acquired WCAP/Washington and broadcast the opening of Congress on December 4, 1923, to a seven station network that reached west to WFAA in Dallas. AT&T was quickly establishing the use of its lines as the network distribution vehicle of greatest quality, dependability and flexibility.

That same December 4 evening, AT&T's WEAF introduced *The Eveready Hour*, named for its battery company sponsor and recognized as radio's first big-time variety program, featuring top Broadway stars. Three months later, March 1, 1924, AT&T put the show on its lines to WJAR/Providence and WGR/Buffalo. *The Eveready Hour* became the first entertainment program heard simultaneously on a chain of stations.

AT&T continued to push its networking advantage with broadcasts of the Republican and Democratic national conventions in the summer of 1924, followed by President Coolidge's inaugural address networked to 24 stations on March 4, 1925. Yet, for all of the company's achievements in the radio industry, Ma Bell still felt like a wallflower at the Broadcasters Ball.

AT&T HANGS UP

AT&T knew that its activities were always in the gunsights of government trust-busters. Already the owner of the near-monopoly in telephone services and part owner of RCA, a legalized monopoly in broadcasting equipment and services, AT&T decided to play it safe — get out of RCA and abandon station ownership.

After several months of negotiations a deal was announced on November 9, 1926. A new entity, The National Broadcasting Company, was incorporated with owners RCA (50 percent), GE (30 percent), and Westinghouse (20 percent). The new NBC agreed to buy AT&T's two stations, WEAF and WCAP for one million dollars, *($12.8 Mil)*. WEAF was designated to become the New York flagship of a new NBC Radio Network.

The plum of the package was the ability granted NBC to lease AT&T's broadcast quality telephone lines for network use — lease fees worth millions to the telephone company. Sarnoff promptly forgot about his network scheme of super-powered stations and Ma Bell left broadcasting counting her cash.

NBC CHIMES IN

Less than a week later on November 15, 1926, NBC inaugurated its network service over AT&T lines to 22 stations with an elaborate four hour broadcast originated before a thousand invited guests in New York's Waldorf-Astoria ballroom. The quickly organized network's publicity department made no secret of the flamboyant event's cost, $50,000 *($640,000)*, of which half was claimed to have been spent on talent.

NBC's new president Merlin Aylesworth opened the proceedings with a speech promising a brilliant future for Network Radio. The program celebrated his promise by delivering a variety of the day's biggest names — Will Rogers, soprano Mary Garden, comedy team Weber & Fields, opera star Titta Ruffo, the New York Symphony, Goldman's Brass Band, a grand and light opera company, plus the popular dance bands led by Vincent Lopez, George Olsen, Ben Bernie and B.A. Rolfe.

The marathon program demonstrated Network Radio's ability to put the world's most popular talents within earshot of any American who purchased a radio that could receive a station linked to NBC.

In addition, Rogers's monologue and Garden's solos originated half a continent away from New York. This use of *reverse* telephone lines underscored network flexibility. Any location east of the Rockies was now able to transmit a broadcast quality signal to the rest of the country — and Hollywood was just beyond the mountains.

If the objective was to promote radio set sales, the expensive program was worth it. NBC had begun to deliver stars into America's living rooms absolutely free. Two million homes were added to the ranks of radio households over the following year, an increase that brought the total to almost seven million homes.

NBC paid all the bills for the historic November 15 inaugural broadcast with no advertising support. That altruistic practice ended five weeks later when the network produced a *twelve* hour special on Christmas Day.

Some of the talent and segments on the marathon Christmas broadcast indicate who was paying for it: *The Colgate Orchestra, The Eveready Novelty Orchestra*, B. A. Rolfe's *Coward Comfort Hour Orchestra*, Walter Damrosch conducting the New York Symphony in the *Bakelite Hour* and the popular singing duo named for cough lozenges, *The Smith Brothers — Trade & Mark*.

NBC was in operation for six weeks and finished 1926 without network competition. Then, on January 1, 1927, it introduced its own competitor — but as it turned out, a competitor of only limited degree which served to create another situation that smacked of monopoly.

THE BIRTH OF THE BLUE

When NBC designated WEAF as its New York anchor station, RCA's WJZ was left out in the cold without network affiliation along with Westinghouse's Pittsburgh, Chicago and Boston stations — KDKA, KYW and WBZ.

NBC established its second network to serve those stations plus others around the country which were shut out of the original network service by local competitors — often more powerful stations which snapped up NBC affiliations in their markets.

The WEAF anchored network was identified as NBC's *Red* Network and the WJZ group became the NBC *Blue* Network. The color-coded identification reportedly originated with the networks' telephone line maps drawn in colored pencils — or their red and blue connection plugs in NBC master control. Whichever was the case, the idea was to differentiate between the two networks.

NBC promptly made it clear that the two networks *would* be different — almost identifying Blue as the ugly duckling of the pair. Blue was to be the home of cultural and informational programming and the repository of Red's overflow programming. In other words, Blue would get Red's unwanted hand-me-downs. In future years Red also stripped Blue of its most popular programs. Blue wasn't competition to Red, it was a supplement — and a secondary source of revenue for owner RCA.

SARNOFF SHOULDN'T HAVE LAUGHED

It's a stroke of irony that NBC's *real* competitor was also conceived in RCA's executive suite in 1926 when Sarnoff rebuffed concert promoter Arthur Judson's proposal to form an in-house talent agency to manage — *and profit from* — performers appearing on the NBC and Blue Networks. Sarnoff added insult to injury when he adopted Judson's idea as his own and laughed when Judson threatened to retaliate by forming a *third* radio network.

Judson and his partners promptly did just that, calling their venture the United Independent Broadcasters — an obvious dig at RCA's monopolistic control of two networks. In constant need of working capital just to get established, Judson's group went through one investor after another, finally selling their network's control and naming rights to the Columbia Phonograph Company for start-up expenses of $163,000 *(2.1 Mil)*. Sarnoff could still laugh at the attempt.

The Columbia Phonograph Company Radio Network went on the air September 19, 1927, with 16 affiliates and lots of glowing promises but not enough cash or advertisers to pay the bills. Within days Columbia abruptly withdrew its support and Judson's search for sponsors and capital resumed. Both were found in Philadelphia.

PALEY'S EXPLODING CIGAR BUSINESS

Young William S. Paley was the college-educated heir and executive whiz kid of his family's Congress Cigar Company. He first came to radio in 1927 as an advertiser who saw encouraging results from sponsoring *The LaPalina Smoker* music programs on WCAU/Philadelphia, the shaky Columbia network's first affiliate whose owners were among the latest of Judson's string of investors.

Increased sales of his cigars convinced Paley to try advertising on the full Columbia chain. LaPalina sales doubled to a million cigars a week and Paley became a believer in Network Radio.

Paley was a serious listener when the owners of WCAU led by Philadelphia industrialist Jerome Louchheim approached him to buy the network that they had taken over and renamed the Columbia Broadcasting System (CBS). The 26-year-old Paley convinced his family to buy CBS for $503,000 *(6.7 Mil)*, on September 12, 1928. By doing so, he greatly expanded the future popularity of Network Radio.

In a related deal, Arthur Judson and Paley created the Columbia Concerts Corporation — a CBS variation of the same talent management idea that Sarnoff rejected and then stole from Judson. Arthur Judson remained with CBS for many years as a major stockholder — sharing in the network's success and getting the last laugh on Sarnoff.

COLUMBIA, THE GEM OF PROMOTION

Bill Paley's Belarusian grandparents hailed from Minsk, David Sarnoff's birthplace. But that's all the two network moguls had in common. Their backgrounds, education

and personalities were totally different.

In 1928, Sarnoff was in his forties, an aloof industrialist whose hirelings ran NBC. Paley became an instant and personable hands-on broadcasting executive before he was 30. Paley immediately toured the stations linked by CBS and renegotiated the affiliate contracts which had financially strapped the network's former owners. The new agreements, similar to NBC and Blue's, paid affiliates an average 30 percent of their published rates for time given to sponsored network programs. Unsponsored — *sustaining* — programs were provided by CBS to its stations at no cost.

One of Paley's first hires was advertising man Paul Kresten who was charged with making CBS *appear* as successful as NBC with a continual bombardment of press releases and expensive promotional pieces to major newspapers, potential sponsors and advertising agencies. The maneuver worked. CBS started to get noticed in the press and attract sponsor interest.

To counter NBC's programs featuring established stars of Vaudeville and movies, Paley was determined to build CBS radio stars from younger, lesser known talent. Bing Crosby, Kate Smith, Morton Downey and the Mills Brothers were prime examples.

Paley figured that he'd simply steal the *really* big stars from NBC when he got his network up to full speed. That day came sooner than he thought.

GO WEST, YOUNG MAN!

NBC had three major advantages over CBS in the summer of 1929 — plenty of cash, powerful station affiliates on the West Coast. and a movie connection thanks to RCA's part ownership of RKO Radio Pictures. Bill Paley concluded that he needed all three to level the playing field. He caught a train to Los Angeles to get them.

Paley scored on two counts by selling 49 percent of CBS to Paramount Pictures for five million dollars *(66.1 Mil)*, just weeks before the stock market crash of October 29. Further, it was the promise of a screen test at Paramount that enabled CBS to outfox NBC for Bing Crosby's debut radio series in 1931.

Three years later in the Depression year of 1932, CBS and Paramount's roles were reversed. Movie attendance had fallen 40 percent and the studios all needed cash to survive. In contrast, the number of radio households had steadily increased to over 16 million — over 55 percent of the nation's homes — and CBS was thriving. Paley bought back total control of his network from Paramount for four million dollars — a cool million dollar profit.

Paley's mid-summer visit to LA in 1929 also resulted in a CBS affiliation contract with the Don Lee Network that linked the flamboyant car dealer's KHJ/Los Angeles and KFRC/San Francisco with a group of key stations up the Pacific coast to Portland, Seattle and Spokane. As a result, CBS could claim nationwide coverage to advertisers.

NETS SET TO GO FOR THE GOLD

When the 1932–33 season opened in September, the two NBC networks had 86 affiliates and the upstart CBS — just four years removed from the brink of bankruptcy — had 84. All shared in 1932's network revenues of 39 million dollars *(644.0 Mil)*. Young Bill Paley had achieved his level playing field for the ratings and revenue battles that lay ahead over the next 21 years of Network Radio's Golden Age.

The gold, of course, was provided by advertisers.

3

If You've Got the Money, I've Got the Time

Now, This Brief Word from Our Sponsor...

Money.

Both familiar and long forgotten consumer brands from the 20th century were the bread and butter of network radio. It didn't take long for manufacturers and their advertising agencies to exploit the money making marketing potential presented by the new nationwide chains of commercial radio stations.

NBC opened its broadcast line to the West Coast and became a complete coast-to-coast network on January 4, 1928. Forty-seven stations were linked for *The Dodge Victory Hour* hosted by Will Rogers to inaugurate the network hookup and introduce the auto maker's new Victory six-cylinder sedan.

NBC claimed the program attracted 35 million listeners — a questionable figure since less than ten million homes had radios in 1928. But apparently the show helped sell automobiles. Dodge returned for a second *Victory Hour* in March — this time originating the show from Hollywood.

Paper Losses

Before 1927, the only means that national advertisers had to reach the entire country with completely controlled messages were national magazines. Network radio offered the same blanket coverage with the added advantages of immediacy and the flexibility to change advertising messages at a moment's notice, opposed to magazines' lead time of days or weeks. Nevertheless, newspapers suffered the greatest revenue losses from radio.

The Radio Committee of the American Newspaper Publishers Association reported that from 1929 to 1930, the 200 leading radio advertisers had reduced their newspaper advertising by $22.4 Million *($303.4 Mil)*, while increasing their

radio budgets by $8.5 Million *(115.1 Mil)*.

Network Radio was simple to buy, growing in audience and where advertisers wanted to hear *their* programs. As a result, network advertising revenues grew at a phenomenal pace — from $3.8 Million in 1927 *(49.4 Mil)* to over $39 Million in 1932 *(644.0 Mil)* — a ten fold increase in just six years with half of them occurring as the nation fell into the Great Depression.

The Wireless Puppets

Program sponsorship meant virtual ownership of a network time period — a throwback to AT&T's original toll-broadcasting concept. Sponsorship extended from the earliest network days when programs were named for their underwriters — *The Eno Crime Club*, *The Cliquot Club Eskimos* and Colgate's *Palmolive Hour* — starring "Paul Oliver" and "Olive Palmer" (singers Frank Munn and Virginia Rea).

Newspaper logs dutifully listed these titles incorporating sponsors' names until publishers banded together and banned the free plugs in the early 1930s. *Gulf Headliners* became *Headliners* in newspaper listings and *The Voice of Firestone* was simply identified as *The Voice*.

Nevertheless, the practice of naming shows for their sponsors continued into Network Radio's peak years, reflecting sponsors' pride of parentage in hits like *Maxwell House Showboat*, *Kraft Music Hall* and *Lux Radio Theater* — and, of course, getting in an extra plug or two wherever possible.

Whether identified in the show's title or not, the sponsor's name was usually the first word(s) from an announcer's mouth when introducing a program. And those first words could often stretch into a ten to 15 second commercial before the program got going.

Sponsors' advertising agencies — not the networks — produced most of the top programs. In some cases, the established stars employed their own writers and produced their shows, but the sponsor and its agency were always in charge.

Remember That Name to Ask for...

Frequency and repetition are keys to successful radio advertising — a fact which network time salesmen were more than happy to point out to advertisers and their agencies. It follows that many of the same brand names popped up as sponsors of the leading programs year after year.

Most of those brands were products manufactured and marketed by only 15 corporations These corporate owners were seldom identified. Yet, during some years of Network Radio's Golden Age, over half of the annual Top 50 programs and up to 80 percent of the Top 20 were sponsored by their various brands.

American Home Products/ Whitehall Pharmacal
Aerowax
Anacin
Bisodol Indigestion Tablets
Black Flag Insecticide
George Washington Coffee
Kolynos Toothpaste
Kolynos Tooth Powder

American Tobacco
Lucky Strike Cigarettes
Pall Mall Cigarettes
Roi Tan Cigars

Andrew Jergens Co
Jergens Lotion
Woodbury Facial Soap & Powder

Bristol-Myers
Ipana Toothpaste
Minit Rub Liniment
Mum Deodorant
Sal Hepatica Laxative
Trushay Hand Lotion
Vitalis Hair Tonic

Brown & Williamson Tobacco

Avalon Cigarettes
Big Ben Tobacco
Bugler Tobacco
Kool Cigarettes
Raleigh Cigarettes
Sir Walter Raleigh Tobacco
Wings Cigarettes

Colgate Palmolive Peet

Cashmere Bouquet Soap
Colgate Dental Cream
Colgate Shave Cream
Colgate Tooth Powder
Halo Shampoo
Lustre Creme Shampoo
Palmolive Shave Cream
Palmolive Beauty Soap
Super Suds Laundry Soap

General Foods

Baker's Chocolate
Birds Eye Frozen Foods
Calumet Baking Powder
Grapenuts Cereal
Grapenuts Flakes Cereal
Huskies Cereal
Jello Gelatin
Jello Puddings
LaFrance Laundry Bluing
Log Cabin Syrup
Maxwell House Coffee
Post Bran Flakes Cereal
Post Raisin Bran Cereal
Post Toasties Cereal
Postum Cereal Beverage
Sanka Coffee
Satina Laundry Starch
Swans Down Cake Flour

Lever Brothers (aka Unilever)

Lifebuoy Deodorant Soap
Lipton Tea (acquired in 1938)
Lipton Instant Soup Mixes

Lux Beauty Soap
Lux Flakes Laundry Soap
Pepsodent Toothpaste (acquired in 1944)
Rayve Home Permanents
Rinso Laundry Soap
Spry Shortening
Surf Laundry Detergent
Swan Soap
Vimms Vitamins

Liggett & Myers

Chesterfield Cigarettes
Fatima Cigarettes

Miles Laboratories

Alka Seltzer
One A Day Vitamins

National Dairy Products Corp. (aka Kraft Foods, 1945)

Kraft Cheese
Miracle Whip Salad Dressing
Parkay Margarine
Philadelphia Brand CreamCheese
Sealtest Dairies
Velveeta Cheese Food

Procter & Gamble

Camay Beauty Soap
Crisco Shortening
Dreft Laundry Soap
Drene Shampoo
Duz Laundry Soap
Ivory Flakes Laundry Soap
Ivory Snow Laundry Soap
Ivory Soap
Lava Hand Soap
Oxydol Laundry Soap
Prell Shampoo
Spic & Span Cleanser
Teel Liquid Dentifrice
Tide Laundry Detergent

RJ Reynolds

Camel Cigarettes
Prince Albert Pipe Tobacco

Standard Brands

Blue Bonnet Margarine
Chase & Sanborn Coffee
Fleischmann's Yeast
Royal Gelatin
Royal Puddings
Tenderleaf Tea

Sterling Drug

Bayer Aspirin
Dr Lyons Tooth Powder
Haley's M-O Laxative
Fletcher's Castoria Laxative
Ironized Yeast
Molle Shaving Cream
Phillips Milk of Magnesia Laxative
Phillips Skin Cream

Many of these brands are long gone but their commercials can still be heard on recordings from the era's programs. And as dated, strange or even silly as they may appear today — like the commercial transcripts found in this book at the beginning of Chapters 5 through 25 — these goods once flew off retailers' shelves and out of dealers' showrooms with the push of Network Radio.

At least radio took credit for these sales successes.

In reality, advertisers had no way of really knowing how many people were actually listening to their programs. That began to change in 1930 when a researcher named Crossley introduced a way to count listeners.

4

Radio's Rulers

THE HIGH PRIESTS OF POPULARITY

"Nothing matters in commercial radio but a Hooper or Crossley rating, whichever one you happen to read. All success is measured by them, most jobs are lost on account of them."— Frederic Wakeman, *"The Hucksters,"* 1946.

Little has been written about Archibald M. Crossley, Claude E. Hooper or Arthur C. Nielsen. Yet, these three pollsters wielded more influence on network radio programming than NBC's Sarnoff or CBS's Paley. Their semi-monthly program popularity surveys in several dozen major cities gave sponsors and their advertising agencies an idea of what their money was buying—by estimating with reasonable accuracy the number of homes where their programs —*more importantly, their commercials*—were heard.

Crossley's *Cooperative Analysis of Broadcasting* reports and the flamboyant Hooper's *Hooperatings* left us with the only measure of program popularity from Network Radio's halcyon days of the '30s and '40s. Nielsen *Audimeter* ratings chronicled its last hurrahs of the late '40s and early '50s. Their thousands of monthly averages allow us to identify network radio's most popular programs and personalities — plus many others that weren't so popular.

How ratings developed is yet another story of high stakes competition. Only this one was among the pollsters, themselves.

BORN IN THE SNITCH OF TIME

Consumer research had taken hold in advertising by 1927. Advertisers and their agencies wanted to know how cost-effectively their sales messages delivered customers. This want would become a need a few years later when the Great Depression slashed consumer spending and advertising budgets.

Archibald Maddock Crossley, a 31-year-old *Literary Digest* magazine research director, had established his own firm specializing in consumer survey services in 1926. An early Network Radio advertiser, Davis Baking Powder Company, commissioned Crossley's researchers in 1927 to confirm the local reception of the Davis program — and its commercials — on stations along the newly established NBC chain of stations.

What Crossley's people discovered was theft.

As Crossley recalled in 1963, "In a number of cities we found local commercials being substituted for the national ones, so the stations were collecting twice. This little bit of sin was brought to the attention of the network, which promptly issued rebates followed by little heart-to-heart talks with the offending stations."

Crossley's whistle-blowing for the baking powder manufacturer caught the attention of other radio advertisers who wondered what happened to *their* programs and commercials once they left the network studios — and, if at all possible, how many people heard them.

In response, Crossley initiated random telephone sampling to estimate program popularity. Crossley coined the word *ratings* to define the percentage of homes that reported listening to specific programs.

As individual sponsors commissioned Crossley for their own studies, demand grew for a continuing service to measure program popularity in major cities on a regular schedule.

```
                          MONDAY EVENING

November 14th and October 31st          Points change from October 31st & Oct. 17th

Amos'n'Andy (Pepsodent)        25.6%    Increases
Myrt & Marge (Wm.Wrigley Jr)   21.2*
Sinclair Wiener Minstrels      20.6*    Myrt & Marge          plus      3.9
The Goldbergs (Pepsodent)      20.1     Kate Smith                      3.6
Kate Smith (La Palina)         18.1     Jones & Hare                    1.9
Lowell Thomas (Sunoco)         14.0     Chandu                          1.8
Fu Manchu (Campana Corp)       12.7     Lowell Thomas                   1.7
Country Doctor (Listerine)     11.3*    Amos'n'Andy                     1.3
Singin' Sam (Barbasol)         10.1     General Electric                1.2
Chandu (Beerhrut & White King) 8.6      Easy Aces                       1.0
Evening in Paris Program       8.6      Fu Manchu                       1.0
Music that Satisfies (Chester) 8.3      Goldbergs                       0.6
Jones & Hare (Best Foods)      8.0      Music that Satisfies            0.5
A & P Gypsies                  7.0
Mills Bros. (P & G Co.)        6.3      Decreases
Easy Aces (Lavoris)            6.2
General Electric Circle        3.1      Mills Bros.           minus     0.1
Pat Barnes (Swift & Co.)       1.9      Sinclair Wiener Minstrels       0.2
Wheatenaville                  1.7      Country Doctor                  0.2
Whispering Jack Smith (Muster.)1.5      Singin' Sam                     0.4
Johnny Hart (Stanco)           1.0      Wheatenaville                   0.4
                                        Johnny Hart                     0.4
                                        Pat Barnes                      0.8
                                        A & P Gypsies                   1.7
                                        Evening in Paris                1.7

* combined with 10/17 due to
political interference 10/31.
```

The October–November 1932 Crossley Ratings from pioneer researcher Archibald Crossley's early surveys for Network Radio advertisers contained scant information — lacking time of broadcast and network identification. But it was only the beginning of audience research *(The Nielsen Company)*.

```
                                                    HOUR EVENING
      A U D I E N C E   T R E N D S   O F   E V E N I N G   P R O G R A M S

                  For Period Ending September 27th

                        60 Minute Programs

          The average (median) of all 60 minute programs is 22.0

  Program                                      Ratings For Report
                                                      Points
                                         #14    #13   Change   #12    #11

      Medians                            22.0   22.1          20.3   20.3

  Major Bowes' Amateur Hour   8:00R  SUN  57.9  54.1   +3.8   45.6   44.7
  (Chase and Sanborn)

  Capt. Henry's Maxwell       9:00R  THU  36.2  30.5   +5.7   28.5   32.2
  House Showboat

  Fleischmann Variety Hour    8:00R  THU  31.5  28.1   +3.4   27.5   27.9

  Whiteman's, Paul, Music    10:00R  THU  26.7  22.6   +4.1   19.8   19.8
  Hall (Kraft-Phenix
  Cheese Corp.)

  Town Hall Tonight           9:00R  WED  26.6  23.0   +3.6   18.5   18.8
  (Bristol-Myers Co.)

  Shell Chateau               9:30R  SAT  25.8  27.8   -2.0   23.1   22.2

  Hollywood Hotel             9:00C  FRI  22.0  21.9   +0.1   23.5   21.2
  (Campbell Soup)

  Palmolive Beauty            9:00B  FRI  21.4  22.3   -0.9   22.8   20.3*
  Box Theatre            11:30 rebroadcast

  National Barn Dance         9:30B  SAT  21.4  19.7   +1.7   20.8   24.4
  (Dr. Miles Laboratories)

  Lux Radio Theatre           9:00C  MON  19.6  17.3   +2.3   15.6

  The Hit Parade              8:00R  SAT  16.8  17.6   -0.8   15.7   15.3
  (Lucky Strike)

  Cities Service Concert      8:00R  FRI  16.2  15.6   +0.6   16.8   15.2

  Waring's, Fred, Pennsyl-    9:30C  TUE  15.6  18.2   -2.6   17.4   17.8
  vanians (Ford Motor Car Co.)

  Uncle Charlie's Tent Show  10:00R  SUN  Off   11.0                 9.3    9.1
  (Ivory Soap)                       the air

  *Changed Day and Network
```

September 1935 Crossley/CAB Ratings illustrate more detail and introduced program rankings when the Cooperative Analysis of Broadcasting, (CAB), was formed by advertising industry groups in 1934 to subsidize Crossley's Network Radio surveys *(The Nielsen Company)*.

With the endorsement of the Association of National Advertisers (ANA), and 30 subscribers each paying $65 a month *($880)*, Crossley's network-wide polling service began on March 1, 1930. The original surveys of radio listening trends in 33 major cities were published three times a year.

Network advertisers finally had estimated numbers of listeners to compare with newspaper and magazine circulation figures.

Crossley's reports became semi-monthly in 1932 at the dawn of Network Radio's Golden Age.

The American Association of Advertising Agencies, (AAAA) joined the ANA in 1934 to create the Cooperative Analysis of Broadcasting (CAB), to finance and market Crossley's surveys. The two sponsoring groups were later joined by the National Association of Broadcasters (NAB).

As a result, the CAB became ruled by a committee of mixed interests and Crossley was merely its employee. The situation eventually led to the CAB's demise. Crossley and the CAB had the field of radio audience research to themselves for just a few months. Then along came a young super-salesman named Hooper.

HOOP ROLLS FROM POTS AND PANS TO FAME AND FORTUNE

"The most powerful voice in radio is the emphatic rumble of a 49 year old New Englander, Claude Ernest Hooper, whose name is a household word and whose semi-monthly Hooperatings are the most eagerly awaited edicts in the frenetic universe of broadcasting."—John Keating, *Esquire*, 1948.

Claude Hooper needed a job.

The 32-year-old "Hoop" once had a promising career during the stock market's heyday as an account executive for Doremus & Co., New York's largest advertising agency specializing in financial and brokerage clients. But in 1931, nobody wanted to be on Wall Street — certainly not Claude Hooper, with a wife and two daughters to support.

Back when Hooper was earning his bachelor's degree from Amherst, the gregarious Baptist minister's son had built a reputation as a tireless cookware salesman working his way through college. But the Depression had made selling advertising campaigns to stock brokers a tougher sell than peddling pots and pans to reluctant New England housewives.

Going over his list of prospective contacts for new opportunities, Hooper came across the name of Dr. Daniel Starch, a once obscure associate professor at Harvard when Hooper was pursuing his MBA. Hooper had enjoyed Starch's courses in Experimental Psychology and Statistical Research.

Starch had since developed an acclaimed newspaper and magazine readership scoring method published in 1923's *Principals of Advertising*. He left Harvard to establish Daniel Starch & Staff, a marketing research firm that enjoyed immediate success. Starch added to his personal resume by moonlighting as Research Director for the AAAA and published a survey of the country's growing radio audience in 1928, shortly after the networks began operating.

That study wasn't lost on Hooper. He did his homework, saw opportunity and called on his former teacher. Starch remembered and liked his former student whom he recognized as a born salesman. Hoop landed a sales job with Starch and remained for two successful years — honing his knowledge of media research and expanding his contacts throughout the advertising and publishing communities.

Along the way he encountered another Amherst grad, L. Montgomery (Monty) Clark, who was employed as a freelance researcher for the ANA. Hooper recruited Clark for the Starch organization and in working together the two eventually developed plans for a business partnership.

Clark-Hooper, Inc., specialists in magazine advertising research and evaluation, was founded on a shoestring in April 1934. With their Starch credentials and personal enthusiasm the pair soon had signed contracts from a roster of women's magazines — *McCall's, Ladies' Home Journal, Woman's Home Companion*, and *Good Housekeeping*— plus the giant of general interest magazines, *The Saturday Evening Post,* which had a weekly circulation over 2.5 million.

MAD MAGAZINES

By 1934, magazine publishers were angered by network radio's claims of circulation — size of audience — based on Crossley's CAB research. They reasoned that something *had* to be wrong with it. They were right. And Clark-Hooper was about to prove it.

Sixty-five percent of American homes had a radio in 1934. As Crossley had determined, almost all of those homes also had a telephone. The use of the telephone for radio audience research purposes was a natural. That was the one area in which Clark-Hooper had no argument with Crossley. However, the partners found two major problems with the CAB reports of broadcast popularity.

First and foremost was its methodology. Crossley used a *Next Day Recall* method, asking respondents by telephone what radio programs they *had listened to the previous day.* The Recall system was rife with the possibility of memory error and was weighted in favor of the most popular and best publicized programs which came imme-

diately to mind — whether heard or not. After all, *everybody* listened to Eddie Cantor, didn't they?

Clark and Hooper conferred with research guru George Gallup who recommended the *Telephone Coincidental* method, originally developed by husband and wife researchers Percy White and Pauline Arnold. Telephone Coincidental surveys asked whoever answered the phone what was being listened to on the home's radio, if anything, *at the moment the phone rang.* Telephone Coincidental removed any need for respondents to either remember or think — just react.

The second problem identified by Clark-Hooper was Crossley's alleged failure to count the number of non-listeners found. It was charged that Crossley simply ignored many respondents who had not listened to the radio from the overall count which inflated both the sets-in-use and ratings figures.

Clark-Hooper's report, *Yardsticks on the Air,* underscored the alleged over-counting of listeners and suggested Telephone Coincidental as a remedy for the problem. Crossley agreed that Telephone Coincidental had merit, but his stubborn CAB board wasn't buying the idea.

Clark and Hooper saw opportunity and seized it. As a result, *magazine* publishers seeking an "honest count" were the first subscribers to the new, independently owned Clark-Hooper *radio* research service, launched in the fall of 1934.

FOUR QUESTIONS WITH MILLIONS OF ANSWERS

During the first week of every month an army of part time Clark-Hooper employees in 30 major cities each made over 150 random phone calls every evening from 6:00 until 10:30, Eastern Time.

The pollsters — many former telephone operators or handicapped persons looking for a bit of extra income — all asked the same four simple questions when they "nickled" a city with calls:

1. "Were you listening to the radio just now?"
2. (If so) "To what program were you listening, please?"
3. "Over what station is the program coming?"

4. "What advertiser puts on the program?"

The first *Clark-Hooper Broadcast Advertising Report* was issued in November 1934. Not surprisingly, its results indicated Network Radio listening — expressed in ratings — were noticeably less than the numbers reported by CAB. Nevertheless, Clark-Hooper's share of audience figures, matching programs versus programs, closely resembled the CAB totals, so rankings of program popularity between the two services were almost identical.

Magazine publishers who underwrote the report were delighted.

Advertisers and their agencies were enlightened.

Now it was the broadcasters' turn to get angry. It was an anger that evolved into an animosity against the Telephone Coincidental system that kept the inferior CAB alive for another dozen years.

A decade later, Arch Crossley confided to his friendly rival Hoop that it was CAB's administration by committee, its internal politics and its reluctance to respond to competitive challenge that prevented him from countering the offensive that began with the first Clark-Hooper report.

Hooper's immediate mission in 1935 was selling the new Clark-Hooper service to advertisers and their agencies as the most accurate means to compare radio's reach to the printed media. It was a tough sell against the established CAB which had the acceptance, support and administration of the advertising and broadcasting industries' most powerful members and trade associations.

As Hooper recalled in 1942, "Advertisers who were friendly to us said, 'Don't go into radio! There are people running the CAB who are politically powerful and jealous of their position of leadership. They'll force you out of business by exerting pressure!' But we were young and foolish in 1934."

Clark-Hooper's broadcast division scrambled for subscribers over the next three years, but its magazine and newspaper divisions continued to flourish and kept the company profitable. However, it became obvious that Hooper was

CO-INCIDENTAL
RADIO ADVERTISEMENT SUMMARY

CLARK-HOOPER, Inc.   January Thru June, 1937

NEW YORK   CHICAGO   SAN FRANCISCO

ALL CALLS MADE IN
BASIC NETWORK AREAS ONLY

ADVERTISER	Pepsodent			Anacin			Wrigley's Gum											
TALENT	Amos & Andy			Easy Aces			Poetic Melodies											
NETWORK AND TIME	RED 7:00-7:15			BLUE 7:00-7:15			C.B.S. 7:00-7:15			RED			BLUE			C.B.S.		
DATE	IDENTIFICATION			IDENTIFICATION			IDENTIFICATION			IDENTIFICATION			IDENTIFICATION			IDENTIFICATION		
	1 PROGRAM	2 PROGRAM	3 SPONSOR	1 PROGRAM	2 PROGRAM	3 SPONSOR	1 PROGRAM	2 PROGRAM	3 SPONSOR	1 PROGRAM	2 PROGRAM	3 SPONSOR	1 PROGRAM	2 PROGRAM	3 SPONSOR	1 PROGRAM	2 PROGRAM	3 SPONSOR
1/5	16.6	49.4	44.8	6.3	20.2	15.4	0.9	2.7	2.7									
1/19	19.9	53.3	47.6	6.5	18.7	15.4	1.7	4.7	4.7									
2/9	19.9	51.9	45.4	6.3	18.3	14.2	2.9	7.3	6.3									
2/23	18.8	61.6	58.1	5.8	20.0	17.1	0.8	2.7	2.7									
3/9	19.4	53.9	48.0	6.9	21.4	11.1	0.8	2.3	1.2									
3/23	18.2	58.8	55.3	4.1	14.0	10.0	1.8	5.7	1.4									
4/6	17.3	62.8	57.7	3.6	14.3	11.0	0.8	2.9	1.5									
4/20	15.7	51.2	45.2	8.0	29.8	21.3	1.7	6.0	3.0									
5/4	7.4	34.1	31.8	7.2	34.2	21.9	1.4	6.3	6.3									
5/18	11.5	48.0	44.0	3.7	18.8	13.0	0.9	3.6	3.6									
6/8	10.4	50.0	45.2	3.1	19.0	10.3	1.8	10.2	2.0									
6/22	7.1	34.1	34.1	4.1	22.4	11.9	0.9	4.0	4.0									
AVERAGES	15.2	50.8	46.4	5.5	20.9	14.4	1.4	4.9	3.3									
(4) SPONSOR	See Weekly Averages.			See Weekly Averages.			See Weekly Averages.											
FOOT NOTES GUEST STARS TALENT CHANGES ETC.	For Weekly Averages see page 60.			For Weekly Averages see page 60.			For Weekly Averages see page 60.											

(1) % Of Total Calls (For Checking Points Receiving Broadcast) Able To Identify Program.
(2) % Of Those Listening To Radio Able To Identify Program. (3) % Of Those Listening To Radio Able To Identify Sponsor
(4) Average % Of Those Listening To Program Able To Identify Sponsor

DAY ___Tuesday 7-7:15___   PAGE ___17___

January through June 1937 Clark-Hooper Ratings reflected the introduction of telephone coincidental surveys — asking what programs were being heard in homes at the time of the calls. The method greatly reduced the inflated totals that resulted from Crossley's recall system which depended on listeners' memories *(The Nielsen Company)*.

more interested in radio than publishing.

This was most evident in 1936 when he convinced Clark to invest company money into the development of *The Programeter*, a mechanical device attached to a radio to record when the radio was on, how long it was on, and to what stations it was tuned when it was on — the prototype of A.C. Nielsen's *Audimeter*.

The two partners stopped short of buying the finished product for $50,000 *($814,000)* — deciding to stick with Telephone Coincidental as their methodology of choice.

Their reasoning was simple. The mechanical system couldn't report if anyone was actually *listening* to the radio when it was on. Hooper would later use this competitive argument when Nielsen introduced its Audimeter in 1946, headlining one of his many memos to clients, "They Have to Be Listening to Be Sold!"

Clark and Hooper decided amicably to part ways in 1938. Hooper

took the nine-employee radio division which accounted for 20 percent of the company's income. Clark kept the larger publishing divisions and 80 percent of the partnership's revenue.

Hooper biographer Frank Nye asked Clark about the split in 1957. Clark recalled, "I always felt about Hoop just as I did after our first meeting — that he was one of the most brilliant and enjoyable characters I have ever known. He was a loyal and honest partner and our five years of intensive business association was one of the most successful partnerships I have ever known about."

HOOPER POLL VAULTS TO PROMINENCE

C.E. Hooper, Inc., funded with loans from Hoop's life insurance, opened its doors for business in May 1938. The monthly Network Radio ratings service didn't miss a beat in its transition of ownership. Several months later Chicago

marketing research giant Arthur Nielsen offered Hooper $250,000 *(4.0 Mil)*, for the business. He turned down the tempting offer but wisely kept the door open — just in case. Then came his epiphany — the turning point in C.E. Hooper's struggle for recognition and acceptance against the larger CAB. It happened when Hoop was having lunch with a prospective subscriber. He was asked to define *in one word* exactly what he was selling.

As Nye reports, Hooper thought for a moment, probably traced a forefinger over his trim moustache, then smiled broadly and said emphatically, "I'm selling *Hooperatings!*"

Claude Hooper had just given himself a brand name, a catchy brand name, and more importantly, the essence of a tangible branded product to publicize and market.

General Foods didn't sell fruit flavored gelatin — it sold *Jello*.

Kimberly-Clark didn't sell paper tissues — it sold *Kleenex*.

Hooper wasn't selling radio

audience research — he was selling *Hooperatings.*

Hoop the pitchman went to work. He courted the press with parties and distributed monthly "First Fifteen" Hooperating rankings for nighttime programs and "Top Ten" Hooperating lists of the most popular daytime shows. Newspapers reprinted the Hooperatings and Hooper's publicity machine began running on a regular schedule, reaching millions of readers every month.

For the first time radio listeners could see how their favorite programs were faring every month in the ratings race — *the Hooperatings race* — and follow them like baseball standings. It didn't take long for radio comedians to pick up on this popularity and jump on Hooper's promotional bandwagon.

Bob Hope said it best, "A Hooperating is an ulcer with a decimal point."

CAB soon found itself playing continual defense against Hooper's publicity barrage and his good-natured digs against its methodology — barbs that had many in the radio industry beginning to question the Crossley system. The reluctant networks and their local affiliates were becoming Hooper converts and subscribers.

QUANTITY TRUMPS QUALITY

A publicity bonus came along when an indignant Eddie Cantor publicly said he could disprove the validity of Hooper research. Cantor had an axe to grind with his Hooperatings which had fallen nearly 40 percent over the course of two seasons. Lacking any evidence to invalidate Hooper's methodology, the comedian accused the ratings service of favoring "lower class" programs over those of "higher quality."

Hooper took Cantor and his other critics to school with his widely circulated response.

"Please remember that ratings aren't intended to, and don't evaluate programs. They are not criticisms. They are measurements. Because a symphony gets a 4.0 rating and *Fibber McGee & Molly* gets a 28.0, we don't say that Fibber is seven times as good. We merely report that seven times as many people listened to him."

HOOPER'S WINNING WAYS

Hooper piled the competitive pressure on CAB in 1938 by extending his network radio polling hours to include daytime programming — all sponsored programs from 9:00 A.M. until 10:30 P.M. The following year his service was expanded to include the West Coast — and tripling the national sampling from 400 to 1,200 calls per half hour, totaling over two million calls annually. Hoop's subscriber list was growing steadily and approaching 100.

Hooper's monthly reports were in a continual state of refinement with increasingly detailed information while CAB fell further behind

ALPHABETIC INDEX			This Report	Last Report	Year Ago	This Report	This Report
PROGRAM - TALENT - NOTES	ADVERTISER, PRODUCT AGENCY PLACING	Network, Day New York Time Size of Network					
ABBOTT AND COSTELLO Marilyn Maxwell, Skinnay Ennis' Orchestra	R. J. REYNOLDS CO. Camel Cigarettes William Esty & Co., Inc.	NBC-Thursday 10:00-10:30 PM (152H)	14.0	15.19	17.7	31.3 (-2.6)	44.8 (+0.2)
A DAY IN THE LIFE OF DENNIS DAY Dink Trout, Paula Winslowe, Jess Kirkpatrick, Sharon Douglas, Victor Miller, Charles Dant's Orchestra	COLGATE-PALMOLIVE-PEET CO. Colgate Dental Cream Ted Bates, Inc.	NBC-Wednesday 8:00-8:30 PM (150H)	13.9	12.4	00	39.0 (+1.5)	35.7 (+2.7)
ADVENTURERS' CLUB	SHEAFFER PEN CO. Russel M. Seeds Co., Inc.	CBS-Saturday 11:30-12:00 N (157c)	6.9	5.9	00	18.8 (-1.4)	36.8 (+7.6)
ADVENTURES OF BULLDOG DRUMMOND Ned Wever, Rod Hendrickson, "The Lost Lady"	AMERICAN TRANSIT ASSOCIATION Owen & Chappell	MBS-Friday 9:30-10:00 PM (41N)	4.1	3.6	5.40	33.7 (+0.3)	12.3 (+1.6)
ADVENTURES OF ELLERY QUEEN Charlotte Keane, Santos Ortega, Ted DeCorsia, "The Adventure of the Man Who Murdered a City", Guests - Bea Wain, Andre Baruch	WHITEHALL PHARMACAL CO. Anacin, Bisodol, Hill's Cold Tablets Sullivan, Stauffer, Colwell & Bayles, Inc.	CBS-Wednesday 7:30-8:00 PM (52N) r	9.6	10.2	10.4	35.7 (+4.4)	27.0 (-5.6)
ADVENTURES OF OZZIE AND HARRIET Ozzie Nelson, Harriet Hilliard, Tommy Bernard, Bee Benadaret, Janet Waldo, John Brown, Con- ductor - Billy May	INTERNATIONAL SILVER CO. International & 1847 Rogers Bros. Silverplate Young & Rubicam, Inc.	CBS-Sunday 6:00-6:30 PM (153H) r	8.2	12.0	8.9	22.7 (-8.7)	36.1 (-2.0)
ADVENTURES OF SAM SPADE Howard Duff, Lurene Tuttle, Jerry Hausner, Lud Gluskin's Orchestra, "House Dick"	WILDROOT CO., INC. Batten, Barton, Durstine & Osborn, Inc.	CBS-Sunday 8:00-8:30 PM (157H) r	11.0	9.7	00	37.5 (-10.8)	29.3 (+9.2)
ADVENTURES OF THE FALCON James Meighan, Organist - Jesse Crawford, Joan Banks, "Death Takes the Stage"	AMERICAN SAFETY RAZOR CORP. Gem Razor Blades Federal Advertising Agency, Inc.	MBS-Tuesday 8:30-9:00 PM (323N) r	10.3	8.9	6.5	41.4 (+4.8)	24.9 (+0.7)

Based on Week Beginning

MONDAY, MARCH 31, 1947

NETWORK
PROGRAM HOOPERATINGS
DAYTIME AND EVENING AUDIENCES

Hooperatings

Average Calls Per Hour

IN EXCESS OF:
Evening = 2,760
M-F Daytime = 13,800

Program Sets In Use *

Share of Audience * *

For Explanation of Symbols See Page III

Page 1

March 1947 Hooperatings published at the height of C.E. Hooper's influence provided detailed information for each program, including the number of network affiliates that carried it *(The Nielsen Company).*

in its feeble, committee-directed reactions. CAB modified its methodology in 1942 to *Same Day Recall*.

Hooper countered by doubling his evening Telephone Coincidental reports, polling both the first and third weeks of every month.

Hooper's operators were now making over four and a half million calls per year.

The race was really over later in 1942 when the radio networks began to withdraw their support from CAB which amounted to 40 per-

cent of its annual $350,000 *(4.9 Mil)*, in revenues.

Hooper continued to apply the marketing pressure, drumming in his "brand" name whenever the occasion arose. For example, the following memo was enclosed in the

---

TABLES 4, 5, 6 & 7

PROGRAM RATINGS

☐ AVERAGE FOR REPORT WEEK ☒ FOR EACH BROADCAST

Arthur Godfrey's Talent Scouts
CBS – MON. – O. 8:30–9:00 PM(2)
R. 11:30–12:00 M(2)
THOMAS J. LIPTON, INC.

TABLE	1948 MONTH / Report Week Ending		JANUARY 10th	24th	FEBRUARY 7th	21st	MARCH 13th	27th	APRIL 10th	24th	MAY 8th	22nd	JUNE (3) 12th	26th
4. TOTAL AUDIENCE	Monday		24.1	26.6	25.7	26.6	28.0	26.1	24.5	25.1	21.4	21.8	17.7	16.5
5. SHARE OF AUDIENCE	Monday		(1) 35.7	(1) 39.2	(1) 39.8	(1) 38.0	(1) 42.0	(1) 41.6	(1) 44.5	(1) 42.9	(1) 41.9	(1) 42.0	(1) 37.7	(1) 37.7
6. HOLDING POWER	Monday		78.5	83.6	84.4	80.3	82.3	78.8	81.4	82.8	81.4	80.0	77.1	74.3
7. AVERAGE AUDIENCE	Monday		18.9	22.2	21.7	21.4	23.0	20.6	19.9	20.8	17.4	17.4	13.6	12.3
	Coverage Factor		91.6	91.5	91.6	91.6	91.6	91.6	91.6	91.6	91.6	91.6	91.6	91.6
	TOTAL AUDIENCE—Full Coverage Basis		26.3	29.1	28.1	29.0	30.6	28.5	26.7	27.4	23.4	23.8	19.3	18.0
	Average Audience—Full Coverage Basis		20.6	24.3	23.7	23.4	25.1	22.5	21.7	22.7	19.0	19.0	14.8	13.4

TABLE 8
PROGRAM COST ANALYSIS
(AVERAGE PER BROADCAST DURING MONTH)

	JANUARY	FEBRUARY	MARCH	APRIL	MAY	JUNE
1. GROSS TIME COST—U.S.A. ...$000	11.1	11.1	11.2	11.2	11.2	12.3
2. NET TIME COST—U.S.A. ...$000	8.3	8.4	8.4	8.4	8.4	9.2
3. TALENT COST—U.S.A. ...$000	9.2	9.2	9.2	9.2	9.2	9.2
4. TOTAL COST—U.S.A. Lines 2 + 3 ...$000	17.5	17.6	17.6	17.6	17.6	18.4
5. TOTAL COST—N.R.I. Area ...$000	10.5	10.5	10.6	10.5	10.5	11.1
6. TOTAL COST—N.R.I. Homes, Line 5 ÷ 18,600 ...$	.565	.566	.568	.567	.566	.598
7. TOTAL COST—N.R.I. Homes, Contiguous Rate ...$	.516	.517	.518	.518	.517	.544
8. N.R.I. HOMES REACHED ...	288	297	308	282	246	194
9. N.R.I. HOMES PER DOLLAR ...	510	525	542	497	435	324
10. N.R.I. HOMES PER DOLLAR—Contiguous Rate ...	558	574	595	544	476	357

(1) Based on original broadcast only.
(2) Prior to Jun. 21, 8:30–8:55 PM; repeat time 11:30–11:55 PM.
(3) Last broadcast Jun. 28.

Tables 4, 5, 6, 7 & 8
Jan.–Jun.

BOR

199–1

January through June, 1948, Nielsen Audience Index summarized returns from A.C. Nielsen's mechanically assisted survey methods, forerunner of today's computerized audience polling. One or two pages of detailed information were devoted to every program, including program costs to determine cost-efficiencies of advertising expenditures *(The Nielsen Company)*.

Hooperating books following a New York elevator operators' strike on September 25, 1945: *"Yes, We Were Struck!— Your advance Hooperatings and this complete report go to you on schedule this week, as usual, because a force of loyal Hooperettes and Hooperites walked 13 flights of stairs at least twice daily to serve you."*

The Cooperative Analysis of Broadcasting finally threw in the towel on July 15, 1946, and negotiated to sell its list of 102 remaining subscribers to Hooper.

The ratings battle was over.

Time reported CAB's collapse in its issue of September 30, 1946: *"Radio's most famous linesman passed into limbo last week. The Cooperative Analysis of Broadcasting, Inc, sponsor of the 'Crossley rating' system, closed its Manhattan office and went out of business. Cause of death: Radiomen decided last summer that the industry-financed CAB was duplicating the independent telephone poll of C.E. Hooper."*

But Hooper's adversaries weren't finished. Shortly after CAB folded, the NAB established the Broadcast Measurement Bureau (BMB) and poured $1,250,000 *(14.5 Mil)*, into a survey mailed to a million households. The experiment was an expensive flop.

Hooper added insult to injury when he told NAB members footing the bill that his firm could have conducted the identical field research for half the cost.

More and more broadcasters, once resentful of Hooper intruding into their business and deflating their cushy CAB ratings, signed local station contracts with the enthusiastic little man whose name had become synonymous with ratings. By 1947, Hooper had over 600 subscribers, each paying from $125 to $1,300 *($1,270–$13,200)*, per month.

The cash flow allowed Hooper to expand into an early Hooperatings service for television in 1948.

KNOW WHEN TO FOLD 'EM

All of this was being closely observed by A.C. Nielsen.

Arthur Nielsen had introduced his company's original service, tracking grocery and drug store purchases, in 1934. It was a phenomenal success. Eight years later Nielsen

expanded into radio audience research with the *Audimeter* system that Clark and Hooper had turned down in 1936.

With television a growing phenomenon in 1948, Nielsen's firm was eager to expand its broadcast ratings business. The fastest way to expand was take over the competition. Nielsen set it sights — again — on C.E. Hooper.

Hooper, meanwhile, was constantly traveling, lecturing and selling. A welcome guest in most any network, station or ad agency executive's office, Hooper picked up the insights of insiders about the future of the broadcast industry. It was knowledge that he would employ when takeover talks with Nielsen got serious.

First reports of Nielsen's attempt to buy Hooper's radio and television rating services surfaced in December 1949. Hooper had seen the handwriting on the wall: Network television programs would soon dwarf the popularity of Network Radio shows. Network Radio would become a supplemental service — primarily of news and special events — to local stations that were expanding in both number and popularity. Local radio was where the action — and clients — would be in the 1950s and beyond.

Hooper sold his national radio and television network rating services to Nielsen in March 1950 for an estimated $650,000 *(6.1 Mil)*— a sum that was up 160 percent from Nielsen's 1938 offer. But Hoop shrewdly kept his company's *local market* radio services where Hooperatings would remain the ratings benchmark for another 20 years.

Claude Hooper had a zest for living as well as working. He was an avid outdoorsman who loved fishing and hunting wherever his business travels would take him. On December 15, 1954, he was hunting from a propeller driven airboat in Utah with a friend from Salt Lake City's KSL Radio. The boat hung up on a sandbar and Hooper jumped out to free it. He fell into the boat's unshielded whirling propeller and was killed instantly.

He was joined in death just a few years later by the kind of Network Radio that made him famous.

THE TOP TEN HIGHEST HOOPERS

The highest rated Network Radio programs during C.E. Hooper's dozen years of polling all had a Hooperating of 50.0 or higher. None were regularly scheduled programs. Only two contained commercials. Eight featured only one voice — seven the were the distinctive addresses of President Franklin Roosevelt and one was a short message delivered in the flat Missouri tones of President Harry Truman. They were **FDR's War Message to the American People** (Dec 9, 1941); rating 79.0; **FDR "Three High Purposes" Speech** (Feb 23, 1942); rating 78.1; **FDR Election Day Address** (Nov 7, 1938); rating 74.8; **FDR Declaration of National Emergency** (May 27, 1941); rating 69.8; **Joe Louis–Billy Conn Heavyweight Championship Fight** (June 19, 1946); rating 67.2; **FDR "Freedom of the Seas" Speech** (Sep 11, 1941); rating 67.0; **Joe Louis-Max Schmeling Heavyweight Championship Fight** (June 22, 1938); rating 63.6; **FDR "Arsenal of Democracy" Speech** (Dec 29, 1940); rating 59.0; **FDR "Stab in the Back" Speech** (June 10, 1940); rating 57.0; **Pres. Truman First Address to U.S. Armed Forces** (Apr 17, 1945); rating 53.6.

President Roosevelt took pride in his Hooperatings. A chart illustrating them — provided by the promotionally minded Hooper — was posted in a White House office. After FDR's death the chart was put on display in the Roosevelt home and museum at Hyde Park, N.Y.

THE REAL WORLD OF RATINGS

In commercial broadcasting, any Network Radio program that earned a rating of 30 or higher was a cause for celebration for its sponsor, agency and network. Only a dozen series were able to maintain this lofty average or higher over a full season: Eddie Cantor (1933–34, 1934–35); *Maxwell House Showboat* (1933–34, 1934–35); Rudy Vallee (1933–34, 1934–35); Ed Wynn (1933–34), *Major Bowes' Original Amateur Hour* (1934–35, 1935–36), Jack Benny (1934–35, 1939–40, 1940–41); Joe Penner (1934–35); Edgar Bergen and

Charlie McCarthy (1937–38, 1938–39, 1939–40, 1942–43); Bob Hope (1941–42, 1942–43, 1943–44); *Fibber McGee & Molly* (1941–42, 1942–43, 1943–44); Red Skelton (1942–43), and *Lux Radio Theater* (1947–48).

A rating above 20 reflected a highly successful program. As many as 15 series, (1933–34 and 1947–48), or as few as two, (1949–50), scored rating averages in the twenties in season-long audience popularity.

None scored a 20 or higher after 1950 when Network Radio's Golden Age was in its decline.

Ratings in the teens usually signaled advertising money very well spent provided the program's budget was within reason for the sponsor.

Most programs — over half of the networks' prime time commercial fare every year — were buried in single digits. Nevertheless, every rating point represented a huge number of listeners — from as few as 184,500 homes (1932–33) to as many as 428,000 homes (1952–53) — all tuned to the same program.

Every season's Top 50 ranking list in this book includes the number of radio households represented by a single rating point during that year. Multiplying the number of homes represented by one point by the rating earned by a program equals the estimated number of homes reached by that program.

THIS GAME'S GROUND RULES

Despite the evolution in rating methodologies from Crossley's Recall system to Hooper's Telephone Coincidental surveys and Nielsen's mechanical devices, four general conditions prevailed throughout Network Radio's Golden Age which create the standards for this account of its history:

1. Network Radio's Golden Age was 1932–33 through 1952–53.

Citing the beginning of Network Radio's greatest popularity is easy. Most of the biggest names from the stage and movies debuted with network series in the fall of 1932. Eddie Cantor, Jack Benny, Fred Allen, Al Jolson and Burns and Allen all lent their star power to radio for handsome fees paid by their sponsors.

The end of the Golden Age is arguable. But by the spring of 1953, most of radio's stars had deserted their radio studios for television — and so did their sponsors.

In 1951, network television advertising revenues had caught up to the radio networks. By 1952, Network TV surpassed Network Radio by almost $100 Million in billings *(853.6 Mil).* The radio networks slashed their evening rates in the fall of 1952 when television had penetrated over half of America's homes.

Network Radio's Golden Age was definitely over in 1953 when the chains began turning the former prime evening hours back to their affiliates for local programming and network revenues dropped beyond the point of competing with television for top dollars.

2. Network Seasons are defined in ten month periods: September through June.

From its earliest days, network radio's biggest attractions took a six to 13 week summer vacation — justified by steep audience declines in July and August. Broadcast seasons have been traditionally defined as the ten months that exclude these two summer months. Accordingly, this study omits July and August ratings.

3. Radio's most popular programs were broadcast from 6:00 to 11:00 P.M., Eastern Time.

Radio listening during the evening hours of the Golden Age was a group experience.

After work, school and household obligations, families relaxed around their homes' living room radios to hear their favorite programs. To estimate the number of listeners to any particular program during this era, the number of homes reached can be conservatively multiplied by 2.5 listeners per home.

Although network radio's daytime programming had millions of listeners and was highly profitable, its ratings paled in comparison to evening programs. For example, the Top 50 Daytime programs of 1946 averaged a 4.9 Hooperating while the Top 50 Evening programs averaged 15.2.

The number one daytime program of that year, *When a Girl Marries,* registered a 7.2 average rating which would have ranked it in a lowly 110th place among evening prime time programs.

4. With rare exception, rating services only tracked sponsored programs.

Unsponsored, or *sustaining,* programs were ignored by the rating books. Networks occasionally commissioned ratings for their sustaining programs in an effort to prove a sizable audience attractive to prospective sponsors. Those findings were withheld from published reports.

HANDICAPPING THE RATINGS RACE

What were the factors that determined a program's success or failure in the ratings?

In his many speeches and memos, Claude Hooper boiled them down to seven:

1. Time of Day of Broadcast. More audience is available and Sets-in-Use is highest when most families settled in for the evening after 8:00 P.M.

2. Day of Week of Broadcast. Sets-in-Use is higher on Sunday through Thursday evenings than on the traditional "nights out" of Friday and Saturday.

3. Season of broadcast. Sets-in-Use is greatest during the colder weather of late fall, winter and early spring months.

4. Program Content.

5. Program Talent.

6. Program Competition.

7. Program Lead-In & Lead-Out. The characteristics and popularity of programs immediately preceding and following on the same and competing stations affect listener restlessness.

Given the perspective of history, one more element can be added to Hooper's list:

8. Consistency of Scheduling. Network Radio's most popular programs could always be heard at the same time on the same night year after year.

Those are the constant rules of the ratings race that have always prevailed — from the days of three wired radio networks into today's world of satellite delivered radio, television and cable programming.

It all began with the first full season of Crossley's semi-monthly ratings in September 1932.

Here's how the race unfolded through Network Radio's Golden Age.

5

The 1932–33 Network Season

Announcer: If you're tired of eating the same old thing day after day, maybe you should try something different ... something delicious ... something with a marvelous flavor that just knocks the socks off any other cereal you've ever tried. Why don't you ask your mother to have a big bowl of crackly, crunchy, golden brown <u>Wheaties Flakes</u> tomorrow morning? Ask your mother to let you have a cereal you'll really like the taste of! Ask her for the big, husky cereal for wide-awake fellows and girls who not only start things, but see them through. Your mother will be mighty glad to let you have Wheaties, too, for most any fellow or girl's mother probably knows that authorities now recognize that <u>Wheaties</u> supplies the very same amount of Heat Producing Units you need to keep your body warm these cold winter days as a cooked cereal does. She'll be glad to let you have all the Wheaties you want to eat this winter <u>if you ask her for them</u>. Remind your mother to always look for the famous <u>Seal of Acceptance</u> of the Committee On Foods by <u>The American Medical Association</u> whenever she buys Wheaties. It tells her that Wheaties are a <u>pure product</u>, <u>honestly advertised</u>. Ask her to get <u>Wheaties</u> the next time she goes to the store. You'll say it's <u>swell</u>!

WHAT DEPRESSION?

There was no depression for network radio in 1932. Sixty percent of America's homes were equipped with radios by the 1932–33 season, all hungry for the free entertainment that the networks offered them — and offered to sponsors at an average $11,000 per prime time hour *($181,650)*.

In the three years since *Variety's* legendary 1929 headline, *Wall Street Lays an Egg,* network revenues had grown a whopping 41 percent — to over 39 million dollars *(644.0 Mil)*. The three chains' combined total revenue had passed the 100 million dollar mark in just four short years. NBC posted its two networks' income at close to 30 million dollars *(495.4 Mil)* in 1932.

Further, NBC's parent company, RCA, was a major player in a manufacturing industry that sold two and a half million radios and 50 million radio tubes in 1932, generating over $72 Million *(1.19 Bil.)* in sales.

In the next six Depression years another 38 million radios and half a *billion* tubes returned gross revenues totaling $766 Million *(12.29 Bil.)*. It's no surprise that David Sarnoff could smile confidently while approving architects' plans for NBC's new eleven story showcase headquarters at Rockefeller

Center. The complex and its neighboring theater would be called *Radio City* in recognition of its high profile occupant.

BIG NEWS DEBUTS

The packaged happiness of variety and comedy shows that the networks fed to Depression weary listeners took the eleven top positions among the season's most popular programs. Star power from the stage and movies came to radio with full force early in the 1932–33 season. The networks gradually replaced patchwork schedules of low cost recitals by studio musicians and singers with appealing variety and drama provided by sponsors eager to sell their goods to the greatest number of listeners.

Fred Allen, Al Jolson and the Marx Brothers made their network series debuts in the fall of 1932. They joined Eddie Cantor, Jack Benny, Jack Pearl, Ed Wynn and George Burns & Gracie Allen, who had made earlier and briefer appearances before committing to full season series in 1932–33. The performers, networks, sponsors and agencies all sought the winning formats to achieve the greatest popularity in the new medium that soaked up material like a sponge. It would become a never-ending search.

The stars were joined during the season by the first nationwide network broadcasts of the long running *Carnation Contented Hour, The Fred Waring Show, Vic & Sade* and *One Man's Family. Variety* released a mid-season poll of listeners' twelve favorite programs. Not surprisingly, Eddie Cantor's Sunday night variety show finished first, followed in order by Ed Wynn, Jack Pearl, *Amos & Andy,* Burns and Allen with Guy Lombardo's Orchestra, Jack

1932–33 Season Scoreboard Mid-Season Totals, December 1932			
		Compared to Year Earlier	
Total U.S. Radio Homes	18.45 Mil	+1.75 Mil	+10.4%
Total U.S. Auto Radios	0.25 Mil	NA	NA
Total U.S. AM Radio Stations	604	(8)	(1.3%)
Total U.S. Radio Network Affiliates	170	+11	+6.9%
1932 Radio Revenues	61.9 Mil	+5.9 Mil	+10.5%
1932 Network Revenues	39.1 Mil	+1.4 Mil	+3.7%
Network Share	63.0%		(4.0%)

Benny, Rudy Vallee, Ben Bernie, Chesterfield Cigarettes' *Music That Satisfies*, Kate Smith, Al Jolson and *Myrt & Marge*.

The personality who would generate the greatest ratings of network radio's early years took to the air on March 12, 1933. Franklin Delano Roosevelt delivered his first *Fireside Chat* on all three networks. The President's series of informally delivered addresses eventually numbered 30, spanning eleven Depression and wartime years. FDR's early speeches didn't appear in the Crossley rating books, but with all the networks preempting regular programming for the addresses, he had little competition for audience.

KIDNAPPING CAPTURES LISTENERS

When the Lindbergh baby was kidnapped on March 1, 1932, the air was saturated with bulletins and updates. By September, the search for the culprit had received heavy radio coverage for over six months and it would continue until Bruno Hauptmann was arrested a year later in September 1934. The hunt for Hauptmann, his subsequent trial and the vigil on the night of his execution all became a string of continuous *radio* events.

Newspapers found themselves repeatedly and increasingly scooped by radio. Their frustration and resentment was heated and would boil over the following year.

THE MONTHLIES

NBC aired the Number One show in all ten months of the 1932–33 season. Sunday was home to radio's most popular program — Eddie Cantor's *Chase & Sanborn Hour* was the top rated show for each of the six months it was broadcast, November through April. *Texaco Fire Chief* Ed Wynn took the top spot in September, October and June when Cantor was on hiatus. Jack Pearl peaked at Number One in May — his first and only monthly win.

Despite Cantor's overwhelming dominance of the Crossley ratings, the remainder of Sunday's Top Ten programs lagged far behind — including those headlined by future

stars Jack Benny, Fred Allen and Walter Winchell. As a result, Crossley reported that Sunday's Top Ten average rating was the season's second *lowest* night in audience popularity.

1932–33 Sunday Night Top Ten Programs
NBC 5, Blue 3, CBS 2
Average 15.0

Eddie Cantor Show	NBC	8:00	55.7
Sunday at Seth Parker's	NBC	10:45	17.7
Jack Benny's Canada Dry Show	CBS	8:00	13.5
Fred Allen's Linit Bath Club Revue	CBS	9:00	11.9
Walter Winchell's Jergens Journal	Blue	9:30	11.6
American Album of Familiar Music	NBC	9:30	10.0
David Lawrence News Commentary	NBC	10:15	8.1
Manhattan Merry Go Round	NBC	9:00	8.0
Silken Strings	Blue	8:00	6.9
The Old Singing Master	Blue	9:15	6.7

STANDARD BRANDS SUNDAY

Standard Brands was formed in 1929 with the merger of Fleischmann Yeast Co., Royal Baking Powder Co. and Chase & Sanborn Coffee Co. Chase & Sanborn promptly became an NBC Sunday night sponsor stayed there through most of the Golden Age. Beginning in 1932–33, its programs in the 8:00 Sunday timeslot were known as *The Chase & Sanborn Hour* and finished among the annual Top Ten for 18 of the next 19 seasons.

The coffee company's first NBC offering in 1929 was modest considering what was to come. *The Chase & Sanborn Orchestra* led by violinist David Rubinoff bounced around several Sunday night timeslots, most often following *Major Bowes' Capitol Theater Family* variety show at 8:30. Sometimes known as *The Chase & Sanborn Choral Orchestra*, the subdued musical variety program drifted along until midway in the 1930–31 season.

By that time, Rudy Vallee had made Fleischmann Yeast a household essential with his Thursday night variety hour. Standard Brands clearly wanted a recognizable star to sell its coffee just like Vallee was selling its yeast.

Maurice Chevalier was signed for 26 weeks beginning on February 8, 1931, for a reported $5,000 (*$74,400*) per week. This was enormous money in the depth of the Depression but illustrates Standard Bands' determined belief in the selling power of popular stage and movie entertainers on radio.

Chevalier took his money and returned to France at the end of June. Again it was up to Rubinoff to fill the Sunday night half hour while Standard Brands sought another star of Chevalier's magnitude who could carry the show for a full hour.

On September 13, 1931, the new *Chase & Sanborn Hour* debuted with its new star, Eddie Cantor.

Cantor, with Rubinoff as his orchestra leader and foil, established the show as a solid hit — but for only five months. Cantor left the show in February 1932 to fulfill personal appearance commitments and film *The Kid from Spain* for Sam Goldwyn.

Rubinoff and a string of guest hosts — George Jessel, singer Harry Richman and comedian Georgie Price — carried the Chase & Sanborn show the next eight months. They were all marking time until Cantor's return on October 30, 1932, as Network Radio's Golden Age was beginning.

The comedian's homecoming was greeted with a 49.4 Crossley rating. His February and March hovered at a stratospheric 60.0. He gave Standard Brands the first of its three top rated Sunday night series of the 1930s. And compared to Chevalier's salary, Cantor's $2,500 a week (*$41,200*) was a bargain.

Proof of Cantor's popularity is found in the show's rating when he left it in May and veteran comic Bert Lahr took over. From Cantor's April average rating of 58.8 the program plummeted to a 28.3 — a 52 percent loss of audience.

FOLLOW THE BOUNCING BENNY

Jack Benny became the first and only major star to have three separate 13-week series of rated shows on all three networks in a single season. His *Canada Dry Show* opened in September on Blue with two shows a week — Monday and Wednesday at 9:30.

The soft drink maker moved the show to CBS in November, again twice per week but at *different* times. Benny's Sunday night show aired at 8:00, opposite Eddie Cantor, and his Thursday show at 10:00, against Jack Pearl. Both Cantor and Pearl were enjoying their seasons of peak popularity on NBC.

Benny's ratings fell 20 percent in the confusing network, day and time switch against two of the season's top three shows. Canada Dry cancelled in January.

The comedian was off the air in February, then debuted a new show for Chevrolet in March — this time just once a week — on NBC's Friday schedule at 10:00. It was a prime timeslot, just vacated by Al Jolson.

Benny's ratings climbed steadily to a 22.2 in May, up 65 percent from his showing on CBS. It was just the beginning to his rise to become Network Radio's most popular comedian.

THE COWBOY AND THE COLUMNIST

One major star didn't qualify for the year's Top 50 programs, despite his ratings in the thirties. Homespun humorist Will Rogers' appearances on *Gulf Headliners* was limited to the last eight weeks of the season. Nevertheless, Rogers boosted Blue's half hour at 9:00 on Sunday from single digits to a May–June rating average of 34.1. It was the best lead-in that Walter Winchell would ever enjoy.

With a year of network exposure on both CBS and NBC behind him, Winchell brought his 15 minutes of rapid fire gossip, news and sound effects to Blue's Sunday night schedule where he would remain until 1955, finishing twelve seasons in the annual Top Ten.

LORD WORKS IN MANY WAYS

Phillips H Lord had created Sunday's biggest surprise three years earlier with his down-home hymn sing, *Sunday at Seth Parker's*. The inspirational half hour beginning at the unusually late time of 10:45, starred the 30 year old Lord as its folksy, and much older, New England host. The show has the distinction of being the only sustaining (unsponsored) series ever to appear in the rating books.

Lord also has the distinction of becoming one of network radio's most successful producers with later hits *We the People, Gangbusters* and *Counterspy.* He also created the short lived multiple run drama *Country Doctor* on Blue's 1932–33 schedule and later claimed naming rights to *Mr. District Attorney.*

Sunday at Seth Parker's was the launching pad for the radio talents of stage actor Bennett Kilpack. Kilpack also had a supporting role — along with 24-year-old Bette Davis — in *Way Back Home,* a 1932 film based on the *Seth Parker* radio series. Five years later Kilpack would originate his long running role as *Mr. Keen, Tracer of Lost Persons* for prolific producers Frank and Anne Hummert.

HUMMERTS' HUM ALONGS

The newlywed Hummerts had music on their minds in the 1932–33 season. In April they moved their *Manhattan Merry Go Round* from Blue's Sunday afternoon schedule to Sunday night on NBC and paired it with their one year old *American Album of Familiar Music* in the nine o'clock spot.

The Hummerts' unabashedly square music formats — "... *With lyrics sung so clearly you can understand every word...*"—may have resulted in the *Tweedle Dee & Tweedle Dum* of music shows, but both drew solid ratings for reasonable budgets provided by Sterling Drug.

Moreover, *Merry Go Round* was the first show to feature the popular music hits of the day which were claimed to be chosen by surveys of retail sales and requests — predating the pop music surveys of *Your Hit Parade* by two seasons and Top 40 radio by over 20 years.

The two studio shows were in Sunday's Top Ten for three consecutive seasons. *Merry Go Round* went around for Sterling's Dr. Lyons Tooth Powder for 17 years, finishing its run with eleven seasons in Sunday's Top Ten. *American Album,* with ten Sunday Top Ten finishes, sold Bayer Aspirin for 19 years.

1932–33 Monday Night Top Ten Programs
Blue 4, NBC 4, CBS 2
Average: 18.9

Amos & Andy*	Blue	7:00	28.6
Sinclair Wiener Minstrels	Blue	9:00	21.8
Voice of Firestone	NBC	8:30	21.8
Myrt & Marge*	CBS	7:00	21.7
Marx Brothers' Flywheel, Shyster & Flywheel	Blue	7:30	18.9
The Goldbergs*	NBC	7:45	18.1
Paul Whiteman Buick Show	NBC	9:30	15.2
Carnation Contented Hour	NBC	10:00	14.7
Fu Manchu Mysteries	CBS	8:30	14.5
Lowell Thomas News*	Blue	6:45	13.7

*Monday–Friday Strip Programs

Sans Strips...

A&P Gypsies	NBC	9:00	11.7
Mysteries in Paris	CBS	9:30	10.8
The Country Doctor	Blue	8:45	10.6
Mills Brothers Show	CBS	9:15	8.5

THE GOLDEN AGE OF STRIP SHOWS

A third of 1932–33's prime time network programming consisted of *Multiple Run* shows, broadcast at the same time on two to six nights a week. *Amos & Andy* and *The Goldbergs* were each broadcast from Monday through Saturday until November 1932, when they were cut back to the five nights a week.

Multiple Run programs broadcast at the same time across consecutive days of the week were identified on programmers' scheduling boards in strips. *Strip Shows* were generally low-budget, 15-minute studio productions without an audience. Strips were always a staple of the networks' daytime programming and for a few of the early years — led by *Amos & Andy, Myrt & Marge* and newscaster Lowell Thomas — they were also a force in the nightly Top Ten ratings.

This was particularly true of Monday. *Amos & Andy* was the night's highest rated program for three consecutive seasons.

Over the course of an average week in the 1932–33 season, Freeman Gosden and Charles Correll's nightly serial racked up an incredible total of 142 rating points. Most of the serial's audience were repeat listeners from night to night. Regardless, their cumulative audience of over 26 million homes and 50+ million listeners per week was a record that no other network program ever came close to matching.

An all-time high six Strip Shows finished among the 1932–33 season's Top 50 programs.

(Note: During the Strips' four years of peak popularity, Crossley reported each night's Multiple Run program ratings individually. Strips are identified in these nightly Top Ten rankings with an asterisk [*]. Below each night's list are the programs pushed out of the Top Ten by Strip Shows.)

MONDAY'S MUSIC MIX

By the 1932–33 season, *The Voice of Firestone* had become a four year classical music fixture on NBC's Monday night schedule. It would stay there for another 21 years. Its headline vocalists included Gladys Swarthout, Richard Crooks and Lawrence Tibbett — all radio favorites. *Voice* would rank among Monday's Top Ten programs ten times.

Swarthout was also heard frequently on Carnation Milk's *Contented Hour* which began its 17 year Monday night run on NBC in a decidedly more classical format than it would adopt in the mid-forties. The program's name was a misnomer — the "hour" was never longer than 30 minutes.

Harry Horlick's eclectic *The A&P Gypsies* might also occasionally toss in a classical number suitable to one of its weekly guest vocalists — often including a very busy Gladys Swarthout. *A&P Gypsies* was one of NBC's first network shows in November 1926, and made history in 1932 for its sponsor, The Great Atlantic & Pacific Tea Company. It became the first nighttime network program on which direct price and item advertising was broadcast.

At the other end of the music spectrum, Blue tied for the night's top rated honors with *The Sinclair "Wiener" Minstrels*. The traditional all-male minstrel show, sponsored by Sinclair Oil, was in the first of its five year run, finishing four times in Monday's Top Ten. The

program's sausage-like identification was the nickname of the station from which it was broadcast, Chicago's WENR.

HARPO ISN'T HEARD OR SEEN

Two of the five Marx Brothers, Julius and Leonard — Groucho and Chico — came to Blue for $6,500 a week *($107,300)* in November with *Flywheel, Shyster & Beagle*—a sitcom about a fast-talking, inept lawyer. It was promptly renamed *Flywheel, Shyster and Flywheel* when an actual attorney named Beagle threatened to sue. The show was cancelled in May.

1932–33 Tuesday Night Top Ten Programs
NBC 5, Blue 3, CBS 2
Average: 22.3

Ed Wynn's Texaco Fire Chief Show	NBC	9:30	40.5
Walter O'Keefe's Lucky Strike Hour	NBC	10:00	33.8
Amos & Andy*	Blue	7:00	28.5
Ben Bernie Show	NBC	9:00	25.6
Myrt & Marge*	CBS	7:00	20.4
The Goldbergs*	NBC	7:45	16.2
Eno Crime Club	Blue	8:00	15.2
Blackstone Plantation	NBC	8:00	15.1
Lowell Thomas News*	Blue	6:45	14.5
Kate Smith's LaPalina Show	CBS	8:00	12.9
Sans Strips....			
The Magic Voice	CBS	8:15	12.5
Easy Aces	CBS	10:15	9.1
Solly Ward Show	CBS	10:00	9.0
Edgar A Guest's Musical Memories	Blue	9:00	6.1

NBC'S WYNN WIN SITUATION

Ed Wynn's clownish persona, *The Perfect Fool*, was given a red helmet, $5,000 *($82,600)* a week and became the *Texaco Fire Chief*— so named for the company's brand of gasoline. Wynn won Tuesday night for the first of two consecutive seasons and began a string of three finishes in the Annual Top Ten.

Wynn's buffoonery, with announcing legend Graham McNamee as his straight man, wore thin after those three seasons. He subsequently moved to CBS and Blue with different formats but his ratings never achieved the lofty 40s of his *Fire Chief* days.

Wynn's life was filled with ups and downs — including a costly, failed attempt at forming his own radio network — the Amalgamated Broadcasting System — in 1933. *Oddly enough, he was starring on NBC at the time.* Twenty-five years later he would close his career as an award winning television and film actor who claimed that he always felt out of place doing radio.

Nevertheless, Wynn can be cited as the first big name comedian to appear on radio. He starred in an adaptation of his Broadway comedy, *The Perfect Fool*, from WJZ's Newark studio on February 19, 1922. The early broadcast is also cited as the first major program to involve a studio audience.

In 1932, Wynn was given a solid Tuesday night lead-in by former vaudevillian Ben Bernie, who had been in radio since 1930 with his popular dance band. The wisecracking, cigar smoking, fiddle playing Bernie would finish six seasons in the annual Top 50.

THE LADY WEIGHS IN

Six of Tuesday's Top Ten were multiple run programs, indicative that network radio had yet to develop its prime time into blocks of hour and half hour weekly programs. Among the multiple runs was Kate Smith's Tuesday through Thursday songfest for CBS boss Bill Paley's LaPalina Cigars. The friendly, 212 pound contralto was riding on the popularity of her Paramount movie, *Hello, Everybody!*, one of many films produced during the Golden Age to capitalize on the public's desire to see and hear their favorite radio stars.

Time magazine began its review of her movie reflecting the print media's disdain of radio, "Produced on the clear assumption that radio listeners are even less intelligent than cinemaddicts.... *Hello, Everybody!* is produced for a moron public."

Smith had the last laugh. The movie made money and her three times a week show finished among the season's Top 50 in 37th place — her launching pad to becoming a Network Radio legend in later years.

1932–33 Wednesday Night
Top Ten Programs
Blue 4, CBS 4, NBC 2
Average: 19.5

Amos & Andy*	Blue	7:00	29.3
Burns & Allen with Guy Lombardo Orchestra	CBS	9:30	26.5
Myrt & Marge*	CBS	7:00	24.1
Adventures of Sherlock Holmes/Richard Gordon	Blue	9:00	21.0
Bing Crosby Music That Satisfies	CBS	9:00	18.5
The Goldbergs*	NBC	7:45	17.6
Fred Waring Old Gold Program	CBS	9:00	16.0
Eno Crime Club	Blue	8:00	15.2
Fanny Brice & George Olsen Orchestra	NBC	8:00	13.6
Lowell Thomas News*	Blue	6:45	13.4
Sans Strips...			
Kate Smith's LaPalina Show	CBS	8:00	12.9
The Shadow	NBC	8:30	11.8
The Country Doctor	Blue	8:45	10.6
Carveth Wells' Exploring America	NBC	10:30	9.8

OH, BROTHER, WHERE ART THOU?

George Burns and Gracie Allen entered their first full Network Radio season with *second billing* to Guy Lombardo's "Sweetest Music This Side of Heaven" orchestra on CBS sponsored by General Cigar's Robert Burns Panatellas.

The pairing of popular dance bands and comedians was common. Fanny Brice was teamed with George Olson's orchestra on the same evening. But few were as successful as the General Cigar show which launched Burns & Allen on an 18 year network radio career and 18 finishes among the season's Top 50 programs.

Burns & Allen's tenth place finish made it CBS' highest rated show of the 1932–33 season. Their success was owed in part to radio's first major publicity stunt involving wholesale cross-promotion among programs. It was concocted by Burns, CBS and General Cigar's agency, J. Walter Thompson, and focused on Gracie's scatterbrained persona.

After several months of set-up gags describing her mythical and equally hare brained brother — *the one who hurt his leg falling off an ironing board while pressing his pants* — she wept and confided on the January 4. 1933, show that her beloved sibling had disappeared and appealed for the public's help to find him.

Gracie's "search" for her missing brother spread to other CBS programs and — thanks to the agency's muscle — to shows on NBC and Blue, as well. Gracie popped-up unannounced, to do a short bit about her missing brother written specifically for the hosting show. Newspapers picked up the story when NBC censors cut the CBS star's "surprise" visit to the Rudy Vallee Show off the air which gave the stunt even more publicity. The wandering Gracie roamed from show to show and kept the running gag alive for months.

Meanwhile, her real brother, a San Francisco accountant, went into hiding. The stunt was a immediate rating bonanza. Burns & Allen's January numbers jumped 32 percent over December's 23.5 to a lofty 31.1. More telling were the ratings before and during the massive promotion. Burns and Allen scored a 19.3 average from September through December and a 31.3 from January through June — a 62 percent increase.

George and Gracie also benefited from solid lead-in shows on CBS. Chesterfield Cigarettes' *Music That Satisfies* with Bing Crosby preceded them until March. Then

Old Gold Cigarettes took over the time period for the popular Fred Waring and his Pennsylvanians. The 32-year-old Waring's group had steadily grown from a small jazz combo of the 1920s to a large show band and chorus. Waring would eventual enjoy seven Annual Top 50 finishes in the 1930s.

WHAT EVIL LURKS IN 40TH PLACE?

The Shadow, alternately voiced by James LaCurto and Frank Readick, made his debut as the narrator of radio adaptations from Street & Smith's *Detective Story* and *Love Story* pulp magazines in 1930. The character caught on with the public and the publisher responded in 1931 with a new monthly dime novel, *The Shadow Magazine*.

After an earlier one-month run trial run of *The Shadow* on CBS, the 1932–33 series on NBC featured Readick in the title role and as a participant in the stories. But the series was still five years away from its run on Mutual when *The Shadow* became Lamont Cranston who discovered the hypnotic secret to, "... Cloud men's minds," and create Sunday afternoon mayhem.

Wednesday was NBC's weakest night of the season. Nevertheless, *The Shadow* earned a respectable double digit rating and placed 40th among the season's Top 50 programs.

1932–33 Thursday Night
Top Ten Program
NBC 4, Blue 3, CBS 3
Average: 21.7

Jack Pearl's Baron Munchausen	NBC	10:00	39.4
Maxwell House Showboat	NBC	9:00	30.5
Rudy Vallee's Fleischmann Hour	NBC	8:00	29.2
Amos & Andy*	Blue	7:00	28.2
Myrt & Marge*	CBS	7:00	21.4
The Goldbergs*	NBC	7:45	17.3
Jack Benny's Canada Dry Show	CBS	10:00	13.5
Lowell Thomas News*	Blue	6:45	13.1
Kate Smith's LaPalina Show	CBS	8:00	12.9
Death Valley Days	Blue	9:00	11.7
Sans Strips...			
Colonel Stoopnagle & Budd	CBS	9:30	9.8
Easy Aces	CBS	10:15	9.1
Mills Brothers Show	CBS	9:15	8.5
Wayne King Orchestra	NBC	8:30	7.0

PEARL'S PEAK

Comic Jack Pearl was on top of the world — starring in the Gershwins' *Pardon My English* on Broadway while his *Baron Munchausen* character with straight man Cliff Hall won Thursday night for NBC. Pearl generated the greatest ratings of his brief network career resulting in a third place finish among the season's Top 50 programs.

To make the season even sweeter, Pearl was voted the favorite radio comic in *The New York World Telegram's* poll of 127 newspaper radio editors. Pearl's variety hour for American Tobacco's Lucky Strike Cigarettes enjoyed the lead-in of two Top Ten shows — *Maxwell House Showboat* and *Rudy Valley's Fleischmann Hour*. The NBC lineup established a pattern for future Thursday nights in which hour-long variety shows would dominate the ratings.

ROLLING ON THE RIVER OF RATINGS

Friday was the traditional grocery shopping day in the 1930s. General Foods joined Standard Brands as a major food advertiser on Thursday night when it staked out the nine o'clock hour on NBC for its *Maxwell House Showboat*. The program's setting, a Mississippi River showboat, and its host, 48-year-old character actor Charles Winninger, were both borrowed from 1929's Jerome Kern/ Oscar Hammerstein II Broadway melodramatic musical hit, *Showboat*, based the Edna Ferber novel. But the similarity ended there. There was no melodrama aboard *The Maxwell House Showboat*.

Instead, Winninger's Captain Henry presided over a large and rollicking radio production that offered music and romance provided by singers Lanny Ross and Muriel Wilson, a weekly parade of guest star "passengers" and comedy from resident blackface comics Pick Malone and Pat Padgett, known on the show as "Molasses 'n' January."

Beginning in January 1933, *Showboat* scored a string of 27 consecutive months when its Crossley ratings never fell below 30, resulting in four straight seasons among the annual Top Five shows. With *Show-*

boat's success, General Foods established itself on NBC's Thursday night schedule with a collection of hit shows that continued over the next 17 seasons.

DEATH BECOMES HER

Pacific Borax, manufacturer of cleansers and laundry additives derived from the borax it mined in the deserts of California and Nevada — 20 Mule Team Borax and Boraxo—cleverly associated its mineral's source with the western anthology series *Death Valley Days* on NBC in 1930. The series was moved to Blue for the 1932–33 season and finished the next four years in the Annual Top 50.

Death Valley Days was scripted by Vassar graduate Ruth Cornwall Woodman, a New York copywriter who made annual treks into the rugged locales of Western desert towns for authentic story material. Her research resulted in hundreds of character driven radio plays, all narrated by "The Old Ranger" — a role held for many years by character actor Jack MacBryde.

Pacific Borax led its mule team across three networks and seven different timeslots in the program's 14 year run which gave it little chance of establishing a sizable base of habitual listeners every week. In its last fifteen seasons it never ranked above 90th.

Nevertheless, Pacific Borax was obviously pleased with the studio show that colorfully depicted the history of the land where its products originated.

---

*1932–33 Friday Night
Top Ten Programs*
NBC 4, Blue 3, CBS 3
Average: 20.0

Al Jolson Show	NBC 10:00	27.8
Amos & Andy*	Blue 7:00	27.6
Myrt & Marge*	CBS 7:00	22.6
Jack Benny's Chevrolet Show	NBC 10:00	22.2
Cities Service Concert	NBC 8:00	20.2
First Nighter	Blue 9:00	17.5
The Goldbergs*	NBC 7:45	16.4
Phil Baker's Armour Jester	Blue 9:30	16.1
The March of Time	CBS 8:30	15.3
Edwin C Hill's Inside Story	CBS 9:30	14.2
Sans Strips...		
Adventures of Charlie Chan	Blue 7:30	10.3
Best Foods Musical Grocery	NBC 9:00	8.2
Ponds Variety Program	NBC 9:30	7.6

JOLSON DRIVES CHEVROLET'S RATINGS

Al Jolson made an immediate impact on the ratings when Chevrolet brought him to NBC's Friday night schedule in late November. He was a show business legend at 46 — a Broadway star for over 20 years who had sold millions of records and already had five movies in sound to his credit — including Warner Brothers' legendary *The Jazz Singer*.

The Chevrolet show was, by design, a limited 15 week series that ran through February — providing a nationwide promotional vehicle for Jolson's film, *Hallelujah, I'm a Bum,* which premiered in theaters on February 3. Jolson starred in three network series at the peak of his career in the 1930s and never fell below the Annual Top 10.

A CLASSICAL GAS

Cities Service Concert, headlined by soprano Jessica Dragonette, celebrated the best ratings of what would become the program's 29 year series of classical, semi-classic, and brass band concerts on NBC. The show finished the season in 16th place with a 20.0 average rating.

Although its ratings sank to single digits after four seasons and the program never again made a season's Top 50 list, *Cities Service Concert—* or *Highways In Melody* and *Band of America* as it was later known — joined *The Voice of Firestone* and *The Telephone Hour* as network radio's three longest running programs in prime time in which sponsors opted for musical prestige over mass popularity.

IT'S ABOUT TIME

Time magazine had jumped into network radio in 1931 with its "newsreel of the air," *The March of Time.* The radio series had begun in 1929 at WLW/Cincinnati and was distributed on discs to stations across the country by the magazine's advertising agency, Batten, Barton, Durstine & Osborne.

By the 1932–33 season it had a year's head start on CBS' Friday schedule. Because radio news was still in its infancy and remote broadcasts of news events as they happened were rare, *The March of Time* boldly *recreated* news events for radio, employing as many as a dozen actors on one program to impersonate the voices of Franklin and Eleanor Roosevelt plus every other newsmaker of the day. Orson Welles, Agnes Moorhead, Art Carney and Arlene Francis were among many young actors who received talent checks from the program. However, the show had one signature voice.

The March of Time's most famous narrator of its network radio and subsequent movie series was (Cornelius) Westbrook Van Voorhis, whose booming and commanding delivery — known in the voiceover trade as "The Voice of God" — belied the fact that he was only 29 years old in 1932.

1932–33 Saturday Night Eight Rated Programs
CBS 4, NBC 3, Blue 1
Average: 11.0

Walter O'Keefe's Lucky Strike Dance Party	NBC	10:00	27.5
Bing Crosby's Music That Satisfies	CBS	9:00	18.5
Saturday Night Dance Party	NBC	10:00	17.2
Oldsmobile Show	NBC	9:30	13.0
The Magic Voice	CBS	8:15	12.5
Easy Aces	CBS	10:15	9.1
Eddie Dooley Football Dope	CBS	6:30	6.1
Cuckoo Program	Blue	10:15	6.0

Between *The March of Time*'s radio and film series, Van Voorhis had a 20 year job reminding millions of Americans that, "TIME ... Marches On!" The program was destined for four consecutive Top 50 finishes on CBS.

RADIO'S AFTERTHOUGHT

Networks, sponsors and agencies always considered Saturday as the movie night, the date night, the party night — anything but the night for radio listening. It took two years for NBC to offer its first and only hour of Saturday night programming to affiliates — *The National*

Symphony Orchestra in December 1928. When the classical music program was cancelled, the network went silent on Saturday nights for another year.

The Saturday slack carried into the 1932–33 season when only eight sponsored programs were rated for 13 weeks or more on the three networks. Although the night would eventually attract millions of listeners with the long running *Truth or Consequences*, *Gangbusters* and *Your Hit Parade*, whenever sponsors and networks cut back programming, Saturday would be first to suffer.

It would happen repeatedly.

LUCKY STRIKES AGAIN AND AGAIN

American Tobacco accomplished a feat that no other sponsor would ever match. The company produced three of the season's Top Ten shows, all under the banner of one brand — Lucky Strike Cigarettes. Tuesday's *Jack Pearl Show*, Thursday's *Lucky Strike Hour*, laden with guest stars and hosted by comedian Walter O'Keefe, and Saturday's *Lucky Strike Dance Bands*, featuring name orchestras and again emceed by O'Keefe, all aired on NBC. The tobacco company would retire from network radio the following season but return in 1934–35 with the longest running Saturday night program of Network Radio's Golden Age, *Your Hit Parade*.

1932–33 Top Ten Multiple Run Programs
CBS 5, Blue 4, NBC 1
Average 15.6

Amos & Andy*	M-F	Blue	7:00	28.9
Myrt & Marge*	M-F	CBS	7:00	23.5
The Goldbergs*	M-F	NBC	7:45	17.2
Eno Crime Club	Tu,W	Blue	8:00	15.2
Lowell Thomas News*	M-F	Blue	6:45	13.7
Kate Smith's LaPalina Show	Tu-Th	CBS	8:00	12.9
Magic Voice	Tu,Sa	CBS	8:15	12.5
Music That Satisfies	M-Sa	CBS	9:00	10.8
Country Doctor	M-W	Blue	8:45	10.6
Just Plain Bill*	M-F	CBS	6:45	10.5

*Monday–Friday Strip Shows

MULTIPLE RUNS' BEST RUN

All of the Top Ten Multiple Run programs reached the season's Top 50 list. It never happened again. Thirty percent of prime time programming consisted of Multiple Run offerings. Of the 107 programs that were rated for a minimum of 13 weeks and ranked, 33 were prime time programs broadcast more than once per week. CBS aired 14, Blue had eleven and NBC presented seven.

In later years the Multiple Runs would be generally confined between 6:00 and 8:00, Eastern Time. But during the 1932–33 season almost all of the CBS prime time schedule was given over to Multiple Runs as the network developed young talent and programs to challenge NBC's monopoly of established stars.

CHICAGO'S SUPPERTIME SHOOT OUT

CBS pioneered the concept of counter-programming in late 1931 and the maneuver paid rating dividends in the 1932–33 season. Blue's previously unbeatable *Amos & Andy* were suddenly faced with the competition from a serial about two Broadway chorus girls, *Myrt & Marge*. It was strictly a Chicago battle for strip show supremacy. The programs and their sponsors, *A&A*'s Pepsodent Toothpaste and *M&M*'s Wrigley Gum, were all based in the Windy City.

Myrt & Marge was both written and performed by the mother/daughter team of Myrtle Vail and Donna Damerel The serial siphoned enough listeners away from *Amos & Andy* to come within 5.4 rating points of the established comedy in the 1932–33 season. The suppertime soap opera drew double digit ratings against *A&A* for three years and became the basis for the 1933 film, *Myrt & Marge*. But unlike its melodramatic inspiration, the movie was a backstage musical comedy featuring The Three Stooges in supporting roles.

Myrt & Marge held

down the 7:00 timeslot on CBS for five years before moving to the network's daytime schedule under the sponsorship of Colgate's Super Suds — thus becoming a soap opera in the truest sense. The series ended tragically when Damerel died in childbirth at age 29 in 1941. Her mother retired a year later.

Oddly, the battle for early evening listeners between *Amos & Andy* and *Myrt & Marge* took place throughout most of the country at 7:00 *except* in their home base of Chicago where both programs were heard in their second feeds to the West Coast.

Amos & Andy was broadcast nightly in Chicago at 10:00 while *Myrt & Marge* was heard at 9:00 until 1935 when it was moved by CBS to 10:00 directly opposite Gosden and Correll's strip.

THE LONERS
FROM DETROIT

George Trendle, owner of early CBS affiliate WXYZ/Detroit, cancelled his station's network affiliation in 1932 and decided to go it alone as an independent station. It was considered a risky, if not a foolish move at the time, but Trendle's daring eventually turned WXYZ into the source of Network Radio's most popular Multiple Run half-hour series.

The Lone Ranger was first broadcast locally by WXYZ on January 10, 1933, establishing a three night a week schedule that it would maintain for the next 21 years — 20 of them at 7:30 every Monday, Wednesday and Friday.

The *Ranger's* title role was originally played by 22-year-old George Stenius. Stenius left the cast after five months and went to Hollywood where he became famous as movie director and Academy Award

winning screenwriter George Seaton, author of the Christmas film classic *Miracle on 34th Street*.

Earl Graser became *The Lone Ranger* on a regional network of Michigan stations in May 1933, when sponsor Bond Bakeries' Silvercup Bread offered listeners the program's first of its many premiums — a pop gun replica of the hero's silver six shooter. The campaign drew almost 25,000 requests — each accompanied by a Silvercup loaf wrapper. The promotion's overwhelming response from *The Lone Ranger's* limited regional audience was the spark that ignited the beginning of the Mutual Broadcasting System in 1934.

When Graser was killed in a 1941 auto accident, the program's announcer, Brace Beemer, 38, became *The Lone Ranger* and remained in the saddle for the show's final 13 seasons of live broadcasts. An expert horseman at a handsome and strapping 6' 3", Beemer was ideally suited for public appearances in which he always appeared in *Lone Ranger* costume — and mask.

The Lone Ranger was really alone at first. His "faithful Indian companion Tonto" — named for Tonto Basin, Arizona — wasn't introduced until the program's twelfth broadcast. Unlike the title role that changed change hands several times, Tonto became steady work for veteran British stage actor John Todd, 56. Todd introduced the character and remained in the role until the program went out of production in 1954 when he was 77.

MUSIC THAT SATISFIES ...
THE BUDGET

Tobacco companies all sponsored music shows and associated themselves with popular singers, creating the impression that vocalists' en-

dorsements of their cigarettes proved their products' safety to their throats and lungs.

While rival American Tobacco spent much larger sums in Network Radio advertising its Lucky Strike brand, Liggett & Myers promoted its Chesterfields with *Music That Satisfies*—a twist on the cigarette's slogan, "They Satisfy." *Music That Satisfies* was a 15 minute show that floated around the CBS prime time schedule until finally becoming a Monday through Saturday strip at 9:00.

It was a simple studio show that rotated a list of headliners of the day including the singing Boswell Sisters, Jane Froman, Arthur "The Street Singer" Tracy and the comedy team of Tom Howard and Gene Sheldon — all backed by Lenny Hayton's CBS house band.

The show's major attraction was Broadway star Ruth Etting — portrayed by Doris Day in the 1955 biopic *Love Me or Leave Me*. Etting attracted the series' largest audience until January 1933 when a newcomer was added to the mix.

Bing Crosby was 29 when he was given *Satisfies*' star billing on Wednesday and Saturday nights. Audience reaction was immediate for a show that seldom scored double digit ratings. Crosby's ratings from January through March averaged a strong 18.5, nearly double Etting's Monday and Thursday night shows.

The series left the air in March, but Liggett & Myers didn't forget its successful experiment in strip programming. The concept was revived with 1939's *Chesterfield Supper Club* which became a ten year fixture on NBC — featuring Fred Waring's orchestra and chorus for its first five seasons until they were replaced in 1944 by another young baritone recording star, Perry Como.

TOP 50 PROGRAMS — 1932–33
NBC 24, CBS 14, Blue 13 (51)*
Average Rating: 18.7, Median: 16.0
18,450,000 Radio Homes / 60.6% Coverage of U.S. Homes / One Rating Point = 184,500 Homes
Source: Crossley Broadcast Advertising Report, Sep 1932–Jun 1933
Total Programs Rated 6–11 P.M.: 147
Programs Rated 13 Weeks & Ranked: 107

	Program	Rtg	Type	Sponsor	Day	Time	Lgth	Net
1	Eddie Cantor Show	55.7	CV	Chase & Sanborn Coffee	Sun	8:00	60	NBC
2	Ed Wynn's Texaco Fire Chief	40.5	CV	Texaco Petroleum	Tue	9:30	30	NBC
3	Jack Pearl's Baron Munchausen	39.4	CV	Lucky Strike Cigarettes	Thu	10:00	60	NBC
4	Lucky Strike Hour/Walter O'Keefe	33.8	MV	Lucky Strike Cigarettes	Tue	10:00	60	NBC

	Program	Rtg	Type	Sponsor	Day	Time	Lgth	Net
5	Maxwell House Showboat	30.5	MV	Maxwell House Coffee	Thu	9:00	60	NBC
6	Rudy Vallee Show	29.2	MV	Fleischmann Yeast	Thu	8:00	60	NBC
7	Amos & Andy	28.9	SC	Pepsodent Toothpaste	M-F	7:00	15	Blue 1
8	Al Jolson Show	27.8	MV	Chevrolet	Fri	10:00	30	NBC
9	Lucky Strike Dance Bands	27.5	MP	Lucky Strike Cigarettes	Sat	10:00	60	NBC
10	Burns & Allen/Guy Lombardo Show	26.5	CV	Robert Burns Cigars	Wed	9:30	30	CBS
11	Ben Bernie Show	25.6	MV	Pabst Beer	Tue	9:00	30	NBC
12	Myrt & Marge	23.5	DCC	Wrigley Gum	M-F	7:00	15	CBS
13t	Sinclair Wiener Minstrels	21.8	MSP	Sinclair Oil	Mon	9:00	30	Blue
13t	Voice of Firestone	21.8	MC	Firestone Tires	Mon	8:30	30	NBC
15	Adventures of Sherlock Holmes	21.0	DCC	George Washington Coffee	Wed	9:00	30	Blue
16	Cities Service Concert/J Dragonette	20.2	MC	Cities Service Petroleum	Fri	8:00	60	NBC
17	Marx Brothers Show	18.9	SC	Standard Oil	Mon	7:30	30	Blue
18	Bing Crosby Music That Satisfies	18.5	MP	Chesterfield Cigarettes	W,Sat	9:00	15	CBS
19	Jack Benny Program	18.3	CV	Chevrolet	Fri	10:00	30	NBC 2,3
20	Sunday at Seth Parker's	17.7	MSP	Sustaining	Sun	10:45	30	NBC
21	First Nighter/Don Ameche	17.5	DA	Campana Balm	Fri	9:00	30	Blue
22t	The Goldbergs/Gertrude Berg	17.2	SC	Pepsodent Toothpaste	M-F	7:45	15	NBC 4
22t	Saturday Night Dancing Party	17.2	MP	Hudson Motors	Sat	10:00	60	NBC
24	Phil Baker the Armour Jester	16.1	CV	Armour Meats	Fri	9:30	30	Blue
25	Fred Waring Show	16.0	MST	Old Gold Cigarettes	Wed	9:00	30	CBS
26	The March of Time	15.3	DA	Time Magazine	Fri	8:30	30	CBS
27t	Eno Crime Club	15.2	DA	Eno Antacid Salts	Tu,Wed	8:00	30	Blue
27t	Paul Whiteman Show	15.2	MV	Buick Motors	Mon	9:30	30	NBC
29	Blackstone Plantation/Crumit, Sanderson	15.1	MST	Blackstone Cigars	Tue	8:00	30	NBC
30	Carnation Contented Hour/Gene Arnold	13.8	MST	Carnation Milk	Mon	10:00	30	NBC
31	Fu Manchu Mysteries	14.5	DCC	Campana Balm	Mon	8:30	30	CBS
32	Inside Story/Edwin C Hill	14.2	DA	Socony Vacuum Oil	Fri	9:30	30	CBS
33	Lowell Thomas News	13.7	NC	Sun Oil	M-F	6:45	15	Blue
34	Fanny Brice & George Olsen Orch	13.6	CV	Chase & Sanborn Tea	Wed	8:00	30	NBC
35t	Armour Program/Leo Reisman Orch	13.0	MV	Armour Meats	Fri	9:30	30	Blue
35t	Ethel Shutta & George Olsen Orch	13.0	MV	Oldsmobile Motors	Sat	9:30	30	NBC
37	Kate Smith Sings	12.9	MP	LaPalina Cigars	Tu-Th	8:00	15	CBS
38	The Magic Voice/E Hitz & N Dawson	12.5	DCC	Ex Lax Laxative	Tu,Sa	8:15	15	CBS
39	Fred Allen Bath Club Revue	11.9	CV	Linit Bath Oil	Sun	9:00	30	CBS
40	The Shadow	11.8	DA	Blue Coal	Wed	8:30	30	NBC
41t	A&P Gypsies	11.7	MSP	A&P Food Stores	Mon	9:00	30	NBC
41t	Death Valley Days	11.7	DA	20 Mule Team Borax Cleaner	Thu	9:00	30	Blue
41t	Mysteries In Paris	11.7	DA	Bourjois Eve in Paris Perfume	Mon	9:30	30	CBS
44	Walter Winchell's Jergens Journal	10.9	NC	Jergens Lotion	Sun	9:30	15	Blue
45	Music That Satisfies/Various Artists	10.8	MP	Chesterfield Cigarettes	M-Sa	9:00	15	CBS
46	Country Doctor/Phillips H Lord	10.6	DCC	Listerine Antiseptic	M-W	8:45	15	Blue
47	Just Plain Bill/Arthur Hughes	10.5	DCC	Kolynos Toothpaste	M-F	6:45	15	CBS
48	Adventures of Charlie Chan	10.3	DCC	Standard Oil	Fri	7:30	30	Blue
49	American Album of Familiar Music	10.0	MST	Bayer Aspirin	Sun	9:30	30	NBC
50t	Carveth Wells Exploring America	9.8	MV	Conoco Petroleum	Wed	10:30	30	NBC
50t	Colonel Stoopnagle & Budd	9.8	CV	Pontiac Motors	Thu	9:30	30	CBS

*Two programs tied for 50th.

	Program			Sponsor	Day	Time	Lgth	Net
1	Amos & Andy		Sep–Nov	Pepsodent Toothpaste	M–Sat	7:00	15	Blue
2	Jack Benny Program		Nov–Feb	Canada Dry	Su,Th	8,10	30	CBS
3	Jack Benny Program		Sep–Nov	Canada Dry	M,W	9:30	30	Blue
4	The Goldbergs		Sep–Nov	Pepsodent Toothpaste	M–Sat	7:45	15	NBC

Key: API — Audience Participation/Interviews   DCC — Drama/Continuing Characters   MV — Music/Variety Show
APQ — Audience Participation/Quiz   MC — Music/Classical, Semi-Classical   NC — News, Commentary
APS — Audience Participation/Stunts   MP — Music/Popular, Contemporary   SC — Situation Comedy
CV — Comedy/Variety Show   MSP — Music/Specialty, Ethnic
DA — Dramatic Anthology   MST — Music/Standard, Traditional

1932–33 Top 50* Favorite Formats

	Programs	Pct
Music — All Categories	23	45%
Drama — Anthology & Continuing	14	27%
Comedy — All Categories	12	24%
News/Commentary	2	4%

*Two programs tied for 50th.

1932–33 Monthly Winners

Sep	Ed Wynn's Texaco Fire Chief	28.2	Feb	Eddie Cantor Show	59.1
Oct	Ed Wynn's Texaco Fire Chief	32.3	Mar	Eddie Cantor Show	60.9
Nov	Eddie Cantor Show	49.4	Apr	Eddie Cantor Show	58.6
Dec	Eddie Cantor Show	47.5	May	Jack Pearl's Baron Munchausen	48.7
Jan	Eddie Cantor Show	58.4	Jun	Ed Wynn's Texaco Fire Chief	38.1

6

The 1933–34 Network Season

Announcer: Not so many years ago, tomato soup and cream of tomato were unusual dishes enjoyed very much but not very often. Today, in most of the world, tomato soup is the one most often served. Is that because women have taken to making tomato soup frequently? No, on the contrary, few housewives ever attempt it anymore. There's just one reason for tomato soup's popularity and it is this ... the magic, matchless flavor of Campbell's Tomato Soup. There's a lively verve and zesting zest about this flavor that people take to at once and come back to enjoy again and again. The first bracing taste of it has a way of arousing a desire to eat and yet there's a pleasant feeling of satisfaction when the last spoonful is gone. So Campbell's Tomato Soup is a happy choice for the main dish at lunchtime or at supper ... and it's also a fine way to start the day's main meal. Serve it sometime, too, as cream of tomato ... made with milk instead of water. You can always be sure that it will be received with pleasure. Because this, of all soups, is the one that people like to have most often ... Campbell's Tomato Soup.

plunged 57 percent since 1929. Against that trend, Network Radio revenues had *grown* 64 percent. For the networks, 1933's income decline — a hefty 19.4 percent — was just a bump in the road that would lead to annual billings of over $100 million by the end of the decade. But newspapers were frustrated.

Even the hundred publishers who owned radio properties — *The Chicago Tribune* (WGN), *The Detroit News* (WWJ), *The St Louis Post-Dispatch* (KSD) and *Louisville Courier-Journal* (WHAS), for example — were stymied by radio's growing competition for local and national advertising dollars.

Radio posed a second threat to newspapers more obvious to the public. Stations and networks alike had increased their daily schedules of up to the minute news summaries. Foremost was Lowell Thomas' nightly newscast on Blue that had become dinnertime listening in several million homes. And radio repeatedly demonstrated its ability to scoop newspapers in breaking news as evidenced by the ongoing Lindbergh baby kidnapping saga.

The 1932 elections further underscored the new medium's advantage. The networks gave blanket coverage to the Roosevelt-Hoover returns as quickly as they were tallied from wire reports.

Newspapers simply couldn't match radio's immediacy in reporting the news. But, publishers figured, they could cut off radio's *supply* of news.

RESERVATIONS AT THE BILTMORE

As early as their 1931 convention, members of the American Newspaper Publishers' Association (ANPA) began to pressure the three major news wire services to refuse service to broadcasters After radio's 1932 election coverage, the pressure exploded into a demand.

The Associated Press, a newspaper cooperative, was first to pull the plug on the networks in early 1933. Hearst's International News Service and Scripps-Howard's United Press followed suite but far more reluctantly as Hearst already owned three radio stations and Scripps-Howard would soon buy its first.

The wire service embargo was complete by late spring. CBS news chief Paul White and NBC's Abe Schlecter retaliated by building their own news departments at a rapid pace, busily recruiting stringers and developing sources. In September CBS announced the formation of the Columbia News Service to compete with the wire services and support two daily five minute newscasts sponsored by General Mills. Operating without the flow of wire service material was a handicap but network news continued to develop and newspapers continued to fume.

Publishers, however, held a trump card. ANPA members had the potential to editorially challenge commercial broadcasting in their 1,800 newspapers and influence regulations governing radio under consideration in Washington. Broadcasters, particularly the networks, feared the political power of the press and sought to appease the newspaper industry while they

---

1933–34 Season Scoreboard
Mid-Season Totals, December 1933

		Compared to Year Earlier	
Total Radio Homes	19.25 Mil	+0.80 Mil	+4.2%
Total Auto Radios	0.5 Mil	+0.25 Mil	+100.0%
Total AM Radio Stations	599	(5)	(0.8%)
Total Radio Network Affiliates	179	+9	+5.3%
1933 Radio Revenues	57.0 Mil	(4.9 Mil)	(7.9%)
1933 Network Revenues	31.5 Mil	(7.6 Mil)	(19.4%)
Network Share	55.0.%		(8.0%)

PAPERS PUT SCREWS ON RADIO NEWS

Advertising was in a slump — total ad spending in all media had

lobbied Congress for favorable legislation.

Radio's willingness to pacify the press was on full display in December 1933, when newspaper and network-led broadcasting representatives signed *The Biltmore Agreement,* named for the New York hotel where they conferred. The radio interests grit their teeth and signed — probably with their fingers crossed.

The pact created the Press Radio Bureau — its top billing reflective of its one-sided conditions. The bureau was intended to become radio's single source for continuing news — providing summaries from the three wire services to its subscribers. But networks and stations were only permitted to broadcast the material *twice a day*—after 9:30 A.M. and 9:00 P.M.— following delivery of morning and afternoon newspapers.

More outrageously, those newscasts could not be sponsored. The networks and participating stations also agreed to discontinue building their own news departments, instead substituting occasional Press Radio Bureau audio bulletins which were always tagged, "...Further details will be found in your newspapers."

The broadcasters did receive several concessions. Newspapers agreed to continue publishing radio program schedules, networks and stations were allowed to cover on-the-scene spot news, and familiar news voices could remain on the air as "commentators" and "interpreters" of the news.

The Lowell Thomas, Boake Carter and Edwin C Hill network newscasts were promptly labeled "Commentary." Newspaper publishers smugly declared a "truce" with broadcasters when the Press Radio Bureau went into operation on March 1, 1934.

A Wire to Wire Race

In quick response to independent broadcasters unwilling to join the Press Radio Bureau flock, former United Press and CBS newsman Herb Moore gathered $150,000 *(2.5 Mil),* from several wealthy station owners and launched an alternative news service, Transradio Press.

Transradio offered national and international news written for radio plus shortwave audio bulletins of breaking news — with no strings attached.

Before long, independent Transradio was feeding copy for complete five and 15 minute newscasts to 150 subscribing stations, more clients than the newspaper controlled Press Radio Bureau. The parade was led by WOR/New York, WLS/Chicago and KNX/Los Angeles. Witnessing Transradio's success and sensing a growing profit center in broadcasting, United Press and INS abandoned *The Biltmore Agreement* and resumed selling news to radio within a year.

With the passage of the Communications Act of 1934 in June — which was generally favorable to commercial broadcasting — the newspapers' editorial and lobbying threats to radio evaporated. The *Biltmore Agreement* became totally impotent and the Press Radio Bureau withered away. Transradio, on the other hand, remained in business until 1951.

More importantly, NBC and CBS were back in the news business. For them, 1933–34's delay in the development of radio news was just another of the season's brief bumps in the road.

Provocations by the Numbers

Both newspapers and magazines were incensed by Crossley's radio audience ratings that the networks happily spread around agencies and advertisers' offices every few weeks. Ratings gave broadcasters quantitative sales ammunition that buyers could compare to the printed media's circulation figures. The numbers could justify — or rationalize — taking the plunge into the new medium. Kraft, Colgate Palmolive and Ford were among the networks' first time advertisers who sponsored shows in the 1933–34 Top 50.

Crossley's ratings continued to raise eyebrows when Eddie Cantor's Sunday show scored a 53.7 average rating for the season, peaking at 57.2 in December 1933. Given the estimated 20 million radio households at the time, the rating infers

that over ten million families listened to Cantor's *Chase & Sanborn Hour* week after week.

High figures like these helped convince magazine publishers to initiate support for the new Clark-Hooper rating service based on coincidental telephone calls as opposed to Crossley's recall system of interviewing.

Table Tops Top Set Sales

Radio receivers continued to sell despite the Depression. A big factor in this trend against the economic tide was the availability of lower priced table model radios. The table top receivers were half the cost or less than the living room console radios generally associated with the era. In 1933, table model radios — often made of Bakelite or other plastics and available since 1929 for under $25 *($435.00)*—outsold consoles by a three to one margin.

Meanwhile, the distant future of radio began to take shape on December 28th when Edwin Armstrong received his first patents for Frequency Modulation broadcasting and reception. FM would be considered a novelty for another quarter century before its popularity made it a viable commercial broadcasting enterprise.

Music's High Note

Network Radio played its part to calm the nerves and lift the spirits of Depression-era America. Music was the major element in 28 of the season's Top 50 programs — an all time high for the Golden Age. For the first and only time, nine shows featuring standard and traditional melodies remindful of better times led the category of programs devoted exclusively to music.

All five of the season's most popular programs, eight of its Top Ten and 21 of the Top 50 were Vaudeville-like variety shows mixing liberal doses of music and comedy. It was obvious that listeners wanted to sing and laugh their troubles away. Network radio was more than willing to help.

The Monthlies

The season produced another sweep for NBC with either Standard Brands or General Foods the proud sponsor of every month's Number One program. Eddie Cantor ran his string to twelve unbeaten months for Standard's Chase & Sanborn Coffee, hitting Number One from November through April, all six months his Sunday night show aired. General Foods's minstrel themed *Maxwell House Showboat* was Number One in the Cantor-free months of September, May and June while Rudy Vallee crooned his way to first place for Standard's Fleischmann Yeast in October.

1933–34 Sunday Night Top Ten Programs
Blue 5, NBC 4, CBS 1
Average 20.7

Eddie Cantor Show	NBC	8:00	53.7
Will Rogers' Gulf Headliners	Blue	9:00	37.0
Joe Penner's Bakers Broadcast	Blue	7:30	24.9
George M Cohan's Gulf Headliners	Blue	9:00	19.5
American Album of Familiar Music	NBC	9:30	14.8
Cadillac Symphony	Blue	6:00	13.2
Lily Pons' Hall of Fame	NBC	10:30	13.2
Manhattan Merry Go Round	NBC	9:00	10.9
Walter Winchell's Jergens Journal	Blue	9:30	10.9
45 Minutes in Hollywood	CBS	10:30	9.3

WHERE THERE'S A WILL THERE'S A RATING

Gulf Headliners was radio's most schizophrenic variety show — featuring one major star and three fill-in hosts covering his absences with fluctuating ratings. *Headliners'* true headliner was Will Rogers, who debuted on the series in May 1933, and returned a 37.8 rating. But Rogers was also working on three movies a year for Fox. To accommodate his film commitments, Gulf Oil came up with a roster of hosts for *Headliners* that can best be described as eclectic.

Vaudeville veteran Fred Stone and his singing daughters hosted *Headliners* in September and October to open its 1933–34 season. Stone was Rogers' closest friend and namesake of the humorist's first born son who died in infancy.

The Stone family act averaged a respectable 17.2 rating for the two autumn months.

Then Rogers took the show in November and *Headliners'* rating more than doubled to a 38.6. Legendary song and dance man George M. Cohan, 55, followed in December and the rating fell 15 points. Rogers came to the rescue again in January and February with 38.9 and 39.9 averages — an excellent promotional lift for his movie *David Harum* which was released in March. Cohan — still eight years from becoming immortalized by James Cagney in Warner Brothers' *Yankee Doodle Dandy*— kept less than half of Rogers' audience with a 17.7 March and April average. Songwriter Irving Berlin's one month *Headliners* appearance in May sank to 13.7. Rogers demonstrated his drawing power again when he returned to close the season in June and the show's rating rebounded to 30.7. *Gulf Headliners* would repeat its rotating host format the following season in this rare example of sponsor deference to its star performer's schedule.

Rogers' appearances continued to benefit Walter Winchell, whose 15 minute *Jergens Journal* immediately followed *Gulf Headliners* on Blue. The columnist's ratings invariably spiked with the momentum provided by Rogers. Winchell completed his first full season on Blue's Sunday night schedule where he would remain until 1955.

PENNER'S SEASON JUST DUCKY

Hungarian immigrant Joe Penner was a Vaudeville and burlesque veteran at 28 when he first appeared on Rudy Vallee's *Fleischmann Yeast Hour* in July 1933. His juvenile persona and cartoonish voice — not unlike Lou Costello or Curly Howard — and his silly catch phrases — "Wanna buy a duck?" and, "You naaaasty man!" — caught on with the public to such an extent that Standard Brands gave Penner his own show in October. *The Bakers' Broadcast,* starring Penner and also under the Fleischmann banner, was broadcast from Los Angeles on Sunday nights at 7:30 on Blue, immediately prior

to Standard's top rated *Chase & Sanborn Hour* with Eddie Cantor on NBC.

Penner, supported by Ozzie Nelson's band and singer Harriet Hilliard (two years before their marriage), started the season slowly with a mere 10.0 rating in October. But his silliness spread quickly and by February Penner enjoyed cushy numbers in the 30s, on his way to a season finish in eleventh place.

FORTY FIVE FOR FILM FANS

CBS began to capitalize on its ties with the movie industry in January with Borden Dairies' *45 Minutes in Hollywood*, a relatively large-scale production created in conjunction with the film fan magazine, *Photoplay*. Although the variety program often featured movie stars in their first appearances before a microphone, it couldn't top the ratings of its 10:00 competition from New York, soprano Lily Pons' *Hall of Fame* on NBC.

45 Minutes in Hollywood was later moved to Thursday nights but never achieved the popularity of its 1934 sound-alike successor, the similarly formatted *Hollywood Hotel*.

MARX MISS MARK

Groucho and Chico Marx, riding high with the November release of their film *Duck Soup*, took a second and last shot at radio together, *The Marx of Time* on CBS. Their time ran out in 13 weeks despite steadily increasing ratings that averaged 9.5, just a shade out of Sunday's Top Ten. The brothers left series radio after the cancellation, remaining on the fringes of radio popularity with guest appearances for the next eight seasons until Groucho took the lead of *Blue Ribbon Town* in 1942.

Groucho was still over a dozen years from teaming with producer John Guedel for their hit comedy quiz, *You Bet Your Life,* in 1947.

1933–34 Monday Night Top Ten Programs
NBC 5, Blue 3, CBS 2
Average: 18.2

Amos & Andy*	Blue	7:00	29.8
Sinclair Wiener Minstrels	Blue	9:00	24.4

Lowell Thomas News*	Blue	6:45	22.0
Myrt & Marge*	CBS	7:00	18.9
Voice of Firestone	NBC	8:30	17.9
Ship of Joy	NBC	9:30	14.9
The Goldbergs*	NBC	7:45	14.6
Carnation Contented Hour	NBC	10:00	13.8
A&P Gypsies	NBC	9:00	13.0
Edwin C Hill News	CBS	8:15	11.5

*Monday–Friday Strip Programs

Sans Strips...

Jack Frost's Melody Moments	Blue	9:30	10.9
Philadelphia Orchestra	CBS	9:00	9.6
Gertrude Nielsen's Ex Lax Big Show	CBS	9:30	9.3
Buck Rogers*	CBS	6:00	6.6

MONDAY'S BLUES

Blue took Monday's top three spots with two Chicago shows, *Amos & Andy* and *Sinclair "Wiener" Minstrels,* plus Lowell Thomas' nightly newscast from New York. The three programs repeated their dominance of Monday the following year — the only times that Blue took the top three positions of any night of any season.

It wasn't until Friday of the 1951–52 season that the WJZ anchored network was able to again score any night's top three programs. By that time the chain had become known as ABC.

THE CAPTAIN'S THINKING SHIP

Del Monte launched Hugh Dobbs' *Ship of Joy* on NBC's Monday schedule. It was network radio's first and only attempt to channel mass mental telepathy via the airwaves.

Dobbs had risen from a local morning exercise program on KPO/San Francisco to become "Captain Dobbsie," a nationally known proponent of positive thinking and goodwill. Every week Dobb's *Ship of Joy* "sailed" from "Good Cheer Dock" and cruised to the "Isle of Happiness," with shipboard music provided by Horace Heidt's orchestra. During each "voyage" the studio and home audiences were urged to think hard and transmit good wishes to sick and troubled friends.

As maudlin as it sounds, *Ship of Joy* developed a loyal following and generated enough ratings for a Top 50 finish before Del Monte sank it after one season.

1933–34 Tuesday Night Top Ten Programs
NBC 5, Blue 3, CBS 2
Average: 23.1

Ed Wynn's Texaco Fire Chief Show	NBC	9:30	32.3
Amos & Andy*	Blue	7:00	30.3
Ben Bernie Show	NBC	9:00	27.8
Palmolive Beauty Box Theater/ Gladys Swarthout	NBC	10:00	26.5
Bing Crosby's Woodbury Show	CBS	9:00	21.5
Cruise of the Seth Parker/Phillips H. Lord	NBC	10:00	21.3
Myrt & Marge*	CBS	7:00	20.3
Lowell Thomas News*	Blue	6:45	20.2
Eno Crime Clues	Blue	8:00	15.4
Blackstone Plantation	NBC	8:00	15.0

Sans Strips...

Wayne King's Lady Esther Serenade	NBC	8:30	14.4
Edgar A. Guest's Musical Memories	Blue	9:00	8.1
Voice of Experience	CBS	8:30	5.7

LADY ESTHER WINS IN A WALTZ

Lady Esther Cosmetics was a relatively small Chicago manufacturer of bargain priced face powders and beauty creams. Chicago agency Lord & Thomas was determined to make Lady Esther as successful as the Chicago based Pepsodent Toothpaste it sold with *Amos & Andy.* It enlisted the house band at Chicago's Aragon Ballroom to do the job beginning in 1931 on NBC.

By the 1933–34 season, Wayne King — "The Waltz King" — scored double digit ratings on Tuesday and Thursday at 8:30 with NBC's *Lady Esther Serenade.* The program was demographically tailored to older women with soft, melodic music and romantic poetry read in the deep, calming baritone of Chicago announcing legend, Franklyn Mac-Cormack. King and MacCormack

also combined talents to create several jukebox hits — including 1942's million-selling *Melody of Love.*

The program became another success story for Lord & Thomas, its Chicago clients and hometown talent. King enjoyed Top 50 annual rankings through the 1930s and Lady Esther became a household name.

SETH SETS SAIL AND SINKS

Phillips H. Lord abandoned his *Sunday at Seth Parker's* hymn sing and its double digit ratings in October. He had a more adventuresome idea for NBC — probably inspired by the hoopla CBS was creating with the launch of the Admiral Byrd Antarctic Expedition and its planned shortwave broadcasts from the South Pole beginning in January.

With the backing of sponsor Frigidaire refrigerators, Lord bought a seaworthy four-mast schooner, renamed it *The Seth Parker,* announced plans for a globe circling cruise and proclaimed that he, too, would broadcast tales of his adventures back to "the folks at home" every week via shortwave radio.

The Seth Parker set sail in December with a full crew and skeleton cast aboard. The voyage began down the eastern seaboard and its Tuesday night remote broadcasts were greeted with Crossley ratings over 20 points. Then the program and the ship hit troubled waters.

Gossip began to spread about wild parties aboard *The Seth Parker* in its ports of call. Crew members reportedly confirmed the rumors and Frigidaire dropped its sponsorship in January, despite ratings that placed *The Cruise of the Seth Parker* among the season's Top 20 programs. NBC cancelled the show in March. Nevertheless, the ship sailed on for another ten months until it was sunk in a south seas gale which newspapers delighted in debunking as a publicity stunt.

Phillips H. Lord survived the shipwreck but *Seth Parker's* wholesome reputation didn't. Several subsequent attempts to revive variations of the original Sunday show on Blue failed.

1933–34 Wednesday
Night Top Ten
Blue 4, NBC 4, CBS 2
Average: 18.7

Burns & Allen and Guy Lombardo Orchestra	CBS	9:30	28.2
Amos & Andy*	Blue	7:00	27.8
Lowell Thomas News*	Blue	6:45	21.2
Myrt & Marge*	CBS	7:00	20.3
Jack Pearl's Baron Munchausen	NBC	8:00	16.1
Fred Allen's Hour of Smiles	NBC	9:00	16.0
Warden Lawes at Sing Sing	Blue	9:00	15.6
John McCormack Sings	Blue	9:30	15.6
Wayne King's Lady Esther Serenade	NBC	7:30	14.4
The Goldbergs*	NBC	7:45	11.9
Sans Strips...			
Edwin C Hill News	CBS	8:15	11.5
Albert Spalding Violin Recitals	CBS	8:30	11.3
Fred Waring Show	CBS	10:00	11.2

PALEY'S FIRST TEAM

Burns and Allen continued on their ratings roll begun with Gracie's "missing brother" stunt of the previous spring. Their popularity was further pushed along by their appearance in Paramount's musical, *College Humor,* released in July. As a result, George and Gracie enjoyed their second Top Ten season and the highest rating they would ever achieve.

Again teamed with Guy Lombardo's orchestra, they gave CBS its first Number One show of a night. Ironically, the win was a mixed blessing for CBS boss Bill Paley. Burns and Allen's sponsor was General Cigar, the biggest competitor to the Paley family's Congress Cigar Co.

1933–34 Thursday
Night Top Ten
NBC 4, Blue 3, CBS 3
Average: 23.4

Maxwell House Showboat	NBC	9:00	44.6
Rudy Vallee's Fleischmann Hour	NBC	8:00	39.8
Amos & Andy*	Blue	7:00	29.0
Paul Whiteman's Kraft Music Hall	NBC	10:00	26.3
Fred Waring Show	CBS	9:30	22.2
Lowell Thomas News*	Blue	6:45	19.2

Myrt & Marge*	CBS	7:00	17.4
Death Valley Days	Blue	9:00	14.6
The Goldbergs*	NBC	7:45	13.3
Glen Gray Orchestra	CBS	10:00	8.0
Sans Strips...			
Eddy Duchin Orchestra	Blue	9:30	7.2
Voice of America (aka The Underwood Hour)	CBS	8:30	6.4
Captain Diamond's Adventures	Blue	8:00	5.4

RADIO'S BIG CHEESE

National Dairy Products, aka Kraft Foods, joined grocery giants General Foods and Standard Brands with its own hour long NBC variety show on Thursday night — the eve of American housewives' traditional Friday food shopping.

Kraft made and marketed Velveeta and a variety of processed cheeses. Its Phenix Foods division produced Philadelphia Cream Cheese and Kraft had just introduced Miracle Whip salad dressing at the Chicago Exposition of 1933.

Paul Whiteman's *Kraft Music Hall*—aka *The Kraft-Phenix Program*—was produced by the J. Walter Thompson agency and featured Al Jolson as Whiteman's guest star for twelve weeks of its 42 week run in 1933–34. The singer's four brief appearances in September, at a reported $5,000 each *($87,000),* spiked the variety show's ratings with a season high 33.2. His return engagements in March averaged 29.0 and April's resulted in 29.9 rating.

Nevertheless, Whiteman, whose *entire group* was paid $4,500 a week *($78,300),* delivered solid ratings in the 20s without Jolson's guest appearances. Their high ratings set the pace for the program. *Kraft Music Hall,* would finish among the Top 15 shows for the next eleven consecutive seasons and in the annual Top Ten in six of those seasons.

1933–34 Friday Night
Top Ten Programs
Blue 4, CBS 3, NBC 3
Average: 19.8

Amos & Andy*	Blue	7:00	28.3
Phil Baker's Armor Jester	Blue	9:30	23.9
First Nighter	NBC	10:00	23.7

Jack Benny Program	NBC	10:00	21.9
Lowell Thomas News*	Blue	6:45	20.1
Cities Service Concert	NBC	8:00	19.6
March of Time	CBS	8:30	18.9
Myrt & Marge*	CBS	7:00	18.6
Phil Harris Orchestra	Blue	9:00	11.7
Edwin C Hill News	CBS	8:15	11.5
Sans Strips...			
Olsen & Johnson's Swift Revue	CBS	10:00	11.1
Waltz Time	NBC	9:00	10.2
Walter O'Keefe's Nestle Show	Blue	8:00	9.2

BLUE'S BEST FOR 14 YEARS

Friday night's win by *Amos & Andy* was the second night of the week won by Gosden and Correll. The pair also won two nights in the 1932–33 season and their ratings held steady into the new season. *A&A*'s nightly strip show combined with Phil Baker's *Armour Jester* variety show, Lowell Thomas's newscasts, and a half hour from Phil Harris's popular dance band to win the night for Blue. The WJZ anchored network wouldn't win Friday night again until 1947–48.

BAKER AND BENNY BUILD

Phil Baker's *Armour Jester* rating shot up 48 percent in its 9:30 timeslot on Blue to a season average of 23.9. It was the highest rating the accordion playing comic would ever register in his long Network Radio career. The *Jester* format involved a butler, a singer and a continual heckler who continually put down the star. Baker's self-deprecation shtick resembled Jack Benny's which was developing on NBC.

Benny continued to his bounce around different timeslots on NBC. After six months on Sunday night for Chevrolet, the violin playing comic was shifted to Friday nights under General Tire sponsorship. Singer Frank Parker and announcer Don Wilson joined Benny's wife — aka Mary Livingston — in support. The familiar Benny cast and format was slowly assembling — although Benny's "valet" and most famous sidekick, Eddie "Rochester" Anderson was still four seasons from his first appearance on the show.

THE LITTLE THEATER OFF LAKE MICHIGAN

It was a down year for radio drama. Half of the previous season's 14 dramatic series dropped out the Top 50, leaving just five anthologies and two scripted dramas with continuing characters.

An exception to the downtrend was *First Nighter,* which jumped from Blue to NBC, registered a 35 percent gain in audience, became the year's top rated dramatic series and moved into the annual Top 15 for the first of five consecutive seasons.

The series of light romantic comedies with an occasional melodrama added for variety was sponsored by Campana Balm — an "Italian" hand lotion manufactured in Batavia, Illinois. Campana's sponsorship of the program began on Blue 1930 and endured for the next 19 years over all four networks — a record for sponsor/program longevity.

First Nighter was an elaborate illusion, creating the atmosphere of an opening night at New York's "Little Theater Off Times Square." In reality, it was *way* off Times Square. The program originated from Chicago for its first 16 years and then moved to Los Angeles.

The two continuing stars of the weekly show for its first four years were versatile Chicago radio actors Don Ameche and June Meredith.

At the time Ameche worked in the shadow of his younger brother Jim, who at 18 played the title role of *Jack Armstrong, All American Boy.* That situation would change in 1937 when the dashing Don left for Hollywood to host the Edgar Bergen and Charlie McCarthy radio show and subsequently become a 20th Century–Fox movie star.

Philadelphia Orchestra	CBS	9:00	9.6
National Barn Dance	Blue	10:30	8.5
Terraplane Travelcade	NBC	9:00	7.8
Eddy Duchin Orchestra	Blue	9:30	7.2
Beatrice Fairfax	NBC	9:30	5.7
Little Jack Little Show	CBS	10:15	3.4

LIVE ... FROM ANTARCTICA!

CBS gave listeners a true reality show on Saturday nights at 10:00. With a buildup that began with his Antarctic expedition's launch in October, Admiral Richard Byrd began a two-year series of live programs via shortwave from his headquarters at Little America II in December.

It was a unique variety show with members of Byrd's crew providing music, CBS staff announcer Charles Murphy reporting news of the expedition and Byrd contributing commentary about the group's adventures in the sub-zero wasteland.

Public curiosity about the expedition — fueled by ample publicity from CBS — propelled the program into Saturday's Top Ten and 26th place in the annual rankings. The novelty wore off the following season when the Byrd broadcasts were moved to Wednesday and ratings fell off by 30 percent.

Nevertheless, the program was an effective advertising vehicle for General Foods' Grape Nuts Cereal and provided a promotional launching pad or a new line of products that the company would begin marketing in 1934 — Birds Eye Frozen Foods.

RIPLEY'S ODDITIES = RADIO COMMODITIES

For half of its 26-week run, Hudson Motors' *Saturday Night Party* featured syndicated cartoonist, author and movie short-subject star Robert L. Ripley whose daily *Believe It or Not* panel of oddities was seen in hundreds of newspapers. It was Ripley's third network radio stop in a broadcast career that began in 1930. There would be many more for the popular world traveler and collector of oddities. He drifted in and out of all four networks' schedules until 1948.

DOWN HOME IN CHICAGO

National Barn Dance became the first Network Radio variety show that appealed directly to rural listeners, featuring "country" or "hillbilly" music and comedy. The hour long *Barn Dance* from WLS/ Chicago debuted on NBC in September — six years ahead of its famous cousin, WSM/Nashville's *Grand Ole Opry.*

Hosted throughout its 15-year network run by jovial Joe Kelly, *National Barn Dance* reached the annual Top 50 only four times yet had the loyalty of its audience *and* sponsor. Miles Laboratories's Alka Seltzer sponsored the show for 14 years.

National Barn Dance is remembered as the incubator for several stars' careers. Gene Autry and his movie sidekick Pat Buttram both appeared on the show before their film careers took off and "Little Georgie" Gobel sang on *Barn Dance* some 20 years before he became an Emmy Award winning television comedian in the mid–1950s.

1933–34 Saturday Night Top Ten Programs
NBC 5, CBS 3, Blue 2
Average: 10.2

Robert Ripley's Saturday Night Party	NBC	10:00	18.6
Byrd Antarctic Expedition	CBS	10:00	17.3
Colgate House Party	NBC	8:00	13.0
Leo Reisman Orchestra	NBC	9:30	10.7

1933–34 Top Ten Multiple Run Programs
CBS 5, NBC 3, Blue 2
Average 14.7

Amos & Andy*	M–F	Blue	7:00	29.8
Lowell Thomas News*	M–F	Blue	6:45	21.0
Myrt & Marge*	M–F	CBS	7:00	19.2
Wayne King's Lady Esther Serenade	Tu,Th	NBC	8:30	14.4
The Goldbergs*	M–F	NBC	7:45	13.6
Edwin C Hill News	M,W,F	CBS	8:15	11.5
Billy Batchelor Sketches*	M–F	NBC	7:15	11.0
Philadelphia Orchestra	M,W,Sa	CBS	9:00	9.8
Boake Carter News*	M–F	CBS	7:45	8.6
Glen Gray Orchestra	Tu,Th	CBS	10:00	8.0

AMOS AND ANDY:
CAB DRIVERS

The proprietors of the Fresh Air Taxi Company scored the highest season's average rating of their careers — albeit with the inflated Crossley/CAB numbers. *Amos & Andy*'s sixth place finish in the annual Top 50 was the highest position they would reach for the next 14 years — after their format had been converted from a strip program to a once a week sitcom. Nev-ertheless, *Amos & Andy* would remain the top rated Multiple Run program for the next four seasons.

THOMAS'S TOP
TEN RECORD RUN

Radio's growing importance as a news source was personified by Blue's Lowell Thomas, whose Crossley average had increased 35 percent and placed his Sun Oil newscast in the Top Ten every night of its broadcast during the 1933–34 season. It was the beginning of Thomas' unmatched record of 13 straight years in the nightly Top Ten, all five nights a week.

News commentaries from Edwin C Hill on CBS and NBC's Boake Carter also finished among the season's Top Ten Multiple Run programs. The number of newscasts on the list would swell to half a dozen by the start of World War II.

TOP 50 PROGRAMS — 1933–34
NBC 27, Blue 13, CBS 11 (51)*
Average Rating: 20.1, Median: 17.9
19,250,000 Radio Homes / 62.5% Coverage of U.S. Homes / One Rating Point = 192,500 Homes
Source: Crossley Broadcast Advertising Report, Sep 1933–Jun 1934
Total Programs Rated 6–11 P.M.: 161
Programs Rated 13 Weeks and Ranked: 123.

		Program	Rtg	Type	Sponsor	Day	Time	Lgth	Net
1	1	Eddie Cantor Show	53.7	CV	Chase & Sanborn Coffee	Sun	8:00	60	NBC
2	5	Maxwell House Showboat	44.6	MV	Maxwell House Coffee	Thu	9:00	60	NBC
3	6	Rudy Vallee Show	39.8	MV	Fleischmann Yeast	Thu	8:00	60	NBC
4	N	Will Rogers' Gulf Headliners	37.0	CV	Gulf Oil	Sun	9:00	30	Blue
5	2	Ed Wynn's Texaco Fire Chief	32.3	CV	Texaco Petroleum	Tue	9:30	30	NBC
6	7	Amos & Andy	29.8	SC	Pepsodent Toothpaste	M-F	7:00	15	NBC
7	10	Burns & Allen/Guy Lombardo Show	28.2	CV	White Owl Cigars	Wed	9:30	30	CBS
8	11	Ben Bernie Show	27.8	MV	Pabst Beer	Tue	9:00	30	NBC
9	N	Beauty Box Theater/G Swarthout	26.5	MST	Palmolive Soap	Tue	10:00	60	NBC
10	27	Paul Whiteman's Kraft Music Hall	26.3	MV	Kraft Cheese	Thu	10:00	60	NBC
11	N	Joe Penner Bakers' Broadcast	24.9	CV	Fleischmann Yeast	Sun	7:30	30	Blue
12	13t	Sinclair Wiener Minstrels	24.4	MSP	Sinclair Oil	Mon	9:00	30	Blue
13	24	Phil Baker The Armour Jester	23.9	CV	Armour Meats	Fri	9:30	30	Blue
14	21	First Nighter/Don Ameche	23.7	DA	Campana Balm	Fri	10:00	30	NBC
15	25	Fred Waring Show	22.2	MST	Ford Motors	Thu	9:30	60	CBS
16	19	Jack Benny Program	21.9	CV	General Tire	Fri	9:30	30	NBC 1
17	18	Bing Crosby Show/Mills Brothers	21.5	MV	Woodbury Soap	Tue	9:00	30	CBS
18	20	Cruise of The Seth Parker	21.3	MV	Frigidaire Refrigerators	Tue	10:00	30	NBC
19	33	Lowell Thomas News	21.0	NC	Sun Oil	M-F	6:45	15	Blue
20	16	Cities Service Concert/J Dragonette	19.6	MC	Cities Service Petroleum	Fri	8:00	60	NBC
21	N	George M Cohan's Gulf Headliners	19.5	MV	Gulf Oil	Sun	9:00	30	Blue
22	12	Myrt & Marge	19.2	DCC	Wrigley Gum	M-F	7:00	15	CBS
23	26	The March of Time	18.9	DA	Remington Rand	Fri	8:30	30	CBS
24	N	Robert Ripley's Saturday Night Party	18.6	MV	Hudson Autos	Sat	10:00	60	NBC
25	13t	Voice of Firestone	17.9	MC	Firestone Tires	Mon	8:30	30	NBC
26	N	Byrd Antarctic Expedition	17.3	MV	Birds Eye Frozen Foods	Sat	10:00	30	CBS
27	3	Jack Pearl's Baron Munchausen	16.1	CV	Royal Gelatin	Wed	8:00	30	NBC 2
28	39	Fred Allen's Hour of Smiles	16.0	CV	Ipana/Sal Hepatica	Wed	9:00	60	NBC 3,4
29t	N	John McCormack Sings	15.6	MST	Vince Mouthwash	Wed	9:30	30	Blue
29t	N	Warden Lawes at Sing Sing	15.6	DA	Sloan's Liniment	Wed	9:00	30	Blue
31	27t	Eno Crime Clues	15.4	DA	Eno Antacid Salts	Tue	8:00	30	Blue
32	29	Blackstone Plantation	15.0	MSP	Blackstone Cigars	Tue	8:00	30	NBC
33	N	Ship of Joy/Hugh Dobbs	14.9	MV	Shell Oil	Mon	9:30	30	NBC
34	49	American Album of Familiar Music	14.8	MST	Bayer Aspirin	Sun	9:30	30	NBC
35	41t	Death Valley Days	14.6	DA	20 Mule Team Borax Cleaner	Thu	9:00	30	Blue
36	N	Wayne King Orch	14.4	MP	Lady Esther Cosmetics	Tu,W	7:30	30	NBC 5
37	30	Carnation Contented Hour/ Gene Arnold	13.8	MST	Carnation Milk	Mon	10:00	30	NBC
38	22	The Goldbergs/Gertrude Berg	13.6	SC	Pepsodent Toothpaste	M-F	7:45	15	NBC
39t	N	The Cadillac Symphony	13.2	MC	Cadillac Automobiles	Sun	6:00	60	Blue
39t	N	Hall of Fame/Lily Pons	13.2	MST	Lysol Disinfectant	Sun	10:30	30	NBC
41t	41t	A&P Gypsies	13.0	MSP	A&P Food Stores	Mon	9:00	30	NBC
41t	N	Colgate House Party/Various Hosts	13.0	MV	Colgate Toothpaste	Sat	8:00	30	NBC
43	N	Let's Listen to Phil Harris	11.7	MP	Cutex Nail Products	Fri	9:00	30	Blue
44	N	Edwin C Hill News	11.5	NC	Barbasol Shave Cream	MWF	8:15	15	CBS

		Program	Rtg	Type	Sponsor	Day	Time	Lgth	Net
45	N	Albert Spalding Violin Recitals	11.3	MC	Fletcher's Castoria Laxative	Wed	8:30	30	CBS
46	25	Fred Waring Show	11.2	MST	Old Gold Cigarettes	Wed	10:00	30	CBS
47	N	Olsen & Johnson's Swift Revue	11.1	CV	Swift Meats	Fri	10:00	30	CBS
48	N	Billy Batchelor Sketches	11.0	DCC	Wheatena Cereal	M–F	7:15	15	NBC
49t	62	Jack Frost's Melody Moments	10.9	MC	Jack Frost Sugar	Mon	9:30	30	CBS
49t	60	Manhattan Merry Go Round	10.9	MP	Dr Lyons Tooth Powder	Sun	9:00	30	NBC
49t	44	Walter Winchell's Jergens Journal	10.9	NC	Jergens Lotion	Sun	9:30	15	Blue

*Three programs tied for 49th

New & Returning Top 50 Programs Underscored

	Program			Sponsor	Day	Time	Lgth	Net
1	Jack Benny Program	Oct–Mar		Chevrolet	Sun	10:00	30	NBC
2	Jack Pearl's Baron Munchausen	Sep–Dec		Lucky Strike Cigarettes	Sat	9:00	30	NBC
3	Fred Allen's Salad Bowl Revue	Sep–Dec		Hellman's Mayonnaise	Fri	9:00	30	NBC
4	Fred Allen's Sal Hepatica Revue	Jan–Mar		Sal Hepatica Laxative	Wed	9:00	30	NBC
5	Wayne King Orch	Sep–Apr		Lady Esther Cosmetics	Tu, W	8:30	30	NBC

Key: API — Audience Participation/Interviews
APQ — Audience Participation/Quiz
APS — Audience Participation/Stunts
CV — Comedy/Variety Show
DA — Dramatic Anthology

DCC — Drama/Continuing Characters
MC — Music/Classical, Semi-Classical
MP — Music/Popular, Contemporary
MSP — Music/Specialty, Ethnic
MST — Music/Standard, Traditional

MV — Music/Variety Show
NC — News, Commentary
SC — Situation Comedy

1933–34 Top 50 Favorite Formats

	Programs	Pct
Music — All Categories	28	56%
Comedy — All Categories	12	20%
Drama — Anthology & Continuing	7	14%
News/Commentary	3	8%

1933–34 Monthly Winners

Sep	Maxwell House Showboat	44.5	Feb	Eddie Cantor Show	56.2
Oct	Rudy Vallee Show	41.6	Mar	Eddie Cantor Show	54.0
Nov	Eddie Cantor Show	48.0	Apr	Eddie Cantor Show	50.2
Dec	Eddie Cantor Show	57.2	May	Maxwell House Showboat	40.3
Jan	Eddie Cantor Show	56.3	Jun	Maxwell House Showboat	43.9

7

The 1934–35 Network Season

Announcer: <u>Feen-A-Mint</u> is the modern laxative in delicious chewing gum. It tastes so good you don't have to coax children to take it. Just let your child chew a piece of delicious, mint-flavored <u>Feen-A-Mint</u> for three minutes or more at bedtime. It'll be a chewing gum treat because Feen-A-Mint has the delicious mint taste that leaves her mouth so clean and fresh tasting. She'll be happy and you'll be confident because science has proved that this chewing actually helps make <u>Feen-A-Mint</u> more thorough and reliable. Feen-A-Mint works gently through the night so next morning your worries are relieved and your youngster's herself again — happy once more, romping and full of fun! For happy smiles tomorrow, be sure you have Feen-A-Mint handy whenever <u>anyone</u> in your family needs its gentle, dependable relief. Ask for the chewing gum laxative ... delicious, mint-flavored <u>Feen-A-Mint</u> at your neighborhood drug counter today!

cent of American homes had invested in radios and the networks' share of the radio industry's total income inched up to 59 percent.

Chicago's Blackett-Sample-Hummert led all advertising agencies in radio spending with over four million dollars in network time bought in 1934 *(67.5 Mil)*. Another twelve agencies spent at least a million dollars with the networks.

A MUTUAL LOVE OF MONEY

A reported $42.6 Million dollars *(719.2 Mil)*, was paid to the three radio networks of a combined 184 affiliates — just 32 percent of the total number of stations. That kind of money led two very independent broadcasters to think about a new, station-owned network of their own.

Bamberger Department Stores' WOR/New York and *The Chicago Tribune*'s WGN had discussed the advantages of a cooperative net-

1929's Quality Broadcasting Group, along with WXYZ/Detroit and WLW/Cincinnati. Quality was meant to be a means for independent stations with high-caliber local programming to swap programs with no network strings attached.

The idea was just a few years ahead of its time.

GETTING A BREAD START

In 1932, WXYZ developed a hot property for Silvercup Bread.

The Lone Ranger was an immediate hit over a regional hookup in Michigan and bread sales grew at a rapid rate. Silvercup wanted to sell bread on WOR WGN and WLW, too.

The three stations were powerhouse clear-channel facilities. WGN and WOR were 50,000 watts each and WLW had begun its five year experiment as the nation's first and only station blasting out 500,000 watts. The three could arguably cover much of the east and Midwest similar to Sarnoff's "super station" network concept of a decade earlier.

WXYZ operated with a modest 5,000 watts but originated the program that the others wanted.

With sponsorship of the one program guaranteed, WGN and WOR incorporated the Mutual Broadcasting System in September 1934 as a cooperative venture involving none of the network obligations required of CBS, NBC or Blue affiliates.

Mutual's first program, *The Lone Ranger*, originated from WXYZ on October 2. The Detroit station would leave the network the following year but continued to feed *Ranger* to Mutual until 1942 when it moved the program to Blue.

Horlick's Malted Milk moved *Lum & Abner* from NBC to Mutual in April. The nightly strip show produced at WGN became

---

1934–35 Season Scoreboard
Mid-season Totals, December 1934

		Compared to Year Earlier	
Total Radio Homes	20.4 Mil	+1.15 Mil	+5.6%
Total Auto Radios	1.25 Mil	+0.75 Mil	+60.0%
Total Radio Stations	583	(16)	(2.7%)
Total Radio Network Affiliates	184	+5	+2.7%
1934 Radio Revenues	72.8 Mil	+15.8 Mil	+21.7%
1934 Network Revenues	42.6 Mil	+11.1 Mil	+26.0%
Network Share	59.0%		+4.0%

RADIO'S REVENUE RENAISSANCE

After a one-year lapse, radio revenues again resumed their healthy growth. A handful of stations couldn't make it through the Depression's hardest years and folded, but the general outlook for the industry was good and getting better. Despite the tough times, 65.2 per-

work venture in early 1934. Both had been early CBS affiliates who objected to relinquishing the time and control that network affiliation required. Yet, they wanted the advantages that a network could provide — the programming and more importantly, the revenue.

WOR had also been part of an earlier, failed networking attempt,

Mutual's first program to appear in the Crossley ratings. Chet Lauck and Norris Goff's daily sketch of life in rural Arkansas finished the season with a 5.5. Although the rating was low by other networks' standards, it was quite respectable for Mutual, which consisted of only four stations at the time.

The Mutual concept was originally a program exchange that allowed advertisers to buy several key markets simultaneously via network lines paid for by the stations. It was never intended to become the world's largest radio network — but Mutual would achieve that status within five years.

Nevertheless, program contributions to the concept were rare and weak. Mutual was never a serious competitor for top prime time ratings. The network profited from its popular news and daytime programming but at night Mutual could often be characterized as either the incubator or graveyard of the other networks' hits.

PALEY GETS PERSONAL

Radio advertising had its share of "personal product" advertisers whose commercials offended the more sensitive listeners. Most notable were the laxatives — Ex Lax, Sal Hepatica, Feen-A-Mint, Fletcher's Castoria and Eno Salts — which all sponsored a string of popular programs.

Newspapers were more than happy to print indignant letters to the editors complaining of such "distasteful" commercials — while running print ads for the very same products.

In response to this hubbub, and in one of his many clever marketing maneuvers, Bill Paley very publicly announced on May 13, 1935, that effective on June 1, CBS would no longer accept new advertising from products of "questionable good taste," meaning laxatives and deodorants.

New was the operative word of Paley's righteous declaration that drew praise from the public, politicians and press for radio's young champion of good taste.

In reality, the statement meant that any manufacturers of the stuff who weren't already CBS adver-

tisers had only two weeks to get on board and stay there — with no lapses during Network Radio's summer months of lower ratings and revenues.

The gambit worked. Laxative and deodorant manufacturers fell into line and signed long-term CBS contracts before Paley's self-imposed "prohibition" took effect.

BLUE HEAVEN

Led by Sunday night's Jack Benny and Joe Penner shows, Blue placed 15 programs in the season's Top 50. It would be an all time high for the WJZ-anchored network, whether known as Blue or ABC. Its more powerful and prestigious sibling, NBC, would soon begin to cherry-pick Blue's lineup of hit programs for its own schedule.

FIRST STEPS TO FAME

Long running programs and personalities made their first ratings showings in 1934–35. Among them were Lucky Strike's *Your Hit Parade,* the Carleton E. Morse family serial, *One Man's Family,* Louella Parson's first series, *Hollywood Hotel,* and *Major Bowes' Original Amateur Hour.*

Bob Hope first appeared in the ratings with *The Intimate Review,* which aired for only five months on Blue but returned dismal ratings that never topped 6.0.

THE MONTHLIES

Eddie Cantor caused the end of two monthly winning streaks at mid-season — NBC's and his own. Cantor's Sunday night *Chase & Sanborn Hour* took monthly honors for NBC when the comedian returned to the network in October and November. But his personal streak of 14 months as Number One whenever he appeared ended with his jump to CBS in February and NBC's Rudy Vallee overtook Cantor to win first place by a scant half of one rating point.

Cantor came back to win March which turned out to be the last time he would ever register a month's Number One show. Ironically, his last monthly win was the first in CBS history and snapped NBC's string at 26 consecutive months of first place

shows that dated back to September 1932.

The ten month season produced five separate monthly winners. *Maxwell House Showboat* continued strong by winning September, December and January. Jack Benny's new Sunday show developed an audience and finished first in April and May giving Blue its first monthly wins. The season's surprise was *Major Bowes' Original Amateur Hour,* which generated an uncommonly high first place rating in June, a 40.1.

Cantor, Bowes and Benny all had ratings exceeding 35, which made Sunday night the highest rated real estate in radio.

1934–35 Sunday Night Top Ten Programs
NBC 4, Blue 3, CBS 3
Average: 24.7

Program	Network	Time	Rating
Eddie Cantor Show	CBS	8:00	41.0
Major Bowes' Original Amateur Hour	NBC	8:00	36.0
Jack Benny Program	Blue	7:00	35.0
Joe Penner's Bakers Broadcast	Blue	7:30	31.3
Will Rogers' Gulf Headliners	CBS	8:30	23.9
Chase & Sanborn Opera Guild	NBC	8:00	22.4
The Gibson Family	NBC	10:00	15.1
Ford Sunday Evening Hour	CBS	9:00	14.7
American Album of Familiar Music	NBC	9:30	13.8
Walter Winchell's Jergens Journal	Blue	9:30	13.7

SUNDAYS AT SEVEN

General Foods hired Jack Benny in October and moved him from NBC's Friday schedule to Sunday evenings at 7:00 on Blue. The comedian, who had been a network nomad for two years, found a home in the time period and wouldn't leave it for the next 24 years that he was on the air.

Although he would change sponsors and networks over the ensuing seasons, he never budged from the timeslot — and with good reason. Benny never finished out of the annual Top Ten while he occupied it, becoming so associated with it that his autobiography coauthored with daughter Joan is titled *Sundays at Seven*.

General Foods knew it had a good thing, too. It employed Benny to sell its flavored gelatin — "*Jello, Everyone!*"—for the next eight years and Grape Nuts cereals for another two.

SUNDAY'S SURPRISES

Sunday continued to be Network Radio's most popular night. Four of Sunday's programs averaged a season rating of 30 or higher and the average rating of Sunday's Top Ten programs reached an all time high.

Yet, there were some shakeups within those numbers.

Fourteen years before Bill Paley's famous 1948–49 talent raid, Eddie Cantor became the first major star to jump from NBC to CBS. He began the season anchoring NBC's Sunday lineup at 8:00 for Chase & Sanborn, averaging a whopping 47.0 Crossley rating in October and November.

Cantor left the show in December and reappeared on CBS in February in the same Sunday 8:00 timeslot — with his show reduced to half an hour. Lehn & Fink, importers of German-made Pebeco Toothpaste, bet the dentifrice's entire advertising budget on Cantor's success. Although he lost 25 percent of his NBC audience in the switch, the comedian still generated an enviable 37.1 average rating during his first three-months on CBS.

WHAT WERE YOU THINKING?

Cantor's departure left NBC and Standard Brands with a big void to fill at 8:00.

John Reber, director of broadcasting at Standard Brands' advertising agency, J. Walter Thompson, was hailed as a programming genius. With support from NBC programming chief, John F. Royal, Reber's staff created some of Network Radio's top hits, including the immensely popular Cantor show.

The pair also concocted one of the biggest turkeys in Network Radio history.

When Cantor left NBC in December, Vaudeville was out and Verdi was in. The comedian was replaced

by *The Chase & Sanborn Opera Guild*—famed operas abridged and sung in English.

The Fat Lady sang quickly for the show. It survived for only 13 weeks.

When their over-estimation of public taste became obvious in the ratings, Reber and Royal again went searching for another way to recapture Sunday night supremacy for Standard Brands.

They found it on a local New York independent station, WHN.

Major Bowes' Original Amateur Hour was given a shot at the Chase & Sanborn hour in March 1935. It was an immediate ratings success. The haughty host and his amateurs would have radio's highest rated program the following season.

Reber and Royal could breathe easier — until Bowes joined Cantor and jumped to CBS in 1936.

AGAIN, WHAT WERE YOU THINKING?

Procter & Gamble's hour long Sunday night entry on NBC for Ivory Soap was *The Gibson Family*—a weekly, serialized, *original musical comedy*. An average of four new songs per week were required from famed songwriters Arthur Schwartz and Howard Deitz at a reported weekly salary of $1,250 *($21,100)*, each. The pair had been responsible for such Tin Pan Alley hits as *Dancing in the Dark, I Found a Million Dollar Baby* and *Something to Remember You by*.

The program gave NBC something else to remember. It simply couldn't live up to its promise and the ratings reflect its downward slide to a final 11.6. The expensive experiment ended after one season with a reported $500,000 *(8.4 Mil)*, in P&G soap money down the drain.

WILL ROGERS SIGNS OFF

Gulf Headliners moved from Blue to CBS in October and occupied no less than six different Sunday night time slots during the 1934–35 season.

Like the previous season, Will Rogers appeared in less than half of *Headliners'* 1934–35 broadcasts. He alternated the series' lead with *Stoopnagle & Budd* (F. Chase Taylor

and Budd Hulick), and character actor Charlie Winninger, a popular personality from his Captain Henry role on NBC's successful *Maxwell House Showboat*. But it was the Oklahoma humorist who drew the big ratings on his *Headliners* broadcasts in October, January, April, May and June.

Rogers bid his final farewell to the *Gulf Headliners* audience on June 9, 1935.

It was more final than anyone could have imagined. Ten weeks later he was dead — killed with aviator Wiley Post in a plane crash near Point Barrow, Alaska.

1934–35 Monday Night Top Ten Programs (11)
Blue 4, CBS 4, NBC 3
Average: 16.2

Amos & Andy*	Blue	7:00	23.2
Lowell Thomas News*	Blue	6:45	21.5
Sinclair Wiener Minstrels	Blue	9:00	20.7
Myrt & Marge*	CBS	7:00	17.3
Kate Smith's New Star Revue	CBS	8:30	14.6
Edwin C Hill News	CBS	8:15	13.5
Red Davis	Blue	8:00	13.5
Voice of Firestone	NBC	8:30	12.8
Block & Sully's Ex Lax Big Show	CBS	9:30	12.7
Carnation Contented Hour	NBC	10:00	12.4
Joe Cook's Colgate House Party	NBC	9:30	12.4

*Monday–Friday Strip Programs

Sans Strips...

Wayne King's Lady Esther Serenade	CBS	10:00	12.0
Dangerous Paradise	Blue	7:45	11.9

BLUE MONDAY FOR NBC

It wasn't supposed to work this way.

NBC's secondary network — the WJZ-anchored Blue chain — and the upstart CBS left the more prestigious NBC with just three also-rans in Monday's Top Ten. What's more, Blue took the top three spots with inexpensively produced programs: *Amos & Andy*, Lowell Thomas News and Chicago's *Sinclair Minstrels*.

Strips aside, musical variety with a capital *V* was Monday's characteristic. The leading programs offered by the three networks seemed to characterize each network's fare during the 1930s — novelty, popular and prestigious.

Blue's top novelty entry, *Sinclair Wiener Minstrels,* was southern-fried specialty music and comedy. It could be likened to another Chicago originated show, *The National Barn Dance*— only in blackface. CBS followed with 27-year-old Kate Smith's popular songs of the day while NBC's prestigious *Voice of Firestone* trailed Smith in the 8:30 timeslot.

Monday's melodic menu also included Carnation Milk's long-running *Contented Hour,* Harry Horlick's eclectic *A&P Gypsies* and the saccharin sweet dance band led by Jan Garber, dubbed "The Idol of the Airlanes."

A ratings tornado called *Lux Radio Theater* was destined to shake up Mondays the following season.

1934–35 Tuesday Night Top Ten Programs
Blue 4, NBC 4, CBS 2
Average: 19.9

Palmolive Beauty Box Theater	NBC	10:00	27.2
Ed Wynn's Texaco Fire Chief Show	NBC	9:30	27.1
Ben Bernie Show	NBC	9:00	23.9
Amos & Andy*	Blue	7:00	22.4
Lowell Thomas News*	Blue	6:45	19.2
Myrt & Marge*	CBS	7:00	17.4
Lawrence Tibbett Program	Blue	8:30	17.0
Wayne King's Lady Esther Serenade	NBC	8:30	15.0
Bing Crosby's Woodbury Show	CBS	9:00	15.3
Eno Crime Clues	Blue	8:00	14.9
Sans Strips...			
Edgar a Guest's Musical Memories	Blue	8:30	7.8
Isham Jones Orchestra	CBS	9:30	7.6
Lavender & Old Lace	CBS	8:00	7.4

*Monday–Friday Strip Shows

THE SUCCESSFUL SOAP OPERETTA

NBC's second attempt at hour long musical comedy in the 1934–35 season had far better success than the *Gibson Family* experiment. *The Palmolive Beauty Box Theater* used material proved successful on the Broadway stage and presented it with top flight talent. Its cast was

headlined by 24-year-old soprano Jessica Dragonette who had first captivated NBC audiences while still a teenager in 1927. Dragonette and company won the night at 10:00 with a 27.2 rating, capping the network's three 20+performances beginning with the 23.9 registered by Ben Bernie's band at 9:00 and continuing with Ed Wynn's 27.1 as *The Texaco Fire Chief* at 9:30.

BING'S BAD SEASON

Bing Crosby's *Woodbury Show* completed its second year on CBS's Tuesday night schedule and suffered a 30 percent loss of audience. Crosby added Cincinnati's popular singing Mills Brothers as his supporting act but continued to trail Ben Bernie's NBC show at 9:00 by a solid 8.6 points — an even greater margin than Bernie's 1933–34 lead of five points. Adding insult to injury, Crosby's show had fewer listeners than operatic baritone Lawrence Tibbett on Blue.

Crosby's fortunes would improve dramatically the next season with a change in network, sponsor and format.

FOUR TIMES IN THREE-QUARTER TIME

Wayne King's broadcast schedule from Chicago was increased to four prime time half hours a week — two on NBC and two on CBS. The "Waltz King's" orchestra with legendary announcer Franklyn MacCormack purring poetry and Lady Esther commercials, had a weekly cumulative audience of an estimated 25 million persons — easily the widest exposure ever given a single dance band on network radio.

Isham Jones's early swing band, fronted later by Woody Herman, earned only half of King's numbers and left the air in February, succeeded by the long running *Hour of Charm* starring Phil Spitalny's all girl orchestra.

Frank and Anne Hummert added their musical touch to Tuesday nights with *Lavender & Old Lace,* another of their formulaic shows featuring singers and studio musicians heard the Hummerts' other shows, led by popular baritone Frank Munn.

1934–35 Wednesday Night Top Ten Programs
NBC 5, Blue 3, CBS 2
Average: 19.6

Fred Allen's Town Hall Tonight	NBC	9:00	29.7
Amos & Andy*	Blue	7:00	21.6
Guy Lombardo's Pleasure Island	NBC	10:00	20.1
Lowell Thomas News*	Blue	6:45	19.9
Mary Pickford & Company	NBC	8:00	19.8
One Man's Family	NBC	9:30	18.7
Burns & Allen Show	CBS	9:30	18.3
Myrt & Marge*	CBS	7:00	18.1
Wayne King's Lady Esther Serenade	NBC	8:30	15.0
Lanny Ross' Log Cabin Orchestra	Blue	8:30	14.8

*Monday–Friday Strip Shows

Sans Strips...			
House of Glass	Blue	8:30	13.7
Edwin C Hill News	CBS	8:15	13.5
Red Davis	Blue	8:00	13.5

EVERYBODY MEETS AT TOWN HALL

NBC expanded its midweek dominance of prime time on Wednesdays with five of the night's Top Ten programs.

Leader of the pack was Fred Allen who nearly doubled his 1933–34 Wednesday night ratings with a new timeslot, sponsor and format. He settled into Texaco's *Town Hall Tonight* and began a string of four consecutive years in the Annual Top Ten.

Mary Pickford's anthology dramas followed by Lanny Ross' half hour of pop vocals set the table for Allen who won the night at 9:00, outdistancing his time period's competition by nearly ten rating points.

HENRY AND FANNY VS. GEORGE AND GRACIE

Half-hour serial drama *One Man's Family*—in its network debut year — lost over a third of Fred Allen's NBC audience at 9:30 opposite CBS's *Burns & Allen Show.* But Henry and Fanny Barbour kept enough listeners to edge out George and Gracie. It was the first of ten consecutive Top 50 seasons for *One Man's Family,* two of them in the Top Ten.

Standard Brands and agency J. Walter Thompson, always aware of trends, picked up sponsorship of the Carleton E. Morse family drama in April and stayed with the program for the next 14 years.

A RECORD BY A SINGER

Lanny Ross, 28, became network radio's most popular singer and achieved a first by starring in two Top 50 programs on two separate networks in the same season. Ross appeared as the romantic singing lead of *Maxwell House Showboat*—second in the Annual Top Ten on NBC — and hosted *Lanny Ross' Log Cabin Syrup Orchestra*—37th in the Annual Top 50 on Blue — both under the corporate sponsorship of General Foods.

The handsome Ross also had two 1934 movies going for him — Paramount's *Melody in Spring* and *College Rhythm*, which also featured radio's Joe Penner and future radio star, Jack Oakie. But the films were lame and Ross' movie career never took off.

Nevertheless, Lanny Ross with his pleasing voice and warm personality enjoyed 20 years of Network Radio popularity — many in 15-minute strip shows.

PEARL DIVING

Jack Pearl's *Baron Munchausen* routine had run its course on NBC. Standard Brands had dropped its sponsorship after Pearl fell from a 39.4 rating and third place in the Annual Top Ten in 1932–33, to a 16.1 rating and 27th place the following season. Pearl moved to CBS and created a new character, *Peter Pfeiffer*—a kinder, gentler variation of *Munchausen*.

Pfeiffer flopped to a 12.7 in its four month run, easily topped by Guy Lombardo's *Pleasure Island* variety show on NBC. Pearl finished the season out of the Top 50 — forever.

NOW FOR SOMETHING COMPLETELY DIFFERENT...

Except for its popular *Amos & Andy* and Lowell Thomas plus the addition singing star Lanny Ross, Blue filled out the night with its typically different programming.

The Goldbergs' Gertrude Berg re-turned to Network Radio with a new serial drama, *The House of Glass* at 8:30. Her semi-autobiographical series lasted less than a year.

Greater staying power was provided by Sing Sing Prison Warden Lewis Lawes. Lawes' stories of crimes, criminals, prisons and prisoners ran for six years. Sometimes known as *Twenty Thousand Years in Sing Sing* (Lawes' book upon which the series was based), *Warden Lawes at Sing Sing* is commonly considered an inspiration for Phillips H. Lord's long running *Gangbusters*.

Shifting gears again, Blue rounded out Wednesday night with legendary Irish tenor John McCormack who was beyond his peak at age 51, but still appealed to a sizable older audience. McCormack had refused to appear on radio a few years earlier because he believed it would jeopardize his concert ticket sales. He changed his tune when Vince Mouthwash sponsored him for two years on Blue.

1934–35 Thursday Night Top Ten Programs
CBS 4, Blue 3, NBC 3
Average: 20.5

Maxwell House Showboat	NBC	9:00	37.8
Rudy Vallee's Fleishmann Hour	NBC	8:00	35.6
Paul Whiteman's Kraft Music Hall	NBC	10:00	22.8
Amos & Andy*	Blue	7:00	21.4
Lowell Thomas News*	Blue	6:45	19.4
Myrt & Marge*	CBS	7:00	17.0
Death Valley Days	Blue	9:00	15.2
Fred Waring Show	CBS	9:30	14.9
Boake Carter News*	CBS	7:45	11.0
Bobby Benson & Sunny Jim*	CBS	6:15	9.5

*Monday–Friday Strip Shows

Sans Strips...

Glen Gray Orchestra	CBS	9:00	9.4
Floyd Gibbons News	Blue	7:30	7.5
Forum of Liberty	CBS	8:30	6.6
Molle Merry Minstrels	NBC	7:30	4.7
Alemite Half Hour	CBS	10:30	4.0

NBC's WINS IN WINDS OF CHANGE

Network Radio's three grocery giants — Standard Brands, General Foods and Kraft — gave NBC continued control of Thursday nights with three strong hour long music/variety shows.

Given Rudy Vallee's strong *Fleishmann Yeast Hour* lead-in, *Maxwell House Showboat* won the night but was showing signs of leaking some of its extremely high ratings. It scored in the 40s for the final time in October. Although Captain Henry's troupe was down 15 percent for the season, it still doubled the ratings of its time period's competition, Blue's *Death Valley Days,* and tripled the numbers posted by Glen Gray's popular "Casa Loma" dance band on CBS.

Paul Whiteman's *Kraft Music Hall* lost 40 percent of *Showboat's* lead-in audience. Whiteman's drop from the mid– to lower 20s gave Kraft and agency J. Walter Thompson thoughts about changing hosts for its high budget production, but *KMH* still had the numbers necessary to give NBC a three hour clean sweep.

The only weak spot in the NBC schedule was the hour preceding Valley, including his 7:30 lead-in, *The Molle Merry Minstrels,* mid-season replacement for another of Molle Shave Cream's southern-fried entries, *The Molle Dixie Dandies.*

1934–35 Friday Night Top Ten Programs
Blue 4, CBS 4, NBC 2
Average: 16.3

First Nighter	NBC	10:00	22.7
March of Time	CBS	9:00	21.5
Amos & Andy*	Blue	7:00	20.4
Phil Baker's Armour Jester	Blue	9:30	19.8
Lowell Thomas News*	Blue	6:45	18.8
Cities Service Concert	NBC	8:00	18.0
Hollywood Hotel	CBS	9:30	17.5
Myrt & Marge*	CBS	7:00	17.1
Edwin C Hill News	CBS	8:15	13.5
Red Davis	Blue	8:00	13.5

*Monday–Friday Strip Shows

Sans Strips...

Court of Human Relations	CBS	8:30	12.5
Beatrice Lillie Show	Blue	9:00	12.4
Dangerous Paradise	Blue	7:45	11.9

HOTEL REGISTERS A HIT

AT&T lowered its long line charges from the West Coast in 1934.

Campbell Soup and CBS were first to jump at the opportunity to capitalize on the glamour of large scale Hollywood originations. *Hollywood Hotel* debuted on Friday nights at 9:30 with Hearst movie columnist Louella Parsons as its gushing hostess and handsome Dick Powell as her co-host and singing star. A flock of film stars paraded through the "hotel lobby" each week to be interviewed by Parsons and sometimes deliver short dramatizations of scenes from their current movies.

Parsons pressured the actors to appear without a fee and would later boast that she had obtained a million dollars worth of talent for nothing.

Despite the show's Hollywood hoopla and the promotion given her program in Parsons' columns that were syndicated to hundreds of newspapers, *Hollywood Hotel* dropped four rating points from its lead-in, *The March of Time*, and trailed its far less costly competition in the same time period, *The Phil Baker Armour Jester Show*, by several points.

Ironically, the highest rated program of the night was Chicago's low-budgeted *First Nighter*, on NBC which repeated as the season's highest rated dramatic series.

1934–35 Saturday Night Top Ten Programs
NBC 5, CBS 3, Blue 2
Average: 15.0

Al Jolson's Shell Chateau	NBC	9:30	25.2
Let's Dance	NBC	10:30	19.4
National Barn Dance	Blue	9:30	19.1
Sigmund Romberg Revue	NBC	8:00	15.6
Your Hit Parade	NBC	8:00	15.5
Radio City Party	Blue	9:00	14.0
Roxy & His Gang	CBS	8:00	13.6
Andre Kostelanetz Orchestra	CBS	9:00	10.3
Songs You Love to Hear	NBC	9:00	9.1
Musical Memories	CBS	8:45	8.3

MUSIC, MUSIC, MUSIC

Every show in Saturday's Top Ten was based in music — jukebox hits, standards, show tunes, the classics, even hillbilly ditties — sung and played by everyone from a legendary star to nameless studio performers. Seven of those programs finished among the season's Top 50.

Al Jolson, cranking out big-budgeted movie musicals for Warner Brothers at the rate of one a year, gave NBC and sponsor Shell Oil one of only three shows to ever to score a rating above 20 on Saturday, the lowest rated night of the week.

Shell Chateau of 1934–35 was the second highest rated Saturday show of the Golden Age era — runner-up only to Walter O'Keefe's *Lucky Strike Dance Party* of 1932–33 and several points ahead of *Truth or Consequences'* biggest season in 1947–48.

From Chicago, Blue's *National Barn Dance* was in the second season of its 15 year Saturday night network run. At the opposite end of the musical spectrum, Sigmund Romberg presented music from his light operettas on NBC and Andre Kostelanetz' CBS studio orchestra played familiar classical and semi-classic melodies.

Dance music — a staple of late night network programming — extended Saturday's prime time to midnight with *Let's Dance*, a 90 minute NBC marathon beginning at 10:30 under Nabisco sponsorship. The format rotated three orchestras in 30 minute segments: Benny Goodman's swing band, Xavier Cugat's Latin group and a studio orchestra led by Al Goodman (no relation to Benny).

The show's one season has been credited with popularizing the distinctive styles of Benny Goodman and Xavier Cugat.

THE SYNCOPATION COMPETITION

Lucky Strike's *Your Hit Parade* started its 18 year multi-network radio run in April 1935 and began to build a following among music fans by presenting the top popular songs of each week according to a "confidential" poll of sheet music and record sales plus disc jockey and dance band requests conducted by American Tobacco's agency, Lord & Thomas.

The popularity competition that eventually featured a dramatic countdown to each week's Number One Song finished among the season's Top 50 programs 16 times and is generally considered the genesis of Top 40 Radio.

1934–35 Top Ten Multiple Run Programs
CBS 5, Blue 4, NBC 1
Average: 14.7

Amos & Andy*	M–F	Blue	7:00	22.3
Lowell Thomas News*	M–F	Blue	6:45	20.0
Myrt & Marge*	M–F	CBS	7:00	18.0
Wayne King's Lady Esther Serenade	Tu,W	NBC	8:30	14.5
Edwin C Hill News	M,W,F	CBS	8:15	13.5
Red Davis	M,W,F	Blue	8:00	13.5
Wayne King's Lady Esther Serenade	Su, M	CBS	8:30	12,0
Dangerous Paradise	M,W,F	Blue	7:45	11.9
Boake Carter News*	M–F	CBS	7:45	10.8
Andre Kostelanetz Orchestra	M,W,Sa	CBS	9:00	10.3

*Monday–Friday Strip Shows

STRIP STRENGTH

Against increasingly stronger prime time competition, low-budgeted Monday through Friday strip programs *Amos & Andy* and, Lowell Thomas News accomplished the rare feat of finishing among the Top Five ratings leaders every weeknight. It would be the last season in which Multiple Run programs enjoyed such popularity.

NEWSCASTERS GETS NOTICED

Listeners were paying more attention to radio news. For the first time newscasters held down three of the Top Ten Multiple Run program rankings. Lowell Thomas —

in the third of his 21 year run among Multiple Run leaders — was joined by Edwin C. Hill and Boake Carter.

Although 1933's *Biltmore Agreement* was in effect and the networks dutifully aired the Press Radio Bureau's five minute digests of dated news, millions of listeners tuned into the three veteran voices whose newscasts were billed as "commen-taries" in accord with the publishers and broadcasters' pact.

THE SHADOW GOES...

Outside the Multiple Runs' Top Ten with a meager 6.5 rating on CBS, *The Shadow* made his second appearance in the Crossley polls. The program had been given limited runs since 1930 and finally introduced its title character as a par-ticipant in the stories and not simply the narrator. Regardless, *The Shadow* lost 20 percent of its lead-in audience from kid shows *Bobby Benson & Sunny Jim* and *Buck Rogers*. The program left the air in March and not return until 1937 when it began its long and legendary Sunday afternoon run on Mutual.

TOP 50 PROGRAMS — 1934–35

NBC 21, Blue 16, CBS 13
Average Rating: 20.6, Median: 19.1
20,400,000 Radio Homes / 66.2% Coverage of US Homes / One Rating Point = 204,000 Homes
Source: Cooperative Analysis of Broadcasting, Sep 1934–Jun 1935
Total Programs Rated 6–11 P.M.: 161
Programs Rated 13 Weeks & Ranked: 135.

		Program	Rtg	Type	Sponsor	Day	Time	Lgth	Net
1	1	Eddie Cantor Show	41.0	CV	Pebeco Toothpaste	Sun	8:00	30	CBS 1
2	2	Maxwell House Showboat	37.8	MV	Maxwell House Coffee	Thu	9:00	60	NBC
3	N	Major Bowes Original Amateur Hour	36.0	TC	Chase & Sanborn Coffee	Sun	8:00	60	NBC
4	3	Rudy Vallee Show	35.6	MV	Fleischmann Yeast	Thu	8:00	60	NBC
5	16	Jack Benny Program	35.0	CV	Jello Gelatin	Sun	7:00	30	Blue 2
6	11	Joe Penner Bakers' Broadcast	31.3	CV	Fleischmann Yeast	Sun	7:30	30	Blue
7	27	Fred Allen's Town Hall Tonight	29.7	CV	Ipana/Sal Hepatica	Wed	9:00	60	NBC
8	8	Beauty Box Theater/G Swarthout	27.2	MST	Palmolive Soap	Tue	10:00	60	NBC
9t	4	Ed Wynn's Texaco Fire Chief	27.1	CV	Texaco Petroleum	Tue	9:30	30	NBC
9t	10	Will Rogers' Gulf Headliners Show	27.1	CV	Gulf Oil	Sun	8:30	30	CBS 3
11	N	Al Jolson's Shell Chateau	25.2	MV	Shell Oil	Sat	9:30	60	NBC
12	7	Ben Bernie Show	23.9	MV	Pabst Beer	Tue	9:00	30	NBC
13	9	Paul Whiteman's Kraft Music Hall	22.8	MV	Kraft Cheese	Thu	10:00	60	NBC
14	14	First Nighter/Don Ameche	22.7	DA	Campana Balm	Fri	10:00	30	NBC
15	N	Chase & Sanborn Opera Guild	22.4	MSP	Chase & Sanborn Coffee	Sun	8:00	60	NBC
16	5	Amos & Andy	22.3	SC	Pepsodent Toothpaste	M–F	7:00	15	Blue
17	22	March of Time	21.5	DA	Remington Rand	Fri	9:00	30	CBS
18	N	Stoopnagle & Budd Gulf Headliners	21.3	CV	Gulf Oil	Sun	9:30	30	CBS 4
19	12	Sinclair Minstrels	20.7	MSP	Sinclair Oil	Mon	9:00	30	Blue
20	N	Guy Lombardo Orch Pleasure Island	20.1	MP	Plough, Inc.	Wed	10:00	30	NBC
21	19	Lowell Thomas News	20.0	NC	Sun Oil	M–F	6:45	15	Blue
22t	N	Mary Pickford & Company	19.8	DA	Royal Gelatin	Wed	8:00	30	NBC
22t	13	Phil Baker The Armour Jester	19.8	CV	Armour Meats	Fri	9:30	30	Blue
24	N	Let's Dance/X Cugat, B Goodman	19.4	MP	Nabisco	Sat	10:30	90	NBC
25	63	National Barn Dance	19.1	MSP	Alka Seltzer	Sat	9:30	60	Blue
26	N	One Man's Family	18.7	DCC	Fleischmann Yeast	Wed	9:30	30	NBC 5
27	6	Burns & Allen Show	18.3	CV	White Owl Cigars	Wed	9:30	30	CBS 6
28t	20	Cities Service Concert/J Dragonette	18.0	MC	Cities Service Petroleum	Fri	8:00	60	NBC
28t	21	Myrt & Marge	18.0	DCC	Wrigley Gum	M–F	7:00	15	CBS
30	N	Hollywood Hotel/Louella Parsons	17.5	MV	Campbell Soup	Fri	9:30	60	CBS
31	N	Lawrence Tibbett Program	17.0	MV	Packard Autos	Tue	8:30	30	Blue
32	N	Sigmund Romberg Revue	15.6	MST	Swift Meats	Sat	8:00	60	NBC
33	N	Your Hit Parade	15.5	MP	Lucky Strike Cigarettes	Sat	8 00	60	NBC
34	17	Bing Crosby Show	15.3	MV	Woodbury Soap	Tue	9:00	30	CBS
35	34	Death Valley Days	15.2	DA	20 Mule Team Borax Cleaner	Thu	9:00	30	Blue
36	N	The Gibson Family	15.1	DCC	Ivory Soap	Sun	10:00	30	NBC 7
37	35	Wayne King Orch	15.0	MP	Lady Esther Cosmetics	Tu–W	8:30	30	NBC
38t	30	Eno Crime Clues	14.9	DA	Eno Antacid Salts	Tue	8:00	30	Blue 8
38t	45	Fred Waring Show	14.9	MST	Ford Motors	Thu	9:30	60	CBS
40	N	Lanny Ross' Log Cabin Orch	14.8	MP	Log Cabin Syrup	Wed	8:30	30	Blue
41	N	Ford Sunday Evening Hour	14.7	MC	Ford Motors	Sun	9:00	60	CBS
42	N	Kate Smith's New Star Revue	14.6	MV	Hudson Autos	Mon	8:30	30	CBS
43	N	Radio City Party/John B Kennedy	14.0	MV	RCA Victor	Sat	9:00	30	Blue
44	33	American Album of Familiar Music	13.8	MST	Bayer Asprin	Sun	9:30	30	NBC
45t	N	House of Glass/Gertrude Berg	13.7	DCC	Palmolive Soap	Wed	8:30	30	Blue
45t	48	Walter Winchell's Jergens Journal	13.7	NC	Jergens Lotion	Sun	9:30	15	Blue
47	N	Roxy & His Gang/Samuel Rothafel	13.6	MV	Fletcher's Castoria Laxative	Sat	8:00	45	CBS

		Program	Rtg	Type	Sponsor	Day	Time	Lgth	Net
48t	43	Edwin C Hill News	13.5	NC	Barbasol Shave Cream	MWF	8:15	15	CBS
48t	95	Red Davis	13.5	DCC	Beechnut Gum	MWF	8:00	15	Blue
50	28	Warden Lawes at Sing Sing	13.1	DA	Sloan's Liniment	Wed	9:00	30	Blue

New & Returning Top 50 Programs Underscored.

	Program	Rtg	Sponsor	Day	Time	Lgth	Net
1	Eddie Cantor Show	Oct–Nov	Chase & Sanborn Coffee	Sun	8:00	60	NBC
2	Jack Benny Program	Sep	General Tire	Fri	10:00	30	NBC
3	Will Rogers' Gulf Headliners	Oct	Gulf Oil	Sun	9:30	30	CBS
4	Stoopnagle & Budd Gulf Headliners	Sep	Gulf Oil	Sun	9:00	30	Blue
5	One Man's Family	Sep–Mar	Kentucky Winner Cigarettes	Wed	10:30	30	NBC
6	aka The Adventures of Gracie						
7	The Gibson Family	Sep–Feb	Ivory Soap	Sat	9:30	60	NBC
8	Eno Crime Clues	Sep–Dec	Eno Antacid Salts	T–W	8:00	30	Blue

Key: API — Audience Participation/Interviews   DCC — Drama/Continuing Characters   MV — Music/Variety Show
APQ — Audience Participation/Quiz   MC — Music/Classical, Semi-Classical   NC — News, Commentary
APS — Audience Participation/Stunts   MP — Music/Popular, Contemporary   SC — Situation Comedy
CV — Comedy/Variety Show   MSP — Music/Specialty, Ethnic   TC — Talent Competition
DA — Dramatic Anthology   MST — Music/Standard, Traditional

1934–35 Top 50 Favorite Formats

	Programs	Pct
Music — All Categories	26	52%
Drama — Anthology & Continuing	11	22%
Comedy — All Categories	10	20%
News/Information	3	6%

1934–35 Monthly Winners

Sep	Maxwell House Showboat	43.0	Feb	Rudy Vallee Show	38.5
Oct	Eddie Cantor Show	44.6	Mar	Eddie Cantor Show	39.0
Nov	Eddie Cantor Show	49.3	Apr	Jack Benny Program	42.3
Dec	Rudy Vallee Show	37.1	May	Jack Benny Program	37.7
Jan	Maxwell House Showboat	38.1	Jun	Major Bowes Amateur Hour	40.1

8

The 1935–36 Network Season

Announcer: <u>Pebeco Toothpaste</u> is the only <u>perfect</u> dentifrice. It's safely and scientifically made, to not only cleanse, whiten and polish the teeth, but also <u>saves</u> them by removing the cause of tooth degeneration — <u>acid</u> <u>mouth</u>! Acid mouth is the condition that leads to unsightly yellowing and painful decay of your teeth. Pebeco isn't one of those "lick and promise" dentifrices that just cleans the surface of the teeth and fool you into thinking everything is all right. <u>Pebeco</u> gets down to the <u>cause of decay</u>, which in 95% of the cases is <u>acid</u> <u>mouth</u> ... bad tasting, bad smelling acid mouth. Pebeco cleans the teeth ... removes tobacco and other odors ... refreshes the mouth ... strengthens the gums and neutralizes the acids that cause acid mouth. <u>Pebeco</u> is the toothpaste that fights acid mouth and leaves your teeth feeling and tasting <u>really clean</u>. So save yourself the embarrassment and the pain that acid mouth can cause. Fight acid mouth with <u>Pebeco</u> ... the <u>perfect</u> dentifrice! <u>Pebeco</u> ... the <u>100%</u> dentifrice! Now in extra-large tubes available at drug counters everywhere. For a <u>free</u> supply of acid test papers to test your mouth for acid, write to Pebeco, that's <u>P-E-B-E-C-O</u> ... in care of this station. Be assured your family is fighting acid mouth with <u>Pebeco</u>!

HOIST THE SALES!

Advertising money flowed into radio in 1935. Total industry revenues sailed past the hundred million dollar mark for the first time and network sales had doubled in two years. It was the greatest one year spurt the business would ever experience after which it would settle back to healthy annual gains — just not as spectacular.

BUT WHERE DID ALL THE LISTENERS GO?

Network radio ratings suffered their first general decline in the 1935–36 season and it was a big one. The seasons' Top 50 program average rating fell 7.3 points — a 36 percent loss of audience.

Despite these losses, nobody panicked. It was simply a change in the methodology employed by Crossley's CAB polling — a change that deflated the ballooning ratings of the early '30s. The switch was championed by researcher Crossley and CAB board member George Gallup who recognized the validity of the new *coincidental* methodology introduced by Clark-Hooper, Inc., in 1934.

CAB operators no longer asked what families listened to the previous day but within the past few hours. (Evening listenership was surveyed the following morning.)

CAB also became less generous with its "Homes Listening" estimates which had swelled in some time periods to over 70 percent in 1934–35.

CAB's change coincided with Clark-Hooper's study, *Yardsticks on the Air,* published in September by its underwriter, the ANPA newspaper alliance. Distributed to advertisers and agencies, *Yardstick*'s findings cast further doubts on Crossley's high figures. Based on a sampling of 400,000 random calls in the winter and early spring months of 1935, Clark-Hooper reported the rating of an "average" prime time program between 7:00 and 10:00 P.M. to be a mere 9.0!

Time magazine reported the findings in late September, obligingly adding, "*Yardsticks on the Air* concluded that most radio advertisers spend a great deal of money competing for an audience which is monopolized by a only few popular programs."

Ironically, *Time* was one of the competitors for audience popularity. Its *March of Time* was entering its fifth season on CBS.

The effect of CAB's new methodology was swift and dramatic. It happened between September and October when ratings historically *increase* as autumn progresses. The 1935–36 season would be the only exception to the rule — and it was a big one as evidenced by the examples at the top of page 49.

Twenty network programs finished the 1934–35 season with an average rating above 20. Only five managed to earn a 20 or greater in 1935–36.

The ratings honeymoon was over.

CBS'S FIRST WINNING SEASON

Despite the loss of Will Rogers, CBS took the season's honors with 20 of the Top 50 most popular pro-

---

1935–36 Season Scoreboard
Mid-season Totals, December 1935

		Compared to Year Earlier	
Total Radio Homes	21.46 Mil	+0.60 Mil	+5.2%
Total Auto Radios	2.0 Mil	+.75 Mil	+37.5%
Total AM Radio Stations	585	+2	+0.3%
Total Radio Network Affiliates	188	+4	+2.2%
1935 Radio Revenues	112.6 Mil	+39.8 Mil	+54.6%
1935 Network Revenues	62.6 Mil	+20.0 Mil	+46.9%
Network Share	55.6%		(3.4%)

Program	Rating Sept 1935	Oct 1935	One Month Difference
Major Bowes' Original Amateur Hour	57.9	31.0	-46.5%
Rudy Vallee Show	35.1	20.1	-42.7%
Maxwell House Showboat	36.2	17.5	-51.7%
Fred Allen's Town Hall Tonight	26.6	17.5	-34.2%
Paul Whiteman's Kraft Music Hall	26.7	14.7	-45.0%
Al Jolson's Shell Chateau	25.8	12.6	-51.2%

grams. The upstart network won three of the nightly Top Ten races and tied for two more.

Monday's Hollywood based *Lux Radio Theater* and Friday's *Hollywood Hotel* established CBS as the network for film stars and listeners responded in a big way.

SPORTS SCORE

The 1935 World Series and two Heavyweight Championship fights coincided with Crossley/CAB survey periods. Their broadcasts had ratings that regular programming only could dream about.

October's World Series was carried on *all* the networks and accounted for a combined rating of 34.7, peaking on Sunday the 6th when the Detroit Tigers and Chicago Cubs attracted a 41.5 rating.

The ratings champ was future Heavyweight Champ Joe Louis, then the up and coming boxing sensation from Detroit. His September 24th fight—a victory over former champion Max Baer—was broadcast on both NBC and Blue, and pulled a combined 45.7 rating.

Louis' surprising loss to another past champion, Max Schmeling, on June 19—again carried by both Blue and NBC—drew an even greater 57.6. And this was in the season of diminished ratings!

THE MONTHLIES

Chase & Sanborn's decision to fill its 8:00 Sunday hour on NBC with *Major Bowes' Original Amateur Hour* proved shrewd. The program was the first to become Number One in all ten months of the season. Nobody came close. The question became how long Bowes could continue his unprecedented streak of first place finishes. Bowes enabled NBC to extend its string of monthly Number One shows to 13.

1935–36 Sunday Night Top Ten Programs
CBS 4, Blue 3, NBC 3
Average: 16.3

Major Bowes' Original Amateur Hour	NBC	8:00	37.5
Jack Benny Program	Blue	7:00	25.8
Robert Ripley's Bakers Broadcast	Blue	7:30	16.0
Eddie Cantor Show	CBS	7:00	14.9
Phil Baker Show	CBS	7:30	14.9
Grace Moore's Vicks Open House	CBS	8:00	12.3
Manhattan Merry Go Round	NBC	9:00	12.0
General Motors Concert	NBC	10:00	11.4
Ford Sunday Evening Hour	CBS	9:00	9.2
Walter Winchell's Jergens Journal	Blue	9:30	9.2

BOWES RUMBLES AND CANTOR TUMBLES

Crossley's switch in interviewing and tabulating had little effect Major Bowes. The 61-year-old ringmaster of amateurs lost less than half a point from his 1934–35 ratings and emerged with the season's only program to finish in the 30s.

Prior to Crossley's adjustments that pushed ratings down, Bowes' *Original Amateur Hour* of September 8th scored a CAB rating in the mid-50s. Winners of the competition that Sunday evening were "Frank Sinatra & the Three Flashes." Bowes renamed the group during the broadcast, "The Hoboken Four."

CBS protected Eddie Cantor from Bowes' first place bulldozer on NBC by shifting his Pebeco Toothpaste show back to 7:00. But in doing so, Cantor ran up against *Blue*'s top rated show and the *second* most listened-to program in the country, Jack Benny's increasingly

popular comedy series. Benny easily topped—and twice doubled—Cantor's ratings in their seven months of head to head competition.

MUTUAL'S FIRST

The fledgling Mutual network, still only a handful of stations, registered its second rated program in February. Ray Perkins' *National Amateur Hour,* a Sunday night transplant from CBS, finished the season with a 6.3. *National,* sponsored by Feen-a-Mint chewing gum laxative, predated Major Bowes' top rated amateur hour on Network Radio by several months. Unlike the Bowes program, the real "original" amateur hour was played for laughs at the expense of its contestants—a predecessor to television's *Gong Show.*

1935–36 Monday Night Top Ten Programs
CBS 5, Blue 3, NBC 2
Average: 10.4

Lux Radio Theater	CBS	9:00	14.6
Amos & Andy*	NBC	7:00	12.7
Grand Hotel	Blue	8:30	11.0
Lowell Thomas*	Blue	6:45	10.8
Voice of Firestone	NBC	8:30	10.7
March of Time*	CBS	10:30	9.9
Boake Carter News*	CBS	7:45	9.4
Pick & Pat	CBS	8:30	8.6
Guy Lombardo Orchestra	CBS	8:00	8.5
Sinclair Minstrels	Blue	9:00	8.0

*Monday–Friday Strip Shows

Sans Strips...

A&P Gypsies	NBC	9:00	7.2
Dangerous Paradise	Blue	7:45	6.9
Uncle Ezra's Radio Station	NBC	7:15	6.8
Fibber McGee & Molly	Blue	8:00	6.6

LUX CLEANS UP IN HOLLYWOOD

Lever Brothers and its agency, J. Walter Thompson, left their mark on radio history when they transplanted *Lux Radio Theater* from New York and Blue's Sunday afternoon schedule to Hollywood and Mondays at 9:00 on CBS.

To reinforce its Hollywood image, the star studded anthology of popular movies adapted for radio was hosted and narrated by legendary film director Cecil B. De-

Mille. DeMille, 54, also conducted curtain call interviews with the stars, chats that always included actresses' glowing endorsements of Lux Beauty Soap.

Lux scored a 14.6 season's average — just one-tenth of one percent higher than its Sunday afternoon rating on Blue a year earlier. That would all change the following year when Lux began a string of 14 straight seasons with average ratings of 20 or better. The show immediately became Monday's highest rated program, a position it would never relinquish during Network Radio's Golden Age by never straying from its format, from CBS or Monday night at 9:00.

NBC HAILS THE FRESH AIR TAXI

NBC took Pepsodent's Amos & Andy from Blue. It was the first in a string of Blue's hits that would shift to the more powerful of RCA's two networks. This larceny, however, might be considered justified.

For six years the program's originating station, NBC's WMAQ, had been required to feed Amos and Andy to the entire Blue network — including its own Chicago competitor, WENR. In a unique arrangement, both stations simultaneously broadcast the program's second (West Coast) feed nightly at 10:00 for five years until WENR took sole custody of the feed in 1934.

Amos & Andy came home to WMAQ's air exclusively on July 15, 1935.

PICK AND PAT'S POPULAR PATTER

Network Radio's other blackface comedy team, Pick Malone and Pat Padgett, known to listeners of Maxwell House Showboat as "Molasses 'n' January," benefited from the success of Lux Radio Theater when sponsor U.S. Tobacco moved their spin-off show from NBC's Friday schedule to CBS on Mondays at 8:30. With the lead-in show to Lux they benefited from early tune-in's for the Hollywood extravaganza.

The move propelled Pick & Pat into the season's Top 50, although the comics trailed both Voice of

Firestone and Grand Hotel in their time period. It was the first of five consecutive Top 50 finishes for Pick & Pat in the cushy time period, although their ratings were always about half of Lux Radio Theater.

FIBBER AND MOLLY'S SLOW START

Jim and Marian Jordan first appeared as Fibber McGee & Molly in the previous May's rating books with a dismal 4.3 average on Blue's Tuesday schedule opposite the 27.4 scored by NBC's top rated Beauty Box Theater. Their 4.3 was the poorest rating ever registered by a future Number One show.

But the program's first Tuesday format hardly resembled that which later became popular with millions. The original FM&M premise placed the bumbling Fibber and his (then) shrewish wife with a thick Irish brogue on a continual car trip, providing announcer Harlow Wilcox with weekly opportunities to pitch Johnson Wax's Car-Nu auto polish at their many stops along the way.

It wasn't until September that Fibber and a much mellower Molly settled in at 79 Wistful Vista and the program began to take shape with its weekly parade of colorful visitors to their front door.

A time change was also due for the developing program. For the 1935–36 season Johnson Wax and Blue moved the McGee's to Mondays at 8:00 where the pair began to steadily build an audience against Guy Lombardo's "Sweetest Music This Side of Heaven" dance band on CBS.

Fibber McGee & Molly finished the season in 62nd place — but better days were ahead. It was the sitcom's last ranking lower than a season's Top 25.

1935–36 Tuesday Night Top Ten Programs
Blue 4, CBS 4, NBC 2
Average: 10.6

Ben Bernie Show	Blue	9:00	13.6
Amos & Andy*	NBC	7:00	12.2
Lowell Thomas News*	Blue	6:45	11.5
Helen Hayes Theater	Blue	9:30	10.9
The March of Time*	CBS	10:30	10.5
Fred Waring Show	CBS	9:30	10.3

Lawrence Tibbett Program	CBS	8:30	9.9
Boake Carter News*	CBS	7:45	9.8
Eno Crime Clues	Blue	8:00	8.7
Wayne King's Lady Esther Serenade	NBC	8:30	8.7

*Monday–Friday Strip Shows

Sans Strips...

Parties at Pickfair	CBS	10:00	8.5
Jimmy Durante's Texaco Jumbo Fire Chief Show	NBC	9:30	7.5
Jane Pickens' Texaco Fire Chief Show	NBC	9:30	7.2
Kate Smith's Coffee Time	CBS	7:30	6.9

TWO TUESDAY TOP TENS TOPPLE

Two of 1934–35's Top Ten shows left NBC's Tuesday lineup for CBS. Palmolive's Beauty Box Theater moved to CBS's Saturday schedule and lost over half of its audience. A worse fate awaited Texaco Fire Chief Ed Wynn who came off three Top Ten NBC seasons and moved to CBS on Thursdays as Gulliver for Chrysler's Plymouth autos opposite NBC's popular Maxwell House Showboat. Wynn lost over 70 percent of his audience and dropped from ninth to 49th in the season's rankings.

DON'T YOU REMEMBER THE GIBSONS?

Meanwhile, Texaco teamed with flamboyant Broadway producer Billy Rose to replace Wynn and create one of the most expensive flops in network history.

The Jumbo Fire Chief Show — so named to coincide with Rose's circus-like stage extravaganza, Jumbo — was a continuing original musical comedy. It was similar in format to the previous season's ratings disappointment, The Gibson Family, only on a larger scale.

Texaco spent $15,000 a week ($247,700), to produce Jumbo Fire Chief, beginning with writers Ben Hecht and Charles MacArthur and composers Richard Rodgers and Lorenz Hart. Beloved comedian Jimmy Durante was the star of the show. With a large cast and orchestra supporting Durante and performing the story and songs written for them by Broadway greats,

Jumbo Fire Chief had everything going for it — except listeners.

Despite a huge promotional push from NBC and Texaco, the program never rose above single digits in the ratings. It was outscored by both Fred Waring's pop concerts on CBS and Helen Hayes' anthology dramas on Blue. *Jumbo Fire Chief* was cancelled at mid-season.

PARSONS PROTESTS PICKFORD'S PARTIES

Legendary screen star Mary Pickford added more glamour to CBS' Hollywood image with *Parties at Pickfair*— radio receptions for film stars supposedly held in the Beverly Hills mansion she shared with husband Douglas Fairbanks, Sr.

Resembling *Hollywood Hotel* in format, the program sparked controversy between Pickford and *Hotel*'s hostess, Hearst columnist Louella Parsons. Parsons complained loudly and threatened to blackball any star who appeared on *Pickfair*.

It wasn't the format similarity that bothered Parsons — it was *Pickfair*'s practice of paying its guests between a thousand and three thousand dollars (*$16,500–49,500*), to appear. Parsons didn't pay *Hollywood Hotel* guests a cent and insisted that Pickford not set a trend that would spoil her free ride.

Pickford's "parties" featured impersonations of movie notables as background chatter performed by radio actors that were panned in the press for their flat-out phoniness.

The entire affair was sponsored by the National Ice Advertisers, an advertising cooperative of ice manufacturers attempting to stem the growing popularity of electric refrigerators with copy points like, "Ice is tops in modern scientific refrigeration," and, "Remember, cold alone is not enough!"

The show suffered a melt-down of its own and left the air after five months.

1935–36 Wednesday Night Top Ten Programs
CBS 4, NBC 4, Blue 2
Average: 12.6

Fred Allen's Town Hall Tonight	NBC	9:00	20.0
Burns & Allen Show	CBS	8:30	18.6
One Man's Family	NBC	9:30	14.0

Amos & Andy*	NBC	7:00	13.7
Lowell Thomas*	Blue	6:45	12.3
Boake Carter News*	CBS	7:45	10.6
The March of Time*	CBS	10:30	10.3
Gangbusters	CBS	10:00	9.3
House of Glass	Blue	8:30	8.9
Wayne King's Lady Esther Serenade	NBC	8:30	8.7

*Monday–Friday Strip Shows

Sans Strips...			
Warden Lawes at Sing Sing	Blue	9:30	7.5
Kate Smith's Coffee Time	CBS	7:30	6.9
Dangerous Paradise	Blue	7:45	6.9
Uncle Ezra's Radio Station	NBC	7:15	6.8

BURNS AND ALLEN STAND OUT

Fred Allen's *Town Hall Tonight* hour won the night for NBC while George Burns and Gracie Allen raised their half hour on CBS a minuscule three-tenths of a rating point over 1934–35. Yet, their small increase was enough to distinguish Burns and Allen as the year's *only* Top 50 program to finish with a higher rating than the previous season.

LORD'S SECOND COMING

Gangbusters (aka *Gang Busters*), was Phillips H. Lord's comeback show.

His *Seth Parker* character sank from popularity with the notorious *Cruise of the Seth Parker* in early 1934 amid gossip of the yacht's wild parties in ports of call and its subsequent, questionable sinking in the South Pacific.

Meanwhile, Warner Brothers had made killings — both on film and at the box office — with violent crime and gangster movies in the early 1930s. Sing Sing prison warden Lewis Lawes had brought stories of crimes and criminals to Network Radio with his popular series, *Twenty Thousand Years in Sing Sing*, in 1933.

Lord decided to capitalize on the "Crime Does Not Pay!" trend and launched *G-Men* on NBC in the summer of 1935 with the reluctant co-operation of J. Edgar Hoover's Bureau of Investigation which would soon become the FBI. Dra-

matizations of the bureau's case histories ran for only 13 weeks but Lord knew he was on to something good.

He converted the format to focus on local law enforcement agencies and changed its name to *Gangbusters*. The program opened on CBS in January 1936 and enjoyed runs on CBS, Blue and ABC for the next 21 years, ranking among the Top 50 programs for twelve seasons of Network Radio's Golden Age.

In a sense, crime *did* pay — and in a big way — for Phillips H. Lord.

1935–36 Thursday Night Top Ten Programs
NBC 5, CBS 3, Blue 2
Average: 13.7

Rudy Vallee's Fleischmann Hour	NBC	8:00	22.4
Maxwell House Showboat	NBC	9:00	20.8
Paul Whiteman's Kraft Music Hall	NBC	10:00	18.2
Bing Crosby's Kraft Music Hall	NBC	10:00	16.9
Amos & Andy*	NBC	7:00	14.4
Lowell Thomas News*	Blue	6:45	11.7
Boake Carter News*	CBS	7:45	9.0
Death Valley Days	Blue	9:00	8.1
Ed Wynn's Gulliver	CBS	9:30	7.8
The March of Time*	CBS	10:30	7.5

*Monday–Friday Strip Shows

Sans Strips...			
Kate Smith's Coffee Time	CBS	7:30	6.9
Glen Gray Orchestra	CBS	9:00	5.9
Edwin C Hill News	NBC	7:15	5.3
Easy Aces	Blue	7:00	4.4

A KRAFTY MOVE

Thursday night on NBC continued to be the grocery store of the air.

Standard Brands, General Foods and Kraft all pitched their products in successful hour long variety formats, led by Rudy Vallee's guest laden *Fleischmann Yeast Hour*. NBC's powerful lineup gathered higher ratings than CBS and Blue combined.

Displaying demographic savvy

in appealing to housewives, Chicago cheese manufacturer J.L. Kraft hired 32-year-old romantic baritone and emerging movie star Bing Crosby to sell its Velveeta processed cheese and its new mayonnaise-like Miracle Whip Salad Dressing.

Crosby replaced rotund orchestra leader Paul Whiteman as the star of *Kraft Music Hall* in January.

It was a gutsy move as Whiteman had taken *Music Hall* to the annual Top Ten in each of the two previous seasons and his September through December run on the show was destined to finish seventh among all programs for the season. Crosby's subsequent 26 week series finished eighth.

Nevertheless, Crosby began a string of eleven seasons among the Top 15 programs, seven of them in the Top Ten.

Charles Winninger left the cast of *Maxwell House Showboat* to reprise his stage role as Captain Andy in the film version of Broadway's *Showboat*. Frank McIntyre became the show's new Captain Henry, sharing host duties with Lanny Ross. Despite Winninger's departure for Hollywood, radio's New York based *Showboat* still managed to finish in fourth place among the season's Top 50.

*1935–36 Friday Night
Top Ten Programs*
CBS 4, NBC 4, Blue 2
Average: 10.7

Hollywood Hotel	CBS	9:30	16.4
First Nighter	NBC	10:00	15.1
Amos & Andy*	NBC	7:00	13.2
Cities Service Concert	NBC	8:00	11.1
Lowell Thomas News*	Blue	6:45	10.4
The March of Time*	CBS	10:30	9.5
Boake Carter News*	CBS	7:45	8.4
Myrt & Marge*	CBS	7:00	7.9
Court of Human Relations	NBC	9:30	7.6
Dangerous Paradise	Blue	7:45	6.9

*Monday–Friday Strip Shows
Sans Strips...

Uncle Ezra's Radio Station	NBC	7:15	6.8
Popeye the Sailor	NBC	7:15	5.9
Fred Waring Show	Blue	9:30	5.8
Broadway Varieties	CBS	8:30	5.8
Flying Red Horse Tavern	CBS	8:00	5.7

Richard Himber Orchestra	CBS	10:00	5.7

MULTIPLE RUNS' MULTIPLE WINS

The March of Time was converted to a 15 minute strip show for the one season. This move led to Friday night in 1935-36 becoming the first and last time that six Multiple Run programs — five of them strip shows — monopolized a single night's Top Ten.

But the conversion of the Westbrook Van Voorhis narrated *March of Time* to its new format began a ratings slide for the elaborately produced docudrama from which it wouldn't recover until 1942.

*1935–36 Saturday
Night Top Ten Programs*
CBS 5, NBC 4, Blue 1
Average: 8.3

Al Jolson's Shell Chateau	NBC	9:30	16.7
Your Hit Parade	NBC	8:00	13.0
Beauty Box Theater	CBS	8:00	12.6
Fanny Brice's Ziegfeld Follies	CBS	8:00	10.9
National Barn Dance	Blue	9:30	10.8
Rubinoff & His Violin	CBS	9:00	10.8
Wallace Beery's Shell Chateau	NBC	9:30	9.9
Bob Hope's Atlantic Family	CBS	7:00	7.7
Dr West's Celebrity Night	NBC	10:30	6.1
Andre Kostelanetz Orchestra	CBS	9:00	5.7

JOLEY SHUNS SHELL

Al Jolson vacated the *Shell Chateau* in March on the eve of the release of his Warner Brothers film, *The Singing Fool*—in which he sang 13 of his most recognizable signature melodies. The public seemingly couldn't get enough of Jolson and made the movie a box office hit. But his departure from the radio show presented the oil company, its J. Walter Thompson advertising agency and NBC with the problem of finding a new host.

They turned to the movies for 51-year-old character actor, Wallace Beery, star of a string of MGM films, and the show was converted from musical variety format to a comedy oriented variety show.

Beery was no Jolson and lost 40 percent of the singer's ratings.

ANOTHER SPARK OF HOPE

Bob Hope's sad six week showing earlier in the year on Bromo Seltzer's *Intimate Revue* didn't deter the busy comedian from trying again. He filmed four shorts for Warner Brothers in 1935, joined Fanny Brice—and future radio stars Eve Arden and Judy Canova—in the cast of Broadway's *Ziegfeld Follies of 1936,* and took on the hosting duties of *The Atlantic (Oil) Family* on CBS.

With blonde Patricia Wilder as his beautiful but dumb southern belle stooge, "Honey Chile," Hope's variety show scored double digit ratings in only one month, yet managed to finish in 50th place for the season. Hope's breakthrough season on radio was still two years away.

BROADCASTING'S BRAT BOWS

Baby Snooks made her radio debut on Fanny Brice's *Ziegfeld Follies* in February in the 8:00 timeslot vacated by *Beauty Box Theater* on CBS. Brice was 47 at the time. The first actor to portray her long suffering "Daddy" was character actor Alan Reed, who later became the voice of *Fred Flintstone*.

Reed was replaced the following season by Hanley Stafford—ten years Brice's junior. The Brice-Stafford team would eventually chronicle *Snooks'* mischief and mayhem across three networks for 15 years, finishing twelve times in the Annual Top 50 and four times in the Top Ten.

WILL'S DELAYED WAKE

Will Rogers' death on August 15th inspired a tribute program in his memory — three months later.

The broadcast honoring Network Radio's first superstar was carried on both Blue and CBS on November 23 in the weakest time period of the week, Saturday night at 10:30. The half hour drew a 7.9 rating — hardly the 30s that the cowboy humorist consistently scored with his *Gulf Headliners* shows.

<table>
<tr><td colspan="5">

1935–36 Top Ten
Multiple Run Programs
CBS 5, NBC 3, Blue 2
Average: 8.7

</td></tr>
</table>

Amos & Andy*	M–F	NBC	7:00	13.1
Lowell Thomas News*	M–F	Blue	6:45	11.2
Boake Carter News*	M–F	CBS	7:45	10.3
March of Time*	M–F	CBS	10:30	9.5
Wayne King's Lady Esther Serenade	Tu,W	NBC	8:30	8.7
Myrt & Marge*	M–F	CBS	7:00	7.4
Dangerous Paradise	M,W,F	Blue	7:45	6.9
Kate Smith's Coffee Time	T,W,T	CBS	7:30	6.9
Uncle Ezra's Radio Station	M,W,F	NBC	7:15	6.8
The Shadow	M,W	CBS	6:30	6.5

*Monday–Friday Strip Shows

THE SUPERSTARS AND THE SPINOFF

To nobody's surprise, NBC captured the Number One Multiple Run spot when it took *Amos & Andy* from Blue before the 1935–36 season began in July. Gosden and Correll were still among the Top Five programs every weeknight while their CBS competition, *Myrt & Marge,* fell from the season's Top 50 rankings.

NBC followed its successful comedy serial three nights a week with another Chicago show, *Uncle Ezra's Radio Station,* a 15 minute program of rural comedy and music. *Ezra* was a pioneering spin-off character, borrowed from Blue's *National Barn Dance.* Pat Barrett played the homespun Ezra with frequent support from musical members of the *Barn Dance* cast. *Ezra* also shared *National Barn Dance's* sponsor, Alka-Seltzer, which targeted rural audiences with its advertising.

THE LAST WALTZ

Wayne King's *Lady Esther Serenade* was the last 30 minute Multiple Run program reported as such in the ratings until *The Lone Ranger* rode into the Hooperatings of 1940. "The Waltz King" would still be heard twice week on NBC for two more seasons but his programs were rated separately.

It was also the last season that Kate Smith, *The March of Time* and *The Shadow* were heard in prime time in Multiple Run formats.

TOP 50 PROGRAMS — 1935–36

CBS 20, NBC 18, Blue 12
Average Rating: 13.0, Median: 11.1
21,456,000 Radio Homes / 67.3% Coverage of U.S. Homes / One Rating Point = 214,560 Homes
Source: Cooperative Analysis of Broadcasting, Sept 1935–June 1936.
Total Programs Rated 6–11 P.M.: 149
Programs Rated 13 Weeks & Ranked: 131.

		Program	Rtg	Type	Sponsor	Day	Time	Lgth	Net
1	3	Major Bowes Original Amateur Hour	37.5	TC	Chase & Sanborn Coffee	Sun	8:00	60	NBC
2	5	Jack Benny Program	25.8	SC	Jello Gelatin	Sun	7:00	30	Blue
3	4	Rudy Vallee Show	22.4	MV	Fleischmann Yeast	Thu	8:00	60	NBC
4	2	Maxwell House Showboat	20.8	MV	Maxwell House Coffee	Thu	9:00	60	NBC
5	7	Fred Allen's Town Hall Tonight	20.0	CV	Ipana/Sal Hepatica	Wed	9:00	60	NBC
6	27	Burns & Allen Show	18.6	CV	Campbell Soup	Wed	8:30	30	CBS
7	13	Paul Whiteman's Kraft Music Hall	18.2	MV	Kraft Cheese	Thu	10:00	60	NBC
8	N	Bing Crosby's Kraft Music Hall	16.9	MV	Kraft Cheese	Thu	10:00	60	NBC
9	11	Al Jolson's Shell Chateau	16.7	MV	Shell Oil	Sat	9:30	60	NBC
10	30	Hollywood Hotel/L Parsons/D Powell	16.4	MV	Campbell Soup	Fri	9:00	60	CBS
11	N	Robert Ripley Bakers' Broadcast	16.0	API	Fleischmann Yeast	Sun	7:30	30	Blue
12	14	First Nighter/Don Ameche	15.1	DA	Campana Balm	Fri	10:00	30	NBC
13t	1	Eddie Cantor Show	14.9	CV	Pebeco Toothpaste	Sun	7:00	30	CBS 1
13t	22t	Phil Baker's Gulf Headliners	14.9	CV	Gulf Oil	Sun	7:30	30	CBS
15	N	Lux Radio Theater/Cecil B. DeMille	14.6	DA	Lux Soap	Mon	9:00	60	CBS
16	26	One Man's Family	14.0	DCC	Tenderleaf Tea	Wed	8:00	30	NBC
17	11	Ben Bernie Show	13.6	MV	American Can Co.	Tue	9:00	30	Blue
18	16	Amos & Andy	13.1	SC	Pepsodent Toothpaste	M–F	7:00	15	NBC
19	33	Your Hit Parade	13.0	MP	Lucky Strike Cigarettes	Sat	8:00	60	NBC
20	8	Beauty Box Theater/G Swarthout	12.6	MST	Palmolive Soap	Sat	8:00	60	CBS 2
21	N	Vick's Open House/Grace Moore	12.3	MV	Vick's Vap-O-Rub	Sun	8:00	30	CBS
22	55	Manhattan Merry Go Round	12.0	MP	Dr Lyons Tooth Powder	Sun	9:00	30	NBC
23	69	General Motors Concert	11.4	MC	General Motors	Sun	10:00	30	NBC
24	21	Lowell Thomas News	11.2	NC	Sun Oil	M–F	6:45	15	Blue
25	28t	Cities Service Concert/J Dragonette	11.1	MC	Cities Service Petroleum	Fri	8:00	60	NBC
26	59	Grand Hotel/Don Ameche	11.0	DA	Campana Balm	Mon	8:30	30	Blue
27t	N	Helen Hayes Theater	10.9	DA	Sanka Coffee	Tue	9:30	30	Blue
27t	N	Fanny Brice Ziegfeld Follies	10.9	CV	Colgate Toothpaste	Sat	8:00	60	CBS
29t	25	National Barn Dance	10.8	MSP	Alka Seltzer	Sat	9:30	60	Blue
29t	N	Rubinoff & His Violin	10.8	MC	Chevrolet Motors	Sat	9:00	30	CBS

	Program	Rtg	Type	Sponsor	Day	Time	Lgth	Net
31 *51*	Voice of Firestone	10.7	MC	Firestone Tires	Mon	8:30	30	NBC
32t *69*	Boake Carter News	10.3	NC	Philco Radios	M–F	7:45	15	CBS
32t *37*t	Fred Waring Show	10.3	MST	Ford Motors	Tue	9:30	60	CBS
34t *31*	Lawrence Tibbett Program	9.9	MV	Packard Motors	Tue	8:30	30	CBS
34t *N*	Shell Chateau/Wallace Beery	9.9	CV	Shell Oil	Sat	9:30	60	NBC
36 *17*	March of Time	9.5	DA	Remington Rand	M–F	10:30	15	CBS
37 *N*	Gangbusters	9.3	DA	Palmolive Shave Cream	Wed	10:00	30	CBS
38t *41*	Ford Sunday Evening Hour	9.2	MC	Ford Motors	Sun	9:00	60	CBS
38t *45*t	Walter Winchell's Jergens Journal	9.2	NC	Jergens Lotion	Sun	9:30	15	Blue
40 *45*t	House of Glass/Gertrude Berg	8.9	DCC	Palmolive Soap	Wed	8:30	30	Blue
41 *44*	American Album of Familiar Music	8.8	MST	Bayer Aspirin	Sun	9:30	30	NBC
42t *38*t	Eno Crime Clues	8.7	DA	Eno Antacid Salts	Tue	8:00	30	Blue
42t *37*	Wayne King Orch	8.7	MP	Lady Esther Cosmetics	Tu–We	8:30	30	NBC
44 *70*	Pick & Pat	8.6	CV	Dill's Best Pipe Tobacco	Mon	8:30	30	CBS
45t *20*	Guy Lombardo Orch	8.5	MP	Esso Petroleum	Mon	8:00	30	CBS
45t *N*	Parties At Pickfair/Mary Pickford	8.5	MV	Ice & Refrigerator Dealers	Tue	10:00	30	CBS
47 *35*	Death Valley Days	8.1	DA	20 Mule Team Borax Cleaner	Thu	9:00	30	Blue
48 *19*	Sinclair Wiener Minstrels	8.0	MSP	Sinclair Oil	Mon	9:00	30	Blue
49 *9*	Ed Wynn's Gulliver	7.8	SC	Plymouth Autos	Thu	9:30	30	CBS
50 *N*	Bob Hope's Atlantic Family	7.7	CV	Atlantic Petroleum	Sat	7:00	30	CBS

New & Returning Top 50 Programs Underscored.

1	Eddie Cantor Show		Oct–Dec	Pebeco Toothpaste	Sun	8:00	30	CBS
2	Beauty Box Theater		Sep–Dec	Palmolive Soap	Fri	9:00	60	Blue

Key: API — Audience Participation/Interviews   DCC — Drama/Continuing Characters   MV — Music/Variety Show
APQ — Audience Participation/Quiz   MC — Music/Classical, Semi-Classical   NC — News, Commentary
APS — Audience Participation/Stunts   MP — Music/Popular, Contemporary   SC — Situation Comedy
CV — Comedy/Variety Show   MSP — Music/Specialty, Ethnic   TC — Talent Competition
DA — Dramatic Anthology   MST — Music/Standard, Traditional

1935–36 Top 50 Favorite Formats

	Programs	Pct
Music — All Categories	25	50%
Comedy — All Categories	11	22%
Drama — Anthology & Continuing	10	20%
News/Commentary	3	6%
Audience Participation/All Categories	1	2%

1935–36 Monthly Winners

Sep	Major Bowes Amateur Hour	57.9	Feb	Major Bowes Amateur Hour	40.5
Oct	Major Bowes Amateur Hour	31.0	Mar	Major Bowes Amateur Hour	37.6
Nov	Major Bowes Amateur Hour	35.2	Apr	Major Bowes Amateur Hour	38.4
Dec	Major Bowes Amateur Hour	34,2	May	Major Bowes Amateur Hour	29.8
Jan	Major Bowes Amateur Hour	40.7	Jun	Major Bowes Amateur Hour	29.2

9

The 1936–37 Network Season

Announcer: You boys and girls won't object to <u>Grove's Emulsified Cold Drops</u>. There's nothing unpleasant about them. They don't run out of your nose and make you messy. They don't run down the back of your throat and make you sickish. What's more, they don't burn or sting the inside of your nose. They quickly check a head cold, yet do it in a <u>nice</u> way. <u>Grove's Emulsified Cold Drops</u> will surprise you by the way they look and act. <u>They don't look, smell or taste like medicine</u>, yet they're highly effective. That's because they are <u>medically</u> <u>superior</u> ... because they stay up in the nose. Any child can understand that nose drops that stay up in the nose can do more good than nose drops that run right out. Impress this fact upon Mother and she'll undoubtedly let you try these new type of nose drops when you have a head cold or stuffed head. All drug stores sell <u>Grove's Emulsified Cold Drops</u>. And they're really more economical than the old fashioned kind because you get more for your money and because you can use less. Ask Mother to get a bottle today!

AUTO AUDIENCE ACCELERATES

More radio stations went on the air and revenues continued climb steadily for both the stations and their networks.

Technology added to radio's popularity for out-of-home listening as the number of automobiles with radios jumped to over 15 percent of the total homes with radios.

First introduced as bulky after-market accessories in 1930 with Crosley's *Roamio* and Galvin Manufacturing's *Motorola*— the smaller and more technically advanced car radios had become standard options in most new cars. The broadcasting industry was given millions of new listeners — plus additional advertisers who appealed to the driving public.

One of those advertisers, automaker Chrysler, would make programming headlines in mid-season by stealing the Number One program from its sponsor and network.

AS CBS GOES, MUTUAL GROWS

CBS had a problem.

Its West Coast group of affiliated stations, the Don Lee Network, was presenting intolerable clearance difficulties for CBS programming and its sponsors. CBS had to have the assurance of unrestricted coverage to be sold as a coast to coast network to advertisers.

When powerful KNX/Los Angeles became available for $1.25 Million *(20.3 Mil)*, in September 1936, Bill Paley snapped it up. In doing so, CBS became the only

network to own a station in California's largest city and America's film capital.

The handwriting was on the wall for Don Lee's KHJ and its affiliation with CBS in Los Angeles. What's more, Paley made no secret of his negotiations with KSFO to replace Lee's KFRC as CBS's San Francisco affiliate. The split between the two chains became effective on December 31.

But the crafty Don Lee wasn't without a backup plan. He was about to make Mutual the fourth nationwide network.

WLW had dropped out of Mutual. Loss of its 500,000 watt Cincinnati powerhouse convinced the network to abandon its clubby super-station cooperative concept and pursue all the affiliates and advertising revenue that it could.

For openers, Mutual received good marks for its 1936 political convention coverage and snared the 17 station Colonial Network in New England as an affiliate along with individual stations in the Midwest and south.

When Don Lee's new Mutual affiliation began on January 1, 1937, MBS became a full coast to coast radio network, boasting a roster of 39 affiliates and a Los Angeles base in Lee's KHJ.

It was just the beginning of growth for the network that became a harbor for stations considered too weak in coverage or rural for the more prestigious CBS, NBC and Blue chains.

LET ME REPEAT THAT...

Your Hit Parade scored twice in the season's Top 50 — Wednesdays on NBC (ranked 17th), and Saturdays on CBS (24th) — both sponsored by American Tobacco's Lucky Strike Cigarettes.

Competitor R.J. Reynolds countered with Russ Morgan's popular

1936–37 Season Scoreboard Mid-Season Totals, December 1936			
		Compared to Year Earlier	
Total Radio Homes	22.87 Mil	+1.41 Mil	+6.6%
Total Auto Radios	3.5 Mil	+1.50 Mil	+75.0%
Total AM Radio Stations	616	+31	+5.3%
Total Radio Network Affiliates	226	+38	+20.2%
1936 Radio Revenues	122.3 Mil	+9.7 Mil	+8.6%
1936 Network Revenues	75.6 Mil	+13.0 Mil	+20.8%
Network Share	61.8%		+6.2%

dance band on NBC's Tuesday schedule (38th), and CBS's Saturday night lineup (61st), both sponsored by Camel Cigarettes.

Ford Motors briefly joined the double-play trend with Fred Waring's musical troupe, the Pennsylvanians. The automaker plugged Waring into CBS on Tuesday and Blue on Friday from September through December.

But Lady Esther remained the queen of repetitive music programming. The Chicago maker of popular priced cosmetics placed *all three* of its weekly *Wayne King Lady Esther Serenade* shows in the season's Top 50—the first and only time a ratings hat trick would be scored.

While most popular dance bands of the day had to settle for late night remote broadcasts from hotels, nightclubs and ballrooms, Wayne King's syrupy sweet *Lady Esther Serenade* of waltzes and novelty tunes accompanied by Franklyn MacCormack's love poems were broadcast in the heart of prime time—twice a week on NBC and once on CBS.

HISTORY REPEATS ITSELF (BY TRANSCRIPTION)

The most famous remote broadcast of the period—and arguably of all time—happened by accident on May 6, 1937, when Herb Morrison of WLS/Chicago was helping test the potential uses of portable recording equipment at Lakehurst, New Jersey, and awaiting the landing of the dirigible *Hindenberg*.

Morrison's report of the airship's sudden explosion and his emotional reaction ("Oh, the humanity!"), were recorded for the ages and deemed important enough that NBC suspended its ban against recorded programming to broadcast the Morrison disc later that day.

SHORTWAVE SHRINKS THE WORLD

With their news operations growing to keep up with fast changing international events—at a pace that newspapers could never match—the networks increased their use of shortwave transmissions to report news as it happened from virtually anywhere in the world.

NBC was first to employ shortwave news coverage in August 1931, with International News Service wire reporter Max Jordan transmitting his first hand accounts of European developments from Switzerland.

In September 1936 CBS dispatched former *Brooklyn Eagle* editor Hans Von (H.V.) Kaltenborn to cover the Spanish Civil War. The feisty Kaltenborn was 58, already a six year veteran of network radio, and soon found himself under gunfire in Spain.

The most famous short waved broadcast of the decade took place on December 12 when England's King Edward VIII delivered his famous "Woman I Love" abdication speech.

NBC continued to follow the royal soap opera by shortwave, climaxing five months later when it broadcast the coronation of his brother, King George VI—all seven consecutive hours of it.

THE MONTHLIES

Major Bowes' *Original Amateur Hour* won September for NBC. It was *Amateur Hour*'s twelfth consecutive month as the country's most popular program.

Then, like Eddie Cantor had done two years earlier, Bowes jumped to CBS in October.

Chrysler assumed Bowes' sponsorship and moved *The Original Amateur Hour* to Thursday nights—and forever out of first place in the monthly rankings.

Jack Benny returned from his summer hiatus in October and won the remaining nine months of the season for his new network, NBC. NBC's run of consecutive monthly winners extended to 21.

1936–37 Sunday Night Top Ten Programs CBS 5, Blue 3, NBC 2 Average: 13.8			
Jack Benny Program	NBC	7:00	28.9
Eddie Cantor Show	CBS	8:30	23.0
Phil Baker Show	CBS	7:30	15.8
Nelson Eddy's Vicks Open House	CBS	8:00	14.9
Walter Winchell Jergens Journal	Blue	9:30	13.1
Robert Ripley's Believe It or Not	Blue	7:30	10.6
Ford Sunday Evening Hour	CBS	9:00	9.2
Do You Want to Be an Actor?	NBC	8:00	8.6
Milton Berle's Gillette Community Sing	CBS	10:00	6.8
Shep Fields Orchestra	Blue	9:00	6.8

NBC STEALS FIRST...

NBC plucked General Foods' *Jack Benny Program* from Blue for an October debut—with obviously no more brotherly spirit than it displayed when it took over *Amos & Andy* the previous season.

With a new production contract worth $390,000 per season *($6.3 Mil)*, Benny and his troupe—now including wife Mary Livingston, announcer Don Wilson, band leader Phil Harris and romantic tenor Kenny Baker—took solid possession of Sundays at 7:00 and gave NBC the season's Number One program.

... AND SUFFERS A MAJOR LOSS

Aside from Benny's top rating, NBC had little to cheer about on Sunday evenings. The network and Standard Brands both lost the previous season's Number One show when Major Bowes signed with Chrysler and defected to CBS's Thursday schedule. *The Original Amateur Hour* remained with CBS for the next nine seasons until Bowes' retirement.

THE PRO BONO NO-NO

The question was what Standard Brands would do with its hour at 8:00 without Bowes hawking Chase & Sanborn Coffee.

Like J. Walter Thompson discovered Bowes' *Original Amateur Hour* on New York's WHN for its client, the agency thought it found another winner on local radio in A.L. Alexander's *Goodwill Court*.

It turned out to be a twelve week wonder that resulted in a brief rating surge that would have placed it in Sunday's Top Ten.

But it also resulted in a lawsuit that forced it off the air.

Goodwill Court had evolved on

WMCA/New York as an hour's worth of free legal advice to guests who presented their problems — sometimes a dozen or more per hour. The program employed lower court judges to dispense the advice and was endorsed by the populist governors of both New York and New Jersey as a public service.

With all of that going for it, what could go wrong?

The human interest program made its NBC debut on September 20, out-rating *Vick's Open House* on CBS at 8:00 and narrowly losing to Eddie Cantor's 8:30 Texaco show in both October and November. *Goodwill Court* was on its way.

Alexander also invited listeners who couldn't afford legal counsel to submit questions and problems by mail for personal answers from his staff. Letters arrived by the thousands.

So did a subpoena from the New York County Lawyers' Association who claimed that *Goodwill Court* implied that legal assistance was expensive. The attorneys took their grievance to the New York Supreme Court's Appellate Division.

Standard Brands and NBC soon found themselves in court trying to defend the *Goodwill Court.*

In a questionable decision, the court ruled in favor of the plaintiffs and forbade all New York State lawyers — *including judges* — from appearing on the program. *Goodwill Court* adjourned on December 20 and never returned.

STALLING FOR TIME

The loss of their second show in the same peak timeslot within 13 weeks left programming chiefs John Reber of J. Walter Thompson and NBC's John Royal with a prime hour to fill at 8:00 for Standard Brands. They needed something fast — and the cheaper the better — while they searched for Bowes' permanent replacement.

Do You Want to Be an Actor? — an amateur hour for actors — debuted on December 27th. The hour long series of hastily written skits were auditions for fledgling actors. Hollywood screen tests were dangled as prizes for winners. The low budgeted hour was hosted by "director" Haven MacQuarrie.

Actor achieved a 10.4 rating in January and then steadily lost a rating point per month — approximately a quarter million radio homes — to limp in with a 6.3 in early May.

The once proud *Chase & Sanborn Hour,* home to radio's Number One shows, had fallen on its hardest times.

But Reber and Royal hadn't given up.

A promising newcomer — a ventriloquist — had made a big impact on another Standard Brands show, Rudy Vallee's Thursday night Fleishmann Yeast variety hour.

On May 19 they gave Sunday's *Chase & Sanborn Hour* to Edgar Bergen and Charlie McCarthy.

CANTOR'S CANADIAN KIDS

Texaco took over sponsorship of Eddie Cantor's CBS show and smartly pulled him out of direct competition with Jack Benny at 7:00. With *Major Bowes' Original Amateur Hour* gone from NBC lineup and the eight o'clock hour up for grabs, the slumping Cantor was inserted into the CBS schedule at 8:30.

Cantor played fatherly host to two young Canadian singers during the late 1930s.

Nine-year-old Bobby Breen from Toronto sang with Cantor for three years and enjoyed a brief film career that was over by the time he was 15.

On the other hand, Deanna Durbin's film career was just beginning at 15 when she joined Cantor's troupe in 1936. The young soprano from Winnipeg was just beginning a series of box office hits for Universal Pictures. Her solos were a weekly highlight of the Cantor shows until 1939. By that time she was making over $250,000 a year *(4.1 Mil),* as one of Hollywood's highest paid female stars.

Out of Benny's shadow and with the talented juveniles at his side, Cantor's rating jumped 54 percent and pushed him back into the season's Top Five. Combined with co-median Phil Baker's 7:30 show and movie singing star Nelson Eddy hosting *Vick's Open House* at 8:00, CBS had a strong Sunday block in

the heart of prime time and easily won the night's most listeners with five of its Top Ten programs.

The CBS reign wouldn't last long.

FIDDLING WITH A FEUD

Radio stars taking good humored shots at each other was nothing new. Walter Winchell and Ben Bernie started a "feud" earlier in the decade that resulted in two 1937 movies, *Wake Up & Live* and *Love & Hisses.* The heckling cross-plugging of each other's shows — both on Blue — was good for ratings.

The mock feud that captured the nation's fancy for 20 years began innocently enough on Jack Benny's program of December 27, when Benny's ineptitude on his beloved violin was the major topic of his Sunday show.

Fred Allen was listening and seized on Benny's fiddling gag to ignite their feud on his *Town Hall Tonight* the following Wednesday night.

1936–37 Monday Night Top Ten Programs
NBC 4, CBS 4, Blue 2
Average: 11.8

Lux Radio Theater	CBS	9:00	21.0
Amos & Andy*	NBC	7:00	15.3
Boake Carter News*	CBS	7:45	12.8
Fibber McGee & Molly	NBC	9:00	11.5
Pick & Pat's One Night Stand	CBS	8:30	11.3
Lowell Thomas News*	Blue	6:45	10.4
Wayne King's Lady Esther Serenade	CBS	10:00	10.1
Uncle Ezra's Radio Station	NBC	7:15	9.2
Lum & Abner*	Blue	7:30	8.8
Voice of Firestone	NBC	8:30	7.4

*Monday–Friday Strip Shows

Sans Strips...

Warden Lawes at Sing Sing	NBC	9:00	6.3
Horace Heidt Orchestra	CBS	8:00	5.2
Carnation Contented Hour	NBC	10:00	4.2
Richard Himber Orchestra	NBC	10:30	3.7
Sinclair Wiener Minstrels	Blue	9:00	3.7

NBC MOVES IN AT 79 WISTFUL VISTA

Blue lost another winner to its big brother when Johnson Wax moved *Fibber McGee & Molly* to NBC for the 1936–37 season.

But the Chicago based sitcom remained in its 8:00 Monday time-slot where it had been developing an audience on Blue.

Jim and Marian Jordan were sailing along, now supported by Ted Weems' popular orchestra featuring future stars Perry Como and Marvel (Marilyn) Maxwell. *FM&M*'s September rating of 7.1 had grown steadily every month to a strong 16.8 in March. Johnson Wax set new sales records and rewarded the couple with a new contract and weekly salary of $2,650 (*$43,100*).

Fibber & Molly won their time period going away and it seemed that nothing could stop their progress — until their own sponsor and network did.

In what can been seen in retrospect as one of the strangest — *if not stupidest*—programming moves of Network Radio's Golden Age, *Fibber McGee & Molly* was moved ahead one hour in April to directly compete for listeners with CBS's runaway hit, *Lux Radio Theater.*

Believing that the simple couple from Wistful Vista and their neighbors could vie for listeners against the likes of Clark Gable and Joan Crawford recreating scenes from their recent movie hits was optimistic absurdity.

Lux doubled *Fibber McGee & Molly*'s ratings and the sitcom fell back to single digit ratings in the May and June surveys.

1936–37 Tuesday Night Top Ten Programs
CBS 5, NBC 3, Blue 2
Average: 11.5

Al Jolson Show	CBS	8:30	15.4
Amos & Andy*	NBC	7:00	15.3
Boake Carter News*	CBS	7:45	12.8
Fred Astaire Show	NBC	9:30	12.5
Ken Murray Show	CBS	8:30	11.0
Lowell Thomas News*	Blue	6:45	10.4
Vox Pop	NBC	9:00	9.7
Jack Oakie's College	CBS	9:30	9.6
Al Pearce Gang	CBS	9:00	9.5
Lum & Abner*	Blue	7:30	8.8

*Monday–Friday Strip Shows
Sans Strips...

Russ Morgan Orchestra	NBC	8:00	8.4
Fred Waring Show	CBS	9:00	8.2
Ben Bernie Show	Blue	9:00	8.1
Wayne King's Lady Esther Serenade	NBC	8:30	7.4

JOLSON TO THE RESCUE

Al Jolson, who vacated the NBC's *Shell Chateau* the previous season, led the five CBS programs in Tuesday's Top Ten. Lever Brothers replaced Hollywood raconteur/comedian Ken Murray with Jolson in January and the singer delivered another show into the season's Top Ten. It was the first of his three consecutive Top Ten seasons at 8:30 for Lever's Lifebuoy deodorant soap.

DANCING ON THE AIR

Fred Astaire was hot when the 1936–37 season arrived.

The 38-year-old song and dance man had just released *Swing Time,* the sixth in his series of legendary RKO Radio musicals co-starring Ginger Rogers in which he crooned the Academy Award–winning *The Way You Look Tonight* to her.

Astaire had also sung the Oscar nominated *Lovely to Look At* and *Cheek to Cheek* from his two 1935 films with Rogers. Yet, he didn't think of himself as much of a singer.

What's more, Astaire didn't consider himself a personality of any great degree. He'd even displayed a bit of mike fright in his early radio appearances. In his own mind, Fred Astaire was nothing more than a hoofer and he was most comfortable playing a role — not by being himself.

Nevertheless, Packard Autos and NBC decided he'd be just dandy on radio — and he was.

Astaire, supported by comedian Charles Butterworth, announcer Ken Carpenter and Johnny Green's big studio orchestra, finished among the season's Top 20 programs — although Astaire reportedly hated every minute of it. He left the show in May and never returned to series radio.

STREET TALKERS

Vox Pop was Network Radio's premier "man on the street" interview show.

For listeners unfamiliar with Latin, the show's title was translated to *Voice of the People* and subtitled *Sidewalk Interviews* in newspaper logs during its early seasons. It provided thousands of guests with a few moments of fame as they talked and joked with its two hosts over the program's 13 year multinetwork run.

Vox Pop was created at KTRH/Houston. Standard Brands transplanted it with hosts Parks Johnson and Jerry Belcher to New York as comedian Joe Penner's summer replacement on Blue in 1935. Sterling Drug's Molle Shave Cream installed *Vox Pop* into NBC's Tuesday schedule midway in the 1935–36 season against the night's top rated *Ben Bernie Show* on Blue.

Despite *Vox Pop*'s dismal rating against Bernie during its first few months, Sterling stayed with the show and let it develop an audience. Belcher was replaced in 1936 by the show's announcer, Wally "The Voice with a Smile" Butterworth.

Both moves paid off. *Vox Pop*'s audience nearly doubled, its ratings overtook Bernie and the show enjoyed the first of an eventual eight seasons in the annual Top 50.

1936–37 Wednesday Night Top Ten Programs
NBC 5, CBS 3, Blue 2
Average: 13.5

Burns & Allen Show	CBS	8:30	20.9
Fred Allen's Town Hall Tonight	NBC	9:00	20.2
Amos & Andy*	NBC	7:00	15.3
One Man's Family	NBC	8:00	13.0
Boake Carter News*	CBS	7:45	12.8
Your Hit Parade	NBC	10:00	12.8
Gangbusters	CBS	10:00	12.0
Lowell Thomas News*	Blue	6:45	10.4
Uncle Ezra's Radio Station	NBC	7:15	9.2
Lum & Abner*	Blue	7:30	8.8

*Monday–Friday Strip Shows
Sans Strips...

Beauty Box Theater	CBS	9:30	7.2
Wayne King's Lady Esther Serenade	NBC	8:30	7.2

Andre Kostelanetz Program	CBS	9:00	6.7
Come, Let's Sing	CBS	9:30	6.5

FRED FIRES FEUD'S FIRST FUSILLADE

Fred Allen's *Town Hall Tonight* was enjoying its third of four consecutive Top Ten seasons with an hour-long variety format that often involved amateur talent. The comedian's show of December 30 featured a revue of talented children — including ten-year-old violin prodigy, Stewart Canin, who flawlessly performed Dvorak's short but difficult *The Bee.*

Allen, playing off Jack Benny's violin gags three nights before, congratulated the youngster and added, "After hearing you play, Jack Benny should hang his head in shame. Benny is the only violinist who makes you feel the strings would sound better back in the cat's intestine."

Benny retorted on his show the following Sunday with cracks about Allen's baggy eyes and nasal voice. The feud was on — each comedian hurling insults at the other and each benefiting from the high ratings their mock battle generated.

Their verbal battle — which some listeners mistook as the real thing — resulted in the 1940 movie *Love Thy Neighbor,* 1945's *It's in the Bag!,* and continued on until Allen's death in 1956.

BURNS AND ALLEN BURNS ALLEN

The public couldn't get enough of ditzy Gracie Allen. She and husband George Burns were in their fifth season on CBS's Wednesday schedule with solid ratings.

They had co-starred with Jack Benny in two films released in the fall 1936, *The Big Broadcast of 1937* and *College Rhythm.* The movies' promotional push helped radio's favorite couple of the decade to edge out Fred Allen's *Town Hall Tonight* as Wednesday's top rated program. George and Gracie finished the season with radio's fifth most popular program, the highest ranking of their 18 year Network Radio career.

LUCKY STRIKES TWICE

American Tobacco's Lucky Strike Cigarettes and its obliging agency, Lord & Thomas, kicked off a summer long promotional campaign linked to *Your Hit Parade* in June that ran into late September. During those weeks, listeners who could predict the show's Top Ten songs in order we awarded free cartons of cigarettes.

Your Hit Parade was broadcast simultaneously over both the NBC and Blue networks on Wednesdays and then repeated Saturdays on CBS at a weekly combined cost of $40,000 *($651,000)*—plus thousands of cigarettes.

Blue was dropped from the Lucky lineup in October but the weekly countdown of hits starring popular baritone Buddy Clark continued in its NBC and CBS editions and both finished among the season's Top 25 rated programs.

1936–37 Thursday Night Top Ten Programs
NBC 5, CBS 3, Blue 2
Average: 12.9

Major Bowes' Original Amateur Hour	CBS	9:00	21.3
Bing Crosby's Kraft Music Hall	NBC	10:00	17.4
Rudy Vallee Varieties	NBC	8:00	16.4
Amos & Andy*	NBC	7:00	15.3
Boake Carter News*	CBS	7:45	12.8
Lowell Thomas News*	Blue	6:45	10.4
Maxwell House Showboat	NBC	9:00	10.1
Kate Smith's A&P Bandwagon	CBS	8:00	8.8
Lum & Abner*	Blue	7:30	8.8
The Voice of Experience	NBC	7:15	7.4

*Monday–Friday Strip Shows

San Strips...			
Floyd Gibbons Show	CBS	10:00	6.9
Then & Now	CBS	10:00	5.2
Ted Husing Sports	CBS	7:15	5.2
Alexander Woolcott, the Town Crier	CBS	7:30	4.1

BOWES TORPEDOES SHOWBOAT

When Chrysler installed *Major Bowes' Original Amateur Hour* into

CBS's struggling Thursday night lineup, the program lost 43 percent of its stratospheric 1935–36 rating. The show fell from the season's Number One ranking to third.

But the maneuver was even more costly to Bowes' 9:00 competition on NBC. *Maxwell House Showboat* lost over half its audience and dropped out of the season's Top 25. It sank from Network Radio altogether two years later.

DUMMY WINS SINGERS' DUEL

Rudy Vallee's variety show for Standard Brands at 8:00 took a hit when Kate Smith's *A&P Bandwagon* was installed opposite him on CBS. Vallee lost 27 percent of his audience and relinquished the night's top spot to *The Original Amateur Hour.* Vallee won the time period but suffered enough loss to propel Smith back into the season's Top 50 where her programs would remain for the next seven years.

The biggest lift Vallee received during the season was the booking of ventriloquist Edgar Bergen on his show of December 17th. Bergen and his Charlie McCarthy were an immediate hit with the audience and critics. The 33-year-old Bergen was signed for a 13-week appearance at mid-season during which Vallee's ratings easily doubled Kate Smith's CBS show.

Standard Brands took the hint and signed Bergen for its ailing Sunday night timeslot in May.

CROSBY'S MUSIC HAUL

The only program from NBC's once dominant Thursday night lineup that escaped damage from the revamped CBS schedule led by Major Bowes and Kate Smith was Bing Crosby's *Kraft Music Hall* at 10:00.

During his second season for Kraft, Crosby had become a full-fledged movie star with three Paramount hits — *Rhythm on the Range, Pennies from Heaven,* in which he sang the Academy Award nominated title song, and *Waikiki Wedding* which featured Crosby crooning the Oscar winning *Sweet Leilani.*

With Hollywood's best songs

going for him, Crosby's records were also selling in the millions.

Kraft Music Hall benefited from Crosby's movie and recording successes. At mid-season the program's ratings broke into the 20s for the first time — a neighborhood that would become very familiar to him the following year.

Crosby's reward for all of this work was a reported 1936 personal income of $320,000 *(5.2 Mil)* — and the best was yet to come.

1936–37 Friday Night Top Ten Programs
CBS 4, NBC 4, Blue 2
Average: 10.6

Amos & Andy*	NBC	7:00	15.3
Hollywood Hotel	CBS	9:00	14.9
First Nighter	CBS	9:30	13.7
Boake Carter News*	CBS	7:45	12.8
Lowell Thomas News*	Blue	6:45	10.4
Uncle Ezra's Radio Station	NBC	7:15	9.2
Lum & Abner*	Blue	7:30	8.8
Court of Human Relations	NBC	9:30	7.5
Hal Kemp & Alice Faye Show	CBS	8:30	6.9
Cities Service Concert	NBC	8:00	6.5

*Monday–Friday Strip Shows

Sans Strips...

Death Valley Days	Blue	8:30	5.7
Jack Pearl Show	Blue	10:00	5.1
Broadway Varieties	CBS	8:00	4.7
Singin' Sam	Blue	8:15	4.5

BYE BYE TO CHI

Their days as a national phenomenon behind them, it was last nightly win for Chicago's *Amos & Andy* in its original 15 minute serial form. Freeman Gosden and Charlie Correll wouldn't win another night until their comeback with a half hour sitcom in the 1943–44 season.

Five of the night's Top Ten were Multiple Run quarter hour programs.

That never happened again.

Four of the Top Ten were Chicago based programs.

That didn't happen again, either.

The shift of programming from Chicago to New York and Los Angeles was well underway.

First Nighter became a Chicago holdout against relocating, although the program lost its leading man to Hollywood before the season began when Don Ameche left to pursue a film career.

It was a season of upheaval for the low budgeted anthology of light dramas.

Les Tremanyne and Barbara Luddy became *First Nighter*'s costars and sponsor Campana Balm moved the Friday show to CBS and a new timeslot, 9:30, in February. Despite the cast, time and network changes, *First Nighter* remained among the season's Top 15 programs and it would continue to originate from Chicago for another ten years.

1936–37 Saturday Night Top Ten Programs
CBS 4, Blue 3, NBC 3
Average: 7.6

Your Hit Parade	CBS	10:00	10.9
Joe Cook's Shell Chateau	NBC	9:30	8.5
Ed Wynn Show	Blue	8:00	8.4
Uncle Jim's Question Bee	Blue	7:30	8.3
Professor Quiz	CBS	8:00	7.7
Floyd Gibbons Show	CBS	9:00	6.7
National Barn Dance	Blue	9:00	6.7
Russ Morgan Orchestra	CBS	8:30	6.6
Saturday Evening Party	NBC	8:00	6.3
Snow Village Sketches	NBC	9:00	5.6

IF YOU CAN'T BEAT HIM...

Your Hit Parade's Wednesday rating of 12.8, plus Saturday's pack leading 10.9 gave sponsor American Tobacco a combined, two show rating of 23.7 for Lucky Strike Cigarettes. *Hit Parade*'s total rating was

second only to Jack Benny's Number One season average of 28.9.

Benny's popularity wasn't lost on American Tobacco's flamboyant president, George Washington Hill. In seven years Benny would also be sponsored by Lucky Strike.

THE QUIZ CRAZE COMMENCES

Network radio discovered a popular new format in September — the quiz show.

Compared to variety and dramatic programming, quizzes were simple and cheap to produce — and listeners liked them. The original two — *Professor Quiz* and *Uncle Jim's Question Bee* — made Saturday's Top Ten and finished in the season's Top 50.

With all of that going for them, it should come as no surprise that within four years a total of 35 quiz shows would be heard on the networks every week.

Generally recognized as first of the breed — although disputed by some historians — Craig Earl's *Professor Quiz* on CBS, was co-hosted early in the show's run by future star Arthur Godfrey. Like Godfrey, Earl hailed from the network's Washington, D.C., outlet, WSJV.

The show's premise was simple — six contestants were asked six questions submitted by a listener. Whichever of the six contestants answered most of the questions correctly won $25 *($407)*. The show enjoyed four consecutive Top 50 seasons as listeners enjoyed playing along with the game.

A week after *Professor Quiz* bowed

1936–37 Top Ten Multiple Run Programs (11)
CBS 5, Blue 3, NBC 3
Average: 8.5

Amos & Andy*	M–F	NBC	7:00	15.3
Boake Carter News*	M–F	CBS	7:45	12.8
Lowell Thomas News*	M–F	Blue	6:45	10.4
Uncle Ezra's Radio Station	M,W,F	NBC	7:15	9.2
Lum & Abner*	M–F	Blue	7:30	8.8
Voice of Experience	T,T	NBC	7:15	7.4
Popeye the Sailor	M,W,F	CBS	7:15	6.7
Easy Aces	T,W,T	Blue	7:00	5.3
Ted Husing Sports	T,T,Sa	CBS	7:15	5.2
Alexander Woolcott, Town Crier	T,T	CBS	7:30	4.1
Ma & Pa*	M–Sa	CBS	7:15	4.1

*Monday–Friday Strip Shows

on CBS, *Uncle Jim's Question Bee* first appeared on Blue with much the same six contestant and $25 prize format. *Question Bee* didn't have the Top 50 success of *Professor Quiz,* but "Uncle Jim" McWilliams later went on to host the popular CBS quiz shows, *Ask It Basket* and *Correction, Please.*

TAKE MY TOWN ... PLEASE

The six top Multiple Run programs finished among the season's Top 50.

Among them, Blue's *Lum & Abner* was on a promotional roll that resulted in the first of its two Top 50 seasons.

Arkansas natives Chet Lauck

(Lum Edwards), and Norris Goff *(Abner Peabody),* introduced their serialized 15 minute sitcom to a regional NBC audience from Chicago in 1931. Despite numerous scheduling shifts across the four networks over the next 22 years, *Lum & Abner* built a loyal following.

They peaked with a 34th place finish among the annual Top 50 in the 1936–37 season.

Lauck and Goff drew most of their program's gentle humor and characterizations from the rural areas of their home state, particularly around the small community of Waters, Arkansas.

Capitalizing on the program's

popularity, the enterprising town council of Waters began a highly publicized and successful move to rename their community Pine Ridge, the fictional home of *Lum & Abner* and their "Jot 'Em Down" store.

The renamed but real Pine Ridge remains to this day in Montgomery County, Arkansas, and has since become home of the Lum & Abner Museum — a lasting tribute to the homespun radio comedy that gave the town its name.

TOP 50 PROGRAMS — 1936–37

CBS 22, NBC 21, Blue 8 (51)*
Average Rating: 12.0, Median: 10.6
22,869,000 Radio Homes / 68.4% Coverage of U.S. Homes / One Rating Point = 228,690 Homes
Source: Clark-Hooper Radio Advertisement Reports, Sep 1936–Jun 1937
Total Programs Rated 6–11 P.M.: 129
Programs Rated 13 Weeks & Ranked: 118.

		Program	Rtg	Type	Sponsor	Day	Time	Lgth	Net
1	2	Jack Benny Program	28.9	SC	Jello Gelatin	Sun	7:00	30	NBC
2	13	Eddie Cantor Show	23.0	CV	Texaco	Sun	8:30	30	CBS
3	1	Major Bowes Original Amateur Hour	21.3	TC	Chrysler Corporation	Thu	9:00	60	CBS
4	15	Lux Radio Theater/Cecil B DeMille	21.0	DA	Lux Soap	Mon	9:00	60	CBS
5	6	Burns & Allen	20.9	CV	Campbell Soup	Wed	8:30	30	CBS
6	5	Fred Allen's Town Hall Tonight	20.2	CV	Ipana/Sal Hepatica	Wed	9:00	60	NBC
7	8	Bing Crosby's Kraft Music Hall	17.4	MV	Kraft Cheese	Thu	10:00	60	NBC
8	3	Rudy Vallee Show	16.4	MV	Royal Gelatin/Fleischmann	Thu	8:00	60	NBC
9	13	Phil Baker's Gulf Headliners	15.8	CV	Gulf Oil	Sun	7:30	30	CBS
10	9	Al Jolson Show	15.4	MV	Lifebuoy Soap/Rinso	Tue	8:30	30	CBS
11	18	Amos & Andy	15.3	SC	Pepsodent Toothpaste	M-F	7:00	15	NBC
12t	10	Hollywood Hotel/Louella Parsons	14.9	MV	Campbell Soup	Fri	9:00	60	CBS
12t	21	Vick's Open House/Nelson Eddy	14.9	MV	Vick's Vap-O-Rub	Sun	8:00	30	CBS
14	12	First Nighter/L Tremayne & B Luddy	13.7	DA	Campana Balm	Fri	9:30	30	CBS 1
15	38	Walter Winchell's Jergens Journal	13.1	NC	Jergens Lotion	Sun	9:30	15	Blue 2
16	16	One Man's Family	13.0	DCC	Tenderleaf Tea	Wed	8:00	30	NBC
17t	32	Boake Carter News	12.8	NC	Philco Radios	M-F	7:45	15	CBS
17t	19	Your Hit Parade/Buddy Clark	12.8	MP	Lucky Strike Cigarettes	Wed	10:00	45	NBC3
19	N	Fred Astaire Show	12.5	MV	Packard Automobiles	Tue	9:30	60	NBC
20	37	Gangbusters	12.0	DA	Palmolive Shave Cream	Wed	10:00	30	CBS
21	62	Fibber McGee & Molly	11.5	SC	Johnson Wax	Mon	9:00	30	NBC 4
22	44	Pick & Pat	11.3	CV	Dill's Best Pipe Tobacco	Mon	8:30	30	CBS
23	71	Ken Murray Show	11.0	CV	Lifebuoy Soap/Rinso	Tue	8:30	30	CBS
24	19	Your Hit Parade/Buddy Clark	10.9	MP	Lucky Strike Cigarettes	Sat	10:00	45	CBS5
25	11	Robert Ripley's Bakers Broadcast	10.6	API	Fleischmann Yeast	Sun	7:30	30	Blue
26	24	Lowell Thomas News	10.4	NC	Sun Oil	M-F	6:45	15	Blue
27t	4	Maxwell House Showboat	10.1	MV	Maxwell House Coffee	Thu	9:00	60	NBC
27t	42	Wayne King Orch	10.1	MP	Lady Esther Cosmetics	Mon	10:00	30	CBS
29	83	Vox Pop Sidewalk Interviews	9.7	API	Molle Shaving Cream	Tue	9:00	30	NBC
30	N	Jack Oakie's College	9.6	CV	Camel Cigarettes	Tue	9:30	30	CBS
31	92	Al Pearce Gang	9.5	CV	Ford Motors	Tue	9:00	30	CBS
32t	38	Ford Sunday Evening Hour	9.2	MC	Ford Motors	Sun	9:00	60	CBS
32t	62	Uncle Ezra's Radio Station	9.2	CV	Alka Seltzer	MWF	7:15	15	NBC
34t	60	Kate Smith's A&P Bandwagon	8.8	MV	A&P Food Stores	Thu	8:00	60	CBS
34t	70	Lum & Abner	8.8	SC	Horlick Malted Milk	M-F	7:30	15	Blue
36	N	Do You Want to Be an Actor?	8.6	TC	Chase & Sanborn Coffee	Sun	8:00	60	NBC

	Program	Rtg	Type	Sponsor	Day	Time	Lgth	Net
37 *34*	Shell Chateau/Joe Cook	8.5	CV	Shell Oil	Sat	9:30	60	NBC
38t *50*	Ed Wynn Show	8.4	CV	Spud Cigarettes	Sat	8:00	30	Blue
38t *23*	General Motors Concert	8.4	MC	General Motors	Sun	10:00	30	NBC
38t *N*	Russ Morgan Orch	8.4	MP	Philip Morris Cigarettes	Tue	8:00	30	NBC
41 *N*	Uncle Jim's Question Bee	8.3	APQ	George Washington Coffee	Sat	7:30	30	Blue
42 *32*	Fred Waring Show	8.2	MST	Ford Motors	Tue	9:00	30	CBS
43 *N*	Professor Quiz/Craig Earl	7.7	APQ	George Washington Coffee	Sat	8:00	30	CBS
44 *17*	Ben Bernie Show	8.1	MV	American Can Co.	Tue	9:00	30	Blue
45 *52*	Court of Human Relations	7.5	DA	True Story Magazine	Fri	9:30	30	NBC
46t *105*	Voice of Experience/Marion Taylor	7.4	API	Lydia Pinkham	T-T	7:15	15	NBC
46t *31*	Voice of Firestone	7.4	MC	Firestone Tires	Mon	8:30	30	NBC
46t *42*	Wayne King Orch	7.4	MP	Lady Esther Cosmetics	Tue	8:30	30	NBC
49t *20*	Beauty Box Theater	7.2	DA	Palmolive Soap	Wed	9:30	30	CBS
49t *27*	Helen Hayes Theater	7.2	DA	Sanka Coffee	Tue	9:30	30	Blue
49t *42*	Wayne King Orch	7.2	MP	Lady Esther Cosmetics	Wed	8:30	30	NBC

*Total: 51. (Three programs tied for 49th.) / New & Returning Top 50 Programs Underscored.

	Program			Sponsor	Day	Time	Lgth	Net
1	First Nighter	Sep–Jan		Campana Balm	Fri	10:00	30	NBC
2	Walter Winchell's Jergens Journal	Sep–Mar		Jergens Lotion	Sun	9:00	15	Blue
3	Your Hit Parade	Sep–Nov		Lucky Strike Cigarettes	Wed	10:00	60	NBC
		Dec–Mar		Lucky Strike Cigarettes	Wed	10:00	30	NBC
4	Fibber McGee & Molly	Sep–Apr		Johnson Wax	Mon	8:00	30	NBC
5	Your Hit Parade	Sep–Nov		Lucky Strike Cigarettes	Sat	10:00	60	CBS
		Dec–Jan		Lucky Strike Cigarettes	Sat	10:00	30	CBS

Key: API — Audience Participation/Interviews   DCC — Drama/Continuing Characters   MV — Music/Variety Show
APQ — Audience Participation/Quiz   MC — Music/Classical, Semi-Classical   NC — News, Commentary
APS — Audience Participation/Stunts   MP — Music/Popular, Contemporary   SC — Situation Comedy
CV — Comedy/Variety Show   MSP — Music/Specialty, Ethnic   TC — Talent Competition
DA — Dramatic Anthology   MST — Music/Standard, Traditional

1936–37 Top 50 Favorite Formats

	Programs	Pct
Music — All Categories	21	42%
Comedy — Variety & Situation	15	29%
Drama — Anthology & Continuing	7	14%
Audience Participation — All Categories	5	10%
News/Commentary	3	6%

*Total 51. (Two programs tied for 50th.)

1936–37 Monthly Winners

Sep	Major Bowes Amateur Hour	21.4	Feb	Jack Benny Program	36.5
Oct	Jack Benny Program	25.6	Mar	Jack Benny Program	35.1
Nov	Jack Benny Program	28.6	Apr	Jack Benny Program	31.3
Dec	Jack Benny Program	29.2	May	Jack Benny Program	27.2
Jan	Jack Benny Program	26.9	Jun	Jack Benny Program	19.7

10

The 1937–38 Network Season

Announcer: Here's a question for homeowners. When you buy a vacuum cleaner or any other household product, you always make sure it's trademarked and therefore guaranteed, then why not take the same precaution when ordering your supply of anthracite? Don't order just any coal. Insist on <u>Blue</u> <u>Coal</u>, the <u>only</u> trademarked <u>anthracite</u>. Order a ton of Blue Coal! Try Blue Coal for a week. See if it doesn't give you more <u>even</u>, <u>dependable</u> and <u>longer lasting</u> heat. That's fair enough, isn't it? Unlike many other anthracites, Blue Coal is a medium, free-burning hard coal. It <u>burns</u> <u>steadily</u> down to a fine, powdery ash, and gives you more useful heat. The finest anthracite money can buy is <u>Blue</u> <u>Coal</u>. Call your dealer tomorrow. And ask him about Blue Coal's automatic heat regulator. This thermostat controls your furnace dampers and enables you to keep your home at a steadier, more even heat, with a minimum of effort and furnace attention. A Blue Coal heat regulator costs but eighteen dollars and ninety-nine cents, plus a nominal installation charge. And it will pay for itself in time and fuel savings for you. Phone your neighborhood <u>Blue</u> <u>Coal</u> Dealer tomorrow for careful, courteous delivery and help for of all your heating problems.

RADIO BAGS
GROCERY MONEY

The networks and its advertisers took a breather. For the first and only time in Network Radio's Golden Age the total number of sponsored programs in prime time fell below 100. Nevertheless, the four chains' size and income continued to grow.

Three giant consumer products manufacturers — General Foods, Standard Brands and Lever Brothers — each sponsored two of the season's Top Ten programs.

Standard had the top rated show in Edgar Bergen and Charlie McCarthy's *Chase & Sanborn Hour* plus Rudy Vallee's variety hour in ninth place.

General Foods' Jello sponsored Jack Benny's second place program and Grape Nuts had Burns and Allen who finished the season in eighth.

Lever's *Lux Radio Theater* rated third and Al Jolson hosted Lifebuoy Soap's tenth place show.

The three conglomerates hit stride among network radio's biggest advertisers. By July they reported spending a combined three and a half million dollars in radio *(55.0 Mil)*, during the first six months of 1937. Each spent more in radio than in national magazine advertising — an inconceiva-

ble thought less than a decade earlier.

General Foods had the greatest ratings success of the group. It controlled three of the season's eleven highest rated programs and seven of the Top 50.

Ironically, the three were all outspent in radio by a sponsor with *no* programs in the Top 50. Procter & Gamble spent most of its radio budget — some four million dollars in 1937 *(62.8 Mil)* — in daytime radio where the Cincinnati soap giant sponsored over a half-dozen weekday strip programs.

THE NETWORKS
MEET AT SUNSET

With combined network revenues approaching a total of 340 million dollars *(5.40 Bil.)*, in the five years since 1932, the chains had plenty of cash to finance new production facilities in Hollywood where most of the top rated prime time shows now originated.

NBC and CBS both broke ground on Sunset Boulevard in Hollywood just a few blocks from each other which made it handy in future years for actors and musicians rushing between shows in the rival's studios.

CBS was first with its new $1.75 Million *(27.5 Mil)*, facility for KNX and network use at Sunset and Gower in April 1937. Not to be outdone, NBC followed with its own two million dollar *(31.4 Mil)*, West Coast headquarters at Sunset and Vine six months later.

NBC, however, would never own a radio station in Los Angeles — depending instead on longtime powerful affiliate KFI as its major outlet in southern California.

1937–38 Season Scoreboard
Mid-season Totals, December 1937

		Compared to Year Earlier	
Total Radio Homes	24.50 Mil	+1.63 Mil	+7.1%
Total Auto Radios	5.0 Mil	+1.50 Mil	+42.9%
Total AM Radio Stations	646	+30	+4.9%
Total Radio Network Affiliates	296	+70	+30.1%
1937 Radio Revenues	164.6 Mil	+42.3 Mil	+34.6%
1937 Network Revenues	88.5 Mil	+12.9 Mil	+17.1%
Network Share	53.8%		(8.0%)

GOING AFRA
THE MONEY

The networks were flush with money and the big name stars were making thousands per broadcast.

Yet, not everyone involved was getting rich. The studio talent — the men and women who worked the shows as announcers and actors, often without name credit — received as little as $2.50 a program or as much as $25 a week *($393)*, which often included days of rehearsal.

Led by comedian and social activist Eddie Cantor, radio performers banded together and formed the American Federation of Radio Artists six weeks before the 1937–38 season began. Cantor was a logical choice for the group — later known as the American Federation of Radio and Television Artists. He had previously served as president of the Screen Actors Guild from 1933 to 1935.

THE LITTLE
NETWORK THAT COULD

Mutual, now with its own Hollywood connection at KHJ, continued to sign affiliates throughout the country. The network finished 1937 with 80 stations, more than doubling its size in a year. It still didn't have much entertainment programming to offer its affiliates besides *The Lone Ranger* and another legendary series launched on the network in September, *The Shadow.*

In later years Mutual would offer a much larger schedule to its stations but even its most popular programs suffered in ratings popularity because of a polling technicality and the regional system by which the network was sold to many of its advertisers.

To meet Hooper reporting standards, a broadcast had to attain a minimum of 600 homes reported listening to a program for *an individual sponsor* in the 30 cities that Hooper surveyed during a rating period. When the same program was sold to *different sponsors* from city to city, it had little chance of making a dent in the ratings.

Mutual was at a further disadvantage in the 30 major markets

surveyed because except for New York, Chicago and Los Angeles, Mutual affiliates were seldom the powerhouse stations that carried NBC, CBS or Blue programming. To make up the difference in coverage Mutual pursued more affiliates by reaching into smaller cities that its competitors dismissed. Because these less populated markets weren't polled by the rating services, Mutual again received short shrift in the rating books.

AND THE BANDS
PLAYED ON ... AND ON...

Over 40 percent of the season's prime time programs were based in music — music of all types.

Benny Goodman and Tommy Dorsey brought swing to network radio with their own series. They were joined by the show bands of Paul Whiteman, Ozzie Nelson and Kay Kyser.

But the sweet bands of Wayne King and Russ Morgan got the most exposure. King was heard three times a week until January, then twice a week with a prime time *Lady Esther Serenade* on both NBC and CBS. Morgan's "wahwah" trombone and orchestra headlined *The Camel Caravan* on both networks every week.

But the big band that grabbed the most headlines was *really* big — 92 musicians.

The NBC Symphony Orchestra debuted in November and its maestro, 70-year-old Arturo Toscanini, made his first appearance on Christmas Eve. The Symphony's 90 minute concerts on Saturday nights at 10:00 were broadcast simultaneously on both the NBC and Blue networks for three months.

The critically acclaimed orchestra remained on NBC for the rest of the season, then moved to co-owned Blue — RCA's "cultural" network — for the next five years of its 17 year run before returning to NBC.

I WITNESS NEWS

NBC hired Max Jordan, 39, as Network Radio's first full time European correspondent in 1934, predating CBS's hiring of the more famed Edward R. Murrow and William L. Shirer by three years. As

a reporter for Hearst's International News Service, the multi-lingual Jordan had free-lanced several stories for NBC since 1931.

Jordan went to work immediately to negotiate contracts that would assure NBC of facilities to short wave his reports to New York from most anywhere on the continent.

His efforts paid their first big dividend on March 12, 1938, when Jordan was first to report directly from Vienna the news of Germany's annexation of Austria. CBS had to settle for Shirer's reports of the event the following day from London. Shirer's dispatches became the foundation for the daily *CBS European Roundup*— later the *CBS World News Roundup*— incorporating short-waved contributions from the network's overseas correspondents and anchored by Robert Trout in New York.

THE BRONX BOMBERS
AND BROWN BOMBER

New York's "subway" World Series between the defending champion Yankees against their crosstown rival Giants was given full coverage by all four networks plus New York independent stations WHN, WINS and WNEW. Both teams were loaded with future Hall of Fame players — Joe DiMaggio, Lou Gehrig, Bill Dickey, Lefty Gomez, Red Ruffing and Tony Lazzeri for manager Joe McCarthy's Yankees and the Giants' Mel Ott, Carl Hubbell, Travis Jackson and player/manager Bill Terry.

The five game series won by the Yankees scored a 25.3 average rating — second only in October to Edgar Bergen and Charlie McCarthy's month leading 26.4.

But the season's ratings winner in sports involved just two men — Heavyweight Champion Joe Louis and the former champion who had knocked him out two years earlier, Max Schmeling. It was a grudge match of the first order — Schmeling representing Nazi Germany and Louis symbolizing American Democracy. Their June 22 rematch was broadcast on both NBC and Blue — all two minutes and four seconds of it. Louis pummeled Schmeling in the first round.

Crossley's CAB survey the following day determined that the bout had a knockout 63.6 rating.

THE MONTHLIES

Standard Brands struck programming gold again. Edgar Bergen and Charlie McCarthy took over the 8:00 Sunday hour on NBC and turned in the Number One rated program for all ten months of the season. NBC's streak of consecutive monthly winners rose to 31.

1937–38 Sunday
Night Top Ten Programs
NBC 5, Blue 3, CBS 2.
Average: 14.5

Edgar Bergen & Charlie McCarthy	NBC	8:00	32.1
Jack Benny Program	NBC	7:00	29.5
Phil Baker Show	CBS	7:30	16.4
Walter Winchell	Blue	9:30	13.7
Hollywood Playhouse	Blue	9:00	10.7
Manhattan Merry Go Round	NBC	9:00	9.8
Interesting Neighbors	NBC	7:30	9.7
Ford Sunday Evening Hour	CBS	9:00	8.4
American Album of Familiar Music	NBC	9:30	8.1
Irene Rich Dramas	Blue	9:45	6.8

BERGEN THROWS VOICE AND MILLIONS CATCH IT

Standard Brands' Chase & Sanborn Coffee installed Edgar Bergen and Charlie McCarthy into the 8:00 Sunday night slot on NBC to replace its short lived *Do Want to Be an Actor?* The time period once again proved to be prime, prime time radio real estate for the ventriloquist just as it had been for Eddie Cantor and Major Bowes before him.

The program was designed to be the cream of radio variety and featured an all-star cast to support Bergen and his wooden ward. Radio veteran Don Ameche, now a leading man in four 20th Century–Fox movies a year, was the show's host. Film star Dorothy Lamour provided its glamour and sang. Legendary comedian W.C. Fields became Charlie's nemesis in an intramural feud of barbs early in the show's run. And the new *Chase*

& Sanborn Hour was well stocked with weekly musical and dramatic guest stars. But the real attraction remained Bergen and the irreverent, horny little adolescent dummy perched on his lap.

Bergen tripled *Do You Want to Be an Actor*'s ratings and began a string of 16 consecutive seasons among the annual Top Ten — never finishing below seventh place.

Edgar Bergen and Charlie McCarthy pushed Hooper's numbers to Crossley-like heights. The highest Hooperatings ever recorded for a weekly series were scored during the debut season of Edgar Bergen's *Chase & Sanborn Hour* on NBC in 1937–38.

On Sunday, January 16th the soft-spoken ventriloquist and his brash Charlie scored a 41.1. The following month on February 6th the Bergen and McCarthy rating rose to a 41.2. It "fell off" to a 40.9 on March 6.

And these numbers were generated after the notorious Mae West incident in December when the program was denounced in the press and pulpits across the country which called for a boycott of the show.

MAE'S WAYS WITH WORDS

Mae West was the original sex symbol of the American stage and movies. In 1937 she had 20 years of sexually oriented roles on Broadway and seven censor-shuddering, but highly profitable films to her credit. She wrote much of her own material and had a way of delivering lines like no other actress — dripping with lasciviousness and spiked with double entendre.

She appeared to be an ageless sex goddess when she was 44 and she made a rare radio appearance on the Bergen/McCarthy *Chase & Sanborn Hour* of December 12th to promote her new movie, *Every Day's a Holiday.*

Her first act in the show was a dialog with Bergen and Charlie in which she recalled a date with Charlie and, "I still have the splinters to remind me of it." It drew howls from the studio audience but shocked some of Sunday night's Sabbath sensitivities around the country.

But the kicker — that got her kicked off NBC for a dozen years — came in the second half hour's *Adam & Eve* sketch co-starring Don Ameche. The script was written by Arch Oboler and seemed perfectly tame on paper when reviewed beforehand by the network and sponsor. Then Mae West took hold of it.

She milked her lines with such over the top sexual innuendo that jaws dropped. By Monday morning everyone involved was condemned by preachers, politicians and papers. As a result, everyone involved apologized profusely — everyone except Mae West.

And within two weeks *The Chase & Sanborn Hour* began to score its record breaking ratings.

IN THE SHADOW OF PRIME TIME

One of network radio's best remembered series, *The Shadow,* is nearly as invisible in this study of prime time programming as he was when Lamont Cranston, "...Clouded men's minds so they could not see him."

Mutual's version of *The Shadow* was a Sunday afternoon series, outside of prime time. But it was one of the most popular mystery melodramas ever to promise a weekly scare for anyone willing to suspend disbelief for half an hour.

It debuted over Mutual at 5:30 on September 26, 1937, with 22-year-old Orson Welles as "Wealthy man about town Lamont Cranston," aka *The Shadow.* Fellow actors from Welles' off–Broadway Mercury Players contributed supporting roles, most notably Agnes Moorhead, 36, who portrayed, "...Cranston's constant companion, the *lovely* Margo Lane."

Moorhead also originated another famous Lane character for radio — "Ace girl reporter Lois Lane" for Mutual's *Adventures of Superman.* Both radio roles — which often involved as much screaming as dialogue — kept the actress busy before her distinguished film career that resulted in four Oscar nominations.

Welles left *The Shadow* and took his troupe to CBS for the 1938–39 season where his *Mercury Theater of the Air* would make headlines with its *War of the Worlds* broadcast.

After Welles and Moorhead left, *The Shadow*'s leads went to a number of radio actors over the next 15 years, most notably Bill Johnstone and Bret Morrison as Lamont and Marjorie Anderson and Gertrude Werner as Margo.

Because of its timeslot and the ratings systems' sporadic reporting of Mutual programming, *The Shadow* never received the scrutiny of prime time programs on the three established networks. It didn't appear in the Hooperatings until four years after its debut on Mutual.

SHADOWING LAMONT'S RATINGS

Had *The Shadow* been grouped with prime time competition, it would have ranked in the season's Top 50 programs only three times. More surprisingly, it would have been among Sunday's Top Ten only twice —1942–43 (7th), and 1943–44 (9th).

BLUE COAL FOR LISTENERS' CHILLS

One can only wonder what *The Shadow* might have done against prime time competition when more homes were using radios on Sunday afternoon as opposed to Sunday evening.

Its weekly parade of sinister villains eerily committing the foulest mayhem — often emphasized by Margo's piercing screams — was radio's answer to pulp fiction. It was easy for critics to dismiss it as simplistic, formulaic and juvenile. But it's longtime sponsor didn't market to juveniles. And the program was doing just fine for the Delaware, Lackawanna & Western Coal Company whose product became known to millions as Blue

Coal, the most famous name in home heating fuel.

Dying anthracite coal blue during its washing process was originated a decade earlier by the Glen Alden Coal Company in upstate New York for its Blue Diamond brand coal. The bluing was simple and cheap — branding every piece of the commodity with no labels required.

Delaware, Lackawanna & Western sponsored *The Shadow* for over a dozen years and sold Blue Coal by the tons — millions of them.

1937–38 Monday Night Top Ten Programs (11)
NBC 5, CBS 4, Blue 2
Average: 12.6

Lux Radio Theater	CBS	9:00	23.4
Burns & Allen Show	NBC	8:00	19.2
Amos & Andy*	NBC	7:00	13.3
Lowell Thomas News*	Blue	6:45	11.3
Boake Carter News	CBS	7:45	10.6
Model Minstrels	CBS	8:30	10.3
Uncle Ezra's Radio Station	NBC	7:15	9.8
Voice of Firestone	NBC	8:30	9.5
Wayne King's Lady Esther Serenade	CBS	10:00	9.4
Hour of Charm	NBC	9:00	8.8
Lum & Abner	Blue	7:30	8.8

*Monday–Friday Strip Shows

Sans Strips...

Grand Hotel	Blue	8:30	8.3
Warden Lawes at Sing Sing	Blue	10:00	5.6

LUX LOOMS LARGER

There was no stopping *Lux Radio Theater* in its march to becoming Monday's all-time ratings champ for Lever Brothers and CBS. During the 1937–38 season alone, *Lux* presented dozens of movie greats its radio adaptations of box office hits. The season's weekly parade of stars included Clark Gable, Spencer Tracy, Bette Davis, Barbara Stanwyck, Gary Cooper, Joan Crawford, Henry

Fonda, Olivia deHavilland, Cary Grant, Claudette Colbert, Errol Flynn and Bing Crosby.

Throughout the remainder of Network Radio's Golden Age no competing program in the 9:00 Monday timeslot would muster even half of *Lux Radio Theater*'s ratings. It proved to be an unmatched dominance.

SPITALNY'S CHARMING COMPETITORS

One of the few ratings "successes" against the Hollywood extravaganza at 9:00 was veteran conductor Phil Spitalny's all girl orchestra and its (30 minute) *Hour of Charm*. The 22 piece ensemble of female musicians and singers — whose highly accomplished members were identified only by their first names — featured Evelyn (Klein) and her "magic" violin. The future Mrs. Spitalny was both highly talented and beautiful.

Despite its musicianship displayed in selections that ranged from standards to symphonic, the female orchestra was considered a novelty act. Far from a disadvantage, the characterization worked to Spitalny's favor that resulted movie appearances plus a ten year sponsorship by General Electric on NBC.

Surprisingly, *Hour of Charm*'s 1937–38 season competing against the unbeatable *Lux Radio Theater* resulted in its only Top 50 season.

NO THANKS, WE'LL WALK

Fortunately for George Burns and Gracie Allen, the new CBS and NBC studios in Hollywood were just a few blocks apart on Sunset Boulevard. They'd make the trip six times.

After five years on the CBS Wednesday schedule, Burns and Allen signed with General Foods for the new season and moved to NBC on Monday against the feint competition of Horace Heidt's "Brigadiers" orchestra. The couple's network hopping lost 10 percent of their audience but they remained in the season's Top Ten for one last time.

They returned to CBS the following season.

The Shadow Season Ratings Averages and Ranking with Prime Time Programs

Season	Rtg	Rank	Season	Rtg	Rank
1941–42	10.9	47t	1947–48	13.1	70t
1942–43	15.5	22t	1948–49	10.4	67
1943–44	13.2	32t	1949–50	9.1	59t
1944–45	9.5	83	1950–51	7.9	54t
1945–46	8.7	78t	1951–52	5.8	51t
1946–47	9.9	60t	1952–53	4.1	64t

MOLLY'S DELICATE CONDITION

Jim Jordan and his writer/partner Don Quinn were dealt a problem in November even greater than being scheduled against Monday's giant, *Lux Radio Theater*. To their credit, *Fibber McGee & Molly* had almost regained the momentum that was quashed when it was pitted against *Lux* for over a year.

But early into the 1937–38 season, Marian Jordan took sick — very sick.

Jim and Marian had been running hard since spring when they filmed their first movie, *This Way Please*. The pressures of their weekly broadcasts, frequent personal appearance commitments and raising two youngsters got to Marian and forced her off the air and into a hospital.

The decision was made that Jim would carry the show by himself until she returned. It would be a longer time than he or Quinn imagined.

Quinn stocked the show with new characters developed from Chicago's company of radio actors and gave Fibber a series of jobs to create new situations every week. And most every week Jim would close the temporarily renamed *Fibber McGee & Company* with a short endearment for his Molly.

Jordan and Quinn finally got a break in mid–March when Johnson Wax and NBC moved the show out of *Lux Radio Theater*'s shadow on Monday night and into its long held 9:30 timeslot on Tuesdays. The move helped raise the show to ratings 20 percent higher than those before the move to Mondays and Marian's absence.

Then Marian managed a brief appearance on the show of June 28 but it would be almost a year until she returned permanently. Meanwhile, it was up to her husband and their trusted writer/partner to keep the program going.

TINSLETOWN TO BIG TOWN

Edward G. Robinson and Claire Trevor became the first major motion picture stars to commit to continuing roles in a dramatic series. Robinson, as "fighting" editor Steve Wilson of *The Illustrated Press*, and Trevor as his star reporter, Lorelei Kilbourne, immediately delivered the newcomer newspaper drama to the season's Top 20. Trevor left the show after two seasons and Robinson stayed for five, yet *Big Town* scored an eventual total of 13 Top 50 seasons.

THE GANG'S ALL HERE

It was billed as *Al Pearce's Gang* and it was exactly that.

Imported by CBS from affiliate KFRC/San Francisco, Ford Motors slotted Pearce and his troupe of supporting players on Wednesday night midway in the previous season. Pearce was ringmaster of the group that included some of radio's most talent comic voices: Arthur Q. Bryan, Morey Amsterdam, Harry Stewart as Scandinavian accented "Yogi Yorgenson," and motor-mouthed Arlene Harris who performed one-way telephone conversations with her silent friend, Masie.

But the star was Pearce who did a regular turn as bashful door-to-door salesman "Elmer Blurt," and whose under-the-breath wish after knocking on doors was, "Nobody's home, I hope, I hope, I hope." The line became national catch phrase.

By fall the show had taken root and scored a 35 percent increase in its second season ratings — its first and only trip to the Top 15.

Unlike most radio stars, Pearce made four movies *after* his prime time glory years and six trips to the Top 50. However, the films were all "quickie" B films produced by Republic Pictures, destined for second billing in double feature houses. Two of the films featured Dale Evans before she hitched up as Roy Rogers' permanent co-star.

IT'S A MATTER OF TIMES...

"I'll mow ya down!"

Charlie McCarthy's weekly threat to W.C. Fields had became a national catch phrase over the summer.

Texaco and CBS saw Edgar Bergen's Sunday night ratings reaper looming and pulled Eddie Cantor out of its path. The comedian was moved from opposite Sunday's *Chase & Sanborn Hour* — which, ironically, was once his own — and into the safe Wednesday timeslot vacated by Burns and Allen who had jumped to NBC for the season.

Cantor returned the favor with Wednesday's most popular program.

... AND A MATTER OF DIMES

The move kept Cantor in the season's Top Five and helped him launch one of the nation's most famous charity drives. AFRA President Cantor was an active and vocal supporter of Franklin Roosevelt, a wheelchair bound victim of what, in 1921, had been diagnosed as paralytic poliomyelitis, more commonly known as polio.

Acting on the President's request, Cantor — with the help of show business luminaries — spearheaded the first fund raising drive for the National Foundation for Infantile Paralysis.

Cantor is credited with calling the campaign, *The March of Dimes* — its similarity to *The March of Time* intended. He introduced it in late January on a special broadcast carried by all four networks. The effort became the most successful charity drive of the pre-war years.

THE OL' MAESTRO AND THE OL' PROFESSOR

Tied in the ratings, bandleaders Ben Bernie and Kay Kyser were both powerful radio personalities. They were 14 years apart in age when their network paths crossed on Wednesday night and their age difference was obvious from their programs.

Bernie, "The Ol' Maestro," was 46. Despite starring in two movies with Walter Winchell in 1937, his radio career was on its downside after two disastrous seasons on Blue. His CBS series for U.S. Rubber was to have been his comeback to the Top Ten. His broadcasts were informal, relaxed and loose, featuring quipster/emcee Bernie talking the lyrics of songs while his orchestra accompanied him in dated standards and novelties — like his own compositions, *Sweet Georgia Brown* and *Who's Your Little Whoosis?*

Kyser, 32, took on a completely opposite persona as "The Ol' Professor" — costumed in cap and gown as the frenetic, fast talking "dean" of the musical comedy quiz, *The Kollege of Musical Knowledge* (aka *The College of Musical Knowledge*). American Tobacco had replaced its Wednesday edition of *Your Hit Parade* on NBC in December with singing movie star Dick Powell for 13 weeks while it honed *Kollege* for the big time on Mutual.

By April, Kyser and his show band presented a tightly formatted, fast paced mix of audience participation, comedy and music for NBC. Kyser's music was definitely of the new order — mixing ballads and novelties of the day with swing instrumentals introduced by Kyser's urging, "C'mon, Students, let's dance!"

Bernie and Kyser both finished the season with a 10.9 average rating, tied for 31st place.

It would be Ben Bernie's last Top 50 season and the first of nine for Kay Kyser, which included two years in the Top Ten.

A BETTER BARBOUR POLL POSITION

One of the first programs to move from NBC's West Coast production headquarters at KPO/San Francisco was the popular Carleton E. Morse continuing drama, *One Man's Family*. The program was transferred to Hollywood in October, before NBC's new studios had been completely finished. The Barbour Family obviously liked their new neighborhood — their rating average increased by nearly 20 percent.

It was the first of four seasons that *One Man's Family* became NBC's most popular dramatic show.

1937–38 Thursday Night Top Ten Programs
NBC 6, CBS 3, Blue 1
Average: 13.6

Bing Crosby's Kraft Music Hall	NBC	10:00	22.7
Major Bowes' Original Amateur Hour	CBS	9:00	19.4
Rudy Vallee Varieties	NBC	8:00	18.6
Good News of 1938	NBC	9:00	16.6
Amos & Andy*	NBC	7:00	13.3
Lowell Thomas News*	Blue	6:45	11.3
Maxwell House Showboat	NBC	9:00	9.8
Kate Smith Hour	CBS	8:00	8.7
We the People	CBS	7:30	8.0
Vocal Varieties	NBC	7:15	6.9

*Monday–Friday Strip Shows

Sans Strips...

Mr. Keen, Tracer of Lost Persons	Blue	7:15	6.5
Easy Aces	Blue	7:00	6.2

GOOD NEWS FOR BING, BUT BAD FOR BOWES

General Foods' Maxwell House Coffee scuttled the aging *Showboat* in November despite the return of host Charlie Winninger as Captain Henry, who went down with his ship. The food conglomerate updated its timeslot's theme from minstrel to movies with MGM's *Good News of 1938*.

Good News was a blatant promotional vehicle for MGM films but a ratings winner. It scored a fast 66 percent jump in audience over the *Showboat* troupe.

Constant in the *Good News* cast among its rotating hosts and visiting stars was veteran MGM character actor and comedian Frank Morgan. He was joined in November by former Ziegfeld star Fanny Brice, who trotted out her *Baby Snooks* character for a skit on each week's show.

Good News' ratings surge opposite Major Bowes' *Original Amateur Hour* combined with Bing Crosby's *Kraft Music Hall* audience increase of 35 percent — thanks in part to *Good News'* strong lead-in — was enough to push Crosby into Thursday's top spot over Bowes and into fourth place among the season's highest rated programs.

It was the first of Crosby's three consecutive Thursday wins and the third of his seven Top Ten seasons.

THE GENERAL'S BATTLE PLAN

Good News was General Foods' second new, hour-long variety show on Thursday night, just before Friday's traditional grocery shopping. The company also picked up sponsorship of Kate Smith's variety hour on CBS at 8:00, beginning a ten year association with the singer. Smith's first season for Swansdown Cake Flour and Calumet Baking Powder was a struggle against Rudy Vallee on NBC, but it paved her way to four consecutive Top 20 finishes beginning the following year.

LORD OF THE PEOPLE

Phillips H. Lord removed himself as host of his CBS hit *Gangbusters* to concentrate on producing and emceeing his new creation on Blue for General Foods, *We the People.*

Never afraid to borrow, adapt and twist others' formats, Lord took parts of *Vox Pop*'s human interest angles, Ripley's *Believe It or Not*'s oddities, *Hollywood Hotel*'s star interviews and concocted his new audience participation program in 1936.

Not content with just two hours of Thursday prime time, General Foods moved the potpourri to CBS at 7:30 in 1937. It also installed a new host, Mutual newscaster Gabriel Heatter, who would remain with the show until 1942.

We the People achieved the Top 50 ranks in only six of its 14 seasons on the air, but the half hour human interest mix remained on CBS at various times for twelve years and spent another two on NBC — all under the sponsorship of General Foods or Gulf Oil.

*1937–38 Friday Night
Top Ten Programs*
NBC 4, Blue 3, CBS 3
Average: 11.0

First Nighter	NBC	10:00	15.1
Hollywood Hotel	CBS	9:00	14.7
Amos & Andy*	NBC	7:00	13.3
Lowell Thomas News*	Blue	6:45	11.3
Boake Carter News	CBS	7:45	10.6
Uncle Ezra's Radio Station	NBC	7:15	9.8
Court of Human Relations	NBC	9:30	9.3
Paul Whiteman Show	CBS	8:30	9.1
Lum & Abner	Blue	7:30	8.8
Death Valley Days	Blue	9:30	8.3

*Monday–Friday Strip Shows

Sans Strips...

Cities Service Concert	NBC	8:00	7.5
Grand Central Station	Blue	8:00	7.1

THE LITTLE THEATER'S LOYAL PATRONS

Friday's top program was the Chicago based, low budgeted *First Nighter* which had been radio's top rated dramatic series for three seasons before *Lux Radio Theater* came along. Longtime sponsor Campana defied programming logic when it shifted the "Little Theater Off Times Square" from NBC to CBS

and a new Friday night timeslot in the middle of the 1936–37 season, then back again to NBC and its original Friday time in the heart of the 1937–38 season. Normally such mid-season dial twisting came at a high cost of ratings.

That wasn't the case with *First Nighter*. In a real test of listener loyalty, the program didn't budge a full point in its two uprootings. It actually gained ground in its second transplant and finished 1937–38 with its sixth season in the annual Top 20.

*1937–38 Saturday Night
Six Rated Programs*
CBS 4, Blue 1, NBC 1
Average: 10.2

Jack Haley Show	NBC	8:30	12.4
Professor Quiz	CBS	9:00	12.4
Your Hit Parade	CBS	10:00	12.4
National Barn Dance	Blue	9:00	9.0
Russ Morgan Orchestra	CBS	8:30	8.4
Saturday Night Serenade	CBS	9:30	6.6

SATURDAY NIGHT IS THE LONELIEST NIGHT

Saturday continued to be the least popular night for Network Radio. The three major networks didn't offer much and Mutual had no sponsored programs to feed to its affiliates

The NBC Symphony, aired at 10:00 on both NBC and Blue from mid–November until late March, then on NBC alone until the end of the season. The classical music series was sustaining. As such, it didn't appear in the Hooperating reports. CBS programmed the highly praised *Columbia Workshop*

on Saturday nights. It, too, was sustaining and unrated.

TIN TIED

In a ratings rarity, three programs tied for Saturday's top honors and 26th place in the season's Top 50.

Jack Haley's comedy based variety show was the newcomer of the three. At 39, Haley already had 13 films to his credit, including 1936's *Poor Little Rich Girl* starring eight-year-old Shirley Temple.

General Foods stocked Haley's half hour with Jack Oakie and Wendy Barrie from the movies and Ted Fio Rito's popular dance band. Haley's best radio seasons were ahead of him as was his immortal *Tin Man* role in the 1939 film classic, *The Wizard of Oz.*

A&A AUDIENCE ATTRITION

Amos & Andy's ratings slide continued.

The legendary strip show remained Network Radio's leading Multiple Run program but slipped below the season's Top 20 for the first time.

Pepsodent pulled out as Gosden and Correll's sponsor in mid-season but Campbell Soup eagerly picked up the tab for the remainder of the serial's downhill ride that would continue for the next five years.

OPPOSITES ATTRACT LISTENERS

Blue made an unusual bid for the early evening audience with two totally different Multiple Run quarter hour shows scheduled back to back three times a week. *Easy*

1937–38 Top Ten Multiple Run Programs
Blue 5, NBC 3, CBS 2
Average: 8.1

Amos & Andy*	M–F	NBC	7:00	13.3
Lowell Thomas News*	M–F	Blue	6:45	11.3
Boake Carter News	M,W,F	CBS	7:45	10.6
Uncle Ezra's Radio Station	M,W,F	NBC	7:15	9.8
Lum & Abner	M,W,F	Blue	7:30	8.8
Vocal Varieties	Tu,Th	NBC	7:15	6.9
Mr. Keen, Tracer of Lost Persons	T,W,T	Blue	7:15	6.5
Easy Aces	T,W,T	Blue	7:00	6.2
George McCall Hollywood News	Tu,Th	CBS	7:15	4.2
Gen Hugh Johnson Commentary	M–Th	Blue	10:00	3.0

*Monday–Friday Strip Shows

Aces and *Mr. Keen, Tracer of Lost Persons* were Network Radio's odd couple. Odder still, both programs were sponsored for many seasons by brands marketed by American Home Products/Whitehall Pharmacal.

Easy Aces was in the second of its seven year run on Blue at 7:00 for Anacin. The program could be considered Burns and Allen for the Mensa set. Former Kansas City newspaperman Goodman Ace wrote the show and, like George Burns, played straight man for his ditzy wife Jane. The Chicago based studio show was simply 15 minutes of conversation between the couple and a few friends — spiked by Jane's frequent and sometimes memorable malapropisms and Goodman's clever puns.

"Time wounds all heels," was just one of her many classics.

Ace wrote for an audience with a love of the language. Although *Easy Aces* never received double digit ratings or cracked a season's Top 50 until it became a half hour sitcom eleven years later, its small audience was appreciative and loyal.

Blue followed Ace's urbane comedy at 7:15 with *Mr. Keen,* Frank and Anne Hummert's major contribution to crime melodrama sponsored by Bisodol indigestion tablets. Veteran radio actor Bennett Kilpack, 54, was cast as "the kindly old investigator," a role he would hold for the next 13 years.

As much as critics praised *Easy Aces*, they panned *Mr. Keen* for its soap opera structure and simplicity of plots. It, too, would never break

out of the single digit ratings in its 15 minute form.

Nevertheless, the two dissimilar Multiple Runs remained paired on Blue for five seasons.

NOT READY FOR PRIME TIME

Buried in the Multiple Run numbers, Arthur Godfrey was given his first solo prime time shot in February for 13 weeks on CBS at 7:15 Tuesdays and Thursdays. Still a local radio personality on WSJV in Washington, Godfrey's 3.4 rating was a fraction of what his breakthrough show *Talent Scouts* would score ten years later.

TOP 50 PROGRAMS — 1937–38

NBC 26, CBS 19, Blue 5
Average Rating: 13.6, Median: 12.5
24,500,000 Radio Homes / 74.0% Coverage of U.S. Homes / One Rating Point = 245,000 Homes
Sources: Clark-Hooper Radio Advertisement Reports, Sep–Dec, 1937
& C.E. Hooper Monthly Network Reports Jan–Jun, 1938
Total Programs Rated 6–11 p.m.: 96
Programs Rated 13 Weeks & Ranked: 94.

		Program	Rtg	Type	Sponsor	Day	Time	Lgth	Net
1	*N*	Edgar Bergen & Charlie McCarthy	32.1	CV	Chase & Sanborn Coffee	Sun	8:00	60	NBC
2	*1*	Jack Benny Program	29.5	SC	Jello Gelatin	Sun	7:00	30	NBC
3	*4*	Lux Radio Theater/Cecil B DeMille	23.4	DA	Lux Soap	Mon	9:00	60	CBS
4	*7*	Bing Crosby's Kraft Music Hall	22.7	MV	Kraft Cheese	Thu	10:00	60	NBC
5	*2*	Eddie Cantor Show	21.6	CV	Texaco Petroleum	Wed	8:30	30	CBS
6t	*6*	Fred Allen's Town Hall Tonight	19.4	CV	Ipana/Sal Hepatica	Wed	9:00	60	NBC
6t	*3*	Major Bowes Original Amateur Hour	19.4	TC	Chrysler Corporation	Thu	9:00	60	CBS
8	*5*	Burns & Allen	19.2	CV	Grape Nuts Cereal	Mon	8:00	30	NBC
9	*8*	Rudy Vallee Show	18.6	MV	Royal Gelatin/Fleischmann	Thu	8:00	60	NBC
10	*10*	Al Jolson Show	18.1	MV	Lifebuoy Soap	Tue	8:30	30	CBS
11	*N*	Good News of 1938/FBrice/ FMorgan	16.6	CV	Maxwell House Coffee	Thu	9:00	60	NBC
12	*9*	Phil Baker's Gulf Headliners	16.4	CV	Gulf Oil	Sun	7:30	30	CBS
13	*16*	One Man's Family	15.3	DCC	Tenderleaf Tea	Wed	8:00	30	NBC
14	*14*	First Nighter/L Tremayne & B Luddy	15.1	DA	Campana Balm	Fri	10:30	30	NBC 1
15	*31*	Al Pearce Gang	14.8	CV	Ford Motors	Tue	9:00	30	CBS
16t	*20*	Gangbusters	14.7	DA	Palmolive Shave Cream	Wed	10:00	30	CBS
16t	*12*	Hollywood Hotel/LParsons/KMurray	14.7	MV	Campbell Soup	Fri	9:00	60	CBS
18t	*N*	Big Town/Edward G Robinson	13.7	DCC	Rinso Laundry Soap	Tue	8:00	30	CBS
18t	*15*	Walter Winchell's Jergens Journal	13.7	NC	Jergens Lotion	Sun	9:30	15	Blue
20	*21*	Fibber McGee & Molly	13.4	SC	Johnson Wax	Tue	9:30	30	NBC 2
21t	*11*	Amos & Andy	13.3	SC	Campbell Soup	M-F	7:00	15	NBC 3
21t	*25*	Robert Ripley's Believe It Or Not	13.3	API	Huskies Cereal	Tue	10:00	30	NBC 4
23	*30*	Jack Oakie's College	13.1	CV	Camel Cigarettes	Tue	9:30	30	CBS
24	*N*	Mardi Gras/Lanny Ross	12.8	MV	Packard Autos	Tue	9:30	30	NBC
25	*N*	Dick Powell Show	12.5	MV	Lucky Strike Cigarettes	Wed	10:00	60	NBC
26t	*N*	Jack Haley Show	12.4	CV	Log Cabin Syrup	Sat	8:30	30	NBC
26t	*42*	Professor Quiz/Craig Earl	12.4	APQ	Nash Kelvinator Refrigerators	Sat	9:00	30	CBS
26t	*24*	Your Hit Parade/Buddy Clark	12.4	MP	Lucky Strike Cigarettes	Sat	10:00	45	CBS
29	*26*	Lowell Thomas News	11.3	NC	Sun Oil	M-F	6:45	15	Blue
30	*28*	Vox Pop	11.1	API	Molle Shaving Cream	Tue	9:00	30	NBC
31t	*43*	Ben Bernie Show	10.9	MV	US Rubber Tires	Wed	8:30	30	CBS

	Program	Rtg	Type	Sponsor	Day	Time	Lgth	Net
31t *N*	Kay Kyser Kollege of Musical Knowledge	10.9	APQ	Lucky Strike Cigarettes	Wed	10:00	60	NBC
33t *N*	Benny Goodman's Swing School	10.7	MV	Camel Cigarettes	Tue	9:30	30	CBS 5
33t *N*	Hollywood Playhouse	10.7	DA	Woodbury Soap	Sun	9:00	30	Blue
35t *17*	Boake Carter News	10.6	NC	Philco Radios	MWF	7:45	15	CBS
35t *17*	Your Hit Parade	10.6	MP	Lucky Strike Cigarettes	Wed	10:00	60	NBC
37 *22*	Pick & Pat's Model Minstrels	10.3	MSP	Model Pipe Tobacco	Mon	8:30	30	CBS
38t *73*	Manhattan Merry Go Round	9.8	MP	Dr Lyons Tooth Powder	Sun	9:00	30	NBC
38t *27*	Maxwell House Showboat	9.8	MV	Maxwell House Coffee	Thu	9:00	60	NBC
38t *32*	Uncle Ezra's Radio Station	9.8	CV	Alka Seltzer	MWF	7:15	15	NBC 6
41 *N*	Interesting Neighbors/Jerry Belcher	9.7	API	Fitch Shampoo	Sun	7:30	30	NBC 7
42 *46*	Voice of Firestone	9.5	MC	Firestone Tires	Mon	8:30	30	NBC
43 *27*	Wayne King Orch	9.4	MP	Lady Esther Cosmetics	Mon	10:00	30	CBS
44 *45*	Court of Human Relations	9.3	DA	True Story Magazine	Fri	9:30	30	NBC
45 *N*	Paul Whiteman Show	9.1	MV	Chesterfield Cigarettes	Fri	8:30	30	CBS
46t *57*	National Barn Dance	9.0	MSP	Alka-Seltzer	Sat	9:00	60	Blue
46t *38*	Russ Morgan Orch	9.0	MP	Philip Morris Cigarettes	Tue	8:00	30	NBC
48t *N*	Hour of Charm/Phil Spitalny	8.8	MST	General Electric	Mon	9:00	30	NBC 8
48t *34*	Lum & Abner	8.8	SC	Horlick Malted Milk	MWF	7:30	15	Blue 9
50 *34*	Kate Smith Hour	8.7	MV	Swansdown/Calumet	Thu	8:00	60	CBS

New & Returning Top 50 Programs Underscored

1	First Nighter	Sep–Dec	Campana Balm	Fri	9:30	30	CBS
2	Fibber McGee & Molly	Sep–Mar	Johnson Wax	Mon	9:00	30	NBC
3	Amos & Andy	Sep–Dec	Pepsodent Toothpaste	M-F	7:00	15	NBC
4	Robert Ripley's Believe It Or Not	Oct–Apr	Huskies Cereal	Sat	8:00	30	NBC
5	Benny Goodman's Swing School	Jan–Mar	Camel Cigarettes	Tue	10:00	30	CBS
6	Uncle Ezra's Radio Station	Sep–Dec	Alka Seltzer	MWF	7:00	15	Blue
7	Interesting Neighbors	Sep–Dec	Fitch Shampoo	Sun	7:45	15	NBC
8	Hour of Charm	Sep–Mar	General Electric	Mon	9:30	30	NBC
9	Lum & Abner	Sep–Nov	Horlick Malted Milk	M-F	7:30	15	Blue

Key: API — Audience Participation/Interviews
APQ — Audience Participation/Quiz
APS — Audience Participation/Stunts
CV — Comedy/Variety Show
DA — Dramatic Anthology

DCC — Drama/Continuing Characters
MC — Music/Classical, Semi-Classical
MP — Music/Popular, Contemporary
MSP — Music/Specialty, Ethnic
MST — Music/Standard, Traditional

MV — Music/Variety Show
NC — News, Commentary
SC — Situation Comedy
TC — Talent Competition

1937–38 Top 50 Favorite Formats

	Programs	Pct
Music — All Categories	21	42%
Comedy — Variety & Situation	14	28%
Drama — Anthology & Continuing	7	14%
Audience Participation — All Categories	5	10%
News/Commentary	3	6%

1937–38 Monthly Winners

Sep	Edgar Bergen & Charlie McCarthy	18.8	Feb	Edgar Bergen & Charlie McCarthy	40.2
Oct	Edgar Bergen & Charlie McCarthy	26.4	Mar	Edgar Bergen & Charlie McCarthy	38.1
Nov	Edgar Bergen & Charlie McCarthy	29.8	Apr	Edgar Bergen & Charlie McCarthy	33.4
Dec	Edgar Bergen & Charlie McCarthy	33.2	May	Edgar Bergen & Charlie McCarthy	33.4
Jan	Edgar Bergen & Charlie McCarthy	37.4	Jun	Edgar Bergen & Charlie McCarthy	30.2

11

The 1938–39 Network Season

Announcer: If you found yourself caught in traffic or just saved yourself from being pulled out to sea by the undertow, you have a right to feel nervous, jumpy and jittery. But when that nervousness is due to little things ... if you jump when somebody speaks to you suddenly ... when you're ready to blow up at the mere sound of the neighbor's piano ... then it's time to look into the cause of that nervousness ... for it might be something you can easily remedy ... something as simple as giving up coffee. Although there are a lot of people who can drink coffee without becoming nervous and jittery, there are many others who can't. So if you suspect coffee upsets your nerves, switch to Postum. Postum contains no caffeine or any other stimulants that could possibly set your nerves on edge. And it's an ideal mealtime beverage ... tempting to look at, fragrant to smell and delicious to taste. What's more, Postum is very economical. You can get it at your grocer's in two convenient forms ... Postum Cereal that you make by boiling or percolating ... and Instant Postum made instantly in the cup. So, if coffee's been making you nervous and jittery, start drinking Postum regularly and see if those nerves of yours don't steady down.

A BIG HAND FOR THE LITTLE NETWORK

A six month slowdown hit the economy in April 1938, and the networks were affected—all but Mutual which continued to carve out its own low budget niche and profit from it.

MBS added the 23 station Texas State Network to its affiliate list bringing its 1938 total up to 107—second only to CBS's 110. Some Mutual affiliates were "secondary"—requiring the network to take a back seat in program clearances to those stations' "primary" network. And much of Mutual's revenue came from regional advertisers who didn't buy the full network. As a result, many of Mutual's programs went unrated.

The four-year-old Mutual earned only a fraction of the revenues raked in by CBS, NBC, and Blue. Nevertheless, Mutual was headed for a its first two and a half million dollar year *(40.1 Mil)*, topping its 1937 income by over 20 percent—while its bigger competitors had to be content with less than a one percent growth.

Yet, any growth was welcome in a slow year. And broadcasting had caught up to magazines in revenues, each earning 17 cents of every advertising dollar spent. Newspapers still led the pack with 59 cents. But momentum was on radio's side, particularly the networks and their affiliates.

The networks continued their steady addition of stations. For the first time, over half of the nation's radio stations—52 percent—were affiliated with one of the four chains.

Time magazine—itself the producer of radio's *March of Time*—reported in September, "Only a few U.S. publishers, Network Radio's chief competitors for advertising contracts, could be supposed last week to be sitting on an eight-month gross so large and comfortable as that enjoyed by the big three broadcasters."

NBC NEWS MAKES NEWS AGAIN

NBC's yeoman European correspondent, Max Jordan, already had one major scoop to his credit from the previous March in Vienna. Six months later he had another exclusive story—this time broadcasting directly from Godesburg, Germany.

Jordan beat his CBS competitor, William L. Shirer, by obtaining the actual text of the infamous September 29 Munich Agreement between British Prime Minister Chamberlin and German dictator Hitler that ceded Czechoslovakia to Germany. Jordan's procuring, reporting and analyzing the verbatim text was a coup in itself.

As a bonus, his four years of pioneering negotiations to transmit dispatches directly from European cities combined with RCA's worldwide shortwave connections gave NBC a technical superiority in receiving and rebroadcasting his reports that CBS couldn't match.

Nearing the eve of World War II, NBC had the advantage in network news coverage—a reputation that CBS would eventually overtake through improved content and continual promotion of its trench-coated overseas reporters as celebrated personalities.

1938–39 Season Scoreboard Mid-season Totals, December 1938			
		Compared to Year Earlier	
Total Radio Homes	26.67 Mil	+2.17 Mil	+8.9%
Total Auto Radios	6.0 Mil	+1.00 Mil	+20.0%
Total AM Radio Stations	689	+43	+6.7%
Total Radio Network Affiliates	359	+63	+21.3%
1938 Radio Revenues	167.1 Mil	+2.5 Mil	+1.5%
1938 Network Revenues	89.2 Mil	+.0.7 Mil	+0.8%
Network Share	53.4%		(0.4%)

As war neared, radio clearly had the advantage over newspapers in reporting and analyzing news events as they happened — often from where they happened. The quality of immediacy deepened the resentment that newspapers held against broadcasting despite the fact that by 1940 nearly 50 percent of the largest dailies held ownership interests in radio stations.

CBS GOES FOR THE RECORDS

Bill Paley wanted a piece of the lucrative phonograph record market that had tripled since 1935 with annual sales around 25 million dollars *(401.1 Mil)*.

RCA Victor alone sold over 13 million discs in 1938. The company's NBC provided exposure to many of the artists and orchestras featured on its three labels — popular music Black, Red Seal classics and budget-priced Bluebird.

CBS bought jukebox giant Wurlitzer's American Record Company for $700,000 *(11.2 Mil)* in late 1938. The sale included American's subsidiary, Columbia Records, from which the Columbia Broadcasting System originally got its name in 1927.

Although Paley was fascinated by the idea of producing complete classical works on a single disc involving the new 33⅓ "Long Playing" recording techniques being developed in laboratories, he knew that 85 percent of the records sold in 1938 were popular swing music.

Accordingly, Paley's new Columbia Records went to work and signed the Benny Goodman, Kay Kyser, Horace Heidt and Orrin Tucker bands as its opening headliners.

Columbia introduced its LP/Microgroove products ten years later.

THE MONTHLIES

The season's Top Four programs finished in the same order as they did the previous year.

In the monthly ratings, Edgar Bergen and his Charlie McCarthy alter-ego did it again. Bergen's *Chase & Sanborn Hour* became the first and only program to be Number One every month for two straight seasons. As a result, NBC's streak of consecutive Number One monthly shows rose to 41.

1938–39 Sunday Night Top Ten Programs (11)
NBC 7, Blue 2, CBS 1
Average: 16.4

Edgar Bergen & Charlie McCarthy	NBC	8:00	32.2
Jack Benny Program	NBC	7:00	27.7
Walter Winchell	Blue	9:30	14.0
Hollywood Playhouse	Blue	9:00	12.7
Fitch Bandwagon	NBC	7:30	12.6
The Circle	NBC	10:00	12.3
Screen Guild Theater	CBS	7:30	9.8
Manhattan Merry Go Round	NBC	9:00	9.6
American Album of Familiar Music	NBC	9:30	9.3
Horace Heidt Orchestra	NBC	10:00	9.3

HE WHO WOOD BE KING

Sunday's two most popular programs originated from NBC's new multi-million dollar Hollywood studios that officially opened for business on October 17. Jack Benny and ventriloquist Edgar Bergen — with his wooden-headed laugh getter Charlie McCarthy — both broadcast from one of the four 350 seat auditoriums in the three story complex at Sunset and Vine. The programs played to standing room only crowds every Sunday.

By this time Benny was making a reported $10,000 a week *($160,450)*, from his radio show.

Meanwhile, Bergen collected $100,000 *($1.6 Mil)*, in annual royalties from the sale of Charlie McCarthy dolls, games and novelties. The February release of Universal's *You Can't Cheat an Honest Man* co-starring W.C. Fields added to Charlie McCarthy's fame and Edgar Bergen's fortune.

Leading fan magazine *Radio Mirror*, in its annual popularity poll among readers, ranked the Bergen and McCarthy *Chase & Sanborn Hour* as the listeners' favorite variety program and Bergen as their favorite comedian. Cast regular Don Ameche was named their favorite radio actor and featured singer Nelson Eddy their "Star of Stars."

Eddy was between the releases of his two 1938 movie hits — both co-starring Jeanette MacDonald — *Girl of the Golden West* and *Sweethearts*. The handsome baritone had signed with the NBC show as its resident singing star until March when he was due to resume working on his two-picture-a-year film contract with MGM.

The *Chase & Sanborn Hour* of October 30th was typical of its star studded variety format with Bergen and McCarthy, Ameche, Eddy, movie queen Dorothy Lamour, the comedy trio of Judy, Annie and Zeke Canova and film star Madeleine Carroll. That night the program scored its fourth highest Hooperating to date — a whopping 34.8.

Yet, an unheralded, unsponsored and unrated program opposite Bergen and McCarthy on the same night stole all the headlines — all because some of its listeners weren't listening closely or couldn't tell fact from fiction.

HISTORIC HALLOWEEN HYSTERIA — OR HYPE?

CBS prided itself on its public affairs and cultural offerings — which were usually placed in its schedule during less popular times or were offered as sustaining sacrificial lambs against competing programs considered unbeatable. Such was the case on Sunday nights when Columbia programmed *The People's Platform* opposite NBC's Jack Benny and Orson Welles' *Mercury Theatre of the Air* against Bergen and McCarthy.

It was Welles' October 30 *Mercury* presentation of H.G. Wells' *War of the Worlds* that caused an uproar which is still the stuff of broadcasting legend.

The powerful update of Wells' 1898 novel scripted by Howard Koch and produced by John Houseman was made to sound like an actual on-the-spot report of a Martian invasion in New Jersey. It was difficult for casual listeners to separate fact from fiction unless they heard the frequent disclaimers before, during and after the broadcast.

Separating the facts of its impact on the radio audience from journalistic fiction is another matter.

The New York Times reported in its lead story the following morning that it was "overwhelmed" with 875 telephone calls as, "A wave of mass hysteria seized thousands of radio listeners between 8:15 and 9:30 o'clock last night when a broadcast of a dramatization of H.G. Wells' fantasy, *The War of the Worlds*, led thousands to believe that an interplanetary conflict had started with invading Martians spreading wide death and destruction in New Jersey and New York."

Headlined, *RADIO LISTENERS IN PANIC TAKING WAR DRAMA AS FACT*—with sub-heads, *Many Flee Homes to Escape "Gas Raid from Mars,"* and, *Phone Calls Swamp Police at Broadcast of Wells' Fantasy*—the story and two related sidebars ran an extraordinary 4,700 words.

Newspapers all over the country jumped on the story with local angles of "panicked" listeners, mass hysteria, heart attacks, traffic accidents and attempted suicides all supposedly the result of the broadcast heard and misinterpreted by "millions."

However, C.E. Hooper never reported how many —*or how few*— listeners actually heard the unrated drama broadcast opposite Network Radio's most popular program. Most reports of its aftermath were later proved to be either exaggerated or false.

Regardless, the print media was more than happy to pile on with "gotchas" against broadcasters who had scooped them with direct reports of the Munich Agreement just a month before. Their message was obvious: *Don't believe everything you hear on the radio.*

Not surprisingly, editorial writers, politicians and the FCC all echoed condemnation of the "hoax."

Welles and CBS apologized profusely — then smiled all the way to the bank.

The extraordinary amount of free publicity given Welles, compounded by an active CBS promotion department, prompted Campbell Soup to pick up sponsorship of *The Mercury Theater* and retitle it *The Campbell Playhouse*. Welles and his troupe were moved into Campbell's fading *Hollywood Hotel* Friday timeslot at 9:00 on CBS following the popular Burns and Allen show and opposite NBC's ratings weak but money making *Waltz Time.*

The Campbell Playhouse opened with a December Hooperating of 17.4, the highest rating it would ever achieve.

Meanwhile, Bergen and McCarthy who continued on their merry way with the nation's Number One program — attacks from Mars notwithstanding

SHAMPOO GETS A HEAD START

There was no better timeslot for a new program than between the season's two most popular programs.

That plum was picked in September by Iowa hair products manufacturer F.W. Fitch for its "dandruff remover" shampoo. *The Fitch Bandwagon,* featuring a different popular dance band each week plus guest stars, settled in for a cushy run at 7:30 between the Jack Benny and Edgar Bergen and Charlie McCarthy shows on NBC. *Bandwagon* lost over half of Benny's audience, never rising above the mid-teens in ratings, yet was solid enough to finish in the season's Top 50 for eight consecutive years.

THE CHARGE OF THE HEIDT BRIGADE

Three music shows rounded out Sunday's Top Ten — Frank and Anne Hummert's *Manhattan Merry Go Round* and *American Album of Familiar Music,* plus a newcomer to the night's schedule, Horace Heidt's "Brigadiers" orchestra.

Heidt and his show band — the "Heidt Brigade"— had been in Network Radio since 1932's *Ship of Joy.* His latest show and bounced around for three seasons, going from CBS to Blue to NBC, all under the sponsorship of Stewart Warner's Alemite automotive oils and chemicals. Although the show finally ranked in the season's Top 50, the sponsor was disappointed with single digit ratings and cancelled in December.

But Heidt wasn't finished. He was a master showman with a keen sense for popular trends and proved it the following September when he and his band became part of the smash hit of the 1939 season, *Pot o' Gold.*

Heidt's vacated 10:00 Sunday timeslot on NBC was taken over by one of the most unusual programs ever attempted, *The Circle.*

WHOSE SOIREE NOW?

The Circle seemed like a good idea when J. Walter Thompson and NBC developed it for Kellogg Corn Flakes: Recruit a group of popular movie and radio personalities known for their "intellect," place them into an hour-long party-like format of conversation led by a star with a British accent to emphasize cultural appeal, add a bit of smart humor, mix in a touch of high-brow music and watch the ratings soar.

The concept appeared to be just what Kellogg needed to combat the highly rated programs on which competitor General Foods' Post cereals were advertised.

The Circle debuted with much fanfare at 10:00 on Sunday, January 15, 1939, featuring host Ronald Colman and guests Cary Grant, Carol Lombard and the two talking Marx brothers, Groucho and Chico. Music was provided by operatic tenor Lawrence Tibbett and a full studio orchestra. The second week's program featured the same "conversationalists"— who actually read from prepared scripts — plus famed classical pianist Jose Iturbi.

But in February it suddenly became a question of, "Suppose you threw a party and nobody came?"

The program's flexible contracts allowed its stars to choose if and when they would grace *The Circle* with their presence.

Despite their lucrative $2,000 to $2,500 talent fees (*$32,100 to $40,100*), most chose not to be bothered — except the Marx brothers who faithfully showed up for the party and their paychecks every week.

British playwright/actor Noel Coward was called in as host on the third show, Colman returned for the fourth and Oscar nominated actor Basil Rathbone took over regular host duties in mid–February.

British born Madeleine Carroll, 1939's highest paid film actress, was added to the permanent cast along with tenor Tibbett and the Marx brothers in April. *The Circle* hobbled along with an assortment of guests who were hardly the major stars originally envisioned for the series. Deems Taylor, Boris Karloff, Irwin S. Cobb, Grantland Rice and Louis Bromfield were the most notable. By June *The Circle*'s ratings had drooped to a meager 11.6 when the party finally ended.

Burned by its experience, Kellogg would never again sponsor a major prime time program.

1938–39 Monday Night Top Ten Programs
CBS 5, NBC 4, Blue 1
Average: 12.7

Lux Radio Theater	CBS	9:00	22.5
Eddie Cantor Show	CBS	7:30	17.3
Lowell Thomas News*	Blue	6:45	14.0
Al Pearce Gang	NBC	8:00	13.3
Amos & Andy*	CBS	7:00	12.1
Guy Lombardo's Lady Esther Serenade	CBS	10:00	10.4
Model Minstrels	CBS	8:30	10.4
Voice of Firestone	NBC	8:30	10.1
Edwin C Hill News	NBC	7:15	9.1
Hour of Charm	NBC	9:00	7.9

*Monday–Friday Strip Shows

Sans Strips...

Cavalcade of America	CBS	8:00	7.7
Eddy Duchin Orchestra	NBC	9:30	6.9
Those We Love	Blue	8:30	6.9

CBS SHOWS LITTLE LOGIC

Eddie Cantor and the night's perennial leader, *Lux Radio Theater,* stood out in a puzzling CBS Monday schedule that defied sequential programming logic.

Cantor's popular variety show, in its third different day and time in three seasons, was slotted at 7:30. Cantor lost some 20 percent of his audience in the move — typical for such switches — but still managed to kick-start the evening for CBS with a healthy 17.3 rating, again finishing in the season's Top Ten.

Cantor was followed at 8:00 by the prestigious historical anthology drama *Cavalcade of America* which lost over half his audience. *Cavalcade* enjoyed an 18 season run under the sponsorship of DuPont Chemical but seldom rose above single digits in ratings. Given high budgets to afford superior writing, celebrated actors and high production values, *Cavalcade* was Network Radio's prime example of image advertising with little, if any, regard given to its popularity.

Cavalcade's rating were nearly doubled by comedian Al Pearce — pulled from Blue to NBC's Monday schedule by General Foods as a replacement for the nomadic Burns and Allen who had jumped back to CBS's Friday schedule.

Following *Cavalcade,* CBS invited audience turnover again by programming *The Model Minstrels* (aka *Pipe Smoking Time*), featuring blackface comedians Pick Malone and Pat Padgett at 8:30. The low-brow comics — whom critics said made *Amos & Andy* appear sophisticated by comparison — struggled along with a 10.4 rating, in a virtual tie opposite NBC's *Voice of Firestone* classical concerts.

Star studded *Lux Radio Theater* followed *Pick & Pat* at 9:00 and doubled their numbers with Monday's only program that averaged over a 20 rating. The question remains how much greater the CBS Monday night audience would have been with a stronger programming hammock between Cantor and *Lux* instead of the hour that sagged.

1938–39 Tuesday Night Top Ten Programs
CBS 6, NBC 3, Blue 1
Average: 13.4

Fibber McGee& Molly	NBC	9:30	17.6
Al Jolson Show	CBS	8:30	17.3
Bob Hope Show	NBC	10:00	15.4
Big Town	CBS	8:00	15.3
Lowell Thomas News*	Blue	6:45	14.0
We the People	CBS	9:00	13.0
Amos & Andy*	CBS	7:00	12.1
Dick Powell Show	CBS	8:30	10.9
Battle of the Sexes	NBC	9:00	9.5
Second Husband	CBS	7:30	9.3

*Monday–Friday Strip Shows

Sans Strips...

Russ Morgan Orchestra	NBC	8:00	8.9
Benny Goodman's Swing School	CBS	9:30	8.6

TUESDAY'S TERRIFIC TWOSOME

Fibber McGee & Molly—transplanted the previous March from an underdog Monday night timeslot opposite CBS's top rated program, *Lux Radio Theater*—took root in NBC's Tuesday night schedule at 9:30 and scored the first of its dozen consecutive Top Ten season finishes.

Jim Jordan began the season solo as *Fibber McGee & Company* with an expanded supporting cast of characters that he and writer Don Quinn had assembled when Marian Jordan was hospitalized early in 1937–38 season. Finally, after an 18 month absence from the air, Marian returned to her husband's side on April 18, 1939.

Fibber McGee & Molly were together again and listeners responded in big numbers.

The couple's sitcom settled into its familiar format which became Tuesday's most popular program for seven of the next 15 seasons. To accommodate Marian's health the show was moved from Chicago to Hollywood.

FM&M provided the lead-in boost for Bob Hope's new *Pepsodent Show.* which finished twelfth among the season's Top 50 programs. Hope's Paramount film, *The Big Broadcast of 1938*, in which he and Shirley Ross sang the poignant Academy Award winning duet, *Thanks for the Memory,* was released in February 1938. The movie made Hope a star and re-launched his radio career after two mediocre seasons on CBS and Blue.

Hope and the Jordan's provided NBC with its long term Tuesday night comedy cornerstone. Between them, the two shows would give the network Tuesday's top rated program for twelve consecutive seasons.

NOT SO FAST

CBS wasn't about to give up Tuesday night leadership without a fight. Its 90 minute block beginning with Edward G. Robinson's newspaper drama *Big Town* at 8:00, followed by Al Jolson's variety show and *We the People,* enabled CBS to stay strong and claim over half of Tuesday's Top Ten programs.

But that situation began to deteriorate when Jolson left radio in April, replaced by singing movie star Dick Powell who lost over 35 percent of Jolson's audience to comedian George Jessel's *For Men Only* on NBC and an interesting newcomer on Blue, *Information Please*.

UNSCRIPTED WITS

The brainchild of producer Dan Golenpaul, *Information Please* was given a trial run on Blue over the summer and its own Tuesday night 8:30 slot opposite Jolson and Jessel in November. Its first month rating of was 5.0—hardly an auspicious beginning for a program that would place among the annual Top 50 over the next five seasons and remain a critical favorite for another five.

Led by host Clifton Fadiman, 34-year-old *New Yorker* book critic, *Information Please* featured a panel of four intellects who laid their knowledge on the line every week by attempting to answer a wide range of questions submitted by listeners for cash and merchandise prizes. Regulars among the rotating panelists included columnists Franklin P. Adams and Walter Kiernan and pianist/actor Oscar Levant. A fourth celebrity panelist was chosen by Golenpaul each week — usually a noted author, politician or show business personality.

Much like NBC's *The Circle*, which was designed to be a popular showcase of wit and intellect but failed, *Information Please* delivered. The panel's responses to questions became springboards from which clever exchanges and puns were the norm. Further, *Information Please* quips were spontaneous, not scripted.

Proving they needed no script, *Circle* regulars Basil Rathbone and Groucho Marx made frequent guest appearances on the *Information Please* panel.

Although the program never reached a season's Top 25, *Information Please* delivered a loyal audience with ratings that generally measured in the low teens.

THE DOCTOR'S INTERNSHIP

In mid–October CBS moved the promising *Dr. Christian* from its Sunday afternoon schedule and put it in direct competition with

NBC's hot newcomer, Bob Hope. The situation drama, starring veteran Danish character actor Jean Hersholt as the kindly doctor of Rivers End, had many things going for it — not the least were fresh plots submitted in a contest among listeners and a top flight supporting cast led by Rosemary DeCamp as the doctor's loyal nurse, Judy Price.

Best of all, *Dr. Christian* had the loyalty of a sponsor who believed in the program, Chesebrough's Vaseline. That loyalty was tested during the program's 26 weeks opposite against radio's most popular new show.

Dr. Christian closed the season with a weak 6.7 average rating. A new day and time was prescribed to save the program the following season.

HEARD BUT NOT SEEN

Helen Menken was a Broadway legend. She received theater's highest recognition, the Antoinette Perry (Tony) Lifetime Achievement Award upon her death in 1966.

Yet, Menken's face wasn't familiar to most of America because the roles she originated on stage always went to others in the movies — Janet Gaynor in *Seventh Heaven*, Katherine Hepburn in *Mary of Scotland* and Bette Davis in *The Old Maid*.

When Menken outgrew her typical ingénue roles she turned to radio and the lead in Frank and Ann Hummert's prime time serial, *Second Husband*—the trials and tribulations related to remarriage.

Menken had experience in the subject. She was in her own second marriage after divorcing Humphrey Bogart.

Following a 13 week split-run on Blue and NBC in the spring, Sterling Drug moved *Second Husband* to CBS where the half hour soap opera took roots at 7:30 for five years — two of them Top 50 seasons. When the serial eventually ran its prime time course down into single digit ratings, Sterling moved the Hummert serial and Menken into weekday, 15-minute form for another four years.

1938–39 Wednesday Night Top Ten Programs
NBC 5, CBS 4, Blue 1
Average: 11.7

Kay Kyser's Kollege of Musical Knowledge	NBC	10:00	16.9
Fred Allen's Town Hall Tonight	NBC	9:00	15.3
One Man's Family	NBC	8:00	14.5
Lowell Thomas News*	Blue	6:45	14.0
Gangbusters	CBS	8:00	12.8
Amos & Andy*	CBS	7:00	12.1
Tommy Dorsey Orchestra	NBC	8:30	10.7
Texaco Star Theater	CBS	9:00	10.0
Edwin C Hill News	NBC	7:15	9.1
Ask It Basket	CBS	7:30	8.1
*Monday–Friday Strip Shows			
Sans Strips...			
Hobby Lobby	Blue	8:30	7.5.
Paul Whiteman Show	CBS	8:30	7.3

KYSER'S KOLLEGE JOINS THE BIG TEN

Bandleader Kay Kyser's *Kollege of Musical Knowledge* was in its sophomore season and rose from 30th to ninth in the annual Top 50. Brought in by Lucky Strike Cigarettes to replace the NBC Wednesday edition of *Your Hit Parade* in March 1938, Kyser's fast paced hour of popular music, comedy and audience participation enjoyed a 55 percent ratings gain and edged out Fred Allen's *Town Hall Tonight* to become Wednesday's ratings leader.

The season was the first of Kyser's seven straight Top 15 seasons, giving NBC a dependable Wednesday night anchor. NBC protected the "The Ol' Professor's" ratings over the years with solid lead-in audiences provided by Fred Allen, Eddie Cantor and *Mr. District Attorney*.

With *One Man's Family* holding its own at 8:00 against *Gangbusters* on CBS, the only weak spot in the NBC lineup was the Tommy Dorsey orchestra at 9:30 for listeners who wanted the new music called Swing.

STAGE VEHICLE RUNS OUT OF GAS

CBS publicists worked overtime to promote the network's new *Tex-*

aco Star Theater, an hour long variety program with dramatic elements supplied by "legitimate" actors John Barrymore, Adolphe Menjou, Una Merkel and Charlie Ruggles, all under the direction of legendary stage director Max Reinhardt. The network boasted that Texaco was footing a talent cost of $18,000 (*$288,800*), per week just to bring this showcase of class to radio.

The 60 minute program was slotted on CBS at 9:30 to siphon audience from Fred Allen's *Town Hall Tonight* and cut into the first half hour of Kay Kyser's *Kollege of Musical Knowledge.*

Instead, *Texaco Star Theater* opened to single digit ratings in October and trended downward.

The strategy to compete with both Allen and Kyser was scrapped in January along with the program's "legitimate" overtones. *Texaco Star Theater* was moved back to 9:00 opposite only Allen and the program took on a decidedly lighter approach with comedian Ken Murray as its host.

The revamp was rewarded when the program came back to place among the season's Top 50 — but still 50 percent short of Fred Allen's ratings.

Texaco dropped the show in June — and picked up sponsorship of Fred Allen a year later.

1938–39 Thursday Night Top Ten Programs
CBS 5, NBC 3, Blue 2
Average: 13.5

Bing Crosby's Kraft Music Hall	NBC	10:00	21.8
Good News of 1939	NBC	9:00	17.3
Major Bowes' Original Amateur Hour	CBS	9:00	16.6
Kate Smith Hour	CBS	8:00	14.5
Rudy Vallee Show	NBC	8:00	14.4
Lowell Thomas News*	Blue	6:45	14.0
Amos & Andy*	CBS	7:00	12.1
Joe Penner Show	CBS	7:30	11.7
Joe E Brown Show	CBS	7:30	9.1
Easy Aces	Blue	7:00	6.5
*Monday–Friday Strip Shows			
Sans Strips...			
Mr. Keen, Tracer of Lost Persons	Blue	7:15	5.7
Vocal Varieties	NBC	7:15	5.5

KATE RATES GREAT

Thursday night was dominated by five hour-long variety shows, four of them sponsored by major food manufacturers. New to the group was Kate Smith, whose CBS show for General Foods jumped over 66 percent in its ratings and edged out Standard Brands' stalwart Rudy Vallee on NBC in their head to head, singer to singer competition at 8:00.

It was Vallee's first fall out of a season's Top Ten and Smith's first of four consecutive Top 20 seasons.

The rotund singer didn't do it alone. Her 1938–39 *Kate Smith Hour* was loaded with new radio talent with bits by former burlesque comedians Bud Abbott and Lou Costello, plus weekly sitcom skits by *The Aldrich Family* starring 21-year-old Ezra Stone. Ironically, Smith's producer/partner Ted Collins had first heard both acts Vallee's show during the previous season.

A song introduced by Smith on her November 10 broadcast to commemorate the 20th anniversary of Armistice Day pushed her popularity beyond that of a pop singer to that of a patriotic icon. Irving Berlin's "God Bless America" became the country's second national anthem.

General Foods scored another win at 9:00 when its *Good News of 1939* for Maxwell House Coffee on NBC topped Major Bowes' *Original Amateur Hour* which suffered its third consecutive season of audience decline on CBS.

A HUSKIES HEX?

On the so-so side of its ledger, General Foods bought another half hour chunk of CBS time at 7:30 to promote its Huskies breakfast cereal.

Joe Penner had just completed two uneventful — and unrated — seasons in a CBS sitcom, *The Park Avenue Penners.*

Penner's return to prime time sponsored by Huskies lasted only 26 weeks. His routines, most all ending with the predictable, "Wanna buy a duck?" punch line, had become stale. He was replaced by movie comedian Joe E. Brown in April.

Meanwhile, Huskies print and radio advertising featured endorsements by baseball star Lou Gehrig, who died less than three years later in 1941 at age 37.

In an odd twist of fate, Joe Penner also died in 1941 at age 36.

1938–39 Friday Night Top Ten Programs
CBS 7, NBC 2, Blue 1
Average: 11.7

Burns & Allen Show	CBS	8:30	15.6
Orson Welles' Campbell Playhouse	CBS	9:00	15.4
Lowell Thomas News*	Blue	6:45	14.0
Hollywood Hotel	CBS	9:00	13.7
Amos & Andy*	CBS	7:00	12.1
First Nighter	CBS	8:00	11.5
Grand Central Station	CBS	10:00	9.1
Jack Haley Show	CBS	7:30	8.8
Guy Lombardo's Lady Esther Serenade	NBC	10:00	8.6
Jimmie Fidler Hollywood News	NBC	7:15	8.1
*Monday–Friday Strip Shows			
Sans Strips...			
Death Valley Days	NBC	9:30	7.4
Cities Service Concert	NBC	8:00	6.2

BURNS AND ALLEN JUMP STARTS WELLES

Burns and Allen switched sponsors, networks, days, and times — and lost nearly 20 percent of their audience.

But the couple retained enough listeners to become Friday's most popular program for CBS against NBC's *Cities Service Concert* at 8:30.

They also gave the 23-year-old new kid on the block a solid lead-in.

Riding high from Halloween's *War of the Worlds* incident, Orson Welles' Mercury Theater troupe took over the 9:00 hour on CBS in December. Campbell Soup replaced its aging *Hollywood Hotel* with the anthology drama and trusted that listener curiosity would provide it with an early promotional boost.

It did.

Campbell Playhouse scored its season high 17.4 in December, placing it among the month's Top

Ten programs. It fell to 21st in January but continued to win its time-slot against NBC's profitable but weak rated *Waltz Time* and *Death Valley Days,* sometimes doubling or tripling the competition's ratings.

It would turn out to be a short lived success for Welles & Co.

HALEY SWITCH TURNS OFF LISTENERS

Jack Haley's top rated Saturday show on NBC the previous season became a Friday night also-ran on CBS. Haley lost 30 percent of his audience in the switch and fell out of the season's Top 50. The comedian's variety show for Wonder Bread left the air after a January through April run in single digits. After the August release of MGM's *The Wizard of Oz* in which he played the Tin Man, Haley became a popular radio guest star, but he didn't return with a series of his own for four years.

When he did, Jack Haley had one of 1943–44's Top Ten shows.

1938–39 Saturday Night Top Ten Programs
CBS 4, NBC 4, Blue 2
Average: 9.6

Your Hit Parade	CBS	10:00	13.6
Tommy Riggs & Betty Lou	NBC	8:00	11.3
Professor Quiz	CBS	8:30	9.9
Fred Waring Show	NBC	8:30	9.4
National Barn Dance	Blue	9:00	9.4
Uncle Jim's Question Bee	Blue	7:30	9.0
Russ Morgan Orchestra	CBS	8:00	8.7
Vox Pop	NBC	9:00	8.0
Phil Baker Show	CBS	9:00	7.6
Avalon Time	NBC	7:00	7.3

PARADE REST

Lucky Strike's *Your Hit Parade* settled in exclusively at CBS for the first of almost ten seasons. Singing host Buddy Clark was replaced by Lanny Ross who had enjoyed top popularity as the romantic singing lead of the former Top Ten entry, *Maxwell House Showboat.* The switch in *Hit Parade* stars was the first of many that would take place over the next 15 years. Ross would remain with the show for only a year. He was replaced during the next season by Barry Wood.

Despite all the switches, *Your Hit*

Parade finished 19 times in the annual Top 50—including twice in two seasons—1936–37 and 1937–38—proving that the real attractions of the program were the music and the weekly competition that the show created among the top hits of the day.

At least, that was the theory until a singer named Sinatra came along in 1943.

WATCH HIS LIPS MOVE!

It was a season for precocious "kids" on radio. Charlie McCarthy and Baby Snooks were both Top Ten stars. Then Quaker Oats brought a new kid to its *Quaker Party* in the form of a 30-year-old man.

Tommy Riggs had a unique vocal condition that was made for radio. He had a natural speaking voice worthy of a network announcer, yet was also able to speak and sing without effort or obvious falsetto as a small girl. His second voice became that of seven-year-old "Betty Lou Barrie."

Not a ventriloquist, Riggs stood at a microphone, obviously speaking both parts. After a season of his double-dialogued repartee with Rudy Vallee, Riggs landed his own variety slot on NBC with support from Zasu Pitts and the Larry Clinton band featuring future *Your Hit Parade* star singer Bea Wain.

Riggs and his very natural little girl's voice scored three Top 50 seasons but never ranked higher than 32nd. Critics later observed that Betty Lou was *too nice* a little girl. She lacked the feisty mean streak found in the other popular kids in radio comedy—Bergen's Charlie McCarthy, Brice's Baby Snooks, or Red Skelton's Mean Widdle Kid.

THE CINCINNATI REDS

Red Skelton's radio career began on powerful WLW/Cincinnati with a limited series in January 1938, headlining country singer Red Foley.

A year later Skelton and Foley were briefly teamed on NBC's *Avalon Time* from Chicago. Skelton was performing in low budget Warner Brothers two-reel shorts when he joined the Avalon Cigarettes show in January.

Like Bob Hope's radio ratings were ignited with his hit movie, *The Big Broadcast of 1938,* the 32-year-old Skelton's film breakthrough, *Whistling in the Dark,* was still two years away.

Ironically, along with Red Skelton and Red Foley, WLW also employed a young sportscaster in 1938 named Red Barber, who broadcast games of the station owned Cincinnati Reds.

Barber later became CBS Radio's Sports Director and a member of Baseball's Hall of Fame.

VOX POOPED? PHIL FINISHED?

NBC and CBS both had problem programs at 9:00 due to switches.

Kentucky Club Pipe Tobacco moved NBC's man on the street interview show, *Vox Pop,* from Tuesday to Saturday and the show dropped from 30th to 62nd place in the season's rankings.

Phil Baker, fresh from three Top 15 seasons with Sunday's *Gulf Headliners* was hired in January to host Dole Pineapple's *Honolulu Bound* variety show and moved into CBS' Saturday schedule. Baker lost over 50 percent of his audience in the switch and plummeted from 12th to 66th.

1938–39 Seven Rated Multiple Run Programs
Blue 3, CBS 2, NBC 2
Average: 8.6

Lowell Thomas News*	M–F	Blue	6:45	14.0
Amos & Andy*	M–F	CBS	7:00	12.1
Edwin C Hill News	M,W	NBC	7:15	9.1
Lum & Abner	M,W,F	CBS	7:15	7.2
Easy Aces	T,W,T	Blue	7:00	6.5
Mr. Keen, Tracer of Lost Persons	T,W,T	Blue	7:15	5.7
Vocal Varieties	T,T	NBC	7:15	5.5

*Monday–Friday Strip Shows

Both the interview show and Baker would recover in their ratings. But both had the bitter memory of the 1938–39 season when they lost their time period to Blue's hayseed frolic from Chicago, *National Barn Dance*.

MULTIPLES SUBTRACTED

Only seven sponsored Multiple Run programs were reported in the ratings — all time low.

Once the champion of Multiple Runs, CBS converted its 7:30 time period to weekly half-hour programs for the next nine seasons. The one year lull in the format can also be traced to the sudden, temporary slowdown in radio advertis-

ing. Broadcast budgets increased the following season and the number of sponsored and rated Multiple Runs returned to normal.

The growing national interest in world news, particularly from Europe, was reflected in Lowell Thomas' 25 percent ratings increase, placing his nightly newscasts above the slipping *Amos & Andy*.

Newscasts would rank as the top Multiple Run program for the next nine seasons, led by Thomas' six.

A&A SLIDE TO CBS

Bill Paley convinced Campbell Soup that a network change could revive *Amos & Andy*'s sagging ratings. The legendary strip show

dropped out of the season's Top Ten in 1935 and showed little promise of returning.

Amos & Andy left NBC on Friday, March 31, 1938, and popped up the following Monday on CBS in its familiar 7:00 timeslot.

First returns weren't very positive. Freeman Gosden and Charlie Correll's first April/May/June rating average on CBS was 10.4, compared to an 11.5 for the same three months the previous season on NBC.

It was the beginning of a dismal four and a half year run for the strip show on CBS.

TOP 50 PROGRAMS — 1938–39

CBS 24, NBC 22, Blue 4
Average Rating: 13.8, Median: 12.8
26,667,000 Radio Homes / 79.2% Coverage of U.S. Homes / One Rating Point = 266,700 Homes
Source: C.E. Hooper Monthly Network Reports. Sept 1938–June 1939
Total Programs Rated 6–11 P.M.: 114
Programs Rated 13 Weeks & Ranked: 99

		Program	Rtg	Type	Sponsor	Day	Time	Lgth	Net
1	1	Edgar Bergen & Charlie McCarthy	32.2	CV	Chase & Sanborn Coffee	Sun	8:00	60	NBC
2	2	Jack Benny Program	27.7	SC	Jello Gelatin	Sun	7:00	30	NBC
3	3	Lux Radio Theater/Cecil B DeMille	22.5	DA	Lux Soap	Mon	9:00	60	CBS
4	4	Bing Crosby's Kraft Music Hall	21.8	MV	Kraft Cheese	Thu	10:00	60	NBC
5	20	Fibber McGee & Molly	17.6	SC	Johnson Wax	Tue	9:30	30	NBC
6t	10	Al Jolson Show	17.3	MV	Lifebuoy Soap	Tue	8:30	30	CBS
6t	5	Eddie Cantor Show	17.3	CV	Camel Cigarettes	Mon	7:30	30	CBS
6t	11	Good News of 1939/FBrice/FMorgan	17.3	CV	Maxwell House Coffee	Thu	9:00	60	NBC
9	31	Kay Kyser Kollege of Musical Knowledge	16.9	APQ	Lucky Strike Cigarettes	Wed	10:00	60	NBC
10	6	Major Bowes Original Amateur Hour	16.6	TC	Chrysler Corporation	Thu	9:00	60	CBS
11	8	Burns & Allen Show	15.6	CV	Chesterfield Cigarettes	Fri	8:30	30	CBS
12t	N	Bob Hope Show	15.4	CV	Pepsodent Toothpaste	Tue	10:00	30	NBC
12t	N	Campbell Playhouse/Orson Welles	15.4	DA	Campbell Soup	Fri	9:00	60	CBS
14t	18	Big Town/Edward G Robinson	15.3	DCC	Rinso Laundry Soap	Tue	8:00	30	CBS
14t	6	Fred Allen's Town Hall Tonight	15.3	CV	Ipana/Sal Hepatica	Wed	9:00	60	NBC
16t	50	Kate Smith Hour	14.5	MV	Swansdown/Calumet	Thu	8:00	60	CBS
16t	13	One Man's Family	14.5	DCC	Tenderleaf Tea	Wed	8:00	30	NBC
18	9	Rudy Vallee Show	14.4	MV	Royal Gelatin/Fleischmann	Thu	8:00	60	NBC
19t	29	Lowell Thomas News	14.0	NC	Sun Oil	M-F	6:45	15	Blue
19t	18	Walter Winchell's Jergens Journal	14.0	NC	Jergens Lotion	Sun	9:30	15	Blue
21	16	Hollywood Hotel/William Powell	13.7	MV	Campbell Soup	Fri	9:00	60	CBS
22	26	Your Hit Parade/Buddy Clark, Lanny Ross	13.6	MP	Lucky Strike Cigarettes	Sat	10:00	45	CBS
23	15	Al Pearce Gang	13.3	CV	Grape Nuts Cereals	Mon	8:00	30	NBC
24	59	We the People/Gabriel Heatter	13.0	API	Sanka Coffee	Tue	9:00	30	CBS
25	16	Gangbusters	12.8	DA	Palmolive Shave Cream	Wed	8:00	30	CBS
26	33	Hollywood Playhouse	12.7	DA	Woodbury Soap	Sun	9:00	30	Blue
27	N	Fitch Bandwagon	12.6	MP	Fitch Shampoo	Sun	7:30	30	NBC
28	N	The Circle	12.3	PS	Kellogg Corn Flakes	Sun	10:00	60	NBC
29	21	Amos & Andy	12.1	SC	Campbell Soup	M-F	7:00	15	CBS 1
30	N	Joe Penner Show	11.7	SC	Huskies Cereal	Thu	7:30	30	CBS
31	14	First Nighter Program	11.5	DA	Campana Balm	Fri	8:00	30	CBS
32	N	Tommy Riggs & Betty Lou	11.3	SC	Quaker Oats	Sat	8:00	30	NBC
33	25	Dick Powell Show	10.9	MV	Lifebuoy Soap	Tue	8:30	30	CBS
34	N	Tommy Dorsey Orchestra	10.7	MV	Raleigh & Kool Cigarettes	Wed	8:30	30	NBC
35t	N	Guy Lombardo Orch	10.4	MP	Lady Esther Cosmetics	Mon	10:00	30	CBS

	Program	Rtg	Type	Sponsor	Day	Time	Lgth	Net
35t *37*	Pick & Pat's Model Minstrels	10.4	MSP	Model Pipe Tobacco	Mon	8:30	30	CBS
37 *42*	Voice of Firestone	10.1	MC	Firestone Tires	Mon	8:30	30	NBC
38 *N*	Texaco Star Theater/Ken Murray	10.0	CV	Texaco	Wed	9:00	60	CBS 2
39 *26*	Professor Quiz/Craig Earl	9.9	APQ	Noxzema Skin Cream	Sat	8:30	30	CBS
40 *N*	Screen Guild Theater/Geo Murphy	9.8	DA	Gulf Oil	Sun	7:30	30	CBS
41 *38*	Manhattan Merry Go Round	9.6	MP	Dr Lyons Tooth Powder	Sun	9:00	30	NBC
42 *N*	Battle of The Sexes/Crumit/ Sanderson	9.5	APQ	Molle Shaving Cream	Tues	9:00	30	NBC
43t *N*	Fred Waring Show	9.4	MST	Bromo Quinine Cold Tablets	Sat	8:30	30	NBC
43t *46*	National Barn Dance	9.4	MSP	Alka-Seltzer	Sat	9:00	60	Blue
45t *58*	American Album of Familiar Music	9.3	MST	Bayer Aspirin	Sun	9:30	30	NBC
45t *83*	Horace Heidt Brigadiers Orch	9.3	MP	Stewart Warner Alemite	Sun	10:00	30	NBC
45t *57*	Second Husband/Helen Menken	9.3	DCC	Bayer Aspirin	Tue	7:30	30	CBS
48t *N*	Edwin C Hill News	9.1	NC	Campbell Soup	M-W	7:15	15	NBC
48t *64*	Grand Central Station	9.1	DA	Listerine Antiseptic	Fri	10:00	30	CBS
48t *N*	Joe E Brown Show	9.1	SC	Post Toasties Cereal	Thu	7:30	30	CBS 3

New & Returning Top 50 Programs Underscored.

1	Amos & Andy	Sep–Mar	Campbell Soup	M-F	7:00	15	NBC
2	Texaco Star Theater	Oct–Dec	Texaco	Wed	9:30	60	CBS
3	Joe E Brown Show	Oct–Mar	Post Toasties Cereal	Sat	7:30	30	CBS

Key: API — Audience Participation/Interviews   DCC — Drama/Continuing Characters   MV — Music/Variety Show
APQ — Audience Participation/Quiz   MC — Music/Classical, Semi-Classical   NC — News, Commentary
APS — Audience Participation/Stunts   MP — Music/Popular, Contemporary   PS — Panel Show Comedy
CV — Comedy/Variety Show   MSP — Music/Specialty, Ethnic   SC — Situation Comedy
DA — Dramatic Anthology   MST — Music/Standard, Traditional   TC — Talent Competition

1938–39 Top 50 Favorite Formats

	Programs	Pct
Music — All Categories	18	36%
Comedy — All Categories	15	30%
Drama — Anthology & Continuing	10	20%
Audience Participation — All Categories	4	8%
News/Commentary	3	6%

1938–39 Monthly Winners

Sep	Edgar Bergen & Charlie McCarthy	33.8	Feb	Edgar Bergen & Charlie McCarthy	35.4
Oct	Edgar Bergen & Charlie McCarthy	31.6	Mar	Edgar Bergen & Charlie McCarthy	34.0
Nov	Edgar Bergen & Charlie McCarthy	34.8	Apr	Edgar Bergen & Charlie McCarthy	34.6
Dec	Edgar Bergen & Charlie McCarthy	34.5	May	Edgar Bergen & Charlie McCarthy	26.1
Jan	Edgar Bergen & Charlie McCarthy	34.4	Jun	Edgar Bergen & Charlie McCarthy	22.8

12

The 1939–40 Network Season

Announcer: This is the time of year when Missus America dons her new chapeau, arranges a snood back over her lovely curls and looks forward to a happy autumn. Mister America acquires the annual snap brim felt hat and an extra spring in his step. This is the time when our new 1940 Plymouth models make their debut. The low priced automobile is one of the greatest contributions ever made to American civilization. The entire continent is your playground. Seven out of every ten cars sold are in the low priced class. The Plymouth advance in popularity is one of the miracles of American industry! And that rise of Plymouth to the peak of popularity can only mean one thing ... it is the utmost automobile value for your dollar. The 1940 Plymouth is much bigger ... the body is completely new ... and you may choose your car with or without a running board. And the Road King, as well as the Deluxe Plymouth, has our marvelous steering wheel gearshift. Gear-shifting is now a pleasure. Oil filters are now standard equipment. Headlamps are the new sealed beam type giving a brighter illumination at night. The 1940 Plymouth is lower without cutting down the headroom. The windshield is wider for better vision. The rear window is curved in one piece for better visibility. As for the new luxury ride, that is, as the debs say, "Something out of this world." If I've been able to impart to you just part of my prideful enthusiasm, you'll wish to go to your Plymouth dealer to see the superb 1940 Plymouth. Why not be the first in town to take a "welcome ride" in our 1940 Plymouth ... the new low priced beauty with the luxury ride.

RADIO REVS UP

The networks and the entire radio industry enjoyed the first of three consecutive years of double digit revenue growth.

To stifle rumbles about over-commercialization, the National Association of Broadcasters skipped a step ahead of public resentment and government scrutiny in July by adopting a Commercial Code for its member stations and networks. The code called for a maximum of three minutes, 15 seconds out of every daytime quarter hour (21.6 percent), to be allowed for advertising. A less generous two minutes, 30 seconds of each quarter hour (16.7 percent), was the allowance for nighttime advertising.

Broadcast lines cost the networks eight to ten dollars a mile per month ($130–163). Nevertheless, the average million dollars a year that each chain paid AT&T was a small cost of doing business with total network billings approaching a hundred million dollars a year.

The networks were riding high

and others wanted a bigger piece of the action.

The newly formed performers' union, AFRA, negotiated a contract calling for a minimum of $15 per network program ($244). It was a long overdue and well deserved guarantee for the talent, but peanuts compared to the major hit planned by ASCAP for all broadcasters on January 1, 1941.

BROADCASTERS COMPOSE THEMSELVES

ASCAP wanted a 50 percent increase in its blanket music license fees for stations and networks, raising the ante from five to seven and a half percent of gross revenues. Based on 1939's revenues, the increase threatened to raise the industry's bill to nearly 14 million dollars a year ($227.9 Mil).

Instead of folding to ASCAP's demands, the National Association of Broadcasters decided to fight. In doing so, they changed the course of popular music by opening its doors to new composers and rhythms.

On September 15, 1939, the NAB established Broadcast Music Incorporated (BMI), as an alternate music licensing source with a fee structure less than half of ASCAP's 1937 rate. The new operation immediately began to collect foreign compositions, update public domain melodies into arrangements for new copyright — and most importantly — invite new compositions from fledgling songwriters who didn't meet ASCAP's clubby standards for membership which favored established composers and virtually shut out newcomers.

The last maneuver resulted in over a thousand new songs *a week* flooding into BMI. Within six months the new organization's inventory and future seemed assured, and over a million dollars of its stock had been sold.

1939–40 Season Scoreboard Mid-season Totals, December 1939			
		Compared to Year Earlier	
Total Radio Homes	27.50 Mil	+0.83 Mil	+3.1%
Total Auto Radios	6.50 Mil	+0.50 Mil	+8.3%
Total AM Radio Stations	722	+33	+4.8%
Total Radio Network Affiliates	396	+37	+10.3%
1939 Radio Revenues	183.8 Mil	+16.7 Mil	+10.0%
1939 Network Revenues	98.6 Mil	+9.4 Mil	+10.5%
Network Share	53.6%		+0.2%

BMI began its licensing operations on April 1, 1940, with a roster of 250 member stations plus all four networks. All agreed to trim their use their of ASCAP music in favor of BMI compositions.

Both sides were girded for the expected battle that was still nine months away.

NO ENCORES FOR SOAP OPERAS

Hill Blackett, head of the Blackett, Sample & Hummert ad agency which was responsible for a flock of daytime serials produced by Frank and Anne Hummert, wanted to syndicate transcriptions of their soap operas for nighttime broadcast on small market independent stations. But NBC and CBS both denied permission to record the broadcasts.

So, Blackett, the Hummerts and a new partner, Elliot Roosevelt, attempted to lease Mutual network circuits for two hours every weeknight to reproduce the serials for prime time audiences. Mutual turned down the proposal.

This led Roosevelt, who headed of the 23 station Texas State Network, to propose an altogether new coast to coast network based on the same idea, the Transcontinental Broadcasting System. The magic of the Roosevelt name helped the President's son sell some $350,000 in stock *(5.7 Mil)*, to fund the startup.

Transcontinental was slated for a January launch but the soap bubble burst from lack of available lines, adequate financing and attractive affiliates.

As a result, daily soap operas were never heard in prime time and *Ma Perkins* never had to work nights.

THE NETWORKS STATION FOR WAR

Germany's September invasion of Poland put the networks' news departments on a wartime stance. with overseas correspondents. All had London, Paris and Berlin bureaus. CBS and NBC also established Rome offices and NBC had additional reporters stationed in Geneva, Shanghai, Tokyo and Danzig (Gdansk), Poland.

NBC maintained larger staffs working in each city but CBS had the stars who were heard with increasing frequency on the network's *Today in Europe,* the twice daily predecessor to *The World Today.* CBS was busily promoting the London Bureau's Edward R. Murrow and H.V. Kaltenborn, plus Eric Sevareid stationed in Paris, William L. Shirer in Berlin and Cecil Brown in Rome.

With Kaltenborn in Europe, CBS filled his New York analyst's position with Elmer Davis. Davis soon became one of the most widely heard newsmen in radio when CBS carved out a five minute slot for his news and comment seven nights a week at 8:55. The first five-minute news capsule in network prime time aired on September 18 and furthered the CBS News image to audiences of popular nighttime fare.

Yet, it was NBC reporter James Bowen who scored the scoop of the year from Montevideo, Uruguay, on December 12 when he described via short wave the scuttling of the German battleship *Graf Spree,* which was barricaded in the harbor by British warships.

Bowen's reports were the first eyewitness descriptions of encounters between World War II combatants.

THE MONTHLIES

Edgar Bergen's string of consecutive monthly wins for Standard Brands continued in September and October. It ended at 22 in November when General Foods' Jack Benny edged out the ventriloquist by two-tenths of a point. The two remained in a close race every month for the rest of the season — the difference often less than a point. The season ended in a virtual tie for Number One — certainly within any pollster's margin of error. Bergen was first in December, January, April, May and June. Benny had the Number One show in February and March.

Both shows aired on NBC which extended its string of consecutive monthly winners to 51.

1939–40 Sunday Night Top Ten Programs (11)
NBC 6, CBS 4, Blue 1
Average: 17.2

Jack Benny Program	NBC	7:00	30.9
Edgar Bergen & Charlie McCarthy	NBC	8:00	30.7
One Man's Family	NBC	8:30	20.3
Walter Winchell's Jergens Journal	Blue	9:00	19.3
Fitch Bandwagon	NBC	7:30	15.2
Screen Guild Theater	CBS	7:30	12.8
Campbell Playhouse	CBS	8:00	11.0
Ford Sunday Evening Hour	CBS	9:00	10.8
American Album of Familiar Music	NBC	9:30	10.7
Gateway to Hollywood	CBS	6:30	10.5
Manhattan Merry Go Round	NBC	9:00	10.5

STANDARD TIME ZONED

General Foods reported that it sold the most goods in its company's history in 1939, netting just over 15 million dollars *(244.1 Mil)*, while advertising more than 80 products on 14 network radio programs.

None of those programs was more important than Jack Benny's Sunday night show for Jello.

And none was more important to Standard Brands than its hour with Edgar Bergen and Charlie McCarthy pushing Chase & Sanborn Coffee. But changes were brewing.

Research confirmed to the sponsor what common sense told them — listeners wanted little more from *The Chase & Sanborn Hour* than the 20 minutes of patter "between" Bergen and McCarthy with frequent guest stars appearing as Charlie's foils.

As a result, the hour long show was cut in half to 30 minutes at mid-season. Don Ameche and Dorothy Lamour left in December to pursue their film careers and Edgar Bergen was on his own, in a manner of speaking.

He still had Charlie McCarthy at his side and brought on a new character for the season to add some variety to his routines, Mortimer Snerd, radio's foremost slow-witted, slow-talking bumpkin.

Bergen's new condensed show attracted 30+ratings until May when the traditional summer slack in listeners began. Standard Brands had created a tighter show, had saved 30 minutes' worth of heavy production costs and had a new half hour at 8:30 at its disposal with a lead-in that was second to none.

HAUL IN THE FAMILY

Standard Brands had a promising program under its Tenderleaf Tea banner considered ready for the Sunday slot.

Carleton E. Morse's *One Man's Family* was pulled from its temporary Thursday timeslot where it had a 16.2 average rating from September through December. Installed following the streamlined Bergen show in January, the Barbour family saga picked up nearly 50 percent more audience and finished in the season's Top Ten.

NBC had put in place a Sunday lineup at mid-season that had staying power: Jack Benny, *Fitch Bandwagon*, Edgar Bergen and Charlie McCarthy, *One Man's Family*, *Manhattan Merry Go Round*, *American Album of Familiar Music* and *The Hour of Charm* remained in that order for the next five years.

WHO'S THE DUMMY NOW?

Encouraged by the previous half season's good ratings against much weaker competition on Friday, Campbell Soup moved *The Campbell Playhouse*, aka Orson Welles and his Mercury Theater troupe, back to where it started. Welles was again pitted against the unbeatable Bergen and McCarthy.

Perhaps the soup maker hoped that amateur magician Welles had another *War of the Worlds* in his bag of tricks. He didn't. The program's ratings sank 30 percent. Welles and Campbell Soup parted company in March.

WW'S DOUBLE DIGITS

Americans were becoming more news hungry as world tensions continued to build. Walter Winchell fed raw meat to the hungry public every Sunday night with his own brand of rapid fire "insider" news and gossip. Blue moved the syndicated columnist's frantic 15 minute

Jergens Journal back from 9:30 to 9:00. Winchell's. rating jumped 38 percent for his first of eight consecutive Top Ten seasons

The program remained at 9:00 for 15 years, registering an overall total of twelve Top Ten finishes.

FUTURE STARS SHINE DIMLY

Sunday was the season's home for Network Radio's biggest hits and the incubator for three series that would run through the next decade. However, none of the rookies approached Sunday's Top Ten in ratings.

Bill Stern's melodramatic *Colgate Sports Newsreel* began unwinding its tall tales of legendary sports heroes on Blue at 9:45 to a meager 4.8 rating—finishing the nine o'clock hour that Walter Winchell opened with a 19.3. Stern never finished in a season's Top 50 in his dozen years on Blue and NBC, yet he was continually voted the most popular sportscaster in fan magazine polls and was heard by millions more with his movie newsreel and two-reel "short subject" narrations.

Gene Autry was the cowboy movie star of eight singing westerns cranked out by Republic Pictures in 1939. Another seven were planned for 1940 when he began his *Melody Ranch* series at 6:30 on CBS for Wrigley in January. The gum manufacturer paid Autry a reported $1,000 a week *($16,275)*. He returned the investment with a 9.6 rating and continued his association with Wrigley and CBS for another twelve years.

Mr. District Attorney debuted on Blue at 7:30 opposite NBC's *Fitch Bandwagon* and *Screen Guild Theater* on CBS. The two programs combined for a 28 rating, leaving little room for the new crime fighter who opened with a 9.1. It would be *Mr. District Attorney's* only finish outside a nightly Top Ten.

Mr. District Attorney became another promising series that was shifted from Blue to NBC. It was given a temporary NBC Thursday timeslot in April then settled into its longtime Wednesday night home the following season where it became a perennial favorite in the annual Top 50.

1939–40 Monday Night Top Ten Programs
CBS 6, Blue 2, NBC 2
Average: 13.1

Lux Radio Theater	CBS	9:00	23.7
Lowell Thomas News*	Blue	6:45	14.5
Guy Lombardo's Lady Esther Serenade	CBS	10:00	13.6
Model Minstrels	CBS	8:30	12.2
Tommy Riggs & Betty Lou	NBC	8:00	12.0
Blondie	CBS	7:30	11.7
Adventures of Sherlock Holmes	Blue	8:00	11.4
Pipe Smoking Time	CBS	8:30	10.8
Amos & Andy*	CBS	7:00	10.8
I Love a Mystery*	NBC	7:15	10.6

*Monday–Friday Strip Shows

Sans Strips...			
Dr IQ	NBC	9:00	10.4
Lum & Abner	CBS	7:15	10.4
Voice of Firestone	NBC	8:30	9.9

REEL RADIO

Lux Radio Theater wasn't the only Monday program to rely on the movies for its stars.

Blondie, starring Penny Singleton and Arthur Lake — recreating the roles they had already established in three Columbia film comedies — debuted on CBS in July at 7:30 as the summer replacement for Eddie Cantor.

The stand-ins became the timeslot's permanent stars when sponsor Camel Cigarettes fired Cantor later in the summer for making political remarks deemed controversial. *Blondie* lost 32 percent of Cantor's ratings in its first season but finished in Monday's Top Ten and among the season's Top 50 programs for the five years of its Monday night run.

The radio sitcom had a ten year multi-network run while Singleton and Lake filmed a total of 28 *Blondie* comedies for Columbia based on the popular Chic Young comic strip.

Similarly typecast from their signature movie roles were Basil Rathbone and Nigel Bruce who starred in 14 *Sherlock Holmes* films for Fox and Universal. The two actors' highly distinctive voices were ideal for radio drama. *The Adventures of Sherlock Holmes'* first season on Blue with Rathbone and Bruce finished in Monday's Top Ten and the season's Top 50. Then, like so many other promising Blue network programs, it was moved to NBC the following season.

1939–40 Tuesday Night Top Ten Programs
NBC 4, Blue 3, CBS 3
Average: 16.0

Fibber McGee & Molly	NBC	9:30	24.8
Bob Hope Show	NBC	10:00	23.1
Pot o' Gold	NBC	8:30	18.0
We the People	CBS	9:00	15.5
Big Town	CBS	8:00	14.9
Lowell Thomas News*	Blue	6:45	14.5
Battle of the Sexes	NBC	9:00	13.1
Information Please	Blue	8:30	13.1
The Aldrich Family	Blue	8:00	12.2
Second Husband	CBS	7:30	11.2

*Monday–Friday Strip Shows

Sans Strips...

Tuesday Night Party	CBS	8:30	10.3

THE BOYS AND NOISE OF WISTFUL VISTA

Fibber McGee & Molly's first full season originating from NBC's Hollywood studios was a big one. The sitcom was becoming a listener favorite in its Tuesday timeslot and its ratings jumped 41 percent for the season. Jim and Marian Jordan and their writer/partner Don Quinn now split $4,000 a week in salary (*$65,100*), a long way from the $125 a week the trio earned just five years earlier. But it was still a terrific bargain for sponsor Johnson Wax.

A new nemesis for Fibber was introduced on September 26 when Throckmorton P. Gildersleeve played by Hal Peary moved in next door to the McGees.

At 31, Peary was an alumnus of Chicago radio and had played a number of characters on *FM&M* since 1937. Fibber and Gildy would go at each other for two seasons before Peary moved on to star in his highly successful spin-off, *The Great Gildersleeve.*

Fibber opened the door to even more laughs on March 5 when one of radio's longest running sound effect gags was born. Without any advance buildup, McGee first opened his infamous hall closet door to a thundering cascade of ac-

cumulated junk. The heap of trash — including oil cans, roller skates, broken dishes, bowling pins, cowbells and Fibber's old mandolin — was pushed down a portable staircase by sound effects technicians and created five seconds of absolute cacophony that was always topped off by the tinkle of a small bell.

Repeated dozens of times over the program's run, it was a virtuoso performance by the NBC sound effects crew, witnessed by hundreds in the studio audience, heard by millions of listeners and enjoyed by all

GETTING UP HOPE

With the push of *Fibber McGee & Molly's* lead-in, Bob Hope's rating shot up 50 percent and placed him in the annual Top Five for the first of ten consecutive seasons. Hope helped his own cause with Paramount Pictures' March release of *The Road to Singapore*, the first of seven musical comedies that teamed him with his pal Bing Crosby.

POT O' GOLD: HOT AND COLD

Bandleader/pianist Horace Heidt was a Network Radio veteran. The 38-year-old Heidt had been frequently, if not steadily employed by different sponsors on CBS, NBC and Blue since 1932.

Like Kay Kyser, Heidt was first and foremost a master of ceremonies fronting a show band of highly skilled musicians. Heidt's *Alemite Brigadiers, Answers by Dancers, Ship of Joy* and *Anniversary Night* orchestras of the 1930s featured future bandleaders Frankie Carle and Alvino Rey and the four singing King Sisters.

Meanwhile, radio producer Ed Byron already had Arlene Francis' quiz, *What's My Name*, on NBC's Friday schedule and Sunday's *Mr. District Attorney* in its first season on Blue when he was given the challenge to create something new and exciting for Lewis-Howe's Tums Antacid Tablets.

Together with Heidt, Byron came up with *Pot o' Gold*, an altogether new and exciting ratings phenomenon — for one season. It

was radio's first giveaway program — awarding three listeners per show a minimum of $1,000 (*$16,275*), for simply answering their telephones when the program called them.

Wheels of chance were spun on stage by Heidt and co-host Ben Grauer to determine the phone book, the page number and the line where each lucky telephone number was found. While Heidt's "Musical Knights" band played, Grauer dialed the number, ready to stop the music and award the cash if somebody answered. If no one answered, the homeowner was sent a hundred dollar consolation prize and the remaining $900 was added to the jackpot. The jackpot never got beyond $2,800 (*$45,575*).

Pot o' Gold was a one season roller coaster of ratings. Its climb started slowly in October with an 8.6. Then word got around about the free money and its November rating jumped 47 percent into double digits. By February the show peaked at 25.4.

Then listeners realized two things. First, the odds against being called were incredibly high. Secondly, winners didn't have to listen to the program to win, just pick up the phone. As a result, the show's downward slide began in March with a 15.5 percent loss of audience and by June its ratings had plummeted to half of its season high.

The show lasted only one season on NBC before it was shuttled off to Blue amid questions about its possible violation of lottery laws.

THE ONE AND ONLY TWO

Married couples were well represented in radio comedy — Jack and Mary Benny, Jim and Marian Jordan, George and Gracie Burns, Fred and Portland Allen, Goodman and Jane Ace — all reading their scripted and rehearsed lines. Only one husband and wife team, Frank Crumit and Julia Sanderson, sang and ad-libbed their way into prime time.

Crumit and his ukulele had taken the Vaudeville route to stardom, accompanying himself on novelty songs he had written. *There Is No One with Endurance Like a Man Who Sells Insurance* was typical of the 250 songs he recorded for RCA and Decca. In 1921 at age 32 he joined the Broadway cast of the musical, *Tangerine*.

Sanderson, 34, had been a Broadway musical star for over a decade when she was cast in the lead of *Tangerine*. Unlike Crumit's ditties, the song most closely identified with her career was Jerome Kern's *They Didn't Believe Me,* which she introduced in 1914.

A backstage romance blossomed between the two and after several years of touring together as a team, Frank and Julia were married in 1927 and ready to settle down. Radio seemed a perfect fit for the fortyish couple and they found work quickly doing network song and patter shows billed as "America's Singing Sweethearts." Two Top 50 seasons during their 1930–34 run on *Blackstone Plantation* were followed with a Sunday afternoon series for another two years.

Crumit and Sanderson returned to prime time in 1939 with *The Battle of the Sexes* for Sterling Drug's Molle Shaving Cream. They reached the season's Top 50 for four consecutive seasons as part of NBC's powerful Tuesday lineup. The quiz show pitted teams of men and women against each other, giving its co-hosts ample opportunity to display their relaxed and friendly rapport with contestants and each other.

INFORMATION FOR THE RECORD

Information Please creator/producer Dan Golenpaul was at a standoff with Blue.

Except for maverick Mutual, which was forced by economies to cut production corners, the networks banned the recording of any programs for delayed broadcast. Their reasoning was based in the inferior technical quality of transcribed programming and the popular appeal of live programs in which anything could happen and sometimes did.

Standard procedure called for many prime time programs to be performed twice, normally three hours apart, which allowed the shows to be scheduled in the key 7:00 to 11:00 time period on both the East and West coasts.

Golenpaul flatly refused a second performance of *Information Please,* arguing that his program wasn't scripted — its content was based on his panel's witty and spontaneous dialogue. There was no way in which a performance of *Information Please* could be duplicated — unless it were recorded.

The feisty producer held all the cards. The program had become a critical favorite with a growing audience. Sponsor Canada Dry and Blue both wanted the program broadcast in prime time on the West coast, not in the late afternoon when it was heard live.

The network caved and on August 15, 1939, *Information Please* became the first major network prime time program to be, "…Transcribed for broadcast at this time."

Golenpaul's stubbornness paid dividends. Moving *Information Please* into prime time on the West coast via recording helped *Information Please* to a 72 percent increase in audience and an all-time high season average rating of 13.1.

1939–40 Wednesday Night Top Ten Programs (11)
CBS 6, NBC 4, Blue 1
Average: 13.4

Kay Kyser's Kollege of Musical Knowledge	NBC	10:00	18.0
Fred Allen Show	NBC	9:00	16.3
Lowell Thomas News*	Blue	6:45	14.5
Burns & Allen Show	CBS	7:30	14.3
Al Pearce Gang	CBS	8:00	13.4
Ken Murray Show	CBS	9:00	12.6
Dr Christian	CBS	8:30	11.7
Hollywood Playhouse	NBC	8:00	11.2
Amos & Andy*	CBS	7:00	10.8
I Love a Mystery*	NBC	7:15	10.6
Ben Bernie Show	CBS	8:00	10.5

*Monday–Friday Strip Shows

Sans Strips…
Lum & Abner	CBS	7:15	10.4
Avalon Time	NBC	8:30	10.4
Quicksilver	Blue	8:30	6.1

THAT'S RIGHT, YOU'RE WRONG!

"Kay Kyser's show band clobbered Glenn Miller's legendary orchestra in the ratings, right?"

It may sound absurd to big band buffs, but it's true.

Liggett & Myers' Chesterfield

Cigarettes brought the Miller band to CBS for a Monday-Wednesday-Friday Multiple Run quarter hour at 10:00. Its Wednesday performance went head to head against Kyser's *Kollege of Musical Knowledge* on NBC.

The final ratings score after their three seasons of direct competition was Kyser, 17.7, Miller, 6.7.

Kyser's cause was helped along with the November release of his first of four RKO movies, *That's Right, You're Wrong!* Unlike most bands whose appearances in films were mere window dressing, Kyser and his troupe of sidemen and singers were central to the cast and plots of his films.

Among them was vocalist Ginny Simms who went on to solo movie and Network Radio careers.

GRACIE'S SURPRISE PARTY

Frequent timeslot hoppers George Burns and Gracie Allen switched day, time and sponsor for the fifth time in eight seasons. The couple made money with every jump — their 1939 radio contract for Hind's Honey & Almond Hand Cream paid them $9,000 per week ($146,500). The pair also appeared in 1939's MGM film *Honolulu,* and Gracie did a solo turn in a Paramount's *Gracie Allen Murder Case.* If and when they had spare time, lucrative personal appearance contracts were theirs for the choosing.

Despite all this success, Burns and Allen were in a three year ratings decline.

George and brother/manager Willie Burns decided it was time for another stunt like 1933's Missing Brother gambit that kept Gracie busy with "surprise" guest appearances on dozens of different programs.

This time they capitalized on the occasion of the 1940 elections by running Gracie for President of the United States.

The idea wasn't original. Will Rogers ran a mock presidential campaign in 1928 and Eddie Cantor repeated the stunt in 1932. Gracie, however, would make a "campaign tour" of other programs to whip up support for her "Surprise Party" nomination at its Omaha convention in May.

The stunt resulted in the desired cross-promotion that helped Burns and Allen establish themselves as CBS' strongest Wednesday entry. But unlike the Missing Brother gag that resulted in an audience surge, Gracie's run for President hardly made a ripple in their ratings which lost a point from the previous season.

THE DOCTOR IS IN

Dr Christian was removed from its uphill Tuesday competition with Bob Hope and given a safer slot in the CBS lineup on Wednesday. Listeners and ratings responded. The Jean Hersholt series scored its first of eight consecutive Top 50 seasons.

Unlike the much-traveled Burns and Allen, *Dr Christian* didn't budge from its familiar network, day and time until it left the air 15 years later.

RED STRIKES GOLD

Red Skelton left *Avalon Time* and Network Radio in December for an extended stage show tour of movie houses accompanied by name bands. Skelton's personal appearance fee had grown to $4,300 a week (*$70,000*), much more than radio was paying. The Avalon show was turned over to comedian Cliff Arquette with little change in its ratings.

Meanwhile, Skelton was a smash hit in his four a day theater grinds. By summer and its high paying state fair shows, he was earning over $7,000 a week (*$113,900*). The comedian stayed out of series radio the following season while he continued to build his fan base with sold out audiences wherever he played. The maneuver engineered by Skelton's wife/manager, Edna, resulted in an MGM film contract offer.

1939–40 Thursday Night Top Ten Programs
NBC 6, CBS 3, Blue 1
Average: 14.0

Bing Crosby's Kraft Music Hall	NBC	10:00	21.1
Major Bowes' Original Amateur Hour	CBS	9:00	18.4
Good News of 1940	NBC	9:00	16.9

Lowell Thomas News*	Blue	6:45	14.5
Rudy Vallee Show	NBC	9:30	13.4
Those We Love	NBC	8:30	12.2
Ask It Basket	CBS	8:00	11.7
Amos & Andy*	CBS	7:00	10.8
George Jessel Show	NBC	8:00	10.6
I Love a Mystery*	NBC	7:15	10.6

*Monday–Friday Strip Shows

Sans Strips...

I Love a Mystery	NBC	8:30	10.3
Vox Pop	CBS	7:30	9.8
Joe Penner Show	Blue	8:30	9.0

YOU'VE BEEN GREAT, YOU'RE FIRED

Two months short of their tenth anniversary together on NBC, Standard Brands cancelled its sponsorship of Rudy Vallee's variety hour in August 1939. The series had been a great success for Standard's Fleischmann Yeast and Royal Gelatin brands since the fall of 1929.

Beginning with Crossley's ratings of 1932–33, Vallee turned in a Top Ten show for six consecutive seasons — but his popularity had slipped steadily to less than half of its peak earlier in the decade.

What followed was a scheduling mess for Standard Brands.

To cover the hour, Standard moved Carleton E. Morse's *One Man's Family* into Vallee's first half at 8:00 and installed another well-traveled serial, *Those We Love,* into the second half at 8:30.

But in January Standard needed the Barbour family to plug Sunday's 8:30 vacancy created by its decision to cut the *Edgar Bergen & Charlie McCarthy Hour* back to 30 minutes.

With both Rudy Vallee and *One Man's Family* gone, Standard released the first half of its long held 8:00 hour on NBC's Thursday schedule. Bristol Myers snapped it up for a short-lived George Jessel entry, *For Men Only,* which it replaced in April by the new and promising *Mr. District Attorney.*

Meanwhile, Standard Brands was left stuck the faltering *Those We Love* in its remaining half hour at 8:30. The company ordered Carleton E. Morse to reformat Fleischmann Yeast's successful strip serial *I Love a Mystery* into a half hour program to replace *Those We Love* in April.

He did and *I Love a Mystery* lost ten percent of the soap opera's audience.

VALLEE'S VENGEANCE

Vallee, still only 39, refused to roll over and play dead with the Standard Brands cancellation.

He vowed to return and signed with Sealtest Dairies for a new half hour variety show beginning in March 1940.

His opportunity became available after General Foods cut its hour-long *Good News* starring Fanny Brice and Frank Morgan back to 30 minutes. That opened the door for Sealtest to buy the 9:30 timeslot for Vallee's new show. Vallee immediately had another of Thursday's Top Ten shows. His ratings continued to climb steadily until he left for military service four years later.

The success of Vallee's new 9:30 program followed by Bing Crosby's hour long *Kraft Music Hall* at 10:00 gave the Sealtest-Kraft conglomerate a solid 90 minutes of NBC advertising exposure on the eve of the week's busiest day for grocery shopping.

NOBODY BOUGHT THE DUCK

Another young man who had experienced a season in the sun with a Top Ten show just four years earlier returned to Blue for a last stab at success.

Joe Penner was only 34 but already considered a radio has-been, always associated with the hackneyed catch-phrase, "Wanna buy a duck?"

His *Tip Top Show* featured Penner as the sad sack lead in a sitcom for Bond Bakeries' Tip Top Bread, slotted at 8:30 against the NBC serial *Those We Love* and CBS' oddity feature, *Strange as It Seems,* which resembled Ripley's *Believe It or Not.*

Penner's comedy, unfortunately, resembled his show that had struggled on CBS the previous season. The program was cancelled in March and Penner left radio forever. He was dead of a heart attack two years later.

1939–40 Friday Night
Top Ten Programs
CBS 7, NBC 2, Blue 1
Average: 12.6

Kate Smith Hour	CBS	8:00	16.8
First Nighter	CBS	9:30	15.4
Lowell Thomas News*	Blue	6:45	14.5
Russ Morgan Orchestra	CBS	9:00	12.6
Grand Central Station	CBS	10:00	11.9
Professor Quiz	CBS	7:30	11.8
Amos & Andy*	CBS	7:00	10.8
What's My Name?	NBC	9:30	10.8
I Love a Mystery*	NBC	7:15	10.6
Lum & Abner	CBS	7:15	10.4

*Monday–Friday Strip Shows

Sans Strips...

Waltz Time	NBC	9:00	8.3
Cities Service Concert	NBC	8:00	7.5
Quixie Doodle Contest	MBS	8:00	6.8

LADIES NIGHT AT THE RADIO

Kate Smith finally arrived as the star of a night's Number One program.

After her three year, head to head ratings battle with Rudy Vallee on Thursdays, General Foods moved Smith's variety show, featuring Abbott and Costello's comedy routines and *Aldrich Family* sitcom skits to CBS's Friday schedule at 8:00 where it would remain for five seasons.

Unlike many schedule switches that backfired, the beloved singer's move into the less competitive Friday time period resulted in a 16 percent audience gain and her all time high 16.8 rating for the season.

It was the first of four Friday night wins for *The Kate Smith Hour.*

General Foods and CBS also kept Smith busy with her daytime assignment, *Kate Smith Speaks,* a weekday, quarter hour talk show that debuted in October. The noontime strip program remained on CBS for eight years and then moved to Mutual for another four.

FIRST NIGHTER'S FIRST LADY

Another CBS switch that paid dividends was moving Campana's *First Nighter* into its sixth timeslot in its nomadic eight season history.

The light anthology drama's audience shot up 35 percent when Kate Smith joined the already strong CBS Friday lineup and *First Nighter* was installed in its 9:30 timeslot.

The show received a bonus at mid-season when the *Radio Mirror* magazine poll of over 800,000 readers named *First Nighter* co-star Barbara Luddy as the fans' favorite radio actress. Luddy was in her third year with the show and would remain with it for the remainder of its long network run.

The versatile Luddy was one of the few radio stars who wasn't active in movies — at least in the typical sense. She made several silents followed by forgettable films in the early 1930s before moving to Chicago for her *First Nighter* role in 1936–37. She returned to Hollywood with the show ten years later but wasn't active in film work until 1955 when she became a leading voiceover talent in Walt Disney animated films, best remembered as the voice of "Lady" in the classic feature *Lady & the Tramp.*

A HALF CENTURY CAREER IN DOUBLE TIME

Like Barbara Luddy, Arlene Francis was another sexy voiced radio pro who contributed a show to Friday's Top Ten. But unlike *First Nighter*'s ten Top 50 seasons, *What's My Name* reached that list only once. A simple quiz that awarded small cash prizes to contestants who could identify famous personalities through a series of clues, *What's My Name* bounced around NBC, Mutual and ABC for ten years like a spare tire — always available to roll when needed.

During the 1940s Francis also stayed active in a number of daytime serial and prime time dramatic roles She served as hostess of the popular *Blind Date* from 1943–46, and as the lead in ABC's private detective series, *The Affairs of Ann Scotland.*

Yet, she was just hitting her stride.

When television arrived Francis was in demand as one of its most versatile and popular performers and ranked among the highest paid women in the industry. She eventually returned to her radio roots

for a weekday talk show on New York's WOR from 1960 through 1983.

1939–40 Saturday Night
Top Ten Programs
CBS 5, NBC 4, Blue 1
Average: 10.2

Gangbusters	CBS	8:00	14.7
Your Hit Parade	CBS	9:00	13.6
Wayne King Orchestra	CBS	8:30	12.6
Stop Me If You've Heard This One	NBC	8:30	11.4
National Barn Dance	Blue	9:00	9.3
Benny Goodman Orchestra	NBC	10:00	8.6
Saturday Night Serenade	CBS	9:45	8.5
Bob Crosby Show	NBC	10:00	8.4
Sky Blazers	CBS	7:30	7.9
Death Valley Days	NBC	9:30	6.7

MAYHEM TRUMPS MUSIC

Against all of the music programming in Saturday's Top Ten, Phillips H. Lord's gritty *Gangbusters* took top honors in the fifth of its eleven Top 50 seasons. The crime drama registered a 15 percent increase in its audience after moving to Saturday from the CBS Wednesday schedule.

Meanwhile, Lucky Strike moved *Your Hit Parade* back an hour to 9:00 on CBS where it remained for seven seasons. The show remained a rarity among network programs at 45 minutes in length. Barry Wood replaced Lanny Ross and mid-season and was joined by the program's first female leads as co-hosts — recording stars Bea Wain and "Wee" Bonnie Baker.

Wain had recorded a number of hits with Larry Clinton's band and was married to *Hit Parade* announcer Andre Baruch, while Baker's baby-voiced recording of *Oh, Johnny, Oh!* elevated her from band singer with Orrin Tucker's orchestra to solo stardom.

Wayne King's sweet band was sandwiched between Saturday's two top shows on CBS. *Radio Guide*'s annual poll of listeners chose "The Waltz King" as its favorite dance orchestra for the seventh consecutive year — beating the likes of Glenn Miller and Benny Goodman. Listeners called by the Hooper pollsters reconfirmed that choice. King's Saturday program for Cashmere Bouquet soap scored 50 percent greater ratings than Goodman's and doubled the audience of Miller's weeknight Multiple Run series.

CAN YOU COP THIS?

Ask any old time radio buff to identify this 1939–40 series:

It was a half hour NBC show heard on Saturday nights. Jokes were solicited from the listening audience for cash prizes. The submitted jokes then became the basis for a competition among a panel of wits including Harry Hirschfield, "Senator" Ed Ford and Ward Wilson.

The answer is obviously *Can You Top This?*— and it's wrong.

Stop Me If You've Heard This One was a short lived series starring comedian Milton Berle. Berle told the listeners' jokes to the panelists who were challenged to beat him to the punch line from their memory of jokes and puns.

The show reached Saturday's Top Five and the season's Top 50 ranks, but only lasted 26 weeks before sponsor Quaker Oats cancelled it.

The joke telling concept inspired panelist Ed Ford to create a twist on the competition and produce *Can You Top This?* which was born in late 1940 on New York's WOR. Ford's show moved up to NBC in 1942 where it became one of Saturday's Top Five and the season's Top 50 for five consecutive years.

THE 7:00 FIGHT...

Amos & Andy continued to lose audience. Its first full season on

CBS resulted in another ten percent erosion of ratings. Nevertheless, the serial continued to provide Campbell Soup and CBS with a Top Ten Multiple Run show.

NBC didn't take its loss of the serial lying down. Liggett & Myers Tobacco picked up sponsorship of *A&A*'s direct competition, a new strip production featuring Fred Waring's "Pennsylvanians" orchestra and chorus.

Waring's *Chesterfield Supper Club* came within a point of *Amos & Andy*'s rating and would continue to nip at the venerable series' popularity for the next three seasons, finally overtaking it four years later.

... AND 7:15 FRIGHT

I Love a Mystery is remembered as one of radio's best crafted adventure dramas.

In Multiple Run strip format for its first six months on NBC, it ranked among the Top Ten programs four nights a week.

Series creator Carleton E. Morse was given free rein by Standard Brands to make *I Love a Mystery* his outlet for everything he couldn't do with *One Man's Family* plots and dialogue. He obviously had fun concocting the wild adventures that confronted his trio of heroes with sinister forces worthy of *The Shadow*'s team of blood thirsty villains.

"Temple of Vampires" was typical of its multiple-chapter story titles.

Morse created *I Love a Mystery*'s three lead characters with specific actors in mind — all college friends from Berkeley and all members of his *One Man's Family* cast.

Michael Raffetto, the Barbour family's eldest son Paul, was Morse's choice for Jack Packard — the straight-arrow, tough-as-nails senior partner of Hollywood's "A-1 Detective Agency."

Barton Yarborough, son Cliff of *One Man's Family*, played Packard's sidekick, Doc Long — a down home Texan, ladies man and comic relief Yarborough recreated the character in Columbia's three low budget movies based on the series — *I Love a Mystery, The Devil's Mask* and *The Unknown* — also written by Morse.

Walter Patterson, a Barbour son in law, doubled as the third of Morse's latter day musketeers, Reggie Yorke, a properly schooled Brit whose clipped dialect provided perfect counterpoint to Doc Long's friendly drawl.

I Love a Mystery gave its fans a prime time rendering of the late afternoon radio serials for kids. Only Morse's spooky fantasies were spiced with an overabundance of gore, violence and chilling effects. Listeners flocked to the often ghoulish goulash that Morse served them at suppertime. The freshman NBC serial's ratings topped its Multiple Run competition on CBS — reliable network talents Lanny Ross and *Lum & Abner* — and Blue's *Mr. Keen.*

The program also attracted protests from parents who objected to such violence interrupting family dinner hours. Standard Brands silenced the complaints with a rare move. It uprooted the 15 minute strip show and converted it to a weekly half hour format on Thursdays at 8:30, replacing the soapy *Those We Love.*

Ratings of the two versions of *I Love a Mystery* were almost identical, reflecting a steady, loyal audience. And although its 10.6 was terrific for a strip show, its 10.3 was disappointing for the Thursday series in the heart of prime time. In a rare, one-time occurrence, the half hour *I Love a Mystery* was edged out of Thursday's Top Ten by itself in its former quarter hour Multiple Run form.

Standard Brands exiled *I Love a Mystery* in half-hour form to Blue's Monday schedule for the next two

1939–40 Top Ten Multiple Run Programs
CBS 4, Blue 3, NBC 3
Average: 9.2

Lowell Thomas News*	M–F	Blue	6:45	14.5
Amos & Andy*	M–F	CBS	7:00	10.8
I Love a Mystery*	M–F	NBC	7:15	10.6
Lum & Abner	M,W,F	CBS	7:15	10.4
Fred Waring Show*	M–F	NBC	7:00	10.1
Lanny Ross Show	T,T	CBS	7:15	8.6
Easy Aces	T,W,T	Blue	7:00	7.0
World News Today	M,W,F	NBC	6:45	6.8
Glenn Miller Orchestra	T,W,T	CBS	10:00	6.6
Mr. Keen, Tracer of Lost Persons	T,W,T	Blue	7:15	6.2

*Monday–Friday Strip Shows

seasons where it rebounded into the night's Top Ten in 1941–42.

The program returned as a quarter hour strip show to CBS for an 18 month run in 1943, and moved on for a three year encore on Mutual beginning in 1949, with a series of past Multiple Run scripts recreated by a new cast.

I Love a Mystery remains a favorite of Network Radio buffs who appreciate Morse's clever writing, his cast's talents and the program's high production values.

ORCHESTRATED COMPETITION

Liggett & Myers Tobacco continued to depend on quarter-hour music shows to push its Chesterfield Cigarettes.

Along with Fred Waring's *Chesterfield Supper Club,* the company also sponsored Glenn Miller's only prime time series, *Chesterfield Serenade.* Both finished in the Multiple Run Top Ten for three consecutive seasons.

Legendary bandsman Miller was given one of the radio's toughest time periods for his 15 minute show

on CBS. His 10:00 timeslot was opposite Bob Hope on Tuesday, Kay Kyser on Wednesday and Bing Crosby on Thursday. Nevertheless, a million and a half homes were reported listening to Miller's medleys of, "…Something old, something new, something borrowed, something blue…," three times a week.

Miller's sidemen were fortunate — as were those who played with Waring, Kyser, Horace Heidt, Guy Lombardo and Wayne King — or any who were members of bands that appeared on sponsored programs. They picked up extra paychecks for their work.

Not so lucky were their brethren who worked the late night shift — playing on unsponsored dance band remotes from hotels, nightclubs and ballrooms.

That was just part of their job.

THE MAN FROM INDIANA

CBS executives Ed Klauber and Paul White had an idea that the promotion minded network embraced immediately. The concept was a Multiple Run, five minute news summary and commentary

carved from the end of the hour at 8:55, five nights a week. They reasoned that it was a service to listeners, a promotional boost for the CBS news image and one that could eventually became another profit source for the network.

They were right on all three counts.

Their choice for the job was neither the mellow-voiced Bob Trout or John Daly, but a newcomer to CBS, 50-year-old former *New York Times* editor, Elmer Davis. The Indiana native didn't have the voice for network radio, but he had the brains.

Davis went on the air in mid–September. His five-minute capsules weren't rated by Hooper but Davis' nasal, matter-of-fact delivery of the news interspersed with incisive comments quickly established him as a major voice in news.

Within several years Davis would have an even greater influence on the news America heard when he became the Director of the U.S. Office of War Information.

TOP 50 PROGRAMS — 1939–40

CBS 28, NBC 17, Blue 5
Average Rating: 15.1, Median: 13.4
27,500,000 Radio Homes / 79.9% Coverage of U.S. Homes / One Rating Point = 275,000 Homes
Source: C.E. Hooper Monthly Network Reports, Sep, 1939–Jun, 1940
Total Programs Rated 6–11 P.M.: 122
Programs Rated 13 Weeks & Ranked: 107

		Program	Rtg	Type	Sponsor	Day	Time	Lgth	Net
1	*2*	Jack Benny Program	30.9	SC	Jello Gelatin	Sun	7:00	30	NBC
2	*1*	Edgar Bergen & Charlie McCarthy	30.7	CV	Chase & Sanborn Coffee	Sun	8:00	30	NBC 1
3	*5*	Fibber McGee & Molly	24.8	SC	Johnson Wax	Tue	9:30	30	NBC
4	*3*	Lux Radio Theater/Cecil B DeMille	23.7	DA	Lux Soap	Mon	9:00	60	CBS
5	*12*	Bob Hope Show	23.1	CV	Pepsodent Toothpaste	Tue	10:00	30	NBC
6	*4*	Bing Crosby's Kraft Music Hall	21.1	MV	Kraft Cheese	Thu	10:00	60	NBC
7	*16*	One Man's Family	20.3	DCC	Tenderleaf Tea	Sun	8:30	30	NBC 2
8	*19*	Walter Winchell's Jergens Journal	19.3	NC	Jergens Lotion	Sun	9:00	15	Blue
9	*10*	Major Bowes Original Amateur Hour	18.4	TC	Chrysler Corporation	Thu	9:00	60	CBS
10t	*9*	Kay Kyser Kollege of Musical Knowledge	18.0	APQ	Lucky Strike Cigarettes	Wed	10:00	60	NBC
10t	*N*	Pot O Gold/Ben Grauer, Horace Heidt	18.0	MV	Tums Antacid Tablets	Tue	8:30	30	NBC
12	*6*	Good News of 1940/F Brice,	16.9	CV	Maxwell House Coffee	Thu	9:00	30	NBC 3
13	*16*	Kate Smith Hour	16.8	MV	Grape Nuts Cereal	Fri	8:00	60	CBS
14	*14*	Fred Allen Show	16.3	CV	Ipana/Sal Hepatica	Wed	9:00	60	NBC
15	*24*	We the People/Gabriel Heatter	15.5	API	Sanka Coffee	Tue	9:00	30	CBS
16	*31*	First Nighter Program	15.4	DA	Campana Balm	Fri	9:30	30	CBS
17	*27*	Fitch Bandwagon	15.2	MP	Fitch Shampoo	Sun	7:30	30	NBC
18	*14*	Big Town/Edward G Robinson	14.9	DCC	Rinso Laundry Soap	Tue	8:00	30	CBS
19	*25*	Gangbusters	14.7	DA	Cue Magazine	Sat	8:00	30	CBS
20	*19*	Lowell Thomas News	14.5	NC	Sun Oil	M-F	6:45	15	Blue
21	*11*	Burns & Allen Show	14.3	CV	Hinds Hand Cream	Wed	7:30	30	CBS

	Program	Rtg	Type	Sponsor	Day	Time	Lgth	Net
22t 35	Guy Lombardo Orch	13.6	MP	Lady Esther Cosmetics	Mon	10:00	30	CBS
22t 22	Your Hit Parade/Lanny Ross, Barry Wood	13.6	MP	Lucky Strike Cigarettes	Sat	9:00	45	CBS
24t 23	Al Pearce Gang	13.4	CV	Camel Cigarettes	Fri	7:30	30	CBS 4
24t 18	Rudy Vallee Show	13.4	MV	Sealtest Dairies	Thu	9:30	30	NBC
24t N	Silver Theater	13.4	DA	International Silver	Sun	6:00	30	CBS
27t 42	Battle of The Sexes/Crumit, Sanderson	13.1	APQ	Molle Shaving Cream	Tues	9:00	30	NBC
27t 66	Information Please	13.1	PS	Canada Dry Ginger Ale	Tue	8:30	30	Blue
29 40	Screen Guild Theater	12.8	DA	Gulf Oil	Sun	7:30	30	CBS
30t N	Ken Murray Texaco Star Theater	12.6	CV	Texaco	Wed	9:00	60	CBS
30t 52	Russ Morgan Orch	12.6	MP	Philip Morris Cigarettes	Fri	9:00	30	CBS
30t N	Wayne King Orch	12.6	MP	Cashmere Bouquet Soap	Sat	8:30	30	CBS
33t N	Aldrich Family/Ezra Stone	12.2	SC	Jello Puddings	Tue	8:00	30	Blue
33t 35	Pick & Pat's Model Minstrels	12.2	MSP	Model Pipe Tobacco	Mon	8:30	30	CBS
33t 76	Those We Love	12.2	DCC	Teel Liquid Dentifrice	Mon	8:30	30	CBS
36 32	Tommy Riggs & Betty Lou	12.0	SC	Quaker Oats	Mon	8:00	30	NBC
37 48	Grand Central Station	11.9	DA	Listerine Antiseptic	Fri	10:00	30	CBS
38 39	Professor Quiz/Craig Earl	11.8	APQ	Teel Liquid Dentifrice	Fri	7:30	30	CBS
39t 59	Ask It Basket/Jim McWilliams	11.7	APQ	Colgate Dental Cream	Thu	8:00	30	CBS
39t N	Blondie/Penny Singleton, Arthur Lake	11.7	SC	Camel Cigarettes	Mon	7:30	30	CBS
39t 79	Dr Christian/Jean Hersholt	11.7	DCC	Vaseline	Wed	8:30	30	CBS 5
42t N	Adventures of Sherlock Holmes	11.4	DCC	Bromo Quinine Cold Tablets	Mon	8:00	30	Blue
42t N	Stop Me If You've Heard This One	11.4	PS	Quaker Oats	Sat	8:30	30	NBC
44t 45	Second Husband/Helen Menken	11.2	DCC	Bayer Aspirin	Tue	7:30	30	CBS
44t 26	Hollywood Playhouse	11.2	DA	Woodbury Soap/Jergens	Wed	8:00	30	NBC
46 12	Campbell Playhouse	11.0	DA	Campbell Soup	Sun	8:00	60	CBS
47t 29	Amos & Andy	10.8	SC	Campbell Soup	M-F	7:00	15	CBS
47t 66	Ford Sunday Evening Hour	10.8	MC	Ford Motor Co	Sun	9:00	60	CBS
47t N	Pipe Smoking Time	10.8	MST	Model Pipe Tobacco	Mon	8:30	30	CBS
47t N	What's My Name?/Arlene Francis	10.8	APQ	Oxydol Laundry Soap	Fri	9:30	30	NBC 6

New & Returning Top 50 Programs Underscored.

1	Edgar Bergen & Charlie McCarthy	Sep–Dec	Chase & Sanborn Coffee	Sun	8:00	60	NBC
2	One Man's Family	Sep–Dec	Tenderleaf Tea	Thu	8:00	60	NBC
3	Good News of 1940	Sep–Mar	Maxwell House Coffee	Thu	9:00	60	NBC
4	Al Pearce Gang	Sep–Mar	Dole Pineapple	Wed	8:00	30	CBS
5	Dr Christian	Nov–Dec	Vaseline	Wed	10:00	30	CBS
6	What's My Name	Sep–Mar	Oxydol Laundry Soap	Sat	7:00	30	NBC

Key: API — Audience Participation/Interviews
APQ — Audience Participation/Quiz
APS — Audience Participation/Stunts
CV — Comedy/Variety Show
DA — Dramatic Anthology

DCC — Drama/Continuing Characters
MC — Music/Classical, Semi-Classical
MP — Music/Popular, Contemporary
MSP — Music/Specialty, Ethnic
MST — Music/Standard, Traditional

MV — Music/Variety Show
NC — News, Commentary
PS — Panel Show Comedy
SC — Situation Comedy
TC — Talent Competition

1939–40 Top 50 Favorite Formats

	Programs	Pct
Drama — Anthology & Continuing	14	28%
Comedy — All Categories	15	30%
Music — All Categories	13	26%
Audience Participation — All Categories	6	12%
News/Commentary	2	4%

1939–40 Monthly Winners

Sep	Edgar Bergen & Charlie McCarthy	22.1	Feb	Jack Benny Program	36.7
Oct	Edgar Bergen & Charlie McCarthy	27.7	Mar	Jack Benny Program	35.4
Nov	Jack Benny Program	34.4	Apr	Edgar Bergen & Charlie McCarthy	35.9
Dec	Edgar Bergen & Charlie McCarthy	31.2	May	Edgar Bergen & Charlie McCarthy	28.3
Jan	Edgar Bergen & Charlie McCarthy	34.6	Jun	Edgar Bergen & Charlie McCarthy	23.7

13

The 1940–41 Network Season

Announcer: Here's a message of importance to millions of people who are continually pale and washed-out, weak and run-down. Doctors will tell you that these conditions are often caused by a <u>deficiency of iron</u> ... the iron you need to build healthy blood, to keep your body functioning properly and to keep you physically fit and mentally alert! <u>Ironized Yeast Tablets</u> provide you with a simple and effective way to get the daily iron that your body requires. <u>Ironized Yeast</u> is a concentrated iron tonic combined with a high potency brewers' yeast, one of the natural sources of <u>Vitamin B-1</u>. And every daily dose of <u>Ironized Yeast</u> gives you more than your daily minimum iron requirement in a form that your body can easily use and put to work. Of course, power and weakness can come from other causes, so see your doctor regularly. But clinical studies show that <u>two</u> <u>out</u> <u>of</u> three <u>women</u> ... particularly those between 15 and 50 ... and many, many men <u>lack sufficient iron</u>! So, if <u>you're</u> not getting the iron <u>your</u> body needs ... if you're <u>weak</u>, <u>run down</u> or easily upset ... get <u>new</u> <u>pep</u>, <u>vigor</u> and <u>color</u> for only a <u>few</u> <u>pennies</u> a <u>day</u>. Start taking <u>Ironized Yeast</u> tomorrow!

THE SWEET SPELL OF SUCCESS

Things couldn't have been going better for the radio industry. Total 1940 revenues went flying by $200 Million *(3.23 Bil.)*, up 30 percent from the 1938 slowdown. The networks kept pace, accounting for over $100 Million in billings — a 27 percent increase in the same two year period.

Hundreds of stations were mandated to shift their frequencies in March 1941, to comply with the Interference Provisions of the North American Radio Agreement. To some stations the shift required major capital investment in equipment and new transmitting towers but the industry took it in stride. Radio was proving to be the business star of an otherwise dismal decade — there was plenty of money coming in to pay for any technical costs.

Further, the industry's preparedness in two critical areas was paying rewards.

EARLY SOUNDS OF WAR REACH AMERICA

The London Blitz began on September 7, 1940, and continued for eight months. The networks had reporters and facilities in place to give their listeners spot coverage of the daily bombings and dogfights over the city. America's entry in World War II was still over a year away but shortwave news reports from the battle fronts and world capitals had established Network Radio as a necessity for news in over 80 percent of the country's homes.

Meanwhile, broadcasters were more directly involved in another war over music and money.

A DUNCE CAP FOR ASCAP

Broadcast Music Inc., created by the industry a year earlier as an alternative to ASCAP and its proposed hike in music fees, had built a catalog of 20,000 songs by September. BMI had opened the doors to country, gospel, rhythm and blues and folk music — genres that ASCAP almost ignored.

BMI music was being recorded, played on radio and accepted by the public. In addition, BMI was buying complete music libraries from publishers. When the networks' ASCAP licenses expired on New Years Eve, 1940, BMI's catalog numbered nearly 50,000 titles.

Radio's boycott of ASCAP music began on January 1, 1941, and was hardly noticed — except by the broadcasters who were vigilant against any of ASCAP's two million songs getting on their air by accident which could result in a $250 fine per station for each violation *($3,850)*. If a network should slip-up, the fine could amount to $20,000 *($307,800)*.

Some local stations, mostly independents which relied on recorded music, signed with ASCAP for the programming advantage its music provided, but the networks hung tough for five months.

Mutual became the first network to negotiate a settlement with ASCAP, which was losing tens of thousands of dollars every day while the boycott lasted. The Society's loss had reached two million dollars in May when Mutual and ASCAP agreed to a new ten year contract calling for an annual blanket fee of only three percent of network revenues — two percent *less* than the previous rate.

1940–41 Season Scoreboard Mid-season Totals, December 1940		Compared to Year Earlier	
Total Radio Homes	28.5 Mil	+1.0 Mil	+3.6%
Total Auto Radios	7.5 Mil	+1.0 Mil	+13.3%
Total AM Radio Stations	765	+43	+6.0%
Total Radio Network Affiliates	454	+58	+14.6%
1940 Radio Revenues	215.6 Mil	+31.8 Mil	+17.3%
1940 Network Revenues	113.3 Mil	+14.7 Mil	+14.9%
Network Share	52.6%		(1.0%)

NBC and CBS took their time and completed the season offering nothing but BMI and public domain music, saving millions in ASCAP royalties.

They'd need the money for yet another legal fight just ahead

A FLY IN THE OINTMENT

FCC Chairman James Fly, an appointee of the Roosevelt administration, issued the commission's 150 page *Report on Chain Broadcasting* in May 1941. The networks knew it was coming — it had been over three years of congressional subcommittee hearings in the making.

But they still didn't understand to what lengths the once passive FCC would go to placate an administration and Congress which were convinced that the networks were just too successful to be legal.

Fly spoke for his four member FCC majority and called the report a "Magna Charta for American Broadcasting Stations."

Broadcasters had different names for it.

NAB President Neville Miller called it, "A usurpation of power that has no justification in Law."

The Report on Chain Broadcasting boiled down to eight edicts dictated to the networks and their affiliated stations to take effect within 90 days. Seven of the eight provisions — dealing with affiliation and territorial exclusivity, length of affiliation contracts, affiliate rights to refuse network programming and multiple station ownership in a single market — turned out to have little effect on what Americans heard or where they heard it.

But one provision was aimed squarely at NBC's ownership of two networks — the Red Network of 74 stations and the Blue chain of 92 affiliates.

The FCC imposed its "trust-busting" ruling through its power to license individual stations.

It decreed that no license would be given or renewed to any station affiliated with a network that simultaneously operated two networks.

The language was awkward but its message was clear: NBC had to dump one of its two networks to stay in business.

CBS and NBC vowed to fight the mandates in court while Mutual relished the prospect of a potentially large pool of program clearances available from their powerful affiliates. The underdog network sided with the FCC.

The battle between the broadcasters and bureaucrats would extend into the following season.

In October 1941, the FCC watered down seven of the eight edicts and temporarily suspended its order that NBC sell one of its two networks. But Blue was already on the auction block.

NBC RED, BLUE AND PURPLE

The Report on Chain Broadcasting suggests that network affiliate rosters were inflexible from one city and program to the next

That wasn't the case.

C.E. Hooper surveyed network program popularity in 30 major cities. Most of the highest rated programs were carried in all 30 markets by the originating network's local affiliate.

But some programs, even Top 50 caliber shows, were not heard on the full networks in all cities.

Sponsors determined the geographical regions for advertising coverage and the networks provided the affiliates to suit those purposes. The 1940–41 season presented the following examples:

Vox Pop was heard in only 19 of Hooper's 30 markets where Kentucky Club Tobacco was sold.

Al Pearce's Gang was broadcast in 23 of the 30 cities per orders of R.J. Reynolds' Camel Cigarettes.

Both shows originated from CBS, which seldom farmed out its programs to alternate, secondary affiliates.

NBC and Blue network programs were something else again.

In the 1940–41 season, Burns and Allen were heard in 26 cities from NBC affiliates and in four markets on Blue network stations.

The new *Rudy Vallee Show* for Sealtest was broadcast by 21 NBC stations, four Blue affiliates and simply wasn't heard in five of the 30 surveyed markets. As always, the sponsor called the shots.

Blue's Lowell Thomas — headed

for NBC in three years — was already heard on five NBC affiliates every weeknight in 1940–41.

Walter Winchell's *Jergens Journal* was Blue's most popular program. But in 13 of Hooper's 30 surveyed cities, Winchell was broadcast on the local NBC station.

Unlike big brother Bing's *Kraft Music Hall* that was heard over the full NBC network, Bob Crosby's Camel Caravan at 7:30 on Thursday was aired by a mix of 13 NBC stations, six Blue affiliates plus one Mutual outlet.

The number of NBC affiliates available to Bob Crosby was limited because the network split on Thursday to feed H.V. Kaltenborn's 7:45 newscast for Pure Oil to nine NBC stations and two Blue affiliates.

What was that again about operating separate networks simultaneously?

THE MONTHLIES

CBS claimed 24 of the season's Top 50 programs and had most of the nightly Top Ten programs. It would be CBS's best ratings season for the next nine years but the network didn't win first place in any the year's monthly ratings.

NBC's Jack Benny and Edgar Bergen competed for the top spot of each month's ratings from September through March. *Fibber McGee & Molly* was the surprising new Number One show in April, Bergen took May and *Fibber* repeated in June.

The three NBC comedies ran the network's string of consecutive monthly wins to 61.

1940–41 Sunday Night
Top Ten Programs (11)
CBS 4, NBC 4, Blue 3
Average: 16.5

Jack Benny Program	NBC	7:00	30.8
Edgar Bergen & Charlie McCarthy	NBC	8:00	27.3
Walter Winchell's Jergens Journal	Blue	9:00	24.1
One Man's Family	NBC	8:30	16.9
Screen Guild Theater	CBS	7:30	15.3
Fitch Bandwagon	NBC	7:30	14.4
The Parker Family	Blue	9:15	13.0
Take It or Leave It	CBS	10:00	12.9
Helen Hayes Theater	CBS	8:00	12.0

| Adventures of Sherlock Holmes | Blue | 8:30 | 10.2 |
| Silver Theater | CBS | 6:00 | 10.2 |

BUCK BENNY'S BIG BUCKS

Jack Benny's repeat with the season's Number One program was helped along with the summer release of Paramount's *Buck Benny Rides Again*, a western spoof that introduced his radio gang — Eddie "Rochester" Anderson, Phil Harris, Dennis Day and Don Wilson — to movie audiences.

General Foods' Jello was in its seventh season of sponsoring the comedian's top rated Sunday night show. The company spent $650,000 *(10.5 Mil)*, for the season's 35 half hours with Benny's troupe on NBC. Of that sum, the comedian took home $350,000 *(5.7 Mil)*.

Late in the season when Benny's ratings had assured him of the season's Number One program, NBC threw a black tie gala honoring his first ten years in Network Radio.

NBC's Hollywood based comedy stars performed at the banquet for 800 invited guests — i.e., sponsors and advertising agencies — held at Hollywood's Biltmore Hotel. Emcee Rudy Vallee introduced Bob Hope, Burns and Allen, Jim and Marian Jordan, Edgar Bergen and Charlie McCarthy and George Jessel who each paid a roast-like tribute to the honoree.

It was also announced that Benny had secured a personal ten-year option on his NBC contract which gave him ownership of his program and the freedom to sell it to the highest bidding sponsor.

NBC President Niles Trammell climaxed the affair by giving Benny two gold keys that would unlock any door in NBC's New York or Hollywood headquarters.

Benny jumped to CBS nine years later and had no need for the keys.

THE QUIPSTER'S QUIZ

At 32, Bob Hawk was already a quick witted, four year veteran of low-budget Mutual quiz shows — *Foolish Questions, Fun Quiz, Name Three,* and *Quixie Doodles*. He was considered a natural for Eversharp Pen & Pencil's new *Take It or Leave*

It on CBS. The audience participation quiz and its grand prize of $64 *($1,034)*, for contestants' correct answers to a sequence of seven questions was slotted against the soft competition of Phil Spitalny's *Hour of Charm* orchestra on NBC and John J. Anthony's tear jerking *Goodwill Hour* on Blue.

It was the first of *Take It or Leave It*'s eight consecutive Top 50 seasons and nine in Sunday's Top Ten.

1940–41 Monday Night Top Ten Programs
CBS 7, NBC 2, Blue 1
Average: 13.2

Lux Radio Theater	CBS	9:00	23.4
Lowell Thomas News*	Blue	6:45	14.2
Guy Lombardo's Lady Esther Serenade	CBS	10:00	13.6
Burns & Allen Show	NBC	7:30	12.8
Gay 90's Revue	CBS	8:30	12.7
Blondie	CBS	7:30	11.8
Those We Love	CBS	8:00	11.6
Amos & Andy*	CBS	7:00	10.8
Dr IQ	NBC	9:00	10.7
Pipe Smoking Time	CBS	8:30	10.5

*Monday–Friday Strip Shows
Sans Strips...

Avalon Showboat	NBC	9:30	10.4
Lanny Ross Show*	CBS	7:15	10.4

IQ OKAY

Doctor IQ was brought to Chicago and the Blue Network by Mars Candies in the spring of 1939 after a successful regional run in Texas.

Like so many promising series first heard on Blue, *Doctor IQ* was moved to NBC where it became the network's needed counter-programming prescription against CBS's *Lux Radio Theater*. The fast paced quiz attracted double digit ratings immediately.

By 1941, *Doctor IQ* had evolved into a permanent road show, originating broadcasts from major city movie palaces from coast to coast where it finished the first of its five seasons as one of Monday's Top Ten programs.

That was a major accomplishment, considering it was slotted against *Lux* for six of its ten seasons on NBC.

Dubbed "The Mental Banker," *Doctor IQ* was the creation of producer Lee Segall and hosted by Lew

Valentine, 26, recruited from WOAI in San Antonio. Valentine, replaced during his military service by an equally talented Jimmy McClain, had the knack of sounding professorial and kindly, yet paced the tightly produced program with over 35 sets of questions and answers per half hour.

Contestants for the rapid fire quiz were audience members chosen by the host's six assistants — local NBC affiliate announcers who roamed the theaters with remote microphones, awarding silver dollars to contestants for correct answers.

Doctor IQ usually attracted an audience that averaged half the size of *Lux Radio Theater*.

But considering that *Lux* cost up to five times as much to produce and *Doctor IQ* regularly reached over three million homes in its peak years, both the candy company and the network had a sweet deal.

RADIO'S PERIPATETIC PAIR

Burns and Allen returned for their second series on NBC, this time for Minnesota meat processor Hormel, makers of SPAM. As so often happened in switches of network, day and time, George and Gracie lost audience. Although the loss was only ten percent it was enough to knock their season ranking down to 30th — the couple's all time low. The bounced back the next season — in yet another new day and time.

THOSE WE SHOVE

Few programs could match Burns and Allen's hopping around the calendars, clocks and networks.

Those We Love did — in spades.

From 1938 until 1941, the half hour soap opera created by Agnes Ridgway had gone through three major corporate sponsors and three networks' prime time schedules. Then, despite two consecutive Top 50 seasons of double digit ratings, it was cancelled in June 1941, and left radio for a year.

Those We Love was eventually brought back in 1942 by Bristol-Myers as Eddie Cantor's Wednesday night summer replacement — picking up the story line that had been interrupted for 13 months.

General Foods then took over *Those We Love* in the fall of 1942 and parked it for three seasons on NBC's Sunday afternoon schedule from September into June. During the summer months General Foods took it off its Sunday afternoon run and used it first as a summer replacement for Jack Benny and then for Frank Morgan.

When *Those We Love* left the air in 1945 it had undergone five network changes and nine jumps in days and times of broadcast — all in a span of seven seasons.

The soap opera's star throughout its tumultuous run was young film actress Nan Grey, who by 1941 at the age of 23 already had 36 B movies — *Dracula's Daughter*, *The Invisible Man Returns*, etc. — to her credit. She married singer Frankie Laine in 1950 and retired, never to know what her radio series might have done had it been given the opportunity to become rooted in a permanent timeslot.

BROWN & WILLIAMSON SPLITS AIRS

Brown & Williamson was an active radio advertiser later associated with Top Ten hits Red Skelton and *People Are Funny*. The tobacco company engineered a interesting maneuver on Monday nights during the 1940–41 season by splitting NBC for two separate programs.

The primary feed, broadcast by 21 NBC affiliates, *The Avalon Showboat*, was a pale copy of the former network hit. The traditional music review was sponsored by B&W's Avalon Cigarettes.

Simultaneously, eight powerful NBC affiliates in the south broadcast Brown &Williamson's *Renfro Valley Folks* starring country singer Red Foley and rural comedian Whitey Ford, aka "The Duke of Paducah." Their down home *Renfro Valley* show pitched B&W's Big Ben brand of loose tobacco for chewers and smokers who rolled their own cigarettes.

Foley and Ford also hosted Brown & Williamson's *Plantation Party* for Bugler Tobacco across the full NBC network on Wednesdays.

Neither *Showboat* nor *Renfro Valley* hit Monday's Top Ten against the second half hour of CBS's top

rated *Lux Radio Theater*. However, it was an early and rare example of demographically targeted programming using split network feeds.

1940–41 Tuesday Night Top Ten Programs
CBS 5, NBC 4, Blue 1
Average: 15.0

Fibber McGee & Molly	NBC	9:30	27.6
Bob Hope Show	NBC	10:00	26.6
We the People	CBS	9:00	15.3
Lowell Thomas News*	Blue	6:45	14.2
First Nighter	CBS	8:30	12.8
HV Kaltenborn News	NBC	7:45	11.6
Amos & Andy*	CBS	7:00	10.8
Court of Missing Heirs	CBS	8:00	10.4
Lanny Ross Show*	CBS	7:15	10.4
Battle of the Sexes	NBC	9:00	10.3

*Monday–Friday Strip Shows

Sans Strips...

Tums Treasure Chest	NBC	8:30	9.7
Grand Central Station	Blue	9:00	9.4
Johnny Presents	NBC	8:00	9.4

THE WIMP OF WISTFUL VISTA

Fibber McGee & Molly turned in Tuesday's most popular program for the third consecutive season and continued the show's climb up to Annual Top 50 to Number Two, behind Jack Benny. The sitcom was destined to finish in second place for a record nine seasons.

Young radio veteran Bill Thompson, 27, had been with the cast of *FM&M* since its Chicago days in 1936, voicing an assortment of characters, most notably the raspy voiced, "Old Timer," who countered Fibber's tall tales with what had become a national catchphrase, "That ain't the way I heerd it."

On April 15, 1941, Thompson introduced one of creator Don Quinn's most endearing characters to Wistful Vista: "Wallace Wimple," the henpecked, mush mouthed bird watcher who was constantly fearful of his, "...big, ol' wife, Sweetie Face" The domineering Cornelia Wimple was never heard, but her acts of spousal abuse were described in detail every week by her meek, secretly vengeful husband who fantasized her doom to the McGee's with an evil chuckle.

Thompson's hilarious Wimple voice inspired legendary MGM cartoon director Tex Avery to create a character to suit it — *Droopy Dog*, the slow talking, slower moving canine detective who always got his critter.

Except for Thompson's leave of absence for military duty, his character remained the McGees' neighbor for the remainder of the show's successful Tuesday night run.

A HOT HEATTER

While *Fibber McGee & Molly* and Bob Hope provided Tuesday's one-two punch for NBC, Gabriel Heatter piloted CBS' *We the People* into becoming the night's third most popular program and another winner for General Foods. The human interest interview potpourri completed its second consecutive season in the annual Top 15. Its ratings averaged over 15 points for those two seasons.

Heatter was also in his fifth year at Mutual and the network's top rated attraction. His weeknight — *except Tuesday*—news and commentary at 9:00 reached some two million homes and five million listeners each night. That number would nearly double before the end of World War II as Heatter became the voice of reasoned optimism. The tide of the war eventually supported his enthusiastic nightly opening, "Ahh, there's good news tonight!"

HORACE'S HEIGHTS

Moving *Pot o' Gold* to Blue's Thursday schedule left sponsor Lewis-Howe's Tums with a hole in NBC's Tuesday lineup. Tums filled the timeslot with Horace Heidt, his "Musical Knights" and what could be implied from its title to be another giveaway show, *Tums Treasure Chest*.

Heidt — still co-hosting *Pot o' Gold* on Blue, was the solo host of *Treasure Chest*, an alluring name for a program that was primarily music, spotlighting soloists from his show band. Heidt became one of the few network stars to simultaneously host two prime time programs on two different networks.

"Tums for the Tummy," kept Heidt in NBC's 8:30 timeslot for

four seasons — a tribute to his showmanship and salesmanship to keep a sponsor happy for a program that never won its time period with ratings that only hovered around a ten.

1940–41 Wednesday Night Top Ten Programs
CBS 6, NBC 3, Blue 1
Average: 13.4

Kay Kyser's Kollege of Musical Knowledge	NBC	10:00	16.6
Big Town	CBS	8:00	16.0
Eddie Cantor's Time to Smile	NBC	9:00	15.0
Mr. District Attorney	NBC	9:30	14.7
Lowell Thomas News*	Blue	6:45	14.2
Fred Allen's Texaco Star Theater	CBS	9:00	13.5
Dr Christian	CBS	8:30	13.3
Amos & Andy*	CBS	7:00	10.8
Lanny Ross Show*	CBS	7:15	10.4
Meet Mr. Meek	CBS	7:30	9.5

*Monday–Friday Strip Shows

Sans Strips...
Hollywood Play-house	NBC	8:00	9.4
Quiz Kids	Blue	8:00	8.7
Plantation Party	NBC	8:30	8.4

CLASS SHOWS

Kay Kyser's *College of Musical Knowledge* continued to lead the pack on Wednesday, helped along by the release of the second of his five musical comedies for RKO Radio Pictures and a patriotic effort that Bob Hope adopted a few months later.

You'll Find Out was released in November and opens with an abbreviated version of Kyser's radio show showcasing the orchestra, singers and comedians whom had become radio and record favorites.

On February 26, 1941, Kyser took his 15 bandsmen and singers on the road to the U.S. Marine Base at San Diego and became the first in a parade of Hollywood-based network stars to originate programs from military installations for the entertainment of the troops.

It was just the first in thousands of shows, both on and off the air, that Kyser and his troupe would perform for servicemen during World War II.

FRED AND ED HEAD TO HEAD

Fred Allen refused Bristol Myers' request to trim his NBC Wednesday night comedy hour back to 30 minutes. He was fired and jumped to the welcoming arms of CBS and Texaco who gladly gave him a full hour at his familiar 9:00 timeslot on Wednesday. He lost nearly 20 percent of his audience in the move and finished behind the two half hour programs that filled the hour he vacated on NBC.

Bristol Myers replaced him on NBC with Eddie Cantor who returned to radio after a year's layoff resulting from a sponsor backlash to his political remarks deemed controversial in 1939. To clinch the deal for his comeback, Cantor came up with a unique offer that he be paid $10,000 per week *($161,600)*, to cover the entire expense of the show, plus a weekly bonus of $200 *($3,200)* for each rating point could he deliver over a base of 20 points.

Cantor never came close to his bonus goal but he did entrench himself into Wednesdays at 9:00 on NBC with a Top 20 program for the next six seasons.

Following Cantor's lead-in, Bristol Myers installed a revamped *Mr. District Attorney* for its Vitalis Hair Tonic. It immediately challenged *Big Town* as Network Radio's highest rated mystery/adventure series The Ed Byron production would call 9:30 on Wednesday its home for twelve seasons and finish in the annual Top Ten three times.

1940–41 Thursday Night Top Ten Programs
NBC 5, CBS 4, Blue 1
Average: 14.7

The Aldrich Family	NBC	8:30	22.1
Major Bowes' Original Amateur Hour	CBS	9:00	18.2
Fanny Brice & Frank Morgan	NBC	8:00	18.0
Bing Crosby's Kraft Music Hall	NBC	9:00	15.6
Rudy Vallee Show	NBC	10:00	14.4
Lowell Thomas News*	Blue	6:45	14.2
HV Kaltenborn News	NBC	7:45	11.6
Vex Pop	CBS	7:30	11.3

Amos & Andy*	CBS	7:00	10.8
Lanny Ross Show*	CBS	7:15	10.4

*Monday–Friday Strip Shows

Sans Strips...
Pot o' Gold	Blue	8:00	9.7
Professor Quiz	CBS	10:15	8.3
Ask It Basket	CBS	8:00	8.0

NBC SHUFFLES ITS LOADED DECK

NBC reshuffled its winning Thursday schedule with moves that continued to win the night and laid the foundation for a complete dominance two years later.

Rudy Vallee's Sealtest show was moved from 8:30 to 10:00.

To accommodate Vallee, Bing Crosby's *Kraft Music Hall* was moved back an hour to 9:00 and into direct competition with *Major Bowes' Original Amateur Hour* on CBS. The shift seemed questionable at first because Crosby lost over 25 percent of his audience along with *Music Hall*'s three year title as Thursday's most popular program.

More surprisingly, Crosby lost his head to head competition with Bowes. The Major's ratings held rock steady despite his new competition from America's most popular crooner.

General Foods made the greatest contribution to NBC's Thursday ratings when it snapped up the 8:00 timeslot vacated by Bristol Myers' cancellation of the weak George Jesse variety show, *For Men Only.*

The half hour became the new home for *Maxwell House Coffee Time* hosted by Frank Morgan and featured Fanny Brice's *Baby Snooks* skits.

Following the Morgan/Brice show at 8:30, General Foods' Jell-O desserts introduced the family sitcom which became the hottest show of the season.

ALDRICH RICH IN RATINGS

The Aldrich Family, based on Clifford Goldsmith's Broadway play, *What a Life*, had scored a 12.2 rating and a 33rd place finish the previous season on Blue. It was Blue's fourth most popular program, aided by Paramount's October 1939, release of *What a Life* starring Jackie Cooper as the comedy's lead character, Henry Aldrich.

But millions of listeners were already familiar with the adolescent-cracking voice of radio's Henry Aldrich, 23-year-old Ezra Stone. Since 1938 *Aldrich Family* skits had been popular features in both the Rudy Vallee and Kate Smith variety hours.

In June 1940, General Foods moved the sitcom from Blue to NBC as Jack Benny's summer replacement. Given that launch and the cushy full season timeslot following Frank Morgan and Fanny Brice, *The Aldrich Family* began a series of four consecutive seasons as Thursday's Number One show and four annual Top Ten finishes among all network programs.

THE END OF THE RAINBOW

Tums moved its *Pot o' Gold* to Blue with predictable results given the program's downward trend in ratings on NBC over the previous season. Listeners had realized by then that they could enjoy *Baby Snooks* and Frank Morgan on NBC without jeopardizing their chances of winning the *Pot o' Gold* jackpot on Blue.

There was, after all, no need to tune into *Pot o' Gold* to win the $1,000 prize — all listeners had to do was be at home and pick up the phone. The program was one of the last to overlook the basic requirement of radio giveaways to accomplish their audience building objective: *Listeners had to listen to win*.

Claims that *Pot o' Gold* violated lottery laws were dismissed in court, ruling that possession of a radio and telephone did not constitute monetary consideration. Although the courts ruled in favor of the program, it was too late — the audience had already ruled against it.

Not even a movie released in April based on the show — *Pot o' Gold*, starring James Stewart, Paulette Goddard and Horace Heist — could revive its ratings. After a dramatic drop from 10th to 53rd in the season's rankings, the show was cancelled.

By the end of its run, *Pot o' Gold* had awarded a total of $89,000 *(1.4 Mil)*, to lucky telephone answerers. Ironically, the last phone call the program made went unanswered

and the remaining jackpot of $1,800 was given to the Red Cross.

An attempt to revive the show six years later on Blue — then known as ABC — failed miserably.

VOX POPULAR AGAIN

Vex Pop was in a slump. The interview show had fallen out of the annual Top 50 in the 1938–39 season and continued to lose audience when sponsor Kentucky Club Tobacco moved it to CBS' Thursday schedule the following season.

Then, beginning in July 1940, the program did an about face and marched back to popularity to a martial beat.

With World War II looming, hosts Parks Johnson and Wally Butterworth took their microphones to the Merchant Marine training ship *Empire State* in New London, Connecticut, and converted the program to a patriotic stance with interviews from military bases and defense plants. *Vex Pop*'s ratings responded immediately and the show was back in the season's Top 50.

Butterworth left the program in 1942 and was replaced by handsome B-movie actor Warren Hull, but the program was on a roll. By the end of 1945, *Vex Pop* had broadcast from over 200 bases, veterans' hospitals and defense factories, scoring double digit ratings and Top 50 finishes throughout the war years.

1940–41 Friday Night
Top Ten Programs
CBS 7, Blue 2, NBC 1
Average: 12.1

Kate Smith Hour	CBS	8:00	16.1
Lowell Thomas News*	Blue	6:45	14.2
Information Please	NBC	8:30	12.9
Campbell Playhouse	CBS	9:30	12.8
Al Pearce Gang	CBS	7:30	12.2
Gangbusters	Blue	9:00	12.0
Amos & Andy*	CBS	7:00	10.8
Lanny Ross Show*	CBS	7:15	10.4
Robert Ripley's Believe It or Not	CBS	10:00	9.9
Russ Morgan Orchestra	CBS	9:00	9.5

*Monday–Friday Strip Shows

Sans Strips...
Waltz Time	NBC	9:00	8.8
Everyman's Theater	NBC	9:30	8.1

Hollywood Premiere	CBS	10:00	8.1

LOLLY POPS UP AGAIN

Hollywood Premiere was Louella Parsons' return to CBS in the March ratings replacing Robert Ripley's *Believe It or Not*. Parson's new show was another *Lux Radio Theater* wannabe — 30 minute audio playlets adapted from current movies followed by interviews with their stars.

"Loveable Lolly" again attempted to coerce movie stars to appear free of charge, using her popular Hearst newspaper column as her weapon. But this time both the Screen Actors Guild and AFRA resisted.

Parsons backed down and begrudgingly paid her guests union scale — but never more than that.

DIVORCE GRANTED

Mutual's dramatic series depicting marital problems, *I Want a Divorce!*, was low on the Friday night ratings chart, scoring a feeble 5.7 at 9:30 against CBS' timeslot winner, *Campbell Playhouse*. The show starred 1930s movie blonde bombshell/comedienne, Joan Blondell, who was an expert on the show's subject — she was married and divorced three times. The program lasted less than her marriages — it was cancelled after 26 weeks.

1940–41 Saturday Night
Top Ten Programs
CBS 5, NBC 5
Average: 9.7

Truth or Consequences	NBC	8:30	13.6
Your Hit Parade	CBS	9:00	13.0
HV Kaltenborn News	NBC	7:45	11.6
Knickerbocker Playhouse	NBC	8:00	10.2
National Barn Dance	NBC	9:00	9.7
Uncle Ezra's Radio Station	NBC	10:00	9.7
Wayne King Orchestra	CBS	7:30	8.5
Saturday Night Serenade	CBS	9:45	8.2
The Marriage Club	CBS	8:00	7.6
Duffy's Tavern	CBS	8:30	6.5

CONSEQUENTIALLY, A HIT

What began as a variation of the Victorian parlor game *Forfeits* in which players were required to perform silly acts, *Truth or Consequences* was the most popular new network program of the 1940–41 season.

The show gave its listeners a zany Saturday night party on NBC for ten years, never dropping out of the Top 50. It was sponsored throughout the decade by Procter & Gamble.

During its peak season, 1947–48, *Truth or Consequences* became a solid Top Ten program in the annual rankings — a rarity for Saturday night shows when fewer homes were using radios.

The audience participation stunt show was created and hosted by glib San Francisco radio announcer Ralph Edwards, 27, whose air talent was cajoling the contestants, egging on the audience and providing a running description of the stunts for listeners — like contestants riding camels, washing elephants, or otherwise making fools of themselves in public.

Edwards' talent as a producer kept his program fresh through its many years with more elaborate stunts and big money giveaways. The giveaways paid off several seasons later when *Truth or Consequences* became the most talked-about program in America for months at a time.

RAISING THE BAR

Ed Gardner had heavyweight comedy and variety credentials as a radio director for the J. Walter Thompson agency, working on Burns and Allen's shows, *Good News* and *Rudy Vallee's Fleischmann Hour.*

As a comedy writer and talent, Gardner created and starred in *Duffy's Tavern,* the long-running ensemble sitcom set in a lower Manhattan pub where, "...The elite meet to eat." Gardner, as "Archie the Manager," played host to a weekly string of guest stars and led a small but memorable cast of barroom regulars into silly plots involving their guests.

Gardner's wife at the time, Shirley Booth, originated the role of the empty headed, man-hungry "Miss Duffy," barfly daughter of the tavern's absentee owner. After

their divorce, Booth left the show to become an award winning stage and film actress, returning to comedy in 1960 as television's *Hazel.*

Popular radio character actor Charlie Cantor, who specialized in "dumb and dumber" comic stooges, brought out his dumbest voice as "Clifton Finnegan," an urban version of Mortimer Snerd who couldn't begin a sentence without the obligatory, "Duhhh...."

Intellectual *Information Please* host Clifton Fadiman came by *Duffy's Tavern* several times to converse with his "namesake" Finnegan.

Eddie Green played Archie's right hand man, "Eddie the Waiter," sometimes the only voice of sanity and reason in the group.

Gardner and his head writer, Abe Burrows, were given a shot on CBS' Saturday night schedule in March. But their chances for success were a long shot in the 8:30 timeslot opposite *Truth or Consequences.*

Duffy's Tavern could only muster a 6.5 rating — less than half of the stunt show's numbers on NBC.

During the next six seasons the sitcom was subjected to two network changes and four different timeslots — enough to kill a weaker program's ratings. But the show's listener loyalty steadily increased throughout the turmoil and *Duffy's Tavern* eventually became a Top 50 program for Bristol Myers over six seasons.

BARN DANCES TO NBC

NBC took *National Barn Dance* from Blue and kept the show in its

familiar 9:00 Saturday timeslot in which it had enjoyed two Top 50 seasons. The Joe Kelly hosted show of rural music and comedy from Chicago continually trailed *Your Hit Parade* in the time period, but had maintained a steady rating hovering around 10.0. More importantly, *National Barn Dance* had a loyal sponsor in Miles Laboratories' Alka-Seltzer which supported the show for ten years.

The loss of *National Barn Dance* left Blue without a Top Ten show on Saturday night. The network wouldn't have another one for the next six years.

FEEDING THE NEWS HUNGRY

Americans were becoming more news conscious as war began to rage in Europe.

The networks and their sponsors responded as the number of rated and ranked news/commentary programs leaped in just one year from three to 13. Seven of the eleven highest rated Multiple Run programs were newscasts.

Lowell Thomas' Monday through Friday newscasts appeared in all five weeknights' Top Ten lists. Thomas turned in Blue's second highest rated program for the season behind Walter Winchell's *Jergens Journal* on Sunday nights.

H.V. Kaltenborn, newly recruited by NBC from CBS, was in Tuesday, Thursday and Saturday's Top Ten — finishing in the season's Top 50 for the first of five consecutive seasons.

Mutual jumped on the news

1940–41 Top Ten Multiple Run Programs (11)
CBS 4, MBS 4, NBC 2, Blue 1
Average: 9.2

Lowell Thomas News*	M–F	Blue	6:45	14.2
HV Kaltenborn News	T,T,Sa	NBC	7:45	11.6
Amos & Andy*	M–F	CBS	7:00	10.8
Lanny Ross Show*	M–F	CBS	7:15	10.4
Fred Waring Show*	M–F	NBC	7:00	9.2
Paul Sullivan News*	M–F	CBS	6:30	8.0
Gabriel Heatter News	M, W–F	MBS	9:00	7.4
Raymond Gram Swing News*	M–F	MBS	10:00	7.1
Arthur Hale Confidentially Yours News	T,T	MBS	7:30	6.9
Glenn Miller Orchestra	T,W,T	CBS	10:00	6.7
Boake Carter News	M,W,Sa	MBS	8:30	6.7

*Monday–Friday Strip Shows

wagon by scheduling a quarter hour newscast in each of the four prime time hours every night. Gabriel Heatter's four-nights-a-week newscasts on Mutual were the highest rated of the 20 MBS programs that appeared in the season's Hooper reports. Heatter took Tuesdays off to emcee the popular *We the People* on CBS.

Dropping to third among the Multiple Runs, *Amos & Andy* held its rating at 10.8 but *A&A's* popularity was in atrophy. Gosden and Correll knew that it was the beginning of the end for their sitcom serial that had steadily lost over 65 percent of its audience in seven seasons.

They also knew that something had to be done or they'd be forced into retirement as has-been, middle aged millionaires.

BEATING THE BIG BAND BANS

They were never rated or ranked because they were broadcast beyond prime time hours and invari-ably sustaining, yet the nightly, late night dance band remote broadcasts from ballrooms, hotels and nightclubs around the country were a network staple for the hours after 11:00 until their affiliates' nightly sign-offs.

It was a cozy arrangement — the bands got free exposure to promote their records and future appearances, the venues got free publicity and the networks got free programming. Dozens of the biggest name bands played the 15 minute and half hour remote sets every week.

Meanwhile, James Caesar Petrillo, autocratic head of the American Federation of Musicians' Chicago local, had been elected National President of the union in July.

Petrillo immediately set about to spread Chicago's "standby" system nationwide.

His plan required local musicians playing on local radio stations to either join the nearest AFM local or the stations would be forced pay an equal number of thumb-twiddling union musicians to "stand by."

Two major stations active in locally produced music programs refused to bow to the featherbedding edict — KSTP, the Minneapolis–St. Paul NBC affiliate and Richmond's CBS station, WRVA.

In retaliation, Petrillo overplayed his hand.

He ordered his members to refuse to play on late night dance band remotes over NBC or CBS that were fed to these two "maverick" affiliates.

The networks cried foul, the bands balked and Mutual came to its competitors' aid by offering its own nightly remotes to CBS and NBC affiliates with no strings attached.

Petrillo's vindictive exertion of power was obvious and his ill-conceived edict was dropped quickly.

The big band's late night remote broadcasts remained a staple of Network Radio throughout its Golden Age and beyond.

TOP 50 PROGRAMS — 1940–41
CBS 24, NBC 21, Blue 5
Average Rating: 14.9, Median: 13.3
28,500,000 Radio Homes / 81.1% Coverage of U.S. Homes / One Rating Point = 285,000 Homes
Source: C.E. Hooper Monthly Network Reports, Sep, 1940 — Jun, 1941
Total Programs Rated 6–11 P.M.: 147
Programs Rated 13 Weeks & Ranked: 133.

		Program	Rtg	Type	Sponsor	Day	Time	Lgth	Net
1	1	Jack Benny Program	30.8	SC	Jello Gelatin	Sun	7:00	30	NBC
2	3	Fibber McGee & Molly	27.6	SC	Johnson Wax	Tue	9:30	30	NBC
3	2	Edgar Bergen & Charlie McCarthy	27.3	CV	Chase & Sanborn Coffee	Sun	8:00	30	NBC
4	5	Bob Hope Show	26.6	CV	Pepsodent Toothpaste	Tue	10:00	30	NBC
5	8	Walter Winchell's Jergens Journal	24.1	NC	Jergens Lotion	Sun	9:00	15	Blue
6	4	Lux Radio Theater/Cecil B DeMille	23.4	DA	Lux Soap	Mon	9:00	60	CBS
7	33	Aldrich Family/Ezra Stone	22.1	SC	Jello Gelatin & Puddings	Thu	8:30	30	NBC
8	9	Major Bowes Original Amateur Hour	18.2	TC	Chrysler Corporation	Thu	9:00	60	CBS
9	N	Fanny Brice & Frank Morgan Show	18.0	CV	Maxwell House Coffee	Thu	8:00	30	NBC
10	7	One Man's Family	16.9	DCC	Tenderleaf Tea	Sun	8:30	30	NBC
11	10	Kay Kyser Kollege of Musical Knowledge	16.6	APQ	Lucky Strike Cigarettes	Wed	10:00	60	NBC
12	13	Kate Smith Hour	16.1	MV	Grape Nuts Cereal	Fri	8:00	60	CBS
13	18	Big Town/Edward G Robinson	16.0	DCC	Rinso Laundry Soap	Wed	8:00	30	CBS
14	6	Bing Crosby's Kraft Music Hall	15.6	MV	Kraft Cheese	Thu	9:00	60	NBC
15t	29	Screen Guild Theater	15.3	DA	Gulf Oil	Sun	7:30	30	CBS
15t	15	We the People/Gabriel Heatter	15.3	API	Sanka Coffee	Tue	9:00	30	CBS
17	N	Eddie Cantor's Time To Smile	15.0	CV	Ipana & Sal Hepatica	Wed	9:00	30	NBC
18	71	Mister District Attorney/Jay Jostyn	14.7	DCC	Vitalis Hair Tonic	Wed	9:30	30	NBC
19t	17	Fitch Bandwagon	14.4	MP	Fitch Shampoo	Sun	7:30	30	NBC
19t	24	Rudy Vallee Show	14.4	MV	Sealtest Dairies	Thu	10:00	30	NBC
21	20	Lowell Thomas News	14.2	NC	Sun Oil	M-F	6:45	15	Blue
22t	22	Guy Lombardo Orch	13.6	MP	Lady Esther Cosmetics	Mon	10:00	30	CBS
22t	N	Truth or Consequences/R Edwards	13.6	APS	Ivory Soap	Sat	8:30	30	NBC
24	14	Fred Allen's Texaco Star Theater	13.5	CV	Texaco	Wed	9:00	60	CBS
25	39	Dr Christian/Jean Hersholt	13.3	DCC	Vaseline	Wed	8:30	30	CBS

	Program	Rtg	Type	Sponsor	Day	Time	Lgth	Net
26t *61*	The Parker Family	13.0	SC	Woodbury Soap	Sun	9:15	15	Blue
26t *22*	Your Hit Parade/Barry Wood, Bea Wain	13.0	MP	Lucky Strike Cigarettes	Sat	9:00	45	CBS
28t *27*	Information Please	12.9	PS	Lucky Strike Cigarettes	Fri	8:30	30	NBC 1
28t *N*	Take It or Leave It/Bob Hawk	12.9	APQ	Eversharp Pens & Pencils	Sun	10:00	30	CBS
30t *21*	Burns & Allen Show	12.8	CV	Hormel Meats	Mon	7:30	30	NBC
30t *46*	Campbell Playhouse	12.8	DA	Campbell Soups	Fri	9:30	30	CBS
30t *16*	First Nighter Program	12.8	DA	Campana Balm	Tue	8:30	30	CBS
33 *N*	Gay 90's Revue/Joe Howard	12.7	MSP	Model Pipe Tobacco	Mon	8:30	30	CBS
34 *24*	Al Pearce Gang	12.2	CV	Camel Cigarettes	Fri	7:30	30	CBS
35t *19*	Gangbusters	12.0	DA	Sloan's Liniment	Fri	9:00	30	Blue
35t *N*	Helen Hayes Theater	12.0	DA	Lipton Tea	Sun	8:00	30	CBS
37 *39*	Blondie/PennySingleton,Arthur Lake	11.8	SC	Camel Cigarettes	Mon	7:30	30	CBS
38t *N*	HV Kaltenborn News	11.6	NC	Pure Oil	T-T-Sat	7:45	15	NBC
38t *33*	Those We Love	11.6	DCC	Teel Liquid Dentifrice	Mon	8:00	30	CBS
40 *66*	Vox Pop	11.3	API	Kentucky Club Tobacco	Thu	7:30	30	CBS
41 *47*	Amos & Andy	10.8	SC	Campbell Soup	M-F	7:00	15	CBS
42 *57*	Doctor IQ/Lew Valentine	10.7	APQ	Mars Candy	Mon	9:00	30	NBC
43 *47*	Pipe Smoking Time/ Howard & Sheldon	10.5	MV	Model Pipe Tobacco	Mon	8:30	30	CBS
44t *89*	Court of Missing Heirs	10.4	API	Ironized Yeast	Tue	8:00	30	CBS
44t *77*	Lanny Ross Show	10.4	MP	Franco American Foods	M-F	7:15	15	CBS
46 *27*	Battle of the Sexes/Crumit, Sanderson	10.3	APQ	Molle Shaving Cream	Tues	9:00	30	NBC
47t *24*	Silver Theater	10.2	DA	International Silver	Sun	6:00	30	CBS
47t *N*	Knickerbocker Playhouse	10.2	DA	Drene Shampoo	Sat	8:00	30	NBC
47t *42*	Adventures of Sherlock Holmes	10.2	DCC	Bromo Quinine Cold Tablets	Sun	8:30	30	Blue
50 *51*	American Album of Familiar Music	10.0	MST	Bayer Aspirin	Sun	9:30	30	NBC

New & Returning Top 50 Programs Underscored.

1	Information Please	Sep — Nov	Sustaining		Tue	8:30	30	Blue

Key: API — Audience Participation/Interviews
APQ — Audience Participation/Quiz
APS — Audience Participation/Stunts
CV — Comedy/Variety Show
DA — Dramatic Anthology

DCC — Drama/Continuing Characters
MC — Music/Classical, Semi-Classical
MP — Music/Popular, Contemporary
MSP — Music/Specialty, Ethnic
MST — Music/Standard, Traditional

MV — Music/Variety Show
NC — News, Commentary
PS — Panel Show Comedy
SC — Situation Comedy
TC — Talent Competition

1940–41 Top 50 Favorite Formats

	Programs	Pct
Drama — Anthology & Continuing	14	28%
Comedy — Variety & Situation	14	28%
Music — All Categories	11	22%
Audience Participation — All Categories	8	16%
News/Commentary	3	6%

1940–41 Monthly Winners

Sep	Edgar Bergen & Charlie McCarthy	21.0	Feb	Jack Benny Program	37.2
Oct	Edgar Bergen & Charlie McCarthy	28.8	Mar	Jack Benny Program	37.2
Nov	Jack Benny Program	32.9	Apr	Fibber McGee & Molly	33.8
Dec	Jack Benny Program	32.9	May	Bob Hope Show	25.5
Jan	Jack Benny Program	36.2	Jun	Bob Hope Show	25.3
				& Walter Winchell's Jergens Journal	25.3

14

The 1941–42 Network Season

Announcer: You know, an old proverb I just thought of, says if you want a whiter wash well done, just leave it to Rinso. How true that is! Why, those quick acting Rinso suds are tough as nails on dirt and grime, yet safe for washable colors. And with Rinso, you can hustle through a load of clothes with as little as a five-minute run in your washer. How's that for saving your clothes and easing up on your trusty machine? That washer's got to last for the duration, you know. Get new Anti-Sneeze Rinso tomorrow. (PAUSE) Morning, evening, noon and night — there are dishes to wash and grease to fight. And that's where the new Anti-Sneeze Rinso is tops! I'm telling you ladies, with those rich go-getter suds in action, every grease-coated pan emerges from the sink with a dazzling sparkle! And Rinso's easy on your hands — it doesn't get them all rough and red. It's all that and thrifty too — less than a cent a day to do your dishes the Rinso way! So get new Anti-Sneeze Rinso tomorrow!

Announcer 2: There's nothing so dismal as a foghorn...

SFX: FOGHORN

Announcer 2: ...unless it's somebody with B-O! Stop B-O! Take a daily bath with the new 1942 Lifebuoy! From head to toe, it stops B-O! Lifebuoy!

THE LAST OF THE GOOD OLD DAYS

The 1941–42 season had two distinct personalities — before and after December 7.

In the three months before Pearl Harbor it was business as usual and business was good.

Both radio industry and network revenues hit new all-time highs Adding to their profitability, CBS and NBC settled with ASCAP at a fraction less than the reduced, three percent of revenue negotiated by Mutual. The total loss to ASCAP in the nine month blackout was a reported two and a half million dollars *(38.4 Mil)*.

Untold millions more would be lost in future income with the broadcasters' creation of ASCAP's major competitor, BMI.

NBC SPLITS, MUTUAL PROFITS

Seven-year-old Mutual quietly became the largest radio network in 1940 with over 160 affiliated stations and doubled its billings to over five million dollars in 1941 *(76.9 Mil)*. The network picked up more affiliates after NBC's establishment of its Blue chain as, "a separate and independent" network in early October. Mutual offered its lines to NBC affiliates who got lost in the shuffle of the separation.

WFBR/Baltimore and WCAE/Pittsburgh were the first to sign with Mutual rather than affiliate with the "new" Blue network without any possible access to NBC programming.

Mutual's selling points were simple. In addition to a steady stream of national and international news, member stations exchanged programs and underwrote network line costs. Most Mutual programs were delivered to stations on the "co-op" basis still popular today — the network profited from half of the commercial availabilities within each program and the other half was available for local sale.

Mutual was the simple, no-frills network that operated with a pre-war staff of only 72 full time employees.

Just to prove it could play ball with the big boys, Mutual and Gillette renewed exclusive broadcast rights to the World Series. The network anticipated another spurt of affiliations from that coup and got them.

FM'S FALSE START

Of the four national chains, Mutual also displayed the most interest in static free *Frequency Modulation* radio, developed by engineering genius Edwin Armstrong in 1935. Mutual's New York flagship station and co-owner, WOR, championed the medium in Manhattan with W71NY, the city's first commercial FM station.

On November 30 W71NY pioneered a wireless FM network broadcast, relaying its powerful signal to FM outlets in Philadelphia, Hartford, Boston, Schenectady, Mount Washington, N.H., and Armstrong's own facility in Alpine, N.J. It was the first serious attempt in a dozen years to link stations without telephone lines

John Shepard III's Boston, Providence, Worcester and Bridgeport stations all had FM operations. Shepard was a major proponent of

1941–42 Season Scoreboard			
Mid-season Totals, December 1941			
		Compared to Year Earlier	
Total Radio Homes	29.30 Mil	+0.80 Mil	+2.8.%
Total Auto Radios	8.75 Mil	+1.25 Mil	+16.7%
Total AM Radio Stations	831	+66	+8.6%
Total Radio Network Affiliates	509	+55	+12.1%
1941 Radio Revenues	247.2 Mil	+31.6 Mil	+14.7%
1941 Network Revenues	125.4 Mil	+12.1 Mil	+10.7%
Network Share	50.7%	(1.9%)	

FM and influenced the move among the 17 affiliates of his regional Yankee Network — Mutual's leg in New England.

Pre-war FM was attracting attention and fans. Some 20 manufacturers were producing combination AM/FM receivers ranging in cost from $70 to $700 *($1,080 to $10,800)*. By late November FM set ownership had increased ten-fold within the year. Over 150,000 homes had FM receivers and the momentum showed no signs of slowing.

But within a few weeks it stopped altogether. FM became a major communications vehicle for the armed forces and production of home receivers was shut down for the duration.

And eventually those thousands of pre-war FM sets were all rendered useless when the FCC ordered the FM broadcast band changed in 1948. With that ruling most broadcasters and listeners lost confidence in the technology.

FM slid into atrophy for another 20 years before confidence in its potential was restored.

TV FIRSTS ON CHANNEL ONE

Two months before the 1941–42 Network Radio season began, commercial television was authorized by the FCC.

NBC's WNBT/New York went on the air as Channel One at 1:30 P.M. on July 1, 1941. CBS owned WCBW became Channel Two a half hour later.

WNBT aired the first television commercial — the video of a clock identified by an announcer as, "B-U-L-O-V-A ... Bulova Watch Time"— for four dollars *($61.50)*.

Lowell Thomas appeared in the first radio/television simulcast when his 6:45 Blue network news was televised by WNBT. The veteran newsman was seen at a desk beside a pyramid of cans of Sun Motor Oil, his longtime radio sponsor. Sun paid $100 *($1,540)*, for the first commercial TV newscast.

WNBT climaxed its first day with a variety program to benefit the USO service clubs. The show featured abbreviated video versions of *Uncle Jim's Question Bee* and the new radio stunt show *Truth or Con-*

sequences. Both Lever Brothers and Procter & Gamble paid $100 for advertising in the fund-raising program that was seen on just a few thousand flickering sets in the city.

Like FM, expansion of television also came to a halt on December 7.

But unlike FM, television came roaring back into popularity immediately after World War II.

SHORTWAVE'S TWO WAY STREET

Competition was keen among the networks to obtain shortwave news dispatches from their correspondents in Europe and the Orient.

However, shortwave transmission originating *from* the United States was a different matter.

The networks and independent shortwave outlets all joined forces in an international war of words months before Pearl Harbor was attacked in December.

Because of its RCA ownership, NBC had the most experience in the long range transmission of news from America to Europe and South America. Its 1941 budget for shortwave operations was $250,000 *(3.8 Mil)*, enough to employ a staff of 65 producers, writers and linguists. The network cited over 10,000 letters from international listeners in 1941 approving of its straight news approach to blunt fascist propaganda beamed from Europe.

CBS — along with Crosley's WLWO/Cincinnati, Westinghouse's WBOS/Boston, GE's WGEO/Schenectady and independent station WURL/Boston — joined NBC in shortwave's battle of broadcasting between the warring Allied and Axis powers — each lobbing hours of programming into the others' backyards.

The New York Times listed the times and frequencies where London, Moscow, Berlin and Rome shortwave broadcasts beamed to North America were available. Its listings later included Berne, Stockholm, Melbourne and Tokyo.

In response, U.S. shortwave broadcasters combined to schedule newscasts every 15 minutes by at least one of the stations from noon until late night in Europe. Each

news report was delivered in one of a dozen different languages.

Meanwhile, GE's powerful KGEI/San Francisco, the only shortwave installation on the West Coast, became an effective tool to broadcast news and strategic communications to remote locations in the Pacific.

Between its periods of news and messages broadcast in nine different languages, the station relayed network programming from NBC and Blue — welcome sounds for American army and navy personnel serving so far from home. It proved to be a forerunner of Armed Forces Radio Service.

In the period immediately prior to World War II, shortwave broadcasting became so important that the FCC advised RCA to hire Pinkerton detectives to guard its main control room. Another squad, armed with machine guns patrolled the grounds and facilities of company's shortwave transmitters.

They were there to prevent sabotage in the international war of words.

THE SHOCK OF '41

For several years, Network Radio had been the verbal battleground between "Isolationists" versus "Interventionists" debating America's involvement in the escalating war. Their argument ended abruptly in early December.

December 7, 1941, was a typically slow Sunday afternoon in the network newsrooms until 1:07 — then all hell broke loose.

The first Associated Press bulletin of the Pearl Harbor attack — from Honolulu reporter Eugene Burns — sent the short handed weekend news staffs into a scramble. But remembering the *War of the Worlds* fiasco, they weren't about to alarm a war-jittery nation without official confirmation.

Their frantic activity continued for over an hour while the last of the "peacetime" programs played on.

NBC offered its affiliates the soft music and poetry of *Sunday Serenade* from Sammy Kaye's popular "Swing & Sway" orchestra. *Great Plays* on Blue featured an hour long adaptation of Oscar Wilde's *The Importance of Being Earnest*. Mutual fed WOR's broadcast of the New York Giants–Brooklyn Dodgers pro football game to any affiliates who wanted it.

The CBS series at 2:00, *The Spirit of '41,* dealt with military and defense preparedness. Newsman John Daly interviewed his guests from the Brooklyn Navy Yard how damaged warships were repaired — unaware that Japanese bombs were falling on the U.S. Pacific Fleet while they talked.

WE INTERRUPT THIS PROGRAM...

At 2:25 — 90 minutes after the first bombs fell — acknowledgment of the attack from the White House cleared the wire services. WOR flashed the news to whatever Mutual affiliates were carrying its football game at 2:26. NBC broke the news on both of its networks simultaneously with a terse, 20-second bulletin read by news writer Bob Eisenbach at 2:29:50. CBS waited until the 2:30 opening of *The World Today* when Daly read the bulletin.

NBC, Blue and Mutual returned to regular programming while their news departments assembled and attempted to reach Honolulu.

CBS already had Daly and commentator Elmer Davis on the air with *The World Today.* Standing by for the program were Robert Trout with reaction from London plus a short wave report from Manila where the Philippines were also reported under pre-invasion attack from Japanese bombers.

At 4:06 NBC scored the first scoop of the day with an eyewitness report from KGU/Honolulu, the same station whose broadcast signal Japanese pilots tuned for radio co-ordinates to reach Pearl Harbor.

December 7 was the afternoon when radio's stature as a news source soared. It was also the turning point in broadcasting history that extended Network Radio's Golden Age by shutting down its competition.

World War II diverted the development of television and FM radio from civilian to military use. The war also delayed the construction of hundreds of new, independent radio stations.

As a result, the existing AM stations and their networks would grow in popularity and revenues — all without serious competition — for the next seven seasons.

WARTIME DUTY

FDR's address to the nation on December 9, 1941, scored an all-time high Hooperating of 79.0. The United States was at war and Americans now depended on radio for immediate news as well as morale boosting entertainment.

The government depended on it, too — for dispersal of official information. The broadcasters were happy to cooperate — they feared another Federal takeover of radio facilities similar to World War I, despite FCC Chairman Fly's assurances that it would never happen.

It never did — but it came close in November 1942.

The networks each pledged, "A generous amount of time," from every prime time program once per month for Government announcements. Every daytime program was committed to carry one public service announcement every two weeks. It was a small price to remain unfettered in the vital and profitable business climate created by war.

Instead of staying at those minimums, the networks exceeded them and became megaphones for patriotism's biggest cheerleaders who sold war bonds, entertained troops and continually promoted the war effort with their programs and personal appearances.

DURATION INNOVATIONS

Daylight Savings Time, usually a point of contention from broadcasters and theater owners, went into effect year round for the duration on February 2 under the name "War Time."

Nobody complained.

With its typical fanfare, CBS arbitrarily cut commercial time inside newscasts by 20 percent — which amounted to roughly 30 seconds in a 15 minute program. The network also prohibited jingles or any other "undue gaiety" to be heard in its newscast commercials.

The NAB chipped in some wartime newscast standards of its own.

Among several gratuitous preachments was, "Don't interrupt a news story with a commercial."

In other words, it was business as usual.

THE MONTHLIES

Edgar Bergen regained ratings momentum with his September start while rivals Jack Benny and *Fibber McGee & Molly* remained on summer hiatus. Bergen gave Chase & Sanborn and NBC the month's Number One program from September through January.

Blue had a rare first place program in December — following America's entry into World War II — when Walter Winchell's Sunday night tabloid newscasts tied Bergen. *Fibber McGee & Molly* reclaimed first place in February, March and April. The Jim and Marian Jordan sitcom provided a golden lead-in for Bob Hope to win May and June.

Although tied in December, NBC's string of consecutive months of Number One shows was extended to 71.

1941–42 Sunday Night *Top Ten Programs* NBC 5, CBS 3, Blue 2 Average: 18.2			
Edgar Bergen & Charlie McCarthy	NBC	8:00	28.0
Jack Benny Program	NBC	7:00	27.2
Walter Winchell	Blue	9:00	26.0
One Man's Family	NBC	8:30	16.5
Fitch Bandwagon	NBC	7:30	15.7
Take It or Leave It	CBS	10:00	14.8
Fred Allen's Texaco Star Theater	CBS	9:00	14.2
Adventures of Sherlock Holmes	NBC	10:30	14.1
Screen Guild Theater	CBS	7:30	13.1
The Parker Family	Blue	9:15	12.8

WW AND WORLD WAR II

Walter Winchell's *Jergens Journal*—a weekly, rapid fire, 15 minute mix of news headlines, gossip, slang, innuendo and opinion punctuated by telegraph key sound effects — had steadily gained audience as the threat of war increased.

Winchell was a hawk — known in the prewar days as an "Interventionist"— who continually warned his listeners of the dangers if America wasn't prepared to defend itself. His Sunday night broadcast of December 7 fell within a Hooper survey week. The saber-rattling gossip columnist suddenly became the prophet patriot and he scored his highest rating to date — a 29.9.

His January and February ratings climbed even higher to 33.1 — territory normally occupied by only the most popular variety shows — before settling back into the 20s for the remainder of the season.

Winchell's 1941–42 season average of 26.0 would be his highest of 21 consecutive Top 50 seasons.

His *Jergens Journal* was easily the most enduring and highest rated program ever originated by the Blue Network.

HAWK WALKS, PHIL FILLS

Bob Hawk had *Take It or Leave It* off to a flying start — helping to push Eversharp Pen & Pencils' comedy quiz into Sunday's Top Ten in its first full season. From its initial short run in the spring of 1940, the show's rating climbed steadily to a 1940–41 rating of 12.9.

Hawk wanted a raise in salary for his performance but Eversharp wasn't about to give him one.

However, R.J. Reynolds Tobacco was.

The glib, 33-year-old quizmaster left *Take It or Leave It* in December 1941 and re-emerged a month later as host of a new quiz for Camel Cigarettes, *How'm I Doin'?*

Eversharp, in need of a fast replacement for Hawk, called on 55-year-old Phil Baker who had been out of radio for over a year since his *Honolulu Bound* disaster in 1939's ratings. Baker brought his accordion and a new kind of humor to *Take It or Leave It*. The Vaudeville veteran improved on Hawk's ratings by 15 percent in his first six months and Baker enjoyed new-found popularity as host of what would eventually become radio's top rated quiz show.

FRED SHEDS RATING WOES

Texaco vacated its CBS Wednesday timeslot opposite NBC's Eddie Cantor and *Mr. District Attorney* in March, moving Fred Allen's *Texaco Star Theater* into a less competitive time period in CBS's Sunday lineup.

Ironically, Texaco had moved Cantor *from* Sunday three years earlier for the same reason.

The 9:00 hour became available when Ford Motors cancelled its long running *Sunday Evening Hour* featuring the Detroit Symphony. It was wartime and the car maker had nothing to sell.

Texaco's move was smart — Allen's ratings improved nearly 20 percent immediately. He benefited from his new timeslot that allowed him to verbally spar with Jack Benny on the same evening. Their "feud" was still very much alive with the 1941 release of Paramount's *Love Thy Neighbor* based on their battle of barbs.

Although CBS missed its chunk of Ford's annual $1,400,000 *(21.5 Mil)*, outlay to sponsor the automaker's hometown symphony, the network could boast of Allen's 15.6 rating in his new time period versus *The Ford Sunday Evening Hour*'s mediocre 8.9.

GILDERSLEEVE
SPINS AND WINS

Throckmorton P. Gildersleeve moved from *Fibber McGee & Molly*'s Wistful Vista and took up residence in nearby Springfield as *The Great Gildersleeve*. Although Hal Peary's new sitcom didn't make Sunday's Top Ten with its 10.3 rating, it nevertheless was among the season's Top 50 — the first of twelve consecutive years — establishing it as the most successful spin-off series in radio history.

The Great Gildersleeve had more than the *McGee* pedigree. The programs shared *FM&M*'s creator, Don Quinn, plus the talents of Gale Gordon, Arthur Q. Bryan and the Billy Mills studio orchestra.

Peary's *Gildersleeve* character was given an extra push in November with a major role in RKO-Radio Pictures' quickie comedy, *Look Who's Laughing*, starring NBC's Edgar Bergen — plus Charlie McCarthy and Mortimer Snerd — and *Fibber McGee & Molly*. The plot was a patchwork of the stars' familiar bits — letting radio audiences see the routines they'd only heard in the past.

The film also featured a 30-year-old Lucille Ball in a supporting role.

GRAPE FLAVORED SOAP

Veteran screen actress Irene Rich, the former favorite leading lady of Will Rogers in movies, was in the last of her eight seasons on Blue, finally settling at 9:30 on Sunday. She headlined a series of weekly, serialized quarter hours under the blanket title, *Irene Rich Dramas*. Her string of melodramatic gems carried chapter titles worthy of romance novels: *Jewels of Enchantment*, *The Lady Counselor*, *Glorious One* and *Dear John*.

Irene Rich Dramas never scored double digit ratings or finished in a season's Top 50, despite enjoying Walter Winchell's *Jergens Journal* as its lead-in for two years. Yet, Rich's program was never in jeopardy of cancellation.

Welch's Grape Juice sponsored her entire run on Blue plus two additional seasons on CBS. Her sponsor's loyalty stemmed from Rich's longtime, widely advertised endorsements of "Welch's Reducing Plan" — claiming that a glass of Welch's before meals and at bedtime enabled her, at 40+years, to have the same figure as she did at 16 — and produced pictures to prove it.

ANOTHER MAN'S FAMILY

Another quarter hour curiosity was programmed following Winchell for three seasons and finished twice in the season's Top 50. *The Parker Family* was a fifteen minute sitcom bearing similarity to *The Aldrich Family* with Leon Janney portraying the clan's perplexed teenaged son, Richard — for some reason tagged, "Richard the Great."

The Parker patriarch, Walter, was a familiar voice to listeners from another role. Jay Jostyn simply softened the forceful delivery he used as *Mr. District Attorney*.

1941–42 Monday Night
Top Ten Programs
CBS 7, Blue 2, NBC 1
Average: 13.4

Lux Radio Theater	CBS	9:00	25.1
Orson Welles	CBS	10:00	16.8
Dramas			

Lowell Thomas News*	Blue	6:45	15.6
Gay 90's Revue	CBS	8:30	13.5
Blondie	CBS	7:30	12.9
Vox Pop	CBS	8:00	12.0
I Love a Mystery	Blue	8:00	9.8
Wayne King's Lady Esther Serenade	CBS	10:00	9.8
Lanny Ross Show*	CBS	7:15	9.7
Dr. IQ	NBC	9:00	9.2

*Monday–Friday Strip Shows

Sans Strips...
| Dr IQ | NBC | 9:00 | 9.2 |
| Cavalcade of America | NBC | 7:30 | 8.8 |

THE LUX LIFE

Lux Radio Theater celebrated its fifth consecutive season as the Columbia network's most popular program. CBS distributed a Gallup research study indicating that on an average Monday five and a half million persons attended the movies while *26 million* stayed at home to *hear* the movies recreated on *Lux*. Future advertising guru David Ogilvy oversaw the study which was more generous than Hooper's figures.

Nevertheless, the point was made — CBS and Lever Brothers had a solid hit.

THE LADY WALTZES AGAIN

Lady Esther temporarily dropped syrupy music programming to sell cosmetics in mid–September and gave the half hour following *Lux* to Orson Welles. Welles, 26, had released his epic *Citizen Kane* four months earlier and was once again a hot property who had made headlines.

The Orson Welles Dramas was an audio encore for many from his *Citizen Kane* cast — Joseph Cotten, Agnes Moorhead, Ray Collins, Paul Stewart, Everett Sloane — all members of his *Mercury Theater* troupe who had participated in his earlier excursions into radio.

Welles' anthology series was the highest ranked new program of the season despite losing half of the *Lux Radio Theater* audience week after week. Surprisingly, the audience attrition was greater than the previous season's drop-off when Lady Esther followed *Lux* with the Guy Lombardo orchestra's "Sweetest Music This Side of Heaven." The

dance bands also came with a far lower production cost than Welles' company of actors and guest stars.

Welles left radio in February to direct his *Kane* follow-up film, *The Magnificent Ambersons*.

With a prime Monday night half hour to fill, Lady Esther turned to the bandleader who brought her to the network dance in the first place, Wayne King. "The Waltz King" and his Chicago based band, complete with Franklyn MacCormack's love poems, finished the season in Lady Esther's Monday timeslot.

1941–42 Tuesday Night Top Ten Programs
NBC 7, CBS 2, Blue 1
Average: 18.5

Fibber McGee & Molly	NBC	9:30	31.7
Bob Hope Show	NBC	10:00	30.7
Red Skelton Show	NBC	10:30	27.7
Burns & Allen Show	NBC	7:30	15.6
Lowell Thomas News*	Blue	6:45	15.6
H.V. Kaltenborn	NBC	7:45	15.2
Bob Burns Show	CBS	8:30	14.0
We the People	CBS	9:00	12.5
Battle of the Sexes	NBC	9:00	11.7
Johnny Presents	NBC	8:00	10.3

*Monday–Friday Strip Shows

Sans Strips...
| Tums Treasure Chest | NBC | 8:30 | 10.0 |
| Are You a Missing Heir? | CBS | 8:00 | 9.7 |

RED'S RATINGS FOLLOW FILM FAME

After two movie shorts and three supporting roles, Red Skelton's first starring film, *Whistling in the Dark,* was released by MGM in August. Riding on the movie's success, Brown & Williamson Tobacco brought Skelton to NBC's Tuesday night comedy lineup in November.

Skelton had the support of Ozzie Nelson, his band and wife/vocalist, Harriet Hilliard, who were no strangers to radio audiences with regular appearances dating back to the mid–1930s. Three years later they would become even more popular with *The Adventures of Ozzie & Harriet.*

Skelton's *Raleigh Cigarette Program* was an immediate hit.

The 9:30 to 11:00 tandem of *Fibber McGee & Molly*, Bob Hope and Red Skelton became the most suc-

cessful 90 minute block in radio history and locked down the top three Tuesday night slots for the next six seasons.

NBC's Tuesday trio of half hour comedies became such a listening habit that during the one season Skelton missed for military service, 1944–45, his replacement show, *Hildegarde's Raleigh Room*, scored a third place finish for the night.

NBC proceeded to dominate Tuesday's Top Ten for the next ten seasons.

LATRIVIA FOR GILDERSLEEVE

Fibber McGee & Molly writer/ partner Don Quinn came up with a new character to replace the couple's volatile neighbor, Throckmorton Gildersleeve. Gale Gordon, a veteran of occurring roles on the show, was elected to play Mayor Charles LaTrivia of Wistful Vista, a weekly caller at their household.

Gordon's LaTrivia found himself in a weekly verbal sparring match of syntax and metaphors with Fibber and Molly that would invariably leave him in frustrated, sputtering confusion. His characterization was the foundation for Gordon's subsequent fame as the pompous Osgood Conklin of *Our Miss Brooks* and as Lucille Ball's foil in two of the comedienne's television series, *The Lucy Show* and *Here's Lucy.*

WE DID I DO'S!

With their fifth new sponsor and fifth different timeslot in five seasons, Burns and Allen moved into NBC's Tuesday schedule. Unlike their four previous scheduling shifts, their new Tuesday night show for Lever Brothers' Swan Soap scored a ratings increase — a hefty 22 percent audience gain over their previous season. It was good news for the couple who were now radio's second most popular husband and wife comedy team behind Jim and Marian Jordan.

But George and Gracie's ratings renaissance was the result of more than a change of venue.

Pragmatic showman that he was, Burns threw out their format of flirtatious "boy and girl" skits that had become stale over ten years of use. Wife Gracie, 46, had complained that her lines in the routines were better suited for an ingénue half her age.

Noting the success that his friend Jack Benny had with a sitcom format filled with continuing characters, Burns restructured the program. The new *Burns & Allen Show* was a sitcom in which he and Gracie played a married couple in weekly domestic situations involving wacky neighbors and visiting guest stars. *They had been married for 16 years at the time.* The show was loaded with top flight supporting character actors including Mel Blanc, Hans Conreid, Gale Gordon, Elvia Allman, announcer Bill Goodwin and Paul Whiteman's orchestra.

The new husband and wife format pushed Burns and Allen back into the season's Top 20 programs and served them throughout the remainder of their radio and television careers.

BOB BURNS UP THE RATINGS

Bing Crosby's sidekick, rural comedian Bob Burns, 51, left *Kraft Music Hall* after five years for a successful solo career. To the delight of CBS and sponsor Campbell Soup, Burns' *Arkansas Traveler* sitcom/variety show featuring Spike Jones' novelty band and singer Ginny Simms became the network's highest rated Tuesday program and began Burns' string of five consecutive Top 50 seasons.

Giving Burns his own show wasn't much of a gamble. By 1941 he had logged three seasons as summer host of *Kraft Music Hall* and was familiar to movie audiences as Crosby's comic co-star in two Paramount musicals, 1936's *Rhythm on the Range* and 1937's *Waikiki Wedding*. In addition, Burns had the lead in eight lesser films, all as the hick hero who outsmarts the city slickers — roles similar to that played by Will Rogers, with whom Burns was invariably compared.

Burns also made headlines early in his show's run. He was sued by Paramount for not reporting for the filming of *Joan of Arkansas* which he claimed was an unfair caricature of his native state. The movie's title also bore a strong resemblance to

Joan of Ozark, a 1942 film starring his ex-wife, Judy Canova.

Burns is forever associated with "The Bazooka"— his homemade, trombone-like novelty instrument fashioned from plumbing pipes and a distilling funnel which he invented when he was 15. Burns toured Vaudeville stages with his jokes and bazooka for ten years before his film and radio careers took off.

Although Burns was too old for military service in World War II, his name "Bazooka" was adopted by the U.S. Army for its newly developed, shoulder-mounted rocket launcher that was able to pierce the enemy's heavily armored vehicles.

MAKING HEIR WAVES

Are You a Missing Heir?—known for its first two seasons as *The Court of Missing Heirs*—was in its third year on CBS. Created and hosted by lawyer James Waters and sponsored by Sterling Drug's Ironized Yeast, *Heirs* was a giveaway program that didn't give away the sponsor's money — a fact that especially appealed to the budget-minded Sterling. Instead, the program attempted to locate heirs for inheritances that were locked in probate without claimants. Two cases involving the known facts were dramatized each week, both leading up to the payoff question, "Are *you* the missing heir?"

The program found over 150 heirs in its three year span and was responsible for the distribution of some $800,000 *(11.1 Mil)*. Over ten percent of the total was awarded to one Chicago couple who didn't listen to the program but were alerted to their windfall by friends who did.

1941–42 Wednesday Night Top Ten Programs
NBC 5, CBS 4, Blue 1
Average: 13.4

Eddie Cantor's Time to Smile	NBC	9:00	18.7
Kay Kyser's Kollege of Musical Knowledge	NBC	10:00	18.4
Mr. District Attorney	NBC	9:30	18.4
Lowell Thomas News*	Blue	6:45	15.6
Meet Mr. Meek	CBS	8:00	12.5

Dr Christian	CBS	8:30	12.2
Adventures of the Thin Man	NBC	8:00	10.1
Amos & Andy*	CBS	7:00	9.6
Uncle Walter's Doghouse	NBC	8:30	9.2
Junior Miss	CBS	9:00	8.9
*Monday–Friday Strip Shows			
Sans Strips...			
Quiz Kids	Blue	8:00	8.2

ANY BONDS TODAY?

When Fred Allen's *Texaco Star Theater* went on summer vacation in June 1941 — six months before Pearl Harbor — Texaco donated a reported $195,000 *(3.0 Mil)*, to the Treasury Department to pay for the CBS hour plus all production costs involved with *Millions for Defense*, a weekly star-studded revue designed to sell U.S. Defense Bonds.

Fred Allen, Jack Benny, Bing Crosby and Bob Hope were among the dozens of film and radio stars who participated in the 13-week series. When Allen reclaimed his Texaco timeslot in September, Bendix Corporation undertook *Millions for Defense*, renamed it *The Treasury Hour* and moved it to Blue's Tuesday schedule.

THE SEXY WHODUNIT'S WHEREABOUTS

When *The Adventures of the Thin Man* debuted on radio, many listeners thought they heard William Powell and Myrna Loy recreating their roles as Nick and Nora Charles, made famous in their string of six MGM mystery/comedies based on Dashiell Hammett's married sleuths.

Instead, radio's Nick and Nora were Les Damon and Claudia Morgan, verbal ringers for Powell and Loy.

Director Himan Brown took radio's portrayal of the sophisticated and sexy couple one step further with prolonged pillow talk accompanied by appropriate murmurs and sighs, concluding each program with Morgan's sultry, "Goodnight, Nicky darling...."

In doing so, Brown let listeners decide if his Nick and Nora were bound by the movies' puritanical "twin-beds" mandate — although he left little doubt that they weren't.

Morgan, the daughter of film actor Ralph Morgan and niece of movie and radio star Frank Morgan, was clearly the star of the program — portraying Nora for the show's entire eight season run in the ratings. She and her Uncle Frank made the season's Top 50 simultaneously three times with their two programs. The role of Nick revolved among Damon, Les Tremayne and David Gothard.

Notorious for its innuendo at the time, *The Adventures of the Thin Man* scored only four Top 50 seasons. Listeners had to be sleuths to find the program. Four different sponsors bounced it around seven separate timeslots on three networks during its eight seasons.

Fans of the series believed that Nick and Nora deserved better.

FRESH AIR TAXI'S LAST STAND

The venerable *Amos & Andy* continued to struggle. Wednesday of the 1941–42 season was the last time their legendary strip show would appear in a nightly Top Ten. Freeman Gosden and Charlie Correll lost another ten percent of their audience and slipped into single digit ratings for the first time. They led their NBC competition, Fred Waring's show band, by less than half a rating point.

Over nine seasons *Amos & Andy* had tumbled from the annual Top Ten and out of the Top 50 altogether into 61st place.

And the worst was yet to come.

MISS MISSES

Child star Shirley Temple was no longer a child — and less of a match for NBC's Eddie Cantor than Fred Allen had been. When Allen's *Texaco Star Theater* was moved to Sunday in March, Procter & Gamble brought in the 13-year-old Temple as the teenaged lead for another of radio's growing list of family sitcoms, *Junior Miss*.

The program cost P&G a reported $12,000 (*$166,550*), per week, much of it taken home by its young star.

Cantor doubled the sitcom's ratings. *Junior Miss* was cancelled after 26 weeks and Temple retired from series radio. *Junior Miss* went on the shelf until 1948 when it was brought back as a feature of CBS's Saturday

morning block of juvenile programs with Barbara Whiting in the title role.

1941–42 Thursday Night Top Ten Programs
NBC 7, CBS 2, Blue 1
Average: 17.3

The Aldrich Family	NBC	8:30	26.6
Fanny Brice & Frank Morgan	NBC	8:00	23.8
Bing Crosby's Kraft Music Hall	NBC	9:00	17.4
Rudy Vallee Varieties	NBC	10:00	16.9
Lowell Thomas News*	Blue	6:45	15.6
Major Bowes' Original Amateur Hour	CBS	9:00	15.3
H.V. Kaltenborn	NBC	7:45	15.2
Big Town	CBS	9:30	14.8
Al Pearce Gang	NBC	7:30	13.6
Frank Fay Show	NBC	10:30	13.3

*Monday–Friday Strip Shows

Sans Strips...
Lanny Ross Show*	CBS	7:15	9.7
Death Valley Days	CBS	8:00	6.6

FOOD FOR RATINGS

NBC's Thursday lineup of winners sponsored by food conglomerates all increased their audiences. Compared to the previous season, Kraft's Bing Crosby and Sealtest's Rudy Vallee scored 15 percent rating gains. General Foods' *Aldrich Family* was up 20 percent to the highest rating of its twelve season run and the Fanny Brice/Frank Morgan *Maxwell House Coffee Time* audience shot up 32 percent.

Crosby's comeback was especially sweet to NBC, reclaiming top spot in the 9:00 time period from *Major Bowes' Original Amateur Hour* which suffered a 15 percent audience loss. CBS and Bowes suffered an even greater loss in February when Chrysler Corporation decided to cut the show back to half an hour. The car maker had shut down its Chrysler, Dodge, DeSoto and Plymouth auto production for the duration which left it nothing to sell to the listening public.

To fill the vacant half hour on CBS following Bowes at 9:30, Lever Brothers moved its successful *Big Town* into the timeslot with only slight ratings harm to the newspaper melodrama starring Ed-

ward G. Robinson. But the loss was enough to push *Big Town* from the season's Top 20 for the first time in its five years on the air.

1941–42 Friday Night Top Ten Programs
CBS 6, NBC 2, Blue 2
Average: 11.8

Kate Smith Hour	CBS	8:00	15.7
Lowell Thomas News*	Blue	6:45	15.6
First Nighter	CBS	9:30	12.9
Information Please	NBC	8:30	12.2
Philip Morris Playhouse	CBS	9:00	11.3
Hollywood Premiere	CBS	10:00	11.2
Gangbusters	Blue	9:00	10.6
Grand Central Station	NBC	7:30	9.9
Lanny Ross Show*	CBS	7:15	9.7
How'm I Doin'?	CBS	7:30	9.2

*Monday–Friday Strip Shows

Sans Strips...
Waltz Time	NBC	9:00	8.5
Wings of Destiny	NBC	10:00	8.5

THE CAMEL SHUFFLE

Bob Hawk and R.J. Reynolds' Camel Cigarettes began their twelve year talent/sponsor association in January with *How'm I Doin'?*, a personality driven audience participation quiz similar to Hawk's *Take It or Leave It*.

Camel's mid-season addition of Hawk's new show set up a three network chain reaction: *How'm I Doin'?* replaced *Al Pearce's Gang* on CBS. Camel moved Pearce to NBC on Thursday, replacing Xavier Cugat's *Rumba Revue*. Then Camel bought a Tuesday night half hour on Blue for Cugat's Latin orchestra.

It was a frustrating exercise. Despite the added elements of Vaughn Monroe's popular band and enthusiastic young announcer Bert Parks, *How'm I Doin'?* could only muster single digit ratings — a few points less than Pearce had generated. It was a shaky start for Hawk and Camels.

A career-saving format change was in order for the following season.

SING QUICKLY, GINNY!

It wasn't sponsored, rated or ranked but deserves note as the shortest musical variety show in Network Radio.

The Ginny Simms Show of 1941–42 was broadcast on CBS every Friday at 9:55 — for five minutes.

1941–42 Saturday Night Top Ten Programs
NBC 6, CBS 4
Average: 11.2

H.V. Kaltenborn	NBC	7:45	15.2
Your Hit Parade	CBS	9:00	14.2
Truth or Consequences	NBC	8:30	13.4
Abie's Irish Rose	NBC	8:00	13.0
Adventures of Ellery Queen	NBC	7:30	10.5
Grand Ole Opry	NBC	10:30	10.0
National Barn Dance	NBC	9:00	9.5
Hobby Lobby	CBS	8:30	9.5
Saturday Night Serenade	CBS	9:45	8.6
Guy Lombardo Orchestra	CBS	8:00	8.4

BETTER LATE THAN NEVER?

The radio extravaganza of the year was broadcast on Saturday, November 15, when NBC celebrated its 15th Anniversary with a two hour, 45-minute salute to itself carried over both its NBC and Blue networks.

Every major star from both chains — from Jack Benny and Bob Hope to the Quiz Kids — plus politicians and network executives appeared in the self-congratulatory marathon which contained the not to subtle message that NBC was doing a great job as a two network operation in spite of the FCC decree that it divest itself of the Blue chain.

The question remains how many people actually heard the broadcast from the combined 243 station hookup. The program began at 11:15 at night and ran on until 2:00 the following morning.

NO COMPETITION, NO SPONSOR, NO RATING

Two months later on Valentine's Day, 1942, the largest ad-hoc network ever assembled — an estimated 700 stations — came on line for a 13-week Saturday night series, *This Is War!* Directed by Norman Corwin, who wrote six of the half-hour dramas, the series was a mix of information and patriotic propaganda presented by a string of distinguished actors, film and radio stars.

The series was "suggested" by the Federal Office of Facts and Figures' radio chief, William Lewis, CBS Vice President of Programming on leave for government duty. Lewis described its objective to, "...Instruct and confirm the American spirit."

The series was translated into a number of foreign languages, performed by separate casts and shortwaved to South America and Europe. *This Is War!* became the most widely circulated radio series in history.

But the program had no commercial sponsor and went unrated by Hooper.

N-B-HAYSEED

NBC went rural on Saturday night, pairing the hour-long *National Barn Dance* from WLS/Chicago with it's 30 minute pickup of the *Grand Ole Opry* from WSM/Nashville.

Miles Laboratories' Alka-Seltzer bought the entire NBC network for the Joe Kelly hosted *Barn Dance* but R.J. Reynolds Tobacco only bought 13 of Hooper's 30 rated markets for *Opry*, sponsored by its Prince Albert Tobacco.

The Nashville program wasn't heard in New York, Los Angeles or other major cities considered too "sophisticated" for country music. For stations in those markets NBC fed *Hot Copy*, a sustaining newspaper crime drama.

Surprisingly, *Grand Ole Opry* turned in a double digit rating, indicating that in those markets where the program was heard, it was *heard*.

1941–42 Top Ten Multiple Run Programs
MBS 4, CBS 3, NBC 3, Blue 1 (11)
Average: 9.5

Lowell Thomas News*	M–F	Blue	6:45	15.6
HV Kaltenborn News	T,T,Sa	NBC	7:45	15.2
Lanny Ross Show*	M–F	CBS	7:15	9.7
Amos & Andy*	M–F	CBS	7:00	9.6
Fred Waring Show*	M–F	NBC	7:00	9.3
Gabriel Heatter News*	M–F	MBS	9:00	8.8
John W Vandercook News of the World*	M–F	NBC	7:15	7.3
The Lone Ranger	M,W,F	MBS	7:30	6.9
Glenn Miller Orchestra	W,Th,F	CBS	10:00	6.6
Raymond Gram Swing News*	M–F	MBS	10:00	6.4
Arthur Hale's Confidentially Yours News	T,T,Sa	MBS	7:30	6.4

*Monday–Friday Strip Shows

THE KNOWS FOR NEWS

Mutual lost its original marquee attraction late in the season when General Mills moved *The Lone Ranger* to Blue on May 4th. Ironically, the western adventure had finally begun to appear in the ratings during the 1941–42 season.

Nevertheless, MBS dominated the Multiple Run Top Ten for the first time with its lineup of nightly newscasts. Mutual aired four the six leading prime time newscasts

Gabriel Heatter, working six nights a week, earned $130,000 a year *(3.0 Mil)*, as Mutual's top attraction. He kept up his schedule of a Monday through Friday strip plus a Sunday newscast for five years.

Newsmen Lowell Thomas on Blue and NBC's H.V. Kaltenborn both set their all time rating records, reaching an estimated 4.5 million homes — over ten million listeners — with each broadcast.

NBC's *News of the World* strip at 7:15 was in its second season. Reported by richly voiced explorer, John W. Vandercook, it remained among the Top Ten Multiple Run programs — with Vandercook and his successor, Morgan Beatty — for the remaining twelve years of Network Radio's Golden Age.

In February Hooper reported that the networks' prime time given to news had risen three hours a week since Pearl Harbor.

Like the war itself, the trend was just beginning.

TOP 50 PROGRAMS —1941–42

Source: C.E. Hooper Monthly Network Reports, Sep 1941–Jun 1942
NBC 26, CBS 21, Blue 4 (51)*
Total Programs Rated 6–11 P.M.: 156
Average Rating: 16.2, Median: 14.2
Programs Rated 13 Weeks & Ranked: 143
29,300,000 Radio Homes / 81.5% Coverage of U.S. Homes / One Rating Point = 293,000 Homes

		Program	Rtg	Type	Sponsor	Day	Time	Lgth	Net
1	2	Fibber McGee & Molly	31.7	SC	Johnson Wax	Tue	9:30	30	NBC
2	4	Bob Hope Show	30.7	CV	Pepsodent Toothpaste	Tue	10:00	30	NBC
3	3	Edgar Bergen & Charlie McCarthy	28.0	CV	Chase & Sanborn Coffee	Sun	8:00	30	NBC
4	N	Red Skelton Show	27.7	CV	Raleigh Cigarettes	Tue	10:30	30	NBC
5	1	Jack Benny Program	27.2	SC	Jello Gelatin	Sun	7:00	30	NBC
6	7	Aldrich Family/Ezra Stone	26.6	SC	Jello Gelatin & Puddings	Thu	8:30	30	NBC
7	5	Walter Winchell's Jergens Journal	26.0	NC	Jergens Lotion	Sun	9:00	15	Blue
8	6	Lux Radio Theater/Cecil B DeMille	25.1	DA	Lux Soap	Mon	9:00	60	CBS
9	9	Fanny Brice & Frank Morgan Show	23.8	CV	Maxwell House Coffee	Thu	8:00	30	NBC
10	17	Eddie Cantor's Time To Smile	18.7	CV	Ipana & Sal Hepatica	Wed	9:00	30	NBC
11t	11	Kay Kyser Kollege of Musical Knowledge	18.4	APQ	Lucky Strike Cigarettes	Wed	10:00	60	NBC
11t	18	Mister District Attorney/Jay Jostyn	18.4	DCC	Vitalis Hair Tonic	Wed	9:30	30	NBC
13	14	Bing Crosby's Kraft Music Hall	17.4	MV	Kraft Cheese	Thu	9:00	60	NBC
14	19	Rudy Vallee Show	16.9	MV	Sealtest Dairies	Thu	10:00	30	NBC
15	N	Orson Welles Dramas	16.8	DA	Lady Esther Cosmetics	Mon	10:00	30	CBS
16	10	One Man's Family	16.5	DCC	Tenderleaf Tea	Sun	8:30	30	NBC
17t	19	Fitch Bandwagon	15.7	MP	Fitch Shampoo	Sun	7:30	30	NBC
17t	12	Kate Smith Hour	15.7	MV	Grape Nuts Cereal	Fri	8:00	60	CBS
19t	30	Burns & Allen Show	15.6	SC	Swan Soap	Tue	7:30	30	NBC
19t	21	Lowell Thomas News	15.6	NC	Sun Oil	M-F	6:45	15	Blue
21	8	Major Bowes Original Amateur Hour	15.3	TC	Chrysler Corporation	Thu	9:00	30	CBS 1
22	38	HV Kaltenborn News	15.2	NC	Pure Oil	T-T-Sa	7:45	15	NBC
23t	13	Big Town/Edward G Robinson	14.8	DCC	Rinso Laundry Soap	Thu	9:30	30	CBS 2
23t	28	Take It or Leave It/B Hawk,P Baker	14.8	APQ	Eversharp Pens & Pencils	Sun	10:00	30	CBS
25t	24	Fred Allen's Texaco Star Theater	14.2	CV	Texaco	Sun	9:00	30	CBS 3
25t	26	Your Hit Parade/B Wood, J Edwards	14.2	MP	Lucky Strike Cigarettes	Sat	9:00	45	CBS
27	47	Adventures of Sherlock Holmes	14.1	DCC	Bromo Quinine Cold Tablets	Sun	10:30	30	NBC
28	N	Bob Burns Show	14.0	CV	Campbell Soups	Tue	8:30	30	CBS
29	34	Al Pearce Gang	13.6	CV	Camel Cigarettes	Thu	7:30	30	NBC
30	33	Gay 90's Revue/Joe Howard	13.5	MSP	Model Pipe Tobacco	Mon	8:30	30	CBS
31	22	Truth or Consequences/R Edwards	13.4	APS	Ivory Soap	Sat	8:30	30	NBC
32	N	Frank Fay Show	13.3	CV	Tums Antacids	Thu	10:30	30	NBC
33	15	Screen Guild Theater	13.1	DA	Gulf Oil	Sun	7:30	30	CBS
34	N	Abie's Irish Rose	13.0	SC	Drene Shampoo	Sat	8:00	30	NBC
35t	37	Blondie/Penny Singleton, Arthur Lake	12.9	SC	Camel Cigarettes	Mon	7:30	30	CBS
35t	30	First Nighter Program	12.9	DA	Campana Balm	Fri	9:30	30	CBS
37	26	The Parker Family	12.8	SC	Woodbury Soap	Sun	9:15	15	Blue
38t	57	Meet Mr Meek/Frank Readick	12.5	SC	Lifebuoy Soap	Wed	8:00	30	CBS
38t	15	We the People/Gabriel Heatter	12.5	API	Sanka Coffee	Tue	9:00	30	CBS
40	47	Silver Theater	12.4	DA	International Silver	Sun	6:00	30	CBS
41t	25	Dr Christian/Jean Hersholt	12.2	DCC	Vaseline	Wed	8:30	30	CBS
41t	28	Information Please	12.2	PS	Lucky Strike Cigarettes	Fri	8:30	30	NBC
43	40	Vox Pop	12.0	API	Bromo Seltzer	Mon	8:00	30	CBS
44	46	Battle of the Sexes/Crumit, Sanderson	11.7	APQ	Molle Shaving Cream	Tues	9:00	30	NBC
45	N	Philip Morris Playhouse	11.3	DA	Philip Morris Cigarettes	Fri	9:00	30	CBS
46	79	Hollywood Premiere/Louella Parsons	11.2	DA	Lifebuoy Soap	Fri	10:00	30	CBS
47	35	Helen Hayes Theater	10.9	DA	Lipton Tea	Sun	8:00	30	CBS
48	35	Gangbusters	10.6	DA	Sloan's Liniment	Fri	9:00	30	Blue
49	N	Adventures of Ellery Queen	10.5	DCC	Bromo Seltzer	Sat	7:30	30	NBC
50t	N	Great Gildersleeve/Hal Peary	10.3	SC	Kraft Cheese	Sun	6:30	30	NBC
50t	60	Johnny Presents/Ray Bloch Orch	10.3	MV	Philip Morris Cigarettes	Tue	8:00	30	NBC

*Total: 51 (Two programs tied for 50th.)
New & Returning Top 50 Programs Underscored.

1	Major Bowes Original Amateur Hour	Sep — Jan	Chrysler Corporation	Thu	9:00	60	CBS
2	Big Town	Oct — Dec	Rinso Laundry Soap	Wed	8:00	30	CBS
3	Fred Allen's Texaco Star Theater	Oct — Mar	Texaco	Wed	9:00	60	CBS

Key: API — Audience Participation/Interviews
APQ — Audience Participation/Quiz
APS — Audience Participation/Stunts
CV — Comedy/Variety Show
DA — Dramatic Anthology

DCC — Drama/Continuing Characters
MC — Music/Classical, Semi-Classical
MP — Music/Popular, Contemporary
MSP — Music/Specialty, Ethnic
MST — Music/Standard, Traditional

MV — Music/Variety Show
NC — News, Commentary
PS — Panel Show Comedy
SC — Situation Comedy
TC — Talent Competition

1941–42 Top 50 Favorite Formats*

	Programs	Pct
Comedy — All Categories	19	37%
Drama — Anthology & Continuing	15	29%
Music — All Categories	8	16%
Audience Participation — All Categories	6	12%
News/Commentary	3	6%

*Total: 51. (Two programs tied for 50th.)

1941–42 Monthly Winners

Sep	Edgar Bergen & Charlie McCarthy	19.4	Feb	Fibber McGee & Molly		38.0
Oct	Edgar Bergen & Charlie McCarthy	28.3	Mar	Fibber McGee & Molly		38.1
Nov	Edgar Bergen & Charlie McCarthy	30.1	Apr	Fibber McGee & Molly		32.3
Dec	Edgar Bergen & Charlie McCarthy	29.9	May	Bob Hope Show		32.9
	& Walter Winchell's Jergens Journal	29.9	Jun	Bob Hope Show		29.5
Jan	Edgar Bergen & Charlie McCarthy	35.2				

The 1942–43 Network Season

Announcer: You know, it's increasingly amazing how many ways are granted us to give our fighting men and women overseas a boost. For instance, <u>waste</u> <u>kitchen</u> <u>fats</u>. It's certainly nothing to us, but they're a vital ingredient in the manufacture of high explosives. That's the stuff that's rocking our enemies right now fore and aft. The OPA has now authorized your butcher to pay you two brown ration points for every pound of fat you save. <u>Two brown points</u> and <u>four cents in cash!</u> That's certainly good pay to help win the war. So keep rendering the fat and pouring it into smooth edged cans and bringing it to your butcher. You'll collect <u>one</u> point for every half to three-quarters of a pound ... <u>two</u> points for every three-quarters of a pound to a pound! These points will be good for any meat or fat purchases. So <u>get</u> <u>your</u> <u>fat</u> <u>in</u>! It's vitally important. To waste fat is unforgivable, so set the patriotic example in your home and be sure to tell others to <u>save</u> <u>fat</u>! (PAUSE) These are days when good nutrition takes on a new importance. It's downright patriotic to know your vitamin alphabet and to see that your three meals are well balanced. <u>America</u> <u>must</u> <u>be</u> <u>strong</u>! And for America to be strong, <u>Americans</u> <u>must</u> <u>be strong</u>!

A Paper Loss, a Radio Gain

The radio industry and networks both saw their revenue growth stall at single digits — its slowest pace in three years. The cutback in advertising was understandable, as 1942 was the chaotic first year of focusing on mobilization for World War II — not consumerism for the pantry, bathroom and garage.

Then, midway in the 1942–43 season — just as business began to recover — radio's biggest competitor for the advertising dollar was dealt a body blow.

Newsprint was rationed.

Paper was needed for the war effort. Manpower and energy shortages had reduced paper mill production. Transportation of newsprint from the mills to publishers had become difficult with gas shortages. As a result, *The Federal Printing & Publishing General Limitation Order of 1942* allowed newspapers to use only as much paper as they ordered for their net circulation in 1941. The rationing would last through the war years.

Some newspapers reduced their size while others ceased publishing on one or two days a week. All of them stopped printing "extra" editions, eliminated sections directed to special interests, condensed headlines, narrowed margins, reduced photographs and did anything else they could to save paper.

Newspaper content — including newspaper advertising — was severely limited.

As a result, local radio advertising salesmen suddenly found doors opening to them that had once been slammed shut.

Magazines were also hit with paper rationing. National publications had to pare their content and pages, which provided a golden opportunity for the networks to introduce their wares to holdout advertisers.

Broadcasting expected a business bonanza.

Going quietly unnoticed in the wave of optimism was the networks' share of total broadcast industry revenues. It was no longer the lion's share. For the first time since 1927, the networks took in less than half the total collected. National, regional and local dollars spent on the growing number of local stations overtook network revenues and the trend was irreversible.

Despite the war, new stations were still springing up around the country faster than one a week — all eager to get into radio's gold rush.

It was during this spurt of profits that the industry also lent its talent and techniques to two immense broadcasting enterprises that never carried a commercial but are definitely parts of its Golden Age — The Voice of America and Armed Forces Radio.

Be Careful What You Wish For...

Radio's news image was boosted another notch in June 1942 when FDR chose one of its own to control the flow of war information and propaganda.

Elmer Davis, 52, had complained

1942–43 Season Scoreboard Mid-season Totals, December 1942			
		Compared to Year Earlier	
Total Radio Homes	30.60 Mil	+1.30 Mil	+4.4.%
Total Auto Radios	9.00 Mil	+0.25 Mil	+2.9%
Total AM Radio Stations	887	+56	+6.7%
Total Radio Network Affiliates	558	+49	+9.6%
1942 Radio Revenues	260.0 Mil	+12.8 Mil	+5.2%
1942 Network Revenues	128.7 Mil	+3.3 Mil	+2.6%
Network Share	49.5%		(1.2%)
Total TV Stations	4	+2	+100%
Total FM Stations	43	+23	+115%

steadily on his nightly 8:55 CBS news broadcasts about the flow and accuracy of war information coming from Washington. Davis groused in his flat Indiana accent that four separate government agencies with bureaucratic titles — *The Office of Facts & Figures, The Office of Government Reports, The Office of the Coordinator of Information* and *The Information Division of the Office of Emergency Management*— plus each of the military services — all tripped over each other in the dissemination of "official" news and announcements. He said the situation led to duplication, contradictions and utter confusion.

Instead, Davis proposed one super-agency to coordinate the flow of information. The President agreed, eliminated the four agencies and created the *Office of War Information.*

Davis was appointed to head the OWI with total responsibility as the government's voice, reporting only to the White House.

Realizing that his talents lay in content and not detail, Davis immediately recruited his boss, CBS Vice President Ed Klauber, to be his administrative assistant. As a result, OWI became a model of bureaucratic efficiency and journalistic integrity, reflecting the best of the industry they represented.

AMERICA GETS A VOICE

Disseminating war news for domestic consumption was only part of the OWI's job.

The agency was also responsible for telling the world.

In the summer of 1942, Hitler's Germany operated over a hundred shortwave installations pumping Nazi propaganda around the globe — including the United States. Great Britain's BBC operated 50 shortwave stations telling its side of the story.

The United States had only 14 privately owned shortwave stations with no common focus.

Short of commandeering the U.S. shortwave facilities — as was the case in World War I — the Office of War Information *leased* all but one of the nation's powerful shortwave installations in November.

In addition, the OWI proposed to build another 20 shortwave stations for the coordinated broadcast of American news, information and entertainment directed to dozens of countries every day.

The project was named after the government's earlier shortwave programming effort, The Voice of America, and was given immediate priority.

By March 1943 the VOA was shortwaving 2,700 programs a week into all parts of the world.

Eighty percent of the programs were newscasts, which Davis ordered to be totally factual and objective — a stark contrast to the boldfaced propaganda beamed from Axis transmitters. Davis contended that America's greatest propaganda tool was the truth. His policy made VOA the preferred choice for news in neutral and occupied countries.

GI DJs

In response to the needs of U.S. armed forces personnel around the world, the War Department began producing programs specifically for them in the spring of 1942. These programs, including the legendary *Command Performance,* were broadcast by the nation's few but powerful, privately owned shortwave stations.

When the OWI leased the stations in November, it inherited the military's programs — plus the needs of a military audience that had become enormous. It was too much of an additional burden for the agency to handle.

Then help arrived from an unexpected source over 4,000 miles north of Washington.

Acting on their own initiative, a group of GI's stationed in Kodiak, Alaska, had rigged up a low-power, "carrier current" radio station transmitter that radiated from powers lines on the base to entertain their buddies with chatter and popular records sent to them by relatives.

The small station's popularity was reported by the wire services and inspired the War Department to create the Armed Forces Radio Service in early 1943.

With OWI's blessing and counsel, AFRS established military op-

erated radio stations wherever American servicemen were sent, supplying them with transcriptions of *Command Performance, GI Jive* and what eventually became over a hundred programs a week produced specifically for them.

AFRS also distributed discs of popular network shows to its stations with all commercials deleted.

A familiar closing line heard at home following popular Network Radio shows during World War II was, "This program is heard by our men and women serving overseas through the facilities of the Armed Forces Radio Network."

Most important to the young audiences stationed in the military outposts were the plastic *V-Discs* of popular hit records distributed for the use of local GI disc jockeys. Armed Forces Radio became the training ground for many talented broadcasters needed during the postwar station boom

AFRS quickly grew to over 29 short-wave stations; 138 AM stations and 37 U.S. expeditionary force (mobile), stations. By the end of 1943, the total number reached 300 separate AFRS outlets. In Great Britain alone, where thousands of American servicemen were staging for the invasion of France, 50 stations were established under the American Forces Network banner.

Along with its primary function of informing and entertaining U.S. servicemen abroad, AFRS also demonstrated to listeners around the world what American radio was all about. All that was missing were the commercials.

WINNING'S THE ONLY THING

In America, radio was all about winning the war. Every network program contained messages directed to that point — in the form of jokes, songs, public service announcements or themes of entire comedy sketches and dramatic plots.

The nation's advertising agencies created the War Advertising Council in February 1942 — a clearing house and distribution point for messages promoting conservation, volunteerism, war bond sales and overall patriotism. Radio did its part by saturating the air with them.

Efforts weren't limited to brief announcements.

At 9:00 on Saturday, August 28, Blue presented the longest program in its history, *I Pledge America*, a seven hour marathon to sell war bonds that continued until 4:00 the following morning.

Red Skelton, Fanny Brice, Gosden and Correll, Bob Burns, Jack Pearl and Edward G. Robinson were among the network stars who volunteered their time to the program, chatting and joking with servicemen via shortwave while urging listeners to order war bonds via telegrams sent to the program.

Within its first two hours the program sold over four million dollars worth of bonds and by sunrise its total exceeded ten million dollars *(138.8 Mil)*.

In October, British born actor Charles Laughton conducted a one man, 17 hour marathon to sell war bonds. Laughton was given time to break into every NBC program with his appeals. When finished with each pitch, he ambled to a telephone bank and spoke directly with listeners responding to his pleas. When his long day ended, Laughton had single handedly sold over $300,00 in bonds *(4.2 Mil)*.

The same month Kate Smith took to CBS and repeated the stunt — going 20 hours, talking to over two thousand listeners who called with pledges and selling over $1,900,000 *(26.4 Mil)*, worth of bonds. She did it again on CBS's WSJV/Washington the following week and continued her crusade at a relentless pace.

Information Please turned in one of the biggest one-night bond sales when the panel show went on the road to Boston's Symphony Hall in December and sold tickets for the broadcast. Tickets were scaled from $50 to $5,000 in war bond purchases *($694 to $69,400)*. The single show resulted in $4,360,000 in sales *(60.5 Mil)*.

TROUPERS FOR THE TROOPS

Before their 1942–43 seasons began, Network Radio stars began their wartime tradition of enter-

taining the troops stationed outside the United States. Bob Hope, Edgar Bergen, Jack Benny and Al Jolson were among the first to make extended tours of bases in Alaska and the Aleutian Islands. All returned with inspiring material for their programs and personal messages for loved ones of servicemen whom they met in their travels. Theirs were experiences that would be repeated countless times as America's war fronts expanded around the globe and more entertainers joined the brigade of morale boosters.

YOU DON'T SAY!

On the home front, all broadcasters observed restrictions that might somehow aid the enemy.

Man on the street programs were severely limited to prevent the leak of any information deemed critical to the war effort. Requests and dedications were eliminated from music shows to preclude the possibility of coded information being relayed among enemy agents. Weather forecasts and references to climate conditions were dropped altogether. Sound effects of sirens that might be confused with air raid warnings were prohibited.

THE MONTHLIES

NBC won the season with 32 of the annual Top 50 programs. It began a four year stretch in which the network had at least 30 programs on the Top 50 list. NBC's string of consecutive months in which it had the Number One show rolled on to 81.

With only one exception, Tuesday night on NBC became the new home of the monthly winners and all. fell within the network's 90-minute period between 9:30 and 11:00. Newcomer Red Skelton took November, January, March and May. Bob Hope won September, February and April. *Fibber McGee & Molly* was first in October and June. The only break in Tuesday's monopoly was NBC's Sunday giant, *Edgar Bergen & Charlie McCarthy*, which took first place in December.

1942–43 Sunday Night Top Ten Programs
NBC 7, CBS 2, Blue 1
Average: 18.2

Edgar Bergen & Charlie McCarthy	NBC	8:00	30.1
Jack Benny Program	NBC	7:00	26.3
Walter Winchell	Blue	9:00	22.9
Take It or Leave It	CBS	10:00	18.1
Fred Allen's Texaco Star Theater	CBS	9:00	17.0
Fitch Bandwagon	NBC	7:30	16.1
The Great Gildersleeve	NBC	6:30	15.1
One Man's Family	NBC	8:30	14.8
Manhattan Merry Go Round	NBC	9:00	11.1
American Album of Familiar Music	NBC	9:30	10.5

VAUDEVILLE VETS VICTORS

Sunday's five top programs were headlined by former Vaudeville performers.

Edgar Bergen, Jack Benny and Walter Winchell had all built successful Sunday radio franchises.

Fred Allen returned to CBS's Sunday schedule where his network career began in 1932.

Phil Baker, once Ben Bernie's Vaudeville partner, had previous CBS Sunday success with *Gulf Headliners*. He was headed for even greater fame with *Take It or Leave It*. The accordion playing comedian's first full season as host of the comedy quiz resulted in a 20 percent ratings jump and the first of five consecutive Top 20 seasons.

GOODBYE, JELLO...

General Foods was one of radio's most successful sponsors with three of the season's Top Ten programs. Its star attraction, Jack Benny, sold Jello gelatin with great success. His weekly, "Jello, again," had signaled the start of his show for eight seasons and Benny was considered responsible for its widespread popularity.

In 1942, General Foods considered him *too* successful.

Jello contained 60 percent sugar. With the war's sugar shortage and rationing, the product couldn't be made or sold in sufficient quantities to justify the expense of sponsoring Benny, who had just signed a new, two-year contract for $770,000 a year *(10.7 Mil)*, one of the highest program prices in radio.

As a result, General Foods swapped sponsorship between two of its Top 50 programs.

Jello was assigned to Kate Smith's Friday night variety hour. To the delight of GF's Post Cereals division, sponsorship of the Benny program was transferred to Grape Nuts and Grape Nuts Flakes for the next two seasons. Benny began selling the breakfast food just as he had Jello — in record quantities.

... HELLO, NEIGHBORS

A comic twist on man on the street interviews was introduced to Fred Allen's show on December 6 when the comedian began the first of his many strolls along "Allen's Alley," knocking on the doors of its residents — all cultural stereotypes with broad accents to match.

Minerva Pious played Jewish housewife, Mrs. Pansy Neusbaum, Alan Reed portrayed bombastic English poet, Falstaff Openshaw, and Charlie Cantor, using one of his many dimwit voices, was Socrates Mulligan whose intelligence matched that of Cantor's Clifton Finnegan of *Duffy's Tavern*. Early inhabitants of Allen's Alley also included character actors Jack Smart, Pat Flick and John Brown.

A STAR EARNS HIS STRIPES

Gene Autry's 6:30 *Melody Ranch* on CBS became *The Sergeant Gene Autry Show* for the season.

The singing cowboy star had enlisted in the U.S. Army Air Corps on his broadcast of July 26, 1942. Autry's show ran the entire 1942–43 season with a respectable 7.6 rating — selling sell war bonds as well as Wrigley's gum — while he trained to be a pilot.

Autry left the air at the end of the season — but only figuratively speaking.

He flew cargo planes in the China-Burma-India war zone for the next three years.

SUNDAY SLUMPS

Gulf Oil picked up sponsorship of the popular CBS Tuesday entry *We the People* and moved it to Sunday at 7:30 against NBC's *Fitch*

Bandwagon. It proved to be a bad move. The Gabriel Heatter hosted human interest program which lost much of its ad-lib elements due to wartime restrictions. It also lost over 20 percent of its audience, dropped out of the nightly Top Ten and the season's Top 50.

Heatter, whose transcribed Mutual newscasts were heard opposite *We the People*, left the interview program at the end of the season.

Sunday's bigger loser was the venerable *First Nighter*, in its eleventh year on the air. After ten consecutive Top 50 seasons, sponsor Campana Balm lifted the anthology drama from its successful four year run on CBS and placed it in Mutual's Sunday night lineup at 6:00.

First Nighter became Mutual's top rated program of the season, but its weak 9.5 rating dropped it down to 70th place. It would never recapture its former popularity.

1942–43 Monday Night Top Ten Programs
CBS 5, NBC 4, Blue 1
Average: 13.5

Lux Radio Theater	CBS	9:00	24.1
Screen Guild Players	CBS	10:00	19.7
HV Kaltenborn News*	NBC	7:45	14.8
Lowell Thomas News*	Blue	6:45	14.0
Vox Pop	CBS	8:00	13.6
Blondie	CBS	7:30	13.4
Gay 90's Revue	CBS	8:30	12.8
Information Please	NBC	10:30	12.6
Cavalcade of America	NBC	7:30	10.5
Fred Waring Show*	NBC	7:00	10.4

*Monday–Friday Strip Shows

Sans Strips...

Dr IQ	NBC	9:30	9.7
Voice of Firestone	NBC	8:30	9.0
Telephone Hour	NBC	9:00	8.0

ACT FAST!

Lady Esther Cosmetics' new ad agency, Young & Rubicam, took over production of *Screen Guild Theater*, removed it from Sunday's 7:30 ratings battle with *Fitch Bandwagon* and placed it in the prime spot of the CBS schedule, following *Lux Radio Theater*. The program's name was changed to *Screen Guild Players* and its format was switched from variety to a carbon

copy of *Lux Radio Theater*'s recreations of movies — only performed in half the time. With time deducted for commercials, interviews, opens and closes, *Players'* radio adaptations of 90 minute movies had to be performed in 22 minutes or less.

Like *Lux*, top stars appeared on the program. But unlike the high talent fees awarded by *Lux*, film stars appeared on *Players* for no pay in return for Lady Esther's weekly donation of $10,000 (*$138,800*), to the Motion Picture Relief Fund's Country Home for aging and indigent actors.

Listeners responded in big numbers. *Screen Guild Players* doubled the previous season's ratings of Wayne King's schmaltzy *Lady Esther Serenades*. Together, the Lux and Lady Esther film-based anthologies combined to give CBS the top two Monday night programs for five consecutive seasons.

SOAP CHIPS

CBS temporarily cancelled its highly acclaimed, much traveled *Columbia Workshop* in early November. The sustaining anthology drama series had been pushed around into eleven different timeslots in its six years on the air. The network decided that it had better use for the valuable half hour at 10:30 following the suddenly popular *Screen Guild Players* — namely the prime time promotion of its daytime programs.

Hooper surveys indicated that the audience growth of Network Radio's daytime serials on CBS and NBC lagged behind the weekday variety programming offered by Blue, Mutual and independent stations. What's more, listeners were spending less time listening to the daily travails of *Ma Perkins, The Romance of Helen Trent, Our Gal Sunday* and their sisters in soap.

To CBS this was a serious matter. The network broadcast 18 soap operas every weekday — all of them sponsored and all lucrative profit centers.

Coupled with NBC's 21 daily soaps, Hooper estimated that the two networks' low-cost studio dramas drew a cumulative audience of 20 million listeners daily.

CBS wanted to protect its turf.

Daytime Showcase debuted in November, its premiere hosted by CBS daytime stars Kate Smith and Ben Bernie who pitched the weekday schedule and promised synopses and snippets of the network's daytime dramas in the shows to come. As promised, capsules of different CBS soaps were presented by their casts each week

The network promotion lasted for 13 weeks — but the sustaining *Columbia Workshop* didn't return to the timeslot. The powerful lead-in ratings provided by *Screen Guild Players* made the time period too valuable for CBS to sacrifice on prestige or promotion.

The half hour was sold to Ballentine Beer for a new show featuring Guy Lombardo's orchestra and humorist/poet Ogden Nash.

1942–43 Tuesday Night Top Ten Programs
NBC 7, CBS 2, Blue 1
Average: 18.6

Bob Hope Show	NBC	10:00	32.3
Red Skelton Show	NBC	10:30	32.3
Fibber McGee & Molly	NBC	9:30	30.7
Burns & Allen Show	CBS	9:00	16.0
HV Kaltenborn News*	NBC	7:45	14.8
Johnny Presents Ginny Simms	NBC	8:00	14.2
Lowell Thomas News*	Blue	6:45	14.0
Al Jolson Show	CBS	8:30	11.1
Fred Waring Show*	NBC	7:00	10.4
Tums Treasure Chest	NBC	8:30	10.3

*Monday–Friday Strip Shows

Sans Strips...

Lights Out	CBS	8:00	10.0
Duffy's Tavern	Blue	8:30	9.7
Battle of the Sexes	NBC	9:00	9.6

HOT COMEDY ON A COLD NIGHT

Bob Hope and Red Skelton had become full fledged movie stars.

MGM released four Skelton comedies in the summer and fall of 1942. Paramount hit paydirt in November with the third Bob Hope/ Bing Crosby pairing, *The Road to Morocco*.

Both Hope and Skelton had reached new heights of popularity and their ratings reflected it when comedy scored its highest Hooperatings of the decade on the winter night of January 19, 1943, during NBC's powerful Tuesday night lineup.

Hope turned in a record Hooperating of 40.9 at 10:00, immediately followed by Skelton's 40.7 at 10:30. Total sets-in-use approached a remarkable 50 percent during both shows and each captured a share of audience that amounted to over 85 percent of all homes listening to the radio.

Both also benefited that night from *Fibber McGee & Molly*'s lead-in at 9:30 and that show's near record 37.7 rating.

Hope and Skelton's numbers on that night can each be translated to an estimated 12,500,000 homes and some 35 million listeners.

No commercial series would ever come close to those numbers again.

HOPE WINS BY A NOSE

Bob Hope and Red Skelton finished the season tied for Number One honors.

In head to head competition it was as close as any race ever seen in prime time radio.

Each led the other's ratings for five of the season's ten months, although Hope won June by default when Skelton left the air for his summer vacation.

Carrying their full season ratings to the next fraction, Hope finished with 32.32 to Skelton's 32.26 — a difference of ⁶⁄₁₀₀ of a point. However, Crossley, Hooper and Nielsen all rounded out their ratings to the nearest tenth of a point — which results in the 1942–43 season's tie for first place.

WHAT'S UP, DOC?

Gale Gordon left the cast of *Fibber McGee & Molly* for Coast Guard service. Gordon's Mayor LaTrivia character had been Fibber's weekly foil since Throckmorton Gildersleeve left Wistful Vista.

In need of another authority figure for verbal jousting with Fibber, writer Don Quinn came up with Dr. George Gamble. Unlike the explosive LaTrivia or Gildersleeve characters, Arthur Q. Bryan's Doc Gamble was a calm, low keyed nemesis who held his own trading barbs with Fibber, much to Molly's giggling delight.

Few listeners recognized Bryan's normal, mellow regular speaking voice. But in a different characterization his voice was known by millions at the movies — that of the relentless and inept "wabbit" hunter of *Bugs Bunny* cartoons, Elmer Fudd.

JOHNNY CALLS FOR GINNY

Philip Morris turned over its *Johnny Presents* show on NBC to former Kay Kyser band singer Ginny Simms who had paid her dues with a weekly five minute show on CBS the previous season.

Johnny Presents was the umbrella title the cigarette manufacturer had given a number of shows since 1934 — all named after the brand's living symbol, a 47-inch tall former hotel bellman, Johnny Rovetini, whose long and shrill page, "Call for Phil-lip Moorr-reeesss!" opened all of its programs.

The glamorous and personable Simms was the singing hostess of a program with strong human interest appeal. Each week three serviceman guests who were allowed to call anyone, anywhere, while the audience eavesdropped. The show resulted in three seasons in Tuesday's Top Ten and the annual Top 50.

Simms' radio popularity was helped along by her brief but high profile movie career.

She had a leading role in RKO's October release, *Here We Go Again*, a sequel to 1941's *Look Who's Laughing*. Both films starred Edgar Bergen and his dummies, Jim and Marian Jordan as *Fibber McGee & Molly*, and Hal Peary as *The Great Gildersleeve*.

The popular low budget movies were among a string produced by RKO to promote and exploit NBC shows. By the time Simms appeared in *Here We Go Again*, she had already been in three RKO comedies featuring Kay Kyser and his NBC show band.

1942–43 Wednesday Night Top Ten Programs
NBC 7, CBS 2, Blue 1
Average: 14.6

Mr. District Attorney	NBC	9:30	21.7

Kay Kyser's Kol-	NBC	10:00	20.5
lege of Musical			
Knowledge			
Eddie Cantor's	NBC	9:00	19.0
Time to Smile			
HV Kaltenborn	NBC	7:45	14.8
News*			
Lowell Thomas	Blue	6:45	14.0
News*			
Mr. & Mrs. North	NBC	8:00	13.7
Dr Christian	CBS	8:30	12.0
Fred Waring	NBC	7:00	10.4
Show*			
Tommy Dorsey	NBC	8:30	10.1
Orchestra			
Mayor of the	CBS	9:00	9.7
Town			

*Monday–Friday Strip Shows

Sans Strips...
Nelson Eddy	CBS	8:00	8.7
Show			
Sammy Kaye	CBS	8:00	6.5
Orchestra			
Manhattan at	Blue	8:30	6.2
Midnight			

CALL ME MISTER

Mr. District Attorney became radio's most popular detective series with its highest rated season and the first of four consecutive years in the annual Top Ten of all programs. In a rare display of sponsor loyalty, Bristol-Myers remained with *Mr. District Attorney* for a remarkable twelve years.

Coupled with Eddie Cantor's popular *Time to Smile*, Bristol-Myers monopolized the hour's ratings for its multiple brands.

Mr. District Attorney unique as the only Network Radio series in which the lead character went nameless. Regardless, the crime fighting prosecutor — who was in more brawls than courtroom debates — eventually became radio's most popular crime fighting hero.

CALL US MISTER AND MISSUS

Andrew Jergens Company, already the sponsor of Walter Winchell's highly rated Sunday broadcasts, hit paydirt again with *Mr. & Mrs. North*, a weekly murder mystery with sitcom elements. Its similarities to *The Adventures of the Thin Man* were unmistakable — it even debuted in the same NBC Wednesday timeslot that Nick and Nora Charles had occupied during the previous season. But *North* topped *Thin Man*'s ratings by 35 percent.

Mr. & Mrs. North was based on the novels written by husband and wife Richard and Frances Lockridge which resulted in Broadway play in 1941 and an MGM film starring Gracie Allen — without George Burns — in 1942.

Jerry and Pam North were amateur detectives given to clever dialogue and quick comebacks. Joseph Curtin and Alice Frost led the cast for nine of the program's eleven year run — all in the seasons' Top 50 — delivering five consecutive finishes for NBC in Wednesday's Top Ten, followed by another six in Tuesday's Top Ten on CBS.

A RECORD WAR RECORD

Unlike his extroverted stage presence, Kay Kyser was in reality a shy and modest individual.

At 38, he was on the outer age limits for the military draft. Yet, he had refused to request a deferment and reported to his hometown draft board at Rocky Mount, N.C., in April 1943.

But the Office of War Information did intervene. The OWI made public for the first time that Kyser and his show band had logged over a thousand performances at 300 military camps since 1941. If that phenomenal record wasn't enough, Kyser's appearances at civilian events had been credited with over 95 million dollars in war bond sales (*1.32 Bil*).

The agency contended that he was more valuable to the war effort outside the military than within it.

Kyser's draft board had another reason to reject him. "The Old Professor" was blind as a bat without his glasses.

UNLUCKY GREEN

Kay Kyser's sponsor, American Tobacco, wasn't as modest as its hard working star.

Billions of the company's Lucky Strike cigarettes were sold every year — all in the familiar dark green packages. For marketing purposes — and to save printing costs — the company switched to white packaging in November 1942. The switch was heralded with the slogan, "Lucky Strike Green has gone to war!"

The slogan was repeated incessantly as commercials explained that the chemicals used to produce the packaging's green ink were needed for the war effort and giving up its use was Lucky Strike's *patriotic* contribution.

The slogan's blitz caused the War Production Board have its say — and it said, "Wrong!"

There was no special war use for the chromium derivative used in green ink that American Tobacco claimed it had so selflessly sent off to serve its country.

The campaign was abruptly halted after two weeks.

Lucky Strike Green never returned from the war.

1942–43 Thursday Night Top Ten Programs
NBC 9, Blue 1
Average: 17.7

The Aldrich	NBC	8:30	25.7
Family			
Fanny Brice &	NBC	8:00	23.2
Frank Morgan			
Abbott & Costello	NBC	10:00	20.5
Rudy Vallee Show	NBC	9:30	20.2
Bing Crosby's	NBC	9:00	20.0
Kraft Music			
Hall			
March of Time	NBC	10:30	17.9
HV Kaltenborn	NBC	7:45	14.8
News*			
Lowell Thomas	Blue	6:45	14.0
News*			
Jimmy Durante	NBC	10:00	14.1
& Garry Moore			
Bob Burns Show	NBC	7:30	13.8

*Monday–Friday Strip Shows

Sans Strips...
Major Bowes'	CBS	9:00	12.4
Original Ama-			
teur Hour			
Stage Door	CBS	9:30	9.4
Canteen			

CBS SHUT OUT

It had never happened before during Network Radio's Golden Age.

CBS had no programs in a nightly Top Ten.

Ironically, NBC's Thursday night dominance was in large part thanks to new properties developed as segments of CBS's *Kate Smith Hour* — *The Aldrich Family* and *The Abbott & Costello Show*. Both were discovered by the singer's manager, producer and talent scout, Ted Collins.

General Foods' *Aldrich Family* kept solid hold of the night's Number One position despite the loss of its star, Ezra Stone, to the Army for two years. Norman Tokar took the lead for the 1942–43 season and then he was also summoned for military duty.

Columbia's top Thursday show was Major Bowes' former ratings giant, *The Original Amateur Hour,* which lost another 20 percent of its audience and sank further behind Bing Crosby's *Kraft Music Hall.*

Crosby was riding high with the November release of Paramount's *The Road to Morocco,* co-starring Bob Hope — their third *Road* comedy in three years. The pair made frequent guest appearances on each other's NBC programs which spiked their ratings and promoted their films.

Yet, NBC's new Thursday ratings winner was the comedy team that sold even more movie tickets than Hope and Crosby — Abbott and Costello.

AC POWERED RATINGS

When comics Bud Abbott, 45, and Lou Costello, 36, delivered the season's most successful new show to NBC, they already had four years of radio guest appearances behind them, plus 13 weeks as Fred Allen's summer replacements in 1940.

More importantly, they had become major motion picture stars.

Between late 1940 and 1942 the burlesque veterans starred in nine low-budget comedies for Universal Pictures — all of them box office hits and widely credited for keeping the studio from financial ruin. Their verbal slapstick and wordplay routines were simple and predictable but audiences couldn't get enough of them.

Abbott and Costello's half hour variety show — with comedic support from Mel Blanc, Frank Nelson and a crew of Hollywood's top character voices — had a solid five year run on NBC, all of them Top 50 seasons.

But the team's first season was cut short when Costello was stricken with rheumatic fever and hospitalized. The show left the air abruptly in March and left its sponsor, R.J. Reynolds' Camel Cigarettes, and its William Esty agency

scrambling for an immediate replacement.

Producer Phil Cohan is credited with saving the day by creating a new comedy team on a week's notice. It was a pairing that solidly established one Network Radio career and rescued another.

LIKE FATHER, LIKE SON

At 27, Garry Moore was already a three year veteran of daytime radio. The glib, crew cut Moore had co-hosted Blue's weekday afternoon variety show, *Club Matinee,* with humorist Ransom Sherman for two years. During this stint his name was changed from Thomas Garrison Morfit to Garry Moore — judged the winning name submitted in a contest among *Club Matinee* listeners.

Moore took the naming contest gimmick to his next assignment, hosting a new NBC morning variety show opposite Blue's popular *Breakfast Club.* His performance on *The Show with No Name* — later changed to the contest-winning *Everything Goes!* — had earned Moore a shot as Abbott and Costello's summer replacement beginning in June 1943.

But when Abbott and Costello left the air abruptly in March, producer Phil Cohan summoned Moore for immediate duty. Nevertheless, Cohan felt that a second, more established marquee name was needed to share the show's billing.

At 50, Jimmy Durante was considered by many to be a show business relic whose time had passed. His exuberance, his mangling of the King's English and his specialty songs were all legendary but of an earlier time. Except for occasional guest shots, Durante had been out of radio since the 1936 flop, *Texaco's Jumbo Fire Chief.* Yet, Durante had the name that Cohan wanted and Durante wanted the job.

Instead of the continually bickering Abbott and Costello — both on and off the air — Durante and Moore genuinely liked each other and it was obvious. Moore treated the veteran comedian with a breezy deference reserved for a father figure. In return, Durante continually addressed Moore as, "Junior." Their routines often involved compli-

cated linguistic setups or punch lines that left Durante's speech in shambles while Moore could untie the toughest tongue-twisters with ease.

Their three months of substituting for Abbott and Costello didn't have the ratings punch that the two movie comedians gave NBC, but Durante and Moore delivered a substantial audience at a fraction of the cost to sponsor R.J. Reynolds. They were rewarded by Reynolds with their own show the following season — on CBS.

The hastily recruited team remained together for five seasons. Their partnership became the springboard for their subsequent, successful solo careers in television.

MY TIME IS MARITIME

Rudy Vallee's ratings snapped back 20 percent, giving the singer his highest numbers in seven years.

The upswing began in November 1941 when Vallee added movie comedienne Joan Davis to his Sealtest Dairies variety show. The gawky redhead had been the star or co-star of eight films since 1939. Her face and comic persona of a man-hungry bachelorette were already popular with millions when her radio career began. By the next season she would be a Top Ten star in her own right.

Vallee sang his familiar theme, "My Time Is Your Time," for the last time on the Sealtest show of July 1, 1943 when the 41-year-old star announced that he was leaving radio to serve his country as a Chief Petty Officer in the U.S. Coast Guard and leader of the Eleventh Naval District band.

Under Vallee's direction the band became a major attraction and fund raiser for the Navy Relief Fund.

1942–43 Friday Night
Top Ten Programs
CBS 5, NBC 4, Blue 1
Average: 12.7

Kate Smith Hour	CBS	8:00	15.5
Adventures of the Thin Man	CBS	8:30	15.1
HV Kaltenborn News*	NBC	7:45	14.8
Lowell Thomas News*	Blue	6:45	14.0
People Are Funny	NBC	10:00	12.1
Tommy Riggs & Betty Lou	NBC	7:30	11.6

Philip Morris Playhouse	CBS	9:00	11.2
That Brewster Boy	CBS	9:30	11.1
Camel Caravan	CBS	10:00	10.7
Fred Waring Show*	NBC	7:00	10.4

*Monday–Friday Strip Shows

Sans Strips...

Waltz Time	NBC	9:00	10.2
Plantation Party/ Whitey Ford, Red Foley	NBC	9:30	10.0
Gangbusters	Blue	9:00	9.6

A FUNNY THING HAPPENED...

Brown & Williamson Tobacco folded its *Wings of Destiny* aviation adventure drama — not so coincidentally sponsored by the company's *Wings Cigarettes* — after a season and a half of single digit ratings.

The tobacco giant took a flyer on newcomers Art Linkletter and John Guedel who proposed an audience participation stunt show, *People Are Funny,* with Linkletter, 30, and seasoned actor/radio personality Art Baker, 44, as its co-hosts.

The program debuted in April 1942, and was immediately popular. B&W sensed it might have another hit like Red Skelton's *Raleigh Cigarette Program.*

The co-host concept was dropped at the end of the season when egotistical Baker delivered a him-or-me ultimatum and insisted that Linkletter be fired.

Linkletter bowed out of the spotlight yet remained Guedel's production partner in the program. Their friendship and successful business relationship flourished for over 50 years, producing *People Are Funny,* the daytime hit *House Party* and Groucho Marx's prime time comedy quiz, *You Bet Your Life.*

People Are Funny was a Top 50 program for eleven consecutive years. But Baker was only around for its first full season's 40th place finish in 1942–43. His personality clashes with producer Guedel backfired and he was fired at the end of the season.

Linkletter took over the following season and hosted the show to its greatest successes.

KIDDING AROUND

It was a period when juvenile humor was in vogue — when laughs were generated from the mouths of fictional adolescents and sub-teens, often played by adults. Edgar Bergen's Charlie McCarthy led a pack of over a dozen comedies designed to get laughs from "kids."

Friday was home to two of the season's crop, both Top 50 shows.

Tommy Riggs and his alter-ego voice, Betty Lou, had been off the air for two seasons when producer Ted Collins signed the act in a new sitcom sketch format for a 1942 spring run on Kate Smith's variety hour. Riggs' return was so well received that Lever Brothers used the sitcom — featuring top character actors Mel Blanc, Verna Felton, Bea Benederet and Wally Maher in support — as a summer replacement for Burns and Allen.

Then, as it had with previous Collins' discoveries on CBS — *The Aldrich Family* and *Abbott & Costello* — NBC stole the show and Riggs enjoyed a final, successful season before enlisting in the Navy.

CBS had lifted *That Brewster Boy* and sponsor Quaker Oats from NBC in March 1942.

Like *The Parker Family* on Blue, *That Brewster Boy* was another *Aldrich Family* wannabe, centered on the tribulations of an awkward teenaged boy. The title role was originated by Eddie Firestone, succeeded by Arnold Stang and Dick York who both went on to successful film and television careers.

That Brewster Boy held its own with double digit ratings until midway into the 1944–45 season when it was suddenly cancelled and morphed into *Those Websters* a week later.

1942–43 Saturday Night Top Ten Programs
NBC 7, CBS 3
Average: 11.7

Truth or Consequences	NBC	8:30	15.4
Abie's Irish Rose	NBC	8:00	14.9
Your Hit Parade	CBS	9:00	14.5
Adventures of Ellery Queen	NBC	7:30	12.1
Can You Top This?	NBC	9:30	11.8
Blue Ribbon Town	CBS	10:15	10.4
National Barn Dance	NBC	9:00	10.4
Grand Ole Opry	NBC	10:30	9.6
Saturday Night Serenade	CBS	9:45	9.3

Bill Stern's Colgate Sports Newsreel	NBC	10:00	8.8

A PENNY FOR YOUR THOUGHT...

A middle-aged New York housewife thought she had the right answer when *Truth or Consequences* host Ralph Edwards asked her, "How many Kings of England had the name Henry?"

She thought wrong, answered five and girded herself for the consequence that the gleeful Edwards had cooked up for her.

To her surprise, the chore was simply to count pennies.

The kicker was that the pennies were to be mailed to her home by the show's listeners. Edwards gave out her address and urged the *Truth or Consequences'* audience to send their pennies to her. He promised that all pennies received would be used to buy war bonds for the woman's son serving in the Marine Corps.

Two days later the first of over 200,000 letters arrived — each containing a penny or more.

The woman reported later to Edwards that she had counted over 300,000 coins — mostly pennies — which bought over $3,000 ($41,600), in war bonds for her son.

The stunt had a happy, heartwarming ending.

It also proved how powerful radio could be.

More than a showman, Edwards was also a shrewd producer. His "Penny" stunt demonstrated the responsiveness of his listeners to Proctor & Gamble — a longtime sponsor of daytime soap operas where mail-in premium offerings were often used as a yardstick of listener response.

The success of Edwards' stunt and his subsequent promotions which all generated national attention, kept P&G's Duz laundry soap a satisfied sponsor of *Truth or Consequences* for ten straight seasons.

... AND NICHOLS FOR A HIT

Procter & Gamble preceded *Truth or Consequences* with the Saturday's second most popular program.

The soap maker had held down the 8:00 timeslot since 1940. The first eighteen months were given to *Knickerbocker Playhouse*, an obvious copy of the low-budgeted, formulaic *First Nighter*, right down to employing many of the same actors. Ratings were mediocre and P&G cancelled the program in January 1941— replacing it with a serial/sitcom adapted from a 1922 Broadway stage hit that ran for over five years and 2,300 performances, *Abie's Irish Rose*.

Playwright Anne Nichols, who wrote the original play, supervised the project.

Like *Knickerbocker*, the program's cast was comprised of solid radio actors, not expensive movie stars. The continuing story of the Irish Catholic girl and her young Jewish husband enjoyed an immediate 60 percent ratings spike into double digits.

Abie's Irish Rose had three Top 50 seasons, all in Saturday's Top Ten leading into *Truth or Consequences*. It was cancelled in 1944 when P&G's Drene shampoo switched its sponsorship to Rudy Vallee's return to radio from military duty.

Nevertheless, author Nichols wasn't finished. Radio had demonstrated continued popularity of her characters which was all the proof she needed to sell a second screen adaptation *Abie's Irish Rose* to the movies. Her 20-year-old idea about enduring love in a marriage between different cultures was translated successfully from the stage to radio and two films. As a result of her concept, Nichols collected over

two million dollars in royalties during her lifetime.

AMOS & ANDY'S ADIEU

Freeman Gosden and Charles Correll said goodbye to listeners of their 15 minute serial on February 19,1943. The once invincible *Amos & Andy* had limped along on CBS in the ratings behind Fred Waring's show band on NBC since the beginning of the season. It was only during the strip's final month on the air, after word got out that the show was closing, when *Amos & Andy*'s ratings jumped 25 percent.

Many listeners who had grown up with the serial wanted one last visit.

Then, after 13½ seasons at 7:00 every weeknight, it was over.

The timeslot was filled the following Monday by *Four to Go*, a low budget studio musical, while *I Love a Mystery* was being prepared for its classic strip format.

But anyone who expected Gosden and Correll to take their money and retire quietly didn't know the pair. They went to work immediately plotting a major comeback.

ME RETIRE? NEVER!

Hans Von Kaltenborn was at the peak of his career and in the second of four consecutive Top 50 seasons. His 7:45 NBC news report and commentary was been expanded from three to five nights a week and overtook Lowell Thomas at the head of the season's Top Ten Multiple Run list.

Kaltenborn, 65, was earning a reported $200,000 *(2.8 Mil)*, from sponsor Pure Oil, for which he

considered himself lucky after years in the lower paying newspaper business.

Time reported a pep talk Kaltenborn gave himself before every broadcast, "Make it good, old boy. It may be your last."

Far from it, Kaltenborn remained a radio and television notable for another decade.

NAMES IN THE NEWS

Kaltenborn founded *The Association of News Analysts* in 1942 — a group 20 Network Radio commentators who took serious and scholarly views of the news — as opposed to Walter Winchell's sensational approach laden with sound effects.

Many of Kaltenborn's association colleagues came from careers as newspaper columnists, reflected in the titles of their programs: *Confidentially Yours* by Arthur Hale; *The Human Side of the News* by Edwin C. Hill; *Monitor Views the News* by Erwin Canham; *Sizing Up the News* by Cal Tinney and Cecil Brown; *Washington Merry Round* by Drew Pearson; *Watch the World Go By* by Earl Godwin, and *Your Land & Mine* by Henry J. Taylor.

Meanwhile, Blue began to assert its status as an "independent" network by signing Godwin and Raymond Gram Swing to compliment its top rated Lowell Thomas — although NBC would snatch Thomas from Blue midway into the following season.

Godwin had the longest work week of all network newscasters. His *Watch the World Go By* news and commentary was heard on Blue at 8:00, seven nights a week.

1942–43 Top Ten Multiple Run Programs CBS 3, NBC 3, Blue 2, MBS 2 Average: 9.5				
HV Kaltenborn News*	M–F	NBC	7:45	14.8
Lowell Thomas News*	M–F	Blue	6:45	14.0
Fred Waring Show*	M–F	NBC	7:00	10.4
Amos & Andy*	M–F	CBS	7:00	9.5
Gabriel Heatter News*	M–F	MBS	9:00	9.4
John W Vandercook News of the World	M–F	NBC	7:15	8.7
Harry James Orchestra	T,W,T	CBS	7:15	7.6
The Lone Ranger	M,W,F	Blue	7:30	7.0
I Love a Mystery*	M–F	CBS	7:00	6.9
John B Hughes News	W,Sa	MBS	10:00	6.5
*Monday–Friday Strip Shows				

Top 50 Programs — 1942–43

NBC 32, CBS 17, Blue 2 (51)*
Average Rating: 17.0, Median: 15.1
30,600,000 Radio Homes / 84% Coverage of U.S. Homes / One Rating Point = 306,000 Homes
Source: C.E. Hooper Semi-Monthly Reports, Sep 1942–Jun 1943
Total Programs Rated 6–11 P.M.: 148
Programs Rated 13 Weeks & Ranked: 141

		Program	Rtg	Type	Sponsor	Day	Time	Lgth	Net
1t	2	Bob Hope Show	32.3	CV	Pepsodent Toothpaste	Tue	10:00	30	NBC
1t	4	Red Skelton Show	32.3	CV	Raleigh Cigarettes	Tue	10:30	30	NBC
3	1	Fibber McGee & Molly	30.7	SC	Johnson Wax	Tue	9:30	30	NBC
4	3	Edgar Bergen & Charlie McCarthy	30.1	CV	Chase & Sanborn Coffee	Sun	8:00	30	NBC
5	5	Jack Benny Program	26.3	SC	Grape Nuts Cereal	Sun	7:00	30	NBC
6	6	Aldrich Family/Norman Tokar	25.7	SC	Jello Gelatin & Puddings	Thu	8:30	30	NBC
7	8	Lux Radio Theater/Cecil B DeMille	24.1	DA	Lux Soap	Mon	9:00	60	CBS
8	9	Fanny Brice & Frank Morgan Show	23.2	CV	Maxwell House Coffee	Thu	8:00	30	NBC
9	7	Walter Winchell's Jergens Journal	22.9	NC	Jergens Lotion	Sun	9:00	15	Blue
10	11	Mister District Attorney/Jay Jostyn	21.7	DCC	Vitalis Hair Tonic	Wed	9:30	30	NBC
11t	N	Abbott & Costello Show	20.5	CV	Camel Cigarettes	Thu	10:00	30	NBC 1
11t	11	Kay Kyser Kollege of Musical Knowledge	20.5	APQ	Lucky Strike Cigarettes	Wed	10:00	60	NBC
13	14	Rudy Vallee Show	20.2	MV	Sealtest Dairies	Thu	9:30	30	NBC
14	13	Bing Crosby's Kraft Music Hall	20.0	MV	Kraft Cheese	Thu	9:00	30	NBC
15	33	Screen Guild Players (Theater)	19.7	DA	Lady Esther Cosmetics	Mon	10:00	30	CBS
16	10	Eddie Cantor's Time to Smile	19.0	CV	Ipana & Sal Hepatica	Wed	9:00	30	NBC
17	23	Take It or Leave It/Phil Baker	18.1	APQ	Eversharp Pens & Pencils	Sun	10:00	30	CBS
18	119	The March of Time	17.9	DA	Time Magazine	Thu	10:30	30	NBC
19	25	Fred Allen's Texaco Star Theater	17.0	CV	Texaco	Sun	9:30	30	CBS
20	17	Fitch Bandwagon	16.1	MP	Fitch Shampoo	Sun	7:30	30	NBC
21	19	Burns & Allen Show	16.0	SC	Swan Soap	Tue	9:00	30	CBS
22	17	Kate Smith Hour	15.5	MV	Sanka Coffee	Fri	8:00	60	CBS
23	31	Truth or Consequences/Ralph Edwards	15.4	APS	Duz Laundry Soap	Sat	8:30	30	NBC
24t	52	Adventures of the Thin Man	15.1	DCC	Woodbury Cosmetics	Wed	8:00	30	CBS
24t	50	Great Gildersleeve/Hal Peary	15.1	SC	Kraft Cheese	Sun	6:30	30	NBC
26	34	Abie's Irish Rose	14.9	SC	Proctor & Gamble	Sat	8:00	30	NBC
27t	22	HV Kaltenborn News	14.8	NC	Pure Oil	M-F	7:45	15	NBC
27t	16	One Man's Family	14.8	DCC	Royal Pudding/Tenderleaf Tea	Sun	8:30	30	NBC
29	25	Your Hit Parade/F Sinatra & J Edwards	14.5	MP	Lucky Strike Cigarettes	Sat	9:00	45	CBS
30	N	Ginny Simms Show	14.2	MV	Philip Morris	Tue	8:00	30	NBC
31	N	Jimmy Durante & Garry Moore Show	14.1	CV	Camel Cigarettes	Thu	10:00	30	NBC
32	19	Lowell Thomas News	14.0	NC	Sun Oil	M-F	6:45	15	Blue
33	28	Bob Burns Show	13.8	CV	Lever Brothers	Thu	7:30	30	NBC 2
34	N	Mr & Mrs North/Joe Curtin, Alice Frost	13.7	DCC	Jergens Lotion	Wed	8:00	30	NBC
35	43	Vox Pop	13.6	API	Bromo Seltzer	Mon	8:00	30	CBS
36	35	Blondie/Penny Singleton, Arthur Lake	13.4	SC	Camel Cigarettes	Mon	7:30	30	CBS
37	30	Gay 90's Revue/Joe Howard	12.8	MSP	Model Pipe Tobacco	Mon	8:30	30	CBS
38	41	Information Please!	12.6	PS	HJ Heinz Foods	Mon	10;30	30	NBC 3
39	21	Major Bowes Original Amateur Hour	12.4	TC	Chrysler Corporation	Thu	9:00	30	CBS
40t	49	Adventures of Ellery Queen	12.1	DCC	Bromo Seltzer	Sat	7:30	30	NBC
40t	N	People Are Funny/Art Baker	12.1	APS	Wings Cigarettes	Fri	9:30	30	NBC
42	41	Dr Christian/Jean Hersholt	12.0	DCC	Vaseline	Wed	8:30	30	CBS
43	N	Can You Top This?	11.8	PS	Colgate Shaving Cream	Sat	9:30	30	NBC
44	N	Tommy Riggs & Betty Lou	11.6	SC	Lever Brothers	Fri	7:30	30	NBC
45	45	Philip Morris Playhouse	11.2	DA	Philip Morris Cigarettes	Fri	9:00	30	CBS
46t	N	Al Jolson Show	11.1	MV	Colgate Palmolive Peet	Tue	8:30	30	CBS
46t	76	Manhattan Merry Go Round	11.1	MP	Dr Lyons Tooth Powder	Sun	9:00	30	NBC
46t	98	That Brewster Boy	11.1	SC	Quaker Oats	Fri	9:30	30	CBS
49	N	Camel Caravan/Herb Shriner	10.7	CV	Camel Cigarettes	Fri	10:00	60	CBS
50t	53	American Album of Familiar Music	10.5	MST	Bayer Aspirin	Sun	9:30	30	NBC
50t	72	Cavalcade of America	10.5	DA	Dupont Chemicals	Mon	8:00	30	NBC

*Two programs tied for 50th.

New & Returning Top 50 Programs Underscored.

1	Abbott & Costello Show	Oct–Dec	Camel Cigarettes	Thu	7:30	30	NBC
2	Bob Burns Show	Oct–Dec	Lever Brothers	Wed	9:00	30	CBS
3	Information Please	Sep–Feb	Lucky Strike Cigarettes	Fri	10:30	30	NBC

Key: API — Audience Participation/Interviews   DCC — Drama/Continuing Characters   MV — Music/Variety Show
APQ — Audience Participation/Quiz   MC — Music/Classical, Semi-Classical   NC — News, Commentary
APS — Audience Participation/Stunts   MP — Music/Popular, Contemporary   PS — Panel Show Comedy
CV — Comedy/Variety Show   MSP — Music/Specialty, Ethnic   SC — Situation Comedy
DA — Dramatic Anthology   MST — Music/Standard, Traditional   TC — Talent Competition

1942–43 Top 50* Favorite Formats

	Programs	Pct
Comedy — All Categories	21	40%
Drama — Anthology & Continuing	11	22%
Music — All Categories	11	22%
Audience Participation — All Categories	5	10%
News/Commentaries	3	6%

*Total: 51 (Two programs tied for 50th.)

1942–43 Monthly Winners

Sep	Bob Hope Show	31.7	Feb	Bob Hope Show	36.6
Oct	Red Skelton Show	29.7	Mar	Red Skelton Show	33.8
Nov	Red Skelton Show	33.7	Apr	Bob Hope Show	32.2
Dec	Edgar Bergen & Charlie McCarthy	36.3	May	Red Skelton Show	28.6
Jan	Red Skelton Show	40.5	Jun	Fibber McGee & Molly	24.8

16

The 1943–44 Network Season

Announcer: It was an Englishman, the Earl of Sandwich, who first invented the portable meal of two bread slices put together with a rich, flavorful filling. But it was we Americans who popularized the handy sandwich. Today, more and more Americans are carrying sandwiches than ever before. And the fillings for those sandwiches are a problem ... quite a problem in these days of wartime rationing. So I want to suggest how to make the points you spend for sandwich fillings do double duty! Use Kraft Cheese Spreads, a spread for the bread and filling for the sandwiches! Kraft gives you a wonderful assortment of cheese spreads ... Pimento, Olive Pimento, Pineapple, Roca and Relish. Kraft Old English Spread takes four ration points but all the rest take only three. And remember, all these are dairy products ... nutritious and wholesome. Let these famous Kraft Spreads help you put variety into the lunch box sandwiches you pack. And let them give you easy refreshment into your holiday parties! Just a few Kraft Cheese Spreads served on a tray with crackers, something hot or cold to drink, and your snack is ready with no trouble at all! Tomorrow, when you're shopping, remember Kraft Cheese Spreads!

A BIG TAX BREAK

Commercial radio had its biggest year since 1937.

The paper rationing that limited newspaper and magazine advertising was only part of the equation leading to broadcasting's record revenues. The Internal Revenue Service ruled that monies spent on advertising were deductible from an excess profits tax imposed for the duration.

Advertisers were given a choice — spend it or send it to the government.

Most chose to spend it.

As a result of the spending spree, two previously unsold network series were sold for more than a million dollars each.

U.S. Rubber paid seven figures for the New York Philharmonic's Sunday afternoon broadcasts on CBS which had gone without a sponsor for 13 years. General Motors paid a million for the NBC Symphony's concerts two hours later.

With so much demand for network time, NBC was able to hang the *Sold Out* sign on its entire 7:00 to 11:00 prime time schedule at the beginning of the 1943–44 season.

CBS wasn't far behind to report a sell-out while Blue and Mutual both registered healthy gains.

Blue's 68 percent revenue in-

crease in the first eight months of 1943 capped its year and a half of independence from NBC during which the castoff network had picked up 30 new affiliates and 20 new sponsors.

Credit goes to Blue's enthusiastic young president, 40-year-old Mark Woods, who was an up and coming NBC executive when he was given the task of heading the new company.

Woods had a vision for the WJZ anchored network free from NBC control.

He began to pattern it after Mutual — allowing the broadcast of phonograph records and transcribed programming, beefing up the news department, encouraging new low-budgeted programs, offering special discounts to advertisers and aggressively pursuing affiliate growth.

Above all, Woods knew that his mission was to make Blue a profitable operation, attractive to prospective buyers.

RCA's asking price for the network was twelve million dollars *(156.9 Mil)*.

At that price, Blue's bottom line had to look good.

THE CANDY MAN CAN!

The Blue network was beginning to look good to Ed Noble after a dozen potential buyers had balked at the price. They were all conservative businessmen and unfamiliar with broadcasting. Noble was neither.

Edward J. Noble was only 30 when he and a partner bought the idea for Life Savers from a Cleveland candy maker in 1913. Thirty years and billions of Life Savers later, Noble's business successes included ownership of WMCA, a popular New York independent station.

Like Woods, Noble saw Blue's

1943–44 Season Scoreboard Mid-season Totals, December 1943			
		Compared to Year Earlier	
Total U.S. Radio Homes	30.80 Mil	+0.2 Mil	+0.7%
Total U.S. Auto Radios	8.00 Mil	(1.0 Mil)	(11.1%)
Total U.S. AM Radio Stations	910	+23	+6.7%
Total U.S. Radio Network Affiliates	620	+62	+11.1%
1943 Radio Revenues	313.6 Mil	+53.6 Mil	+20.6%
1943 Network Revenues	156.5 Mil	+27.8 Mil	+21.6%
Network Share	49.9%		+0.4%
Total TV Stations	8	+/-0	+/-0%
Total FM Stations	52	+6	+6.1%

potential. He further believed that he could get a lower price if he simply waited.

In the summer of 1943, Noble offered RCA eight million dollars for the network and its three owned stations — WJZ/New York, KGO/San Francisco and WENR/Chicago, which split time on its 890 frequency with WLS.

Sold!

Under the FCC's duopoly provision limiting owners to one AM station per market, Noble sold WMCA and took control of Blue in January. His first acts were to retain Woods as his CEO and sell a 12½ percent interest in the network to Time, Incorporated.

Noble then used the FCC's duopoly edict to his advantage.

He went to work on West Coast Packard automobile dealer Earle C. Anthony to sell one of his two Los Angeles stations to his new American Broadcasting Company. For years Anthony had resisted NBC's attempts to buy his powerful KFI.

Instead, Noble set his sights on Anthony's other station, his namesake KECA. With Anthony under the government gun to sell, Noble got it. The station eventually became KABC.

"C" for Caesar and Czar

Musicians' union boss James C. Petrillo had called another strike a year earlier, forbidding AFM players to perform in any recording sessions except for V-Discs — made specifically for Armed Forces Radio.

At issue was Petrillo's insistence that record companies somehow prevent their discs from being played on radio or jukeboxes. His demand was ruled unenforceable by the courts which revealed Petrillo's real motive.

He wanted a piece of the action — approximately one percent of the price of every record sold — to be paid into a union welfare fund that he alone would administer. The AFM's boycott of recording studios was the leverage Petrillo used to get it.

In response, record companies stockpiled hundreds of sides before the July 31, 1942, walkout, but their inventories were running out by mid–1943.

Local radio stations around the country — and their listeners — clamored for new records that featured more than the novelty sounds of harmonicas and ukuleles which the union didn't consider to be musical instruments.

As the strike dragged on through the summer of 1943, Petrillo rebuffed a personal plea from President Roosevelt to end the boycott. The union leader became seen as a petty dictator — mere mention of his name on comedy shows brought laughs and catcalls.

Decca Records — a lower cost label that recorded Bing Crosby — was losing millions in sales and became the first to capitulate to Petrillo's demands in October. Other companies slowly followed suite.

Major labels RCA Victor and Columbia held out for another year before caving in to the union boss who had defied public derision and government pressure in order to make millions for "his boys."

Radio's D-Day

The most historic broadcast of the season began in the midnight hours of June 6, 1944, when most of America slept.

Wire services began flashing the bulletins at 12:37 A.M. (Eastern War Time), citing German sources which reported that the long awaited Allied invasion of Europe had begun. Radio Berlin immediately began a running account of the early paratroop landings and bombardment of the northern coastal areas of France.

Unlike Pearl Harbor, the networks had months to prepare for D-Day. When it finally came — even in the dead of night — they were fully staffed and ready. Aware of a false alarm dispatched by the Associated Press two days earlier, the network newsmen cautiously cited enemy shortwave as their source of information. Finally, after three hours of winging it with German reports, shortwave confirmation came from General Eisenhower's headquarters in London that the invasion was indeed underway.

Then the networks went about the business of describing the 5,000 vessel armada crossing the English Channel with 150,000 Allied troops headed for the beaches of Normandy.

The "D" in D-Day has no definition, military or otherwise. But it was the Day of Deliverance for broadcasting from the shadow of newspapers as a primary source for news.

NBC's Wright Bryan had flown over the area with an early wave of paratroopers, carrying a recorder for an on-the-spot report. The network ban of transcribed material was shoved aside and his report via shortwave from London was the first eyewitness account of D-Day action to be broadcast.

Equally dramatic were the recordings made in a landing craft by Blue's London Bureau chief, George Hicks. Richard C. Hottelet's described the scene from an Allied bomber on CBS, and Mutual's Larry Meier witnessed a beachhead landing.

Few listeners heard these reports when first broadcast before sunrise. But as America awoke and realized what was happening, the transcriptions added vivid dimension to the continuous coverage that took over Network Radio for the day without commercial interruption.

A special Hooper survey commissioned by CBS estimated that radio listening on D-Day was 82 percent higher than normal. President Roosevelt's address to the nation that evening resulted in a 45.2 rating.

Both overseas and at home, the networks were on top of the story of D-Day and the ensuing campaigns across Europe.

In London, competing correspondents shared information and facilities. With the exception of occasional scoops, a spirit of cooperation thrived to get the story straight and straight to the listener.

The overall tone of "facts first" and putting journalistic egos aside was bluntly defined by CBS news chief Paul White, who told his staff shortly before D-Day, "Remember, winning the war is a hell of a lot more important than reporting it."

The Fourth Chime

NBC's famous three note melody struck on chimes that concluded all of its network programs since 1929 — *G, E, C* — was altered for the first hours of the network's D-Day coverage. The network had devised a separate use for the familiar system-cue that signaled local affiliates to cut away from the network and alerted its own engineers to begin necessary switching for the next network program.

The additional in-house purpose — for which the chimes had seldom been used — was to alert NBC executives and news personnel out of telephone reach to contact the office immediately and possibly report for duty. For this function a fourth note was added to the melody which became *G-E-C-C.*

The fourth chime was heard several times in the early morning hours of June 6 when it became apparent that D-Day was a reality. But given the urgency of the broadcast, it seems hardly necessary that NBC newsmen should have been told to come to work early.

THE 30-DAY BONDBARDMENT

Radio continued to devote more total time to selling war bonds than any other single product.

The second highest rating of the season was 44.4, scored on Monday, January 17, when *Let's All Back the Attack!* was broadcast on all four networks at 9:00, preempting *Lux Radio Theater, The Telephone Hour, Dr. IQ,* Gabriel Heatter's news and ventriloquist Paul Winchell.

Attack was an hour-long kickoff to the Fourth War Loan war bond drive with a goal of $14 Billion *(183.08 Bil).* Suave Conrad Nagel hosted the movie and radio star gala with transcribed remarks from General Dwight Eisenhower and Admiral Chester Nimitz. A total of $65 Million worth of advertising time and space *(850.0 Mil),* was pledged to the drive by the broadcast, print and outdoor media.

The 30 day campaign exceeded its goal by nearly 10 percent.

AS SEEN ON TV — BUT NOT HEARD

NBC and Philco were both pioneers in early television. The war had severely limited development of the medium, but the two companies accomplished the first publicized attempt to link two stations on May 25, 1944.

WNBT's signal from New York City was picked up by a relay tower in New Jersey and pushed on to Philco's WPTZ in Philadelphia. In effect, television networking was born with the transmission.

But it didn't come without some labor pains.

NBC's Eddie Cantor appeared on television's inaugural chain hookup and launched into a duet of "We're Having a Baby, My Baby and Me" from his 1942 Broadway musical, *Banjo Eyes.* TV's first "network" censors found the lyrics objectionable and cut the telecast's sound midway through the song.

The act embarrassed and angered both Cantor and Philco. In retaliation, Philco invited Cantor to appear on its *Radio Hall of Fame* show on Blue the following Sunday night.

He did and sang the song in its entirety.

THE MONTHLIES

NBC continued to dominate the ratings with the season's Top Five programs and eight of the first eleven.

NBC's Tuesday night comedy block again provided each month's Number One program — running the network's string up to 91 consecutive monthly winners.

Fibber McGee & Molly won five months, Bob Hope was first in four and. Red Skelton completed the Tuesday sweep by tying with Sunday's Edgar Bergen and Charlie McCarthy in September.

The three Tuesday programs ran in a tightly knit pack. The difference between first and second place was half a rating point or less in October, November, February and April.

---

*1943–44 Sunday Night
Top Ten Programs*
NBC 5, CBS 4, Blue 1
Average: 18.1

Edgar Bergen & Charlie McCarthy	NBC	8:00	26.8
Jack Benny Program	NBC	7:00	23.7
Walter Winchell's Jergens Journal	Blue	9:00	21.4
Take It or Leave It	CBS	10:00	19.2
Fred Allen's Texaco Star Theater	CBS	9:30	18.0
The Great Gildersleeve	NBC	6:30	16.3
Adventures of the Thin Man	CBS	10:30	15.0
Fitch Bandwagon	NBC	7:30	14.8
One Man's Family	NBC	8:30	13.1
Crime Doctor	CBS	8:30	13.0

ONCE IN 120 MONTHS

Sunday's Top Five finished in the same order as the previous season. It was the first time in the dozen years since ratings were first published that any night's Top Five repeated in order from one season to the next.

The same names would continue appearing in Sunday's top tier of programs for the next three seasons with one notable exception, Fred Allen.

ALLEN'S ILLS

Fred Allen wasn't a well man. His high blood pressure led to heart problems in 1943 and delayed his return from "summer" vacation until December. Texaco covered the 9:30 timeslot on CBS with tenor James Melton and a half hour of light classics and standards. The fill-in *Texaco Star Theater* registered a meager 8.5 rating in early December.

Allen's homecoming show later in the month scored 20.4, his highest rating in five years. He went on to enjoy his best rated season since 1939–40. But by June, the responsibility of writing and starring in the weekly show took its toll again.

Doctors ordered Allen off the air for the entire following season during which Melton would again deliver single-digit ratings.

Fred Allen never returned to CBS.

PHILCO'S VARIETY VARIETY SHOW

Philco had no love for RCA although the former Philadelphia Storage Battery Company had become the nation's leading home and auto radio manufacturer, outselling the giant RCA by more than two to one when the war started.

A dispute over radio tubes in 1930 started their feud and

prompted Philco to pull its concert series from RCA-owned NBC and move it to CBS. Nearly fourteen years later, Philco's ill feelings toward RCA and NBC still lingered and Blue's new management team, mostly former NBC executives, took advantage of it.

They sold Philco two high profile programs during Blue's early years as an independent competitor to NBC. The first was *Radio Hall of Fame* in 1943. It was Blue's only attempt at a full hour, major league variety show with big name guest stars.

Radio Hall of Fame was produced in conjunction with show business trade journal *Variety. Variety*'s influence and Philco's top dollar talent fees assured the show of headline talent every week. Philco reportedly budgeted a million and a half dollars annually for the program *(19.6 Mil)*, and Blue scheduled it at 6:00 on Sunday, considered a safe hour before the competition for listeners from NBC and CBS got stiff.

Virtually every top name from radio, movies and the stage appeared on *Radio Hall of Fame* over its three season run. *Time* magazine hailed its December 1943 premiere starring Bob Hope and Jimmy Durante as promising, "...The most entertaining hour in U.S. radio."

Entertaining or not, *Radio Hall of Fame* was a ratings dud — never getting as high as one of the season's Top 100 programs. It was outscored by a three to one margin by NBC's *Great Gildersleeve*, while sitcoms *The Adventures of Ozzie & Harriet* and Fanny Brice's *Baby Snooks* on CBS kept it buried in a distant third place during its time period. *Radio Hall of Fame* was cut to 30 minutes in its third season and quietly left the air in April 1946.

Nevertheless, Philco didn't give up on the new Blue network. The two concocted another new show in October 1946 that literally turned the tables on network radio, Bing Crosby's *Philco Radio Time*.

DOCTORING THE RATINGS
Network stars commonly appeared in films — it was good for the box office and for ratings.

But film producers seldom took the chance of basing a movie on an also-ran radio property — until *Crime Doctor* came along.

Philip Morris established *Crime Doctor* on the CBS Sunday schedule in 1940 where it remained for seven seasons at 8:30. The first three seasons were an uphill fight against the NBC favorite *One Man's Family* which benefited from Edgar Bergen's powerful lead-in.

During the period *Crime Doctor*'s title role had been handed down from Ray Collins to John McIntyre to Brian Donlevy — all returning only single digit rating results.

Then, in the summer of 1943, Columbia Pictures released the first in its series of ten *Crime Doctor* movies, low-budget film noir mysteries starring Warner Baxter as the psychologist/detective. The movie and its first sequel in December gave the radio series the promotional push it needed — a 40 percent ratings increase into the first of three consecutive Top 50 seasons.

Six months before the first film's release, *Crime Doctor*'s radio role was given to *Mercury Theater* veteran Everett Sloane who shared in the show's newly found popularity for its final four seasons.

IF A FORD CAN AFFORD IT...
Auto magnate Henry Ford had a soft spot for Greenfield, Michigan, his home town.

This was no more evident than when Ford Motors bought 15 minutes on Blue's Sunday night schedule to present the Greenfield Chapel Children's Choir. The company had bought weekday and Sunday time for the hymn singers beginning in 1937. The question was if they were ready for prime time — opposite *Edgar Bergen & Charlie McCarthy* at 8:00.

The choral concerts began in January 1944 and remained on Blue's schedule for 18 months, but only once generated a rating over a 3.0. The Greenfield Choir became network radio's longest running, lowest rated, sponsored program.

But Henry Ford paid his bills promptly and that was important to the new network. *Besides, what's a network to do against Bergen and McCarthy?*

Surprisingly, Blue answered its own question five years later with a giveaway show called *Stop the Music.*

KIDS WHIZ QUIZZES
Stop the Music's future creator, Chicago based producer Louis G. Cowan, already had a show going on Blue — one of only ten programs that the network placed in the season's Top 100.

The Quiz Kids was Cowan's weekly contest that pitted a panel of four or five juvenile geniuses, ages six to 16, against questions submitted by listeners and often against teams of adult experts and educators.

A team of network news commentators — Earl Godwin, H.R. Baukhage, Leland Stowe and John W. Vandercook — took on a panel of *Quiz Kids* in 1943 and were shut out. The average age of the kids' panel on that broadcast was ten.

Over 200 children and teenagers appeared on the program during its twelve year run, all hosted by jovial Joe Kelly and all sponsored by Miles Laboratories' Alka Seltzer — the same host and sponsor of Saturday night's *National Barn Dance.*

The Quiz Kids enjoyed a six year prime time run on Blue and hit its rating high of 9.5 during the 1943–44 season at 7:30. The show never achieved Top 50 status but it delivered a respectable rating and a reliable advertiser for the network — until NBC stole both for its Sunday afternoon schedule in 1946.

1943–44 Monday Night Top Ten Programs
CBS 5, NBC 5
Average: 14.0

Lux Radio Theater	CBS	9:00	23.3
Screen Guild Players	CBS	10:00	20.5
Blondie	CBS	7:30	15.4
HV Kaltenborn News*	NBC	7:45	13.4
Lowell Thomas News*	NBC	6:45	12.7
Vox Pop	CBS	8:00	12.7
Information Please	NBC	10:30	11.5
Gay 90's Revue	CBS	8:30	11.1
Dr IQ	NBC	9:30	9.8
Cavalcade of America	NBC	7:30	9.4

*Monday–Friday Strip Shows

Sans Strips...

Blind Date	Blue	8:30	9.0

| Adventures of Sherlock Holmes | MBS | 8:00 | 8.7 |

BLUE LOSES VOICE IN DIVORCE

Blue lost a dependable weeknight Top Ten program when NBC took full custody of Lowell Thomas in January during Blue's transition from a co-owned to a competing network. Between his nightly newscasts and twice weekly narration of Fox *Movietone* newsreels, Thomas had one of America's most familiar voices. Although his program was already broadcast by a number of NBC affiliates in scattered markets, his departure formally ended a 13 year association with Blue.

It also marked the first time that Blue had been totally shut out of a weeknight's Top Ten.

Thomas joined some heavyweight company. Top Ten hits Jack Benny, *Fibber McGee & Molly, The Aldrich Family* and *Mr. District Attorney*— plus a host of other programs from *Information Please* to *The National Barn Dance*— who were all alumni of Blue and graduated to the more powerful NBC. With Thomas gone, Blue was left with only two Top 50 programs for the season — Walter Winchell's Sunday *Jergens Journal* and *Duffy's Tavern* on Tuesday.

And one of those would leave for NBC the following year.

IT TAKES A PUN TO KNOW ONE...

Stripped by NBC, the new Blue was scrapping for new programming like the expansion team that it was during its first year. The network began experimenting with weekly half hour shows at 7:00 to counter the Multiple Runs offered by the other networks.

One of its first offerings in January was *Heidt Time for Hires* packaged by bandleader Horace Heidt who was never without a gimmick to keep his show band employed. His past gigs included *Answers by the Dancers, Anniversary Night with Horace Heidt, Pot o' Gold* and *Tums Treasure Chest.*

The new show's title was a multiple play on words conveying his name, his sponsor's name — Hires Root Beer — and the show's theme, "It's high time to hire returning servicemen!"

Interspersed with pop tunes from his "Musical Knights" band — formerly the "Heidt Brigade" — the enthusiastic Heidt interviewed returning veterans from the war who had received early discharges — often from wounds suffered in battle. With their life and war stories told, attempts were made to solicit jobs for the vets from employers who were listening and moved to call the program.

Not many employers were listening — or anyone else. *Heidt Time for Hires* was buried in the ratings.

Adding to the show's troubles, two of the featured "GI's back from the war" turned out to be phonies who had lied their way onto the program before its producers had the opportunity to check their stories.

The show left the air after a year. Always resilient, Horace Heidt would return two years later with his biggest hit of all.

1943–44 Tuesday Night Top Ten Programs
NBC 6, CBS 3, Blue 1
Average: 18.3

Bob Hope Show	NBC	10:00	31.7
Fibber McGee & Molly	NBC	9:30	31.3
Red Skelton Show	NBC	10:30	29.9
Burns & Allen Show	CBS	9:00	17.0
HV Kaltenborn News*	NBC	7:45	13.4
Johnny Presents Ginny Simms	NBC	8:00	13.0
Lowell Thomas News*	NBC	6:45	12.7
Judy Canova Show	CBS	8:30	11.7
Duffy's Tavern	Blue	8:30	11.5
Big Town	CBS	8:00	10.9

*Monday–Friday Strip Shows

Sans Strips...

| Tums Treasure Chest | NBC | 8:30 | 9.9 |
| Molle Mystery Theater | NBC | 9:00 | 9.5 |

FILLING THE HOPE CHEST

Lever Brothers bought Chicago toothpaste manufacturer Pepsodent and inherited sponsorship of Bob Hope's top rated program. Always the opportunist, Hope negotiated a new contract that paid him $15,000 a week (*$196,000*), to deliver the show. The comedian reportedly netted over half for himself.

Lever Brothers spent money to make money. With the highly budgeted *Lux Radio Theater* and Hope, the company had the Number One program on both Monday and Tuesday nights.

And Lever had a third winner up its sleeve for Friday, as well.

MAID TO ORDER LAUGHS

Marlin Hurt was a 39-year-old journeyman saxophonist, vocalist and sometimes character actor in late 1943 when he caught Don Quinn's ear. Quinn was continually scouting for new characters to drop into his *Fibber McGee & Molly* scripts. World War II service had removed Bill Thompson and Gale Gordon from the cast and Quinn needed fresh foils for Fibber.

Hurt had the unique ability to switch his voice into a totally believable, throaty and jovial falsetto shaded with a stereotypical *Aunt Jemima* dialect. His character was introduced to the show at midseason as Beulah, the McGees' maid — never explaining how the McGees could afford a maid.

Hurt's opening shout every week, "Somebody bawl fo' Beulah?" brought down the house. The character's catch-phrase, "Love dat man!," caught on immediately.

Fibber McGee & Molly finished the season less than a rating point behind Bob Hope's Number One program. It was the first of an unmatched six consecutive seasons that Jim and Marian Jordan's sitcom would finish in second place.

Beulah remained a popular member of the McGee household through the 1944–45 season when it was decided that Hurt could carry a spinoff show on his — or her — own.

A BIG TOWN IN THE YEAST

Big Town returned to CBS after a year's hiatus following the departure of its star, Edward G. Robinson.

Creator Jerry McGill brought Broadway actors Ed Pawley and Fran Carlon into the lead roles and the pair struggled in their first season. The former Top 20 program fell out of the season's Top 50, losing more than 30 percent of Robinson's audience. But Sterling Drug's Ironized Yeast stayed with the low budget newspaper melodrama. It bounced back into the Top 50 the following year and became CBS's highest Tuesday program for four consecutive seasons.

UNCLE MILTIE — TUESDAY'S POOR RELATIVE

Milton Berle was only 35 but a 20 year veteran of show business and still looking for his big break.

He had starred in two low-budget 20th Century–Fox mystery-comedies in 1942, *Whispering Ghosts* and *Over My Dead Body.* But Berle is best remembered in films as the hero's wisecracking sidekick with names like Frosty, Nifty and Lucky.

His radio career had followed suite with a mediocre resume that included 1936's *Gillette Community Sing* and the short lived *Stop Me if You've Heard This One* in 1940.

When Blue began experimenting with weekly half hour programs at 7:00, Eversharp bought a new concept starring Berle, *Let Yourself Go.* The pen and pencil manufacturer was riding high with Sunday's hit, *Take It or Leave It* and was a believer in the comedian-hosted audience participation format. Unfortunately, *Let Yourself Go* was no *Take It or Leave It,* and Milton Berle was no Phil Baker.

Go's format invited contestants and celebrities alike to fulfill a fond desire — the sillier the better — and hopefully make fools of themselves in the process. Guest stars over the show's first weeks included movie character actors Ned Sparks, Roland Young and Patsy Kelly — hardly big name guests.

The best rating Berle could deliver with the absurdity was a lowly 3.0 — on the same night that his contemporaries, Bob Hope and Red Skelton, were racking up 30s. Berle's attempts to compete for Tuesday's radio audience with *Let Yourself Go* was a dismal failure. Ironically, Berle returned to Tuesday night four years later with television's *Texaco Star Theater.* TV made him the hottest comedian in show business and he stole Network Radio's audience by the millions.

BLUE'S LAST ROUND

After four seasons, three sponsors and two networks, producer/star Ed Gardner pushed *Duffy's Tavern* into Tuesday's Top Ten with annual ratings gains averaging 20 percent. The Blue network sitcom continued to build audience against stiff competition from CBS and NBC, scoring the first of six consecutive Top 50 seasons.

Then, like so many other promising hits developed on Blue, sponsor Bristol-Myers moved the program to NBC at the end of the season. *Duffy's Tavern* became the Blue Network's last Top 50 comedy/variety show. By the time the network had another hit two years later, the it was known as ABC.

JUDY PUNCHES IN

Gardner's wise-cracking, big city sitcom was programmed against a new, similarly structured sitcom on CBS with a completely opposite setting and appeal.

Judy Canova was a pig-tailed 30-year-old who had years of stage experience, a dozen movies and scores of radio guest appearances to her credit when her own show was scheduled on CBS in 1943. A singer/comedienne given to both ballads and yodeling, Canova became known as "Queen of the Hillbillies" from her films.

The Judy Canova Show, a rural sitcom with music, shot immediately into the season's Top 50 and stayed there for nine years. After her first season's success, sponsor Colgate packed up the show and moved it to NBC — where former competitors Judy Canova and Ed Gardner both became part of the network's comedy monopoly.

1943–44 Wednesday Night Top Ten Programs
NBC 8, CBS 2
Average: 13.3

Mr. District Attorney	NBC	9:30	21.4
Kay Kyser's Kollege of Musical Knowledge	NBC	10:00	19.1
Eddie Cantor's Time to Smile	NBC	9:00	16.8
Mr. & Mrs. North	NBC	8:00	14.1
HV Kaltenborn News*	NBC	7:45	13.4
Dr Christian	CBS	8:30	13.2
Lowell Thomas News*	NBC	6:45	12.7
Frank Sinatra Show	CBS	9:00	12.2
Beat the Band	NBC	8:30	10.2
Fred Waring Show*	NBC	7:00	9.4

Monday–Friday Strip Shows

Sans Strips...

Jack Carson Show	CBS	9:30	8.0
Sammy Kaye & Monty Wooley Show	CBS	8:00	7.9
First Nighter	MBS	9:30	5.9

SINATRA'S DOUBLE SIDED HITS

CBS always had an ear for young singers.

It had nurtured Bing Crosby and Kate Smith to radio stardom in the early 1930s, then caught Frank Sinatra at the height of his "bobbysox" popularity in 1943 when American Tobacco made Sinatra the star of Lucky Strike's *Your Hit Parade* with immediate ratings success.

Less than two years after leaving the Tommy Dorsey band for a solo career, the 28-year-old Sinatra was given his own variety as the mid-season replacement for *Mayor of the Town,* starring screen legend Lionel Barrymore, 66, which was nudged over to the network's Saturday schedule.

Sinatra's first month on the air attracted 50 percent more audience than the aging Barrymore could muster. The singer was on his way to accomplishing a rare feat — starring in two Top 50 shows in the same season.

BONDING WITH LISTENERS

Despite Sinatra's success with CBS, his Wednesday competitor on NBC at 9:00, Eddie Cantor, attracted almost 40 percent more audience.

Cantor, 52, proved that he still had his energy and a persuasive pull with listeners by executing a memorable stunt in early 1944.

At six in the morning on Saturday, January 29, 1944, Cantor began a 33 hour marathon broadcast from NBC's KPO/San Francisco. It was a big show, complete with a full orchestra and backup singers with the objective to sell war bonds.

Cantor's broadcast originated from a theater with seating for a rotating audience who purchased war bonds to attend an hour's portion of the show. Over 17,000 bonds were sold as his fans flocked in to see Cantor sing, dance and joke with the crowd over the long stretch.

But that was just a trickle compared to the flood of response that flowed from the KPO listening audience. When all bond sales resulting from the broadcast were tallied, they totaled an astonishing 40 million dollars *(514.2 Mil)*.

A RARE MEDIUM? WELL, DUNNINGER...

Joseph "The Master Mind" Dunninger — once known on the Vaudeville circuits as "Master Joseph Dunninger, Child Magician" — toured the nation's theaters and night clubs with a popular mind reading act.

The 50-year-old jack of all illusions offered a $10,000 reward to anyone who could prove that he employed plants or accomplices of any kind as he surveyed his audiences and dramatically related answers to questions they had secretly written down which allowed him to, "Lock into their thoughts."

Sherwin-Williams Paints bought the idea for radio and Blue scheduled Dunninger on Wednesday at 9:00 opposite NBC's Eddie Cantor and Frank Sinatra on CBS.

Of all people, a mystic should have foreseen the ratings wreck ahead.

After a respectable opening in January, the novelty of a magic act on radio wore off quickly. Dunninger finished the season with a feeble 3.9. Nevertheless, his sponsor was somehow convinced to stuck with him until midway through the next season.

But then, Dunninger was also a hypnotist.

1943–44 Thursday Night Top Ten Programs
NBC 10
Average: 17.2

The Aldrich Family	NBC	8:30	22.3
Abbott & Costello	NBC	10:00	21.3

Sealtest Village Store	NBC	9:30	21.3
Fanny Brice & Frank Morgan	NBC	8:00	19.9
Bing Crosby's Kraft Music Hall	NBC	9:00	19.6
March of Time	NBC	10:30	16.0
Bob Burns Show	NBC	7:30	15.6
HV Kaltenborn News*	NBC	7:45	13.4
Lowell Thomas News*	NBC	6:45	12.7
Fred Waring Show*	NBC	7:00	9.4

*Monday–Friday Strip Shows

Sans Strips...

Major Bowes' Original Amateur Hour	CBS	9:00	9.3
Suspense	CBS	8:00	8.3
Death Valley Days	CBS	8:30	7.4

N ... B ... SWEEP!

NBC swept the nightly Top Ten — a feat that would never be duplicated.

It was also the second season that the network fed two of Thursday's Top Ten programs simultaneously to different parts of the country. The Chicago-based Pure Oil Company's sponsorship of H.V. Kaltenborn's nightly 7:45 newscast extended only to the Midwest and south where Pure Oil gas stations were located. For eastern and West Coast audiences, Lever Brothers' Lifebuoy Soap picked up the entire 7:30 half hour for Bob Burns' weekly variety show. Both sides of the split-feed were strong enough to finish in the annual Top 50 for two seasons.

RUDY WHO?

Joan Davis made sponsor Sealtest forget Rudy Vallee.

With *Wizard of Oz* "Tin Man" Jack Haley as her co-star, Davis held her own in the strong NBC lineup with her newly formatted *Sealtest Village Store* sitcom. Davis and Haley pushed their way into the season's Top Ten, something that Vallee was unable to do in his three years of Sealtest sponsorship.

It was the first of two Top Ten and four Top 50 seasons for the comedienne.

A MAJOR COLLAPSE

Major Bowes' Original Amateur Hour took the biggest fall of the

season, dropping 25 percent of its audience in one year and a full 50 percent in three seasons. The former Number One program finished the season in 71st place with less than half of Bing Crosby's *Kraft Music Hall* rating. The question became how long Chrysler Corporation — with nothing to sell to the public but its name for the remainder of World War II — would remain the sponsor of Bowes' fading show.

1943–44 Friday Night Top Ten Programs
CBS 5, NBC 5
Average: 12.2

Amos & Andy	NBC	10:00	14.6
Kate Smith Hour	CBS	8:00	14.1
HV Kaltenborn News*	NBC	7:45	13.4
Lowell Thomas News*	NBC	6:45	12.7
Jimmy Durante & Garry Moore	CBS	10:00	12.1
Stage Door Canteen	CBS	10:30	11.6
People Are Funny	NBC	9:30	11.5
Philip Morris Playhouse	CBS	9:00	11.0
That Brewster Boy	CBS	9:30	10.8
Bill Stern's Colgate Sports Newsreel	NBC	10:30	10.1

*Monday–Friday Strip Shows

Sans Strips...

Gangbusters	Blue	9:00	10.0
Waltz Time	NBC	9:00	10.0

THE BIG COMEBACK

Freeman Gosden and Charles Correll staged the fastest and biggest comeback in Network Radio history.

When *Amos & Andy* finished its weeknight quarter hour run on CBS the previous February, the two radio veterans quickly went to work reinventing their format.

The cozy little two man studio show was out — replaced by a weekly sitcom performed before an audience with a stage full of actors and musicians — almost all of them black performers. *Amos & Andy* was suddenly a major production with a staff of writers, producers and directors.

Lever Brothers' Rinso laundry soap brought the pair back to NBC's Friday schedule after their seven months in exile. Listeners found their familiar favorites in new situations with new characters and fresh, crisply delivered material. They liked what they found.

From their last, dismal half-season's 9.5 rating in the old format, *Amos & Andy* rebounded with a 14.6, their highest rating in seven years.

And after two season finishes below the annual Top 50, the crafty Gosden and Correll were first in Friday's ratings and headed back to the annual Top Ten.

LADY LIBERTY'S A CONTRALTO

Kate Smith duplicated her war bond selling marathon of 1942 with another 20 hour appeal broadcast by CBS on September 28, 1943, which netted $39 Million in sales *(510.0 Mil)*. Smith was continually pitching bonds on her weekly variety show, her daily CBS daytime program, *Kate Smith Speaks*, and her countless personal appearances where she was forever singing "God Bless America."

By the end of the war, Kate Smith was reported to have personally participated in the sale of $600 Million *(7.54 Bil)*, in bonds.

1943–44 Saturday Night Top Ten Programs
NBC 7, CBS 3
Average: 12.1

Your Hit Parade	CBS	9:00	16.7
Truth or Consequences	NBC	8:30	14.7
Can You Top This?	NBC	9:30	13.2
Abie's Irish Rose	NBC	8:00	12.3
Grand Ole Opry	NBC	10:30	11.8
Adventures of Ellery Queen	NBC	7:30	11.3
Million Dollar Band aka Palmolive Party	NBC	10:00	10.8
National Barn Dance	NBC	9:00	10.7
Saturday Night Serenade	CBS	9:45	9.4
Blue Ribbon Town	CBS	8:00	9.3

SINATRA LEADS THE PARADE

Your Hit Parade's twelfth season was its best ever.

Frank Sinatra joined Lucky Strike's weekly countdown of pop music hits during the previous February as its co-star with Joan Edwards. His presence became felt in 1943–44 when the program broke into the season's Top 20 for the first time in nine years.

It stayed there for two seasons — until Sinatra left.

The singer was just eight years removed from his first radio appearance on Major Bowes' amateur show in 1935 with the Hoboken Four quartet. His rise through the Harry James and Tommy Dorsey orchestras into a shrewdly managed solo career paid off in a reported 1943 income of $100,000 *(1.3 Mil)*.

Sinatra's first starring film, RKO's *Higher & Higher,* was released in December and his crooning its Oscar-nominated "I Couldn't Sleep a Wink Last Night" was a smash with his bobby-sox following. As a result, *Your Hit Parade* featured Sinatra singing his own hit song every week in early 1944.

MAKING LISTENERS GAG

When NBC's *Stop Me if You've Heard This One* was cancelled in 1940, panelist "Senator" Ed Ford believed its concept — a group of veteran storytellers swapping jokes from memory — had more potential than the 26 weeks that sponsor Quaker Oats had given it. The short lived show had come from nowhere to place in the season's Top 50 before it was cancelled and Ford saw opportunity.

A master at switching jokes to fit different situations, Ford switched the format of *Stop Me if You've Heard This One* and came up with *Can You Top This?* He sold it to Colgate for a trial run on New York's WOR in late 1940.

The show was simple and cheap to produce. Listeners were given five dollars for jokes they submitted that were read on the air by comedian/dialectician Peter Donald. Then it was up to Ford, 56, and his longtime pals from the Lambs Club — cartoonist Harry Hirschfield, 58, and comedian/author Joe Laurie, Jr., 50 — to each "top" the listeners' jokes with one of their own in the same general category, ad-libbed from memory. The trio claimed a mental inventory of over 15,000 jokes.

Winners were determined by a decibel meter reading of studio audience laughter and resulting scores were displayed on the studio's "laugh meter." Whenever one of the three pros failed to top a listener's joke, another two dollars was added to the contestant's five dollar prize.

Can You Top This? was in the second of its five year run on WOR sponsored by Colgate's regionally marketed Kirkman's Laundry Soap, when the parent company took the show to NBC's Saturday schedule — and kept it on WOR, as well. For the next three seasons two different performances of *Can You Top This?* were heard in New York City every week.

The show made its greatest ratings increase during the 1943–44 season, its second of five in the annual Top 50. It eventually played on three networks in weekly or Multiple Run form over a 14 year span. As time went by, the prize money increased but not by much. The prize wasn't as important as the punch lines and laughs.

Ed Ford's faith in the discarded program concept gave him the last laugh — all the way to the bank.

MR. FORD'S MUSIC FOR SQUARES

Henry Ford's heavy foot stepped on the toes of J. Walter Thompson when his new ad agency signed Tommy Dorsey's popular orchestra for a 13 week Saturday night series on Blue. The auto magnate wanted nothing to do with the "Devil's Music!" that Dorsey represented.

Ford had his Sunday night hymns from Blue's lowly rated Greenfield Chapel Children's Choir. He determined to have "his kind" of music on Saturday nights, too — music for square dancing.

Early American Dance Music featured "The Ford Early American Dance Orchestra" — a dulcimer, a cymbal, a violin and bass — plus a "caller" for those dancing along at home — which probably included the entire Ford household but not many more. It was among the season's lowest rated programs.

OBJECTIONABLE OBJECTIVITY

Five of the highest rated Multiple Run programs were newscasts from NBC and Mutual.

1943–44 Top Ten Multiple Run Programs (11)
NBC 4, CBS 3, MBS 3, Blue 1
Average: 8.5

HV Kaltenborn News*	M–F	NBC	7:45	13.4
Lowell Thomas News*	M–F	NBC	6:45	12.7
Fred Waring Show*	M–F	NBC	7:00	9.4
Gabriel Heatter News*	M–F	MBS	9:00	9.2
I Love a Mystery*	M–F	CBS	7:00	8.0
Harry James Orchestra	T,W,T	CBS	7:15	7.6
John W Vandercook News of the World*	M–F	NBC	7:15	7.5
The Lone Ranger	M,W,F	Blue	7:30	7.2
Fulton Lewis Jr. News*	M–F	MBS	7:00	5.1
Gracie Fields Victory Show*	M–F	MBS	9:15	5.1
John Nesbitt's Passing Parade	T,W,T	CBS	7:15	5.1

*Monday–Friday Strip Shows

CBS was conspicuously missing. *The World Today* with Joseph C. Harsch — the network's former Rome and Berlin correspondent — could only muster a third of Lowell Thomas' ratings on NBC when the two were pitted against each other at 6:45.

The CBS promotion department went to work attempting to elevate its news department's image with a full page ad in metropolitan newspapers. The ad proclaimed that neither the network nor its newscasters and commentators would ever express editorial opinion.

Speaking for his Association of Radio News Analysts, NBC's H.V. Kaltenborn expressed outrage by saying, "No newsman worth his salt could or would be completely neutral or objective!"

Taking the offense personally, CBS newsman Cecil Brown quit the network. Brown was the voice of the network's nightly *Johns-Manville News* which CBS had smartly carved out of its prime-time programming every night at 8:55.

Brown left for Mutual where he would remain for the next dozen years.

The CBS ad was never seen again.

Top 50 Programs — 1943–44
NBC 30, CBS 18, Blue 2
Average Rating: 16.7, Median: 15.0
30,800,000 Radio Homes / 83.6% Coverage of U.S. Homes / One Rating Point = 308,000 Homes
Source: C.E. Hooper Semi-Monthly Reports, Sep 1943–Jun 1944.
Total Programs Rated 6–11 P.M.: 188
Programs Rated 13 Weeks & Ranked: 183

		Program	Rtg	Type	Sponsor	Day	Time	Lgth	Net
1	1	Bob Hope Show	31.7	CV	Pepsodent Toothpaste	Tue	10:00	30	NBC
2	3	Fibber McGee & Molly	31.3	SC	Johnson Wax	Tue	9:30	30	NBC
3	2	Red Skelton Show	29.9	CV	Raleigh Cigarettes	Tue	10:30	30	NBC
4	4	Edgar Bergen & Charlie McCarthy	26.8	CV	Chase & Sanborn Coffee	Sun	8:00	30	NBC
5	5	Jack Benny Program	23.7	SC	Grape Nuts Cereal	Sun	7:00	30	NBC
6	7	Lux Radio Theater/Cecil B DeMille	23.3	DA	Lux Soap	Mon	9:00	60	CBS
7	6	Aldrich Family/Dickie Jones	22.3	SC	Jello Gelatin & Puddings	Thu	8:30	30	NBC
8t	10	Mister District Attorney/Jay Jostyn	21.4	DCC	Vitalis Hair Tonic	Wed	9:30	30	NBC
8t	9	Walter Winchell's Jergens Journal	21.4	NC	Jergens Lotion	Sun	9:00	15	Blue
10t	11	Abbott & Costello Show	21.3	CV	Camel Cigarettes	Thu	10:00	30	NBC
10t	N	Joan Davis/Jack Haley Village Store	21.3	SC	Sealtest Dairies	Thu	9:30	30	NBC
12	15	Screen Guild Players	20.5	DA	Lady Esther Cosmetics	Mon	10:00	30	CBS 1
13	8	Fanny Brice & Frank Morgan Show	19.9	CV	Maxwell House Coffee	Thu	8:00	30	NBC
14	14	Bing Crosby's Kraft Music Hall	19.6	MV	Kraft Cheese	Thu	9:00	30	NBC
15	17	Take It or Leave It/Phil Baker	19.2	APQ	Eversharp Pens & Pencils	Sun	10:00	30	CBS
16	11	Kay Kyser Kollege of Musical Knowledge	19.1	APQ	Lucky Strike Cigarettes	Wed	10:00	60	NBC
17	19	Fred Allen's Texaco Star Theater	17.3	CV	Texaco	Sun	9:30	30	CBS
18	21	Burns & Allen Show	17.0	SC	Swan Soap	Tue	9:00	30	CBS
19	16	Eddie Cantor's Time to Smile	16.8	CV	Ipana & Sal Hepatica	Wed	9:00	30	NBC
20	29	Your Hit Parade/F Sinatra & J Edwards	16.7	MP	Lucky Strike Cigarettes	Sat	9:00	45	CBS
21	24	Great Gildersleeve/Hal Peary	16.3	SC	Kraft Cheese	Sun	6:30	30	NBC
22	18	March of Time	16.0	DA	Time Magazine	Thu	10:30	30	NBC
23	33	Bob Burns Show	15.6	CV	Lifebuoy Soap	Thu	7:30	30	NBC
24	36	Blondie/Penny Singleton, Arthur Lake	15.4	SC	Camel Cigarettes	Mon	7:30	30	CBS
25	24	Adventures of Thin Man	15.0	DCC	Post Toasties Cereal	Sun	10:30	30	CBS
26	20	Fitch Bandwagon	14.8	MP	Fitch Shampoo	Sun	7:30	30	NBC
27	23	Truth or Consequences/R Edwards	14.7	APS	Duz Laundry Soap	Sat	8:30	30	NBC
28	N	Amos & Andy	14.6	SC	Rinso Laundry Soap	Fri	10:00	30	NBC
29t	22	Kate Smith Hour	14.1	MV	Sanka Coffee	Fri	8:00	60	CBS
29t	34	Mr & Mrs North/Joe Curtin, Alice Frost	14.1	DCC	Woodbury Soap	Wed	8:00	30	NBC

	Program	Rtg	Type	Sponsor	Day	Time	Lgth	Net
31 *27*	HV Kaltenborn News	13.4	NC	Pure Oil	T-T-Sat	7:45	15	NBC
32t *43*	Can You Top This?	13.2	PS	Colgate Shaving Cream	Sat	9:30	30	NBC
32t *42*	Dr Christian/Jean Hersholt	13.2	DCC	Vaseline	Wed	8:30	30	CBS
34 *27*	One Man's Family	13.1	DCC	Royal Pudding/Tenderleaf Tea	Sun	8:30	30	NBC
35t *75*	Crime Doctor/Everett Sloane	13.0	DCC	Philip Morris Cigarettes	Sun	8:30	30	CBS
35t *30*	Ginny Simms Show	13.0	MV	Philip Morris Cigarettes	Tue	8:00	30	NBC
37t *32*	Lowell Thomas News	12.7	NC	Sun Oil	M-F	6:45	15	NBC 2
37t *35*	Vox Pop	12.7	API	Bromo Seltzer	Mon	8:00	30	CBS
39 *26*	Abie's Irish Rose	12.3	SC	Drene Shampoo	Sat	8:00	30	NBC
40 *N*	Frank Sinatra Show	12.2	MV	Vimms Vitamins	Wed	9:00	30	CBS
41 *31*	Jimmy Durante &Garry Moore Show	12.1	CV	Camel Cigarettes	Fri	10:00	30	CBS
42 *65*	Grand Ol Opry	11.8	MSP	Prince Albert Tobacco	Sat	10:30	30	NBC
43 *N*	Judy Canova Show	11.7	CV	Colgate Tooth Powder	Tue	8:30	30	CBS
44 *72*	Stage Door Canteen/Bert Lytell	11.6	MV	Corn Products Refining	Fri	10:30	30	CBS
45t *61*	Duffy's Tavern/Ed Gardner	11.5	SC	Minit-Rub & Sal Hepatica	Tue	8:30	30	Blue
45t *38*	Information Please	11.5	PS	HJ Heinz Foods	Mon	10;30	30	NBC
45t *40*	People Are Funny/Art Linkletter	11.5	APS	Wings Cigarettes	Fri	9:30	30	NBC
48 *40*	Adventures of Ellery Queen	11.3	DCC	Bromo Seltzer	Sat	7:30	30	NBC
49 *37*	Beatrice Kay's Gay 90's Review	11.1	MSP	Model Pipe Tobacco	Mon	8:30	30	CBS
50 *45*	Philip Morris Playhouse	11.0	DA	Philip Morris Cigarettes	Fri	9:00	30	CBS

New & Returning Top 50 Programs Underscored

1	aka Screen Guild Theater						
2	Lowell Thomas News	Sep–Jan 24	Sun Oil	M–F	6:45	15	Blue

Key: API — Audience Participation/Interviews   DCC — Drama/Continuing Characters   MV — Music/Variety Show
     APQ — Audience Participation/Quiz   MC — Music/Classical, Semi-Classical   NC — News, Commentary
     APS — Audience Participation/Stunts   MP — Music/Popular, Contemporary   SC — Situation Comedy
     CV — Comedy/Variety Show   MSP — Music/Specialty, Ethnic   SP — Sports
     DA — Dramatic Anthology   MST — Music/Standard, Traditional   TC — Talent Competition

1943–44 Top 50 Favorite Formats

	Programs	Pct
Comedy — All Categories	22	44%
Drama — Anthology & Continuing	11	22%
Music — All Categories	9	18%
Audience Participation — All Categories	5	10%
News/Commentary	3	6%

1943–44 Monthly Winners

Sep	Bob Hope Show	25.1	Feb	Bob Hope Show		36.2
Oct	Fibber McGee & Molly	29.5	Mar	Bob Hope Show		35.6
Nov	Fibber McGee & Molly	31.8	Apr	Fibber McGee & Molly		33.9
Dec	Fibber McGee & Molly	32.1	May	Red Skelton Show		29.1
Jan	Bob Hope Show	34.6	Jun	Fibber McGee & Molly		24.8

17

The 1944–45 Network Season

Announcer: Soon you'll be able to walk into your Admiral dealer's store and confidently buy the style of radio or radio-phonograph that you want. The selection of <u>Admiral</u> radios will be complete. There'll be radio-phonographs with the famous <u>Admiral exclusive features</u> ... <u>Slide-Away</u> that makes loading and unloading your record changer so easy ... and the <u>foolproof Admiral Automatic Record Changer</u>. There'll be consoles and table models ... in cabinets of fine woods and modern plastics. There'll be fun sets and portables, including the popular <u>Admiral Bantam</u>, the camera-type radio that operates on alternating current, direct current, or <u>self-contained batteries!</u> There'll be new electronic refinements in AM, FM and shortwave reception. And now about <u>Television!</u> Admiral's extensive research assures television receivers with true Admiral quality. So, whatever you want in radio ... or television ... you'll find it in an <u>Admiral</u> ... <u>America's Smart Set!</u> You can get a good idea of what Admiral will offer if you'll write for a free copy of the new, full-color booklet, entitled, "<u>It's a Promise</u>" from Admiral. Just write your name and address on a penny postcard and mail it to "Admiral" in care of this radio station ... that's all! "<u>It's a Promise</u>" ... from Admiral!

DIALING FOR DOLLARS

Radio was rolling in wartime advertising revenues while newspapers and magazines continued to struggle with paper rationing.

In four short years commercial radio's income had grown by over 80 percent to nearly $400 Million *(5.14 Bil)*. The four networks shared almost $200 million of that total, a 70 percent leap since 1940.

During that same period, network affiliate lists grew by over 60 percent, although the war had halted new station construction in 1943. Existing stations wanted network news connections, preferably with few strings attached. That's exactly what Mutual offered, resulting in its surge of 85 new affiliates in 48 months.

Blue didn't aggressively enter the competition for new affiliates until 1943 when it broke free of NBC and Mark Woods' team began to rebuild it from the news department up. The new Blue added 57 stations to its chain in just two years — surpassing both NBC and CBS in its number of affiliates.

MOURNING RADIO

By mid-season America was entering its fourth year of World War II and network programming reflected the public's demands of radio. Five of the season's Top 50 programs were newscasts reporting

the increasing momentum toward an Allied victory.

Meanwhile, 36 of the Top 50 were devoted to light comedy and music intended to relieve the nation's listeners *from* the worries war, if for only a few minutes at a time.

But on Thursday, April 12, 1945, all the music and laughter stopped in sudden shock.

The first network bulletins of President Franklin Roosevelt's death were broadcast at 5:49 P.M., in the middle of soap opera *Front Page Farrell* on NBC, and kid shows *Captain Midnight* on Blue and Mutual's *Tom Mix*. The news plunged the country into four days of disbelief and mourning.

All network entertainment programs and commercials were immediately cancelled through the following Sunday night. Only news and memorial programming was broadcast in tribute to the fallen President.

At 4:00 on Saturday afternoon all radio stations in the country observed a minute of silence in tribute to Roosevelt as his funeral service began at the White House.

The following Tuesday night, newly inaugurated President Harry Truman spoke briefly to the country on all the networks and to United States service personnel via Voice of America and Armed Forces Radio. His message reaffirmed the nation's determination to win World War II.

Truman's address drew a 53.6 rating.

V-E DAY — VERY EARLY

Less than a month following FDR's death, the networks reported the story that they'd waited for years to broadcast. And they broke the story a day ahead of its planned announcement.

The Associated Press was first with the news. Its bulletin from

1944–45 Season Scoreboard Mid-season Totals, December 1944			
		Compared to Year Earlier	
Total Radio Homes	32.5 Mil	+1.7 Mil	+5.5%
Total Auto Radios	7.0 Mil	(1.0 Mil)	(12.5%)
Total AM Radio Stations	910	+/-0	+/-0%
Total Radio Network Affiliates	694	+74	+11.9%
1944 Radio Revenues	393.5 Mil	+79.9 Mil	+25.5%
1944 Network Revenues	191.8 Mil	+35.3 Mil	+22.6%
Network Share	48.7%		(1.2%)
Total TV Stations	8	+/-0	+/-0%
Total FM Stations	52	+6	+6.1%

131

General Eisenhower's Allied headquarters in Reims, France, cleared the wires at 9:35 A.M. on May 7, 1945.

Germany had signed its surrender documents with the Americans, British and French in the early morning hours of May 7. Victory in Europe had been achieved.

The networks hit the air with the story and cancelled all regular programming — including commercials — and immediately began a round of shortwave reports from their European correspondents.

All that was needed was formal word from the White House to make V-E Day official.

News departments expected the announcement at any minute while word of victory in Europe spread quickly and celebrations began.

But the minutes of waiting dragged into hours and doubts began to arise about the validity of the story. The networks sheepishly resumed regular programming — with commercials.

President Truman finally dropped the other shoe at 9:00 the *next* morning and delivered a five minute address announcing Germany's surrender to Allied forces.

By this time radio had made the delayed announcement anti-climactic.

It was later learned that the United States, Great Britain, France and the Soviet Union had agreed earlier to designate May 8 as the official date of V-E Day which gave the Soviets time to sign their own separate surrender document with Germany.

May 8, 1945, would forever be known as V-E Day.

THE TAIL OF TWO STATIONS

V-E Day meant the conversion of one powerful broadcaster to opposite propaganda purposes and the beginning of the end for another — but for altogether different reasons.

The first, Radio Berlin, had been severely limited with its daily barrage of Nazi propaganda since April. Its powerful transmitters in Hamburg and Bremen followed suit. With Germany's surrender and the division of the country by its con-

querors, Radio Berlin became a Soviet propaganda operation and Radio Hamburg-Bremen began to speak for the three Western powers.

Meanwhile, Nazi Germany's biggest competitor for European listeners, the American Broadcasting Station in Europe — ABSIE — prepared to shut down.

ABSIE was established and operated by the Elmer Davis–led Office of War Information. It had broadcast news in seven languages to the European continent eight hours a day for 14 months from twelve powerful BBC transmitters in Great Britain. It was a massive operation with a staff of 250 run by Davis's former employer, CBS chief Bill Paley — Colonel William S. Paley for the duration.

Per agreement with its British hosts, the American Broadcasting Station in Europe signed-off the air 90 days after V-E Day and returned control of the stations back to the BBC.

BYE, BYE BLUE

Meanwhile at home, the American Broadcasting Company had problems with identifying itself by its full name or simply, "ABC." Storer Broadcasting owned the name American Broadcasting System from an earlier networking failure. Presenting several regional issues, the Arizona Broadcasting Company and Michigan's Associated Broadcasting Corporation both called themselves ABC.

Negotiations for name clearance dragged on through the 1944–45 season while the chain continued to identify itself as the Blue Network.

Finally, on June 15, 1945 — two long years after Ed Noble began his short two month negotiation to buy the network — Blue became known on the air as, "The ABC Radio Network."

The call-sign of the network's New York anchor remained WJZ until March 1953 when it became WABC — calls vacated by CBS in 1946 when its New York station adopted WCBS. NBC's flagship, WEAF/New York, also took its parent network name in 1946, becoming WNBC.

NOISE ABOUT NEWS

World War II went on in the Pacific and the sellers' market continued for Network Radio. Feeling its oats, NBC publicly requested its newscast sponsors to eliminate their commercials inside the news. It wasn't the patriotic, altruistic move that it was painted to be — advertisers simply padded their opening and closing commercials around the news.

CBS, which had cut back commercial time within newscasts by 20 percent in 1942 — again padding opening and closing advertising messages — refused to go along with the NBC plan. Instead, the network issued a press release promising that commercials wouldn't interrupt any *important* war news — without defining "important."

Less known outside the advertising industry, CBS sponsors were flatly prohibited from plugging any of their programs broadcast on rival networks. Meanwhile, Blue quietly asked its sponsors to relinquish the last ten seconds of their programs to allow the network to promote the next program on its schedule.

THE MONTHLIES

NBC was at the peak of its popularity.

The network dominated the ratings with 33 of the season's Top 50 programs. Equally impressive were its 18 programs placed in the Top 25. Its top Tuesday entries extended NBC's string of consecutive monthly winners to 101 with nothing in sight to challenge its comedy and variety heavyweights.

Bob Hope's weekly shows, mostly performed before military audiences, were the highest rated programs in nine of the season's ten months. *Fibber McGee & Molly* edged out Hope in October by less than half a point.

1944–45 Sunday Night
Top Ten Programs
NBC 6, CBS 3, Blue 1
Average: 16.0

Walter Winchell's Jergens Journal	Blue	9:00	22.8
Edgar Bergen & Charlie McCarthy	NBC	8:00	22.0
Jack Benny Program	NBC	7:00	20.4

Take It or Leave It	CBS	10:00	16.4
The Great Gilder-sleeve	NBC	6:30	13.9
We the People at War	CBS	10:30	13.6
Fitch Bandwagon	NBC	7:30	13.0
Eddie Bracken Show	NBC	8:30	12.9
Crime Doctor	CBS	8:30	12.7
American Album of Familiar Music	NBC	9:30	12.0

A PATCH OF BLUE

Walter Winchell's *Jergens Journal* became the first Blue Network program in nine years to win a nightly ratings race. The 47-year-old Winchell was at the top of his game. It was his fifth consecutive season with ratings in the 20s and his sixth straight finish in the annual Top Ten.

Winchell's quarter-hour of rapid fire news, gossip and opinion punctuated with a telegraph key was Blue's only Top 50 program as the network worked to rebuild itself.

One step was capitalizing on Winchell's numbers with a show following his quarter hour to keep listeners tuned to the network.

Its 1944 attempt was *Hollywood Mystery Time,* a half hour drama at 9:15 that incorporated snippets of Hollywood gossip from columnist Louella Parsons. The hybrid Hollywood show lost over half of the ratings it inherited from Winchell and was cancelled in December.

VENGEANCE, THY NAME IS JELLO!

Jack Benny and General Foods split after ten years of his popularizing Jello and Grape Nuts for the company.

Benny's half-hour at 7:00 on NBC — which he controlled — was sold to the highest bidder. American Tobacco won the bidding and began Benny's ten year sponsorship by Lucky Strike Cigarettes.

General Foods didn't take Benny's exit graciously and decided to take aim at its former star. It bought the time period on CBS opposite him. Then the company uprooted Kate Smith's highly rated CBS variety hour from Friday and assigned her to the network's 7:00 Sunday timeslot directly against Benny.

Kate Smith's untiring efforts to

sell war bonds — singing *God Bless America* countless times — had made her a national institution with ten Top 50 seasons and millions of records to her credit.

If anyone could take down Benny, it would be America's most beloved singer — or so it was thought.

It turned out to be a suicide mission. Benny kept his ratings in the 20s while Smith was swamped and lost 40 percent of her Friday show's audience. Her hour dropped from 29th most popular in 1943–44, to 93rd place.

General Foods pulled its singing star the following season and moved her back to Friday, but the damage had been done.

Kate Smith never again had another Top 50 show.

SNOOKS SLIPS

General Foods made another questionable move by breaking up its successful Thursday night *Maxwell House Coffee Time* comedy team on NBC — Frank Morgan and Fanny Brice.

Brice was moved to CBS and became the star of *Toasties Time* for General Foods' Post Cereals at 6:30 leading into Kate Smith's new show opposite Benny. Brice split the half hour into two skits — one as *Baby Snooks* and the other as her new character, *Irma Potts,* a lisping store clerk.

Less than 50 percent of her audience followed Brice to her new show which could only generate a 9.6 rating against NBC's *The Great Gildersleeve.* After four Top Ten seasons plus another three in the Top 15, Fanny Brice failed to make the annual Top 50, dropping to a humiliating 79th in the season's rankings.

BUMSTEADS' BUMMER

As Blondie and Dagwood Bumstead, Penny Singleton and Arthur Lake had steadily built a Monday audience for *Blondie* on CBS over five consecutive Top 50 seasons. Nevertheless, R.J. Reynolds' Camel Cigarettes dropped the sitcom in 1944 to make room for Bob Hawk's comedy quiz, *Thanks to the Yanks.*

Hawk lost 20 percent of *Blondie's* ratings.

Meanwhile, Colgate picked up

Blondie for its Super Suds laundry detergent. Following a short summer run on Blue, the soap company slotted the show in another suicide spot on CBS's Sunday schedule, opposite NBC's *Edgar Bergen & Charlie McCarthy* at 8:00. *Blondie* took a 35 percent ratings hit into single digits, dropping to 73rd in the annual rankings. Bergen, meanwhile, dropped 20 percent of his audience from the sitcom's challenge, but remained comfortably in the season's Top Ten.

WEE PEEPS AT WAR

To make room for its expanded Kate Smith variety hour, General Foods moved Phillips H. Lord's *We the People* from 7:30 to the less competitive 10:30 timeslot. The program's ratings surged 50 percent into the mid and high teens. But its time shift wasn't the only reason *We the People* jumped back into the middle of the season's Top 50. Thanks to the easing of network bans against recorded elements, the show brought the reality of World War II closer to home than any other program.

The CBS show had been re-titled *We the People at War* in 1942 and was given a new host a short time later, actor Milo Boulton.

In the summer of 1944, it did take its listeners to war via radio. Two Marines covered the invasion and subsequent battles for the South Pacific island of Saipan — reporting and recording the battles throughout the campaign with portable wire recorders.

When their 20 hours of recordings were edited for broadcast, *We the People at War* was acclaimed by *Time* as, "...Putting home-fronters just about as close to the battle as they could get without participating in it."

BRACKEN'S NO BERGEN

Standard Brands pulled *One Man's Family* in January to make way for a much heralded new sitcom following *Edgar Bergen & Charlie McCarthy.* The *Eddie Bracken Show* starred the 30-year-old Paramount contract actor whose comic bumbling innocence had propelled him to the lead or co-starring roles in twelve movies since 1940—teamed four times with Paramount's "Blonde Bombshell," Betty Hutton. Two of Bracken's 1944 films, *Miracle at Morgan's Creek* and *Hail the Conquering Hero* earned Oscar nominations for writer/director Preston Sturges.

Bracken was a hot Hollywood property and his sitcom was boosted with the talents of familiar movie stars Ann Rutherford and William Demarest, plus a cast to top radio character actors. Nevertheless, the new show made hardly a ripple in the ratings compared to *One Man's Family*, losing close to half of the lead-in audience left by Bergen.

The Eddie Bracken Show was cancelled four months after its debut.

NOT SO SUPER BOWL I

The National Football League championship game's first Hooperating was posted on Sunday, December 17th when Blue broadcast the game between the Green Bay Packers and New York Giants. The afternoon game resulted in a feeble 4.3 rating for sponsor Wilson Sporting Goods.

*1944–45 Monday Night
Top Ten Programs*
CBS 6, NBC 3, MBS 1
Average: 14.7

Lux Radio Theater	CBS	9:00	23.0
Screen Guild Players	CBS	10:00	20.6
Burns & Allen Show	CBS	8:30	14.7
HV Kaltenborn News*	NBC	7:45	14.7
Lowell Thomas News*	NBC	6:45	13.6
Vox Pop	CBS	8:00	13.0
Thanks to the Yanks	CBS	7:30	12.4
Bill Henry Johns Manville News*	CBS	8:55	12.0
Dr IQ	NBC	10:30	11.4
Gabriel Heatter News*	MBS	9:00	11.4

*Monday–Friday Strip Shows

Sans Strips...

Cavalcade of America	NBC	8:00	10.8
Information Please	NBC	9:30	10.7
Adventures Sherlock Holmes	MBS	8:30	10.0
Blind Date	Blue	8:30	8.6

DEMILLE DEPARTS DEFIANTLY

Cecil B. DeMille had an easy job with *Lux Radio Theater*, on which he was introduced as, "Your director." He actually did little more than narrate the show and conduct the scripted closing interviews with each week's stars—interviews that always included hefty plugs for Lever Brother's Lux Beauty Soap.

For this appearance he was paid $2,500 a week *($32,135)*, 39 weeks a year.

Meanwhile, radio talent union AFRA had assessed all of its members one dollar in 1944 to lobby against a proposed ban on closed-shop rules which prohibited any non-union talent from working in Network Radio. DeMille, a reluctant union member to begin with, refused to pay the dollar, saying it was against his principle to support a cause in which he didn't believe.

He took the case to court and lost.

It became a contest of wills. AFRA wanted DeMille's dollar—a dollar that Lever or CBS would gladly have contributed to keep him on the air—but he refused.

As a consequence, DeMille was booted from the union and lost his *Lux* job on January 22 after nine years with the show.

Lux tried various replacement hosts for the remainder of the season. All lacked DeMille's polish, but the show surprisingly lost no ground in its ratings. Instead, the program advanced in the season's rankings from sixth to third.

DeMille, then 63, devoted the rest of his career to full time film making and turned out notable pictures including the Academy Award winning *Greatest Show on Earth* in 1952. Ironically that was the same year that *Lux Radio Theater* celebrated its fifth consecutive season as Network Radio's most popular program—all hosted by DeMille's permanent replacement, William Keighley.

*1944–45 Tuesday Night
Top Ten Programs*
NBC 8, CBS 2
Average: 16.3

Bob Hope Show	NBC	10:00	29.6
Fibber McGee & Molly	NBC	9:30	28.3
Hildegarde's Raleigh Room	NBC	10:30	16.6
HV Kaltenborn News*	NBC	7:45	14.7
Lowell Thomas News*	NBC	6:45	13.6
Big Town	CBS	8:00	12.8
A Date with Judy	NBC	8:30	12.5
Bill Henry Johns Manville News*	CBS	8:55	12.0
Molle Mystery Theater	NBC	9:00	11.6
Johnny Presents Ginny Simms	NBC	8:00	11.5

*Monday–Friday Strip Shows

Sans Strips...

Gabriel Heatter News*	MBS	9:00	11.4
Theater of Romance	CBS	8:30	10.5
Inner Sanctum	CBS	9:00	10.0
One Man's Family	Blue	7:30	9.4

MAKE ROOM FOR HILDY

NBC's Tuesday lineup took a hit in early June 1944 when Red Skelton left his show for military duty.

Brown & Williamson Tobacco gave his 10:30 half hour—and its nearly 30 rating—to Skelton's summer replacement and its former star of *Beat the Band*, "The Incomparable" Hildegarde.

Born Loretta Sell of Milwaukee, the 38-year-old Hildegarde was an elegant and bubbly chanteuse who had become the country's most successful night club entertainer. *Raleigh Room*, recreated her night club act—a briskly paced but gentle mix of her songs and audience interviews.

Hildegarde's *Raleigh Room* was the most popular new show of the season but it was a hollow victory. Hildy's charm couldn't match Skelton's broad comedy. His 29.9 season average of 1943–44 became her 16.6 of 1944–45—a 45 percent drop. Only half of Bob Hope's lead-in audience remained tuned to NBC for *The Raleigh Room*.

Nevertheless, Brown & Williamson kept the show at 10:30 until Skelton's return in December 1945.

JUDY OUTDATES HEIDT

NBC's breakout hit of the year was *A Date with Judy* which jumped into the season's Top 50 after three of summer replacement duty for

Bob Hope and Eddie Cantor and a half season of gaining traction after Tums Antacid Tablets brought the sitcom into NBC's Tuesday comedy lineup in January 1944. The show replaced Horace Heidt's *Tums Treasure Chest*, which couldn't crack the season's Top 50 for four years. The *Treasure Chest* format was stale and ratings had declined steadily.

A Date with Judy's Judy Davis was considered the female counterpart to Henry Aldrich. The title role was given to 16-year-old Louise Erickson in 1944. She remained with the show throughout its Tuesday night run — five consecutive Top 50 seasons including two among the annual Top 20.

The sitcom's final season on ABC's Thursday schedule in 1949–50 was a disaster — falling from 13th to 100th place in the ratings when pitted opposite NBC's *Father Knows Best* and *Mr. Keen* on CBS.

TO BLUE — TOO BAD

Trade paper *Radio Daily* polled a thousand newspaper and magazine radio editors, critics and reporters in January who reported that their favorite serial drama on radio was *One Man's Family*.

Two weeks later, Standard Brands evicted *One Man's Family* from its cushy, Sunday night home of five years following *Edgar Bergen & Charlie McCarthy* on NBC to make room for its new sitcom starring Eddie Bracken.

One Man's Family was shifted off to Blue on Tuesday at 7:30 — a timeslot that belonged to *The Lone Ranger* on Monday, Wednesday and Friday.

The Barbour clan took an immediate 25 percent hit in its ratings, falling from 34th to 83rd in the season's rankings. Standard rescued the serial from Blue at the end of the season and moved it to NBC's Sunday afternoon schedule where it remained for five years before it became a highly successful quarter-hour Multiple Run strip on NBC in 1950 with a new sponsor, Miles Laboratories.

1944–45 Wednesday Night Top Ten Programs
NBC 6, CBS 3, MBS 1
Average: 14.6

Mr. District Attorney	NBC	9:30	21.3
Eddie Cantor's Time to Smile	NBC	9:00	17.9
Kay Kyser's Kollege of Musical Knowledge	NBC	10:00	17.2
HV Kaltenborn News*	NBC	7:45	14.7
Mr. & Mrs. North	NBC	8:00	14.0
Lowell Thomas News*	NBC	6:45	13.6
Dr Christian	CBS	8:30	13.1
Bill Henry Johns Manville News*	CBS	8:55	12.0
Gabriel Heatter News*	MBS	9:00	11.4
Frank Sinatra Show	CBS	9:00	11.0

*Monday–Friday Strip Shows

Sans Strips...

Carton of Cheer	NBC	8:30	9.8
Adventures of Ellery Queen	CBS	7:30	9.7
Counterspy	Blue	8:30	8.9
Which Is Which?	CBS	9:30	8.8

SASS OVER CLASS

The Electric Companies of America opened the 30 minute *Electric Hour* at 10:30 on CBS in September with as much promotion as the sponsor and network could muster. The image-minded utilities offered a refined program of classical and semi-classical music, headlined by handsome baritone Nelson Eddy, who had a dozen MGM operetta hits to his credit — often teamed with soprano Jeanette MacDonald.

Eddy received a reported $5,000 per week (*$64,270*), to compete for audience with Kay Kyser's *Kollege of Musical Knowledge* on NBC.

It was no contest.

Eddy's *Electric Hour* recitals with guest stars generally unknown outside the concert world, could only generate a 6.6 rating against Kyser's averages in the high teens and 20s. *The Electric Hour* was moved to the cultural ghetto of CBS's Sunday afternoon schedule following New York Philharmonic concerts in December.

Eversharp filled the 10:30 Wednesday void on CBS with Milton Berle's *Let Yourself Go* which had been struggling on Blue's Tuesday schedule. Berle opened with a sur-

prisingly strong 8.0 rating in January. But once CBS listeners got a sample of *Let Yourself Go*'s nonsensical format, the show sank quickly.

Kay Kyser regularly doubled and tripled Berle's ratings with ease.

Eversharp cancelled *Let Yourself Go* in June.

1944–45 Thursday Night Top Ten Programs
NBC 9, CBS 1
Average: 16.0

Bing Crosby's Kraft Music Hall	NBC	9:00	22.2
Sealtest Village Store	NBC	9:30	21.5
Abbott & Costello	NBC	10:00	19.1
Dinah Shore Show	NBC	8:30	15.4
Bob Burns Show	NBC	7:30	14.9
HV Kaltenborn News*	NBC	7:45	14.7
Frank Morgan Show	NBC	8:00	13.7
Lowell Thomas News*	NBC	6:45	13.6
Rudy Vallee Show	NBC	10:30	12.7
Bill Henry Johns Manville News*	CBS	8:55	12.0

*Monday–Friday Strip Shows

Sans Strips...

Gabriel Heatter News*	MBS	9:00	11.4
Suspense	CBS	8:00	11.1
Death Valley Sheriff	CBS	8:30	10.1
Mr. Keen, Tracer of Lost Persons	CBS	7:30	8.3

MORGAN'S BRICELESS RATINGS

Frank Morgan was working solo for the first time after a seven year partnership with Fanny Brice on *Good News* and *Maxwell House Coffee Time*. General Foods split the pair and shipped Brice off to a disastrous season on CBS' Sunday schedule where she lost half her audience.

By comparison Morgan had only a disappointing season, losing 30 percent of the ratings the two had enjoyed during the previous season. Nevertheless, General Foods cancelled Morgan in May.

But the 55-year-old comic actor staged a comeback the following season that would have made his *Wizard of Oz* proud — when Bing Crosby walked off *Kraft Music Hall* and Morgan took over the show.

SWITCH TURNS ON DINAH

Nowhere was a switch in networks more of an advantage than to Dinah Shore.

The 28-year-old singer from Nashville already had four network series to her credit — plus a year as vocalist with Eddie Cantor's *Time to Smile*—when General Foods starred her in *Birds Eye Open House* for its frozen foods division in September 1943.

The show was placed on CBS's Thursday schedule at 9:30— opposite the hottest new show of the year, NBC's *Sealtest Village Store* starring Joan Davis and Jack Haley. Shore was buried in the 1943–44 ratings with only a third of the sitcom duo's audience.

But Birds Eye had faith in Shore. She had a string of hit records and projected a genuinely warm personality in her program's interview segments with guest stars. She was rewarded in 1944 with a transfer to NBC's Thursday schedule at 8:30, replacing *The Aldrich Family* which General Foods moved to Friday in the company's continual chess game among competing sponsors.

Dinah's *Birds Eye Open House*— identical to the CBS show — zoomed 120 percent in the ratings, from 7.1 to 15.4. Her climb in the season's ratings from 104th to 16th was one of the most dramatic turnabouts in Network Radio history.

SWITCH TURNS OFF TIME

Nowhere was a switch in networks more of a disadvantage than to *The March of Time*.

Time magazine moved its highly rated Thursday entry from NBC to the new American Broadcasting Company's Blue Network in November. The magazine's parent, Time, Incorporated, owned a 12½ percent of ABC's stock.

The program remained on Thursday at 10:30, but the move cost *The March of Time* over half of its audience. Radio's original docudrama plunged from a 16.0 to a 7.7 rating — from 22nd place to 103rd in the season's rankings.

The 14-year-old program was cancelled in July and was never heard again.

Time also sold its stock in ABC.

A SHOWER BEFORE RETIRING

Bing Crosby's *Kraft Music Hall* on NBC continued to dominate *The Original Amateur Hour* at 9:00, pushing the onetime ratings champ of CBS out of Thursday's Top Ten. Major Edward Bowes, now 70, scuttled his amateurs in December 1944 and launched into a series of shows dedicated to various charitable causes — the Red Cross, March of Dimes and Navy Relief.

His ratings slid even further.

He followed that attempt in February with the short lived *Major Bowes' Shower of Stars,* featuring Morton Gould's studio orchestra and guest vocalists from the operatic world. The refined program had no chance against Crosby's high powered half hour.

Bowes quietly disappeared from his *Shower of Stars* in May 1945 and died 14 months later.

WARING OUT

The Blue Network continued to explore for breakthroughs in popularity at 7:00 by scheduling weekly half hour shows in what had always been the province of 15 minute strip shows since the heyday of *Amos & Andy*.

Monday's weekly half hour entry at 7:00 was Horace Heidt's *Heidt Time for Hires* which had struggled with low single digit ratings since its inception earlier in the year.

But the network had bigger plans for Thursday by signing Fred Waring's Pennsylvanians orchestra and chorus for a half hour sponsored by Owens-Illinois Glass.

Unlike the contrived Heidt show, Waring's concerts had been popular with listeners since 1932 and the group had just finished a successful five year run for Leggett & Myers on NBC, headlining *The Chesterfield Supper Club* every weeknight at 7:00.

Blue had every reason to believe Waring would succeed in his new network home at the same time.

He didn't. Waring lost over two-thirds of his NBC audience in the switch.

Blue gave up on its 7:00 experiments in January. Heidt was cancelled and Waring's half hour was moved up to 10:00— directly opposite NBC's ratings hit, *Abbott & Costello.*

Fred Waring had seven Top 50 seasons to his credit but finished the 1944–45 season in 157th place with the lowest ratings his career.

A NEW SHERIFF IN TOWN

Western anthology *Death Valley Days,* had enjoyed a continuous 14 year multi-network run, four of them in a season's Top 50. But its ratings had sagged into single digits after five network and time shifts.

Pacific Coast Borax pulled the plug on the anthology series in August and replaced it with a new western mystery series set in the present day, *Death Valley Sheriff,* a lawman who preferred psychology to bullets. The new CBS entry was pitted against NBC's Dinah Shore variety show and turned in a respectable 10.1 rating — almost a 40 percent increase over *Death Valley Days'* last season.

Nevertheless, Borax moved the program to Blue before the following season where it remained for the final six years of its run, known simply as *The Sheriff.* It never budged from its Blue/ABC Friday timeslot at 9:30— part of a lineup that the network would develop into a winning schedule in three years.

---

*1944–45 Friday Night
Top Ten Programs*
NBC 5, CBS 4, MBS 1
Average: 13.3

The Aldrich Family	CBS	8:00	15.1
Amos & Andy	NBC	10:00	15.1
HV Kaltenborn News*	NBC	7:45	14.7
Lowell Thomas News*	NBC	6:45	13.6
Duffy's Tavern	NBC	8:30	13.5
People Are Funny	NBC	9:30	13.4
Adventures of the Thin Man	CBS	8:30	12.4
Bill Henry Johns Manville News*	CBS	8:55	12.0
Jimmy Durante & Garry Moore	CBS	10:00	11.7
Gabriel Heatter News*	MBS	9:00	11.4

*Monday–Friday Strip Shows

Sans Strips...
Waltz Time	NBC	9:00	10.7
Danny Kaye Show	CBS	10:30	10.6

Bill Stern Colgate Sports Newsreel	NBC	10:30	10.4
Stage Door Canteen	CBS	10:30	10.4

WYNN'S BUBBLES BURST

Ed Wynn made his comeback to Network Radio after a seven year absence in September He was the creator and star in the third of Blue's weekly half hour shows at 7:00—*Happy Island.*

Wynn portrayed "King Bubbles" who roamed "Worry Park" of the fantasy island, making life happier for his subjects. Borden Dairies picked up the bills for the show—a fully costumed stage production performed before a theater audience that Wynn envisioned to be destined for television after its certain success in radio.

He was wrong.

Happy Island never received a rating higher than 4.1. Borden shut down the show in January.

Blue and sponsor Borden then moved the 58-year-old comedian—with a scaled back format known simply as *The Ed Wynn Show*—to one of Network Radio's surest spots for failure. He was slotted on Monday at 9:00 opposite *Lux Radio Theater.* Predictably, Wynn's new show was a failure and he left series radio forever in February.

KAYE NOT OKAY

Danny Kaye was 31 and Hollywood's hottest new star with the release of *Up in Arms* in 1944, the first of his 17 hit movies. The young comic's novelty songs and rapid fire, tongue twisting routines seemed a natural for radio. Pabst Beer signed Kaye for a weekly variety show on CBS beginning in January 1945.

Opening with much fanfare on Saturdays at 8:00—a soft spot in both the NBC and Blue schedules—Kaye was supported in his half hour variety show with reliable movie comedians Lionel Stander and Eve Arden plus music from Harry James' popular orchestra. The new show seemed a Top Ten cinch against the nostalgia-driven *Gaslight Gaieties* on NBC and Blue's *Early American Dance Music.*

Kaye won his time period, but not by the expected margins—and

as the season wore on, his ratings drifted further downward.

Pabst and CBS came to Kaye's "rescue" in April and moved his show to another soft time period, Friday at 10:30—vacated by the fading *Stage Door Canteen.* Kaye's only Friday competition was Bill Stern's *Colgate Sports Newsreel* on NBC and Blue's Gillette Friday night fights.

Nevertheless, Friday was another disappointment for the comedian.

Kaye finished the season in single digits—out of Friday's Top Ten and the season's Top 50.

SPORTS OF SORTS STEM FROM STERN

At 37, sportscaster/raconteur Bill Stern was the most popular voice in radio who never cracked a season's Top 50. He broadcast major college football games for NBC, narrated sports segments in MGM newsreels and was the voice of a string of sports shorts produced by Columbia Pictures.

Yet, Stern was best known for his weekly *Sports Newsreel,* a quarter hour of over-the-top human interest stories—"Some true, some legend, some hearsay..."—that Colgate Shave Cream sponsored on NBC's Friday schedule at 10:30 from 1941 to 1951 following a two year run on Blue.

Sports Newsreel was a fully scripted production written by Mac Davis. Stern's melodramatic narration of tall tales involving famous and obscure athletes was punctuated with liberal doses of scoring provided by an organ and male quartet. Adding glitz to the program were weekly guests from the sports world or show business with their own stories related to sports—and often presenting scripter Davis with a far-reaching challenge.

For example, the 1944–45 season—*Sports Newsreel*'s peak in the ratings—Stern's guests included singers Lawrence Tibbett and Lena Horne, comedians Milton Berle and Henny Youngman, mind reader Dunninger, teenage movie star Jane Withers and newscaster H.V. Kaltenborn. That kind of diverse variety of guests called for both research and imagination from Davis—plus Stern keeping a straight face.

FAMILY FEUDS

General Foods gave CBS Friday's Number One program when it moved *The Aldrich Family* over from NBC to plug the hole left at 8:00 when it shifted Kate Smith's Friday show to Sunday and her doomed match-up against Jack Benny.

Meanwhile, Quaker Oats dropped *Aldrich Family* wannabe *That Brewster Boy* in March and replaced it on the CBS Friday schedule at 9:30 with *Those Websters,* yet another family sitcom resembling *The Aldrich Family.*

Much of *Brewster*'s cast was retained for the new show with the key addition of Willard Waterman, who both looked and sounded like Hal Peary—a resemblance that would pay off for Waterman in 1950 when he replaced Peary as *The Great Gildersleeve.*

But as George Webster, Waterman headed a household troubled by ratings.

Those Websters lost 25 percent of *That Brewster Boy*'s audience and couldn't generate half the ratings registered by *The Aldrich Family*—Network Radio's all-time ratings champ of family sitcoms.

Quaker shipped *Those Websters* off to Mutual the following year for three more dismal seasons.

*1944–45 Saturday Night
Top Ten Programs*
NBC 7, CBS 3
Average: 12.1

Your Hit Parade	CBS	9:00	15.3
Truth or Consequences	NBC	8:30	14.5
Can You Top This?	NBC	9:30	13.6
Judy Canova Show	NBC	10:00	13.2
Palmolive Party	NBC	10:00	11.2
Grand Ole Opry	NBC	10:30	11.0
The Saint	NBC	7:30	11.0
National Barn Dance	NBC	9:00	10.5
Ned Calmer Parker Pen News	CBS	8:55	10.4
FBI in Peace & War	CBS	8:30	10.2

POP GOES THE OPERA

Lucky Strike Cigarettes had a good deal going with Frank Sinatra's weekly appearances on *Your Hit Parade.* The program was based in New York, but Sinatra's film career required his presence in

Hollywood working on MGM's *Anchors Aweigh*. To be in both places at once, Sinatra was forced to pay the weekly line charges from Los Angeles to New York — reportedly double the amount of his $2,000 weekly salary from American Tobacco *($25,700)*.

With his own CBS program in Wednesday's Top Ten, Sinatra figured that Saturday's *Your Hit Parade* needed him more than he needed the program's costly exposure.

He threatened to quit the show in December unless he received more money.

The sponsor called his bluff — but Sinatra wasn't given to bluffing. He left *Your Hit Parade* on December 30.

His replacement on the pop music show came as a complete surprise to *Hit Parade* fans — operatic baritone Lawrence Tibbett, who found himself singing such popular favorites as "Don't Fence Me In" and "Ac-cent-cheu-ate the Positive."

Your Hit Parade's ratings were an even greater surprise. Its numbers went up then leveled off to compare favorably with the period that Sinatra headlined the show. By late spring it began to appear that the $3,500 a week Tibbett demanded *($45,000)*, might be a good investment.

But by fall the novelty of a 50-year-old classically trained voice singing juke box hits had worn thin and the show's ratings trailed off. Tibbett left the show in late 1945.

SERIAL STUNTS

Ralph Edwards proved the audience drawing power of elaborate stunts stretched out over consecutive weeks when he "randomly" selected a contestant from his studio audience by name on his November 4 *Truth or Consequences* broadcast. The pre-selected contestant, Rudolph Wickel, was a New Jersey mechanical engineer who became the subject of a stunt that was weeks in planning and execution.

Edwards grandly announced that the program was giving Wickel $1,000 *($12,850)*, and handed him a shovel as the key to his prize — two bags containing 500 silver dollars each which were buried in a

Holyoke, Massachusetts, vacant lot. Edwards announced the address of the lot and wished Wickel good luck in finding the cash.

Wikel reported to Edwards the following week that *Truth or Consequences* listeners in Holyoke had beaten him to the vacant lot by hours and found the prize within minutes.

With mock apologies Edwards gave his patsy a check for $1,000 — with no bank name on it but just enough clues to keep Wikel hooked into the stunt trying to locate the bank.

The gag continued from week to week incorporating Confederate money, a seven ton safe and a parrot. It climaxed in December when Edwards told Wikel that he would finally receive the missing half of a genuine thousand dollar bill that he'd already found — located between pages 12 and 13 of a book that would be mailed to his home.

When the contestant was led off-stage and out of earshot, Edwards urged his listeners to mail their old books to Wikel's home address. He promised that they'd be collected for the Victory Book Drive and donated to servicemen and veterans' hospitals.

Over 18,000 books flooded into Wikel's house.

Wikel's prize was finally found in the book sent to him by the program, wrapped in plain brown paper without a return address — an edition of Winston Churchill's *Blood, Sweat & Tears*.

Edwards' put his popularity to a test again in January, when a ten-year-old boy recovering from polio sang "Over the Rainbow" on *Truth*

or Consequences. Moved by the performance, Edwards promised to give the youngster a $1,000 war bond if listeners would contribute a total of $10,000 to the polio-fighting March of Dimes. Listeners responded with nearly $140,000 *(1.8 Mil)*, the largest single donation the charity had ever received.

NEWS RULES

For the first time and only time, four newscasts led the season's Multiple Run programs and seven of the Top Ten Multiple Runs were news reports.

The H.V. Kaltenborn, Lowell Thomas, Bill Henry and Gabriel Heatter news strips all made the season's Top 50 and were also among the nightly Top Ten of all programs four nights a week.

Heatter's nightly newscast became the first Mutual program to finish the season with a double digit rating and the first Mutual entry to ever crack the season's Top 50 list. Heatter's rating achievement is even more impressive considering his heavyweight competition at 9:00 every night. To siphon off an estimated nine million listeners from the likes of *Lux Radio Theater*, Bing Crosby and Eddie Cantor was no small achievement.

CBS replaced the disgruntled and departed Cecil Brown with West Coast newscaster Bill Henry for its 8:55 *Johns-Manville* news strip which became a Hooper rated and ranked program in September. The nation's obsession with news resulted in Henry's career-high ratings and only trip to a season's Top 50.

1944–45 Multiple Run Top Ten Programs
NBC 4, MBS 3, CBS 2, Blue 1
Average: 9.5

H.V. Kaltenborn News*	M–F	NBC	7:45	14.7
Lowell Thomas News*	M–F	NBC	6:45	13.6
Bill Henry Johns Manville News*	M–F	CBS	8:55	12.0
Gabriel Heatter News*	M–F	MBS	9:00	11.4
Chesterfield Supper Club*	M–F	NBC	7:00	9.1
John W Vandercook News of the World*	M–F	NBC	7:15	8.3
The Lone Ranger	M,W,F	Blue	7:30	7.3
Music That Satisfies	T,W,T	CBS	7:15	6.5
Cecil Brown Sizing Up the News	M,W,F	MBS	8:00	6.4
Fulton Lewis Jr. News*	M–F	MBS	7:00	6.0

*Monday–Friday Strip Shows

TOP 50 PROGRAMS — 1944–45

NBC 33, CBS 15, Blue 1, MBS 1
Average Rating: 15.6, Median: 13.9
32,500,000 Radio Homes / 87.6% Coverage of U.S. Homes / One Rating Point = 325,000 Homes
Source: C.E. Hooper Semi-Monthly Reports, Sept 1944–June 1945
Total Programs Rated 6–11 P.M.: 223
Programs Rated 13 Weeks & Ranked: 194

		Program	Rtg	Type	Sponsor	Day	Time	Lgth	Net
1	1	Bob Hope Show	29.6	CV	Pepsodent Toothpaste	Tue	10:00	30	NBC
2	2	Fibber McGee & Molly	28.3	SC	Johnsons Wax	Tue	9:30	30	NBC
3	6	Lux Radio Theater/Various Hosts	23.0	DA	Lux Soap	Mon	9:00	60	CBS
4	8	Walter Winchell's Jergens Journal	22.8	NC	Jergens Lotion	Sun	9:00	15	Blue
5	15	Bing Crosby's Kraft Music Hall	22.2	MV	Kraft Cheese	Thu	9:00	30	NBC
6	4	Edgar Bergen & Charlie McCarthy	22.0	CV	Chase & Sanborn Coffee	Sun	8:00	30	NBC
7	10	Joan Davis/Jack Haley Village Store	21.5	SC	Sealtest Dairies	Thu	9:30	30	NBC
8	8	Mister District Attorney/Jay Jostyn	21.3	DCC	Vitalis Hair Tonic	Wed	9:30	30	NBC
9	12	Screen Guild Players	20.6	DA	Lady Esther Cosmetics	Mon	10:00	30	CBS
10	5	Jack Benny Program	20.4	SC	Lucky Strike Cigarettes	Sun	7:00	30	NBC
11	10	Abbott & Costello Show	19.1	CV	Camel Cigarettes	Thu	10:00	30	NBC
12	20	Eddie Cantor's Time to Smile	17.9	CV	Trushay & Sal Hepatica	Wed	9:00	30	NBC
13	14	Kay Kyser Kollege of Musical Knowledge	17.2	APQ	Colgate Dental Cream	Wed	10:00	60	NBC
14	N	<u>Hildegarde's Raleigh Room</u>	16.6	MV	Raleigh Cigarettes	Tue	10:30	30	NBC
15	16	Take It or Leave It/Phil Baker	16.4	APQ	Eversharp Pens & Pencils	Sun	10:00	30	CBS
16	105	<u>Dinah Shore Show</u>	15.4	MV	Birds Eye Frozen Foods	Thu	8:30	30	NBC
17	18	Your Hit Parade/Sinatra,Tibbett, Edwards	15.3	MP	Lucky Strike Cigarettes	Sat	9:00	45	CBS
18t	7	Aldrich Family/Dickie Jones	15.1	SC	Postum Beverage	Fri	8:00	30	CBS
18t	28	Amos & Andy	15.1	SC	Rinso Laundry Soap	Fri	10:00	30	NBC
20	23	Bob Burns Show	14.9	CV	Lifebuoy Soap	Thu	7:30	30	NBC
21t	18	Burns & Allen	14.7	SC	Swan Soap	Mon	8:30	25	CBS 1
21t	31	HV Kaltenborn News	14.7	NC	Pure Oil	M-F	7:45	15	NBC
23	27	Truth or Consequences/R Edwards	14.5	APS	Duz Laundry Soap	Sat	8:30	30	NBC
24	29	Mr & Mrs North/Joe Curtin, Alice Frost	14.0	DCC	Woodbury Soap	Wed	8:00	30	NBC
25	21	Great Gildersleeve/Hal Peary	13.9	SC	Parkay Margarine	Sun	6:30	30	NBC
26	13	Frank Morgan Show	13.7	CV	Maxwell House Coffee	Thu	8:00	30	NBC
27t	32	Can You Top This?	13.6	PS	Colgate Shaving Cream	Sat	9:30	30	NBC
27t	37	Lowell Thomas News	13.6	NC	Sun Oil	M-F	6:45	15	NBC
27t	74	<u>We the People at War/Milo Boulton</u>	13.6	API	Gulf Oil	Sun	10:30	30	CBS
30	45	Duffy's Tavern/Ed Gardner	13.5	SC	Minit-Rub & Vitalis	Fri	8:30	30	NBC
31	45	People Are Funny/Art Linkletter	13.4	APS	Wings Cigarettes	Fri	9:30	30	NBC
32	43	Judy Canova Show	13.2	CV	Colgate Tooth Powder	Sat	10:00	30	NBC
33	32	Dr Christian/Jean Hersholt	13.1	DCC	Vaseline	Wed	8:30	25	CBS
34t	26	Fitch Bandwagon/Dick Powell	13.0	MP	Fitch Shampoo	Sun	7:30	30	NBC
34t	37	Vox Pop	13.0	API	Bromo Seltzer	Mon	8:00	30	CBS
36	N	<u>Eddie Bracken Show</u>	12.9	SC	Fleischmann's Yeast	Sun	8:30	30	NBC
37	51	<u>Big Town/Ed Pawley</u>	12.8	DCC	Ironized Yeast	Tue	8:00	30	CBS
38t	35	Crime Doctor/Everett Sloane	12.7	DCC	Philip Morris Cigarettes	Sun	8:30	30	CBS
38t	N	<u>Rudy Vallee's Villa Vallee</u>	12.7	MV	Drene Shampoo	Thu	10:30	30	NBC
40	79	<u>A Date with Judy/Louise Erickson</u>	12.5	SC	Tums Antacid	Tue	8:30	30	NBC
41t	25	Adventures of Thin Man	12.4	DCC	Grapenuts Cereal	Fri	8:30	25	CBS
41t	74	<u>Thanks to the Yanks/Bob Hawk</u>	12.4	APQ	Camel Cigarettes	Mon	7:30	30	CBS
43t	53	<u>American Album of Familiar Music</u>	12.0	MST	Bayer Aspirin	Sun	9:30	30	NBC
43t	N	<u>Bill Henry Johns-Manville News</u>	12.0	NC	Johns Manville Insulation	M-F	8:55	05	CBS
45	41	Jimmy Durante &Garry Moore Show	11.7	CV	Rexall Drugs	Fri	10:00	30	CBS 2
46t	66	<u>Molle Mystery Theater</u>	11.6	DA	Molle Shaving Cream	Tue	9:00	30	NBC
46t	35	Ginny Simms Show	11.6	MV	Philip Morris Cigarettes	Tue	8:00	30	NBC
48t	64	<u>Doctor IQ /Jimmy McClain</u>	11.4	APQ	Mars Candy	Mon	10:30	30	NBC
48t	74	<u>Gabriel Heatter News</u>	11.4	NC	Various	M-F	9:00	15	MBS
50	N	<u>Palmolive Party/Barry Wood</u>	11.2	MV	Palmolive Soap	Sat	10:00	30	NBC

New & Returning Top 50 Programs Underscored.

1	Burns & Allen Show	Oct-Jan	Swan Soap	Tue	9:00	30	CBS
2	Jimmy Durante & Garry Moore Show	Oct-Mar	Camel Cigarettes	Fri	10:00	30	CBS

Key:

API — Audience Participation/Interviews	DCC — Drama/Continuing Characters	MV — Music/Variety Show
APQ — Audience Participation/Quiz	MC — Music/Classical, Semi-Classical	NC — News, Commentary
APS — Audience Participation/Stunts	MP — Music/Popular, Contemporary	SC — Situation Comedy
CV — Comedy/Variety Show	MSP — Music/Specialty, Ethnic	SP — Sports
DA — Dramatic Anthology	MST — Music/Standard, Traditional	TC — Talent Competition

1944–45 Top 50 Favorite Formats

	Programs	Pct
Comedy — All Categories	19	38%
Drama — Anthology & Continuing	9	18%
Music — All Categories	9	18%
Audience Participation — All Categories	8	16%
News/Commentary	5	10%

1944–45 Monthly Winners

Sep	Bob Hope Show	23.5	Feb	Bob Hope Show	34.7
Oct	Fibber McGee & Molly	25.6	Mar	Bob Hope Show	30.6
Nov	Bob Hope Show	31.3	Apr	Bob Hope Show	30.5
Dec	Bob Hope Show	31.7	May	Bob Hope Show	27.4
Jan	Bob Hope Show	35.5	Jun	Bob Hope Show	25.2

18

The 1945–46 Network Season

Announcer: This year, for the first time in recorded history, it's the men who are complaining that they have positively nothing to wear! As one soldier wrote to his wife from overseas, "I'll need clothes the way a newborn baby needs them. Buy me a complete layette." (CHUCKLE) The perfect answer for him and for millions of men fresh off the transports is Textron Men's Wear. For Textron shorts and Textron pajamas bring to life the comfort and masculine smartness your new civilians used to just dream about those past nights in far-off foxholes. Textron pajamas are generously proportioned throughout, with trousers that fit and hang like slacks ... and jackets so handsomely cut and finished, you could wear them for sports shirts! As for the colors ... whether stripes or prints or solids ... they'll satisfy every man's desire for brightness and conservatism combined. And they're all cut and tailored with the same masterful precision Textron used in making parachutes for war! So build your lucky man's postwar wardrobe on a Textron foundation. For fit, for comfort and for style, he'll toast both Textron and you.

JORDAN SCORES AGAIN

The biggest news story since Pearl Harbor broke in mid–August 1945, and NBC had it first.

Neutral Switzerland brokered the surrender negotiations between the Allies and Japan. All communications between the combatants went thru Geneva.

Once again — as he had been in Munich at the war's start — NBC's Max Jordan was also on the spot at its finish.

Chronicled by broadcast historian Elizabeth McLeod, NBC News pre-empted soap opera *Stella Dallas* at 4:18 P.M. Eastern War Time on August 14th for Jordan's first word that the Japanese government's coded message accepting surrender terms had been received in Geneva. Jordan's scoop was an exclusive for a long two hours and forty-five minutes until United Press cleared its bulletin that World War II was over.

Ironically, the outstanding war reporter became a man of peace. Jordan retired from NBC in 1947 at the age of 52. A PhD in religious philosophy, he become a Benedictine priest — a position in which he served for the remaining 31 years of his life.

TIME'S UP!

War Time — the designation given to year round Daylight Savings during the duration — was declared officially over on September 30th. Some localities reverted to Standard Time while others waited

until later in the year. Standardization of the beginning and end dates of Daylight Savings in the United States didn't take effect until 1966. But even then, enough loopholes were in the bill to allow local options which could confuse the broadcast schedules from one municipality to another.

BROADCASTING'S BIG BUSINESS BOOM

The networks were sold-out from wall to wall as the nation transitioned to peacetime.

A record 232 sponsored programs were rated in the season's prime time Hooperatings — the all-time high between 6:00 and 11:00 P.M.

In the five years since the beginning of World War II, total annual radio revenues had doubled and the networks were approaching the $200 Million mark in sales *(2.51 Bil)*. The tax breaks given to advertisers and paper rationing that limited print competition created a bonanza for broadcasters.

The FCC shook its finger at the industry in March 1946 when it issued a 140 page report that complained of over-commercialization. It was strictly for show purposes.

A DAY ON THE DIAL

The highly publicized FCC report which the press was happy to report and editorially praise, also complained of "too many" soap operas on the networks.

The 1945–46 season was typical of the decade — strips of highly profitable serials dominated daytime programming.

NBC had 22 soap operas in the Hooperatings and CBS scheduled 17. The 39 soaps absorbed nearly ten hours of airtime every weekday.

A ten month Hooper snapshot of 1946 — January through June and September through December —

1945–46 Season Scoreboard
Mid-season Totals, December 1945

		Compared to Year Earlier	
Total Radio Homes	33.1 Mil	+0.6 Mil	+18.5%
Total Auto Radios	6.0 Mil	(1.0 Mil)	(14.3%)
Total AM Radio Stations	919	+9	+1.0%
Total Radio Network Affiliates	874	+180	+25.9%
1945 Radio Revenues	423.9 Mil	+30.4 Mil	+7.7%
1945 Network Revenues	197.9 Mil	+6.1 Mil	+3.2%
Network Share	46.7%		(2.0%)
Total TV Stations	8	+/-0	+/-0%
Total FM Stations	54	+2	+3.8%

credits Procter & Gamble's *Ma Perkins* and *The Road of Life* with the highest daytime ratings — noting that each program was broadcast *twice a day*— once on CBS and once on NBC. *Perkins* scored a prime time-like 12.5 combined rating over the year, *Road* trailed with 9.3.

Virginia Payne was the undisputed Queen of the Soaps with her 23 year portrayal of the kindly, wise widow Perkins in the Frank and Anne Hummert production for P&G's Oxydol laundry soap.

Close on her heels was Mary Jane Higbee of *When a Girl Marries*, daytime radio's highest rated single-broadcast program with a 7.2 rating.

Of the Top 25 weekday programs, 22 were soaps with an average rating of 5.9 — a mediocre number by prime time standards, yet it represented nearly two million homes every weekday. The audience was comprised primarily of women who listened to the daytime serials and responded to the sponsors' targeted marketing.

ABC DEFIES BIG GUYS

Surprisingly, the program that won second place among all daytime programs wasn't a soap opera. Jovial Tom Brenaman's audience participation show, ABC's *Breakfast in Hollywood,* scored the second largest weekday audience with a 7.0 rating. The show's popularity was exploited by the 1946 low budget film comedy, *Breakfast in Hollywood.*

ABC had dropped serials and countered with weekday variety programming — Don McNeill's long running *Breakfast Club* opened its weekday schedule, followed by *Breakfast in Hollywood*. The Cliff Arquette sitcom, *Glamour Manor* and the heartwarming wedding-of-the-day reality series, *Bride & Groom* continued ABC's daily variety fare.

During the 1946 ratings snapshot, McNeill's hour-long *Breakfast Club* from Chicago enjoyed a 5.0 rating, Arquette scored 3.7. and John Nelson's daily wedding party trailed at 3.0.

Bride & Groom gave away over a half million dollars' worth of prizes

a year to its many newlywed couples, but it was scheduled opposite another human interest/giveaway show — Mutual's *Queen for a Day,* hosted by an enthusiastically empathetic Jack Bailey who delivered a 4.1 rating.

Although daytime radio was monopolized by soap operas, these five variety and audience participation programs — plus Art Linkletter's *House Party, The Fred Waring Show,* Johnny Olsen's *Ladies Be Seated* and the quarter hour songfests by Morton Downey and Jack Berch — all had one thing in common. Like the soaps, they were all fully sponsored and making money for everyone involved.

THE MAGNIFICENT SEVEN

Industry trade journal *Broadcasting* reported that the four networks received 60 percent of their 1945 revenue from manufacturers of foods and beverages, soaps, patent medicines and toiletries.

Seven of these major corporations sponsored half the 1945–46 season's Top 50 programs.

Procter & Gamble ranked first by spending $14.9 Million *(187.3 Mil),* for a mix of programming.

The Cincinnati soap giant had four prime time shows that made the season's Top 50: *Truth or Consequences, The Life of Riley, The Rudy Vallee Show* and *The FBI in Peace & War.*

In addition to sponsoring half of *Breakfast in Hollywood,* P&G block — programmed CBS for an hour every day at 1:00 with *Life Can Be Beautiful,* followed by "Oxydol's Own" *Ma Perkins, Young Doctor Malone* and *The Road of Life.* It followed with a second hour-long buy on NBC at 3:00 with *Woman of America,* the *Ma Perkins* repeat broadcast, *Pepper Young's Family* and *The Right to Happiness.*

Sterling Drug spent $8.25 Million *(103.7 Mil),* for a program mix supplied mostly by producers Frank and Anne Hummert — soap operas *Stella Dallas, Lorenzo Jones, Backstage Wife* and *Young Widder Brown,* plus Hummert music shows *Manhattan Merry Go Round, The American Album of Familiar Music* and *Waltz Time,* which all made the

season's Top 50 in prime time. Sterling also sponsored the long running Top 50 hit *Big Town,* which wasn't a Hummert production.

General Foods spent a fraction over eight million *(100.5 Mil),* for soaps *When a Girl Marries, Portia Faces Life, The Second Mrs. Burton* plus four Top 50 programs: *Burns & Allen, The Aldrich Family,* Fanny Brice as *Baby Snooks* and *The Dinah Shore Show.* The conglomerate also extended its long-time sponsorship of Kate Smith's prime time show which had dropped off the season's Top 50 list — plus her daily 15 minute noonday talk show on CBS that delivered a strong 6.3 rating.

For a chunk of its $7.2 Million *(90.5 Mil),* Lever Brothers got two of the season's Top Five prime time programs, *The Bob Hope Show* and *Lux Radio Theater.* The company also had Top 50 winners in *Amos & Andy* and *The Bob Burns Show.* Unlike Procter & Gamble's strong daytime presence, Lever sponsored only two soaps, *Big Sister* and *Aunt Jenny's True Life Stories.*

Although not ranked among the biggest spenders, Brown & Williamson Tobacco, Colgate Palmolive Peet and Bristol Myers each sponsored three shows ranked in the season's Top 50.

NEWCOMERS KNIT INTO NETS

The total number of network affiliated stations jumped 25.9 percent — a record high annual growth. Ninety-five percent of America's commercial AM radio stations were linked to one of the four networks.

Mutual remained the largest network in terms of affiliates by offering a strong news lineup, a menu of variety programming and few strings attached. The network grew by 139 new outlets in 1945 for a total of 384 affiliates, followed by ABC's 195 stations, NBC's 150 and CBS's 145.

ABC added to its string of owned-and-operated stations with the purchase of George W. Trendle's WXYZ/Detroit in May 1946. Ed Noble floated 950,000 shares of ABC stock to pay for WXYZ and his network's first steps into television.

The ABC purchase of WXYZ didn't include the shrewd Trendle's program properties, *The Lone Ranger, The Green Hornet,* and *Challenge of the Yukon.* Trendle netted three million dollars in 1949 *(28.5 Mil),* for television rights to *The Lone Ranger.*

PALEY'S BATTLE PLAN

In audience popularity, NBC had registered twice the number of programs in the annual Top 50 than CBS for two consecutive seasons.

CBS boss Bill Paley, returned from two years of Army service, was determined to put an end to NBC's dominance of prime time ratings. With newly appointed network president Frank Stanton at his side, Paley told the press that CBS would counter NBC's powerful comedy shows — eleven of the season's Top 15 programs — by concentrating on, "...News, drama, public service programming and music."

He neglected to mention some clever talent piracy — which would make CBS the most popular network by the end of the decade.

TV TESTS TUBES AND TOLLS

CBS and General Electric successfully tested their color television system in October and demonstrated it to the press in February. The technique, invented by 39-year-old Peter Goldmark was hailed for its quality. But Goldmark's technology was incompatible with the black and white television system already in use.

Led by RCA, manufacturers employing the existing system promised consumers that new, postwar model black and white television sets would be in the stores and in good supply by summer. By flooding the market, they planned to make any conversion to the CBS system unacceptable to the public.

Earlier in the season NBC had transmitted the Army-Navy football game over a 90 mile coaxial cable from Philadelphia to New York. In February, the cable extended another 135 miles to Washington and Lincoln Day ceremonies were relayed to New York.

As it was in early network radio, AT&T's wires were again the choice to link networks and stations for the grainy television images.

NBC's first television station, WNBT/New York, issued its first rate card for programming that was still limited to a few hours every evening. Eight dollars *($100.55)* bought a one-minute commercial. Television still had a long way to go to pay for its expensive development.

Until then it was up to radio to support the new medium.

THE MONTHLIES

As it had the previous season, NBC claimed two-thirds — 33 — of the seasons Top 50 programs. It was the greatest dominance a network would ever enjoy over its competitors.

NBC's string of consecutive monthly winners reached 111 and was becoming an old story. The only excitement was the ping-pong game between Bob Hope and his Tuesday night lead-in, *Fibber McGee & Molly,* for the monthly crown.

Hope won September, December, February, April, May and June. Jim and Marian Jordan's homespun heroes of Wistful Vista finished first in October, November, January and March.

1945–46 Sunday Night Top Ten Programs
NBC 7, CBS 2, ABC 1
Average: 16.6

Edgar Bergen & Charlie McCarthy	NBC	8:00	22.4
Jack Benny Program	NBC	7:00	21.3
Fred Allen Show	NBC	8:30	21.1
Walter Winchell's Jergens Journal	ABC	9:00	19.8
Take It or Leave It	CBS	10:00	16.5
Fitch Bandwagon	NBC	7:30	14.8
The Great Gildersleeve	NBC	6:30	14.6
American Album of Familiar Music	NBC	9:30	11.7
Blondie	CBS	7:30	11.7
Manhattan Merry Go Round	NBC	9:00	11.7

BENNY'S VAULT TO HIGHER RATINGS

Jack Benny's ratings had slowly slipped 35 percent since 1941. His tenth place finish in the 1944–45 season was the lowest in ten years. Nevertheless, Benny's Sunday show had never slipped below a 20 rating and he wanted to keep it that way.

To stir things up and reverse the trend, Benny pulled a switch in character on his November 25 program: The world's cheapest man announced that he would remove $10,000 *($125,700),* from his subterranean vault and award U.S. Savings Bonds to listeners who best completed the statement, "*I can't stand Jack Benny because...*" in 50 words or less.

The six week contest drew over 275,000 entries vying for the $2,500 top prize. More importantly, the stunt got widespread publicity and helped reverse Benny's slide in popularity.

THIN MAN MURDERED!

General Foods pulled Kate Smith's CBS variety show out of Jack Benny's line of fire at 7:00, trimmed it 30 minutes and swapped her Sunday timeslot with its successful Friday night detective series, *The Adventures of the Thin Man,* a Top 50 program on CBS for three consecutive seasons.

The move became another of General Foods' futile attempts to compete with its former star salesman on NBC. Pitted against Benny on Sunday, *The Thin Man* lost a third of its Friday ratings and plummeted from 41st to 78th in the season's rankings.

ALLEN'S HEALTHY RATINGS

After four seasons on CBS, Fred Allen returned from a year's sabbatical for his ailing health to a prime spot on the NBC schedule. His year of "rest" included writing and co-starring with Jack Benny in the movie comedy, *It's in the Bag!*

Standard Brands signed Allen for its half hour immediately following *Edgar Bergen & Charlie McCarthy.* His 21.1 season average was his highest rating in eleven years and the first of three consecutive seasons in the annual Top Ten.

The best of times lay ahead of Allen in those three seasons.

Along for the comedian's high ratings ride were his wife, Portland, and his most memorable *Allen's*

Alley cast — Minerva Pious in her twelfth season with Allen as Mrs. Pansy Neusbaum, Peter Donald as Irishman Ajax Cassidy, Parker Fennelly as New Englander Titus Moody and Kenny Delmar as Senator Beauregard Claghorn.

Delmar, who doubled as the show's announcer and spokesman for Standard's Tenderleaf Tea, was such a hit as the blustery, southern-fried politician that he starred in the 1947 low budget film, *It's a Joke, Son!* The film launched Delmar's 20 year career as a television actor and voice talent.

Mel Blanc's close impersonation of Delmar's Claghorn character is still heard today from the beak of "Foghorn Leghorn" in Warner Brothers cartoons.

BACKING UP TO A COMEBACK

Colgate rescued *Blondie* after its disastrous 1944–45 season opposite Edgar Bergen. All it took was moving the series back half an hour to 7:30 on the CBS schedule.

The Penny Singleton/Arthur Lake sitcom began its comeback against NBC's *Fitch Bandwagon* and its new hostess, comedienne Cass Daley. *Blondie*'s ratings increased 20 percent and the show scored the first of three consecutive Top 50 seasons, all of them as one of Sunday's Top Ten programs.

By 1948, *Blondie* was Top 25 show again, doubling the ratings it generated opposite Bergen. But not everyone learned to stay away from the soft spoken Swede and his sharp-tongued adolescent alter ego.

A HEARTBREAKER

Marlin Hurt created a character that outlived him.

After a strong season and a half as *Fibber McGee & Molly*'s maid, Hurt's Beulah was considered prime spinoff material. The first spinoff series from Wistful Vista, Hal Peary's *Great Gildersleeve*, had proved to be consistent Top 25 show on Sunday and the same success was predicted for Hurt. *FM&M* assistant writer Phil Leslie was charged with writing the series scheduled for a fall debut.

Unfortunately, *The Marlin Hurt*

& Beulah Show was doomed from the start.

Just like Kraft had placed *Gildersleeve* on Sunday, sponsor Tums also scheduled *Beulah* on Sunday — but on CBS at 8:00 — a suicide slot opposite *Edgar Bergen & Charlie McCarthy.*

Sunday's Number One program trampled *Beulah*'s ratings by a three to one margin.

Beulah left the air suddenly in March — but for a reason far more compelling than low ratings.

Marlin Hurt dropped dead of a heart attack at the age of 41 and the show was cancelled.

Nevertheless, his character was resurrected 18 months later when *The Beulah Show* returned as a CBS strip sitcom with veteran black screen actress Hattie McDaniel in the lead. The series enjoyed a successful six year run and became the highest rated Multiple Run program of 1950–51.

It would have made Hurt's heart proud.

1945–46 Monday Night Top Ten Programs (12)
CBS 6, NBC 5, MBS 1
Average: 13.5

Lux Radio Theater	CBS	9:00	21.9
Screen Guild Players	CBS	10:00	19.7
Joanies Tea Room	CBS	8:30	14.4
Vox Pop	CBS	8:00	13.2
Thanks to the Yanks & Bob Hawk Show	CBS	7:30	12.4
Lowell Thomas News*	NBC	6:45	12.0
Bill Henry Johns Manville News*	CBS	8:55	10.6
Dr IQ	NBC	10:30	10.5
HV Kaltenborn News*	NBC	7:45	10.3
Adventures Sherlock Holmes	MBS	8:30	10.1
Chesterfield Supper Club*	NBC	7:00	10.1
Information Please	NBC	9:30	10.1
*Monday–Friday Strip Shows			
Sans Strips...			
Cavalcade of America	NBC	8:00	9.3
Carnation Contented Hour	NBC	10:00	8.3

JOANIE'$ TEA ROOM

It was a maneuver that Paley's CBS publicity corps had to love...

Lever Brothers signed comedienne Joan Davis to a "Million Dol-

lar" contract and gave her the half hour on CBS leading into its perennial Monday leader, *Lux Radio Theater.* Industry sources were quick to point out that the million dollars was to cover all of her new show's talent and production costs for two years — but why let details clutter up a good fan magazine headline.

Davis was touted with the publicists' title, "Radio's Highest Paid Female Performer," worthy of the million dollars after scoring two Top Ten seasons co-starring with Jack Haley on the NBC sitcom *Sealtest Village Store.*

Her new CBS show, *Joanie's Tea Room*, was a similar format — the weekly misadventures of the man hungry, wise-cracking, twang-talking Davis supported by some of Hollywood's best radio character actors. Handsome romantic baritone Andy Russell, 26, replaced Haley as her co-star — a move Davis predicted would lure the "bobbysox." audience.

It didn't.

Davis lost a third of her *Village Store* audience with the new show. *Joanie's Tea Room* slipped below the ratings posted in the timeslot a year earlier by Burns and Allen, who had skipped back to NBC.

Nevertheless, Davis kept *Tea Room* in the mid-teens and Monday's Top Ten for two seasons when Lever Brothers let her highly publicized contract expire to make way for a new and much cheaper new show hosted by a local radio personality, *Arthur Godfrey's Talent Scouts.*

MR. C SINGS FOR SUPPER

When Liggett & Myers Tobacco cancelled the Fred Waring troupe in 1944 after five seasons on its *Chesterfield Supper Club,* the company took a calculated risk and gave the show to 33-year-old baritone Perry Como on Monday, Wednesday and Friday.

Como's Monday *Supper Club* became the first non-news Multiple Run program to crack a nightly Top Ten in two years.

NAME CHANGE = NO CHANGE

Bob Hawk's comedy quiz *Thanks to the Yanks* changed its name in mid-season to *The Bob Hawk Show* and changed its rules of play — awarding cash prizes to civilians instead of Camel cigarettes to servicemen. Despite the name and format changes, one thing didn't change: Hawk's average rating for the season, 12.4, was exactly the same as the previous season — a rarity among Top 50 programs.

1945–46 Tuesday Night Top Ten Programs (11)
NBC 7, CBS 4
Average: 16.6

Bob Hope Show	NBC	10:00	27.7
Fibber McGee & Molly	NBC	9:30	27.1
Red Skelton Show	NBC	10:30	23.1
Amos & Andy	NBC	9:00	16.8
Big Town	CBS	8:00	13.7
Date with Judy	NBC	8:30	12.3
Lowell Thomas News*	NBC	6:45	12.0
Inner Sanctum	CBS	9:00	11.9
Bill Henry Johns Manville News*	CBS	8:55	10.6
HV Kaltenborn News*	NBC	7:45	10.3
Theater of Romance	CBS	8:30	10.3

*Monday–Friday Strip Shows

Sans Strips...

Johnny Presents Johnny Desmond	NBC	8:00	10.0
His Honor the Barber	NBC	7:30	9.5

NBC's Happy Returns

Red Skelton returned from military duty and was back on the air in December. His 18 month absence from radio cost 20 percent of his audience, but his ratings remained the season's third best behind his Tuesday night NBC teammates, Bob Hope and *Fibber McGee & Molly*.

FM&M regained its peak form during the season. Gale Gordon returned from the Coast Guard and his Mayor LaTrivia character resumed his weekly verbal bouts with Fibber in October. Wistful Vista neighbors Wallace Wimple and the Old Timer were welcomed back in January with Bill Thompson's release from the Navy.

NBC's Tuesday comedy lineup got still another lift when Lever Brothers moved the resurgent *Amos & Andy* from Friday into the 9:00 Tuesday slot before *Fibber McGee*

& Molly. The Vaudeville and radio veterans gave NBC two solid hours of Tuesday dominance on their climb back to popularity. *Amos & Andy* would be among the annual Top Ten by the following season.

CBS chairman Paley's strategy to counter-program comedy with drama produced three shows in Tuesday's Top Ten. It was formula that eventually overtook NBC five years later.

From Barbours to Barber

One Man's Family creator Carleton E. Morse launched another NBC series, *His Honor the Barber*. Unlike typical Morse productions, *His Honor* featured a movie star, veteran character actor Barry Fitzgerald. The crusty Fitzgerald, 57, had won an Oscar earlier in the year for his supporting role in 1944's *Going My Way* — becoming the only actor ever nominated for both Best Actor and Best Supporting Actor in the same role. His voice was unmistakable and he a natural for another Morse family-oriented series.

But *His Honor* never got a fair trial. The program was only heard in parts of the country as NBC split the network at 7:30 to accommodate H.V. Kaltenborn's news commentary at 7:45 in areas where Pure Oil products were sold.

Unlike the Barbour family's 27 years on the air, Fitzgerald's barber left after 26 weeks.

1945–46 Wednesday Night Top Ten Programs
NBC 7, CBS 3
Average: 13.1

Mr. District Attorney	NBC	9:30	19.6
Eddie Cantor's Time to Smile	NBC	9:00	17.1
Dr Christian	CBS	8:30	13.9
Kay Kyser's Kollege of Musical Knowledge	NBC	10:00	13.4
Mr. & Mrs. North	NBC	8:00	12.1
Hildegarde's Raleigh Room	NBC	8:30	12.0
Lowell Thomas News*	NBC	6:45	12.0
Bill Henry Johns Manville News*	CBS	8:55	10.6
Frank Sinatra Show	CBS	9:00	10.3

HV Kaltenborn News*	NBC	7:45	10.3

*Monday–Friday Strip Shows

Sans Strips...

Adventures of Ellery Queen	CBS	7:30	9.6
Jack Carson Show	CBS	8:00	9.4
An Evening with Romberg	NBC	8:30	9.2

Wed Locked Too Long?

Show business trade paper *Variety* had criticized Network Radio early in the season for its lack of new programs to attract listeners. Wednesday was a prime example of the resulting audience attrition forecast by the trade paper. The average rating for the night's veteran Top Ten shows sank to its lowest level in seven years.

Of Wednesday's Top Ten prime time programs, Kay Kyser's *Kollege of Musical Knowledge* had been on the list for nine consecutive seasons, *Doctor Christian* for seven, Eddie Cantor for six, *Mr. District Attorney* for five, *Mr. & Mrs. North* for four and Frank Sinatra for three.

Outside of entertainment programming, newscasters H.V. Kaltenborn and Lowell Thomas had been among Wednesday's Top Ten for 5 and 14 consecutive years, respectively.

The only newcomer to Wednesday's list was a transplant from Tuesday, *Hildegarde's Raleigh Room*, pushed out of its timeslot when Red Skelton returned from the Navy in December. Sponsor Brown & Williamson also had a Wednesday time period available on NBC at 8:30 which it had filled with veteran composer/conductor Sigmund Romberg's semi-classical concerts. Romberg, 58, had a history of Network Radio shows dating back to 1934.

When *Raleigh Room* was displaced, B&W moved the "Incomparable" Hildy's breezy music and audience participation show into Romberg's timeslot. Hildegarde raised the time period's ratings by 30 percent, resulting in her second Top 50 season.

Nevertheless, Hildegarde was out at the end of the season and Wednesday was due for a shakeup the following fall.

JOE'S CONN JOB
IS A KNOCKOUT

The all-time high Hooperating for a commercial broadcast was set on Wednesday, June 19, 1946, when Joe Louis and Billy Conn fought for the Heavyweight Championship in Yankee Stadium. It was a rematch of their fierce 1941 bout won by Louis in 13 rounds.

The second fight had been delayed for five years by the fighters' service in World War II and was eagerly awaited. It was the first championship bout ever televised — but television was still a few years away from nationwide network coverage.

Most of America — registering a whopping 71.6 percent of homes using radio and a 93.8 share of audience — was tuned to ABC's hookup of 224 stations for Don Dunphy's piercing machine gun call of the fight and commentary by Bill Corum, the gravel voiced boxing reporter for Hearst's *New York Journal-American*. The pair also announced ABC's weekly Friday night fights for Gillette — a series that averaged less than ten percent of the 67.2 rating scored on that special night when Louis knocked out Conn in the eighth round.

1945–46 Thursday Night
Top Ten Programs
NBC 9, CBS 1
Average: 14.6

Bing Crosby's Kraft Music Hall	NBC	9:00	21.5
Sealtest Village Store	NBC	9:30	16.9
Frank Morgan's Kraft Music Hall	NBC	9:00	16.7
Abbott & Costello Show	NBC	10:00	16.4
Dinah Shore Show	NBC	8:30	13.1
Bob Burns Show	NBC	7:30	12.9
Burns & Allen Show	NBC	8:00	12.8
Suspense	CBS	8:00	12.5
Lowell Thomas News*	NBC	6:45	12.0
Rudy Vallee Show	NBC	10:30	11.4

*Monday–Friday Strip Shows

Sans Strips...

FBI in Peace & War	CBS	8:30	11.3

THURSDAY'S DISTANT
THUNDER

NBC's continued to dominate Thursday night ratings despite disruptions in its leading shows sponsored by food companies.

General Foods' Maxwell House Coffee dumped Frank Morgan and brought in Burns & Allen from CBS for its half hour at 8:00. Ratings dropped a fraction in George and Gracie's fifth jump between the two networks.

Joan Davis checked out of Sealtest's *Village Store* at 9:30 in her "million dollar" jump to the CBS Monday schedule. Sealtest paired Jack Haley with a new co-star, movie actress/comedienne Eve Arden. As a result, *Village Store* suffered a 25 percent loss in audience.

Abbott and Costello followed Haley and Arden at 10:00 and lost 15 percent of their previous season's ratings.

But NBC's greatest concern was Bing Crosby' walkout from *Kraft Music Hall* at 9:00.

Crosby, 1945's Oscar winning actor for *Going My Way*, quit *Music Hall* in a dispute over his demand to pre-record his shows. Neither the sponsor nor NBC would allow it, so the star simply didn't report for work in October. Kraft sued Crosby for breach of contract and turned to the deposed Frank Morgan who was without a Thursday night radio job for the first time seven years.

While the Crosby-Kraft battle dragged on in the courts, Morgan kept *Music Hall* open through January with guest stars and Eddy Duchin's orchestra. The show's ratings drifted down from the 20s into the mid-teens.

Crosby finally came to separation terms with Kraft and returned to *Music Hall* in February for a 13 week encore run. His ratings were 30 percent higher than Morgan's but it would be the last time that the singer's numbers would score in the twenties.

The season was a bitter taste of ratings to come for *Kraft Music Hall* and NBC and Crosby.

CBS STICKS TO
THE SCRIPTS

True to Bill Paley's prediction, CBS was building audience with drama — he just didn't say what *kind* of drama.

He certainly didn't mean Shakespeare.

Thursday's CBS inroads were led by *Suspense* and *The FBI in Peace & War*, both newcomers to the seasons' list of Top 50 programs. Both stayed there for eight years.

Suspense hit the fall season running with its fourth (live), repeat in two years of *Sorry, Wrong Number* featuring the virtuoso almost-solo performance of Agnes Moorhead. She would repeat it again three times during the program's lengthy run. The *Suspense* blend of headline stars given excellent scripts and direction, is hailed by many critics as the best mystery series of the Golden Age.

The FBI in Peace & War was popular, yet forgettable, stock melodrama best remembered for its signature opening — a booming bass voice chanting the sponsor's name to the accompanying beat on a kettle-drum, "L-A-V-A ... L-A-V-A!" Procter & Gamble's agency, Biow Company, was responsible for the memorable opening that literally drummed home the name of the program's heavy-duty hand soap sponsor, pumice-laden Lava Soap.

This business was followed Prokofiev's heavy handed march from *Love for Three Oranges* which set the program's "documentary" feel — made popular in World War II crime and espionage fighting movies.

CBS would continue to develop its relatively inexpensive studio dramas opposite NBC's aging variety shows and claim most of Thursday's Top Ten programs in just two years.

1945–46 Friday Night
Top Ten Programs
NBC 6, CBS 4
Average: 11.6

Aldrich Family	CBS	8:00	14.2
People Are Funny	NBC	9:00	13.2
Duffy's Tavern	NBC	8:30	12.7
Lowell Thomas News*	NBC	6:45	12.0
Waltz Time	NBC	9:30	11.1
Danny Kaye Show	CBS	10:30	10.8

Jimmy Durante & Garry Moore	CBS	10:00	10.8
Bill Henry Johns Manville News*	CBS	8:55	10.6
Molle Mystery Theater	NBC	10:00	10.6
HV Kaltenborn News*	NBC	7:45	10.3

*Monday–Friday Strip Shows

Sans Strips...

Kate Smith Sings	CBS	8:30	10.1
Ginny Simms Show	CBS	7:30	8.7
Maisie	CBS	10:30	8.5

TOO LATE FOR KATE

After its failed attempt to challenge Jack Benny with Kate Smith on Sunday the previous season, General Foods attempted to revive the CBS ratings of "Radio's First Lady" by moving her back to Friday following its top rated *Aldrich Family.*

The beloved singer's ratings picked up 20 percent from her Sunday night debacle, yet she lost 30 percent of her lead-in's ratings as most of the audience shifted to *Duffy's Tavern* on NBC.

SWITCH AVOIDS FRIDAY'S FIZZLES

Ratings of returning programs dropped across the board in Friday's Top Ten during the first full postwar Network Radio season. Families were reunited, weekend social activities resumed and radio listening became secondary.

The only exception to the drop was Frank and Anne Hummert's bland production, *Waltz Time,* featuring Abe Lyman's NBC studio orchestra, tenor Frank Munn and a string of female vocalists who had all been serenading listeners for Sterling Drug's Phillips Milk of Magnesia laxative for twelve seasons.

It was the first time since 1933 that *Waltz Time* had been ranked among Friday's Top Ten or the season's Top 50.

The show's boost was a matter of scheduling. *Waltz Time* swapped timeslots with *People Are Funny.* Art Linkletter's successful stunt show became the lead into Hummerts' half hour of soft music. Both shows benefited from the switch. Given the comedy lead-in of *Duffy's Tavern, People Are Funny*

moved up to 28th in the season's rankings and *Waltz Time* scored the highest rating and ranking that it ever enjoyed. The maneuver also allowed NBC to hold its lead on Friday night for one last season.

PABST TAPS FOR KAYE

Pabst Beer kept comedian Danny Kaye on the CBS Friday schedule for a second year and moved his show back to 10:00 in the 1945–46 season to capitalize on the comedy lead-in provided by Jimmy Durante and Garry Moore. The shift was rewarded with an improvement in Kaye's ratings beyond the single digits of the previous season.

But *The Danny Kaye Show* was a costly production that included high-priced writing talents of Goodman Ace and Abe Burrows. Then Kaye's personal appearance commitments forced the show to move from Hollywood to New York in March which called for an entirely new supporting cast led by Kenny Delmar to replace Eve Arden and Lionel Stander whose careers were based in Hollywood.

The two versions of *The Danny Kaye Show* combined to finish in Friday's Top Ten but still failed to reach the season's Top 50 and Pabst cancelled the program in June.

Although he continued to become a major film and television star who won Golden Globe and Emmy awards plus honorary Oscars, Danny Kaye never returned to series radio.

1945–46 Saturday Night Top Ten Programs
NBC 6, CBS 4
Average: 11.7

Truth or Consequences	NBC	8:30	14.6
Judy Canova Show	NBC	10:00	13.8
Can You Top This?	NBC	9:30	13.4
Life of Riley	NBC	8:00	13.2
Your Hit Parade	CBS	9:00	13.0
Mayor of the Town	CBS	8:30	10.5
Grand Ole Opry	NBC	10:30	10.3
First Nighter	CBS	7:30	9.6
Saturday Night Serenade	CBS	9:45	9.3
National Barn Dance	NBC	9:00	9.0

HUSH MONEY

Ralph Edwards was up to his serial stunt tricks again with a twist that propelled *Truth or Consequences* into the annual Top 20 for the first of three consecutive seasons — a feat that no other Saturday night program would ever match.

A famous but unidentified celebrity was introduced by Edwards on his December 29th show as "Mister Hush." The first *T or C* contestant to correctly identify him would win a jackpot of prizes. The secret celebrity read the prerecorded clues to his identity every week while more prizes were piled into the jackpot with every incorrect guess.

The concept wasn't new. Arlene Francis' *What's My Name?* had been based on a similar idea since 1938 — only with far fewer and smaller prizes than the bonanza that *Truth or Consequences* offered.

What made Edwards' take on the concept so special was the magnitude of the prizes he gleefully dangled before his growing audience every week, all hungry for the merchandise that was denied them during World War II.

He promised a new, 1946 Mercury automobile, a fur coat, a diamond ring, a piano, a Bendix washer, Crosley refrigerator, Tappan kitchen range, RCA Victor console radio-phonograph — and two years' supply of nylon stockings. Edwards obtained all the merchandise in exchange for healthy plugs on *Truth or Consequences.*

After five weeks, the jackpot reached $13,000 worth of prizes ($150,800), when "Mister Hush" was correctly identified as legendary heavyweight boxing champion Jack Dempsey.

Edwards had introduced *really* big giveaway jackpots to radio that resulted in press coverage, listener conversation and higher ratings.

He was just beginning.

Before he was finished, Edwards repeated the gimmick over the next two seasons and, with yet another twist, he raised millions of dollars for worthy causes in the process.

RILEY GETS NEW LIFE

Actor William Bendix was 39 with 17 films to his credit including one that won an Oscar nomination for his supporting role in 1942's *Wake Island*. He originated the role most associated with him, *The Life of Riley*'s Chester A. Riley, on Blue (as ABC was still known), in January 1945. The sitcom had a shaky start. It hobbled along in the Sunday ratings for six months opposite the CBS comedy quiz, *Take It or Leave It*.

Procter & Gamble rescued the show in September by moving it to Saturday at 8:00 on NBC, immediately prior to its hit, *Truth or Consequences*. The Bendix sitcom doubled its ratings and vaulted into 28th place for the season.

It was the first of six consecutive Top 50 seasons for Riley, his family and neighbors — most notably character actor John Brown's Digby (Digger) O'Dell, "The Friendly Undertaker." During those six years Bendix also appeared in another 25 movies, including the 1949 Universal exploitation film based on the series, *The Life of Riley*.

GOOD NEWS IS BAD FOR NEWS

The good news was that the war was over. Yet, the world was still in turmoil and a record 29 separate prime time news programs appeared in the season's rating books.

The bad news was that newscast ratings were rapidly sinking.

Only one Multiple Run newscast, Lowell Thomas' 6:45 strip on NBC, made the season's Top 50—but the veteran newsman fell from 27th to 40th in the rankings with his lowest rating in eight years.

H.V. Kaltenborn lost 30 percent of his audience and dropped out of the season's Top 50 for the first time in five years. He would never return.

Most dramatic of the drops was Gabriel Heatter's fall from 48th to 117th in the rankings, the result of losing over 45 percent of his 9:00 nightly audience on Mutual — an estimated four million listeners — to the other networks' entertainment programming

Veteran newscaster Elmer Davis returned to radio after his successful service as Director of the Office of War Information. Wary of the new "objective" climate at CBS News that prompted his colleague Cecil Brown to leave the network in 1944, Davis signed with ABC for $1,500 per broadcast (*$18,850*)— and a clause in his contract that allowed him to editorialize if he so desired.

15 MINUTES OF FAME FOR FIVE YEARS

Liggett & Myers and NBC caught rising stars at 7:00 with two former band singers who were building successful solo careers as the big band era drew to a close.

Perry Como, 33, headlined *The Chesterfield Supper Club* on Monday, Wednesday and Friday. Jo Stafford, 28, hosted the quarter hour of pop music on Tuesday and Thursday. The pair enjoyed five seasons in the Multiple Runs' Top Ten.

While rival American Tobacco's *Your Hit Parade* marketed Lucky Strike cigarettes with hit music

once a week, Liggett & Myers relied on the new generation of hit makers every weeknight.

Como had sung with Ted Weems' dance band for six years, including its two seasons with *Fibber McGee & Molly* in the sitcom's Chicago days. When Weems disbanded his group in 1942, Como began looking for work — but not for long. He signed on with *Supper Club* in December 1944. The personable Como's five year success on *Supper Club* was mirrored by his successful recording career.

Como's "Till the End of Time"— with melody provided by Chopin's "Polonaise"— was 1945's Number One record. His three-times a week *Supper Club* led to an NBC-TV version of the program in 1949, and a succession of highly popular weekly television variety hours.

Como's success was shared by Jo Stafford who had left Tommy Dorsey's band in 1942 and spent two years performing countless USO camp shows where she earned the nickname, "GI Jo." Stafford later became Columbia Records' best selling female vocalist. When she departed *Supper Club*'s Thursday shows in 1948, Capitol Records' top female singer, Peggy Lee, took over.

As it had with the first rush of Bing Crosby's popularity in 1932, and the Glenn Miller band in 1939, Liggett & Myers proved that it still had an ear for musical talent and trends. It smartly identified its Chesterfield brand with the three top vocalists of the immediate postwar years.

BIG SPENDER SPLITS CBS

The year's biggest broadcast advertising spender, Procter & Gamble, split the CBS network at 7:00 for two quarter hour strips sponsored by Ivory Soap.

Half the network was fed *The Jack Kirkwood Show*, a 15 minute variety series starring the comedian, his wife Lillian Leigh and a supporting cast that included radio veterans Herb Sheldon and Ransom Sherman.

For regions where Kirkwood's off-the-wall humor wasn't considered a good fit, CBS stations car-

---

1945–46 Top Ten Multiple Run Programs
CBS 4, NBC 4, ABC 1, MBS 1
Average: 8.7

Lowell Thomas News*	M–F	NBC	6:45	12.0
Bill Henry/Johns Manville News*	M–F	CBS	8:55	10.6
HV Kaltenborn News*	M–F	NBC	7:45	10.3
Chesterfield Supper Club/Como/ Stafford*	M–F	NBC	7:00	10.1
Ned Calmer Parker Pen News	Sa,Su	CBS	8:55	8.6
Jack Smith Show*	M–F	CBS	7:15	7.8
The Lone Ranger/Brace Beemer	M,W,F	ABC	7:30	7.7
John W Vandercook News of the World*	M–F	NBC	7:15	7.3
Gabriel Heatter News*	M–F	MBS	9:00	6.2
Jack Kirkwood Show*	M–F	CBS	7:00	5.9

*Monday–Friday Strip Shows

ried *Mommie & the Men*, a soap opera featuring busy radio actors Elspeth Eric, Lon Clark and Jackie Grimes.

Both programs were cancelled in March, replaced on the full CBS network by *The Mystery of the Week*— detective stories told in five nightly chapters, starring Harold Huber as Agatha Christie's sleuth, Hercule Poirot.

But none of these efforts could beat the Perry Como/Jo Stafford pop music combination on NBC.

THE SAME TIME, THE SAME PLACE...

Procter & Gamble had better luck with its 7:15 strip on CBS when it signed handsome, 29-year-old tenor Jack Smith for 15 minutes of upbeat pop tunes. Smith had over a decade of radio experience leading up to his first starring vehicle. He had logged the first six months of 1945 as vocalist for the soap company's popular weekday show, *Glamour Manor*.

The new *Jack Smith Show* proved to be a smart move. Smith appealed to the same audience as *Chesterfield Supper Club*—listeners who went dial twisting when NBC programmed news at 7:15.

Smith could sing the opening line from his closing theme, "...The same time, the same place, tomorrow night...," with confidence. He had a two year contract from Procter & Gamble.

But with the solid ratings that Smith's program produced, his contract was extended three times.

The Jack Smith Show was among the Multiple Runs' Top Ten for eight consecutive seasons.

TOP 50 PROGRAMS—1945–46

NBC 33, CBS 16, ABC 1
Average Rating: 15.3, Median: 13.7
33,100,000 Radio Homes / 88.0% Coverage of U.S. Homes / One Rating Point = 331,000 Homes
Source: C.E. Hooper, Inc. Semi-monthly Reports, Sep 1945 — Jun 1946
Total Programs Rated 6–11 P.M.: 232
Programs Rated 13 Weeks & Ranked: 193

		Program	Rtg	Type	Sponsor	Day	Time	Lgth	Net
1	*1*	Bob Hope Show	27.7	CV	Pepsodent Toothpaste	Tue	10:00	30	NBC
2	*2*	Fibber McGee & Molly	27.1	SC	Johnson Wax	Tue	9:30	30	NBC
3	*N*	Red Skelton Show	23.1	CV	Raleigh Cigarettes	Tue	10:30	30	NBC
4	*6*	Edgar Bergen & Charlie McCarthy	22.4	CV	Chase & Sanborn Coffee	Sun	8:00	30	NBC
5	*3*	Lux Radio Theater/William Keighley	21.9	DA	Lux Soap	Mon	9:00	60	CBS
6	*5*	Bing Crosby's Kraft Music Hall	18.3	MV	Kraft Cheese	Thu	9:00	30	NBC 1
7	*10*	Jack Benny Program	21.3	SC	Lucky Strike Cigarettes	Sun	7:00	30	NBC
8	*N*	Fred Allen Show	21.1	CV	Tenderleaf Tea	Sun	8:30	30	NBC
9	*4*	Walter Winchell's Jergens Journal	19.8	NC	Jergens Lotion	Sun	9:00	15	ABC
10	*9*	Screen Guild Players	19.7	DA	Lady Esther Cosmetics	Mon	10:00	30	CBS
11	*8*	Mister District Attorney/Jay Jostyn	19.6	DCC	Vitalis Hair Tonic	Wed	9:30	30	NBC
12	*12*	Eddie Cantor's Time to Smile	17.1	CV	Trushay & Sal Hepatica	Wed	9:00	30	NBC
13	*7*	Jack Haley/Eve Arden Village Store	16.9	SC	Sealtest Dairies	Thu	9:30	30	NBC
14	*18*	Amos & Andy	16.8	SC	Rinso Laundry Soap	Tue	9:00	30	NBC
15	*N*	Frank Morgan Kraft Music Hall	16.7	CV	Kraft Cheese	Thu	9:00	30	NBC
16	*15*	Take It or Leave It/Phil Baker	16.5	APQ	Eversharp Pens & Pencils	Sun	10:00	30	CBS
17	*11*	Abbott & Costello Show	16.4	CV	Camel Cigarettes	Thu	10:00	30	NBC
18	*34*	Fitch Bandwagon/Cass Daley	14.8	CV	Fitch Shampoo	Sun	7:30	30	NBC
19t	*25*	Great Gildersleeve/Hal Peary	14.6	SC	Parkay Margarine	Sun	6:30	30	NBC
19t	*23*	Truth or Consequences/Ralph Edwards	14.6	APS	Duz Laundry Soap	Sat	8:30	30	NBC
21	*N*	Joanie's Tea Room/Joan Davis	14.4	SC	Swan Soap	Mon	8:30	25	CBS
22	*18*	Aldrich Family/Raymond Ives, Ezra Stone	14.2	SC	Grapenuts Cereal	Fri	8:00	30	CBS
23	*33*	Dr Christian/Jean Hersholt	13.9	DCC	Vaseline	Wed	8:30	25	CBS
24	*32*	Judy Canova Show	13.8	CV	Colgate Tooth Powder	Sat	10:00	30	NBC
25	*37*	Big Town/Ed Pawley	13.7	DCC	Ironized Yeast	Tue	8:00	30	CBS
26t	*27*	Can You Top This?	13.4	PS	Colgate Shaving Cream	Sat	9:30	30	NBC
26t	*13*	Kay Kyser Kollege of Musical Knowledge	13.4	APQ	Colgate Dental Cream	Wed	10:00	60	NBC
28t	*120*	Life of Riley/William Bendix	13.2	SC	Teel Liquid Dentifrice	Sat	8:00	30	NBC
28t	*31*	People Are Funny/Art Linkletter	13.2	APS	Raleigh Cigarettes	Fri	9:00	30	NBC
28t	*34*	Vox Pop	13.2	API	Bromo Seltzer	Mon	8:00	30	CBS
31	*16*	Dinah Shore Show	13.1	MV	Birds Eye Frozen Foods	Thu	8:30	30	NBC
32	*17*	Your Hit Parade/DickTodd, JoanEdwards	13.0	MP	Lucky Strike Cigarettes	Sat	9:00	45	CBS
33	*20*	Bob Burns Show	12.9	CV	Lifebuoy Soap	Thu	7:30	30	NBC
34	*21*	Burns & Allen Show	12.8	SC	Maxwell House Coffee	Thu	8:00	30	NBC
35	*30*	Duffy's Tavern/Ed Gardner	12.7	SC	Ipana & Vitalis	Fri	8:30	30	NBC

	Program	Rtg	Type	Sponsor	Day	Time	Lgth	Net
36 51	Suspense	12.5	DA	Roma Wines	Thu	8:00	30	CBS
37 41	Bob Hawk Show	12.4	APQ	Camel Cigarettes	Mon	7:30	30	CBS 2
38 40	A Date with Judy/Louise Erickson	12.3	SC	Tums Antacid	Tue	8:30	30	NBC
39 24	Mr & Mrs North/Joe Curtin, Alice Frost	12.1	DCC	Woodbury Soap	Wed	8:00	30	NBC
40t 14	Hildegarde's Raleigh Room	12.0	MV	Raleigh & Kool Cigarettes	Wed	8:30	30	NBC 3
40t 27	Lowell Thomas News	12.0	NC	Sun Oil	M-F	6:45	15	NBC
42 71	Inner Sanctum	11.9	DA	Lipton Tea	Tue	9:00	30	CBS
43t 43	American Album of Familiar Music	11.7	MST	Bayer Aspirin	Sun	9:30	30	NBC
43t 73	Blondie/Penny Singleton, Arthur Lake	11.7	SC	Super Suds Laundry Soap	Sun	7:30	30	CBS
43t 79	Manhattan Merry Go Round	11.7	MP	Dr Lyons Tooth Powder	Sun	9:00	30	NBC
46 38	Rudy Vallee's Villa Vallee	11.4	MV	Drene Shampoo	Thu	10:30	30	NBC
47t 38	Crime Doctor/Everett Sloane	11.3	DCC	Philip Morris Cigarettes	Sun	8:30	30	CBS
47t N	The FBI in Peace & War	11.3	DCC	Lava Hand Soap	Thu	8:30	25	CBS
49 79	Fanny Brice/Baby Snooks Show	11.2	SC	Sanka Coffee	Sun	6:30	30	CBS
50 58	Waltz Time	11.1	MSP	Phillips Milk of Magnesia	Fri	9:30	30	NBC

New & Returning Top 50 Programs Underscored.

1	Frank Morgan Kraft Music Hall	Oct–Jan	Kraft Cheese	Thu	9:00	30	NBC
2	aka Thanks To The Yanks	Oct–Dec	Camel Cigarettes	Mon	10:00	30	CBS
3	Hildegarde's Raleigh Room	Sep–Nov	Raleigh Cigarettes	Tue	10:30	30	NBC

Key: API — Audience Participation/Interviews
APQ — Audience Participation/Quiz
APS — Audience Participation/Stunts
CV — Comedy/Variety Show
DA — Dramatic Anthology

DCC — Drama/Continuing Characters
MC — Music/Classical, Semi-Classical
MP — Music/Popular, Contemporary
MSP — Music/Specialty, Ethnic
MST — Music/Standard, Traditional

MV — Music/Variety Show
NC — News, Commentary
PS- Panel Show Comedy
SC — Situation Comedy
TC — Talent Competition

1945–46 Top 50 Favorite Formats

	Programs	Pct
Comedy — All Categories	24	48%
Drama — Anthology & Continuing	10	20%
Music — All Categories	8	16%
Audience Participation — All Categories	6	12%
News/Commentary	2	4%

1945–46 Monthly Winners

Sep	Bob Hope Show	20.6	Feb	Bob Hope Show	31.2
Oct	Fibber McGee & Molly	28.3	Mar	Fibber McGee & Molly	29.0
Nov	Fibber McGee & Molly	27.0	Apr	Bob Hope Show	27.9
Dec	Bob Hope Show	31.7	May	Bob Hope Show	26.9
Jan	Fibber McGee & Molly	30.9	Jun	Bob Hope Show	26.0

19

The 1946–47 Network Season

Announcer: Here's something that's really a matter of <u>life</u> <u>and</u> <u>death</u> ... and that's a <u>blowout!</u> Did you ever stop to think that if you're driving at today's top speed of <u>35</u> <u>miles</u> <u>per</u> <u>hour</u> and a blowout swerves your car into an oncoming truck which travels at the same speed, the resulting crash has the force of <u>70</u> <u>miles</u> <u>per</u> <u>hour</u>! That's enough to double you over the steering wheel and push the engine through the dash. Yet, there is no need for a blowout to throw your car out of control ... not if your car is equipped with <u>Goodyear</u> <u>Life</u> <u>Guards</u>. For the Life Guard is an <u>inner-tire</u> ... a two-ply safety tire within a tube ... it replaces the conventional inner-tube and if your outer tire and inner-tube blow, the inner-tire ... the <u>Life Guard</u> ... <u>remains</u> <u>inflated</u> and holds the car steady so you can come to a sure, safe stop. That's the kind of blowout protection your family needs! It's such sure protection that never once has a <u>Goodyear</u> <u>Life Guard</u> been reported to fail ... <u>never</u> <u>once</u>! Think it over. Then ask your Goodyear dealer if he has any Life Guards. If so, equip your car with Life Guards which are now <u>ration-free</u>. Remember, when your tire blows out, the <u>Goodyear</u> <u>Life Guard</u> never lets <u>you</u> <u>down</u>!

GOIN' FISHIN'

New stations coming on the air and the wartime boom in business had helped push broadcasting's total revenues up steadily for two years. But the networks were virtually sold out and had little left to sell. With empty shelves, the chains slowed to their lowest revenue gain since 1938.

It seemed hypocritical to broadcasters when CBS chief Bill Paley lectured November's National Association of Broadcasters convention on the evils of over-commercialization.

It was also a difficult time for broadcasters to raise prices. Shedding the wartime handicap of paper rationing gave newspapers and magazines new life as radio's competitors for the advertising dollar.

The networks were left with just one alternative to increase revenues — attract more affiliates to justify higher rates.

They all went trolling in 1946 for stations in markets where they lacked coverage and came back with a huge catch by the end of the following year.

THE TRANSCRIPTION TRANSFORMATION

Bing Crosby left NBC's *Kraft Music Hall* in May 1946 determined to record his programs.

It didn't take long for him to find a new sponsor with deep pockets and a new network with a deep need for his star-power.

Philadelphia radio and television manufacturer Philco wanted Crosby.

And Mark Woods at ABC would take Crosby on *any* terms — in person or on disc. ABC had no policy against transcribed programs. Just the opposite, ABC had encouraged the technology earlier in the year by introducing a recording/re-broadcasting technique to its affiliates in an effort to avoid the confusion caused by Daylight Savings Time differences among cities.

Meanwhile, CBS and NBC continued to forbid the recorded production of prime time programs for broadcast, claiming a fear of losing live shows' superior technical quality, timeliness and spontaneity.

What the networks *really* feared was losing their monopoly of big name stars and big buck sponsors to transcribed shows distributed on disc directly to local stations — cutting the networks out of the picture altogether.

Nevertheless, Woods had nothing to lose. Bing Crosby's *Philco Radio Time* began its three year transcribed spin on ABC on October 16. The program's first two seasons were broadcast from disc and the third from tape.

It was another turning point for the new ABC which was becoming a viable competitor. In the five years since its split from NBC, followed by its sale to Ed Noble in 1943, the network had grown to 250 affiliates and a 1946 income over $40 Million (*464.1 Mil*).

On a larger scale, Bing Crosby's *Philco Radio Time* was a turning point for Network Radio.

NBC and CBS would reluctantly embrace the new technology and slowly shift to pre-recorded programming.

1946–47 Season Scoreboard Mid-season Totals, December 1946			
		Compared to Year Earlier	
Total Radio Homes	34.0 Mil	+0.90 Mil	+2.7%
Total Auto Radios	7.0 Mil	+1.0 Mil	+16.7%
Total AM Radio Stations	948	+29	+3.2%
Total Network Affiliates	881	+7	+0.8%
1946 Radio Revenues	454.4 Mil	+30.5 Mil	+7.2%
1946 Network Revenues	199.6 Mil	+1.7 Mil	+0.9%
Network Share	43.9%		(2.8%)
Total TV Homes	14,000		
Total TV Stations	9	+1	+12.5%
Total FM Stations	57	+3	+5.5%

Networks and producers came to rely on the tape recording equipment provided by industry pioneer Ampex. The exclusive West Coast distributor for Ampex was a newcomer in the electronics field, Bing Crosby Enterprises.

A NETWORK OF RECORD

Transcribed network programming had been the backbone of the Keystone Broadcasting System since 1940. Founded by entrepreneur Michael M. Sillerman, Keystone was a flexible "network" of small market rural stations Sillerman offered his stations in tailored groups to NBC and CBS advertisers for transcribed repeats of their existing programs into areas where network reception was spotty. Among Keystone's featured programs in 1947 were General Foods' *Burns & Allen Show* and Miles Laboratories' *Lum & Abner.*

NO SIN IN SYNDICATION

The fear that NBC and CBS harbored of transcribed programs cutting into their control of popular programming was heightened in April when NBC's owned and operated Chicago outlet, WMAQ, aided the "enemy" and began airing discs of the syndicated *Favorite Story* starring distinguished actor Ronald Colman.

Colman had signed a $150,000 (*1.7 Mil*) contract with Frederick Ziv's production and syndication firm.

Ziv offered 23 different series of programs to local stations and advertisers with a roster of stars that included network favorites Wayne King, Kenny Baker, *Easy Aces* and *Philo Vance.* Over 200 stations bought Ziv shows in 1946 resulting in an income of $7.5 million dollars (*87.0 Mil*).

Newly licensed stations began to pop up after World War II, providing a growing market for the syndicators and more competition for network affiliates. The country's 950 AM stations would nearly double in three years.

Adding to the program options available to stations, the Lang-Worth, World, RCA-Thesaurus and Atlas transcription services all offered pre-packaged transcribed programs and scripts to stations for their sale to local advertisers.

As it turned out, neither transcribed nor syndicated programming really threatened the networks' ratings or revenues. Network ratings held steady and the chains' revenues increased over the next three years.

The real threat to Network Radio was found lurking in the living rooms of a mere 12,000 homes — television.

That number would explode to four million by 1949.

WHOSE HUES?

Television had been stalled.

Licenses for 44 new stations had been issued, but the industry was on hold, waiting for an FCC landmark decision. Would the country's video standard remain the RCA system of electronic television that could only promise color in several years? Or would it switch to the incompatible CBS part-mechanical system that already produced color but would render all past equipment useless?

The decision was finally handed down after 14 weeks of hearings and testimony — RCA won. Current station and set owners could breath easier.

New station construction got underway at full speed and receivers priced from $225 to $2,500 (*$2,610–$29,000*), began flying out of stores in New York, Philadelphia, Schenectady, Washington, Chicago and Los Angeles — the six cities that had operating television stations.

To provide programming fodder, all three New York baseball teams signed home game television contracts for the 1947 season — the Giants with WNBT-TV, the Dodgers with WCBS-TV and the Yankees with DuMont's WABD-TV.

Terms weren't disclosed, but the three broadcasters promised to pay the teams more money if they could find sponsors for the games. They promptly did — Camel, Chesterfield and Old Gold cigarettes.

TO BE OR NOT TV

Musicians union boss James Caesar Petrillo was at it again.

AFM members were prohibited from performing on television until a fee structure could be created. Petrillo's edict not only kept union musicians off live television but also prevented the televising of any motion pictures that had employed AFM members — so none of the major studios' films could be shown.

The boycott remained in effect until March 1948.

This move coincided with an earlier ban against performances on AM/FM simulcasts unless musicians were paid double. The two barriers helped push broadcasters — especially local stations — toward greater use of recorded music and pushed union musicians out of work.

THE MONTHLIES

NBC's string of consecutive monthly winners had begun with Major Bowes' amateur show in June 1935. It encompassed Edgar Bergen and Charlie McCarthy's two season sweeps of the late thirties, the frequent firsts by Jack Benny and extended through the glory days of Tuesday's terrific trio — Bob Hope, *Fibber McGee & Molly* and Red Skelton.

The streak reached a whopping 120 months — the equivalent of twelve consecutive ten month seasons — when the inevitable finally happened.

CBS snapped it when *Lux Radio Theater*—the only hour-long program in the season's Top 50— produced the month's highest ratings in June 1947.

That, in turn, began a string of 15 consecutive monthly wins for *Lux*— the longest since Edgar Bergen's 22 month streak on NBC from 1937 to 1939.

Earlier in the season, Red Skelton set a record of a different kind. Skelton's 15.3 in September was the lowest rating yet recorded for a month's Number One show. It was a glimpse of things to come.

NBC comedy continued to sweep first place for the next eight months. *Fibber McGee & Molly* won October and NBC's Sunday programs were represented by Jack Benny's win in November and Edgar Bergen's in December. Bob Hope's Tuesday show took first place from January through May before *Lux* finally won for CBS in June.

1946–47 Sunday Night Top Ten Programs
NBC 6, CBS 3, ABC 1
Average: 17.2

Jack Benny Program	NBC	7:00	25.8
Fred Allen Show	NBC	8:30	23.4
Edgar Bergen & Charlie McCarthy	NBC	8:00	22.8
Walter Winchell's Jergens Journal	ABC	9:00	20.8
Phil Harris & Alice Faye	NBC	7:30	17.9
Take It or Leave It	CBS	10:00	14.5
Blondie	CBS	7:30	12.4
Manhattan Merry Go Round	NBC	9:00	11.8
American Album of Familiar Music	NBC	9:30	11.4
We the People	CBS	10:30	11.0

SPIN AND WIN

Phil Harris had been with Jack Benny since 1936, serving as the comedian's wise-cracking band leader and establishing his supporting character as a hard drinking ladies' man.

NBC scored a the season's biggest win by a new program when Harris walked across the hall moments after his appearances with Benny to co-star with his wife, movie musical queen Alice Faye, in their new sitcom immediately following Benny's Number One program.

Hair tonic manufacturer F.W. Fitch had drifted away from its eight-year-old *Fitch Bandwagon* format the previous season when the program's focus shifted from a rotation of popular dance bands to comedy.

Comedienne Cass Daley pushed *Bandwagon*'s ratings into the season's Top 20 in 1945–46. But the idea of segueing from the top rated Benny show into its own spinoff was too hard for Fitch and NBC to resist.

The brash Harris and his beautiful, soft-spoken wife debuted late September in a sitcom format that gave each of them a solo musical number at breaks in the storyline. The couple went on to chalk up six Top 50 seasons, beginning with two years in which their program

remained *The Fitch Bandwagon* in name only. Rexall Drugs assumed their sponsorship in 1948 and the series became *The Phil Harris & Alice Faye Show*.

Despite the spin-off's success, Harris continued his role on the Benny show until 1952.

JACK'S BACK

Jack Benny boosted his ratings another 20 percent to his first Number One finish on Sunday in six years.

After two seasons and sacrificing the ratings of Kate Smith and *Adventures of the Thin Man*, General Foods gave up its CBS timeslot opposite Benny and removed whatever competition those programs offered. Wrigley took the half hour on CBS for *Gene Autry's Melody Ranch* which appealed more to kids than adult audiences.

Benny's writers kept his show fresh with stunts — like his March 16th broadcast when he assembled a "Million Dollar Quartet" — singers Bing Crosby, Dick Haymes, Andy Russell and Dennis Day — for only $3,000 ($30,400). Russell, the only member of the quartet without a radio show of his own on which Benny could make a reciprocal appearance, was the only guest Benny had to pay. The show drew a healthy chunk of publicity and a 28.5 rating.

THE SONGBIRD'S SWAN SONG

Kate Smith was radio's "grand old lady" at 39. General Foods brought Smith back to Sunday's CBS schedule opposite NBC's Bob Burns at 6:30. It was the singer's last attempt to recapture the popularity that had led to ten Top 50 seasons on CBS including four in the Top 20.

It failed. Her half hour variety show could only manage single digit ratings.

General Foods cancelled both Smith's Sunday show and her weekday quarter hour chat programs in June, thus ending their decade-long sponsor/star relationship.

She also left CBS Radio forever after 16 consecutive years with the network.

But "The Songbird of the South"

was far from finished. Smith moved on to Mutual, ABC and NBC with a half dozen different talk and music shows — many of them sustaining — until 1958. Meanwhile, she enjoyed a decade of television popularity with a constant stream of daytime and prime time shows on NBC-TV and CBS-TV throughout the 1950s.

A CBS DOUBLE DIP

Hildegarde's *Raleigh Room* format was moved intact from NBC's Wednesday schedule to Sunday at 9:00 on CBS. Hildegarde's new soup-sponsored *Campbell Room* suffered the season's worst drop of a Top 50 star. The "incomparable" one lost half her NBC audience and fell from 40th to 126th place. Her show was cancelled in April with a measly 5.9 average rating for its abbreviated season.

Texaco picked up another NBC orphan to replace its struggling *Texaco Star Theater* headlining tenor James Melton at 9:30 on CBS. Eddie Bracken was still a Paramount Films comedy star and his earlier NBC series was a Top 50 entry before Standard Brands cancelled it in May 1945.

Bracken was another ratings disappointment for CBS — losing a third of his earlier NBC audience and falling from 39th to 83rd place.

Like Hildegarde, Bracken was gone from Network Radio in April. Neither returned except for an occasional guest appearance

THERE'S NO MYSTERY TO IT

Woodbury had cancelled *Hollywood Mystery Time* as its follow-up to Walter Winchell's *Jergens Journal* the previous January. But the company kept one element of the program for a new quarter hour show on ABC at 9:15 — Louella Parsons' Hollywood news and interviews with the stars. The syndicated columnist had no problem lining up headline guests and registered double digit ratings over her first full season as a solo. She remained in the timeslot for seven seasons, recording Top 50 finishes twice.

A Rookie Sings, Ratings Surge

Henry Ford didn't care about ratings. Ford Motors, after all, was the company that had sponsored the Greenfield Chapel Children's Choir and *Early American Dance Music* in prime time. Both were rating disasters.

Nevertheless, Ford had also sponsored the Detroit Symphony's *Sunday Evening Hour* concerts on CBS for eight seasons and the program returned a respectable 9.8 average. The hour was dropped in 1942 when the car company cut back its consumer advertising for the duration.

The series was revived in 1946 on ABC, averaging a meager 2.1 rating against Edgar Bergen's 22.8.

Yet, on the night of March 3, 1947, the symphony's rating shot up to an 18.0.

The sudden 900 percent surge in popularity was created by the program's guest, Margaret Truman. The President's 22-year-old daughter had a soprano singing voice of which her father was fiercely proud but had met with mixed critical response. The public was obviously curious.

1946–47 Monday Night Top Ten Programs
CBS 6, NBC 4
Average: 13.4

Lux Radio Theater	CBS	9:00	21.9
Screen Guild Players	CBS	10:00	20.0
Joanie's Tea Room	CBS	8:30	13.9
Inner Sanctum	CBS	8:00	13.3
Bob Hawk Show	CBS	7:30	13.1
Lowell Thomas News*	NBC	6:45	11.3
Dr IQ/Lew Valentine	NBC	10:30	10.9
Chesterfield Supper Club*	NBC	7:00	10.5
Bill Henry Johns Manville News*	CBS	8:55	9.7
Cavalcade of America	NBC	8:00	9.3

*Monday–Friday Strip Shows

Sans Strips...
Voice of Firestone	NBC	8:30	9.1
Telephone Hour	NBC	9:00	8.4
Carnation Contented Hour	NBC	10:00	7.2

Boo!

Born on Blue in 1940 and shuffled around the CBS schedule since 1943, *Inner Sanctum* was given new life to scare its listeners to death when Emerson Drugs' Bromo Seltzer cancelled *Vox Pop* and moved the spooky anthology into the strong CBS Monday lineup where it became a Top 20 program for three seasons.

Inner Sanctum was *Suspense* with its tongue in cheek. Narrator "Raymond the (G)Host" was played for macabre laughs by Paul McGrath while some of radio's best studio actors played *Sanctum*'s stories for every blood-curdling chill they could wring out of the scripts and organist Lew White scored every story to its fullest melodramatic peak.

Veteran radio director Himan Brown took credit for *Inner Sanctum*'s memorable opening and closing to Raymond's chamber of horror stories—a loud, elongated squeaking door.

Emerson ad agency BBDO is credited with the sponsor's unforgettable signature, a locomotive that seemingly chanted, "Bromo Seltzer ... Bromo Seltzer ... Bromo Seltzer," produced with engineer Gilbert Wright's "Sonovox" process in which sounds were given speech by placing handheld speakers against the larynx of an actor mouthing the desired words.

Mixing Milk with Pop

Monday had become NBC's repository for institutional advertisers DuPont, Firestone, Bell Telephone and Carnation—all sponsoring prestige programming that drew single digit ratings against the powerful CBS schedule.

Like Bell's *Telephone Hour*, Carnation's *Contented Hour* was never longer than 30 minutes but it had one of the longest runs in network history. Sponsored by the Pacific Coast Condensed Milk Company of Seattle, the series began in 1932 as programs of light classics featuring soloists from the concert stage and opera.

Contented Hour enjoyed two Top 50 seasons before pop music began squeezing out the classics in ratings. By the mid-thirties *Contented* was regularly beaten in its 10:00 time-slot by the Guy Lombardo and Wayne King orchestras' syrupy *Lady Esther Serenade* on CBS.

In response, *Contented Hour* began leaning more toward standard and traditional music—then into pop when Canadian arranger/conductor Percy Faith took over the show in 1941. The conversion was completed in 1946 when singer Buddy Clark joined the cast as its singing co-host.

But the competition had gotten tougher. Lady Esther Cosmetics replaced its saccharin *Serenade* with *Screen Guild Players*. The new CBS show buried Faith and Clark in the ratings.

Nevertheless, the two made beautiful music together and apart. Clark had three hit records in the spring and summer of 1947, including the million selling *Linda*. Faith had several hit singles and a dozen best selling albums.

Ironically, both stars of Carnation's NBC show recorded for the same label, Columbia Records—owned by CBS.

1946–47 Tuesday Night Top Ten Programs
NBC 8, CBS 2
Average: 16.7

Bob Hope Show	NBC	10:00	27.6
Fibber McGee & Molly	NBC	9:30	26.4
Red Skelton Show	NBC	10:30	22.2
Amos & Andy	NBC	9:00	22.1
Big Town	CBS	8:00	13.7
Date with Judy	NBC	8:30	13.1
Lowell Thomas News*	NBC	6:45	11.3
Chesterfield Supper Club*	NBC	7:00	10.5
Rudy Vallee Show	NBC	8:00	10.3
Bill Henry Johns Manville News*	CBS	8:55	9.7

*Monday–Friday Strip Shows

Sans Strips...
Milton Berle Show	NBC	8:00	9.3
Adventures of the Falcon	MBS	8:30	8.6
American Melody Hour	CBS	7:30	8.5
Hollywood Players	CBS	9:30	8.5

NBC's Block Party

Tuesday's Top Seven programs finished in the same order as they did the previous season. NBC had established Tuesday as the night for comedy much as CBS dramas dominated Mondays.

The NBC comedy block had been anchored for ten years by *Fibber McGee & Molly*. Jim and Marian Jordan celebrated their 500th broadcast as Wistful Vista's leading citizens in February. Bob Hope joined the NBC block in 1938 and Red Skelton came along in 1941.

With the additions of *A Date with Judy* in 1944 and *Amos & Andy* a year later, NBC had a solid lock on two and a half consecutive hours of Tuesday prime time.

It would take another four seasons for CBS to catch up.

MY TIME WAS YOUR TIME

At 45, Rudy Vallee's time had passed. His Top Ten ratings of the thirties and Top 20s of the early forties had steadily sunk since he returned from Coast Guard duty in 1944.

Philip Morris cancelled handsome 27-year-old crooner Johnny Desmond in 1946 and moved Vallee into its vacant 8:00 timeslot on NBC.

Unlike Vallee's earlier days when his program was known for introducing young new stars to radio, his continuing co-star on this show was 50-year-old Ruth Etting, another voice from the past looking for a comeback. Their effort was met with listener apathy, losing the time period to the CBS newspaper drama *Big Town* which didn't budge from its previous season's rating.

Sponsor Philip Morris pulled the plug in April and replaced "The Vagabond Lover" with comedian Milton Berle. Vallee left Network Radio after 13 seasons.

He returned to CBS in 1955 — as a disc jockey.

1946–47 Wednesday Night Top Ten Programs
NBC 7, CBS 2, ABC 1
Average: 13.6

Mr. District Attorney	NBC	9:30	18.5
Bing Crosby's Philco Radio Time	ABC	10:00	17.6
Duffy's Tavern	NBC	9:00	16.9
Great Gildersleeve	NBC	8:30	15.2
A Day in the Life of Dennis Day	NBC	8:00	12.5
Mr. & Mrs. North	NBC	8:00	12.3
Dr Christian	CBS	8:30	11.7
Lowell Thomas News*	NBC	6:45	11.3
Chesterfield Supper Club*	NBC	7:00	10.5

Frank Sinatra Show	CBS	9:00	9.9

*Monday–Friday Strip Shows

Sans Strips...			
Frank Morgan's Fabulous Dr. Tweedy	NBC	10:00	9.8
Kay Kyser's Kollege of Musical Knowledge	NBC	10:30	9.7

CROSBY BRIMS WITH HOPE

Bing Crosby's weekly price of $35,000 ($406,050), for his transcribed half hour series on ABC was considered worth the expense by Philco to introduce its new line of postwar television sets. Philco was fresh from a three year sponsorship of ABC's all-star variety show, *Radio Hall of Fame*—a costly flop in the ratings and never a match for its Sunday competition. The company needed Crosby's audience and endorsement value for the high stakes game of marketing television sets against industry pioneer RCA.

Philco Radio Time's mid–October premiere on ABC paired the 43-year-old crooner with guest Bob Hope, his sidekick in Paramount's successful *Road* comedies and star of the season's Number One radio show. Their fourth film together, *The Road to Utopia*, had been released in late spring and they were already promoting their next, *The Road to Rio*.

ABC told the press beforehand that the two stars' ad-lib antics ran the first recorded show two minutes overtime — but sponsor Philco generously edited out its commercials so listeners could enjoy the Crosby and Hope merriment without interruption.

The program's stars, hype and listener curiosity resulted in a 24.0 rating — the highest figure that ABC had drawn for a variety show since the height of its Blue Network days in the early 1930s.

Crosby gave ABC October's fourth most popular program and he appeared to be headed for his third consecutive Top Ten season.

But *Philco Radio Time*'s ratings dropped 40 percent over subsequent weeks with low priced guests Spike Jones, the Les Paul Trio, trumpeter Rafael Mendez, Ezio Pinza and folk singer Burl Ives. The

show got back on track in late November with a succession of headliners — Judy Garland, Jimmy Durante, Al Jolson and Maurice Chevalier. Crosby finished the season in 13th place among the Top 50 shows and ABC had cause to celebrate.

The celebration didn't last long — the worst season of Crosby's 21 year network career was just ahead.

A BIG NAME AND BIG RATINGS

Dennis Day was the second member of Jack Benny's cast to spin off into his own NBC sitcom in 1946 while remaining with the cast of Benny's highly rated Sunday night show.

A Day in the Life of Dennis Day had the longest title in Network Radio and enjoyed five consecutive Top 50 seasons. Like Phil Harris, the 30-year-old Day played his spinoff sitcom in the same character he established on the Benny show. Day portrayed a naive, dim-witted lad with a golden Irish tenor's voice in a format that allowed him a song or two in every show.

Colgate's Lustre Creme Shampoo debuted the NBC show on Thursday at 7:30 then upgraded its timeslot to Wednesday at 8:00 in January 1947, when Jergens Lotion cancelled *Mr. & Mrs. North* and vacated the time period.

Day held his own in NBC's strong Wednesday lineup but the network would regret the loss of sleuths Pam and Jerry North the following season.

COLLEGE DROP OUTS

American Tobacco used a new Frank Morgan vehicle, *The Fabulous Doctor Tweedy*, as Jack Benny's 1946 summer replacement with satisfactory results. The tobacco company and NBC agreed that the sitcom with a college setting would be a natural lead-in for Wednesday's slowly fading *Kay Kyser Kollege of Musical Knowledge*.

Kyser's Colgate show was cut to 30 minutes and pushed ahead on NBC's schedule to 10:30, making room for Morgan's absent minded Professor Tweedy character at 10:00 — sponsored by American's Pall Mall Cigarettes. Morgan gave his new comedy the old college try against Bing Crosby's *Philco Radio Time* on ABC but fell short. He lost over 40 percent of his previous season's *Kraft Music Hall* audience — when, ironically, he filled in for Crosby.

Without the strong lead-in provided for six seasons by *Mr. District Attorney,* Kyser's *Kollege* lost 30 percent of its 1945–46 ratings.

Both Morgan and Kyser were ten year veterans of Network Radio. Both dropped out of the season's Top 50 for the only time in their network careers.

THE OTHER MORGAN

At 31, Henry Morgan was considered by ABC to be the modern day Fred Allen — a cynic with a cerebral sense of humor. Morgan's barbs — often directed against sponsors — been the cause for a career full of firings by advertisers and stations around the country. His early network attempts on Mutual and ABC were critical successes but developed little more than a cult audience.

Morgan was given ABC's best timeslot in January — following Crosby's *Philco Radio Time.* The comedian's off the wall half hour featuring sidekicks Arnold Stang and Art Carney was sponsored by Eversharp's Shick razors and blades. Despite the network's high hopes and hype, *Here's Morgan* lost 50 percent of the Crosby lead-in audience and was gone at the end of the season.

SHORE LEAVES

Ford picked up Dinah Shore and moved her Top 50 NBC show to CBS on Wednesday, pitting the popular singer against the radio's highest rated crime series, *Mr. District Attorney.* Shore's lead-in, Frank Sinatra, had dipped to single digit ratings and she couldn't do any better, losing 35 percent of her NBC audience and dropping to 83rd place for the season.

Shore left Ford and CBS at the end of the season. Four years later she re-emerged in her most renowned role — as an NBC-TV singing star and spokesperson for Ford's arch-competitor, Chevrolet.

WEDNESDAY'S WINNER

The highest rated broadcast of the year aired on ABC on Wednesday, September 18, when Heavyweight Champ Joe Louis defended his title against challenger Tami Mauriello at Yankee Stadium. Gillette sponsored the fight that recorded a 33.0 Hooperating. But the razor blade company didn't get much of Don Dunphy's blow-by-blow report for its money — Louis knocked out Mauriello in the first round.

1946–47 Thursday Night Top Ten Programs
NBC 6, CBS 4
Average: 13.0

Burns & Allen	NBC	8:30	15.2
Eddie Cantor Show	NBC	10:30	14.4
Suspense	CBS	8:00	13.5
Abbott & Costello	NBC	10:00	13.3
Aldrich Family	NBC	8:00	13.2
FBI in Peace & War	CBS	8:30	13.0
Sealtest Village Store	NBC	9:30	12.3
Casey Crime Photographer	CBS	9:30	11.8
Dick Haymes Show	CBS	9:00	11.7
Kraft Music Hall	NBC	9:00	11.6

THE NEWS IS OUT

For the first time since Friday of the 1932–33 season no news program ranked in a weeknight Top Ten. It was also the first time that a Multiple Run program failed to make the weeknight list.

HAYMES OVER HALL'S RATINGS

CBS was still scouting for new singers and packaged a winner for automotive equipment manufacturer Autolite.

Dick Haymes, 30, was the former band singer with Benny Goodman, Tommy Dorsey and Harry James with a budding film career as the crooning leading man in 20th Century–Fox musicals. Haymes was supported in his radio new show by popular vocalist Helen Forrest and Gordon Jenkins' studio orchestra. The three scored their first of two Top 50 seasons on Thursday night at 9:00.

Haymes edged out *Kraft Music Hall* which dropped nearly half the ratings that were generated by Bing

Crosby when he left the show in May. Thursday's Number One show of the previous two seasons, *Music Hall* struggled with comedians Edward Everett Horton and Eddie Foy, Jr., supported by Eddy Duchin's band and guests stars with bigger box office names than their hosts.

1946–47 Friday Night Top Ten Programs
CBS 4, NBC 4, ABC 2
Average: 11.1

Fanny Brice Baby Snooks Show	CBS	8:00	13.2
People Are Funny	NBC	9:00	12.7
Lowell Thomas News*	NBC	6:45	11.3
Adventures of the Thin Man	CBS	8:30	11.1
Jimmy Durante & Garry Moore	CBS	9:30	10.9
Molle Mystery Theater	NBC	10:00	10.7
Chesterfield Supper Club*	NBC	7:00	10.5
The Fat Man	ABC	8:00	10.4
This Is Your FBI	ABC	8:30	10.2
It Pays to Be Ignorant	CBS	10:00	9.9

*Monday–Friday Strip Shows

Sans Strips...

Maisie	CBS	10:30	9.6
Break the Bank	ABC	9:00	9.5
Waltz Time	NBC	9:30	9.5

THE NAMES SOUND FAMILIAR...

While NBC and CBS tangled in a tight race at the top of Friday's ratings, ABC was investing in its future with two studio crime dramas.

This Is Your FBI, sponsored by the Equitable Life Assurance Society, was ABC's sound alike to *The FBI in Peace & War,* but unlike the CBS show, it was endorsed by the Federal agency. The program's creator, Jerry Devine, was a welcome guest in the bureau's Washington headquarters to research its cases and techniques.

During the two series' runs their ratings were close — *The FBI in Peace & War* scored an average 11.2 to *This Is Your FBI's* 10.8. But the ABC show accomplished something on Friday that its higher rated twin couldn't match on Thursday — it eventually became its night's Number One program.

General Foods gave up trying to

fight Jack Benny's Sunday show and pulled *The Adventures of the Thin Man* back to the safety of CBS on Friday and back into the season's Top 50.

Less than a point behind *The Thin Man* in Friday's ratings was another detective series loosely based on Dashiell Hammett's writings, ABC's *The Fat Man*.

In reality, the overweight sleuth was created by producer Ed Rosenberg. Hammett only collected royalties for the use of his name and the "inspiration" for the character, based on Sidney Greenstreet's fat villain, Kasper Gutman, in the film version of Hammett's *The Maltese Falcon*.

The Fat Man enjoyed four Top 50 seasons and was Friday's Number One program twice, all sponsored by Norwich Pharmacal's Pepto Bismol. Veteran radio actor J. Scott (Jack) Smart was typecast as the show's hero — Smart he stood only 5' 9" tall and weighed 270 pounds.

Smart was a natural to star in the 1951 Universal film, *The Fat Man*, co-starring two young studio contract players, Rock Hudson and Julie London.

THERE HE IS...

Bristol Myers and ABC took a struggling quiz with rotating hosts from Mutual, *Break the Bank*, and made it the showcase for their "new" postwar star, 32-year-old Bert Parks.

Actually, Parks was no stranger to Network Radio — he had become the youngest CBS staff announcer in 1933 at age 19. By 24 he was the announcer/singer and foil for Eddie Cantor. When he enlisted in the Army in 1940, Parks had seven years of network experience to his credit. But few of his assignments allowed him do what he did best — host programs and interact with contestants with his gift of ad-lib.

Joining the Army as a private, Parks emerged four years later as a captain with a Bronze Star for service under fire in the Burmese/Indo-China theater, setting up communications links for forces under the command of General "Vinegar Joe" Stillwell.

Break the Bank was a simple general knowledge quiz for teams of two contestants — often married couples. It was similar to the *Take It or Leave It* format that awarded mounting cash prizes for each correct answer — but with one important difference. Phil Baker's quiz topped off at $64 — a paltry sum where Parks and his contestants were just getting started toward *Bank*'s jackpot of $1,000 or more — often much more.

The show made news during its first ABC season by awarding nearly $5,800 *($67,300)*, to one couple who remembered the last line to "The Night Before Christmas." It was the largest cash amount yet awarded by a radio program.

Within a year *Break the Bank* would be among the season's Top 50 shows and part of ABC's winning Friday lineup.

1946–47 Saturday Night Top Ten Programs
NBC 7, ABC 2, CBS 1
Average: 11.3

Truth or Consequences	NBC	8:30	14.8
Judy Canova Show	NBC	10:00	13.5
Life of Riley	NBC	8:00	13.2
Your Hit Parade	NBC	9:00	12.6
Can You Top This?	NBC	9:30	11.6
Gangbusters	ABC	9:00	11.2
Grand Ole Opry	NBC	10:30	9.6
Roy Rogers Show	NBC	9:00	9.2
Mayor of the Town	CBS	8:30	9.0
Murder & Mr. Malone	ABC	9:30	8.4

MORE HUSH MONEY

Ralph Edwards had created a monster with the previous season's "Mr. Hush" contest.

He topped it with "Mrs. Hush" by allowing the *Truth or Consequences* listeners to participate in the game and adding a charity angle to the giveaway.

In early 1947, Edwards invited his home audience into the chase for the contest's mounting jackpot of prizes, telling them to submit letters that completed the sentence, "*We should all support the March of Dimes because....*"

He coyly added that although it wasn't *really* necessary, donations to the charity would be gratefully accepted with the listeners' contest entries.

Each week three letters were chosen and those listeners were given a crack at identifying the mystery woman from clues she had recorded in hushed tones. With every incorrect answer the jackpot grew to include a new Ford convertible, a Cessna airplane, a mink coat and diamond ring, a camping trailer and a television set. By mid-March the jackpot contained 23 huge prizes with a total value over $17,500 *($177,535)*, when a Chicago housewife correctly revealed "Mrs. Hush" to be Clara Bow, the "It Girl" of silent films.

The *real* winners of the contest were Edwards and the March of Dimes. Before Bow was identified *Truth or Consequences* ratings had jumped into the 20s and the charity had collected $555,000 *(5.6 Mil)* from over 700,000 contest entries.

PARADE'S MARCH IN APRIL

Three months short of ten full seasons on CBS, American Tobacco abruptly moved *Your Hit Parade* to NBC in April. It also shifted the show's production from New York to Hollywood — a concession in its rumored negotiations to bring Frank Sinatra back as its star the following season. The rumor proved to be true.

Time for the Lucky Strike program on NBC was cleared when *The Roy Rogers Show* left the air. The overworked "King of the Cowboys" had been cranking out musical adventures for Republic Pictures at a clip of one every seven weeks for three years after the studio lost his stable mate Gene Autry in a contract dispute.

Rogers' 9.2 rating for Miles Laboratories' Alka Seltzer was little better than the 9.0 registered by the final NBC season of *National Barn Dance*, which Miles cancelled in September after 13 years.

Your Hit Parade hardly missed a beat in its network switch, delivering a 30 percent increase in ratings over Rogers' show to NBC. The weekly countdown of hits would remain a Saturday Top Ten show in its new home for the next five seasons.

NEWS BEHIND THE NEWS

Seven of the Top Ten Multiple Run programs were news and news

1946–47 Top Ten Multiple Run Programs NBC 4, CBS 3, MBS 2, ABC 1 Average: 8.4				
Lowell Thomas News*	M–F	NBC	6:45	11.3
Chesterfield Supper Club*	M–F	NBC	7:00	10.5
Bill Henry Johns Manville News*	M–F	CBS	8:55	9.7
HV Kaltenborn News*	M–F	NBC	7:45	8.8
The Lone Ranger	M,W,F	ABC	7:30	8.6
Ned Calmer Parker Pen News	Sa,Su	CBS	8:55	8.4
Jack Smith Show*	M–F	CBS	7:15	8.1
Morgan Beatty News of the World*	M–F	NBC	7:15	7.1
Gabriel Heatter News*	M–F	MBS	9:00	5.9
Fulton Lewis, Jr., News*	M–F	MBS	7:00	5.6
*Monday–Friday Strip Shows				

commentaries. But the ratings of those newscasts had dwindled since the end of World War II. Lowell Thomas turned in his lowest season rating in nine years, H.V. Kaltenborn and Gabriel Heatter had their lowest in seven and NBC's *News of the World* with John W. Vandercook and Morgan Beatty finished with its lowest rating since its inception five years earlier. Only Mutual's conservative voice, Fulton Lewis, Jr., had a fractional gain in his numbers.

News would always have a presence in Multiple Run programming but it was the final season in which Thomas or any of his colleagues would be Number One in the category.

TOP 50 PROGRAMS — 1946–47

NBC 29, CBS 18, ABC 3
Average Rating: 15.2, Median: 13.3
33,998,000 Radio Homes / 89.9% Coverage of U.S. Homes / One Rating Point = 340,000 Homes
Source: C.E. Hooper, Semi-monthly Reports, Sep 1946–Jun 1947
Total Programs Rated 6–11 P.M.: 199
Programs Rated 13 Weeks & Ranked: 169

		Program	Rtg	Type	Sponsor	Day	Time	Lgth	Net
1	1	Bob Hope Show	27.6	CV	Pepsodent Toothpaste	Tue	10:00	30	NBC
2	2	Fibber McGee & Molly	26.4	SC	Johnson Wax	Tue	9:30	30	NBC
3	6	Jack Benny Program	25.8	SC	Lucky Strike Cigarettes	Sun	7:00	30	NBC
4	8	Fred Allen Show	23.4	CV	Tenderleaf Tea	Sun	8:30	30	NBC
5	4	Edgar Bergen & Charlie McCarthy	22.8	CV	Chase & Sanborn Coffee	Sun	8:00	30	NBC
6	3	Red Skelton Show	22.2	CV	Raleigh Cigarettes	Tue	10:30	30	NBC
7	14	Amos & Andy	22.1	SC	Rinso Laundry Soap	Tue	9:00	30	NBC
8	5	Lux Radio Theater/William Keighley	21.9	DA	Lux Soap	Mon	9:00	60	CBS
9	9	Walter Winchell's Jergens Journal	20.8	NC	Jergens Lotion	Sun	9:00	15	ABC
10	10	Screen Guild Players	20.0	DA	Lady Esther Cosmetics	Mon	10:00	30	CBS
11	11	Mister District Attorney/Jay Jostyn	18.5	DCC	Vitalis Hair Tonic	Wed	9:30	30	NBC
12	N	Phil Harris & Alice Faye	17.9	SC	Fitch Shampoo	Sun	7:30	30	NBC
13	6	Bing Crosby Philco Radio Time	17.6	MV	Philco Radios & Refrigerators	Wed	10:00	30	ABC
14	35	Duffy's Tavern/Ed Gardner	16 9	SC	Ipana & Vitalis	Wed	9:00	30	NBC
15t	34	Burns & Allen Show	15.2	SC	Maxwell House Coffee	Thu	8:30	30	NBC
15t	19	Great Gildersleeve/Hal Peary	15.2	SC	Parkay Margarine	Wed	8:30	30	NBC
17	19	Truth or Consequences/ Ralph Edwards	14.8	APS	Duz Laundry Soap	Sat	8:30	30	NBC
18	16	Take It or Leave It/Phil Baker	14.5	APQ	Eversharp Pens & Pencils	Sun	10:00	30	CBS
19	12	Eddie Cantor Show	14.4	CV	Pabst Beer	Thu	10:30	30	NBC
20	21	Joanie's Tea Room/Joan Davis	13.9	SC	Swan Soap	Mon	8:30	25	CBS
21	25	Big Town/Ed Pawley	13.7	DCC	Ironized Yeast	Tue	8:00	30	CBS
22t	24	Judy Canova Show	13.5	CV	Halo Shampoo	Sat	10:00	30	NBC
22t	36	Suspense	13.5	DA	Roma Wines	Thu	8:00	30	CBS
24t	42	Inner Sanctum	13.3	DA	Bromo Seltzer	Mon	8:00	30	CBS
24t	17	Abbott & Costello Show	13.3	CV	Camel Cigarettes	Thu	10:00	30	NBC
26t	22	Aldrich Family/Ezra Stone	13.2	SC	Grapenuts Cereal	Thu	8:00	30	CBS
26t	49	Fanny Brice Baby Snooks Show	13.2	SC	Jello Gelatin & Puddings	Fri	8:00	30	CBS
26t	28	Life of Riley/William Bendix	13.2	SC	Dreft Laundry Soap	Sat	8:00	30	NBC
29t	37	Bob Hawk Show	13.1	APQ	Camel Cigarettes	Mon	7:30	30	CBS
29t	38	A Date with Judy/Louise Erickson	13.1	SC	Tums Antacid	Tue	8:30	30	NBC
31	47	The FBI in Peace & War	13.0	DCC	Lava Hand Soap	Thu	8:30	25	CBS
32	28	People Are Funny/Art Linkletter	12.7	APS	Raleigh Cigarettes	Fri	9:00	30	NBC
33	32	Your Hit Parade/Andy Russell	12.6	MP	Lucky Strike Cigarettes	Sat	9:00	30	NBC 1
34	N	A Day in the Life of Dennis Day	12.5	SC	Lustre Cream Shampoo	Wed	8:00	30	NBC 2
35	43	Blondie/Penny Singleton, Arthur Lake	12.4	SC	Super Suds Laundry Soap	Sun	7:30	30	CBS
36t	13	Jack Haley/Eve Arden Village Store	12.3	SC	Sealtest Dairies	Thu	9:30	30	NBC
36t	39	Mr & Mrs North/Joe Curtin, Alice Frost	12.3	DCC	Woodbury Soap	Wed	8:00	30	NBC
38t	N	Casey Crime Photographer	11.8	DCC	Anchor Hocking Glass	Thu	9:30	30	CBS

	Program	Rtg	Type	Sponsor	Day	Time	Lgth	Net
38t 43	Manhattan Merry Go Round	11.8	MP	Dr Lyons Tooth Powder	Sun	9:00	30	NBC
40t 84	Dick Haymes Show	11.7	MV	Autolite Spark Plugs	Thu	9:00	30	CBS
40t 23	Dr Christian/Jean Hersholt	11.7	DCC	Vaseline	Wed	8:30	25	CBS
42t 26	Can You Top This?	11.6	PS	Colgate Shaving Cream	Sat	9:30	30	NBC
42t N	Kraft Music Hall/Ed Ev Horton, Ed Foy	11.6	MV	Philadelphia Cream Cheese	Thu	9:00	30	NBC
44 43	American Album of Familiar Music	11.4	MST	Bayer Aspirin	Sun	9:30	30	NBC
45 40	Lowell Thomas News	11.3	NC	Sun Oil	M-F	6:45	15	NBC
46 85	Gangbusters	11.2	DA	Waterman Pens	Sat	9:00	30	ABC
47 78	Adventures of the Thin Man	11.1	DCC	Sanka Coffee	Fri	8:30	25	CBS
48 53	We the People/Milo Boulton	11.0	API	Gulf Oil	Sun	10:30	30	CBS
49t 56	Doctor IQ/Lew Valentine	10.9	APQ	Mars Candies	Mon	10:30	30	NBC
49t 49	Jimmy Durante & Garry Moore Show	10.9	CV	Rexall Drugs	Fri	9:30	30	CBS

New & Returning Top 50 Programs Underscored.

1	Your Hit Parade		Sep–Mar	Lucky Strike Cigarettes	Sat	9:00	45	CBS
2	A Day in the Life of Dennis Day		Sep–Dec	Lustre Cream Shampoo	Thu	7:30	30	NBC

Key: API — Audience Participation/Interviews
APQ — Audience Participation/Quiz
APS — Audience Participation/Stunts
CV — Comedy/Variety Show
DA — Dramatic Anthology

DCC — Drama/Continuing Characters
MC — Music/Classical, Semi-Classical
MP — Music/Popular, Contemporary
MSP — Music/Specialty, Ethnic
MST — Music/Standard, Traditional

MV — Music/Variety Show
NC — News, Commentary
PS — Panel Show Comedy
SC — Situation Comedy
TC — Talent Competition

1946–47 Top 50 Favorite Formats

	Programs	Pct
Comedy — All Categories	24	48%
Drama — Anthology & Continuing	12	24%
Music — All Categories	6	12%
Audience Participation — All Categories	6	12%
News/Commentary	2	4%

1946–47 Monthly Winners

Sep	Red Skelton Show	15.3	Feb	Bob Hope Show	32.0
Oct	Fibber McGee & Molly	25.9	Mar	Bob Hope Show	30.9
Nov	Jack Benny Show	27.6	Apr	Bob Hope Show	31.0
Dec	Edgar Bergen & Charlie McCarthy	28.0	May	Bob Hope Show	25.8
Jan	Bob Hope Show	31.7	Jun	Lux Radio Theater	20.1

20

The 1947–48 Network Season

BOY: Gee! Imagine, Quaker Puffed Wheat and Quaker Puffed Rice are offering everyone a complete model farm!

GIRL: Gol-lee! Swell models right here on eight new packages!

Announcer: Yes, kids, anyone can build these exciting models of farm buildings, equipment and animals simply by getting these new packages of Quaker Puffed Wheat and Quaker Puffed Rice. There are as many as six colorful models printed on a single package! And they don't cost a single, extra penny! There's no waiting and no box tops to send in!

GIRL: Look at all the models you get just on Package Number One!

BOY: You get the farmhouse, the garage, the pickup truck...

GIRL: ... and milk and hay wagon, and Dobbin the horse, Queenie the collie and Bossie the cow!

Announcer: What's more, these models are easy to build! All packages are pre-cut and scored. Tell Mom that no paste or glue is necessary!

GIRL: Gee, what fun you can have with this Quaker model farm!

Announcer: What could be sweller? Mind you, they come only with Quaker Puffed Wheat and Quaker Puffed Rice. So get busy!

For fun, games and excitement, start building your Quaker model farm right now!

BABIES BOOM AND RATINGS BLOOM

The 1947–48 season provided Network Radio's Golden Age with its last hurrah.

Revenues broke the $200 Million mark *(2.03 Bil)*. In a sudden reversal of a four year downtrend, Network Radio's Top 50 average program rating jumped a whopping 23 percent, representing well over a million homes. The nightly Top Ten programs' season ratings grew an even more impressive 25 percent.

In terms of total audience, 1947–48 can be recognized as the most popular season of the Golden Age.

The sharp ratings increase came after four seasons of trickling decline — a decline that resumed again the following season. The one-season spike can be attributed to two factors.

The industry ratings standard became A.C. Nielsen's mechanical, "Audimeter" methodology which proved to be more generous in its count than C.E. Hooper's telephone coincidental polls. However, Claude Hooper personally issued a notice to his subscribers in January that cited "violent fluctuations" and

an abnormally high *Sets in Use* reported by listeners.

The other cause for the higher ratings began in the bedrooms of America in late 1945 and resulted in a population surge that columnist Sylvia Porter dubbed, "The Baby Boom."

By January 1948, nearly eleven million babies had been born in the U.S. since the end of World War II. The young parents of these infants were staying at home in droves to tend their young.

While radio ratings boomed, movie attendance bombed.

Movie ticket sales dropped ten percent in 1947, down nearly half a *billion* tickets. It's no coincidence that Network Radio's greatest ratings gains were scored on Friday and Saturday — the traditional "nights out" for singles and young couples.

Most of those stay-at-homes were listening to their radios — and hearing the first commercials about the new phenomenon in home entertainment that was still on the far horizon for most of America, television.

NET GROWTH

The networks' year-long hunt for new affiliates was led by Mutual, adding 104 stations for a total of 488. ABC signed 27 new affiliates, bringing it up to 222 and NBC added six for a total of 161. CBS continued to trail the group by taking on ten new stations to reach 157

As a result, 97 percent of the country's commercial AM stations had affiliated with a network — an all time high.

Outspoken Mutual boss Ed Koback used none of the typical programming platitudes or self-serving promises of public service when discussing his network's intentions. "We're not going to fuss

---

1947–48 Season Scoreboard
Mid-season Totals, December 1947

		Compared to Year Earlier	
Total Radio Homes	35.9 Mil	+1.90 Mil	+5.6%
Total Auto Radios	9.0 Mil	+2.0 Mil	+28 6%
Total AM Radio Stations	1,062	+114	+12.0%
Total Radio Network Affiliates	1,028	+147	+16.7%
1947 Radio Revenues	506.4 Mil	+52.0 Mil	+11.4%
1947 Network Revenues	201.2 Mil	+1.6 Mil	+0.8%
Network Share	39.7%		(4.2%)
Total TV Homes	172,000	+158,000	+1,128.5%
Total TV Stations	19	+10	+111.1%
Total FM Stations	150	+93	+163.1%

around with highbrow programs" he told *Time* magazine in February, "We're primed for battle with the other networks for mass audience."

Mutual seldom produced a program that made the season's Top 50, but it did make money with Koback at the helm. The network's billings jumped 30 percent to nearly $26 Million *(263.8 Mil)*, in his first two years and he was just getting started.

BIG MAC'S WHOPPER OF A NETWORK

Gordon McLendon took after his wealthy father who owned a chain of theaters in Texas.

He was a showman.

Who but a showman would train a parrot to recite his station's call letters on cue?

The 25-year-old McLendon did just that at his KLIF/Dallas in 1947.

In March 1948, McLendon launched the Liberty Broadcasting System from KLIF. It became the most viable new national radio network since Mutual was formed in 1934. Liberty programs were heard from nearly 500 stations before its collapse in 1952.

Liberty was based in baseball — play by play broadcasts of major league games recreated from Western Union reports and fed to Liberty affiliates in minor league cities throughout America. In 1948, only the ten cities that were homes to the 16 major league teams were out of bounds to McLendon.

The recreation technique had been used in radio since its earliest days — but McLendon's production touches made it a broadcast art. Mixed with the appropriate sound effects, Liberty's recreations were difficult to tell from the real thing.

The young network executive, who took to the air himself as "The Old Scotchman," headed a team of sportscasters in their twenties that included future greats Lindsey Nelson, Don Wells, Buddy Blattner and Jerry Doggett. The group was skilled at the extemporaneous speaking demands necessary to create colorful word pictures from the barest of information.

Liberty operated only in the daytime hours with its baseball broadcasts, but McLendon had his

sights set on its becoming a full time, full service network. This was a special concern to Mutual as it pondered what to do about the upstart network that threatened its territory in small and medium sized markets.

The situation would come to a head four years later.

THE BEGINNING OF THE END

Network Television was officially born on Friday, June 27, 1947, when NBC fed a special three hour block of programs — a speech, a short film, a variety show and a boxing match — to stations in New York, Philadelphia, Washington and Schenectady. Baltimore and Boston were added to the chain later in the year.

The June event passed with little notice — but it was the genesis of Network Radio's decline.

Television was still a novelty and seemed no immediate threat to radio — reaching less than 200,000 homes with patchwork programming several hours a day.

But video's growth trend was inescapable.

By March 1948, 16 stations were on the air across the United States with another 82 under construction.

To meet the growing demand for receivers, 31 different manufacturers reported turning out 33,000 new sets in February. Most popular were the ten-inch screen table models produced by RCA and Philco with an average price tag of $350 *($3,550)*.

NBC reported that its 1947 television operations lost $2,700,000 *(27.4 Mil)*. It was understood that its radio division would cover the loss plus the additional five million dollars that the network projected to lose before the new medium turned its first profit.

In effect, Network Radio was buying the bullets for its own execution.

THE MONTHLIES

Lux Radio Theater was radio's Number One rated program for ten consecutive months and gave CBS its first season sweep. Nothing came close to the star-studded

Monday night adaptations of Hollywood films hosted by William Keighley. Easily the most popular program of the year, *Lux Radio Theater* of the 1947–48 season was the last series of Network Radio's Golden Age to finish its season with an average rating of 30 or higher.

1947–48 Sunday Night Top Ten Programs
NBC 6, CBS 3, ABC 1
Average: 18.9

Edgar Bergen & Charlie McCarthy	NBC	8:00	22.7
Fred Allen Show	NBC	8:30	22.3
Phil Harris & Alice Faye	NBC	7:30	22.1
Jack Benny Program	NBC	7:00	21.9
Blondie	CBS	7:30	18.1
Adventures of Sam Spade	CBS	8:00	17.8
Walter Winchell's Jergens Journal	ABC	9:00	17.2
Manhattan Merry Go Round	NBC	9:00	17.1
Take It or Leave It	NBC	10:00	16.0
Meet Corliss Archer	CBS	9:00	15.6

NBC TAKES IT, BAKER LEAVES IT

NBC had a lock on the two hour period between 7:00 and 9:00 with all four of its comedy programs scoring ratings in the 20s and finishing in the season's Top Ten. But CBS was laying plans to upset listening habits the following season.

Meanwhile, Eversharp Pens moved its popular quiz *Take It or Leave It* from CBS to NBC and fired the show's host of seven years, Phil Baker. Baker was replaced by 32-year-old Garry Moore, fresh from five Top 50 seasons teamed with Jimmy Durante on CBS's Friday schedule.

With Moore's high energy, fast talking approach, the quiz show's rating increased from 14.5 to 16.0. But in a season of widespread rating increases, the show dropped from 18th to 40th in the season's Top 50.

SPADE DIGS IN

Even in a season of inflated ratings, one of the big surprises was *The Adventures of Sam Spade*, which nearly doubled its CBS rating to a

17.8 against NBC's *Edgar Bergen & Charlie McCarthy* at 8:00. It was the first of three Top 50 seasons for the slick private eye series starring Howard Duff and produced by William Spier. Spier was also responsible for the successful *Suspense* mysteries on CBS.

Like *The Adventures of the Thin Man,* the *Spade* series was based upon a detective hero created by author Dashiell Hammett. However, Hammett had nothing to do with the program or its success against Bergen.

But both *Sam Spade* and Edgar Bergen were headed for a showdown with a newcomer from ABC, *Stop the Music.*

STOP STARTS

ABC needed a mid-season replacement at 8:00 for its low rated and costly Detroit Symphony broadcasts.

Ford Motors had dropped sponsorship of its hometown symphony orchestra when Henry Ford died. The company became free to appeal to popular taste with its radio advertising instead of bowing to its founder's dictates which included buying prime time for the Greenfield Chapel Children's Choir and *Early American Dance Music.*

Ford snapped up Fred Allen's show on NBC when Standard Brands dropped it in late December.

As a result, ABC was looking for something inexpensive to produce that would appeal more to listeners and advertisers than Ford's Detroit Symphony broadcasts — which could mean most anything.

Stop the Music—offering a mountain of merchandise prizes similar to *Truth or Consequences*' "Hush" contests — was the brainchild of bandleader Harry Salter and *Quiz Kids* producer Louis Cowan. The show's weekly production budget was low but its "Mystery Melody" jackpot sometimes bulged with $30,000 in prizes (*$304,300*)— mostly merchandise obtained in exchange for glowing promotional plugs rattled off by host Bert Parks and announcer Don Hancock.

The game was simple. Popular and traditional songs were played by Salter's orchestra or sung without title identification by singers

Kay Armen and Dick Brown who would hum over titles in lyrics. Parks would break into songs shouting, "Stop the Music!," which indicated he had a contestant on the line whose telephone number had been picked at random. If the contestant correctly identified the song, a single prize was awarded — plus the opportunity to identify the jackpot's "Mystery Melody," usually a vaguely familiar folk or classical selection with an obscure title. Every incorrect answer added another prize to the jackpot.

The show made headlines in May by showering a North Carolina couple with a jackpot touted to be worth $17,000 (*$172,500*).

Stop the Music was trend setter. It introduced *forced listening* contests to Network Radio. Contestants had be listening to the program to win — a device employed by broadcasters ever since.

ABC also sold the program in a unique manner, offering 15 minute segments for sponsorship to separate, non-competing advertisers. The sale of participating sponsorships in network programs had long been practiced in daytime programming. *Stop the Music* was the first major prime time show to be sold in pieces.

Stop the Music was first broadcast on March 21, 1948, but didn't appear in the Nielsen reports until June when the giveaway show scored an initial 12.6 rating.

By June, Edgar Bergen had taken Charlie McCarthy and left on summer vacation from his NBC timeslot at 8:00. Bergen's departure stranded Fred Allen at 8:30 with the feeble lead-in of Bergen's summer replacement, the Robert Shaw Chorale's concerts of traditional music.

Without Bergen's powerful escort, Allen's season long average rating of 22.7 sank to a 9.4 in June against the second half hour of *Stop the Music.*

It was a sign of things to come.

YOUTH MUST BE SERVED

Horace Heidt returned to Network Radio after a two year layoff with *The Youth Opportunity Program*— a talent competition for singers and musicians that bor-

rowed its format and judging standards from *The Original Amateur Hour.* Broadcasting from different major cities every week, à la *Dr. IQ,* Heidt and his orchestra traveled from city to city where the troupe performed for a week in downtown theaters and broadcast the program on Sunday nights.

Heidt hit the air running on his first show in December by introducing a handsome, 18-year-old accordion virtuoso to the contest, Dick Contino. Contino won the program's weekly first prize of $250 (*$2,535*), for 13 consecutive weeks and took home the season's grand prize of $5,000 (*$50,700*).

As a result of the show, Contino became a teen idol. Sales of accordions and accordion lessons soared and Heidt was off to a five season run for Philip Morris cigarettes.

FOR CRYING OUT LOUD

Prime time radio had no tear-jerking reality programming since John J. Anthony took his sobbing guests — "No tears, please..." — to Mutual's daytime schedule in 1945.

Break the Bank producer Walt Framer filled that void with *Strike It Rich,* the quiz show that dwelled on the "true life experiences" of its needy contestants who spilled out their problems to host Todd Russell. The more tragic their stories leading to their seeking help from the program, the better. All candidates were screened and selected by Framer's staff to meet that criteria.

Pleas to appear on the program flowed in by the thousands. All requested jobs, housing, transportation, medical treatment, artificial limbs, false teeth or whatever else the applicants might need to evade poverty, pain or worse.

Santa Claus had come to Network Radio.

The quiz, which offered a top prize of $800 (*$8,100*), was secondary to the show's "Heartline" telephone which rang with offers to help the contestants escape whatever dire straits that had brought them to *Strike It Rich.* The show was awash in tears of self-pity converted to cries of joy when the Heartline and its pre-arranged benefactors came to the contestants' rescue — on Framer's cue.

Russell, the two year veteran of Mutual's *Double or Nothing*, was host during the program's first and only prime time season on CBS. It scored a respectable 10.9 season rating against Horace Heidt's new *Youth Opportunity* talent show on NBC.

Strike It Rich was moved to Sunday afternoon the following season with a new host, Warren Hull from *Vox Pop*. Hull remained with the show through its subsequent seven year weekday run on NBC Radio and CBS Television.

As a result, Walt Framer cried all the way to the bank.

FIDLER'S DUETS

Among his Hollywood reporter competitors, including Louella Parsons and Hedda Hopper, Jimmie Fidler was the most controversial with his often sarcastic and biting commentaries on the work and personal lives of the movie colony's elite. His rapid-fire 15 minute Network Radio series dating back to 1934 were never ranked in the season's Top 50, but Fidler became unique in 1947 when his program was broadcast twice on Sunday nights over two different networks—first on Mutual and two hours later on ABC.

The unusual double dip, underwritten by drug manufacturer Carter-Wallace for its Carter's Little Liver Pills laxative and Arrid deodorant, scored a total rating in double digits for two consecutive seasons.

MUTUAL'S NEAT NICK

Nick Carter, Master Detective finished the season with a 13.0 rating—the all time high for any prime time program on Mutual. The detective series was similar in its melodramatic format and heavy organ scoring to Mutual's Sunday afternoon pulp-fiction block—*House of Mystery*, *True Detective Mysteries* and *The Shadow*. With popular radio actor Lon Clark in the title role, *Nick Carter* had a solid five year run at 6:30 for Cudahy Packing's Old Dutch Cleanser but never cracked a season's Top 50 or a Sunday Top Ten.

*1947–48 Monday Night
Top Ten Programs*
CBS 6, ABC 2, NBC 2
Average: 17.9

Lux Radio Theater	CBS	9:00	31.2
My Friend Irma	CBS	10:00	22.2
Arthur Godfrey's Talent Scouts	CBS	8:30	21.9
Screen Guild Players	CBS	10:30	18.9
Inner Sanctum	CBS	8:00	18.6
The Lone Ranger	ABC	7:30	16.4
Cavalcade of America	NBC	8:00	14.0
Voice of Firestone	NBC	8:30	12.2
Cliff Arquette's Point Sublime	ABC	8:00	12.1
Bill Henry Johns Manville News*	CBS	8:55	11.7

*Monday–Friday Strip Shows

Sans Strips...
Telephone Hour	NBC	9:00	10.7

LEVER LEVERAGE

Lever Brothers and CBS co-owned Network Radio's highest rated two hour block.

Lux Radio Theater was the centerpiece—scoring its all-time highest ratings and the first of five consecutive seasons as Network Radio's most popular program.

Lever's Lipton Tea and Pepsodent brands book-ended *Lux* with two newcomers—Arthur Godfrey's *Talent Scouts* at 8:30 and *My Friend Irma* at 10:00. Both new shows shot into the year's Top Ten along with *Lux,* making 1947–48 the first season in a decade that CBS had as many as three programs in the annual Top Ten.

It was Lever Brothers' big year. It owned five of the season's Top Ten programs under its corporate sponsorship. In addition to Monday's leaders, the company—known to the rest of the world as Unilever—also sponsored Bob Hope and *Amos & Andy* on NBC's Tuesday schedule.

GODFREY'S TEA PARTY

After 13 years on the air, *Lux Radio Theater* became the only dramatic series to ever rank as a season's Number One program.

All it took was a lead-in boost from a 44-year-old ukulele playing disc jockey who brought the first talent competition back to Network Radio since Major Bowes' amateurs left the air in 1945.

Arthur Godfrey's Talent Scouts, produced by CBS, had kicked around the network's schedule without a sponsor for over a year. Lever Brothers picked up the show for its Lipton Tea division in September to replace the disappointing—and highly expensive—Joan Davis sitcom, *Joanie's Tea Room.*

Godfrey had been on the CBS payroll since 1934—as a popular early morning disc jockey on the network's Washington, D.C., and New York City stations. He was so popular that beginning in 1941, Godfrey was heard in both cities every weekday morning.

But he never clicked on the full network until June 1947 when the informal, mid-morning *Arthur Godfrey Time* debuted Monday through Friday on CBS.

Nevertheless, Godfrey kept his "day job" with the two local stations in New York and Washington until November 1948.

Talent Scouts was an immediate hit in the Monday timeslot. Godfrey's first season resulted in a rating that was over 50 percent higher than *Joanie's Tea Room* could score for Lever. It was the first of five consecutive Top Ten seasons for *Talent Scouts.*

IRMA LA DUNCE

Marie Wilson was 31 and a beautiful, busty, wide-eyed blonde. She had appeared in 40 films in supporting roles—yet few knew her name outside Hollywood where she had starred in comedian Ken Murray's long-running stage revue *Blackouts* since 1941.

That all changed when the comedienne became *My Friend Irma* immediately following *Lux Radio Theater* on CBS in 1947. Lever Brothers snatched up the prime timeslot when *Screen Guild Players* was pushed up to 10:30 by its new sponsor, Camel Cigarettes.

My Friend Irma was created by writer-producer Cy Howard and starred Wilson as Irma Peterson, the warm hearted, empty headed, dumb blonde extraordinaire—an extension of her stage and movie persona.

With support from top radio talents Cathy Lewis, Hans Conreid, John Brown and Alan Reed, *My*

Friend Irma became one of Network Radio's highest rated sitcoms, scoring four consecutive Top Ten seasons.

SMART SHOW, STUPID MOVE

Doctor IQ had enjoyed four seasons as one of Monday's Top Ten programs.

The rapid fire quiz show was NBC's top rated entertainment program on Monday for all four years, consistently scoring double digit ratings in its 10:30 timeslot.

In 1947, after a two year hiatus, Mars Candy resumed sponsorship of the quiz show that traveled from city to city to originate its remote broadcasts from theaters packed with eager potential contestants seeking the silver dollars awarded for correct answers.

Then, in a maneuver nuttier than its Mars Bars, the candy company moved the NBC winner back one hour to 9:30, opposite the second half of *Lux Radio Theater*, Monday's perennial leader since the 1935–36 season.

Lux had grown even stronger since *Doctor IQ* first faced off against it in 1940 and lost its time period by better than a two-to-one margin. Their rematch was even more one-sided.

Doctor IQ fell from Monday's Top Ten and plummeted in the season's rankings from 49th to 108th place among all prime time programs. The Lew Valentine quiz was battered by *Lux* for two seasons until Mars and NBC dropped the show in 1949.

*1947–48 Tuesday Night
Top Ten Programs (11)*
NBC 6, CBS 5
Average: 19.0

Fibber McGee & Molly	NBC	9:30	26.1
Amos & Andy	NBC	9:00	24.1
Bob Hope Show	NBC	10:00	22.5
Red Skelton Show	NBC	10:30	20.4
Big Town	CBS	8:00	19.5
Date with Judy	NBC	8:30	19.0
Mr. & Mrs. North	CBS	8:30	17.1
Milton Berle Show	NBC	8:00	15.4
Bill Henry Johns Manville News*	CBS	8:55	11.7
Adventures of Christopher Wells	CBS	9:30	11.3
We the People	CBS	9:00	11.3

*Monday–Friday Strip Shows

KILLING TIME

NBC's veteran comedy lineup took Tuesday's Top Four positions — with *Amos & Andy* scoring its highest rating since 1934.

But CBS continued to counter with the drama that Bill Paley promised it would against the highly rated NBC laugh getters. Scripted crime and detective melodramas of different types were relatively inexpensive for sponsors and generators of solid ratings for the network.

It was smart programming for CBS because NBC outlawed any crime or murder mystery dramas to be broadcast before 9:30.

Big Town beat NBC's Milton Berle at 8:00. *Mr. & Mrs. North* was brought to CBS by Colgate and nipped at *A Date with Judy* at 8:30. *The Adventures of Christopher Wells* was a one season attempt to siphon listeners from *Fibber McGee & Molly*.

CBS continued its practice into other nights with familiar titles like *The Adventures of Sam Spade, Mr. Keen, The FBI in Peace & War* and *Casey, Crime Photographer*—all broadcast before 9:30. As a result, the network placed eight of its low-budget, low-risk dramas in the season's Top 50.

RIGHT DAY, RIGHT TIME, WRONG PLACE

Milton Berle finally scrambled into the season's Top 50 with a variety show that featured some of radio's top comedic studio talent—Arnold Stang, Pert Kelton, Arthur Q. Bryan, Jack Albertson, Ed Begley and announcer/foil Frank Gallop.

In its second season in NBC's 8:00 timeslot the show's audience jumped 40 percent and scored double digit ratings against *Big Town* on CBS. Nevertheless, Berle and sponsor Philip Morris parted company in April and he was gone from NBC Radio.

Ironically, Tuesday at 8:00 brought Berle his greatest triumph — on television.

He first appeared as guest host of NBC-TV's new *Texaco Star Theater* on June 8, 1948. It was the preview of a program would make

entertainment history over the following season.

*1947–48 Wednesday Night
Top Ten Programs*
NBC 6, ABC 3, CBS 1
Average 16.5

Mr. District Attorney	NBC	9:30	21.1
Duffy's Tavern	NBC	9:00	20.0
Great Gildersleeve	NBC	8:30	19.1
The Lone Ranger	ABC	7:30	16.4
The Big Story	NBC	10:00	16.1
A Day in the Life of Dennis Day	NBC	8:00	16.1
Mayor of the Town	ABC	8:00	14.8
Bing Crosby's Philco Radio Time	ABC	10:00	13.9
Dr Christian	CBS	8:30	13.9
Jimmy Durante Show	NBC	10:30	13.9

THE CROONER'S SWOON

Bing Crosby made big news earlier in the year by signing Al Jolson to a $50,000 contract (*$507,250*), for ten *Philco Radio Time* guest appearances during the season.

The ink was barely dry when Jolson signed another contract — to host Crosby's former NBC hit, *Kraft Music Hall*. Jolson showed up for just one *Philco Radio Time* appearance.

Crosby was forced to scramble and rely on a mix of movie star guests — actors Jimmy Stewart, Claudette Colbert and Barry Fitzgerald among them — and "casual drop-in guests" from other ABC shows like *Lone Ranger* Brace Beemer and *Breakfast in Hollywood*'s Tom Breneman.

In a season of inflated ratings Crosby's suffered a 20 percent loss of audience, falling out of the season's Top 50 for the first and only time in his 21 years on the air.

THE BIG STORY IS CROSBY'S DOWNFALL

Buried in the ratings by Crosby during its first season, NBC's studio drama *The Big Story* doubled its audience and became the first program to beat Crosby in his time period since 1941 when Major Bowes pulled a one season upset.

Inspired by actual newspaper reporters' investigative tactics and their resulting true stories — while never allowing the facts to get in the way of an even better tale — *The Big Story* dramatized the stories and awarded the reporters responsible for them with a weekly prize of $500 ($5,070).

The series became a Wednesday fixture on the NBC schedule for eight years, all of them under the sponsorship of American Tobacco's Pall Mall and Lucky Strike cigarettes.

INKA DINKA DID!

Rating woes were forecast for Jimmy Durante without Garry Moore, his partner for five years who had gone solo to host *Take It or Leave It.* But failure was always predicted for the 54-year-old Durante since his *Jumbo Fire Chief* fiasco of 1935–36.

Durante-Moore sponsor Rexall Drugs, moved Durante and his "Inka Dinka Doo" theme song to NBC's Wednesday schedule at 10:30. The comedian fooled everyone by posting a solid three point gain over the team's final season together.

With or without Moore, Durante finished in the season's Top 50 five times and was never out of a nightly Top Ten from 1942 through 1950 when he retired from series radio for even greater success in television.

MAYOR BARRYMORE AND MR. SCROOGE

Screen legend Lionel Barrymore was 69 and had over 200 films to his credit along with five network seasons as *Mayor of the Town* on CBS. Sponsor Noxema Skin Cream moved the heartwarming family series to ABC with better than expected results.

Mayor of the Town became the first program to ever increase its ratings by moving *to* ABC *from* NBC or CBS. The series topped its CBS ratings by a stunning 65 percent.

Barrymore played the widowed mayor of a small town much like his Dr. Gillespie character in 15 of MGM's *Dr. Kildare* movies — a gruff but tender hearted patriarch with a booming laugh Agnes Moorhead headed a strong supporting cast as Hizzoner's housekeeper, Marilly.

Mayor of the Town was best known for its annual departure from format when Barrymore became "Ebenezer Scrooge" in his annual holiday presentation of *A Christmas Carol.* He performed his radio adaptation of the Dickens classic over a dozen times.

Barrymore's success at 8:00 was followed by *Vox Pop* which was picked up after eight seasons on CBS and moved to ABC's Wednesday lineup at 8:30. The Parks Johnson and Warren Hull human interest/interview show recorded a 40 percent jump in its ratings.

NOTHING FUNNY ABOUT IT

Abbott and Costello weren't as lucky in their move to ABC.

The comics and Reynolds' Camel Cigarettes had parted company in June after five successful seasons as part of NBC's potent Thursday lineup. ABC scooped them up as a bridge between *Vox Pop* and the new Groucho Marx comedy quiz, *You Bet Your Life,* at 10:00.

The new *Abbott & Costello Show* on ABC was offered to affiliates on a co-op basis, with half its commercial minutes sold nationally and the other half made available for local sale.

Without the powerful support of NBC's *Sealtest Village Store* and Eddie Cantor surrounding them, Abbott and Costello's ABC show — with its familiar format and top flight supporting cast held over from its NBC run — dropped from 24th to 105th in the season's rankings.

1947–48 Thursday Night Top Ten Programs
CBS 5, NBC 5
Average: 16.3

Al Jolson's Kraft Music Hall	NBC	9:00	18.9
Aldrich Family	NBC	8:00	18.5
Burns & Allen	NBC	8:30	18.0
Mr. Keen Tracer of Lost Persons	CBS	8:30	16.7
FBI in Peace & War	CBS	8:00	15.7
Casey Crime Photographer	CBS	9:30	15.6
Dick Haymes Show	CBS	9:00	15.3
Suspense	CBS	8:00	15.0
Bob Hawk Show	NBC	10:00	14.6
Sealtest Village Store	NBC	9:30	14.5

JOLSON SINGS AGAIN

Kraft had seen its *Music Hall* ratings drop to half the levels that Bing Crosby averaged before he jumped to ABC. The low-budgeted replacement pairing of comedians Edward Everett Horton and Eddie Foy with Eddy Duchin's orchestra struggled to stay in double digits. As a result, the cheese company decided to open its checkbook for a headliner who approached Crosby's stardom.

Meanwhile, Al Jolson was hot again after the success of his filmed biography, *The Jolson Story,* a year earlier. The movie earned six Academy Award nominations and won two Oscars. A sequel, *Jolson Sings Again,* was already in the works at Columbia Pictures and his records were selling again.

Jolson demanded and got $7,500 (*$76,100*), per week to sign on as the new host of *Kraft Music Hall.*

It proved to be a good investment for Kraft. The 60-year-old singer, paired with pianist-comedian Oscar Levant, pumped the show back into first place on Thursday and a return into the season's Top 20.

CBS PLAYS CATCH UP

Just two years after placing only one program in Thursday's Top Ten, CBS pulled even with NBC.

The network's strategy was long term, counter-programming that landed most of its prime time entries into Thursday's Top Ten.

Against the aging Jolson's *Kraft Music Hall,* CBS and Autolite countered with a variety show hosted by 32-year-old movie singing star Dick Haymes. Opposite the frivolous *Aldrich Family,* CBS presented the well acted *Suspense,* replaced at mid-season by *The FBI in Peace & War.* Against the still popular comedy of Burns and Allen, CBS offered the melodrama of *Mr. Keen, Tracer of Lost Persons* and *Casey, Crime Photographer* beat Jack Carson and Eve Arden's *Sealtest Village Store* at 9:30.

Although neither CBS anthology series finished in Thursday's Top Ten, *First Nighter* helped push Eddie Cantor out of the season's Top 50 for the first time in his long career and *Radio Readers Digest* took audience from Bob Hawk who was moved to NBC for the season by Camel Cigarettes to replace Abbott and Costello.

Momentum was on CBS's side against the long running shows on NBC.

SUSPENDED SUSPENSE

One glitch in the CBS Thursday schedule was the November cancellation of *Suspense* by Roma Wines.

The network moved the mystery anthology — a Top 50 hit for three seasons — to Saturdays for the remainder of the season as a sustaining, hour-long feature hosted by Hollywood star Robert Montgomery. It remained unsponsored, unrated and apparently unwanted until mid–May when CBS shelved the show and waited for another sponsor to come along. It wasn't a long wait before Autolite automotive products picked up *Suspense* for the following season and returned it to the CBS Thursday schedule.

JUMPING JACK

Movie comedian Jack Carson was at the height of his Warner Brothers film career and had logged four years on CBS with his own Wednesday night sitcom dating back to the 1943–44 season. Despite his growing movie fame and skilled comedic support on his radio show provided by Dave Willock, Arthur Treacher, Mel Blanc and Agnes Moorhead, Carson could never win his time period against NBC's *Mr. & Mrs. North*.

Carson left CBS to join Eve Arden as co-host of NBC's *Sealtest Village Store* when Jack Haley left the show in 1947. Coincidentally, both Carson and Arden had strong supporting roles to Oscar winning Joan Crawford in 1945's *Mildred Pierce*.

The move provided Carson with his only double digit rating although *Sealtest* lost its time period to the CBS potboiler, *Mr. Keen, Tracer of Lost Persons*. The comedian jumped back to NBC and his old format the following season. Once again he lost his time period to a mystery — ABC's *The Fat Man* — and retired from radio to

focus on his still strong screen career.

DARTING IN AND OUT OF PRIME TIME

A dart game on radio made about as much sense as putting a ventriloquist on radio.

Except *Darts for Dough* didn't get anywhere near Edgar Bergen's ratings.

Soft drink Dr. Pepper promoted its hometown's local radio favorite, *Darts for Dough*, from WFAA/Dallas to Blue's Sunday afternoon schedule in 1944 to replace Al Pearce who had jumped to CBS. Hosted by friendly Orval Anderson, the combination quiz and stunt show's contestants threw darts for cash prizes including a grand prize of $100 *($1,014)*, for hitting a bulls eye and setting off a crescendo of bells and whistles.

The show's large on-stage dartboard was highlighted by segments marked *10, 2* and *4*—the times of day when the sponsor recommended a bottle of Dr. Pepper for a workday energy rush of sugar.

Darts for Dough enjoyed its three year Sunday run until October 1947 when it was slotted into ABC's Thursday schedule at 9:30 to replace *Mr. President*, a biographical series starring character actor Edward Arnold.

The dart game didn't have a chance against two of Thursday's Top Ten programs in the same half hour — *Casey, Crime Photographer* and the Jack Carson and Eve Arden *Sealtest Village Store*. It lasted for three months and scored a dismal 3.5 rating at 9:30.

1947–48 Friday Night
Top Ten Programs
ABC 4, CBS 3, NBC 3
Average: 15.9

This Is Your FBI	ABC	8:30	18.0
Fanny Brice Baby Snooks Show	CBS	8:00	17.3
People Are Funny	NBC	9:00	16.7
The Lone Ranger	ABC	7:30	16.4
Break the Bank	ABC	9:00	16.1
Waltz Time	NBC	9:30	16.1
The Fat Man	ABC	8:00	15.7
It Pays to Be Ignorant	CBS	10:00	14.3
Adventures of the Thin Man	CBS	8:30	14.1
Can You Top This?	NBC	8:30	13.9

13TH YEAR'S GOOD LUCK

The average rating for Friday night's Top Ten soared 43 percent to the highest level since 1934–1935. Coincidentally, ABC won the night with four programs in the Top Ten — its best showing since Monday of 1934–1935 in its Blue Network days.

This Is Your FBI became ABC's first program to win a night since Walter Winchell took first place on Sunday in 1944–45. With its twin, *The FBI in Peace & War* on CBS, the two G-Man shows turned in a combined 33.7 rating for the season.

MAKE ROOM FOR DANNY

Danny Thomas was the hottest comedian on the nightclub circuit and General Foods wanted a replacement for *The Adventures of the Thin Man* at 8:30. Thomas was no stranger to radio — he had played ongoing supporting roles for *Baby Snooks* and *The Bickersons* since 1944.

The new Danny Thomas Show debuted in January against two of Friday's Top Ten — *This Is Your FBI* and *Can You Top This?* The Thomas variety show lost its time period to both with a 13.7 rating and the comedian left series radio in June, never to return.

Four years later Thomas turned up on television with his legendary sitcom, *Make Room for Daddy*, and teamed with Sheldon Leonard to produce a string of television's most popular comedies including *The Andy Griffith Show* and *The Dick Van Dyke Show*.

IGNORANCE IS BLISS

It was a classic choice for listeners: brains or buffoonery.

Mutual picked up *Information Please* for co-op sponsorship — half network sponsored, half locally sponsored. The highly praised intellectual panel quiz led by Clifton Fadiman had enjoyed five seasons as a Top 50 program in its nine year history on Blue, NBC and CBS. It was slotted at 9:30 on Mutual.

Meanwhile, CBS scheduled *It Pays to Be Ignorant* at 10:00.

To label *It Pays to Be Ignorant* as one of radio's dumbest shows would disappoint its husband and wife creators, Bob and Ruth Howell. Their objective was to present *the* dumbest show ever heard. They did and their reward was a sporadic nine year run beginning in 1942.

With veteran Vaudeville comic Tom Howard asking truly stupid questions like, "Who's buried in Grant's Tomb?,," his panel of blithering numbskulls played by Vaudeville vets Gene Sheldon, Harry McNaughton and Lulu McConnell — all formally addressed as "Mister" or "Miss" à la *Information Please*—would go off on rambling, nonsensical tangents but never answer the question. It was a half hour of verbal baggy pants slapstick, full of cheap jokes and insults — the total antithesis of *Information Please*.

The season's final ratings gave *Information Please* a 4.7 — *It Pays to Be Ignorant* a 14.3.

NOT EVERYBODY WON

Despite the popularity of *It Pays to Be Ignorant*, sponsor Philip Morris pulled the plug on the silliness in February and replaced it with *Call for Music*, headlining Dinah Shore, Johnny Mercer and the Harry James orchestra. The show didn't dent the ratings and was shipped off to Saturdays in April, requiring yet another replacement program.

Phil Baker, out of work for eight months after leaving *Take It or Leave It,* was brought in to host the cigarette maker's *Everybody Wins,* a conventional audience participation quiz. The program drew a disappointing 11.5 rating and was gone in the fall. With its cancellation, Phil Baker retired from series radio.

Now You See It

Gillette's *Cavalcade of Sports*— aka *Friday Night Boxing* on ABC — became the first network radio series to be televised on a regular basis — seen weekly on NBC-TV. Nevertheless, radio still ruled the ratings.

Don Dunphy's audio account the Joe Louis/Jersey Joe Walcott Heavyweight Championship fight on June 25, 1948, drew a whopping 59.5 rating. The fight was a re-

match of their December 1947 bout won by Louis in a controversial decision. Louis settled the rematch with an 11th round knockout.

1947–48 Saturday Night Top Ten Programs
NBC 7, ABC 3
Average: 15.8

Truth or Consequences	NBC	8:30	22.3
Life of Riley	NBC	8:00	20.1
Your Hit Parade	NBC	9:00	20.0
Judy Canova Show	NBC	9:30	17.3
Kay Kyser's Kollege of Musical Knowledge	NBC	10:00	15.9
Grand Ole Opry	NBC	10:30	14.0
Curtain Time	NBC	7:30	12.6
Gangbusters	ABC	9:00	11.9
Murder & Mr. Malone	ABC	9:30	11.9
Famous Jury Trials	ABC	7:30	11.7

SATURDAY UP, CBS OUT

Saturday's Top Ten average rating shot up 40 percent to its highest point ever recorded — even bigger than during the early Crossley years when double digit ratings were common. NBC claimed the seven top shows while ABC took the remaining three spots of the Top Ten with its crime oriented studio dramas.

CBS was shut out of a nightly Top Ten for only the second time in its history.

EDWARDS WALKS INTO TOP TEN

Among the millions of random phone calls made by his operators over the years, C.E. Hooper himself was called once. It happened on a Saturday night in May 1948. He reported that he was listening to *Truth or Consequences.*

He wasn't alone.

Truth or Consequences was in its peak season — scoring the highest rating and ranking of any audience participation show — ever.

Ralph Edwards spiked his fall ratings with the third of his big jackpot giveaways, "Miss Hush," again suggesting that listeners' entries be accompanied by donations to the March of Dimes. Before dancer Martha Graham was identified six weeks later, the bounty of cash and merchandise prizes had grown to over $20,000 (*$202,900*),

and the charity had collected an astounding $880,000 (*8.9 Mil*).

Edwards followed that success in late December with "The Walking Man"— a mystery celebrity whose identity was disclosed in a series of clues — similar to the "Hush" contests. But only "The Walking Man's" recorded footsteps were heard while Edwards read the clues.

This time Edwards solicited donations for the fledgling American Heart Association. Contest entries containing contributions — sometimes over 100,000 envelopes per day — poured in for ten weeks while Edwards lured listeners with a jackpot that swelled to $22,500 (*$228,259*), in cash and merchandise.

When Jack Benny was finally identified as "The Walking Man" in March, the American Heart Association had collected over $1,750,000 (*17.8 Mil*) in donations.

Edwards continued his secret identity contests well into the next season. "Mr. and Mrs. Hush" were identified as playwright Moss Hart and his actress wife Kitty Carlisle. The dance team of Veloz and Yolanda were "Mama and Papa Hush," and popular poet Edgar A. Guest was "Mr. Heartbeat."

Jeanette MacDonald rounded out the secret identity group as "The Whispering Woman" in early 1949 — by which time giveaways had worn thin with the public's taste and the FCC's patience.

NBC'S RECORD PARTY

Led by *Truth or Consequences,* NBC's entire Saturday lineup benefited from the listening boom.

The Life of Riley, The Judy Canova Show, Your Hit Parade, The Grand Ole Opry and *Curtain Time* all recorded their highest ever ratings.

Colgate rescued Kay Kyser's *Kollege of Musical Knowledge* from Wednesday's debacle of the previous season when Kyser's half hour was paired with the failed Frank Morgan sitcom, *The Fabulous Dr. Tweedy.* In his new Saturday timeslot Kyser inherited the powerful lead-in provided by Colgate's Judy Canova. "The Ol' Professor's" ratings leaped 65 percent, propelling his musical comedy quiz back into the season's Top 50.

NBC had more reason to celebrate when Frank Sinatra returned to *Your Hit Parade* after a two year absence and his fans responded in huge numbers. They accounted for a 60 percent ratings surge and a record high ranking in the Top 15 for Lucky Strike's weekly countdown of hits.

"I'M NOBODY'S SWEETHEART"

Joan Davis couldn't have picked a better theme song.

Evicted from *Joanie's Tea Room* by Lever Brothers, the comedienne was moved by CBS to Saturday at 9:00 in one of the network's first experiments in co-op sponsorship — affiliated stations received commercial availabilities within the program instead of cash payment from the network for carrying the show. *Joan Davis Time* was slotted opposite two of Saturday's Top Ten programs occupying the same half hour — NBC's *Your Hit Parade*, which celebrated Frank Sinatra's return as its singing host, and the gritty *Gangbusters* on ABC. The two programs accounted for 31.9 rating points which didn't leave much audience left for Davis. Her sitcom registered a meager 5.1 — down over 60 percent from *Joanie's Tea Room.*

Her sitcom quietly left the air at the end of the season.

SHOOTING UP THE RATINGS WITH SILVER BULLETS

All but one of the Multiple Run Top Ten programs was a Monday through Friday strip.

The lone exception was *The Lone Ranger,* the Number One Multiple Run. After 15 years in the same Monday-Wednesday-Friday timeslot, "The Masked Rider of the Plains" out-distanced his nearest competition on CBS by a wide margin and finished among the Top Ten of all prime time programs on each of the three nights it was broadcast.

The General Mills sponsored series from WXYZ/Detroit almost doubled its previous season's rating and made its first of two appearances in the annual Top 50.

It remained the Number One Multiple Run program for three consecutive seasons.

THOMAS JUMPS AND FALLS

After 13 years with the Blue Network and four with NBC, Lowell Thomas jumped to CBS for a reported $10,000 per week *($101,500),* from Procter & Gamble. Keeping him in his 6:45 timeslot of 17 years, P&G owned a 45 minute block of CBS time — following the nightly Thomas newscast with *Beulah* at 7:00 and the Jack Smith songfest at 7:15.

During the season when other programs enjoyed record gains in ratings, Thomas lost 30 percent of his NBC audience, fell out of the season's Top 50 for the first time in his long career and never returned. Nevertheless, the veteran newscaster remained with CBS in the 6:45 timeslot until his retirement in 1976 when he was 84 years old.

SOAPY AND SOUPY SALES

Despite Thomas's slip in popularity, CBS achieved a rarity by placing its entire block of five strip programs from 6:45 to 8:00 in the Multiple Run Top Ten. Two advertisers, Procter & Gamble and Campbell Soups, sponsored the entire block.

CBS hadn't programmed Multiple Runs in the 7:30 time period since 1938, opting instead for weekly half hour programs with different degrees of success. The network returned to the Multiple Run race in 1947 with Campbell Soups' *Club 15* starring Bob Crosby and the singing Andrew Sisters at 7:30 followed by a quarter-hour newscast by Edward R. Murrow, also sponsored by Campbell.

Singing bandleader Crosby had become popular with radio audiences for a dozen years, shedding any notion that he benefited from his brother Bing's coat tails.

Murrow's popularity was boosted by the Columbia Records' release of *I Can Hear It Now,* a unique, best-selling audio history series co-written and narrated by Murrow.

The Murrow and Thomas newscasts, Crosby and Smith music shows plus *Beulah* would all repeat as Multiple Run Top Ten programs for five consecutive seasons.

BEULAH BACK BIG TIME

The big surprise was Procter & Gamble's revival of a former programming failure with a new format and familiar face.

Hattie McDaniel, 54, won the Academy Award for Best Supporting Actress in 1939's *Gone with the Wind* and had another 18 featured movie roles to her credit — all in the stereotyped role as a fat and jolly family maid. Her radio experience was limited to reoccurring parts in the 1937 revival of *Showboat* and the cast of the Eddie Cantor Show five years later.

In November she won the title role of the newly reformatted sitcom, *Beulah,* based on the character created two years earlier by the late Marlin Hurt. As a strip show, *Beulah* became a Multiple Run Top Ten hit for five years and for three seasons was among the annual Top 50 programs.

1947–48 Top Ten Multiple Run Programs				
CBS 6, NBC 2, ABC 1, MBS 1				
Average: 11.1				
The Lone Ranger	M,W,F	ABC	7:30	16.4
Bill Henry Johns Manville News*	M–F	CBS	8:55	11.7
Edward R Murrow News*	M–F	CBS	7:45	11.6
Chesterfield Supper Club*	M–F	NBC	7:00	10.7
Club 15*	M–F	CBS	7:30	10.6
Jack Smith Show*	M–F	CBS	7:15	9.9
Beulah*	M–F	CBS	7:00	9.6
Morgan Beatty News of the World*	M–F	NBC	7:15	8.5
Lowell Thomas News*	M–F	CBS	6:45	8.2
Gabriel Heatter News*	M–F	MBS	9:00	6.8
*Monday–Friday Strip Shows				

TOP 50 PROGRAMS—1947–48
NBC 27, CBS 17, ABC 6
Average Rating: 18.7, Median: 18.0
35,900,000 Radio Homes / 93.1% Coverage of U.S. Homes / One Rating Point = 359,000 Homes
Source: A.C. Nielsen Radio Index Service, Sept 1947–June 1948
Total Programs Rated, 6–11 P.M.: 162
Programs Rated 13 Weeks & Ranked: 156

		Program	Rtg	Type	Sponsor	Day	Time	Lgth	Net
1	8	Lux Radio Theater/William Keighley	31.2	DA	Lux Soap	Mon	9:00	60	CBS
2	2	Fibber McGee & Molly	26.1	SC	Johnson Wax	Tue	9:30	30	NBC
3	7	Amos & Andy	24.1	SC	Rinso Laundry Soap	Tue	9:00	30	NBC
4	5	Edgar Bergen & Charlie McCarthy	22.7	CV	Chase & Sanborn Coffee	Sun	8:00	30	NBC
5	1	Bob Hope Show	22.5	CV	Pepsodent Toothpaste	Tue	10:00	30	NBC
6t	4	Fred Allen Show	22.3	CV	Ford Motors	Sun	8:30	30	NBC 1
6t	17	Truth or Consequences/ Ralph Edwards	22.3	APS	Duz Laundry Soap	Sat	8:30	30	NBC
8	N	My Friend Irma/Marie Wilson	22.2	SC	Pepsodent Toothpaste	Mon	10:00	30	CBS
9	12	Phil Harris & Alice Faye	22.1	SC	Fitch Shampoo	Sun	7:30	30	NBC
10t	N	Arthur Godfrey's Talent Scouts	21.9	TC	Lipton Tea	Mon	8:30	30	CBS
10t	3	Jack Benny Program	21.9	SC	Lucky Strike Cigarettes	Sun	7:00	30	NBC
12	11	Mister District Attorney/Jay Jostyn	21.1	DCC	Vitalis Hair Tonic	Wed	9:30	30	NBC
13	6	Red Skelton Show	20.4	CV	Raleigh Cigarettes	Tue	10:30	30	NBC
14	26	Life of Riley/William Bendix	20.1	SC	Dreft Laundry Soap	Sat	8:00	30	NBC
15t	14	Duffy's Tavern/Ed Gardner	20 0	SC	Ipana & Vitalis	Wed	9:00	30	NBC
15t	33	Your Hit Parade/Frank Sinatra	20.0	MP	Lucky Strike Cigarettes	Sat	9:00	30	NBC
17	21	Big Town/Ed Pawley	19.5	DCC	Ironized Yeast	Tue	8:00	30	CBS
18	15	Great Gildersleeve/Hal Peary	19.1	SC	Parkay Margarine	Wed	8:30	30	NBC
19	29	A Date with Judy/Louise Erickson	19.0	SC	Tums Antacid	Tue	8:30	30	NBC
20t	N	Al Jolson's Kraft Music Hall	18.9	MV	Kraft Cheese	Thu	9:00	30	NBC
20t	10	Screen Guild Players	18.9	DA	Camel Cigarettes	Mon	10:30	30	CBS
22	24	Inner Sanctum	18.6	DA	Bromo Seltzer	Mon	8:00	30	CBS
23	26	Aldrich Family/Ezra Stone	18.5	SC	Grapenuts Cereal & Jello	Thu	8:00	30	NBC
24	35	Blondie/Penny Singleton, Arthur Lake	18.1	SC	Super Suds Laundry Soap	Sun	7:30	30	CBS
25t	15	Burns & Allen Show	18.0	SC	Maxwell House Coffee	Thu	8:30	30	NBC
25t	58	This Is Your FBI	18.0	DCC	Equitable Life Insurance	Fri	8:30	30	ABC
27	62	Adventures of Sam Spade/H Duff	17.8	DCC	Wildroot Cream Oil	Sun	8:00	30	CBS
28t	26	Fanny Brice Baby Snooks Show	17.3	SC	Jello Gelatin & Puddings	Fri	8:00	30	CBS
28t	22	Judy Canova Show	17.3	CV	Halo Shampoo	Sat	10:00	30	NBC
30	9	Walter Winchell's Jergens Journal	17.2	NC	Jergens Lotion	Sun	9:00	15	ABC
31t	38	Manhattan Merry Go Round	17.1	MP	Dr Lyons Tooth Powder	Sun	9:00	30	NBC
31t	36	Mr & Mrs North/Joe Curtin, Alice Frost	17.1	DCC	Halo Shampoo	Tue	8:30	30	CBS
33t	51	Mr Keen/Bennett Kilpack	16.7	DCC	Kolynos Toothpaste	Thu	8:30	30	CBS
33t	32	People Are Funny/Art Linkletter	16.7	APS	Raleigh Cigarettes	Fri	9:00	30	NBC
35	86	The Lone Ranger/Brace Beemer	16.4	DCC	Cheerios Cereal	MWF	7:30	30	ABC
36t	81	The Big Story	16.1	DA	Pall Mall Cigarettes	Wed	10:00	30	NBC
36t	71	Break The Bank/Bert Parks	16.1	APQ	Vitalis Hair Oil	Fri	9:00	30	ABC
36t	34	A Day in the Life of Dennis Day	16.1	SC	Lustre Cream Shampoo	Thu	7:30	30	NBC
36t	71	Waltz Time	16.1	MSP	Phillips Milk of Magnesia	Fri	9:30	30	NBC
40	18	Take It or Leave It/Garry Moore	16.0	APQ	Eversharp Pens & Pencils	Sun	10:00	30	NBC
41	65	Kay Kyser Kollege of Musical Knowledge	15.9	APQ	Colgate Dental Cream	Sat	10:00	30	NBC
42t	55	The Fat Man/J Scott Smart	15.7	DCC	Pepto Bismol	Fri	8:00	30	ABC 2
42t	31	The FBI in Peace & War	15.7	DCC	Lava Hand Soap	Thu	8:00	25	CBS
44t	38	Casey Crime Photographer	15.6	DCC	Anchor Hocking Glass	Thu	9:30	30	CBS
44t	122	Meet Corliss Archer/Janet Waldo	15.6	SC	Campbell Soup	Sun	9:00	30	CBS
46	74	Milton Berle Show	15.4	CV	Philip Morris Cigarettes	Tue	8:00	30	NBC
47t	40	Dick Haymes Show	15.3	MV	Autolite Spark Plugs	Thu	9:00	30	CBS
47t	96	Theater Guild on the Air	15.3	DA	US Steel	Sun	10:00	60	ABC 3
49	N	The Man Called X/Herbert Marshall	15.2	DCC	Frigidaire Refrigerators	Sun	8:30	30	CBS 4
50	22	Suspense	15.0	DA	Roma Wines	Thu	8:00	30	CBS 5

New & Returning Top 50 Programs Underscored.

1	Fred Allen Show	Oct–Dec	Tenderleaf Tea	Sun	8:30	30	NBC
2	The Fat Man	Sep–Dec	Pepto Bismol	Mon	8:30	30	ABC
3	aka: US Steel Hour						
4	The Man Called X	Sep–Nov	Frigidaire Refrigerators	Thu	10:00	30	CBS
5	Suspense	Jan–Jun	Sustaining (Unrated, Unranked)	Sat	8:00	60	CBS

Key: API — Audience Participation/Interviews
APQ — Audience Participation/Quiz
APS — Audience Participation/Stunts
CV — Comedy/Variety Show
DA — Dramatic Anthology

DCC — Drama/Continuing Characters
MC — Music/Classical, Semi-Classical
MP — Music/Popular, Contemporary
MSP — Music/Specialty, Ethnic
MST — Music/Standard, Traditional

MV — Music/Variety Show
NC — News, Commentary
PS — Panel Show Comedy
SC — Situation Comedy
TC — Talent Competition

1947–48 Top 50 Favorite Formats

	Programs	Pct
Comedy — Variety & Situation	21	42%
Drama — Anthology & Continuing	17	34%
Music — All Categories	6	12%
Audience Participation — All Categories	5	10%
News/Commentary	1	2%

1947–48 Monthly Winners

Sep	Lux Radio Theater	24.0	Feb	Lux Radio Theater	38.5
Oct	Lux Radio Theater	30.4	Mar	Lux Radio Theater	34.2
Nov	Lux Radio Theater	31.4	Apr	Lux Radio Theater	32.0
Dec	Lux Radio Theater	30.5	May	Lux Radio Theater	30.2
Jan	Lux Radio Theater	34.5	Jun	Lux Radio Theater	26.6

21

The 1948–49 Network Season

Announcer: I'd like to say something to the ladies. You know, one of the rules of modern life is perfect cleanliness. For instance, years ago women would have been horrified with the thought of washing their hair every day as many of our Hollywood stars do. But then, they didn't have Fitch's Emulsified Coconut Oil Shampoo. If they had, I'll wager that they'd have used it frequently. Because Fitch's Emulsified Coconut Oil Shampoo always leaves the hair lustrous and easy to set. Made from pure vegetable and mild coconut oils, it won't dry the air or make it harsh feeling. It cleanses thoroughly, too, with loads of fluffy lather that leaves your hair fragrant and sparkling clean. Ask for a professional application of Fitch's Emulsified Coconut Oil Shampoo at your beauty or barber shop or buy an economical bottle at your drug or toilet goods counter. Look for the bottle with the bright yellow label. Fitch's Emulsified Coconut Oil Shampoo. (PAUSE) If dandruff is your problem, ask for Fitch's Dandruff Remover Shampoo ... the only shampoo whose guarantee to remove dandruff is backed by one of the world's largest insurance firms! No other shampoo can make this statement! Ask for Fitch's Dandruff Remover Shampoo. Fitch is spelled, F-I-T-C-H.

WHAT, WE WORRY?

Network Radio opened the 1948–49 season flush with the sense of renewed popularity and its 14th consecutive year of record high earnings.

The percentage of total stations affiliated with the networks had plunged from 97 percent to 68 percent. But the drop was easily attributed to the postwar surge of new AM stations the air — 559 in 1948 alone. The networks, limited to just one affiliate per city, added 76 of the newcomers to their flocks.

Almost unnoticed was the growth of FM radio which had leaped in number to almost 500. But the importance of FM was still a thing of the distant future.

Of greater concern to radio's immediate future was the rapid growth of television.

By December 1948 another 33 television stations had begun operations with 50 more under construction.

New television stations attracted new viewers. TV penetration grew faster than 10,000 new homes per month in 1948. Momentum for set ownership snowballed to avalanche proportions in early 1949 and a million households were soon in sight. It was still less than three percent of the radio homes, but advertisers were beginning to use the new medium.

Television was the new nightly center of family gatherings and neighborhood parties. By coincidence — or perhaps not — the Top 50 Network Radio programs' average audience dropped over a million homes during the season.

Merlin Aylesworth, NBC's founding president from 1926 to 1932, predicted in the spring that television would wipe out radio as America knew it within three years.

He wasn't far off the mark.

PALEY GETS HIS PIECE OF THE ROCK

In the four seasons since Bill Paley's return from World War II with his vow to take CBS to the top of the ratings, the network had averaged a scant 18 shows in the annual Top 50.

Paley had America's most popular program in *Lux Radio Theater* and there were encouraging signs from the CBS stable of home grown shows — most notably *Arthur Godfrey's Talent Scouts, My Friend Irma* and *The Adventures of Sam Spade*.

But NBC's comedy stars continued to dominate the Top Ten year after year.

Paley's network lacked the power and prestige of radio's biggest names. He determined to get them for CBS — and with an eye to the future, lock them up for CBS-TV which required huge amounts of capital to compete with NBC. To accomplish the job he borrowed five million dollars *(46.9 Mil)*, from Prudential Insurance.

His first target was the resurgent *Amos & Andy* — which had scrambled back into the annual Top Ten since its conversion to an NBC half hour sitcom in 1943.

Freeman Gosden and Charles Correll owned their program and its characters. Paley convinced them to sell their property to CBS

1948–49 Season Scoreboard			
Mid-season Totals, December 1948			
		Compared to Year Earlier	
Total Radio Homes	37.6 Mil	+1.70 Mil	+4.7%
Total Auto Radios	11.0 Mil	+2.0 Mil	+22 2%
Total AM Radio Stations	1,621	+559	+52.6%
Total Radio Network Affiliates	1,104	+76	+7.4%
1948 Radio Revenues	561.6 Mil	+55.2 Mil	+10.9%
1948 Network Revenues	210.6 Mil	+9.4 Mil	+4.7%
Network Share	37.5%		(2.2%)
Total TV Homes	940,000	+768,000	+446.5%
Total TV Stations	52	+33	+173.7%
Total FM Stations	473	+323	+215.3%

for $2,000,000 *($18.8 Mil)*, in September. Their windfall from the sale was subject to a capital gains tax of 25 percent instead of an income tax that could soar close to 80 percent.

Then CBS captured the team's NBC sponsor—Lever Brothers' Rinso laundry soap—and paid Gosden and Correll an additional fee as "technical advisors" to their own program. It was a win-win situation for the comedians and the network.

The losers were NBC and the Internal Revenue Service.

WHEN YOU DISS UPON A STAR...

With *Amos & Andy* in his fold, Bill Paley landed an even bigger prize—his friend Jack Benny.

The pair floated another capital gains deal similar to the *Amos & Andy* coup, but the IRS refused the idea. It ruled that *Amos & Andy* were fictional characters and the program was indeed a property that could conceivably exist without Gosden and Correll—a point that television later proved.

Benny was different—he was an actual person and without him, his program was worthless.

Benny's move to CBS was costly. to the comedian. As 60 percent owner of his program's production company, Benny's personal tax liability after signing with Paley was just over a million dollars *(9.4 Mil)*—more than three times the amount that a capital gains deal would have been.

Although the sum was undoubtedly covered by CBS, Benny jumped networks for personal reasons.

Unlike CBS chief Paley who displayed true interest in Benny's welfare, NBC's David Sarnoff refused to personally meet with his star of over a decade in an attempt to keep him in the fold. Instead, Sarnoff assigned an RCA staff lawyer to negotiate with Benny—a former federal prosecutor against whom Benny had a rare personal grudge stemming back to an overblown jewelry smuggling charge in the 1930s. Sarnoff's thoughtless insults pushed Benny to CBS.

Jack Benny was highly respected in the entertainment community.

With his endorsement, the personable Paley lured Edgar Bergen, Red Skelton and Burns and Allen from NBC plus Bing Crosby and Groucho Marx from ABC for his 1949–50 schedule.

Paley's loan from Prudential was paid off promptly while Sarnoff's insensitive blunder with Benny eventually cost NBC millions of dollars in radio and television revenue.

A REVOLUTIONARY BATTLEGROUND

Sarnoff and Paley took their battle into the phonograph and recording industries when Columbia Records introduced the 33⅓ revolutions-per-minute, microgroove "Long Playing" disc on June 21, 1948. CBS had offered to share the technology with RCA, but Sarnoff rejected the idea.

Instead, RCA came out with its own 45 r.p.m. system seven months later.

The battle of systems went on for several years until the record buying public decided the issue, preferring the seven inch, 45s for singles and the twelve inch, 33⅓ discs for albums That forced both companies to share their technologies.

The bulky 78 r.p.m. records that had been popular for decades were on their way out and sales of phonographs employing the new slower playing records boomed.

THE FEDERAL PARTY POOPER

The FCC complained in August that Network Radio schedules contained 40 quiz and giveaway programs that awarded a total of $150,000 in prizes *($1.4 Mil)* every month. Particular targets of the complaint were ABC's *Stop the Music* and *Truth or Consequences* on NBC. It went conveniently unmentioned that the *Truth or Consequences* promotions also raised over three million dollars for charities.

The commission floated a broad reinterpretation of the 1934 antilottery statutes which it directed at giveaway and quiz shows. The bureaucrats proposed to outlaw *any* effort on the part of listeners as a

requirement to win a radio contest—writing a letter, answering the telephone or listening to a specific program.

Although there were wide loopholes in the edict, ABC, CBS and NBC prepared to file injunctions against it. The giveaways continued as the argument continued during a year of hearings.

Only Mutual complied immediately, piously observing that giveaway programs, "Were not healthy for radio."

That said, Mutual cancelled its only prime time giveaway show, *Three for the Money*, which had been unable to attract a sponsor for three months and was thus deemed, "Not healthy for radio."

TV FREEZES AND EXPANDS

Television's growth was stalled in September when the FCC "froze" all pending television station applications while it considered ways to alter its 1945 rules regarding channel usage and TV signal separation distances between cities.

The freeze, originally projected at 90 days, lasted for four years.

But the freeze didn't effect television stations already established or under construction. By early 1949, new stations were coming on the air at the rate of one every week.

Meanwhile, AT&T officially opened coaxial cable networking from the east coast to the Midwest in January 1949. The video chains were linked as far west as St. Louis and live network programming became available to most of the country's largest markets.

TELEVISION WRESTLES WITH PROGRAMMING

ABC and CBS began regularly scheduled television programming in 1948, joining the year-old NBC and DuMont networks.

All four were wrestling with their program schedules—or boxing with them, depending on the night.

NBC televised boxing on Monday and Friday nights, wrestling on Tuesday. Both CBS and DuMont scheduled boxing against ABC's wrestling shows on Wednesday.

Combined, the four networks logged eight boxing or wrestling shows a week in the prime time 10 o'clock hour. It was this kind of programming that prompted Fred Allen to quip, "Imitation is the sincerest form of television."

Nevertheless, boxers and wrestlers provided the networks with cheaply produced "reality" programming while network and agency producers scrambled for ideas to create programs likely to attract audience interest and advertising investment.

LOOK, DON'T LISTEN

For a decade the networks had taken radio income in huge chunks to finance television's technological development. Now they looked to radio to provide television with programming content beyond the "saloon" appeal of boxing, wrestling, baseball and Roller Derby.

The networks' cannibalization of radio programming to feed television began with just a few nibbles.

Arthur Godfrey's Talent Scouts was the sudden new radio hit for CBS a year earlier, finishing in the season's Top Ten. It was a simple studio show with a small audience that could easily be covered with just two or three cameras. CBS-TV began simulcasting *Talent Scouts* on December 6 — replacing Roller Derby.

The radio version of Godfrey's show lost almost ten percent of its previous season's rating in the process, but the maneuver gave CBS and sponsor Lipton Tea a solid foothold in the new medium.

CBS then simulcast *We the People* on Tuesday night. *People's* radio ratings slid 12.5 percent.

ABC simulcast *Break the Bank* on Friday nights, losing 20 percent of its radio audience. The network's long running public affairs feature, *America's Town Meeting* was simulcast on Tuesday and lost 17 percent.

The pioneering but short-lived Dumont Television Network (1946–56), produced only one program on Sunday nights, a video version of *The Original Amateur Hour* hosted by Ted Mack. ABC Radio broadcast a separate production of the program on Wednesdays.

Simultaneous video of ABC Radio's *Friday Night Boxing*, aka *Gillette Cavalcade of Sports*, had first appeared on NBC-TV a year earlier. NBC's television network borrowed just one more program from radio in 1948–49 — Mutual's *Meet the Press*, with co-creators Martha Rountree and Lawrence Spivak. The program was first seen in November on Sunday nights at 8:30.

Meet the Press remains on NBC-TV's Sunday television schedule to this day — but nowhere near prime time.

NBC was slow to translate its own radio favorites to television. That would all change in a big way the following season when advertising executive Pat Weaver was appointed President of NBC Television.

Regardless of the danger to Network Radio's ratings, the adaptation of radio favorites to television inspired imitation — and lots of it.

THE MONTHLIES

Lux Radio Theater continued its winning ways as radio's Number One show from September through December, plus April and May. Jack Benny, who began the season on NBC then jumped to CBS at mid-season, tied for first place in January with ABC's Walter Winchell. Winchell snapped the CBS string of consecutive monthly wins at 16 by taking sole possession of first in February, March and June.

The sharp tongued columnist gave ABC the greatest number of monthly wins that the network ever experienced.

1948–49 Sunday Night
Top Ten Programs
NBC 4, CBS 3, ABC 3
Average: 16.3

Jack Benny Program	CBS	7:00	22.9
Walter Winchell's Journal	ABC	9:00	21.7
Edgar Bergen & Charlie McCarthy	NBC	8:00	20.1
Amos & Andy	CBS	7:30	17.1
Phil Harris & Alice Faye	NBC	7:30	15.4
Stop the Music	ABC	8:00	15.2
Louella Parsons' Hollywood News	ABC	9:15	13.3
The Adventures of Sam Spade	CBS	8:00	12.6
Fred Allen Show	NBC	8:00	12.5
Manhattan Merry Go Round	NBC	9:00	12.5

PALEY'S LUCKY BET

Bill Paley's acquisition of Jack Benny for CBS didn't mean that sponsor Lucky Strike would automatically follow its star to his familiar Sunday time period on a different network. So Paley guaranteed American Tobacco that Benny's program on CBS would either match or better his NBC ratings — or CBS would refund $1,000 *($9,400)* for every rating point that the show lost.

Paley didn't refund a penny.

Benny's audience moved with him. The comedian's October through December NBC ratings averaged 22.7 — his January through June average on CBS was 22.9 His defection to CBS gave the network its first Sunday night leader since 1935 when Eddie Cantor became the first major star to jump from NBC to CBS.

The Lucky Strike Program starring Jack Benny was a CBS fixture at 7:00 for the next seven seasons.

BENNY BREAKS *A&A*'S
FALL FALL

Jack Benny gave CBS additional value as a lead-in for its Sunday programming.

Amos & Andy premiered on CBS at 7:30 on October 10th, three months before Benny arrived with his show at 7:00. For those three months Gosden and Correll were stuck with *Gene Autry's Melody Ranch* as their lead-in — a program that appealed primarily to juvenile fans of the cowboy hero.

The veteran comedy duo lost 25 percent of their audience from the same three months on NBC the previous season. *Amos & Andy* lost their time period, too, lagging behind Phil Harris and Alice Faye's sitcom which still had Benny as its lead-in on NBC.

The situation was reversed in January when Benny joined CBS and became *Amos & Andy*'s lead-in. Harris and Faye lost a whopping 42 percent of their audience on the month he left while *Amos & Andy* recovered for a third consecutive Top Ten season.

WELCOME TO
THE CLUBBING

Horace Heidt joined a sadder-but-wiser group that included Eddie Cantor, Kate Smith and Gene Autry, plus detectives *The Thin Man* and *Sherlock Holmes*. Over the years all had been programmed against Jack Benny on Sundays at 7:00 and none had succeeded.

Heidt's *Youth Opportunity Program* was doing nicely on NBC's Sunday schedule at 10:30. Then the network convinced Heidt and his sponsor Philip Morris to move the show back to 7:00, vacated when Benny left in January.

The result was an immediate 40 percent loss of audience against Benny's show on CBS and a drop into single digit ratings for the next four months. To cut their losses, the network and sponsor moved the show back to 10:30 in late April.

The cigarette maker and its star rectified the mistake to an even greater degree the following season.

They joined Benny and jumped to CBS's Sunday schedule where Horace Heidt's *Youth Opportunity Program* enjoyed three consecutive Top 50 seasons.

STOP'S SUMMERTIME STATS

By the beginning of the 1948–49 season, ABC's *Stop the Music* had been on the air for six months and had awarded three jackpot prizes averaging nearly $20,000 in retail value (*$187,700*). The show continued to make news with its pyramiding piles of prizes which spurred accusations that it "bought" its audience and further emboldening the FCC to redefine prohibited lotteries to new dimensions.

Stop the Music remained on the air through the summer of 1948 to build a following and attract major sponsors for each of its four quarter-hour segments. Lorillard's Old

Gold Cigarettes bought two of the segments while Smith Brothers Cough Drops and Spiedel Watch Bands each sponsored one.

Prospects were even rosier for *Stop the Music* when Edgar Bergen went on vacation in June and left his 8:00 timeslot on NBC to his summer replacement, the bland Robert Shaw Chorale.

Regardless, CBS won the summertime 8:00 half hour with *The Adventures of Sam Spade* starring Howard Duff as producer William Spier's wise-cracking version of Dashiell Hammett's classic detective. *Spade* consistently won its time period in July, August and September with 7.5, 9.4 and 9.7 ratings against *Stop the Music*'s 5.9, 6.3 and 8.3.

COWAN VS. COWAN

Ford and NBC brought in a summer replacement for the sophisticated humor of Fred Allen at 8:30 against *Stop the Music* that can only be termed puzzling.

RFD America was a simplistic quiz show that featured farmers as contestants.

More puzzling was the fact that *RFD America* was created by *Stop the Music*'s producer, Louis Cowan. As a result, Cowan's two shows were programmed opposite each other on competing networks.

Against NBC's rural quiz and actor Herbert Marshall's espionage drama, *The Man Called X* on CBS, *Stop the Music* easily won the 8:30 time period.

BERGEN BEATS THE BAND

The real Sunday night battle resumed in October when Edgar Bergen and Fred Allen returned after summer hiatus.

Well publicized momentum appeared to be on *Stop the Music*'s side. But the half hour charts for

the last quarter of 1948 tell a different story. See the chart below.

Despite *Stop the Music*'s also-ran ratings, ABC had every right to be delighted with its hour-long giveaway show that attracted headlines, listeners and advertising revenue.

Then in late 1948, CBS Chairman Paley did a huge favor for *Stop the Music*. He hired Edgar Bergen away from NBC and broke up the Bergen-Allen ratings tandem in January 1949. The ventriloquist left the air for the rest of the season before joining the CBS Sunday lineup at 8:00 ten months later.

Bergen's long absence was the giveaway show's big break. Whether he was at NBC or CBS, the soft spoken Scandinavian and his popular alter egos consistently stopped *Stop the Music* in its tracks.

THE WIT'S END

The same wasn't true for Fred Allen in his fight against *Stop the Music*.

NBC and Allen's sponsor, Ford Motors, seemed to be at a loss when Bergen left in January. Instead of keeping Allen in his familiar timeslot of three and a half years and supporting him with a suitable lead-in that could attract respectable numbers, the network moved him into Bergen's vacated half hour at 8:00 with disastrous consequences.

Rating breakouts for the time period illustrate Allen's decline. See the chart at the top of page 175.

Some reports claim that Allen welcomed the fight. Indeed, he did offer a tongue-in-cheek reward of $5,000 (*$46,900*), to any listeners who could prove that they missed a shot at *Stop the Music*'s jackpot by listening to his show.

But by June and five straight months of third place finishes, Allen was discouraged, bitter and

		October		November		December	
		8:00	8:30	8:00	8:30	8:00	8:30
NBC	Edgar Bergen & Charlie McCarthy	18.9	—	19.8	—	21.7	—
CBS	Adventures of Sam Spade	15.6	—	15.8	—	18.4	—
ABC	Stop the Music	11.6	—	12.2	—	13.0	—
NBC	Fred Allen	—	17.5	—	18.6	—	20.0
ABC	Stop the Music	—	15.2	—	17.2	—	17.1
CBS	Cabin B-13 (Sustaining and Not Rated)	—	NA	—	NA	—	NA

		Jan	*Feb*	*Mar*	*Apr*	*May*	*Jun*
ABC	Stop the Music	16.3	16.8	17.6	14.6	9.8	8.8
CBS	Adventures of Sam Spade	10.7	12.5	11.3	9.5	10.1	8.3
NBC	Fred Allen	11.7	11.3	9.4	8.9	9.5	5.8

once again in ill-health. The 55-year-old comedian abandoned his weekly series on June 26th, closing out a 17 year career in Network Radio.

Stop the Music's 1948–49 full-hour ratings record was truly remarkable. It reflects an unmatched popularity growth in which the show added at least one rating point each month — over 376,000 homes per point — for six consecutive months from September through March, rising from an 11.3 to a 20.4.

It was all downhill from there. But it was a great ride while it lasted for the ABC giveaway show that stopped Fred Allen — with strong assists from both CBS and NBC.

WINCHELL GETS A GRAND DEAL

After a successful 16 year association, Jergens Lotion and Walter Winchell parted company in December, ending the longest sponsor-program relationship in prime time radio.

The columnist — reported to be another target of the CBS talent raid — became radio's first "Thousand Dollar a Minute" star when he signed a widely publicized 90 week, $1,350,000 *(12.7 Mil)* contract with ABC which had sold his broadcasts to Kaiser-Frazer automobiles in December.

With a push from *Stop the Music*'s strong lead-in, Winchell's ratings rose 25 percent over the season but the automaker saw no results from his endorsements and dropped his Sunday broadcasts after 26 weeks.

ABC was left with the problem of finding a sponsor — any sponsor — who would pick up the high-priced tab for its expensive and increasingly controversial star's program.

HOLLYWOOD HIGHS

Although Jergens pulled out of the high-priced Winchell broadcasts, it held onto its sponsorship of Louella Parsons following Winchell at 9:15. For the first time since her *Hollywood Hotel* days a decade earlier, Parsons returned to the season's Top 50 with her film colony news and movie star interviews.

Meanwhile, Jimmie Fidler continued his two quarter hour Sunday shows on ABC and Mutual.

Parsons and Fidler combined to produce a aggregate total of 23.8 rating points on Sunday, evidence that the public was still hungry for Hollywood news and gossip in the postwar years before television drove movie attendance down.

ABC'S STEEL PLATE OF PRESTIGE

ABC had a record high nine programs in the season's Top 50 — four of them were broadcast on Sunday.

The network's fourth winner followed its successful 90 minute block of *Stop the Music*, Walter Winchell and Louella Parsons. It was a complete change of pace — the prestigious *Theater Guild on the Air*, aka *The U.S. Steel Hour*.

Unlike its Hollywood counterpart *Lux Radio Theater* which adapted familiar film stories and depended heavily on the box office appeal of its stars, *Theater Guild on the Air* adapted what its producers considered to be the finest plays of Broadway's "legitimate" stage, featuring highly skilled, if not immensely popular actors.

The program was introduced to the ABC Sunday schedule at 10:00 in 1945 and started slowly with single digit ratings for two seasons against radio favorites *Take It or Leave It*, *We the People* and *The Bickersons*.

It was moved back 30 minutes in September 1947 to take advantage of Winchell and Parsons' lead-in and nearly doubled its audience. By the 1948–49 season it was an established hit for ABC, topping all competition in its time period.

Unfortunately for ABC, its suc-cessful Sunday lineup was fragile. *Theater Guild* sponsor United States Steel moved the program to NBC the following season.

1948–49 Monday Night Top Ten Programs
CBS 8, ABC 1, NBC 1
Average: 14.6

Lux Radio Theater	CBS	9:00	25.5
Arthur Godfrey's Talent Scouts	CBS	8:30	21.9
My Friend Irma	CBS	10:00	19.5
Inner Sanctum	CBS	8:00	15.0
The Bob Hawk Show	CBS	10:30	14.1
The Lone Ranger	ABC	7:30	11.7
Beulah*	CBS	7:00	10.0
The Jack Smith Show*	CBS	7:15	9.8
Club 15/Bob Crosby*	CBS	7:30	9.5
Cavalcade of America	NBC	8:00	9.1

*Monday–Friday Strip Shows

Sans Strips...

The Railroad Hour	ABC	8:00	8.6
Dr IQ	NBC	9:30	8.4
The Telephone Hour	NBC	9:00	8.1

MONDAY AWASH WITH HITS

CBS's domination of Monday seemed like it would never end — and it never did as long as the Golden Age lasted. The network's peak was 1948–49 when it won every time period from 7:00 until 11:00.

Lever Brothers and CBS repeated with Monday's Top Three programs packaged from 8:30 to 10:30 — *Lux Radio Theater*, *Arthur Godfrey's Talent Scouts* and *My Friend Irma*. The three were again in the season's Top Ten and Lever again had five of the season's Top Ten most popular programs.

HAWK RETURNS TO THE NEST

After one year on NBC's Thursday schedule and a fall from the season's Top 50, R.J. Reynolds Tobacco moved *The Bob Hawk Show* comedy quiz back to CBS where it had been a fixture for five years. The quipping quizmaster remained on CBS with Camel Cigarettes sponsorship for the next five seasons, all rated in Monday's Top Ten and the annual Top 50.

RAILROADS EXPRESS STYLE

The National Association of Railroads introduced its stylish *Railroad Hour* on ABC in October. The program featured handsome baritone Gordon MacRae, 27, as host and singing lead in each week's presentation of a Broadway operetta or a Hollywood musical with popular guest stars from the stage and screen. MacRae was a best selling artist for Capitol Records and just beginning a film career that peaked seven years later when he starred in the movie versions of *Oklahoma* and *Carousel.*

Like its predecessors *Telephone Hour* and *Carnation Contented Hour, The Railroad Hour* was never an hour in length. It began as one of network radio's few 45 minute programs. The "hour" was further reduced in April when it was shortened to 30 minutes.

Unfortunately for ABC, the railroad association, like U.S. Steel, moved its prestigious theatrical presentation and its sponsorship money to NBC the next season.

1948–49 Tuesday Night
Top Ten Programs
NBC 6, CBS 4
Average: 15.3

Fibber McGee & Molly	NBC	9:30	23.5
The Bob Hope Show	NBC	9:00	19.8
People Are Funny	NBC	10:30	17.1
A Date with Judy	NBC	8:30	16.4
Mystery Theater	CBS	8:00	15.2
Big Town	NBC	10:00	14.8
Mr. & Mrs. North	CBS	8:30	13.7
This Is Your Life	NBC	8:00	11.1
Hit the Jackpot	CBS	10:00	11.0
Beulah*	CBS	7:00	10.0

*Monday–Friday Strip Shows

Sans Strips...
We the People	CBS	9:00	9.9

NBC LAUGHS OFF TUESDAY

Three of Tuesday's Top Ten shows — comedies headlining *Amos & Andy,* Red Skelton and Milton Berle — were gone from the NBC schedule.

Amos & Andy jumped to CBS.

Brown & Williamson Tobacco curiously swapped Tuesday's *Red Skelton Show* with its Friday success, *People Are Funny.* The Art Linkletter stunt show picked up a

fraction of a point and finished in the season's Top Ten, but Skelton lost 30 percent of his audience on Friday and his season rating fell below 20.0 for the first time in seven years.

Meanwhile, Texaco installed Milton Berle as permanent host of NBC-TV's *Texaco Star Theater* on September 21— in the same 8:00 timeslot on Tuesday that he had occupied on NBC Radio the previous season.

Berle's television success was rapid and legendary — forever leaving the question of why NBC allowed Berle's television comedy hit to be programmed against its own Tuesday comedy lineup on radio.

In yet another questionable maneuver, NBC reversed the decade-old scheduling order of its two reliable Tuesday hits, *Fibber McGee & Molly* and Bob Hope. Although *FM&M* held its own as Tuesday's Number One program, Hope dropped from the season's Top Five for the first time in nine years and his annual rating fell into the teens.

The decline of Hope's radio popularity had just begun.

One maneuver that did pay off for NBC was Lever Brothers' Lifebuoy Soap takeover of *Big Town* — a ten year hit on CBS — and moving it to NBC. The newspaper drama lost 25 percent of its audience in the shift but remained in Tuesday's Top Ten, winning its time period against a CBS entry in the big money quiz craze — *Hit the Jackpot,* hosted by a glib newcomer, 28-year-old Bill Cullen.

THE SURPRISE HIT

This Is Your Life grew out of a *Truth or Consequences* segment from 1946 when the U.S. Army asked Ralph Edwards to "do something" for a despondent paraplegic veteran. Edwards hit on the idea of profiling the young man's life on the air — with surprise appearances and tributes from his family and friends. The idea was to bridge the soldier's happier past with the promise of better things to come beginning with a parcel of gifts presented by Edwards.

The segment drew immediate praise and inspired a new program based on the biographical concept.

This Is Your Life, which usually surprised its unsuspecting guests of honor, had a two year radio run for Philip Morris cigarettes and became a nine year television hit for Edwards beginning in 1952.

LISTENERS TURN TUMS DOWN

Tums gave itself unnecessary ratings heartburn in January. The antacid tablets cancelled *A Date with Judy* starring Louise Erickson at midseason. The sitcom had passed perennial favorite *Aldrich Family* as radio's most popular teen comedy the previous season with a Top 20 finish. It had another one in the works with 16.4 average rating when it was abruptly shut down in January.

Tums replaced *A Date with Judy* with *The Alan Young Show*—a sitcom starring the 29-year-old Canadian comedian. Curiously, it co-starred the displaced Erickson in the role of Young's girlfriend. Listeners obviously missed her as Judy. *The Alan Young Show* limped in with a 9.6 average and was cancelled at the end of the season.

1948–49 Wednesday Night
Top Ten Programs
NBC 5, CBS 3, ABC 2
Average: 13.3

Duffy's Tavern	NBC	9:00	16.7
Mr. District Attorney	NBC	9:30	16.6
The Great Gildersleeve	NBC	8:30	13.4
The Big Story	NBC	10:00	13.3
Your Song & Mine	CBS	9:00	13.3
Bing Crosby's Philco Radio Time	ABC	10:00	12.6
Mr. Chameleon	CBS	8:00	12.3
You Bet Your Life	ABC	9:30	12.1
Curtain Time	NBC	10:30	11.9
Dr Christian	CBS	8:30	11.7

THE BEACHED BLONDE

When *Amos & Andy* moved their highly rated Lever Brothers show to the CBS Sunday schedule, the shift bumped another Lever hit, *Blondie,* out of its timeslot.

The sitcom starring Penny Singleton and Arthur Lake had enjoyed nine seasons on CBS, eight of them in the annual Top 50. The 1947–48 season was its highest rated yet, finishing 24th in the annual Top 50.

Besides their radio success, Singleton and Lake had starred in two dozen of an eventual 28 *Blondie* movies for Columbia Pictures all based on the immensely popular Chic Young comic strip.

Lever uprooted *Blondie* from its network home and put it into NBC's Wednesday schedule where it floundered, losing 37 percent of its CBS audience.

Singleton left the radio series at mid-season and was replaced by movie star Ann Rutherford.

Blondie's short-lived run on NBC was cancelled at the end of the season and the sitcom left radio.

MATINEE IDOL IN DISGUISE

Blondie lost her 8:00 time period ratings to another blonde, handsome Karl Swenson, star of Frank and Anne Hummert's detective series, *Mr. Chameleon*, on CBS.

Swenson was one of daytime radio's busiest actors — the male lead in the Hummerts' afternoon soap operas *Our Gal Sunday* and *Lorenzo Jones*.

His *Chameleon* sleuth was described as a "master of disguises." To match each disguise that he used to catch the killer du jour, Swenson would employ one of his many character voices and neatly wrap up each week's potboiler in a predictable, formulaic fashion.

The format was virtually identical to the Hummerts' simplistic but successful *Mr. Keen, Tracer of Lost Persons*. Not surprisingly, both programs were sponsored by products from Sterling Drug, the biggest booster of Frank Hummert's philosophy to keep his programs simple and repetitive as not to challenge or confuse even the most backward or casual listeners.

Like *Mr. Keen*, *Mr. Chameleon* was a program that critics loved to hate. It was confounding to them when the show became one of the season's Top Ten programs two years later.

MR. TELEVISION MISSES RADIO

Despite his smash success on NBC-TV's *Texaco Star Theater*, Milton Berle hadn't given up on radio.

Berle's television popularity was so great that Texaco gladly picked up the tab for a radio version of *Texaco Star Theater* which was placed with ABC on Wednesday at 9:00 opposite NBC's *Duffy's Tavern* and the classically themed *Your Song & Mine* starring concert baritone Thomas L. Thomas on CBS.

To insure his radio success, Berle retained much of his cast from the previous two seasons on NBC and beefed up his comedy writing crew with Nat Hiken and brothers Danny and Neil Simon. Berle expressed confidence that he was ready to conquer radio like he had television.

But the show failed. Berle and company could only generate a 9.6 rating, losing the time period to both *Duffy's* comedy and the CBS recitals.

"Mr. Television" left series radio for good — his own good — in June.

ABC'S WEDNESDAY WINS AND WOES

Bing Crosby was in the last of his three-year *Philco Radio Time* contract on ABC.

After two seasons of mediocre ratings with few signs of improvement, it became common knowledge within the industry that Crosby wanted out, while both CBS and NBC wanted him back despite his demand to pre-record his programs.

NBC Vice President Sid Eiges, licking the wounds from his network's loss of its top comedy stars to CBS, told the press, "NBC is negotiating with the greatest name in the entertainment world, an international figure." It was no secret that he was referring to Crosby — who undoubtedly appreciated the accolades but nevertheless signed with CBS.

Ironically, Crosby finished his last season on ABC back in the annual Top 50 as did his lead-in, Groucho Marx's comedy quiz, *You Bet Your Life*.

Then Marx followed Crosby's lead and signed with CBS, too.

A DRAMATIC COMEBACK

For the first time in 14 years CBS won Thursday and did it in dramatic style by winning every time period from 7:00 until 11:00.

The returning *Suspense* topped Al Jolson's *Kraft Music Hall* at 9:00. The mystery anthology scored its highest-ever rating and became one of the year's Top 15 programs. Jolson lost a third of his previous season's audience and left the show in May. The long-running *Music Hall* itself folded four months later.

The FBI in Peace & War beat NBC's *Aldrich Family* at 8:00. *FBI* established itself as a solid Top 25 hit while the family sitcom starring Ezra Stone lost a third of its ratings and barely remained in the season's Top 50.

Mr. Keen, Tracer of Lost Persons outrated Burns and Allen at 8:30 and became one of the season's Top 15 programs. It was George and Gracie's last series for NBC before heading back to CBS for their final Network Radio season and subsequent hit series on CBS-TV.

Casey, Crime Photographer destroyed Dorothy Lamour's *Sealtest Show* at 9:30. *Casey* bounded into the season's Top 20 while the beautiful movie star took the once strong Sealtest half hour into single digit ratings. Sealtest then joined co-owned Kraft Foods and left Network Radio at the end of the season.

Newcomer *Hallmark Playhouse* edged NBC's transplant from CBS, *Screen Guild Players*, at 10:00 and the long running anthology of light drama, *First Nighter*, beat Fred Waring's Pennsylvanians at 10:30.

The CBS publicity department crowed the Thursday triumph while those who scoffed at Bill Paley's concept of 1946 that CBS could beat NBC's hit variety shows with drama were forced to eat crow.

TO CARE ENOUGH TO AIR THE VERY BEST

Kansas City greeting card giant Hallmark entered Network Radio in 1946, taking on sponsorship of the CBS series *Radio Readers Digest*, based on material found in the popular monthly magazine. *Digest* was a respectable program but never reached a season's Top 50 in its five year run.

Hallmark Greeting Cards founder Joyce Hall often said that good quality was good business, leading to his company's slogan, "When you care enough to send the very best."

He was determined to prove it in the programs that carried his company's name too. *Digest* was replaced on CBS in 1948 with *The Hallmark Playhouse*, weekly half hour radio adaptations of classic and popular novels.

British author James Hilton was chosen to host and select the books used in the series. Hilton's credits included the best selling *Goodbye Mr. Chips, Random Harvest* and *Lost Horizon*. Hilton also won a 1942 Oscar for co-writing the screenplay for MGM's *Mrs. Miniver*.

Hallmark Playhouse was the surprise hit of the year. Opposite longtime listener favorite *Screen Guild Players* on NBC, *Hallmark* immediately established itself as one of the season's Top 50 programs and remained on the list for the next five years.

More importantly, *Hallmark Playhouse* set the pattern for broadcast quality that Hallmark Cards would follow in its many years of television programming that succeeded its radio series.

1948–49 Friday Night Top Ten Programs
ABC 4, NBC 4, CBS 2
Average: 12.7

This Is Your FBI	ABC	8:30	14.6
Red Skelton Show	NBC	9:30	14.4
Life of Riley	NBC	10:00	13.9
The Fat Man	ABC	8:00	13.7
Break the Bank	ABC	9:00	12.8
Mr. Ace & Jane aka Easy Aces	CBS	8:30	12.2
Eddie Cantor Show	NBC	9:00	11.7
The Lone Ranger	ABC	7:30	11.7
Ford Theater	CBS	9:00	11.3
Jimmy Durante Show	NBC	8:30	10.3

FRIDAY'S FLIPS AND FLOPS

Listening tastes were changing and Friday was in turnover.

Six of the previous season's most popular shows of the night were gone.

Illness forced Fanny Brice's *Baby Snooks* off the air for a year. *People Are Funny* was moved to Tuesday. *Waltz Time* was cancelled after its best rating and ranking in 14 seasons. The same fate was suffered by *It Pays to Be Ignorant* after five seasons. *The Adventures of the Thin Man* and *Can You Top This?* were both relegated to Mutual's home for aging programs.

Only ABC held steady with its four proven winners — three low cost dramas and a big money quiz.

In response to the upstart ABC, NBC programmed what would have been an unbeatable comedy lineup just a few seasons earlier — Eddie Cantor, Red Skelton and Jimmy Durante plus William Bendix in *The Life of Riley*. But they simply weren't the drawing cards they once were.

Television, however, would be a different story for all four.

EASY DOES IT — FINALLY

One fascinating exception to Friday's demise of veteran comics was *Easy Aces* — identified during its final season on the air as *Mr. Ace & Jane*. Goodman and Jane Ace had logged twelve multi-network seasons when CBS brought them back after a three year absence for an encore.

Jane continued to earn her title, the Queen of Malapropisms, uttering such lines as, "We're insufferable friends," or, "Familiarity breeds attempt," or, "We're all cremated equal."

Goodman portrayed her patient and long suffering husband. Although he actually wrote her material, he muttered asides to the lis-

tener in response to her lines like, "Isn't that awful?"

Easy Aces was quiet little program from which the industry didn't expect much. The Aces had the last laugh — finishing for the first time ever in a night's Top Ten and the season's Top 50.

Nevertheless, General Foods cancelled *Easy Aces* at mid-season to make way for a new sitcom from which great things *were* expected — *My Favorite Husband* starring Lucille Ball.

Lucy's radio predecessor to her television classic could only score half of *Easy Aces'* ratings.

As Jane might have said of the network and sponsor that cancelled her show, "You certainly hit the nail on the thumb that time!"

ANOTHER SHOT AT FORD'S THEATER

Ford Motors had decided in 1947 to pursue prestige with *The Ford Theater*, a late Sunday afternoon hour comparable to U.S. Steel's successful Sunday night anthology, *Theater Guild on the Air*. NBC and the auto maker boasted that no expense would be spared to bring adaptations of the finest Broadway plays to listeners, interpreted through the talents of radio's best actors. And Ford delivered. Critics agreed that the program was highly commendable.

Unfortunately, listeners far preferred the cheap thrills offered by *The Shadow* on Mutual and ABC's *Counterspy*. Ford Theater was destroyed in the ratings and the automaker went back to the drawing board.

Following *Lux Radio Theater's* successful lead of 1935, Ford abandoned New York for Hollywood, moved to CBS and opened the 1948–49 season with a carbon copy of radio's most popular program: hour-long adaptations of popular films performed by Hollywood's biggest stars.

The new *Ford Theater* opened with a flourish but finished third in its time period behind ABC's *Break the Bank* and Eddie Cantor on NBC.

It became painfully obvious that Americans didn't *listen* to the movies on Friday night — they *went* to the movies on Friday night.

The program was cancelled at the end of the season.

1948–49 Saturday Night Top Ten Programs
NBC 5, CBS 4, MBS 1
Average: 11.3

A Day in the Life of Dennis Day	NBC	10:00	14.6
Judy Canova Show	NBC	9:30	13.9
Your Hit Parade	NBC	9:00	13.8
Truth or Conse-quences	NBC	8:30	13.7
Grand Ole Opry	NBC	10:30	11.0
Vaughn Monroe's Camel Caravan	CBS	7:30	10.6
Gangbusters	CBS	9:00	9.6
Gene Autry's Melody Ranch	CBS	8:00	9.1
Spike Jones' Spot-light Revue	CBS	7:00	8.9
Twenty Questions	MBS	8:00	7.9

SATURDAY NIGHT BECOMES DAY TIME

A major change in its Saturday schedule didn't dislodge NBC from the Top Five positions.

Missing after eleven seasons and ten Top 50 finishes, Kay Kyser was gone from NBC and prime time radio with Colgate's cancellation. Kyser's *Kollege of Musical Knowledge* was picked up in November by Pillsbury for a seven month run on ABC's weekday schedule where it finished a poor second to NBC's long running soap operas, *Backstage Wife* and *Stella Dallas*.

To replace Kyser, Colgate moved *A Day in the Life of Dennis Day* from NBC's Wednesday schedule to Saturday and paired the singer's sitcom with its successful *Judy Canova Show*. As a result, Day and Canova rose to the top of Saturday's ratings.

The big loser in Saturday's situation was *Truth or Consequences*. The FCC's far-fetched lottery edict prohibiting giveaways spooked Ralph Edwards and sponsor Procter & Gamble into abandoning the secret identity contests that had scored big ratings and raised millions for charity. The stunt show lost nearly 40 percent of its audience, falling from sixth to 30th in the season's rankings.

A BANG UP SATURDAY ON CBS

CBS recovered from its 1947–48 Saturday shutout by placing four programs in Saturday's Top Ten. Among them was the gunshot-filled *Gangbusters*, which the network lifted from ABC at mid-season for Procter & Gamble sponsorship.

Another was the wildest music show ever broadcast, hosted by a dead-panned bandleader dressed in a clownish suit who addressed his audience as, "Music lovers."

By his late 20s Spike Jones was regarded as one of the best studio drummers in radio, performing anonymously, but profitably, in John Scott Trotter's *Kraft Music Hall* orchestra and Billy Mills' *Fibber McGee & Molly* band. He was also known among his peers as a comedian — just like his fellow bandsman, trombonist Jerry Colonna.

Jones' big break came in 1942 when he gathered a group of studio players and recorded *Der Fuehrer's Face* for RCA's Bluebird label. The anti–Nazi novelty became an instant hit and led to the formation of Spike Jones' "City Slickers"— a group of highly skilled musicians who doubled on washboards, cowbells, auto horns, sirens, pistols filled with blanks and most anything else that could lead to musical mayhem.

Two years on the Bob Burns Show followed along with a string hit records — all parodies of familiar classical and popular songs — most notably *The William Tell Overture* and *Cocktails for Two* — plus the holiday novelty *All I Want for Christmas Is My Two Front Teeth* featuring the falsetto voice of trumpeter George Rock.

Coca-Cola and CBS gave Jones his own Friday timeslot in the 1947–48 season. The show was moved briefly to Sunday at 6:30 in January 1949 and two months later to Saturday at 7:00 — opposite the NBC Symphony under the direction of Arturo Toscanini.

Spike Jones won the time period.

THE FAMILY THAT PLAYS TOGETHER...

Mutual's *Twenty Questions* was a family game in the truest sense of the term.

It was brought to radio by WOR/Mutual newsman Fred VanDeven-ter and played every Saturday night by VanDeventer, his wife Florence, their teenage son Bobby, and sometimes their college age daughter, Nancy. The show's producer, Herb Polesie, and a celebrity guest filled out the weekly panel.

Twenty Questions was an old parlor game of deduction. Its object was to identify an object — which could be anything or anyone — within 20 questions answered "yes" or "no" by the show's host, Mutual sportscaster Bill Slater. The only clue given panelists was whether the mystery subject was animal, vegetable, mineral or a combination of the elements.

Listeners nominated subjects to be identified for prizes — pocket cigarette lighters from sponsor Ronson Lighters. Silver plated table lighters awarded to those which stumped the panel — which was seldom.

In one episode they identified "Lincoln, Nebraska" in nine questions, "Jimmy Valentine" in 13, "A Dentist's Chair" in 14, "The Ice Cream in Pie à la Mode" in 15, but missed "Pete" in "Oh, for Pete's Sake."

The VanDeventer family and Polesi displayed quick wit and humor remindful of *Information Please*, yet the game and subject matter were within the grasp of average listeners whose response kept *Twenty Questions* a fixture on Mutual's Saturday night schedule for eight years.

MULTIPLES RUN OUT OF THE MONEY

For the first time and only time, no Multiple Run program finished among the season's Top 50.

Nevertheless, CBS continued to place its entire 6:45 to 8:00 block in the Multiple Runs' Top Ten.

Serial sitcom *Beulah* became the first CBS program in six seasons to beat NBC's *Chesterfield Supper Club* and win prime time's keynote quarter hour at 7:00.

ABC set new marks for its early evening programming by placing both of its alternating half-hour adventure dramas in the Multiple Run Top Ten. *The Lone Ranger* was in the second of its three year run topping the list. *Counterspy*, a crime

1948–49 Top Ten Multiple Run Programs
CBS 5, NBC 3, ABC 2
Average: 8.9

The Lone Ranger	M,W,F	ABC	7:30	11.7
Beulah*	M–F	CBS	7:00	10.0
Jack Smith Show*	M–F	CBS	7:15	9.8
Club 15*	M–F	CBS	7:30	9.5
Counterspy	Tu,Th	ABC	7:30	9.4
Edward R Murrow News*	M–F	CBS	7:45	9.0
Lowell Thomas News*	M–F	CBS	6:45	8.4
Chesterfield Supper Club*	M–F	NBC	7:00	8.3
Morgan Beatty News of the World*	M–F	NBC	7:15	6.8
HV Kaltenborn & Richard Harkness News*	M–F	NBC	7:45	6.5

*Monday–Friday Strip Shows

fighter from a different era, filled the 7:30 timeslot on Tuesday and Thursday.

FROM SUPER SPY TO SOAPER STAR

Radio actor Don MacLaughlin was 35 when he was cast as David Harding, *Counterspy*, in 1942. It turned out to be one of the steadiest jobs in Network Radio—he held it for 15 years. *Counterspy* was producer Phillips H. Lord's interpretation of the government agents fighting espionage genre—it predated both *The FBI in Peace & War* and *This Is Your FBI* by several years.

The purely fictional *Counterspy* was supposed to be to G-Men what Lord's *Gangbusters* was to local police. MacLaughlin had played various roles in *Gangbusters* melodramas since the show's inception.

Counterspy bounced around the Blue/ABC prime time and Sunday afternoon schedules for seven seasons before achieving its highest ratings on the network in the two years when it alternated with *The Lone Ranger* at 7:30 under Pepsi Cola sponsorship.

Pepsi took the show to NBC's Thursday schedule in 1950 and Gulf Oil took over its sponsorship the following season. But after two years of disappointing ratings *Counterspy* was relegated to NBC's Sunday afternoon schedule and offered to participating sponsors.

Counterspy's final stop was Mutual in 1953 where it was programmed in various time periods under participating and co-op sponsorship for four and a half years.

MacLaughlin's tour of duty with the fictional government crime

fighting unit ended in 1957, but he was busier than ever. A year earlier he originated the role of lawyer Chris Hughes on CBS-TV's *As the World Turns*—a part he played for 32 years until his death in 1986 at age 78.

Don MacLaughlin knew how to keep a job.

HENRY'S LEADS TURN TO LEAD

Veteran West Coast newsman Bill Henry had reported the 8:55 *Johns-Manville News* strip on CBS since 1943 when Cecil Brown walked out in a dispute over the network's editorial policy. Henry had averaged double digit ratings in the timeslot and constantly placed in the Multiple Runs' Top Ten.

But interest in news had waned since the end of World War II — evidenced by the absence of any newscasts in the season's Top Five Multiple Run programs. It was the first time that had ever happened.

CBS anticipated the drop-off and discontinued Henry's popular news strip in August 1948. His *Johns-Manville News* immediately began a new five year run on Mutual, but not to the 11.7 rating he had enjoyed on CBS with lead-in's provided by the likes of Arthur Godfrey and *Mr. Keen*.

His first season on Mutual averaged a 2.6 rating — down 80 percent.

TOP 50 PROGRAMS—1948–49
NBC 23, CBS 18, ABC 9
Average Rating: 15.2, Median: 14.4
37,623,000 Radio Homes / 94.2% Coverage of U.S. Homes / One Rating Point = 376,230 Homes
Sources: .A. C Nielsen Radio Index Serv, Sep 1948 — Dec 1948
& C.E. Hooper Semi-Monthly Reports, Jan 1949 — June 1949
Total Programs Rated, 6–11 PM: 164
Programs Rated 13 Weeks & Ranked: 148

		Program	Rtg	Type	Sponsor	Day	Time	Lgth	Net
1	1	Lux Radio Theater/William Keighley	25.5	DA	Lux Soap	Mon	9:00	60	CBS
2	2	Fibber McGee & Molly	23.5	SC	Johnson Wax	Tue	9:30	30	NBC
3	10	Jack Benny Program	22.9	SC	Lucky Strike Cigarettes	Sun	7:00	30	CBS 1
4	30	Walter Winchell's Journal	21.7	NC	Kaiser-Frazer Autos	Sun	9:00	15	ABC 2
5t	10	Arthur Godfrey's Talent Scouts	20.1	TC	Lipton Tea	Mon	8:30	30	CBS
5t	4	Edgar Bergen & Charlie McCarthy	20.1	CV	Chase & Sanborn Coffee	Sun	8:00	30	NBC
7	5	Bob Hope Show	19.8	CV	Swan Soap	Tue	9:00	30	NBC
8	8	My Friend Irma/Marie Wilson	19.5	SC	Pepsodent Toothpaste	Mon	10:00	30	CBS
9t	3	Amos & Andy	17.1	SC	Rinso Laundry Soap	Sun	7:30	30	CBS
9t	33	People Are Funny/Art Linkletter	17.1	APS	Raleigh Cigarettes	Tue	10:30	30	NBC
11	15	Duffy's Tavern/Ed Gardner	16.7	SC	Vitalis & Trushay	Wed	9:00	30	NBC
12	12	Mister District Attorney/Jay Jostyn	16.6	DCC	Ipana & Sal Hepatica	Wed	9:30	30	NBC
13t	19	A Date with Judy/Louise Erickson	16.4	SC	Tums Antacid	Tue	8:30	30	NBC

	Program	Rtg	Type	Sponsor	Day	Time	Lgth	Net
13t *50*	Suspense	16.4	DA	Autolite Spark Plugs	Thu	9:00	30	CBS
15 *33*	Mr Keen/Bennett Kilpack	16.0	DCC	Kolynos Toothpaste	Thu	8:30	30	CBS
16 *44*	Casey Crime Photographer	15.7	DCC	Toni Home Permanents	Thu	9:30	30	CBS
17 *9*	Phil Harris & Alice Faye	15.4	SC	Rexall Drug Stores	Sun	7:30	30	NBC
18t *N*	Mystery Theater	15.2	DCC	Bayer Aspirin	Tue	8:00	30	CBS
18t *N*	Stop The Music/Bert Parks	15.2	APQ	Participating Sponsors	Sun	8:00	60	ABC
20 *22*	Inner Sanctum	15.0	DA	Bromo Seltzer	Mon	8:00	30	CBS
21 *17*	Big Town/Ed Pawley	14.8	DCC	Lifebuoy Soap	Tue	10:00	30	NBC
22t *36*	A Day in the Life of Dennis Day	14.6	SC	Palmolive Soap	Sat	10:00	30	NBC
22t *42*	The FBI in Peace & War	14.6	DCC	Lava Hand Soap	Thu	8:00	30	CBS
22t *25*	This Is Your FBI	14.6	DCC	Equitable Life Insurance	Fri	8:30	30	ABC
25 *13*	Red Skelton Show	14.4	CV	Raleigh Cigarettes	Fri	9:30	30	NBC
26 *55*	Bob Hawk Show	14.1	APQ	Camel Cigarettes	Mon	10:30	30	CBS
27t *28*	Judy Canova Show	13.9	CV	Halo Shampoo	Sat	9:30	30	NBC
27t *14*	Life of Riley/William Bendix	13.9	SC	Prell Shampoo	Fri	10:00	30	NBC
29 *15*	Your Hit Parade/Frank Sinatra	13.8	MP	Lucky Strike Cigarettes	Sat	9:00	30	NBC
30t *42*	The Fat Man/J Scott Smart	13.7	DCC	Pepto Bismol	Fri	8:00	30	ABC
30t *31*	Mr & Mrs North/JoeCurtin, Alice Frost	13.7	DCC	Halo Shampoo	Tue	8:30	30	CBS
30t *6*	Truth or Consequences/ Ralph Edwards	13.7	APS	Duz Laundry Soap	Sat	8:30	30	NBC
33 *18*	Great Gildersleeve/Hal Peary	13.4	SC	Parkay Margarine	Wed	8:30	30	NBC
34t *36*	The Big Story	13.3	DA	Pall Mall Cigarettes	Wed	10:00	30	NBC
34t *76*	Louella Parsons Hollywood News	13.3	NC	Jergens Lotion	Sun	9:15	15	ABC
34t *N*	Your Song & Mine/Thomas L Thomas	13.3	MST	Borden Dairies	Wed	9:00	30	CBS
37 *25*	Burns & Allen Show	13.0	SC	Maxwell House Coffee	Thu	8:30	30	NBC
38t *20*	Al Jolson Kraft Music Hall	12.8	MV	Kraft Cheese	Thu	9:00	30	NBC
38t *36*	Break The Bank/Bert Parks	12.8	APQ	Ipana/Sal Hepatica	Fri	9:00	30	ABC
40t *27*	Adventures of Sam Spade/H Duff	12.6	DCC	Wildroot Cream Oil	Sun	8:00	30	CBS
40t *62*	Bing Crosby Philco Radio Time	12.6	MV	Philco Radios & Televisions	Wed	10:00	30	ABC
42t *6*	Fred Allen Show	12.5	CV	Ford Motors	Sun	8:00	30	NBC 3
42t *31*	Manhattan Merry Go Round	12.5	MP	Dr Lyons Tooth Powder	Sun	9:00	30	NBC
44 *N*	Mr Chameleon/Karl Swenson	12.3	DCC	Bayer Aspirin	Wed	8:00	30	CBS
45 *N*	Mr Ace & Jane (Easy Aces)	12.2	SC	Sanka Coffee	Fri	8:30	30	CBS
46t *47*	Theater Guild on the Air	12.1	DA	US Steel	Sun	9:30	60	ABC
46t *72*	You Bet Your Life/Groucho Marx	12.1	APQ	Elgin-American Costume Jwlry	Wed	9:30	30	ABC
48 *53*	Hallmark Playhouse	12.0	DA	Hallmark Cards	Thu	10:00	30	CBS
49t *23*	Aldrich Family/Ezra Stone	11.9	SC	Grapenuts Cereal & Jello	Thu	8:00	30	NBC
49t *76*	Curtain Time	11.9	DA	Mars Candy	Wed	10:30	30	NBC

New & Returning Top 50 Programs Underscored.

1	Jack Benny Program			Oct–Dec	Lucky Strike Cigarettes	Sun	7:00	30	NBC
2	Walter Winchell			Sep–Dec	Jergens Lotion	Sun	9:30	15	ABC
3	Fred Allen Show			Oct–Dec	Ford Motors	Sun	8:30	30	NBC

Key: API — Audience Participation/Interviews   DCC — Drama/Continuing Characters   MV — Music/Variety Show
APQ — Audience Participation/Quiz   MC — Music/Classical, Semi-Classical   NC — News, Commentary
APS — Audience Participation/Stunts   MP — Music/Popular, Contemporary   SC — Situation Comedy
CV — Comedy/Variety Show   MSP — Music/Specialty, Ethnic   SP — Sports
DA — Dramatic Anthology   MST — Music/Standard, Traditional   TC — Talent Competition

1948–49 Top 50 Favorite Formats

	Programs	Pct
Comedy — Variety & Situation	18	36%
Drama — Anthology & Continuing	18	36%
Music — All Categories	6	12%
Audience Participation — All Categories	6	12%
News/Commentary	2	4%

1948–49 Monthly Winners

Sep	Lux Radio Theater	22.2	Feb	Walter Winchell's Journal	26.5
Oct	Lux Radio Theate	28.6	Mar	Walter Winchell's Journal	26.8
Nov	Lux Radio Theater	33.2	Apr	Lux Radio Theater	23.7
Dec	Lux Radio Theater	32.3	May	Lux Radio Theater	22.0
Jan	Jack Benny Program		Jun	Walter Winchell's Journal	14.8
	& Walter Winchell's Journal	28.3			

22

The 1949–50 Network Season

Announcer: Ladies, what's your complexion problem?

LADY 1: My skin's so dingy...

LADY 2: Mine's oily...

LADY 3: My skin is dull and coarse looking.

Announcer: For a lovelier complexion, stop improper cleansing! Instead, use Palmolive Soap the way doctors advise. Leading skin specialists have proved the Palmolive Plan, using nothing but Palmolive Soap, can bring you a fresher, brighter complexion regardless of age, condition of skin or previous beauty care. Now here's what these doctors advise...

LADY 1: Wash your face with Palmolive Soap ... massaging for one minute with Palmolive's soft, lovely lather. This cleansing massage brings your skin Palmolive Soap's full, beautifying effect. Rinse. Do this three times a day for fourteen days. It's that simple!

Announcer: Remember, 36 doctors, leading skin specialists, advised this for 1, 285 women with all types of skin and proved this plan using Palmolive alone ... nothing else ... really works for two out of three. So, for a lovelier complexion, forget all other beauty care. Instead, do as these doctors advise. Use Palmolive for a fresher, brighter complexion!

WHAT GOES UP...

Network Radio revenues dropped for the first time since 1933.

Competition for the broadcast advertising dollar had become keener with over 2,600 AM and FM stations vying for audience and revenues. The United States spent the first ten months of 1949 in a recession which contributed to the radio industry's lowest revenue growth rate in eleven years.

But at least it grew, which was more than the networks could say.

Television was becoming a serious threat to prime time Network Radio.

Over a hundred TV stations were on the air, all siphoning off radio's nighttime audience. Television's growing impact helped drive radio's Top 50 program average rating down 30 percent in two seasons to its lowest level since 1936–37.

When the season ended and audience statistics were tallied, only two Network Radio shows remained with ratings in the 20s — CBS's Jack Benny on Sunday and *Lux Radio Theater* on Monday. Just two years earlier, 15 programs had averaged a season's rating of 20.0 or better.

Meanwhile, the television networks reported a combined income of 29.4 million dollars *(279.5 Mil)*.

But advertisers were learning that television production costs

were much greater than radio. The extra money had to come from somewhere — and radio budgets were the likely source.

STATUS QUOTE

NBC reacted defiantly to the loss of its major comedy stars — Jack Benny, Edgar Bergen, Red Skelton, Burns and Allen and *Amos & Andy*— to CBS.

Time magazine reported that NBC Executive Vice President Charles Denny flatly told his network's affiliates in 1949 that NBC would remain the Number One network. "It has the money and the resources to back up its plans," he said, "And above all it has the resolve to use its money, its experience and its every effort for that purpose."

President Nils Trammell told the same group, "Radio can't be satisfied indefinitely with the same material, the same performers and the same programs."

Vice President of Programs Sid Eiges added, "We have new programs in the works — new shows of all kinds, including comedy."

That said, it was announced that NBC had signed new multi-year contracts with Bob Hope, *Fibber McGee & Molly*, *Duffy's Tavern* and Phil Harris and Alice Faye — none of whom were hardly new to radio.

All four programs suffered significant audience losses in the 1949–50 season and CBS dominated the season's Top 50 for the first time in nine years.

NBC never regained its stature as America's most popular radio network.

OLD FRIENDS IN NEW NEIGHBORHOODS

Radio listeners had cause for confusion —15 prime time programs switched networks for the new season.

1949–50 Season Scoreboard
Mid-season Totals, December 1949

		Compared to Year Earlier	
Total Radio Homes	39.3 Mil	+1.70 Mil	+4.5%
Total Auto Radios	14.0 Mil	+3.0 Mil	+27.2%
Total AM Radio Stations	1,912	+291	+18.0%
Total Radio Network Affiliates	1,132	+28	+2.5%
1949 Radio Revenues	571.0 Mil	+9.4 Mil	+1.7%
1949 Radio Network Revenues	203.0 Mil	(7.6 Mil)	(3.6%)
Network Share	35.5%		(2.0%)
Total TV Homes	3.4 Mil	+2.5 Mil	+261.7%
Total TV Stations	101	+49	+94.2%
Total FM Stations	727	+254	+53.7%

CBS took Bing Crosby and Groucho Marx from ABC to add to its newly acquired Edgar Bergen and Charlie McCarthy, Red Skelton, Burns and Allen, *Horace Heidt's Youth Opportunity Program* and *Carnation Contented Hour* from NBC.

Only Crosby, Marx and Heidt gained audience in their first CBS season.

ABC picked up *The Adventures of Ozzie & Harriet*, *A Date with Judy*, *Blondie* and *Dr. IQ*, all from NBC.

All lost ratings in the switch.

The best NBC could do in the shuffle was add *Break the Bank*, *Theater Guild on the Air* and *The Railroad Hour* from ABC, plus *The Adventures of Sam Spade* and *We the People* from CBS.

All lost audience in their jump to NBC.

NBC also landed Fanny Brice's *Baby Snooks* sitcom, last heard on CBS before the 57-year-old star's 18 month sabbatical for health reasons.

To Air on the Side of Caution

The Top 50 programs of the season were evidence of network and sponsor reluctance to invest in new radio efforts. Only two "new" programs made the list — Fanny Brice's *Baby Snooks*, returning to NBC after a season off the air and *Life with Luigi*, a sitcom that CBS had broadcast for over a year in search of a sponsor before landing Wrigley Gum which resulted in the show's first appearance in the ratings.

The other seven newcomers to the season's Top 50 were all veteran programs and personalities with a range of five to 16 years' experience on the air. All had slipped out of the Top 50 for one or more seasons.

MGM Lion Down on Radio

Against the tide of the networks' diminished original programming, Metro-Goldwyn-Mayer jumped into radio with four new transcribed series intended for syndication.

The movie studio led with *MGM's Musical Comedy Theater*, an hour long anthology similar to *Lux Radio Theater* featuring adaptations of its past film hits and starring its contract players.

MGM followed with three half-hour shows based on its low-budget but highly popular and profitable movie series, *Dr. Kildare*, *The Hardy Family* and *Maisie*. To insure success of the programs, each series was headlined by their movies' continuing stars — Lew Ayres and Lionel Barrymore of *Kildare*, Mickey Rooney and Lewis Stone as Andy Hardy and his father, and Ann Sothern reprised her title role in *The Adventures of Maisie*.

After initial broadcast on the studio's WMGM/New York (formerly and subsequently known as WHN), the programs were put into syndication. Sales to individual stations were dismal in the recessionary year when broadcast advertising revenues were flat.

MGM finally farmed out the programs to Mutual where, despite their high production values, they found little audience acceptance.

The movie studio abandoned its radio projects in 1952 and reluctantly turned its attention to the production of filmed television programming.

Ford Motors into 1950

Ford Motors began January with one of the most unique time buys in Network Radio history.

To push its 1950 models to the country emerging from a recession, Ford bought the sponsorship of 23 sustaining programs on CBS and Mutual *for two weeks*. Among the familiar titles were *Can You Top This*, *Blondie*, *Lum & Abner*, *Escape*, *The Saint*, *Hawaii Calls*, *Philip Marlow* and *Peter Salem*.

The automaker repeated the stunt later in the month with five otherwise sustaining television programs.

The month-long blitz, carrying a combined cost of $500,000 *(4.8 Mil)*, was an early example of an advertiser buying prime time Network Radio and TV like local media — to specifically coordinate with marketing campaigns of limited duration. It was a sign of things to come as advertisers began to abandon sponsorships of entire programs and the networks reacted by offering time in increments of 30 and 60 second spots.

An F for Effort

The FCC pushed ahead with its proposed limits on giveaway and quiz shows with a year of hearings that most broadcasters considered a kangaroo court.

The commission subsequently ruled that effective on October 1, 1949, any broadcast game that offered: (1) A *Prize*, and (2) Any degree of *Chance* involved in winning the prize, and (3) Any *Consideration* required from a contestant to become eligible to win the prize, constituted a *Lottery* and was therefore illegal.

Nobody argued with that classic and accepted definition of a lottery — as far as it went.

It was the commission's new definition of *consideration* that was objectionable. The term originally meant money changing hands. The FCC ruled that any *effort* on the part of a contestant — even the requirement of listening to a specific program — would henceforth be ruled *consideration*.

ABC took the lead for the networks and filed suit against the ruling, specifically citing the commission's far-fetched definition of *consideration*. A temporary injunction was obtained to stall the edict while the broadcasters prepared to battle with the FCC in court.

With the FCC enjoined from stopping them, 16 prime time giveaway and quiz shows were rated and ranked during the 1949–50 season. Six reached the in the season's Top 50.

The networks' fight with the commission dragged on for four years, finally working its way up to the U.S. Supreme Court where the FCC lost an embarrassing unanimous verdict.

It was a hollow victory for Network Radio. By that time most of the giveaways had lost their popularity and had left the air.

"Stop Staring at Your Radio!"

That command was the advertising slogan used by Earl "Mad Man" Muntz to sell his low-cost, big picture *(16 inch)*, television sets.

It was also the message that newly installed NBC-TV chief Pat Weaver sent to NBC's radio listeners.

Both men were marketing geniuses and both had the same motive — to sell television sets.

Muntz — a longtime Los Angeles car dealer whose antics and name were made famous by Hollywood-based *radio* comedians — marketed his stripped-down television sets designed for metropolitan areas where video signals were strong. He wanted a piece of the action dominated by RCA, Admiral, Philco and Motorola who were selling over 2,000 new television sets a day.

Weaver — a former American Tobacco and Young & Rubicam advertising executive — was charged by RCA to make television set ownership as desirable as possible and as quickly as possible. He moved quickly and NBC became the first network to fully exploit radio's potential as an attractive programming source for television and a lure for new viewers.

NBC-TV adapted or simulcast over a dozen familiar Network Radio titles for television in the 1949–50 season — including the first video version of *The Life of Riley*, starring an obscure comic actor in the title role, Jackie Gleason.

Besides the *Riley* sitcom, Weaver's 1949–50 NBC-TV schedule opened with video versions of *The Aldrich Family*, *The Big Story*, *Chesterfield Supper Club*, *Leave It to the Girls*, *Lights Out*, *Meet the Press*, *The Original Amateur Hour*, *The Quiz Kids* and *We the People*.

In addition, NBC simulcast three of its Network Radio series — *The Voice of Firestone*, *Cities Service Band of America* and *Break the Bank*, plus a video version of ABC's Friday night boxing bouts, *The Gillette Cavalcade of Sports*.

The 17 programs amounted to 38 percent of NBC-TV's 25½ hours of prime time service in 1949–50. Weaver's use of familiar radio properties to fill his television schedule would spread to ABC and CBS the following season.

CBS scheduled only five radio-to-television conversions in 1949–50. It continued to simulcast

Arthur Godfrey's Talent Scouts, and debuted television versions of *The Goldbergs* and *Suspense*. It also packaged radio veterans Ed Wynn and Fred Waring in new television formats.

ABC telecast video versions of *Stop the Music* and *Blind Date* while the small DuMont network picked up *Famous Jury Trials* and *The Fishing & Hunting Club of the Air*.

Programs made popular on radio were responsible for 15 hours of the television networks' 65½ hours of weekly prime time programming in the 1949–50 season.

Boxing, wrestling and Roller Derby accounted for 14 hours.

THE MONTHLIES

For only the second time since 1932, CBS had the winning program of every month.

Jack Benny and *Lux Radio Theater* battled for first place for nine months and a newcomer slipped in on the tenth.

Lux won September, October, November, March, April and May. Benny turned in the highest ratings for December, January and February. Both shows went on an early summer vacation which allowed Marie Wilson's sitcom, *My Friend Irma*, to take first place in June with a mediocre 12.1 rating.

1949–50 Sunday Night Top Ten Programs
CBS 6, ABC 2, NBC 2
Average: 13.6

Jack Benny Program	CBS	7:00	20.7
Walter Winchell's Journal	ABC	9:00	16.3
Edgar Bergen & Charlie McCarthy	CBS	8:00	16.0
Amos & Andy	CBS	7:30	15.7
Red Skelton Show	CBS	8:30	13.5
Horace Heidt Youth Opportunity Program	CBS	9:30	12.2
Our Miss Brooks	CBS	6:30	11.0
Take It or Leave It	NBC	10:00	10.9
Louella Parsons Hollywood News	ABC	9:15	10.1
Theater Guild on the Air	NBC	8:30	9.8

HAIL TO THE THIEF!

Bill Paley's broad smile was no longer confined to broadcasting

trade journals and Manhattan society pages. The CBS Chairman's grin had spread to the front pages of newspapers and weekly news magazines where he was hailed as "Radio's Robin Hood" — stealing headline talent from the powerful NBC for his "underdog" network.

CBS dominated Sunday's Top Ten for the first time in a dozen years and did it with programs developed on NBC.

Amos & Andy were the first to succumb to Paley's capital gains lure in 1947.

Then Jack Benny jumped midway in the 1948–49 season.

By the 1949–50 season, Edgar Bergen, Red Skelton and Horace Heidt's *Youth Opportunity Program* talent show were all Sunday newcomers on CBS from NBC.

Only Eve Arden's sitcom, *Our Miss Brooks*, was a CBS original in the network's Sunday lineup.

All six were among Sunday's Top Ten and the season's Top 40 programs.

AN APPLE FOR EVE THE TEACHER

Eve Arden was 40 in 1948 and had plugged along in radio just as she had in the movies — mostly in supporting roles to the stars. She won an Academy Award nomination as Best Supporting Actress for her role in 1945's *Mildred Pierce*.

The beautiful redhead had three seasons as co-star of NBC's *Sealtest Village Store* when she was offered the lead in the CBS sitcom, *Our Miss Brooks*. She was considered ideal for the title role of the lovesick high school English teacher with a warm heart, sharp wit and snappy comebacks.

Arden's only condition to do the show was that it be pre-recorded so she wouldn't be away from her young children at night. CBS and sponsor Colgate agreed to break the once inviolate network ban against transcribed shows.

Our Miss Brooks debuted by transcription on the CBS Monday schedule in July 1948 as a summer replacement for half of *Lux Radio Theater's* time period. Two months later the show took its first full season spot on the network at 9:30 on Sundays. But 1948–49 was an uphill season for the sitcom as it suffered from the weak lead-in provided by actress Helen Hayes' dramatic anthology series, *The Electric Theater.*

With the revamped CBS Sunday schedule of 1949–50, *Our Miss Brooks* was moved back to 6:30 where it became the lead-in to Jack Benny. The sitcom broke into Sunday's Top Ten and the season's Top 50, beginning its four year climb to the annual Top Ten among all prime time programs.

WHAT'S MISSING?

Five programs from the Sunday Top Ten of the previous season were gone from the 1949–50 list.

Without Jack Benny's lead-in, Phil Harris and Alice Faye lost nearly 40 percent of their NBC audience.

Edgar Bergen and Red Skelton did what the FCC couldn't do — they shut down ABC's *Stop the Music.* The giveaway show lost 40 percent of its ratings against the CBS tandem of comedians, dropping from 18th to 57th place in the season's rankings.

NBC acquired *The Adventures of Sam Spade* from CBS and scheduled it opposite Bergen. The private eye series lost 25 percent of its audience and sank into single digit ratings.

NBC lost Fred Allen to retirement and *Manhattan Merry Go Round* was cancelled after its 16 years of sponsorship by Sterling Drug's Dr. Lyons Tooth Powder...

Another missing Sunday star was Garry Moore, who was replaced as host of NBC's *Take It or Leave It* by Eddie Cantor. Cantor found himself out of place as an ad-libbing quiz master, bantering with contestants. He left at the end of the season while Moore moved into an hour long weekday variety show on CBS and eventually became one of the network's most enduring prime time television personalities.

HOLLYWOOD CRAWLING

NBC wasn't going to take the loss of Jack Benny lying down — it was determined to get even.

To do the job the network called in Louis Cowan, whose *Stop the Music* was credited with driving

NBC's Fred Allen off the air earlier in the year. The king of giveaways was commissioned to design a new show with glamour, excitement, polish and prizes that would make Benny sorry he ever jumped to CBS.

Hollywood Calling had the glamour of Hollywood guest stars hosted by veteran actor George Murphy, the excitement of a game for listeners at home, the polish of a 35 piece orchestra and chorus, and a jackpot of prizes worth over $30,000 ($285,200).

What it didn't have was listeners.

The network and sponsor Gruen Watches debuted the hour-long production on Sundays at 6:30 in mid–July — designed to build an audience during Benny's summer vacation.

But neither NBC nor Cowan had anticipated the overkill that some 30 combined daytime and prime time network quiz and giveaway shows had created.

Hollywood Calling was an expensive flop. When it was cancelled, the lavish giveaway show crawled in with a December rating of 4.2.

Jack Benny, who gave his listeners nothing but laughs, scored a 25.4 during the same month.

A SUDDEN DEATH LOSS

Carnation's *Contented Hour* hadn't pulled a double digit rating since 1935. Yet it had been a constant source of NBC revenue for 18 years. With singing host Buddy Clark, musical guest stars and Percy Faith's large studio orchestra, it was a well produced and profitable half hour.

CBS pursued the program as an extra gotcha to the NBC balance sheet and convinced the evaporated milk company to switch networks for the 1949–50 season.

Contented Hour was scheduled to debut on CBS at 10:00 on Sunday, October 2.

But on the evening of Saturday, October 1st, Buddy Clark, 37, was killed in a private plane crash when returning to Los Angeles from the Stanford-Michigan football game at Palto Alto. The first CBS broadcast of the show was cancelled.

Singers Tony Martin and Jo Stafford took over *Contented Hour* the

following week. During the following months, Doris Day, Dick Haymes and Jack Smith were among a parade of singers who appeared on the show. Stafford became its permanent hostess in March, co-starring with Haymes for the rest of the season.

Contented Hour finished the season with a 6.8 rating, nearly 40 percent less than the audience of Eddie Cantor's *Take It or Leave It* on NBC. But with Jo Stafford as its star, the show began to build a pop music fan following that resulted in a Top 50 finish two years later.

1949–50 Monday Night Top Ten Programs
CBS 8, ABC 1. NBC 1
Average: 12.9

Lux Radio Theater	CBS	9:00	22.3
Arthur Godfrey's	CBS	8:30	18.4
Talent Scouts			
My Friend Irma	CBS	10:00	17.4
Bob Hawk Show	CBS	10:30	13.0
Inner Sanctum	CBS	8:00	13.0
The Lone Ranger	ABC	7:30	10.0
Beulah*	CBS	7:00	9.8
Jack Smith Show*	CBS	7:15	9.1
Club 15*	CBS	7:30	7.9
Railroad Hour	NBC	8:00	7.9

*Monday–Friday Strip Shows

Sans Strips...
Telephone Hour	NBC	9:00	7.1
Voice of Firestone	NBC	8:30	7.1
Cities Service Band	NBC	9:30	5.3
of America			

GODFREY CRANKS UP HIS VOLUME

Arthur Godfrey was reported to be the highest paid CBS talent at $420,000 a year (4.0 Mil).

The network depended on Godfrey to carry over seven hours of its radio programming every week — 75 minutes every weekday midmorning for its highly profitable *Arthur Godfrey Time,* plus Monday's half hour radio/television simulcast of *Talent Scouts* and the new *Godfrey Digest,* 30 minutes of taped highlights from the week's morning shows broadcast on Saturday night.

In addition, CBS-TV added the hour-long *Arthur Godfrey & His Friends* variety show to its Wednesday prime time schedule.

At a little over a thousand dollars an hour, CBS got a bargain in Godfrey.

In contrast, Procter & Gamble

reportedly paid newscaster Lowell Thomas over $400,000 a year for his 15 minute radio broadcast every weeknight.

MONDAY'S MUSICAL MONEY MACHINE

NBC was almost shut out of Monday's Top Ten — and cried all the way to the bank.

Only NBC's newcomer from ABC, *The Railroad Hour*, made the list.

Nevertheless, NBC had its long running string of three high class, low-rated concerts which all were prestigious showcases for their loyal sponsors and reliable sources of income for the network.

The Telephone Hour was in its tenth of 18 seasons on NBC's Monday schedule.

The Voice of Firestone had been a Monday fixture for 18 of an eventual 22 seasons and was simulcast on NBC-TV beginning in 1949.

Cities Service Band of America was the latest variation of the petroleum company's weekly concerts that NBC had broadcast since 1927.

All three were beaten in the ratings by a ratio of three or four to one against the powerful CBS Monday block. But NBC realized that if the night had to be written off, it was best to do it with black ink instead of red.

---

*1949–50 Tuesday Night
Top Ten Programs*
NBC 5, CBS 4, ABC 1
Average: 12.9

Fibber McGee & Molly	NBC	9:30	17.7
Bob Hope Show	NBC	9:00	15.0
People Are Funny	NBC	10:30	13.7
Fanny Brice as Baby Snooks	NBC	8:30	13.3
Mystery Theater	CBS	8:00	13.3
Big Town	NBC	10:00	12.7
Mr. & Mrs. North	CBS	8:30	12.3
Life with Luigi	CBS	9:00	11.9
Beulah*	CBS	7:00	9.8
Counterspy	ABC	7:30	9.4

*Monday–Friday Strip Shows

Sans Strips...

Cavalcade of America	NBC	8:00	7.7

HOPE FOR TELEVISION

Bob Hope's radio ratings for the season had dropped his annual

ranking to tenth place — the lowest point in a dozen years

Yet, television's biggest event of the season was NBC-TV's 90 minute Easter Sunday special, *Bob Hope's Star Spangled Revue*.

The unparalleled popularity of Hope's occasional television specials and his continually strong movie box office appeal indicated that the comedian's weakened radio ratings could be blamed on the general decline of Network Radio.

After a dozen years of his selling Pepsodent Tooth Paste and Swan Soap, Lever Brothers cancelled Hope's series at the end of the season. But Hope wasn't about to give up the radio show that pumped nearly $35,000 a week (*$332,700*), into his production company. Radio continued to be a profit center for Hope for another seven years — by which time he had become television's top attraction.

AN EYE ON MISS RYAN

Irene Noblette Ryan is the least remembered of Bob Hope's female stooges. Ironically, she became the most famous and wealthiest of the string that included Patricia "Honey Chile" Wilder in the 1930s and Barbara Jo Allen as "Vera Vague" during the war years.

Irene Ryan replaced Allen's man-hungry Vague character in 1948. Her mousy "Miss Ryan" character told Hope week after week that she was, "Feeling about as well as could be expected," before launching into a string of hypochondriac jokes.

Irene Noblette and husband Tim Ryan went into radio in 1933 after a Vaudeville and minor movie career doing a Burns and Allen type of "Dumb Dora" act. They kept busy in radio for ten years, four of them as stars of their own shows, including 1937's *Royal Crown Revue*.

After their divorce in 1943, Irene kept the Ryan name and worked in some 20 low budget movie comedies and shorts plus occasional radio roles. While with Hope's troupe she continued her screen work and drifted into occasional television roles in the 1950s.

In 1962, at age 60 and ready to retire as a relative unknown, Irene Ryan was cast as "Granny" Daisy

Mae Moses in a new television sitcom, *The Beverly Hillbillies*. The show was an immediate hit that endured for nine seasons on CBS-TV.

In 1972, by which time she was 70, she co-starred on Broadway in the musical hit *Pippin*. She collapsed on stage a year later and died of a stroke, leaving a million dollars of her estate to the Irene Ryan Foundation which provides scholarships to collegiate acting students.

Irene Ryan is a forgotten star of Network Radio who remains well remembered in the annals of television and theater.

NAUGHTY GIRL'S NICE NUMBERS

Fanny Brice returned from her year's sabbatical to join the NBC Tuesday lineup for Tums sponsorship.

The 58-year-old star's comeback — limited to 26 weeks to conserve her strength — was a roaring success. The *Baby Snooks* sitcom finished in the season's Top 20, Brice's highest ranking in five years. With renewed strength and confidence she planned an extended nine month season the following year.

Fate would have another idea.

FAD FADES FAST

Another sign that the giveaway fad was fading was the 35 percent drop in audience suffered by the Mark Goodson/Bill Todman production, *Hit the Jackpot*.

The program wasn't helped by news reports about one of the show's big winners of a jackpot with an announced value of $28,000 (*$266,150*). Selling his prizes for cash to pay taxes on the loot, the "lucky" winner could on get 25 cents on the dollar — before taxes.

The bad ratings and bad press prompted Chrysler to cancel *Hit the Jackpot* in December.

THE TRUMAN SHOWS

President Harry Truman's 1950 State of the Union address drew an 18.3 rating in January. His subsequent speech in February in reaction to a Soviet Union/Communist China military alliance treaty was rated at 22.2.

Meanwhile, the President's 24-year-old daughter once again worked her ratings magic for a lowly ranked ABC concert series. Her beneficiary in late December was American Oil's *Carnegie Hall* on ABC which drew an all time high 10.0 rating when Margaret Truman appeared as guest soloist. Her encore performance in February scored a respectable 7.7.

Without her, *Carnegie Hall* was just another prestigious image builder for the network and sponsor. The Tuesday night program finished the season with a 3.5 rating—136th of the season's 156 rated and ranked programs.

1949–50 Wednesday Night Top Ten Programs
NBC 5, CBS 5
Average: 12.6

Bing Crosby Show	CBS	9:30	15.8
You Bet Your Life	CBS	9:00	14.9
Mr. Chameleon	CBS	8:00	13.4
Great Gildersleeve	NBC	8:30	12.5
Mr. District Attorney	NBC	9:30	12.5
The Big Story	NBC	10:00	12.2
Burns & Allen Show	CBS	10:00	12.0
Curtain Time	NBC	10:30	11.3
Dr Christian	CBS	8:30	11.3
Break the Bank	NBC	9:00	10.3

CROSBY'S TAPE MEASURED FIRST

CBS pulled even with NBC in Wednesday's Top Ten for the first time in nine years with the addition of two hits lifted from ABC and a third from NBC.

Bing Crosby's tape recorded show for Chesterfield Cigarettes topped his ABC ratings by 25 percent and vaulted him back into the season's Top Ten. He also gave CBS its first Number One show on Wednesday since Eddie Cantor in 1937–38.

It was the breakthrough that the networks had insisted for years would never happen — Crosby's *recorded* program had achieved the popularity that only *live* performances were supposed to reach.

Groucho Marx's *You Bet Your Life*—also recorded and highly edited — gained almost 25 percent more audience in its switch from ABC to CBS. Groucho was right on Crosby's heels in second place with the highest rating the comedian ever scored as a solo act.

Marx pulled what was considered an upset when his comedy quiz attracted nearly 50 percent more audience in its time period than NBC's big money quiz, *Break the Bank*.

The third Tuesday show stolen by CBS was in its final Network Radio season by design.

Burns and Allen, newly arrived from four seasons on NBC, had worked steadily in prime time series since 1932. They said goodbye to their listeners in May 1950 and returned five months later to CBS-TV where George and Gracie's sitcom would be a popular fixture for another eight years.

FIRST NIGHTER'S FIRST COUSIN

First Nighter left the air in October. But listeners didn't have to go far for their weekly "theater experience."

Curtain Time was a carbon copy of *First Nighter*'s format and setting. It had been open for business on NBC since 1946 after a short run on ABC. The half hour anthology of light dramas with permanent co-stars Harry Elders and Nanette Sargent was introduced every week by host Patrick Allen guiding listeners to their "seats" accompanied by the realistic sounds of a theater preparing for the evening's performance.

Curtain Time delivered two Top 50 seasons for Mars Candy before leaving the air in March 1950.

CHAMPAGNE ON A BEER BUDGET

For many years Pabst Blue Ribbon was the only beer with any advertising presence on Network Radio. In 1949, Pabst's Milwaukee neighbor, Miller Brewing, took its first steps as a network advertiser for its featured product, Miller Hi-Life, "The Champagne of Bottled Beer."

The brewer sponsored the "Champagne Music" of Chicago based Lawrence Welk's popular dance band for a two year run on ABC at 10:00. Welk's champagne went flat its first season with a 1.6 rating and didn't do much better in its second year at 2.3.

Welk left Chicago for the West

Coast in 1951 and re-emerged on ABC-TV in 1955, where his weekly dance parties became a highly-rated 16 year fixture, followed by an eleven years as successful syndicated series.

1949–50 Thursday Night Top Ten Programs
CBS 7, NBC 2, ABC 1
Average: 11.2

Mr. Keen	CBS	8:30	13.9
Suspense	CBS	9:00	13.3
Casey Crime Photographer	CBS	9:30	12.9
FBI in Peace & War	CBS	8:00	12.3
Hallmark Playhouse	CBS	10:00	11.9
Beulah*	CBS	7:00	9.8
Aldrich Family	NBC	8:00	9.5
Counterspy	ABC	7:30	9.4
Father Knows Best	NBC	8:30	9.4
Jack Smith Show*	CBS	7:15	9.1

*Monday–Friday Strip Shows

Sans Strips...

Screen Guild Theater	NBC	9:00	8.9
Dragnet	NBC	10:30	8.5

THE FAMILY HOUR

When *Kraft Music Hall* with summertime host Nelson Eddy quietly left the air in September after its 16 year run, General Foods was left as the only major food sponsor on NBC's Thursday night schedule. It countered the top rated CBS wave of crime programs at 8:00 with two family sitcoms. One had been king of radio's popular teen comedies of the early 1940s. The other was a series that would become the stereotype for 1950s family values.

The Aldrich Family had been a prime time staple for General Foods since 1939. The company also sponsored a separately cast video version of *The Aldrich Family* on NBC TV's Sunday night schedule. But the radio show's ratings had tumbled since 1946 when it was Friday's Number One program on CBS. Nevertheless, it was still a strong entry with a loyal following.

Meanwhile, longtime Hollywood star Robert Young, 41, made his radio series debut with *Father Knows Best*. At first, the show was a cookie-cutter sitcom that portrayed father as a bumbling fathead.

But as the series evolved into a

more realistic reflection of Young's movie persona and postwar family life, it developed an audience who related to it and became a Top 20 program within two years.

Both *The Aldrich Family* and *Father Knows Best* lost their time periods to CBS crime melodramas but remained within Thursday's Top Ten. However, both finished outside the season's Top 50 for the first and only times of their Network Radio runs.

The Aldrich Family was seen for four so-so seasons on television while Young moved *Father Knows Best* to television with a new cast in 1954 and became the icon of wise and patient fatherhood for six highly successful seasons.

DISCS DON'T FLY

CBS won the night with scripted drama, leading the competition from 8:00 until 10:00 by a sizeable margin. But 10:30 was a different matter.

When Campana cancelled *First Nighter* in October, CBS allowed the program and its double digit ratings to disappear. Its lead actress, Barbara Luddy, retired from series radio after 16 years with the show and became a star voice actress for Walt Disney's animated features. Her co-star, Olan Soule, went into movie and television work.

For two months the network filled the timeslot with *Pursuit*, a much traveled sustaining series.

However, the 11.9 rating delivered by *Hallmark Playhouse* as a lead-in to the 10:30 timeslot became attractive to Best Foods, the manufacturer of Skippy Peanut Butter.

Best Foods had sponsored producer C.P. MacGregor's transcribed series, *Skippy Hollywood Theater* and syndicated it to local stations since 1941—when recorded programming was rejected by NBC and CBS.

But times had changed by 1949 and the networks were hungry.

CBS gladly sold its 10:30 half hour to Best Foods for Skippy's polished transcribed series featuring top Hollywood stars.

Skippy Hollywood Theater lost 40 percent of *First Nighter*'s audience and became the only CBS series

of the night to lose its time period.

The time period was won by a new and different crime series on NBC, *Dragnet*.

FRIDAY BEGINS ON THURSDAY

World War II veteran Jack Webb was 29 with only four years of San Francisco radio experience when he recreated his popular ABC/West Coast regional network character, *Pat Novak for Hire*, on the full ABC network in February 1949. The private detective series ran on a sustaining and co-op basis for six months while Webb moonlighted, preparing a series of his own creation called *Dragnet*.

His new police drama was picked up by NBC in June 1949 and roamed the network schedule over the summer, gathering listeners and critical acclaim. It attracted the sponsorship of Liggett & Myers' Fatima Cigarettes in October and was slotted on Thursday at 10:30.

Dragnet was an original. As Sergeant Joe Friday, Webb led listeners in flat, low-keyed, documentary delivery, through each week's case taken from the files of the Los Angeles Police Department. Produced in cooperation with the LAPD, *Dragnet*'s terse realism and underplayed dialog stood out in a field of melodramatic crime fighters who populated the dial on Thursday, led by the night's Number One show, *Mr. Keen, Tracer of Lost Persons*.

Webb and his co-star Barton Yarborough were supported by Hollywood's top radio actors.

All were on their way to establishing *Dragnet* as one of Network Radio's last great series of the Golden Age.

DUFFY'S TABERNA

Ed Gardner moved *Duffy's Tavern* to Puerto Rico—literally.

The sitcom's creator/producer/star with three Top 15 seasons on NBC's Wednesday night schedule to his credit, Gardner took advantage of Puerto Rico's generous tax breaks to establish residency and a production company on the island.

He packed up his cast and crew and moved to San Juan. They recorded *Duffy's Tavern* every week

for shipment back to New York and broadcast in a new NBC Thursday timeslot at 9:30, pitted against *Casey, Crime Photographer*, in the heart of CBS's two hour block of hit mysteries.

But Gardner faced a bigger problem he hadn't considered in his move to the Caribbean.

Duffy's Tavern storylines were based on each week's big name guest star. Persuading those busy film and radio stars to interrupt their schedules for the long trip to Puerto Rico—over a thousand miles from Miami—was almost impossible.

As a result, Wednesday's Number One show of 1948–49 lost over half its audience and became a Thursday also-ran in 1949–50, dropping in the season's rankings from eleventh to 69th place.

Duffy's Tavern left the air a year later.

1949–50 Friday Night Top Ten Programs
ABC 5, CBS 3, NBC 2
Average: 9.8

The Fat Man	ABC	8:00	11.9
This Is Your FBI	ABC	8:30	11.8
Life of Riley	NBC	10:00	10.2
The Lone Ranger	ABC	7:30	10.0
Jimmy Durante Show	NBC	9:30	9.9
Beulah*	CBS	7:00	9.8
Jack Smith Show*	CBS	7:15	9.1
Adventures of Ozzie & Harriet	ABC	9:00	8.9
Leave It to Joan	CBS	9:00	8.8
The Sheriff	ABC	9:30	7.3

*Monday–Friday Strip Shows

Sans Strips...			
Screen Directors Playhouse	NBC	9:00	7.1
Halls of Ivy	NBC	8:00	6.5

ABC WINS AND EVERYBODY LOSES

ABC had reason to celebrate.

For the very first time since its 1927 inception as NBC's Blue Network, it placed five programs in a night's Top Ten.

And for the first time since its Blue Network days in 1933–34, ABC won a night outright.

But Network Radio's total ratings for the night were more a cause for concern than celebration.

For the first time in ratings history, the average rating for a night's

Top Ten dropped below double digits to 9.8. Unfortunately for the networks, the single digit average wasn't an aberration, it was the beginning of a trend.

CBS LEAVES JOAN ALONE

Except for Procter & Gamble's two successful strips, *Beulah* and Jack Smith's quarter hour songfests, CBS had just one program in Friday's Top Ten.

Joan Davis reemerged with a new sitcom, *Leave It to Joan*, for a six week summer run as vacation fill-in for half of *Lux Radio Theater*. For the fall season her show was given a questionable placement by American Tobacco's Lucky Strike and Pall Mall cigarettes.

Leave It to Joan was scheduled opposite two other sitcoms at 9:00 — NBC's *Life of Riley* and *The Adventures of Ozzie & Harriet*, newly arrived on ABC from a year on NBC. Although *Riley* was moved up to 10:00 at mid-season, it was an uphill battle for the comedienne.

Leave It to Joan left the air in March. Davis filled in for *My Friend Irma* during the following summer and then retired from series radio.

She had better luck with television and a three year run of *I Married Joan*, NBC TV's knock-off of *I Love Lucy* beginning in 1952.

MOVIE MAGIC: A DISAPPEARING ACT

With Red Skelton's defection to CBS and Eddie Cantor's departure to host Sunday's *Take It or Leave It*, NBC lost two of Friday's Top Ten shows from the previous season.

The network temporarily plugged Skelton's 9:00 timeslot with *The Life of Riley* and moved Jimmy Durante's Camel Cigarettes show up to 9:30, while it honed a major new Friday effort, *Screen Directors' Playhouse* — a program that could have been a big hit only ten years earlier.

But when *Playhouse* debuted in January, the concept of major Hollywood stars appearing in 30 minute adaptations of familiar movies was simply too little, too late. Although the program was critically praised for its scripts, acting and production values, *Screen Directors' Playhouse* never made it into a season's Top 50.

1949–50 Saturday Night Top Ten Programs
CBS 5, NBC 5
Average: 10.1

A Day in the Life of Dennis Day	NBC	9:30	12.6
Judy Canova Show	NBC	10:00	12.0
Gangbusters	CBS	9:00	11.5
Truth or Consequences	NBC	8:30	11.4
Your Hit Parade	NBC	9:00	10.4
Gene Autry's Melody Ranch	CBS	8:00	9.4
Vaughn Monroe Show	CBS	7:30	9.4
Grand Ole Opry	NBC	10:30	8.5
Sing It Again	CBS	10:00	8.2
Arthur Godfrey Digest	CBS	9:30	7.8

GANG BUSTS UP PARADE

When Frank Sinatra left *Your Hit Parade* the show lost 25 percent of its audience. It was exactly the opening that *Gangbusters* needed to win the 9:00 time period. The ratings boost back into double digits propelled Phillips H. Lord's weekly shootout back into the season's Top 50 for the first time in two years. As *Hit Parade* continued to lose audience, *Gangbusters* increased its ratings advantage even further.

Lucky Strike eventually moved its long running Saturday countdown of the week's hits to NBC's Thursday schedule and out of competition with the crime series in 1951.

By the 1952–53 season, *Gangbusters* again became Saturday's Number One program — a position it hadn't held for 13 seasons.

EDWARDS PUTS HIS SHOW ON THE MAP

Ralph Edwards opened the *Truth or Consequences* season with another big money, secret identity contest. "The Laughing Boy" was correctly identified in late October as Milton Berle by a Milwaukee housewife who won $2,500 (*$23,800*). Nevertheless, the show's ratings were off over 30 percent.

To celebrate his program's tenth anniversary — and spike its sagging ratings — Edwards immortalized *Truth or Consequences* with a unique offer.

Edwards promised that he would originate a broadcast of his show from any village, town or city that would permanently rename itself *Truth or Consequences*.

To everyone's surprise — except perhaps the crafty Edwards — the voters of Hot Springs, New Mexico, voted to do exactly that by a margin of 1300 to 300.

Protests were filed by irate Hot Springs residents and another election was conducted. The name change was upheld by another four to one vote.

True to his word, Edwards brought *Truth or Consequences* to the renamed Truth or Consequences, New Mexico, in April — and kept returning for an annual civic celebration for the next 50 years.

Edwards had yet another stunt of a different kind up his sleeve. *Truth or Consequences* would begin its eleventh season with a new sponsor on CBS.

LISTENERS HEAR MORE SEYMOUR

Dan Seymour's voice was familiar to millions.

The season's host of *We the People* had been a first-call network announcer since 1938 when he read the disclaimers that nobody seemed to hear on Orson Welles' *War of the Worlds* broadcast. He'd worked a number of programs since, becoming best known as "Danny," the weekday announcer and daily visitor to the kitchen of *Aunt Jenny*, where the kindly matron spun her *Real Life Stories* while invariably baking or frying with Lever Brothers' Spry Shortening. The show was steady work for Seymour for 19 years.

Not so steady was *Sing It Again*, a Saturday night CBS knock-off of *Stop the Music* hosted by Seymour that dangled a jackpot prize worth at least $1,000 to its listeners each week, topping off at a $28,000 peak (*$266,150*).

Sing It Again was scheduled opposite NBC's "hick hour" of Judy Canova's sitcom and *The Grand Ole Opry*. The CBS show produced a respectable 8.2 rating in its first rated season but fell to a 5.4 over the following year and was cancelled.

But Dan Seymour—*not to be confused with the movie character actor of the same name*—did all right for himself. He began moonlighting from radio in 1949 when he joined the radio/television department of Young & Rubicam Advertising. That began a quarter century career that eventually led him to becoming Chairman of the Board of J. Walter Thompson Advertising in 1972.

ARTHUR AFTER HOURS

CBS forgot about any restrictions against recorded programming when it scheduled *The Arthur Godfrey Digest*, taped highlights of the star's weekday morning show edited into a half hour package.

The network was obviously unconcerned about any overexposure of Godfrey—and with good reason.

Opposite Saturday's Number One program, *A Day in the Life of Dennis Day*, Godfrey's taped compilation trailed in the ratings by 38 percent but still finished in the night's Top Ten—and made money.

SINATRA'S RATINGS GO UP IN SMOKE

Liggett & Myers moved Perry Como's *Chesterfield Supper Club* to NBC-TV, opening the door for American Tobacco to obtain the 7:00 quarter hour on NBC Radio. American pulled Frank Sinatra off Lucky Strike's *Your Hit Parade* and

installed him as singing host of *Light Up Time*.

Sinatra's movie career at MGM had peaked with the 1949 release of hit musicals *Take Me Out to the Ballgame* and *On the Town*, both co-starring Gene Kelly. But Sinatra's outspoken political activities and stormy personal life were fodder for tabloid headlines that soured his once adoring bobby-sox fans.

Compounding the problem, Met Opera soprano Dorothy Kirsten was made Sinatra's *Light Up Time* co-star. It was another quirky casting move by Lucky Strike—remindful of its naming opera star Lawrence Tibbett as singing host of *Your Hit Parade* in 1945.

The pairing didn't work. *Light Up Time* lost 30 percent of Como's *Supper Club* ratings and nearly 60 percent of the audience Sinatra enjoyed on *Your Hit Parade*. The show was cancelled at the end of the season.

Meanwhile, top selling record artists were doing nicely on CBS.

Procter & Gamble's Jack Smith added Dinah Shore and Margaret Whiting to his cast while Campbell Soups loaded its *Club 15* at 7:30 with hit makers Dick Haymes, the Andrew Sisters, Evelyn Knight and the Modernaires.

1949–50 Top Ten Multiple Run Programs
CBS 5, NBC 3, ABC 2
Average: 7.8

The Lone Ranger	M,W,F	ABC	7:30	10.0
Beulah*	M–F	CBS	7:00	9.8
Counterspy	Tu,Th	ABC	7:30	9.4
Jack Smith Show*	M–F	CBS	7:15	9.1
Club 15*	M–F	CBS	7:30	7.9
Lowell Thomas News*	M–F	CBS	6:45	7.7
Edward R Murrow News*	M–F	CBS	7:45	7.5
Light Up Time*	M–F	NBC	7:00	5.9
Morgan Beatty News of the World*	M–F	NBC	7:15	5.5
HV Kaltenborn & Richard Harkness News*	M–F	NBC	7:45	5.4

*Monday–Friday Strip Shows

TOP 50 PROGRAMS—1949–50
CBS 26, NBC 20, ABC 5 (51)*
Average Rating: 13.1, Median: 12.5
39,300,000 Radio Homes / 94.8% Coverage of U.S. Homes / One Rating Point = 393,000 Homes
Sources: CE. Hooper Semi-Monthly Reports, Sept 1949 — Feb 1950
& A.C. Nielsen Radio Index Serv, Mar 1950–June 1950
Total Programs Rated, 6–11 P.M.: 182
Programs Rated 13 Weeks & Ranked: 136

		Program	Rtg	Type	Sponsor	Day	Time	Lgth	Net
1	1	Lux Radio Theater/William Keighley	22.3	DA	Lux Soap	Mon	9:00	60	CBS
2	3	Jack Benny Program	20.7	SC	Lucky Strike Cigarettes	Sun	7:00	30	CBS
3	5	Arthur Godfrey's Talent Scouts	18.4	TC	Lipton Tea	Mon	8:30	30	CBS
4	2	Fibber McGee & Molly	17.7	SC	Johnson Wax	Tue	9:30	30	NBC
5	8	My Friend Irma/Marie Wilson	17.4	SC	Pepsodent Toothpaste	Mon	10:00	30	CBS
6	4	Walter Winchell's Journal	16.3	NC	Richard Hudnut Cosmetics	Sun	9:00	15	ABC
7	5	Edgar Bergen & Charlie McCarthy	16.0	CV	Coca-Cola	Sun	8:00	30	CBS
8	40	Bing Crosby Show	15.8	MV	Chesterfield Cigarettes	Wed	9:30	30	CBS
9	10	Amos & Andy	15.7	SC	Rexall Drug Stores	Sun	7:30	30	CBS
10	7	Bob Hope Show	15.0	CV	Swan Soap	Tue	9:00	30	NBC
11	46	You Bet Your Life/Groucho Marx	14.9	APQ	DeSoto & Plymouth Autos	Wed	9:00	30	CBS1
12	15	Mr Keen/Bennett Kilpack	13.9	DCC	Kolynos Toothpaste	Thu	7:30	30	CBS
13	9	People Are Funny/Art Linkletter	13.7	APS	Raleigh Cigarettes	Tue	10:30	30	NBC
14	25	Red Skelton Show	13.5	CV	Tide Laundry Detergent	Sun	8:30	30	CBS
15	44	Mr Chameleon/Karl Swenson	13.4	DCC	Bayer Aspirin	Wed	8:00	30	CBS
16t	N	Fanny Brice Baby Snooks Show	13.3	SC	Tums Antacid Tablets	Tue	8:30	30	NBC
16t	18	Mystery Theater	13.3	DCC	Bayer Aspirin	Tue	8:00	30	CBS
16t	13	Suspense	13.3	DA	Autolite Spark Plugs	Thu	9:00	30	CBS

Program	Rtg	Type	Sponsor	Day	Time	Lgth	Net
19t *26* Bob Hawk Show	13.0	APQ	Camel Cigarettes	Mon	10:30	30	CBS
19t *20* Inner Sanctum	13.0	DA	Bromo Seltzer	Mon	8:00	30	CBS
21 *16* Casey, Crime Photographer	12.9	DCC	Philip Morris Cigarettes	Thu	9:30	30	CBS
22 *21* Big Town/Ed Pawley	12.7	DCC	Lifebuoy Soap	Tue	10:00	30	NBC
23 *22* A Day in the Life of Dennis Day	12.6	SC	Lustre Creme Shampoo	Sat	9:30	30	NBC
24t *33* Great Gildersleeve/Hal Peary	12.5	SC	Parkay Margarine	Wed	8:30	30	NBC
24t *12* Mister District Attorney/Jay Jostyn	12.5	DCC	Vitalis Hair Tonic	Wed	9:30	30	NBC
26t *22* The FBI in Peace & War	12.3	DCC	Lava Hand Soap	Thu	8:00	30	CBS
26t *30* Mr & Mrs North/Joe Curtin, Alice Frost	12.3	DCC	Halo Shampoo	Tue	8:30	30	CBS
28t *34* The Big Story	12.2	DA	Pall Mall Cigarettes	Wed	10:00	30	NBC
28t *61* <u>Horace Heidt Youth Oppty Program</u>	12.2	TC	Philip Morris Cigarettes	Sun	9:30	30	CBS
30t *37* Burns & Allen Show	12.0	SC	Pycopay Tooth Powder	Wed	10:00	30	CBS
30t *27* Judy Canova Show	12.0	CV	Colgate Dental Cream	Sat	10:00	30	NBC
32t *30* The Fat Man/J Scott Smart	11.9	DCC	Pepto Bismol	Fri	8:00	30	ABC
32t *48* Hallmark Playhouse	11.9	DA	Hallmark Cards	Thu	10:00	30	CBS
32t *N* <u>Life With Luigi/J.Carrol Naish</u>	11.9	SC	Wrigley Chewing Gum	Tue	9:00	30	CBS
35 *22* This Is Your FBI	11.8	DCC	Equitable Life Assurance	Fri	8:30	30	ABC
36 *75* <u>Gangbusters</u>	11.5	DA	Grape Nuts Cereal	Sat	9:00	30	CBS
37 *30* Truth or Consequences/ Ralph Edwards	11.4	APS	Duz Laundry Soap	Sat	8:30	30	NBC
38t *52* <u>Dr. Christian/Jean Hersholt</u>	11.3	DCC	Vaseline	Wed	8:30	30	CBS
38t *49* Curtain Time	11.3	DA	Mars Candy	Wed	10:30	30	NBC
40 *56* <u>Our Miss Brooks/Eve Arden</u>	11.0	SC	Lustre Creme Shampoo	Sun	6:30	30	CBS
41 *51* Take It or Leave It/Eddie Cantor	10.9	APQ	Eversharp Pens & Pencils	Sun	10:00	30	NBC
42 *29* Your Hit Parade/Eileen Wilson	10.4	MP	Lucky Strike Cigarettes	Sat	9:00	30	NBC
43 *38* Break the Bank/Bert Parks	10.3	APQ	Vitalis Hair Tonic	Wed	9:00	30	NBC
44 *27* Life of Riley/William Bendix	10.2	SC	Pabst Beer	Fri	10:00	30	NBC
45 *34* Louella Parsons Hollywood News	10.1	NC	Jergens Lotion & Woodbury	Sun	9:15	15	ABC
46 *52* <u>The Lone Ranger/Brace Beemer</u>	10.0	DCC	Cheerios Cereal	M-W-F	7:30	30	ABC
47 *67* <u>Jimmy Durante Show</u>	9.9	CV	Camel Cigarettes	Fri	9:30	30	NBC
48t *69* <u>Beulah/Hattie McDaniel</u>	9.8	SC	Dreft Laundry Soap	M-F	7:00	15	CBS
48t *46* Theater Guild on the Air	9.8	DA	US Steel	Sun	8:30	60	NBC
50t *40* Adventures of Sam Spade/H Duff	9.6	DCC	Wildroot Cream Oil	Sun	8:00	30	NBC
50t *17* Phil Harris & Alice Faye Show	9.6	SC	Rexall Drug Stores	Sun	7:30	30	NBC

*Two programs tied for 50th.
New & Returning Top 50 Programs <u>Underscored.</u>

1 You Bet Your Life/Groucho Marx	Oct–Dec	Elgin-American Costume Jwlry	Wed	9:00	30	CBS

Key: API — Audience Participation/Interviews
APQ — Audience Participation/Quiz
APS — Audience Participation/Stunts
CV — Comedy/Variety Show
DA — Dramatic Anthology

DCC — Drama/Continuing Characters
MC — Music/Classical, Semi-Classical
MP — Music/Popular, Contemporary
MSP — Music/Specialty, Ethnic
MST — Music/Standard, Traditional

MV — Music/Variety Show
NC — News, Commentary
SC — Situation Comedy
SP — Sports
TC — Talent Competition

1949–50 Top 50* Favorite Formats

	Programs	Pct
Drama — Anthology & Continuing	21	40%
Comedy — Variety & Situation	18	36%
Audience Participation — All Categories	6	12%
Music — All Categories	4	8%
News/Commentary	2	4%

Total: 51 (Two programs tied for 50th.)

1949–50 Monthly Winners

Sep	Lux Radio Theater	17.3	Feb	Jack Benny Program		25.2
Oct	Lux Radio Theater	20.5	Mar	Lux Radio Theater		24.4
Nov	Lux Radio Theater	25.4	Apr	Lux Radio Theater		23.2
Dec	Jack Benny Program	25.4	May	Lux Radio Theater		19.8
Jan	Jack Benny Program	25.6	Jun	My Friend Irma		12.1

23

The 1950–51 Network Season

GIRL: (SINGS) Bit O Honey, so delicious... / Bit O Honey, so nutritious... / So rich and chewy, sweeter than sweet... / So butter smoothie, oh, what a treat! / Bit O Honey at your candy store, / Bit O Honey, you'll want some more ... beecuzzz / It's a honey of a candy bar, and only <u>five cents</u>!

Announcer: Did you ever walk up to a display of candy bars and think...

GIRL: (FILTER MIKE, AS TO SELF) I want a candy bar ... but I don't know what kind. I'd like a change. Something different and <u>refreshing</u>.

Announcer: I'll bet you have that feeling sometimes ... and here's the answer! When you want a refreshing <u>change</u> in candy, then get a famous <u>Bit O Honey</u> candy bar. It's delightfully pleasant with a mild <u>honey</u> flavor, filled all through with crunchy, fresh toasted almonds. You'll like it as a frequent, refreshing change from chocolate bars. <u>Bit O Honey</u> is unusual ... and unusually delicious. Get <u>Bit O Honey</u>. Taste it and you'll agree...

GIRL: (SINGS) It's a honey of a candy bar, and only <u>five cents</u>!

Your Slips Are Showing

Television was hot and getting hotter.

In a period remindful of radio's growth spurt 20 years earlier, every family wanted a television receiver and 8,000 new sets were being delivered to American homes every day. By mid–1950, TV was boasting a reach that was double the size of the most widely circulated magazine, *Reader's Digest*.

Audience surveys estimated up to four viewers in every TV household every evening — four less listeners for prime time radio.

Audiences deserting to television and competition from independent stations began to take a heavy toll on the Network Radio. The season's Top 50 average program rating was down 20 percent and for the first time since audience polling began, none of radio's most popular programs achieved a season average rating of 20 or higher.

The season's Top 50 programs had a combined rating average of only 10.4 — a new low.

More telling, by mid-season radio network revenues had slipped below the 200 million dollar mark *(1.88 Bil)* — while the entire radio industry's total income *increased* to over 600 million *(5.63 Bil)*.

The reaction from ABC, CBS and NBC to this crisis was concern — but backed with little action.

Their attention had turned to television, too. Network television revenues for 1950 were reported at 85 million dollars *(797.9 Mil)*. The amount was less than half of the radio networks' income for the year, but it had climbed by 190 percent in just one year.

The question was no longer *if* television network revenues would overtake network radio, but *when*.

ABC Goes to the Movies

Like his famous Life Savers, candy millionaire Ed Noble's pockets had holes.

Noble's plans to expand ABC into television required more working capital than anticipated and the network needed cash to catch up with NBC and CBS. Just as Paramount Pictures had come to the aid of CBS in 1929, its spinoff company, United Paramount Theaters, rescued ABC in May 1951. The merger was worth $25 Million *(234.7 Mil)* to the network. It also provided ABC with a new president, Leonard Goldenson, 45, who would successfully lead the company for the next 30 years.

Hummerts' Finest Hour and a Half

CBS monopolized the annual Top 50 list as no network had since NBC in the 1945–46 season.

Three of the 30 CBS hits — indeed, three of the season's Top 15 shows — were produced by Frank and Anne Hummert, famous for their low-budget, formulaic programs which critics were quick to dismiss as simplistic garbage similar to their stable of soap operas — with little appeal to "intelligent" listeners.

Regardless, Hummerts' *Mystery Theater* was Tuesday's Number One program and eleventh in the season rankings.

Their *Mr. Chameleon* broke into the season's Top Ten and placed

1950–51 Season Scoreboard Mid-season Totals, December 1950			
		Compared to Year Earlier	
Total Radio Homes	40.7 Mil	+1.40 Mil	+3.6%
Total Auto Radios	18.0 Mil	+4.0 Mil	+28 5%
Total AM Radio Stations	2,086	+174	+9.1%
Total Radio Network Affiliates	1,170	+38	+3.4%
1950 Radio Revenues	605.4 Mil	+34.4 Mil	+6.0%
1950 Network Revenues	196.3 Mil	(6.7 Mil)	(3.3%)
Network Share	32.4%		(3.1%)
Total TV Homes	9.8 Mil	+6.5 Mil	+190.8%
Total TV Stations	110	+9	+8.9%
Total FM Stations	781	+27	+7.4%

second on Wednesday, just two-tenths of a point behind Groucho Marx's *You Bet Your Life*.

And *Mr. Keen, Tracer of Lost Persons*, in it's 14th year, was Thursday's most popular program, finishing the season in 15th place among all shows.

All three Hummert programs were sponsored by Sterling Drug which had first call on all of the couple's prime time offerings since the earliest days of Network Radio.

NETS' WORTH

Johnson Wax cancelled its 15 year sponsorship of *Fibber McGee & Molly* and sent shock waves through the industry. Advertisers were taking a closer, critical look at Network Radio costs.

Nielsen introduced program costs provided by cooperating networks and sponsors to its rating reports The figures enable observers to determine the cost efficiencies of sponsors' investments by dividing the cost of each broadcast by the program's rating, resulting in a *Cost Per* (rating) *Point*.

Program costs were the total of two items.

The first, *Network Time Charges*, was based on program length to cover AT&T line costs and the number of affiliate stations paid to carry the program. The average time charge for a half hour prime time program was in the neighborhood of $535 per minute *($5,020)*, for a 30 minute total of $16,000 *($150,195)*.

With falling ratings, the networks were under pressure to lower their charges.

A bigger variance lay in the *Talent & Production Charges* associated with the different programs. These charges could range from less than $5,000 *($46,935)*, to almost $35,000 *($328,550)*. This was the area under closest scrutiny by advertisers scrambling to find money to invest in television.

WHAT PRICE GLORY?

How much did it actually cost the sponsoring advertisers to reach their shares of Network Radio's dwindling prime time audience?

The average charge to produce and broadcast a half hour prime

Network Radio Prime Time Program Costs—1950–51 Season				
	Time Charge (000)	Talent & Prod (000)	Total Cost (000)	Rating Avg	Cost Per Point
Adventures of Ozzie & Harriet	$17.9	$10.9	$28.8	8.7	$3,310
The Aldrich Family	16.0	7.5	23.5	9.1	2,582
American Album Familiar Music	16.0	4.0	20.0	4.9	4,081
Amos & Andy	16.7	28.8	45.5	14.0	3,250
Arthur Godfrey's Talent Scouts	16.8	10.4	27.2	13.4	2,029
Bing Crosby Show	17.7	34.5	52.2	9.8	5,327
Bob Hawk Show	17.1	6.9	24.0	10.5	2,286
Bob Hope Show	16.5	34.5	51.0	9.6	5,313
Carnation Contented Hour	16.7	9.2	25.9	7.3	3,548
Casey Crime Photographer	16.2	4.6	20.8	10.0	2,080
Cities Service Band of America	12.6	7.5	20.1	4.7	4,277
Club 15 (15 Min)	12.6	7.5	20.1	7.2	2,792
A Day in the Life of Dennis Day	15.3	13.8	29.1	8.8	2,560
Dr Christian	17.7	4.6	22.3	10.2	2,186
Dragnet	16.5	4.6	21.1	8.7	2,425
Edgar Bergen & Charlie McCarthy	18.5	25.9	44.4	14.7	3,020
Fanny Brice as Baby Snooks	15.8	7.5	23.3	9.7	2,402
The Fat Man	16.8	5.8	22.6	10.5	2,152
Father Knows Best	16.3	8.6	24.9	9.5	2,621
Fibber McGee &Molly	15.8	26.5	42.3	11.1	3,811
Gangbusters	16.1	5.8	21.9	10.1	2,168
Gene Autry's Melody Ranch	17.3	17.3	34.6	10.2	3,392
Grand Ole Opry	16.1	5.2	21.3	8.0	2,663
Great Gildersleeve	16.1	11.5	27.6	9.7	2,845
Hallmark Playhouse	17.6	11.5	29.1	9.7	3,000
Hollywood Star Playhouse	16.5	6.9	23.4	10.3	2,272
Horace Heidt Youth Oppty Prog	17.7	11.5	29.2	9.7	3,010
Jack Benny Program	16.3	28.8	45.1	15.6	2,891
Judy Canova Show	15.9	10.9	27.8	9.4	2,957
The Life of Riley	15.6	10.9	26.5	8.1	3,272
Life with Luigi	17.2	7.5	24.7	11.1	2,225
Lowell Thomas News (15 Min)	7.4	1.4	8.8	7.1	1,239
Lux Radio Theater (60 Min)	29.3	20.1	49.4	17.9	2,760
Meet Corliss Archer	16.7	4.6	21.3	9.3	2,290
Mr. & Mrs. North	15.3	7.5	22.8	11.2	2,036
Mr. District Attorney	16.7	7.4	24.1	10.7	2,252
Mr. Keen, Tracer of Lost Persons	16.6	4.6	21.2	10.7	1,981
My Favorite Husband	16.5	8.1	20.1	8.8	2,284
My Friend Irma	17.6	10.9	28.5	13.3	2,143
News of the World (15 Min)	10.4	0.9	11.3	6.0	1,883
Nick Carter, Master Detective	12.0	2.5	14.5	6.7	2,164
One Man's Family (15 Min)	10.6	1.4	11.4	6.3	1,810
Our Miss Brooks	14.4	8.6	23.0	9.8	2,347
People Are Funny	16.4	8.6	25.0	10.3	2,427
The Railroad Hour	16.9	14.4	31.3	8.3	3,771
Red Skelton Show	16.5	21.0	37.5	11.9	3,151
Richard Diamond, Private Detective	16.6	5.2	21.8	8.2	2,659
Roy Rogers Show	14.3	8.3	22.6	8.1	2,790
Suspense	17.1	8.1	25.2	9.3	2,710
The Telephone Hour	16.4	13.8	30.2	6.6	4,576
Theater Guild on the Air (60 Min)	27.6	20.5	48.1	8.1	5,938
Truth or Consequences	16.0	10.9	26.9	9.0	2,989
Vaughn Monroe Show	17.1	11.6	28.7	8.6	3,337
Voice of Firestone	15.2	12.0	27.2	7.2	3,778
Walter Winchell (15 Min)	13.0	8.5	21.5	12.4	1,734
You Bet Your Life	16.8	13.2	30.0	11.8	2,542
Your Hit Parade	16.1	12.7	28.8	7.7	3,740

time network program was $27,750 *($260,500)*.

The average Cost Per Point to reach one-percent of homes with radios with a was $2,930 *($27,500)*.

Two of the higher priced pro-

grams on a Cost Per Point basis, *The American Album of Familiar Music* and *The Life of Riley*, were gone from Network Radio at the end of the season.

One of the best buys wasn't a

major network prime time show, but lowly Mutual's late Sunday afternoon offering, *The Shadow.* With a 7.9 rating and total cost of $12,600 *($118,280)*, Lamont Cranston and company registered a Cost Per Point of less than $1,600 *($15,020).*

COSTS TO THE POINT OF CANCELLATION

Three programs stood out from all others with a Nielsen-reported Cost Per Point in excess of $5,000 *($46,935).*

U.S. Steel's hour long *Theatre Guild on the Air* was expensive because of its length and production charges. But NBC didn't worry as long as the sponsor was happy. The steelmaker finally cancelled the high priced, prestigious program at the end of the 1952–53 season.

The half hour shows hosted by Bing Crosby and Bob Hope also cracked the $5,000 mark with ratings that sank to single digits.

"ABC" ON NBC AND CBS

Liggett & Myers Tobacco was on an advertising splurge for its major brand, Chesterfield Cigarettes.

Bob Hope's falling NBC radio ratings didn't seem to be of any concern to the tobacco company, any more than Bing Crosby's tumble on CBS.

Liggett & Myers bought both shows — Network Radio's most expensive properties — to push its slogan, "A-B-C ... Always Buy Chesterfields." The fact that ABC was also the identity of their up and coming competitor was of no concern to the two networks. The sponsor's money was good and that was all that mattered.

What mattered to Chesterfield was the endorsement value of the two stars in full color, full page ads that were splashed across the back covers of the country's leading magazines — and on Christmas gift cartons of cigarettes that bore their pictures.

Regardless of Hope and Crosby's popularity, Liggett & Myers dropped both shows in 1952.

1932 REDEUX

Jack Benny and Eddie Cantor were among a handful of Network

Radio's first stars from the 1932–33 season who began appearing regularly on the flickering television screens that were rapidly filling America's living rooms.

George Burns, 54, and 55-year-old Gracie Allen launched their familiar radio sitcom on CBS-TV.

Gertrude Berg, 52, brought her *Goldbergs* family to television for a weekly reunion.

Fifty-year-old Fred Waring fronted a far larger orchestra and choral group on television than appeared on his first radio shows 18 years earlier.

Bandleader Wayne King, also 50, was still serenading viewers with romantic waltzes on TV as he had at the dawning of Network Radio's Golden Age in 1932.

Sixty-year-old Paul Whiteman was even busier than his days in early radio, performing 90 minutes of live television on ABC-TV every weekend.

And comedian Ed Wynn, 64, who made his first radio appearance in 1922, won the second annual Emmy as, "Television's Most Outstanding Live Personality."

AS SEEN ON TV...

The three television networks opened the 1950–51 season with 46 series rooted in Network Radio. The adaptations and simulcasts accounted for a third of TV's prime time programming.

CBS took its cue from NBC-TV's heavy conversion of familiar radio titles to television the previous season. The CBS-TV schedule boasted 16 shows familiar to radio audiences: *The Alan Young Show, Arthur Godfrey's Talent Scouts* (simulcast), *Big Town, Blue Ribbon Bouts, The Burns & Allen Show, Perry Como's Chesterfield Supper Club, The Frank Sinatra Show, The Fred Waring Show, The Gene Autry Show, The Goldbergs, The Horace Heidt Show, The Jack Benny Program, Lux Video Theater, Sing It Again* (simulcast), *Truth or Consequences* and *The Vaughn Monroe Show.*

NBC-TV continued to draw from radio popularity with 16 programs: *The Aldrich Family, The Big Story, Break the Bank, Friday Night Boxing, Kay Kyser's Kollege of Mu-*

sical Knowledge, Leave It to the Girls, Lights Out, Martin Kane Private Eye, One Man's Family, The Original Amateur Hour, The Quiz Kids, The Voice of Firestone (simulcast), *Wayne King's Serenade, We the People, You Bet Your Life* and *Your Hit Parade.*

ABC-TV trailed with a dozen: *Beulah, Blind Date, Buck Rogers, Can You Top This?, Chance of a Lifetime, Dick Tracy, Don McNeill's TV Club, First Nighter, Life Begins at 80, The Lone Ranger, Stop the Music,* and *Twenty Questions.*

The struggling DuMont Television Network added two more: *Famous Jury Trials* and *The Adventures of Ellery Queen.*

As listeners became viewers and flocked to see their radio favorites on television, Network Radio was left to wonder what to do about its loss of popularity and profits.

THE LAST OF THE MEDICINE SHOWS

Ironically, as Network Radio pondered its future, a ghost from its structure's past appeared, remindful of the era when wagons of entertainers roamed the country offering free shows in return for the chance to pitch their dubious tonics and remedies. For two nights in January, ABC and Mutual carried the first — and last — of the medicine shows.

Buried in the season's unranked programs are the two one-shot offerings — *The LeBlanc Hollywood Party* on Mutual, Friday, January 12, starring Judy Garland, Groucho Marx, Vic Damone, Victor Moore and Minnie Pearl. The show was repeated on ABC the following night with the cumbersome title, *The LeBlanc Comedy & Musical Show.*

The shows carried the name of self-promoting Louisiana State Senator Dudley J. LeBlanc, the Barnum-like manufacturer of Hadacol, a cure-all tonic supposedly laced with vitamins.

The elixir — which was 12 percent alcohol — was advertised as, "An effective treatment and cure for scores of ailments and diseases ... and makes you boogie-woogie all the time!"

The radio programs promoted

The Hadacol Caravan, a $350,000 (3.3 Mil) traveling show starring Mickey Rooney and singer Connee Boswell with occasional major guest stars the likes of Jimmy Durante, Bob Hope and Lucille Ball. Admission to the shows was a two Hadacol boxtops.

The tour played to huge audiences in arenas and ballparks. By March, LeBlanc reported annual sales over three million dollars *(28.2 Mil)*.

Six months later Hadacol was charged with false and deceptive advertising by the Federal Trade Commission.

LeBlanc didn't care—he had sold the company a month earlier for over eight million dollars *(69.6 Mil)*. He was off the hook and his medicine shows were off the air.

THE MONTHLIES

CBS Radio again swept the season with the Number One show in all ten months, extending its string of consecutive winning months to 20.

Lux Radio Theater continued to dominate with eight first place finishes from September through December and February through May. Jack Benny beat *Lux* by one-tenth of a point to win January. Both programs were edged out in June by Benny's fellow defectors from NBC to CBS, Edgar Bergen and Charlie McCarthy and *Amos & Andy*, which tied for first.

1950–51 Sunday Night Top Ten Programs
CBS 7, ABC 1, MBS 1, NBC 1
Average: 11.4

Jack Benny Program	CBS	7:00	15.6
Edgar Bergen & Charlie McCarthy	CBS	8:00	14.7
Amos & Andy	CBS	7:30	14.0
Walter Winchell	ABC	9:00	12.4
Red Skelton Show	CBS	8:30	11.9
Our Miss Brooks	CBS	6:30	9.8
Horace Heidt Youth Opportunity Program	CBS	9:30	9.7
Meet Corliss Archer	CBS	9:00	9.3
Roy Rogers Show	MBS	6:00	8.1
Theater Guild on the Air	NBC	8:30	8.1

TV TAKES TOLL

CBS dominated Sunday with seven of the Top Eight programs—five of them lifted from NBC.

Nevertheless, ratings continued to fall as television loaded Sunday with top attractions.

Radio was faced with competition from some of its own with NBC-TV's *Colgate Comedy Hour* at 8:00, starring rotating hosts Eddie Cantor, Fred Allen and Bob Hope. The Colgate lineup also featured the hot new comedy team, Dean Martin and Jerry Lewis, whose NBC radio show was having a hard time catching on.

The 8 o'clock hour on Sunday had been radio's peak prime time just two years earlier when Edgar Bergen, Fred Allen and *Stop the Music* combined for 47.8 rating points. By 1950–51 only Bergen was left and his season's average rating fell to a personal low 14.7.

CBS-TV added to its Sunday star power on October 28 with the first of Jack Benny's four television shows of the season. The programs were simply adaptations of his popular radio format, co-starring Eddie "Rochester" Anderson, singer/stooge Dennis Day and announcer/foil Don Wilson. Benny's television schedule would gradually increase to a bi-weekly basis in 1953—immediately following his 7:00 CBS radio show.

THE BIG FLOP

NBC-TV chief Pat Weaver was given the added responsibility to run NBC Radio in the fall of 1951.

His biggest and most expensive blunder in Network Radio was *The Big Show*.

Weaver called his 90 minute extravaganza, "NBC's Sunday Spectacular at Six." It was intended to blunt the rating damage done by the defections of Jack Benny, Edgar Bergen and *Amos & Andy* to CBS. *The Big Show* was hosted by Broadway actress Tallulah Bankhead with Meredith Willson's orchestra and chorus, and a weekly guest star list of famous singers, comedians and actors that would have scored double digit ratings—before television came along to steal radio's audience.

The Big Show opened on No-

vember 5, 1950, backed by multiple, participating sponsors and a guest lineup that included Jimmy Durante, Fred Allen, Danny Thomas and singers Ethel Merman and Frankie Laine. Despite heavy advertising and its roster of stars, the show scored a disappointing 5.7 rating. It peaked the following month with an 8.0 and finished the season with a meager 5.5 average.

Adding insult to injury, *The Big Show* finished dead last in its 90 minute time period, beaten by CBS's *Our Miss Brooks* and Jack Benny, ABC's Drew Pearson commentary and Don Gardiner newscast *plus* Mutual's *Roy Rogers Show* and *Nick Carter, Master Detective*.

The Big Show sagged even further in the ratings the following season to a sorrowful 5.2 when NBC finally pulled the plug on the highly expensive failure in April 1952.

NEAT CORLISS ARCHER

Bouncing into Sunday's Top Ten was the night's only program that gained audience over its previous season, albeit only one-tenth of a rating point. *Meet Corliss Archer*, was a family sitcom with 32-year-old Janet Waldo in the title role of a breezy teenager. The show had kicked around the CBS schedule since 1943 before settling in for a five year stand on Sunday and three Top 50 seasons.

Meet Corliss Archer remained with CBS for another year before moving on to a final season on ABC.

However, Waldo's young voice and unique delivery forever typecast her as a teenager. She was featured in scores of animated television shows including a 13 year run as Judy Jetson, the teenaged daughter of *The Jetsons*.

Janet Waldo was in her fifties and sixties at the time.

HAPPY TRAILS TO THE TOP 50

Television brought new popularity to movie cowboy heroes.

Roy Rogers starred in eight Republic westerns during the 1950–51 season, all directed to the Saturday afternoon kids' matinee audience with titles pegged to each film's locale, *Twilight in the Sierras, Sunset in the West, North of the Great Divide, In Old Amarillo,* etc. In reality, most were filmed in Hollywood's backyard, the San Fernando Valley.

The Roy Rogers Show became Mutual's third prime time program to reach a season's Top 50. The combination adventure and music show, similar in format to *Gene Autry's Melody Ranch,* was sponsored by Quaker Oats. And like most of Rogers' movies, the show co-starred his wife, singer Dale Evans.

The couple's closing duet, "Happy Trails," written by Evans, became their signature song over the program's seven year, two network run, bouncing between Mutual and NBC. The two were supported in the show by their movies' sidekick comedians and musical groups.

"The King of the Cowboys" and his wife jumped back to NBC the following season which coincided with the debut of their half-hour filmed adventure series that ran for six years on NBC-TV.

THE ALBUM'S LAST PAGE

Sterling Drug's Bayer Aspirin had sponsored *The American Album of Familiar Music* on NBC's Sunday schedule since 1931 where it had finished in the season's Top 50 nine times. For 17 of the its 19 years it had been a fixture at 9:30 — in nine of those years it was among Sunday's Top Ten programs.

The drug company abruptly ended the NBC association in mid–November when it shifted Frank and Anne Hummert's concert of standards to the same time period on ABC without any appreciable loss of its dwindling ratings.

Nevertheless, the program quietly left the air in June.

WILD ROOTED IN COMMERCIALS

Wildroot Cream Oil replaced its popular *Adventures of Sam Spade* on NBC with a new detective series carrying the blatantly commercial title, *Charlie Wild, Private Detective.* It's no coincidence that the milky hair tonic's jingle, already familiar to millions, began, "Ya better get Wildroot Cream Oil, Chaaarlie!"

Listeners didn't sing along. The half hour camouflaged commercial lost over half of *Spade*'s ratings.

It was moved to CBS at 6:00 in January and became the only program to be out-rated by NBC's lowly *Big Show.*

HELLO, AMERICANS!

Chicago based newscaster Paul Harvey, 33, began his legendary network broadcasting career over 119 ABC stations on December 10. His late Sunday night news and commentary drew a 2.3 rating for the season

The distinctive Harvey added his long running series of weekday newscasts on April 2, 1951, replacing veteran commentator H.R. Bauckage on ABC's midday schedule. He remained there for the next 58 years.

1950–51 Monday Night Top Ten Programs (11)
CBS 8, NBC 2, ABC 1
Average: 10.6

Lux Radio Theater	CBS	9:00	17.9
Arthur Godfrey's Talent Scouts	CBS	8:30	13.4
My Friend Irma	CBS	10:00	13.3
Bob Hawk Show	CBS	10:30	10.5
Hollywood Star Playhouse	CBS	8:00	10.3
Beulah*	CBS	7:00	9.4
Railroad Hour	NBC	8:00	8.3
Jack Smith Show*	CBS	7:15	7.8
The Lone Ranger	ABC	7:30	7.5
Club 15*	CBS	7:30	7.2
Voice of Firestone	NBC	8:30	7.2

*Monday–Friday Strip Shows

Sans Strips...

Telephone Hour	NBC	9:00	6.6
NBC Symphony	NBC	10:00	5.2
Cities Service Band of America	NBC	9:30	4.7

THE PRICE IS RIGHT

Lever Brothers happily endured the high costs of *Lux Radio Theater* that approached $50,000 a week (*$435,000*), because radio's Number One program carried a Cost Per Point that was just slightly above programs that were half its length and nowhere near its popularity.

For the fourth consecutive season Lever and CBS dominated Monday with *Lux, Arthur Godfrey's Talent Scouts,* and *My Friend Irma*

in the Top Three positions. Camel Cigarettes' Bob Hawk quiz show repeated as the runner-up behind the Lever's top trio, while a short-lived newcomer, *Hollywood Star Playhouse,* replaced *Inner Sanctum* to round out Monday's Top Five.

THE REAL MYSTERY IS WHY...

Emerson Drugs' Bromo Seltzer abruptly cancelled its long running *Inner Sanctum* in April 1950 and replaced it with yet another mystery anthology series, *Hollywood Star Playhouse.*

It was a questionable move because *Inner Sanctum* had enjoyed four consecutive seasons as a Top 25 program since moving to the CBS Monday schedule in 1946. It had placed among Monday's Top Five in each of those seasons.

Hollywood Star Playhouse hit the air running in late April with original playlets starring Academy Award winners Jimmy Stewart, Broderick Crawford, Ray Milland and Claire Trevor. But was a tough and expensive act to follow.

The show opened the 1950–51 season featuring lesser names from the movies like Richard Widmark, Mercedes McCambridge, Anne Bancroft and Ida Lupino, but continued to present solid material with high production values.

Despite its quality, *Hollywood Star Playhouse* lost 20 percent of *Inner Sanctum*'s ratings and was cancelled at the end of the season.

Meanwhile, *Inner Sanctum* was picked up by Mars Candy and moved to ABC in the 8:00 timeslot opposite *Hollywood Star Playhouse* on CBS and NBC's high powered musical series, *The Railroad Hour.*

Inner Sanctum lost 65 percent of its audience in the move and was cancelled after its one season run on ABC.

THE BANDS PAY ON

NBC expanded Monday's prestigious and profitable music programming of earlier seasons and slotted the NBC Symphony under the direction of Fritz Reiner into the ten o'clock hour against *My Friend Irma* and *The Bob Hawk Show* on CBS.

The concerts hardly dented the

ratings but were underwritten by drug manufacturer Squibb and rounded out four hours of classical, semi-classical and show music in NBC's prime time that were fully sponsored by image seeking advertisers who obligingly footed the bills.

1950–51 Tuesday Night Top Ten Programs
CBS 5, NBC 5
Average: 10.2

Mystery Theater	CBS	8:00	11.4
Mr. & Mrs. North	CBS	8:30	11.2
Fibber McGee & Molly	NBC	9:30	11.1
Life with Luigi	CBS	9:00	11.1
People Are Funny	NBC	10:30	10.3
Fanny Brice as Baby Snooks	NBC	8:30	9.7
Bob Hope Show	NBC	9:00	9.6
Beulah*	CBS	7:00	9.4
Big Town	NBC	10:00	9.4
Truth or Consequences	CBS	9:30	9.0

*Monday–Friday Strip Shows

Sans Strips...

Cavalcade of America	NBC	8:00	7.1

BYE, BYE, BABY

Fanny Brice joined Will Rogers and Joe Penner as another of radio's great early comedians to die before the end of the Golden Age. Fresh from her comeback season on NBC when *Baby Snooks* finished in the annual Top 20 against the popular *Mr. & Mrs. North* on CBS, Brice didn't quite make it to the end of the 1950–51 season.

Her last performance as *Baby Snooks* was on May 22. She succumbed to a cerebral hemorrhage one week later.

On that evening's memorial broadcast her longtime co-star, "Daddy" Hanley Stafford, eulogized the 59-year-old Brice as "...a very real, a very warm and very wonderful person."

MILKING THE LAUGHS

Fibber McGee & Molly didn't miss a beat when Johnson Wax cancelled its sponsorship of the venerable sitcom after 15 years. Pet Evaporated Milk promptly picked up the show that was coming off three consecutive seasons as Tuesday's Number One program.

The show didn't change in the least with its new sponsor and it re-mained NBC's top Tuesday entry. But *Fibber McGee & Molly* lost over 35 percent of its ratings and dropped out of the season's Top Ten for the first time in a dozen years. A major reason for the sitcom's loss of audience was the new competition offered in its time period by CBS, *Truth or Consequences*.

THE TRUTH BE GOIN'

Ralph Edwards' *Truth or Consequences* had become a Saturday night fixture on NBC for ten years, all of them sponsored by Procter & Gamble's Duz laundry soap. The show had slipped since its Top Ten season in 1947–48 and P&G cancelled it in June 1950.

Philip Morris Cigarettes picked up the show and moved it to the CBS Tuesday schedule. The maneuver set up a unique situation in which both of Network Radio's big stunt shows, *Truth or Consequences* and *People Are Funny* were broadcast on the same night within half an hour of each other.

Both finished in Tuesday's Top Ten.

But pitted against the stiff competition of *Fibber McGee & Molly* on NBC, *Truth or Consequences'* rating fell into single digits and its lowest-ever ranking, barely remaining in the season's Top 50. Edwards, Philip Morris and CBS parted ways at the end of the season.

Ironically, *Truth or Consequences* popped up next on NBC in the summer of 1952 as the vacation replacement for its former competition, *Fibber McGee & Molly*.

THANKS FOR THE MEMORY OF FIRST PLACE

Fibber McGee & Molly bounced back into the next season's Top Ten after its one year drop in ratings.

The same wasn't true for Bob Hope, whose Tuesday show had either preceded or followed Jim and Marian Jordan's sitcom on NBC's Tuesday schedule since 1938.

Over the dozen years, Hope had five Number One seasons. From 1941 to 1947, Hope and *Fibber McGee & Molly* were radio's unbeatable Tuesday combination that led NBC's greatest years of dominance.

Hope was popular as ever in his films, his increasing television schedule and his stage appearances. But the comedian's radio ratings plummeted over 35 percent during the season into single digits, pushing him down to 33rd place in the annual rankings.

More embarrassing to the comedian, his show finished second in its time period to a simplistic, low budget sitcom on CBS, *Life with Luigi*.

HOWARD'S HAPPY HITS

Cy Howard was the creator of two CBS comedy hits — Monday's *My Friend Irma* and the Tuesday show that took down Bob Hope, *Life with Luigi*.

The story of a humble Italian immigrant learning the ways of his new country in Chicago's Little Italy district, *Life with Luigi* was dependent on the dialectal skills of its cast, headed by J. Carroll Naish in the title role.

Naish's versatility in ethnic characteristics was on full display as Chief Sitting Bull in MGM's 1950 musical *Annie Get Your Gun* and as television's *Charlie Chan* in the late 1950s. He was supported in *Life with Luigi* by character actors Alan Reed and Hans Conreid, both also members of *My Friend Irma*'s cast.

The strength of Howard's *Irma* convinced CBS to put *Luigi* on the network schedule as a sustaining feature in 1948 and carry it until Wrigley Gum picked up its sponsorship in 1950.

The network's faith in the show paid off.

Life with Luigi was given a timeslot that was once considered suicide opposite Bob Hope. Instead, the Italian accented sitcom developed a following against the overexposed comedian that resulted in a successful four year run and two finishes in the annual Top Ten.

1950–51 Wednesday Night Top Ten Programs
CBS 5, NBC 4, ABC 1
Average: 9.9

You Bet Your Life	NBC	9:00	11.8
Mr. Chameleon	CBS	8:00	11.6
Mr. District Attorney	NBC	9:30	10.7
The Big Story	NBC	10:00	10.4
Dr Christian	CBS	8:30	10.2

Bing Crosby Show	CBS	9:30	9.8
Great Gildersleeve	NBC	8:30	9.7
Beulah*	CBS	7:00	9.4
Jack Smith Show*	CBS	7:15	7.8
The Lone Ranger	ABC	7:30	7.5

*Monday–Friday Strip Shows

Sans Strips...
| Halls of Ivy | NBC | 8:00 | 6.6 |
| Blue Ribbon Boxing | CBS | 10:00 | 5.6 |

HELLO, I MUST BE GOING...

Groucho Marx made it a hat trick by jumping to his third network in three years.

The move to NBC pushed his *You Bet Your Life* comedy quiz into the season's Top Ten — helped along by producer John Guedel's insightful insistence that the show remain in the same Wednesday night time slot that it had occupied on CBS.

Marx's long term contract with NBC also included a television version of *You Bet Your Life*, which debuted on Thursdays in October 1950. Both the radio and television editions of the quiz were sponsored by Chrysler Motors' DeSoto and Plymouth automobiles.

With *You Bet Your Life* going for him on both radio and television, Marx was one of the few stars from radio's earliest days whose popularity increased as Network Radio's Golden Age slowly passed into history.

You Bet Your Life became Wednesday's top rated radio show for three consecutive years, during which it also finished among the seasons' Top Ten programs.

BING'S SONGS FALL FLAT

Without the solid lead-in provided by Groucho Marx the previous season, Bing Crosby's ratings on CBS at 9:30 suffered a 40 percent hit. Wednesday's Number One show of 1949–50 fell into single digits — an all time low for Crosby's Network Radio career that dated back to 1932.

Like his friend Bob Hope on Tuesday, Crosby found himself a runner-up in his time period — in this case to NBC's *Mr. District Attorney*.

The 47-year-old singer's radio popularity would never again reach its earlier heights. One reason for

his loss of audience can be attributed to the feeble lead-in provided by a rotund comedian who didn't know how good he had it as *The Great Gildersleeve* on NBC and jumped to CBS in a new role — Hal Peary.

WEARY PEARY WALKS INTO FAILURE

Hal Peary had grown tired of his title role as *The Great Gildersleeve* which had become a fixture on the NBC schedule under Kraft Foods sponsorship since its spinoff from *Fibber McGee & Molly* in 1941.

The sitcom had been a Top 50 show in each of its nine seasons, reaching the Top 25 in seven of them. In addition, Peary had been featured as Throckmorton P. Gildersleeve in nine film comedies. Nevertheless, the 42-year-old Peary left *Gildersleeve* and signed with CBS to star in a new sitcom he had created for himself, *Honest Harold* — a character in plots both remarkably similar to *Gildersleeve*.

In a questionable scheduling move, CBS never gave *Honest Harold* a chance, slotting it in the 9:00 time period opposite Groucho Marx's top rated *You Bet Your Life*. Unsponsored and unrated, *Honest Harold* left the air after one season.

WATERMAN FOR WATER COMMISSIONER

Meanwhile, NBC had an immediate replacement for *The Great Gildersleeve*'s title role when Hal Peary left. Willard Waterman was a veteran radio actor who both sounded and looked like Peary. Waterman made the most of his opportunity to star as the blustery water commissioner of Summerfield, keeping *The Great Gildersleeve* a solid ratings contender for the remaining seven years of its NBC radio run. Waterman also starred in 1955's television version of the sitcom on NBC-TV.

1950–51 Thursday Night Top Ten Programs
CBS 6, NBC 4
Average: 9.2

Mr. Keen	CBS	8:30	10.7
FBI in Peace & War	CBS	8:00	10.2
Hallmark Playhouse	CBS	9:30	9.7

Father Knows Best	NBC	8:30	9.5
Beulah*	CBS	7:00	9.4
Suspense	CBS	9:00	9.3
The Aldrich Family	NBC	8:00	9.1
Dragnet	NBC	9:00	8.7
Screen Directors Playhouse	NBC	10:00	7.9
Jack Smith Show*	CBS	7:15	7.8

*Monday–Friday Strip Shows

Sans Strips...
| Original Amateur Hour | ABC | 9:00 | 6.7 |
| Philip Morris Playhouse | CBS | 10:00 | 6.6 |

TWO OF THREE ISN'T BAD

Only three of the year's Top 50 weekly programs could boast rating increases over the previous season. Two were on NBC's Thursday schedule. *Father Knows Best* added one tenth of a point and *Dragnet*'s rating was two-tenths higher. The increases were minimal but they were still better than the CBS competition fared.

Father Knows Best was slotted against Thursday's Number One program, *Mr. Keen*, which clung to first place despite a 23 percent loss of audience. Meanwhile, *Suspense* lost 30 percent opposite *Dragnet*.

The overall downward trend was obvious and would become more so the following season.

HEAR SPOT!

Although it didn't reach and season's Top 50 and never would, *Screen Directors' Playhouse* showed a rare rating increase of 11 percent and broke into Thursday's Top Ten. It was cancelled at the beginning of the following season.

Nevertheless, the program made history within the industry as one of NBC Radio's first prime time shows to be offered to a group of non-competing, participating advertisers for their spot announcements as opposed to a single advertiser's sponsorship of entire programs. Within a few years virtually all radio and television programs would be sold in the same manner.

CASEY STRIKES OUT

Casey, Crime Photographer had bounced around the CBS schedule since 1943, often used as a sustaining filler. The newspaper crime drama, featuring unique jazz piano interludes at the hero's favorite hangout bar, *Casey* finally snared Anchor Hocking Glass as its sponsor in 1947 and scored the first of four consecutive Top 50 seasons, all of them ranking among Thursday's Top Ten.

The glass company dropped the program after one season but CBS had no problem in selling it to Toni Home Permanents for two years and Philip Morris Cigarettes beginning in 1949. The formulaic series starring veteran radio actor Staats Cotsworth as the sleuthing photographer was a ratings and commercial success.

Casey was on its way to its fifth successful season, registering a 10.0 rating two months into the 1950–51 season, when it was cancelled by Philip Morris. Instead of carrying the show on a sustaining basis and using its proven track record as the lure for a new sponsor, CBS dumped the program. The network reasoned that post-war listeners wanted realistic crime dramas — evidenced by NBC's *Dragnet*— not the simplistic, pulp fiction plots and heroes that were popular during the 1930s and '40s.

Nevertheless, CBS-TV programmed a video version of *Casey, Crime Photographer* the following year and the radio series returned for 14 month encore run in 1954.

COPY CAT COPS?

Hallmark Playhouse was moved back to 9:30. Its former timeslot at 10:00 was given to a new police drama stressing realistic situations and dialogue, *The Lineup*. Coming when it did on the CBS schedule, a half-hour following NBC's *Dragnet*, comparisons between the two cop shows were natural.

The Lineup was given strong a strong cast which included some of Hollywood's best radio actors behind star Bill Johnstone — Joseph Kearns, Wally Maher, Raymond Burr, John McIntire and Sheldon Leonard.

Despite its high production values, *The Lineup* was always considered a CBS attempt to cash in on Jack Webb's ground-breaking approach to police drama in *Dragnet*. *The Lineup* remained on the CBS schedule for two and a half

years. All but two months of the program's run were unsponsored — a reflection that Network Radio was becoming a tough sell.

1950–51 Friday Night Top Ten Programs
ABC 5, CBS 4, NBC 1
Average: 8.3

The Fat Man	ABC	8:00	10.5
This Is Your FBI	ABC	8:30	8.8
Beulah*	CBS	7:00	9.4
Adventures of Ozzie & Harriet	ABC	9:00	8.7
Richard Diamond, Private Detective	ABC	8:00	8.2
Life of Riley	NBC	9:00	8.1
Jack Smith Show*	CBS	7:15	7.8
The Lone Ranger/ Brace Beemer	ABC	7:30	7.5
Club 15*	CBS	7:30	7.2
Lowell Thomas News*	CBS	6:45	7.1

*Monday–Friday Strip Shows

Sans Strips...

Duffy's Tavern	NBC	9:30	6.4
The Sheriff	ABC	9:30	6.1
Friday Night Boxing	ABC	10:00	5.9
Bill Stern's Colgate Sports Newsreel	NBC	10:30	4.4

RAISING A FAMILY TAKES TIME

A whimsical family sitcom finally made the season's Top 50 after six years of trying. Few would have thought that it could become the basis for a legendary television series except its creator, Ozzie Nelson.

Like Rudy Vallee, Nelson was a singing saxophone player who formed a dance band in college to make ends meet. A born promoter, Nelson took his band on the road and by 1932 became a headline attraction when he hired a girl singer, Harriet Hilliard. The pair's sweetheart duets had an effect — they were married in 1935, the same year their prime time radio careers began — providing the music for the Joe Penner *Bakers' Broadcast*, then a Top Ten program.

For the next ten years Harriet sang with the band, gave birth to the couple's two sons, David and Ricky, and pursued a movie career. The most notable of her 16 films was the 1936 Fred Astaire/Ginger Rogers military musical, *Follow the*

Fleet. The remainder were B grade quickies. Ozzie appeared with her in three of the films — *Campus Sweethearts*, *Take It Big* and *Hi, Good Lookin'*—titles indicative of their content and quality.

The Nelsons' next big broadcast break came in 1941 when they were signed for the new *Raleigh Cigarette Program* starring Red Skelton, an immediate Top Five hit for three seasons until Skelton was drafted It was generally assumed that Ozzie and Harriet would take the show until the comedian's return.

But the cigarette maker opted instead for *Hildegarde's Raleigh Room*, which put the Nelsons out of work — and lost 45 percent of Skelton's ratings.

Meanwhile, Ozzie had the idea for a sitcom loosely based on the couple's real family life and was encouraged to develop it by his friend, *People Are Funny* and *You Bet Your Life* producer John Guedel.

The Adventures of Ozzie & Harriet spent four so-so years on CBS and another on NBC before Heinz Foods moved it into ABC's powerful Friday lineup in 1949 where it remained for five seasons.

In 1952, the program was adapted for television. It became an ABC-TV staple for the next 14 years, joining *Father Knows Best* and *Make Room for Daddy* as symbols of 1950s family values.

NUMBER ONE TO NUMBER NONE

Author Dashiell Hammett was radio poison. The political faction he headed, the Civil Rights Congress of New York, was branded a Communist front group by the Attorney General's office in 1947.

One by one, the programs with which Hammett's name was associated, all disappeared.

The Adventures of the Thin Man was gone in 1949, *The Adventures of Sam Spade* followed in 1950 and in January 1951, it was *The Fat Man*'s turn despite its Number One ranking on Friday. It was moved to Wednesday, vanished from the Nielsen ratings and was gone nine months later.

DICK'S ANOTHER NAME FOR DETECTIVE

When ABC's 8:00 timeslot became available with the departure of *The Fat Man*, Camel Cigarettes plucked *Richard Diamond, Private Detective* from NBC and moved it into the upstart network's popular Friday lineup.

The series was created by Blake Edwards who later contributed suave *Peter Gunn* to television and Peter Sellers' bumbling Inspector Clouseau to films. Edwards tailored *Richard Diamond* for the talents of Dick Powell, Warner Brothers' leading musical comedy star of the 1930s who was reshaping his image as a tough guy in a series of film noir mysteries for RKO.

Richard Diamond combined the two Powell persona. It was a light-hearted mystery series in which the happy go lucky hero would invariably break into a song before or after the business of pursuing the villain of the week. The smartly written show — with support given to Powell by some of Hollywood's best radio actors — and finished in the season's Top 50 for two consecutive years before the star turned his attention to television's *Four Star Playhouse* in 1952.

1950–51 Saturday Night Top Ten Programs
CBS 5, NBC 5
Average: 8.7

Gene Autry's Melody Ranch	CBS	8:00	10.2
Gangbusters	CBS	9:00	10.1
Hopalong Cassidy	CBS	8:30	9.8
Judy Canova Show	NBC	10:00	9.4
A Day in the Life of Dennis Day	NBC	9:30	8.8
My Favorite Husband	CBS	9:30	8.8
Vaughn Monroe Show	CBS	7:30	8.6
Grand Ole Opry	NBC	10:30	8.0
Your Hit Parade	NBC	9:00	7.7
The Man Called X	NBC	8:30	5.9

RIDE 'EM COWBOYS!

CBS corralled the television's cowboy craze for Network Radio on Saturday night.

Gene Autry's Melody Ranch was one of only a few weekly prime time programs to show a ratings increase over the previous season. After eight years on the air without a Top 50 finish, the singing cowboy vaulted into the season's 22nd place with double digit ratings.

Like Roy Rogers, who would later have a radio and television contract with NBC, Autry already had his own deal with CBS. His weekly half-hour filmed western adventure series debuted on CBS-TV's prime time Sunday schedule in July 1950 and remained with the network for six seasons.

The synergy between radio and television to propel the popularity of cowboy movie stars was never more evident than the unlikely star who followed Autry on Saturday nights.

HIP HOPPY

Handsome, silver haired William Boyd had starred in 66 low budget *Hopalong Cassidy* westerns from 1935 through 1948.

The 53-year-old Boyd saw the potential of television in 1948 and borrowed $350,000 *(3.3 Mil)*, to purchase the television rights to his 13 year library of films. He then successfully syndicated his movies to television stations which hungered for programming.

Boyd was discovered by a new generation of fans and was on his way to becoming a multi-millionaire. Black clad *Hopalong Cassidy* aboard his white horse Topper was suddenly as popular with juvenile audiences as Roy Rogers and Trigger or Gene Autry and Champion.

The flood of revenue from his old movies, personal appearances and merchandise sales enabled Boyd to produce another 54 hour and half hour adventures for television. His 1950–51 Sunday series on NBC-TV ranked ninth among all television programs for the season.

General Foods and its ad agency, Foote, Cone & Belding, were quick to hop on Hoppy's wagon with a nine month Sunday afternoon radio run on Mutual in early 1950. General's Grape Nuts cereal moved the show to CBS in September to follow *Gene Autry's Melody Ranch* on Saturday at 8:30.

The transcribed *Hopalong Cassidy* adventures from syndicator Commodore Productions, literally shot their way into Saturday's Top Ten and the annual Top 30 for two years until the cowboy fad ran its course.

TO MAKE A LONG TITLE SHORT

A Day in the Life of Dennis Day was faced with new competition when CBS and General Foods slotted Lucille Ball's *My Favorite Husband* against the Irish singer/comedian in September.

The 9:30 time period became a ratings race between the two sitcoms until midway through the season when Colgate decided that Day's format with the long-winded title had run its course after four Top 50 seasons and two consecutive Top 25 finishes. The show was converted to a variety format in January and became *The Dennis Day Show*, with the singer as its host.

The mid-season switch didn't work. Day's ratings sank 30 percent.

The maneuver also handed Ball the time period's sitcom audience. As a result, the two shows finished the season in a dead heat. The tie was enough to give the redheaded comedienne her only Top 50 season.

Nevertheless, Lucille Ball left radio in April. Taking her radio show's producer Jess Oppenheimer and writers Bob Carroll and Madelyn Pugh with her, she and husband Desi Arnaz introduced their legendary CBS-TV sitcom, *I Love Lucy*, seven months later.

REPEATS BUILD RATINGS

People Are Funny and *You Bet Your Life* producer John Guedel is rightfully hailed as an innovator.

One of his ideas, however, didn't seem to work at the time. In retrospect, he was simply ahead of his time.

Guedel was a pioneer in transcribed programming. His productions were recorded, edited and polished on tape as quickly as technology and network permission allowed. But Guedel also saw an additional benefit to recorded programs — repeat broadcasts.

He and his *People Are Funny* host/partner Art Linkletter introduced taped rebroadcasts of their Tuesday hit to NBC's Saturday schedule in September 1950.

The concept provided sponsor Brown & Williamson Tobacco with relatively inexpensive programming that lacked most of its original production costs. It also gave NBC the revenue of 30 minutes' network time that might have otherwise gone unsold faced with television's increasing competition for Saturday night's audience.

The one year run of *People Are Funny* rebroadcasts on NBC's Saturday schedule averaged only a 3.7 rating. But combined with *People's* Tuesday rating of 10.3, the two broadcasts' total rating of 14.0 would have pushed *People Are Funny* into the season's Top Five at a bargain basement price.

Regardless, Brown & Williamson cancelled at the end of the season.

Although abandoned at the time, Guedel's concept to build cumulative rating points through repeat programming is common in both broadcast and cable television today.

A CBS First

Amos & Andy couldn't do it. Neither could *Myrt & Marge* nor *I Love a Mystery*.

But *Beulah* did.

The serialized sitcom became the first program broadcast by CBS to ever reach Number One in the Multiple Run category. Hattie Mc-

Daniel's portrayal of the jolly and warm-hearted housemaid led CBS to its third of six consecutive seasons dominating the Multiple Run Top Ten.

Henry and Fanny's Golden Years

One Man's Family had enjoyed a peaceful three year semi-retirement on NBC's Sunday afternoon schedule until Standard Brands dropped the show in 1949. The network carried the serial as a sustaining Sunday feature through the 1949–50 season but cancellation was imminent.

Then, Miles Laboratories came to its rescue in June 1950 and thrust the Barbour family back into prime time as a Monday through Friday strip at 7:45.

The success of the program's conversion from a weekly half hour to the new nightly quarter hour format was immediate. Henry and Fanny Barbour's clan broke into the Multiple Run Top Ten, edging out the CBS competition in their time period, newscaster Edward R. Murrow.

One Man's Family outlived Network Radio's Golden Age by half a dozen years, remaining in the 7:45 NBC timeslot until May 1959. Its creator, Carleton E. Morse, supervised the entire 27 year run — all 3,256 episodes of the family saga.

How to Kill a Hero

ABC and sponsor General Mills broke the spirit of America's favorite late afternoon adventure serial in 1947. *Jack Armstrong, the All American Boy* was converted from a daily 15 minute strip to half-hours of self-contained stories, alternating every other day with another conversion to the 30 minute format, *Sky King.*

Gone were the extended stories that could drag on for months and the cliff hanging Friday episodes that kept kids hooked on the shows over weekends. The network and sponsor rebuffed these two soap opera elements that also contributed to listener loyalty among juvenile serial fans.

Nevertheless, the two watered-down half hour melodramas remained on the ABC schedule for three seasons until June 1950 when *Sky King* moved to Mutual, where it stayed alive for four more years.

Jack Armstrong wasn't so lucky.

After a three month hiatus over the summer of 1950, "The All American Boy" suddenly grew up as *Armstrong of the SBI* and moved into ABC's primetime on Tuesday and Thursday at 7:30, alternating with *The Lone Ranger's* Monday-Wednesday-Friday broadcasts. Both shows were sponsored by General Mills.

Charles Flynn had played teenager *Jack Armstrong* since 1939. At age 30 he could finally use his adult speaking voice as a government agent in pursuit of villains for the "Scientific Bureau of Investigation."

But listeners didn't buy the new storyline.

Armstrong of the SBI trailed *The Lone Ranger's* ratings in the 7:30 time period by over 25 percent, sinking into low single digits. The series was cancelled in June and the once legendary role-model for kids was gone.

1950–51 Multiple Run Top Ten Programs CBS 5, ABC 2, NBC 2, MBS 1 Average: 6.7				
Beulah*	M–F	CBS	7:00	9.4
Jack Smith Show*	M–F	CBS	7:15	7.8
The Lone Ranger	M,W,F	ABC	7:30	7.5
Club 15*	M–F	CBS	7:30	7.2
Lowell Thomas News*	M–F	CBS	6:45	7.1
One Man's Family*	M–F	NBC	7:45	6.3
Morgan Beatty News of the World*	M–F	NBC	7:15	6.0
Edward R Murrow News*	M–F	CBS	7:45	5.6
Armstrong of the SBI	Tu,Th	ABC	7:30	5.5
Gabriel Heatter News*	M–F	MBS	7:30	4.4
*Monday–Friday Strip Shows				

TOP 50 PROGRAMS—1950–51

CBS 30, NBC 16, ABC 5, MBS 1 (52)*
Average Rating: 10.5, Median: 10.1
40,700,000 Radio Homes / 94.7% Coverage of U.S. Homes / One Rating Point = 407,000 Homes
Source: A.C. Nielsen Radio Index Serv, Sept 1950–June 1951
Total Programs Rated, 6–11 P.M.: 163
Programs Rated 13 Weeks & Ranked: 126

		Program	Rtg	Type	Sponsor	Day	Time	Lgth	Net
1	1	Lux Radio Theater/William Keighley	17.9	DA	Lux Soap	Mon	9:00	60	CBS
2	2	Jack Benny Program	15.6	SC	Lucky Strike Cigarettes	Sun	7:00	30	CBS
3	7	Edgar Bergen & Charlie McCarthy	14.7	CV	Coca-Cola	Sun	8:00	30	CBS
4	9	Amos & Andy	14.0	SC	Rexall Drug Stores	Sun	7:30	30	CBS
5	3	Arthur Godfrey's Talent Scouts	13.4	TC	Lipton Tea	Mon	8:30	30	CBS
6	5	My Friend Irma/Marie Wilson	13.3	SC	Pepsodent Toothpaste	Mon	10:00	30	CBS
7	6	Walter Winchell's Journal	12.4	NC	Richard Hudnut Cosmetics	Sun	9:00	15	ABC
8	14	Red Skelton Show	11.9	CV	Tide Laundry Detergent	Sun	8:30	30	CBS
9	11	You Bet Your Life/Groucho Marx	11.8	APQ	DeSoto & Plymouth Autos	Wed	9:00	30	CBS 1
10	15	Mr Chameleon/Karl Swenson	11.6	DCC	Bayer Aspirin	Wed	8:00	30	CBS
11	16	Mystery Theater	11.4	DCC	Bayer Aspirin	Tue	8:00	30	CBS
12	26	Mr & Mrs North/Joe Curtin, Alice Frost	12.3	DCC	Halo Shampoo	Tue	8:30	30	CBS
13t	4	Fibber McGee & Molly	11.1	SC	Pet Milk	Tue	9:30	30	NBC
13t	32	Life with Luigi/J.Carrol Naish	11.1	SC	Wrigley Chewing Gum	Tue	9:00	30	CBS
15t	24	Mr District Attorney/Jay Jostyn	10.7	DCC	Vitalis Hair Tonic	Wed	9:30	30	NBC
15t	12	Mr Keen/Arthur Hughes	10.7	DCC	Kolynos Toothpaste	Thu	7:30	30	CBS
17t	19	Bob Hawk Show	10.5	APQ	Camel Cigarettes	Mon	10:30	30	CBS
17t	32	The Fat Man/J Scott Smart	10.5	DCC	Pepto Bismol	Fri	8:00	30	ABC
19	28	The Big Story	10.4	DA	Pall Mall Cigarettes	Wed	10:00	30	NBC
20t	N	Hollywood Star Playhouse	10.3	DA	Bromo Seltzer	Mon	8:00	30	CBS
20t	13	People Are Funny/Art Linkletter	10.3	APS	Raleigh Cigarettes	Tue	10:30	30	NBC
22t	38	Dr. Christian/Jean Hersholt	10.2	DCC	Vaseline	Wed	8:30	30	CBS
22t	26	The FBI in Peace & War	10.2	DCC	Lava Hand Soap	Thu	8:00	30	CBS
22t	53	Gene Autry's Melody Ranch	10.2	DCC	Wrigley Chewing Gum	Sat	8:00	30	CBS
25	36	Gangbusters	10.1	DA	Grape Nuts Cereal	Sat	9:00	30	CBS
26t	8	Bing Crosby Show	9.8	MV	Chesterfield Cigarees	Wed	9:30	30	CBS
26t	N	Hopalong Cassidy/William Boyd	9.8	DCC	Grape Nuts Cereal	Sat	8:30	30	CBS
26t	40	Our Miss Brooks/Eve Arden	9.8	SC	Lustre Creme Shampoo	Sun	6:30	30	CBS
29t	16	Fanny Brice Baby Snooks Show	9.7	SC	Tums Antacid Tablets	Tue	8:30	30	NBC
29t	24	Great Gildersleeve/Willard Waterman	9.7	SC	Parkay Margarine	Wed	8:30	30	NBC
29t	32	Hallmark Playhouse/James Hilton	9.7	DA	Hallmark Cards	Thu	9:30	30	CBS
29t	28	Horace Heidt Youth Oppty Program	9.7	TC	Philip Morris Cigarettes	Sun	9:30	30	CBS
33	10	Bob Hope Show	9.6	CV	Swan Soap	Tue	9:00	30	NBC
34	53	Father Knows Best/Robert Young	9.5	SC	Grape Nuts Cereal & Jello	Thu	8:30	30	NBC
35t	48	Beulah/Hattie McDaniel	9.4	SC	Dreft Laundry Soap	M–F	7:00	15	CBS
35t	22	Big Town/Ed Pawley	9.4	DCC	Lifebuoy Soap	Tue	10:00	30	NBC
35t	30	Judy Canova Show	9.4	CV	Colgate Dental Cream	Sat	10:00	30	NBC
38t	58	Meet Corliss Archer/Janet Waldo	9.3	SC	Electric Companies Co-op	Sun	9:00	30	CBS
38t	16	Suspense	9.3	DA	Autolite Spark Plugs	Thu	9:00	30	CBS
40	52	Aldrich Family/Ezra Stone	9.1	SC	Grape Nuts Cereal & Jello	Thu	8:00	30	NBC
41	37	Truth or Consequences/ Ralph Edwards	9.0	APS	Philip Morris Cigarettes	Tue	9:30	30	CBS
42t	23	The Dennis Day Show	8.8	CV	Lustre Creme Shampoo	Sat	9:30	30	NBC 2
42t	85	My Favorite Husband/Lucille Ball	8.8	SC	Maxwell House Coffee	Sat	9:30	30	CBS
42t	35	This Is Your FBI	8.8	DCC	Equitable Life Assurance	Fri	8:30	30	ABC
45t	60	Adventures of Ozzie & Harriet	8.7	SC	Heinz Foods	Fri	9:00	30	ABC
45t	64	Dragnet/Jack Webb	8.7	DCC	Fatima Cigarettes	Thu	9:00	30	NBC
47	53	Vaughn Monroe Show	8.6	MV	Camel Cigarettes	Sat	7:30	30	CBS
48	70	The Railroad Hour/Gordon MacRae	8.3	DA	American Railroad Assn	Mon	8:00	30	NBC
49	N	Richard Diamond, Priv Det/ Dick Powell	8.2	DCC	Camel Cigarettes	Fri	8:00	30	ABC 3
50t	44	Life of Riley/William Bendix	8.1	SC	Pabst Beer	Fri	10:00	30	NBC
50t	66	Roy Rogers Show	8.1	DCC	Quaker Oats	Sun	6:00	30	MBS
50t	48	Theater Guild on the Air	8.1	DA	US Steel	Sun	8:30	60	NBC

*Three programs tied for 50th.
New & Returning Top 50 Programs Underscored.

1	You Bet Your Life/Groucho Marx	Oct–Dec	Elgin Watches	Wed	9:00	30	CBS
2	A Day in the Life of Dennis Day	Oct–Jan	Lustre Creme Shampoo	Sat	9:30	30	NBC
3	Richard Diamond, Private Detective	Sep–Dec	Rexall Drug Stores	Wed	10:30	30	NBC

Key: API — Audience Participation/Interviews
APQ — Audience Participation/Quiz
APS — Audience Participation/Stunts
CV — Comedy/Variety Show
DA — Dramatic Anthology

DCC — Drama/Continuing Characters
MC — Music/Classical, Semi-Classical
MP — Music/Popular, Contemporary
MSP — Music/Specialty, Ethnic
MST — Music/Standard, Traditional

MV — Music/Variety Show
NC — News, Commentary
SC — Situation Comedy
SP — Sports
TC — Talent Competition

1950–51 Top 50* Favorite Formats

	Programs	Pct
Drama — Anthology & Continuing	23	44%
Comedy — Variety & Situation	20	38%
Audience Participation — All Categories	4	8%
Music — All Categories	4	8%
News/Commentary	1	2%

*Total: 52 (Three programs tied for 50th.)

1950–51 Monthly Winners

Sep	Lux Radio Theater	15.9	Feb	Lux Radio Theater	21.3
Oct	Lux Radio Theater	18.4	Mar	Lux Radio Theater	19.2
Nov	Lux Radio Theater	20.2	Apr	Lux Radio Theater	17.8
Dec	Lux Radio Theater	21.0	May	Lux Radio Theater	14.4
Jan	Jack Benny Program	19.8	Jun	Edgar Bergen & Charlie McCarthy	11.8
				& Amos & Andy	11.8

24

The 1951–52 Network Season

Announcer: When you want expert opinion you go to the experts. When the Camel people wanted expert opinion on cigarette mildness they went to noted throat specialists ... leaders in their profession. These specialists made weekly examinations of hundreds of men and women who smoked only Camels for thirty days. The smokers included heavy smokers and light smokers ... people in different climates, in different parts of the country. The specialists made over two thousand careful examinations and they reported not one single case of throat irritation due to smoking Camels! Try Camels for yourself! Smoke only Camels for thirty days and see how mild Camels are ... how well they agree with your throat, pack after pack. You'll enjoy Camel's flavor, too ... rich, full flavor that you won't find in any other cigarette. You'll see why Camel is by far America's most popular cigarette!

ANNC 2: Doctors in every branch of medicine, in all parts of the country, were asked: "What cigarette do you smoke, Doctor?" The brand named most was Camel. Yes, according to this nationwide survey, more doctors smoke Camels than any other cigarette!

TV COOKS WITH MICROWAVE

Television continued to grow rapidly in technical development and popularity.

AT&T completed the installation of over a hundred microwave towers that traversed 3,000 miles, crossed the Rockies and linked both coasts with live video transmission. The path was cleared for live variety and dramatic show TV production from Hollywood — an advantage previously exclusive to Network Radio.

And as had been the case with radio, prime time television production would begin to shift from low-cost Chicago and Broadway-oriented New York to the glamour and glitz of the movie capital.

Improved programming and production techniques sold television sets at the rate of over 400,000 units per month. A third of America's homes had become television households.

RADIO CHAINS LINKED TO LOSSES

Adding to Network Radio's woes, increased competition from over a thousand AM stations newly licensed since 1947 — mostly independent outlets — cut further into the audience of established network affiliates.

For the first time, the average rating of the season's Top 50 and nightly Top Ten Network Radio shows fell into single digits, a new low.

People Are Funny, Groucho Marx's *You Bet Your Life, Dragnet, The Adventures of Ozzie & Harriet* and *Hopalong Cassidy* became Network Radio's first programs to win their respective nights with less than a ten rating — numbers that only two years earlier would have barely scratched the season's Top 50.

As ratings went, so went revenues. To stay competitive, all four radio networks cut their evening rates from 15 to 25 percent.

The radio chains finished 1951 with their greatest drop in income since 1933 in the depths of the Great Depression. Network Radio took a $16.8 Million hit *(146.2 Mil),* totaling a 15.5 percent revenue decrease in three years.

For the first time since the networks were established 24 years earlier, their share of total U.S. radio income dropped below 30 percent — and there seemed no way to reverse the trend.

Meanwhile, the networks' television billings leaped to $180.8 Million in 1951 *(1.57 Bil),* up an astounding 112 percent in just one year and passing the radio networks by $1.3 Million *(11.3 Mil).*

DREAM, WEAVER

Like Bill Paley at CBS, NBC's Pat Weaver was a strong proponent of the networks producing the programs they aired, not just providing their facilities for shows provided by advertisers and their agencies. In doing so, he advanced a new way to sell radio and television network advertising.

Citing the high production costs inherent to television, Weaver argued that underwriting sponsor-

1951–52 Season Scoreboard			
Mid-season Totals, December 1951			
		Compared to Year Earlier	
Total Radio Homes	41.9 Mil	+1.20 Mil	+2.9%
Total Auto Radios	21.0 Mil	+3.0 Mil	+16 7%
Total AM Radio Stations	2,232	+146	+7.0%
Total Radio Network Affiliates	1,210	+40	+3.4%
1951 Radio Revenues	606.3 Mil	+0.9 Mil	+0.1%
1951 Network Revenues	179.5 Mil	(16.8 Mil)	(8.6%)
Network Share	29.6%		(2.8%)
Total TV Homes	15.1 Mil	+5.2 Mil	+53.1%
Total TV Stations	111	+1	+0.9%
Total FM Stations	749	(32)	(4.1%)

ships of entire programs would become economically infeasible. Instead of offering network time to individual advertisers in 30 or 60 *minute* chunks, Weaver proposed selling commercials within network produced programs to multiple advertisers in 30 and 60 *second* units Already practiced to a limited degree in Network Radio, Weaver wanted to make it routine.

He called the concept *magazine* advertising. It was already known and wide spread in local market radio and television as *spot* advertising — more formally, *participating* advertising.

NBC introduced spot advertising to network television in January 1952 with the debut of Weaver's ground breaking morning program, *Today*.

The network produced program and its new way of selling commercial time both had their critics.

Nevertheless, *The Today Show* is still a fixture on NBC-TV and virtually all radio and television advertising is now sold in spots.

Weaver also foresaw a new kind of Network Radio program. His autobiography dates the idea back to the spring of 1952 when he first proposed *Monitor*, a 40 hour weekend marathon mosaic of entertainment, news, sports and feature segments anchored by popular network personalities. It took three years to put all the pieces together.

Monitor finally hit the air in June 1955 and remained on the NBC weekend schedule for 20 years.

RCA's David Sarnoff and his son Robert still controlled NBC, however. The elder Sarnoff's ego was bruised when Weaver was hailed in the press for his many innovations. The pair rewarded the former advertising man who turned NBC's fortunes around by pushing him out of network power in 1956.

GIVE ME LIBERTY ... ER ... GIVE ME DEBT

Gordon McLendon's Liberty Broadcasting System, with its daily mix of live and recreated baseball games, had grown to 481 affiliates in the summer of 1951, second only to Mutual in size.

Mutual and major league baseball had long-standing association

with the network's exclusive coverage of the annual All-Star game and World Series. They decided that something had to be done about the maverick from Texas who was leeching broadcast rights to big league games for a mere $1,000 a year ($8,700).

Adding insult to injury, *The Sporting News* named Gordon McLendon as, "America's Outstanding Sports Broadcaster of the Year" in 1951.

Mutual retaliated first in 1950 with its own *Game of the Day*— play-by-play broadcasts featuring sportscasters Al Helfer, Gene Kirby and Art Gleeson originating their reports directly from the ballparks, not a studio in Dallas. Then Mutual went after McLendon's primary sponsor, Falstaff Beer.

Organized Baseball followed with a demand that McLendon pay an annual $250,000 (2.2 Mil), in rights fees and prohibited Liberty baseball broadcasts in any city that had a major *or* minor league team, claiming that Liberty's radio broadcasts of major league games weakened minor league attendance.

Faced with these impossible obstacles plus the loss of its key sponsor, Liberty began to hemorrhage money and shut down operations in May 1952. McLendon sued baseball for twelve million dollars in damages (104.4 Mil).

"The Old Scotchman" settled out of court for $200,000 (1.7 Mil), three years later. By that time the crafty McLendon had become a successful early proponent of Todd Storz' Top 40 format at his Dallas, Houston and San Antonio radio stations. He later pioneered the "good music" and all-news radio formats in what became his ten city chain of a dozen AM and FM independent stations.

Mutual continued its daily baseball broadcasts until 1960. At its peak, *Game of the Day* had 458 affiliates, several dozen shy of Liberty's record when McLendon and his young crew created play-by-play broadcasts with wire reports and colorful imaginations.

THE EYES HAVE IT

Television continued to offer a familiar and formidable lineup of

programs appealing to Network Radio audiences.

Radio properties converted to television remained the fastest, most convenient — and sometimes cheapest — means that the television networks had to lure new viewers, push their ratings and attract bigger advertising dollars.

ABC-TV offered *The Amazing Mr. Malone, Beulah, Chance of a Lifetime, Charlie Wild Private Eye, The Clock, The Lone Ranger, Mr. District Attorney* and *Stop the Music*.

CBS-TV countered with *Amos & Andy, Arthur Godfrey's Talent Scouts, Big Town, Blue Ribbon Bouts, Burns & Allen, Casey, Crime Photographer, The Frank Sinatra Show, The Fred Waring Show, The Garry Moore Show, The Jack Benny Program, Lux Video Theater, Perry Como's Chesterfield Supper Club, The Sammy Kaye Show, Songs for Sale, Strike It Rich* and *Suspense*.

CBS also introduced *I Love Lucy* in 1951, a variation of Lucille Ball's CBS radio sitcom, *My Favorite Husband*.

NBC-TV boasted *The Aldrich Family, The Big Story, Break the Bank, You Bet Your Life, The Kate Smith Hour, Leave It to the Girls, Lights Out, Martin Kane Private Eye, One Man's Family, The Original Amateur Hour, The Quiz Kids, The Voice of Firestone, The Wayne King Show, We the People* and *Your Hit Parade*.

Some of the conversions went on to successful television runs — including a few legends. Others were simply filling time until something better came along. All further lessened whatever unique programming that remained on Network Radio.

INFOMERCIAL PLEAS

Mutual introduced another innovation to Network Radio in 1951— programs of solid commercial appeals with the sole purpose of moving merchandise — known today as *infomercials*.

Homecraft Industries presented *How to Play the Piano*, which popped up occasionally in prime time to sell piano lesson books. Meanwhile, Mutual's 9:30 to 10:00 timeslot weekday mornings was briefly given over to pitches for "Charles Antell's Formula Nine" hair pomade and National Health Aids vitamins in back to back 15 minute segments.

THE MONTHLIES

CBS pushed its number of consecutive month-winning programs to 30.

Lux Radio Theater won six of the season's ten months and Jack Benny captured three. *Amos & Andy* won March — providing Freeman Gosden and Charles Correll their first outright monthly win in their 23 year Network Radio career.

1951–52 Sunday Night
Top Ten Programs
CBS 7, NBC 2, ABC 1
Average: 9.1

Amos & Andy	CBS	7:30	13.4
Jack Benny Program	CBS	7:00	12.9
Edgar Bergen & Charlie McCarthy	CBS	8:00	11.2
Walter Winchell's Journal	ABC	9:00	9.2
Horace Heidt Youth Opportunity Program	CBS	8:30	8.8
Our Miss Brooks	CBS	6:30	8.6
Theater Guild on the Air	NBC	8:30	7.8
Philip Morris Playhouse on Broadway	CBS	8:30	7.3
Carnation Contented Hour	CBS	9:30	6.4
Phil Harris & Alice Faye	NBC	8:00	6.4

A&A PLUS

Amos & Andy not only captured its first monthly win in March but also registered the program's first nightly win since Monday of the 1934–35 season when it was the giant among 15 minute Multiple Run programs.

Only eight years had passed since Freeman Gosden, 53, and Charles Correll, 62, were considered washed up in radio when the quarter hour *Amos & Andy* dropped to 70th place in the season's rankings. Their remarkable comeback in half-hour sitcom format rewarded Lever Brothers' Rinso laundry soap with the season's second highest rated program — just half a rating point behind Lever's *Lux Radio Theater*.

Gosden and Correll were also rewarded with the loyalty of CBS which kept them on the radio network long after the sitcom had run its course in 1955. Their *Amos & Andy's Music Hall*, a glorified disc jockey show, ran as a nightly strip show of 30 and 45 minutes with participating sponsors until November 1960.

WINCHELL'S ILLS

Walter Winchell, citing a "complete rest" ordered by his doctors after a second nervous breakdown within a year, cut his broadcast season short and left the air after his March 23 ABC broadcast. The columnist was in the midst of his twelfth and last Top Ten season at the time.

The bombastic Winchell had proclaimed himself—like Wisconsin Senator Joe McCarthy—a "Crusading commie fighter," and flung innuendo-laden accusations with abandon in his newspaper columns and weekly broadcasts. His list of formidable critics and enemies grew to include leaders of both political parties, the NAACP and most every other influential syndicated columnist. Winchell found himself in a constant state of self-created public and private battles — more than enough to give anyone a nervous breakdown.

Winchell's broadcasts were filled following his departure by Erwin Canham and then Taylor Grant before Drew Pearson took over for the rest of the season in April. Despite Pearson's popularity, Winchell sponsor Richard Hudnut Cosmetics immediately cancelled its $500,000 annual contract *(4.4 Mil)*.

Winchell returned to his Sunday program six months later but never regained his former popularity.

WHAT WERE YOU SMOKING?

Philip Morris Cigarettes had sponsored *The Philip Morris Playhouse* on CBS for five years — three of which were Top 50 seasons. The program was renamed *The Philip Morris Playhouse on Broadway* in September and moved to NBC for four months. It was pulled from the network and moved back to CBS in January.

To make room for *Playhouse on Broadway* on CBS — and make the situation even more unusual — Philip Morris cancelled Horace Heidt's *Youth Opportunity Program* talent show — a Top 30 program for two consecutive seasons.

At season's end, Heidt's cancelled series finished in his career high 13th place — *Philip Morris Playhouse on Broadway*'s ratings trailed Heidt by 20 percent and finished 30th.

GI JO WINS LAST HOUR BATTLE

Former Tommy Dorsey band singer Jo Stafford had carved out a successful solo career for herself in both records and radio since 1944 when she became a favorite entertainer of American servicemen stationed overseas who dubbed her "G.I. Jo."

The beautiful 34-year-old Stafford had co-hosted NBC's *Chesterfield Supper Club* with Perry Como for five seasons. Leaving the show in 1949, she returned to radio as permanent co-host of Carnation's *Contented Hour* on CBS in March 1950.

Stafford and her co-star, veteran film actor/singer Tony Martin, pushed *Contented Hour*'s ratings back into contention. The long running show placed 40th in the 1951–52 season — its first Top 50 finish in 17 years.

Yet, Carnation cancelled *Contented Hour* in December.

Eight months later, Jo Stafford became an international star with the release of *You Belong to Me*, the Number One record in both the United States and Great Britain. Stafford's string of hits made her Columbia Records' top selling female artist of the early 1950s and the company's first recording star to sell over 25 million records.

TUNE IN TURNOVER

Contented Hour was one of Sunday's seven former Top Ten shows that disappeared from the schedule over the course of the season. Red Skelton moved to CBS on Wednesday, *Meet Corliss Archer* left for ABC on Friday and Mutual's Roy Rogers rode off to NBC's Friday schedule. *The American Album of Familiar Music*, Horace Heidt's

Youth Opportunity Program and Louella Parsons' *Hollywood News* joined *Contented* as December cancellations.

IRMA'S WIN STREAKS MEET ENNDS

Lever Brothers' Pepsodent Toothpaste surprisingly cancelled *My Friend Irma* in June.

The sitcom had ranked among Monday's Top Ten the season's Top Ten programs for four consecutive years since its debut on CBS in 1947.

The show was picked up by a small independent drug firm, Pearson Pharmacal, manufacturers of Ennds Chlorophyl Tablets, touted to rid its consumers of bad breath, perspiration odors *and* smelly feet.

Pearson was a forerunner in a short lived fad of the early 1950s during which a number of toothpastes, soaps and chewing gums became green in color to promote their "new and improved" formulas containing chlorophyl, billed as "Nature's Deodorant."

Pearson moved *My Friend Irma* from the heart of Monday prime time to the CBS Sunday schedule at 6:00. Without the powerful lead-in provided by Monday's *Lux Radio Theater*, the one joke sitcom starring Marie Wilson lost over 55 percent of its audience, failed to reach Sunday's Top Ten and dropped out of the season's Top 50.

1951–52 Monday Night Top Ten Programs
CBS 5, NBC 4, ABC 1
Average: 7.4

Lux Radio Theater	CBS	9:00	13.9
Arthur Godfrey's Talent Scouts	CBS	8:30	9.7
Bob Hawk Show	CBS	10:00	9.1
Suspense	CBS	8:00	9.0
Railroad Hour	NBC	8:00	7.2
Beulah*	CBS	7:00	6.6
Voice of Firestone	NBC	8:30	6.4
One Man's Family*	NBC	7:45	5.9
The Lone Ranger	ABC	7:30	5.8
Telephone Hour	NBC	9:00	5.8

*Monday–Friday Strip Shows

Sans Strips...

Cities Service Band of America	NBC	9:30	4.3
Henry J Taylor Your Land & Mine News	ABC	8:00	2.7

A DRAMATIC CLIMAX

Lux Radio Theater led a pack of 24 scripted dramas — the highest number of dramatic series that would ever rank among a season's Top 50 programs.

Lux celebrated its fifth and final season as the country's Number One program. Although its ratings had dropped over 55 percent since the advent of television in 1948, Lever Brothers' *Lux Radio Theater* would always rank Network Radio's most popular dramatic series.

KING ARTHUR'S CAMELOT

Arthur Godfrey's *Talent Scouts* lost nearly 30 percent of its previous season's radio audience and dropped into single digit ratings for the first time in its five year run. But nobody at CBS or Lever Brothers' Lipton Tea division panicked — instead they cheered.

Simulcast with CBS-TV, the low cost *Talent Scouts* became the season's Number One *television* program with a weekly audience estimated by Nielsen at over eight million. Combined with the show's Nielsen radio audience average of over four million homes — and an estimated eight million or more listeners in those homes — *Talent Scouts* became the leading simulcast program of all time.

In addition to *Talent Scouts,* Godfrey continued to host his popular mid-morning CBS radio show and a Wednesday night variety show on CBS-TV — both highly rated and sold out with advertisers waiting in line. For his weekly marathon of broadcasts Godfrey's pay was upped to approximately a million dollars a year by CBS *(8.7 Mil).*

The 47-year-old redhead was worth every red cent to his network and sponsors.

WHAT A DIFFERENCE A DAY MAKES

Suspense scored the season's biggest comeback when Autolite moved the nine-year-old series from Thursday to Monday, replacing the cancelled *Hollywood Star Playhouse.* Introduced every week by host Harlow Wilcox as, "Radio's out-

standing Theater of Thrills," *Suspense* climbed from 38th to twelfth in the annual rankings.

Suspense was the year's top mystery/crime drama in a season when the genre accounted for over 20 percent of the Top 50 programs. It was a sweet comeback for the program that had been erased from the CBS schedule in 1948 for lack of a sponsor.

1951–52 Tuesday Night Top Ten Programs
CBS 5, NBC 5
Average: 7.8

People Are Funny	CBS	8:00	9.6
Fibber McGee & Molly	NBC	9:30	9.3
Life with Luigi	CBS	9:00	9.1
Mr. & Mrs. North	CBS	8:30	8.6
Bob Hope Show	NBC	9:00	7.8
Pursuit	CBS	9:30	6.7
Tums Hollywood Theater	NBC	8:30	6.7
Beulah*	CBS	7:00	6.6
Cavalcade of America	NBC	8:00	6.2
Eddie Cantor's Show Biz Old & New	NBC	10:00	6.2

*Monday–Friday Strip Shows

Sans Strips...

Barrie Craig, Confidential Investigator	NBC	8:30	5.4

POWER TO THE PEOPLE!

Ralph Edwards' *Truth or Consequences* left CBS in May 1951 after just one season.

Its departure left CBS without one of its Top Ten programs on Tuesday.

Meanwhile, Mars Candy picked up *People Are Funny* when Brown & Williamson Tobacco cancelled its sponsorship of Art Linkletter's stunt show after nine successful seasons on NBC. *People* had outscored *Truth or Consequences'* ratings for four years, including their coincidental scheduling on Tuesday night the previous season.

The candy company kept *People Are Funny* on Tuesday but moved it from NBC to CBS.

Listeners followed. *People Are Funny* became Tuesday's most popular program and jumped back into the season's Top Ten after a two year absence from the list.

THE REAL MYSTERY IS WHY

People Are Funny replaced Tuesday's Number One program of the previous season on CBS when Sterling Drugs moved *Mystery Theater* to ABC's Wednesday schedule.

Beginning in 1943 on NBC as Sterling's *Molle Mystery Theater,* the program was often compared to *Suspense* as a top notch mystery anthology. *Molle* was dropped from the title in 1948 when Sterling switched sponsorship of the show from its Molle Shave Cream to its Bayer Aspirin and Phillips Milk of Magnesia laxative and moved the program to CBS.

Of greater consequence, Sterling assigned production of the program to Frank and Anne Hummert and it became another of the couple's simplistic character-driven series, sometimes known as *Hearthstone of the Death Squad.*

Nevertheless, it was popular.

Mystery Theater/Hearthstone registered three consecutive seasons on CBS among the annual Top 20 programs, finishing in eleventh place in 1950–51.

In its subsequent move to ABC in 1951, *Mystery Theater/Hearthstone* became known as *Mark Sabre*—yet another of Hummerts' formulaic productions. The program lost 55 percent of its CBS ratings and dropped out of the annual Top 50.

Meanwhile, Sterling Drug remained on the CBS Tuesday schedule with *Pursuit,* sponsored by Molle.

Pursuit had traveled over five separate CBS timeslots in two years as a sustaining fill-in and summer substitute before Sterling picked it up. The detective series starring Ben Wright was considered *Suspense* with a British accent — following the adventures of a Scotland Yard inspector.

Pursuit wasn't a Hummert production. Instead, it sounded more like *Suspense* with sharp writing, plus the same meticulous supervision of William Robson and Elliot Lewis, and the same support of Hollywood's best radio actors.

Nevertheless, *Pursuit* lost over 40 percent of *Mystery Theater/Hearthstone*'s audience. Sterling cancelled it before the end of the season.

REPORTS OF MY DEATH...

Eddie Cantor left radio in 1950 to concentrate on his twelve *Colgate Comedy Hour* television shows per season plus another half dozen TV guest shots. The 59-year-old comedian was briefly hospitalized in May 1951 with a ruptured blood vessel in his vocal chords, prompting false reports that he had died.

Proving the reports totally wrong, Cantor bounced back to his television work immediately and signed a new radio contract with Philip Morris Cigarettes for the 1951–52 season. The cigarette maker had jumped on the "mildness" advertising bandwagon and Cantor's endorsement following throat surgery was considered a coup.

Eddie Cantor's *Show Business— Old & New* debuted in October on NBC's Sunday night schedule, then moved to Tuesdays in January. The recorded program with no studio audience was a total departure for Cantor. It featured phonograph records by Cantor's show business friends, providing a springboard for his reminiscing about them.

Philip Morris dropped the show after one season, but disc jockey/raconteur Cantor enjoyed doing it — even for little money *Show Business — Old & New* remained on NBC as a sustaining program until June 1954.

THEATER DEAD AND BARRIED

Lewis Howe's Tums antacid tablets replaced the expensive *Hollywood Theater,* an anthology series featuring film stars, with *Barrie Craig, Confidential Investigator* in mid–March.

Craig starred Hollywood tough guy William Gargan who had enjoyed a 20 year career in the movies playing police and detective types. Gargan had left his radio and television role as *Martin Kane, Private Eye* three months earlier in a dispute over script quality.

Barrie Craig began slowly but steadily built a following and remained on the NBC schedule until 1955.

TUESDAY'S HOPELESS

Bob Hope, 49, had been a Tuesday night fixture on NBC for 14 years. His half hour comedy/variety show had been radio's Number One program for five consecutive seasons from 1942 through 1947.

Liggett & Myers' Chesterfield Cigarettes cancelled Hope's expensive show at the end of the season. His final Tuesday night program was broadcast on June 24, 1952, resulting in a final month's rating of 5.0.

Hope's timeslot was filled over the next 13 weeks by an audience participation quiz, *Meet Your Match,* starring another fast talking comedian, 36-year-old Jan Murray.

Hope would return the following season on Wednesdays.

But Tuesday night radio was never the same again.

1951–52 Wednesday Night Top Ten Programs
NBC 5, CBS 5
Average: 7.4

You Bet Your Life	NBC	9:00	9.6
Dr Christian	CBS	8:30	8.4
The Big Story	NBC	9:30	8.0
Bing Crosby Show	CBS	9:30	7.9
Great Gildersleeve	NBC	8:30	7.6
Big Town	CBS	8:00	7.4
Halls of Ivy	NBC	8:00	6.7
Beulah*	CBS	7:00	6.6
Blue Ribbon Boxing	CBS	10:00	6.0
One Man's Family*	NBC	7:45	5.9

*Monday–Friday Strip Shows

Sans Strips...

The Lone Ranger	ABC	7:30	5.8
Mystery Theater	ABC	8:00	5.4

RED WEDS A DISASTER

Procter & Gamble cancelled Red Skelton's Sunday show and CBS moved the suddenly sustaining Skelton into Wednesday at 9:00 to replace Hal Peary's poorly received *Honest Harold.* CBS had carried Peary's sitcom for a year in search of a sponsor without success.

Skelton's sponsor-less program went unrated until March when Norge Appliances picked it up. It would have been better if Skelton had stayed under Nielsen's radar during the show's final four months of the 1951–52 season

The comedian's ratings dropped over 65 percent. He fell from 8th to 86th place in the season's ranking.

It can only be assumed that the

program would have registered a higher rating if its sustaining months during the fall and winter had been rated when listenership was traditionally higher.

However, Skelton's six films in two years and his highly rated NBC-TV variety show every week beginning in the fall of 1951 suggest that the comedian's decline in radio popularity was the result of overexposure.

More evidence of this was found the following season when Skelton jumped back to NBC Radio's Tuesday schedule with little improvement in his dismal rating.

NBC RUNS OUT OF TOWN

Lever Brothers struck a double blow to NBC in December when it pulled *Big Town* from the network's Tuesday schedule where it had registered three consecutive Top 50 seasons after its jump from CBS in 1948.

Lever returned *Big Town* to CBS and a new Wednesday timeslot which did more than harm NBC's ratings. The switch removed all Lever Brothers' advertising from the NBC prime time radio schedule.

A BOUT WINNING

Pabst Blue Ribbon Beer was a longtime Network Radio sponsor dating back to *The Ben Bernie Show* of 1932–33. The Milwaukee brewer returned to the season's Top 50 with its sponsorship of *Blue Ribbon Bouts* on the CBS Wednesday schedule—a series of weekly boxing matches simulcast by Pabst on CBS-TV.

What differed the CBS/Pabst boxing shows from Friday's long running Gillette *Cavalcade of Sports* on ABC Radio and NBC-TV, was its willingness to follow the boxing headliners of the day—Rocky Marciano, Ezzard Charles, Sugar Ray Robinson, Rocky Graziano, Jake LaMotta, Kid Gavilan, etc.—to arenas around the country, while the Gillette bouts were generally confined to New York's Madison Square Garden.

As a result, the Pabst matches reported by Russ Hodges scored steady ratings and finished in Wednesday's Top Ten. Television stole

its audience the following season. *Blue Ribbon Bouts'* radio ratings collapsed, Pabst cancelled its sponsorship and the program went off the air in December 1952.

DEGREES OF CONSISTENCY

Another Milwaukee brewer, Schlitz, took a different approach to its radio advertising.

Academy Award winner Ronald Colman and his wife, Benita Hume, had been frequent and popular guests on Jack Benny's Sunday show, portraying the comedian's polite but embarrassed British neighbors in posh Beverly Hills.

In 1949, *Fibber McGee & Molly* creator Don Quinn proposed that they star in his new weekly series, *The Halls of Ivy,* an urbane sitcom about a college professor and his wife. After a slow start in January 1950, the Schlitz Beer program broke into the season's Top 50 in 1951–52.

Halls of Ivy earned a steady, consistent following that grew, however slightly, during its three seasons on the air. While most every other programs lost audience, *Halls* edged up in ratings from 6.5 to 6.6 to 6.7.

It left radio in June 1952 and was converted to television for a 39 week run in 1954–55.

TOP TO BOTTOM

When *The Fat Man* was permanently pulled from ABC's schedule in September, the program's head writer, Richard Ellington, had another series prepared for its star, J. Scott Smart.

The Top Guy was the continuing story of a two-fisted police commissioner who spent more time in the trenches fighting criminals than he did behind his desk. The melodrama bore a strong resemblance to *Mr. District Attorney,* complete to the presence of *Mr. DA*'s star, Jay Jostyn, in a supporting role.

Unfortunately, *The Top Guy* was slotted against two of Wednesday's Top Ten programs, NBC's *The Great Gildersleeve* and *Dr. Christian* on CBS. *Top Guy* couldn't muster half of *The Fat Man*'s ratings and limped in at 71st place in the season's rankings. The series was shuffled around the ABC schedule over the next season as a spot carrier

for participating advertisers until it left the air in May 1953.

1951–52 Thursday Night Top Ten Programs
NBC 6, CBS 4
Average: 7.0

Dragnet	NBC	9:00	8.7
Father Knows Best	NBC	8:00	8.4
FBI in Peace & War	CBS	8:00	7.9
Mr. Keen	NBC	8:30	7.8
Hallmark Playhouse	CBS	9:30	6.7
Beulah*	CBS	7:00	6.6
Your Hit Parade	NBC	10:00	6.4
Mr. Chameleon	CBS	9:00	5.9
One Man's Family*	NBC	7:45	5.9
Morgan Beatty News of the World*	NBC	7:30	5.7

*Monday–Friday Strip Shows

Sans Strips...			
Counterspy	NBC	9:30	5.6
Original Amateur Hour	ABC	9:00	5.2
Defense Attorney	ABC	8:30	4.4

WEBB COPS A HIT

Dragnet was in its third season and became Thursday's Number One show by holding the same 8.7 rating it had earned the previous season. Jack Webb's low keyed police drama jumped from 45th to 14th in the season's Top 50. It remained a fixture on the NBC radio schedule for the next six seasons.

Webb took *Dragnet* to NBC-TV in January where it enjoyed an eight year run and became the network's most popular dramatic series in concurrent radio and television runs—all sponsored by Liggett & Myers Tobacco.

CBS never shared in *Dragnet*'s rating success but still profited from it.

Webb's Mark VII Productions filmed all of the series' 276 TV installments at the CBS Television City Studios in Hollywood.

A FAMILIAR VOICE FADES

Barton Yarborough was one of Network Radio's many studio actors whose voice was familiar but his face wasn't. The native Texan was 31 when he landed his first major radio role as Cliff in Carleton E. Morse's original San Francisco cast of *One Man's Family* in 1932. He remained with the series for 19 years.

Yarborough's infectiously friendly drawl was also featured as Doc Long in Morse's *I Love a Mystery*. He recreated the role in three low budget Columbia movie adaptations of the legendary series. The films were far from major attractions and Yarborough remained just another face in the crowd.

In 1949, Jack Webb, another veteran of San Francisco radio, chose Yarborough for the role of his Los Angeles police detective sidekick, Ben Romero, on *Dragnet*. The realistic police drama became a hit and was destined for television.

After two and a half seasons of *Dragnet*'s increasingly popular radio run, Yarborough was eager to share in the success and fame that the program's television adaptation promised.

It was never to be.

Five days after filming the second episode of the *Dragnet* television series Barton Yarborough dropped dead of a heart attack at age 51.

HUMMERTS' MISTERS OF MYSTERY MOVE

Sterling Drug slashed its radio advertising schedule and pulled the rug out from under three of the previous season's Top 15 programs on CBS — all mysteries produced by Frank and Anne Hummert.

In addition to moving Tuesday's Number One program, *Mystery Theater*, to ABC as *Mark Sabre*, Sterling dropped *Mystery*'s first spin-off, *Hearthstone of the Death Squad*. *Hearthstone* was shuffled around the network as an unrated spot carrier for the remainder of the 1951–52 season.

Sterling's Bayer Aspirin also cancelled Wednesday's Top Ten melodrama, *Mr. Chameleon*, in December. CBS exiled the Hummert series to Sunday afternoons for a month until General Foods and Wrigley Gum joined to bring the show back to the network's prime time schedule on Thursday.

Mr. Chameleon lost half its audience in the three moves and dropped to 49th for the season.

Sterling's Kolynos Toothpaste cancelled Thursday's top rated *Mr. Keen, Tracer of Lost Persons* in June 1951. Liggett & Myers' Chesterfield Cigarettes picked it up and moved it to NBC's Thursday schedule. *Keen* fared better than the other Hummert programs, losing only 27 percent of its previous season's ratings.

Despite their programs' ratings losses, the Hummerts finished the 1951–52 season in a unique position. They produced two of Thursday's Top Ten programs on two separate networks.

PARADE OF HITS RUNS AND AIRS ON THURSDAY

After 17 consecutive seasons as a Saturday night staple, American Tobacco uprooted Lucky Strike's *Your Hit Parade* and moved it to NBC's Thursday schedule. The weekly countdown of popular hits had hopped between CBS and NBC over the years, but could always be heard on Saturdays.

The move to Thursday was considered necessary by the tobacco giant and its agency, BBDO. They had discarded the idea of simulcasting the radio show and its television adaptation which was entering its second season as a Saturday night feature on NBC-TV.

A complete divorce between the two versions of the program was ordered. That also meant two completely different casts. Television's *Your Hit Parade* took the show's young lead singers, Snooky Lanson and Dorothy Collins, which forced the radio version to look for a new and fresh headliner.

But instead of enlisting young star vocalists as it had in the past, the radio show turned to 49-year-old Guy Lombardo, his Royal Canadians orchestra and their "Sweetest Music This Side of Heaven," — a band that had been heard on various network shows since 1928.

The top hits of the day played and sung in Lombardo's much ridiculed "square" treatment of earlier decades was often a study in contrasts. But to the surprise of many, Lombardo's troupe pushed radio's *Your Hit Parade* back into the season's Top 50 and kept the program alive for its final 18 months.

ABC'S ONE NIGHT STAND

It had never happened before, not even in its peak Blue Network days of the 1930s.

ABC won every prime time half-hour from 8:00 through 11:00, led by its Friday mix of scripted shows.

The lineup included four of the season's Top 50 shows — Dick Powell's *Richard Diamond, Private Eye*, *This Is Your FBI*, *Mr. District Attorney*, and *The Adventures of Ozzie & Harriet*.

The Lone Ranger provided a substantial lead into the powerful ABC schedule with a ratings tie against NBC's strip shows, *One Man's Family* and *News of the World*. All three were among Friday's Top Ten.

ABC's dominance of Friday lasted for only one season but stands as a tribute to the network that rose from a shell — methodically stripped of its headline attractions and sold by NBC in 1943 — to become a strong competitor in the high stakes arena of Network Radio in just eight years.

DUNPHY PUTS UP A FIGHT

Gillette's *Cavalcade of Sports* Friday night boxing shows followed the ABC lineup of scripted winners at 10:00. The series didn't gain a Top 50 rating, but won its time period from the diminished and sustaining opposition offered by CBS and NBC.

Don Dunphy's exciting blow-by-blow radio accounts of the weekly fights was also opposed by NBC's telecasts of the same contests, and yet another television attraction that siphoned Network Radio's audience during the time period — *Cavalcade of Stars* on the fledgling DuMont TV Network, starring comic actor Jackie Gleason, former star of television's *Life of Riley*, who was fast becoming one of video's top headliners.

Nevertheless, the Gillette boxing show posted two of the season's biggest ratings. Dunphy's description of the Joe Louis/Rocky Marciano bout in October scored a 10.6 and the Joe Walcott/Ezzard Charles Heavyweight Championship match in June hit 14.1.

Unlike Pabst's Wednesday night fights that left the air the following season, Gillette's Friday night *Cavalcade of Sports* continued on year after year. The program moved from ABC to NBC in September 1954 and remained a Friday night radio fixture until the summer of 1960.

Throughout his 19 years of describing Gillette's weekly boxing matches — including some 200 championship bouts — Don Dunphy was arguably the most widely heard sportscaster of Network Radio's Golden Age.

DA BECOMES DOA

Bristol-Myers' Vitalis Hair Tonic evicted *Mr. District Attorney* from its eleven year home on NBC's Wednesday schedule — all of them Top 50 seasons — and moved the melodrama to Friday on ABC. The crime fighting DA played by Jay Jostyn had compiled an enviable track record on NBC. It scored three Top Ten seasons and another six among radio's 15 most popular programs.

Mr. District Attorney lost 35 percent of its audience in the move to ABC, but managed to hold its own with the network's powerful Friday lineup that took four of the night's Top Five slots.

Despite its decent showing, Bristol-Myers cancelled the program at the end of the season and radio's most popular detective series of the Golden Age was gone.

THE TROUBLED TENOR'S TUMBLE

Handsome operatic tenor Mario Lanza was only 29 and on top of the show business world.

His meteoric MGM film career began with 1949's *That Midnight Kiss,* continued with *The Toast of Orleans* a year later and peaked with *The Great Caruso* in 1951. Readers of movie fan magazine *Photoplay* voted Lanza "The Most Popular Male Star of the Year" and critics hailed his incredibly powerful yet romantic voice that sold millions of RCA Victor records.

Lanza's radio career began with a CBS summer replacement show for Edgar Bergen and Charlie Mc-Carthy in June 1951, sponsored by Coca-Cola. The soft drink maker gave the tenor his own NBC program in September on Monday at 10:00. It was a logical extension of the network's Monday block of quality musical shows, but unfortunate for ratings against the powerful CBS Monday lineup.

Lanza's October through January rating was a disappointing 5.7. The show was moved in February to Friday at 9:00 against ABC's top rated *Adventures of Ozzie & Harriet* and fell even further to 3.7 over the next five months. The NBC program was cancelled in June and Lanza returned to CBS, again as the summer replacement for Bergen and McCarthy.

It was Lanza's last Network Radio series. Mediocre ratings weren't his only problem — he was legally forbidden from returning to radio in September 1952.

A month earlier Lanza had walked off the set of MGM's *The Student Prince* in a dispute with its director. The studio retaliated by obtaining an injunction that prohibited him from *any* public appearances — including radio — until the dispute with its talented but temperamental tenor was settled. The situation was finally resolved in May 1953.

But by that time, negative pub-

licity fueled by reports of the singer's increasing problems with alcohol and his ballooning weight had virtually killed his career.

Mario Lanza took his family and moved to Italy where he died six years later at the age of 38.

DUFFY AIN'T HERE ANYMORE

After eleven seasons over three networks, Ed Gardner's familiar opening line to *Duffy's Tavern,* "Duffy ain't here...," had another meaning in late 1951. The sitcom which had scored three consecutive Top 15 seasons just five years earlier had drifted into unrated participating sponsorship on NBC and was cancelled at mid-season.

Also gone from NBC's Friday schedule were Bill Stern's *Colgate Sports Newsreel* after a ten year run and the William Bendix sitcom, *The Life of Riley,* which had enjoyed six Top 50 seasons.

An even longer network program ended on ABC when *The Sheriff* was cancelled. The western series was the successor to Pacific-Borax's *Death Valley Days,* a pioneering network drama that began in 1930.

1951–52 Saturday Night Eight Rated Programs
CBS 4, NBC 2, ABC 1, MBS 1
Average: 5.9

Hopalong Cassidy	CBS	8:30	8.7
Gangbusters	CBS	9:00	8.2
Gene Autry's Melody Ranch	CBS	8:00	7.9
Vaughn Monroe Show	NBC	10:00	5.5
Grand Ole Opry	NBC	9:30	5.4
Sanka Salutes	ABC	7:55	5.3
Tarzan	CBS	8:30	3.6
Cecil Brown News	MBS	7:55	2.4

SATURDAY'S LISTLESS

Only eight prime time Network Radio programs were sponsored and qualified to be rated and ranked on Saturday.

Saturday had become a stay at home night for millions of television viewers attracted by NBC-TV's block of *All Star Revue* and *Your Show of Shows,* both developed under Pat Weaver's leadership of the network. The *Revue* hour was hosted by rotating comedians Jimmy Durante, Danny Thomas,

Ed Wynn, Jack Carson and Martha Raye. *Show of Shows* was a 90 minute marathon of variety starring Sid Caesar and Imogene Coca.

It was tough for radio advertisers to compete as sponsors. So they didn't. Most of Saturday's programming was sustaining and available to participating advertisers.

Network Radio's only rated popular music offering of the night was R.J. Reynolds' *Vaughn Monroe Show*, aka *The Camel Caravan*. Reynolds abruptly pulled the show from CBS in December and moved it to NBC.

GETTING THE GATE

Colgate was spending a large budget in television and cancelled two of Saturday's top radio shows.

The soap company dropped *The Judy Canova Show* during the summer of 1951 despite her seven consecutive seasons among Saturday's Top Ten. The hillbilly comedienne/singer was off the air until December when NBC brought her sitcom back on a sustaining basis and retained its strong supporting cast intact, including the voice of Warner Brothers' cartoons, Mel Blanc

Without a fulltime sponsor for the rest of the season, *The Judy Canova Show* went unrated by Nielsen, breaking its string of eight consecutive Top 50 finishes. But the popular Judy wasn't to be ignored for long.

She returned with participating sponsors in October 1952 and an encore Top 50 season.

Colgate also cancelled *The Dennis Day Show* in June. The singer had compiled five consecutive Top 50 seasons. The soap company had designs on a television show for the

handsome Day, but the project never got beyond the pilot stage.

THE BEULAH CURSE?

Marlin Hurt created *Beulah* and died before the character's first complete season as a half hour sitcom. In her fifth season in the title role, Hattie McDaniel was forced by illness to leave *Beulah* on November 14. She died of cancer eleven months later at the age of 59.

McDaniel was widely criticized by civil rights groups for her stereotyped role as a housemaid. In her own defense she retorted, "I'd rather *play* a maid for seven hundred dollars a week than *be* a maid for seven dollars a week."

The veteran actress was actually paid a $1,000 a week *($8,700)*, and considered worth every penny by CBS, sponsor Procter & Gamble and her millions of listeners. McDaniel was replaced at mid-season by another veteran black actress, Lillian Randolph — who survived until 1980.

THE OTHER AMECHE

Adventure shows *The Silver Eagle* and *Mr. Mercury* had alternated

with *The Lone Ranger* in ABC's 7:30 timeslot on Tuesday and Thursday after the ill-conceived *(Jack) Armstrong of the SBI* was cancelled in June 1951.

Mercury starred busy radio, television and stage actor Staats Cotsworth who had held the title role of *Casey, Crime Photographer* on CBS for seven years. When *Mr. Mercury* left the air at mid-season, *Silver Eagle* became a multiple run series on both Tuesday and Thursday.

The Silver Eagle, aka Canadian Mountie Jim West, was played by veteran radio actor Jim Ameche — who ironically originated the role of Jack Armstrong in 1933.

Jim Ameche always lived in the shadow of his older brother Don. The Ameche brothers both looked and sounded alike, but only Don went on to huge Network Radio and movie stardom.

Jim remained as *The Silver Eagle* under General Mills sponsorship for five seasons and later became the morning disc jockey on WHN/New York.

```
                1951–52 Top Ten Multiple Run Programs
                     CBS 5, ABC 2, NBC 2, MBS 1
                            Average: 5.4
```

Program				
Beulah*	M–F	CBS	7:00	6.6
One Man's Family*	M–F	NBC	7:45	5.9
The Lone Ranger	M,W,F	ABC	7:30	5.8
Morgan Beatty News of the World/*	M–F	NBC	7:30	5.7
Jack Smith Show*	M–F	CBS	7:15	5.5
Club 15*	M–F	CBS	7:30	5.4
Edward R Murrow News*	M–F	CBS	7:45	5.4
Lowell Thomas News*	M–F	CBS	6:45	5.3
Silver Eagle	Tu,Th	ABC	7:30	4.2
Gabriel Heatter News*	M–F	MBS	7:30	4.1

Monday–Friday Strip Shows

TOP 50 PROGRAMS — 1951–52

CBS 27, NBC 18, ABC 5
Average Rating: 8.0, Median: 7.8
41,900,000 Radio Homes / 95.5% Coverage of U.S. Homes / One Rating Point = 419,000 Homes
Source: A.C. Nielsen Radio Index Serv, Sep 1951–Jun 1952
Total Programs Rated, 6–11 P.M.: 136
Programs Rated 13 Weeks & Ranked: 105

		Program	Rtg	Type	Sponsor	Day	Time	Lgth	Net
1	*1*	Lux Radio Theater/William Keighley	13.9	DA	Lux Soap	Mon	9:00	60	CBS
2	*4*	Amos & Andy	13.4	SC	Rexall Drug Stores	Sun	7:30	30	CBS
3	*2*	Jack Benny Program	12.9	SC	Lucky Strike Cigarettes	Sun	7:00	30	CBS
4	*3*	Edgar Bergen & Charlie McCarthy	11.2	CV	Coca-Cola	Sun	8:00	30	CBS
5	*5*	Arthur Godfrey's Talent Scouts	9.7	TC	Lipton Tea	Mon	8:30	30	CBS

	Program	Rtg	Type	Sponsor	Day	Time	Lgth	Net
6t 20	People Are Funny/Art Linkletter	9.6	APS	Mars Candy	Tue	8:00	30	CBS
6t 9	You Bet Your Life/Groucho Marx	9.6	APQ	DeSoto & Plymouth Autos	Wed	9:00	30	NBC
8 13	Fibber McGee & Molly	9.3	SC	Pet Milk	Tue	9:30	30	NBC
9 7	Walter Winchell's Journal	9.2	NC	Richard Hudnut Cosmetics	Sun	9:00	15	ABC
10t 17	Bob Hawk Show	9.1	APQ	Camel Cigarettes	Mon	10:30	30	CBS
10t 13	Life With Luigi/J. Carrol Naish	9.1	SC	Wrigley Gum	Tue	9:00	30	CBS
12 38	Suspense	9.0	DA	Autolite Spark Plugs	Mon	8:00	30	CBS
13 29	Horace Heidt Youth Oppty Program	8.8	TC	Philip Morris Cigarettes	Sun	9:30	30	CBS
14t 45	Dragnet/Jack Webb	8.7	DCC	Chesterfield Cigarettes	Thu	9:00	30	NBC
14t 26	Hopalong Cassidy/William Boyd	8.7	DCC	Grape Nuts Cereal	Sat	8:30	30	CBS
16t 12	Mr & Mrs North/Joe Curtin, Alice Frost	8.6	DCC	Halo Shampoo	Tue	8:30	30	CBS
16t 26	Our Miss Brooks/Eve Arden	8.6	SC	Lustre Creme Shampoo	Sun	6:30	30	CBS
18t 22	Dr. Christian/Jean Hersholt	8.4	DCC	Vaseline	Wed	8:30	30	CBS
18t 34	Father Knows Best/Robert Young	8.4	SC	General Foods	Thu	8:00	30	NBC
20 25	Gangbusters	8.2	DA	Grape Nuts Cereal	Sat	9:00	30	CBS
21 19	The Big Story	8.0	DA	Pall Mall Cigarettes	Wed	9:30	30	NBC
22t 26	Bing Crosby Show	7.9	MV	Chesterfield Cigarettes	Wed	9:30	30	CBS
22t 22	FBI In Peace & War	7.9	DCC	Wildroot Cream Oil	Thu	8:00	30	CBS
22t 22	Gene Autry's Melody Ranch	7.9	DCC	Wrigley Chewing Gum	Sat	8:00	30	CBS
25t 33	Bob Hope Show	7.8	CV	Chesterfield Cigarettes	Tue	9:00	30	NBC
25t 15	Mr Keen/Arthur Hughes	7.8	DCC	Chiclets Chewing Gum	Thu	8:00	30	NBC 1
25t 50	Theater Guild on the Air	7.8	DA	US Steel	Sun	8:30	60	NBC
28 29	Great Gildersleeve/Willard Waterman	7.6	SC	Parkay Margarine	Wed	8:30	30	NBC
29 35	Big Town/Ed Pawley	7.4	DCC	Lifebuoy Soap	Wed	8:00	30	CBS 2
30 67	Philip Morris Playhouse on Broadway	7.3	DA	Philip Morris Cigarettes	Sun	8:30	30	CBS 3
31t 45	Adventures of Ozzie & Harriet	7.2	SC	Heinz Foods	Fri	9:00	30	ABC
31t 48	The Railroad Hour/Gordon MacRae	7.2	DA	American Railroad Assn	Mon	8:00	30	NBC
31t 42	This Is Your FBI	7.2	DCC	Equitable Life Assurance	Fri	8:30	30	ABC
34 15	Mr District Attorney/Jay Jostyn	6.8	DCC	Vitalis Hair Tonic	Fri	9:30	30	ABC
35t 29	Hallmark Playhouse	6.7	DA	Hallmark Cards	Thu	8:30	30	CBS
35t 67	Halls of Ivy/Ronald Colman	6.7	SC	Schlitz Beer	Wed	8:00	30	NBC
35t N	Pursuit/Ben Wright	6.7	DCC	Molle Shaving Cream	Tue	9:30	30	CBS
35t N	Tums Hollywood Theater	6.7	DA	Tums Antacid Tablets	Tue	8:30	30	NBC
39 35	Beulah/Hattie McDaniel, Lillian Randolph	6.6	SC	Dreft Laundry Soap	M–F	7:00	15	CBS
40t 59	Carnation Contented Hr/Stafford, Martin	6.4	MP	Carnation Milk	Sun	9:30	30	CBS
40t N	Phil Harris & Alice Faye Show	6.4	SC	RCA Victor Radios & TV	Sun	8:00	30	NBC
40t 49	Richard Diamond, Priv Det/ Dick Powell	6.4	DCC	Rexall Drug Stores	Fri	8:00	30	ABC
40t 60	Voice of Firestone	6.4	MC	Firestone Tire & Rubber	Mon	8:30	30	NBC
40t 56	Your Hit Parade/Guy Lombardo Orch	6.4	MP	Lucky Strike Cigarettes	Thu	10:00	30	NBC
45 38	Meet Corliss Archer/Janet Waldo	6.3	SC	Electric Companies Co-op	Sun	9:00	30	CBS
46t 62	Cavalcade of America	6.2	DA	DuPont Chemicals	Tue	8:00	30	NBC
46t N	Eddie Cantor's Show Biz Old & New	6.2	MV	Philip Morris Cigarettes	Tue	10:00	30	NBC 4
48 80	Blue Ribbon Bouts	6.0	SP	Pabst Beer	Wed	Var	60	CBS
49t 10	Mr Chameleon/Karl Swenson	5.9	DCC	Post Cereal/Wrigley Gum	Thu	9:00	30	CBS
49t 72	One Man's Family	5.9	DCC	Alka Seltzer	M–F	7:45	15	NBC

New & Returning Top 50 Programs Underscored.

1	Mr Keen, Tracer of Lost Persons	Sep–Mar	Chesterfield Cigarettes	Thu	8:30	30	NBC
2	Big Town	Sep–Dec	Lifebuoy Soap	Tue	10:00	30	NBC
3	Philip Morris Playhouse on Broadway	Sep–Dec	Philip Morris Cigarettes	Tue	10:30	30	NBC
4	Eddie Cantor's Show Biz Old & New	Oct–Jan	Philip Morris Cigarettes	Sun	9:30	30	NBC

Key: API — Audience Participation/Interviews
APQ — Audience Participation/Quiz
APS — Audience Participation/Stunts
CV — Comedy/Variety Show
DA — Dramatic Anthology

DCC — Drama/Continuing Characters
MC — Music/Classical, Semi-Classical
MP — Music/Popular, Contemporary
MSP — Music/Specialty, Ethnic
MST — Music/Standard, Traditional

MV — Music/Variety Show
NC — News, Commentary
SC — Situation Comedy
SP — Sports
TC — Talent Competition

1951–52 Top 50 Favorite Formats

	Programs	Pct
Drama — Anthology & Continuing	24	48%
Comedy — Variety & Situation	14	28%

	Programs	Pct
Music — All Categories	7	14%
Audience Participation — All Categories	3	6%
News/Commentary	1	2%
Sports	1	2%

1951–52 Monthly Winners

Mon	Program	Rating	Mon	Program	Rating
Sep	Lux Radio Theater	11.5	Feb	Lux Radio Theater	15.4
Oct	Lux Radio Theater	15.3	Mar	Amos & Andy	15.0
Nov	Jack Benny Program	16.5	Apr	Lux Radio Theater	11.4
Dec	Lux Radio Theater	15.7	May	Lux Radio Theater	10.5
Jan	Jack Benny Program	15.7	Jun	Jack Benny Program	8.8

25

The 1952–53 Network Season

JINGLE: Each year more people buy RCA Victor than any other TV!

Announcer: Give your family the luxury of RCA Victor Television!

WOMAN: New Lo-Boy models ... long ... low ... lovely. New full door consoles ... the ultimate in fine furniture in Modern, Contemporary, Colonial, Provincial, Regency and Empire styling...

Announcer: ... and mahogany, limed oak, walnut, maple or cherry finish ... 42 different styles and finishes. Now as low as 199.95 including Federal Excise Tax and a one-year picture tube warranty.

WOMAN: With RCA's new optional, UHF-VHF Tuner, just turn one knob and "click," there's your station!

Announcer: RCA's new "Magic Monitor" circuit system brings in the best TV pictures possible and holds them at their best automatically. It screens out static and interference automatically. It tunes in the best sound ... RCA's "Golden Throat" Sound ... automatically.

WOMAN: Ask your RCA Victor dealer about his expert installation and RCA Victor Factory Service contract, available only to RCA Victor owners. See your RCA Victor dealer and you'll learn why...

JINGLE: Each year more people buy RCA Victor than any other TV!

THE PARTY'S OVER

Any question that Network Radio's Golden Age had ended at 21 years was answered decisively by the 1952–53 audience ratings and advertising revenue figures.

Television had taken over radio's role as the primary source of free entertainment in almost half of America's homes — spurred on by the establishment of 125 new TV stations during the season. In addition, over 60 more stations would go on the air by the end of 1953. As smaller markets like Duluth, Topeka and Peoria came on line, television was no longer confined to America's largest cities.

And while the television audience ballooned to greater proportions, Network Radio's nighttime ratings continued to shrink. It was no longer the prime time that advertisers coveted.

Nielsen estimated that Network Radio's leading attraction, Jack Benny, was heard in approximately 4.7 million homes each week. Meanwhile, Benny's new bi-weekly series on CBS-TV was viewed in *eight* million homes.

Topping Benny, Lucille Ball's sitcom *I Love Lucy*, television's highest rated program, was seen every week in nearly 14 million homes.

Network Radio's Top 50 programs generated a season average

Nielsen rating of only 6.3, the lowest ever recorded.

Where 49 programs had averaged double digit Crossley ratings in the 1932–33 season, just four network shows reached that mark in Nielsen's 1952–53 surveys.

BAD NEWS AND GOOD NEWS

When listeners abandoned nighttime radio to watch television, advertisers followed.

As a result of audience declines, Network Radio revenues dropped another ten percent to their lowest level since 1943. Another round of discounts for Network Radio advertisers became effective on October 1st. CBS announced evening rates for its continuing advertisers would be cut from 20 to 30 percent.

Network Radio's Golden Age of dominance was over but the networks didn't mourn its passing — their combined television billings grew another 42 percent to $256.4 Million *(2.19 Bil)*.

For NBC, CBS and ABC, the Golden Age of Television had just begun.

THE AUDIENCE PLAYS FAVORITES

Program popularity continued its crossover from radio to television. Audiences wanted to see their favorite programs as well as hear them.

Nine of the season's Top 15 Network Radio programs were also among Nielsen's Top 25 television shows.

Only Arthur Godfrey's Monday night *Talent Scouts* was a simulcast, offering a direct comparison between the two versions of the identical program available to both radio and television audiences at the same time. The ratings provide another clear indication that TV

1952–53 Season Scoreboard
Mid-season Totals, December 1952

		Compared to Year Earlier	
Total Radio Homes	42.8 Mil	+0.90 Mil	+2.1%
Total Auto Radios	23.5 Mil	+2.5 Mil	+11.9%
Total AM Radio Stations	2,331	+99	+4.4%
Total Radio Network Affiliates	1,247	+37	+3.1%
1952 Radio Revenues	624.1 Mil	+17.8 Mil	+2.9%
1952 Radio Network Revenues	161.5 Mil	(18.0 Mil)	(10.0%)
Network Share	25.9%		(3.7%)
Total TV Homes	20.4 Mil	+5.3 Mil	+35.1%
Total TV Stations	125	+14	+12.6%
Total FM Stations	722	(27)	(3.6%)

had overtaken radio in audience popularity for Network Radio's favorite programs.

Ranked by Nielsen's estimate of their weekly audiences in terms of households reached, the figures in the chart at the bottom of this page illustrate how television dominated radio among America's most popular programs.

Two more programs with concurrent radio and television runs made TV's Top 30 and Network Radio's Top 50 for the season — *The Red Skelton Show* and *What's My Line.*

Meanwhile, *The Lone Ranger,* Pabst Beer's *Blue Ribbon Bouts* and Gillette's Friday night *Cavalcade of Sports* boxing bouts were among television's 30 favorite programs but failed to place in radio's Top 50.

Regardless of ranking, the story was the same: More people watched the their favorite programs on television than listened to their radio predecessors.

RADIO'S EXPANSION = NETWORKS' LOSSES

Radio's audience was moving out of homes and into cars. Over 90 percent of all new automobiles featured AM radios as standard equipment. The number of cars and trucks equipped with radio had surged from six million to nearly 25 million in the seven years since the end of World War II.

Unfortunately for broadcasters, only the lesser-regarded Pulse ratings, which employed a variation of the defunct Crossley recall system, attempted to count the audience in cars and trucks.

Within American homes, con-

sole radios in living rooms were rapidly replaced by bulky, furniture-styled television sets and continually smaller, lower cost, portable radios in kitchens and bedrooms.

Still another advance in radio portability was introduced in November when RCA previewed the first hand-held radio incorporating germanium transistors developed by Bell Laboratories. Transistors eliminated the need for vacuum tubes and cleared the path for pocket-sized radios later in the decade.

Radio listening was fast becoming a fragmented, personal experience dictated by individual tastes best served by local, independent stations which had sprouted like weeds since 1946. Indies had grown to outnumber network affiliates by almost two to one in 1952.

Local independent stations were the very antithesis of Network Radio's traditional programming which served the entire nation with schedules directed to four immense groups of listeners with common tastes.

That role had been usurped by the television networks.

THE CBS MARCH TO A RATINGS RECORD

CBS closed out Network Radio's Golden Age with eleven of the season's Top Twelve programs.

The network reached a new height of superiority in March 1953 when Nielsen reported that CBS accounted for the month's Top Ten shows in both evening and daytime radio.

Nighttime programs leading the month were Jack Benny, *Amos & Andy,* Edgar Bergen and Charlie

McCarthy, Eve Arden's *Our Miss Brooks, Lux Radio Theater, People Are Funny, My Little Margie, Arthur Godfrey's Talent Scouts, Suspense* and *Gene Autry's Melody Ranch.*

CBS Daytime could claim Frank and Anne Hummert's *Romance of Helen Trent* as the Number One show and the couple's *Our Gal Sunday* in third place. Soap operas *Aunt Jenny's Real Life Stories, The Guiding Light* and *Wendy Warren & the News* were sixth, eighth and tenth, respectively.

The remaining five spots in the Weekday Top Ten were the domain of CBS Radio's prize personality, Arthur Godfrey. All 15 minute segments of Godfrey's informal mid-morning variety show, were among Daytime's Top Ten. The first half hour of *Arthur Godfrey Time* every morning at 10:00 was also seen on CBS-TV, and like his Monday night *Talent Scouts* show, it was a simulcast hit on both radio and television.

In total, the 49-year-old Godfrey accounted for eight hours of CBS radio time and four hours of the network's television programming every week — all fully sponsored. He was fully worth the nearly two million dollars paid him annually by the network *(17.1 Mil)* at his peak of popularity.

Capitalizing on its dominance, CBS increased its daytime radio rates by five percent.

THE PILE OF AUTUMN LEAVES

Sixteen of the previous season's Top 50 programs were gone from the list in when 1952–53 began — among them were eight series that left the air permanently.

The Carnation Contented Hour disappeared after 20 seasons and three Top 50 finishes.

Big Town was cancelled at the end of its 14th season, 13 of them in the Top 50.

The most successful of the retirees was *Mr. District Attorney,* which registered ten Top 25 seasons in its 13 years on the air.

Shorter-term favorites permanently shelved were *Horace Heidt's Youth Opportunity Program* and *Mr. Chameleon,* after four seasons each. Movie stars

| | Radio | | Television | | Combined | |
	Rtg	Rank	Rtg	Rank	Total HH's	Pct TV
Arthur Godfrey's Talent Scouts	7.3	12	54.7	2	14,283,200	78.1%
Jack Benny Program	11.0	1	39.0	12	12,664,000	62.8%
Dragnet	6.7	15	46.8	4	12,414,800	76.9%
Groucho Marx's You Bet Your Life	7.9	7	41.6	9	11,877,600	71.4%
Gangbusters	7.4	9	42.4	8	11,816,800	73.2%
Amos & Andy	10.8	2	34.4	25	11,640,000	60.3%
Life with Luigi	7.7	8	38.5	13	11,149,60	70.4%
Our Miss Brooks	8.4	6	35.0	22t	10,735,200	66.5%
The Big Story	7.2	13	35.0	22t	10,221,600	69.9%

Ronald Colman's *Halls of Ivy*, William Boyd's *Hopalong Cassidy* and Dick Powell's *Richard Diamond, Private Detective* were all gone after three solid seasons

THE MONTHLIES

CBS entered the season with a string of 30 consecutive months of first place programs.

Jack Benny and *Lux Radio Theater* tied for honors in September, Benny pulled ahead to win October through December and was tied for first by *Amos & Andy* in January. Benny then won February and March outright

NBC finally broke CBS's total dominance of first place finishes in April when Groucho Marx's comedy quiz *You Bet Your Life* tied *Lux Radio Theater*.

It was the first time in 59 long months that NBC, which had once dominated Network Radio, could boast of even a tie for a month's Number One program.

Lux won May and Benny closed out the season by winning June.

As the Golden Age came to an end, CBS had run up 40 straight months of winning or tying for Number One monthly finishes.

*1952–53 Sunday Night
Top Ten Programs (11)*
CBS 6, NBC 4, ABC 1
Average: 7.5

Jack Benny Program	CBS	7:00	11.0
Amos & Andy	CBS	7:30	10.8
Edgar Bergen & Charlie McCarthy	CBS	8:00	10.6
Our Miss Brooks	CBS	6:30	8.4
My Little Margie	CBS	8:30	7.4
Dragnet	NBC	9:30	6.7
Theater Guild on the Air	NBC	8:30	6.4
Barrie Craig, Confidential Investigator	NBC	10:00	5.8
Hallmark Playhouse/Hall of Fame	CBS	9:00	5.2
Phil Harris & Alice Faye Show	NBC	8:00	5.2
Walter Winchell's Journal	ABC	9:00	5.2

BETTER LATE THAN NEVER

CBS accomplished an unprecedented feat on Network Radio's most popular night.

It was the first time any network delivered Sunday's Top Five shows and placed all five in the season's Top Ten with Jack Benny leading the pack.

Four of the five were also among CBS-TV's top rated shows.

The only holdout from television was Edgar Bergen. Although popular in films and as a television guest, the ventriloquist never converted his radio variety show into a TV series.

SO LONG DOESN'T MEAN GOODBYE

Freeman Gosden and Charles Correll didn't appear in the television adaptation of *Amos & Andy*. They had avoided any visual depiction of their characters since their 1930 film, *Check & Double Check*, in which Network Radio's most popular pair of the day were reduced to secondary characters performing stilted roles in blackface.

Instead, they wisely stayed with radio ... and stayed ... and stayed.

Gosden and Correll's program of November 23, 1952, celebrated their 10,000th broadcast. It recalled their 25 years of local and network performances as *Amos & Andy*. The nostalgia-laden show prompted the press and many of their fans to presume that it also signaled their last season on the air.

Such fears were premature — by eight years, almost to the day.

The half hour sitcom was last heard in 1955, but Gosden and Correll didn't bid a final goodbye to their fans until November 25, 1960, when their nightly strip show featuring records and guests, *Amos & Andy's Music Hall*, was cancelled.

GALE STORMS INTO RADIO

My Little Margie was one of the simplest of television's simple sitcoms of the 1950s.

The misadventures of a pert young woman and her befuddled father was loaded with silly situations and their making even sillier faces in reaction to them.

Syndicated columnist John Crosby labeled *My Little Margie*, "My Little Stinker."

Yet, the sitcom was historic in broadcasting annals.

My Little Margie was the first television series that transitioned into Network Radio's Top Ten.

Both the radio and television versions of the sitcom starred Gale Storm, 31, a veteran of over 30 low budgeted movies in which she portrayed bright ingénues similar to *My Little Margie*'s title character, 21-year-old Margie Albright.

Her clueless father was played by handsome silent film star Charles Farrell who returned to acting from a successful business career in Palm Springs, California.

My Little Margie was one of television's most traveled series. It debuted on CBS-TV in June 1952, as the summer substitute for Lucille Ball's top rated *I Love Lucy*. It bounced back and forth between CBS-TV and NBC-TV three times until its 126th and final episode in May 1955.

Unlike its television inspiration, the radio adaptation of *My Favorite Margie* opened on CBS in December 1952 and remained on the network until June 1955.

WINCHELL'S RANTING AND RATING WOES

Walter Winchell returned to the air in October after a six month leave of absence to recover from a nervous breakdown.

He was welcomed back two months later with a $1.525 Million *(18.7 Mil)* lawsuit filed against him, ABC and Winchell's sponsor, Gruen Watch Company, by *The New York Post*.

Hearst Newspapers — owner Winchell's flagship tabloid, *The New York Mirror,* and Hearst's King Features syndication subsidiary — were also named in the libel suit.

The action was the culmination of a year long feud begun when *The Post* published a 24-part series highly critical of Winchell's methods and ethics.

In angry response, Winchell accused *The Post*, its publishers and editors of Communist leanings. He referred to the rival tabloid as, "That pinko-stinko sheet," "The New York Pravda," and "The New York Com-post."

Winchell's continued smears in his newspaper columns and radio commentaries led *The Post* to take the fight into court.

Never one to back down from a fight, Winchell countersued *The Post* for libel, demanding two million dollars *(17.1 Mil)* in damages.

Radio "feuds" had traditionally fueled higher radio ratings. Winchell himself had been involved in a phony feud with bandleader Ben Bernie in the 1930s which predated the Jack Benny/Fred Allen and Bob Hope/Bing Crosby verbal battles. All were played for laughs.

But this was different and it had a different outcome.

The public wanted no part of it. Winchell's ratings plunged 40 percent over the season. His Top Ten ranking of four consecutive seasons dropped to a tie for 36th place. Gruen cancelled its sponsorship of his Sunday show at the end of the season.

The Post won the suit two years later — settling for $30,000 in court costs *($256,100)*, and a retraction/apology from Winchell.

The settlement was paid by ABC and Hearst. But the obstinate Winchell refused to say a word about the verdict. An ABC staff announcer was assigned read the apology on his broadcast of March 16, 1955.

Winchell's penalty came three months later — the loss of his high paying ABC contract, ending his 23-year run on the network.

He was replaced on July 3, 1955, by ABC's promising young newscaster, Paul Harvey.

WITH FRIENDS LIKE THESE...

Walter Winchell and Drew Pearson had been friends and political allies.

Both were 55 years old, widely read left-wing leaning newspaper columnists with Sunday night newscast/commentaries on ABC.

Pearson joined the Blue network in 1941. His outspoken opinions often mirrored Winchell's throughout the decade.

Their combined and relentless barrage questioning the patriotism of James Forrestal, the United States' first Secretary of Defense, was blamed by many in the press to have contributed to Forrestal's dismissal from the post by President Truman in March 1949 and his apparent suicide three months later.

Their split began in April 1952, when Winchell suffered the nervous breakdown that forced him off the air for six months. ABC temporarily moved Pearson's news commentary ahead three hours from 6:00 to cover Winchell's 9:00 timeslot which reached a much larger audience.

Unlike Winchell, Drew Pearson was highly critical of Senator Joe McCarthy. In 1951, he debunked the Wisconsin lawmaker's accusations against suspected communists within government — predating by three years Edward R. Murrow's widely recognized rebuke of McCarthy on CBS-TV.

McCarthy's response to Pearson was a series of high profile attacks from the floor of the Senate, branding him a communist sympathizer. The Senator called for his followers to bombard ABC and sponsor Adam Hats with letters and calls demanding that Pearson be silenced.

It worked, but only in part.

Adam Hats cancelled its sponsorship. However, ABC stood by Pearson and quickly sold his program to Carter Products, manufacturers of various patent medicines.

Pearson's victory was only temporary.

He continued to question McCarthy's tactics in Winchell's timeslot during the spring and summer 1952. The controversial senator furiously demanded that ABC fire his "commie loving" critic.

It was generally expected that ABC, his sponsor and his friend Winchell would all spring to Pearson's defense against McCarthy's rele,ntless attacks that continued into 1953.

But Winchell turned and championed McCarthy's cause *against* Pearson.

ABC and Carter Products stood silent, apparently fearful of the Wisconsin senator's wrath.

Drew Pearson's final ABC broadcast for Carter's Serutan Laxative — "Serutan, Nature's Spelled Backwards"— aired on March 29, 1953. He reportedly offered to continue his broadcasts on ABC at no charge until a new sponsor could be found but the network refused.

McCarthy had won the battle and banished his critic from Network Radio.

Nevertheless, Pearson won the war of words by establishing his own syndicated network of over 150 stations to carry his weekly commentaries. The 15-minute programs were delivered to the stations on tape and sponsored by local advertisers who collectively paid Pearson far more than his ABC contract.

Meanwhile, McCarthy was censured by the Senate in 1954 and died three years later.

Walter Winchell left Network Radio in 1961.

Drew Pearson remained on the air with his wealth-producing syndicated programs until 1968.

1952–53 Monday Night Top Ten Programs
CBS 5, NBC 5
Average: 6.2

Lux Radio Theater	CBS	9:00	10.4
Suspense	CBS	8:00	7.4
Arthur Godfrey's Talent Scouts	CBS	8:30	7.3
Bob Hawk Show	CBS	10:00	6.6
Railroad Hour	NBC	8:00	5.7
One Man's Family*	NBC	7:45	5.3
Morgan Beatty News of the World*	NBC	7:30	5.0
Voice of Firestone	NBC	8:30	4.9
Club 15	CBS	7:30	4.8
Telephone Hour	NBC	9:00	4.8

*Monday–Friday Strip Shows

Sans Strips...			
Cities Service Band of America	NBC	9:30	3.2
The Falcon	MBS	8:00	2.9

LUX LOSES TO LUCY'S LABOR

Lux Radio Theater lost over 25 percent of its ratings in two seasons. After five consecutive years as Network Radio's Number One program, it remained Monday's audience favorite, but dropped from first to fourth in the season's overall rankings.

The major factor to the popularity decline of CBS Radio's longtime favorite was its competition from television — its own CBS Television network.

Lux had the misfortune of being scheduled against CBS-TV's *I Love Lucy*, the Lucille Ball/Desi Arnaz runaway hit that scored a phenomenal 67.3 Nielsen season rating in the nation's millions of television homes — capped by a 71.7 for the January episode depicting the birth of the couple's son.

Lux Radio Theater still dominated its Network Radio time period with over double the audience of NBC's *Telephone Hour* and *Voice of Firestone*, but its glory days were gone.

Network Radio's all time favorite dramatic series remained on CBS for one more year, then moved to NBC's Tuesday schedule for an encore season in 1954. It left the air on June 6, 1955, at the completion of its 927th broadcast.

CBS WINS A
DOUBLEHEADER

Despite the decline in radio audience, CBS presented Monday's overwhelming winning lineups on both nighttime radio and television from 8:00 until 10:30.

CBS-TV's *Lux Video Theater*, *Arthur Godfrey's Talent Scouts*, *I Love Lucy*, *Life with Luigi* and *Studio One* were all Number One in their television time periods as were CBS Radio's *Suspense*, *Godfrey's Talent Scouts* simulcast, *Lux Radio Theater*, and *The Bob Hawk Show* on radio.

It was another first for CBS in broadcasting history.

1952–53 Tuesday Night
Top Ten Programs
CBS 5, NBC 5
Average: 6.4

People Are Funny	CBS	8:00	8.7
Life with Luigi	CBS	9:00	7.7
Mr. & Mrs. North	CBS	8:30	6.6
My Friend Irma	CBS	9:30	6.5
Fibber McGee & Molly	NBC	9:30	6.3
Yours Truly, Johnny Dollar	CBS	9:00	6.3
Martin & Lewis Show	NBC	9:00	5.9
One Man's Family*	NBC	7:45	5.3
Cavalcade of America	NBC	8:00	5.1
Two for the Money	NBC	10:00	5.1

*Monday–Friday Strip Shows

Sans Strips...

Red Skelton Show	NBC	8:30	5.0
Morgan Beatty News of the World	NBC	7:30	5:0

THE BLONDE'S BOMBSHELL

R.J. Reynolds' Camel Cigarettes rescued *My Friend Irma* from its disastrous season on CBS Radio's Sunday schedule. The Cy Howard sitcom starring Marie Wilson as the quintessential dumb blonde was moved to CBS on Tuesday at 9:30, following Howard's hit, *Life with Luigi*—the show that had beaten Bob Hope for two consecutive seasons.

My Friend Irma returned with a slight ratings increase. But in a season when most other programs suffered rating losses, the show's gain was enough to push *Irma* up from 51st to 19th in the annual rankings.

Of greater note, the show edged out *Fibber McGee & Molly* in the ratings.

My Friend Irma became the first program in 15 years to beat Jim and Marian Jordan's legendary sitcom in its Tuesday time period.

FIBBER AND MOLLY GET
THE LAST LAUGHS

Jim and Marian Jordan retired from Tuesday night radio after their disappointing 1952–53 season.

The couple had enjoyed a successful quarter century in radio comedy, capped by their 18 years as *Fibber McGee & Molly*—a Top Ten program for 13 seasons. They were both in their late fifties, wealthy and tired of the grind — particularly Marian, whose health had always been frail.

Molly bid her traditional, "G'night, all," for what they thought was the last time on June 30, 1953.

But NBC had different ideas. The network lured them back with a scaled down *Fibber McGee & Molly*—just 15 minutes a day, transcribed at their convenience and without the pressure of a major production with a studio audience.

The new shows, written by Don Quinn's successor Phil Leslie and his assistants, returned to the NBC evening schedule as a Monday through Friday nighttime strip at 10:00 in October 1953. It became a Sunday through Thursday feature

in August 1954 when Gillette moved its Friday night *Cavalcade of Sports* boxing shows from ABC to NBC Radio.

The Sunday installment of *FM&M* was dropped in late June 1955, but a concurrent run of the transcribed series was added to the network's weekday morning schedule at 11:45. The commercially successful double run of *Fibber McGee & Molly* remained in the two timeslots until late March 1956, when — after recording 577 of the quarter hour shows — the Jordans again called it quits, said goodbye to their fans and retired.

And again, NBC had different ideas.

This time the network offered them a series of *five minute*, transcribed, two-person *Fibber McGee & Molly* conversational inserts to be incorporated into NBC's marathon weekend program, *Monitor*, beginning in June 1957.

The two-year contract called for ten vignettes per week, all written by an NBC team headed by Tom Koch. Each four minutes of dialogue allowed for 60 seconds of commercial time which NBC had no problem selling in advance to major advertisers including General Mills, Pepsi Cola and Liggett & Myers Tobacco.

Jim and Marian recorded over a thousand original *Monitor* segments during the two year period. They finally retired in 1959 but occasional repeats extended their run as *Fibber McGee & Molly* on *Monitor* until 1961.

Meanwhile, the show that ended their Tuesday dominance in the 1952–53 season, *My Friend Irma*, had disappeared from Network Radio seven years earlier.

WHATEVER HAPPENED
TO MY PAL, SPIKE?

As a teenager, Jim Jordan loved sports and played on his Spalding Institute high school basketball team in Peoria with a bright and popular neighborhood pal, Spike Sheen. Following graduation Jim went to work and Spike left for college with hopes of entering the ministry.

The two kids from the same neighborhood never lost touch as

each in his own time became popular with millions of Americans on Tuesday nights.

Jim, of course, was *Fibber McGee.* Spike became New York Auxiliary Bishop Fulton J. Sheen, who hosted *The Catholic Hour* on NBC Radio for 20 years and whose simple and absorbing chalk talks, *Life Is Worth Living,* were a ratings phenomenon on the lowly DuMont Television Network from 1952 to 1957. Sheen's weekly sermons became DuMont's most popular series, drawing between ten and 20 million viewers a week against NBC-TV's once unbeatable *Texaco Star Theater* starring Milton Berle.

In February 1953, Sheen was presented with an Emmy as television's "Most Outstanding Personality."

BETTER SEEN THAN HEARD

Despite his faltering radio ratings, Bob Hope had provided solid ratings leading into *Fibber McGee & Molly* since 1948. When Hope left NBC's Tuesday schedule at the end of the 1951–52 season, his timeslot was filled by another variety show, headlined by the hottest new comedy team of the decade, Dean Martin and Jerry Lewis.

The handsome romantic baritone Martin, 35, and his 26-year-old manic comedian partner were wildly successful in nightclub, stage and television appearances. But their slapstick act didn't translate to radio. After a stumbling starts on NBC's Sunday, Monday and Friday schedules beginning in 1949, Martin and Lewis were moved to Tuesdays for the 1952–53 season as Bob Hope's replacement.

They lost 25 percent of Hope's ratings and left radio at the end of the season.

Dean Martin and Jerry Lewis remained a team until 1956 when each went on to highly successful solo careers.

Ironically, their 1952–53 Network Radio series was outrated by a low cost CBS studio drama starring the handsome movie actor who had appeared with them in their 1949 movie debut, *My Friend Irma,* John Lund. Lund was better known to radio fans as *Yours Truly, Johnny Dollar.*

CBS GETS ITS DOLLAR'S WORTH

Yours Truly, Johnny Dollar had been on CBS schedules since 1949. Except for a brief summer run in 1950, the program was sustaining. As such, the program was non-existent in the Nielsen ratings until 1952 when Wrigley Gum picked up the series with Paramount film star John Lund in the title role.

The adventures of the freelance insurance investigator with, "...The action packed expense account!" replaced *Life with Luigi* on the CBS schedule at 9:00 in March and broke into the season's list of Top 25 programs.

Johnny Dollar had originally been created for actor Dick Powell who opted instead to become radio's singing sleuth, *Richard Diamond, Private Detective.* When Powell rejected the *Dollar* role it was passed on to Charles Russell for a season, Edmond O'Brien for two and finally Lund until Wrigley's cancellation in 1954.

Yours Truly, Johnny Dollar was the last dramatic series of Network Radio's Golden Age.

It returned as a CBS Monday-Friday strip series in 1955 and reverted to its half-hour form in 1956. The title role was subsequently taken by Bob Bailey, Bob Readick and Mendel Kramer for the remainder of its remarkable run of 13 years that extended into 1962.

YOU CAN'T GO HOME AGAIN

After three sorry seasons on CBS that saw his ratings drop to single digits, Red Skelton returned the scene of his past radio glories — NBC's Tuesday night schedule where he and Bob Hope had tied as Network Radio's Number One attractions in the 1942–43 season with 32.3 Hooperatings.

What had been considered Skelton's fluke rating of only 3.9 his previous season at CBS, only improved by a disappointing 1.1 point.

Skelton's MGM films continued to be box office hits and his weekly NBC-TV show scored big ratings, but the Tuesday radio audience deserted him to watch comedians Milton Berle on NBC-TV and Red Buttons on CBS-TV, both opposite his radio series.

Ironically, Skelton's 1952–53 season rating again tied with Bob Hope's new Wednesday show on NBC.

Both registered a sad 5.0 Nielsen rating — and a tie for 46th place in the season's rankings.

As Bob Hope had done in June 1952, Red Skelton joined *Fibber McGee & Molly* and left NBC Radio's Tuesday schedule after the 1952–53 season.

Network Radio's most unbeatable trio of comedy hits became relics the Golden Age.

A SHORT DAY'S JOURNEY INTO NIGHT

More proof that movie popularity no longer translated to Network Radio success was found in Tuesday's *Doris Day Show* on CBS.

The 30-year-old former singer with Les Brown's band on the Bob Hope Show had graduated to solo careers as a highly popular Columbia Records artist and Warner Brothers film star. By 1952 she had a string of hit records and movies to her credit and was on her way to becoming a superstar of the decade.

The transcribed *Doris Day Show* supported by participating sponsors appeared in the Nielsen ratings for only four months of the 1952–53 season, scoring a dismal 2.9 against NBC's quiz, *Two for the Money.*

The blonde singing sweetheart of the movies left series radio after one season.

TWO FOR THE SHOWS

Mark Goodson and Bill Todman were producers specializing in game shows.

Their radio credits dated back to *Winner Take All* in 1946 hosted by Bill Cullen and Bud Collyer. They followed with 1948's *Catch Me if You Can* and *Hit the Jackpot* with Cullen, plus *Time's a Wastin',* and a short-lived radio version of their later TV hit *Beat the Clock,* starring Collyer.

All were CBS Radio series that met with only moderate success.

In 1952 they moved to NBC and introduced *Two for the Money,* a comedy quiz à la *You Bet Your Life* starring 34-year-old homespun comedian Herb Shriner. The radio/television simulcast was sponsored by Lorrilard's Old Gold Cigarettes. After one season Lorrillard moved the show to CBS where it remained a popular Saturday night simulcast for two more years.

Goodson and Todman also moved to CBS-TV where they established a string of prime time hits including *What's My Line?*, *I've Got a Secret* and *To Tell the Truth*.

1952–53 Wednesday Night Top Eleven Programs
NBC 6, CBS 5
Average: 6.1

You Bet Your Life	NBC	9:00	7.9
Great Gildersleeve	NBC	8:30	7.6
The Big Story	NBC	9:30	7.2
Dr. Christian	CBS	8:30	6.4
Philip Morris Playhouse on Broadway	CBS	9:00	6.3
FBI in Peace & War	CBS	8:00	6.0
Walk a Mile	NBC	8:00	5.4
One Man's Family*	NBC	7:45	5.3
What's My Line	CBS	9:30	5.1
Bob Hope Show	NBC	10:00	5.0
Morgan Beatty News of the World*	NBC	7:30	5.0

*Monday–Friday Strip Shows

Sans Strips...
Club 15	CBS	7:30	4.8
Mystery Theater	ABC	8:00	3.9

DOUBLING BETS

Four years earlier producer John Guedel was one of the first to capitalize on the potential of tape recording when he edited Groucho Marx's lengthy contestant interviews into the compact, laugh-filled *You Bet Your Life*.

Guedel and partner Art Linkletter advanced their belief in the technology — in wholesale — on NBC in the 1950–51 season by repeating broadcasts of Tuesday's *People Are Funny* on the following Saturday nights.

On June 17, 1953, Guedel introduced summer reruns to Network Radio and television.

He selected the funniest broadcasts of Groucho Marx's Top Ten comedy quiz *You Bet Your Life* from the 1952–53 season and repeated them as *The Best of Groucho* in the

program's Wednesday night timeslot through the summer.

Although he pioneered them in radio, Guedel's concepts of highly edited programs, canned laughter and repeat broadcasts remain integral parts of television programming to this day.

LINE UP FOR RADIO

Mark Goodson and Bill Todman's game show *What's My Line?* was the first hit program that successfully transitioned *from* television *to* Network Radio. It preceded *My Little Margie* on the CBS Radio schedule by six months, debuting in June 1952.

The panel show hosted by former CBS newsman John Daly featured Arlene Francis, Dorothy Kilgallen, Bennett Cerf and Hal Block — all veterans of Network Radio. On *What's My Line?* they were faced with the challenge of deducing the occupations of three guest contestants a week plus the identity of a celebrity "Mystery Guest."

The radio version of *What's My Line?* lasted for only the one season while its television inspiration remained a Sunday night staple on CBS-TV until 1967.

HOPE FOR DAYTIME

Bob Hope's sabbatical from Network Radio didn't last long after Liggett & Myers cancelled his 14-year-old Tuesday night series in June. Hope finished work on Paramount Pictures' *The Road to Bali* with Bing Crosby, left for the summer in Europe and planned to devote time to his monthly *Colgate Comedy Hour* on NBC-TV along with his increasing schedule of high paying personal appearances.

Then General Foods called with the offer he couldn't refuse — a two-year, two million dollars a year contract *(17.1 Mil)* to transcribe a daily, 15-minute *daytime* monologue/interview series beginning in November, *plus* another million dollars to resume his weekly nighttime variety show from January through June. Both series were sponsored by Jello gelatin and puddings.

Both were rating disasters. Hope's Wednesday night show averaged a mere 5.0 rating and his mid-morning series opened with a meager 2.3.

Hope left daytime radio counting his cash in 1954. Meanwhile, his nighttime radio show was picked up in late 1953 by the American Dairy Association and was shuffled around NBC's schedule for two seasons until it was cancelled.

Hope called his radio career quits after 17 years in late April 1955, concluding a run that included five Number One seasons, six more seasons in the Top Ten and a few that are best forgotten.

1952–53 Thursday Night Top Ten Programs
NBC 7, CBS 3
Average: 5.1

Father Knows Best	NBC	8:30	6.0
Bing Crosby Show	CBS	9:30	5.8
Truth or Consequences	NBC	9:00	5.8
One Man's Family*	NBC	7:45	5.3
Meet Millie	CBS	8:00	5.1
Roy Rogers Show	NBC	8:00	5.1
Morgan Beatty News of the World*	NBC	7:30	5.0
Judy Canova Show	NBC	10:00	4.8
Log Cabin News	NBC	8:25	4.3
Horace Heidt's the American Way	CBS	10:00	4.2

*Monday–Friday Strip Shows

Sans Strips...
Official Detective	MBS	8:00	3.2
Modern Adventures of Casanova	MBS	8:00	2.4

FATHER DOES BEST

Father Knows Best, starring popular 45-year-old film actor Robert Young, had matured from a broad *Blondie* and *Life of Riley* comedy into a warm, well written sitcom to which millions of American families could relate. And, thanks to the postwar Baby Boom, the number of those families was continually growing.

The show told the story of a typical American family named Anderson — an insurance agent, his wife and three children — who lived in a typical Midwestern town named Springfield. They faced everyday life with the typical situations and problems confronting all young families and always resolved them to everyone's satisfaction within the allotted half hour.

In its fourth and final radio season before graduating to its legendary nine year television run, *Father Knows Best* became the first family sitcom to win or tie for first place on Thursday since *The Aldrich Family*'s four year run as the night's Number One show that ended in 1944. General Foods sponsored both NBC series.

By coincidence, Young's career path would cross that of another Friday radio sitcom star 16 years later when he and Elena Verdugo played a family doctor and his nurse in the hit television series, *Marcus Welby, M.D.*

MILLIE DIVES INTO THE SECRETARIAL POOL

MGM contract actress Audrey Totter originated the role of wisecracking office secretary Millie Bronson, on the CBS sitcom *Meet Millie*, which debuted as a sustaining show in search of a sponsor in 1951. Procter & Gamble picked up the show in 1952 and installed it into the network's Thursday schedule.

The show was considered a cross between *My Friend Irma* and *The Adventures of Maisie* which also revolved around the misadventures of less than bright blonde secretaries.

When CBS announced plans to create a television version of the show, Totter's movie commitments prohibited her from continuing in the role. In search of a replacement, *Millie*'s producers came up with 32-year-old Elena Verdugo, a beautiful veteran of 20th Century–Fox films and Universal horror movies in which her talent for screaming came into good use.

It turned out that she also had a flair for comedy and made *Millie* her own through the remaining two years of its radio run and its four years on CBS-TV.

The role elevated Verdugo's popularity to such a degree that she came into in demand for a number of short term television supporting roles and guest appearances. She joined the cast of *Marcus Welby, M.D.*, in 1969 as Robert Young's co-star for the television series' entire 170 episode, seven year run.

THURSDAY SOUNDS LIKE SATURDAY

NBC's Thursday schedule contained two past hits from the network's Saturday lineup.

Ralph Edwards returned his *Truth or Consequences* to NBC for the full season under Pet Milk sponsorship. After his dismal 1950–51 season at CBS, Edwards came back in the summer of 1952 as summer replacement for Pet's *Fibber McGee & Molly*.

The stunt show still had appeal. It won its time period and bounced back into the 1952–53 season's Top 30. Despite its one bad season on CBS, *Truth or Consequences* nevertheless registered twelve straight years as a Top 50 program and remained on the air with multiple sponsorships until 1956.

Judy Canova had enjoyed eight consecutive seasons on NBC's Saturday schedule with a Top 50 show until Colgate pulled its sponsorship after the 1950–51 season and her rural musical/sitcom was brought back by the network during the following year as a sustaining show and was thus ignored in the Nielsen ratings.

Her comeback in 1952–53 was under the participating sponsorships of Emerson Drug's Bromo Seltzer, Smith Brothers' Cough Drops and General Motors. She won her time period against Horace Heidt's short-lived, patriotically themed *The American Way*—not so coincidentally sponsored by American Tobacco on CBS.

But Canova missed making the season's Top 50 list. She left Network Radio at the end of the season and resumed her movie career.

1952–53 Friday Night Top Ten Programs
ABC 4, CBS 3, NBC 3
Average: 4.9

Adventures of Ozzie & Harriet	ABC	9:00	5.3
One Man's Family*	NBC	7:45	5.3
Mr. Keen	CBS	8:00	5.1
This Is Your FBI	ABC	8:30	5.1
Morgan Beatty News of the World*	NBC	7:30	5.0
Your Hit Parade	NBC	8:00	4.8
Club 15	CBS	7:30	4.8
Beulah*	CBS	7:00	4.7

The Lone Ranger	ABC	7:30	4.6
Crime Letter from Dan Dodge	ABC	8:00	4.5
*Monday–Friday Strip Shows			
Sans Strips...			
Friday Night Boxing	ABC	10:00	4.2
Meet Corliss Archer	ABC	9:30	4.1
Adventures of Maisie	MBS	8:00	2.4

FRIDAY NIGHT BECOMES FAMILY NIGHT

The Adventures of Ozzie & Harriet beat out crime melodramas for a second consecutive season as Friday's Number One show, although the nine-year-old family sitcom had to share first place with a much older, much traveled family serial.

In its 20th season, *One Man's Family* became the first strip show in 18 years to either capture first place or tie for first place on any night of the week. The feat hadn't been accomplished since the 1934–35 season when *Amos & Andy* won Monday night outright.

The popularity of the Nelson and Barbour families reflected the trend toward family oriented dramas and sitcoms that would populate television schedules throughout the remainder of the decade.

MARSHALL DILLON SLOW ON HIS DRAW

Gunsmoke began its nine year run on CBS Radio in late April of the 1951–52 season, unsponsored and unrated. Nevertheless, critics and fans alike recognized the gritty stories of life after the Civil War in Dodge City, Kansas, to be classic radio drama.

It finally appeared in the ratings on November 21, 1952, sponsored for only one broadcast by Chrysler's Plymouth automobiles.

Developed by Norman MacDonnell and John Meston, and starring William Conrad as Marshall Matt Dillon, *Gunsmoke* scored a respectable 5.0 against *This Is Your FBI* which was in its final months on ABC.

Gunsmoke disappeared again from the ratings until eleven months later when General Foods' Post Toasties cereal assumed its sponsorship. The inability of CBS to sell *Gunsmoke* for 18 months illustrates the tough sell that nighttime Network Radio had become in the wake of television.

Ironically, television proved to be *Gunsmoke's* greatest triumph. The video version of the series debuted on CBS-TV in 1955. It became television's most popular program from 1957 through 1961, and remained on the network's schedule until 1975.

Although Bill Conrad lost the role of television's Matt Dillon to James Arness, he was nevertheless seen in every episode — as the villain gunned down by Marshall Dillon in *Gunsmoke's* opening.

SOTHERN'S RADIO RATINGS GO SOUTH

Blonde and breezy comedienne Ann Southern had great luck in the movies portraying a pert and smart talking secretary, Maisie Revier.

The 42-year-old Sothern had starred in MGM's ten successful *Maisie* films since 1939. A sitcom based on the series of B movies was featured on CBS Radio from 1945 through 1947. Despite Sothern's movie popularity, the radio show was unable to crack Friday's Top Ten or the seasons' Top 50 lists.

Regardless of its mediocre ratings history, MGM gave new life to the radio adaptation of Sothern's movie series, renamed the freshly produced sitcom *The Adventures of Maisie* and packaged it with the studio's three other transcribed programs intended for the syndication market — *MGM's Theater of the Air, Dr. Kildare* and *The Hardy Family*.

Like its three companion MGM series, *The Adventures of Maisie* wound up in a sporadic run on Mutual and left the air in late 1952.

Her mediocre radio career behind her, Sothern left MGM and moved into television as the bright *Private Secretary,* an immediate and immensely popular CBS-TV Sunday night series that ran for four successful seasons.

1952–53 Saturday Night Eight Rated Programs CBS 5, MBS 2, NBC 1 Average: 4.9			
Gangbusters	CBS	9:00	7.4
Gene Autry's Melody Ranch	CBS	8:00	6.6
Vaughn Monroe Show	CBS	7:30	5.4
Tarzan	CBS	8:30	5.3
Sanka Salutes	CBS	9:25	5.1
Grand Ole Opry	NBC	10:30	4.1
Twenty Questions	MBS	8:00	3.5
Cecil Brown News	MBS	7:55	2.1

CBS RADIO WINS BY DEFAULT

Television had taken Saturday night's audience with NBC-TV's *My Little Margie, The All Star Revue* with rotating headline comedians, *Your Show of Shows* starring Sid Caesar and Imogene Coca and *Your Hit Parade.*

Meanwhile CBS-TV countered with its up and coming lineup of *Beat the Clock,* the new *Jackie Gleason Show,* singer Jane Froman's new musical revue and *Meet Millie.*

As a result, only CBS Radio was able to provide a full three hours of sponsored network programming to its affiliates and in doing so claimed all five of the night's top programs.

Meanwhile, ABC turned all Saturday night programming back to its affiliates and NBC scheduled an eclectic mix that began with the sustaining NBC Symphony from 6:30 until 8:00 and followed with the Pee Wee King and *Grand Ol' Opry* country music shows.

It was a sign of things to come.

NO SCRIPTS, NO CAST AND NO MERCY

Sandwiched within NBC's odd musical mix was an unrated gem, which like the legendary *Gunsmoke,* went unsponsored and unnoticed by most listeners except critics and a small but growing following.

Bob Elliott was only 28 and his partner Ray Goulding, 29, when NBC's New York flagship station, WNBC, brought them in them from WHDH/Boston for its 6:00 to 8:30 morning show in late August 1951.

The team had become popular with New England audiences for their low-key, high satire of Network Radio programs in general and soap operas in particular. Without scripts or supporting cast, Bob and Ray verbally reflected popular radio favorites through a fun house mirror — much as Stan Freberg had done with his Capitol Records' spoof of *Dragnet.*

But unlike Freberg's limited output of satirical recordings, Bob and Ray were on the job five mornings a week on WNBC and then hosted a compilation of their best routines, *Inside Bob & Ray,* which was broadcast on the full NBC network on Saturday night.

Nothing was out of bounds to the pair who took on every leading format and personality in Network Radio and twisted them into hilarity.

Elliott and Goulding left the WNBC morning show in August 1952. Their sustaining Saturday show was cancelled ten months later. Nevertheless, their iconoclastic satire had become a cult favorite with younger audiences.

Bob and Ray subsequently moved on to daytime runs with Mutual and CBS, returning to NBC's *Monitor* in 1955, and finishing their radio career with National Public Radio in 1987. Recordings of their skits remain big sellers to this day.

1952–53 Top Ten Multiple Run Programs CBS 4, ABC 3, NBC 2, MBS 1 Average: 4.4				
One Man's Family*	M–F	NBC	7:45	5.3
Morgan Beatty News of the World*	M–F	NBC	7:30	5.0
Club 15	M,W,F	CBS	7:30	4.8
Beulah*	M–F	CBS	7:00	4.7
The Lone Ranger	M,W,F	ABC	7:30	4.6
Jack Smith Show*	M–F	CBS	7:15	4.3
Lowell Thomas News*	M–F	CBS	6:45	4.2
Gabriel Heatter News*	M–F	MBS	7:30	4.0
Silver Eagle	Tu,Th	ABC	7:30	4.0
Les Griffith News*	M–F	ABC	7:55	3.1
*Monday–Friday Strip Shows				

THE NIELSENS BECOME THE BARBOURS' BEST FRIENDS

One Man's Family hadn't been so successful since its Top Ten seasons in 1939–40 and 1940–41.

Carleton E. Morse's clan ended the season as the year's Number One Multiple Run program, ranked among the Top Ten every night of its broadcast and its twelfth Top 50 finish since going on the full NBC Network 19 years earlier.

It had seemed like curtains for the long-running family saga three years earlier when its sponsor of 14 years, Standard Brands, cancelled the program and NBC was left to carry it on Sunday afternoons as a sustaining feature.

The network and Morse saved *One Man's Family* by converting it to a quarter hour strip and selling it to Miles Laboratories for sponsorship by Alka Seltzer and One A Day vitamins. The serial was slotted weeknights at 7:45 following the Miles Laboratories' increasingly popular *News of the World* with Morgan Beatty which made all but one of the nightly Top Ten's.

One Man's Family remained in its Multiple Run home at 7:45 until May 1959 when it retired from the air after a remarkable 27-year run.

SO LONG UNTIL TOMORROW...

Lowell Thomas closed out the 21 years of Network Radio's Golden Age with an unmatched record.

The 61-year-old newscaster finished every season in the Multiple Runs' Top Ten.

His string included six seasons as the category's most popular program and five finishes in second place.

The Golden Age was over but Thomas wasn't done yet.

He went on to set another record for consistency and longevity. Throughout his entire Network Radio career — a record 46 years that began two years before the Golden Age began and extended 23 years beyond it — Lowell Thomas was heard every weeknight at 6:45.

He said his last, "So long until tomorrow!," on Thursday, May 13, 1976, and bid a final farewell to his millions of listeners the following night.

With his departure the last remnant of Network Radio's Golden Age left the air.

TOP 50 PROGRAMS — 1952–53

CBS 27, NBC 20, ABC 3
Average Rating: 6.4, Median: 6.0
42,800,000 Radio Homes / 95.6% Coverage of U.S. Homes / One Rating Point = 428,000 Homes
Source: A.C. Nielsen Radio Index Serv, Sept 1952–June 1953
Total Programs Rated, 6–11 P.M.: 137
Programs Rated 13 Weeks & Ranked: 108

		Program	Rtg	Type	Sponsor	Day	Time	Lgth	Net
1	3	Jack Benny Program	11.0	SC	Lucky Strike Cigarettes	Sun	7:00	30	CBS
2	2	Amos & Andy	10.8	SC	Rexall Drug Stores	Sun	7:30	30	CBS
3	4	Edgar Bergen & Charlie McCarthy	10.6	CV	Richard Hudnut Cosmetics	Sun	8:00	30	CBS
4	1	Lux Radio Theater/Irving Cummings	10.4	DA	Lux Soap	Mon	9:00	60	CBS
5	6	People Are Funny/Art Linkletter	8.7	APS	Mars Candy	Tue	8:00	30	CBS
6	16	Our Miss Brooks/Eve Arden	8.4	SC	Lustre Creme Shampoo	Sun	6:30	30	CBS
7	6	You Bet Your Life/Groucho Marx	7.9	APQ	DeSoto & Plymouth Autos	Wed	9:00	30	NBC
8	10	Life With Luigi/J Carrol Naish	7.7	SC	Wrigley Chewing Gum	Tue	9:00	30	CBS
9t	12	Suspense	7.4	DA	Autolite Spark Plugs	Mon	8:00	30	CBS
9t	20	Gangbusters	7.4	DA	Grape Nuts Cereal	Sat	9:00	30	CBS
9t	N	My Little Margie/Gale Storm	7.4	SC	Philip Morris Cigarettes	Sun	8:30	30	CBS
12	5	Arthur Godfrey's Talent Scouts	7.3	TC	Lipton Tea	Mon	8:30	30	CBS
13	21	The Big Story	7.2	DA	Pall Mall Cigarettes	Wed	9:30	30	NBC
14	28	Great Gildersleeve/Willard Waterman	7.0	SC	Parkay Margarine	Wed	8:30	30	NBC
15	14	Dragnet/Jack Webb	6.7	DCC	Chesterfield Cigarettes	Sun	9:30	30	NBC
16t	10	Bob Hawk Show	6.6	APQ	Camel Cigarettes	Mon	10:00	30	CBS
16t	22	Gene Autry's Melody Ranch	6.6	DCC	Wrigley Chewing Gum	Sat	8:00	30	CBS
16t	16	Mr & Mrs North/Joe Curtin, Alice Frost	6.6	DCC	Halo Shampoo	Tue	8:30	30	CBS
19	51	My Friend Irma/Marie Wilson	6.5	SC	Camel Cigarettes	Tue	9:30	30	CBS
20t	18	Dr. Christian/Jean Hersholt	6.4	DCC	Vaseline	Wed	8:30	30	CBS
20t	25	Theater Guild on the Air	6.4	DA	US Steel	Sun	8:30	60	NBC
22t	8	Fibber McGee & Molly	6.3	SC	Reynolds Aluminum	Tue	9:30	30	NBC
22t	30	Philip Morris Playhouse on Broadway	6.3	DA	Philip Morris Cigarettes	Sun	8:30	30	CBS
22t	N	Yours Truly, Johnny Dollar/ John Lund	6.3	DCC	Wrigley Chewing Gum	Tue	9:00	30	CBS
25t	18	Father Knows Best/Robert Young	6.0	SC	General Foods	Thu	8:30	30	NBC
25t	22	FBI In Peace & War	6.0	DCC	Nescafe Coffee	Wed	8:00	30	CBS 1
27	58	Martin & Lewis Show	5.9	CV	Chesterfield Cigarettes	Tue	9:00	30	NBC
28t	61	Barrie Craig/William Gargan	5.8	DCC	Bromo Seltzer	Sun	10:00	30	NBC
28t	22	Bing Crosby Show	5.8	MV	General Electric	Thu	9:30	30	CBS

	Program	Rtg	Type	Sponsor	Day	Time	Lgth	Net
28t *N*	Truth or Consequences/R Edwards	5.8	APS	Pet Milk	Thu	9:00	30	NBC
31 *31*	The Railroad Hour/Gordon MacRae	5.7	DA	American Railroad Assn	Mon	8:00	30	NBC
32t *N*	Walk a Mile/John Henry Faulk	5.4	APQ	Camel Cigarettes	Wed	8:00	30	NBC
32t *N*	Vaughn Monroe Show	5.4	MV	Camel Cigarettes	Sat	7:30	30	CBS
34t *31*	Adventures of Ozzie & Harriet	5.3	SC	Participating Sponsors	Fri	9:00	30	ABC
34t *49*	One Man's Family	5.3	DCC	Alka Seltzer	M-F	7:45	15	NBC
34t *N*	Tarzan/James Pierce	5.3	DCC	Post Toasties Cereal	Sat	8:30	30	CBS
37t *35*	Hallmark Playhouse & Hall of Fame	5.2	DA	Hallmark Cards	Sun	9:00	30	CBS
37t *40*	Phil Harris & Alice Faye Show	5.2	SC	RCA Victor Radios & TV	Sun	8:00	30	NBC
37t *9*	Walter Winchell's Journal	5.2	NC	Gruen Watches	Sun	9:00	15	ABC
40t *N*	Meet Millie/Elena Verdugo	5.1	SC	Procter & Gamble	Thu	8:00	30	CBS
40t *25*	Mr Keen/Arthur Hughes	5.1	DCC	Procter & Gamble	Fri	8:00	30	CBS
40t *60*	Roy Rogers Show	5.1	DCC	Post Toasties	Thu	8:00	30	NBC
40t *N*	Sanka Salutes/Win Elliot	5.1	SP	Sanka Coffee	Sat	9:25	5	CBS
40t *31*	This Is Your FBI	5.1	DCC	Equitable Life Assurance	Fri	8:30	30	ABC
40t *N*	Two for the Money/Herb Shriner	5.1	APQ	Old Gold Cigarettes	Tue	10:00	30	NBC
40t *N*	What's My Line/John Daly	5.1	PS	Stopette Deodorant	Wed	9:30	30	CBS
47t *25*	Bob Hope Show	5.0	CV	General Foods	Wed	10:00	30	NBC
47t *54*	News of the World/Morgan Beatty	5.0	NC	Alka Seltzer	M-F	7:30	15	NBC
47t *86*	Red Skelton Show	5.0	CV	Bromo Seltzer	Tue	8:30	30	NBC
50 *40*	Voice of Firestone	4.9	MC	Firestone Tire & Rubber	Mon	8:30	30	NBC

New & Returning Top 50 Programs Underscored.

1	The FBI in Peace & War		Sept–Dec	Lucky Strike Cigarettes	Wed	8:00	30	CBS

Key: APl — Audience Participation/Interviews   DCC — Drama/Continuing Characters   MV — Music/Variety Show
APQ — Audience Participation/Quiz   MC — Music/Classical, Semi-Classical   NC — News, Commentary
APS — Audience Participation/Stunts   MP — Music/Popular, Contemporary   PS — Panel Show Comedy
CV — Comedy/Variety Show   MSP — Music/Specialty, Ethnic   SC — Situation Comedy
DA — Dramatic Anthology   MST — Music/Standard, Traditional   SP — Sports
TC — Talent Competition

1952-53 Top 50 Favorite Formats

	Programs	Pct
Drama — Anthology & Continuing	20	40%
Comedy — All Categories	17	34%
Audience Participation — All Categories	6	12%
Music — All Categories	4	8%
News/Commentary	2	4%
Sports	1	2%

1952-53 Monthly Winners

Sep	Jack Benny Program	8.8	Feb	Jack Benny Program	13.9
	& Lux Radio Theater	8.8	Mar	Jack Benny Program	12.8
Oct	Jack Benny Program	11.6	Apr	Lux Radio Theater	8.4
Nov	Jack Benny Program	12.9		& You Bet Your Life/	8.4
				Groucho Marx	
Dec	Jack Benny Program	13.0	May	Lux Radio Theater	9.8
Jan	Jack Benny Program	13.9	Jun	Jack Benny Program	7.0
	& Amos & Andy	13.9			

26

Network Radio's All Time Favorites

RIGHT BACK WHERE WE STARTED FROM

This lengthy chronicle of Network Radio's Golden Age began as a simple search to identify its most popular programs and personalities.

It resulted in the ratings compilation and analysis of an average 158 programs per year broadcast from 1932 to 1953. You can see them for yourself in the appendix — nearly 20,000 monthly entries that give us the definitive answers we sought.

Crossley, Clark-Hooper, Hooper and Nielsen ratings crowned Network Radio's royalty.

They're identified by a simple point system applied against each season's Top 50 rankings. Their final positions are determined by the total number of points scored by each program or personality.

This method rewards their performances against their contemporaries regardless of the methodology employed by the ratings service at the time. It also recognizes their longevity in the Top 50 rankings. The more seasons a program remained in the annual Top 50, the greater its final score.

Two hundred and sixty-five separate programs and personalities made the Annual Top 50 at least once over the 21-year span.

Only two individuals made the Annual Top 50 in all 21 seasons — Jack Benny and Walter Winchell.

AND THE WINNERS ARE...

Each season's Top 50 report in this book contains a "Favorite Formats" section that itemizes the percentage of programs which fall into five general categories.

Comedy includes three sub-categories. Comedy/Variety programs starred comedians with heavy doses of music and miscellany. Situation Comedies are self-explanatory, and

Panel Shows were always light-hearted and played for laughs — even the intellectually bent *Information Please.*

By far the most popular format, Comedy shows made the season's Top 50 356 times over the 21 years of Network Radio's Golden Age. Here's how they finished in order of their rankings history:

1. Jack Benny
2. Edgar Bergen and Charlie McCarthy
3. *Fibber McGee & Molly*
4. *Amos & Andy*
5. Bob Hope
6. Eddie Cantor
7. Burns and Allen
8. Fred Allen
9. Fanny Brice as *Baby Snooks*
10. Red Skelton

Drama includes Anthologies of different stories every week and Situation series with continuing characters from episode to episode. Drama was the runner-up to Comedy in popularity with 285 Top 50 entries during the Golden Age. In the postwar years, Drama overtook Comedy as the favorite format, evidenced in the 1951–52 season when 24 dramatic programs made the annual Top 50.

These Dramas were the Top Ten most enduring favorites:

1. *Lux Radio Theater*
2. *Mr. District Attorney*
3. *Big Town*
4. *One Man's Family*
5. *Screen Guild Players*
6. *First Nighter*
7. *Gangbusters*
8. *Mr. & Mrs. North*
9. *Dr. Christian*
10. *Suspense*

Music was offered to listeners in six different sub-categories and got a head start as listeners' favorite format. Over half of the season's Top 50 programs in 1933–34 and 1934–35 offered their audiences music of one kind or another in these formats:

Music/Variety mixed its musical host's talents with comedy and/or dramatic skits. Popular Music shows focused on song hits of the day or recent past. Specialty Music was found in the ethnic offerings of gypsy, minstrel and country music shows. Standard/Traditional Music formats were the "oldies but goodies" of their day. Classical Music programs leaned heavily on well-known classical and operatic works. Talent Competitions were primarily contests among singers and instrumental soloists.

Although these sub-categories made Music the most popular format of the 1930s, it finished in third place behind Comedy and Drama with 267 Top 50 programs during the Golden Age. Leading the pack were these favorites:

1. Bing Crosby
2. Rudy Vallee
3. *Your Hit Parade*
4. *Major Bowes' Original Amateur Hour*
5. Al Jolson
6. *Arthur Godfrey's Talent Scouts*
7t. *Fitch Bandwagon*
7t. Kate Smith
9. *Maxwell House Showboat*
10. Guy Lombardo Orchestra

Audience Participation shows trailed in fourth place with 95 Top 50 finishes during the Golden Age. Programs involving members of their audiences depended on their fast-thinking hosts' abilities to ad-lib and move the shows along at a brisk pace. The category is divided into the three sub-categories. Interviews were generally of a human interest nature. Quiz shows offered both large and small prizes to their contestants. Stunt shows were few in number but big in ratings.

Audience Participation was the latecomer to Network Radio. None appeared in a season's Top 50 until the 1935–36 season. At their peak of popularity, eight Audience Participation shows made the annual Top 50 in the 1940–41 and 1944–45 seasons.

These were the ten most popular as determined by their annual rankings:

1. *Kay Kyser's Kollege of Musical Knowledge*
2. *Truth or Consequences*
3. *People Are Funny*
4. *Take It or Leave It*
5. *Bob Hawk Show* aka *Thanks to the Yanks*
6. *You Bet Your Life*
7. *We, the People*
8. *Vox Pop*
9. *Professor Quiz*
10. *Battle of the Sexes*

News/Sports placed only 54 programs in the annual Top 50 rankings from 1932 to 1953. Its peak came near the end of World War II in 1944–45 when five of its News/Commentary sub-category placed among the annual Top 50. It's also a sub-category that could make a serious journalist cringe with its inclusion of Blue/ABC's dynamic duo on Sunday nights, sensationalistic Walter Winchell and gushy Hollywood columnist Louella Parsons — more proof that listeners wanted to be entertained.

Sports received little attention in Network Radio's prime time *except* when Heavyweight Championship fights were involved. Nevertheless, Pabst's *Blue Ribbon Bouts* and Win Elliot's *Sanka Salutes* sports capsules both reached News/Sports All Time Top Ten.

In order of their popularity:

1. *Walter Winchell's Journal*
2. Lowell Thomas News
3. H.V. Kaltenborn News
4. Boake Carter News
5. Edwin C. Hill News
6. Win Elliot *Sanka Salutes Sports*
7. Bill Henry *Johns-Manville News*
8. Morgan Beatty *News of the World*
9. Louella Parsons Hollywood News
10t. Gabriel Heatter News
10t. *Blue Ribbon Bouts*

WE'RE A LITTLE LATE, FOLKS ... SO, GOODNIGHT!

Jack Benny's familiar sign-off to listeners — used when his Sunday night program often ran overtime — is a fitting close to this work that evolved into hundreds of stories about Network Radio's Golden Age.

Our research has uncovered many more forgotten stories about the people and their programs of the era. But they'll have to wait for another day — or another book.

As put forth early in this text, they all contributed to a phenomenon so popular at its peak that it dominated American media as none other ever had or ever will again. It was also an industry in which billions of dollars changed hands over its 21 years of greatest influence.

But more importantly, Network Radio kept its listeners informed of the latest news and boosted their spirits with entertainment throughout the darkest days of the 20th century.

And that is the true legacy of its Golden Age.

Appendices

The following pages contain the monthly and annual averages of all Network Radio programs broadcast and rated between 6:00 and 11:00 P.M. (Eastern Time), during the September through June broadcast seasons of 1932 through 1952. Averages were calculated from the semi-monthly survey reports issued by Crossley Research, Inc.; The Co-operative Analysis of Broadcasting (CAB); Clark-Hooper, Inc.; C.E. Hooper, Inc., and The Nielsen Company, Inc. All ratings incorporated in these averages is copyrighted information of The Nielsen Company, licensed for use herein.

TRANSLATING RATING POINTS

Unlike today's radio and television ratings expressed in numbers of listeners and viewers, ratings of the Golden Age era were limited to the estimated number of homes in which the programs were heard. One rating point represents one-percent of the number of radio households in a given year. As the number of radio households grew every year, so did the value of each rating point:

Broadcast Season	One Rating Point Equals
1932–33	184,500 Homes
1933–34	192,500 Homes
1934–35	204,000 Homes
1935–36	214,560 Homes
1936–37	228,690 Homes
1937–38	245,000 Homes
1938–39	266,700 Homes
1939–40	275.000 Homes
1940–41	285,000 Homes
1941–42	293,000 Homes
1942–43	306,000 Homes
1943–44	308,000 Homes
1944–45	325,000 Homes
1945–46	331,000 Homes
1946–47	340,000 Homes
1947–48	359,000 Homes
1948–49	376,230 Homes
1949–50	393,000 Homes
1950–51	407,000 Homes
1951–52	419,000 Homes
1952–53	428,000 Homes

Estimating the number of listeners within those homes is pure conjecture. Nevertheless, this book has used a conservative "guesstimate" of 2.5 listeners per home. Therefore, if a program registered a 9.8 rating during the 1947–48 season, for example, its rating translates into 3,518,200 homes and 8,795,500 listeners.

NETWORK ABBREVIATIONS

A = The American Broadcasting Company (ABC).

B = The Blue Network, identified until 1941 as the NBC Blue Network.

C = The Columbia Broadcasting System (CBS).

M = The Mutual Broadcasting System (MBS).

N = The National Broadcasting Company (NBC), identified until 1941 as the NBC Red Network.

SCHEDULING CHANGES

In cases of mid-season changes in a program's day or time of broadcast, or its network of origin, as a general rule the information contained in that season's April rating report used.

BLANK MONTHS

Months in which no rating is reported signifies that the program was not rated because it was either not broadcast or not sponsored. With rare exception, only sponsored programs were included in rating reports.

A: Year-by-Year Monthly and Annual Ratings of All Prime-Time Programs

(next page)

1932-33 Crossley Ratings 6-11 P.M.

Program				Sept. 32	Oct. 32	Nov. 32	Dec. 32	Jan. 33	Feb. 33	March 33	April 33	May 33	June 33	1932-33 Avg
A&P Gypsies	N	Mon	9:00	8.1	11.9	7.0	11.2	12.4	12.6	15.5	12.6	13.6	12.4	11.7
Abe Lyman Orch	C	Tu,Th	8:45		3.7	4.1	6.1	3.1	3.8	3.5	2.8	3.0		4.1
Adventures in Good Health	B	Tu,Fr	8:30	2.4	2.2	1.6	1.2	2.3	3.7	2.3			1.6	2.3
Adventures of Charlie Chan	B	Fri	7:30				6.8	7.5	11.8	13.0	14.5	8.4		10.3
Adventures of Sherlock Holmes	N	Wed	9:00	21.2	21.2	17.2	19.9	25.5	21.6	20.8	21.4	20.2		21.0
Al Jolson Show	N	Fri	10:00				23.2	29.7	30.5					27.8
All American Football Show	C	Fri	9:30		9.3	6.9	5.1							7.1
American Album of Familiar Music	B	Sun	9:30	6.8	10.0	10.0	6.6	8.6	13.9	11.6	12.2	9.8	10.9	10.0
Amos & Andy	B	M-F	7:00	26.1	29.1	25.7	28.8	30.6	30.9	30.6	29.4	30.4	27.1	28.9
Angelo Patri's Your Child	C	Wed	7:45			2.2	2.3	2.3	1.7	1.9				2.3
Angelo Patri's Your Child	C	Sun	7:45		3.6	4.4	3.9				2.5	1.6		2.7
Armour Program Leo Reisman Orch	B	Fri	9:30	10.3	13.4	16.2	13.9	12.8	11.4					13.0
Ben Bernie Show	N	Tue	9:00		20.5	22.9	24.4	26.4	25.7	25.2	33.7	26.6	25.3	25.6
Best Foods Musical Grocery	N	Fri	9:00							6.8	7.5	9.9	8.4	8.2
Big Time	N	Wed	7:00	4.8										4.8
Bing Crosby Music That Satisfies	C	W,Sa	9:00	15.2	13.8	13.6	14.3	18.4	18.5	18.5	19.3	14.6	10.0	18.5
Blackstone Plantation/Crumit & Sandsn	N	Tue	8:00					12.9	19.3	18.2				15.1
Blue Coal Musical Review	N	Sun	7:00		3.4	3.4		2.7						3.4
Boake Carter News	C	M-F	7:45				6.7		3.6	8.4	9.9	7.5		6.3
Buck Rogers	C	M-F	7:15						7.0	7.8	8.0	6.6	5.9	7.4
Burns & Allen & Guy Lombardo Orch	C	Wed	9:30	18.2	15.4	20.0	23.5	31.1	30.1	32.8	33.3	31.8	28.4	26.5
Captain Diamond's Adventures	B	Thu	8:00				5.3	2.4	3.8	4.3	3.4	3.8	3.8	3.8
Carborundum Band	C	Sat	9:30					4.1						4.1
Carnation Contented Hour	N	Mon	10:00	5.8	10.5	10.5	8.9	10.6	13.8	16.6	19.6	18.6	14.9	14.7
Carson Robison Buckeroos	C	Fri	8:30				1.6							1.6
Carveth Wells Exploring America	N	Wed	10:30					10.9	11.0	9.9	7.2	9.1		9.8
Chase & Sanborn Hour Bert Lahr	N	Sun	8:00									28.3	30.7	29.5
Chase & Sanborn Hour Georgie Price	N	Sun	8:00	24.5	30.4	30.4	10.5							27.5
Chandu the Magician	S	M-Sa	Var	3.9	7.9	7.9	10.3	7.9	7.4	7.0	8.6	8.8		7.9
Cities Service Concert	N	Fri	8:00	16.1	19.3	18.2	17.5	23.9	25.5	20.4	23.3	21.3	16.4	20.2
Cliquot Club Eskimos	B	Mon	8:00	9.2	8.8	8.7	8.3	10.6	7.0	8.8	8.6	6.9	6.7	8.4
Colonel Howe	N	Sun	10:30										7.4	7.4
Colonel Stoopnagle & Budd	C	Thu	9:30	5.5	3.6	3.3	7.7	8.0	8.3	9.7	10.7	12.1		9.8
Corn Cob Pipe Club	N	Wed	10:00	9.9	10	11.5	10.8	7.9	7.5	9.7	7.7	7.5	7.2	6.8
Country Doctor	B	M-W	8:45			4.2	7.9	10.8	7.5	6.3	8.9	2.2	3.5	10.6
Cuckoo Program Ray Knight	B	Sat	10:15	5.6	5.6				5.8					6.0
DW Griffith Hollywood News	B	Su,W	10:00				7.8	5.0	8.3	8.0	8.3	8.6		5.5
David Lawrence News Commentary	N	Sun	10:15	6.0	9.2	9.2		8.5	12.0	15.4	11.0	10.8	10.5	8.1
Death Valley Days	B	Thu	9:00	8.5	8.5	12.7	11.6	13.2						11.7
"Dr Haggard's Devils, Drugs & Doctors"	N	Sun	7:15				1.2	1.2	1.2	0.0	0.0	0.0		0.5
Easy Aces	C	T,T,Sa	10:15	5.4	5.4	5.8	7.5	7.5	11.3	10.5	12.1	12.3		9.1
Ed Wynn Texaco Fire Chief	N	Tue	9:30	28.2	32.3	40.7	44.3	45.8	41.3	47.1	44.8	41.9	38.1	40.5
Eddie Cantor Chase & Sanborn Hour	N	Sun	8:00			49.4	47.5	58.4	59.1	60.9	58.6			55.7
Eddie Dooley Football Dope	C	Sat	6:30	5.5	6.1	6.1	6.5							6.1
Edgar Guest Musical Memories	N	Tue	9:00	3.5	2.4	3.7	4.9	8.0	6.8	8.1	7.4	6.8	9.8	6.1
Edwin C Hill News	C	MWF	10:30	9.8	9.8									9.8
Elgin Adventurers' Club Floyd Gibbons	N	Fri	10:30			6.4	9.1							7.8
Emma Jettick Melodies	B	Mon	6:30	3.3	4.6	4.6	4.7							4.3

1932-33 Crossley Ratings 6-11 P.M.				Sept. 32	Oct. 32	Nov. 32	Dec. 32	Jan. 33	Feb. 33	March 33	April 33	May 33	June 33	1932-33 Avg
Eno Crime Club	B	Tu,W	8:00	18.2	14.6	17.4	18.2	13.0	16.7	15.5	13.5	13.1	11.3	15.2
Ernest Hutcheson Concerts	C	Sun	10:30		8.2	5.0	1.8	4.2	6.3	4.8				5.1
Fanny Brice & Geo Olsen Orch	N	Wed	8:00								13.6	13.1	14.1	13.6
Ferde Grofe Orch	N	M,W,Sa	7:45									3.6	2.2	2.9
First Nighter	N	Fri	9:00	13.1	14.9	13.5	19.0	20.3	16.7	19.8	21.5	19.1	17.4	17.5
Five Star Theater	N	Thu	7:30				12.4	5.6						9.0
Five Star Theater	N	Fri	7:30				8.2							8.2
Floyd Gibbons News	B	Su,T,T	8:45										5.9	5.9
Fred Allen Linit Bath Club Revue	C	Sun	9:00			10.0	10.0	12.6	13.1	13.7				11.9
Fred Waring Old Gold Program	N	Wed	9:00							13.2	17.2	17.2	16.4	16.0
Friendship Town	B	Tue	9:30	4.5	3.5	2.9	6.7							4.4
Fu Manchu Mysteries	C	Mon	8:30	11.7		12.7	14.8	17.5	15.5	14.9				14.5
Gem Highlights	C	Sun	9:00	8.7										8.7
General Electric Circle	N	MWF	6:30	1.4	2.8	2.2	2.6							2.3
General Electric Concert	B	Sun	8:00						23.9	23.4				23.7
Gold Medal Musical Fast Freight	C	Tu,W	8:45	4.2	5.6			4.8						4.9
The Goldbergs	N	M-F	7:45	18.5	22.0	18.6	17.2	18.5	18.3	18.3	16.3	13.5	11.2	17.2
Great Moments in History	B	Sun	7:30		4.8	4.6	4.7	6.3	6.3	8.1	7.9	6.3		6.1
Hot from Hollywood	C	TWT	7:45								3.3	2.9	3.0	3.1
Howard Thurston the Magician	B	Th,Fr	8:45			3.9	5.3		5.3	3.3				4.5
Inside Story Edwin C Hill	C	Fri	9:30						10.5	13.7	16.0	16.4		14.2
Irwin S Cobb Commentary	C	W,F	9:00									12.6	8.8	10.7
Jack Benny Canada Dry Show	B	M,W	9:30	18.9	14.8									16.9
Jack Benny Canada Dry Show	C	Su,Th	8/10			13.5	12.9	14.0						13.5
Jack Benny Chevrolet Show	N	Fri	10:00						20.3	20.3	22.0	24.4	24.4	22.2
Jack Benny Show Total	All	Var	Var	18.9	14.8	13.5	12.9	14.0	20.3	20.3	22.0	24.0		18.3
Jack Dempsey's Gymnasium	C	T,T,Sa	6:30	2.4							2.2	3.5		2.9
Jack Frost's Melody Moments	B	Mon	9:30					6.1	7.0	7.1	11.9	11.1		7.6
Jack Pearl as Baron Munchausen	N	Thu	10:00	22.4	25.3	31.0	43.3	53.8	41.4	41.5	47.2	48.7	9.9	39.4
Johnny Hart in Hollywood	B	M-F	7:45		2.3	2.1	0.7							1.7
Jones & Hare	C	MWF	7:30	5.9	7.5	8.0								7.1
Just Plain Bill	B	M-F	6:45						10.2	8.6	11.9	11.1		10.5
Kate Smith LaPalina Show	C	Tu-Th	8:00	12.7	12.3	14.8	17.2	14.2	12.7	12.3	12.6	10.0	9.8	12.9
"Keller, Sargent & Ross"	C	Tu,Th	7:30						0.0	1.4				0.7
Ken Murray Royal Gelatin Show	C	Wed	8:00						4.1	8.9				6.5
Lifetime Revue	B	Sun	9:45	3.8	5.5	4.6	3.8							4.4
Lives at Stake	C	Tue	10:00									10.9	9.2	10.1
Love Story Program	C	Thu	9:30	11.1										11.1
Lowell Thomas News	B	M-F	6:45	13.8	11.7	12.5	11.9	12.3	13.7	15.7	16.0	14.0	14.9	13.7
Lucky Strike Hour Walter O'Keefe	N	Tue	10:00			25.8	26.9	33.3	41.4	41.5				33.8
Lucky Strike Dance Bands	C	Sat	10:00	25.1	26.4	26.9	30.4	28.9						27.5
Magic Voice Hitz & Dawson	C	Tu,Sa	8:15			12.2	12.2	13.2	11.9	13.8	12.4	11.7		12.5
Manhattan Merry Go Round	N	Sun	9:00								10.2	7.0	6.8	8.0
March of Time	C	Fri	8:30	17.5	17.5	14.9	13.4							15.3
Marx Brothers Show	B	Mon	7:30				16.7	17.9	17.2	21.4	22.1	18.3		18.9
Maud & Cousin Bill	B	M-W	6:00						1.6	0.0	0.0	2.4		1.0
Maxwell House Show Boat	N	Thu	9:00	20.3	20.3	24.9	28.4	32.2	31.6	32.7	34.6	37.8	32.0	30.5
Memories in Melody	C	Sun	7:30		2.7	2.7	1.8							2.3

1932-33 Crossley Ratings 6-11 P.M.

Program	Net	Days	Time	Sept. 32	Oct. 32	Nov. 32	Dec. 32	Jan. 33	Feb. 33	March 33	April 33	May 33	June 33	1932-33 Avg
Mills Brothers	C	M,Th	9:15	10.8	10.1	5.8	8.8	8.7	7.5	7.9				8.5
Morton Downey Sings	B	Wed	9:30		9.4	9.2	10.6	12.7	11.2	10.4				8.9
Music That Satisfies – Various Artists	C	M-Sa	9:00	10.5		11.5			12.3	11.9	5.6	4.6		10.8
Myrt & Marge	C	M-F	7:00		25.7	21.6	22.5	22.8	24.5	23.8				23.5
Mysteries in Paris	C	Mon	9:30				11.1	12.1	12.8	10.7				11.7
Ohman & Arden	N	Sun	9:45			2.9	1.0							2.0
Old Singing Master	B	Sun	9:15	7.7		4.9								6.7
Oldsmobile Show Ethel Shutta	N	Sun	9:30		7.4		5.0	12.6	13.5	13.0				13.0
Omar Khayam	C	Sat	9:30		4.1	4.4								4.5
Our Daily Food	B	Thu	9:30						0.0	1.3				0.7
Parade of States	N	Fri	6:00			0.6								
Pat Barnes	B	Mon	9:30	12.2	16.3									14.3
Patri's Dreams of Childhood	B	M-W	8:45		4.9	3.9	3.9			1.9				2.9
Paul Whiteman Rhythmic Concert	C	Sun	7:45		3.6	4.4		2.3	1.7	1.9	2.5	1.6		2.7
Paul Whiteman Buick Show	B	Sun	6:30	13.1		8.8	8.8	8.8						8.8
Pennzoil Parade of Melodies	N	Mon	9:30	5.5	7.6	15.9	15.6	13.5	16.2	15.4				15.2
Phil Baker the Armour Jester	B	Fri	10:00							11.8	20.5	15.9	16.3	16.1
Phil Cook's Ingram Shavers	B	Fri	9:30							8.4	8.4	6.0	4.2	6.2
Phil Harris Orch	B	M,W	8:45	2.9	4.0	3.6					3.5	3.5	5.3	5.3
Phil Spitalny Nestle Chocolateers Orch	N	Fri	9:00		1.6	2.9		2.9	2.5	2.5	3.5			2.9
Philadelphia Symphony Orch	B	Fri	8:00			7.0	8.9	12.6	10.9	7.2	6.9	6.2	5.2	15.9
Ponds Variety Program	C	Sat	9:00											7.6
Ray Perkins	N	Fri	9:30	5.4	5.4									4.9
Richfield Country Club	N	Tu,Th	7:30	5.3	4.5	4.8								4.0
Rin Tin Tin Thriller	B	Fri	10:30				4.7	3.9	6.4	6.4	1.9	4.6		4.5
Romantic Bachelor Sings	B	Thu	8:30					3.8	5.4	5.6	4.3	4.5		4.9
Roxy Theater Revue	C	Wed	9:15	2.9	4.0	3.6	4.3	3.6						4.9
Royal Vagabonds	N	Sun		4.2	2.7	5.5	3.3	3.8						3.8
Rudy Vallee Show	B	Thu	7:15	26.1	26.1	26.1	26.2	31.2	30.0	34.6	33.9	31.5	28.0	29.2
Saturday Night Dancing Party	N	Thu	8:00					18.3	12.5	16.8	18.7	16.6	16.6	17.2
Sealed Power Program	B	Sat	10:00					2.4	1.4	2.7				2.2
The Shadow	N	Sun	6:00						12.5	16.1				11.8
Silken Strings	B	Wed	8:30				9.9		6.4	7.1	6.6	7.3	7.0	6.9
Sinclair Minstrels	N	Sun	8:00	21.0	20.8	20.6	23.3	22.1	23.6	20.7	22.7	24.0	18.8	21.8
Singin' Sam	B	Mon	9:00	8.9	9.1	8.8	8.2	9.5	8.1	8.1	7.2	7.6	6.0	8.2
Smith Brothers – Trade & Mark	C	MWF	7:00			2.0	1.8	2.4	2.7	3.2				2.4
Solly Ward Show	NC	Su,Fri					7.1	9.6	7.9	8.2				9.0
Stebbins Boys	C	Var	10:00	9	7.9						9.0	12.4		8.5
Street Singer	B	Tu-Fr	7:30		7.9									7.3
Sunday at Seth Parker's	C	MWF	8:15	24.2	19.0	18.7	16.3	16.9	20.2	14.6	16.5	14.2		17.7
Thompkins Corners	N	Sun	10:45	8.5										8.5
Threads of Happiness	C	Thu	9:30		2.5	2.2	2.6	3.9	4.1	4.7	3.6	4.9		3.6
Three X Sisters	C	Tue	9:15		2.5	2.2	2.8							2.8
To the Ladies Woodbury Show	B	MWF	6:30	2.1	8.9	10.0	8.4							7.4
Townsend Murder Mystery	C	Fri	9:30					1.3		4.8				4.8
Tydol Jubilee Freddy Martin Orch	B	T,T,Sa	7:15								0.0	1.8	1.8	1.0
Voice of Experience	C	MWF	7:30				1.3	1.3	1.2	0.0	0.0	2.5	1.9	2.2
Voice of Firestone	N	Mon	8:30			22.9	20.8	21.3	22.0	22.0				21.8

1932-33 Crossley Ratings 6-11 P.M.

Program	Net	Day	Time	Sept. 32	Oct. 32	Nov. 32	Dec. 32	Jan. 33	Feb. 33	March 33	April 33	May 33	June 33	1932-33 Avg
Waldorf Astoria Orch	N	Tu,Th	6:00	1.9	3.2	2.5	3.5							2.8
Walter Winchell Jergens Journal	B	Sun	9:30				8.7	12.3	13.8	12.9	11.5	10.5		11.6
Warden Lawes at Sing Sing	B	Sun	9:00						6.0	7.8				6.9
Wayne King Orch	B	Tu,Th	8:30			2.3	6.3	5.8	5.3	8.2	10.7	9.2	8.0	7.0
Wheatenaville	N	Su-Th	7:15		3.3	2.2	2.9	3.8	4.9	5.6				3.8
Whispering Jack Smith	C	M,W	8:00			1.7	3.3	3.4						2.8
Whitman Sampler Program	N	W,Th,Th	7:30			4.7	4.0							4.4
Will Rogers Gulf Headliners Show	B	Sun	9:00									37.8	30.3	34.1

1933-34 Crossley Ratings 6-11 P.M.

Program	Net	Day	Time	Sept. 33	Oct. 33	Nov. 33	Dec. 33	Jan. 34	Feb. 34	March 34	April 34	May 34	June 34	1933-34 Avg
A&P Gypsies	N	Mon	9:00	13.5	13.8	14.8	13.8	14.5	13.3	14.8	9.0	11.9	10.7	13.0
Accordiana	B	Tue	6:45									4.5	4.3	4.4
Adventures in Good Health	B	T,T	8:30	2.1	2.9	3.4	3.3	2.3	2.9	3.3	1.5	1.2	1.7	2.5
Albert Spalding Violin Recitals	C	Wed	8:30		8.2	10.5	14.6	12.5	12.6	11.0	13.1	9.7	9.5	11.3
All American Football	C	Fri	9:30	8.1	7.3	7.6	7.8							7.7
American Album of Familiar Music	N	Sun	9:30	15.6	14.0	16.7	14.6	13.0	14.2	17.1	17.8	12.1	13.2	14.8
American Musical Revue E Waters	C	Sun	7:00			3.6	4.3	6.5	6.5					5.2
Amos & Andy	B	M-F	7:00	34.1	29.6	26.9	30.0	30.0	27.7	31.8	30.3	30.5	27.5	29.8
Armco Iron Master Brass Band	B	Fri	10:00			4.8	5.5							5.2
Babe Ruth	B	MWF	8:45							3.8	3.7	3.7	4.1	3.8
Baby Rose Marie Sings	B	T,T	6:30					3.4			5.5	5.4	5.4	4.7
Beatrice Fairfax	N	Sat	9:30				5.1			5.7	6.3			5.7
Beauty Box Theater	N	Tue	10:00						27.7		22.5	25.9	31.0	26.5
Ben Bernie Show	N	Tue	9:00	29.4	23.8	29.3	30.8	29.9	14.6	31.9	26.5	22.9	25.5	27.8
Billy Batchelor Sketches	N	M-F	7:15		7.4	8.4	11.6	12.9						11.0
Bing Crosby Woodbury Show	C	Tue	9:00		20.2	18.4	17.2	23.1	24.5	21.7	25.1			21.5
Blackstone Plantation	C	Tue	8:00	15	13.9	18.2	12.9							15.0
The Blue Coal Program	N	Sun	7:00		2.2	1.3	3.6							2.4
Boake Carter News/Comment	C	M-F	7:45	7.1	8.1	10.6	10.9	8.6	10.8	9.9	8.1	6.1	5.8	8.6
Bobby Benson & Sunny Jim	C	M-F	6:15		4.3	5.3	4.6	5.3	6.3	7.9	8.7	8.8	8.5	6.6
Broadway Vanities Ev Marshall	C	Wed	8:30									4.1	3.0	3.6
Buck Rogers	C	M-Th	6:00		3.5	5.4	6.3	7.8	6.2	7.1	8.6	7.5	6.8	6.6
Burns & Allen w/ Guy Lombardo	C	Wed	9:30	31.3	28.8	24.9	28.4	28.8	25.5	27.8	30.2	20.1	11.4	28.2
Byrd Antarctic Expedition	C	Sat	10:00				13.0	16.8	20.2	20.7	19.1			17.3
Cadillac Symphony	C	Sun	6:00				13.8	13.8	12.1					13.2
Captain Diamond's Adventures	B	Thu	8:00	7.6	4.8	7.6	5.2	1.4	5.7					5.4
Carborundum Band	C	Sat	9:30			5.1	7.6							6.4
Carnation Contented Hour	N	Mon	10:00	15.9	13.4	12.5	15.5	14.9	14.4	12.9	9.9	11.9	16.9	13.8
The Chevrolet Program	N	Sun	10:00								10.9	7.2	8.7	8.9
Circus Days	N	T,T	7:30		2.3	2.7	2.7	2.9	2.3					2.6
Cities Service Concert	N	Fri	8:00	25.9	20.6	20.4	19.2	20.1	20.6	15.6	21.3	17.8	14.4	19.6
Colgate House Party	N	Sat	8:00							13.4	13.8	13.2	11.4	13.0
Colonel Howe	N	Sun	10:30	3.8	5.2									4.5
Colonel Stoopnagle & Budd	C	W,Sa	9:15					7.6	8.8	6.3	10.3			8.2
Conoco Tourist Adventures	N	Wed	10:30									9.3		8.3
Corn Cob Pipe Club	N	Wed	10:00					8.6	9.3	7.8	10.3			8.6
Court of Human Relations	N	Sun	7:00	9.4	7.6			6.2	8.1	9.1	10.1	9.0	7.6	8.1
Cruise of the Seth Parker	N	Tue	10:00					19.4	22.3					21.3

1933-34 Crossley Ratings 6-11 P.M.

Program	Net	Day	Time	Sept. 33	Oct. 33	Nov. 33	Dec. 33	Jan. 34	Feb. 34	March 34	April 34	May 34	June 34	1933-34 Avg
Cuckoo Program Ray Knight	B	Wed	9:00	7.6	4.5			2.0	1.5	10.5	10.2	8.9	8.2	8.3
Cyrena Van Gordon Sings	B	Mon	8:30					2.0	1.5					1.8
Dangerous Paradise	B	W,F	8:30		5.9		6.3	8.3	9.7					7.6
Death Valley Days	B	Thu	9:00	14.7	15.6	12.4	17.4	14.9	13.5	13.9	14.7	15.1	13.7	14.6
Dill's Best	N	Sat	6:45				1.9	2.6	1.9					2.1
Dixie Circus	N	Mon	8:00										1.1	1.1
Don Carney's Dog Stories	B	Tue	7:45	1.2	1.5									1.4
Don Quixote	B	ThFSa	7:15				3.6	2.2	3.1					3.0
Dorris Lorraine Sings	C	Thu	10:30									3.6	1.4	2.5
Easy Aces	C	WThF	8:15									5.2	4.8	5.0
Ed Wynn Texaco Fire Chief	N	Tue	9:30	20.3	19.3	36.1	40.3	37.6	36.6	36.6	31.6			32.3
Eddie Cantor Show	N	Sun	8:00			48.0	57.2	56.3	56.2	54.0	50.2			53.7
Eddie Dooley Sports	C	ThFSa	6:30	3.4	3.4									3.4
Eddy Duchin Orchestra	N	Wed	9:30					4.7	7.3	6.2	8.4	8.3	8.5	7.2
Edgar Guest Musical Memories	B	Tue	9:00	7.9	6.3	8.6	6.8	9.5	8.6	7.7	9.2	8.3	8.3	8.1
Edwin C Hill News/Comment	C	MWF	8:15	11.6	10.9	12.8	11.5	12.2	12.7	15.1	11.5	8.8	7.7	11.5
Eno Crime Clues	B	Tue	8:00	10.9	15.6	14.8	15.4	17.9	18.6	16.1	17.9	13.7	13.4	15.4
Evening in Paris	C	Sun	8:00	5.2	6.1	1.6	2.1	2.8	3.7	2.8	4.9			3.7
First Nighter	C	Fri	10:00	20.7	21.7	23.0	23.1	25.7	24.0	24.9	28.0	23.1	23.1	23.7
45 Minutes in Hollywood	C	Sun	10:30					9.6	12.9	14.9	4.8	6.6	7.0	9.3
Fred Allen Hour of Smiles	N	Wed	9:30	18.1	16.3	16.3			14.1	16.0	18.5	18.3	17.6	16.0
Fred Stone Gulf Headliners	B	Sun	9:00	16.7		16.7								17.2
Fred Waring Show	C	Thu	9:30	31.5	26.7	22.6	21.2	22.1	18.1	17.9	17.4			22.2
Fred Waring Show	N	Wed	10:00							10.0	11.0	12.1	11.4	11.2
Gems of Melody	N	Sun	6:45		1.1	1.7	2.0	1.4	1.7					1.6
Gene & Glenn	N	M-F	7:15								4.0	8.0	8.4	6.8
George M Cohan Gulf Headliners	B	Sun	9:00							21.2	17.8			19.5
Gertrude Nielsen Ex Lax Big Show	C	Mon	9:30		11.7	8.0	8.8	5.8	10.6	9.1	10.9	7.8	11.2	9.3
Glen Gray Orch Camel Caravan	C	T,T	10:00				7.1	7.0	8.6	7.9	9.4			8.0
The Goldbergs	C	M-F	7:45	15.9	16.9	14.9	13.8	13.8	12.2	13.2	13.2	11.3	11.1	13.6
Hall of Fame	N	Sun	10:30					13.9	11.1	12.9	11.8	14.0	15.6	13.2
Happy Wonder Bakers	N	Tue	8:00	2.9	3.9	5.4	5.5	5.8	5.6	6.7	5.5			5.2
Hudson Vocalians	B	Tue	8:30	4.5										4.5
Ipana Troubadours	N	Wed	9:00	10.4	10.4	9.7	9.2	10.1	14.7					10.8
Irene Rich Dramas	N	Wed	7:45					3.3	3.0	1.8	2.6	3.4		2.9
Irving Berlin Gulf Headliners	B	Sun	9:00									13.7		13.7
Irwin S Cobb	C	W,F	9:00	12.9	9.3									11.1
Jack Benny Program	N	Fri	9:30		16.7	18.8	19.5	22.7	23.0	22.8	25.3	23.2	24.7	21.9
Jack Denny Orch	B	Wed	10:30								10.5		9.9	9.7
Jack Frost's Melody Moments	N	Mon	9:30	13.0	12.2	9.8	10.4	14.2	11.5	9.2	10.7	8.6	8.9	10.9
Jack Pearl's Baron Munchausen	N	Wed	8:00		13.8	12.7	12.2	23.5	18.4	18.6	18.0	15.2	12.5	16.1
Jan Garber Yeast Foamers Orch	B	Mon	8:00								3.7	2.4	3.9	3.3
Joe Penner Bakers' Broadcast	B	Sun	7:30	10.0	13.2	19.8	19.8	25.8	32.5	33.0	35.2	29.1	25.9	24.9
John McCormack Sings	B	Wed	9:30	17.9		19.3	18.9	15.2	15.2	11.5	11.3			15.6
Just Plain Bill	C	M-F	7:15	8.5	8.5	6.7	6.2	7.1	8.4	7.3	9.1	7.5	7.2	7.6
King's Henchmen	C	Sat	7:30	6.3	6.3									6.3
Leo Reisman Orch	N	Sat	9:30	10.6	10.6	11.1	10.3							10.7
Leo Reisman Orch	N	Tue	8:00	4.3	2.9	3.3	3.3	6.5	5.8	5.3	7.1	3.5	4.5	4.8

1933-34 Crossley Ratings 6-11 P.M.

Program				Sept. 33	Oct. 33	Nov. 33	Dec. 33	Jan. 34	Feb. 34	March 34	April 34	May 34	June 34	1933-34 Avg
Literary Digest	B	Wed	6:15									1.4	1.6	1.5
Little Italy	C	T,T	6:45						3.3			3.0	2.7	3.2
Little Jack Little	C	Sat	10:15		2.3	2.6	3.8	4.1	4.5	4.2	2.4			3.4
Lives at Stake	C	Tue	10:00	10.8	8.4									9.6
Love Story Program	B	Wed	9:30									6.1	5.0	5.6
Lowell Thomas News	B	M-F	6:45	19.7	20.4	20.2	22.3	22.1	23.1	24.9	21.6	20.3	15.1	21.0
Lum & Abner	N	M-Th	7:30	6.4	6.1	7.6	10.1							7.6
Madame Schumann-Heink Sings	B	Sun	9:00									6.9	11.5	9.2
Madame Sylvia Hollywood News	N	T,T	10:30		3.2	3.5	4.3	3.5	4.0					3.7
Magic Carpet Program	N	Sat	9:00			39.5	36.1							37.8
Manhattan Merry Go Round	N	Sun	9:00	13.9	11.8	11.6	10.5	10.3	11.8	9.6	11.8	7.9	9.4	10.9
Maple City Four	B	MWF	7:30									1.4	1.7	1.6
March of Time	C	Fri	8:30		17.8	18.4	18.8	21.6	17.8					18.9
Marvelous Melodies	C	Fri	9:30						6.4	5.9	5.8			6.0
Marx Brothers Show	N	Sun	7:00						8.3	9.1	10.1			9.2
Maxwell House Show Boat	N	Thu	9:00	44.5	41.5	43.2	43.7	49.7	44.6	48.4	45.9	40.3	43.9	44.6
Minneapolis Symphony	N	Sun	10:30						6.9	6.9	10.9			8.9
Molle Show Shirley Howard	N	MWTh	7:30					1.3	1.7	1.3	1.3	1.3	1.3	1.4
Music by Gershwin	N	M,F	7:30											4.7
Music on the Air	C	MWF	7:30	2.9	1.1	4.6	4.2	3.4	5.2	4.0	4.9	2.4	2.9	3.2
Musical Cruise Vincent Lopez Orch	C	MWF	7:30						6.5	4.5	2.8	8.3	7.3	6.3
Myrt & Marge	B	Wed	10:00	20.4	20.4	20.9	18.9	19.6	18.5	17.9	18.5			19.2
Mysterious Island	C	M-F	7:00	2.4	2.4	3.7	4.3			5.0				3.5
Nat Shilkret Orch	N	TuFSa	6:00						1.8					1.8
National Barn Dance	B	Sun	9:45	6.7	6.7	7.3	7.3	8.4	8.9	8.9	11.3	9.6	8.6	8.5
Olsen & Johnson Swift Revue	C	Sat	10:30	11.9	11.8	11.6	11.6	9.6	10.5					11.1
Palmer House Program	B	Tue	10:00							3.3	4.7			4.8
Patri's Dreams of Childhood	C	Sun	10:00	4.2	4.8	4.4	4.4	3.8	3.9	3.1	3.9			4.0
Paul Whiteman Kraft Music Hall	N	Thu	10:00	33.2	25.5	23.4	22.7	25.2	23.4	29.0	29.9	26.3	24.2	26.3
Phil Baker the Armour Jester	B	Fri	9:30	21	19.7	23.8	23.6	25.8	26.2	29.5	27.1	24.4	17.8	23.9
Phil Harris Orch	B	Fri	9:00	9.6	9.2	10.2	9.6	12.9	16.5	13.6	12.7	12.0	10.2	11.7
Phil Spitalney Ensemble	C	Wed	7:00										1.6	1.6
Philadelphia Symphony Orch	C	MWSa	9:00				10.9	9.3	8.6		11.5	9.7	9.0	9.8
Pick & Pat One Night Stands	N	Fri	9:30							5.7	6.9	8.1	9.8	7.6
Pond's Players	B	Fri	9:30	6.3	5.2	4.7	5.4	9.1	10.3					6.8
Potash & Perlmutter	N	MWF	7:30	3.9	3.9	3.0	2.7	2.7	3.7					3.3
Program of the Week	C	Fri	10:00								3.7			3.7
Red Davis	B	MWF	8:45	2.3	2.3		4.4	5.5	6.9					4.5
Richard Himber Orch	N	Mon	8:00									4.5	4.3	4.4
Richfield Country Club	B	Mon	7:30	3.0	2.9									3.0
Rin Tin Tin	B	MWF	8:45			1.4	1.9	1.9	2.5	1.1	1.4			1.7
Robert Benchley Buick Show	C	T,T	9:15					3.6	4.4					4.0
Robert Ripley Saturday Night Party	N	Sat	10:00	20.5	18.1	17.4	18.6	18.8	18.1					18.6
Romantic Melodies	B	Thu	7:30							1.9	2.8			2.4
Rudy Vallee Show	N	Thu	8:00	37.3	41.6	41.1	42.9	44.8	42.4	44.1	39.0	30.7	33.8	39.8
Sealed Power Side Show	N	Mon	8:00		5.3	5.3	4.2	3.6	6.2					4.8
Seven Star Revue	C	Sun	9:00	8.0	5.7	5.7	6.2	6.9	6.6					6.7
Ship of Joy Hugh Dobbs	N	Mon	9:30	12.7	12.7	12.7	12.9	17.2	17.2	17.8	13.7			14.9

1933-34 Crossley Ratings 6-11 P.M.

Program		Day	Time	Sept. 33	Oct. 33	Nov. 33	Dec. 33	Jan. 34	Feb. 34	March 34	April 34	May 34	June 34	1933-34 Avg
Silken Strings	B	Sun	8:00	6.2	8.2	8.9	6.5	6.1	10.6	11.4	5.9	5.9	6.1	7.6
Silver Dust Serenaders	C	MWF	7:30						5.1	4.6	3.2	2.0	2.8	3.5
Sinclair Minstrels	N	Mon	9:00	24.7	25.8	25.2	23.8	25.6	26.5	24.7	25.1	24.2	18.5	24.4
Singin' Sam	C	Mon	10:30	6.9	5.4									6.2
Smilin' Ed McConnell	C	Sun	6:30	1.5	2.5	2.9	1.7	1.9	2.7	3.3	1.7	1.1	3.0	2.2
Smith Brothers	C	Fri	7:30		1.3	1.6	2.2	1.6	2.0					1.7
Songs My Mother Used to Sing	C	Sun	6:00					1.1	3.0					2.1
Stories That Should Be Told	B	Fri	10:00											2.2
Sunday at Seth Parker's	N	Sun	10:45	19.6	17.3									18.5
Tastyeast Theater	B	Sun	9:45		2.2						3.1	3.1	1.7	2.6
Terraplane Travelcade	N	Sat	9:00								7.8	9.9	5.8	7.8
Threads of Happiness	C	Fri	9:15		4.5	2.8	4.3							3.9
Treasure Island	B	MWF	7:15								2.2	1.9	2.4	2.2
Vince Program	B	Wed	9:30							11.5	11.3			11.4
Voice of America	C	Thu	9:30			4.8	8.0	6.8	7.0	6.3	5.3		6.1	6.4
Voice of Experience	C	Tue	8:30	5.2	5.7	5.1	5.3	6.9	6.3	5.1	5.7	5.3	7.3	5.7
Voice of Firestone	N	Mon	8:30				23.9	20.2	18.8	17.3	17.3	20.6		17.9
Walter Damrosch Music App Hour	B	Fri	11:00	6.2	6.4	6.9	10.5	10.5	13.3	10.9	9.2			9.2
Walter O'Keefe Nestle Show	B	Fri	8:00	7.8	8.7	6.4	11.5	13.2	13.5	14.2	10.7	8.9	7.7	9.2
Walter Winchell Jergens Journal	B	Sun	9:30					10.4	8.2	10.9	11.6			10.9
Waltz Time	N	Fri	8:00	14	6.1	15.0	14.0	17.0	18.7		10.9	9.7	10.9	10.2
Warden Lawes at Sing Sing	B	Wed	9:00	13.3	13.3		14.1	16.1	15.5			5.5		15.6
Ward's Family Theater	C	Sun	6:30	1.5				4.2	2.5	2.7	2.2		4.7	3.8
Wayne King Orch	N	Tu,We	7:30	15.0	15.0	13.8				18.2	17.4	13.0	6.6	14.4
Wendell Hall Sings	N	Sun	6:45		1.5	2.5	1.5			2.9	4.9	4.2	4.0	3.1
Will Rogers Gulf Headliners	B	Sun	9:00			38.6		38.9	39.9				30.7	37.0
Zoel Parenteau Orch	C	Fri	6:45						1.2					1.2

1934-35 Crossley/CAB Ratings 6-11 P.M.

Program		Day	Time	Sept. 34	Oct. 34	Nov. 34	Dec. 34	Jan. 35	Feb. 35	March 35	April 35	May 35	July 35	1934-35 Avg
A&P Gypsies	N	Mon	9:00	10.2	10.2	11.7	12.4	11.0	14.0	9.5	10.9	15.3	11.3	11.7
Adventures of Sherlock Holmes	B	Sun	9:45					7.1	7.7	8.7	8.4	9.2		8.2
Al Jolson Shell Chateau	N	Sat	9:30								22.5	26.0	27.1	25.2
Alemite Half Hour	C	Thu	10:30							4.6	3.3	3.2	4.7	4.0
Alexander Woolcott	C	Sun	7:00		4.4	8.8	7.9	6.9	10.8					7.8
American Album of Familiar Music	N	Sun	9:30	13.0	14.2	13.6	14.9	13.2						13.8
American Musical Revue	N	Sun	9:30						11.5	12.1	9.9	9.7	8.9	10.4
Amos & Andy	B	M-F	7:00	24.4	23.8	24.8	21.8	21.3	22.6	22.3	20.9	21.2	19.5	22.3
Andre Kostelanetz Orch	C	MWSa	9:00		9.3	9.8	10.5	9.3	10.9	11.2	11.0		10.5	10.3
Armco Iron Master Brass Band	N	Sun	6:30			1.5	1.7	2.9	2.6					2.2
Atwater Kent Radio Hour	C	Mon	8:30	1.7										1.7
Beatrice Lillie Show	B	Fri	9:00					10.0	11.7	15.7	15.1	11.6		12.4
Beauty Box Theater	N	Tue	10:00	26.9	24.9	28.9	28.4	27.4	25.8	28.4	26.8	27.4	27.4	27.2
Ben Bernie Show	N	Tue	9:00		22.0	20.1	22.0	20.3	22.8	26.9	27.2	25.4	28.5	23.9
Billy Batchelor Sketches	N	M-F	6:45	4.2	4.8	5.9	6.1	7.3	5.7	5.7				5.7
Bing Crosby Woodbury Show	C	Tue	9:00	14.9	13.9	15.7	17.1	17.1	15.5	16.2	16.6	13.9	12.2	15.3
Block & Sully Ex Lax Big Show	C	Mon	9:30	7.0	6.6	10.8	11.8	14.0	15.6	16.2	15.4	15.9	13.8	12.7
Boake Carter News	C	M-F	7:45	6.0	7.5	7.7	6.5	5.5	18.9	14.3	12.8	8.8	9.6	10.8
Bob Hope Intimate Revue	B	Fri	8:30	2.5	2.5	2.7	3.7		6.0					4.1

1934-35 Crossley/CAB Ratings 6-11 P.M.

Program	Net	Day	Time	Sept. 34	Oct. 34	Nov. 34	Dec. 34	Jan. 35	Feb. 35	March 35	April 35	May 35	July 35	1934-35 Avg
Bobby Benson & Sunny Jim	C	M-F	6:15	6.2	6.0	7.5	8.8	8.8	7.9	11.6	10.9	11.3	8.5	8.8
Broadway Varieties	C	Wed	8:30	4.7	6.2	5.4	6.0	5.6	4.9	6.2	5.4	3.5	3.5	5.1
Buck Rogers	C	M-Th	6:00	6.3	8.0	10.7	8.7	8.3	8.9	9.5	8.0	8.1	7.2	8.4
Burns & Allen Show	C	Wed	9:30	16.1	16.5	16.7	16.5	16.4	19.6	19.2	21.0	19.8	21.4	18.3
Byrd Antartic Expedition	C	Wed	10:00	8.4	10.8	12.5	9.8	14.1	14.5					11.7
Carborundum Band	C	Sat	9:00			4.1	6.9							5.5
Carefree Carnival Gene Arnold	B	Mon	8:30					5.4	7.0	5.6				6.0
Carnation Contented Hour	N	Mon	10:00	8.4	13.6	13.4	15.8	10.3	12.9	11.0	12.5	14.2	11.9	12.4
Charlie Winninger Gulf Headliners	N	Sun	7:30						20.5	18.9				19.7
Chase & Sanborn Opera Guild	N	Sun	8:00				26.8	22.0	18.4					22.4
Circus Nights in Silvertown	N	Fri	10:30										13.1	9.4
Cities Service Concert	N	Fri	8:00	20.2	18.2	19.4	19.8	16.5	19.8	16.8	17.6	15.8	16.0	18.0
Club Romance	C	Sun	8:00					5.0	8.1					6.6
Court of Human Relations	C	Fri	8:30	8.6	11.1	12.8	11.7	15.5	11.5	13.4	13.0	13.2	14.0	12.5
Dangerous Paradise	B	MWF	7:45		7.8	9.3	9.7	12.7	12.3	19.0	16.3	11.6	8.4	11.9
Death Valley Days	B	Thu	9:00	14.3	16	13.3	16.8	13.1	15.8	16	17.6	13.5	15.6	15.2
Dennis King	B	Wed	10:00	5.4	4.2									4.8
Diane's Life Saver Musical Comedy	C	M,W	8:00					1.7	2.3					2.0
Dick Liebert Organ Melodies	N	Fri	8:15				1.1	1.9	1.6					1.5
Easy Aces	B	MTuW	7:30						4.5	3.4	2.8			4.6
Ed Wynn Texaco Fire Chief Show	N	Tue	9:30	26.4	26.4	28.0	28.6	26.4	25.8	27.8	27.1	26.3	27.2	27.1
Eddie Cantor Show	C	Sun	8:00	44.6	44.6	49.3			38.0	39.0	34.3			40.0
Eddie Dooley Sports	C	Sat	6:30	1.2	3.7	7.3	6.9	4.1	3.3					4.4
Edgar A Guest Musical Memories	B	Tue	8:30	7.8	3.6	9.1	12.7	7.8	6.8	8.3	8.3	9.0	6.7	8.0
Edwin C Hill News/Comment	C	MWF	8:15	12.4	12.8	12.8	11.9	14.5	16.4	14.1	13.1			13.5
Eleanor Roosevelt	C	Fri	8:00							6.8				6.8
Eno Crime Clues	B	Tue	8:00	14.5	13.2	18.5	20.1	16.4	16.4	14.0	13.6	11.1	11.6	14.9
Fibber McGee & Molly	B	Tue	10:00								4.3	4.3	4.6	4.5
Fireside Recitals	N	Sun	7:30		3.1	2.0	1.4	1.0	1.4	1.0	1.8	1.6	1.1	1.6
First Nighter	N	Fri	10:00	24.9	20.7	22.5	24.3	21.7	20.5	22.3	22.6	24.5	22.8	22.7
Floyd Gibbons News/Comment	B	Thu	7:30	7.6	8.8									7.5
Ford Sunday Evening Hour	C	Sun	9:00		10.7	9.8	15.7	14.3	15.3	18.2	17.5	16.9	14.0	14.7
Forum of Liberty	C	Thu	8:30			5.1	6.3	6.5	7.2	8.0				6.6
45 Minutes in Hollywood	C	Thu	10:00	8.2	9.4									8.8
Frank Buck	N	M-F	7:45	10.5	5.1									7.8
Fred Allen Town Hall Tonight	N	Wed	9:00	23.6	23.4	23.9	27.4	26.6	32.0	35.3	33.1	33.8	37.6	29.7
Fred Waring Show	C	Thu	9:30	10.2	13.5	12.2	12.8	17.0	16.9	16.9	15.1	17.2	17.5	14.9
Gems of Melody	B	Thu	7:15			3.6	4.2	2.9	3.6	2.9				3.4
General Motors Concert	B	Sun	8:00		9.9	6.9	7.1	13.8	9.9	12.2	13.8			10.5
Gibson Family	N	Sun	10:00	16.1	13.1	15.7	17.9	18.8	19.1	14.4	12.2	12.3	11.6	15.1
Glen Gray Orch Camel Caravan	C	T,T	10&9		7.3	8.6	9.2	9.8	11.4	9.5	10.0	9.6	9.6	9.4
Grand Hotel	B	Sun	6:30	7.8	7.6	9.8	9.0	12.2	14.4	17.2	17.3	15.0	12.5	12.3
Guy Lombardo Orch Pleasure Isle	N	Wed	10:00	20.1	18.7	21.1	24.6	21.3	23.5	16.9	18.1	19.4	17.6	20.1
Hal Kemp Orch	B	Wed	8:00							7.9	6.2	2.5	3.4	5.0
Harry Richman Show	B	Wed	10:30	11.9	5.0	9.2	5.5	6.4						7.6
Hollywood Hotel	C	Fri	9:30		11.7	16.9	16.6	18.0	17.5	17.4	19.8	18.6	21.1	17.5
Hour of Charm	C	Tue	9:30					4.1	4.7	6.5	9.1	9.8	8.8	7.2
House of Glass	B	Wed	8:30								11.2	13.3	16.7	13.7

1934-35 Crossley/CAB Ratings 6-11 P.M.				Sept. 34	Oct. 34	Nov. 34	Dec. 34	Jan. 35	Feb. 35	March 35	April 35	May 35	July 35	1934-35 Avg
Irene Rich Dramas	B	Fri	8:00	1.7	2.9	4.1	3.5	2.9	5.3	7.1	6.4	4.3		4.2
Isham Jones Orch	C	Tue	9:30		6.1	6.9	9.0	9.2	6.9					7.6
Jack Benny Show	C	Sun	7:00		22.9	30.0	35.3	35.8	36.4	38.1	42.3	37.7	36.5	35.0
Jack Pearl as Peter Pfeiffer	C	Wed	10:00						13.4	12.7	12.4	12.2		12.7
Jan Garber Orch Supper Club	B	Mon	8:00	6.0	6.7	8.6	8.8	6.7	7.7	9.7				7.7
Jimmie Fidler Hollwood News	B	Wed	10:00					4.4	3.1	3.9	2.8	1.5		3.1
Jimmy Durante Show	N	Sun	8:00	28.5										28.5
Joe Cook Colgate House Party	N	Mon	9:30	10.7	11.9	14.5	14.0	11.1						12.4
Joe Penner Bakers' Broadcast	N	Sun	7:30		29.3	38.8	36.5	30.0	30.3	36.5	34.1	23.5	23.0	31.3
John Charles Thomas Sings	N	Wed	10:00					12.2	10.2					11.2
John McCormack Sings	B	Wed	9:30	12.8	16.0	13.6	9.0			12.8	11.2			12.6
Johnnie & The Foursome	C	Wed	8:00									1.1	1.1	1.1
Just Plain Bill	C	M-F	7:15	4.7	7.0	8.3	7.8	8.1	8.6	9.1	9.9	8.0	7.1	7.9
Kate Smith New Star Revue	C	Mon	8:30					14.8	15.0	13.8	16.6	12.9		14.6
Kellogg College Prom	B	Fri	8:30					5.8	3.7	3.4	4.9	4.9	3.8	4.4
Lanny Ross' Log Cabin Orch	B	Wed	8:30		14.8	16.1	15.0	13.4	11.1	18.4				14.8
Lavender & Old Lace	C	Tue	8:00	5.8	6.8	7.7	8.0	8.0	7.0	8.5	8.6	7.2	6.8	7.4
Lawrence Tibbett Sings	B	Tue	8:30	16.6	18.6	11.9	18.9	18.0	18.0					17.0
Leo Reisman Orch	N	Tue	8:00	4.7	5.7	7.8	6.9	8.2	6.7	10.0	8.3	6.3	6.4	7.1
Let's Dance XCugat, BGoodman	N	Sat	10:30				16.2	18.0	19.8	20.1	20.3	22.0		19.4
Lilac Time A Murray & Night Singer	C	Mon	10:30				2.5	3.3	4.1	5.1	3.7	7.3	6.7	4.7
Little Jackie Heller	B	Mon	10:00					2.6	4.0	4.0	3.8	1.9		3.3
Lowell Thomas News	B	M-F	6:45	13.6	21.8	19.1	17.7	22.9	23.1	25.0	23.0	16.0	17.8	20.0
Lucky Smith	N	Mon	10:30									7.5		7.5
Ludens Musical Revue	C	Sat	8:45					3.5	6.3	6.7	6.3	5.0	5.2	5.4
Lum & Abner	M	M-F	6:15			5.0	6.1	5.8	4.5					5.5
Madame Sylvia Hollywood News	B	Wed	10:15		2.4	2.4	2.0	1.4	1.8					2.0
Major Bowes Amateur Hour	N	Sun	8:00								31.1	36.5	40.1	36.0
Manhattan Merry Go Round	N	Sun	9:00	11.1	14.0	14.6	13.5	10.7	11.8	12.0	11.7	13.4	11.1	12.4
March of Time	C	Fri	9:00		18.6	20.1	21.2	24.1	20.9	23.7	21.8			21.5
Mary Pickford & Co	N	Wed	8:00		18.6	19.0	18.2	18.6	22.5					19.8
Maxwell House Show Boat	N	Thu	9:00	43.0	44.3	38.1	36.6	38.1	37.3	37.4	36.9	33.2	32.9	37.8
Melodiana	C	Tue	8:30		3.3	6.7	6.9	7.1	7.4	6.2	7.8	7.2	6.1	6.5
Mexican Musical Tours	B	Thu	9:30								2.3	3.0	1.9	2.4
Molle Dixie Dandies	N	Thu	7:30	1.9		1.7	3.7							2.4
Molle Merry Minstrels	N	Thu	7:30					2.6	5.7	8.0	6.3	2.6	3.2	4.7
Morton Downey Sings	B	Fri	8:15				8.1	5.0	5.6	4.0	5.9	5.9	6.8	5.9
Music at the Hadyn's	N	Mon	9:30						13.5	11.7	10.1	11.8	8.5	11.1
Music by Gershwin	N	Sun	6:00	2.4										2.4
Myrt & Marge	C	M-F	7:00		17.4		16.9	18.0	16.5	19.1	19.9			18.0
National Amateur Night	C	Sun	6:00					2.8	5.4	7.9	8.6	7.6	7.8	6.7
National Barn Dance	B	Sat	9:30	15.2	15.7	15.5	18.7	17.3	16.8	22.7	24.5	22.7	22.3	19.1
The O'Flynn's	C	Fri	10:30				1.9	1.9	2.2					2.0
One Man's Family	N	Wed	9:30			15.3	17.3	17.6	18.6		22.3	18.9	20.7	18.7
The O'Neill's	C	MWF	7:30				4.3	4.1	5.3	12.6	14.6	9.5	10.2	8.7
Our Home on the Range	B	Wed	9:00									7.6	11.0	9.3
Outdoor Girl Beauty Parade	C	Sat	7:30					3.1	3.4	4.0	3.4			3.5
Paul Whiteman Kraft Music Hall	N	Thu	10:00	22.1	22.0	23.1	21.0	21.8	22.5	26.0	21.8	24.4	22.8	22.8

1934–35 Crossley/CAB Ratings 6–11 P.M.

Program	Net	Day	Time	Sept. 34	Oct. 34	Nov. 34	Dec. 34	Jan. 35	Feb. 35	March 35	April 35	May 35	July 35	1934–35 Avg
Pause That Refreshes	N	Fri	10:30				10.4	11.1	11.5	12.8	12.9			11.7
Penthouse Party Mark Hellinger	B	Wed	8:30					6.2	3.9					5.1
Phil Baker the Armour Jester	B	Fri	9:30	15.8	19.7	21.2	17.8	20.5	22.5	21.8	22.4	17.4	19.1	19.8
Phil Harris Orch	B	Fri	9:00	8.8	9.6	8.4	10.3	11.3	10.6	11.9	9.3	12.4	8.6	9.2
Pick & Pat One Night Stands	B	Fri	9:30	11.5	9.4									10.4
Plantation Echos	B	MWF	7:15		2.1	2.5	3.6	4.6	5.0	7.4	4.4			4.2
Pontiac Program Jane Froman	N	Sun	10:00		5.9	5.9	8.2	7.4	8.4					7.2
Princess Pat Players	B	Mon	9:30	7.9	6.2	5.9	7.4	10.8	9.9	9.1	8.2	10.2	8.1	8.4
Radio City Party	B	Sat	9:00	14.2	15.0	11.0	16.7	15.7	13.8	12.7	13.1	13.7	13.7	14.0
Ray Noble Orch	B	Wed	10:30							9.9	10.7	11.0	13.4	11.3
Red Davis	N	MWF	8:00			10.3	12.9	14.1	14.3	17.7	17.0	14.2	9.2	13.5
Red Grange Sports	N	ThFSa	6:30	3.5	4.2									3.9
Red Trails	B	Tue	9:00		7.6									5.3
Rhythm at Eight	C	Sun	8:00						2.0	6.1	5.0	4.2		4.3
Richard Himber Orch	C	Mon	8:00	6.1	5.2	5.8	8.1	7.8	5.9	7.0	6.4	4.9	3.7	6.6
Richard Himber Orch	C	Fri	10:00							5.9	6.3	7.1	6.3	6.9
Roxy & His Gang Samuel Rothafel	C	Sat	8:00	10.4	12.2	13.5	15.5	16.3	14.9	13.2	12.4	8.2	7.1	13.6
Rudy Vallee Show	N	Thu	8:00	31.5	39.0	35.5	37.1	36.6	38.5	38.7	37.6	32.8	28.8	35.6
The Shadow	C	M,W	6:30		3.1	8.0	8.0	5.8	7.6					6.5
Sigmund Romberg Revue	B	Sat	8:00		13.8	14.5	14.3	16.6	17.5	16.9				15.6
Silken Strings	B	Sun	9:00	5.5	7.5	7.9	10.2	9.6	9.5	8.2	7.5	7.4	8.7	8.2
Silver Dust Serenaders	C	MWF	7:30	1.2	3.1									2.2
Sinclair Minstrels	B	Mon	9:00	21.9	21.9	21.0	22.8	21.7	20.8	19.2	18.7	19.9	18.8	20.7
Smilin' Ed McConell	C	Sun	6:30	1.3	1.6	1.6	3.3	2.4	2.7	2.9	3.0	2.4	2.2	2.3
Soconyland Sketches	C	Sat	7:00	11.7	16.4									14.1
Songs You Love to Hear	N	Sat	9:00		7.8	8.4	9.2	10.9	9.2					9.1
Stoopnagle & Budd Gulf Headliners	C	Sun	9:30	23.3		20	20.5							21.3
Stoopnagle & Budd	N	Fri	10:30										5.1	5.1
Stories of the Black Chamber	N	MWF	7:15					2.0	2.0	4.1	3.9	3.3		2.9
Tastyeast Theater	B	Sun	9:45	1.5				2.6	3.3	3.3	2.0	2.1	2.0	2.0
Thornton Fisher Briggs Sports Rpt	B	Sat	6:45		2.5	3.3	1.5						2.3	2.5
Tony & Gus	B	M-F	7:15									8.9	8.3	8.6
Uncle Ezra's Radio Station	N	MWF	7:45			1.3	1.4	1.2	2.3	3.4	2.8	3.0	2.3	2.3
Vera Brodsky & Harold Triggs	B	Sun	10:15								1.7	3.3	1.7	2.2
Vicks Open House Grace Moore	B	Tue	9:00					15.3	18.5					16.9
Voice of Experience	C	Sun	6:45	2.3	2.3		2.6	3.0	4.7	4.2	4.6	4.3		3.3
Voice of Firestone	B	Mon	8:30	8.6	8.9	16.5	15.5	13.4	16.0	13.9	13.5	10.7		12.8
Walter Winchell Jergens Journal	B	Sun	9:30	11.8	10.1	13.0	14.9	15.6	13.8	17.0	16.8	16.0	10.5	13.7
Waltz Time	N	Fri	9:00	9.9	10.7	10.5	10.7	12.5	12.5	9.9	9.0		7.6	10.1
Warden Lawes at Sing Sing	B	Wed	9:00	11.8	12.0	13.0	11.8	13.6	11.6	16.6	14.6	8.1	6.8	13.1
Wayne King Orch	C	Sun	10:00	9.5	9.5	10.0	10.0	9.9	9.9	11.6	11.4	12.4	7.6	10.2
Wayne King Orch	N	Su,M	8:30	14.6	14.6	16.4	16.4	14.8	14.8	16.7	15.8	13.5	12.0	15.0
Wendell Hall Sings	N	Tu,W	7:45	4.2	4.0	3.0	3.6	4.0	3.2	3.8	6.0	5.7	2.9	4.0
Whispering Jack Smith	N	Sun	7:15	1.7	2.8			2.0	2.5	1.9				2.2
Will Rogers Gulf Headliners	C	T,T,Sa	8:30		34.7			30.5			25.3	24.1	20.8	27.1
Your Hit Parade	N	Sat	8:00								13.2	16.6	16.7	15.5

1935-36 Crossley/CAB Ratings 6-11 P.M.

				Sept. 35	Oct. 35	Nov. 35	Dec. 35	Jan. 36	Feb. 36	March 36	April 36	May 36	June 36	1935-36 Avg
A&P Gypsies	N	Mon	9:00	10.1		7.5	7.4	8.5	9.1	6.2	6.5	5.6	4.3	7.2
Al Jolson's Shell Chateau	B	Sat	9:30	25.8	12.6	13.6	14.7	15.6	17.9	16.9				16.7
Al Pearce Gang	B	Fri	9:00					5.3	5.6	5.1	4.6			5.2
Alexander Woolcott	C	Sun	7:00		5.0	5.1	5.1							5.1
American Album of Familiar Music	N	Sun	9:30		7.5	10.7	8.8	11.1	9.5	8.6	10.1	6.8	6.8	8.8
Amos & Andy	N	M-F	7:00	17.9	12.6	12.0	12.4	14.5	14.4	13.7	13.0	11.2	8.9	13.1
Andre Kostelanetz Orch	C	W,Sat	9:00		5.4	6.4	5.5	7.1	7.2	5.8	5.8	4.5	4.0	5.7
Armco Iron Master Brass Band	B	Wed	8:30				2.1	2.9	1.6	1.5				2.0
Atwater Kent Radio Hour	C	Thu	8:00		3.0	3.1	3.0							3.0
Beauty Box Theater	C	Sat	9:00	21.4	10.3	10.0	8.6	13.5	15.2	15.1	14.0	11.9		12.6
Ben Bernie Show	B	Tue	9:00	19.3	11.4	15.0	12.0						8.8	13.6
Bing Crosby's Kraft Music Hall	N	Thu	10:00					15.2	20.1	17.0	19.4	17.2	12.3	16.9
Boake Carter News/Comment	C	M-F	7:45	9.1	9.3	10.0	9.9	12.4	11.8	12.6	14.6	6.9	6.1	10.3
Bob Crosby Orch	B	Fri	8:15			2.2	2.8							2.6
Bob Hope Atlantic Family	C	Sat	7:00		6.5	8.5	8.5	9.3	6.3	8.3	10.3	7.3	4.0	7.7
Bobby Benson & Sunny Jim	C	MWF	6:15		4.3	3.8	4.6	5.5	5.1	5.4	4.9	2.2	1.5	4.1
Briggs Sports Review	N	Sat	7:45	2.1										2.1
Broadway Varieties	C	Fri	8:30	4.7	4.9	5.1	6.4	7.7	6.8	7.5	7.0	4.3	3.3	5.8
Buck Rogers	C	MWF	6:00	5.2	4.7	4.5	4.9	4.4	3.7	3.6	4.2			4.4
Burns & Allen Show	C	Wed	8:30	25.5	15.8	16.4	15.5	21.4	22.6	20.4	18.6	15.5	14.6	18.6
Campus Review	N	Fri	10:30		4.4	5.6	4.4							4.8
Captain Tim Healy	B	MWF	7:15		2.3	2.3	2.8	2.2	3.0	3.2				2.6
Carborundum Band	N	Sat	7:30		4.3	4.4	4.2	8.2	5.8					5.4
Carnation Contented Hour	N	Mon	10:00	8.1	5.9	5.9	7.5	7.4	6.8	6.9	6.6	5.5	4.7	6.5
Cavalcade of America	C	Wed	8:00		3.9	3.9	3.7	6.5	6.7	6.1	5.4	3.7	4.3	4.9
Chrysler Air Show	C	Thu	8:00							2.5	2.5	1.8		2.3
Cities Service Concert	N	Fri	8:00	16.2	9.9	12.6	11.1	11.1	12.9	9.1	10.3	9.2	8.1	11.1
Corn Cob Pipe Club	B	Wed	9:00			5.1	5.7	5.6	4.3	5.1	3.4			4.9
Court of Human Relations	C	Fri	9:30	11.3	6.0	6.7	5.8	8.0	9.4	7.5	8.7	6.7	5.4	7.6
Crumit & Sanderson	C	Sun	7:30									10.4	10.7	10.6
Dangerous Paradise	B	MWF	7:45	6.9	7.5	6.2	7.0							6.9
Death Valley Days	B	Thu	9:00	14.7	7.3	8.6	8.4	7.9	7.5	8.2	7.1	5.8	5.7	8.1
Dr West's Celebrity Night	B	Sat	10:30							8.0	6.0	4.4		6.1
Easy Aces	B	TWT	7:00			4.7	3.8	3.5	5.0	5.2	4.9	4.0	3.8	4.4
Ed Wynn's Gulliver	C	Thu	9:30						7.1	7.4	5.7	10.4	8.5	7.8
Eddie Cantor Show	C	Sun	7:00		14.5	11.7	13.6	15.5	18.1	16.3	16.5	13.3		14.9
Eddie Dowling Elgin Revue	N	Tue	10:00							6.1	6.1	4.5		5.6
Eddy Duchin Show	N	Tue	9:30	11.5										11.5
Edgar A Guest Welcome Valley	B	Tue	8:30	8.3				6.9	6.5	6.9	7.4	4.5	3.7	6.3
Edwin C Hill News/Comment	N	T,T,Sa	7:15						6.5	5.2	6.8	4.8	3.4	5.3
Eno Crime Clues	B	Tue	8:00	10.6	7.0	8.0		8.9	9.8	10.2	10.5	7.9	6.2	8.7
Evening in Paris	B	Mon	8:30	3.6	3.2	4.5		3.5	4.3	3.8	4.3			3.9
Fanny Brice Ziegfeld Follies	C	Sat	8:00					13.1	9.8	10.8	10.9	10.0		10.9
Fibber McGee & Molly	N	Mon	8:00	9.1	5.2	5.1	6.3	7.3	6.9	7.0	8.5	5.5	4.6	6.6
Fireside Recitals	N	Sun	7:30	1.2	2.4	2.4	2.4	1.5	1.6	2.3	1.9	1.6	1.4	1.9
First Nighter	N	Fri	10:00	23.6	14.2	13.3	12.4	15.0	15.4	12.9	14.2			15.1
Flying Red Horse Tavern	N	Fri	8:00		4.6	4.6	5.5	6.7	7.2	8.8	6.8	3.9	3.4	5.7
Folies de Paree	B	Wed	8:00								2.3	1.5	2.5	2.1

1935-36 Crossley/CAB Ratings 6-11 P.M.

Program	Net	Time	Day	Sept. 35	Oct. 35	Nov. 35	Dec. 35	Jan. 36	Feb. 36	March 36	April 36	May 36	June 36	1935-36 Avg
Ford Sunday Evening Hour	C	9:00	Sun		9.4	9.8	11.2	9.2	9.5	8.2	10.1	8.2	7.1	9.2
Frank Fay Calling	N	9:00	Sat									6.6	3.9	5.3
Fred Allen Town Hall Tonight	B	9:00	Wed	26.6	17.5	16.7	19.1	21.6	19.9	19.1	21.8	19.8	17.9	20.0
Fred Waring Show	C	9:30	Fri							5.8	6.9	5.2	4.8	5.8
Fred Waring Show	N	9:00	Tue	15.6	8.5	9.5	11.6	12.5	9.1	9.4	10.4	8.8	7.5	10.3
G Men	C	9:00	Sat	17.1										17.1
Gangbusters	C	10:00	Wed					9.3	10.8	9.4	10.7	8.0	7.6	9.3
General Motors Concert	C	10:00	Sun		10.0	11.9	11.0	12.8	12.1	13.2	11.2	10.8	9.3	11.4
Glen Gray Orch	C	9:00	T,T					7.1	6.0	6.3	6.5	4.6	5.0	5.9
Goodwill Hour John J Anthony	M	10:30	Sun										3.8	3.8
Grand Hotel	B	8:30	Mon	13.1	6.9	10.3	11.4	12.3	11.9					11.0
Guy Lombardo Orch	C	8:00	Mon	16.2	8.3	5.8	8.3	10.1	9.5	4.8	8.3	7.9	6.2	8.5
Hammerstein's Music Hall	N	8:00	Mon		3.8	7.6	5.8	5.8	7.1	5.9	5.7	3.7	4.3	5.5
Harv & Esther	B	8:00	Thu	1.2				2.6	2.0					1.9
Helen Hayes Theater	B	9:30	Tue		7.2	11.0	10.8	10.1	13.5	12.8		11.3		10.9
Hollywood Hotel	C	9:00	Fri	22.0	14.4	15.1	15.2	17.7	17.4	18.6	17.8	13.7	12.4	16.4
Horace Heidt Brigadiers Orch	C	10:00	Thu	4.2	3.8	2.4	2.2	3.5	4.2	3.9	2.7	2.9	2.9	3.3
Hour of Charm	C	6:00	Sun							3.8	3.8	1.8	3.0	3.1
House of Glass/Gertrude Berg	B	8:30	Wed	17.1	5.6	7.0	5.9							8.9
Husbands & Wives	C	7:30	Sun	11.8								11.3	12.0	11.7
Imperial Hawaiian Band	B	6:45	Thu			3.1	3.6	3.1	1.0	2.2				2.6
Irene Rich Dramas	B	8:00	Fri		2.5	3.1	3.6	3.9	3.2	3.5	3.9	2.1	2.5	3.3
Jack Benny Program	B	7:00	Sun		24.7	27.9	28.1	27.1	25.4	22.9	24.2			25.8
Jack Hylton Continental Revue	N	9:00	Sun		5.0	5.8	5.4	5.4	6.9	5.5	6.5	4.4	4.4	5.5
Jello Summer Show	N	7:00	Sun									17.1	20.9	19.0
Jimmie Fidler Hollywood News	B	10:30	Tue			2.6	3.6	2.6	2.7	3.4	3.4			3.1
Jimmy Durante Texaco Fire Chief	C	9:30	Tue	1.5										1.5
John Charles Thomas Sings	B	10:00	Wed		7.0	7.0	8.4	4.9	4.7	5.5	4.1			5.7
Johnnie & The Foursome	C	8:00	Wed		4.3									1.5
Kate Smith Coffee Time	B	8:00	T,W,T			7.7	6.3	8.5	8.7	7.9	7.7	4.7	3.4	6.9
Kellogg College Prom	C	7:30	Fri	5.4	2.2	2.6	2.9	4.0	3.0	2.2				3.1
Ken Murray Show	C	8:30	Tue							6.6	6.3	5.2	5.6	5.9
Lanny Ross' State Fair	C	7:00	Sun	12.7										12.7
Lavender & Old Lace	N	8:00	Tue	5.6	3.9	5.7	6.1	7.4	5.2	4.3	6.1			5.5
Lawrence Tibbett	C	8:30	Tue		9.1	9.7	9.8	10.9	10.1					9.9
Lazy Dan the Minstrel Man	N	8:00	Sun	8.6	5.2	6.1	6.1		6.3	6.8	5.7	5.0		5.7
Leo Reisman Orch	B	8:00	Tue		5.0		6.1			7.2				5.6
Leslie Howard Program	C	8:30	Tue	4.6	5.0	4.7	6.7	5.6	7.7					5.3
Log Cabin Revue	N	10:00	Sun			6.7		6.7			6.9			6.1
Lowell Thomas News	N	6:45	M-F	17.7	11.6	11.4	11.1	12.4	11.6	12.1	10.9	7.0	6.1	11.2
Lum & Abner	B	7:30	M-F	5.9	4.2	6.1	6.0	6.1	6.7	7.4	6.9	5.1	5.3	6.0
Lux Radio Theater	C	9:00	Mon	19.6	10.8	13.8	11.6	14.1	16.2	14.9	16.3	12.6	16.2	14.6
Major Bowes Amateur Hour	N	8:00	Sun	57.9	31.0	35.2	34.2	40.7	40.5	37.6	38.4	29.8	29.2	37.5
Manhattan Merry Go Round	N	9:00	Sun	12.5	8.4	13.4	14.2	15.3	12.7	12.4	13.2	9.0	9.1	12.0
March of Time	C	10:30	Fri	15.3	7.5	8.0	7.9	10.4	11.1	9.2	9.9	8.9	6.7	9.5
Marion Talley	N	10:30	Thu								5.0	4.2	3.8	4.3
Maxwell House Show Boat	C	9:00	Thu	36.2	17.5	19.8	20.0	21.3	21.8	18.9	20.2	17.5	15.0	20.8
Melodiana	B	8:30	Mon									1.6	2.5	2.1

1935-36 Crossley/CAB Ratings 6-11 P.M.

Program				Sept. 35	Oct. 35	Nov. 35	Dec. 35	Jan. 36	Feb. 36	March 36	April 36	May 36	June 36	1935-36 Avg
Melody Master	N	Sun	11:00				1.2	1.5	1.5	1.2	2.2			1.5
Musical Toast	C	T,T	7:15					3.7	3.1	4.2	2.4	1.3		2.9
Myrt & Marge	C	M-F	7:00		7.4	7.1	6.6	7.8	8.0	7.6	7.3			7.4
National Amateur Night	M	Sun	6:00	8.7	5.0	6.6	7.6	8.1	7.3	6.5	7.7	3.0	2.1	6.3
National Barn Dance	B	Sat	9:30	21.4	9.8	9.6	9.3	10.5	11.1	10.2	11.1	7.8	7.3	10.8
Neila Goodelle	B	Sun	9:45		1.3	2.0	2.6							2.0
News of Youth	C	T,T,Sa	6:15					1.0	1.4	1.9	2.1			1.6
Nine to Five	B	Thu	7:15					1.5	1.3					1.4
NTG & His Girls	N	Tue	9:00	6.5	4.2	4.4	5.7							5.2
Old Gold Sports Page	N	Sat	7:00		3.8									3.8
One Man's Family	N	Wed	8:00	22.2	12.4	13.1	13.9	13.5	14.1	14.0	13.9	11.1	11.4	14.0
Paris Night Life	C	Fri	7:30					5.1	6.3	6.6	6.5	2.8	2.3	4.9
Parties at Pickfair	C	Tue	10:00						11.6	9.3	8.9	9.6	3.0	8.5
Paul Whiteman's Kraft Music Hall	N	Thu	10:00	26.7	14.7	16.1	15.4							18.2
Paul Whiteman Varieties	B	Sun	9:45					6.1	7.1	6.9	7.7	7.6	6.5	7.0
Phil Baker's Gulf Headliners	C	Sun	7:30	10.7	11.4	11.1	12.5	17.5	18.5	15.1	18.1	5.2	6.3	14.9
Pick & Pat	C	Mon	8:30		8.9	8.0	8.4	10.2	10.3	8.0	9.5	2.3		8.6
Pittsburgh Symphony	B	Thu	8:00	2.1	4.3					3.0	3.8			3.0
Popeye the Sailor	N	T,T,Sa	7:15	6.2	3.2	3.6	5.1	7.5	8.0	7.5				5.9
Princess Pat Tales of Today	B	Mon	9:30		3.2	5.3	6.0	3.9	3.4	2.9	2.1	2.5		3.7
Refreshment Time Ray Noble Orch	C	Wed	9:30					5.9	6.5					5.9
Rendezvous	B	Wed	8:00				1.3		3.0	2.3	2.3	2.1	2.3	2.3
Renfrew of the Mounted	C	M-F	6:45		1.9			3.1						2.3
Richard Himber Orch	C	Fri	10:00		10.4	4.9	4.1	4.7	5.1	5.9	5.8	5.9	4.5	5.7
Robert Ripley Bakers' Broadcast	B	Sun	7:30		15.8	15.5	15.5	16.6	16.9	18.6	18.0			16.0
Rubinoff & His Violin	C	Sat	9:00			10.1	10.7	10.7	11.2	11.5	10.6			10.8
Rudy Vallee Show	N	Thu	8:00	35.1	20.1	22.9	20.3	24.2	24.1	23.7	21.2	17.2	15.2	22.4
Shell Chateau Wallace Beery	N	Sat	9:30		5.5	5.6	7.3	5.6	6.4	6.5	11.8	9.6	8.4	9.9
Sigmund Romberg Studio Party	N	Mon	9:30								7.6	5.6		6.3
Silken Strings	B	Sun	9:00	9.0	9.4	6.4	7.0		8.5	7.4	7.4	4.5	5.5	9.0
Sinclair Minstrels	B	Mon	9:00	16.2	5.6	5.3	5.5		6.1	5.5	5.7			8.0
Singin' Sam	C	Mon	7:30						3.4	3.4	3.6	1.8		5.7
Smilin' Ed McConell	C	Sun	6:30		3.0	3.5	3.2							3.0
Sunbrite Junior Nurse Corps	C	MWF	6:15							2.0	1.2			1.6
Sunset Dreams	N	Sun	7:45	2.0					2.2	2.4	2.1	3.4	3.4	2.8
Ted Husing & Charioteers	C	Mon	7:15						4.5	3.5	3.7	2.6	2.2	3.3
Texaco Fire Chief Variety Show	N	Tue	9:30						6.1	6.4	8.4			7.2
To Arms for Peace	N	Thu	9:30			4.0	3.5							3.8
Tony & Gus	B	MWF	7:15	7.7								5.4	4.6	7.7
Uncle Ezra's Radio Station	N	MWF	7:15	3.0				8.0	9.0	8.3	9.2			6.8
Vanished Voices	C	M,W	6:35		2.1	2.2	2.6	3.3	3.2					2.8
Vick's Open House	C	Sun	8:00			10.1	12.6	12.5	14.5	11.8				12.3
Voice of Experience	C	Sun	6:45	2.8	2.7	3.8	4.5	3.9	4.1	4.2	5.1	2.9		3.8
Voice of Firestone	N	Mon	8:30	10.8	11.8	11.9	11.5	11.1	13.9	11.8	12.5	9.2	8.8	10.7
Voice of the People	B	Tue	7:30	11.2					9.2	9.4	9.5	8.5	7.3	11.2
Vox Pop	N	Tue	9:00						6.2			6.2	5.1	5.6
Walter Winchell Jergens Journal	B	Sun	9:30	14.7	8.4	8.4	8.2	9.8	9.2	9.4	6.1	3.9	4.3	9.2
Waltz Time	N	Fri	9:00	6.8	3.3	5.4	4.7	5.1	5.0	4.5				4.9

1935-36 Crossley/CAB Ratings 6-11 P.M.

Program	Net	Day	Time	Sept. 35	Oct. 35	Nov. 35	Dec. 35	Jan. 36	Feb. 36	March 36	April 36	May 36	June 36	1935-36 Avg
Warden Lawes at Sing Sing	B	Wed	9:30	11.6	5.8	7.5	6.8	6.4	7.9	9.2	8.6	6.8	6.7	7.5
Wayne King Orch	C	Sun	8:30	12.1	6.4	6.8	6.6	8.2	9.8	6.9	6.1	6.8	6.1	7.6
Wayne King Orch	N	Tu,W	8:30		9.1	8.1	8.6	9.0	9.1	9.1	9.0			8.7
Wendell Hall Sings	B	Fri	8:15			2.5	2.9	2.3	2.6	1.3	2.8			2.4
Your Hit Parade	N	Sat	8:00	16.8	12.5	12.0	14.3	12.4	16.0	13.1	11.3	11.4	9.8	13.0

Special Broadcasts

Program	Net	Date	Sept. 35	Oct. 35	Nov. 35	June 36	1935-36 Avg
Boxing; Joe Louis/Max Baer	N,B	9/24	45.7				
World Series: Detroit/ChiCubs	All	10/4		32.6			
World Series: Detroit/ChiCubs	All	10/6		36.6			34.7
World Series: Detroit/ChiCubs	All	10/6		41.5			
World Series: Detroit/ChiCubs	All	10/7		28.2			
Will Rogers Memorial Program	C	11/23			7.9		
Boxing; Joe Louis/Max Schmeling	N,B	6/19				57.6	

1936-37 Clark-Hooper Ratings 6-11 P.M.

Program	Net	Day	Time	Sept. 36	Oct. 36	Nov. 36	Dec. 36	Jan. 37	Feb. 37	March 37	April 37	May 37	June 37	1936-37 Avg
Al Jolson Show	C	Tue	8:30					18.3	18.0	16.7	17.8	11.2	10.4	15.4
Al Pearce Gang	C	Tue	9:00					8.4	10.6	10.5	10.6	9.5	7.3	9.5
Alexander Woolcott	C	T,T	7:30					4.7	4.9	4.8	3.9	4.0	2.3	4.1
All Star Cycle	B	Thu	7:15								0.6	1.2	0.3	0.7
American Album of Familiar Music	N	Sun	9:30	4.7	5.2	4.9	5.6	3.9	4.3	4.2	3.9	4.0	3.2	4.4
Amos & Andy	N	M-F	7:00	11.9	15.0	16.6	17.1	17.5	19.9	18.9	16.5	10.3	9.3	15.3
Andre Kostelanetz Orch	C	Wed	9:00	5.9	7.1	7.8	6.0	10.2	5.8	6.6	6.9	6.2	4.8	6.7
Armco Iron Master Brass Band	B	Tue	10:00					1.1	1.5					1.3
Bar Z Dude Ranch	B	Tue	8:00		3.3	3.4	3.4	4.6	4.6	5.6				4.2
Beauty Box Theater	C	Wed	9:30					7.9	7.4	7.7	7.8	6.9	5.6	7.2
Ben Bernie Show	B	Tue	9:00	6.3	7.3	8.1	7.1	8.4	10.4	10.5	9.5	7.5	5.5	8.1
Bing Crosby Kraft Music Hall	N	Thu	10:00	15.0	15.6	18.0	15.2	21.0	19.3	20.9	18.9	16.5	13.5	17.4
Boake Carter News/Comment	C	M-F	7:45	10.8	13.5	13.4	14.3	15.3	15.5	13.6	13.1	10.3	8.6	12.8
Broadway Merry Go Round	B	Wed	8:00					6.4	4.2	5.5	6.1	4.8	3.0	5.0
Broadway Varieties	C	Fri	8:00				4.2	4.8	7.4	5.9	4.1	2.8		4.7
Burns & Allen Show	C	Wed	8:30	16.1	20.5	20.9	19.5	23.5	24.4	21.6				20.9
Carborundum Band	C	Sat	7:30		1.0	1.5	2.6	3.8	2.0	3.0				2.4
Carnation Contented Hour	N	Mon	10:00	5.0	4.6	5.0	3.8	3.9	5.0	3.2	3.9	3.8	3.6	4.2
Cavalcade of America	C	Wed	8:00	3.4	5.5	5.9	5.7	6.8	6.5	5.7	5.1	3.8	3.3	5.2
Cities Service Concert	N	Fri	8:00	6.5	7.8	7.9	7.0	8.0	6.4	6.5	6.0	4.3	4.1	6.5
"Clara, Lu & Em"	B	Fri	9:30	1.9										1.9
"Come, Let's Sing"	C	Wed	9:30	6.6	6.2	6.4	6.6	7.9	8.0	7.7	8.8	7.5	5.8	6.5
Court of Human Relations	N	Fri	9:30	5.9	8.3	7.7	7.2	6.9	7.7	7.6	7.8	4.4		7.5
Death Valley Days	B	Fri	8:30	4.6	2.3	5.9	5.4							5.7
Deems Taylor	B	Fri	9:30								1.2	1.2	0.8	1.1
Easy Aces	B	TWT	7:00	4.2	4.9	6.5	5.0	6.1	6.0	6.0	5.8	4.4	3.6	5.3
Ed Wynn Show	B	Sat	8:00			8.3	9.4	10.7	10.0	8.2	6.4	5.6		8.4
Eddie Cantor Show	C	Sun	8:30	16.8	20.0	20.6	25.0	25.3	28.0	27.2	24.6	19.3		23.0
Eddie Rickenbacker	C	W,F	7:30							1.3				1.3
Edgar Guest	B	Tue	8:30		4.0	4.0	4.3	4.9	4.0	5.7				4.0
Edwin C Hill News/Comment	B	Sun	9:45	3.1	3.9	4.7	4.5	6.9	7.4	5.6	4.7	3.0	2.3	5.5

1936-37 Clark-Hooper Ratings 6-11 P.M.

Program	Net	Day	Time	Sept. 36	Oct. 36	Nov. 36	Dec. 36	Jan. 37	Feb. 37	March 37	April 37	May 37	June 37	1936-37 Avg
Eleanor Roosevelt	B	Wed	7:15					4.8	4.2	4.6	8.0	5.2	2.9	5.4
Ethel Barrymore Theater	B	Wed	8:30								4.1	3.3	2.8	4.0
Fibber McGee & Molly	N	Mon	9:00	7.1	9.5	11.8	10.0	12.4	14.5	16.8	15.0	8.9	9.1	11.5
Fireside Recitals	N	Sun	7:30		1.6	3.7	3.6	2.4	3.0	3.9	2.3	1.8	1.8	2.7
First Nighter	C	Fri	9:30	9.0	10.0	12.1	12.8	15.3	17.7	15.9	16.8	14.2	12.7	13.7
Floyd Gibbons Show	C	Sat	9:00			5.2	5.8	8.0	7.4	7.2				6.7
Floyd Gibbons Show	C	Thu	10:00					8.4	6.7	7.8	7.1	6.6	5.0	6.9
Football Review	C	Sat	8:30		4.2	3.5	3.1							3.6
Ford Sunday Evening Hour	C	Sun	9:00	7.0	8.2	7.8	9.4	10.0	11.6	9.7	10.8	8.3		9.2
Fred Allen Town Hall Tonight	N	Wed	9:00		19.1	20.7	18.4	21.0	25.3	22.0	22.5	18.1	15.0	20.2
Fred Astaire Show	N	Tue	9:30	11.4	11.1	13.2	12.7	11.7	14.8	12.8	12.6	12.3		12.5
Fred Waring Show	B	Fri	9:00	3.8	3.8	4.8	4.2							4.2
Fred Waring Show	C	Tue	9:00	7.2	8.2	9.7	7.5							8.2
Gangbusters	C	Wed	10:00	8.7	11.2	10.2	10.6	14.8	13.6	14.3	13.9	12.9	10.2	12.0
General Motors Concert	B	Sun	8:00	7.9	7.5	8.3	10.0	6.7	10.3	8.2	8.4			8.4
Gillette Community Sing	C	Sun	10:00	6.2	7.2	6.6	5.9	6.6	7.8	7.3		7.8	4.2	6.8
Gladys Swarthout Sings	N	Sun	10:00								4.9	4.6		4.8
Glen Gray Orch	C	Tue	9:30	4.0	6.4	7.2	6.2							6.0
Goodwill Court AL Alexander	N	Sun	8:00		15.8	18.1								17.0
Goose Creek Parson	C	MWF	7:30	1.6	2.6	3.0	2.8							2.5
Hal Kemp & Alice Faye	C	Fri	8:30	6.2	7.4	7.8	6.7	7.2	8.4	8.5	7.5	5.2	4.8	6.9
Hammerstein's Music Hall	C	Tue	8:00	7.9	6.5	5.9	7.4	8.0	7.7	6.5	6.3	5.0	3.4	6.5
Helen Hayes Theater	B	Tue	9:30					8.7	6.5					7.2
Hollywood Hotel Louella Parsons	C	Fri	9:00	12.5	13.0	14.4	16.5	18.7	17.8	15.8	16.2	12.8	11.6	14.9
Horace Heidt Brigadiers Orch	C	Mon	8:00	4.5	4.5	4.7	5.1	5.6	6.0	6.8	6.1	4.5	4.6	5.2
Hour of Charm	N	Mon	9:30									2.8	3.8	3.3
Husbands & Wives	B	Tue	9:30		4.6	5.0	4.4	5.7	6.4	7.3	6.6	4.9	3.5	5.4
Irene Rich Dramas	B	Fri	8:00	1.5	4.2	3.1	8.0	6.0	5.1	5.7	4.9	2.8	2.5	4.4
Jack Benny Show	N	Sun	7:00		25.6	28.6	29.2	26.9	36.5	35.1	31.3	27.2	19.7	28.9
Jack Oakie's College	C	Tue	9:30		8.6	6.5	5.6	8.9	10.5	10.5	9.8	8.6	9.2	9.6
Jack Pearl Show	B	Fri	10:00			8.8	8.6	6.2	5.5	5.4	3.9	4.5	3.3	5.1
Kate Smith A&P Bandwagon	C	Thu	8:00	7.5			11.2	12.3	10.6	9.8	8.8	6.9	5.9	8.8
Ken Murray Show	C	Tue	8:30	9.1	11.8	11.8								11.0
Lavender & Old Lace	C	Wed	8:30	2.3	4.3	3.0	2.8							3.1
Leo Reisman Orch	N	Tue	8:00	5.6	6.9	7.0	7.8							6.8
Literary Digest Political Poll	B	MWF	7:15	3.8	5.4									4.6
Louis Armstrong Orch	B	Fri	9:00								2.4	1.6	1.0	1.7
Lowell Thomas News	B	M-F	6:45	7.6	10.6	12.4	12.7	11.9	12.1	12	12.4	5.6	6.8	10.4
Lum & Abner	B	M-F	7:30	7.1	8.8	9.2	9.3	10.2	9.9	10.3	9.6	7.7	6.1	8.8
Lux Radio Theater	C	Mon	9:00	15.9	19.0	19.4	19.2	22.3	25.1	26.3	24.6	22.6	15.4	21.0
Ma & Pa	C	M-Sat	7:15					3.9	5.8	4.4	4.3	3.2	2.8	4.1
Major Bowes Amateur Hour	C	Thu	9:00	21.4	18.7	22.1	18.2	23.9	23.9	24.2	25.5	19.3	16.1	21.3
Manhattan Merry Go Round	N	Sun	9:00	6.3	6.8	6.1	4.9	5.5	4.6	4.4	4.4	4.3	5.2	5.3
Maxwell House Show Boat	N	Thu	9:00	11.8	9.6	11.5	9.0	11.0	12.8	11.2	9.8	8.3	6.4	10.1
Melodiana	B	Mon	8:30	2.5	3.8	4.6	2.6	3.0						3.4
Mortimer Gooch	C	Fri	7:00			1.8	1.1		2.8	2.7	1.5	0.9	0.9	1.8
National Barn Dance	B	Sat	9:00	4.9	5.6	6.2	7.4	7.6	7.2	7.8	8.4	6.4	5.7	6.7
One Man's Family	N	Wed	8:00	9.6	13.2	14.0	11.8	15.0	13.6	15.2	15.3	12.1	9.8	13.0

1936-37 Clark-Hooper Ratings 6-11 P.M.

Program		Day	Time	Sept. 36	Oct. 36	Nov. 36	Dec. 36	Jan. 37	Feb. 37	March 37	April 37	May 37	June 37	1936-37 Avg
Phil Baker's Gulf Headliners	C	Sun	7:30		17.9	18.2	16.5	16.9	18.0	17.2	14.9	14.2	8.4	15.8
Philadelphia Symphony	C	Fri	10:00			4.2	3.8	2.9	4.2	3.6	3.4	2.1	1.0	3.2
Pick & Pat	C	Mon	8:30	9.8	12.1	11.6	11.7	13.3	12.4	12.4	12.5	9.2	7.9	11.3
Poetic Melodies	C	MTWT	7:00			0.7	1.5	2.1	2.0	1.5	1.2	1.2	1.2	1.4
Popeye the Sailor	C	MWF	7:15	3.9	5.8	6.6	6.6							6.7
Professor Quiz	N	Sat	8:00				5.6	8.9	8.5	8.1	9.3	6.4	7.1	7.7
Red Grange Sports	C	Sat	7:00	3.6	4.2	5.8								4.5
Red Horse Tavern	B	Fri	8:00	5.4	4.8	5.1								5.4
Revue de Paree	N	Wed	8:00	2.2	4.3	4.2	4.0	3.0						4.4
Richard Himber Orch	B	Mon	10:30	4.4				3.7			1.9			3.7
Robert Ripley's Bakers Broadcast	B	Sun	7:30		8.5	9.5	11.6	13.7	13.3	13.2	10.7	8.9	6.3	10.6
Rudy Vallee Show	N	Thu	8:00	14.8	17.0	17.0	15.1	16.3	20.3	19.2	19.2	14.1	11.0	16.4
Russ Morgan Orch	C	Sat	8:30		5.9	6.2	6.6	8.7	6.2	7.1	7.6	4.5		6.6
Russ Morgan Orch	N	Tue	8:00			3.7	3.2	7.9	9.4	9.3	9.3	8.6		8.4
Saturday Evening Party	C	Sat	8:00	5.9			8.2	3.0	7.5	6.4	5.6			6.3
Saturday Night Serenade	N	Sat	9:30	2.6	2.6	3.7	1.8		4.0	4.2	3.0	3.1	2.9	3.3
Shell Chateau	C	Sat	9:30	8.0	6.9	8.8	8.2	11.3	9.3	9.7	9.2	7.3	6.4	8.5
Shep Fields Orch	N	Sun	9:00	2.8	2.8	2.7	1.8	9.8	10.2	10.4	9.6	8.0	5.8	6.8
Sinclair Minstrels	B	Mon	9:00	4.2	3.4	4.3	3.7	2.7		5.9	4.1			3.7
Singin' Sam	B	Fri	8:15	2.5	2.9	3.6	3.9	7.7	7.2	6.0	5.3	2.8	3.7	4.5
Snow Village Sketches	N	Sat	7:15		5.0	7.3	5.6	5.9		0.5				5.6
Stainless Show	B	Fri	10:00					1.2	0.9		0.9	0.5		0.8
Sunday Night Party	B	Sun	7:45	5.4				1.7	4.1	3.1	4.7	2.7	3.6	3.6
Sunset Dreams	N	Sun	8:30		3.2	4.4		2.2	2.6	3.6	3.1	1.8	3.2	3.7
Sweetest Love Songs	N	Mon	7:15						3.7		3.4	1.9		2.5
Tastyeast Original Jesters	B	TWT	7:15						3.9					3.3
Ted Husing Sports	C	TTSat	10:00	6.6	6.6	5.3	3.6							5.2
Then & Now	C	Thu	7:00	6.0	5.1	4.7	4.8							5.2
Tic Toc Revue	B	Mon	9:30	1.6		1.8	1.3					1.5	1.8	1.3
Twin Stars	N	Fri	7:15										1.1	3.0
Uncle Ezra's Radio Station	B	MWF	7:30	8.2		10.1	9.9	10.6	10.5	11.3	10.8	8.1	6.1	9.2
Uncle Jim's Question Bee	B	Sat	9:00	6.3				9.2	8.0	9.6	7.6	9.0	6.5	8.3
Universal Rhythm	B	Fri	7:15				2.3	2.3	2.2	2.0	2.1			2.2
Unsung Champions	B	TWT	7:30			2.6	2.3							2.6
Vee Lawnhurst	C	Thu	10:00		1.5		2.6							2.1
Vic & Sade	B	Wed	8:00	1.5						1.7				1.8
Vick's Open House	C	Sun	7:15	12.5	13.3	13.3	16.3	14.8	15.4	17.3				14.9
Vocal Varieties	N	T,T	7:15						3.9	3.7	4.2	2.2	2.8	3.4
Voice of Experience	N	T,T	8:30	4.7	6.7	7.9	8.0	9.9						7.4
Voice of Firestone	N	Mon	9:00	5.9	5.9	7.4	7.4	8.5	9.6	9.5	8.0	7.0	5.0	7.4
Vox Pop Sidewalk Interviews	N	Tue	9:30	7.7	10.7	10.0	10.9	8.3	12.2	10.5	9.6	8.8	8.6	9.7
Walter Winchell Jergens Journal	B	Sun	9:00	8.3	12.4	12.2	15.2	14.2	15.5	15.3	14.1	13.6	10.0	13.1
Waltz Time	N	Fri	8:00	3.7	3.8	4.8	2.4	5.6	5.1	5.2	4.4	3.6	3.2	4.2
Want to Be an Actor?	N	Sun	8:00				9.9	10.4	9.5	8.0	7.2	6.3		8.6
Warden Lawes at Sing Sing	C	Mon	9:00		4.8	5.5	5.8	7.0	8.1	7.6	5.0			6.3
Wayne King Orch	N	Mon	10:00	8.7	9.2	10.1	9.1	11.1	12.5	11.0	10.4	10.0	8.7	10.1
Wayne King Orch	N	Tue	8:30	6.7	8.6	9.5	7.7	8.2	6.5	8.4	8.0	5.3	4.6	7.4
Wayne King Orch	N	Wed	8:30	5.9	6.8	6.6	7.7	7.5	6.9	7.5	8.7	7.4	6.5	7.2

1936-37 Clark-Hooper Ratings 6-11 P.M.

Program	Net	Day	Time	Sept. 36	Oct. 36	Nov. 36	Dec. 36	Jan. 37	Feb. 37	March 37	April 37	May 37	June 37	1936-37 Avg
William Hard Commentary	C	M-F	7:00		2.9	4.1								3.5
Your Hit Parade	C	Sat	10:00	11.6	11.0	12.0	10.7	9.8	11.5	10.3	13.0	10.3	8.6	10.9
Your Hit Parade	N	Wed	10:00	14.5	12.3	13.1	13.1	14.0	14.6	13.4	11.8	11.8	9.6	12.8

Special Broadcasts

Program	Net	Date	May 37	June 37
Kentucky Derby	B	5/8	14.0	
Boxing: Joe Louis/JJ Braddock	N,B	6/22		57.6

1937-38 Clark-Hooper Ratings 6-11 P.M.

Program	Net	Day	Time	Sept. 37	Oct. 37	Nov. 37	Dec. 37	Jan. 38	Feb. 38	March 38	April 38	May 38	June 38	1937-38 Avg
Al Jolson Show	C	Tue	8:30	12.4	15.0	19.0	21.0	23.2	22.4	19.0	19.7	16.3	13.2	18.1
Al Pearce Gang	C	Tue	9:00	10.0	12.3	14.2	16.3	16.9	17.8	17.7	16.7	15.2	11.2	14.8
Alias Jimmy Valentine	B	Tue	9:30					3.5	3.7	4.7	5.7			4.4
American Album of Familiar Music	N	Sun	9:30	6.2	6.9	9.1	8.2	8.2	10.1	8.7	7.8	7.3	7.3	8.1
Amos & Andy	N	M-F	7:00	9.7	12.0	12.4	15.1	15.1	17.7	15.0	14.0	11.4	9.0	13.3
Andre Kostelanetz Orch	C	Wed	9:00	6.7	8.1	6.8	8.3	8.3	10.1	10.3	9.9	6.8	6.1	8.4
Arthur Godfrey	C	M,F	7:15							3.1	4.3			3.4
Ben Bernie Show	C	Wed	9:30		8.1	8.7	11.3	11.3	13.6	10.6	13.2	9.2	7.4	10.9
Benny Goodman Orch	C	Tue	9:30	8.1		10.4	9.7	9.7	9.7	12.3	11.2	11.1	10.6	10.7
Big Town	C	Tue	8:00		8.7	10.4	11.3	14.9	13.6	16.6	16.2	14.6	13.3	13.7
Bing Crosby Kraft Music Hall	N	Thu	10:00	8.4	18.5	20.5	18.6	18.6	24.6	23.6	25.4	22.0	21.1	22.7
Boake Carter News/Comment	C	MWF	7:45		8.4	10.5	10.6	10.9	12.2	11.0				10.6
Burns & Allen Show	N	Mon	8:00	14.1	14.1	17.5	19.6	22.1	25.6	20.9	17.4	16.9	13.8	19.2
Carborundum Band	C	Sat	7:30						4.8	5.4				5.1
Carnation Contented Hour	N	Mon	10:00	5.3	5.3	6.0	6.0	6.0	6.0	5.4	4.0	4.5	4.7	5.3
Cavalcade of America	C	Wed	8:00	6.0	6.0	7.4	7.4	7.4	9.0	7.9	7.1	6.1	4.2	7.3
Cities Service Concert	N	Fri	8:00	6.6	6.7	7.8	7.6	7.6	8.2	8.1	8.4	7.4	6.2	7.5
Court of Human Relations	N	Fri	9:30	9.6	9.6	8.0	9.5	9.5	9.3	9.1	9.4	8.6		9.3
Dale Carnegie	N	Sat	8:30											4.7
Death Valley Days	B	Fri	9:30	4.6	8.8			6.4	10.2	9.0		6.7	4.7	8.3
Dick Powell Show	N	Wed	10:00				5.2	13.4	11.6	11.4	11.2		6.8	12.7
Easy Aces	B	TWT	7:00	4.4	4.4		5.6	5.6	7.5	7.8	7.0	5.1	4.8	6.2
Eddie Cantor Show	C	Wed	8:30	18.8	20.0	17.3	21.9	21.9	22.9	23.2				21.6
Edgar Bergen & Charlie McCarthy	N	Sun	8:00		26.4	29.8	33.2	33.2	37.4	38.1	33.4	33.4	30.2	32.1
Edgar A Guest	B	Tue	8:30		4.8	4.1	4.7	4.7	4.0	4.1				4.2
Fibber McGee & Molly	N	Tue	9:30	12.0	13.7	13.1	12.6	12.6	13.7	13.0	15.4	14.8	11.2	13.4
First Nighter	C	Fri	10:00	14.7	16.2	15.5	12.9	12.9	14.4	12.9	18.2	15.1	13.9	15.1
Ford Sunday Evening Hour	C	Sun	9:00	7.3	7.5	8.3	9.6	9.6	9.3	9.5	8.8	7.9	6.0	8.4
Fred Allen Town Hall Tonight	N	Wed	9:00	12.9	15.3	18.9	23.4	23.4	22.0	20.0	21.6	18.4	18.5	19.4
Gangbusters	C	Wed	10:00	12.9	13.7	13.9	14.1	14.1	13.7	16.5	15.3	14.3	16.0	14.7
General Hugh Johnson Commentary	B	M-Th	10:00	5.9	2.4	2.4	2.1	2.1	2.5	2.0				3.0
George McCall Hollywood News	C	T,T	7:15		4.1	4.1	3.6	3.6	4.2	4.3	5.7	3.7	3.6	4.2
Good News of 1938	N	Thu	9:00		13.9	13.9	13.9	13.9	14.5	17.1	19.7	17.5	15.0	16.6
Grand Central Station	B	Fri	8:00		6.6	6.6	6.6	6.6	7.7	8.4	9.6	8.5	6.8	7.1
Grand Hotel	B	Mon	8:30	4.0	7.3	8.8	8.8	8.8	10.8	12.2				8.3
Hammerstein's Music Hall	C	Fri	8:00	6.6	7.6	8.8	7.2	7.2	6.4	6.6				6.9
Harriet Parsons Hollywood News	B	Wed	8:30				2.6	2.6	2.6	2.3	2.5	2.2	1.2	2.2
Hobby Lobby	C	Wed	7:15		3.8	3.8	4.5	4.5	4.4	6.9				5.0

1937-38 Clark-Hooper Ratings 6-11 P.M.

Program	Net	Day	Time	Sept. 37	Oct. 37	Nov. 37	Dec. 37	Jan. 38	Feb. 38	March 38	April 38	May 38	June 38	1937-38 Avg
Hollywood Hotel	C	Fri	9:00	12.9	13.1	15.1	15.4	18.7	18.7	14.8	15.2	12.1	11.2	14.7
Hollywood Playhouse	B	Sun	9:00	9.0	7.7	9.2	12.0	11.2	13.5	14.1	10.7	10.8	8.5	10.7
Horace Heidt Brigadiers Orch	B	Tue	9:00				8.5	5.0	4.4	5.2	5.6	4.5	3.1	4.6
Hour of Charm	N	Mon	9:00	9.2	7.7	9.1	8.6	10.0	10.2	9.8	6.2			8.8
Interesting Neighbors	N	Sun	7:30	7.1	8.0	9.2	8.6	11.7	13.6	11.4	10.0	8.0	9.2	9.7
Irene Rich Dramas	B	Sun	9:45	4.4	5.5	6.4	7.8	6.9	8.3	6.8	6.5	9.3	6.1	6.8
Jack Benny Show	N	Sun	7:00		23.5	28.7	31.7	32.2	32.6	33.1	29.9	28.6	25.1	29.5
Jack Haley Show	N	Sat	8:30		11.0	10.4	11.9	14.1	13.8	13.2				12.4
Jack Oakie Show	C	Tue	9:30		10.1	12.0	11.7	15.5	15.5	13.5				13.1
Just Entertainment	C	M-F	7:00					3.4	3.0	3.3	3.0	3.0	3.0	3.1
Kate Smith Hour	C	Thu	8:00		8.7	7.0	9.3	10.2	9.6	9.3	10.8	7.5	6.2	8.7
Kay Kyser Kollege Mus Knowledge	N	Wed	10:00								11.5	11.1	10.0	10.9
Lowell Thomas News	B	M-F	6:45	8	11.3	11	11.5	14.2	13.8	14	13.6	7.4	7.8	11.3
Lum & Abner	B	M-F	7:30	6.4	8.0	9.3	8.7	10.7	9.6					8.8
Lux Radio Theater	B	Mon	9:00	17.8	18.7	21.9	22.7	25.2	24.5	25.8	28.3	26.2	22.9	23.4
Major Bowes Amateur Hour	C	Thu	9:00	18.1	20.8	19.4	22.2	22.0	23.6	20.2	18.4	15.7	13.7	19.4
Manhattan Merry Go Round	N	Sun	9:00	8.3	9.1	9.4	9.9	9.6	11.4	10.6	9.6	9.9	10.2	9.8
March of Time	B	Thu	8:00		3.5	3.5	3.6	4.1	4.7	5.7	5.2	3.7	3.2	4.1
Mardi Gras	N	Tue	9:30	12.5	11.6	13.4	13.1	13.2	13.2					12.8
Maxwell House Show Boat	N	Thu	9:00	8.2	9.6	11.6	11.6	11.6						9.8
Melody Puzzles	B	Mon	8:00					4.4	5.0	6.0	5.4			5.2
Mr Keen	B	TWT	7:15		3.4	3.8	6.1	7.4	9.0	7.4	10.1	5.8	5.2	6.5
National Barn Dance	B	Sat	9:00	8.6	9.0	9.7	8.8	9.8	10.4	9.1	9.7	7.4	7.6	9.0
One Man's Family	N	Wed	8:00	11.3	12.3	12.1	15.3	17.0	18.3	18.9	17.2	16.2	14.0	15.3
Ozzie Nelson Show	N	Sun	7:30	3.3	5.9	6.5	6.6	7.2	7.1	6.2	5.3	5.0	4.4	5.8
Paul Whiteman Show	C	Fri	8:30					11.0	10.9	9.2	9.1	8.2	6.9	9.1
Phil Baker's Gulf Headliners	C	Sun	7:30	15.9	15.4	16.0	16.1	20.5	20.6	20.1	15.2	13.7	10.4	16.4
Philadelphia Symphony	C	Mon	9:00		2.5	2.3	2.6	2.5	2.7	3.0	3.5			2.7
Pick & Pat's Model Minstrels	B	Mon	8:30	8.9	12.2	11.0	11.8	11.6	9.4	10.4	11.9	8.3	7.9	10.3
Professor Quiz	C	Sat	9:00	9.8	10.2	12.0	11.7	13.4	15.5	14.1	14.2	11.9	10.7	12.4
Rising Musical Stars	C	Sun	10:00		6.3	5.2	6.2	6.5	6.4	6.2	6.5	5.2	7.6	6.2
Robert Ripley Show	N	Tue	10:00		9.7	12.6	12.2	16.1	15.4	15.5	14.2	14.0	14.0	13.3
Royal Crown Revue	B	Fri	9:00							4.8	6.2	5.0	2.6	4.7
Rudy Vallee Show	N	Thu	8:00	15.7	18.4	19.2	20.9	21.6	21.4	18.8	20.8	15.0	14.1	18.6
Russ Morgan Orch	N	Sat	8:30	9.3	7.6	7.9	7.0	9.1	9.2	8.0	11.0	8.8	6.5	8.4
Russ Morgan Orch	C	Tue	8:00	8.9	11.1	9.7	8.7	9.9	10.9	9.0	9.1	7.3	5.3	9.0
Saturday Night Serenade	C	Sat	9:30		6.2	6.0	6.2	7.4	7.2	7.0	7.2	5.6	5.3	6.6
Second Husband/Helen Menken	C	Tue	7:30	3.6	4.9	8.6	8.9	8.4	11.0	11.1	9.8	8.3	7.7	8.2
Song Shop	C	Fri	10:00	6.9	5.6	6.0	5.4	4.4	7.9	5.2	7.0	5.0	5.7	5.9
Those We Love	B	Tue	8:00			4.1	3.9	3.1	2.3	2.5	3.5	5.0	4.2	3.7
Time to Shine	C	Tue	10:00					4.4	9.2	9.3	9.5	7.1	6.5	7.7
Tommy Dorsey Orch	N	Wed	8:30	1.8	10.9	10.1	10.8	12.5	9.2	10.1	13.0	10.4	11.6	7.0
Uncle Ezra's Radio Station	N	MWF	7:15	7.6	7.4	6.8	6.3	7.7	11.4	6.7	7.6	7.1	7.6	9.8
Vick's Open House	C	Sun	7:00	7.3	8.2	7.5	8.0	7.7	7.2	10.0	7.6	4.6	4.6	7.1
Vocal Varieties	N	T,T	7:15	4.7	8.8	8.7	9.9	11.6	9.5	11.6	7.6	9.3	4.6	6.9
Voice of Firestone	N	Mon	8:30	7.8	10.8	11.2	11.1	12.7	11.0	10.0	10.3	10.5	7.3	9.5
Vox Pop	N	Tue	9:00	9.3	6.7	11.0	9.9	12.7	13.7	11.6	12.3	10.5	7.7	11.1
Walter Winchell Jergens Journal	B	Sun	9:30	13.2			14.8	14.7	19.0	17.9	13.1	13.7	13.2	13.7

1937-38 Clark-Hooper Ratings 6-11 P.M.

				Sept. 37	Oct. 37	Nov. 37	Dec. 37	Jan. 38	Feb. 38	March 38	April 38	May 38	June 38	1937-38 Avg
Waltz Time	N	Fri	9:00	5.0	6.4	6.9	8.8	9.7	7.6	6.6	6.2	6.8	4.5	6.9
Warden Lawes at Sing Sing	B	Mon	10:00		6.2	5.2	6.6	9.3	5.4	4.7	4.0	4.5	4.7	5.6
Wayne King Orch	C	Mon	10:00	7.9	9.0	8.0	10.6	8.4	10.0	9.5	9.1	11.3	10.2	9.4
Wayne King Orch	N	Tue	8:30	6.9	8.9	7.8	7.6	8.1	8.2	7.3	7.8	7.7	6.3	7.7
Wayne King Orch	N	Wed	8:30	9.9	6.8	7.0	9.3	8.6						8.3
We the People	N	Thu	7:30		6.7	6.3	8.0	7.6	9.2	9.5	9.8	7.1		8.0
You Said It	C	Mon	8:00							4.7	8.2	4.1	4.5	5.4
Your Hit Parade	C	Sat	10:00	11.8	11.5	14.3	11.7	13.8	12.5	13.5	12.9	11.4	10.6	12.4
Your Hit Parade	N	Wed	10:00	10.2	10.4	11.3								10.6
Zenith Radio Foundation	C	Sun	10:00	2.8	3.4	4.5	6.5	4.0	5.7	5.6				4.6

Special Broadcasts

				Sept. 37	Oct. 37	Nov. 37	Dec. 37	Jan. 38	Feb. 38	March 38	April 38	May 38	June 38	1937-38 Avg
World Series: NYYanks - NYGiants	All	10/6	CAB		27.2									
World Series: NYYanks - NYGiants	All	10/7	CAB		26.1									
World Series: NYYanks - NYGiants	All	10/8	CAB		20.6									25.3
World Series: NYYanks - NYGiants	All	10/9	CAB		27.2									
Boxing: James Braddock/Tom Farr	B	1/22	CAB					35.9						
Boxing: Joe Louis/Nathan Mann	B	2/23	Hoop						28.5					
Boxing: Joe Louis/Max Schmeling	N,B	6/22	CAB										63.6	

1938-39 Hooper Ratings 6-11 P.M.

				9/38	10/38	11/38	12/38	1/39	2/39	3/39	4/39	5/39	6/39	1938-39 Avg
Al Jolson Show	C	Tue	8:30	19.5	14.4	17.3	16.8	16.3	18.5	18.2	12.7	10.1		17.3
Al Pearce Gang	N	Mon	8:00			14.4	14.3	15.2	17.7	14.4			7.5	13.3
Alias Jimmy Valentine	B	Mon	7:00		3.5	2.7	3.5	3.9	4.9					3.7
American Album of Familiar Music	N	Sun	9:30		8.8	13.0	10.3	8.9	11.2	9.2	8.0	9.2	8.4	9.3
Amos & Andy	C	M-F	7:00	6.3	12.5	11.9	12.5	13.3	15.1	14.5	14.9	9.4	7.0	12.1
Ask It Basket	C	Wed	7:30	9.8	7.1	8.0	7.0	9.0	11.2	9.2	9.5	6.8	4.8	8.1
Battle of the Sexes	N	Tue	9:00	9.1	10.1	2.7	11.2	10.0	11.3	12.7	11.5	9.3	7.3	9.5
Benny Goodman Orch	C	Tue	9:30	11.9	8.7	11.6	9.5	8.7	7.7	8.7	7.7	6.0	5.8	8.6
Bert Lytell Show	B	Fri	7:00							2.6	1.5			2.1
Big Game Hunt	N	Wed	9:00	12.4										12.4
Big Town	C	Tue	8:00	15.1	14.8	16.3	15.1	18.5	16.5	18.0	15.5	13.1	9.8	15.3
Bing Crosby's Kraft Music Hall	N	Thu	10:00			23.2	23.1	22.3	24.1	21.1	24.1	20.6	15.1	21.8
Bob Burns Show	N	Thu	10:00	22.2	22.2									22.2
Bob Hope Show	C	Tue	10:00		13.3	14.2	16.1	20.2	20.7	12.7	15.1	13.3	12.4	15.4
Burns & Allen Show	C	Fri	8:30		15.2	17.4	17.2	14.5	16.2	16.2	15.7	13.2	8.4	15.6
Campbell Playhouse	C	Fri	9:00				17.4			14.8	14.8	6.8		15.4
Carnation Contented Hour	N	Mon	10:00	4.5	5.4	7.8	7.4		6.9	7.5	5.9	6.1	5.9	6.5
Carson Robison Show	B	Mon	8:00			3.5	1.9	2.7	2.8	3.6	3.2			3.0
Cavalcade of America	C	Mon	8:00						7.3	8.2	8.4			7.7
The Circle	N	Sun	10:00			6.4	9.5	6.5	11.8	12.3	12.8	13.4	11.6	12.3
Cities Service Concert	N	Fri	8:00	7.2	5.6		6.5	6.0	6.8	6.9	6.3	6.4	4.2	6.2
Death Valley Days	N	Fri	9:30	8.4	7.4	7.2	8.3	9.0	7.4	5.3	6.3	7.4	7.6	7.4
Dick Powell Show	C	Tue	8:30								14.0	9.4	9.2	10.9
Dick Tracy	N	Sat	7:00									5.5		5.5
Dr Christian	C	Tue	10:00					6.6	7.8	7.0	6.7			6.7
Dr Rockwell	B	Tue	9:30			6.1	6.1					1.0		1.0

1938-39 Hooper Ratings 6-11 P.M.

Program	Net	Time	Day	9/38	10/38	11/38	12/38	1/39	2/39	3/39	4/39	5/39	6/39	1938-39 Avg
Easy Aces	B	7:00	TWT	7.2	6.5	7.4	7.1	7.3	7.0	8.2	5.0	5.1	3.8	6.5
Eddie Cantor Show	C	7:30	Mon		19.0	17.0	17.7	18.0	19.4	18.0	19.1	13.9	13.8	17.3
Eddy Duchin Orch	N	9:30	Mon	4.6	5.7	7.3	9.5	5.8	6.8	7.7		8.0		6.9
Edgar Bergen & Charlie McCarthy	N	8:00	Sun	33.8	31.6	34.8	34.5	34.4	35.4	34.0	34.6	26.1	22.8	32.2
Edwin C Hill News/Comment	N	7:15	M-W		8.1	8.9	8.5	9.6	9.7	9.8				9.1
Fibber McGee & Molly	N	9:30	Tue	14.0	15.3	16.2	18.4	17.5	22.8	21.5	18.1	17.3	14.6	17.6
First Nighter	C	8:00	Fri	11.5	11.3	12.4	13.0	13.0	13.2	13.4	9.6	9.8	7.3	11.5
Fitch Bandwagon	N	7:30	Sun	8.1	12.8	15.6	17.0	10.0	13.4	15.6	14.0	9.8	9.7	12.6
For Men Only	N	8:30	Tue	10.7	6.1	7.1	7.4	6.2	6.8	7.2	7.0	6.4	5.4	7.0
Ford Sunday Evening Hour	C	9:00	Sun	6.8	6.6	7.0	7.8	6.8	8.0	8.6	7.5	6.8	6.6	7.6
Fred Allen Town Hall Tonight	N	9:00	Wed		16.6	16.8	14.9	16.4	17.4	17.0	15.6	14.4	8.8	15.3
Fred Waring Show	N	8:30	Sat		8.6	8.6	9.5	10.1	10.2					9.4
Fulton Oursler	N	9:30	Tue										1.9	1.9
Gangbusters	C	8:00	Wed	13.1	12.7	12.9	12.5	15.0	15.3	13.7	13.7	9.2	10.2	12.8
Gateway to Hollywood	C	7:00	Sun								4.8			4.8
George McCall Hollywood News	C	7:15	TT		3.7	5.3								4.5
Good News of 1939	N	9:00	Thu	17.3	17.1	15.6	17.1	18.9	19.5	20.0	18.3	17.0	11.7	17.3
Goodwill Hour John J Anthony	C	9:00	Sun	10.9	7.0	9.7	7.1	8.6	8.9	8.2	8.4	6.7	7.8	8.2
Grand Central Station	M	10:00	Fri		4.2	7.6	9.7	8.7	9.7	11.9	9.1	9.8	6.8	9.1
Guy Lombardo Orch	C	10:00	Mon	11.2		9.9	9.2	11.6	9.9	13.2	11.1	10.4	8.9	10.4
Guy Lombardo Orch	C	10:00	Fri			8.6	9.3	8.3	7.6	9.0	9.3	8.2	5.6	8.6
Hobby Lobby	N	8:30	Wed			6.9	7.7	8.0	8.9	8.8	7.7	5.7		7.5
Hollywood Hotel	B	9:00	Fri	12.2	14.7	14.3	13.2							13.7
Hollywood Playhouse	C	9:00	Sun		9.6	13.5	8.5	11.8	15.6	13.6	14.2	11.6	11.1	12.7
Horace Heidt Brigadiers Orch	B	10:00	Mon	9.6	8.6	10.6	8.9	9.0	8.2	8.7	7.5	7.7	6.5	9.3
Hour of Charm	N	9:00	Tue		6.1	7.3	5.0	7.6	8.6	9.4	7.8	8.5		7.9
Information Please	B	8:30	Tue					8.7	8.5	8.3				7.6
Inside Story	B	8:00	Sun								3.0	2.1	2.4	2.5
Irene Rich Dramas	B	9:45	Wed	7.0	8.0	7.7	9.5				9.0	9.9	8.6	8.5
It Can Be Done	C	10:00	Sun				3.2	3.9	4.5				1.9	3.4
Jack Benny Program	N	7:00	Sun		28.3	28.0	30.3	30.2	30.9	32.1	27.5	21.4	20.3	27.7
Jack Haley Show	C	7:30	Fri		10.3	8.8	7.3	7.7	10.7	9.2	9.2	6.2	5.6	8.8
Jimmie Fidler Hollywood News	C	7:15	Tue		8.0	9.6	7.9	10.7	10.0	7.5	5.5	7.5	6.0	8.1
Jimmie Fidler Hollywood News	C	7:15	Thu				7.1	7.8	8.9	7.5	9.4	8.1	6.7	7.7
Joe E Brown Show	C	7:30	Thu				8.3	9.9	9.6	8.6				9.1
Joe Penner Show	C	7:30	Thu		11.9	12.0	10.2	10.8	12.1	12.9	12.8			11.7
John Nesbitt's Passing Parade	C	7:30	Sun	3.1	6.3	5.1	4.9							4.9
Kate Smith Hour	C	8:00	Thu	17.2	12.5	13.6	12.8	15.7	17.0	17.5	18.3	12.8	10.2	14.5
Kay Kyser Kollege Mus Knowledge	N	10:00	Wed		14.9	14.0	17.4	18.2	18.8	18.6	19.6	17.2	13.3	16.9
Lowell Thomas News	B	6:45	M-F		13.5	14.3	12.9	14.1	16.0	15.7	16.4	11.7	10.8	14.0
Lum & Abner	C	7:15	MWF		6.6	7.0	6.1	7.1	8.4	7.5	10.3	7.1	5.1	7.2
Lux Radio Theater	C	9:00	Mon	29.0	23.0	20.6	23.6	24.3	23.7	25.3	21.1	17.8	16.6	22.5
Major Bowes Amateur Hour	C	9:00	Thu	14.2	16.9	18.7	18.9	18.9	18.4	17.4	17.8	14.0	10.8	16.6
Manhattan Merry Go Round	N	9:00	Sun	7.9	10.7	12.3	11.9	9.9	9.0	10.7	9.3	7.7	6.6	9.6
March of Time	B	9:30	Fri	7.2	4.6	3.8	3.7	2.7	4.3	5.6	4.4			5.2
Mary & Bob	B	9:00	Tue									2.5		3.6
Matty Melnick Orch	C	7:15	Thu								3.6		3.6	3.6
Mr District Attorney	N	7:00	M-F			3.8			4.6	4.3		5.1		5.1

1938-39 Hooper Ratings 6-11 P.M.

Program	Net	Day	Time	9/38	10/38	11/38	12/38	1/39	2/39	3/39	4/39	5/39	6/39	1938-39 Avg
Mr Keen	B	TWT	7:15	6.0	5.1	6.4	5.8	6.7	6.2	8.2	5.5	4.4	3.1	5.7
Monday Night Show	C	Mon	8:00		6.6	5.9								6.3
National Barn Dance	B	Sat	9:00	7.3	8.4	9.6	10.2	9.7	11.0	10.7	11.4	9.0	7.0	9.4
99 Men & a Girl Hildegarde	C	Wed	10:00							4.4	4.7	4.5	4.4	4.5
One Man's Family	N	Wed	8:00	13.9	13.1	14.9	14.7	14.2	18.0	16.4	16.6	12.6	10.9	14.5
Orphans of Divorce	B	Wed	7:00							3.8	3.4	3.0	2.8	3.3
Paul Whiteman Show	C	Mon	8:30	7.1	6.8	7.8	7.1	7.8	8.6	8.9	7.9	6.3	4.3	7.3
Phil Baker's Honolulu Bound Show	C	Wed	9:00					11.0	7.1	8.3	7.0	6.4	5.6	7.6
Pick & Pat Model Minstrels	B	Sat	8:30	12.2	11.4	10.0	10.9	11.8	11.4	9.4	10.9	8.7	6.9	10.4
Plantation Party	C	Wed	9:00				2.5	4.2	3.8	4.6	4.0	3.3	3.6	3.7
Professor Quiz	N	Sat	8:30	11.9	9.8	10.3	9.9		11.2	13.2	8.6	8.3	6.3	9.9
Red Skelton Avalon Variety Show	C	Sat	7:00		5.5	6.9	7.6	7.8	8.9	8.0	8.4	6.1	6.8	7.3
Robert Benchley Show	N	Sat	10:00				5.7	6.9	5.8	5.7	4.7	5.8	3.9	5.5
Robert Ripley Believe It or Not	N	Mon	8:00	14.6	13.4									14.0
Rudy Vallee Show	C	Thu	8:00	19.1	14.7	15.7	16.6	16.1	17.0	13.5	12.8	11.1	7.6	14.4
Russ Morgan Orch	N	Sat	8:00	9.9	7.1	9.2	7.6	9.6	7.8	11.7	10.3	7.2	6.8	8.7
Russ Morgan Orch	C	Tue	9:30	7.7	8.5	11.0	9.4	8.3	9.2	7.3	7.2	6.9	7.0	8.9
Saturday Night Serenade	C	Sun	7:30											7.0
Screen Guild Theater	C	Sun	7:30					13.7	11.5	10.2	9.0	7.7	6.8	9.8
Second Husband Helen Menken	B	Tue	7:30	8.6	8.2	10.7	9.8	11.4	9.8	9.8	8.8	8.8	6.8	9.3
Seth Parker Show	C	Sun	9:00				9.8	7.9	6.9	8.0				8.1
Texaco Star Theater	B	Wed	9:00	6.4	9.7	8.1	9.6	11.0	10.9	12.4	10.9	10.3	6.7	10.0
Those We Love	C	Mon	8:30	8.5	6.9		6.4			7.5				6.9
Time to Shine	N	Tue	10:00									4.8	4.3	6.2
Tommy Dorsey Orch	N	Wed	8:30	10.6	11.3	10.9	10.8	12.0	10.9	12.1	10.9	9.5	7.5	10.7
Tommy Riggs & Betty Lou	B	Sat	8:00	10.7	8.7	10.4	12.8	12.6	14.4	11.4	11.0			11.3
True or False	C	Mon	10:00		7.2	5.4	6.9	5.6	8.0	6.7	6.5	7.0	4.3	6.8
Tune Up Time	B	Thu	10:00					6.7	5.2	4.7	5.0	5.3		5.4
Uncle Jim's Question Bee	N	Thu	7:30					8.8	9.5	9.6	10.7	9.2	5.9	9.0
Vocal Varieties	N	TT	7:15	3.2	6.3	7.3	6.1	6.9	7.3	7.2	6.6	1.3	2.9	5.5
Voice of Firestone	N	Mon	8:30	8.2										10.1
Vox Pop	C	Sat	9:00											8.0
Walter Winchell Jergens Journal	B	Sun	9:30	11.5	12.9	18.0	14.8	12.7	14.7	15.3	13.6	14.7	11.4	14.0
Waltz Time	N	Fri	9:00	5.7	5.1	5.9	5.3	7.6	6.3	6.9	6.0			6.1
Warden Lawes at Sing Sing	B	Fri	8:00								4.6	6.9	5.7	5.2
Wayne King Orch	N	Fri	10:00	9.0										9.0
Wayne King Orch	B	Mon	10:00	11.1	10.3									10.7
We the People	C	Tue	10:00			12.2	14.3	15.5	15.2	14.8	14.3	11.6	8.5	13.0
Win Your Lady	C	Tue	9:00	9.3										9.3
Your Hit Parade	B	Sat	10:00	13.0	10.5	10.9	16.1	15.3	16.3	14.1	14.6	14.0	11.6	13.6

Special Broadcast

Program	Net	Date	11/38
Pres Roosevelt Political Address	BCM	11/4	22.2

1939-40 Hooper Ratings 6-11 P.M.

Program	Net	Day	Time	Sept. 39	Oct. 39	Nov. 39	Dec. 39	Jan. 40	Feb. 40	March 40	April 40	May 40	1939-40 Avg
Adventures of Ellery Queen	C	Sun	7:30		10.2	11.8	12.9	9.1	12.7	11.4	10.1	9.2	9.5
Adventures of Sherlock Holmes	B	Mon	8:00							11.4			11.4

1939-40 Hooper Ratings 6-11 P.M.

Program	Net	Day	Time	Sept. 39	Oct. 39	Nov. 39	Dec. 39	Jan. 40	Feb. 40	March 40	April 40	May 40	April 40	1939-40 Avg
Al Pearce Gang	C	Fri	7:30		14.2	13.5	13.1	13.7	17.4	16.2		9.3	9.6	13.4
Alec Templeton Show	N	Mon	9:30		8.4	10.7	9.8	10.6	8.9	11.4	8.8	9.4	6.9	9.4
Aldrich Family	B	Tue	8:00	10.4	8.5	10.1	11.3	12.4	14.0	15.6	16.2	11.3		12.2
American Album of Familiar Music	N	Sun	9:30	9.6	11.8	12.2	14.0	12.3	10.4	9.8	10.1	9.9	7.1	10.7
Amos & Andy	N	M-F	7:00		10.5	10.9	12.5	11.6	12.5	11.0	10.9	9.1	8.4	10.8
Ask It Basket	C	Thu	8:00		9.7	11.8	11.3	15.7	13.8	14.4	13.1	8.5	6.6	11.7
Battle of the Sexes	N	Tue	9:00		11.0	15.0	15.2	17.5	15.1	14.4	14.0	12.0	10.2	13.1
Beat the Band	N	Sun	6:30	6.9								6.2	6.1	8.6
Ben Bernie Show	N	Wed	8:00						9.9	10.2	10.5	10.0	9.2	10.5
Benny Goodman Orch	C	Sat	10:00	7.9	9.5	8.0	8.9				12.2			8.6
Big Town	C	Tue	8:00		12.9	15.4	13.9	17.5	18.4	17.4	15.7	11.2	11.3	14.9
Bill Stern Colgate Sports Newsreel	B	Sun	9:45		4.2	3.1		4.3	5.4	5.2	6.1	6.7	3.3	4.8
Bing Crosby's Kraft Music Hall	N	Thu	10:00		19.6	22.3	20.5	23.3	25.7	24.3	20.5	18.9	14.4	21.1
Blondie	C	Mon	7:30		10.8	11.1	12.6	11.4	14.1	13.5	13.0	10.0	10.3	11.7
Bob Crosby Show	N	Sat	10:00	9.9	6.7	8.3	6.3	12.1	10.1	9.4	8.5	7.8	8.2	8.4
Bob Hope Show	N	Tue	10:00	6.9	15.3	19.1	23.7	25.0	29.5	26.5	26.1	22.9	20.1	23.1
Breezing Along	B	Wed	8:00											4.2
Bugler Showboat	B	Fri	9:00			3.6	4.4	4.7	3.7	4.7	4.3		3.8	4.9
Burns & Allen Show	C	Wed	7:30	7.6	14.1	15.3	16.1	15.8	16.6	16.7	14.5	6.0	8.2	14.3
Campbell Playhouse	C	Sun	8:00	7.5	8.9	10.4	10.9	12.8	12.4	13.7		11.7		11.0
Carnation Contented Hour	N	Mon	10:00		7.0	6.4	8.5	7.4	7.9	7.3	6.1			7.1
Carson Robison Show	B	Fri	8:30		4.3	4.0	3.9	2.5	6.1	4.4			5.7	4.2
Cavalcade of America	B	Tue	9:00	6.4	8.8	7.6	8.1							7.0
Cities Service Concert	N	Fri	8:00					6.5	6.1	9.3	8.0	7.1	4.9	7.5
Court of Missing Heirs	C	Tue	8:30					9.2	7.6	8.2	7.6	6.8	6.9	7.0
Death Valley Days	C	Sat	9:30		5.6	7.5	6.0	6.8	8.0	8.8	6.9	6.5	5.1	6.7
Dr Christian	C	Wed	8:30			9.0	8.4	7.4	9.8	6.9	8.8	4.8	3.8	11.7
Dr IQ	N	Mon	9:00	7.6	9.0	13.4	12.4	13.4	14.7	13.4	12.6	13.3	8.9	10.4
Don Ameche Show	N	Fri	10:00					11.8	11.6	12.0	10.7	7.8	7.9	9.0
Easy Aces	B	TWT	7:00		5.7	6.7	6.7	9.6	7.9	9.2	6.9	5.5	5.1	7.0
Edgar Bergen & Charlie McCarthy	N	Sun	8:00	22.1	27.7	34.2	31.2	34.6	34.5	35.1	35.9	28.3	23.7	30.7
Fibber McGee & Molly	N	Tue	9:30	13.9	20.5	23.4	24.2	30.6	29.2	29.0	31.0	23.8	22.4	24.8
First Nighter	C	Fri	9:30	10.1	12.9	14.9	17.4	17.1	19.1	16.2	17.8	12.8		15.4
Fitch Bandwagon	N	Sun	7:30	9.6	11.2	18.1	15.4	22.4	17.1	15.0	19.0	13.0		15.2
Ford Sunday Evening Hour	C	Sun	9:00	7.1	10.8	10.1	12.4	13.1	10.2	11.9	11.9	9.3	10.7	10.8
Fred Allen Show	N	Wed	9:00	16.4	16.4	17.5	16.1	16.6	17.1	16.4	17.3	17.7	11.7	16.3
Fred Waring Show	N	M-F	7:00		7.9	10.1	9.9	11.5	12.1	11.9	10.4	8.1	9.0	10.1
Fun in Print	C	Sun	6:00										5.7	5.7
Gangbusters	C	Sat	8:00			14.9	13.7	17.5	16.6	16.8	15.5	12.4	9.9	14.7
Gateway to Hollywood	C	Sun	6:30		8.9	10.6	12.0	10.7					5.7	10.5
Gene Autry's Melody Ranch	C	Sun	6:30					10.3	14.7	11.5	10.4	5.0	6.1	9.6
George Jessel Show	N	Thu	8:00	11.1	6.8	10.5	9.1		13.2	12.4	10.4	6.8	5.2	10.6
Glenn Miller Orch	C	TWT	10:00					6.2	7.4	7.4	6.4	6.8	5.2	6.6
Good News of 1940	N	Thu	9:00	12.9	14.9	20.1	17.5	17.7	19.5	19.5	19.6	16.1	10.9	16.9
Goodwill Hour John J Anthony	M	Sun	10:00	8.4	9.8	7.6	8.2	9.0	7.9	8.6	9.9	9.5	8.7	8.8
Grand Central Station	N	Fri	10:00		10.1	11.7	14.0							11.9
Grouch Club	C	Sun	6:30		5.2	9.7	7.9	14.4	8.5		12.7	12.9	9.0	9.0
Guy Lombardo Orch	C	Mon	10:00	11.4	12.0	15.1	15.2		12.9	14.9	16.8	12.6		13.6

1939-40 Hooper Ratings 6-11 P.M.

Program	C	Day	Time	Sept. 39	Oct. 39	Nov. 39	Dec. 39	Jan. 40	Feb. 40	March 40	April 40	May 40	April 40	1939-40 Avg
Hedda Hopper Hollywood News	C	MWF	6:15	7.8	11.0	5.0	5.1	5.4	7.2	6.8	5.2	6.2	4.5	5.7
Hobby Lobby	B	Wed	8:30	11.3							14.0			7.8
Hollywood Playhouse	N	Wed	8:00		9.2	12.9	10.9	13.0	10.9	11.3	11.6	9.7	9.1	11.2
Hour of Charm	N	Sun	10:00		5.6	10.5	9.8	11.7	8.5	8.4		11.3	8.2	9.9
I Love a Mystery	N	M-F	7:15			8.7	9.9	11.2	13.0	15.1				10.6
I Love a Mystery	N	Thu	8:30	7.3	7.7	9.5	6.8	8.6	10.6	10.3	13.5	9.4	8.4	10.3
Information Please	B	Tue	8:30	14.9	14.2	13.6	13.8	12.3	12.4	14.0	13.2	12.4	10.2	13.1
Irene Rich Dramas	N	Sun	9:30								13.3	8.9	8.4	9.1
Jack Benny Program	N	Sun	7:00		24.8	34.4	30.1	34.1	36.7	35.4	35.3	26.2	21.2	30.9
Jimmie Fidler Hollywood News	C	Tue	7:15		9.3	8.9	10.0	10.0	10.5	10.3	9.3			9.5
Joe E Brown Show	C	Thu	7:30	8.0	8.2									8.0
Joe Penner Show	B	Thu	8:30	8.0	7.5	8.0	7.5	9.0	12.4	8.2	10.0			9.0
Johnny Presents	N	Tue	8:00	9.7		8.6	8.6	9.8	9.8	7.9	7.1	6.2	7.3	8.3
Kate Smith Hour	C	Fri	8:00		16.3	16.5	16.8	19.6	18.8	17.5	19.3	15.0	11.4	16.8
Kay Kyser Kollege Mus Knowledge	N	Wed	10:00	17.5	16.4	17.6	15.8	21.2	22.8	18.8	18.0	18.8	12.6	18.0
Ken Murray Show	C	Wed	9:00	10.2	11.1	14.0	14.3	16.4	13.9	14.1	12.8	11.4	8.0	12.6
Lanny Ross Show	C	M-F	7:15		5.4	5.3					10.3	8.0	7.4	8.6
Larry Clinton Orch	N	Mon	7:30	7.5										4.6
Lowell Thomas News	C	M-F	6:45		14.0	13.2	14.8	15.0	16.3	15.2	16.4	11.5	14.1	14.5
Lum & Abner	C	MWF	7:15		9.1	10.1	8.9	11.2	12.6	10.6				10.4
Lux Radio Theater	C	Mon	9:00	21.1	24.1	24.0	25.3	26.9	26.2	24.2	29.7	19.2	16.7	23.7
Major Bowes Amateur Hour	C	Thu	9:00	13.2	16.4	17.5	21.0	21.6	21.1	20.4	20.7	18.0	14.2	18.4
Manhattan Merry Go Round	N	Sun	9:00	8.9	10.4	13.7	12.1	14.3	10.8	10.6	9.4	7.9	6.8	10.5
Melody & Madness	B	Tue	9:00	7.2	5.0									6.1
Mr District Attorney	N	Thu	9:00	12.5	6.8	8.2	6.9	6.1	9.4	9.5	14.5	9.9	6.7	9.1
Mr Keen	B	TWT	7:15		5.1	5.9	7.4	6.7	6.7	6.7	8.3	4.7	4.2	6.2
Pick & Pat Model Minstrels	C	Mon	8:30	9.4	12.4	10.3	12.1	13.8	13.6	13.8				12.2
Musical Americana	B	Thu	8:00						3.0	2.7	3.7	4.0	2.7	3.2
National Barn Dance	B	Sat	9:00	8.0	7.9	10.3	10.9	10.9	11.5	8.9	10.0	7.6	6.9	9.3
One Man's Family	N	Sun	8:30	14.1	17.9	15.9	16.7	28.4	22.0	25.3	24.6	19.4	18.8	20.3
Parker Family	B	Sun	9:15	3.8	7.7	9.7	12.1	10.2	13.1	10.8	12.3	10.6	10.6	10.1
Paul Sullivan News/Comment	C	M-F	6:30									6.5	7.6	7.1
Paul Whiteman Show	C	Wed	8:30	7.2	10.2									10.2
Phil Baker Show	C	Wed	8:00		4.5	4.6	5.9	5.3	7.4	4.1				7.2
Pipe Smoking Time	C	Mon	8:30								14.6	10.0	7.9	10.8
Plantation Party	B	Fri	9:00		8.2						6.0	8.2	5.9	5.8
Pot O Gold	N	Tue	8:30		12.9	15.4	18.8	21.1	25.4	21.7	22.2	14.8	14.4	18.0
Professor Quiz	C	Fri	7:30			13.0	12.6	13.5	14.2	13.3	13.6	7.3	5.8	11.8
Quicksilver	B	Wed	8:30			6.7	6.5	5.3	5.9	6.1	5.9			6.1
Quixie Doodle Contest	M	Fri	8:00			4.9	5.4	6.1	7.0	9.8	7.7			6.8
Red Skelton Avalon Time	N	Wed	8:30		9.6	10.5	10.3	10.2	11.0	11.7	9.3			10.4
Rudy Vallee Varieties	N	Thu	9:30	12.7	11.6	13.9	11.3	14.9	15.1	15.4	15.1	14.3	9.3	13.4
Russ Morgan Orch	C	Fri	9:00	9.1						13.0	15.6	12.0	9.5	12.6
Sammy Kaye Orch	N	Mon	7:30			7.3	8.7	8.0	6.6	8.3	8.8	7.7	6.2	7.6
Saturday Night Serenade	C	Sat	9:45			9.2	12.5	8.7	10.3	8.1	7.9	9.8	8.2	8.5
Screen Guild Theater	C	Sun	7:30					13.0	13.9	15.6	14.2			12.8
Second Husband Helen Menken	C	Tue	7:30	8.0	11.0	11.1	12.2	11.3	14.1	14.7	11.7	8.6	8.8	11.2
Silver Theater	C	Sun	6:00		10.8	13.7	13.9	15.5	17.4	15.1	12.6	8.4		13.4

1939-40 Hooper Ratings 6-11 P.M.

Program	Net	Day	Time	Sept. 39	Oct. 39	Nov. 39	Dec. 39	Jan. 40	Feb. 40	March 40	April 40	May 40	June 40	1939-40 Avg
Sky Blazers	C	Sat	7:30				6.9	6.8	9.5	9.2	10.9	6.6	5.7	7.9
Stop Me If You Heard This One	N	Sat	8:30		13.0	8.5	11.3	11.8	12.2					11.4
Strange as It Seems	C	Thu	8:30		10.5	10.2		12.8	11.9	9.8	10.7	7.8	8.0	10.1
Swingo/Musical Game	C	Thu	8:30	6.5										6.5
Take It or Leave It	C	Sun	10:00										5.1	7.8
Telephone Hour	N	Mon	8:00									6.7	8.9	5.3
This Amazing America	B	Fri	8:00							3.0	2.4		5.3	3.5
Those We Love	N	Thu	8:30			12.5	13.0	11.3	12.8	13.8		5.4	3.3	12.2
Time to Shine	C	Tue	10:00		9.7									6.3
Tommy Dorsey Orch	N	Wed	8:30		4.9									10.2
Tommy Riggs & Betty Lou	N	Mon	8:00		9.6	12.6	11.1	13.1	13.5	12.9				12.0
True or False	B	Mon	8:30		8.2	7.6	9.5		9.6	11.8	11.5	7.4	4.8	8.9
Tuesday Night Party	C	Tue	8:30		11.0	9.0	10.9	9.3	11.4	9.9	12.2			10.3
Tune Up Time	C	Mon	8:00		6.9	8.1	6.9	9.5	10.3	9.2	8.9	8.9	6.8	8.8
Voice of Firestone	N	Mon	8:30		9.8	13.3	12.3	12.1	13.0	11.9	14.1	8.7	6.5	9.9
Vox Pop	C	Thu	7:30		8.9	9.5	9.1	10.8				9.4	4.7	9.8
Walter Winchell Jergens Journal	B	Sun	9:00		17.4	20.4	20.9	20.0	20.9	20.9	20.7	18.5	18.4	19.3
Waltz Time	N	Fri	9:00		6.2	8.7	9.6	8.8	8.6	10.5	8.4	7.6	5.4	8.3
Wayne King Orch	C	Sat	8:30			13.2	11.0	11.0	13.1	15.8	15.4	11.7	9.6	12.6
We the People	C	Tue	9:00		14.7	15.4	16.8	16.9	20.2	16.2	16.2	15.5	11.9	15.5
What Would You Have Done?	B	Fri	9:30						4.9	2.9	3.4	3.8	3.2	3.6
What's My Name?	N	Fri	9:30			13.8	11.9	12.1	12.7	8.9	9.8	9.1	7.8	10.8
World Today News	C	MWF	6:45								8.4	5.7	6.2	6.8
Your Hit Parade	C	Sat	9:00		10.8	14.3	13.7	14.1	16.3	15.8	14.6	14.4	11.7	13.6
Youth Vs Age	N	Sat	9:00						8.2	6.2	5.0			6.5

Special Broadcasts

Program	Net	Date	Jan. 40	Feb. 40
Pres Roosevelt Address	BCM	1/8	27.5	
Boxing: Joe Louis/Arturo Godoy	B	2/9		39.1

1940-41 Hooper Ratings 6-11 P.M.

Program	Net	Day	Time	Sept. 40	Oct. 40	Nov. 40	Dec. 40	Jan. 41	Feb. 41	March 41	April 41	May 41	June 41	1940-41 Avg
Adventures of Bulldog Drummond	M	Sun	6:30								6.4			6.4
Adventures of Ellery Queen	C	Sun	7:30	8.6	8.2	9.1								8.6
Adventures of Sherlock Holmes	B	Sun	8:30				10.1	10.2	12.8	10.8				10.2
Al Pearce Gang	C	Fri	7:30	8.7	10.6	12.2	14.1	13.8	12.4	13.2	12.8	11.8		12.2
Alec Templeton Show	N	Fri	7:30	6.3	7.7	6.5	9.1	7.1	9.1	6.9	6.3			7.4
Aldrich Family	N	Thu	8:30	16.0	21.8	17.2	23.1	26.3	23.9	27.6	24.4	21.1	19.3	22.1
Amazing Mr Smith	M	Mon	8:00								3.0	3.0	3.2	3.1
American Album of Familiar Music	N	Sun	9:30	7.8	8.4	11.1	12.8	11.4	11.4	11.7	9.2	8.2	8.0	10.0
Amos & Andy	C	M-F	7:00	8.2	9.4	12.1	11.8	11.9	14.4	12.4	12.5	7.7	7.7	10.8
Arthur Hale News/Comment	M	T;T	7:30		8.3		7.2	7.4	6.0	7.0	8.2	4.7	4.5	6.9
Ask It Basket	C	Thu	8:00		6.8	9.2	8.5	8.2	9.3	7.3	7.3			8.0
Avalon Showboat	N	Mon	9:30	9.0	7.5	7.3	9.3	7.9	7.5		7.2			7.9
Battle of the Sexes	N	Tue	9:00	7.6	10.2	7.7	12.2	11.2	12.1	8.6	9.8	7.8	8.7	10.3
Beat the Band	N	Sun	6:30	9.1	9.9	10.9	8.1	10.5	9.5	11.2				9.2
Ben Bernie Show	B	Tue	8:00	7.7	10.3	9.9	9.3	10.2	9.9	8.3	8.0	5.8	3.3	8.2
Big Town	C	Wed	8:00		14.8	16.2	15.3	18.3	18.4	16.9	19.2	12.5	12.0	16.0

1940-41 Hooper Ratings 6-11 P.M.	Net	Day	Time	Sept. 40	Oct. 40	Nov. 40	Dec. 40	Jan. 41	Feb. 41	March 41	April 41	May 41	June 41	1940-41 Avg
Bill Stern Colgate Sports Newsreel	B	Sun	9:45	5.6	4.8	4.2		5.2	8.2	6.5	6.5	6.1	4.8	5.8
Bing Crosby's Kraft Music Hall	N	Thu	9:00		14.8	12.2	17.6	18.6	16.7	18.3	14.9	13.9	13.1	15.6
Blondie	C	Mon	7:30	8.9	10.3	10.5	12.4	12.7	12.2	13.1	15.0	12.7	9.8	11.8
Boake Carter News/Comment	M	MW/Sa	8:30		8.8		6.1	6.0			7.1	5.5		6.7
Bob Crosby Show	N	Thu	7:30	6.4	5.9	5.4	7.1	7.3						6.4
Bob Hope Show	N	Tue	10:00	11.9	22.9	25.0	26.4	28.2	29.6	29.4	27.3	25.5	25.3	26.6
Burns & Allen Show	N	Mon	7:30		10.2	11.3	13.5	14.9	14.1	13.6	14.9	11.9	7.2	12.8
Campbell Playhouse	C	Fri	9:30	6.1		7.5	11.3	15.7	14.2	14.4	5.2	3.3	5.2	12.8
Carnation Contented Hour	N	Mon	10:00		6.9	9.0	7.5	6.8	6.9	7.9	5.9	5.2	6.2	6.3
Cavalcade of America	N	Wed	7:30		6.7		7.7	7.9	5.3	7.1				6.8
Chamber Music Soc Low Basin St	B	Mon	9:30							2.0				2.0
Cities Service Concert	N	Fri	8:00	5.7	4.8	6.8	5.3	7.6	8.6	7.7	7.9	5.3	5.1	6.5
City Desk	C	Thu	8:30					6.6	9.0	6.7	7.5	4.8	5.3	6.7
Court of Missing Heirs	C	Tue	8:00	8.6	8.7	10.1	11.7	10.8	13.3	12.5	11.0	9.3	8.3	10.4
Crime Doctor	C	Sun	8:30	6.8	7.5	6.2	7.7	9.3	10.3	8.6	9.7	9.6	5.6	8.1
Danger Is My Business	M	Wed	10:15										2.5	2.5
Death Valley Days	B	Fri	8:30	6.8	7.5	7.3	8.0	10.1	9.3	8.1	9.2	5.4	4.2	7.6
Dr Christian	C	Wed	8:30	10.2	12.9	12.2	14.9	15.2	15.9	16.7	13.7	10.6	10.7	13.3
Dr IQ	N	Mon	9:00	10.7	10.2	10.7	12.8	11.2	11.4	12.8	11.1	8.4	7.4	10.7
Dr IQ Junior	N	Sun	6:30										4.0	4.0
Dorothy Thompson News/Commnt	M	Sun	8:45					4.4	5.8	5.5	5.7	6.7	4.2	5.2
Double or Nothing	M	Sun	6:00		5.9	5.2	7.7	7.9	7.2	7.5	6.6	7.1	6.0	6.4
Duffy's Tavern	C	Sat	8:30							6.2	4.8	4.2	4.5	6.5
Easy Aces	B	TWT	7:00	6.2	6.1	6.9	7.8	8.0	6.9	7.2				6.3
Eddie Cantor Time to Smile	N	Wed	9:00	11.9	16.6	13.4	13.9	14.7	17.6	16.0	17.6	14.4	13.5	15.0
Edgar Bergen & Charlie McCarthy	N	Sun	8:00	21.0	28.8	31.9	30.4	32.2	32.8	28.5	25.7	21.7	20.3	27.3
Everyman's Theater	N	Fri	9:30		5.2	9.6	8.5	8.0	9.9	7.6	4.2			8.1
Fame & Fortune	B	Thu	8:30			6.2		5.6	5.0	5.9				5.4
Famous Jury Trials	B	Mon	10:00				6.0	8.1	9.3	7.1	6.3	6.6	5.0	6.9
Fanny Brice & Frank Morgan	N	Thu	8:00	15.4	15.0	15.5	18.5	23.4	19.4	20.8	21.2	15.0	15.6	18.0
Fibber McGee & Molly	N	Tue	9:30		25.9	25.2	29.5	27.4	29.2	33.3	33.8	21.0	22.9	27.6
First Nighter	C	Tue	8:30	8.4	12.2	13.4	14.0	13.8	15.4	16.2	14.2	11.6	8.6	12.8
Fitch Bandwagon	N	Sun	7:30	8.4	15.9	16.8	17.7	17.8	16.8	14.7	13.8	10.6	11.4	14.4
Ford Sunday Evening Hour	C	Sun	9:00	6.8	10.2	9.7	10.1	10.1	10.2	10.4	10.9	8.2	6.5	9.3
Fred Allen Texaco Star Theater	C	Wed	9:00	8.3	13.8	15.0	15.4	16.1	15.3	14.8	12.6	12.8	10.8	13.5
Fred Waring Show	N	M-F	7:00	10.0	9.7	9.5	10.0	9.7	9.5	9.8	9.4	7.5	7.3	9.2
Fulton Lewis Jr News/Comment	M	M-F	7:00		2.6	2.5	2.8	3.8	4.2	4.2	3.9	3.3	3.2	3.4
Gabriel Heatter News/Comment	M	MWF	9:00		4.4	9.2	8.0	10.1	7.3	9.2	7.1	6.2	4.9	7.4
Gangbusters	B	Fri	9:00		9.2	9.3	13.7	12.2	14.0	12.7	13.2			12.0
Gay Nineties Revue	C	Mon	8:30							15.4	13.8	10.3	11.2	12.7
Glenn Miller Orch	C	TWT	10:00	7.8	6.9	8.0	6.8	6.8	6.7	5.7	5.3	6.7	6.0	6.7
Goodwill Hour John J Anthony	B	Sun	10:00	6.8	8.4	5.9	9.2	8.7	9.5	7.2	10.2	7.7	6.9	8.1
Grand Central Station	B	Tue	9:00	11.9	11.4	8.8	8.7	8.4	10.0	10.8	8.7	7.5	7.4	9.4
Great Moments Great Plays	C	Fri	9:00								7.7	8.6	6.6	7.6
Guy Lombardo Orch	C	Mon	10:00	9.2	11.6	14.7	15.8	15.5	13.6	14.8	13.7	14.9	12.3	13.6
HV Kaltenborn News/Comment	N	TTSa	7:45	10.3	11.8	13.6	11.8	16.2	13.0	11.8	11.0	8.4	8.1	11.6
Hedda Hopper Hollywood News	C	MWF	6:15	6.6	6.3	6.7	6.4	7.7	7.4	5.5	6.2	5.1	4.9	6.3
Helen Hayes Theater	C	Sun	8:00		11.8	11.0	12.1	14.4	12.8	14.3	13.7	9.4	8.9	12.0

1940-41 Hooper Ratings 6-11 P.M.

Program		Day	Time	Sept. 40	Oct. 40	Nov. 40	Dec. 40	Jan. 41	Feb. 41	March 41	April 41	May 41	June 41	1940-41 Avg
Hollywood Playhouse	N	Wed	8:00	9.9	9.7	8.3	9.7	10.3			8.3	9.0	7.1	9.4
Hollywood Premiere	C	Fri	10:00		8.6	9.3	8.2	6.1	7.9	8.4	7.9	6.4	8.0	8.1
Hour of Charm	N	Sun	10:00	8.2				10.0	6.3	5.2	4.9	4.2	5.5	8.3
How Did You Meet?	B	Wed	8:15		7.9	7.8	7.7	3.9			9.3	7.7	5.9	6.4
I Love a Mystery	M	Mon	8:00	7.9		5.3	5.7		10.9	11.1	4.9			8.7
I Want a Divorce	M	Fri	9:30						6.8	7.4				5.7
Imperial Time	M	Mon	10:15										3.4	3.4
Information Please	N	Fri	8:30	12.0	15.9		12.0	15.0	14.9	13.2	12.5	11.2	9.7	12.9
Inner Sanctum	B	Sun	8:30			4.3	2.7	2.4	3.2	2.8	5.8	4.6	5.1	4.0
Inside of Sports	M	TTSa	7:45					3.6	2.8	3.7	3.4	3.0	2.7	3.3
Irene Rich Dramas	B	Sun	9:30	5.8	8.6	9.8	10.4	11.4	11.8	13.1	10.7	9.1	8.4	9.9
Jack Benny Program	N	Sun	7:00		27.1	32.9	32.9	36.2	37.2	37.2	30.5	21.1	22.5	30.8
Johnny Presents	N	Tue	8:00		10.1	11.2	11.3	9.8	9.6	9.7	9.9	6.9	6.4	9.4
Kate Smith Hour	C	Fri	8:00		15.2	17.7	18.5	18.1	19.3	17.8	16.7	12.1	9.6	16.1
Kay Kyser Kollege Mus Knowledge	N	Wed	10:00	14.8	15.5	14.2	19.6	18.8	19.0	20.3	14.6	14.6	14.7	16.6
Knickerbocker Playhouse	N	Sat	8:00		8.1	9.0	11.7	13.3	11.5	10.0	10.9	7.3		10.2
Lanny Ross Show	C	M-F	7:15	8.7	9.9	10.1	11.5	12.3	13.0	11.8	10.5	8.6	7.1	10.4
The Lone Ranger	M	MWF	7:30									5.3	4.8	5.1
Lowell Thomas News	B	M-F	6:45	14.6	15.0	16.8	14.9	16.0	16.3	14.0	12.8	12.1	9.9	14.2
Lux Radio Theater	C	Mon	9:00	17.2	23.2	24.3	26.1	26.8	27.1	26.2	23.4	20.5	19.3	23.4
Major Bowes Amateur Hour	C	Thu	9:00	18.2	19.4	19.1	20.3	19.8	21.3	19.8	17.3	14.4	12.6	18.2
Manhattan at Midnight	B	Wed	8:30	4.4	4.5	3.7	5.6	7.5	6.9	6.6	6.8	5.7	5.7	5.7
Manhattan Merry Go Round	N	Sun	9:00	7.0	6.6	8.4	8.5	9.6	8.1	8.3	7.6	7.5	6.5	7.8
Marriage Club	C	Sat	8:00	5.0	7.5	8.8	7.4	9.1	8.9	9.0	7.7	6.1	6.0	7.6
Meet Mr Meek	C	Wed	7:30	6.3	9.0	7.2	11.3	10.0	13.2	10.5	12.4	7.7	7.2	9.5
Gene Autry's Melody Ranch	C	Sun	6:30	5.3	8.7	12.8	12.0	12.9	14.7	8.3	9.2	5.7	5.0	9.5
Mr District Attorney	N	Wed	9:30	14.9	12.7	14.0	12.8	14.1	15.0	19.1	16.2	14.1	14.0	14.7
Mr Keen	B	TWT	7:15	5.1	6.4	7.2	6.2	7.4	7.7	6.2	7.1	4.8	3.7	6.2
Musical Americana	B	Tue	9:00	5.4				11.2						5.4
National Barn Dance	N	Sat	9:00	8.1	11.0	10.4			11.8	10.1	9.9	7.7	5.2	9.7
News for the Americas	N	Sun	7:30							2.4	5.5	2.6		3.5
Newsroom of the Air	B	M-F	7:15					7.0			6.3	4.3	4.8	5.6
One Man's Family	N	Sun	8:30	15.4	19.5	20.1	20.1	17.6	16.7	17.0	17.3	13.6	11.5	16.9
Parker Family	B	Sun	9:15	7.1	12.3	13.3	14.4	12.7	16.0	16.2	13.1	12.0	12.5	13.0
Paul Sullivan News/Comment	C	M-F	6:30	8.1	8.4	9.2	8.6	7.7	9.8	7.0	8.1	7.2	5.9	8.0
Pipe Smoking Time	C	Mon	8:30	8.7	12.6	12.7	10.2	9.3	9.7					10.5
Plantation Party	N	Wed	8:30	9.1	9.0	9.2	10.7	9.6	8.1	8.3	8.2	6.6	5.5	8.4
Play Broadcast	M	Mon	8:00		5.5	6.0	6.0	4.9	4.9	5.3	2.7	1.9		4.7
Pot O Gold	B	Thu	8:00	11.2	9.4	14.3	11.9	10.2	11.0	8.9	8.0	6.4	5.8	9.7
Professor Quiz	C	Thu	10:15	13.7	7.6	8.6	8.8	7.1	8.5	7.2	6.4	7.2	7.7	8.3
Quiz Kids	B	Wed	8:00	5.1	7.8	9.1	8.5	9.5	10.0	11.5	9.8	8.7	6.8	8.7
Raymond Gram Swing News/Com	M	M-F	10:00	8.1	7.2	6.6	7.9	6.4	7.4	7.7	7.3	5.0	7.6	7.1
Renfro Valley Folks	N	Mon	9:30		7.5	7.5	7.4	6.5	7.4	7.2	7.5			7.3
Robert Ripley Show	N	Fri	10:00		10.7	8.3	10.7							9.9
Rudy Vallee Varieties	N	Thu	10:00	9.9	13.5	12.4	17.8	17.2	16.6	16.0	13.8	12.8	13.8	14.4
Russ Morgan Orch	C	Fri	9:00	10.1	10.1	10.2	9.9	8.7	9.2	9.1			9.5	9.5
Saturday Night Serenade	C	Sat	9:45	9.5	6.0	9.5	8.6	10.3	7.7	10.2	8.4	7.2	5.9	8.2
Screen Guild Theater	C	Sun	7:30	8.4	12.5	14.1	13.1	16.2	19.8	15.3	16.3			15.3

1940-41 Hooper Ratings 6-11 P.M.

Program	Net	Day	Time	Sept. 40	Oct. 40	Nov. 40	Dec. 40	Jan. 41	Feb. 41	March 41	April 41	May 41	June 41	1940-41 Avg
Second Husband Helen Menken	C	Tue	7:30	5.7	9.7	10.7	9.7	10.3	12.0	12.1	10.3	4.8	5.7	9.1
Show of the Week	M	Sun	6:30			5.1	4.8	5.2	4.7	6.1				5.2
Silver Theater	C	Sun	6:00		10.6	12.7	12.3	14.0	12.9	9.3	11.9	4.7	3.4	10.2
Speak Up America	B	Sun	7:30			3.3	3.3							3.3
Spin & Win	B	Wed	9:30							2.9				2.9
Spotlight	C	Thu	8:00									4.0	3.5	3.8
Star Spangled Theater	B	Sun	8:00							1.8				1.8
Strange as It Seems	C	Thu	8:30	7.2	8.7	7.9	7.5							7.8
Take It or Leave It	C	Sun	10:00		11.9	10.8	14.6	11.7	14.9	15.1	14.0	11.3	11.7	12.9
Telephone Hour	N	Mon	8:00	7.4	7.3	9.8	10.5	9.7	8.5	9.5	9.0	6.9	6.4	8.5
Those We Love	C	Mon	8:00		9.7	12.4	12.0	10.8	13.0	12.7	14.6	9.9	9.7	11.6
Tony Martin Show	N	Wed	8:00					7.0	6.6	5.8	5.9	6.4	5.8	6.3
True or False	B	Mon	8:30	5.8	8.2	9.1	10.3	11.1	13.3	12.1	8.7	7.1	6.7	9.2
Truth or Consequences	N	Sat	8:30	9.8	12.3	12.7	15.0	18.4	15.7	17.7	14.8	10.9	8.8	13.6
Tums Treasure Chest	N	Tue	8:30	9.3	10.3	11.7	11.6	11.5	9.7	10.4	9.4	7.3	5.9	9.7
Uncle Ezra's Radio Station	N	Sat	10:00	9.0	8.7	9.8	9.8	12.2	8.7	12.5	10.2	8.5	7.2	9.7
Uncle Jim's Question Bee	B	Tue	8:30	8.4	6.9	7.4	7.3	7.1	8.9	7.9	6.2	5.4	4.9	7.0
Uncle Walter's Doghouse	N	Fri	9:30									7.7	6.3	7.0
Voice of Firestone	N	Mon	8:30	8.4	7.3	10.5	14.2	10.3	9.4	8.8	9.9	7.2	6.8	9.3
Voice of Liberty	M	Th,Sa	9:00			6.5	7.6	7.3	6.3	8.6				7.3
Vox Pop	C	Thu	7:30	8.0	9.7	12.2	14.3	11.9	15.2	13.5	13.1	7.7	7.3	11.3
Wake Up America	M	Mon	9:15							4.2	2.1	2.0		2.7
Walter Winchell Jergens Journal	B	Sun	9:00	17.3	25.5	22.4	23.9	24.8	26.9	23.9	27.8	22.8	25.3	24.1
Waltz Time	N	Fri	9:00	8.9	6.6	9.0	9.4	10.6	10.7	10.0	8.1	7.4	7.0	8.8
Wayne King Orch	C	Sat	7:30		9.0	10.4	9.8	11.0		9.4	7.5	6.5	4.0	8.5
We the People	N	Tue	9:00	11.8	17.0	15.6	17.7	15.8	16.9	17.1	15.4	13.0	12.4	15.3
What's Your Idea?	C	Sun	6:30							6.9	4.2	4.0		5.0
Who Knows?	M	Mon	10:15							3.8	3.2	2.5		3.2
Wings of Destiny	N	Fri	10:00		5.3	7.2	7.4	10.5	11.4		5.1	7.3		8.0
World News Tonight	C	Sun	7:30	5.5	5.1	5.3	4.1	4.2	3.8	4.1		4.6	6.4	5.2
Wythe Williams News/Comment	M	T,T	8:00								6.2	5.3	5.7	5.0
Xavier Cugat Orch	N	Thu	7:30						6.5	7.3	6.2	5.3	6.2	6.3
Your Happy Birthday	B	Fri	9:30					5.6	5.2	3.6	6.9	4.1	3.8	4.9
Your Hit Parade	C	Sat	9:00	12.1	11.3	15.5	13.6	15.9	13.0	13.1	13.2	11.3	9.0	13.0

Special Broadcasts

Program	Net	Date	Rating
Boxing: Max Baer/Lou Nova	B	4/4	19.0 (April 41)
Kentucky Derby	C	5/3	11.1 (May 41)

1941-42 Hooper Ratings 6-11 P.M.

Program	Net	Day	Time	Sept. 41	Oct. 41	Nov. 41	Dec. 41	Jan. 42	Feb. 42	March 42	April 42	May 42	June 42	1941-42 Avg
Abie's Irish Rose	N	Sat	8:00						11.7	14.1	13.8	13.6	11.7	13.0
Adventures of Bulldog Drummond	M	Sun	6:30						9.5	8.3				8.9
Adventures of Ellery Queen	N	Sat	7:30						10.9	9.7	13.3	12.0	6.5	10.5
Adventures of Sherlock Holmes	N	Sun	10:30			10.1	13.5	14.6	15.0	17.5				14.1
Adventures of the Thin Man	N	Wed	8:00	5.9	9.6	10.2	7.7	12.0	13.1	11.3	9.4	11.5	10.1	10.1
Al Pearce Gang	N	Thu	7:30		11.3	11.5	11.2	18.5	16.8	16.6	14.5	12.2	9.9	13.6
Aldrich Family	N	Thu	8:30	16.3	25.6	28.2	27.8	30.9	33.6	31.0	25.8	25.8	21.4	26.6

1941-42 Hooper Ratings 6-11 P.M.	Net	Time	Day	Sept. 41	Oct. 41	Nov. 41	Dec. 41	Jan. 42	Feb. 42	March 42	April 42	May 42	June 42	1941-42 Avg
American Album of Familiar Music	N	9:30	Sun	8.0	9.5	11.4	13.8	11.6	11.7	11.4		8.5	7.0	10.0
American Melody Hour	B	9:00	Wed			1.9	1.4	2.4	2.5	2.6	3.3	5.5	4.8	3.1
Amos & Andy	C	7:00	MWF	6.5	8.9	10.4	10.2	11.5	11.5	10.4	9.4	8.4	8.6	9.6
Are You a Missing Heir?	C	8:00	Tue	7.0	10.4	9.8	10.5	11.9	12.5	10.7	9.0	7.6	7.3	9.7
Arthur Hale News/Comment	M	7:30	T,T,Sa					7.9	7.4	7.8	5.5	5.6	3.9	6.4
Auction Quiz	B	8:00	Fri					2.9						2.9
Battle of the Sexes	N	9:00	Tue	8.2	9.6	12.2	12.3	11.8	15.2	13.4	13.2	12.0	9.4	11.7
Big Town	C	9:30	Thu			14.3	17.7	17.0	17.2	14.7	13.2	13.5	11.1	14.8
Bill Stern Colgate Sports Newsreel	N	10:00	Sat	4.8	6.8	7.6	7.1	10.1	11.1	7.4	7.4	8.8	5.9	7.7
Bing Crosby's Kraft Music Hall	N	9:00	Thu	11.5	13.4	17.3	16.6	21.1	21.0	19.7	19.0	18.3	15.6	17.4
Birth of the Blues	M	9:00	Sat			4.9								4.9
Blondie	C	7:30	Mon	8.7	12.1	13.3	14.1	15.0	15.3	14.5	12.0	12.0	12.0	12.9
Bob Burns Show	C	8:30	Tue		12.6	15.0	12.9	16.2	18.0	14.5	12.0	10.7		14.0
Bob Hope Show	N	10:00	Tue		25.4	27.7	28.8	31.7	34.5	35.2	30.9	32.9	29.5	30.7
Burns & Allen Show	N	7:30	Tue		15.3	16.2	14.1	19.3	18.3	17.4	14.8	13.4	11.9	15.6
Cal Tinney News/Comment	M	8:00	MWF	2.7	3.0	2.6	3.7	6.0	5.4	6.0	4.9	5.0	4.2	4.4
Captain Flagg & Sgt Quirt	N	10:00	Fri		3.5	4.3	7.6	7.1		12.3	11.7			7.8
Carnation Contented Hour	N	10:00	Mon	4.6	6.3	4.9	5.8							5.4
Cavalcade of America	N	7:30	Mon	5.2	6.1	8.2	10.1	11.9	11.7	10.8	9.6	7.4	6.6	8.8
Cities Service Concert	N	8:00	Fri	5.3	7.4		6.0	8.1	4.7	6.1	6.6	6.0	5.2	6.2
Crime Doctor	C	8:30	Sun	5.0	7.1	9.1	14.6	10.8	10.2	10.3	9.2	7.8	7.3	9.1
Danger Is My Business	M	9:15	Wed		1.9	2.3								2.1
Death Valley Days	C	8:00	Thu	5.2	8.2	7.6	7.3	6.7	7.5	6.9	5.9	5.8	4.4	6.6
Dinah Shore Sings	B	9:45	Sun			7.5	7.2	8.9	5.8	8.4	2.7	3.0	4.1	6.0
Dr Christian	C	8:30	Wed	7.7	12.0	15.1	14.0	14.7	15.2	14.3	10.9	10.0	7.6	12.2
Dr IQ	N	8:00	Mon	6.5	8.8	8.5	11.6	11.0	10.2	8.9	9.5	8.7	8.7	9.2
Dorothy Thompson News	B	8:45	Thu								2.8	2.7		2.8
Double or Nothing	M	6:00	Sun	6.3	6.2	5.6	8.3	7.2	7.8	6.3	4.1	6.2	4.7	6.3
Drew Pearson & Robt Allen News	B	6:30	Sun				6.5	8.6	5.7	4.7	5.1	4.2	5.5	5.8
Duffy's Tavern	C	9:00	Tue			6.0	6.1	6.7	6.4	7.5	10.8	10.1	9.7	7.8
Easy Aces	B	7:00	TWT	4.3	4.6	6.5	5.9	7.5	7.2	5.9	5.0	4.9	3.8	5.6
Eddie Cantor Time to Smile	N	9:00	Wed	14.6	17.0	19.3	18.3	22.2	22.6	19.6	16.8	20.0	16.3	18.7
Edgar Bergen & Charlie McCarthy	N	8:00	Sun	19.4	28.3	30.1	29.9	35.2	35.8	31.0	24.5	24.8	20.6	28.0
Edward R Murrow in London	C	6:00	Sun								4.9	4.9	7.0	6.0
Eleanor Roosevelt	B	6:45	Sun	3.4		4.0	9.2	7.8	4.4	4.2	2.2			5.0
Elsa Maxwell Party Line	B	10:00	Fri					5.6	6.1	6.0	3.3	3.5	3.1	4.6
Famous Jury Trials	B	9:00	Tue	5.8	5.8	4.9	7.4	5.9	7.7		7.7	6.2	5.7	6.5
Fanny Brice & Frank Morgan	N	8:00	Thu	13.9	25.2	23.3	23.7	28.9	27.4	26.8	21.9	23.1		23.8
Fibber McGee & Molly	N	9:30	Tue		27.7	29.0	28.7	33.3	38.0	38.1	32.3	30.9	26.9	31.7
First Line of Defense	C	10:15	Thu					5.5	3.9	5.2	4.2	5.1	4.4	4.7
First Nighter	N	9:30	Fri	8.4	9.5	12.1	14.9	17.5	14.9	14.5	12.9	11.4		12.9
Fitch Bandwagon	N	7:30	Sun	8.3	14.4	16.6	18.8	19.8	18.9	19.0	12.5	16.2	12.5	15.7
Ford Sunday Evening Hour	C	9:00	Sun	5.8	8.5	8.2	13.0	9.9	8.5	8.6				8.9
Frank Fay Show	N	10:30	Thu			9.6	10.7	16.2	15.1	14.9				13.3
Frank Parker Sings	C	6:30	MWF				4.9	8.1	5.5	6.1	3.6	5.2		5.6
Frazier Hunt News/Comment	C	6:00	TTSa							5.5	5.5	6.0	5.0	5.5
Fred Allen Texaco Star Theater	C	9:00	Sun		12.1	12.0	14.5	14.4	13.7		16.5	16.5	13.8	14.2
Fred Waring Show	N	7:00	M-F	5.6	9.3	9.2	9.6	12.6	11.4	9.9	8.2	8.1	8.9	9.3

1941–42 Hooper Ratings 6–11 P.M.				Sept. 41	Oct. 41	Nov. 41	Dec. 41	Jan. 42	Feb. 42	March 42	April 42	May 42	June 42	1941–42 Avg
Friday Night Boxing	B	Fri	10:00							6.4	4.7	4.4	4.7	6.4
Fulton Lewis Jr News/Comment	M	M-F	7:00	2.9	3.4	2.7	3.8	6.1	4.4	5.2				4.2
Gabriel Heatter News/Comment	M	M-F	9:00		7.6	6.6	7.8	11.3	10.2	12.2	8.2	5.9	9.2	8.8
Gabriel Heatter News/Comment	M	Sun	8:45					9.7	10.3		8.4	4.0	6.7	8.2
Gangbusters	B	Fri	9:00		10.1	9.9	9.9	10.0	11.8	11.6	10.0	10.1		10.6
Gay Nineties Revue	C	Mon	8:30	10.0	13.2	13.2	13.0	18.1	18.2	17.3	12.5	5.5		13.5
Gene Autry's Melody Ranch	C	Sun	6:30	4.2	6.6	7.8	10.2	10.6	9.9	9.2	5.5	7.1	11.2	7.5
Glenn Miller Orch	C	WThF	10:00	5.8	5.4	6.0	6.5	7.6	6.2	7.8	6.6	8.1	5.7	6.6
Golden Treasury of Song	C	MWF	6:30		4.2	5.4					6.6		6.9	4.8
Good Will Hour John J Anthony	B	Sun	10:00	5.9	6.3	8.9	8.6	9.5	8.4	9.2		8.3		7.8
Grand Central Station	N	Fri	7:30	7.4	10.7	8.0	8.1	13.1	11.2	12.1	9.8	11.8	6.1	9.9
Grand Ole Opry	N	Sat	10:30	9.6	7.4	8.6	9.5	11.2	12.6	8.7	8.9	9.6	10.6	10.0
Great Gildersleeve	N	Sun	6:30	5.2	13.1	9.0	11.4	12.7	14.7	11.7	11.9		8.6	10.3
Great Moments of Great Plays	C	Fri	9:00	6.5									9.2	9.8
Great Moments in Music	C	Wed	10:15					5.0	4.8	4.3	2.7	3.5		4.1
Guy Lombardo Orch	C	Sat	8:00	6.5	8.8	9.7	10.5	8.8	10.5	7.0	8.2	6.9	6.8	8.4
HV Kaltenborn News/Comment	N	TTSa	7:45		15.7	14.6	12.2	17.5	23.1	16.0	11.6	13.5	12.9	15.2
Hedda Hopper Hollywood News	C	MWF	6:15		5.2	6.2	6.2	6.2	6.9	5.7	4.9	5.4	5.5	5.8
Helen Hayes Theater	C	Sun	8:00		9.4	9.9		12.6	11.5		9.7	8.8		10.9
Hillman & Clapper News/Comment	B	Thu	9:00		2.0	3.9	0.9							2.3
Hobby Lobby	C	Sat	8:30		7.3	7.9	9.2	11.7	13.1	10.2	7.8	6.8	7.2	9.5
Hollywood Premiere	C	Fri	10:00	8.6	10.7	14.3	12.9	10.8	9.9					11.2
Hour of Charm	N	Sun	10:00	3.5	7.3	8.3	11.2	11.5	10.9	10.2	8.9	8.2	6.5	8.4
How Am I Doin'?	C	Fri	7:30					12.9	11.6	9.3	9.3	8.0	8.8	9.2
I Love a Mystery	B	Mon	8:00		8.5	10.3		12.1	13.8	10.3	11.4	11.3	7.5	9.8
Information Please	N	Fri	8:30	10.9	12.8	13.9	12.6		11.7	11.9	9.1	9.5	10.8	12.2
Inner Sanctum	B	Sun	8:30	6.3	7.2	8.1	7.9			8.9			8.0	8.9
Inside of Sports	M	TTSa	7:45	2.0	2.4	2.5	2.4	3.2	2.6	3.0	2.9	2.3	2.7	2.6
Irene Rich Dramas	B	Sun	9:30	7.8	8.5	10.1	9.1	12.2	8.0	9.9	5.6	5.2	5.5	8.2
Jack Benny Show	N	Sun	7:00		20.5	27.6	27.1	31.0	35.5	26.6	22.4	26.5		27.2
Jimmie Fidler Hollywood News	B	Mon	7:00							5.4	4.2	2.5	4.3	4.1
John B Hughes News/Comment	M	Tu,W	10:00								2.7	4.6	5.8	4.4
Johnny Presents	N	Tue	8:00	5.6	10.3	10.2	10.1	13.4	12.1	12.0	10.8	8.6	9.5	10.3
Junior Miss	C	Wed	9:00							13.6	7.3	7.2	7.3	8.9
Kate Smith Hour	C	Fri	8:00		14.3	16.8	15.8	19.3	18.8	16.9	14.9	13.4	10.9	15.7
Kay Kyser Kollege Mus Knowledge	N	Wed	10:00	12.6	14.9	17.3	18.3	22.3	22.6	21.0	17.5	19.6	17.6	18.4
Knickerbocker Playhouse	N	Sat	8:00	5.0	8.8	10.1	8.1	10.6	11.9		7.7	3.3		8.0
Lanny Ross Show	C	M-F	7:15	6.7	9.0	10.5	11.6	9.4	9.4	9.5	6.9			9.7
Lone Ranger	M	MWF	7:30	5.4	6.4	7.0	7.7			9.2			4.1	6.9
Lowell Thomas News	B	M-F	6:45		12.9	14.3	15.9	20.1	18.9	16.8	12.3	14.1	14.9	15.6
Lum & Abner	B	M-F	6:30		5.8	6.4	6.1	5.9	5.6	5.7	5.4	5.4	5.5	5.8
Lux Radio Theater	C	Mon	9:00	17.1	22.3	26.4	27.1	30.8	30.6	27.7	24.0	23.3	21.8	25.1
Major Bowes Amateur Hour	C	Thu	9:00	10.3	15.8	17.4	18.9	20.7	17.8	15.2	13.2	14.1	9.9	15.3
Manhattan at Midnight	B	Wed	8:30	4.0	4.9	6.1	7.3	8.6	7.7	7.5	4.6	7.5	5.0	6.3
Manhattan Merry Go Round	N	Sun	9:00	5.8	8.8	10.1	9.2	8.7	11.5	9.7	7.4	8.4	5.7	8.5
March of Time	B	Fri	9:30		5.9	5.9	5.2	5.8	6.6	6.1	5.7	3.9		5.4
Maudie's Diary	C	Thu	7:30	4.7	5.8	6.6				7.6	6.5			6.5
Meet Mr Meek	C	Wed	8:00		6.6		6.9	13.5	9.3	12.3		7.7	6.5	12.5

1941-42 Hooper Ratings 6-11 P.M.

Program	Net	Day	Time	Sept. 41	Oct. 41	Nov. 41	Dec. 41	Jan. 42	Feb. 42	March 42	April 42	May 42	June 42	1941-42 Avg
Michael & Kitty	B	Fri	9:30	12.3	16.2	3.3	2.9	4.7	4.1	21.6	20.2	21.1	17.3	3.8
Mr District Attorney	N	Wed	9:30	3.9	5.2	18.3	16.7	19.7	20.9	5.4	3.9	4.7	4.1	18.4
Mr Keen	B	TWT	7:15			5.9		5.6	4.9	3.7	2.3			4.8
Monday Merry Go Round	B	Mon	10:00		9.7	3.1	2.9	3.6	4.5	3.7	2.3			3.4
National Barn Dance	N	Sat	9:00	6.3		10.1	10.8	11.2	11.1	10.0	9.1	9.4	7.0	9.5
Nelson Eddy Show	C	Wed	8:00									7.6	7.4	7.5
New Old Gold Show	B	Fri	8:00			6.0	4.6	5.8	5.2	5.0	4.5	7.2		5.2
News of the World/JW Vandercook	N	M-F	7:15	4.7	6.4	5.8	7.8	9.9	8.4	8.7	6.5	7.2	7.2	7.3
One Man's Family	N	Sun	8:30	11.6	16.8	16.8	18.4	20.0	21.9	17.6	14.5	15.8	11.7	16.5
Ontario Show	N	Fri	7:00								2.9	2.3	2.6	2.6
Orson Welles Dramas	C	Mon	10:00		11.0	18.0	17.8	20.2	16.8	13.8	10.1	8.5	7.6	16.8
Parker Family	B	Sun	9:15	10.8	10.7	16.5	17.5	16.4	15.9					12.8
Penthouse Party	B	Wed	9:30	4.1		2.4	1.5							2.7
People Are Funny	N	Fri	10:00			12.6	11.8	11.5	13.4	10.1	8.9	11.1	8.6	9.9
Philip Morris Playhouse	C	Fri	9:00	5.0	8.6	9.1	11.5	11.3	11.6	6.1	7.4	11.7	10.0	11.3
Plantation Party	N	Fri	9:30			7.5	5.5	5.5	7.6	6.7	7.4	8.8	7.1	8.7
Portraits in Music	N	Mon	10:00		8.7	8.3	8.2	9.0	10.7	8.4	8.3	5.7	6.7	6.6
Quiz Kids	B	Wed	8:00	7.0		6.7	6.2	7.6	10.3	9.5	5.6	6.2	6.9	8.2
Ransom Sherman Show	C	Wed	9:30	2.4	5.9	20.6	22.3	28.0	7.2	9.0	5.3	5.5	7.1	7.6
Raymond Gram Swing News/Comm	M	M,Th	10:00			15.3	17.5	19.6	30.7	32.5	31.7	7.0	6.5	6.4
Red Skelton Show	N	Tue	10:30	10.7	15.1	7.5	9.8	11.7	19.9	18.7	19.8	28.3		27.7
Rudy Vallee Show	N	Thu	10:00	5.4	6.9	15.1	13.5	14.2	10.2	9.8	7.9	17.0	15.4	16.9
Saturday Night Serenade	C	Sat	9:45		11.1	7.9	8.7	8.8	14.1	12.8	10.7	9.2	7.2	8.6
Screen Guild Theater	C	Sun	7:30	5.2	8.5	2.2	2.3	2.8	8.1	8.0	6.1			13.1
Second Husband/Helen Menken	C	Tue	7:30		2.7	10.6	12.5		2.1	1.6				7.7
Service with a Smile	B	Thu	8:30		9.7		14.7							2.3
The Shadow	M	Sun	5:30	4.4		10.3	15.2	15.1	12.9	12.2				10.9
Shirley Temple Time	C	Sun	10:00		8.5	3.9	5.7	4.9	4.5	3.0	3.0			14.7
Silver Theater	C	Sun	6:00				4.5	4.8	3.4	2.8	2.8	3.0		12.4
Spotlight Bands	M	Sat	9:30			14.7	18.5	15.1	17.3	14.9	15.3	15.6	15.0	4.0
Spotlight Bands	M	M-F	9:30	9.2	12.3	9.8	8.6	10.8	9.7	9.3	6.4	5.8	5.9	3.7
Take It or Leave It	C	Sun	10:00	6.0	8.7	5.1	7.0	5.9	7.2	6.8	8.3		9.9	14.8
Telephone Hour	N	Mon	8:00	5.0	4.5	3.5	5.0	5.0	4.1	4.5	4.4	3.4		8.1
That Brewster Boy	N	Mon	9:30		4.3				3.1	3.5	2.0	2.0	3.7	6.6
Three Ring Time	B	Tue	8:30	4.4	7.4	6.7	7.1							4.2
Treasure Hour of Song	M	Sat	8:00	4.4	12.1	8.3	9.1	10.0	9.6	9.4	9.5	7.1	5.9	2.9
Treasury Hour	B	Tue	8:00	7.3	9.6	12.8	14.7	14.6	16.2	16.2	13.8	15.6	10.8	6.1
True or False	B	Mon	8:30	5.9	3.1	9.2	11.8	12.2	11.5	11.5	9.3	8.5	10.1	8.1
Truth or Consequences	N	Sat	8:30		9.6	3.2								13.4
Tums Treasure Chest	N	Tue	8:30											10.0
Twenty Grand Club	M	Mon	9:15											3.2
Uncle Walter's Doghouse	N	Wed	8:30	7.7	7.8	9.6	7.3	10.1	9.9	11.9	9.9	9.5	8.1	9.2
Voice of Broadway/D Kilgallen	C	Tue	6:15		3.3	3.3	3.8	5.6	6.0	5.5	4.8	3.4	4.8	4.5
Voice of Firestone	N	Mon	8:30	7.1	6.8	7.6	9.1	9.9	10.4	9.1	6.6	7.0	7.6	8.1
Vox Pop	B	Mon	8:00	8.9	11.0	11.1	13.7	14.6	13.5	15.2	12.8	9.4	9.6	12.0
Walter Winchell Jergens Journal	B	Sun	9:00	18.3	21.4	28.6	29.9	33.1	33.1	29.7	23.7	22.0	20.0	26.0
Waltz Time	N	Fri	9:00	7.2	9.3	8.7	8.9	9.8	8.1	9.0	7.6	8.6	7.8	8.5
Wayne King Orch	C	Mon	10:00	4.2	7.7	9.4	8.5	10.1	9.4	14.4	10.6	12.3	11.5	9.8

1941–42 Hooper Ratings 6–11 P.M.

	Net	Day	Time	Sept. 41	Oct. 41	Nov. 41	Dec. 41	Jan. 42	Feb. 42	March 42	April 42	May 42	June 42	1941–42 Avg
We the People	C	Tue	9:00	8.5	11.5	12.7	15.7	17.7	17.8	14.1		7.3	6.8	12.5
What's My Name?	M	Tue	8:00					7.8	6.5	7.3	5.0	5.5	5.9	6.3
Wings of Destiny	N	Fri	10:00	5.6	6.7	7.6	7.7	12.7	10.5					8.5
The World Today News	C	M-F	6:45						7.3	5.5	5.1	5.0	5.1	5.6
Xavier Cugat Orch	B	Tue	8:00	5.7	9.7	9.7	11.5	3.9	4.7	4.1	3.6	4.1	2.7	6.0
Your Hit Parade	C	Sat	9:00	9.1	12.4	12.1	13.6	17.4	18.4	17.3	14.6	15.1	12.2	14.2

Special Broadcasts

	Net	Day	Sept. 41	Oct. 41	Nov. 41	Dec. 41	Jan. 42	Feb. 42
Pres Roosevelt War Declaration	All	12/8				79.0		
FDR 3 High Purposes Speech	All	2/23						78.1

1942–43 Hooper Ratings 6–11 P.M.

	Net	Day	Time	Sept. 42	Oct. 42	Nov. 42	Dec. 42	Jan. 43	Feb. 43	March 43	April 43	May 43	June 43	1942–43 Avg
Abbott & Costello Show	N	Thu	10:00		15.7	18.0	19.8	24.6	22.9	22.1	15.2	14.9	10.7	20.5
Abie's Irish Rose	N	Sat	8:00	11.6	13.5	15.4	15.9	17.1	17.3	17.6	13.2	11.6	9.4	14.9
Adventures of Ellery Queen	N	Sat	7:30		11.1	10.2	12.4	13.5	13.3	13.9		5.1	3.5	12.1
Adventures of Sherlock Holmes	M	Fri	8:30											4.3
Adventures of the Thin Man	C	Fri	8:00	13.3	15.9	16.4	17.8	18.5	15.8	15.7	15.1	13.4	8.9	15.1
Al Jolson Show	C	Tue	8:30	11.9	10.8	10.7	11.8	13.2	12.5	12.6	9.7	10.0	7.6	11.1
Aldrich Family	N	Thu	8:30	22.4	25.9	27.4	30.4	30.8	30.2	28.7	27.1	23.6	17.3	25.7
American Album of Familiar Music	N	Sun	9:30	9.2	11.1	10.2	10.9	12.4	10.8	10.4	10.2	9.4		10.5
American Melody Hour	C	Tue	7:30	5.9	6.5	8.6	7.8	7.4	12.5	7.8	7.5	6.1	3.4	9.1
Amos & Andy	C	M-F	7:00	8.1	7.7	9.0	9.5	10.0	10.2	10.3				9.5
Arthur Hale News/Comment	M	T,T,Sa	7:30	6.7	8.0	7.2	7.3	6.9	5.7	6.3	5.3	5.0	4.0	6.2
Battle of the Sexes	N	Tue	9:00	9.4	9.4	11.5	10.6	10.0	10.3	11.3	9.5	7.7	6.8	9.6
Better Half	M	Mon	8:30									4.1	2.8	3.5
Bill Stern Colgate Sports Newsreel	N	Sat	10:00	6.5	7.3	8.6	10.8	8.6			8.6	7.6	8.2	8.8
Bing Crosby's Kraft Music Hall	N	Thu	9:00	16.5	19.9	22.8	22.8	23.6	23.4	21.0	20.3	17.3	12.7	20.0
Blondie	C	Mon	7:30	7.9	12.1	14.0	14.4	16.0	15.8	14.5	14.9	13.7	11.0	13.4
Blue Ribbon Town/Groucho Marx	C	Sat	10:15								11.1	11.2	8.8	10.4
Bob Burns Show	N	Thu	7:30	10.9	10.3	9.1	12.0	18.4	18.0	18.7	15.9	13.3		13.8
Bob Hope Show	N	Tue	10:00	31.7	29.3	32.4	36.2	38.9	36.6	33.1	32.2	28.2	24.6	32.3
Burns & Allen Show	C	Tue	9:00	15.3	14.1	16.3	17.1	19.2	17.3	18.1	15.3	14.4	13.2	16.0
Cal Tinney News/Comment	M	MWF	8:00	4.2	5.0	5.9	5.3	6.2	5.7	6.3	5.6	5.4	4.0	5.4
Camel Caravan	C	Fri	10:00	7.8	8.6	9.0	11.3	11.3	12.3	13.0	11.5	10.5	11.2	10.7
Campana Serenade	N	Sat	10:15				7.4	7.9	9.1	8.0	7.7			8.1
Can You Top This?	N	Sat	9:30	7.7	9.0	11.0	13.2	13.1	13.0	14.9	12.2	13.8	10.1	11.8
Carnation Contented Hour	N	Mon	10:00	6.8	7.4	7.2	7.2	8.7	7.3	7.1	6.4	6.3		7.2
Carnival	C	Wed	10:30		4.3	3.4	4.0	4.4	4.9	3.1	4.6	4.7		4.3
Cavalcade of America	N	Mon	8:00	9.6	10.9	11.2	10.6	12.3	11.8	11.7	10.3	10.0	5.0	10.5
Ceiling Unlimited	C	Mon	7:15			5.4	6.7	8.1	9.1	5.6	5.3	5.2	6.9	6.2
Chamber Music Soc Lower Basin St	B	Sun	9:15								10.9	12.0	4.4	10.3
Cities Service Concert	N	Fri	8:00	7.1	7.3		7.1	7.5	7.1	6.6	6.0	5.4	8.0	6.5
Counterspy	B	Mon	9:00	5.5	4.8		6.6	8.1	7.0	7.4	7.3	7.1	4.6	6.6
Crime Doctor	C	Sun	8:30	8.6	8.8	9.6	9.9	10.7	10.5	10.4	9.9	8.4	5.8	9.2
Crummit & Sanderson *	C	Sat	8:00	4.4	5.3	6.7	7.9	7.4	6.8	8.2	6.9	5.0	5.6	5.8
Death Valley Days	C	Thu	8:30	5.3	5.6	6.8	6.9	5.8	7.3	6.7	5.8	5.4	4.6	6.0
Dinah Shore Sings	B	Fri	8:15		3.8	4.6	4.3	4.5	3.5	4.3	3.8		4.0	4.1

1942-43 Hooper Ratings 6-11 P.M.				Sept. 42	Oct. 42	Nov. 42	Dec. 42	Jan. 43	Feb. 43	March 43	April 43	May 43	June 43	1942-43 Avg
Dr Christian	C	Wed	8:30	9.7	11.7	12.2	13.1	14.3	14.7	14.4	11.2	11.1	8.0	12.0
Dr IQ	N	Mon	9:30	9.0	9.2	10.0	10.4	12.3	9.7	10.5	9.0	8.6	7.9	9.7
Don Winslow of the Navy	B	M-F	6:15		2.2	2.9	3.9							3.0
Dorothy Thompson News/Comment	B	Sun	9:45	6.8	4.5						5.4	5.5	3.9	5.2
Double or Nothing	M	Fri	9:30	4.5	4.6	6.3	6.1	7.9	5.8	6.6	5.6	5.2	5.1	5.8
Drew Pearson News/Comment	B	Sun	7:00	5.7	6.5		6.3	6.3	5.9	6.8	5.8	7.0	6.0	6.3
Duffy's Tavern	B	Tue	8:30	6.1	6.3	7.9	9.2	11.4	12.5	12.6	12.2	10.4	8.5	9.7
Earl Godwin News/Comment	B	Su-Sa	8:00	3.4	4.0	5.6		6.2	6.0	5.7	5.2	5.3	4.6	5.1
Easy Aces	C	WThF	7:30	3.3	4.3	6.7	7.2	8.5	8.2	6.9	5.9	5.1	4.4	6.1
Eddie Cantor Time to Smile	N	Wed	9:00	18.3	18.7	21.1	22.6	22.0	21.3	21.1	17.1	15.3	12.5	19.0
Edgar Bergen & Charlie McCarthy	N	Sun	8:00	24.8	28.9	30.4	36.3	34.5	31.7	30.5	28.5	25.0		30.1
Edward R Murrow News	C	Sun	6:00	4.0	6.1	9.0	7.9	8.1	9.2	8.0	4.9	7.0	6.3	7.1
Edwin C Hill News/Comment	C	Tue	6:15	3.4	3.9	6.1	7.1	5.6	5.9	5.4	6.2	4.7	4.6	5.3
Famous Jury Trials	B	Tue	9:00	5.7	6.7	9.6	10.1	9.4	11.1		10.4	8.5	6.1	8.6
Fanny Brice & Frank Morgan	N	Thu	8:00	19.4	23.6	25.2	27.5	26.1	26.5	25.6	22.8	20.7	14.7	23.2
Fibber McGee & Molly	N	Tue	9:30	28.8	28.4	30.4	33.1	35.7	34.5	33.5	30.7	27.1	24.8	30.7
First Line of Defense	C	Thu	10:00	4.5	4.5	4.2	5.3	7.7	4.8	6.8	6.5	4.7	4.5	5.4
First Nighter	M	Sun	6:00	8.4	8.0	9.4	10.8	10.9	9.3	10.8	8.3			9.5
Fitch Bandwagon	N	Sun	7:30	12.8	15.6	17.2	21.8	21.3	18.7	15.9	14.5	14.6	8.4	16.1
Frazier Hunt News/Comment	C	T,T,Sa	6:00	4.8	4.9	7.2	6.6	5.9	6.8	6.1	6.5	6.3		6.1
Fred Allen Texaco Star Theater	C	Sun	9:30	11.2	15.6	17.6	17.9	19.7	19.9	20.3	18.4	16.8	13.0	17.0
Fred Waring Show	N	M-F	7:00	8.1	9.8	10.7	11.4	11.9	11.2	12.6	10.1	9.8	8.6	10.4
Fulton Lewis Jr News/Comment	M	M-F	7:00	4.4	4.1	5.3	5.2	6.4	5.7	6.0	4.8	4.6	4.3	5.1
Gabriel Heatter News/Comment	M	M-F	7:00	10.9	10.5	9.4	9.3	9.5	9.9	9.6	8.1	8.9	7.8	9.4
Gabriel Heatter News/Comment	M	Sun	8:45	7.8	7.7	8.0	7.9	8.0	8.4	7.7	6.5	6.5		7.6
Gangbusters	B	Fri	9:00	7.8	9.3	10.3	10.5	12.3	9.5	11.5	9.8	8.1	6.6	9.6
Gay Nineties Revue	C	Mon	8:30	12.7	11.7	13.5	14.3	16.0	14.6	13.0	12.7	10.9	8.5	12.8
Ginny Simms Show	N	Tue	8:00	11.3	12.8	16.4	14.6	16.4	15.8	15.2	15.4	13.0	11.4	14.2
Goodwill Hour/John J Anthony	B	Sun	10:00	6.6	6.9	7.9	8.4	8.5	8.5	7.7		8.9	6.9	7.8
Gracie Fields	B	M-F	10:15					4.2	3.6	3.4	4.3	3.8	2.9	3.7
Grand Ole Opry	N	Sat	10:30	8.0	8.4	10.1	10.9	9.4	11.5	11.6	8.4	8.0	9.2	9.6
Great Gildersleeve	N	Sun	6:30	9.1	11.6	16.0	18.1	17.3	17.0	18.5	15.9	14.8	13.0	15.1
Great Moments in Music	C	Wed	10:00	3.8	5.4	4.2	6.0	4.7	4.5	4.5	4.8	4.0	6.2	4.8
HV Kaltenborn News/Comment	N	M-F	7:45	12.6	14.5	18.5	17.6	17.5	16.8	14.5	13.3	12.1	10.2	14.8
Harry James Orch	C	T,W,T	7:15	5.1	5.5	7.9	8.2	8.8	9.9	8.1	8.3	7.8	6.7	7.6
Hedda Hopper Hollywood News	C	MWF	6:15	4.4	5.0									4.7
Here's to Romance	B	Sun	6:00									3.1	2.7	2.9
Hobby Lobby	C	Sat	8:30	6.9	7.8	8.8	9.4	10.3	10.4	10.3	8.8	8.0	6.7	8.7
Hour of Charm	N	Sun	10:00	8.7	9.6	9.9	11.2	9.9	10.1	9.4	9.5	8.6	8.7	9.6
I Love a Mystery	C	M-F	7:00								7.7	6.9	6.2	6.9
Information Please	N	Mon	10:30	10.1	10.1	12.5	14.3	14.3	15.7	13.7	12.9	11.7	10.3	12.6
Inner Sanctum	B	Sun	8:30	7.7	8.3	10.6	11.1	12.2	10.6	10.8	9.6	9.1	6.5	9.7
Irene Rich Dramas	C	Sun	6:15	5.0	5.2	4.9	6.0	6.0	4.8	5.8	4.6	4.9	3.7	5.1
Jack Benny Show	N	Sun	7:00	24.8	24.9	27.1	29.1	32.3	27.5	24.4	23.5	23.1		26.3
Jack Carson Show	C	Wed	9:30										5.0	5.0
Jimmie Fidler Hollywood News	B	Sun	9:30	7.7	8.9	8.6	9.3	8.7	7.4	7.2	7.3	8.7	5.1	7.9
Jimmy Durante & Garry Moore	N	Thu	10:00								17.2	13.2	12.0	14.1
John B Hughes News/Comment	M	W,Sa	10:00	27.0	3.5	5.4	4.1	5.2	5.4	4.0	3.6	4.0	3.1	6.5

1942-43 Hooper Ratings 6-11 P.M.				Sept. 42	Oct. 42	Nov. 42	Dec. 42	Jan. 43	Feb. 43	March 43	April 43	May 43	June 43	1942-43 Avg
John B Kennedy News/Comment	C	T,T	6:30									4.2	4.6	4.0
Kate Smith Show	C	Fri	8:00	13.4	15.8	17.1	17.2	19.1	17.5	17.2	15.3	12.0	10.5	15.5
Kay Kyser Kollege Mus Knowledge	N	Wed	10:00	16.7	17.7	23.1	22.1	24.8	22.4	23.5	20.2	19.2	15.5	20.5
Keep Working Keep Singing	C	MWF	6:30	4.1	4.6	5.6	4.9	5.1	5.5	3.9	3.6	3.3		4.5
Lights Out	C	Tue	8:00	9.6	9.1	10.1	10.6	12.3	13.5	11.5	8.5	8.5	6.2	10.0
The Lone Ranger	B	MWF	7:30	4.9	5.4	6.4	6.7	9.0	9.3	8.6	7.6	6.6	5.3	7.0
Lowell Thomas News	B	M-F	6:45	11.9	12.8	14.8	16.4	15.4	16.3	15.1	13.8	12.7	11.0	14.0
Lum & Abner	B	MTWT	8:15	4.1	4.1	4.5	5.6	5.5	5.2	5.8	5.3	4.5	4.2	4.9
Lux Radio Theater	C	Mon	9:00	22.3	24.7	25.2	23.7	25.7	27.7	25.1	26.0	22.3	18.6	24.1
Major Bowes Amateur Hour	C	Thu	9:00	11.7	13.4	12.6	14.3	15.1	13.6	12.5	12.2	9.5	9.3	12.4
Man Behind the Gun	C	Sun	9:00							8.5	8.4	10.6		9.2
Manhattan at Midnight	B	Wed	8:30	4.9	6.7	5.9	6.6	6.8	7.8	7.2	7.0	5.2	4.3	6.2
Manhattan Merry Go Round	N	Sun	9:00	10.3	11.7	11.2	13.8	14.4	10.6	11.2	10.5	9.9	7.2	11.1
March of Time	N	Thu	10:30	14.5	17.6		20.4	20.2	21.0	19.2	17.1	17.2	13.9	17.9
Mayor of the Town	B	Wed	9:00	7.9	8.2	8.2	12.2	10.9	11.2	10.5	10.6	9.0	8.1	9.7
Meet Your Navy	B	Fri	8:30	2.8	3.2	3.0	3.6	3.5	3.5	3.8	3.4			3.4
Metropolitan Auditions	C	Sun	6:30				3.9	3.8	2.9					3.5
Milton Berle Show	B	Wed	9:30							8.0	7.5	7.3		7.6
Mr & Mrs North	N	Wed	8:00					16.1	15.3	15.6	14.1	11.9	9.1	13.7
Mr District Attorney	N	Wed	9:30	17.5	18.7	22.1	21.1	26.8	26.1	25.3	22.1	20.0	17.4	21.7
Mr Keen	C	WThF	7:45	4.1	4.1	5.7	6.4	7.6	7.3	5.9	5.1	5.4		5.7
National Barn Dance	N	Sat	8:00	9.2	9.2	7.6	11.8	12.6	12.8	10.3	11.2	9.8	6.9	10.4
Nelson Eddy Show	C	Wed	8:00	7.9	8.7	10.3	8.7	10.4	9.5	8.8	8.1			8.7
News of the World/JW Vandercook	N	M-F	7:15	8.0	8.3		9.5	10.2				7.7	6.8	8.7
One Man's Family	N	Sun	8:30	14.7	16.8	14.2	17.7	16.7	15.6	15.0	13.9	13.3	9.9	14.8
Our Secret Weapon	C	Fri	7:15		4.0			5.5	6.2	6.0	5.1	4.6	5.0	5.4
Parker Family	B	Sun	9:15	9.8	12.2	11.3	10.4	10.5	10.2		12.2	4.5	3.3	9.5
People Are Funny	N	Fri	9:30	11.2	10.7	11.7	14.0	15.3	12.1	13.7	11.1	11.3	9.1	12.1
Philip Morris Playhouse	C	Fri	9:00	10.2	10.8	11.8	11.7	12.5	13.2	13.8		10.2	8.1	11.2
Plantation Party	B	Fri	9:30	9.3	9.6	9.8	10.0	11.2	9.3	12.3	9.7			10.0
Quiz Kids	B	Sun	7:30	4.8	5.9	6.3	7.6	8.3	10.0	10.2		10.2	8.2	7.9
Radio Readers Digest	C	Sun	9:00	7.4	7.8	9.3	10.5	11.8		9.3		9.2	5.8	9.1
Ransom Sherman Show	C	Thu	8:00					3.6	3.4	4.2	3.4	2.8		3.6
Raymond Clapper News/Comment	M	M,Th	10:00	4.7	4.7	3.7	4.0	5.6		3.5	3.6	3.9	3.4	3.9
Raymond Gram Swing News/Comm	B	MTWT	10:00	4.8	4.6	5.4	4.2		5.5	4.8	4.9	4.9	3.3	4.8
Raymond Paige Orch	N	Tue	7:30									5.5	5.3	5.4
Red Skelton Show	N	Tue	10:30	23.7	29.7	33.7	34.4	40.5	35.4	33.8	30.6	28.6		32.3
Rudy Vallee Show	N	Thu	9:30	16.5	18.3	20.3	21.5	24.1	23.6	23.5	21.5	19.1	13.9	20.2
Sammy Kaye Orch	C	Wed	8:00						7.4	7.1	6.5	7.1	4.6	6.5
Saturday Night Serenade	C	Sat	9:45	9.4	9.0	9.2	9.7	10.5	11.5	8.6	10.0	8.6	6.5	9.3
Screen Guild Theater	C	Mon	10:00		15.7	18.1	20.6	20.9	25.1	21.4	20.0	19.8	15.8	19.7
Sergeant Gene Autry	C	Sun	6:30	7.2	7.6	6.1	7.7	9.7	10.3	8.0	7.2	6.9	5.6	7.6
The Shadow	M	Sun	5:30				15.0	16.5	15.0					15.5
Singin Sam	M	T,T	8:00			3.7	3.7	3.3	3.9	3.4	3.1	3.7	3.2	3.4
Spotlight Bands	B	M-Sa	9:30	3.1	3.6			4.0	3.6	3.8	3.1	2.9	2.4	3.4
Stage Door Canteen	C	Thu	9:30	9.3	9.8	9.2	8.8	9.9	10.8	9.7	9.9	9.5	6.6	9.4
Take It or Leave It	C	Sun	10:00	14.0	15.7	17.2	18.8	21.9	20.6	20.3	20.3	18.2	13.7	18.1
Telephone Hour	N	Mon	9:00	7.2	8.3	9.3	8.5	9.4	8.7	8.4		7.5	5.1	8.0

1942-43 Hooper Ratings 6-11 P.M.

Program	Time	Net	Day	Sept. 42	Oct. 42	Nov. 42	Dec. 42	Jan. 43	Feb. 43	March 43	April 43	May 43	June 43	1942-43 Avg
Terry & The Pirates	6:00	B	M-F						4.6	4.6	4.0	7.1	6.9	4.4
Thanks to the Yanks	7:30	C	Sat		9.4	9.3	9.8	9.9	9.8	9.6	6.9	9.8	7.6	8.7
That Brewster Boy	9:30	C	Fri		8.6	12.2	11.8	13.3	13.9	12.4	11.6	9.8	7.6	11.1
Today at Duncan's	6:15	C	Fri			3.9	4.2	4.6	4.2	4.0	3.1	2.8	2.1	3.6
Tommy Dorsey Orch	8:30	N	Wed	9.5	10.3	11.5	11.0	10.8	11.8	9.5	10.6	8.9	7.0	10.1
Tommy Riggs & Betty Lou	7:30	N	Fri			11.4	11.7	14.5	12.2	12.6	12.4	10.7		11.6
Treasure Hour of Song	9:30	N	Thu						1.6	3.2	1.9	2.1		2.2
True or False	8:30	M	Mon	5.9	6.1	6.7	6.8	7.0	7.6	6.2	5.7	7.3		6.6
Truth or Consequences	8:30	B	Sat	13.1	14.1	15.5	15.0	17.1	16.2	18.3	17.0	16.8	10.6	15.4
Tums Treasure Chest	8:30	N	Tue	10.4	10.5	12.4	12.3	12.4	10.5	10.7	10.1	7.3	6.4	10.3
Upton Close News/Comment	8:30	M	Sat							2.7	2.7	2.6		2.7
Upton Close News/Comment	6:30	M	Sun						4.9	4.9	4.9	4.8	4.4	4.8
Voice of Firestone	8:30	N	Mon	8.5	8.6	9.1	9.4	11.6	10.3	8.8	8.4	7.9	6.9	9.0
Vox Pop	8:00	C	Mon		11.9	13.5	16.1	15.7	15.5	12.7	14.1	11.7	11.4	13.6
Walter Winchell Jergens Journal	9:00	B	Sun	21.4	24.4	25.3	22.4	24.1	24.1	25.4	23.9	22.8	16.5	22.9
Waltz Time	9:00	N	Fri	9.0	9.5	11.0	10.6	11.2	10.8	11.2	11.0	9.6	7.6	10.2
We the People at War	7:30	C	Sun	9.1	9.4	10.7	11.2	10.3	11.9	11.2	10.0	9.1	5.8	9.9
Your All Time Hit Parade	8:30	N	Fri								10.4	10.1	7.2	9.2
Your Hit Parade	9:00	C	Sat	13.6	14.0	15.9	16.5	16.4	16.4	12.1	15.5	13.9	10.9	14.5

*aka Mr Adam & Mrs Eve

Special Broadcasts

Program	Net	Date	Rating
Community Chest Drive	All	10/5	29.5
Aunt Jenny Special Broadcast	C	1/6	8.2
Herbert Hoover Speech	N	1/21	17.5
Mme Chiang Kai-Shek Speech	CM	3/2	14.1
Pres Roosevelt Speech from Mexico	All	4/20	44.1

1943-44 Hooper Ratings 6-11 P.M.

Program	Time	Net	Day	Sept. 43	Oct. 43	Nov. 43	Dec. 43	Jan. 44	Feb. 44	March 44	April 44	May 44	June 44	1943-44 Avg
Abbott & Costello Show	10:00	N	Thu	12.2	13.3	21.1	23.0	24.1	24.5	21.8	21.6	18.1	17.9	21.5
Abie's Irish Rose	8:00	N	Sat	7.9	11.4	14.2	14.2	13.0	14.1	12.4	12.9	9.6	7.4	12.3
Adventures of Ellery Queen	7:30	N	Sat	5.6	9.2	12.8	11.4	10.9	13.2	15.0	12.2	10.1	8.2	11.3
Adventures of Sherlock Holmes	8:30	M	Mon	11.1	11.7	8.9	10.3	10.8	9.4	10.0	9.5	7.0	6.5	8.7
Adventures of the Thin Man	10:30	C	Sun			12.7	17.8	15.9	18.0	18.1	16.1	13.8		15.0
Alexander's Mediation Board	8:00	M	Sun	3.4	4.2	4.4	5.0	4.2	4.0	4.2	4.4	3.8	3.7	4.1
Aldrich Family	8:30	N	Thu	19.2	22.5	24.2	25.1	26.5	27.9	21.6	21.8	20.1	14.3	22.3
Alan Young Show	9:00	N	Wed			5.8	5.9	6.0			6.8	5.6	5.8	5.8
Allan Jones & Frankie Carle	8:00	C	Wed						4.4	4.9	4.2	4.1	4.3	5.6
America in the Air	6:30	C	Sun	4.7	5.2	5.8	5.9						3.8	4.9
American Album of Familiar Music	9:30	N	Sun	9.1	12.7	13.4	12.0	9.9	11.1	9.5	11.6	9.2	9.4	10.8
American Melody Hour	7:30	C	Tue	5.2	7.6	8.5	8.3	8.9	8.5	7.8	6.5	6.1	5.2	7.3
Amos & Andy	10:00	N	Fri		13.8	14.3	14.0	16.3	15.9	14.7	15.2	14.1	13.2	14.6
Arch Ward Sports	10:15	M	Fri			2.4	2.4	2.1	2.1	1.9				2.0
Arthur Hale News/Comment	7:30	M	T,T,Sa	4.3	3.4	3.7	4.0	3.1	3.0	3.8	2.5	2.7	3.1	3.2
Battle of the Sexes	8:30	N	Wed	3.9	4.0			4.5	4.3					4.0
Beat the Band	8:30	B	Wed	9.3	10.2	11.0	12.4	11.3	13.5	11.0	10.4	7.9	4.6	10.2
Big Town	8:00	N	Tue			11.3	12.4	12.5	12.9	11.6	10.7	8.8	5.8	10.9
Bill Stern Colgate Sports Newsreel	10:30	N	Fri	10.7	11.1	8.7	11.4	10.7	9.8	10.1	11.2	8.6	8.8	10.1

1943-44 Hooper Ratings 6-11 P.M.				Sept. 43	Oct. 43	Nov. 43	Dec. 43	Jan. 44	Feb. 44	March 44	April 44	May 44	June 44	1943-44 Avg
Bing Crosby's Kraft Music Hall	N	Thu	9:00	15.6	20.6	20.4	22.2	23.9	24.1	20.0	18.8	17.6	13.4	19.6
Blind Date	B	Mon	8:30			6.9	8.5	11.4	9.7	11.9	10.6	7.7	5.4	9.0
Blondie	C	Mon	7:30	13.2	14.5	16.2	14.1	17.1	15.4	17.4	16.9	15.0	13.8	15.4
Blue Ribbon Town/Groucho Marx	C	Sat	8:00	7.6	8.8	10.7	11.1	11.1	10.8	11.4	9.2	6.7	5.1	9.3
Bob Becker Outdoors & Dogs	C	Thu	6:15			2.9	2.6	1.8	2.3	2.1				2.3
Bob Burns Show	N	Thu	7:30			17.5	15.9	18.4	17.2	17.7	13.8	13.1	11.4	15.6
Bob Crosby Show	N	Sun	10:30	10.3	10.8	11.6	11.6	13.0	10.4	10.7	10.4	8.9	8.8	10.7
Bob Hope Show	N	Tue	10:00	25.1	29.4	31.6	31.2	34.6	36.2	35.6	33.8	27.8		31.7
Boston Blackie	N	Fri	10:00										6.9	6.9
Boston Symphony & Boston Pops	B	Sat	8:30					2.6	2.7	2.7	2.5	2.9	2.7	2.7
Burns & Allen Show	C	Tue	9:00	13.7	17.0	19.7	17.9	18.3	19.3	17.7	16.4	13.4		17.0
Cal Tinney News/Comment	M	MWF	8:00	3.9	4.6	4.7	3.9	4.5	5.0	5.3	4.5	4.0	4.5	4.5
Can You Top This?	N	Sat	9:30	12.0	13.3	13.1	14.4	13.3	16.2	13.6	14.5	11.8	9.9	13.2
Carnation Contented Hour	N	Mon	10:00	5.8	5.4	7.1	7.8	7.2	6.5	7.4	7.8	6.7	6.8	6.9
Carnival	C	Wed	10:30	4.9	5.1	5.1	6.3	4.9	6.1	4.6	5.5	3.4		5.1
Cavalcade of America	N	Mon	8:00		9.4	11.3	8.2	10.9	10.7	10.5	10.3	7.4	5.6	9.4
Cedric Foster News	M	Sun	10:00	3.9	2.6	3.5	3.5	2.8	4.2	4.7	3.2	3.3	2.9	3.5
Chamber Music Soc Low Basin St	B	Sun	9:15	7.9	9.7	10.9	10.1	10.0	8.1	8.6	7.9	7.4	6.2	8.7
Cities Service Concert	N	Fri	8:00	7.9	5.6	6.8	7.4	7.6	7.0	7.5	6.0	6.3	5.4	6.8
Correction Please	C	Sat	10:15			7.3	9.7	7.7	9.0	8.6	8.2	7.2	4.9	7.8
Counterspy	B	Mon	9:00	6.7	7.3	7.1	7.7	7.4	7.8	8.6	7.8	6.7	6.4	7.4
Crime Doctor	C	Sun	8:30	10.8	13.1	13.5	14.2	14.7	14.1	15.3	15.0	12.3	6.5	13.0
Dale Carnegie	M	Thu	10:15	2.6	1.6	3.2	3.0	2.0	3.1	2.6	2.1	2.5		2.5
Date with Judy	N	Tue	8:30	9.1				8.9	9.6	9.1	9.8	8.3		9.1
Dateline	C	Fri	7:15		5.1	5.2	6.3						4.6	5.3
Death Valley Days	C	Thu	8:30	6.6	6.6	6.3	8.5	8.4	9.0	7.7	6.4	7.3	4.5	7.4
Dinah Shore Show	C	Thu	9:30		6.8	7.7	6.6	8.0	9.0	7.7	6.4	6.4	5.6	7.1
Dr Christian	C	Wed	8:30	10.0	13.4	12.9	14.8	14.8	13.9	14.5	14.7	12.4	10.5	13.2
Dr IQ	N	Mon	10:30	9.7	9.4	9.2	9.4	10.5	8.6	11.1	11.5	8.4	10.0	9.8
Dorothy Thompson News/Comment	B	Sun	7:15		3.8	4.2	4.5				3.9	3.8		4.0
Double or Nothing	M	Fri	9:30	4.9	5.6	5.8	6.2	6.2	5.4	6.0	5.6	4.5	3.9	5.4
Drew Pearson News/Comment	B	Sun	7:00	6.7	8.5	6.8	8.0	7.6	7.3	6.9	7.0	6.9	7.0	7.3
Duffy's Tavern	B	Tue	8:30		10.2	10.8	11.7	13.8	14.6	12.4	11.4	10.7	7.9	11.5
Dunninger the Mentalist	B	Wed	9:00					5.3	4.3	4.2	3.4	3.4	3.0	3.9
Earl Godwin News/Comment	B	M-F	8:00	5.0	5.6	5.9	5.2	4.4	5.0	4.1	4.5	2.5	3.2	4.6
Early American Dance Music	B	Sat	8:00			4.2	4.5	4.4	3.4	2.7	2.9	2.9	2.3	3.1
Easy Aces	C	Wed	7:30	5.1	5.7	5.3	5.1	6.5	5.9	5.7	4.0	4.8	5.0	5.2
Ed Sullivan Entertains	C	Mon	7:15	5.4	4.9	6.8	4.9	6.8	6.1	5.0	4.0	3.9	4.0	5.2
Eddie Cantor Time to Smile	N	Wed	9:00		17.8	17.9	20.6	17.8	18.1	15.3	16.8	13.2	13.5	16.8
Edgar Bergen & Charlie McCarthy	N	Sun	8:00	22.6	25.3	30.4	30.1	29.6	27.9	26.7	27.1	21.4		26.8
Edwin C Hill News/Comment	C	Tue	6:15	5.4	4.6	6.6	4.8	5.3	4.8	4.6	4.4	4.2	4.1	4.9
Famous Jury Trials	B	Tue	9:00	7.3	7.1	7.7	7.5	7.7	8.9		7.8	6.2	5.8	7.4
Fanny Brice & Frank Morgan	N	Thu	8:00	17.1	19.6	22.4	23.2	23.7	23.8	20.2	17.8	16.8	13.9	19.9
Fibber McGee & Molly	N	Tue	9:30		29.5	31.8	32.1	32.7	35.7	33.4	33.9	27.9	24.8	31.3
First Line of Defense	C	Thu	10:00	5.8	5.3	4.6	5.7	5.4	6.2	5.8	5.9	4.3	4.7	5.4
First Nighter	M	Wed	9:30			6.0	7.4	6.4	8.1	6.0	4.8	3.3	4.8	5.9
Fitch Bandwagon	N	Sun	7:30	9.0	11.5	17.7	18.5	16.2	14.8	17.8	16.6	12.5	12.9	14.8
Fitch Bandwagon	B	Wed	9:00	2.6	2.5	2.8	4.0							3.0

1943-44 Hooper Ratings 6-11 P.M.				Sept. 43	Oct. 43	Nov. 43	Dec. 43	Jan. 44	Feb. 44	March 44	April 44	May 44	June 44	1943-44 Avg
Frank Sinatra Show	C	Wed	9:00					16.0	14.0	11.9	11.3	10.4	9.6	12.2
Frank Singiser News	M	T,T,Sa	8:00									3.0	3.5	3.3
Fred Allen Texaco Star Theater	C	Sun	9:30				20.4	19.5	18.7	20.5	17.6	17.4	11.8	18.0
Fred Waring Show	M	M-F	7:00	8.7	8.9	9.7	10.0	9.5	10.7	10.6	8.8	8.7	8.4	9.4
Freedom of Opportunity	C	Fri	8:30					2.6	3.1	1.3	2.9	1.9	1.4	2.2
Friday on Broadway	C	Fri	7:30				5.0	4.8	5.3	5.1	5.4	3.6	3.6	4.7
Fulton Lewis Jr News/Comment	M	M-F	7:00	4.3	5.1	5.5	6.0	6.6	4.4	4.9	5.1	4.5	4.5	5.1
Fulton Oursler	M	M-F	8:15			3.3	2.7	3.5	3.0	3.7	2.9			3.2
Gabriel Heatter News/Comment	M	M-F	9:00		10.0	9.6	9.3	8.6	9.4	9.8	8.7	8.6	8.5	9.2
Gabriel Heatter News/Comment	M	Sun	8:45	8.8	8.6	9.4	8.2	8.4	9.6	8.3	7.2	7.3	8.7	8.4
Gangbusters	B	Fri	9:00		9.3	9.7	10.5	11.5	12.4	11.7	10.6	8.4	7.0	10.0
Gay Nineties Revue	C	Mon	8:30	10.2	13.5	12.0	10.5	13.4	12.5	10.7	10.2	8.0	9.7	11.1
Gertrude Lawrence Show	B	Thu	10:30		3.7	4.6	3.6	4.1	4.8	5.0				4.3
Ginny Simms Show	N	Tue	8:00	11.8	12.7	15.4	16.3	13.9	14.6	13.0	12.4	10.2	9.2	13.0
Goodwill Hour/John J Anthony	M	Sun	10:15				6.5	4.8	4.9	5.7	4.1	5.1	5.3	5.2
Gracie Fields Show	N	Sun	8:00										11.4	11.4
Gracie Fields Victory Show	N	M-F	9:15	8.5			4.8							5.1
Grand Ole Opry	M	Sat	10:30	10.8	11.6	13.0	12.7	12.6	13.6	12.7	12.7	9.9	8.5	11.8
Great Gildersleeve	N	Sun	6:30	12.2	14.2	18.1	18.1	16.5	19.0	18.4	17.9	16.0	13.0	16.3
Great Moments in Music	N	Wed	10:00	4.3	4.6	6.2	5.2	5.8	7.1	4.8	5.5	5.2	5.1	5.4
Greenfield Village Chapel Choir	C	Sun	8:00											2.3
Guy Lombardo Orch	B	Sun	10:30					2.5	2.7	1.9	1.7	2.2	2.7	3.1
HV Kaltenborn News/Comment	N	M-F	7:45	11.8	14.2	16.3	15.7	14.7	16.0	12.2	11.8	10.8	10.2	13.4
Harry James Orch	C	T,W,T	7:15	7.3	7.0	8.9	7.8	7.3	7.5	7.6				7.6
Harry Savoy Show	M	Thu	10:00										8.7	8.7
Henry Gladstone News/Comment	M	M,Th	10:00							3.5	2.1	1.8	2.8	2.6
Here's to Romance	C	Thu	10:30	2.3	5.3	5.2	7.3	7.3	6.5	6.1	6.0	6.1	4.4	5.7
Hildegarde's Raleigh Room	N	Tue	10:30										14.7	14.7
Horace Heidt Orch	B	Mon	7:00						4.2	3.9	2.8	2.5	3.0	3.3
Hour of Charm	C	Sun	7:00	8.2	9.5	10.3	11.3	9.1	8.2	8.7	9.9	9.6	7.1	9.2
I Love a Mystery	C	M-F	7:00	5.8	7.4	8.4	8.4	8.0	9.1	9.1	8.1	10.0	5.5	8.0
Information Please	N	Mon	10:30	10.0	11.7	13.3	13.7	10.1	9.1	11.9	11.5	9.7	10.1	11.5
Inner Sanctum	C	Sat	8:30	7.0	7.8	8.6	10.1	11.7	12.7	10.7	10.8	9.1	6.5	9.2
It Pays to Be Ignorant	C	Fri	9:00						10.1	8.6	8.5	7.7	6.2	7.8
Jack Benny Show	N	Sun	7:00	23.9	23.9	24.6	26.0	26.5	26.1	25.4	23.8	20.1	16.8	23.7
Jack Carson Show	C	Wed	9:30	5.4	7.4	8.1	8.4	9.4	9.5	9.7	9.4	7.5	5.5	8.0
Jimmy Durante & Garry Moore	C	Fri	10:00	13.7	11.8	12.8	12.1	14.3	13.8	11.6	12.5	9.8	9.1	12.1
Jimmie Fidler Hollywood News	B	Sun	9:45	9.0	9.3	11.3	10.3	8.2	6.3	7.9	7.7	5.3	4.0	7.9
Joan Davis & Jack Haley	N	Thu	9:30	17.6	18.9	18.5	22.5	25.1	25.7	24.0	22.9	20.1	17.3	21.3
John Gunther News/Comment	B	F,Sat	10:00			3.5	4.9	4.3						4.2
John B Hughes News/Comment	M	W,Sat	7:15			3.1	4.0							3.6
John Nesbit's Passing Parade	C	T,W,T	8:30	3.3	3.9						5.7	5.2		5.1
Judy Canova Show	C	Tue	8:00		14.8	13.5	11.7	12.4	12.6	13.8	11.5	9.0	4.5	11.7
Kate Smith Hour	C	Fri	8:00	9.9	14.4	14.4	15.6	16.9	16.2	14.9	13.8	11.8	8.5	14.1
Kay Kyser Kollege Mus Knowledge	N	Wed	10:00	15.6	20.4	18.2	22.9	21.4	20.2	20.8	19.5	17.4	15.0	19.1
Keepsakes	B	Sun	8:30	4.3	4.1	5.0	5.0	5.2	5.5	4.9	5.0	3.7	2.7	4.5
Leon Henderson News	B	Sat	6:45	2.1	2.7	2.5	2.6	2.3	3.2	2.6	2.2	1.7	1.5	2.3
Let Yourself Go	B	Tue	7:00							3.3	3.5	2.9	2.2	3.0

1943-44 Hooper Ratings 6-11 P.M.

Show	Net	Day	Time	Sept. 43	Oct. 43	Nov. 43	Dec. 43	Jan. 44	Feb. 44	March 44	April 44	May 44	June 44	1943-44 Avg
Little Show	M	Sun	6:45			2.7	1.8	2.3						2.3
The Lone Ranger	B	MWF	7:30	5.5	7.0	7.2	7.9	8.6	8.6	8.5	7.6	6.1	5.2	7.2
Lowell Thomas News	N	M-F	6:45	11.7	12.2	14.4	15.0	13.6	12.6	13.8	11.0	10.9	11.4	12.7
Lum & Abner	B	M-Th	8:15	4.4	4.8	5.4	5.0	5.6	5.5	4.9	4.7	3.8	3.6	4.8
Lux Radio Theater	C	Mon	9:00	20.1	22.0	24.7	24.4	25.4	27.2	26.5	23.9	20.0	18.3	23.3
Lyn Murray Show	C	MWF	6:15							2.0	2.1	2.4	2.6	2.3
Major Bowes Amateur Hour	C	Thu	9:00	8.3	9.9	9.9	8.6	10.8	10.7	10.4	9.8	8.1	6.2	9.3
Man Behind the Gun	C	Sat	7:00	4.2	4.3	6.5	4.7							4.9
Manhattan Merry Go Round	N	Sun	9:00	6.7	8.4	9.5	10.2	10.2	8.1	9.5	10.7	9.8	7.5	9.1
March of Time	N	Thu	10:30	13.2	16.0	16.8	20.0	17.8	18.0	17.2	16.4	12.2	12.6	16.0
Mayor of the Town	C	Sat	7:00	8.9	10.6	11.6	10.8			9.3	7.6	7.3	5.6	9.0
Meet Your Navy	B	Fri	8:30		4.2	3.6	3.1	4.0	5.2	2.9	3.6	2.8	2.7	3.6
Million Dollar Band/Palmolive Party	N	Sat	10:00	8.9	9.6	11.5	12.3	10.5	11.7	12.0	13.0	9.1	9.1	10.8
Mr & Mrs North	N	Wed	8:00		12.3	15.1	16.0	16.4	15.3	16.3	14.3	8.8	12.1	14.1
Mr District Attorney	N	Wed	9:30	16.1	23.3	22.5	23.3	23.8	24.0	22.7	23.1	18.4	17.1	21.4
Mr Keen	C	Thu	7:30	4.3	5.4	5.7	7.5	6.9	7.5	9.3	7.2	6.6	5.5	6.6
Molle Mystery Theater	N	Tue	9:00	6.8	10.1	9.4	9.6	9.9	10.1	11.7	10.5	9.5	7.2	9.5
Music America Loves Best	B	Sat	7:30							4.6	3.0	2.4	1.5	2.9
My Best Girls	B	Wed	8:30						4.6	3.2	3.6	1.8	2.4	3.1
National Barn Dance	N	Sat	9:00	8.3	11.0	12.1	12.0	14.2	11.3	11.5	11.4	9.2	6.1	10.7
Nero Wolfe	B	Fri	7:00					4.2	4.3	4.2	3.6	4.4	3.5	4.0
News of the World/JW Vandercook	N	M-F	7:15	7.1	7.1	7.4	7.8	8.2	8.1	9.9	8.4	5.1	5.9	7.5
One Man's Family	N	Sun	8:30	11.2	13.3	13.9	17.5	14.7	13.9	13.4	13.1	12.4	8.0	13.1
Parker Family	B	Fri	8:15	3.9	4.9	4.6	4.9	4.2	5.8	4.2	3.9	2.9	2.8	4.2
People Are Funny	N	Fri	9:30	9.5	10.9	11.4	11.7	11.8	14.8	12.1	12.7	10.7	9.7	11.5
Philip Morris Playhouse	C	Fri	9:00	8.7	11.5	9.8	11.4	12.2	12.6					11.0
Pick & Pat	M	Tue	8:30					2.6	3.9	2.8	3.4	2.6	3.5	3.1
Quiz Kids	B	Sun	7:30	8.6	8.6	10.3	10.2	10.3	10.1	10.9	9.7	6.2	7.8	9.5
Radio Hall of Fame	B	Sun	6:00				6.7	6.3	5.7	6.8	5.0	5.5	4.1	5.7
Radio Readers Digest	C	Sun	9:00	7.7	10.7	8.2	11.2	10.0	10.6	10.6	10.5	9.1	7.0	9.4
Raymond Clapper News/Comment	M	M,Th	10:00	4.6	2.2	3.1	3.3	3.0						3.2
Raymond Gram Swing News/Com	B	M-Th	10:00	5.1	4.6	4.1	3.3	4.8	4.7	3.5	4.7	4.1	5.3	4.4
Raymond Paige Orch	N	Tue	7:30	6.0	6.8	8.7	6.7							7.1
Red Skelton Show	N	Tue	10:30	22.6	29.0	29.9	30.5	33.4	32.6	32.4	29.9	29.1		29.9
Report to the Nation	C	Tue	9:30	7.3	5.0	5.9	5.1	5.3	5.6	4.3	4.9	4.5	6.7	5.5
Robert Ripley	N	M-F	9:15					4.6	4.1	5.1				4.6
Ronald Colman	N	Tue	7:30					13.6	12.9	10.4	8.5	7.9	3.4	9.9
"Ruggles, Astor & Auer"	C	Thu	8:00		4.9	5.9								5.1
Sammy Kaye Orch	C	Wed	8:00	4.5	7.3	7.7	8.9	10.2	10.0	7.2	10.0	7.7	6.6	7.9
Saturday Night Serenade	C	Sat	9:45	5.4	9.0	10.4	9.9		11.1	11.2				9.4
Screen Guild Players	C	Mon	10:00	7.6	18.7	21.9	21.5	21.1	24.0	22.1	22.1	19.0	18.2	20.5
The Shadow	M	Sun	5:30	16.1	8.2	10.6	12.8		14.9	14.1	13.6	13.6		13.2
Silver Theater	C	Sun	6:00	6.4	3.3	8.9	6.7	9.0	7.6	8.2	9.8	6.8	6.3	7.8
Spotlight Bands	B	M-Sat	9:30	3.5		3.4	3.1	3.0	2.6	3.1	2.2	2.8	2.6	3.0
Stage Door Canteen	C	Fri	10:30	5.5	12.8	10.8	14.0	14.1	14.9	12.1	13.1	10.4	8.6	11.6
Star & The Story	C	Sun	8:00						8.4	7.8	6.6	5.6	4.6	6.6
Star for a Night	B	Wed	10:30										2.9	2.9
Stop or Go	B	Thu	10:30					2.2	3.2		3.4	3.8	3.4	3.5

1943-44 Hooper Ratings 6-11 P.M.

Program	Net	Day	Time	Sept. 43	Oct. 43	Nov. 43	Dec. 43	Jan. 44	Feb. 44	March 44	April 44	May 44	June 44	1943-44 Avg
Suspense	C	Thu	8:00				8.2	8.5	9.1	9.5	9.7	6.8	6.0	8.3
Take It or Leave It	C	Sun	10:00	14.5	16.1	18.1	20.7	20.9	22.2	22.5	22.6	19.6	15.0	19.2
Telephone Hour	N	Mon	9:00	7.9	7.2	7.1	7.1	7.8	6.7	6.4	7.1	6.6	5.7	7.0
Terry & The Pirates	B	M-F	6:00	2.9	3.1	3.0	4.3	4.9	5.1	3.6	3.5	3.4		3.8
Texaco Star Theater	C	Sun	9:30	7.4	8.7	8.5								8.2
Thanks to the Yanks	C	Sat	7:30	9.8	9.5	8.9	8.9	10.4	9.5	9.8	9.4	8.0	7.7	9.2
That Brewster Boy	C	Fri	9:30	9.4	12.2	9.5	13.9	12.8	12.3	11.9	9.7	8.8	7.3	10.8
That's a Good One	B	Sun	9:30	2.7	3.0	2.1								2.6
To Your Good Health	C	MWF	8:15		3.5	3.0	2.6	2.6						2.9
Top of the Evening	B	MWF	6:15							2.6	2.1	1.5		2.1
Treasure Chest	N	Tue	10:15	9.7	9.2	9.7	10.8							9.9
Treasure Hour of Song	M	Thu	8:30			2.8	2.5	3.2	3.6	3.4	2.3	2.5	2.9	2.9
Truth or Consequences	N	Sat	9:30	12.5	14.8	16.0	16.7	16.9	17.7	15.9	16.4	11.2	9.1	14.7
Upton Close News/Comment	M	Sun	8:30	5.8	5.6	5.7	5.2	5.4	4.3	4.9	5.6	3.4	3.2	4.9
Voice of Firestone	N	Mon	6:30	7.8	9.5	8.2	9.0	7.1	7.4	7.1	8.6	7.9	4.9	7.8
Vox Pop	C	Mon	8:30	10.3	12.8	13.7	13.2	15.4	14.2	14.9	11.4	11.9	8.7	12.7
Walter Winchell Jergens Journal	B	Sun	8:00	17.2	21.3	22.0	23.8	22.0	25.6	25.8	23.6	16.2	16.6	21.4
Waltz Time	N	Fri	9:00	11.2	10.7	9.6	11.1	10.7	11.0	9.8	9.0	9.6	7.6	10.0
We the People at War	C	Sun	9:00	9.1	10.8	9.5	8.9	7.3	10.7	10.6	9.5	8.5	7.4	9.2
We Who Dream	C	Fri	7:30	4.4	4.7							3.2	3.2	3.4
What's New?	B	Sat	7:15	10.2		4.2	4.7	4.4	4.0	3.9	3.9	3.6	5.5	4.4
William L Shirer News/Comment	C	Sun	7:00	4.6	4.5		4.1	4.1	3.9	5.0	3.9	4.1	4.3	4.3
World Today News	C	M-Sat	7:00			4.8	4.1	5.3	4.7	5.5	4.1	3.9	4.0	4.6
Xavier Cugat Orch	M	Wed	6:45					5.6	4.8	5.1	4.0			4.6
Your All Time Hit Parade	N	Fri	8:30	9.5	11.4	8.6	10.1	11.1	10.7	10.7	8.0	7.1	8.3	9.6
Your Hit Parade	C	Sat	9:00	14.4	16.9	17.0	18.5	20.1	19.7	18.0	17.3	13.6	11.2	16.7

Special Broadcasts

Program	Net	Date	Rating
Pres Roosevelt Speech	All	10/5	37.4
Wendell Wilkie Speech	N	10/15	9.5
Tehran Conference News Roundup	C	12/1	7.4
Secy of State Byrnes Speech	C	12/7	5.0
Christmas Variety Show	C	12/21	12.9
Admiral Halsey Speech	N	1/7	7.4
Fourth War Bond Appeal	All	1/17	44.4
Bakers' Salute to Armed Forces	N	6/4	20.2
Pres Roosevelt D-Day Statement	All	6/5	45.2

1944-45 Hooper Ratings 6-11 P.M.

Program	Net	Day	Time	Sept. 44	Oct. 44	Nov. 44	Dec. 44	Jan. 45	Feb. 45	March 45	April 45	May 45	June 45	1944-45 Avg
Abbott & Costello Show	N	Thu	10:00		16.4	20.5	19.7	21.1	21.1	21.3	17.9	17.7	16.5	19.1
Adventures of Ellery Queen	C	Wed	7:30	8.9	11.4	12.4	12.4		7.8	8.5	8.7	8.8	8.6	9.7
Adventures of Ozzie & Harriet	C	Sun	6:00		7.6	8.7	9.0	9.5	9.3	9.0	7.9	6.1	6.9	8.2
Adventures of Sherlock Holmes	M	Mon	8:30	8.3	11.0	9.8	9.0	9.8	11.3	10.0	10.4	10.2		10.0
Adventures of the Thin Man	C	Fri	8:30	10.0	12.4	11.6	13.5	15.9	16.8	12.5	11.0	10.8	9.4	12.4
Adventures of Topper	N	Thu	8:30										7.1	7.1
Al Pearce Gang	C	Sat	10:15	8.1					8.5	7.7	8.8	7.1	6.9	7.8
Alan Young Show	B	Tue	8:30			4.2	4.6	5.2	4.9	4.3	4.2	4.0	4.2	4.5

1944-45 Hooper Ratings 6-11 P.M.				Sept. 44	Oct. 44	Nov. 44	Dec. 44	Jan. 45	Feb. 45	March 45	April 45	May 45	June 45	1944-45 Avg
Aldrich Family	C	Fri	8:00	11.3	13.9	17.1	16.5	17.9	18.3	17.0	13.3	13.7	11.9	15.1
Alexander's Mediation Board	M	Sun	8:00	4.1	5.2	4.5	5.1	7.6	8.4	6.5	6.7	5.7	7.4	6.1
Allan Jones & Frankie Carle	C	Wed	8:00	5.3	5.7									5.5
America in the Air	C	Sat	7:30	4.4	4.5	5.8	5.6	6.6	7.0	5.6	5.4	5.1	4.3	5.4
American Album of Familiar Music	N	Sun	9:30	9.0	11.2	12.0	12.3	13.5	14.4	12.7	11.6	12.1	11.5	12.0
American Melody Hour	C	Tue	7:30	6.2	7.5	8.9	8.3	8.3	8.4	7.6	7.2	7.0	7.2	7.7
America's Town Meeting	B	Thu	8:30	3.8	4.1	4.7	4.4	4.4	6.1	4.6	4.0	5.5	4.7	4.6
Amos & Andy	N	Fri	10:00		12.7	14.7	14.1	16.9	17.4	16.9	15.7	14.2	12.9	15.1
Arthur Hale News/Comment	M	T,T,Sa	10:30	2.9	3.1	5.3	3.4	4.5	4.0	4.9	4.7	5.9	4.1	4.3
Beatrice Kay's Gaslight Gaieties	N	Sat	8:00			8.1	10.5	11.5	10.5	8.5	7.9	7.2	7.2	8.9
Big Town	C	Tue	8:00	10.1	12.1	12.6	12.4	14.9	15.4	13.6	12.5	12.0	12.7	12.8
Bill Henry Johns Mansville News	C	M-F	8:55		11.4	13.1	11.5	11.2	13.1	13.3	12.5	11.3	10.5	12.0
Bill Stern Colgate Sports Newsreel	N	Fri	10:30	9.9	12.0	10.0	11.3	12.4	10.0	10.3	10.3	9.5	8.6	10.4
Billie Burke Show	N	Wed	8:30							9.1	9.1	8.0	8.0	8.4
Bing Crosby's Kraft Music Hall	N	Thu	9:00			22.6	23.5	25.2	24.5	21.9	20.9	21.5	17.8	22.2
Blind Date	B	Mon	8:30	7.2		9.5	10.2	10.0	9.0	9.1	8.5	7.5	6.5	8.6
Blondie	C	Sun	8:00	6.2	9.0	10.6	10.5	12.2	11.4	9.9	10.3	9.0	9.5	9.9
Bob Burns Show	N	Thu	7:30		12.2	16.3	14.9	18.3	16.5	14.7	14.5	14.6	11.7	14.9
Bob Hope Show	N	Tue	10:00	23.4	25.2	31.3	31.7	35.5	34.7	30.6	30.5	27.4	25.2	29.6
Boston Blackie	N	Fri	10:00	8.2										8.2
Boston Symphony & Boston Pops	B	Sat	8:30		3.2	3.2	2.6	2.7	2.9	2.4	2.5	3.2	3.0	2.9
Burns & Allen Show	C	Mon	8:30	11.9	13.8	15.1	15.3	17.4	16.6	15.0	12.8	14.8	14.0	14.7
Can You Top This?	N	Sat	9:30	10.7	12.7	13.7	13.6	16.7	15.9	14.9	13.0	12.5	12.6	13.6
Carnation Contented Hour	N	Mon	10:00	6.4	7.3	9.1	8.4	7.6	8.5	6.4	6.3	7.1	7.2	7.4
Carton of Cheer	N	Wed	8:30	8.1	8.6	10.0	10.7	10.9	11.0	9.4				9.8
Cavalcade of America	N	Mon	8:00	7.9	12.6	11.2	11.0	12.0	13.4	11.0	10.5	9.4	9.1	10.8
Cecil Brown News/Comment	M	MWF	8:00	4.9	6.9	5.1	6.6	6.9	7.0	6.1	6.3	7.3	6.4	6.4
Cedric Foster News	M	Sun	9:30	4.4	5.0	5.0	4.0	3.5	4.1	3.5	4.7	4.1	3.1	4.1
Chamber Music Soc Low Basin St	B	Sun	9:15	6.8										6.8
Charlie Chan	N	Thur	7:30	8.4										8.4
Charlotte Greenwood Show	N	Tue	10:00	10.2										10.2
Chesterfield Supper Club	N	M-F	7:00		7.3		7.6	9.0	10.8	9.6	8.6	9.2	8.9	9.1
Cities Service Concert	N	Fri	8:00	6.2			7.8	7.3	8.5	6.9	8.2	10.4	9.1	6.8
Cities Service Highways in Melody	N	Fri	8:00			7.1	12.4	12.0	9.5	8.7	6.8	7.4	7.9	8.2
Comedy Theater	N	Sun	10:30		6.6	10.5								9.4
Correction Please	C	Sat	10:15	7.1	6.6	7.1								6.9
Counterspy	B	Wed	8:30	6.6		8.2	8.0	8.7	8.6	10.0	10.3	10.4	9.4	8.9
Crime Doctor	C	Sun	8:30	10.2	12.9	14.3	15.1	14.6	14.0	13.1	10.4	11.0	11.6	12.7
Danny Kaye Show	C	Fri	10:30					12.5	13.0	10.0	10.2	9.5	8.1	10.6
Date with Judy	N	Tue	8:30	9.8	9.2	12.2	12.3	12.7	15.9	14.2	12.9	12.4	10.9	12.5
Death Valley Sheriff	C	Thu	8:30	8.7	8.7	9.9	9.3	10.9	11.2	11.2	10.4	10.6	9.1	10.1
Detroit Symphony	M	Sat	8:30	2.7	2.7	1.9	2.5	3.0	2.3	2.0	2.0	2.2		2.4
Dick Brown Sings	M	Sun	6:45	2.1	2.0	2.3	3.3	2.2	2.7	2.6	2.2	2.2	3.1	2.5
Dick Haymes Show	N	Tue	7:30	7.1	9.7	9.6	8.5	10.3	8.7	9.2	7.5	9.6	8.1	8.8
Dinah Shore Show	N	Thu	8:30		14.4	17.8	15.9	17.5	16.7	13.9	13.5	13.6		15.4
Dr Christian	C	Wed	8:30	11.6	13.7	16.1	12.5	14.9	14.6	13.0	12.5	10.9	9.9	13.1
Dr IQ	N	Mon	10:30	9.7	13.2	12.5	13.5	13.4	11.4	11.2	9.8	9.8	10.0	11.4
Don Gardiner News	B	Sun	7:15	6.3	4.9	6.4	4.6	6.2	6.3	5.8	6.4	6.8	7.4	6.1

1944-45 Hooper Ratings 6-11 P.M.

Program				Sept. 44	Oct. 44	Nov. 44	Dec. 44	Jan. 45	Feb. 45	March 45	April 45	May 45	June 45	1944-45 Avg
Dorothy Thompson News/Comment	B	Sun	8:15		1.6	3.0	3.1					3.8	3.1	2.9
Double or Nothing	M	Fri	9:30	5.0	5.9	6.1	5.2	6.4	6.2	6.1	5.9	5.5	4.6	5.7
Drew Pearson News/Comment	B	Sun	7:00	9.3	10.4	10.4	8.6	9.8	11.1	9.3	10.3	9.6	9.2	9.8
Duffy's Tavern	N	Fri	8:30	11.3	12.0	13.6	13.4	16.2	15.7	15.8	12.6	12.5	11.4	13.5
Dunninger the Mentalist	B	Wed	9:00	3.5	2.8	3.4	3.6							3.3
Earl Godwin News/Comment	B	M-F	8:00	3.6	3.5	5.5	3.4	3.5	5.4	3.7	5.1	4.9	4.3	4.3
Earl Wilson on Broadway	M	Sun	10:00					1.5	2.6	1.4	1.7	3.2	1.4	2.0
Early American Dance Music	B	Sat	8:00	3.3	3.6	4.8	4.6	4.8	4.6	4.2	3.9	4.4	4.0	4.2
Easy Aces	C	Wed	7:30	4.7	4.7	5.5	5.8	5.3						5.2
Ed Wynn Show	B	Mon	9:00	3.0	3.5	4.1	3.8	4.4	3.3					3.7
Eddie Bracken Show	N	Sun	8:30						15.2	13.3	11.9	11.0		12.9
Eddie Cantor Show	N	Wed	9:00	18.1	16.3	19.3	19.7	20.8	19.8	17.4	17.3	14.6	15.7	17.9
Edgar Bergen & Charlie McCarthy	N	Sun	8:00		22.5	22.7	25.0	25.8	25.2	20.9	18.5	19.3		22.0
Edwin C Hill News/Comment	C	Tue	6:15	4.7	4.0	6.3	4.8	6.2	5.3	4.0	4.3	6.9	3.7	5.0
Famous Jury Trials	B	Fri	9:00	5.1	5.0	4.6	4.6	6.6	7.9	11.6	7.6	6.5	6.5	6.6
Fanny Brice Baby Snooks Show	C	Sun	6:30	8.4	9.1	10.3	9.5	12.0	11.7	10.2	9.4	7.5	8.2	9.6
FBI in Peace & War	C	Sat	8:30					11.0	13.0	9.8	10.1	8.7	8.7	10.2
Fibber McGee & Molly	N	Tue	9:30		25.6	28.8	30.5	30.6	31.7	28.6	28.9	26.3	24.0	28.3
First Line of Defense	C	Thu	10:00	5.3	3.9	4.8	5.3	5.1	5.4	5.1	5.4	5.3	4.4	5.0
First Nighter	M	Wed	9:30	2.9	5.2	5.2								4.1
Fitch Bandwagon	N	Sun	7:30	7.8	13.6	15.6	17.7	15.8	14.7	12.6	11.3	11.1	9.8	13.0
Frances Langford & Spike Jones	N	Sun	8:00										15.0	15.0
Frank Morgan Show	N	Thu	8:00	11.8	14.2	14.1	15.0	14.7	16.9	13.0	11.3	12.6		13.7
Frank Sinatra Show	C	Wed	9:00	11.5	10.6	12.0	12.2	10.6	10.8	11.1	9.1	10.9		11.0
Frank Singiser News	M	T,T,Sa	8:00	3.3	5.1	4.6	5.2	4.4	5.0	4.7	4.9	5.3	4.2	4.7
Fred Waring Show	B	Thu	10:00	2.6	2.7	3.5	4.0	4.6	4.6	4.0	4.2	4.1		3.8
Freedom of Opportunity	M	Fri	8:30	2.6	2.1	2.6	2.3	2.2	3.4	2.7	3.3	2.8	2.4	2.6
Fresh Up Show	M	Wed	8:30					3.0	3.5	3.4	2.9	3.2	2.7	3.0
Friday Night Boxing	M	Fri	10:00	3.0	2.8	3.0	2.9					2.7	2.8	3.0
Friday on Broadway	C	Fri	7:30	4.0	4.9	5.2	5.7	6.2	5.4	5.2	4.5	5.9	5.2	5.2
Fulton Lewis Jr News/Comment	M	M-F	7:00	5.5	5.4	6.5	4.9	6.2	5.6	5.5	6.6	7.7	6.3	6.0
Gabriel Heatter News/Comment	M	M-F	9:00	10.8	10.7	10.4	9.3	11.1	12.7	11.5	13.2	13.9	10.8	11.4
Gabriel Heatter News/Comment	M	Sun	8:45	8.2	9.1	10.1	10.6	10.3	11.0	9.3	10.3	9.9	8.9	9.8
Gangbusters	B	Fri	9:00	9.4	8.9	11.0	11.2							10.1
Gay Nineties Revue	C	Mon	8:30	7.4	8.2									7.8
Ginny Simms Show	N	Tue	8:00	10.8	11.3	11.2	13.1	11.8	13.5	11.6	11.0	10.5	9.7	11.5
Goodwill Hour John J Anthony	M	Sun	10:15	7.2	7.8	5.8								6.9
Gracie Fields Show	B	Tue	9:00			4.9	4.3	6.7						5.3
Grand Ole Opry	N	Sat	10:30	8.3	11.4		14.4	12.2	12.1	9.8	10.5	10.5	9.9	11.0
Great Gildersleeve	N	Sun	6:30	10.8	11.8	15.6	14.9	16.2	16.1	14.2	13.3	13.6	12.7	13.9
Great Moments in Music	C	Wed	10:00	5.4	5.1	6.0	6.5	7.1	6.9	6.5	5.0	6.5	5.8	6.1
Greenfield Village Chapel Choir	B	Sun	8:00	1.5	1.9	1.5	2.6	2.4	3.3	2.8	1.4	1.1	1.9	2.0
Guy Lombardo Orch	B	Mon	10:00	3.2	4.8	3.9	3.9	5.2	5.6	4.8	4.5	4.9	5.2	4.6
HV Kaltenborn News/Comment	N	M-F	7:45	13.2	14.2	15.1	13.9	15.1	16.3	14.9	15.5	16.6	12.3	14.7
Hal MacInyre Orch	B	Tue	10:30					3.1						3.1
Harry Savoy Show	N	Thu	10:00	11.6										11.6
Hedda Hopper Hollywood News	C	Mon	7:15		5.4	7.1	5.5	9.2	7.4	6.8	6.9	6.7	6.6	6.8
Henry Gladstone News/Comment	M	M,Th	10:00	3.0	2.8	4.2	2.5							3.1

1944-45 Hooper Ratings 6-11 P.M.				Sept. 44	Oct. 44	Nov. 44	Dec. 44	Jan. 45	Feb. 45	March 45	April 45	May 45	June 45	1944-45 Avg
Here's to Romance Robert Ripley	C	Thu	10:30	5.3	5.3	5.8	5.3	4.3	4.5	4.3				5.0
Hildegarde's Raleigh Room	N	Tue	10:30	8.4	16.8	17.3	21.6	22.3	17.8	15.2	16.0	16.6	13.7	16.6
Hollywood Mystery Time	B	Sun	9:15		10.1	8.9	9.9	10.9	11.2	9.8	10.3	10.8	9.9	10.2
Horace Heidt Orch	B	Mon	7:00	3.1	2.7	3.2	3.8	4.8						3.5
Hour of Charm	N	Sun	10:00	7.2	9.4	11.0	10.8	10.3	10.7	10.0	9.1	9.3	8.6	9.6
I Love a Mystery	B	Wed	10:00	5.5	7.0	7.1	8.0							6.9
Ice Box Follies	B	Wed	10:00						3.5	2.7	2.8	2.3	2.4	2.7
Information Please	N	Mon	9:30	11.0	11.8	11.3	10.4	12.4	10.1	9.4	10.4	10.1	10.1	10.7
Inner Sanctum	C	Tue	9:00	7.9	10.3	10.6	9.1	12.2	9.6	10.7	10.7	10.3	9.0	10.0
It Pays to Be Ignorant	C	Fri	9:00	6.7	8.8	10.1	9.6	11.6	12.6	11.6	11.0	9.8	8.7	10.1
Jack Benny Program	N	Sun	7:00		19.8	21.1	23.1	24.2	23.0	19.2	16.7	15.8		20.4
Jack Carson Show	C	Wed	8:00	7.9	9.9	8.2	7.0	9.1	10.2	9.5	8.6	7.3	6.3	8.4
Jack Kirkwood Show	C	M-F	7:00					6.2	6.3	5.5	5.9	5.3	4.3	5.6
James Melton Show	C	Sun	9:30	7.2	8.7	9.1	9.4	9.2	9.1	8.8	7.0	7.1	7.2	8.3
Jerry Cooper Show	M	Sun	9:45			3.8	2.2	2.4	1.7	1.9				2.4
Jerry Wayne Sings	B	Mon	9:00							3.1	3.8	2.9	2.8	3.2
Jimmie Fidler Hollywood News	B	Sun	9:45	8.4	9.4	8.6	12.0	13.6	12.4	12.1	11.5			11.0
Jimmy Carroll Sings	C	MWF	6:15							3.3	3.3	3.9	2.9	3.4
Jimmy Durante & Garry Moore	C	Fri	10:00	7.5	10.7	11.5	11.8	12.8	13.4	11.9	13.6			11.7
Joan Davis & Jack Haley	N	Thu	9:30	16.4	17.4	22.2	23.7	23.4	24.0	21.5	23.1	21.6		21.5
John Nesbit's Passing Parade	C	TWT	7:15	5.1										5.1
Johnny Mercer Show	N	M-F	7:00		9.2	8.3								8.8
Joseph C Harsch BF Goodrich News	C	M-F	6:55	5.6	5.1	5.8	4.4	5.5	5.5	5.4	6.8	6.2	4.3	5.5
Judy Canova Show	C	Sat	10:00					15.0	14.8	13.7	11.2	12.5	11.9	13.2
Kate Smith Hour	C	Sun	7:00	10.7	7.2	8.3	8.7	9.0	9.4	8.2	7.5	6.9	8.2	8.4
Kay Kyser Kollege Mus Knowledge	N	Wed	10:00		16.7	16.2	20.4	20.8	17.9	17.7	15.8	15.8	13.6	17.2
Keep Up with the World	B	Wed	9:00	3.3	3.3	3.5	3.5	2.4	3.1	3.2	2.9			3.2
Keepsakes	B	Sun	8:30	3.1										3.1
Kenny Baker Show	C	Sat	8:00	5.8	7.6	9.5	9.8							8.1
Kraft Music Hall Summer Show	C	Thu	9:00	11.4	14.2									12.8
Leland Stowe News/Comment	B	Sat	7:15	2.8	2.5	2.8	2.1	2.8	2.4	2.5	3.0	3.4	2.2	2.7
Let Yourself Go	C	Wed	10:30	6.7	5.1	4.1	4.1	8.0	5.8	5.8	5.0	6.5	6.7	5.8
Life of Riley	B	Sun	10:00		4.7	5.6	5.9	7.2	7.3	7.2	6.5	7.1	7.3	6.5
Little Known Facts Dale Carnegie	M	Wed	10:00				2.3	2.6	3.9	3.2	2.8	2.3	2.4	2.8
The Lone Ranger	B	MWF	7:30	5.3	6.5	7.5	8.2	9.2	8.9	7.8	6.6	6.8	6.4	7.3
Lowell Thomas News	B	M-F	6:45	11.9	13.2	15.1	13.3	13.5	15.9	13.4	12.7	14.8	11.7	13.6
Lum & Abner	B	M-Thu	8:15	4.0	4.6	4.2	5.7	4.8	5.0	5.3	4.9	5.2	4.2	4.8
Lux Radio Theater	C	Mon	9:00	16.9	20.8	23.5	22.5	23.3	27.0	26.6	23.2	24.4	21.3	23.0
Lyn Murray	C	MWF	6:15	2.5	2.7	3.3	2.5	3.2	2.7	3.1				2.9
Major Bowes Amateur Hour	C	Thu	9:00	9.4	11.4	9.4	8.3	6.8	5.9	5.2	4.0			7.6
Man Called X	B	Sat	10:30	6.1	4.8	2.8	4.5	7.3	4.6					5.0
Manhattan Merry Go Round	N	Sun	9:00	7.6	9.6	11.9	9.6	9.7	12.3	9.4	8.0	9.6	8.6	9.6
March of Time	B	Thu	10:30	12.8	13.8	7.2	6.3	6.7	6.6	6.7	6.0	6.3	4.4	7.7
Mayor of the Town	C	Sat	7:00	7.2	8.8	9.0	10.1	11.4	12.0	10.1	9.4	9.8	9.8	9.8
Meet Corliss Archer	C	Thu	9:30	5.9	8.5	7.4	5.6	8.3	7.9	7.2	6.2	7.1	6.4	7.1
Meet Your Navy	B	Sat	7:30	2.4	3.1	3.4	3.2	3.3	4.1	2.8	2.8	3.3	3.1	3.2
Mr & Mrs North	N	Wed	8:00	11.9	14.4	14.6	14.8	15.1	15.5	14.4	14.1	13.8	11.7	14.0
Mr District Attorney	N	Wed	9:30	16.6	17.8	24.6	20.9	25.0	23.9	22.7	21.5	19.8	19.9	21.3

1944-45 Hooper Ratings 6-11 P.M.

Program				Sept. 44	Oct. 44	Nov. 44	Dec. 44	Jan. 45	Feb. 45	March 45	April 45	May 45	June 45	1944-45 Avg
Mr Keen	C	Thu	7:30	5.5	8.1	8.9	7.7	8.6	9.5	8.5	9.8	8.6	7.4	8.3
Molle Mystery Theater	N	Tue	9:00	7.9	10.1	11.7	12.5	13.3	13.3	13.4	12.0	11.1	10.5	11.6
Music by Morton Gould	C	Thu	9:00									4.0	3.9	4.0
Music by Raymond Paige	B	Fri	9:00								2.3	2.4	2.0	2.2
Music That Satisfies	C	T,W,T	7:15		6.4	6.7	6.3	7.6	7.5	6.2	6.6	5.8	5.4	6.5
My Best Girls	B	Wed	8:30	11.4	3.4	2.6	3.6							5.3
National Barn Dance	N	Sat	9:00	7.5	11.3	12.7	11.4	11.8	11.9	11.6	8.9	9.4	8.9	10.5
Ned Calmer Parker Pen News	C	Sa,Su	8:55	10.2	10.4	10.9	11.3	13.7	11.1	8.8	10.2	8.9	8.5	10.4
Nelson Eddy Show	C	Wed	10:30	7.1	6.4	6.4								6.6
News of the World	N	M-F	7:15	6.9	6.9	9.9	8.5	8.7	9.0	7.5	8.3	9.6	7.5	8.3
Old Gold Program	N	Sun	10:30	7.9	8.3									8.1
One Man's Family	B	Tue	7:30	9.2	12.0		13.4	12.5		7.2			7.5	9.4
Palmolive Party	N	Sat	10:00	10.1	9.7		11.7		9.2	7.2	7.2	8.6	5.6	11.2
Parker Family	B	Fri	8:15	2.2	3.5									2.9
People Are Funny	N	Fri	9:30	8.5	12.2	12.6	14.2	15.6	15.6	14.2	14.0	14.5	12.9	13.4
Philco Summer Hour	B	Sun	6:00	4.2							6.6	6.6	5.3	6.0
Phil Harris Show	N	Wed	10:00	12.8										12.8
Quick as a Flash	M	Sun	6:00	1.9	3.4	4.2	5.7	5.8	7.3	6.1	4.0	4.1	5.0	4.8
Quiz Kids	B	Sun	7:30	9.0	8.7	11.3	9.3	10.1	10.5	10.5	8.6	9.1	7.5	9.4
Radio Hall of Fame	B	Sun	6:00		5.4	6.8	7.0	8.1	9.0	6.6	6.2			7.0
Radio Readers Digest	C	Sun	9:00	6.2	8.3	10.0	9.0	12.5	9.0	9.4	8.7	6.2	7.1	8.6
Ransom Sherman Show	B	Tue	8:30	4.2	4.0	4.6								4.2
Ray Noble by Request	C	Wed	9:00			5.1						5.0	5.0	5.0
Raymond Gram Swing News/Com	B	M-F	7:15	5.4	4.0		4.4		4.0		3.5	4.3	2.8	4.1
Road Ahead	B	Wed	9:00									3.2	2.6	2.9
Romance Rhythm & Robt Ripley	C	Thu	10:30								4.4	4.8	4.4	4.5
Roy Rogers Show	M	Tue	8:30		5.1		5.0	5.3	6.0	6.4	5.5	4.5		5.4
Rudy Vallee Show	N	Thu	10:30	10.1	12.3	12.3	15.0	15.2	15.2	14.5	11.8	11.5	10.8	12.7
The Saint	N	Sat	10:30	10.7	10.7			12.4	10.8	9.7				11.0
Sammy Kaye Orch	B	Fri	7:30	4.9	3.7	3.8	3.6	4.2	4.2	2.8	2.7	3.8		3.7
Saturday Night Serenade	C	Sat	10:00	7.5	8.5	10.5	10.5	10.6	9.8	9.8	9.3	10.2	8.8	9.6
Scramby Amby	B	Wed	9:45	2.4	4.0	2.8	3.4	2.0	2.6	2.7				2.9
Screen Guild Players	C	Mon	10:00	15.3	17.7	21.7	20.6	20.8	23.7	23.4	22.3	21.9	20.6	20.6
Screen Test	M	M-F	9:15	3.3	4.0	3.6	2.9	3.4	3.1	3.5	4.0		3.6	3.6
Service to the Front	C	Tue	10:00	4.2	3.6	3.0	8.9	10.4	10.4	9.3	10.4			3.6
The Shadow	M	Sun	5:30		9.3	8.0							3.2	3.4
Silver Theater	C	Sun	6:00	7.0		8.0								9.5
Spotlight Bands Victory Parade	B	M-Sat	9:30	3.5	3.3	3.6	3.3	3.4	3.1	3.2	2.8	2.9		3.2
Stage Door Canteen	C	Fri	10:30	8.8	10.4	10.8	13.1	14.0	11.1	10.5	9.6			11.0
Stars of the Future	B	Fri	8:00			2.1	3.7	3.0	2.6	2.7				3.0
Starlight Serenade	M	Thu	9:30	3.6	3.4	3.2	2.2	2.1	2.2	2.2	1.7	2.1	2.1	2.8
Steel Horizons	M	Sun	9:30		2.2		2.2	2.1	2.2	2.2				2.2
Stop or Go	B	Sun	8:30	5.1	5.3	6.3	7.9	7.0	6.1	5.5				6.2
Stop That Villain	M	Sun	8:30	3.6	3.7	4.0								3.8
Story Teller Marvin Miller	B	M-F	9:55	3.3	4.2	3.0	3.3	3.6	2.8	2.6	2.6	2.4	2.6	3.0
Sumner Welles Commentary	C	Wed	10:00		3.0	4.7	2.7	3.1						3.4
Suspense	C	Thu	8:00	8.6	9.7	10.4	10.1	12.8	11.2	13.6	11.7	11.9	11.0	11.1
Swing's the Thing	M	Thu	10:30					3.5	2.0	2.3	1.4	1.9	1.8	2.2

1944-45 Hooper Ratings 6-11 P.M.

Program	Net	Day	Time	Sept. 44	Oct. 44	Nov. 44	Dec. 44	Jan. 45	Feb. 45	March 45	April 45	May 45	June 45	1944-45 Avg
Symphony of the Americas	M	Sat	8:30									1.8	2.0	1.9
Take It or Leave It	C	Sun	10:00	14.4	15.7	18.0	18.4	18.4	18.5	15.9	14.6	14.8	14.8	16.4
Ted Malone	B	MWF	8:00	3.4	3.4	3.1	3.4	4.1	3.8	4.6	4.8	4.3	3.6	3.9
Telephone Hour	N	Mon	9:00	5.9	7.2	7.0	7.7	8.3	8.6	7.4	8.5	7.8	7.0	7.5
Thanks to the Yanks	C	Mon	7:30	8.0	12.2	11.4	14.0	13.2	13.6	14.0	12.0	13.2	11.9	12.4
That Brewster Boy	C	Fri	9:30	6.8	8.9	10.7	11.6	11.5	11.6	10.9	10.3	11.0		10.2
Theater of Romance	C	Tue	8:30	8.6	10.2	11.7	10.7	12.6	9.8				9.2	10.5
This Is Helen Hayes	M	Sun	10:15							1.8	1.1	1.5	1.2	1.4
This Is My Best	C	Tue	9:30	7.7	8.0	7.1	6.1	6.9	9.1	7.1	6.2	6.9		7.2
This Is Your FBI	B	Fri	8:30									5.5	5.3	5.4
Those Websters	C	Fri	9:30							8.1	8.9	7.2	6.6	7.7
Treasure Hour of Song	M	Thu	9:30				3.8	2.3	3.3	3.9	3.2			3.4
Truth or Consequences	N	Sat	8:30	10.5	14.4	16.2	15.8	16.5	16.2	14.7	12.7	14.4	13.2	14.5
Upton Close News/Comment	M	Sun	6:30	3.6	3.9	4.3	5.0	4.6	6.6	5.1	3.2	5.3	4.4	4.6
Voice of Firestone	N	Mon	8:30	6.3	10.5	7.2	8.0	7.8	7.1	7.0	7.4	6.6	6.4	7.4
Vox Pop	C	Mon	8:00	9.7	11.5	13.6	13.8	16.0	16.0	12.7	12.5	12.2	11.5	13.0
Walter Winchell Jergens Journal	B	Sun	9:00	17.6	23.9	20.9	24.5	24.6	23.9	23.6	26.6	21.5	21.3	22.8
Waltz Time	N	Fri	9:00	8.1	9.9	10.9	12.3	11.9	13.1	11.4	10.6	10.6	8.6	10.7
We the People at War	C	Sun	10:30		13.1	12.7	14.5	16.0	13.2	14.3	12.9	13.7	12.4	13.6
We Who Dream	C	Fri	7:15	2.9										2.9
Which Is Which?	C	Wed	9:30	4.9	10.1	10.1	7.6	9.2	10.0	8.7	8.7	9.0	6.7	8.8
World Today News/Doug Edwards	C	M-F	6:45		5.7	5.7	5.2	5.0	5.2	4.7	5.4	5.8	4.7	5.1
Your All Time Hit Parade	N	Sun	7:00	7.5										7.5
Your Hit Parade	C	Sat	9:00	12.8	15.2	15.2	16.6	18.7	17.7	15.5	15.5	13.2	12.5	15.3

Special Broadcasts

Program	Net	Date	Rating
Thomas Dewey Political Speech	N	9/7	20.1
Thomas Dewey Political Speech	C	9/18	13.9
Thomas Dewey Political Speech	N	9/19	18.4
Pres Roosevelt Political Speech	BN	10/14	31.7
Thomas Dewey Political Speech	BN	10/20	15.3
Thomas Dewey Political Speech	BN	10/23	21.3
Sixth War Loan Drive Bob Hope	N	11/18	15.0
NFL Champ GreenBay vs NYGiants	B	12/17	4.3
Pres Truman Address on FDR Death	All	4/17	53.6

1945-46 Hooper Ratings 6-11 P.M.

Program	Net	Day	Time	Sept. 45	Oct. 45	Nov. 45	Dec. 45	Jan. 46	Feb. 46	March 46	April 46	May 46	June 46	1945-46 Avg
Abbott & Costello Show	N	Thu	10:00		16.4	17.2	19.2	19.4	18.6	15.0	16.2	15.5	10.4	16.4
Academy Award Theater	C	Sat	7:00								5.6	6.0	4.5	5.4
Adventures of Bulldog Drummond	M	Mon	8:00	6.9	4.8	4.8	4.4	6.1	6.8	6.7	6.0	6.4	5.4	5.8
Adventures of Ellery Queen	C	Wed	7:30	5.8	9.4	10.2	10.4	10.4	11.8	11.3	10.1	9.0	6.8	9.6
Adventures of Ozzie & Harriet	C	Sun	6:00	7.0	8.8	10.1	11.8	9.9	9.2	9.3	8.4	7.0	6.8	8.7
Adventures of Sherlock Holmes	M	Mon	8:30	5.7	10.0	11.1	11.2	11.6	10.5	9.9	10.2	9.3		10.1
Adventures of the Falcon	M	Tue	8:30		5.2	5.0	5.3	6.6	7.6	7.1	6.3	5.6	5.7	6.0
Adventures of the Thin Man	C	Sun	7:00	8.9	9.3	8.2	10.2	9.5	8.7	9.0	7.2	7.4	8.6	8.7
Alan Young Show	A	Fri	9:00	3.7	3.9	4.4	4.0	5.0	6.6	6.4	5.2	5.3	4.7	4.9
Aldrich Family	C	Fri	8:00	9.9	13.6	15.8	17.4	15.6	17.9	16.1	13.4	12.8	9.9	14.2

1945-46 Hooper Ratings 6-11 P.M.		Day	Time	Sept. 45	Oct. 45	Nov. 45	Dec. 45	Jan. 46	Feb. 46	March 46	April 46	May 46	June 46	1945-46 Avg
Alec Templeton Show	N	Sun	8:00										10.0	10.0
Alexander's Mediation Board	M	Sun	8:15	7.3	5.4	5.8	5.0	5.6	7.0	6.1				6.0
Amazing Mrs Danbury	C	Sun	8:00								4.2	4.4	6.1	4.9
American Album of Familiar Music	C	Sun	9:30	9.3	11.4	11.3	13.0	14.4	12.6	12.6	11.0	10.6	10.3	11.7
American Melody Hour	A	Tue	7:30	6.2	8.4	8.2	9.2	8.6	9.9	10.1	7.1	7.2	5.1	8.0
America's Town Meeting	N	Thu	8:30	3.8	4.8	4.8								5.7
Amos & Andy	N	Tue	9:00	16.7	16.7	15.8	16.8	17.3	19.4	17.5	17.6	15.3	14.5	16.8
An Evening with Romberg	C	Wed	8:30	9.3	9.3	10.6	7.4						7.7	9.2
Andre Kostelanetz Orch	C	Thu	9:00	5.7	6.2	6.4	6.6	7.4	5.7	5.1	4.4	4.7		5.8
Andrews Sisters Show	M	Wed	10:30	5.2	5.0	5.4	6.6	4.1	6.1	5.1				5.6
Arthur Hale News/Comment	N	TTSa	7:30	4.0	4.6	4.6	4.4	4.0	3.4	4.5	3.4	4.4	3.6	4.1
Ask Me Another	C	Sun	6:30										5.6	5.6
Beulah	C	Sun	8:00	6.2	7.6	8.9	9.2	8.9	7.6	8.0				8.1
Big Town	C	Tue	8:00	9.8	14.4	14.8	15.2	15.5	17.5	14.6	14.3	11.0	9.4	13.7
Bill Henry Johns Manville News	N	M-F	8:55	10.2	12.4	11.2	12.0	12.2	12.2	11.2	9.8	8.0	6.5	10.6
Bill Stern Colgate Sports Newsreel	N	Fri	10:30	5.6	5.9	4.7	8.3	8.8	8.2		8.1	7.8	4.8	6.9
Bing Crosby Kraft Music Hall	N	Thu	9:00	20.6					24.3	22.4	21.7	17.4		21.5
Blind Date	A	Fri	8:00	4.7										6.5
Blondie	C	Sun	7:30	8.2	13.1	14.6	14.3	14.6	13.3	14.7	11.6	11.3	8.5	11.7
Bob Burns Show	N	Thu	7:30		13.2	14.2	15.5	13.3	15.2	14.7	13.1		7.5	12.9
Bob Crosby Show	N	Wed	9:30		8.9	8.9	8.5	4.7	3.9	7.0	7.6	8.9	6.2	6.5
Bob Hope Show	A	Tue	10:00		27.1	26.8	31.7	30.5	31.2	28.0	27.9	26.9	26.0	27.7
Boston Symphony & Boston Pops	M	Sat	9:30		2.3	2.2	2.8	2.6	2.6	2.7	2.4	2.3	2.5	2.5
Break the Bank	N	Sat	9:30			2.4	4.6	4.6	5.0	5.0	5.1			4.5
Burns & Allen Show	N	Thu	8:00	10.0	13.1	14.6	14.8	14.8	15.1	14.1	11.8	9.7	9.7	12.8
Can You Top This?	N	Sat	9:30	10.7	13.0	15.0	15.1	15.2	14.2	14.8	13.1	12.1	10.8	13.4
Carnation Contented Hour	M	Mon	10:00	6.7	8.9	8.9	8.5	11.2	8.6	8.1	7.5	7.6	6.6	8.3
Casebook of Gregory Hood	N	Mon	8:30							8.1	7.5	7.6	6.1	6.1
Cavalcade of America	N	Mon	8:00	7.0	10.1	10.1	9.8	10.5	10.0	10.2	9.4	9.1	7.1	9.3
Cedric Foster News/Comment	M	Sun	6:30	3.0	3.0	4.3	3.4	4.9	4.5	3.2	3.6	2.4	4.8	3.7
Celebrity Club	C	Sat	10:15						7.3	5.9	6.2	6.5	6.4	6.7
Charles Collingwood News	C	Sat	6:45				8.2	6.2			2.7	4.8	2.6	3.4
Chester Morrison News	A	M-F	9:55						2.8	3.2	3.0			3.0
Chesterfield Supper Club	N	Fri	7:00	8.4	9.9	10.6	11.5	11.8	12.0	10.6	9.5	8.9	8.0	10.1
Cities Service Highways in Melody	A	M-F	8:00	6.0	8.3	8.1	8.1	8.0	7.8	7.6	6.8	6.4	5.1	7.1
Counterspy	A	Wed	10:00	6.5	7.1	7.7	9.2							7.6
County Fair	A	Sun	5:30	3.5		3.1			6.1	6.4	4.9		5.8	5.6
Crime Doctor	C	Sun	7:30	9.9	9.7	13.1	14.3	13.6	13.4	12.6	9.3	7.8	9.0	11.3
Curtain Time	A	Thu	8:30	3.2	2.8	4.4	4.6	3.9	4.4	5.2	3.4	4.7	3.9	4.1
Danny Kaye Show	C	Fri	10:00	10.0	9.7	9.5	11.4	11.2	12.0	11.4	10.7	11.7	11.7	10.8
Date with Judy	N	Tue	10:30		12.7	12.7	14.0	15.4	12.9	12.9	12.4	10.1	9.3	12.3
Detect & Collect	A	Thu	8:30		4.1	4.4	4.6	4.6	4.0	4.6	3.8	4.6	3.9	4.2
Detroit Symphony	M	Sun	8:30	3.3										3.3
Dick Haymes Show	C	Sat	8:00		8.5	9.0	8.8	8.4	8.3	9.3	8.1	7.0	7.9	8.4
Dick Tracy	A	Sat	8:00		3.9	4.0	4.6	5.5						4.5
Dinah Shore Show	N	Thu	8:30	9.0	13.2	13.7	15.7	14.3	15.0	14.0	12.8	11.8	11.8	13.1
Dr Christian	C	Wed	8:30	11.3	14.2	15.2	15.2	16.6	17.0	14.5	14.8	12.0	8.6	13.9

1945-46 Hooper Ratings 6-11 P.M.

Program	Net	Time	Day	Sept. 45	Oct. 45	Nov. 45	Dec. 45	Jan. 46	Feb. 46	March 46	April 46	May 46	June 46	1945-46 Avg
Dr IQ	N	10:30	Mon	8.7	10.0	9.0	11.3	11.8	12.3	10.9	11.3	10.0	9.7	10.5
Doctors Talk It Over	A	9:30	Tue	2.2	1.6	1.9	1.7	1.3	1.2	1.8	1.3	0.9	1.3	1.5
Don Gardiner News	A	7:15	Sun	6.4	5.1	5.9	6.2	6.7	4.8	6.0	4.4	4.6	4.9	5.5
Double or Nothing	M	9:30	Sun	4.7	6.0	6.1	6.3	8.5	8.9	9.5	7.5	9.1	7.1	7.4
Drew Pearson News/Comment	A	7:00	Sun	7.9	8.4	8.9	9.1	9.0	8.9	9.8	6.6	6.2	8.3	8.3
Duffy's Tavern	N	8:30	Fri	11.2	12.6	13.9	14.5	15.4	15.3	12.7	12.2	10.9	8.7	12.7
Dunninger the Mentalist	N	10:00	Fri	8.1									9.5	8.8
Earl Godwin News/Comment	A	8:15	Thu	2.9	2.9	2.7	3.4	2.8	3.8	3.2	2.8	2.3	2.9	3.0
Ed Sullivan	A	9:00	Tue								2.0	1.7	1.3	1.7
Eddie Cantor Show	N	9:00	Wed		15.8	17.1	19.2	20.2	18.8	17.5	16.7	14.9	14.0	17.1
Edgar Bergen & Charlie McCarthy	N	8:00	Sun	14.6	21.6	23.0	26.3	26.9	26.6	25.5	22.4	19.0	18.8	22.4
Edward Maher News/Comment	A	10:00	Mon										1.1	1.1
Edwin C Hill News/Comment	C	6:15	Tue	4.9	5.1	5.5	5.5							5.3
Encore Theater	C	9:30	Tue										6.7	6.7
Erwin Canham News/Comment	A	6:15	Sat				2.2	2.0	2.1	1.9	1.6	2.0		2.0
Everything for the Boys	N	7:30	Tue	6.0										6.0
Exploring the Unknown	M	9:00	Sun			2.9	2.9	2.6	3.5	2.6	2.3	2.5	2.9	2.8
Famous Jury Trials	A	9:00	Fri	6.0	7.1	8.5	7.9	9.7	9.1					8.1
Fanny Brice Baby Snooks Show	C	6:30	Sun	8.2	12.0	11.1	14.2	13.4	12.2	12.5	11.1	8.7	8.8	11.2
FBI in Peace & War	C	8:30	Thu	8.2	10.4	11.1	12.2	13.6	14.8	13.6	10.6	9.3	9.5	11.3
Fibber McGee & Molly	N	9:30	Tue		28.3	27.0	28.8	30.9	31.0	29.0	27.3	23.2	18.5	27.1
First Line of Defense	C	10:00	Thu	4.8	4.6	2.6								4.0
First Nighter	C	7:30	Sat		7.2	8.7	10.9	10.7	11.2	9.0	9.6			9.6
Fishing & Hunting Club	A	8:30	Wed	1.9	1.8	2.4	1.9	2.4	2.9	3.2	2.1	2.0	2.9	2.4
Fitch Bandwagon	N	7:30	Sun		14.3	14.7	18.0	18.2	17.9	15.8	12.7	12.4	9.1	14.8
Fitch Bandwagon Mysteries	N	7:30	Sun	6.8										6.8
Follies of 1946/Philip Morris Frolics	C	8:00	Tue						10.4	9.0	7.7	7.6	6.0	8.1
Ford Show	C	10:00	Tue		2.9	3.2	3.4					2.7	2.8	3.2
Ford Sunday Evening Hour	A	8:00	Sun		3.3	3.1	4.1	3.5	3.1	3.1	3.8			3.3
Forever Ernest	C	8:00	Mon									5.8	4.1	5.0
Frank Morgan Kraft Music Hall	N	9:00	Thu		15.1	16.3	17.4	18.1						16.7
Frank Morgan Show	N	7:00	Sun										7.6	7.6
Frank Sinatra Show	C	9:00	Wed	10.5	9.4	9.8	11.9	10.5	12.8	11.2	10.0	9.3	7.2	10.3
Frank Singiser News	M	8:00	TTSa	3.9	3.4	3.9	3.1	3.6	3.9	3.1				3.6
Fred Allen Show	N	8:30	Sun		20.9	19.6	22.6	23.9	24.2	23.7	20.9	19.2	15.3	21.1
Fred Waring Show	N	9:30	Tue										10.5	10.5
Freedom of Opportunity	M	10:00	Sun	2.0	2.0	2.0	1.7	1.3	1.6	1.4	1.0	1.6	2.1	1.7
Fresh Up Show Bert Lahr	M	8:30	Wed	3.5	4.1	4.0	3.7	3.8	3.7	4.4	3.4	3.3	3.8	3.8
Friday Night Boxing	A	10:00	Fri	3.2	2.9	3.9	4.8	5.6	6.3	5.4	4.3	5.9	3.9	4.6
Front Page News Paul Barnes	A	9:55	M-F			1.9	3.0	3.1						2.7
Fulton Lewis Jr News/Comment	M	7:00	M-F	4.4	5.0	5.7	5.7	6.0	6.3	5.7	4.4	4.2	3.7	5.1
Fulton Lewis Jr News/Comment	M	6:45	Sun		3.2	4.2	5.8	4.3	4.4					4.4
Gabriel Heatter News/Comment	M	9:00	M-F	8.0	7.6	5.7	6.2	6.5	6.4	6.3	5.6	5.8	4.3	6.2
Gabriel Heatter News/Comment	M	8:45	Sun	8.4	5.5	5.1	4.9	5.5	4.9	5.8	4.2	3.3	3.4	5.1
Gangbusters	A	9:00	Sat	5.1	6.8	7.6	8.6	8.3	9.2	10.2	9.3	8.1	9.3	8.3
Gene Autry's Melody Ranch	C	7:00	Sun										5.0	5.0
Ginny Simms Show	C	7:30	Fri		8.2	9.0	7.7	10.2	10.1	8.9	6.2	9.0		8.7
Grand Ole Opry	N	10:30	Sat	7.9	9.2	8.6	13.0	11.5	11.3	9.9	10.7	11.3	9.5	10.3

1945-46 Hooper Ratings 6-11 P.M.

Program				Sept. 45	Oct. 45	Nov. 45	Dec. 45	Jan. 46	Feb. 46	March 46	April 46	May 46	June 46	1945-46 Avg
Great Gildersleeve	N	Sun	6:30	9.8	14.3	15.6	18.3	17.7	16.4	15.9	13.7	13.1	11.4	14.6
Great Moments in Music	C	Wed	10:00	4.4	4.5	5.2	5.0	7.0	7.8	7.0	6.8	5.3	4.2	5.7
Guy Lombardo Orch	A	Tue	9:00	5.9	5.2	5.7	6.3	6.6	4.9	5.7				5.8
HV Kaltenborn News/Comment	N	M-F	7:45	11.7	10.6	11.7	12.7	13.9	10.6	9.9	7.7	8.0	6.6	10.3
Harry James Orch	C	Fri	10:30	5.7										5.7
Harry Wismer Sports	A	Fri	9:55										5.8	5.8
Headline Edition News/Taylor Grant	A	M-F	7:00		3.7	2.3	3.6	3.8		4.2				3.4
Hedda Hopper Hollywood News	A	Mon	8:15	4.8	3.2	4.1	3.6	4.3	3.0		3.7	2.8	2.3	3.6
Helen Hayes Theater	C	Sat	7:00	6.2	7.2	7.5	7.8	8.9	8.0	6.8				7.5
Henry J Tayler Your Land & Mine	M	M,F	7:30				0.9	0.9	1.4	1.6	1.9	1.7	2.2	1.6
Hildegarde's Raleigh Room	N	Wed	8:30	11.0	15.5	14.3	13.9	13.0	12.1	11.4	11.6	8.3	8.8	12.0
His Honor the Barber	N	Tue	7:30			8.7	10.4	8.3	10.3	9.4	9.9			9.5
Hobby Lobby	C	Thu	9:30	6.7	5.8	5.6	6.8	7.8	6.2	7.1	5.6	5.2		6.2
Holiday & Company	C	Fri	9:00						6.7	5.9				5.9
Holiday for Music	C	Wed	10:30								5.0	5.1	3.6	5.0
Hollywood Mystery Time	A	Sun	9:15	8.4	7.8	9.4	9.1							8.7
Hour of Charm Phil Spitalny	N	Sun	10:00	8.3	9.2	10.7	11.0	10.1	10.5	10.5	8.9	9.3	7.7	9.6
Hour of Mystery	A	Sun	10:00										5.0	5.0
Human Adventure	M	Sun	9:00		2.3	2.5								2.4
Information Please	N	Mon	9:30	9.9	9.9	10.8	10.8	10.3	10.8	11.3	10.6	8.8	8.1	10.1
Inner Sanctum	C	Tue	9:00	12.1	10.7	12.7	12.2	12.8	12.3	12.2	13.1	10.6	10.1	11.9
Inside of Sports Bill Brandt	M	M-F	7:45	2.5	2.5	2.0	2.4	2.9	2.8	2.4	2.3	2.2	3.2	2.5
Island Venture	C	Thu	10:00			3.6	4.9	3.7	4.3	5.6	4.4	4.9	4.0	4.4
It Pays to Be Ignorant	C	Fri	9:00	8.6	9.0	8.5	10.5	8.7			7.1	7.1	5.0	8.2
Jack Benny Show	N	Sun	7:00	21.7	21.7	21.6	24.8	25.9	24.6	22.3	17.0	18.3	15.6	21.3
Jack Carson Show	C	Wed	8:00	10.7	10.7	9.0	10.7	10.9	11.8	10.0	8.5	8.1	6.8	9.4
Jack Haley & Eve Arden	N	Thu	9:30	12.0	15.8	16.2	17.1	19.8	21.5	18.7	18.7	16.6	12.7	16.9
Jack Kirkwood Show	C	M-F	7:00	7.5	5.7	5.6	6.1	6.8	6.5	6.7	9.0	7.0	6.6	5.9
Jack Smith Show	C	M-F	7:15	4.1	7.2	7.7	9.2	8.5	9.0	9.1	7.6	6.5	5.4	7.8
James Melton Show	N	Sun	9:30	5.0	6.9	7.9	9.4	9.1	8.1	7.9	9.0			7.6
Jan Savitt Orch	C	Sun	10:30	6.7							4.7		4.5	4.5
Jerry Wayne Show	C	Fri	7:30	5.1										5.1
Jimmy Durante & Garry Moore	C	Fri	10:00	11.3	9.6	11.6	13.8	12.3	12.3	10.1		9.6	8.5	10.8
Jimmie Fidler Hollywood News	A	Sun	9:45	8.4	8.8	8.8	8.4	6.0	6.3	8.5		7.1	4.9	7.2
Joan Davis & Andy Russell	C	Mon	8:30	11.5	16.0	15.8	16.8	17.7	17.5	14.1	14.9	10.2	9.8	14.4
Johnny Presents	N	Tue	8:00	9.4	9.8	9.8	10.2	10.9						10.0
Judy Canova Show	C	Sat	10:00	13.3	12.5	13.7	14.6	14.7	15.1	14.3	14.3	13.2	12.0	13.8
Just Entertainment	C	Sat	7:30	4.9										4.9
Just Entertainment	C	Tue	10:00	4.2										4.2
Kate Smith Sings	C	Fri	8:30	11.4	10.2	10.8	11.1	10.1	10.9	10.7	8.3	9.5	7.8	10.1
Kay Kyser Kollege Mus Knowledge	N	Wed	10:00	10.0	12.1	12.9	14.5	16.0	15.5	14.9	13.6	15.3	9.6	13.4
Keep Working Keep Singing	C	MWF	6:15	3.2	3.5	3.7	3.8	3.8	3.4	3.0				3.5
Kraft Music Hall Eddy Duchin Orch	N	Thu	9:00	12.0										12.3
Kraft Music Hall Edw Everett Horton	N	Thu	9:00									12.3	7.8	9.9
Laguardia Speaks for Liberty	A	Sun	9:30					9.6	6.2	5.4	4.8	5.8		6.4
Lanny Ross Show	C	M-F	7:00								5.5	5.4	5.2	5.4
Life of Riley	C	Sat	8:00	10.2	12.3	12.9	16.0	15.6	15.8	15.1	12.5	11.9	9.8	13.2
Listen to a Love Song Tony Martin	C	Sat	7:30								6.2	7.5	5.5	6.4

1945-46 Hooper Ratings 6-11 P.M.				Sept. 45	Oct. 45	Nov. 45	Dec. 45	Jan. 46	Feb. 46	March 46	April 46	May 46	June 46	1945-46 Avg
Lone Ranger	A	MWF	7:30	4.7	7.1	7.2	8.4	9.6	9.9	9.1	8.3	6.2	6.4	7.7
Louella Parsons Hollywood News	A	Sun	9:15					9.9	11.3	11.2	8.1	7.4	8.8	9.5
Lowell Thomas News	N	M-F	6:45	12.9	13.0	13.4	12.8	13.6	14.5	12.4	11.1	8.0	8.3	12.0
Lum & Abner	N	M-Th	8:00	3.2	4.3	4.0	4.6	5.9	5.6	5.2	4.3	3.5	3.7	4.4
Lux Radio Theater	C	Mon	9:00	18.2	21.1	23.6	24.2	27.2	24.9	22.6	22.1	19.9	14.8	21.9
Maisie	C	Fri	10:30	6.3	8.5	7.4	9.2	9.3	9.8	7.9	8.9	9.7	8.1	8.5
Man Called X	N	Tue	10:00										9.5	9.5
Manhattan Merry Go Round	N	Sun	9:00	8.6	12.0	12.7	13.4	14.0	12.3	12.3	11.2	10.9	9.9	11.7
Mayor of the Town	C	Sat	8:30	9.5	9.5	11.5	11.9	12.5	11.6	9.9	10.2	10.9	7.9	10.5
Meet Corliss Archer	C	Sun	9:00									6.3	4.6	5.5
Meet Me at Parky's	N	Sun	10:30	5.6	8.0	7.9	9.9	8.6	7.6	8.9	7.0	8.2	7.2	7.9
Meet Your Navy	A	Mon	8:30	1.7										1.7
Mercury Summer Theater	C	Fri	10:00									5.5	5.5	5.5
Meredith Willson Show	C	Thu	8:30									5.3	5.3	5.3
Mr & Mrs North	N	Wed	8:00	11.6	13.0	12.8	13.9	13.3	13.5	12.2	11.9	9.6	9.2	12.1
Mr District Attorney	N	Wed	9:30	17.2	18.9	20.3	22.8	21.4	20.5	20.8	19.5	18.6	15.9	19.6
Mr Keen	C	Thu	7:30	8.4	9.0	9.1	8.8	9.6	11.4	11.1	9.0	8.1	6.6	9.1
Molle Mystery Theater	C	Fri	10:00		11.5	10.2	10.3	11.7	11.6	11.2	9.0	10.4	9.3	10.6
Mommie & The Men	C	M-F	7:00	2.6	4.9	5.6	5.3	5.4	7.6	5.4	5.0	3.2		5.3
Mutual Fight of the Week	M	Mon	10:15				2.0	1.2	1.7				3.3	2.7
Mystery in the Air	N	Thu	10:00	9.8										9.8
Mystery of the Week	N	M-F	7:00							5.7	5.7	6.5	4.5	5.6
National Barn Dance	C	Sat	9:00	8.5	8.2	9.4	10.1	10.4	10.9	10.5	9.1	6.1	6.5	9.0
Ned Calmer Parker Pen News	C	S-S	8:55	9.5	8.2	9.4	11.1	10.3	9.2	9.1	7.2	5.3	6.5	8.6
News of the World John Vandercook	N	M-F	7:15	6.3	8.3	8.0	8.6	9.3	7.9	7.1	6.6	5.8	5.4	7.3
One Man's Family	N	Sun	3:30	6.6	6.6	9.3	10.8	11.0	10.8	9.4	8.9	8.4	7.3	8.9
People Are Funny	N	Fri	9:00	12.1	11.2	12.5	13.9	14.3	16.0	15.2	14.8	12.9	9.2	13.2
Philo Vance	N	Thu	7:30	8.2										8.2
Powder Box Theater	C	Thu	10:30		4.9	3.2	6.6	5.5	7.2	4.3	4.9	2.6		5.2
Professor Quiz	A	Thu	7:30						2.9	3.6	2.9	1.7	2.7	2.9
Quentin Reynolds News/Comment	M	Sun	6:45							2.5	2.6			2.3
Quick as a Flash	M	Sun	6:00	3.1	4.9	6.6	7.1							5.4
Quick as a Flash	M	Sun	5:30					6.9	6.7	7.2	5.4	5.1	4.2	5.7
Quiz Kids	A	Sun	7:30	7.1	8.5	8.1	8.5	8.8	8.8	8.0	7.3	6.0	8.0	7.9
Radio Auction Show	M	Mon	10:00	2.8	3.0	2.2	3.1	2.8	3.3	3.3				2.9
Radio Hall of Fame	A	Sun	6:00		5.8	6.1	7.1	7.2	5.5	6.8	6.4			6.4
Radio Readers Digest	C	Sun	9:00											
Raymond Gram Swing News/Com	A	M-Th	7:15			2.8			3.5	3.0	1.8	2.2	2.2	2.7
Real Stories from Real Life	M	M-F	9:15	3.9	4.2	3.5	4.2	4.2	3.9	3.6	3.7	3.1	3.3	3.8
Red Skelton Show	N	Tue	10:30				24.5	25.3	25.6	22.5	21.1	23.4	19.5	23.1
Report to the Nation John Daly	C	Sat	10:30				5.1							5.3
Request Performance	C	Sun	9:00		7.4	8.2	9.1	9.0	8.2	7.7				8.0
Robert Trout News	C	M-F	6:45								3.1	3.6	3.4	3.4
Rogues Gallery	M	Thu	8:30	3.4	3.2	3.7	3.9	4.5	5.1	4.8	4.0	5.0	5.2	4.4
Romance Rhythm & Robert Ripley	C	Thu	10:30											3.4
Rudy Vallee Show	N	Thu	10:30	8.2	10.7	12.0	12.1	13.0	12.7	12.1	11.6	13.1	8.5	11.4
The Sad Sack	C	Wed	9:00										5.6	5.6
Saturday Night Serenade	C	Sat	9:45	6.6	9.8	9.8	11.5	9.9	9.5	9.5	9.8	8.8	7.3	9.3

1945–46 Hooper Ratings 6–11 P.M.

Program				Sept. 45	Oct. 45	Nov. 45	Dec. 45	Jan. 46	Feb. 46	March 46	April 46	May 46	June 46	1945–46 Avg
Screen Guild Players	C	Mon	10:00		18.3	18.9	22.2	22.0	21.4	22.0	19.5	19.3	14.0	19.7
The Shadow	M	Sun	5:00		7.5	7.4	9.9	9.2	10.3	10.5	7.8	7.2	8.3	8.7
The Sheriff	A	Fri	9:30	5.6	8.0	8.6	8.9	9.8	8.8	8.6	8.3	7.0	5.5	7.9
Spotlight Bands	M	MWF	9:30	3.1	3.2	3.0	3.5	2.7	3.3	3.0	3.3	3.3	3.2	3.2
Stairway to Stars	A	Sun	6:00		3.7	3.0							4.2	4.3
Starlight Serenade	M	Thu	9:30	2.7										3.1
Steel Horizons	M	Sun	9:00	1.7										1.7
Story Teller Marvin Miller	A	M-F	9:55	2.0										2.0
Sunday Evening Party	A	Sun	6:30	3.7	4.0	4.8	4.5	4.4	3.9	3.9	4.0	3.6	4.3	4.1
Suspense	C	Thu	8:00	8.7	11.9	12.6	12.4	15.0	14.2	14.3	13.7	11.2	11.4	12.5
Swing's the Thing	M	Thu	10:30	2.7		2.3	2.3							2.4
Take It or Leave It	C	Sun	10:00	14.1	17.0	17.2	19.5	19.0	17.2	17.0	15.7	15.3	13.1	16.5
Telephone Hour	N	Mon	9:00	6.5	8.1	8.5	6.7	9.3	8.1	9.2	9.2	9.1	7.0	8.2
Thanks to Yanks /Bob Hawk Show	C	Mon	7:30	9.8	13.3	12.6	12.7	14.2	14.2	13.3	12.6	12.9	8.6	12.4
Theater Guild on the Air	A	Sun	10:00	2.8	4.6	4.3	6.1	4.6	5.3	5.8	4.3	5.6	5.6	4.9
Theater of Romance	C	Tue	8:30	8.0	10.2	10.9	11.9	11.1	12.0	11.3	11.4	8.4	7.5	10.3
This Is My Best	C	Tue	9:30	14.6	6.0	8.1	8.9	7.2	8.2	7.7	7.5	7.0	6.2	8.1
This Is Your FBI	A	Fri	8:30	4.9	8.0	7.9	9.3	11.0	11.7	8.2	8.5	6.4	5.5	8.1
Those Websters	C	Sun	6:00	6.2	8.4	7.8	7.5	8.6	7.3	5.0	3.4	4.5	3.2	6.2
Tom Harmon Sports	M	Sat	7:45		3.2	2.7	2.6	3.0						2.9
Tommy Riggs & Betty Lou	C	Fri	7:30									7.1	6.0	6.6
Treasure Hour of Song	M	Thu	8:30						3.1	2.8	2.3	2.9	3.5	2.9
Truth or Consequences	N	Sat	8:30	9.2	14.2	14.0	18.2	17.5	18.7	15.0	15.9	13.0	10.7	14.6
Upton Close News/Comment	M	Tue	10:15							2.5	1.7	1.7	3.8	2.4
Vic & Sade	C	M-F	7:15	3.0	3.8	5.9	6.2							4.7
Victor Borge	N	Tue	9:30	11.7										11.7
Voice of Firestone	N	Mon	8:30	7.6	8.8	9.0	9.3	8.9	7.8	8.5	7.2	7.8	6.3	8.1
Vox Pop	C	Mon	8:00	9.9	14.6	12.9	14.8	14.2	12.7	13.6	12.6	13.2		13.2
Walter Winchell Jergens Journal	A	Sun	9:00	16.2	19.3	22.8	22.1	19.4	20.9	23.6	19.3	18.3	16.4	19.8
Waltz Time	N	Fri	9:30	9.1	10.8	10.9	12.4	13.9	13.8	13.3	12.2	7.8	7.2	11.1
Wayne King Orch	N	Sun	7:00	6.6										6.6
We the People	C	Sun	10:30	11.4							9.4	11.8	10.5	10.6
Wednesday with You	N	Wed	9:00	8.1										8.1
Woody Herman Orch	A	Fri	8:00		3.3		3.5	2.8	3.9	3.6	3.2	3.6	2.9	3.3
World Today News	C	M-F	6:45	4.3	4.6	4.4								4.4
Your Hit Parade	C	Sat	9:00	12.6	13.0	13.7	13.9	14.7	13.6	13.4	12.4	11.7	10.8	13.0

Special Broadcasts

Program	Net	Date	Sept. 45	Oct. 45	Nov. 45	Dec. 45	Jan. 46	Feb. 46	March 46	April 46
Official Japanese Surrender	All	9/1	43.7							
President Truman Announcement	All	9/1	46.8							
President Truman Address	All	9/2	31.3							
AFRS Victory Program	All	9/2	29.8							
World Series: Det/ChiCubs 2 Games	N	10/6&7		13.1						
NFL Champ: Washington/Cleveland	A	12/16				7.1				
All American Jazz Show	A	1/16					2.2			
General Eisenhower Address	C	1/18					10.6			
Winston Churchill Address	N,M	3/15							19.6	
All Star Cancer Fund Appeal	M	4/19								4.5

Special Broadcasts

	Net	Date	April 47	June 47
European Food Crisis Pres Truman	All	4/19	20.1	
US Open Golf Tournament	A	6/15		1.0
Boxing: Joe Louis/Billy Conn	A	6/19		67.2

1946-47 Hooper Ratings 6-11 P.M.

Program	Net	Day	Time	Sept. 46	Oct. 46	Nov. 46	Dec. 46	Jan. 47	Feb. 47	March 47	April 47	May 47	June 47	1946-47 Avg
Abbott & Costello Show	N	Thu	10:00		13.0	14.7	13.9	15.5	12.9	16.1	14.6	9.7	9.3	13.3
Academy Award Theater	C	Wed	10:00	5.2	6.0	8.1	8.5							7.0
Adventures of Bulldog Drummond	M	Fri	9:30	6.2	5.8				4.1	4.1	3.9	3.6	3.9	4.6
Adventures of Ellery Queen	C	Wed	7:30			9.3	9.3	9.7	10.2	10.6	9.9	8.4	4.5	9.0
Adventures of Ozzie & Harriet	C	Sun	6:00	5.6	8.9	13.0	13.0	12.1	11.0	12.6	10.1	7.5	6.7	10.1
Adventures of Sam Spade	A	Fri	8:00	5.0	5.3									5.2
Adventures of Sam Spade	C	Sun	8:00		7.3	9.8	10.7	10.6	11.2	11.3	10.4	8.4	8.9	9.8
Adventures of Sherlock Holmes	A	Mon	8:30		7.2	7.5	7.9	8.6	7.7	6.9	6.9	4.4	4.4	6.8
Adventures of the Falcon	M	Tue	8:30	6.8	9.2	8.8	10.6	9.3	10.5	9.8	9.6	6.7	5.1	8.6
Adventures of the Thin Man	C	Fri	8:30	8.1	11.2	11.1	11.7	14.2	12.1	12.3	10.9	8.3		11.1
Affairs of Ann Scotland	A	Wed	9:00		8.3	4.6	4.5	5.9						5.0
Alan Young Show	N	Fri	8:30	7.3	13.5	8.7	10.4	9.8	11.0	10.2	9.1	7.7	6.2	8.9
Aldrich Family	N	Thu	8:00	8.0	11.4	14.1	13.9	16.8	15.6	15.9	15.1	9.9	8.9	13.2
American Album of Familiar Music	N	Sun	9:30	9.6	9.5	12.6	12.3	12.9	11.5	12.5	11.1	10.9	9.3	11.4
American Melody Hour	C	Tue	7:30	5.7	18.0	10.2	8.7	10.0	10.3	10.2	9.5	5.6	5.6	8.5
America's Town Meeting of Air	A	Thu	8:30					6.4	4.5	4.9	5.2	4.0	4.1	4.9
Amos & Andy	N	Tue	9:00	18.0		20.9	22.3	23.4	28.9	23.9	23.9	19.3	18.2	22.1
An Evening with Romberg	N	Tue	10:30	10.0										10.0
Arthur Hale News/Comment	M	Tu,Th	7:30	2.5	4.7	4.7	4.0	4.6	5.7	4.6	4.7	3.9	2.2	4.2
Ask Me Another	N	Sun	6:30	5.1										5.1
Benny Goodman Orch	N	Mon	9:30	6.0										6.0
Best Things in Life	A	Thu	9:30											2.8
The Bickersons	N	Sun	10:00	6.4	6.7	6.8	6.9	8.8	6.9	10.4	8.2	2.9	2.7	7.5
The Big Story	N	Wed	10:00								8.1	7.8	6.4	8.9
Big Town	C	Tue	8:00	9.8	13.8	14.8	15.2	15.2	17.0	15.9	14.9	9.9	8.6	13.7
Bill Henry Johns Manville News	C	M-F	8:55	7.5	10.2	9.4	11.8	12.0	11.2	10.2	10.8	10.5	9.4	9.7
Bill Stern Colgate Sports Newsreel	N	Fri	10:30	6.6	5.3	8.7	5.8		8.7	7.6	8.1	8.0	6.3	6.9
Bing Crosby Philco Radio Time	A	Wed	10:00		24.0	13.9	14.6	18.4	16.8	19.4	21.5	16.0	5.1	17.6
Blondie	C	Sun	7:30	8.6	11.9	14.2	14.4	16.4	13.9	14.2	11.8	9.1	13.6	12.4
Bob Burns Show	N	Sun	6:30		9.3	9.9	11.4	9.8	10.6	9.6	8.0	6.4	9.1	9.4
Bob Hawk Show	C	Mon	7:30	8.2	13.1	13.9	13.2	16.0	13.8	15.3	14.7	11.3	11.1	13.1
Bob Hope Show	N	Tue	10:00		24.6	27.1	26.4	31.7	32.0	30.9	31.0	25.8	19.1	27.6
Boston Symphony & Boston Pops	A	Tue	8:30					3.6	2.6	2.5	2.4			2.8
Break the Bank	A	Fri	9:00	7.9	7.2	7.0	9.7	11.3	11.7	11.1	10.5	10.4	8.5	9.5
Burl Ives Show	M	Fri	8:00		2.8	2.3	2.6	2.6	2.5	1.9	2.9	1.8	2.1	2.4
Burns & Allen Show	N	Thu	8:30	11.3	14.4	17.1	16.4	17.5	17.9	16.2	15.1	11.1		15.2
By Popular Demand	M	Thu	9:30	3.4	2.3	3.2								3.0
Can You Top This?	N	Sat	9:30	8.5	11.4	12.6	11.7	12.0	12.6	13.1	12.2	11.7		11.6
Carnation Contented Hour	N	Mon	10:00	5.6	6.6	7.3	6.9	8.0	7.8	8.4	7.9	7.4	10.1	7.2
Casebook of Gregory Hood	M	Mon	8:30	4.0	6.1	7.0	6.1	6.8	7.4	7.8	7.8	5.0	6.0	6.4
Casey Crime Photographer	C	Thu	9:30		9.6	11.6	10.9	14.1	15.1	12.6	12.4	11.7	8.6	11.8
Cavalcade of America	N	Mon	8:00	5.9	9.4	9.8	9.2	11.4	9.9	11.9	11.2	7.2	7.3	9.3
Chesterfield Supper Club	N	M-F	7:00	7.8	9.6	10.8	12.1	12.0	11.9	11.1	10.5	11.1	8.0	10.5

1946-47 Hooper Ratings 6-11 P.M.	Net	Day	Time	Sept. 46	Oct. 46	Nov. 46	Dec. 46	Jan. 47	Feb. 47	March 47	April 47	May 47	June 47	1946-47 Avg
Counterspy	A	Sun	5:30	6.2	7.5	8.6	8.7	8.9	8.9	10.3	7.2	5.1	5.2	7.7
Crime Doctor	C	Sun	8:30	10.0	10.9	10.6	11.2	11.2	12.0	10.7	9.6	8.1	9.2	10.4
Curtain Time	N	Sat	7:30	4.5	6.2	8.0	7.9	9.4	10.0	9.3	8.4	6.6	6.5	7.7
A Date with Judy	N	Tue	8:30	7.5	12.8	13.8	14.5	15.9	15.6	15.6	15.5	10.9	8.9	13.1
A Day in the Life of Dennis Day	N	Wed	8:00		11.3	14.1	12.4	14.4	13.9	13.2	13.2	11.5	8.9	12.5
Detect & Collect	A	Sat	9:30	4.2										4.2
Detroit Symphony Sunday Eve Hour	A	Sun	8:00										2.1	2.1
Dick Haymes Show	C	Thu	9:00		9.6	10.4	11.2	13.2	14.1	13.1	11.9	10.4		11.7
Dinah Shore Ford Show	C	Wed	9:30	9.0	7.1	10.0	10.4	9.4	9.3	9.4	9.4	8.0	6.4	8.8
Dr Christian	C	Wed	8:30	10.0	11.9	12.2	12.6	13.9	14.9	13.4	12.1	9.0	6.8	11.7
Dr IQ	N	Mon	10:30	10.2	11.5	10.1	13.2	10.8	11.9	11.0	11.8	9.8	8.4	10.9
Doctors Talk It Over	A	Mon	10:00	1.7	1.3	1.5	0.9	1.2	1.6	2.0	1.6	1.5	1.6	1.5
Don Gardiner News	A	Sun	6:15		4.8	4.7	4.9	5.7	5.3	5.7	5.5	4.9	4.6	5.1
Double or Nothing	M	Sun	9:30	6.6	7.2	7.1	8.0	7.3	8.6	7.9	7.0	6.0	6.5	7.2
Drew Pearson News/Comment	N	Sun	6:00	6.2	7.5	8.8	9.6	8.0	8.5	10.9	8.2	7.0	6.0	8.1
Duffy's Tavern Ed Gardner	N	Wed	9:00	15.9	15.9	16.9	15.9	19.2	21.4	18.7	19.8	13.0	11.3	16.9
Ed Sullivan	A	Mon	8:15	2.8										2.8
Eddie Bracken Show	C	Sun	9:30		7.8	8.4	10.1	8.5	9.0	9.1	8.4			8.8
Eddie Cantor Show	N	Thu	10:30	14.7	14.7	15.1	13.9	15.6	14.3	18.2	15.0	11.9	10.5	14.4
Edgar Bergen & Charlie McCarthy	N	Sun	8:00	14.3	24.4	25.2	28.0	27.7	25.7	23.1	19.8	17.4		22.8
Elmer Davis News/Comment	A	M-F	7:15	2.3	3.4	3.7	4.0	3.2	2.4	2.4	2.9	3.2	1.9	2.9
Eric Sevareid News/Comment	C	M-F	6:00		2.4				2.1	2.3	2.5	2.5	2.6	2.4
Erwin Canham News/Comment	A	Thu	8:15	2.2	2.4	2.1	1.9	2.3	2.0	2.4	2.5	2.0	1.9	2.2
Exploring the Unknown	M	Sun	9:00	3.3	3.8	4.1	4.9	4.5	5.2	3.5	3.3	3.7	3.2	4.0
Fanny Brice Baby Snooks Show	A	Fri	8:00	9.6	13.0	14.6	15.9	15.9	13.5	13.7	12.5	10.1		13.2
The Fat Man	A	Fri	8:00						11.9	11.2	10.5	9.1	9.3	10.4
FBI in Peace & War	C	Thu	8:30	9.8	11.9	14.8	14.8	14.5	16.5	13.5	13.1	9.8	10.8	13.0
Festival of American Music	A	Sun	8:00	2.7										2.7
Fibber McGee & Molly	N	Tue	9:30	25.9	25.9	25.6	27.6	30.5	31.6	28.5	26.7	25.6	15.3	26.4
The Fighting Senator	A	Mon	8:30	6.1										6.1
Fishing & Hunting Club	M	Mon	10:00	2.6	1.9	2.9	2.6	3.0	2.4	2.6	2.6	1.9	2.1	2.5
Frank Morgan Show	N	Wed	10:00	5.5	10.2	9.3	10.0	9.4	10.9	10.6	12.1	9.6		9.8
Frank Sinatra Show	C	Wed	9:00	10.0	9.5	11.3	9.3	10.4	9.2	10.0	9.8	9.6	6.7	9.9
Fred Allen Show	N	Sun	8:30	24.8	24.8	27.3	26.8	25.8	25.9	25.8	21.7	19.2	13.6	23.4
Fred Waring Show	N	Tue	9:30	9.2										9.2
Friday Night Boxing	A	Fri	10:00	4.4	5.2	6.3	7.1	6.2	5.8	5.1	4.8	5.6	5.5	5.6
Fulton Lewis Jr News & Comment	M	M-F	7:00	4.7	6.4	6.8	5.7	6.4	5.9	6.1	5.9	4.3	4.2	5.6
Gabriel Heatter News & Comment	M	M-F	9:00	5.7	6.6	6.7	6.5	6.2	6.5	6.2	5.8	4.7	4.0	5.9
Gabriel Heatter Behind Front Page	M	Sun	10:00		2.7	2.7	2.4	2.4	2.1	1.8	1.8	2.5	2.4	2.3
Gangbusters	A	Sat	9:00	8.5	9.9	11.1	12.6	12.8	12.6	12.2	13.2	10.1	9.2	11.2
Gene Autry's Melody Ranch	C	Sun	7:00	5.4	4.5	5.9	7.0	7.2	5.4	6.9	5.7	3.8	5.0	5.7
Ginny Simms Show	N	Fri	9:00	7.4	8.0	8.4	10.6	9.0	8.0	7.2	5.8	5.9	3.9	7.4
Grand Marquee	N	Thu	7:30						9.9	8.6	7.6	6.0	4.7	7.4
Grand Ole Opry	N	Sat	10:30	8.6	11.1	9.5	10.9	11.5	10.6	10.4	8.4	7.9	7.4	9.6
The Great Gildersleeve	N	Wed	8:30	10.5	16.7	16.2	17.9	17.2	17.1	17.6	17.6	11.2	10.6	15.2
Greatest Story Ever Told	A	Sun	6:30							4.4	3.8	3.1	3.1	3.6
The Green Hornet	A	Tue	7:30										4.5	4.5
HV Kaltenborn News/Comment	N	M-F	7:45	6.6	9.2	11.2	11.7	10.2	10.2	8.5	8.3	7.6	4.7	8.8

1946-47 Hooper Ratings 6-11 P.M.	Net	Day	Time	Sept. 46	Oct. 46	Nov. 46	Dec. 46	Jan. 47	Feb. 47	March 47	April 47	May 47	June 47	1946-47 Avg
Hedda Hopper This Is Hollywood	C	Sat	10:15		5.0	6.3	8.7	9.3	7.5	7.7	7.3	5.4	4.6	6.9
Henry J Taylor News/Comment	M	M,F	7:30	2.4	3.1	3.0	2.3	2.8	2.3	3.2	2.7	2.2	1.5	2.6
Henry Morgan Show	A	Wed	10:30		11.1	7.4	8.1	9.5	8.6	9.4	9.1	10.5	8.6	9.1
Highways in Melody	N	Fri	8:00	4.7	7.4	8.1	8.1	8.1	7.9	7.4	7.0	5.8		7.0
Hildegarde's Campbell Room	C	Sun	9:00		5.7	6.0	5.9	5.8	6.5	6.1	5.5			5.9
Holiday for Music	C	Wed	10:30	5.5										5.5
Hollywood Players	C	Tue	9:30	11.7	7.2	8.8	7.7	7.6	7.8					8.5
Hollywoood Star Time	C	Sat	8:00				7.8	7.0	7.2		7.0			7.3
Hour of Charm Phil Spitalny	C	Sun	4:30			6.0	7.5	7.1	6.4	7.0	6.7	5.0	3.8	6.2
Hour of Charm Phil Spitalny	N	Sun	10:00	8.4	4.2									6.3
Hour of Mystery	A	Sun	10:00	5.9										5.9
I Deal in Crime	A	Sat	8:30		6.8	6.7	8.8	10.0	8.8	8.6	7.4	6.8		8.0
Information Please	C	Wed	10:30		8.6	8.3	9.5	8.2	10.2	6.2	7.2	7.0	5.9	7.9
Inner Sanctum	C	Mon	8:00	8.3	12.8	13.6	15.1	15.7	16.2	16.0	14.7	11.3	9.6	13.3
Inside of Sports Bill Brandt	M	M-F	7:45	2.4	2.5	3.0	2.2	2.5	2.5	2.7	2.4	2.4	2.4	2.5
It Pays to Be Ignorant	C	Fri	10:00	7.3	9.2	9.6	11.3	12.5	11.9	11.8	8.6	9.3	7.0	9.9
It's Up to Youth	M	Wed	8:00		2.3	3.1	2.5	2.7	3.2	2.3	2.0			2.6
Jack Benny Program	N	Sun	7:00		21.5	27.6	27.5	28.5	28.4	29.0	25.0	19.2		25.8
Jack Carson Show	C	Wed	8:00		8.5	10.7	9.7	11.6	11.5	11.1	10.4	7.3	5.8	9.6
Jack Haley & Eve Arden	C	Thu	9:30	8.6	12.8	12.9	13.8	14.4	15.2	13.4	13.1	11.3	7.3	12.3
Jack Smith Show	C	M-F	7:15	5.3	8.0	8.9	8.7	9.2	9.8	9.4	8.9	6.8	6.0	8.1
James Melton Show	C	Sun	9:30	5.7										5.7
Jan Savitt Orch	C	Sun	10:30	5.2										5.2
Jean Sablon Sings	N	Sat	7:15									4.2		6.0
Jimmy Durante & Garry Moore	C	Fri	9:30	8.7	10.6	12.5	13.0	12.9	13.2	11.1	10.3	9.4	6.8	10.9
Jimmie Fidler Hollywood News	A	Sun	9:30	7.3	7.7	8.7	9.7	9.8	8.3	9.5	8.3	7.4	7.7	8.4
Joan Davis Show	C	Mon	8:30		12.9	13.8	15.0	15.1	15.9	16.5	16.7	10.1	9.4	13.9
Judy Canova Show	N	Sat	10:00	11.8	13.2	16.4	14.1	15.5	15.0	15.2	13.1	11.1	9.4	13.5
Kate Smith Sings	C	Sun	6:30		8.9	10.8	11.9	11.4	10.4	12.2	9.7	6.7	5.9	9.8
Kay Kyser Kollege Mus Knowledge	N	Wed	10:30	9.1	9.1	8.6	9.3	9.6	11.5	11.4	10.6	9.5	8.1	9.7
Kraft Music Hall/EdHorton/Ed Foy	N	Thu	9:00	8.4	12.4	13.9	12.1	13.1	15.1	12.2	12.1	8.7	7.5	11.6
Life of Riley	N	Sat	8:00	9.9	12.6	13.4	14.0	14.7	15.5	15.5	15.0	11.7	9.7	13.2
Lone Ranger	A	MWF	7:30	5.6	8.3	8.5	9.5	10.0	9.9	9.7	9.9	7.4	7.1	8.6
Louella Parsons Hollywood News	A	Sun	9:15	7.8	10.1	11.1	12.2	11.4	10.7	14.2	12.9	8.5	7.8	10.7
Lowell Thomas News	N	M-F	6:45	7.8	11.8	12.5	15.5	12.7	12.3	12.9	12.3	8.4	7.2	11.3
Lum & Abner	M	M-Th	8:00	3.2	3.9	4.4	4.7	5.2	5.6	4.6	4.8	2.9	2.6	4.2
Lux Radio Theater	C	Mon	9:00	13.9	21.2	22.6	23.4	24.8	22.8	24.6	24.4	21.6	20.1	21.9
Maisie	C	Fri	10:30	9.4	7.9	10.1	9.4	10.8	11.7	9.6	7.6			9.6
Man Called X	N	Tue	10:00	10.7										10.7
Man Called X	C	Thu	10:30									7.9	7.0	7.5
Manhattan Merry Go Round	N	Sun	9:00	8.5	11.6	12.6	13.3	14.0	12.5	13.6	12.1	10.6	9.6	11.8
Margaret Whiting Show	N	Tue	8:00	5.2										5.2
Mayor of the Town	C	Sat	8:30	7.9	8.9	8.3	11.0	9.1	10.8	10.0	8.6	6.6		9.0
McGarry & His Mouse	M	Mon	8:00					4.7	3.9	3.6	3.6			4.0
Meet Corliss Archer	C	Sun	9:00							6.5	6.5	6.2	6.3	6.4
Meet Me at Parky's	C	Sun	10:30	6.7	5.9	7.0	7.3	7.8	7.3	8.5	7.2			7.2
Mel Blanc Show	C	Tue	8:30	6.6	6.9	8.9	7.2	8.0	9.1	7.6	7.9	5.4	5.9	7.4
Mercury Summer Theater	C	Fri	10:00	6.2										6.2

1946-47 Hooper Ratings 6-11 P.M.

Program	Net	Day	Time	Sept. 46	Oct. 46	Nov. 46	Dec. 46	Jan. 47	Feb. 47	March 47	April 47	May 47	June 47	1946-47 Avg
Michael Shane Private Detective	M	Tue	8:00			5.5	5.5	6.1						5.7
Milton Berle Show	N	Tue	8:00	9.1	13.4	13.3	13.2	12.7		11.1	10.4	8.7	7.0	9.3
Mr & Mrs North	N	Wed	8:00	14.0	17.4	20.2	19.2	21.0	20.6	21.1	20.0	17.2	14.0	12.3
Mr District Attorney	N	Wed	9:30	8.3	9.2	10.8	12.2	13.3	13.1	13.3	12.0	8.2	7.1	18.5
Mr Keen	C	Thu	7:30	8.7	10.8	10.6	11.3	13.0	13.4	11.7	11.3	9.1	7.1	10.8
Molle Mystery Theater	N	Fri	10:00					7.0	8.3	9.2	9.2	8.6	8.1	10.7
Murder & Mr Malone	A	Sat	9:30		4.0									8.4
Mystery Is My Hobby	M	Sun	10:00	3.9	4.9	6.2	6.0	6.5	6.4	6.5	5.8	4.3	4.3	4.0
Mystery of the Week	C	M-F	7:00	3.5										5.4
National Barn Dance	N	Sat	9:00	6.3										6.3
Ned Calmer Parker Pen News	C	Sa,Su	8:55		8.6	8.8	10.9	10.2	8.4	8.9	8.8	6.6	4.8	8.4
News of the World/Morgan Beatty	N	M-F	7:15	7.7	6.9	8.0	9.2	8.7	7.8	6.9	7.1	5.5	5.0	7.1
Nick Carter Master Detective	M	Sun	6:30	5.4	6.7	8.0	7.8	9.5	7.8	9.0	6.7	5.2	4.5	7.0
One Man's Family	N	Sun	3:30	5.2	8.0	10.7	9.7	9.9	10.1	10.9	9.9	7.2	5.9	8.9
People Are Funny	N	Fri	9:00	6.3	11.1	13.0	12.1	13.7	15.1	15.7	14.7	10.7	8.0	12.7
Phil Harris & Alice Faye	N	Sun	7:30		18.4	21.0	21.1	20.4	21.1	19.8	17.6	13.7	8.4	17.9
Policewoman	A	Sun	9:45	5.7	6.2	5.3	7.2	7.8	7.4	6.0	6.8	6.2	6.5	6.5
Pot O Gold	A	Wed	9:30		6.0	4.9	5.3	5.8	6.2	5.8	5.6			5.7
Professor Quiz	A	Sat	10:00	3.9	3.1	3.0	2.7	4.9	4.6		4.8	3.8	4.8	4.0
Quick as a Flash	N	Sun	5:30	4.3	6.4	6.7	7.4	7.0	7.5	7.0	5.9	5.1	5.6	6.3
Quiz Kids	N	Sun	4:00	6.6	6.9	6.9	7.1	8.0	8.4	8.7	7.4	7.1	5.4	7.3
Radio Readers Digest	C	Thu	10:00	7.9	8.1	9.6	9.9	11.4	11.9	10.3	9.7	9.2	8.7	9.7
Raymond Gram Swing News/Com	A	WThF	7:15	3.0	2.9	2.5	2.2	2.5						2.6
Red Skelton Show	M	M-F	9:15	3.2	3.5	3.9	3.9	3.7	4.0	3.9	3.8	3.4	3.4	3.6
Robert Trout News	C	M-F	10:30	15.3	19.9	22.4	22.9	25.5	26.1	25.3	24.7	21.8	18.4	22.2
Rogues Gallery	N	Sun	6:45	2.7	4.6	4.7	5.3	5.4	4.8	4.6	4.5	3.2	2.7	4.3
Roy Rogers Show	N	Sun	7:30	7.4										7.4
Rudy Vallee Show	N	Sat	9:00	6.8	8.5	8.5	8.5	8.9	9.1	10.0	10.6			9.2
The Sad Sack	C	Tue	8:00	7.7	10.2	11.5	9.6	11.9	10.5	11.4				10.3
Saturday Night Serenade	C	Wed	9:00	7.6	7.7	8.3	10.6	9.8	9.1	10.5	9.4	5.0	4.6	7.7
Screen Guild Players	C	Sat	9:45	14.5	18.5	20.0	22.1	24.0	20.9	22.3	21.7	18.1	17.8	8.3
The Shadow	C	Mon	10:00	6.3	9.4	9.9	10.8	11.6	11.9	13.1	9.1	8.9	8.1	20.0
The Sheriff	M	Sun	5:00	8.4	7.6	7.9	8.3	9.5	8.9	9.9	0.3	8.2	6.6	9.9
Sparkle Time	A	Fri	9:30		5.7	6.6	7.4	7.9	8.0	8.3	9.1			7.6
Special Investigator	A	Fri	7:30	3.1	1.8	2.2	2.5	2.2	3.3	2.2	4.1			7.6
Spotlight Bands	M	Sun	8:30	3.5	3.0	3.2								2.8
Spotlight on America/Geo Putnam	M	MWF	9:30	1.8	1.5	2.3	1.5	1.5	1.9			3.4	3.2	3.2
Sunday Evening Party	M	Fri	10:00	3.3	5.4	4.9	4.4	4.4						1.8
Suspense	A	Sun	6:00	11.3	14.0	13.5	15.5	16.6	15.2	15.0	14.1	11.1	8.7	4.5
Take It or Leave It	C	Thu	8:00	10.3	14.7	16.2	17.3	15.4	17.8	16.3	14.8	10.8	11.0	13.5
Taylor Grant Headline Edition News	C	Sun	10:00				1.3	2.2	2.2	2.2	1.8	2.0	2.2	14.5
Telephone Hour	A	M-F	7:00			8.3	8.3	9.4	9.4	11.1	10.0	7.0	5.9	2.0
That's Finnegan	N	Mon	9:00	7.8	7.4	5.5	5.5	5.9	6.0	5.7	5.5	8.1		8.4
Theater Guild on the Air	C	Thu	10:30	6.6	3.4	5.1	7.4	9.3	7.7	8.6	9.4		8.0	5.5
This Is Your FBI	A	Fri	8:30	6.3	7.3	7.0	9.2	12.1	12.4	12.4	12.0	10.6	8.9	8.1
Those Websters	M	Sun	6:00	6.6	9.1	8.8	9.3	9.3						10.2
Tommy Dorsey Orch	N	Sun	8:30	3.4	4.9	5.8	5.7	6.6	6.3	6.3	4.1	3.6	4.4	5.1

1946–47 Hooper Ratings 6–11 P.M.

Program	Time	Net	Day	Sept. 46	Oct. 46	Nov. 46	Dec. 46	Jan. 47	Feb. 47	March 47	April 47	May 47	June 47	1946-47 Avg
Tommy Riggs & Betty Lou	7:30	C	Fri	4.6							7.1	6.9	5.6	4.6
Tony Martin Sings	7:30	C	Sat	5.5							2.9	2.6	2.7	6.6
Tony Martin Sings	9:30	C	Sun		7.6									6.5
Treasure Hour of Song	9:30	M	Thu			4.0	2.8	3.5	4.7	3.0				3.3
Truth or Consequences	8:30	N	Sat			14.8	14.0	16.0	15.6	20.9	19.8	13.0	10.4	14.8
Twenty Questions	8:00	M	Sat			4.9	5.9	4.8	6.0	5.0	5.5	4.6	4.2	4.9
Upton Close News/Comment	10:15	M	Tue			2.8	3.3	2.6	3.4					3.2
Vacation with Music	9:00	N	Fri											5.4
Vaughn Monroe Show	7:30	C	Sat			7.6	9.3	9.1	11.0	9.1	7.6	6.1	4.2	8.1
Vic & Sade	8:30	M	Thu	2.1										2.1
Victor Borge & Benny Goodman	9:30	N	Mon	6.8		7.0	7.0	6.5	7.7	6.4	6.4	5.5	3.8	6.4
Voice of Firestone	8:30	N	Mon	7.8		9.9	11.2	9.1	10.2	10.0	9.6	7.6	6.2	9.1
Vox Pop	9:00	C	Tue	8.5		9.5	8.3	7.9	7.9	8.4	7.7	6.8		8.3
Walter Winchell Jergens Journal	9:00	A	Sun	13.2		21.8	23.1	21.8	21.0	24.6	21.9	17.1		20.8
Waltz Time	9:30	N	Fri	6.3		10.0	9.9	11.1	9.9	11.3	10.6	7.4		9.5
Wayne King Orch	9:30	N	Fri	5.5										5.5
We the People	10:30	C	Sun	10.7		11.1	11.5	11.9	12.6	11.7	10.1	10.8		11.0
The Whistler	10:00	C	Wed	8.8							5.3	7.8		6.6
Your Hit Parade	9:00	N	Sat	11.6		12.7	13.2	13.8	12.7	13.6	13.1	13.0	11.7	12.6

Special Broadcasts

Program	Net	Date	Month	Rating
Boxing Joe Louis/Tami Mauriello	A	9/18	Sept. 46	33.0
NL Playoffs 2 Games StL/Brooklyn	M	10/18&2	Oct. 46	9.0
World Series: NLStLouis/ALBoston	M	10/7	Oct. 46	11.1
NFL Champ: NYGiants/ChicagoBears	A	12/15	Dec. 46	9.8
Pres Truman Address	AMN	4/5	April 47	20.5
Kentucky Derby	C	5/3	May 47	19.0
US Open Golf	A	6/15	June 47	1.9
Pres Truman Address	All	6/20	June 47	30.7

1947–48 Nielsen Ratings 6–11 P.M.

Program	Time	Net	Day	Sept. 47	Oct. 47	Nov. 47	Dec. 47	Jan. 48	Feb. 48	March 48	April 48	May 48	June 48	1947-48 Avg
Abbott & Costello Show	9:00	A	Wed	10.6		9.3	9.9	11.8	12.3	10.0	6.9	6.5	4.3	10.4
Abe Burrows Show	7:30	C	Sat											8.0
Adventures of Charlie Chan	8:30	M	Mon		10.6	9.6	9.8	10.5	11.8	8.1	8.7	8.1	7.4	9.5
Adventures of Christopher Wells	9:30	C	Tue		8.3	8.9	10.6	10.8	10.8	9.6	12.6	12.6	12.9	11.3
Adventures of Ellery Queen	6:30	N	Sun	6.4				9.2	13.9	12.7				6.4
Adventures of Ozzie & Harriet	9:30	C	Fri	7.6	12.1	14.8	15.5	16.0	16.6	14.4	13.5	13.3	10.6	13.4
Adventures of Sam Spade	8:00	C	Sun	13.7	19.2	17.7	21.0	22.6	20.6	19.2	16.2	15.1	13.0	17.8
Adventures of Sherlock Holmes	7:00	C	Sun		9.5	10.2	12.1	11.7	12.6	10.9	8.6	7.7	5.4	9.9
Adventures of the Falcon	8:30	M	Tue	9.8										9.8
Adventures of the Thin Man	8:30	C	Fri	13.0		15.6	14.9							14.1
Al Jolson Kraft Music Hall	9:00	N	Thu	10.9	18.7	21.5	17.1	23.5	22.4	21.2	20.2	18.0	15.1	18.9
Aldrich Family	8:00	N	Thu	10.6	18.5	21.9	17.5	22.2	22.2	19.7	18.5	16.2	10.0	18.5
American Album of Familiar Music	9:30	N	Sun		13.6	14.6	17.1	17.5	15.6	17.3	14.8	13.8	12.0	14.7
American Forum of the Air	10:00	M	Tue			3.2	3.4							3.3
American Melody Hour	8:00	C	Wed	9.0	11.0	12.4	13.6	12.1	13.1	13.0	10.4	10.0	8.4	11.3
Amos & Andy	9:00	N	Tue	15.9	22.9	28.0	26.9	28.3	30.1	28.4	23.3	22.7	14.3	24.1

1947-48 Nielsen Ratings 6-11 P.M.

Program	Net	Day	Time	Sept. 47	Oct. 47	Nov. 47	Dec. 47	Jan. 48	Feb. 48	March 48	April 48	May 48	June 48	1947-48 Avg
Arthur Gaeth Commentary	A	Mon	10:00					2.3	2.4	2.2	2.6	2.2	2.6	2.4
Arthur Godfrey's Talent Scouts	C	Mon	8:30	15.4	19.4	21.4	20.8	25.4	26.2	27.1	24.8	21.6	17.1	21.9
Beulah	C	M-F	7:00				9.3	10.9	12.0	10.4	9.1	8.9	6.9	9.6
The Bickersons	C	Fri	9:00	15.0	12.6	13.9	14.8	14.3	14.6	12.7	11.7	11.4	8.8	13.0
The Big Break	C	Sun	10:30	11.3	11.7	12.2	15.0							11.7
The Big Story	N	Wed	10:00	14.3	14.7	16.6	15.0	18.7	18.3	18.0	13.4	15.7	16.6	16.1
Big Town	C	Tue	8:00	14.5	17.8	21.0	21.4	22.5	24.6	22.2	20.0	16.9	13.7	19.5
Bill Henry Johns Manville News	C	M-F	8:55	8.6	10.8	12.5	12.3	14.2	14.3	12.9	12.4	10.6	8.6	11.7
Bill Stern Colgate Sports Newsreel	C	Fri	10:30	7.7	8.7	9.5	9.6	10.8	10.5	9.6	10.3	9.1	4.9	9.1
Billy Rose Commentary	M	T,T	8:55		5.9	5.6	5.1	5.5	5.3	6.1	5.1	5.9	6.0	5.6
Bing Crosby Philco Radio Time	A	Wed	10:00	13.6		12.7	14.3	15.3	16.5	14.5	13.6	13.2		13.9
Blondie	C	Sun	7:30	13.0	18.5	18.7	20.9	22.6	21.8	19.5	17.9	14.7	12.4	18.1
Bob Hawk Show	N	Thu	10:00	13.2	13.6	14.8	11.5	18.1	18.0	16.7	15.1	13.6	11.9	14.6
Bob Hope Show	N	Tue	10:00	11.2	22.8	25.0	27.1	25.4	28.5	26.7	21.5	20.6	14.3	22.5
The Borden Program	C	Wed	9:00	13.6	10.6	11.6	11.5	12.4	13.3	11.7	10.7			11.6
Break the Bank	A	Fri	9:00		14.2	15.8	17.8	18.2	18.5	17.9	16.0	13.9	15.3	16.1
Burl Ives Show	M	Fri	8:00	3.2	3.7	4.0	3.4	3.4	4.2	2.7	3.3			3.5
Burns & Allen Show	N	Thu	8:30	11.7	18.4	21.4	17.2	22.5	22.6	19.6	17.7	16.7	12.6	18.0
Call for Music	N	Tue	8:00		13.4	14.3	15.0	15.9	14.3	12.8	11.2	12.0	9.6	12.0
Can You Top This?	N	Fri	8:30	14.1	15.6	16.6	13.0	18.8	16.1	14.8	13.4	12.8	8.8	13.9
Casey Crime Photographer	C	Thu	9:30	15.7	10.0	11.7	10.0	11.4	17.1	15.6	14.7	15.3	13.3	15.6
Carnation Contented Hour	N	Mon	10:00	9.1	13.9	15.4	14.5	15.9	9.6	11.6	9.1	7.8	6.8	9.7
Cavalcade of America	N	Mon	8:00	10.7	8.2	8.0	10.4	10.5	15.3	15.9	14.5	12.8	10.8	14.0
Champion Roll Call	A	Fri	9:55	5.8	10.8	12.4	12.4	12.9	10.8	10.0	9.3	8.1	13.5	9.5
Chesterfield Supper Club	N	M-F	7:00	9.4	10.5	11.2	11.4	12.7	11.8	11.6	9.6	9.5	6.6	10.7
Club 15	C	M-F	7:30	6.9	11.2	12.3	13.0	14.1	12.9	11.7	10.2	8.2		10.6
Counterspy	A	Sun	5:30	10.3	17.4				14.4	12.7	10.7	9.4	8.3	11.6
Crime Doctor	C	Sun	8:30	15.0	15.0	13.6	15.2	16.6	16.1	12.1	12.1	8.8		16.2
Curtain Time	N	Sat	7:30	9.9				16.7	16.2	14.4	11.9	12.0	6.1	12.6
Danny Thomas Show	C	Fri	8:30			13.6							8.1	13.2
Darts for Dough	N	Thu	9:30	3.6	3.6	4.0	2.8							3.5
Date with Judy	N	Tue	8:30	12.2	17.7	21.6	22.0	21.7	22.7	21.6	19.8	18.1	12.3	19.0
A Day in the Life of Dennis Day	N	Wed	8:00	13.2	16.1	18.3	15.2	18.2	19.2	18.5	17.1	15.0	10.1	16.1
Dick Haymes Show	C	Thu	9:00	15.5	14.1	16.7	14.2	17.7	18.3	16.0	14.8	12.9	12.3	15.3
Dr Christian	C	Wed	8:30	11.2	12.2	15.2	15.9	14.9	17.7	15.1	12.5	13.0	11.1	13.9
Dr IQ	N	Mon	9:30	8.4	9.1	10.4	9.9	11.4	10.0	12.0	11.5	10.4	8.2	10.1
Doctors Talk It Over	A	Mon	10:00	2.9	3.2									3.1
Don Gardiner Mon Morn Headlines	A	Sun	6:15	7.4	8.8	8.7	9.9	12.2	11.9	10.9	10.9	7.8	6.5	9.5
Drew Pearson News/Comment	A	Sun	6:00	9.5	10.8	11.9	12.4	14.4	14.4	14.4	12.5	10.7	7.7	11.9
Duffy's Tavern	N	Wed	9:00	15.0	19.1	22.4	17.6	23.9	25.4	22.5	19.3	19.1	16.0	20.0
Eddie Cantor Show	N	Thu	10:30	8.6	12.4	16.3	12.7	17.2	15.4	15.8	13.1	12.2	15.9	14.0
Edgar Bergen & Charlie McCarthy	N	Sun	8:00	14.5	21.5	23.4	27.6	27.2	26.3	25.3	20.7	17.8		22.7
Edward R Murrow News/Comment	C	M-F	7:45		10.8	12.0	11.5	13.3	12.8	12.3	11.2	9.0		11.6
Eric Sevareid News/Comment	C	M-F	6:00					2.4	2.2	2.4	2.0	1.9	1.7	2.1
Erwin Canham News/Comment	A	Tue	8:15	3.9	2.9		4.3	3.4	3.6	2.9	3.4	3.4	2.9	3.5
Everybody Wins	C	Fri	10:00			4.4					13.4	12.2	9.0	11.5
Family Hour of Stars	C	Sun	6:00					11.7	8.7	8.7	6.7	7.2	5.0	8.0
Famous Jury Trials	A	Sat	7:30	8.1	14.4	14.4	13.2	13.7	13.9	13.2	11.8	10.0	5.3	11.7

1947-48 Nielsen Ratings 6-11 P.M.

Program	Net	Day	Time	Sept. 47	Oct. 47	Nov. 47	Dec. 47	Jan. 48	Feb. 48	March 48	April 48	May 48	June 48	1947-48 Avg
Fanny Brice Baby Snooks Show	C	Fri	8:00	14.2	15.4	18.2	17.4	20.7	21.4	18.1	16.6	13.9	11.3	17.3
The Fat Man	A	Fri	8:00	12.5	14.1	14.6	17.8	18.3	20.1	18.2	17.0	12.8	11.7	15.7
FBI in Peace & War	C	Thu	8:00	10.2	12.4	13.9	16.1	21.5	20.0	20.3	17.3	14.0		15.7
Fibber McGee & Molly	N	Tue	9:30	14.3	23.9	27.5	29.9	29.5	31.6	29.7	24.2	24.4		26.1
First Nighter	C	Thu	10:30		9.3	9.7	9.8	11.3	13.4	10.7	8.5	9.4	9.6	10.2
Fishing & Hunting Club	M	Mon	10:00	4.5	3.6	2.5	3.0	2.4	2.0	2.6	1.7	2.2	1.6	2.6
Fred Allen Show	N	Sun	8:30		21.6	23.5	27.4	27.8	25.5	25.1	22.0	18.8	9.4	22.3
Friday Night Boxing	A	Fri	10:00	7.4	9.2	10.4	12.7	13.0	13.2	14.0	9.5	9.0	32.7	13.1
Fulton Lewis Jr News/Comment	M	M-F	7:00		2.5	2.9	3.1	3.0	4.9	4.6	3.6	3.0	2.9	3.4
Gabriel Heatter News/Comment	M	M-F	9:00	6.3	7.0	6.8	6.3	7.2	7.8	7.9	6.7	6.1	5.9	6.8
Gabriel Heatter Behind Front Page	M	Sun	7:30					7.4	8.6	7.4	6.7	5.7	6.1	7.0
Gabriel Heatter Brighter Tomorrow	M	Sun	7:30	6.7	6.5	7.0	8.3							7.1
Gangbusters	C	Sat	9:00	11.1	13.3	15.8	16.3	16.9	18.1	7.9	7.9	6.4	5.6	11.9
Gene Autry's Melody Ranch	C	Sun	7:00	10.0	12.7	14.6	17.2	16.6	15.6	14.5	12.1	9.9	7.9	13.1
Grand Ole Opry	N	Sat	10:30	9.9	8.7	13.2	15.0	18.3	18.8	16.2	15.0	13.2	11.8	14.0
The Great Gildersleeve	N	Wed	8:30	14.5	18.6	21.6	18.1	19.5	21.9	21.4	18.6	18.1		19.1
Greatest Story Ever Told	A	Sun	6:30	6.6	8.4	8.0	9.8	11.0	10.6	10.6	8.9	7.9	7.1	8.9
The Green Hornet	A	Tue	7:30	9.5	10.5	12.2	13.5	14.2	14.0	13.4	12.0	9.9	7.5	11.7
HV Kaltenborn News/Comment	C	M-F	7:45	1.6	2.7	2.7	2.5							2.4
Harvest of Stars	C	Wed	9:30					11.7	9.7	10.6	7.7	10.5	8.4	9.8
Henry Morgan Show	A	Thu	7:30	6	9	10.2	12.7		11.1	11	9.9	8.9	6.5	9.5
Henry J Taylor News/Comment	M	M,F	7:30	3	4.3	5.1	4.4							4.2
Highways in Melody	N	Fri	8:00	6	9.2	8.6	8.9	8.8	9.2	8.1	8.2	6.4	5.8	7.9
Hollywood Star Preview	N	Sun	6:00		11.1	13.7	14.1	13.4	12.8	13	9.3	8.9	6.5	11.4
Horace Heidt Youth Oppty Program	N	Sun	10:30				14.9	15.1	16.1	16.2	14.7	13.6	13.9	14.9
Information Please	M	Fri	9:30		4.9	5.6	5.3	5.1	4.2	5.2	4	3.3	4.5	4.7
Inner Sanctum	C	Mon	8:00	13.7	19.5	19.3	19	22.6	22.2	20.7	19.3	16.7	13.3	18.6
Inside of Sports Bill Brandt	M	M-F	7:45	2.6	3.3	3.7	3.3	3.3	3.4	3.3	2.8	2.4	3	3.1
It Pays to Be Ignorant	C	Fri	10:00	10.9	11.9	14.1	14.1	17.3	17.4					14.3
Jack Benny Program	N	Sun	7:00		20.2	22	24.8	24.4	24.7	26.1	22.2	18.7	13.7	21.9
Jack Carson Show	N	Thu	9:30	9.1	12.6	16.1	13.3	18.5	17.5	16.6	15.5	13.6	12.2	14.5
Jack Paar Show	A	Wed	9:30		11.3	9.9	10.9							10.7
Jack Smith Show	C	M-F	7:15	6	9.3	10.5	10.7	11.8	12.6	11.5	10.6	8.9	6.6	9.9
Jan August Show	M	Thu	8:00	1.8	4.1	4.4	4	3.6	3.5					3.6
Jim Backus Show	M	Sun	9:30	5.3	5.8	6	7.2	7.3	7.1	7.3	5.3	5.1		6.3
Jimmie Fidler Hollywood News	A	Sun	10:30	5.7	5.7	5.9	7.6	7.4	7.9	7.3	5.3	6.3	3	6.2
Jimmie Fidler Hollywood News	M	Sun	8:30	4.2	7.3	6.3	8	8.6	7.9	6.7	7.1	4.8	4	6.5
Jimmy Durante Show	N	Wed	10:30	12.2	11.7	13.5	13.6	16.7	18	16	11.5	13.4	12.6	13.9
Joan Davis Show	C	Sat	9:00		5.3	5.8	6.7	5.2	5.8	5.5	4.4	3.7	3.1	5.1
Judy Canova Show	N	Sat	9:30	13.6	16.4	17.6	18	20.6	19.9	19.5	17.8	15.4	13.8	17.3
Kay Kyser Kollege Mus Knowledge	N	Sat	10:00		15.3	17.2	15.7	19.2	18.2	17.3	15.7	12.8	11.8	15.9
Life of Riley	N	Sat	8:00	16.8	20	20.8	23.2	25.1	25.3	23.2	19.8	14.8	12	20.1
The Lone Ranger	A	MWF	7:30	12.8	16.2	17.2	16.9	19.7	20.6	19.5	17.3	13.1	10.3	16.4
Louella Parsons Hollywood News	A	Sun	9:15	8.8	11.5	11.1	13.9	13.3	12.8	15.8	13.8	12		12.6
Lowell Thomas News	M	M-F	6:45	2.3	8.1	9.3	8.9	10.7	10.7	9.6	8.7	7.6	6.2	8.2
Lux Radio Theater	C	Mon	9:00	24	30.4	31.4	30.5	34.5	38.5	34.2	32	30.2	26.6	31.2
Man Called X	C	Sun	8:30	12.1	10.9	17.6	19.6	19.3	19.7	17.5	12.8	13.1	9.7	15.2
Manhattan Merry Go Round	N	Sun	9:00	11.3	16.3	17.5	20.5	21.7	19.2	19.6	17.7	15.9	11.5	17.1

1947-48 Nielsen Ratings 6-11 P.M.

Program	Net	Time	Day	Sept. 47	Oct. 47	Nov. 47	Dec. 47	Jan. 48	Feb. 48	March 48	April 48	May 48	June 48	1947-48 Avg
Mayor of the Town	A	8:00	Wed		15.7	13.9	14.2	17.5	18.9	18.4	14.3	11.8	8.5	14.8
Meet Corliss Archer	C	9:00	Sun	13.9	14.5	14.3	16.8	17.4	17	15.2				15.6
Milton Berle Show	N	8:00	Tue	9	14.3	17.9	17.5	18.4	16.6	15.6	13.9			15.4
Mr & Mrs North	C	8:30	Tue	12.7	16.3	18.2	19.9	21.5	20.5	19.3	16	14.9	11.8	17.1
Mr District Attorney	N	9:30	Wed	16.7	21.3	23.6	20.1	24.6	25.4	23	19.5	20.2	16.2	21.1
Mr Keen	C	8:30	Thu	14.6	13.9	17.6	15.7	19.8	21.4	19.7	17.3	14.5	12.1	16.7
Molle Mystery Theater	N	10:00	Fri	11	14.4	14.5	14.4	15.9	16.4	14.5	13.3	13.2	8.1	13.6
Murder & Mr Malone	A	9:30	Sat	9.2	11.4	13.4	13.2	13.0	13.1	12.1	12.0	9.3		11.9
My Friend Irma	C	10:00	Mon	16.2	21.1	22.3	21.9	23.9	28.3	23.4	22.2	22.5	19.9	22.2
Mystery of the Week	C	7:00	M-F	4.2	7.5	8.2								6.0
Ned Calmer News	C	8:55	Sun	8.5	9.1	9.4	10.4	12.7	12.1	10.4				10.4
News of the World/ Morgan Beatty	N	7:15	M-F	5.9	9.0	10.1	9.6	9.8	9.1	9.8	8.3	7.5	6.3	8.5
Newscope*	M	7:30	Sa,Su			5.6	4.4	6.1	5.0	5.2	4.4	3.7		4.9
Nick Carter Master Detective	M	6:30	Sun	9.0	12.0	13.2	15.1	16.9	16.7	15.3	13.1	11.1	6.7	13.0
Official Detective	M	8:30	Tue					5.2	8.8	10.3	8.8	8.7	7.8	8.3
One Man's Family	N	3:30	Sun	9.1	8.9	10.6	12.7	11.8	12.6	11.9	10.1	8.7	7.9	10.4
Pause That Refreshes	C	6:30	Sun	8.3	13.2	16.0	16.5	12.2	10.9	9.3	7.4	8.2	6.2	10.8
People Are Funny	N	9:00	Fri	14.4	16.0	18.3	18.7	19.8	20.1	17.3	16.3	15.1	11.0	16.7
Phil Harris & Alice Faye	N	7:30	Sun	11.3	20.9	22.2	25.5	25.3	25.1	26.0	23.3	19.2		22.1
Point Sublime	A	8:00	Mon						13.9	13.7	12.2	8.7	10.4	12.1
Radio Readers Digest	C	10:00	Thu	12.8	13.0	14.0	12.2	16.6	18.1	14.2	14.8	14		14.0
Real Stories from Real Life	M	9:15	M-F	3.0	3.4	3.6	3.2							3.3
Red Skelton Show	N	10:30	Tue	15.4	20.0	23.0	26.6	25.2	23.8	22.2	17.7	18.6	11.0	20.4
Saturday Night Serenade	C	10:00	Sat	7.1	8.1	8.4	8.6	9.4	9.8	9.4	8.4	8.6	6.7	8.5
Screen Guild Players	M	10:30	Mon					19.8	22.7	19.7	18.2	19.5	13.3	18.9
The Shadow	M	5:00	Sun			14.5	14.5	15.8	15.1	13.4	9.7	10.3	10.1	13.1
The Sheriff	A	9:30	Fri	9.6	11.5	12.3	16.2	16.2	16.7	15.0	13.8	12.3	3.3	13.4
Songs by Morton Downey	N	11:15	T,T,Sa			1.1	1.4	1.4	0.6	1.1				1.5
Spike Jones Spotlight Revue	C	10:30	Fri		10.8	11.4	11.1	14.6	12.8	10.6	10.9	11.1	11.0	11.6
Stop the Music	A	8:00	Sun							11.7	13.8	11.0	12.6	12.6
Strike It Rich	C	10:30	Sun			8.8	12.1	11.3	12.4	11.7	10.0			10.9
Sunday Evening Hour	A	8:00	Sun			8.5	9.9	10.1					9.9	9.5
Suspense	C	8:00	Thu	15.1	13.3	16.6								15.0
Take It or Leave It	N	10:00	Sun	13.1	14.2	15.2	17.7	18.4	17.7	16.7	17.7	14.9	14.3	16.0
Tales of Willie Piper	A	9:00	Thu	7.9	9.0	9.2	8.1	10.2	10.8	10.1	8.8	10.0		9.3
Telephone Hour	N	9:00	Mon	8.4	10.5	11.5	11.7	13.2	13.6	11.9	10.3			10.7
Texaco Star Theater/James Melton	C	9:30	Sun	11.8	11.9	12.4	13.7							12.6
Texaco Star Theater/Tony Martin	A	10:30	Wed					10.3	10.5	10.0	10.3	13.0	11.0	10.7
Theater Guild on the Air	A	9:30	Sun	12.8	14.4	13.6	16.9	17.1	16.7	18.0	14.9	13.0		15.3
This Is Your FBI	A	8:30	Fri	14.6	15.5	17.6	19.7	21.1	22.0	20.4	18.3	15.2	15.7	18.0
Those Websters	M	6:00	Sun	8.8	9.7	11.3	12.9	17.3	17.0	15.3	11.0	10.4	7.3	12.1
Three Star Extra News	N	6:45	M-F		4.7	5.1	4.9	5.2	4.6	4.5	4.0	3.6	2.9	4.4
Truth or Consequences	N	8:30	Sat	16.2	20.6	24.4	24.5	27.1	28.0	27.3	22.5	19.1	13.0	22.3
Twenty Questions	M	8:00	Sat	6.2	7.5	7.8	7.6	8.4		8.3	7.2	5.7		7.1
Vaughn Monroe Show	C	9:30	Sat	9.1	7.7	9.6	9.9							9.1
Voice of Firestone	N	8:30	Mon	9.7	12.2	13.1	13.3	14.1	14.9	13.7	12.1	10.7		12.2
Vox Pop	A	8:30	Wed		11.4	10.9	11.5	13.9	17.2	13.1	9.8	8.9	9.4	11.8
Walter Winchell	A	9:00	Sun	11.6	15.3	15.1	17.6	18.3		21.0	21.0	18.3	16.3	17.2

1947-48 Nielsen Ratings 6-11 P.M.

Program	Net	Day	Time	Sept. 47	Oct. 47	Nov. 47	Dec. 47	Jan. 48	Feb. 48	March 48	April 48	May 48	June 48	1947-48 Avg
Waltz Time	N	Fri	9:30	10.4	15.9	18.6	17.8	19.0	18.9	17.6	16.0	14.8	12.3	16.1
We the People	C	Tue	9:00	9.8	10.1	11.1	13.3	14.6	13.0	12.2	10.8	10.1	8.1	11.3
The Whistler	C	Wed	10:00	7.4	6.1	6.5	7.6	6.8		6.5	5.2	6.4	6.1	6.6
You Bet Your Life/Groucho Marx	A	Wed	9:30											
Your Hit Parade	N	Sat	9:00	16.2		11.7	12.9	13.1	15.5	13.4	11.4			13.0
*Sunday Broadcast Time	M	Sun	8:45		18.9	21.3	20.0	24.3	23.2	24.5	20.2	18.7	13.1	20.0

Special Broadcast

Program	Net	Date	June 48
Boxing: Joe Louis/Joe Walcott	A	6/25	59.5

1948-49 Nielsen/Hooper Ratings 6-11 P.M.

Program	Net	Day	Time	Sept. 48	Oct. 48	Nov. 48	Dec. 48	Jan. 49	Feb. 49	March 49	April 49	May 49	June 49	1948-49 Avg
Abbott & Costello Show	A	Thu	8:00	9.9	8.9	15.1	17.0	9.2	4.6	5.6	8.4	7.1	4.8	5.1
Adventures of Archie Andrews	N	Wed	8:30											4.8
Adventures of Ozzie & Harriet	C	Sun	6:30	13.3	15.6	15.8	18.4	10.7	8.9	9.7	9.5		4.8	10.5
Adventures of Sam Spade	C	Sun	8:00	8.4	8.8	10.5	10.9	6.9	12.5	11.3	4.9		8.3	12.6
Adventures of Sherlock Holmes	M	Mon	8:30					4.8	5.2	6.1			3.4	7.0
Adventures of the Thin Man	M	Thu	10:00	9.0	15.4	14.5	17.8	13.8						6.9
Al Jolson's Kraft Music Hall	N	Thu	9:00						14.2	12.0	10.4	8.5	4.8	12.8
Alan Young Show	N	Tue	8:30					14.9	12.0	10.0	9.0	6.6	6.3	9.6
Aldrich Family	N	Thu	8:00	8.7	15.8	14.7	18.2	11.6	11.7	11.2	10.4	7.3	4.6	11.9
American Album of Familiar Music	N	Sun	9:30		14.1	14.2	15.8	9.7	9.9	7.3	6.5	6.8		9.8
American Forum of the Air	M	Mon	10:00		2.3	2.2	2.8	2.5	2.7	2.4	2.3	1.3		2.3
America's Town Meeting of Air	A	Tue	8:30						3.9	4.3	3.3	4.7	4.4	4.1
Amos & Andy	C	Sun	7:30	18.0	18.0	19.1	20.3	19.6	18.8	16.3	13.8	10.6	2.6	17.1
Arthur Gaeth News	A	Mon	10:00	2.9	2.3	2.4	2.9	1.7	1.6	1.9	1.2	1.2		2.1
Arthur Godfrey's Talent Scouts	C	Mon	8:30	17.9	22.6	26.8	26.5	20.5	21.4	23.4	18.6	17.4	12.6	20.1
The Better Half	M	Thu	8:30	5.0	3.6	4.1	4.9	4.9						4.4
Beulah	C	M-F	7:00	6.9	10.9	13.7	14.1	14.1	11.2	10.2	8.6	7.4	6.1	10.0
Big Story	N	Wed	10:00	13.1	12.8	16.1	16.9	14.6	13.0	13.2	12.7	10.6	10.2	13.3
Big Town	N	Tue	10:00	15.0	16.3	19.6	20.2	16.4	16.3	13.3	12.0	11.3	7.8	14.8
Bill Henry Johns Manville News	M	M-F	9:55	3.5	3.3	3.3	3.6	2.4	2.3	1.9	1.8	2.0	2.2	2.6
Bill Stern Sports Newsreel	N	Fri	10:30	9.5	10.8	11.8	11.3	9.6	8.1	6.9	8.2	5.3	5.7	8.7
Bing Crosby Philco Radio Time	A	Wed	10:00		12.5	12.9	15.0	15.9	14.6	14.8	10.7	9.7	7.0	12.6
Blondie	N	Wed	8:00	12.9	15.9	16.4	16.9	16.2	10.6	10.6	8.5	6.4	5.5	11.4
Bob Hawk Show	C	Mon	10:30	8.9	15.5	18.3	19.0	10.4	14.1	14.3	12.6	12.5	9.2	14.1
Bob Hope Show	N	Tue	9:00	15.4	23.5	25.0	25.3	23.2	21.2	21.3	17.0	13.7	12.0	19.8
Break the Bank	A	Fri	9:00	15.8	15.2	16.4	14.1	12.9	11.5	12.3	11.4	10.0	8.0	12.8
Burns & Allen Show	N	Thu	9:00	8.7	16.4	15.7	19.5	15.4	15.2	13.2	11.1	8.1	7.1	13.0
Can You Top This?	N	Sat	9:30	11.8	9.3									11.8
Carnation Contented Hour	N	Mon	10:00	7.9	4.3	9.3	10.7	6.4	7.4	6.6	6.0	5.7	4.2	7.4
Carnegie Hall	A	Sun	7:30			3.3	3.5	3.2	2.6	3.0	2.5	2.8	2.3	3.1
Casey Crime Photographer	C	Thu	9:30	16.8	17.9	17.2	18.4	15.6	16.6	15.8	14.4	12.5	11.3	15.7
Cavalcade of America	N	Mon	8:00	10.0	13.3	12.5	13.8	8.2	7.5	8.4	6.4	6.6	4.7	9.1
Champion Roll Call	A	Fri	9:55	5.5	7.0	7.3	6.9							6.7
Chesterfield Supper Club	N	M-F	7:00	7.8	9.9	10.3	10.4	8.8	8.6	8.2	6.9	6.6	5.2	8.3
Cities Service Band of America	N	Fri	8:00	7.8	8.4	9.9	9.9	6.7	7.6	5.9	4.9	4.1	2.7	6.8
Club 15	C	M-F	7:30	7.7	11.1	12.7	12.8	10.4	10.5	9.2	8.7	5.8	5.8	9.5

1948-49 Nielsen/Hooper Ratings 6-11 P.M.

Program		Time	Day	Sept. 48	Oct. 48	Nov. 48	Dec. 48	Jan. 49	Feb. 49	March 49	April 49	May 49	June 49	1948-49 Avg
Counterspy	A	7:30	T,T	9.2	11.1	12.7	13.4	7.9	9.6	9.7	8.3	6.3	5.6	9.4
County Fair	C	9:00	Wed				7.3	6.7	6.9	6.7	5.6	4.9	5.3	6.2
Curtain Time	N	10:30	Wed	7.7	12.2	16.1	15.3	12.9	12.2	11.8	11.2	9.9	9.8	11.9
A Date with Judy	N	8:30	Tue	11.8	18.5	19.3	19.1	13.2	15.0	14.2	13.4	11.7	9.5	16.4
A Day in the Life of Dennis Day	N	10:00	Sat	14.0	16.2	18.5	17.5	15.6	15.0	10.8	9.7	11.7	7.6	14.6
Dr Christian	C	8:30	Wed	14.1	14.5	16.4	16.0	16.0	10.0	8.0	7.3	7.8	4.9	11.7
Dr IQ	N	9:30	Mon	8.2	10.0	9.7	11.0	10.0	9.2	6.7	7.4	7.3	4.7	8.4
Don Gardiner Mon Morn Headlines	A	6:15	Sun	5.7	9.2	10.5	10.8	8.6	7.9	9.8	7.7	5.4	6.9	7.7
Drew Pearson News/Comment	A	6:00	Sun	7.5	11.0	13.3	12.5	8.5	11.2	9.8	7.7	8.3	9.1	9.9
Duffy's Tavern	N	9:00	Wed	12.3	20.9	22.4	21.9	18.8	17.9	17.7	14.4	11.3	6.5	16.7
Eddie Cantor Show	N	9:00	Fri	10.2	14.5	15.6	15.9	10.9	12.1	11.1	9.7	9.2	4.6	11.7
Edgar Bergen & Charlie McCarthy	N	8:00	Sun		18.9	19.8	21.7	12.1						20.1
Edward R Murrow News/Comment	C	7:45	M-F	8.4	11.4	13.3	13.3	9.3	9.0	8.9	6.6	5.4	1.4	9.0
Edwin C Hill News/Comment	A	7:00	M-F	2.2	3.7	4.6	4.6	3.9	3.3	3.6	2.7	2.3	2.9	3.2
Eric Sevareid News/Comment	C	6:00	M-F	1.4	1.8	2.4	2.4	4.1	4.1	3.7	4.1	3.6	1.5	3.0
Erwin Canham News/Comment	A	9:30	Tue	2.1	2.8	2.3	2.9	2.1	2.3	2.1	1.8	1.7	4.0	2.2
Family Hour of Stars	C	6:00	Sun	4.6	8.6	10.8	12.3	6.7	7.5	5.9	4.2	4.9	9.0	7.0
The Fat Man	A	8:00	Fri	14.3	16.0	18.1	15.7	13.7	13.6	13.5	13.2	9.9	8.9	13.7
FBI in Peace & War	C	8:00	Thu	16.5	18.1	19.2	20.7	14.0	14.9	13.4	11.1	9.4		14.6
Fibber McGee & Molly	C	9:30	Tue		24.4	25.2	26.6	26.0	25.8	24.3	19.9	15.8	8.9	23.5
First Nighter	C	10:30	Thu		12.6	12.6	14.2	12.7	11.7	11.4	11.7	10.7	7.4	11.7
Fishing & Hunting Club	M	9:30	Mon	2.1	2.7	2.5	2.7	1.3	1.6	1.7	1.2	1.3	1.0	1.8
Ford Theater	C	9:00	Fri		14.5	15.5	16.4	11.3	10.4	11.4	8.3	7.0	7.1	11.3
Fred Allen Show	N	8:00	Sun	14.5	17.5	18.6	20.0	11.7	11.3	9.4	8.9	9.5	5.8	12.5
Fred Waring Show	N	10:30	Thu	17.5	10.7	9.4	12.6	7.1	7.6	6.6	5.7	4.4	4.1	7.6
Friday Night Boxing	A	10:00	Fri	10.7	7.9	10.8	11.0	4.8	5.5	5.3	4.9	3.3		6.9
Fulton Lewis Jr News/Comment	M	7:00	M-F	7.9	3.1	3.7	4.1	5.1	5.0	4.8	3.4			3.7
Gabriel Heatter Behind Front Page	M	7:30	Sun	8.9	8.7	9.2	11.0	11.8	12.6	11.8	10.8	9.2	7.8	9.3
Gabriel Heatter News/Comment	M	7:30	M-F	3.7	5.8	5.3	5.7	8.7	8.3	8.4	7.7	5.8	4.1	4.8
Gangbusters	C	9:00	Sat	8.4	8.0	9.3	8.6	10.0	10.7	9.3	8.1	7.4		9.6
Gene Autry's Melody Ranch	C	9:00	Sat	6.6	13.3	14.0	13.2	13.8	14.0	13.0	11.9	8.9	8.1	9.1
Grand Ole Opry	N	8:00	Sat	6.5	13.7	16.5	15.8	2.5	2.5	5.3	4.1	5.8	4.1	11.0
Great Gildersleeve	N	8:30	Wed	7.6	17.0	17.6	18.4	13.8	6.6	5.2	5.2	7.4	5.5	13.4
Great Scenes from Great Plays	M	8:00	Fri	13.1	5.1	5.3	5.9	3.9	6.3	6.1	11.5	9.3	8.1	4.3
Greatest Story Ever Told	A	6:30	Sun	11.7	8.0	9.9	10.8	2.7	6.6	3.2	4.5	4.3	4.2	6.4
Guy Lombardo Orch	M	9:30	Sat							5.3	6.1	5.4		2.7
HV Kaltenborn/Richard Harkeness	C	7:45	M-F	6.6	15.1	14.0	16.4	7.6	6.3	8.0	5.2	5.4		6.5
Hallmark Playhouse	C	10:00	Thu		11.3	9.5	10.4	11.3	11.5	11.1	11.5	9.3	6.7	12.0
Harvest of Stars*	A	9:30	Wed					4.7	4.7	5.2	4.5	4.3		7.2
Headline Edition News/Taylor Grant	A	7:05	M-F	13.1	13.8	14.0	16.9	8.3	8.6	6.1	1.6	1.6	1.6	1.6
Helen Hayes Electric Theater	C	9:00	Sun					2.5	3.4	3.2	6.7	6.7		10.1
Henry J Taylor News/Comment	A	8:45	Mon		12.2	13.9	16.2	11.2	3.4	3.2	2.1	1.6	1.6	2.4
Hit the Jackpot	C	10:00	Tue				9.5	9.3	10.5	11.7	8.1	7.8	5.6	11.0
Hollywood Star Theater	N	8:00	Sat	13.8	13.1	14.8	17.1	10.4	7.2	9.7	7.2	5.5	3.6	7.4
Horace Heidt Youth Oppty Program	N	10:30	Sun	12.2	20.5	20.8	19.7	13.9	9.7	7.4	7.8	10.0	8.6	15.0
Inner Sanctum	C	8:00	Mon	13.1	3.4	2.9	3.3	2.1	14.6	15.6	13.3	9.7	8.4	2.5
Inside of Sports Joe Cummisky	M	7:45	M-F	13.6					2.3	2.2	2.0	2.0	1.7	
Jack Benny Program	C	7:00	Sun	2.7	20.3	22.1	25.8	28.3	26.2	23.1	19.3	17.9		22.9

1948-49 Nielsen/Hooper Ratings 6-11 P.M.				Sept. 48	Oct. 48	Nov. 48	Dec. 48	Jan. 49	Feb. 49	March 49	April 49	May 49	June 49	1948-49 Avg
Jack Carson Show	C	Fri	8:00		10.7	12.2	12.9	9.3	8.3	7.3	7.8	5.5	4.7	8.7
Jack Smith Show	C	M-F	7:15	7.5	10.4	12.5	12.9	11.0	11.2	10.3	9.1	6.7	6.1	9.8
Jimmie Fidler Hollywood News	A	Sun	10:30	3.7	5.8	7.9	7.7	6.7	6.3	7.7	5.1	5.1	4.5	6.1
Jimmie Fidler Hollywood News	M	Sun	9:30	5.1	5.2	5.4	6.7	3.7	4.0	4.6	3.3	3.3	3.0	4.4
Jimmy Durante Show	N	Fri	8:30		12.5	13.3	14.3	10.3	11.0	11.5	8.3	6.5	5.2	10.3
Jo Stafford Show	A	Thu	9:30			4.5	4.3	2.8	2.4	3.4	2.6	2.1		3.2
Judy Canova Show	N	Sat	9:30		14.0	18.5	16.6	13.0	14.0	14.3	13.5	11.1	9.9	13.9
King's Men Quartet	N	Tue	9:30										6.4	6.4
Leave It to the Girls	M	Fri	8:30	3.8	4.0	4.7								4.2
A Life in Your Hands	N	Tue	10:30									7.2	7.2	7.2
Lawrence Welk Show	A	Wed	9:30									3.5	3.5	3.5
Life of Riley	N	Fri	10:00	14.2	15.7	16.7	17.9	12.4	14.5	12.7	11.3	9.9		13.9
Little Herman	A	Tue	8:00					4.2	4.6	4.4	3.4	3.6	3.9	4.0
Lone Ranger	A	MWF	7:30	10.9	15.0	16.5	15.5	11.2	11.5	11.3	10.9	7.7	6.3	11.7
Louella Parsons Hollywood News	A	Sun	9:15	9.3	13.2	16.3	16.7	13.3	15.4	17.3	9.4	12.2	9.5	13.3
Lowell Thomas News	C	M-F	6:45	6.7	10.1	11.9	12.8	8.5	8.5	8.4	6.6	5.8	5.1	8.4
Lum & Abner	C	Sun	10:00		10.4	12.2	11.6	8.5	7.9	7.3	7.7	8.0	5.6	8.8
Lux Radio Theater	C	Mon	9:00	22.2	28.6	33.2	32.3	27.9	25.3	25.4	23.7	22.0	14.7	25.5
Man Called X	C	Sun	8:30	12.8										12.8
Manhattan Merry Go Round	N	Sun	9:00	7.7	16.8	16.7	17.0	7.7	9.0					12.5
Mayor of the Town	M	Sun	7:30					4.3	4.1	5.2	3.2	3.4		4.0
Meet the Boss	M	Sat	9:30		6.2	8.4	5.4							6.7
Meet the Stars	A	Thu	8:55				2.8							2.8
Mel Allen Sports	M	Sat	7:45	3.7	4.0	5.6	7.7							5.3
Meredith Willson Show	A	Wed	10:30		8.4	9.0	10.0	5.4	4.8	5.5				7.2
Milton Berle Show	A	Wed	9:00	10.6	9.7	10.7	12.4	9.4	10.0	9.7	8.2	8.4	6.9	9.6
Mr Ace & Jane (Easy Aces)	C	Fri	8:30	10.3	11.8	13.1	13.4							12.2
Mr & Mrs North	C	Tue	8:30	15.1	17.5	19.5	18.6	12.5	14.1	12.9	11.1	8.6	7.2	13.7
Mr Chameleon	C	Wed	8:00	12.9	13.2	15.2	15.7	12.6	11.1	12.4	11.5	9.2	9.2	12.3
Mr District Attorney	N	Wed	9:30	15.5	19.3	20.8	21.7	18.5	17.4	16.1	14.4	11.8	10.7	16.6
Mr Keen	C	Thu	8:30	19.6	19.3	18.4	20.7	15.0	17.0	15.8	13.2	11.5	9.7	16.0
My Favorite Husband	C	Fri	8:30					7.9	6.9	7.3	6.0	6.5	5.4	6.7
My Friend Irma	C	Mon	10:00	13.5	19.5	23.5	24.2	22.1	20.5	21.2	19.4	18.3	13.2	19.5
Mystery Theater	C	Tue	8:00	15.5	20.0	22.1	19.8	15.6	16.0	14.1	12.1	8.7	8.1	15.2
Name the Movie	A	Thu	9:30									2.6	1.8	2.2
National Barn Dance	A	Sat	10:00								3.3	4.0	3.3	3.5
NBC Symphony	N	Sat	8:30										3.4	3.4
News of the World/Morgan Beatty	N	M-F	7:15	6.4	8.6	9.2	9.8	7.1	6.8	6.3	4.9	4.4	4.3	6.8
Nick Carter Master Detective	M	Sun	6:30	8.3	13.3	12.7	16.1	7.8	8.0	8.1	5.4	5.2	5.2	9.0
One Man's Family	N	Sun	3:30	7.0	8.6	9.6	11.0	6.8	7.2	7.7	8.2			8.3
Original Amateur Hour	N	Wed	8:00		16.0	16.2	17.7	9.6	9.7	9.0	8.9	6.6	5.3	11.0
Our Miss Brooks	C	Sun	9:30		13.5	14.3	16.4	10.0	11.1	10.6	9.3	10.2	8.6	11.6
Pause That Refreshes	C	Sun	6:30	5.7	10.5	10.3	12.5	5.5	7.0					8.6
People Are Funny	N	Tue	10:30	14.3	16.8	19.4	21.6	18.7	17.6	17.0	15.4	13.5		17.1
Pet Milk Show	N	Sat	7:30		10.6	13.6	12.4	7.0	6.1	5.5	5.6	3.7	3.4	7.5
Phil Harris & Alice Faye	N	Sun	7:30		21.2	20.8	26.0	15.1	15.1	13.7	11.4	8.8	6.6	15.4
Philip Morris Playhouse	C	Fri	10:00			11.6	10.7	9.5	9.8	8.9	8.1	6.2	7.5	9.0
Railroad Hour	A	Mon	8:00		12.9	13.3	13.6	7.5	7.1	6.8	6.6	5.7	4.1	8.6

1948-49 Nielsen/Hooper Ratings 6-11 P.M.

Program	Net	Day	Time	Sept. 48	Oct. 48	Nov. 48	Dec. 48	Jan. 49	Feb. 49	March 49	April 49	May 49	June 49	1948-49 Avg
Red Skelton	N	Fri	9:30	14.5	15.9	17.4	19.5	13.8	14.8	12.2	11.4	9.8		14.4
Revere All Star Revue	M	Thu	9:30	3.2	3.8									3.6
Roy Rogers Show	M	Sun	6:00	8.1	14.2	13.6	17.8	9.0	8.7	7.8	6.2	5.0	4.4	9.5
Saturday Night Serenade	C	Sat	7:30	6.9										6.9
Screen Guild Players	N	Thu	10:00	11.0	14.5	12.8	16.0	12.5	10.1	11.3	8.7	7.8	6.4	11.1
Sealtest Variety Show	N	Thu	9:30	7.9	12.9	11.6	14.8	11.6	10.7	6.0	9.3	6.8	5.3	9.7
The Shadow	M	Sun	5:00	5.3	9.4	9.9	13.5	12.9	13.6	14.6	10.6	7.0	6.7	10.4
The Sheriff	A	Fri	9:30	11.5	10.1	11.9	10.8	8.1	6.4	8.9	7.1	4.9	5.1	8.5
Songs by Morton Downey	N	TTSa	11:15	3.5	3.8	4.6	5.1							4.3
Spike Jones Spotlight Review	C	Sat	7:00	9.3	10.7	11.6	11.2	10.6	9.7	8.3	6.7	5.8	5.3	8.9
Stop the Music	A	Sun	8:00	11.3	13.4	14.6	15.5	18.9	19.4	20.4	16.4	11.7	9.9	15.2
Suspense	C	Thu	9:00	18.5	18.6	18.3	21.9	15.5	17.6	14.9	14.1	13.6	11.2	16.4
Take a Number	M	Sat	8:30					3.3	4.4	4.2	4.0	3.2	2.2	3.6
Take It or Leave It	C	Sun	10:00	11.4	13.4	14.4	16.7	13.8	11.7	10.8	8.3	10.2	7.3	11.8
Tales of Fatima	C	Sat	9:30					5.9	5.7	5.6	7.0	6.9	5.0	6.0
Telephone Hour	N	Mon	9:00	8.1	9.7	10.0	12.0	6.4	8.5	6.4	7.2	7.3	5.4	8.1
Theater Guild on the Air	A	Sun	9:30	11.1	14.7	17.5	18.0	10.6	11.2	11.5	8.7	9.4	7.8	12.1
Theater USA	A	Thu	8:30					3.8	3.0	3.7	2.8	2.7	1.8	3.0
This Is Your FBI	N	Fri	8:30	17.3	17.1	19.2	16.2	15.3	15.0	13.9	13.7	9.8	8.4	14.6
This Is Your Life	N	Tue	8:00			17.4	16.1	11.1	10.4	10.7	9.7	7.4	6.0	11.1
Three Star Extra News	N	M-F	6:45	3.0	4.2	4.8	4.7	4.9	5.0	5.0	4.4	4.2	3.4	4.4
Truth or Consequences	N	Sat	8:30	13.4	15.0	18.4	17.4	13.9	14.8	14.8	12.4	10.0	6.9	13.7
Twenty Questions	M	Sat	8:00	6.6	7.8	9.6	8.4	8.4	8.0	8.8	8.0	8.4	5.2	7.9
Vaughn Monroe Show	C	Sat	7:30		11.7	13.1	13.7	10.6	11.2	10.4	10.7	7.8	5.9	10.6
Voice of Firestone	N	Mon	8:30	7.8	12.8	11.7	12.6	6.4	5.7	6.8	5.8	6.2	4.6	8.0
Walter Winchell Journal	A	Sun	9:00	14.9	15.4	23.4	23.1	28.3	26.5	26.8	23.3	20.3	14.8	21.7
We the People	C	Tue	9:00	11.8	11.5	12.0	13.3	8.4	10.3	9.6	9.5	6.9	5.5	9.9
The Whistler	C	Wed	10:00	6.3										6.3
Whiz Quiz	A	Sat	10:00	5.6	7.4	7.7								6.9
You Bet Your Life/Groucho Marx	A	Wed	9:30		10.8	12.7	13.0	12.5	11.7	13.9	12.2	10.1		12.1
Your Hit Parade	N	Sat	9:00	12.9	12.8	19.2	17.7	13.7	14.6	13.7	12.5	11.9	8.5	13.8
Your Hit Parade on Parade	N	Sun	7:00										5.3	5.3
Your Song & Mine	C	Wed	9:00	13.5	13.4	12.5	13.6							13.3
Yours for a Song	M	Fri	8:30				2.0	1.6	1.1	1.3	1.4	1.9		1.6

Special Broadcasts

Program	Net	Date	Sept. 48	Oct. 48	Nov. 48	Dec. 48	Jan. 49	Feb. 49	March 49	April 49	May 49	June 49	1948-49 Avg
Pres Truman State of Union	All	1/5					26.0						
Pres Truman Speech	All	4/4								12.9			
Hope & Crosby Baseball Special	C	4/17								11.8			
Kentucky Derby	C	5/7									13.0		

1949-50 Hooper/Nielsen Ratings 6-11 P.M.

Program	Net	Day	Time	Sept. 49	Oct. 49	Nov. 49	Dec. 49	Jan. 50	Feb. 50	March 50	April 50	May 50	June 50	1949-50 Avg
ABC's of Music	C	Wed	9:30										7.0	7.0
Adventures of the Falcon	M	Sun	7:00					6.6	6.2	8.9				7.2
Adventures of Ozzie & Harriet	A	Fri	9:00		5.9	8.9	7.4	9.8	10.2	12.1	11.7	7.5	6.7	8.9
Adventures of Philip Marlow	C	Wed	10:00										4.7	4.7
Adventures of Sam Spade	N	Sun	8:00	10.1	8.4	10.9	11.0	11.5	11.0	9.7	8.8	6.4	7.9	9.6

1949-50 Hooper/Nielsen Ratings 6-11 P.M.				Sept. 49	Oct. 49	Nov. 49	Dec. 49	Jan. 50	Feb. 50	March 50	April 50	May 50	June 50	1949-50 Avg
Adventures of Sherlock Holmes	A	Wed	9:00	5.2	4.2	5.0	4.4	5.1	7.9	4.6	3.3	3.1	3.0	4.6
Adventures of the Thin Man	A	Fri	9:00										6.2	6.2
Aldrich Family	N	Thu	8:00		8.7	9.4	9.9	10.3	11.3	11.2	10.7	9.0	5.2	9.5
Alexander's Mediation Board	M	Sun	8:00							1.8	1.3	0.9	1.6	1.4
Allen Jackson News	C	M-F	6:00								1.6	1.3	1.0	1.3
American Album of Familiar Music	N	Sun	9:30	5.4	6.7	6.7	8.7	7.9	8.8	5.8	6.4	5.0	4.7	6.6
Amos & Andy	C	Sun	7:30	13.4	14.8	18.2	17.1	17.5	17.0	15.9	11.7			15.7
Arthur Gaeth News/Comment	A	Mon	10:00	1.8	1.1	1.1	1.6	1.8						1.7
Arthur Godfrey Digest	C	Sat	9:30						9.7	8.0	8.8	6.6	5.9	7.8
Arthur Godfrey's Talent Scouts	C	Mon	8:30	14.7	18.1	20.8	19.7	22.2	22.8	20.4	18.8	14.8	11.5	18.4
Beulah	C	M-F	7:00	6.2	8.2	10.6	10.5	11.4	11.6	14.0	11.3	10.7	6.6	9.8
The Big Story	N	Wed	10:00	11.5	10.9	13.0	12.6	15.7	14.0	13.3	11.2	10.7	9.2	12.2
Big Town	N	Tue	10:00	10.6	12.5	14.1	15.7	17.5	14.6	12.2	11.7	8.8	9.1	12.7
Bill Henry Johns Manville News	N	M-F	8:55	2.4	2.4	2.8	3.4	2.6	3.1	4.2	3.3	3.0	2.7	3.0
Bill Stern Colgate Sports Newsreel	M	Fri	10:30	4.3	5.1	7.6	6.6	6.6	6.8	6.1	7.2	4.4	4.3	5.9
Bing Crosby Show	C	Wed	9:30	12.8	11.0	16.0	18.7	21.4	19.0	16.4	15.6	11.1		15.8
Blondie	C	Thu	8:00						7.0					7.0
Bob Hawk Show	A	Mon	10:30	11.1	11.8	13.9	15.2	17.1	14.7	13.3	12.1	10.5	10.4	13.0
Bob Hope Show	C	Tue	9:00	16.2	16.9	15.7	17.2	17.4	19.0	15.4	14.7	9.3	7.7	15.0
Break the Bank	N	Wed	9:00	8.4	10.1	11.9	11.5	11.6	11.0	13.3	10.6	7.8	7.1	10.3
Burns & Allen Show	N	Wed	10:00	11.6	9.0	11.8	13.5	14.1	14.4	12.1	11.6	10.1		12.0
Call the Police	C	Sun	7:30	5.0										5.0
Can You Top This?	C	Wed	8:00					3.4						3.4
Carnation Contented Hour	A	Sun	10:00	4.0	7.3	5.7	7.5	6.6	6.3	8.6	7.7	6.8	7.2	6.8
Carnegie Hall	A	Tue	8:00	2.5	5.4	4.0	7.4	4.6	5.8	1.4	1.7	0.7	1.1	3.5
Casey Crime Photographer	N	Thu	9:30	11.7	12.6	15.6	13.9	15.6	14.7	13.4	12.9	9.9	9.1	12.9
Cavalcade of America	C	Tue	8:00	5.2	6.0	9.1	8.8	7.6	9.2	10.9	8.3	5.8	6.1	7.7
Champion Roll Call	A	Fri	9:55							4.8	4.3	3.5	1.9	3.6
Chance of a Lifetime	M	Sun	9:30	5.2	6.6	7.0	7.9	8.5	8.9	6.8	7.6	6.8		7.3
Chesterfield Supper Club	N	Thu	10:00	6.0	6.2	8.7	7.9	9.6	10.0	9.4	7.6	7.3		8.1
Cities Service Band of America	A	Mon	9:30	4.8	4.3	5.5	6.8	6.8	7.0	4.7	4.7	4.6	4.2	5.3
Club 15	N	M-F	7:30	5.6	7.3	8.9	9.3	9.1	8.6	9.9	8.8	6.1	5.1	7.9
Counterspy	C	Tu,Th	7:30	7.1	8.5		10.8	10.5	11.2	12.8	10.8	7.1	5.7	9.4
Crime Fighters	A	Mon	9:30					4.5						4.5
Curtain Time	M	Wed	10:30	10.7	10.6	11.1	11.4	13.5	10.3	11.5				11.3
Dangerous Assignment	N	Wed	10:30									8.8	8.0	8.4
A Date with Judy	A	Thu	8:30			5.2	5.3	5.8	6.3			8.8		5.7
A Day in the Life of Dennis Day	N	Sat	9:30	10.2	11.0	15.1	13.2	14.9	14.6	15.0	13.4	11.5	7.5	12.6
Dr Christian	C	Wed	8:30	8.9	9.9	12.6	11.3	14.0	11.2	13.6	13.0	10.6	8.1	11.3
Dr IQ	A	Wed	8:00	6.5	7.9			5.4	5.9	5.6	3.8	3.3	2.7	4.5
Don Gardiner Mon Morn Headlines	A	Sun	6:15	5.0									4.4	6.1
Dragnet	N	Thu	10:30			8.2	9.0	11.5	9.3	9.3	8.0	8.0	6.5	8.5
Drew Pearson News/Comment	A	Sun	6:00	5.3	7.5	8.9	9.0	11.5	9.3	9.3	8.3	8.0	5.3	7.4
Duffy's Tavern	N	Thu	9:30		8.2	8.5	7.4	7.4	8.7	8.6	8.3	6.3	4.4	8.0
Edgar Bergen & Charlie McCarthy	C	Sun	8:00				17.6	16.9	16.4	18.3	16.0	13.6		16.0
Edwin C Hill News/Comment	A	M-F	7:45	5.4	6.5	7.5	8.6	8.9	9.3	9.2	8.9	6.1	5.1	7.5
Edward R Murrow News/Comment	A	M-F	7:00						4.0	3.6	1.9	2.2	1.6	3.2
Eric Sevareid News/Comment	C	M-F	6:00	3.1	3.1	3.3	4.1	4.3	4.1	1.6				3.4

1949-50 Hooper/Nielsen Ratings 6-11 P.M.

Program	Net	Day	Time	Sept. 49	Oct. 49	Nov. 49	Dec. 49	Jan. 50	Feb. 50	March 50	April 50	May 50	June 50	1949-50 Avg
Erwin Canham News/Comment	A	Tue	9:30	1.0	1.5	2.0	2.3	2.6	2.3	0.8	0.7	0.5	0.7	1.4
Escape	C	Tue	9:30					10.6						10.6
The Falcon	N	Wed	8:30										5.5	5.5
Family Hour of Stars	C	Sun	6:00	2.9	5.4	5.3	6.6	6.0	5.3					5.3
Fanny Brice as Baby Snooks	C	Tue	8:30			11.5	12.9	13.8	12.1	14.6	14.6			13.3
The Fat Man	A	Fri	8:00	10.5	10.3	14.3	13.9	14.5	14.3	12.9	12.4	8.5	7.1	11.9
Father Knows Best	N	Thu	8:30	5.8	8.5	9.7	9.4	11.0	10.1	13.0	11.3	8.9	6.0	9.4
FBI in Peace & War	C	Thu	8:00	10.7	11.6	15.1	13.9	14.0	12.4	14.1	13.3	9.6	8.4	12.3
Fibber McGee & Molly	N	Tue	9:30	16.1	16.9	18.5	20.4	20.9	20.0	17.5	17.5	11.1		17.7
First Nighter	C	Thu	10:30	9.8	8.5									9.2
Fishing & Hunting Club	M	Thu	8:30	2.1	0.9	1.8	1.6							1.6
Frank Edwards News/Comment	M	M-F	10:00					2.3	2.6	2.0	1.6	1.8	1.5	2.0
Frank Sinatra Light Up Time	N	M-F	7:00		5.9	6.5	7.0	7.1	5.9	5.8	4.6	4.0		5.9
Fred Waring Show	N	Thu	10:30	4.5										4.5
Friday Night Boxing	A	Fri	10:00		4.9	4.5	5.5	4.8		9.2	6.6	5.4		5.8
Fulton Lewis Jr News/Comment	M	M-F	7:00							3.3	3.3	2.2	1.8	2.7
Gabriel Heatter News/Comment	M	M-Th	7:30	3.5	3.4	4.7	4.7	4.8	5.4	4.8	4.0	3.6	2.7	4.2
Gangbusters	C	Sat	9:00		10.5	11.6	12.5	14.3	13.4	11.6	11.7	9.0	8.8	11.5
Gene Autry's Melody Ranch	C	Sat	8:00	6.0	7.2	8.7	10.1	9.0	9.4	13.9	12.6	9.1	7.7	9.4
Get More Out of Life	A	Sun	10:15						1.9	1.6	2.0	2.3		2.0
Goldbergs	C	Fri	8:00	5.3	5.0	5.9	6.0	5.4	7.1	8.5	8.3	4.8	4.4	6.1
Grand Ole Opry	N	Sat	10:30	4.8	7.1	9.7	9.0	9.1	8.6	11.4	10.4	8.6	6.3	8.5
Great Gildersleeve	N	Wed	8:30	12.3	11.0	13.0	13.5	16.2	15.0	14.9	12.0	8.9	8.5	12.5
Guy Lombardo Orch	N	Sun	7:30	4.5										4.5
Guy Lombardo Orch	N	Sun	7:00										8.7	8.7
HV Kaltenborn/Rich Harkeness News	N	M-F	7:45	3.8	5.2	6.3	5.4	6.0	5.9					5.4
Hallmark Playhouse	C	Thu	8:00	11.2	11.0	12.0	12.1	14.1	13.3	11.9	11.6	10.0		11.9
Halls of Ivy	N	Fri	8:00					9.0	7.3	7.1	6.9	4.6	3.9	6.5
Hawaii Calls	M	Sat	7:00					3.5						3.5
Henry J Taylor News/Comment	A	Mon	8:30	1.9	1.1	2.3	1.4	2.6	2.9	3.6	3.8	2.3	2.3	2.4
Henry Morgan Show	N	Wed	9:00	9.5										9.5
Hit the Jackpot	C	Tue	10:00	5.7	7.2	8.2	8.6						6.1	7.2
Hollywood Calling	N	Sun	7:00	3.8	3.3	4.3	4.2							3.9
Hollywood Star Playhouse	C	Mon	8:00									10.5	8.6	9.6
Hollywood Star Theater	N	Sat	8:00	5.1	7.1	8.2	7.2	8.7	7.7	9.0				7.6
Hogan's Daughter	N	Wed	8:00	4.1										4.1
Horace Heidt Youth Oppty Program	C	Sun	9:30	10.8	12.1	13.9	13.8	13.2	12.3	13.7	11.5	10.7	10.0	12.2
Inner Sanctum	C	Mon	8:00	10.6	13.9	14.0	14.0	14.5	12.6	12.0	12.1			13.0
Inside of Sports/Joe Cummisky	M	M-F	7:45	2.0										2.0
Jack Benny Program	C	Sun	7:00	14.7	20.3	22.1	25.4	25.6	25.2	20.3	19.0	13.7		20.7
Jack Smith Show	C	M-F	7:15	5.8	7.8	10.0	11.4	11.2	11.0	11.7	9.9	6.4	5.3	9.1
Jergens/Woodbury Journal News	A	Sun	9:15							10.2	9.5	8.5	6.5	8.7
Jimmie Fidler Hollywood News	A	Sun	10:00	5.3	5.0	6.1	6.8	6.6	7.9	4.7	4.4	4.3		5.7
Jimmy Durante Show	N	Fri	9:30		9.7	11.9	11.0	12.1	11.9	10.5	10.2	6.7	5.5	9.9
John B Kennedy News/Comment	M	Sat	7:55							5.1				5.1
Johnny Desmond Show	A	Wed	9:25							3.5				3.5
Judy Canova Show	N	Sat	10:00		9.7	13.8	11.8	13.7	13.6	14.2	12.7	10.9	7.9	12.0
Kraft Music Hall/Nelson Eddy	N	Thu	9:00	5.2										5.2

1949-50 Hooper/Nielsen Ratings 6-11 P.M.

	Net	Day	Time	Sept. 49	Oct. 49	Nov. 49	Dec. 49	Jan. 50	Feb. 50	March 50	April 50	May 50	June 50	1949-50 Avg
Lawrence Welk Show	A	Wed	10:00		1.1	2.3	2.6	1.8	2.1	1.2	1.1	0.6		1.6
Leave It to Joan/Joan Davis	C	Fri	9:00		7.7	8.2	7.1	11.1	10.0					8.8
A Life in Your Hands	N	Tue	10:30	8.1										8.1
Life of Riley	C	Fri	10:00		9.6	9.2	10.1	14.4	12.2	11.2	10.8	7.5	8.0	10.2
Life with Luigi	C	Tue	9:00			10.3	10.8	12.9	13.2	14.1	12.8	10.5	6.5	11.9
Lone Ranger	A	MWF	7:30			10.7	14.0	13.0	11.5	13.5				10.0
Louella Parsons Hollywood News	A	Sun	9:15	7.0	9.7	8.0	8.7	9.7	12.9	10.2	10.2	7.1	7.7	10.1
Lowell Thomas News	C	M-F	6:45	4.9	9.1			5.2	8.8	9.5	9.5	8.5	5.6	7.7
Lum & Abner	C	Wed	10:30		6.7				8.4		7.5	5.8	6.5	6.8
Lux Radio Theater	C	Mon	9:00	17.3	20.5	25.4	21.5	24.5	23.7	24.4	23.2	19.8		22.3
Me & Janie	N	Tue	8:30	4.7	5.3	6.2								5.4
Meet Corliss Archer	C	Sun	9:00	8.5	6.6	8.7	9.0	8.6	9.5	11.7	11.2	9.3	9.2	9.2
Meet the Press	N	Fri	9:30							1.4	1.3	0.5		1.1
Meredith Willson Show	C	Thu	8:00	4.2										4.2
Mr & Mrs North	C	Tue	8:30	11.2	11.3	13.7	11.4	14.9	11.9	12.3	12.7	11.2		12.3
Mr Chameleon	C	Wed	8:00	9.9	12.1	14.1	16.3	16.0	17.4	14.8	13.4	10.9	8.7	13.4
Mr District Attorney	N	Wed	9:30	11.2	11.8	12.9	14.0	14.7	14.6	14.8	11.9	10.3	9.1	12.5
Mr Keen	C	Thu	8:30	12.5	14.2	15.0	15.2	16.8	15.3	15.3	14.4	10.9	9.5	13.9
Music with the Hormel Girls	A	Sun	6:30			2.1	3.6	2.6	3.2	3.3	2.8	2.5	3.1	2.9
My Favorite Husband	C	Sun	6:00	6.8	6.4	8.6	7.9	8.7	10.7	6.6	6.8	4.5	4.8	7.2
My Friend Irma	C	Mon	10:00	14.8	16.2	20.5	19.1	21.4	20.9	17.8	16.8	14.2	12.1	17.4
Mystery Theater	C	Tue	8:00	11.1	12.7	12.4	13.7	14.9	16.6	17.1	14.9	11.0	8.9	13.3
Name the Movie	A	Thu	9:45	3.2	2.2	3.0	2.4							2.8
National Barn Dance	A	Sat	10:00	2.1	3.2	2.5		3.2	3.1	1.9				2.6
NBC Symphony	N	Sun	8:30	2.7										3.7
News of the World/Morgan Beatty	N	M-F	7:15	4.6	5.1	6.2	5.9	6.3	5.9	6.5	5.9	4.8	4.6	5.5
Nick Carter Master Detective	M	Sun	6:30	7.1	7.0	7.5	8.3	9.2	7.8	10.6	8.3	6.1	4.0	7.8
Nightbeat Frank Lovejoy	N	Mon	10:00									6.0	6.0	6.0
Official Detective	M	Tue	8:30					6.1	6.4				6.0	6.3
One Man's Family	N	M-F	7:00										3.9	3.9
Original Amateur Hour/Ted Mack	A	Thu	9:00	4.8	5.6	7.7	7.7	9.3	9.1	11.0	8.7	6.4	4.7	7.5
Our Miss Brooks	C	Sun	6:30	7.0	9.6	11.6	12.1	13.5	13.4	12.5	11.1	8.0		11.0
Pause That Refreshes	C	Sun	8:00										6.1	6.1
Penny Singleton Story	N	Tue	9:00										6.4	6.4
People Are Funny	N	Tue	10:30	12.8	13.7	14.9	14.7	17.1	16.2	14.0	13.5	10.0	10.4	13.7
Pet Milk Show/Bob Crosby	N	Sun	10:30	6.2	5.5	7.9	9.5	9.1	7.8	9.4	8.6	6.1	6.9	7.7
Peter Salem	M	Mon	8:30					5.8	4.5					5.2
Phil Harris & Alice Faye	N	Sun	7:30	9.2	9.3	12.0	11.5	12.2	13.3	9.1	8.5	5.5	5.8	9.6
Philip Marlow	C	Sat	8:30				8.2	10.0	11.2					10.0
Quick as a Flash	M	Sat	7:30	3.7	3.7	4.2	4.2							4.0
Railroad Hour	N	Mon	8:00	3.8	7.6	8.6		10.6		9.0	8.3	6.6	5.5	7.9
Rebuttal/John W Vandercook	M	Sun	9:15						1.7					1.7
Red Barber's Clubhouse Sports	C	Sat	6:30	2.2										2.2
Red Skelton	C	Sun	8:30	13.1	13.1	13.7	13.6	14.2	15.4	15.6	13.8	12.0	9.8	13.5
Rex Allen Show	N	Fri	10:00							1.2	2.5	2.2	2.2	2.0
Richard Diamond, Private Detective	N	Wed	10:30										8.6	8.6
Robert Montgomery Comments	A	Thu	9:45	2.4	1.9	2.9	4.4	5.0	6.4	5.6	5.1	3.9	1.8	3.9
Roy Rogers Show	M	Sun	6:00	5.1	6.9	8.9	9.1	8.1	9.2	11.6	9.7	6.9	6.3	8.2

1949–50 Hooper/Nielsen Ratings 6–11 P.M.

Program	Net	Day	Time	Sept. 49	Oct. 49	Nov. 49	Dec. 49	Jan. 50	Feb. 50	March 50	April 50	May 50	June 50	1949–50 Avg
The Saint	M	Sun	7:30					5.9						5.9
Sara's Private Caper	N	Thu	10:30									5.2	4.3	4.3
Satan's Waitin'	C	Tue	8:30										8.0	8.0
Screen Directors' Playhouse	N	Fri	9:00	4.5				10.6		8.0	8.1	7.2	4.8	7.1
Screen Guild Theater	N	Thu	9:00		8.4	8.3	7.7	10.5	8.4	10.2	9.4	6.1		8.9
The Shadow	M	Sun	5:00	9.6	7.3	10.3	10.3	11.0	9.4	10.8	8.5		6.4	9.1
Share the Weath	A	Mon	8:00		3.7	3.4	3.1	4.4						3.7
The Sheriff	A	Fri	9:30	7.1	7.2	8.1	9.4	9.9	10.4	7.2	6.9	4.7	3.6	7.3
Sing It Again	C	Sat	10:00		7.1	10.1	10.4	10.9	8.5	7.7	6.1	5.6	5.5	7.3
Skippy Hollywood Theater	C	Thu	10:30				9.3	9.0	10.1	6.8	6.7	5.9	5.1	8.2
Songs by Morton Downey	N	TTSa	11:15						8.3			2.4	2.0	7.3
Sports for All	M	Thu	8:30					1.2		3.0	2.7	0.5	0.4	2.5
Starlight Concert	N	Tue	8:30						1.0	1.6	1.1			1.0
Steve Allen Show	C	Sun	6:30									5.5	4.8	5.2
Stop the Music	A	Sun	8:00		8.1	10.4	10.8	11.8					6.6	6.6
Suspense	C	Thu	9:00	8.5	13.6	14.7	15.4	15.8	12.2	9.8	9.3	5.7	6.3	9.3
Take It or Leave It	N	Sun	10:00	14.1	9.4	13.7	12.1	12.4	14.6	12.9	13.1	9.7	9.0	13.3
Tales of Fatima	C	Sat	9:30	10.5	7.3	7.4	8.5	9.1	12.5	10.8	11.0	8.6	7.9	10.9
Telephone Hour	N	Mon	9:00	7.2	7.6	12.1	10.9	10.7	8.4	7.4	7.3	5.6	5.2	7.3
Theater Guild on the Air	N	Sun	8:30	4.6	8.9	12.7	14.6	13.9	11.7	10.5	10.2	8.2	8.7	7.1
This Is Your FBI	A	Fri	8:30	6.5	10.6	8.7	9.9	8.7	12.6	13.4	13.2	8.8	8.4	9.8
This Is Your Life	N	Wed	8:00	10.1	7.5	5.0	4.7	13.8	11.4	10.3	8.8	7.1		11.8
Three Star Extra News	N	M-F	6:45	6.3		12.9	11.3	8.7	6.0	8.6		2.1	2.1	8.7
Truth or Consequences	N	Sat	8:30	3.2	4.5			4.7	7.4	3.1	2.3	2.1	6.2	3.8
Twenty Questions	M	Sat	8:00	7.9	10.8	8.7	9.7	11.3	14.8	15.0	11.9	9.1	4.4	11.4
Vaughn Monroe Show	C	Sat	7:30	5.9	7.2	7.7	10.5	8.7	10.0	8.9	6.8	5.9	5.9	7.6
Voice of Firestone	N	Mon	8:30	4.9	8.7	8.3	8.2		11.9	11.1	10.2	6.2	5.1	9.4
Walter Winchell Journal	A	Sun	9:00	15.0	15.4	19.1	17.0	19.4	18.7	17.7	16.5	13.1	11.4	16.3
We the People	N	Fri	8:30	7.3	6.2	5.0	7.9	7.7	7.5	5.4	4.6	2.6	2.2	5.8
You Bet Your Life/Groucho Marx	C	Wed	9:00		11.3	15.4	16.5	18.5	17.6	17.5	15.4	12.3	9.7	14.9
Your Hit Parade	N	Sat	9:00	7.6	10.4	11.6	11.0	12.9	11.8	11.5	11.1	8.9	6.7	10.4
Your Hit Parade on Parade	C	Sun	7:00	4.0										4.0
"Yours Truly, Johnny Dollar"	C	Thu	10:00											6.5

Special Broadcasts

Program	Net	Date	Rating	Month
Pres Truman Speech	C	11/3	9.4	Nov. 49
NFL Champ Philadelphia/LARams	M	12/18	7.1	Dec. 49
Pres Truman Speech	All	1/4	18.3	Jan. 50
Pres Truman Speech	All	2/16	22.2	Feb. 50

1950–51 Nielsen Ratings 6–11 P.M.

Program	Net	Day	Time	Sept. 50	Oct. 50	Nov. 50	Dec. 50	Jan. 51	Feb. 51	March 51	April 51	May 51	June 51	1950–51 Avg
ABC's of Music	C	Wed	9:30	6.3										6.3
Adventures of Ozzie & Harriet	A	Fri	9:00	8.8	7.5	9.9	10.2	9.7	10.1	10.6	8.6	6.3	5.2	8.7
Adventures of Sam Spade	N	Sun	8:00	8.5	8.6	8.5	11.4	11.4	10.7	10.7	8.4	6.9	5.6	8.5
Aldrich Family	N	Thu	8:00	9.1										9.1
Alexander's Mediation Board	M	Sun	8:30						0.9	0.6				0.8
Allen Jackson News	C	M-F	6:00	1.5	1.4	2.0	2.6	2.0	1.5	1.3	1.4	1.2	1.1	1.6

1950–51 Nielsen Ratings 6–11 P.M.

Program		Day	Time	Sept. 50	Oct. 50	Nov. 50	Dec. 50	Jan. 51	Feb. 51	March 51	April 51	May 51	June 51	1950–51 Avg
American Album of Familiar Music	A	Sun	9:30	5.4	4.7	5.3	5.5	5.7	4.1	4.7	3.8	4.4	5.3	4.9
Amos & Andy	C	Sun	7:30		12.7	16.4	15.7	17.0	16.4	14.6	11.9	9.5	11.8	14.0
Armstrong of the SBI	A	T;T	7:30	6.0	5.8	6.0	6.9	6.4	6.6	5.6	4.8	3.4	3.3	5.5
Arthur Godfrey's Talent Scouts	C	Mon	8:30	10.8	13.9	14.8	16.4	15.5	15.5	15.3	13.4	10.3	7.9	13.4
Beulah	C	M-F	7:00	7.6	9.4	10.8	11.9	11.2	11.2	10.4	9.3	6.3	5.4	9.4
The Bickersons	C	Tue	9:30										5.9	5.9
The Big Show	N	Sun	6:00			5.7	8.0	5.0	5.6	5.7	4.5	4.3	7.4	5.5
The Big Story	N	Wed	10:00	10.0	10.4	11.5	12.3	12.8	11.5	9.9	9.9	8.0	6.0	10.4
Big Town	N	Tue	10:00	8.7	9.5	9.0	10.8	12.0	11.0	10.4	9.6	6.9	2.5	9.4
Bill Henry Johns Manville News	M	M-F	8:55	3.4	2.8	3.2	3.4	3.0	3.2	2.8	2.8	2.4	3.6	3.0
Bill Stern Colgate Sports Newsreel	N	Fri	10:30	3.0	3.5	4.0	5.3	4.7	5.7	5.3	4.7	4.0	3.1	4.4
Bing Crosby Show	C	Wed	9:30	9.5	8.5	11.4	13.5	11.1	11.0	10.7	9.4	6.7	5.6	9.8
Blatz Reporter News	A	Tu-F	10:00										0.9	0.9
Blatz Reporter News	N	M-F	10:45										0.4	0.4
Blue Ribbon Bouts	C	Wed	Var		4.2	4.4	6.1	4.5	4.9	5.0	4.4	3.8	2.3	5.6
"Bob Barclay, American Agent"	A	Wed	8:00					5.8	4.9	5.1	4.5	3.9	2.4	4.4
Bob Hawk Show	C	Mon	10:30	11.8	10.0	11.2	12.8	11.6	11.1	10.9	10.7	8.7	7.5	10.5
Bob Hope Show	N	Tue	9:00	10.0	10.0	11.2	11.4	12.3	10.1	9.1	9.2	7.3	5.6	9.6
Boston Pops Orch	N	Mon	10:00						4.6	4.3	3.6	4.4	2.3	3.8
Botany Song Shop	A	Sun	10:00		1.9	2.1	2.8	2.5	2.0					2.2
Break the Bank	N	Wed	9:00	10.3										10.3
Can You Top This?	A	Tue	8:00					4.1	4.4	5.0	4.4	2.2	2.3	3.7
Carmen Dragon Orch	C	Tue	8:30										4.9	4.9
Carnation Contented Hour	C	Sun	10:00	6.0	7.6	8.0	9.8	7.5	7.4	8.0	7.0	6.3	5.3	7.3
Casey Crime Photographer	C	Thu	9:30	10.0										10.0
Cavalcade of America	N	Tue	8:00	6.1	7.4	8.6	8.6	8.1	8.3	6.8	6.6	6.3	4.3	7.1
Cecil Brown News/Comment	M	Sat	10:45								1.4	1.9	1.9	1.7
Cecil Brown News/Comment	M	Sat	7:55	3.8	3.3									3.6
Champion Roll Call	A	Fri	9:55	3.1	3.3									4.1
"Charlie Wild, Private Detective"	C	Sun	6:00									3.3	3.1	4.6
Cities Service Band of America	N	Mon	9:30	4.9	5.1	4.8	6.0	4.9	5.2	4.7	4.5	3.3	3.1	4.7
Club 15	C	M-F	7:30	6.2	7.0	8.0	9.0	8.7	8.3	8.2	7.1	5.5	4.3	7.2
Counterspy	N	Thu	9:30	7.1										5.7
Dangerous Assignment	N	Wed	10:30	5.3										7.1
David Rose Orchestra	C	Sun	8:30											5.3
Dennis Day Show	N	Sat	9:30		8.9	10.1	10.1	9.9	8.7	8.1	8.9	7.2	7.1	8.8
Dr Christian	C	Wed	8:30	10.3	11.1	12.1	13.1	10.7	10.7	11.0	9.0	7.4	7.0	10.2
Dr IQ	A	Wed	8:00	3.4	3.9	3.5								3.6
Don Gardiner Mon Morn Headlines	A	Sun	6:15	4.6	4.7	5.4	6.4	6.7	6.0	4.6	5.5	4.6	4.1	5.3
Dragnet	N	Thu	9:00	7.5	7.5	8.0	9.6	10.3	10.6	9.7	8.2	8.5	7.0	8.7
Drew Pearson News/Comment	A	Sun	6:00	6.2	7.5	7.7	8.3	8.5	7.7	6.9	5.9	6.0	4.2	6.6
Duffy's Tavern	N	Fri	9:30	5.2	5.6	6.6	6.3	7.4	6.4	6.9	5.9	6.0		6.4
Edgar Bergen & Charlie McCarthy	C	Sun	8:00	13.6	13.6	16.2	16.9	16.2	16.4	15.6	14.2	11.6	11.8	14.7
Edward R Murrow News/Comment	C	M-F	7:45	7.0	7.7	7.7	9.1	9.4	8.9	8.9	7.7	5.9	4.4	7.5
Edwin C Hill News/Comment	A	M-F	7:00	1.8	1.8	1.9	2.4	1.8	1.6	1.7	1.5	1.1		1.7
Erwin Canham News/Comment	A	Tue	9:30	0.7	0.5	0.5	1.1	0.9	0.9	0.7				0.8
Fanny Brice as Baby Snooks	N	Tue	8:30	8.5	10.5	10.8	10.8	11.9	9.7	9.5	9.8	6.5		9.7
The Fat Man	A	Fri	8:00	9.4		11.6	10.6							10.5

1950-51 Nielsen Ratings 6-11 P.M.

Program	Net	Day	Time	Sept. 50	Oct. 50	Nov. 50	Dec. 50	Jan. 51	Feb. 51	March 51	April 51	May 51	June 51	1950-51 Avg
Father Knows Best	N	Thu	8:30	9.6	9.7	9.5	11.4	11.9	10.8	10.2	8.9	7.5	5.7	9.5
FBI in Peace & War	C	Thu	8:00	9.4	10.5	10.0	13.6	11.3	12.0	10.7	9.8	7.5	7.1	10.2
Fibber McGee & Molly	N	Tue	9:30	10.5	11.3	13.1	13.4	12.9	11.6	11.1	11.0	8.3	7.5	11.1
Frank Edwards News/Comment	M	M-F	10:00	2.2	1.6	1.9	2.2	1.7	1.8	1.5	1.7	1.6	1.6	1.8
Friday Night Boxing	A	Fri	10:00	3.3	4.9	7.0	6.1	8.6	6.4	5.7	5.2			5.9
Fulton Lewis Jr News/Comment	M	M-F	7:00	2.8	2.8	2.6	3.4	3.4	2.4	2.3	2.7	1.9	1.5	2.6
Gabriel Heatter News/Comment	M	Sun	9:30	2.4	2.7	2.3	2.6	3.1	3.0					2.7
Gabriel Heatter News/Comment	M	M-F	7:30	4.7	4.2	4.7	4.7	4.0	4.9	4.5	4.9	3.6	3.3	4.4
Gangbusters	C	Sat	9:00	10.1	10.0	11.7	10.5	10.7	11.2	11.0	10.3	8.5	6.6	10.1
Gene Autry's Melody Ranch	C	Sat	8:00	9.5	10.4	11.9	12.0	11.8	10.8	10.7	10.1	8.1	6.5	10.2
Get More Out of Life	C	Sun	9:45					0.7						0.7
Grand Ole Opry	N	Sat	10:30	3.8	9.4	9.5	9.4	9.2	9.3	8.1	8.2	6.8	5.9	8.0
Great Gildersleeve	N	Wed	8:30	8.9	9.6	10.5	11.1	11.1	10.8	9.3	9.2	7.2		9.7
Guy Lombardo Orch	C	Sun	7:00	6.7									4.5	5.6
Hal Peary Show	C	Wed	9:00					8.6	7.5					8.1
Hallmark Playhouse	N	Thu	9:30	9.1	9.4	9.4	12.7	11.4	9.5	9.1	9.0	7.5		9.7
Halls of Ivy	A	Wed	8:00	5.8	5.0	7.9	8.0	7.9	7.3	8.0	6.9	5.3	4.3	6.6
Henry J Taylor News	C	Mon	8:30	3.3	3.0	3.7	3.1	3.4	3.1	2.9	2.5	2.6		3.1
Hollywood Star Playhouse	C	Mon	8:00	10.0	11.7	11.1	12.4	12.0	10.4	11.3	10.5	8.0	6.0	10.3
Hopalong Cassidy	A	Sat	8:30			11.6	10.7	10.3	10.8	11.3	10.1	7.5	6.3	9.8
Horace Heidt Youth Oppty Program	C	Sun	9:30	7.3	9.1	12.0	12.1	10.5	11.0	11.9	9.5	7.4	6.6	9.7
Inner Sanctum	C	Mon	9:00					5.0	5.7	5.9	4.5	3.2	2.6	4.5
It Pays to Be Ignorant	A	Wed	9:00	9.5										9.5
Jack Benny Program	C	Sun	7:00	10.1	15.8	18.8	19.2	19.8	19.5	15.3	14.8	11.8	10.6	15.6
Jack Pearl Show	N	Tue	9:30											3.9
Jack Smith Show	C	M-F	7:15	6.5	7.7	9.0	10.0	9.6	9.4	8.8	7.4	5.6	4.4	7.8
John B Kennedy News/Comment	A	M-Th	10:30	0.9	1.0	1.3	1.6	1.1	1.2					1.2
Judy Canova	N	Sat	10:00		10.6	10.5	9.8	10.8	10.1	8.4				9.4
Larry LeSueur News	C	Tue	10:25								2.2	1.2	2.2	1.9
Larry LeSueur News	C	Thu	10:30								2.3	2.3	2.6	2.4
Larry LeSueur News	C	Sat	7:25					2.9			3.7	2.5	2.1	2.8
LeBlanc's Comedy & Musical Show	A	Sat	9:00					3.3						2.9
LeBlanc's Hollywood Party	M	Fri	8:55											3.3
Les Griffith News	A	Wed	8:00								3.9	3.9	2.2	3.1
Les Griffith News	A	Thu	10:00								4.2	2.8	2.2	2.3
Lawrence Welk's Highlife Revue	A	Wed	10:30		1.7	2.1	2.4	3.0	2.2	2.4				2.3
A Life in Your Hands	N	Tue												2.4
Life of Riley	N	Fri	10:00	7.3										7.3
Life with Luigi	C	Tue	9:00	12.0	12.6	12.0	12.6	12.2	12.7	11.7	10.4	7.7	7.3	11.1
Lineup	C	Thu	10:00					8.2	8.1	6.8				7.5
The Lone Ranger	A	MWF	7:30	6.9	7.5	9.1	8.5	8.5	8.1	8.7	7.1	5.8	4.7	7.5
Longine Choraliers	C	Sun	10:35		6.2	5.9	7.7	5.5	6.0	6.3	5.2	5.0	3.6	5.7
Longine Symphonette	A	M-Th	10:30		1.0	1.6	1.5							1.4
Longine Symphonette	A	Sun	10:30											3.3
Louella Parsons Hollywood News	A	Sun	9:15		6.7	8.6	8.6	7.9	6.8	6.9	6.3	5.1	4.4	6.8
Lowell Thomas News	C	M-F	6:45	5.7	6.7	8.5	9.3	8.6	8.4	7.4	6.8	5.2	4.6	7.1
Lux Radio Theater	C	Mon	9:00	15.9	18.4	20.2	21.0	19.7	21.3	19.2	17.8	14.4	11.4	17.9
Man Called X	N	Sat	8:30		6.3	6.3	6.4	5.7	6.3	6.0	5.7	5.6	4.9	5.9

1950–51 Nielsen Ratings 6–11 P.M.

Program		Day	Time	Sept. 50	Oct. 50	Nov. 50	Dec. 50	Jan. 51	Feb. 51	March 51	April 51	May 51	June 51	1950–51 Avg
Mario Lanza Show	C	Sun	8:00										4.3	4.3
Meet Corliss Archer	C	Sun	9:00	7.4	9.3	11.0	10.7	9.9	11.3	11.2	8.5	7.6	6.2	9.3
Mindy Carson Sings	N	TTSa	11:15	1.0										1.0
Mr & Mrs North	C	Tue	8:30	12.1	12.0	12.2	12.6	12.6	12.6	11.4	9.9	8.2	8.1	11.2
Mr Chameleon	C	Wed	8:00	12.2	12.5	13.6	13.9	12.6	13.5	11.5	10.6	8.2	7.3	11.6
Mr District Attorney	N	Wed	9:30	10.6	11.7	11.5	11.6	12.1	12.2	12.0	11.0	7.8	6.9	10.7
Mr Keen	C	Thu	8:30	10.9	10.5	10.1	13.0	11.7	12.7	11.1	10.5	9.2	7.7	10.7
Musical Merry Go Round	N	Sat	8:00									3.2	2.9	3.1
My Favorite Husband	C	Sat	9:30	6.9	8.3	9.2	9.0	9.2	9.7	9.4				8.8
My Friend Irma	C	Mon	10:00	12.6	13.7	14.0	16.1	14.8	15.2	14.2	13.0	10.7	8.6	13.3
Mystery Theater	C	Tue	8:00	11.6		13.0	13.7	12.5	12.7	11.6	10.3	8.6	8.5	11.4
NBC Symphony	N	Mon	10:00	7.1		4.0	5.0	4.5						5.2
NBC Symphony	N	Sat	6:30					6.1						5.6
NBC Symphony	N	Sat	8:30	5.4					5.1					4.2
News of the World/Morgan Beatty	N	M-F	7:15	5.4	5.7	6.6	6.9	7.3	6.9	6.4	5.9	4.5	4.2	6.0
News of Tomorrow	A	M-Th	10:30							1.0	1.3	1.1	1.2	1.2
Nick Carter Master Detective	M	Sun	6:30	5.5	7.0	8.5	8.3	7.5	7.5	7.7	6.1	4.9	4.1	6.7
One Man's Family	N	M-F	7:45	5.2	5.9	6.7	6.9	7.8	7.4	7.3	6.2	5.1	4.1	6.3
Original Amateur Hour	A	Thu	9:00	7.0	6.9	5.8	8.3	7.1	8.5	7.2	7.1	5.3	4.8	6.7
Our Miss Brooks	C	Sun	6:30	6.4	9.4	12.7	12.3	11.2	12.6	9.9	11.4	7.4	4.1	9.8
Paul Harvey News/Comment	A	Sun	10:15				2.4	2.1	1.9	2.2	2.7	2.8		2.3
Pause That Refreshes	C	Sun	8:00	4.5	8.1	5.0	4.8							6.3
Peggy Lee Show	C	Sun	7:30										2.9	2.9
People Are Funny	N	Sat	7:30	4.1				3.7	4.4	3.5	2.5	2.3		3.7
People Are Funny	N	Tue	10:30	8.6	10.0	11.0	12.5	12.5	11.2	9.8	10.8	6.7		10.3
Pet Milk Show Bob Crosby	N	Sun	10:30	6.0										6.0
Phil Harris Show	N	Sun	7:30						6.8		8.0	4.6	6.2	6.3
Philip Morris Playhouse	C	Thu	10:00											6.6
Private Files of Rex Saunders	N	Wed	10:30								7.7	5.6	5.7	5.7
Railroad Hour	N	Mon	8:00	7.3	8.3	9.3	9.7	9.0	9.8	9.0	8.7	6.5	5.3	8.3
Ralph Flanagan Orch	A	Mon	10:00					1.6	2.3	2.0	2.3	1.9	1.3	1.9
Red Skelton Show	C	Sun	8:30		10.3	14.2	14.4	13.4	13.4	13.3	11.3	9.5	7.1	11.9
Refreshment Time	C	Sat	10:30	4.8	4.8	5.2	4.8	5.0	5.6	6.1	4.0	3.5	4.5	4.8
Rex Allen Show	C	Fri	10:00	2.2	2.2	3.5	3.1	2.7	2.6	2.0	2.5	2.3	1.9	2.6
"Richard Diamond, Private Detective"	A	Fri	8:00	8.0	8.4	9.9	10.9	8.5	9.3	8.5	7.8	5.9	4.4	8.2
Robert Montgomery Comments	A	Thu	9:45	3.7	3.8	3.7	5.2	4.9	5.5	4.5	4.5	4.2	3.2	4.3
Roy Rogers Show	M	Sun	6:00	6.4	7.0	9.1	9.9	8.6	9.2	8.6	7.1	6.6		8.1
Screen Directors' Playhouse	N	Thu	10:00			5.6	10.8	8.1	8.3	9.0	6.8	6.4		7.9
The Shadow	M	Sun	5:00	6.0	6.2	7.4	9.2	8.2	9.3	8.7	7.8	5.8	4.1	6.1
The Sheriff	A	Fri	9:30	5.8	4.9	6.1	7.1	7.3	6.5	6.5	6.7	4.3	3.6	5.4
Sing It Again	C	Sat	10:00	5.8	5.8	5.7	6.1	6.2	5.8	5.8	4.4	4.7	5.3	7.7
$64 Question (Take It or Leave It)	N	Sun	10:00	6.7	6.9	8.7	9.4	9.5	9.3	8.7				6.1
Skippy Hollywood Theater	C	Thu	10:30	6.1				5.6						5.6
Songs for Sale	C	Fri	8:30		6.1	7.8	9.0	7.3	6.2	5.4	2.9			5.9
Starlight Concert	C	Tue	8:30	5.7	6.9					6.4	5.4	2.9	3.1	6.2
Stop the Music	A	Sun	8:00	7.2	10.1	9.1	11.4	10.8	10.2	9.1	9.3	7.3	6.4	9.3
Suspense	C	Thu	9:00	9.0										6.2
Telephone Hour	N	Mon	9:00	6.6	6.5	6.8	8.2	7.6	7.0	6.3	5.7	4.6		6.6

1950-51 Nielsen Ratings 6-11 P.M.

Program	Net	Day	Time	Sept. 50	Oct. 50	Nov. 50	Dec. 50	Jan. 51	Feb. 51	March 51	April 51	May 51	June 51	1950-51 Avg
Theater Guild on the Air	N	Sun	8:30	10.9	8.2	7.4	8.3	9.2	8.9	8.3	8.3	6.2	5.0	8.1
This Is Your FBI	A	Fri	8:30	9.1	9.0	11.4	10.6	9.1	9.7	8.9	8.7	6.8	4.9	8.8
Three Star Extra News	N	M-F	6:45	2.2	2.5	2.4	3.1	3.0	2.7	2.6	2.0	1.6	1.5	2.4
Truth or Consequences	C	Tue	9:30	9.4	8.9	8.7	10.2	11.1	9.4	8.8	8.1	6.0		9.0
Twenty Questions	M	Sat	8:00	5.0	5.5	7.3	6.1	6.6	5.9	5.3	5.2	4.1	3.8	5.5
Vaughn Monroe Show	C	Sat	7:30	8.5	9.1	10.9	9.8	10.2	9.1	8.4	8.2	6.5	5.2	8.6
Voice of Firestone	N	Mon	8:30	6.9	8.1	7.8	8.3	7.7	7.9	7.3	7.1	6.5	4.4	7.2
Walter Winchell	A	Sun	9:00	8.9	12.8	13.6	16.3	14.5	14.2	13.3	12.1	10.3	7.9	12.4
We the People	N	Thu	9:30	3.7	3.6	4.1	4.2	4.9						4.1
Wild Bill Hickock	M	Sun	7:00								2.1	1.9	2.7	2.2
You Bet Your Life/Groucho Marx	N	Wed	9:00		12.1	12.0	13.8	13.7	13.8	12.2	12.4	8.4	8.2	11.8
Your Hit Parade	N	Sat	9:00	7.3	8.1	9.6	8.9	8.7	7.6	6.8	8.1	6.0	5.8	7.7

Special Broadcasts

Program	Net	Day	Time	Sept. 50	Oct. 50	Nov. 50	Dec. 50	Jan. 51	Feb. 51	March 51	April 51	May 51	June 51	1950-51 Avg
Boxing: Ezzard Charles/Joe Wolcott	C	3/7								16.8				
Gen McArthur Homecoming Events	A	4/20									4.4			

1951-52 Nielsen Ratings 6-11 P.M.

Program	Net	Day	Time	Sept. 51	Oct. 51	Nov. 51	Dec. 51	Jan. 52	Feb. 52	March 52	April 52	May 52	June 52	1951-52 Avg
Adventures of Maisie	M	Fri	8:00								1.5	2.4	1.8	1.9
Adventures of Ozzie & Harriet	A	Fri	9:00	1.2	7.8	7.8	7.6	9.2	7.3	7.3	6.8	5.5	5.4	7.2
Allen Jackson News	C	M-F	6:00		1.8	1.8	1.6	1.8	1.5	1.7	1.1	1.0	0.9	1.4
Amos & Andy	C	Sun	7:30	8.6	14.0	14.9	14.8	15.5	14.2	15.0	8.3	10.1		13.4
Arthur Godfrey's Talent Scouts	C	Mon	8:30		11.8	12.3	11.7	11.0	10.8	9.7	7.0	8.2	5.5	9.7
Barrie Craig Confidtal Investigator	N	Tue	8:30				7.2				4.0	5.1	5.4	5.4
Beulah	C	M-F	7:00	5.3	8.0	9.1	8.4	8.1	7.8	7.5	4.2	4.1	3.5	6.6
The Big Show	N	Sun	6:00	6.9	5.2	5.1	5.4	5.6	5.1	4.5	7.8		5.6	5.2
The Big Story	N	Wed	9:30	6.1	7.6	8.2	8.8	10.2	8.7	8.5	6.5	7.4	4.4	8.0
Big Town	C	Wed	8:00	2.9	7.8	9.3	9.8	8.1	8.8	8.6	6.5	5.0	2.1	7.4
Bill Henry Johns Manville News	M	M-F	9:00		2.7	2.9	3.3	2.8	2.9	2.5	2.1	2.1	5.1	2.6
Bing Crosby Show	C	Wed	9:30		9.6	9.3	9.1	9.1	8.3	9.1	6.3	5.5	2.6	7.9
Black Museum	M	Tue	8:00								1.4	2.0		2.0
Blue Ribbon Bouts	C	Wed	10:00	7.0	6.4	6.1	6.6	5.6	5.6	6.8	5.0	6.0		6.0
Bob Hawk Show	N	Mon	10:00		9.8	10.7	10.0	10.4	9.6	9.5	7.6	6.9		9.1
Bob Hope Show	N	Tue	9:00		8.4	9.3	8.7	9.5	8.7	9.0	5.8	6.1	5.0	7.8
Boston Pops Orch	N	Mon	10:00	3.5										3.5
Broadway Is My Beat	C	Mon	9:30			7.1	6.5							6.2
Carnation Contented Hour	C	Sun	9:30	5.4	6.6	7.6	7.2	7.8	6.7	5.9			6.2	6.4
Casebook of Gregory Hood	A	Wed	8:30		4.2									4.2
Cavalcade of America	N	Tue	8:00	5.4	8.0	7.6	7.2				4.1	5.5	4.0	6.2
Cecil Brown News	M	Sat	7:50	2.3	3.1			2.9						2.7
Cecil Brown News	M	Sat	7:55			2.6	3.5							2.4
Cecil Brown/Cedric Foster News	M	Sun	6:55		4.5	4.7	4.2	3.8	3.1	3.7	2.4	1.8	1.4	3.4
Champion Roll Call	A	Fri	9:55	2.7	5.1	4.2	4.7				2.2	2.4	1.8	4.2
Cities Service Band of America	N	Mon	9:30	3.2	5.1	4.3	4.6	4.7	4.2	5.7	3.4	4.5	2.8	4.3
Citizen Views the News	N	M-F	10:30					2.7	2.5	2.8	1.8	1.6	1.4	2.1
Club 15	C	M-F	7:30	4.5	6.6	6.9	6.7	6.3	6.1	5.9	3.9	4.2	3.1	5.4
Counterspy	N	Thu	9:30	5.4	6.2	5.8	6.3	6.5	6.2	6.3	5.2	4.2	3.4	5.6

1951–52 Nielsen Ratings 6–11 P.M.

Program				Sept. 51	Oct. 51	Nov. 51	Dec. 51	Jan. 52	Feb. 52	March 52	April 52	May 52	June 52	1951-52 Avg
Defense Attorney	A	Thu	8:30	2.4	4.9	4.4	5.1	5.6	5.3	4.3	4.4	4.5	3.1	4.4
Dr Christian	C	Wed	8:30	8.0	9.2	9.6	9.1	9.7	9.2	10.4	7.6	6.0	4.8	8.4
Don Gardiner Mon Morn Headlines	A	Sun	6:15		4.9	6.0		6.1	6.3	5.9	2.7	1.9		4.8
Doris Day Show	C	Sun	7:30										4.4	4.4
Dragnet	N	Thu	9:00	7.8	9.2	9.1	9.8	10.3	9.3	10.4	8.5	6.8	5.7	8.7
Drew Pearson News/Comment	A	Sun	6:00	3.6	5.5	6.7	6.6	6.3	6.8	5.3	5.3	5.4	4.8	5.6
Eddie Cantor's Show Biz Old & New	N	Tue	10:00		6.6	5.8	6.2	6.2	5.7	6.5	6.0			6.2
Edgar Bergen & Charlie McCarthy	C	Sun	8:00		12.3	13.3	12.0	13.3	12.8	11.5	8.6	9.6	7.6	11.2
Edward R Murrow News/Comment	C	M-F	7:45	5.5	6.0	7.2	6.3	6.0	5.5	5.6	3.6	3.8	3.2	5.3
The Fat Man	A	Fri	8:00	2.1										2.1
Father Knows Best	N	Thu	8:00	7.3	8.9	7.3	8.8	9.2	8.8	8.8				8.4
FBI in Peace & War	C	Thu	8:00	7.7	8.1	7.1	8.1	8.8	9.8	8.0		7.6	5.4	7.9
Fibber McGee & Molly	C	Tue	9:30		9.6	11.5	11.3	10.7	9.1	9.2	7.7	6.8	6.8	9.3
Frank Edwards News/Comment	M	M-F	10:00	1.6	1.3	1.6	1.4	1.2	1.5	1.1	1.3	1.2	1.2	1.3
Friday Night Boxing	A	Fri	10:00	3.0	7.8	5.2	5.9	5.1	5.7	5.1	3.5	4.2	3.8	4.9
Fulton Lewis Jr News/Comment	M	M-F	7:00	2.1	2.8	2.5	2.9	3.9	3.7	3.5	2.4	2.6	2.2	2.9
Gabby Hayes Show	M	Sun	6:00					4.6	4.0	4.6	2.7			4.0
Gabriel Heatter News/Comment	M	M-F	7:30	3.7	4.2	4.6	4.3	5.2	5.0	4.5	2.9	3.5	3.1	4.1
Gangbusters	M	Sat	9:00	8.8	9.3	9.7	10.2	9.8	8.2	8.4	7.0	5.7	4.9	8.2
Gene Autry's Melody Ranch	C	Sat	8:00	7.5	9.0	9.4	10.8	9.7	8.3	7.9	7.0	4.5	5.0	7.9
Goodwill Hour/John J Anthony	M	Sun	9:30					3.4	2.2	2.4	3.2	2.0	1.7	2.5
Grand Ole Opry	N	Sat	10:30	3.7	5.3	5.5	6.5	6.3	7.0	6.3	5.3	3.8	4.0	5.4
Grantland Rice Sports	C	Fri	8:00		2.2	2.3								2.3
Great Gildersleeve	N	Wed	8:30	5.3	8.3	8.6	8.8	8.5	8.6	8.2	7.1	7.0	6.0	7.6
Guy Lombardo Orch	C	Sun	7:00	4.5										4.5
Hallmark Playhouse	C	Thu	8:30	6.7	7.7	6.9	8.2	8.3	7.2	5.7	5.5	4.1		6.7
Halls of Ivy	N	Wed	8:00		7.5	7.8	7.9	7.8	6.9	6.8	5.6	6.1	4.1	6.7
Hearthstone of the Death Squad	C	Thu	9:00				5.9							5.9
Henry J Taylor News	A	Mon	8:00	2.3	2.9	2.7	3.0	3.2	3.7	3.3	2.1	2.3	1.8	2.7
Hollywood Stars on Stage	A	Sun	9:30		3.1	3.3	4.1							3.5
Hopalong Cassidy	C	Sat	8:30	7.4	8.8	9.2	9.1	9.8	8.6	8.1				8.7
Horace Heidt Youth Oppty Program	C	Sun	8:30	6.4	9.1	10.1	9.6							8.8
Homecraft's How to Play the Piano	A	Var	Var			1.8	1.7	1.8						1.8
It Pays to Be Ignorant	C	Wed	9:00	5.3										5.3
Jack Benny Program	C	Sun	7:00	9.8	14.6	16.5	15.4	15.7	14.5	14.9	8.9	10.1	8.8	12.9
Jack Pearl Show	N	Tue	9:30	5.0										5.0
Jack Smith Show	C	M-F	7:15	4.5	6.9	7.6	6.5	6.9	6.2	6.0	3.8	3.7	3.1	5.5
Law & You	A	Sun	9:30	1.3										1.3
A Life in Your Hands	A	Fri	9:00	4.9	5.5	5.5								5.2
Life with Luigi	A	Tue	9:00	7.7	10.3	10.6	10.1	10.4	9.0	8.5	7.6	7.3	6.2	9.1
The Lineup	C	Tue	9:00											6.2
The Lone Ranger	A	MWF	7:30	5.3	6.6	6.3	6.8	7.3	6.6	6.5	4.6	4.3	3.3	5.8
Longine Choraliers	C	Sun	10:30	4.1	4.6	5.5	6.1	5.0	4.4	4.3	3.9	3.1	3.3	4.4
Louella Parsons Hollywood News	A	Sun	9:15	4.0	4.5	5.0	5.4							4.7
Louella Parsons Hollywood News	A	Tue	9:30							3.8	3.8	3.5	3.7	3.7
Lowell Thomas News	C	M-F	6:45	4.0	6.3	7.0	6.8	6.8	6.2	5.9	3.8	3.5	3.1	5.3
Lux Radio Theater	C	Mon	9:00	11.5	15.3	16.3	15.7	14.6	15.4	14.2	11.4	10.5		13.9
Magnificent Montague	N	Sat	8:30	3.6										3.6

1951-52 Nielsen Ratings 6-11 P.M.		Day	Time	Sept. 51	Oct. 51	Nov. 51	Dec. 51	Jan. 52	Feb. 52	March 52	April 52	May 52	June 52	1951-52 Avg
Mario Lanza Show	N	Fri	9:00	6.0	6.2	4.8	6.1	5.7	5.2	4.1	3.3	3.0	2.9	4.7
Martin & Lewis Show	N	Fri	8:30		6.1	5.5	5.6	6.0	5.2	4.7				5.5
Meet Corliss Archer	C	Sun	9:00	6.0	7.4	7.9	8.0	7.7	8.7	6.5	4.2	4.1	2.7	6.3
Meredith Willson's Music Room	N	Wed	10:30	3.8	5.8	4.5	5.8						2.1	4.4
MGM Musical Comedy Theater	M	Wed	8:00									2.3	2.4	2.4
Mr & Mrs North	C	Tue	8:30	8.8	10.5	10.8	10.2	10.7	8.6	9.0	6.2	6.1	4.8	8.6
Mr Chameleon	C	Thu	9:00					7.2	6.8	5.4	5.6	5.4	5.2	5.9
Mr District Attorney	A	Fri	9:30	6.5	7.3	7.5	7.9	8.4	7.7	7.0	5.3	5.2	5.4	6.8
Mr Keen	N	Thu	8:30	7.6	9.6	7.8	8.6	9.2	9.5	9.6		5.0	3.7	7.8
Mr Mercury	A	Tue	7:30	3.6	4.3	4.3	5.0							4.3
Modern Adventures of Casanova	N	Thu	8:00							2.5	1.5	2.0	2.1	2.0
Musical Merry Go Round	N	Sat	9:00	3.8										3.8
My Friend Irma	C	Sun	6:00		6.5	7.5	6.2	7.9	5.8	5.7	4.3	4.0	4.4	5.8
Mystery Theater	A	Wed	8:00		6.5	5.2	6.8	6.8	5.5	5.6	4.5	4.1	3.4	5.4
NBC Symphony	N	Sun	8:30	4.5										4.5
News of the World/Morgan Beatty	N	M-F	7:30	4.7	6.1	6.5	7.0	6.7	7.0	5.8	4.2	4.4	4.3	5.7
News of Tomorrow	A	M-Th	10:30	1.1										1.1
Nick Carter Master Detective	M	Sun	6:30				6.4							6.4
One Man's Family	N	M-F	7:45	4.8	6.2	6.5	7.3	7.3	6.6	6.4	4.8	5.0	4.3	5.9
Original Amateur Hour	C	Thu	9:00	4.8	5.8	5.2	5.8	5.8	5.6	5.8	4.4	3.7	4.7	5.2
Our Miss Brooks	C	Sun	6:30		8.7	10.6	10.5	11.2	8.4	8.4	7.5	7.1	5.2	8.6
Paul Harvey News/Comment	A	Sun	10:00	1.4	1.9	2.6	2.6	2.7	2.5	2.5	2.2	2.5	1.8	2.3
People Are Funny	C	Tue	8:00		9.7	11.7	11.6	12.1	11.1	12.7	7.9	5.4	4.5	9.6
Phil Harris & Alice Faye Show	N	Sun	8:00		7.2	6.8	7.2	7.3	6.7	7.4	4.7	3.8		6.4
Philip Morris Playhouse on Bdwy	C	Sun	8:30	6.0	7.3	7.8	8.4	8.6	9.3	8.1	5.6	6.2	5.8	7.3
Pursuit	C	Tue	9:30	6.3	6.3	6.9	6.2	7.2	7.3	6.4				6.7
Railroad Hour	N	Mon	8:00	6.2	8.7	8.8	8.4	8.1	7.5	7.9	6.1	6.3	4.4	7.2
Red Skelton Show	C	Wed	9:00							8.7	2.5	2.4	2.0	3.9
Rex Allen Show	C	Fri	8:30	2.5	3.0	2.8	3.2	2.7	2.6	3.2	2.3	1.6	1.4	2.5
Roy Rogers Show	N	Fri	8:00		6.7	6.8	7.1	7.9	7.8	6.2	5.8	4.5	4.9	6.4
Sanka News Roundup	A	Fri	9:55		6.0	6.7	6.3	6.8	5.3	6.5	4.0	3.8	3.3	5.4
Sanka Salutes/Win Elliot	A	Sat	10:00					5.0	4.6	4.4	3.4	3.4	3.1	4.0
Screen Directors' Playhouse	N	Fri	8:30	5.1					6.4	6.9	5.1	4.5	3.7	5.3
The Shadow	M	Sun	5:00		6.5	6.9	7.6	7.1	6.7	6.8	3.4	3.7	3.1	5.1
The Sheriff	A	Fri	9:30	2.2				1.7						5.8
Sidney Walton News/Comment	A	M,T	8:00				2.4							2.2
Sidney Walton News/Comment	A	Thu	9:45				2.6							2.1
Silver Eagle	A	T,T	7:30	3.5	4.2	3.8	4.7	5.3	5.3	5.1	3.7	3.5	2.8	2.6
Songs for Sale	C	Sun	10:00	4.9										4.2
Stop the Music	A	Sat	10:00	4.0										4.9
Stop the Music	A	Sun	8:00	3.2	4.6	5.8	5.3	6.3	6.5	5.6	3.4	3.6	3.3	4.0
Suspense	C	Mon	8:00	6.5	9.2	10.7	10.9	11.3	10.5	9.6	6.9	7.3	7.2	4.8
Tarzan	C	Sat	8:30								3.9	3.9	3.0	9.0
Telephone Hour	N	Mon	9:00	5.2	6.5	6.4	6.3	6.5	6.2	6.0	5.2	5.5	4.2	3.6
Theater Guild on the Air	N	Sun	8:30	7.4	8.3	8.6	8.9	8.6	8.5	9.5	5.5	6.5	5.8	5.8
This Is Your FBI	A	Fri	8:30	6.4	7.9	8.2	8.2	9.3	8.1	7.0	5.8	5.0	6.0	7.8
Three Star Extra News	N	M-F	6:45	1.8	2.2	2.3	2.3	2.5	2.2	2.1	1.6	1.9	1.5	7.2

1951-52 Nielsen Ratings 6-11 P.M.

Program	Net	Day	Time	Sept. 51	Oct. 51	Nov. 51	Dec. 51	Jan. 52	Feb. 52	March 52	April 52	May 52	June 52	1951-52 Avg
Top Guy	A	Wed	8:30		4.6	5.2	5.5	6.3	5.8	4.9	3.9	3.7	3.6	4.8
Truth or Consequences	C	Tue	9:30										4.0	4.0
Tums Hollywood Theater	N	Tue	8:30	5.7	6.9	6.5	7.1	7.5	6.2	7.2	3.7	2.4	3.6	6.7
Vaughn Monroe Show	N	Sat	10:00		7.7	8.1	7.3	5.5	5.7	5.4				5.5
Voice of Firestone	N	Mon	8:30	5.2	7.2	7.2	8.0	6.9	7.4	7.5	4.6	5.6	4.4	6.4
Walk a Mile	C	Mon	10:00										5.0	5.0
Walter Winchell	A	Sun	9:00	7.0	9.6	9.9	11.0	11.2	9.1	6.5				9.2
What's My Line?	N	Tue	10:00									5.8	4.5	5.2
Wild Bill Hickock	M	Sun	7:00	3.9	3.2	3.9								3.7
Woman of the Year	M	Mon	8:00				3.8					2.2		2.2
You Bet Your Life/Groucho Marx	N	Wed	9:00		9.4	10.3	10.9	11.1	10.6	9.4	9.5	8.2	7.1	9.6
Your Hit Parade	N	Thu	10:00	6.0	7.1	6.2	7.5	7.4	7.6	7.0	5.6	4.6	4.5	6.4

Special Broadcasts

Program	Net	Date	Time	Sept. 51	Oct. 51	Nov. 51	Dec. 51	Jan. 52	Feb. 52	March 52	April 52	May 52	June 52	1951-52 Avg
World Series: NYYankees/NYGiants	M	10/8,9,10			17.4									17.4
Boxing: Joe Louis/Rocky Marciano	A	10/26			10.6									
Belmont Stakes	N	6/7											1.1	
Gnl Eisenhower Political Speech	C	6/21											3.1	
Boxing: Joe Walcott/Ezzard Charles	A	6/5											14.1	

1952-53 Nielsen Ratings 6-11 P.M.

Program	Net	Day	Time	Sept. 52	Oct. 52	Nov. 52	Dec. 52	Jan. 53	Feb. 53	March 53	April 53	May 53	June 53	1952-53 Avg
Adventures of Maisie	M	Fri	8:00		2.3	2.4	2.4							2.4
Adventures of Ozzie & Harriet	A	Fri	9:00		5.4	5.5	5.1	5.7	6.7	6.9	4.2	4.5	3.4	5.3
Aldrich Family	N	Sun	7:30			1.9								1.9
Allen Jackson News	C	M-F	6:00	1.0	1.1	1.3	1.2	1.2	1.3	1.3	0.9	0.9	0.9	1.1
The American Way/Horace Heidt	C	Thu	10:00					5.3	4.2	3.9	3.6	4.7	3.2	4.2
Amos & Andy	C	Sun	7:30	6.4	10.8	12.5	12.2	13.9	12.8	10.5	6.5	7.1		10.8
Arthur Godfrey's Talent Scouts	C	Mon	8:30		8.0	6.5	7.5	8.5	9.0	9.4	6.5	6.7	4.2	7.3
Bakers' Theater of Stars	C	Sun	6:00								2.3	2.3		2.3
Barrie Craig Private Investigator	N	Sun	10:00		5.3	5.2	5.8	6.1	6.4	6.9	5.5	4.9		5.8
Best of Groucho (Repeat Bdcsts)	N	Wed	9:00										5.1	5.1
Beulah	C	M-F	7:00	3.4	5.0	5.4	5.0							4.7
The Big Story	N	Wed	9:30		7.0	7.0	7.2	8.0	8.1	8.1	7.2	6.6	5.4	7.2
Bill Henry Johns Manville News	M	M-F	9:00	2.5	2.5	2.5	2.4	2.7	3.2	2.9	1.9	2.1	2.0	2.5
Bing Crosby Show	C	Thu	9:30		6.5	5.9	5.1	7.9	6.8	6.7	4.3	5.3	4.1	5.8
Blue Ribbon Bouts	C	Wed	10:00		3.8	3.4	3.3							3.5
Bob Hawk Show	C	Mon	10:00	6.1	7.0	6.8	6.7	7.7	7.0	8.5	5.6	5.7	4.6	6.6
Bob Hope Show	N	Wed	10:00					5.2	6.3	5.8	4.9	4.2		5.0
Bob Trout News	C	Sun	10:00		2.8	3.3								3.1
Bob Trout News	C	Thu	10:00				3.1							3.1
Cafe Istanbul	A	Sun	8:30				3.1	3.4						3.4
Cavalcade of America	N	Tue	8:00	5.3	4.7	5.0	4.2	4.9	4.6	4.8				4.8
Cecil Brown News/Comment	M	Sat	7:55	2.4	2.0	2.2	2.2	2.7	2.3	2.4	1.8	1.7	1.6	2.1
Cecil Brown News/Comment	M	Sun	6:25	2.9	2.6	3.2	3.5	4.0	4.5	3.8	2.4	2.7	2.4	3.2
Champion Roll Call	A	Fri	9:55											
Cedric Adams Commentary	C	Mon	10:35				2.5	3.1	2.7	3.4	2.8	2.9	2.2	2.8
Cities Service Band of America	N	Mon	9:30	3.3	4.1	3.3	4.1	3.4	3.8	3.4	2.6	2.1	2.1	3.2

1952-53 Nielsen Ratings 6-11 P.M.

Program	Net	Day	Time	Sept. 52	Oct. 52	Nov. 52	Dec. 52	Jan. 53	Feb. 53	March 53	April 53	May 53	June 53	1952-53 Avg
Club 15	C	MWF	7:30	3.5	5.2	4.7	5.0	5.6						4.8
Coca-Cola Show	N	Fri	9:00	3.4										3.4
Coke Time	N	Tu,F	8:00									2.9	2.8	2.9
Counterspy	N	Thu	9:30	4.6										4.6
Crime Files of Flamond	M	Wed	8:00					2.9	2.7	3.0				2.5
Crime Letter from Dan Dodge	A	Fri	8:00	3.5		4.5	4.1	5.0	4.9	4.9				4.5
Defense Attorney	A	Thu	8:30	3.4										3.4
Dinah Shore Show	N	M,F	10:00								1.6	2.0	1.3	1.6
Dr Christian	C	Wed	8:30	7.3	6.7	6.8	6.5	7.5	7.4	7.3	5.5	5.0	3.9	6.4
Don Gardiner Mon Morn Headlines	A	Sun	6:15			3.3	3.1	3.4	4.8	4.2	2.7	2.6	2.3	3.3
Doris Day Show	C	Tue	10:05			2.2	2.9	3.1	3.5					2.9
Dragnet	N	Sun	9:30	6.4	6.9	5.9	6.5	8.3	7.8	8.5	6.2	6.3	4.2	6.7
Drew Pearson News/Comment	A	Sun	6:00	4.2	3.7	3.9	4.2	4.4	5.4	4.6				4.3
Edgar Bergen & Charlie McCarthy	C	Sun	8:00		10.1	11.0	12.0	13.0	12.9	11.0	6.7	7.7		10.6
Edward R Murrow News/Comment	C	M-F	7:45	1.7	3.2	5.6	2.5	5.7	2.7	2.7	2.1	1.8	1.3	2.9
Edwin C Hill News/Comment	A	M-F	10:30	0.8	0.5	0.7	1.0	0.8	0.6	0.9	1.0	0.8	0.8	0.8
The Falcon	M	Mon	8:00				2.7							2.9
Family Skeleton	C	M-F	7:15			1.9								2.0
Father Knows Best	N	Thu	8:30	5.5	6.3	6.3	5.4	7.2	8.0	6.0	6.7	4.8	4.2	6.0
FBI in Peace & War	C	Wed	8:00	5.0	6.3	6.7	6.1	8.0	7.1	7.2	4.5	4.5	4.2	6.0
Fibber McGee & Molly	N	Tue	9:30		7.8	6.9	6.6	6.8	6.5	6.5	5.4	5.4	4.5	6.3
First Nighter	N	Tue	10:35		1.7	1.9	2.7	3.2	2.7	2.0				2.4
Frank Edwards News/Comment	M	M-F	10:00	1.3	1.0	1.2	1.2	1.0	1.4	1.2	1.3	1.3	1.4	1.2
Friday Night Boxing	A	Fri	10:00	2.1	4.6	7.7	3.3	4.9	4.5	4.7	3.5	3.5	3.1	4.2
Fulton Lewis Jr News/Comment	M	M-F	7:00	2.9	3.4	3.8	3.4	3.0	3.0	3.1	1.5	1.4	1.2	2.7
Gabriel Heatter News/Comment	M	M-F	7:30	3.9	4.0	4.1	3.8	4.9	4.9	5.1	3.2	2.8	3.2	4.0
Gangbusters	C	Sat	9:00	5.9	5.7	7.2	7.9	8.4	7.9	8.7				7.4
Gene Autry's Melody Ranch	C	Sat	8:00	5.2	5.9	7.1	7.7	8.6	9.2	8.7	4.4	5.2	3.8	6.6
Goodwill Hour/John J Anthony	M	Sun	9:30		1.9	2.4	2.7							2.3
Grand Ole Opry	N	Sat	9:30	3.8	4.5	5.3	4.5	4.6	4.9	4.7	3.7	2.6	2.4	4.1
Great Gildersleeve	N	Wed	8:30	6.7	8.0	7.7	6.8	7.6	7.7	7.8	6.7	6.5	4.7	7.0
Gunsmoke	C	Fri	8:30			5.0								5.0
Guy Lombardo Orch	C	Sun	7:00										3.6	3.6
Hallmark Playhouse/Hall of Fame	C	Sun	9:00	5.4	5.3	4.9	6.2	5.8	6.6	4.4	3.6	4.3		5.2
Henry J Taylor News/Comment	A	Mon	8:00	2.3	1.9	2.5	2.5	3.0	2.9	2.5	2.4	2.8	2.2	2.5
It Happens Every Day	A	T,T	10:35	0.8										0.8
Jack Benny Program	C	Sun	7:00	8.8	11.6	12.9	13.0	13.9	13.9	12.8	7.4	8.2	7.0	11.0
Jack Smith Show	C	M-F	7:15	3.0	4.5	4.8	4.7							4.3
Jason & The Golden Fleece	N	Wed	10:00			5.7								5.7
John Cameron Swayze News	N	M-F	10:30			2.4	2.3	3.1	2.7	2.7				2.6
John Daly News	A	M-F	10:00	1.1	0.8	1.4	1.3							1.2
Bill Henry Johns Manville News	M	M-F	9:00	2.5	2.5	2.5	2.4	2.7	3.2	2.9	1.9	2.1	2.0	2.5
Judy Canova Show	N	Thu	10:00				4.8							4.8
Junior Miss	C	Thu	8:30											4.7
Les Griffith News	A	M-F	7:55						3.8	4.0	2.8	3.0	1.8	3.1
Life Begins at 80	A	Wed	8:30						1.4	1.7	2.1			1.7
Life Is Worth Living	M	Thu	9:05									2.4		2.4
Life with Luigi	C	Tue	9:00	6.6	6.8	7.2	6.8	9.1	9.0	8.2	7.4	8.2	7.0	7.7

1952-53 Nielsen Ratings 6-11 P.M.

Program	Net	Day	Time	Sept. 52	Oct. 52	Nov. 52	Dec. 52	Jan. 53	Feb. 53	March 53	April 53	May 53	June 53	1952-53 Avg
The Lineup	C	Wed	9:00			5.1								5.1
Log Cabin News	N	Thu	8:25	4.2	4.6	4.8	4.4	4.7	5.0	3.7	4.0	3.9	3.4	4.3
The Lone Ranger	A	MWF	7:30	4.0	4.9	5.2	5.0	5.8	5.4	5.3	3.6	3.9	2.4	4.6
Longine Choraliers	C	Sun	10:05	2.6	3.4	2.4	3.6							3.0
Louella Parsons Hollywood News	C	Tue	10:00	3.3	3.5	4.0	3.9	4.9	4.9	5.0	2.2	3.2	2.2	3.7
Lowell Thomas News	C	M-F	6:45	3.6	4.9	4.8	4.5	5.7	5.2	4.8	3.2	2.9	2.8	4.2
Lux Radio Theater	C	Mon	9:00	8.8	10.6	10.3	10.1	11.7	11.2	12.4	8.4	9.8		10.4
Lux Summer Theater	C	Mon	9:00										7.1	7.1
Martin & Lewis Show	N	Tue	9:00	6.7	6.7	5.8	5.8	6.5	5.4	7.4	5.4	5.4	4.0	5.9
Meet Corliss Archer	A	Fri	9:30		4.1	4.3	4.3	4.1	5.1	5.0	3.8	3.8	2.7	4.1
Meet Millie	C	Thu	8:00		5.1	5.0	4.5	6.0	6.8	6.2	4.8	4.7	2.5	5.1
Meredith Willson's Music Room	N	Mon	10:00	3.1		3.0								3.0
MGM Musical Comedy Theater	M	Wed	8:00		2.7	3.1	3.2							3.0
Mr & Mrs North	C	Tue	8:30	5.6	6.7	7.6	6.7	7.4	8.4	7.8	5.3	6.5	4.1	6.6
Mr Chameleon	C	Fri	9:00			5.0	5.2							5.0
Mr Keen	C	Thu	8:00	4.4	4.5	5.8	2.4	6.5	6.3	5.9	4.6	4.5	3.7	5.1
Modern Adventures of Casanova	M	Fri	8:00		2.7	2.0								2.4
Movie Quiz	M	Tue	8:00					1.9	2.2	2.4				2.2
My Friend Irma	C	Sun	9:30		6.7	6.5	5.9	8.4	7.5	7.6	4.8	5.9	4.9	6.5
My Little Margie	C	Sun	8:30					9.3	10.0	7.7	5.4	5.7	4.2	7.4
Mystery Theater	A	Wed	8:00		4.0	4.6	4.3	4.6	4.1	4.0	4.0	3.1	2.3	3.9
News of the World/Morgan Beatty	N	M-F	7:30	5.0	5.8	5.9	4.8	4.9	5.0	5.5	4.6	4.6	3.6	5.0
News of Tomorrow	A	M-Th	10:00									1.3		1.3
Norman Brokenshire Show	A	Sun	6:15									0.2		0.2
Official Detective	M	Thu	8:00	5.3	5.6	5.6	5.3	3.3	4.3	3.5	3.2	2.5	2.2	3.2
One Man's Family	N	M-F	7:45					5.5	5.6	5.9	5.2	4.8	3.9	5.3
Original Amateur Hour	A	Thu	9:00	3.3										3.3
Our Miss Brooks	C	Sun	6:30		8.5	10.4	9.8	10.4	11.4	10.3	4.8	5.7	4.3	8.4
Paul Harvey News/Comment	A	Sun	10:00	1.8	1.8	1.6								1.7
People Are Funny	C	Tue	8:00	7.0	8.0	9.1	8.7	10.8	10.9	10.5	7.8	7.9	6.0	8.7
Phil Harris & Alice Faye Show	N	Sun	8:00		5.7	5.4	5.9	6.0	6.3	6.4	3.9	4.3	3.2	5.2
Philip Morris Playhouse on Bdwy	C	Wed	9:00	6.5	7.5	8.1	5.6	7.6	7.2	6.5	4.4	5.3	3.8	6.3
Railroad Hour	N	Mon	8:00	5.8	7.4	5.3	6.7	7.0	4.7	7.5	5.0	4.5	3.2	5.7
Red Skelton Show	N	Tue	8:30		5.4	5.8	4.8	5.5	5.1	4.9	4.3	4.4		5.0
Richard Diamond Pvt Detective	N	Sun	7:30										4.1	4.1
Robert Q's Waxworks	C	Sun	10:00										0.6	0.6
Roy Rogers Show	N	Thu	8:00	4.7	6.3	6.0	5.3	5.2	6.1	4.9	4.6	4.2	3.5	5.1
Sanka Salutes/Win Elliot	C	Sat	9:25	4.6	4.4	5.4	6.5	6.9	6.1	7.5	3.6	3.3	2.5	5.1
The Shadow	M	Sun	5:00	4.4	3.4	3.8	4.5	4.8	5.9	5.3	3.3	3.1	2.5	4.1
Silver Eagle	A	T,T	7:30	3.5	4.4	4.5	4.1	4.7	4.5	4.7	2.5	2.8		4.0
Suspense	C	Mon	8:00	6.9	8.3	7.3	8.1	9.4	9.1	8.7	6.1	5.7	4.6	7.4
Take a Number	M	Fri	8:30								1.5	2.3	1.3	1.7
Tarzan	C	Sat	8:30	3.3	5.9	7.1	7.0	6.5	6.9	6.8	3.4	3.4	3.0	5.3
Taylor Grant News/Comment	A	Sun	9:15			3.8	3.5	3.7	3.4	4.0	3.2	3.2	3.2	3.5
Telegram for You	A	Sun	8:55								1.4	1.7	2.1	1.7
Telephone Hour	N	Mon	9:00	4.9	5.8	4.6	5.8	5.3	4.1	5.8	4.3	4.2	3.3	4.8
That Hammer Guy/Mickey Spillane	M	Tue	8:00					3.3	4.2	3.8	2.9	3.5	2.6	3.4
Theater Guild on the Air	N	Sun	8:30	6.1	7.1	6.4	7.0	8.1	7.6	7.6	5.0	6.0	3.5	6.4

1952-53 Nielsen Ratings 6-11 P.M.

Program	Net	Day	Time	Sept. 52	Oct. 52	Nov. 52	Dec. 52	Jan. 53	Feb. 53	March 53	April 53	May 53	June 53	1952-53 Avg
This Is Your FBI	A	Fri	8:30	5.3	5.1	5.2	4.7							5.1
Three Star Extra News	N	M-F	6:45	1.6	1.9	1.7	1.6	1.7	1.6	1.8	1.5	1.3	1.1	1.6
Titus Moody	M	Tu,Th	7:55		2.5	2.8	2.0	2.4	2.5	2.2	2.1	2.5	1.4	2.3
Top Guy	A	Fri	8:00	4.6										4.6
Truth or Consequences	N	Thu	9:00	5.3	6.7	6.7	5.0	7.1	6.8	5.7	6.1	4.4	3.9	5.8
Twenty Questions	M	Sat	8:00		4.2	3.5	4.5	4.3	3.3	4.2	2.7	2.8	2.4	3.5
Two for the Money	N	Tue	10:00		5.3	5.2	5.1	5.8	4.9	5.4	5.6	4.7	4.1	5.1
Vaughn Monroe Show	C	Sat	7:30	4.7	5.3	6.0	6.4	6.9	7.4	7.1	3.1	3.4	3.6	5.4
Voice of Firestone	N	Mon	8:30	4.6	5.6	5.0	5.6	5.3	4.6	5.8	4.3	4.2	3.5	4.9
Walk a Mile	N	Wed	8:00		6.3	5.6	5.1	5.8	5.8	6.5	5.4	4.7	3.4	5.4
Walter Winchell	A	Sun	9:00		6.1	6.5	5.3	6.3	5.8	5.4	3.4	4.3	4.1	5.2
What's My Line?	C	Wed	9:30	4.4	5.3	5.3	5.1	6.2	6.7	6.1	4.2	4.3	3.6	5.1
Woman of the Year	M	Mon	8:00		2.5	3.2	2.0							2.6
You Bet Your Life/Groucho Marx	N	Wed	9:00	7.1	8.8	8.7	6.9	8.8	9.0	9.1	8.4	7.0	4.8	7.9
Your Hit Parade	N	Fri	8:00	4.9	5.1	5.1	4.5	4.4						4.8
Yours Truly Johnny Dollar	C	Tue	9:00								5.9	7.3	5.8	6.3

Special Broadcasts

Program	Net	Date	Sept. 52	Oct. 52	Nov. 52	Dec. 52	Jan. 53	May 53	June 53
Nixon Checkers Political Speech	All	9/23	16.8						
World Series: NY Yankees-Brooklyn	M	10/5-7		18.1					
Eisenhower Nixon Speech	All	11/3			13.3				
Speeches for Stevenson	All	11/3			14.3				
Election Returns	A	11/4			12.9				
Election Returns	C	11/4			16.7				
Election Returns	M	11/4			14.9				
Election Returns	N	11/4			18.4				
Football: Blue-Gray All Star Game	M	12/27				5.0			
Football: East-West Shrine Game	M	12/27				6.4			
Inaguration Day Ceremonies	A	1/20					10.4		
Inaguration Day Ceremonies	C	1/20					9.5		
Inaguration Day Ceremonies	N	1/20					10.4		
Racing: Preakness Stakes	C	5/23						1.8	
Racing: Belmont Stakes	C	6/13							2.0

B: Rated (13+ Weeks per Season) Prime-Time Programs, 1932–1953

= Sunday afternoon programs not ranked
(Program stars or hosts in parenthesis)

6–11 P.M., Sept through June Programs Rated 13 Weeks or More

	Season	Rank	Rtg	Net	Day	Time
A&P Gypsies (Harry Horlick Orch)	32–33	41t	11.7	N	Mon	9:00
A&P Gypsies (Harry Horlick Orch)	33–34	41t	13.0	N	Mon	9:00
A&P Gypsies (Harry Horlick Orch)	34–35	62t	11.7	N	Mon	9:00
A&P Gypsies (Harry Horlick Orch)	35–36	56t	7.2	N	Mon	9:00
Abbott & Costello Show (Bud Abbott & Lou Costello)	42–43	11t	20.5	N	Thu	10:00
Abbott & Costello Show (Bud Abbott & Lou Costello)	43–44	10t	21.3	N	Thu	10:00
Abbott & Costello Show (Bud Abbott & Lou Costello)	44–45	11	19.1	N	Thu	10:00
Abbott & Costello Show (Bud Abbott & Lou Costello)	45–46	17	16.4	N	Thu	10:00
Abbott & Costello Show (Bud Abbott & Lou Costello)	46–47	24t	13.3	N	Thu	10:00
Abbott & Costello Show (Bud Abbott & Lou Costello)	47–48	105t	10.4	A	Wed	9:00
Abe Burrows Show	47–48	127t	8.0	C	Sat	7:30
Abe Lyman Orch	32–33	89	4.1	C	Tu,Th	8:45
Abie's Irish Rose (Sidney Smith & Betty Winkler)	41–42	34	13.0	N	Sat	8:00
Abie's Irish Rose (Sidney Smith & Betty Winkler)	42–43	26	14.9	N	Sat	8:00
Abie's Irish Rose (Sidney Smith & Betty Winkler)	43–44	39	12.3	N	Sat	8:00
Academy Award Theater	45–46	132t	5.4	C	Sat	7:00
Academy Award Theater	46–47	114t	7.0	C	Wed	10:00
Adventures in Good Health (Dr Herman Bundesen)	32–33	101t	2.3	B	Tu,Fr	8:30
Adventures in Good Health (Dr Herman Bundesen)	33–34	115	2.5	B	Tu,Th	8:30
Adventures of Bulldog Drummond (Ned Weaver)	45–46	124t	5.8	M	Mon	8:00
Adventures of Bulldog Drummond (Ned Weaver)	46–47	140	4.6	M	Fri	9:30
Adventures of Charlie Chan (Walter Connolly)	32–33	48	10.3	B	Fri	7:30
Adventures of Charlie Chan (Ed Begley/Santos Ortega)	47–48	114t	9.5	M	Mon	8:30
Adventures of Christopher Wells (Myron McCormick)	47–48	94t	11.3	C	Tue	9:30
Adventures of Ellery Queen (Hugh Marlowe)	41–42	49	10.5	N	Sat	7:30
Adventures of Ellery Queen (Carleton Young)	42–43	40t	12.1	N	Sat	7:30
Adventures of Ellery Queen (Sidney Smith)	43–44	48	11.3	N	Sat	7:30
Adventures of Ellery Queen (Sidney Smith)	44–45	78	9.7	C	Wed	7:30
Adventures of Ellery Queen (Sidney Smith)	45–46	67t	9.6	C	Wed	7:30
Adventures of Ellery Queen (Sidney Smith)	46–47	79t	9.0	C	Wed	7:30
Adventures of Maisie (Ann Sothern)	51–52	102	1.9	M	Fri	8:00
Adventures of Maisie (Ann Sothern)	52–53	92t	2.4	M	Fri	8:00
Adventures of Ozzie & Harriet (Ozzie & Harriet Nelson)	44–45	99t	8.2	C	Sun	6:00
Adventures of Ozzie & Harriet (Ozzie & Harriet Nelson)	45–46	78t	8.7	C	Sun	6:00
Adventures of Ozzie & Harriet (Ozzie & Harriet Nelson)	46–47	59	10.1	C	Sun	6:00
Adventures of Ozzie & Harriet (Ozzie & Harriet Nelson)	47–48	67t	13.4	C	Fri	9:30
Adventures of Ozzie & Harriet (Ozzie & Harriet Nelson)	48–49	66	10.5	N	Sun	6:30
Adventures of Ozzie & Harriet (Ozzie & Harriet Nelson)	49–50	60t	8.9	A	Fri	9:00
Adventures of Ozzie & Harriet (Ozzie & Harriet Nelson)	50–51	45t	8.7	A	Fri	9:00
Adventures of Ozzie & Harriet (Ozzie & Harriet Nelson)	51–52	31t	7.2	A	Fri	9:00
Adventures of Ozzie & Harriet (Ozzie & Harriet Nelson)	52–53	34t	5.3	A	Fri	9:00
Adventures of Sam Spade (Howard Duff)	46–47	62t	9.8	C	Sun	8:00
Adventures of Sam Spade (Howard Duff)	47–48	27	17.8	C	Sun	8:00
Adventures of Sam Spade (Howard Duff)	48–49	40t	12.6	C	Sun	8:00
Adventures of Sam Spade (Howard Duff)	49–50	50t	9.6	N	Sun	8:00
Adventures of Sherlock Holmes (Richard Gordon)	32–33	15	21.0	B	Wed	9:00
Adventures of Sherlock Holmes (Louis Hector)	34–35	81t	8.2	B	Sun	9:45
Adventures of Sherlock Holmes (Basil Rathbone & Nigel Bruce)	39–40	42t	11.4	B	Mon	8:00
Adventures of Sherlock Holmes (Basil Rathbone & Nigel Bruce)	40–41	47t	10.2	B	Sun	8:30
Adventures of Sherlock Holmes (Basil Rathbone & Nigel Bruce)	41–42	27	14.1	N	Sun	10:30
Adventures of Sherlock Holmes (Basil Rathbone & Nigel Bruce)	43–44	82t	8.7	M	Mon	8:30
Adventures of Sherlock Holmes (Basil Rathbone & Nigel Bruce)	44–45	71t	10.0	M	Mon	8:30
Adventures of Sherlock Holmes (Basil Rathbone & Nigel Bruce)	45–46	62t	10.1	M	Mon	8:30
Adventures of Sherlock Holmes (Tom Conway & Nigel Bruce)	46–47	119	6.8	A	Mon	8:30
Adventures of Sherlock Holmes (John Stanley)	47–48	109t	9.9	M	Sun	7:00
Adventures of Sherlock Holmes (John Stanley)	48–49	107t	7.0	M	Mon	8:30
Adventures of Sherlock Holmes (Ben Wright)	49–50	107	4.6	A	Wed	9:00
Adventures of the Falcon (James Meighan)	45–46	120t	6.0	M	Tue	8:30
Adventures of the Falcon (James Meighan)	46–47	86t	8.6	M	Tue	8:30

6–11 P.M., Sept through June Programs
  Rated 13 Weeks or More

	Season	Rank	Rtg	Net	Day	Time
Adventures of the Falcon (Les Tremayne)	49–50	85t	7.2	M	Sun	7:00
Adventures of the Falcon (Les Damon)	52–53	82t	2.9	M	Mon	8:00
Adventures of the Thin Man (Les Damon & Claudia Morgan)	41–42	52	10.1	N	Wed	8:00
Adventures of the Thin Man (Les Damon & Claudia Morgan)	42–43	24t	15.1	C	Fri	8:00
Adventures of the Thin Man (Les Tremayne & Claudia Morgan)	43–44	25	15.0	C	Sun	10:30
Adventures of the Thin Man (David Gothard & Claudia Morgan)	44–45	41t	12.4	C	Fri	8:30
Adventures of the Thin Man (Les Tremayne & Claudia Morgan)	45–46	78t	8.7	C	Sun	7:00
Adventures of the Thin Man (Les Damon & Claudia Morgan)	46–47	47	11.1	C	Fri	8:30
Adventures of the Thin Man (Les Damon & Claudia Morgan)	47–48	57	14.1	C	Fri	8:30
Adventures of the Thin Man (Les Tremayne & Claudia Morgan)	48–49	109t	6.9	M	Thu	10:00
Affairs of Ann Scotland (Arlene Francis)	46–47	137	5.0	A	Wed	9:00
Al Jolson Show	32–33	8	27.8	N	Fri	10:00
Al Jolson Shell Chateau	34–35	11	25.2	N	Sat	9:30
Al Jolson Shell Chateau	35–36	9	16.7	N	Sat	9:30
Al Jolson Show	36–37	10	15.4	C	Tue	8:30
Al Jolson Show	37–38	10	18.1	C	Tue	8:30
Al Jolson Show	38–39	6t	17.3	C	Tue	8:30
Al Jolson Show	42–43	46t	11.1	C	Tue	8:30
Al Jolson Kraft Music Hall	47–48	20t	18.9	N	Thu	9:00
Al Jolson Kraft Music Hall	48–49	38t	12.8	N	Thu	9:00
Al Pearce Gang	35–36	91t	5.2	B	Fri	9:00
Al Pearce Gang	36–37	31	9.5	C	Tue	9:00
Al Pearce Gang	37–38	15	14.8	C	Tue	9:00
Al Pearce Gang	38–39	23	13.3	N	Mon	8:00
Al Pearce Gang	39–40	24t	13.4	C	Fri	7:30
Al Pearce Gang	40–41	34	12.2	C	Fri	7:30
Al Pearce Gang	41–42	29	13.6	N	Thu	7:30
Al Pearce Gang	44–45	102	7.8	C	Sat	10:15
Alan Young Show	44–45	149t	4.5	B	Tue	8:30
Alan Young Show	45–46	142t	4.9	A	Fri	9:00
Alan Young Show	46–47	81t	8.9	N	Fri	8:30
Alan Young Show	48–49	75t	9.6	N	Tue	8:30
Albert Spalding Violin Recitals	33–34	45	11.3	C	Wed	8:30
Aldrich Family (Ezra Stone)	39–40	33t	12.2	B	Tue	8:00
Aldrich Family (Ezra Stone)	40–41	7	22.1	N	Thu	8:30
Aldrich Family (Ezra Stone)	41–42	6	26.6	N	Thu	8:30
Aldrich Family (Norman Tokar)	42–43	6	25.7	N	Thu	8:30
Aldrich Family (Dickie Jones)	43–44	7	23.2	N	Thu	8:30
Aldrich Family (Dickie Jones)	44–45	18t	15.1	C	Fri	8:00
Aldrich Family (Raymond Ives, Ezra Stone)	45–46	22	14.2	C	Fri	8:00
Aldrich Family (Ezra Stone)	46–47	26t	13.2	N	Thu	8:00
Aldrich Family (Ezra Stone)	47–48	23	18.5	N	Thu	8:00
Aldrich Family (Ezra Stone)	48–49	49t	11.9	N	Thu	8:00
Aldrich Family (Ezra Stone)	49–50	52	9.5	N	Thu	8:00
Aldrich Family (Ezra Stone)	50–51	40	9.1	N	Thu	8:00
Alec Templeton Show	39–40	70	9.4	N	Mon	9:30
Alec Templeton Show	40–41	92t	7.4	N	Fri	7:30
Alemite Half Hour	34–35	116t	4.0	C	Thu	10:30
Alexander Woolcott	34–35	85	7.8	C	Sun	7:00
Alexander Woolcott	35–36	93	5.1	C	Sun	7:00
Alexander Woolcott	36–37	91t	4.1	C	Tu,Th	7:30
Alexander Woolcott	37–38	83t	7.8	C	Sun	7:00
Alexander's Mediation Board (A L Alexander)	43–44	145	4.1	M	Sun	8:00
Alexander's Mediation Board (A L Alexander)	44–45	124t	6.1	M	Sun	8:00
Alexander's Mediation Board (A L Alexander)	45–46	120t	6.0	M	Sun	8:15
Alexander's Mediation Board (A L Alexander)	49–50	132t	1.4	M	Sun	8:00
Alias Jimmy Valentine (Bert Lytell)	37–38	85	4.4	B	Tue	9:30
Alias Jimmy Valentine (Bert Lytell)	38–39	93t	3.7	B	Mon	7:00
All American Football Show	32–33	66t	7.1	C	Fri	9:00
All American Football Show	33–34	70	7.7	C	Fri	9:30
All Star Cycle	36–37	118	0.7	B	Thu	7:15
Allan Jones & Frankie Carle	43–44	113	5.6	C	Wed	8:00
Allen Jackson News	49–50	134	1.3	C	M-F	6:00
Allen Jackson News	50–51	122	1.6	C	M-F	6:00
Allen Jackson News	51–52	104	1.4	C	M-F	6:00
Allen Jackson News	52–53	107	1.1	C	M-F	6:00
Amazing Mr Smith (Keenan Wynn)	40–41	131	3.1	M	Mon	8:00
Amazing Mrs Danbury (Agnes Moorhead)	45–46	142t	4.9	C	Sun	8:00
America in the Air	43–44	127t	4.9	C	Sun	6:30

**6–11 P.M., Sept through June Programs
Rated 13 Weeks or More**

	Season	Rank	Rtg	Net	Day	Time
America in the Air	44–45	132t	5.4	C	Sat	7:30
American Album of Familiar Music (Frank Munn & Gus Haenschen Orch)	32–33	49	10.0	N	Sun	9:30
American Album of Familiar Music (Frank Munn & Gus Haenschen Orch)	33–34	34	14.8	N	Sun	9:30
American Album of Familiar Music (Frank Munn & Gus Haenschen Orch)	34–35	44	13.8	N	Sun	9:30
American Album of Familiar Music (Frank Munn & Gus Haenschen Orch)	35–36	41	8.8	N	Sun	9:30
American Album of Familiar Music (Frank Munn & Gus Haenschen Orch)	36–37	84t	4.4	N	Sun	9:30
American Album of Familiar Music (Frank Munn & Gus Haenschen Orch)	37–38	58	8.1	N	Sun	9:30
American Album of Familiar Music (Frank Munn & Gus Haenschen Orch)	38–39	45t	9.3	N	Sun	9:30
American Album of Familiar Music (Frank Munn & Gus Haenschen Orch)	39–40	51	10.7	N	Sun	9:30
American Album of Familiar Music (Frank Munn & Gus Haenschen Orch)	40–41	50	10.0	N	Sun	9:30
American Album of Familiar Music (Frank Munn & Gus Haenschen Orch)	41–42	53t	10.0	N	Sun	9:30
American Album of Familiar Music (Frank Munn & Gus Haenschen Orch)	42–43	50t	10.5	N	Sun	9:30
American Album of Familiar Music (Frank Munn & Gus Haenschen Orch)	43–44	52t	10.8	N	Sun	9:30
American Album of Familiar Music (Frank Munn & Gus Haenschen Orch)	44–45	43t	12.0	N	Sun	9:30
American Album of Familiar Music (Gus Haenschen Orch & Soloists)	45–46	43t	11.7	N	Sun	9:30
American Album of Familiar Music (Gus Haenschen Orch & Soloists)	46–47	44	11.4	N	Sun	9:30
American Album of Familiar Music (Abe Lyman Orch & Soloists)	47–48	53	14.7	N	Sun	9:30
American Album of Familiar Music (Abe Lyman Orch & Soloists)	48–49	72t	9.8	N	Sun	9:30
American Album of Familiar Music (Abe Lyman Orch & Soloists)	49–50	92	6.6	N	Sun	9:30
American Album of Familiar Music (Abe Lyman Orch & Soloists)	50–51	88	4.9	A	Sun	9:30
American Forum of the Air (Theodore Granik)	48–49	144	2.3	M	Mon	10:00
American Melody Hour (Vivian della Chiesa)	41–42	137	3.1	B	Wed	9:00
American Melody Hour (Vivian della Chiesa)	42–43	79t	9.1	C	Tue	7:30
American Melody Hour (Bob Hannon & Evelyn MacGregor)	43–44	100t	7.3	C	Tue	7:30
American Melody Hour (Bob Hannon & Evelyn MacGregor)	44–45	103t	7.7	C	Tue	7:30
American Melody Hour (Bob Hannon & Evelyn MacGregor)	45–46	96t	8.0	C	Tue	7:30
American Melody Hour (Bob Hannon & Evelyn MacGregor)	46–47	88t	8.5	C	Tue	7:30
American Melody Hour (Bob Hannon & Evelyn MacGregor)	47–48	94t	11.3	C	Wed	8:00
American Musical Revue (Ethel Waters)	33–34	88t	5.2	C	Sun	7:00
American Musical Revue (Frank Munn)	34–35	69t	10.4	N	Sun	9:30
America's Town Meeting of the Air (George V Denny)	44–45	146t	4.6	B	Thu	8:30
America's Town Meeting of the Air (George V Denny)	45–46	127t	5.7	A	Thu	8:30
America's Town Meeting of the Air (George V Denny)	46–47	138t	4.9	A	Thu	8:30
America's Town Meeting of the Air (George V Denny)	48–49	130	4.1	A	Tue	8:30
Amos & Andy (Freeman Gosden & Charles Correll)	32–33	7	28.9	B	M-F	7:00
Amos & Andy (Freeman Gosden & Charles Correll)	33–34	6	29.8	B	M-F	7:00
Amos & Andy (Freeman Gosden & Charles Correll)	34–35	16	22.3	B	M-F	7:00
Amos & Andy (Freeman Gosden & Charles Correll)	35–36	18	13.1	N	M-F	7:00
Amos & Andy (Freeman Gosden & Charles Correll)	36–37	11	15.3	N	M-F	7:00
Amos & Andy (Freeman Gosden & Charles Correll)	37–38	21t	13.3	N	M-F	7:00
Amos & Andy (Freeman Gosden & Charles Correll)	38–39	29	12.1	C	M-F	7:00
Amos & Andy (Freeman Gosden & Charles Correll)	39–40	47t	10.8	C	M-F	7:00
Amos & Andy (Freeman Gosden & Charles Correll)	40–41	41	10.8	C	M-F	7:00
Amos & Andy (Freeman Gosden & Charles Correll)	41–42	61	9.6	C	M-F	7:00
Amos & Andy (Freeman Gosden & Charles Correll)	42–43	70t	9.5	C	M-F	7:00
Amos & Andy (Freeman Gosden & Charles Correll)	43–44	28	14.6	N	Fri	10:00
Amos & Andy (Freeman Gosden & Charles Correll)	44–45	18t	15.1	N	Fri	10:00
Amos & Andy (Freeman Gosden & Charles Correll)	45–46	14	16.8	N	Tue	9:00
Amos & Andy (Freeman Gosden & Charles Correll)	46–47	7	22.1	N	Tue	9:00
Amos & Andy (Freeman Gosden & Charles Correll)	47–48	3	24.1	N	Tue	9:00

6–11 P.M., Sept through June Programs
  Rated 13 Weeks or More

	Season	Rank	Rtg	Net	Day	Time
Amos & Andy (Freeman Gosden & Charles Correll)	48–49	9t	17.1	C	Sun	7:30
Amos & Andy (Freeman Gosden & Charles Correll)	49–50	9	15.7	C	Sun	7:30
Amos & Andy (Freeman Gosden & Charles Correll)	50–51	4	14.0	C	Sun	7:30
Amos & Andy (Freeman Gosden & Charles Correll)	51–52	2	13.4	C	Sun	7:30
Amos & Andy (Freeman Gosden & Charles Correll)	52–53	2	10.8	C	Sun	7:30
An Evening with Sigmund Romberg	45–46	75	9.2	N	Wed	8:30
Andre Kostelanetz Orch	34–35	71	10.3	C	MWSa	9:00
Andre Kostelanetz Orch	35–36	76t	5.7	C	We,Fr	9:00
Andre Kostelanetz Orch	36–37	57t	6.7	C	Wed	9:00
Andre Kostelanetz Orch	37–38	51t	8.4	C	Wed	9:00
Andre Kostelanetz Orch	45–46	124t	5.8	C	Thu	9:00
Andre Kostelanetz Pause That Refreshes	47–48	100	10.8	C	Sun	6:30
Andrews Sisters Show	45–46	129t	5.6	C	Wed	10:30
Angelo Patri's Your Child	32–33	99	2.7	C	Sun	7:45
Angelo Patri's Dreams of Childhood	33–34	97	4.0	C	Sun	10:00
Arch Ward Sports	43–44	183	2.0	M	Fri	10:15
Are You a Missing Heir? aka Court of Missing Heirs (James Waters)	39–40	90t	7.0	C	Tue	8:30
Are You a Missing Heir? aka Court of Missing Heirs (James Waters)	40–41	44t	10.4	C	Tue	8:00
Are You a Missing Heir? aka Court of Missing Heirs (James Waters)	41–42	59t	9.7	C	Tue	8:00
Armco Iron Master Brass Band (Frank Simon)	34–35	129t	2.2	N	Sun	6:30
Armco Iron Master Brass Band (Frank Simon)	35–36	125t	2.0	B	Wed	8:30
Armour Program (Leo Reisman Orch)	32–33	35t	13.0	B	Fri	9:30
Armstrong of the SBI (Charles Flynn)	50–51	82t	5.5	A	Tu,Th	7:30
Arthur Gaeth News & Comment	47–48	153t	2.4	A	Mon	10:00
Arthur Gaeth News & Comment	48–49	146	2.1	A	Mon	10:00
Arthur Gaeth News & Comment	49–50	129	1.7	A	Mon	10:00
Arthur Godfrey	37–38	90	3.4	C	M,Fr	7:15
Arthur Godfrey Digest	49–50	72t	7.8	C	Sat	9:30
Arthur Godfrey's Talent Scouts	47–48	10t	21.9	C	Mon	8:30
Arthur Godfrey's Talent Scouts	48–49	5t	20.1	C	Mon	8:30
Arthur Godfrey's Talent Scouts	49–50	3	18.4	C	Mon	8:30
Arthur Godfrey's Talent Scouts	50–51	5	13.4	C	Mon	8:30
Arthur Godfrey's Talent Scouts	51–52	5	9.7	C	Mon	8:30
Arthur Godfrey's Talent Scouts	52–53	12	7.3	C	Mon	8:30
Arthur Hale Confidentially Yours News	40–41	98t	6.9	M	Tu,Th	7:30
Arthur Hale Confidentially Yours News	41–42	103t	6.4	M	T,T,Sa	7:30
Arthur Hale Confidentially Yours News	42–43	107t	6.2	M	T,T,Sa	7:30
Arthur Hale Confidentially Yours News	43–44	158t	3.2	M	T,T,Sa	7:30
Arthur Hale Confidentially Yours News	44–45	151t	4.3	M	T,T,Sa	10:30
Arthur Hale Confidentially Yours News	45–46	155t	4.1	M	T,T,Sa	7:30
Arthur Hale Confidentially Yours News	46–47	143t	4.2	M	Tu,Th	7:30
Ask It Basket (Jim McWilliams)	38–39	59t	8.1	C	Wed	7:30
Ask It Basket (Jim McWilliams)	39–40	39t	11.7	C	Thu	8:00
Ask It Basket (Ed East)	40–41	83t	8.0	C	Thu	8:00
Atwater Kent Radio Hour	35–36	112t	3.0	C	Thu	8:30
Avalon Showboat (Carleton Brickert & Marlin Hurt)	40–41	44t	10.4	N	Mon	9:30
Avalon Time (Red Skelton & Red Foley)	38–39	71t	7.3	N	Sat	7:00
Avalon Time (Red Skelton/Cliff Arquette)	39–40	57t	10.4	N	Wed	8:30
Babe Ruth Show	33–34	99t	3.8	B	MWF	8:45
Baby Rose Marie Sings	33–34	93t	4.7	B	Tu,Th	6:30
Bar Z Dude Ranch	36–37	87t	4.2	B	Tue	8:00
"Barrie Craig, Confidential Investigator (William Gargan)"	51–52	60t	5.4	N	Tue	8:30
"Barrie Craig, Confidential Investigator (William Gargan) "	52–53	28t	5.8	N	Sun	10:00
Battle of the Sexes (Frank Crumit & Juia Sanderson)	38–39	42	9.5	N	Tue	9:00
Battle of the Sexes (Frank Crumit & Juia Sanderson)	39–40	27t	13.1	N	Tue	9:00
Battle of the Sexes (Frank Crumit & Juia Sanderson)	40–41	46	10.3	N	Tue	9:00
Battle of the Sexes (Frank Crumit & Juia Sanderson)	41–42	44	11.7	N	Tue	9:00
Battle of the Sexes (Walter OKeefe & JC Flippen)	42–43	66t	9.6	N	Tue	9:00
Battle of the Sexes (Walter OKeefe & JC Flippen)	43–44	146t	4.0	B	Wed	8:30
Beat the Band (Garry Moore)	39–40	78t	8.6	N	Sun	6:30
Beat the Band (Garry Moore)	40–41	65t	9.2	N	Sun	6:30
Beat the Band (Hildegarde)	43–44	57	10.2	N	Wed	8:30
Beatrice Fairfax Advice to Lovelorn	33–34	85t	5.7	N	Sat	9:30
Beatrice Kay's Gaslight Gaieties	44–45	87t	8.9	N	Sat	8:00
Beatrice Lillie Show	34–35	56t	12.4	B	Fri	9:00
Beauty Box Theater (Gladys Swarthout)	33–34	9	26.5	N	Tue	10:00
Beauty Box Theater (Gladys Swarthout)	34–35	8	27.2	N	Tue	10:00
Beauty Box Theater (Otto Harbach)	35–36	20	12.6	C	Sat	8:00
Beauty Box Theater (Jessica Dragonnete)	36–37	49t	7.2	C	Wed	9:30

6–11 P.M., Sept through June Programs
Rated 13 Weeks or More

	Season	Rank	Rtg	Net	Day	Time
Ben Bernie Show	32–33	11	25.6	N	Tue	9:00
Ben Bernie Show	33–34	8	27.8	N	Tue	9:00
Ben Bernie Show	34–35	12	23.9	N	Tue	9:00
Ben Bernie Show	35–36	17	13.6	B	Tue	9:00
Ben Bernie Show	36–37	43	8.1	B	Tue	9:00
Ben Bernie Show	37–38	31t	10.9	C	Wed	9:30
Ben Bernie Show	39–40	54t	10.5	C	Wed	8:00
Ben Bernie Show	40–41	77t	8.2	B	Tue	8:00
Benny Goodman Orch	37–38	33t	10.7	C	Tue	9:30
Benny Goodman Orch	38–39	55t	8.6	C	Tue	9:30
Benny Goodman Orch	39–40	78t	8.6	N	Sat	10:00
Best Foods Musical Grocery (Tom Howard)	32–33	57t	8.2	B	Fri	9:00
Better Half (Tiny Ruffner)	48–49	124t	4.4	M	Thu	8:30
Beulah (Marlin Hurt)	45–46	90t	8.1	C	Sun	8:00
Beulah (Hattie McDaniel)	47–48	113	9.6	C	M–F	7:00
Beulah (Hattie McDaniel)	48–49	69	10.0	C	M–F	7:00
Beulah (Hattie McDaniel)	49–50	48t	9.8	C	M–F	7:00
Beulah (Hattie McDaniel)	50–51	35t	9.4	C	M–F	7:00
Beulah (Hattie McDaniel, Lillian Randolph)	51–52	39	6.6	C	M–F	7:00
Beulah (Lillian Randolph, Amanda Randolph)	52–53	56	4.7	C	M–F	7:00
The Bickersons aka Don Ameche & Frances Langford Show	46–47	105	7.5	N	Sun	10:00
The Bickersons aka Don Ameche & Frances Langford Show	47–48	72t	13.0	C	Fri	9:00
The Big Break (Eddie Dowling)	47–48	86t	11.7	N	Sun	10:30
The Big Show (Tallulah Bankhead)	50–51	82t	5.5	N	Sun	6:00
The Big Show (Tallulah Bankhead)	51–52	68t	5.2	N	Sun	6:00
The Big Story (Bob Sloane)	46–47	81t	8.9	N	Wed	10:00
The Big Story (Bob Sloane)	47–48	36t	16.1	N	Wed	10:00
The Big Story (Bob Sloane)	48–49	34t	13.3	N	Wed	10:00
The Big Story (Bob Sloane)	49–50	28t	12.2	N	Wed	10:00
The Big Story (Bob Sloane)	50–51	19	10.4	N	Wed	10:00
The Big Story (Bob Sloane)	51–52	21	8.0	N	Wed	9:30
The Big Story (Bob Sloane)	52–53	13	7.2	N	Wed	9:30
Big Town (Edward G Robinson & Claire Trevor)	37–38	18t	13.7	C	Tue	8:00
Big Town (Edward G Robinson & Claire Trevor)	38–39	14t	15.3	C	Tue	8:00
Big Town (Edward G Robinson & Ona Munson)	39–40	18	14.9	C	Tue	8:00
Big Town (Edward G Robinson & Ona Munson)	40–41	13	16.0	C	Wed	8:00
Big Town (Edward G Robinson & Ona Munson)	41–42	23t	14.8	C	Thu	9:30
Big Town (Ed Pawley & Fran Carlon)	43–44	51	10.9	C	Tue	8:00
Big Town (Ed Pawley & Fran Carlon)	44–45	37	12.8	C	Tue	8:00
Big Town (Ed Pawley & Fran Carlon)	45–46	25	13.7	C	Tue	8:00
Big Town (Ed Pawley & Fran Carlon)	46–47	21	13.7	C	Tue	8:00
Big Town (Ed Pawley & Fran Carlon)	47–48	17	19.5	C	Tue	8:00
Big Town (Ed Pawley & Fran Carlon)	48–49	21	14.8	N	Tue	10:00
Big Town (Ed Pawley & Fran Carlon)	49–50	22	12.7	N	Tue	10:00
Big Town (Ed Pawley & Fran Carlon)	50–51	35t	9.4	N	Tue	10:00
Big Town (Walter Greaza & Fran Carlon)	51–52	29	7.4	C	Wed	8:00
Bill Henry Johns Manville News	44–45	43t	12.0	C	M–F	8:55
Bill Henry Johns Manville News	45–46	53t	10.6	C	M–F	8:55
Bill Henry Johns Manville News	46–47	65t	9.7	C	M–F	8:55
Bill Henry Johns Manville News	47–48	86t	11.7	C	M–F	8:55
Bill Henry Johns Manville News	48–49	141	2.6	M	M–F	9:55
Bill Henry Johns Manville News	49–50	119	3.0	M	M–F	8:55
Bill Henry Johns Manville News	50–51	107	3.0	M	M–F	8:55
Bill Henry Johns Manville News	51–52	93	2.6	M	M–F	9:00
Bill Henry Johns Manville News	52–53	89t	2.5	M	M–F	9:00
Bill Stern Colgate Sports Newsreel	39–40	102	4.8	B	Sun	9:45
Bill Stern Colgate Sports Newsreel	40–41	115	5.8	B	Sun	9:45
Bill Stern Colgate Sports Newsreel	41–42	91t	7.7	N	Sat	10:00
Bill Stern Colgate Sports Newsreel	42–43	82	8.8	N	Sat	10:00
Bill Stern Colgate Sports Newsreel	43–44	58	10.1	N	Fri	10:30
Bill Stern Colgate Sports Newsreel	44–45	63t	10.4	N	Fri	10:30
Bill Stern Colgate Sports Newsreel	45–46	110	6.9	N	Fri	10:30
Bill Stern Colgate Sports Newsreel	46–47	117t	6.9	N	Fri	10:30
Bill Stern Colgate Sports Newsreel	47–48	120t	9.1	N	Fri	10:30
Bill Stern Colgate Sports Newsreel	48–49	89t	8.7	N	Fri	10:30
Bill Stern Colgate Sports Newsreel	49–50	96t	5.9	N	Fri	10:30
Bill Stern Colgate Sports Newsreel	50–51	93t	4.4	N	Fri	10:30
Billie Burke Show	44–45	93t	8.4	N	Wed	8:30
Billy Batchelor Sketches	33–34	48	11.0	N	M–F	7:15

6–11 P.M., Sept through June Programs
  Rated 13 Weeks or More

	Season	Rank	Rtg	Net	Day	Time
Billy Batchelor Sketches	34–35	102	5.7	N	M-F	6:45
Billy Rose Commentary	47–48	139	5.6	M	Tu,Th	8:55
Bing Crosby Music That Satisfies	32–33	18	18.5	C	We,Sa	9:00
Bing Crosby Woodbury Show	33–34	17	21.5	C	Tue	9:00
Bing Crosby Woodbury Show	34–35	34	15.3	C	Tue	9:00
Bing Crosby Kraft Music Hall	35–36	8	16.9	N	Thu	10:00
Bing Crosby Kraft Music Hall	36–37	7	17.4	N	Thu	10:00
Bing Crosby Kraft Music Hall	37–38	4	22.7	N	Thu	10:00
Bing Crosby Kraft Music Hall	38–39	4	21.8	N	Thu	10:00
Bing Crosby Kraft Music Hall	39–40	6	21.1	N	Thu	10:00
Bing Crosby Kraft Music Hall	40–41	14	15.6	N	Thu	9:00
Bing Crosby Kraft Music Hall	41–42	13	17.4	N	Thu	9:00
Bing Crosby Kraft Music Hall	42–43	14	20.0	N	Thu	9:00
Bing Crosby Kraft Music Hall	43–44	14	19.6	N	Thu	9:00
Bing Crosby Kraft Music Hall	44–45	5	22.2	N	Thu	9:00
Bing Crosby Kraft Music Hall	45–46	6	21.5	N	Thu	9:00
Bing Crosby Philco Radio Time	46–47	13	17.6	A	Wed	10:00
Bing Crosby Philco Radio Time	47–48	62t	13.9	A	Wed	10:00
Bing Crosby Philco Radio Time	48–49	40t	12.6	A	Wed	10:00
Bing Crosby Show	49–50	8	15.8	C	Wed	9:30
Bing Crosby Show	50–51	26t	9.8	C	Wed	9:30
Bing Crosby Show	51–52	22t	7.9	C	Wed	9:30
Bing Crosby Show	52–53	28t	5.8	C	Thu	9:30
Black Museum (Orson Welles)	51–52	99t	2.0	M	Tue	8:00
Blackstone Plantation (Frank Crumit & Julia Sanderson)	32–33	29	15.1	N	Tue	8:00
Blackstone Plantation (Frank Crumit & Julia Sanderson)	33–34	32	15.0	N	Tue	8:00
Blind Date (Arlene Francis)	43–44	80t	9.0	B	Mon	8:30
Blind Date (Arlene Francis)	44–45	91t	8.6	B	Mon	8:30
Blind Date (Arlene Francis)	45–46	112t	6.5	A	Fri	8:00
Block & Sully Ex Lax Big Show	34–35	52t	12.7	C	Mon	9:30
Blondie (Penny Singleton & Arthur Lake)	39–40	39t	11.7	C	Mon	7:30
Blondie (Penny Singleton & Arthur Lake)	40–41	37	11.8	C	Mon	7:30
Blondie (Penny Singleton & Arthur Lake)	41–42	35t	12.9	C	Mon	7:30
Blondie (Penny Singleton & Arthur Lake)	42–43	36	13.4	C	Mon	7:30
Blondie (Penny Singleton & Arthur Lake)	43–44	24	15.4	C	Mon	7:30
Blondie (Penny Singleton & Arthur Lake)	44–45	73	9.9	C	Sun	8:00
Blondie (Penny Singleton & Arthur Lake)	45–46	43t	11.7	C	Sun	7:30
Blondie (Penny Singleton & Arthur Lake)	46–47	35	12.4	C	Sun	7:30
Blondie (Penny Singleton & Arthur Lake)	47–48	24	18.1	C	Sun	7:30
Blondie (Penny Singleton/Ann Rutherford & Arthur Lake)	48–49	57	11.4	N	Wed	8:00
Blue Coal Program	33–34	116	2.4	N	Sun	7:00
Blue Ribbon Bouts	50–51	80t	5.6	C	Wed	10:00
Blue Ribbon Bouts	51–52	48	6.0	C	Wed	10:00
Blue Ribbon Bouts	52–53	71t	3.5	C	Wed	10:00
Blue Ribbon Town (Groucho Marx)	42–43	52t	10.4	C	Sat	10:15
Blue Ribbon Town (Groucho Marx)	43–44	71t	9.3	C	Sat	8:00
Boake Carter News & Comment	32–33	72	6.3	C	M-F	7:45
Boake Carter News & Comment	33–34	62t	8.6	C	M-F	7:45
Boake Carter News & Comment	34–35	67	10.8	C	M-F	7:45
Boake Carter News & Comment	35–36	32t	10.3	C	M-F	7:45
Boake Carter News & Comment	36–37	17t	12.8	C	M-F	7:45
Boake Carter News & Comment	37–38	35	7.1	C	MWF	7:45
Boake Carter News & Comment	40–41	101t	6.7	M	MWSa	8:30
Bob Barclay, American Agent	50–51	93t	4.4	A	Wed	8:00
Bob Becker Outdoors & Dogs	43–44	176t	2.3	C	Thu	6:15
Bob Burns Show	41–42	28	14.0	C	Tue	8:30
Bob Burns Show	42–43	33	13.8	N	Thu	7:30
Bob Burns Show	43–44	23	15.6	N	Thu	7:30
Bob Burns Show	44–45	20	14.9	N	Thu	7:30
Bob Burns Show	45–46	33	12.9	N	Thu	7:30
Bob Burns Show	46–47	73	9.4	N	Sun	6:30
Bob Crosby Show	39–40	82	8.4	N	Sat	10:00
Bob Crosby Show	40–41	106t	6.4	N	Thu	7:30
Bob Crosby Show	43–44	55t	10.7	N	Sun	10:30
Bob Crosby Show	45–46	112t	6.5	C	Wed	9:30
Bob Hawk's Thanks to the Yanks	42–43	83t	8.7	C	Sat	7:30
Bob Hawk's Thanks to the Yanks	43–44	73t	9.2	C	Sat	7:30
Bob Hawk's Thanks to the Yanks	44–45	41t	12.4	C	Mon	7:30
Bob Hawk's Thanks to the Yanks & Bob Hawk Show	45–46	37	12.4	C	Mon	7:30

6–11 P.M., Sept through June Programs
Rated 13 Weeks or More

	Season	Rank	Rtg	Net	Day	Time
Bob Hawk Show	46–47	29t	13.1	C	Mon	7:30
Bob Hawk Show	47–48	54	14.6	N	Thu	10:00
Bob Hawk Show	48–49	26	14.1	C	Mon	10:30
Bob Hawk Show	49–50	19t	13.0	C	Mon	10:30
Bob Hawk Show	50–51	17t	10.5	C	Mon	10:30
Bob Hawk Show	51–52	10t	9.1	C	Mon	10:00
Bob Hawk Show	52–53	16t	6.6	C	Mon	10:00
Bob Hope Intimate Review	34–35	115	4.1	B	Fri	8:30
Bob Hope Atlantic Family	35–36	50	7.7	C	Sat	7:00
Bob Hope Show	38–39	12t	15.4	N	Tue	10:00
Bob Hope Show	39–40	5	23.1	N	Tue	10:00
Bob Hope Show	40–41	4	26.6	N	Tue	10:00
Bob Hope Show	41–42	2	30.7	N	Tue	10:00
Bob Hope Show	42–43	1t	32.3	N	Tue	10:00
Bob Hope Show	43–44	1	31.7	N	Tue	10:00
Bob Hope Show	44–45	1	29.6	N	Tue	10:00
Bob Hope Show	45–46	1	27.7	N	Tue	10:00
Bob Hope Show	46–47	1	27.6	N	Tue	10:00
Bob Hope Show	47–48	5	22.5	N	Tue	10:00
Bob Hope Show	48–49	7	19.8	N	Tue	9:00
Bob Hope Show	49–50	10	15.0	N	Tue	9:00
Bob Hope Show	50–51	33	9.6	N	Tue	9:00
Bob Hope Show	51–52	25t	7.9	N	Tue	9:00
Bob Hope Show	52–53	47t	5.0	N	Wed	10:00
Bobby Benson & Sunny Jim (Billy Halop)	33–34	80t	6.6	C	M-F	6:15
Bobby Benson & Sunny Jim (Billy Halop)	34–35	77	8.8	C	M-F	6:15
Bobby Benson & Sunny Jim (Billy Halop)	35–36	102	4.1	C	MWF	6:15
Borden Program (Mark Warnow Orch)	47–48	90t	11.6	C	Wed	9:00
Boston Pops Orch	50–51	99	3.8	N	Mon	10:00
Boston Symphony & Boston Pops	43–44	172	2.7	B	Sat	8:30
Boston Symphony & Boston Pops	44–45	177t	2.9	B	Sat	8:30
Boston Symphony & Boston Pops	45–46	183t	2.5	A	Sat	9:30
Boston Symphony & Boston Pops	46–47	155t	2.8	A	Tue	8:30
Botany Song Shop (Ginny Simms)	50–51	116t	2.2	A	Sun	10:00
Break the Bank (Various Hosts)	45–46	147t	4.5	M	Sat	9:30
Break the Bank (Bert Parks)	46–47	71t	9.5	A	Fri	9:00
Break the Bank (Bert Parks)	47–48	36t	16.1	A	Fri	9:00
Break the Bank (Bert Parks)	48–49	38t	12.8	A	Fri	9:00
Break the Bank (Bert Parks)	49–50	43	10.3	N	Wed	9:00
Breezing Along (Jack Smith)	39–40	104t	4.2	B	Wed	8:00
Broadway Merry Go Round (Beatrice Lillie)	36–37	80	5.0	B	Wed	8:00
Broadway Varieties (Helen Morgan)	34–35	106	5.1	C	Wed	8:30
Broadway Varieties (Victor Arden Orch)	35–36	74t	5.8	C	Fri	8:30
Broadway Varieties (Victor Arden Orch)	36–37	81	4.7	C	Fri	8:00
Buck Rogers (Curtis Arnall)	32–33	64t	7.4	C	M-F	7:15
Buck Rogers (Curtis Arnall)	33–34	80t	6.6	C	M-Th	6:00
Buck Rogers (Matt Crowley)	34–35	79t	8.4	C	M-Th	6:00
Buck Rogers (Matt Crowley)	35–36	99t	4.4	C	MWF	6:00
Burl Ives Show	46–47	162t	2.4	M	Fri	8:00
Burl Ives Show	47–48	146t	3.5	M	Fri	8:00
Burns & Allen w/Guy Lombardo Orch	32–33	10	26.5	C	Wed	9:30
Burns & Allen w/Guy Lombardo Orch	33–34	6	28.2	C	Wed	9:30
Burns & Allen Show (George Burns & Gracie Allen)	34–35	27	18.3	C	Wed	9:30
Burns & Allen Show (George Burns & Gracie Allen)	35–36	6	18.6	C	Wed	8:30
Burns & Allen Show (George Burns & Gracie Allen)	36–37	5	20.9	C	Wed	8:30
Burns & Allen Show (George Burns & Gracie Allen)	37–38	8	19.2	N	Mon	8:00
Burns & Allen Show (George Burns & Gracie Allen)	38–39	11	15.6	C	Fri	8:30
Burns & Allen Show (George Burns & Gracie Allen)	39–40	21	14.3	C	Wed	7:30
Burns & Allen Show (George Burns & Gracie Allen)	40–41	30t	12.8	N	Mon	7:30
Burns & Allen Show (George Burns & Gracie Allen)	41–42	19t	15.6	N	Tue	7:30
Burns & Allen Show (George Burns & Gracie Allen)	42–43	21	16.0	C	Tue	9:00
Burns & Allen Show (George Burns & Gracie Allen)	43–44	18	17.0	C	Tue	9:00
Burns & Allen Show (George Burns & Gracie Allen)	44–45	21t	14.7	C	Mon	8:30
Burns & Allen Show (George Burns & Gracie Allen)	45–46	34	12.8	N	Thu	8:00
Burns & Allen Show (George Burns & Gracie Allen)	46–47	15t	15.2	N	Thu	8:30
Burns & Allen Show (George Burns & Gracie Allen)	47–48	25t	18.0	N	Thu	8:30
Burns & Allen Show (George Burns & Gracie Allen)	48–49	37	13.0	N	Thu	8:30
Burns & Allen Show (George Burns & Gracie Allen)	49–50	30t	12.0	C	Wed	10:00
By Popular Demand (Bud Collyer)	46–47	153	3.0	M	Thu	9:30

	Season	Rank	Rtg	Net	Day	Time
Byrd Antarctic Expedition	33–34	26	17.3	C	Sat	10:00
Byrd Antarctic Expedition	34–35	62t	11.7	C	Wed	10:00
Cadillac Symphony	33–34	39t	13.2	B	Sun	6:00
Call for Music (Dinah Shore, Johnny Mercer, Harry James Orch)	47–48	81	12.0	N	Tue	8:00
Camel Caravan (Herb Shriner)	42–43	49	10.7	C	Fri	10:00
Campana Serenade (Dick Powell)	42–43	88	8.1	N	Sat	10:15
Campbell Playhouse (Orson Welles)	38–39	12t	15.4	C	Fri	9:00
Campbell Playhouse (Orson Welles)	39–40	46	11.0	C	Sun	8:00
Campbell Playhouse	40–41	30t	12.8	C	Fri	9:30
Campus Review (Hal Totten, Art Kassel Orch)	35–36	98	4.8	N	Fri	10:30
Can You Top This? (Ward Wilson)	42–43	43	11.8	N	Sat	9:30
Can You Top This? (Ward Wilson)	43–44	32t	13.2	N	Sat	9:30
Can You Top This? (Ward Wilson)	44–45	27t	13.6	N	Sat	9:30
Can You Top This? (Ward Wilson)	45–46	26t	13.4	N	Sat	9:30
Can You Top This? (Ward Wilson)	46–47	42t	11.6	N	Sat	9:30
Can You Top This? (Ward Wilson)	47–48	62t	13.9	N	Fri	8:30
Can You Top This? (Ward Wilson)	50–51	100t	3.7	A	Tue	8:00
Captain Diamond's Adventures (Al Swenson)	32–33	91t	3.8	B	Thu	8:00
Captain Diamond's Adventures (Al Swenson)	33–34	87	5.4	B	Thu	8:00
Captain Flagg & Sgt Quirt (Victor McLaglen & Edmund Lowe)	41–42	88t	7.8	N	Fri	10:00
Captain Tim Healy	35–36	118t	2.6	B	MWF	7:15
Carborundum Band (Francis Bowman)	35–36	88	5.4	C	Sat	7:30
Carborundum Band (Francis Bowman)	36–37	109	2.4	C	Sat	7:30
Carefree Carnival (Gene Arnold)	34–35	100	6.0	B	Mon	8:30
Carnation Contented Hour (Gene Arnold & Morgan Eastman Orch)	32–33	30	14.7	N	Mon	10:00
Carnation Contented Hour (Gene Arnold & Morgan Eastman Orch)	33–34	37	13.8	N	Mon	10:00
Carnation Contented Hour (Morgan Eastman Orch)	34–35	56t	12.4	N	Mon	10:00
Carnation Contented Hour (Morgan Eastman Orch)	35–36	63	6.5	N	Mon	10:00
Carnation Contented Hour (Vivienne della Chiesa & Frank Black Orch)	36–37	87t	4.2	N	Mon	10:00
Carnation Contented Hour (Vivienne della Chiesa & Frank Black Orch)	37–38	79	5.3	N	Mon	10:00
Carnation Contented Hour (Opal Craven & Marek Weber Orch)	38–39	80t	6.5	N	Mon	10:00
Carnation Contented Hour (Opal Craven & Josef Pasternack Orch)	39–40	89	7.1	N	Mon	10:00
Carnation Contented Hour (Louise King & Percy Faith Orch)	40–41	109t	6.3	N	Mon	10:00
Carnation Contented Hour (Percy Faith Orch)	41–42	119t	5.4	N	Mon	10:00
Carnation Contented Hour (Percy Faith Orch)	42–43	97	7.2	N	Mon	10:00
Carnation Contented Hour (Percy Faith Orch)	43–44	106	6.9	N	Mon	10:00
Carnation Contented Hour (Percy Faith Orch)	44–45	108t	7.4	N	Mon	10:00
Carnation Contented Hour (Percy Faith Orch)	45–46	85t	8.3	N	Mon	10:00
Carnation Contented Hour (Buddy Clark & Percy Faith Orch)	46–47	110t	7.2	N	Mon	10:00
Carnation Contented Hour (Buddy Clark & Percy Faith Orch)	47–48	112	9.7	N	Mon	10:00
Carnation Contented Hour (Buddy Clark & Percy Faith/ Ted Dale Orch)	48–49	103t	7.4	N	Mon	10:00
Carnation Contented Hour (Jo Stafford & Dick Haymes)	49–50	91	6.8	C	Sun	10:00
Carnation Contented Hour (Jo Stafford & Tony Martin)	50–51	59	7.3	C	Sun	10:00
Carnation Contented Hour (Jo Stafford & Tony Martin)	51–52	40t	6.4	C	Sun	9:30
Carnegie Hall Concerts	48–49	138	3.1	A	Sun	7:30
Carnegie Hall Concerts	49–50	116	3.5	A	Tue	8:00
Carnival (Morton Gould Orch)	42–43	130	4.3	C	Wed	10:30
Carnival (Morton Gould Orch)	43–44	122t	5.1	C	Wed	10:30
Carson Robison Show	38–39	98	3.0	B	Mon	8:00
Carson Robison Show	39–40	104t	4.2	B	Fri	8:30
Carton of Cheer (Henny Youngman)	44–45	74t	9.8	N	Wed	8:30
Carveth Wells' Exploring America	32–33	50t	9.8	N	Wed	10:30
Casebook of Gregory Hood (Gale Gordon)	46–47	122t	6.4	M	Mon	8:30
Casey Crime Photographer (Staats Cotsworth)	46–47	38t	11.8	C	Thu	9:30
Casey Crime Photographer (Staats Cotsworth)	47–48	44t	15.6	C	Thu	9:30
Casey Crime Photographer (Staats Cotsworth)	48–49	16	15.7	C	Thu	9:30
Casey Crime Photographer (Staats Cotsworth)	49–50	21	12.9	C	Thu	9:30
Cavalcade of America	35–36	94t	4.9	C	Wed	8:00
Cavalcade of America	36–37	75t	5.2	C	Wed	8:00
Cavalcade of America	37–38	63	7.3	C	Wed	8:00
Cavalcade of America	38–39	64t	7.7	C	Mon	8:00
Cavalcade of America	39–40	90t	7.0	B	Tue	9:00
Cavalcade of America	40–41	100	6.8	N	Wed	7:30
Cavalcade of America	41–42	72t	8.8	N	Mon	7:30
Cavalcade of America	42–43	50t	10.5	N	Mon	8:00
Cavalcade of America	43–44	67t	9.4	N	Mon	8:00

6–11 P.M., Sept through June Programs *Rated 13 Weeks or More*	Season	Rank	Rtg	Net	Day	Time
Cavalcade of America	44–45	57	10.8	N	Mon	8:00
Cavalcade of America	45–46	73t	9.3	N	Mon	8:00
Cavalcade of America	46–47	74t	9.3	N	Mon	8:00
Cavalcade of America	47–48	58t	14.0	N	Mon	8:00
Cavalcade of America	48–49	82t	9.1	N	Mon	8:00
Cavalcade of America	49–50	74t	7.7	N	Tue	8:00
Cavalcade of America	50–51	62t	7.1	N	Tue	8:00
Cavalcade of America	51–52	46t	6.2	N	Tue	8:00
Cavalcade of America	52–53	51t	4.8	N	Tue	8:00
Cecil Brown News	50–51	102t	3.6	M	Sat	7:55
Cecil Brown News	51–52	96	2.4	M	Sat	7:55
Cecil Brown News	52–53	76t	3.2	M	Sun	6:25
Cecil Brown News	52–53	98	2.1	M	Sat	7:55
Cecil Brown/Cedric Foster News	51–52	90	3.4	M	Sun	6:55
Cedric Adams Commentary	52–53	85	2.8	C	Mon	10:35
Cedric Foster News	43–44	153t	3.5	M	Sun	10:00
Cedric Foster News	44–45	155t	4.1	M	Sun	9:30
Cedric Foster News	45–46	161	3.7	M	Sun	6:30
Ceiling Unlimited (Orson Welles, Patrick McGeehan)	42–43	107t	6.2	C	Mon	7:15
Celebrity Club (Margaret Whiting & Jackie Kelk)	45–46	111	6.7	C	Sat	10:15
Chamber Music Society of Lower Basin Street (Milton Cross)	42–43	55t	10.3	B	Sun	9:15
Chamber Music Society of Lower Basin Street (Milton Cross)	43–44	82t	8.7	B	Sun	9:15
Champion Roll Call (Harry Wismer)	47–48	114t	9.5	A	Fri	9:55
Champion Roll Call (Harry Wismer)	48–49	114t	6.7	A	Fri	9:55
Champion Roll Call (Harry Wismer)	49–50	115	3.6	A	Fri	9:55
Champion Roll Call (Harry Wismer)	50–51	97t	4.1	A	Fri	9:55
Champion Roll Call (Harry Wismer)	51–52	81t	4.2	A	Fri	9:55
Chance of a Lifetime (John Reed King)	49–50	82t	7.3	A	Sun	9:30
Chandu the Magician (Gayne Whitman)	32–33	61	7.9	Syn	M–Sat	Var
Charles Collingwood News	45–46	165t	3.4	C	Sat	6:45
Charlie Wild, Private Detective (George Petrie)	50–51	91	4.6	C	Sun	6:00
Chase & Sanborn Opera Guild (Deems Taylor)	34–35	15	22.4	N	Sun	8:00
Chester Morrison News	45–46	173t	3.0	A	M–F	9:55
Chesterfield Supper Club (Fred Waring)	39–40	62t	10.1	N	M–F	7:00
Chesterfield Supper Club (Fred Waring)	40–41	65t	9.2	N	M–F	7:00
Chesterfield Supper Club (Fred Waring)	41–42	64	9.3	N	M–F	7:00
Chesterfield Supper Club (Fred Waring)	42–43	52t	10.4	N	M–F	7:00
Chesterfield Supper Club (Fred Waring)	43–44	67t	9.4	N	M–F	7:00
Chesterfield Supper Club (Perry Como & Jo Stafford)	44–45	86	9.1	N	M–F	7:00
Chesterfield Supper Club (Perry Como & Jo Stafford)	45–46	62t	10.1	N	M–F	7:00
Chesterfield Supper Club (Perry Como & Jo Stafford)	46–47	54	10.5	N	M–F	7:00
Chesterfield Supper Club (Perry Como & Jo Stafford)	47–48	100t	10.7	N	M–F	7:00
Chesterfield Supper Club (Perry Como, Jo Stafford & Peggy Lee)	48–49	96	8.3	N	M–F	7:00
Chesterfield Supper Club (Peggy Lee)	49–50	68	8.1	N	Thu	10:00
Chevrolet Program (Victor Young Orch)	33–34	61	8.9	N	Sun	10:00
Chrysler Air Show (Charles Hanson Towne)	35–36	121t	2.3	C	Thu	8:00
The Circle	38–39	28	12.3	N	Sun	10:00
Circus Days	33–34	113t	2.6	N	Fr,Sa	7:30
Circus Nights in Silvertown (Joe Cook)	34–35	74t	9.4	N	Fri	10:30
Cities Service Concert (Jessica Dragonette)	32–33	16	20.2	N	Fri	8:00
Cities Service Concert (Jessica Dragonette)	33–34	20	19.6	N	Fri	8:00
Cities Service Concert (Jessica Dragonette)	34–35	28t	18.0	N	Fri	8:00
Cities Service Concert (Jessica Dragonette)	35–36	25	11.1	N	Fri	8:00
Cities Service Concert (Jessica Dragonette)	36–37	62t	6.5	N	Fri	8:00
Cities Service Concert (Lucille Manners & Frank Black Orch)	37–38	62	7.5	N	Fri	8:00
Cities Service Concert (Lucille Manners & Frank Black Orch)	38–39	82t	6.2	N	Fri	8:00
Cities Service Concert (Lucille Manners & Frank Black Orch)	39–40	87	7.5	N	Fri	8:00
Cities Service Concert (Lucille Manners & Frank Black Orch)	40–41	104t	6.5	N	Fri	8:00
Cities Service Concert (Lucille Manners & Frank Black Orch)	41–42	108	6.2	N	Fri	8:00
Cities Service Concert (Lucille Manners & Frank Black Orch)	42–43	103t	6.5	N	Fri	8:00
Cities Service Concert (Lucille Manners & Frank Black Orch)	43–44	107	6.8	N	Fri	8:00
Cities Service Highways in Melody (Paul Lavalle Orch)	44–45	99t	8.2	N	Fri	8:00
Cities Service Highways in Melody (Paul Lavalle Orch)	45–46	109	7.1	N	Fri	8:00
Cities Service Highways in Melody (Paul Lavalle Orch)	46–47	114t	7.0	N	Fri	8:00
Cities Service Highways in Melody (Paul Lavalle Orch)	47–48	129	7.9	N	Fri	8:00
Cities Service Band of America (Paul Lavalle Orch)	48–49	113t	6.8	N	Fri	8:00
Cities Service Band of America (Paul Lavalle Orch)	49–50	105t	5.3	N	Mon	9:30
Cities Service Band of America (Paul Lavalle Orch)	50–51	90	4.7	N	Mon	9:30
Cities Service Band of America (Paul Lavalle Orch)	51–52	79t	4.3	N	Mon	9:30

6–11 P.M., Sept through June Programs
Rated 13 Weeks or More

	Season	Rank	Rtg	Net	Day	Time
Cities Service Band of America (Paul Lavalle Orch)	52–53	76t	3.2	N	Mon	9:30
A Citizen Views the News (Robert Montgomery)	51–52	98	2.1	N	M-F	10:30
City Desk (James Meighan & Gertrude Warner)	40–41	101t	6.7	C	Thu	8:30
Cliquot Club Eskimos (Harry Reser Orch)	32–33	56	8.4	B	Mon	8:00
Club 15 (Bob Crosby)	47–48	104	10.6	C	M-F	7:30
Club 15 (Bob Crosby)	48–49	78t	9.5	C	M-F	7:30
Club 15 (Dick Haymes)	49–50	70t	7.9	C	M-F	7:30
Club 15 (Bob Crosby)	50–51	60t	7.2	C	M-F	7:30
Club 15 (Bob Crosby)	51–52	60t	5.4	C	M-F	7:30
Club 15 (Bob Crosby)	52–53	51t	4.8	C	MWF	7:30
Colgate House Party (Various Hosts)	33–34	41t	13.0	N	Sat	8:00
Colgate House Party (Joe Cook)	34–35	56t	12.4	N	Mon	9:30
Colonel Stoopnagle & Budd (F Chase Taylor & Budd Hulick)	32–33	50t	9.8	C	Thu	9:30
Come, Let's Sing (Homer Rodeheaver)	36–37	62t	6.5	C	Wed	9:30
Comedy Theater (Harold Lloyd)	44–45	83t	9.4	N	Sun	10:30
Corn Cob Pipe Club	32–33	70	6.8	N	Wed	10:00
Corn Cob Pipe Club	33–34	62t	8.6	N	Wed	10:00
Corn Cob Pipe Club	35–36	94t	4.9	B	Wed	9:00
Correction Please (Jim McWilliams)	43–44	91t	7.8	C	Sat	10:15
Correction Please (Jay C Flippen)	44–45	114t	6.9	C	Sat	10:15
Counterspy (Don MacLaughlin)	42–43	101t	6.6	B	Mon	9:00
Counterspy (Don MacLaughlin)	43–44	97t	7.4	B	Mon	9:00
Counterspy (Don MacLaughlin)	44–45	87t	8.9	B	Wed	8:30
Counterspy (Don MacLaughlin)	45–46	102t	7.6	A	Wed	10:00
Counterspy (Don MacLaughlin)	45–46	##	5.6	A	Sun	5:30
Counterspy (Don MacLaughlin)	46–47	##	7.7	A	Sun	5:30
Counterspy (Don MacLaughlin)	47–48	##	11.6	A	Sun	5:30
Counterspy (Don MacLaughlin)	48–49	80	9.4	A	Tu,Th	7:30
Counterspy (Don MacLaughlin)	49–50	53t	9.4	A	Tu,Th	7:30
Counterspy (Don MacLaughlin)	50–51	78t	5.7	N	Thu	9:30
Counterspy (Don MacLaughlin)	51–52	55t	5.6	N	Thu	9:30
Country Doctor (Phillips H Lord)	32–33	46	10.6	B	M-W	8:45
County Fair (Jack Bailey)	45–46	185t	2.4	A	Tue	7:30
County Fair (Win Elliot)	48–49	119	6.2	C	Wed	9:00
Court of Human Relations (Percy Hemus)	33–34	66t	8.1	N	Sun	7:00
Court of Human Relations (Percy Hemus)	34–35	55	12.5	C	Fri	8:30
Court of Human Relations (Percy Hemus)	35–36	51t	7.6	N	Fri	9:30
Court of Human Relations (Percy Hemus)	36–37	45	7.5	N	Fri	9:30
Court of Human Relations (Percy Hemus)	37–38	44	9.3	N	Fri	9:30
Court of Missing Heirs aka Are You a Missing Heir? (James Waters)	39–40	90t	7.0	C	Tue	8:30
Court of Missing Heirs aka Are You a Missing Heir? (James Waters)	40–41	44t	10.4	C	Tue	8:00
Court of Missing Heirs aka Are You a Missing Heir? (James Waters)	41–42	59t	9.7	C	Tue	8:00
Crime Doctor (Ray Collins)	40–41	79t	8.1	C	Sun	8:30
Crime Doctor (John McIntyre)	41–42	68	9.1	C	Sun	8:30
Crime Doctor (Brian Donlevy, Everett Sloane)	42–43	76t	9.2	C	Sun	8:30
Crime Doctor (Everett Sloane)	43–44	35t	13.0	C	Sun	8:30
Crime Doctor (Everett Sloane)	44–45	38t	12.7	C	Sun	8:30
Crime Doctor (Everett Sloane)	45–46	47t	11.3	C	Sun	8:30
Crime Doctor (Everett Sloane)	46–47	55t	10.4	C	Sun	8:30
Crime Files of Flamond (Arthur Wyatt)	52–53	89t	2.5	M	Wed	8:00
Crime Letter from Dan Dodge (Myron McCormick)	52–53	58	4.5	A	Fri	8:30
Cruise of the Seth Parker (Phillips H Lord)	33–34	18	21.3	N	Tue	10:00
Crumit & Sanderson Quiz (aka Mr Adam & Eve)	42–43	113t	5.8	C	Sat	8:00
Cuckoo Program (Ray Knight)	32–33	76	6.0	B	Sat	10:15
Cuckoo Program (Ray Knight)	33–34	65	8.3	B	Wed	9:00
Curtain Time (Harry Elders & Nannette Sargent)	45–46	155t	4.1	A	Thu	10:00
Curtain Time (Harry Elders & Nannette Sargent)	46–47	102	7.7	N	Sat	7:30
Curtain Time (Harry Elders & Nannette Sargent)	47–48	75t	12.6	N	Sat	7:30
Curtain Time (Harry Elders & Nannette Sargent)	48–49	49t	11.9	N	Wed	10:30
Curtain Time (Harry Elders & Nannette Sargent)	49–50	38t	11.3	N	Wed	10:30
Dale Carnegie Commentary	43–44	175	2.5	M	Thu	10:15
Dangerous Paradise (Elsie Hitz & Nick Dawson)	33–34	71t	7.6	B	We,Fr	7:45
Dangerous Paradise (Elsie Hitz & Nick Dawson)	34–35	61	11.9	B	MWF	7:45
Dangerous Paradise (Elsie Hitz & Nick Dawson)	35–36	60	6.9	B	MWF	7:45
Danny Kaye Show	44–45	60	10.6	C	Fri	10:30
Danny Kaye Show	45–46	51t	10.8	C	Fri	10:30
Danny Thomas Show	47–48	69	13.2	C	Fri	8:30
Darts for Dough (Orval Anderson)	47–48	146t	3.5	A	Thu	9:30
Date with Judy (Louise Erickson)	43–44	78t	9.1	N	Tue	8:30

6–11 P.M., Sept through June Programs
Rated 13 Weeks or More

	Season	Rank	Rtg	Net	Day	Time
Date with Judy (Louise Erickson)	44–45	40	12.5	N	Tue	8:30
Date with Judy (Louise Erickson)	45–46	38	12.3	N	Tue	8:30
Date with Judy (Louise Erickson)	46–47	29t	13.1	N	Tue	8:30
Date with Judy (Louise Erickson)	47–48	19	19.0	N	Tue	8:30
Date with Judy (Louise Erickson)	48–49	13t	16.4	N	Tue	8:30
Date with Judy (Louise Erickson)	49–50	100t	5.7	A	Thu	8:30
Dateline (Robert Trout)	43–44	118	5.3	C	Fri	7:15
David Lawrence Commentary	32–33	59	8.1	N	Sun	10:15
A Day in the Life of Dennis Day	46–47	34	12.5	N	Wed	8:00
A Day in the Life of Dennis Day	47–48	36t	16.1	N	Wed	8:00
A Day in the Life of Dennis Day	48–49	22t	14.6	N	Sat	10:00
A Day in the Life of Dennis Day	49–50	23	12.6	N	Sat	9:30
A Day in the Life of Dennis Day/The Dennis Day Show	50–51	42t	8.8	N	Sat	9:30
Death Valley Days (Jack MacBryde)	32–33	41t	11.7	B	Thu	9:00
Death Valley Days (Jack MacBryde)	33–34	35	14.6	B	Thu	9:00
Death Valley Days (Jack MacBryde)	34–35	35	15.2	B	Thu	9:00
Death Valley Days (Jack MacBryde)	35–36	47	8.1	B	Thu	9:00
Death Valley Days (Jack MacBryde)	36–37	68	5.7	B	Fri	8:30
Death Valley Days (Jack MacBryde)	37–38	54t	8.3	B	Fri	9:30
Death Valley Days (Jack MacBryde)	38–39	70	7.4	N	Fri	9:30
Death Valley Days (Jack MacBryde)	39–40	95	6.7	N	Sat	9:30
Death Valley Days (Jack MacBryde)	40–41	89t	7.6	B	Fri	8:30
Death Valley Days (Jack MacBryde)	41–42	97t	6.6	C	Thu	8:00
Death Valley Days (Jack MacBryde)	42–43	112	6.0	C	Thu	8:30
Death Valley Days (Jack MacBryde)	43–44	97t	7.4	C	Thu	8:30
Death Valley Sheriff (Robert Haag)	44–45	68t	10.1	C	Thu	8:30
Deems Taylor	36–37	116	1.1	B	Fri	9:30
Defense Attorney (Mercedes McCambridge)	51–52	76t	4.4	A	Thu	8:30
Detect & Collect (Fred Uttal & Wendy Barrie)	45–46	153	4.2	A	Thu	9:30
Detroit Symphony	44–45	187t	2.4	M	Sat	8:30
Dick Brown Sings	44–45	186	2.5	M	Sun	6:45
Dick Haymes Show	44–45	89t	8.8	N	Tue	7:30
Dick Haymes Show	45–46	84	8.4	C	Sat	8:00
Dick Haymes Show	46–47	40t	11.7	C	Thu	9:00
Dick Haymes Show	47–48	47	15.3	C	Thu	9:00
Dick Liebert Organ Melodies	34–35	135	1.5	B	Fri	8:15
Dick Powell Show	37–38	25	12.7	N	Wed	10:00
Dick Powell Show	38–39	33	10.9	C	Tue	8:30
Dick Tracy (Ned Weaver)	45–46	147t	4.5	A	Sat	8:00
Dill's Best (Pick & Pat)	33–34	119	2.1	N	Sat	6:45
Dinah Shore Sings	41–42	110t	6.0	B	Sun	9:45
Dinah Shore Sings	42–43	131	4.1	B	Fri	8:15
Dinah Shore Show	43–44	103t	7.1	C	Thu	9:30
Dinah Shore Show	44–45	16	15.4	N	Thu	8:30
Dinah Shore Show	45–46	31	13.1	N	Thu	8:30
Dinah Shore Ford Show	46–47	83t	8.8	C	Wed	9:30
Dinah Shore Show	52–53	103t	1.6	N	Mo,Fr	10:00
Doctor Christian (Jean Hersholt)	38–39	79	6.7	C	Tue	10:00
Doctor Christian (Jean Hersholt)	39–40	39t	11.7	C	Wed	8:30
Doctor Christian (Jean Hersholt)	40–41	25	13.3	C	Wed	8:30
Doctor Christian (Jean Hersholt)	41–42	41t	12.2	C	Wed	8:30
Doctor Christian (Jean Hersholt)	42–43	42	12.0	C	Wed	8:30
Doctor Christian (Jean Hersholt)	43–44	32t	13.2	C	Wed	8:30
Doctor Christian (Jean Hersholt)	44–45	33	13.1	C	Wed	8:30
Doctor Christian (Jean Hersholt)	45–46	23	13.9	C	Wed	8:30
Doctor Christian (Jean Hersholt)	46–47	40t	11.7	C	Wed	8:30
Doctor Christian (Jean Hersholt)	47–48	62t	13.9	C	Wed	8:30
Doctor Christian (Jean Hersholt)	48–49	52t	11.7	C	Wed	8:30
Doctor Christian (Jean Hersholt)	49–50	38t	11.3	C	Wed	8:30
Doctor Christian (Jean Hersholt)	50–51	22t	10.2	C	Wed	8:30
Doctor Christian (Jean Hersholt)	51–52	18t	8.4	C	Wed	8:30
Doctor Christian (Jean Hersholt)	52–53	20t	6.4	C	Wed	8:30
Doctor Haggard's Devils, Drugs & Doctors	32–33	107	0.5	B	Sun	7:15
Doctor IQ (Lew Valentine)	39–40	57t	10.4	N	Mon	9:00
Doctor IQ (Lew Valentine)	40–41	42	10.7	N	Mon	9:00
Doctor IQ (Lew Valentine)	41–42	65t	9.2	N	Mon	9:00
Doctor IQ (Jimmy McClain)	42–43	62t	9.7	N	Mon	9:30
Doctor IQ (Jimmy McClain)	43–44	63	9.8	N	Mon	10:30
Doctor IQ (Jimmy McClain)	44–45	48t	11.4	N	Mon	10:30

6–11 P.M., Sept through June Programs
　Rated 13 Weeks or More

Program	Season	Rank	Rtg	Net	Day	Time
Doctor IQ (Jimmy McClain)	45–46	56t	10.5	N	Mon	10:30
Doctor IQ (Lew Valentine)	46–47	49t	10.9	N	Mon	10:30
Doctor IQ (Lew Valentine)	47–48	108	10.1	N	Mon	9:30
Doctor IQ (Lew Valentine)	48–49	94t	8.4	N	Mon	9:30
Doctor IQ (Lew Valentine)	49–50	108	4.5	A	Wed	8:00
Doctor IQ (Lew Valentine)	50–51	102t	3.6	A	Wed	8:00
Doctor West's Celebrity Night (Ethel Shutta)	35–36	67t	6.1	N	Sat	10:30
Doctors Talk It Over (Milton Cross)	45–46	194	1.5	A	Tue	9:30
Doctors Talk It Over (Milton Cross)	46–47	169	1.5	A	Mon	10:00
Don Ameche & Frances Langford Show aka The Bickersons	46–47	105	7.5	N	Sun	10:00
Don Ameche & Frances Langford Show aka The Bickersons	47–48	72t	13.0	C	Fri	9:00
Don Gardiner Monday Morning Headline News	44–45	124t	6.1	B	Sun	7:15
Don Gardiner Monday Morning Headline News	45–46	131	5.5	A	Sun	7:15
Don Gardiner Monday Morning Headline News	46–47	135t	5.1	A	Sun	6:15
Don Gardiner Monday Morning Headline News	47–48	114t	9.5	A	Sun	6:15
Don Gardiner Monday Morning Headline News	48–49	100	7.7	A	Sun	6:15
Don Gardiner Monday Morning Headline News	49–50	94t	6.1	A	Sun	6:15
Don Gardiner Monday Morning Headline News	50–51	86	5.3	A	Sun	6:15
Don Gardiner Monday Morning Headline News	51–52	71t	4.8	A	Sun	6:15
Don Gardiner Monday Morning Headline News	52–53	75	3.3	A	Sun	6:15
Don Quixote	33–34	111	3.0	B	ThFSa	7:15
Don Winslow of the Navy (Bob Guilbert)	42–43	140	3.0	B	M–F	6:15
Doris Day Show	52–53	82t	2.9	C	Tue	10:05
Dorothy Thompson News & Comment	40–41	120t	5.2	M	Sun	8:45
Dorothy Thompson News & Comment	42–43	120	5.2	B	Sun	9:45
Dorothy Thompson News & Comment	43–44	146t	4.0	B	Sun	7:15
Dorothy Thompson News & Comment	44–45	177t	2.9	B	Sun	8:15
Double or Nothing (Walter Compton)	40–41	106t	6.4	M	Sun	6:00
Double or Nothing (Walter Compton)	41–42	105t	6.3	M	Sun	6:00
Double or Nothing (Walter Compton)	42–43	113t	5.8	M	Fri	9:30
Double or Nothing (John Reed King)	43–44	115t	5.4	M	Fri	9:30
Double or Nothing (John Reed King)	44–45	129	5.7	M	Fri	9:30
Double or Nothing (Todd Russell)	45–46	106	7.4	M	Sun	9:30
Double or Nothing (Todd Russell)	46–47	110t	7.2	M	Sun	9:30
Dragnet (Jack Webb)	49–50	64t	8.5	N	Thu	10:30
Dragnet (Jack Webb)	50–51	45t	8.7	N	Thu	9:00
Dragnet (Jack Webb)	51–52	14t	8.7	N	Thu	9:00
Dragnet (Jack Webb)	52–53	15	6.7	N	Sun	9:30
Drew Pearson & Robt Allen News & Comment	41–42	112t	5.8	B	Sun	6:30
Drew Pearson News & Comment	42–43	106	6.3	B	Sun	7:00
Drew Pearson News & Comment	43–44	100t	7.3	B	Sun	7:00
Drew Pearson News & Comment	44–45	74t	9.8	B	Sun	7:00
Drew Pearson News & Comment	45–46	85t	8.3	A	Sun	7:00
Drew Pearson News & Comment	46–47	96t	8.1	A	Sun	6:00
Drew Pearson News & Comment	47–48	82t	11.9	A	Sun	6:00
Drew Pearson News & Comment	48–49	70t	9.9	A	Sun	6:00
Drew Pearson News & Comment	49–50	81	7.4	A	Sun	6:00
Drew Pearson News & Comment	50–51	67t	6.6	A	Sun	6:00
Drew Pearson News & Comment	51–52	55t	5.6	A	Sun	6:00
Drew Pearson News & Comment	52–53	59t	4.3	A	Sun	6:00
Duffy's Tavern (Ed Gardner)	40–41	104t	6.5	C	Sat	8:30
Duffy's Tavern (Ed Gardner)	41–42	88t	7.8	C	Tue	9:00
Duffy's Tavern (Ed Gardner)	42–43	62t	9.7	B	Tue	8:30
Duffy's Tavern (Ed Gardner)	43–44	45t	11.5	B	Tue	8:30
Duffy's Tavern (Ed Gardner)	44–45	30	13.5	N	Fri	8:30
Duffy's Tavern (Ed Gardner)	45–46	35	12.7	N	Fri	8:30
Duffy's Tavern (Ed Gardner)	46–47	14	16.9	N	Wed	9:00
Duffy's Tavern (Ed Gardner)	47–48	15t	20.0	N	Wed	9:00
Duffy's Tavern (Ed Gardner)	48–49	11	16.7	N	Wed	9:00
Duffy's Tavern (Ed Gardner)	49–50	69	8.0	N	Thu	9:30
Duffy's Tavern (Ed Gardner)	50–51	71	6.4	N	Fri	9:30
Dunninger the Mentalist	43–44	149	3.9	B	Wed	9:00
Dunninger the Mentalist	44–45	167	3.3	B	Wed	9:00
DW Griffith Hollywood News	32–33	79	5.5	B	Su,W	10:00
Earl Godwin Watch the World Go by News	42–43	121t	5.1	B	Su–Sa	8:00
Earl Godwin Watch the World Go by News	43–44	133t	4.6	B	M–F	8:00
Earl Godwin Watch the World Go by News	44–45	153t	4.2	B	M–F	8:00
Earl Godwin News & Comment	44–45	151t	4.3	B	Thu	8:00
Earl Godwin News & Comment	45–46	173t	3.0	A	Thu	8:15

6–11 P.M., Sept through June Programs Rated 13 Weeks or More	Season	Rank	Rtg	Net	Day	Time
Earl Wilson on Broadway	44–45	192t	2.0	M	Sun	10:00
Early American Dance Music	43–44	161t	3.1	B	Sat	8:00
Early American Dance Music	44–45	153t	4.2	B	Sat	8:00
Easy Aces (Goodman & Jane Ace)	32–33	52	9.1	C	T,T,Sa	10:15
Easy Aces (Goodman & Jane Ace)	34–35	110	4.6	N	MTuW	7:30
Easy Aces (Goodman & Jane Ace)	35–36	99t	4.4	B	TWT	7:00
Easy Aces (Goodman & Jane Ace)	36–37	73t	5.3	B	TWT	7:00
Easy Aces (Goodman & Jane Ace)	37–38	73t	6.2	B	TWT	7:00
Easy Aces (Goodman & Jane Ace)	38–39	80t	6.5	B	TWT	7:00
Easy Aces (Goodman & Jane Ace)	39–40	90t	7.0	B	TWT	7:00
Easy Aces (Goodman & Jane Ace)	40–41	109t	6.3	B	TWT	7:00
Easy Aces (Goodman & Jane Ace)	41–42	115t	5.6	B	TWT	7:00
Easy Aces (Goodman & Jane Ace)	42–43	110t	6.1	C	WThF	7:30
Easy Aces (Goodman & Jane Ace)	43–44	119t	5.2	C	Wed	7:30
Easy Aces (Goodman & Jane Ace)	44–45	136t	5.2	C	Wed	7:30
Easy Aces aka Mr Ace & Jane (Goodman & Jane Ace)	48–49	45	12.2	C	Fri	8:30
Ed Sullivan Entertains	43–44	119t	5.2	C	Mon	7:15
Ed Sullivan's Broadway	45–46	191t	1.7	A	Tue	9:00
Ed Wynn Texaco Fire Chief	32–33	2	40.5	N	Tue	9:30
Ed Wynn Texaco Fire Chief	33–34	5	32.3	N	Tue	9:30
Ed Wynn Texaco Fire Chief	34–35	9t	27.1	N	Tue	9:30
Ed Wynn's Gulliver	35–36	49	7.8	C	Thu	9:30
Ed Wynn Show	36–37	38t	8.4	B	Sat	8:00
Ed Wynn Show	44–45	159t	3.7	B	Mon	9:00
Eddie Bracken Show	44–45	36	12.9	N	Sun	8:30
Eddie Bracken Show	46–47	83t	8.8	C	Sun	9:30
Eddie Cantor Show	32–33	1	55.7	N	Sun	8:00
Eddie Cantor Show	33–34	1	53.7	N	Sun	8:00
Eddie Cantor Show	34–35	1	41.0	C	Sun	8:00
Eddie Cantor Show	35–36	13t	14.9	C	Sun	7:00
Eddie Cantor Show	36–37	2	23.0	C	Sun	8:30
Eddie Cantor Show	37–38	5	21.6	C	Wed	8:30
Eddie Cantor Show	38–39	6t	17.3	C	Mon	7:30
Eddie Cantor Time to Smile	40–41	17	15.0	N	Wed	9:00
Eddie Cantor Time to Smile	41–42	10	18.7	N	Wed	9:00
Eddie Cantor Time to Smile	42–43	16	19.0	N	Wed	9:00
Eddie Cantor Time to Smile	43–44	19	16.8	N	Wed	9:00
Eddie Cantor Show	44–45	12	17.9	N	Wed	9:00
Eddie Cantor Show	45–46	12	17.1	N	Wed	9:00
Eddie Cantor Show	46–47	19	14.4	N	Thu	10:30
Eddie Cantor Show	47–48	58t	14.0	N	Thu	10:30
Eddie Cantor Show	48–49	52t	11.7	N	Fri	9:00
Eddie Cantor Show (Take It or Leave It)	49–50	41	10.9	N	Sun	10:00
Eddie Cantor's Show Business Old & New	51–52	46t	6.2	N	Tue	10:00
Eddie Dooley Football Dope	32–33	74t	6.1	C	Sat	6:30
Eddie Dooley Sports	34–35	111t	4.4	C	Sat	6:30
Eddie Dowling Elgin Revue	35–36	82t	5.6	N	Tue	10:00
Eddy Duchin Orch	33–34	76	7.2	B	T,T,Sa	9:30
Eddy Duchin Orch	38–39	76t	6.9	N	Mon	9:30
Edgar A Guest Musical Memories	32–33	74t	6.1	B	Tue	9:00
Edgar A Guest Musical Memories	33–34	66t	8.1	B	Tue	9:00
Edgar A Guest Musical Memories	34–35	83	8.0	B	Tue	8:30
Edgar A Guest Welcome Valley	35–36	64t	6.3	B	Tue	8:30
Edgar A Guest Welcome Valley	36–37	93t	4.0	B	Tue	8:30
Edgar A Guest It Can Be Done	37–38	86t	4.2	B	Tue	8:30
Edgar A Guest It Can Be Done	38–39	96	3.4	C	Wed	10:00
Edgar Bergen & Charlie McCarthy	37–38	1	32.1	N	Sun	8:00
Edgar Bergen & Charlie McCarthy	38–39	1	32.2	N	Sun	8:00
Edgar Bergen & Charlie McCarthy	39–40	2	30.7	N	Sun	8:00
Edgar Bergen & Charlie McCarthy	40–41	3	27.3	N	Sun	8:00
Edgar Bergen & Charlie McCarthy	41–42	3	28.0	N	Sun	8:00
Edgar Bergen & Charlie McCarthy	42–43	4	30.1	N	Sun	8:00
Edgar Bergen & Charlie McCarthy	43–44	4	27.3	N	Sun	8:00
Edgar Bergen & Charlie McCarthy	44–45	6	22.0	N	Sun	8:00
Edgar Bergen & Charlie McCarthy	45–46	4	22.4	N	Sun	8:00
Edgar Bergen & Charlie McCarthy	46–47	5	22.8	N	Sun	8:00
Edgar Bergen & Charlie McCarthy	47–48	4	22.7	N	Sun	8:00
Edgar Bergen & Charlie McCarthy	48–49	5t	20.1	N	Sun	8:00
Edgar Bergen & Charlie McCarthy	49–50	7	16.0	C	Sun	8:00

6–11 P.M., Sept through June Programs
Rated 13 Weeks or More

	Season	Rank	Rtg	Net	Day	Time
Edgar Bergen & Charlie McCarthy	50–51	3	14.7	C	Sun	8:00
Edgar Bergen & Charlie McCarthy	51–52	4	11.2	C	Sun	8:00
Edgar Bergen & Charlie McCarthy	52–53	3	10.6	C	Sun	8:00
Edward R Murrow News & Comment	42–43	98	7.1	C	Sun	6:00
Edward R Murrow News & Comment	47–48	90t	11.6	C	M-F	7:45
Edward R Murrow News & Comment	48–49	84t	9.0	C	M-F	7:45
Edward R Murrow News & Comment	49–50	79t	7.5	C	M-F	7:45
Edward R Murrow News & Comment	50–51	80t	5.6	C	M-F	7:45
Edward R Murrow News & Comment	51–52	65t	5.3	C	M-F	7:45
Edward R Murrow News & Comment	52–53	82t	2.9	C	M-F	7:45
Edwin C Hill Human Side of the News	33–34	44	11.5	C	MWF	8:15
Edwin C Hill Human Side of the News	34–35	48t	13.5	C	MWF	8:15
Edwin C Hill Human Side of the News	35–36	89t	5.3	N	T,T,Sa	7:15
Edwin C Hill Human Side of the News	36–37	70	5.5	B	Sun	9:45
Edwin C Hill Human Side of the News	38–39	48t	9.1	N	M-W	7:15
Edwin C Hill Human Side of the News	42–43	119	5.3	C	Tue	6:15
Edwin C Hill Human Side of the News	43–44	127t	4.9	C	Tue	6:15
Edwin C Hill Human Side of the News	44–45	139t	5.0	C	Tue	6:15
Edwin C Hill Human Side of the News	45–46	135t	5.3	C	Tue	6:15
Edwin C Hill Human Side of the News	48–49	136t	3.2	A	M-F	7:00
Edwin C Hill Human Side of the News	49–50	118	3.2	A	M-F	7:00
Edwin C Hill Human Side of the News	50–51	121	1.7	A	M-F	7:00
Edwin C Hill Human Side of the News	52–53	108	0.8	A	M-F	10:30
Eleanor Roosevelt Commentary	36–37	71t	5.4	B	Wed	7:15
Eleanor Roosevelt Commentary	41–42	122	5.0	B	Sun	6:45
Elmer Davis News & Comment	46–47	154	2.9	A	M-F	7:15
Elsa Maxwell Party Line	41–42	125	4.6	B	Fri	10:00
Enna Jettick Melodies	32–33	88	4.3	B	Mon	6:30
Eno Crime Club (Edward Reese)	32–33	27t	15.2	B	Tu,W	8:00
Eno Crime Clues (Edward Reese)	33–34	31	15.4	B	Tue	8:00
Eno Crime Clues (Clyde North)	34–35	38t	14.9	B	Tue	8:00
Eno Crime Clues (Clyde North)	35–36	42t	8.7	B	Tue	8:00
Eric Sevareid News & Comment	46–47	162t	2.4	C	M-F	6:00
Eric Sevareid News & Comment	47–48	155	2.1	C	M-F	6:00
Eric Sevareid News & Comment	48–49	139t	3.0	C	M-F	6:00
Eric Sevareid News & Comment	49–50	117	3.4	C	M-F	6:00
Ernest Hutcheson Concerts	32–33	80	5.1	C	Sun	10:30
Erwin Canham Monitor Views the News	45–46	190	2.0	A	Sat	6:15
Erwin Canham Monitor Views the News	46–47	165	2.2	A	Thu	8:15
Erwin Canham Monitor Views the News	47–48	146t	3.5	A	Tue	8:15
Erwin Canham Monitor Views the News	48–49	145	2.2	A	Tue	9:30
Erwin Canham Monitor Views the News	49–50	132t	1.4	A	Tue	9:30
Erwin Canham Monitor Views the News	50–51	126	0.8	A	Tue	9:30
Eve Arden & Jack Haley Sealtest Village Store	45–46	13	16.9	N	Thu	9:30
Eve Arden & Jack Haley Sealtest Village Store	46–47	36t	12.3	N	Thu	9:30
Eve Arden & Jack Carson Sealtest Village Store	47–48	56	14.5	N	Thu	9:30
Evening in Paris (Odette Myrtil)	33–34	101t	3.7	C	Sun	8:00
Everybody Wins (Phil Baker)	47–48	93	11.5	C	Fri	10:00
Exploring the Unknown (Charles Irving)	45–46	179	2.8	M	Sun	9:00
Exploring the Unknown (Charles Irving)	46–47	145t	4.0	M	Sun	9:00
Fame & Fortune (Tommy Dorsey Orch)	40–41	119	5.4	B	Thu	8:30
Family Hour of Stars (Gladys Swarthout)	47–48	127t	8.0	C	Sun	6:00
Family Hour of Stars (Truman Bradley)	48–49	107t	7.0	C	Sun	6:00
Family Hour of Stars (Truman Bradley)	49–50	105t	5.3	C	Sun	6:00
Famous Jury Trials (Maurice Franklin)	40–41	98t	6.9	B	Mon	10:00
Famous Jury Trials (Maurice Franklin)	41–42	101t	6.5	B	Tue	9:00
Famous Jury Trials (Maurice Franklin)	42–43	87	8.6	B	Tue	9:00
Famous Jury Trials (Maurice Franklin)	43–44	97t	7.4	B	Tue	9:00
Famous Jury Trials (Maurice Franklin)	44–45	118t	6.6	B	Fri	9:00
Famous Jury Trials (Maurice Franklin)	45–46	90t	8.1	A	Fri	9:00
Famous Jury Trials (Maurice Franklin)	47–48	86t	11.7	A	Sat	7:30
Fanny Brice & George Olsen Orch	32–33	34	13.6	N	Wed	8:00
Fanny Brice Ziegfeld Follies	35–36	27t	10.9	C	Sat	8:00
Fanny Brice Revue de Paree aka Folies de Paris	36–37	84t	4.4	B	Wed	8:00
Fanny Brice & Frank Morgan (Good News of 1938)	37–38	11	16.6	N	Thu	9:00
Fanny Brice & Frank Morgan (Good News of 1939)	38–39	6t	17.3	N	Thu	9:00
Fanny Brice (Good News of 1940)	39–40	12	16.9	N	Thu	9:00
Fanny Brice & Frank Morgan Show	40–41	9	18.0	N	Thu	8:00
Fanny Brice & Frank Morgan Show	41–42	9	23.8	N	Thu	8:00

6–11 P.M., Sept through June Programs
Rated 13 Weeks or More

	Season	Rank	Rtg	Net	Day	Time
Fanny Brice & Frank Morgan Show	42–43	8	23.2	N	Thu	8:00
Fanny Brice & Frank Morgan Show	43–44	13	19.9	N	Thu	8:00
Fanny Brice Baby Snooks Show	44–45	79t	9.6	C	Sun	6:30
Fanny Brice Baby Snooks Show	45–46	49	11.2	C	Sun	6:30
Fanny Brice Baby Snooks Show	46–47	26t	13.2	C	Fri	8:00
Fanny Brice Baby Snooks Show	47–48	28t	17.3	C	Fri	8:00
Fanny Brice Baby Snooks Show	49–50	16t	13.3	N	Tue	8:30
Fanny Brice Baby Snooks Show	50–51	29t	9.7	N	Tue	8:30
The Fat Man (J Scott Smart)	46–47	55t	10.4	A	Fri	8:00
The Fat Man (J Scott Smart)	47–48	42t	15.7	A	Fri	8:00
The Fat Man (J Scott Smart)	48–49	30t	13.7	A	Fri	8:00
The Fat Man (J Scott Smart)	49–50	32t	11.9	A	Fri	8:00
The Fat Man (J Scott Smart)	50–51	17t	10.5	A	Fri	8:00
Father Knows Best (Robert Young)	49–50	53t	9.4	N	Thu	8:30
Father Knows Best (Robert Young)	50–51	34	9.5	N	Thu	8:30
Father Knows Best (Robert Young)	51–52	18t	8.4	N	Thu	8:00
Father Knows Best (Robert Young)	52–53	25t	6.0	N	Thu	8:30
FBI in Peace & War (Martin Blaine & Donald Briggs)	44–45	65t	10.2	C	Sat	8:30
FBI in Peace & War (Martin Blaine & Donald Briggs)	45–46	47t	11.3	C	Thu	8:30
FBI in Peace & War (Martin Blaine & Donald Briggs)	46–47	31	13.0	C	Thu	8:30
FBI in Peace & War (Martin Blaine & Donald Briggs)	47–48	42t	15.7	C	Thu	8:00
FBI in Peace & War (Martin Blaine & Donald Briggs)	48–49	22t	14.6	C	Thu	8:00
FBI in Peace & War (Martin Blaine & Donald Briggs)	49–50	26t	12.3	C	Thu	8:00
FBI in Peace & War (Martin Blaine & Donald Briggs)	50–51	22t	10.2	C	Thu	8:00
FBI in Peace & War (Martin Blaine & Donald Briggs)	51–52	22t	7.9	C	Thu	8:00
FBI in Peace & War (Martin Blaine & Donald Briggs)	52–53	25t	6.0	C	Wed	8:00
Fibber McGee & Molly (Jim & Marian Jordan)	35–36	62	6.6	B	Mon	8:00
Fibber McGee & Molly (Jim & Marian Jordan)	36–37	21	11.5	N	Mon	9:00
Fibber McGee & Molly (Jim & Marian Jordan)	37–38	20	13.4	N	Tue	9:30
Fibber McGee & Molly (Jim & Marian Jordan)	38–39	5	17.6	N	Tue	9:30
Fibber McGee & Molly (Jim & Marian Jordan)	39–40	3	24.8	N	Tue	9:30
Fibber McGee & Molly (Jim & Marian Jordan)	40–41	2	27.6	N	Tue	9:30
Fibber McGee & Molly (Jim & Marian Jordan)	41–42	1	31.7	N	Tue	9:30
Fibber McGee & Molly (Jim & Marian Jordan)	42–43	3	30.7	N	Tue	9:30
Fibber McGee & Molly (Jim & Marian Jordan)	43–44	2	31.3	N	Tue	9:30
Fibber McGee & Molly (Jim & Marian Jordan)	44–45	2	28.3	N	Tue	9:30
Fibber McGee & Molly (Jim & Marian Jordan)	45–46	2	27.1	N	Tue	9:30
Fibber McGee & Molly (Jim & Marian Jordan)	46–47	2	26.4	N	Tue	9:30
Fibber McGee & Molly (Jim & Marian Jordan)	47–48	2	26.1	N	Tue	9:30
Fibber McGee & Molly (Jim & Marian Jordan)	48–49	2	23.5	N	Tue	9:30
Fibber McGee & Molly (Jim & Marian Jordan)	49–50	4	17.7	N	Tue	9:30
Fibber McGee & Molly (Jim & Marian Jordan)	50–51	13t	11.1	N	Tue	9:30
Fibber McGee & Molly (Jim & Marian Jordan)	51–52	8	9.3	N	Tue	9:30
Fibber McGee & Molly (Jim & Marian Jordan)	52–53	22t	6.3	N	Tue	9:30
Fireside Recitals	34–35	134	1.6	N	Sun	7:30
Fireside Recitals	35–36	127t	1.9	N	Sun	7:30
Fireside Recitals	36–37	106	2.7	N	Sun	7:30
First Line of Defense	41–42	124	4.7	C	Thu	10:15
First Line of Defense	42–43	116t	5.4	C	Thu	10:00
First Line of Defense	43–44	115t	5.4	C	Thu	10:00
First Line of Defense	44–45	139t	5.0	C	Thu	10:00
First Line of Defense	45–46	158	4.0	C	Thu	10:00
First Nighter (Don Ameche & June Meredith)	32–33	21	17.5	B	Fri	9:00
First Nighter (Don Ameche & June Meredith)	33–34	14	23.7	N	Fri	10:00
First Nighter (Don Ameche & June Meredith)	34–35	14	22.7	N	Fri	10:00
First Nighter (Don Ameche & Betty Lou Gerson)	35–36	12	15.1	N	Fri	10:00
First Nighter (Les Tremayne & Barbara Luddy)	36–37	14	13.7	C	Fri	9:30
First Nighter (Les Tremayne & Barbara Luddy)	37–38	14	15.1	N	Fri	10:00
First Nighter (Les Tremayne & Barbara Luddy)	38–39	31	11.5	C	Fri	8:00
First Nighter (Les Tremayne & Barbara Luddy)	39–40	16	15.4	C	Fri	9:30
First Nighter (Les Tremayne & Barbara Luddy)	40–41	30t	12.8	C	Tue	8:30
First Nighter (Les Tremayne & Barbara Luddy)	41–42	35t	12.9	C	Fri	9:30
First Nighter (Les Tremayne & Barbara Luddy)	42–43	70t	9.5	M	Sun	6:00
First Nighter (Olan Soule & Barbara Luddy)	43–44	110	5.9	M	Wed	9:30
First Nighter (Olan Soule & Barbara Luddy)	45–46	67t	9.6	C	Sat	7:30
First Nighter (Olan Soule & Barbara Luddy)	47–48	107	10.2	C	Thu	10:30
First Nighter (Olan Soule & Barbara Luddy)	48–49	52t	11.7	C	Thu	10:30
First Nighter (Olan Soule & Barbara Luddy)	52–53	92t	2.4	N	Tue	10:35
Fishing & Hunting Club (Dave Newell & Jim Hurley)	45–46	185t	2.4	A	Wed	8:30

6–11 P.M., Sept through June Programs
Rated 13 Weeks or More

	Season	Rank	Rtg	Net	Day	Time
Fishing & Hunting Club (Dave Newell & Jim Hurley)	46–47	160t	2.5	M	Mon	10:00
Fishing & Hunting Club (Dave Newell & Jim Hurley)	47–48	152	2.6	M	Mon	10:00
Fishing & Hunting Club (Dave Newell & Jim Hurley)	48–49	147	1.8	M	Mon	9:30
Fishing & Hunting Club (Dave Newell & Jim Hurley)	49–50	130t	1.6	M	Thu	8:30
Fitch Bandwagon	38–39	27	12.6	N	Sun	7:30
Fitch Bandwagon	39–40	17	15.2	N	Sun	7:30
Fitch Bandwagon	40–41	19t	14.4	N	Sun	7:30
Fitch Bandwagon	41–42	17t	15.7	N	Sun	7:30
Fitch Bandwagon	42–43	10	16.1	N	Sun	7:30
Fitch Bandwagon	43–44	26	14.8	N	Sun	7:30
Fitch Bandwagon (Tom Reddy & Freddy Martin Orch)	43–44	165t	3.0	B	Wed	9:00
Fitch Bandwagon (Dick Powell)	44–45	34t	13.0	N	Sun	7:30
Fitch Bandwagon (Cass Daley)	45–46	18	14.8	N	Sun	7:30
Floyd Gibbons News	34–35	89	7.5	B	Thu	7:30
Floyd Gibbons Show	36–37	57t	6.7	C	Sat	9:00
Floyd Gibbons' Your True Adventures	36–37	52t	6.9	C	Thu	10:00
Flying Red Horse Tavern (Beatrice Lillie)	35–36	76t	5.7	C	Fri	8:00
Folies de Paree (Willie & Eugene Howard)	35–36	124	2.1	B	Wed	8:00
Folies de Paree (Willie & Eugene Howard)	36–37	84t	4.4	B	Wed	8:00
Follies of 1946/Philip Morris Frolics	45–46	90t	8.1	N	Tue	8:00
Football Review	36–37	98	3.6	C	Sat	8:30
For Men Only (George Jessel)	38–39	74t	7.0	N	Tue	8:30
Ford Show (Lawrence Brooks)	45–46	170t	3.2	C	Tue	10:00
Ford Sunday Evening Hour (Detroit Symphony)	34–35	41	14.7	C	Sun	9:00
Ford Sunday Evening Hour (Detroit Symphony)	35–36	38t	9.2	C	Sun	9:00
Ford Sunday Evening Hour (Detroit Symphony)	36–37	32t	9.2	C	Sun	9:00
Ford Sunday Evening Hour (Detroit Symphony)	37–38	51t	8.4	C	Sun	9:00
Ford Sunday Evening Hour (Detroit Symphony)	38–39	66t	7.6	C	Sun	9:00
Ford Sunday Evening Hour (Detroit Symphony)	39–40	47t	10.8	C	Sun	9:00
Ford Sunday Evening Hour (Detroit Symphony)	40–41	63t	9.3	C	Sun	9:00
Ford Sunday Evening Hour (Detroit Symphony)	41–42	69t	8.9	C	Sun	9:00
Ford Sunday Evening Hour (Detroit Symphony)	45–46	168t	3.3	A	Sun	8:00
Ford Sunday Evening Hour (Detroit Symphony)	46–47	166	2.1	A	Sun	8:00
Ford Sunday Evening Hour (Detroit Symphony)	47–48	114t	9.5	A	Sun	8:00
Ford Theater (Howard Lindsay)	48–49	58	11.3	C	Fri	9:00
Forum of Liberty (Edwin C Hill)	34–35	96t	6.6	C	Thu	8:30
Forty-Five Minutes in Hollywood	33–34	57t	9.3	C	Sun	10:30
Frank Edwards News & Comment	49–50	126t	2.0	M	M-F	10:00
Frank Edwards News & Comment	50–51	120	1.8	M	M-F	10:00
Frank Edwards News & Comment	51–52	105	1.3	M	M-F	10:00
Frank Edwards News & Comment	52–53	105t	1.2	M	M-F	10:00
Frank Fay Show	41–42	32	13.3	N	Thu	10:30
Frank Morgan & Fanny Brice (Good News of 1938)	37–38	11	16.6	N	Thu	9:00
Frank Morgan & Fanny Brice (Good News of 1939)	38–39	6t	17.3	N	Thu	9:00
Frank Morgan & Fanny Brice Show	40–41	9	18.0	N	Thu	8:00
Frank Morgan & Fanny Brice Show	41–42	9	23.8	N	Thu	8:00
Frank Morgan & Fanny Brice Show	42–43	8	23.2	N	Thu	8:00
Frank Morgan & Fanny Brice Show	43–44	13	19.9	N	Thu	8:00
Frank Morgan Show	44–45	26	13.7	N	Thu	8:00
Frank Morgan's Kraft Music Hall	45–46	15	16.7	N	Thu	9:00
Frank Morgan as the Fabulous Doctor Tweedy	46–47	62t	9.8	N	Wed	10:00
Frank Parker Sings	41–42	115t	5.6	C	MWF	6:30
Frank Sinatra Show	43–44	40	12.2	C	Wed	9:00
Frank Sinatra Show	44–45	52t	11.0	C	Wed	9:00
Frank Sinatra Show	45–46	58t	10.3	C	Wed	9:00
Frank Sinatra Show	46–47	60t	9.9	C	Wed	9:00
Frank Sinatra Light Up Time	49–50	96t	5.9	N	M-F	7:00
Frank Singiser News & Comment	43–44	156t	3.3	M	T,T,Sa	8:00
Frank Singiser News & Comment	44–45	145	4.7	M	T,T,Sa	8:00
Frank Singiser News & Comment	45–46	162t	3.6	M	T,T,Sa	8:00
Frazier Hunt News & Comment	41–42	118	5.5	C	T,T,Sa	6:00
Frazier Hunt News & Comment	42–43	110t	6.1	C	T,T,Sa	6:00
Fred Allen's Linit Bath Club Revue	32–33	39	11.9	C	Sun	9:00
Fred Allen's Hour of Smiles	33–34	28	16.0	N	Wed	9:30
Fred Allen's Town Hall Tonight	34–35	7	29.7	N	Wed	9:00
Fred Allen's Town Hall Tonight	35–36	5	20.0	N	Wed	9:00
Fred Allen's Town Hall Tonight	36–37	6	20.2	N	Wed	9:00
Fred Allen's Town Hall Tonight	37–38	6t	19.4	N	Wed	9:00
Fred Allen's Town Hall Tonight	38–39	14t	15.3	N	Wed	9:00

6–11 P.M., Sept through June Programs
Rated 13 Weeks or More

	Season	Rank	Rtg	Net	Day	Time
Fred Allen's Town Hall Tonight aka Fred Allen Show	39–40	14	16.3	N	Wed	9:00
Fred Allen's Texaco Star Theater	40–41	24	13.5	C	Wed	9:00
Fred Allen's Texaco Star Theater	41–42	25t	14.2	C	Sun	9:00
Fred Allen's Texaco Star Theater	42–43	19	17.0	C	Sun	9:30
Fred Allen's Texaco Star Theater	43–44	17	18.0	C	Sun	9:30
Fred Allen Show	45–46	8	21.1	N	Sun	8:30
Fred Allen Show	46–47	4	23.4	N	Sun	8:30
Fred Allen Show	47–48	6t	22.3	N	Sun	8:30
Fred Allen Show	48–49	42t	12.5	N	Sun	8:00
Fred Astaire Show	36–37	19	12.5	N	Tue	9:30
Fred Waring Show	32–33	25	16.0	C	Wed	9:00
Fred Waring Show	33–34	15	22.2	C	Thu	9:30
Fred Waring Show	33–34	46	11.2	C	Wed	10:00
Fred Waring Show	34–35	38t	14.9	C	Thu	9:30
Fred Waring Show	35–36	74t	5.8	B	Fri	9:30
Fred Waring Show	35–36	32t	10.3	C	Tue	9:30
Fred Waring Show	36–37	42	8.2	C	Tue	9:00
Fred Waring Show	36–37	87t	4.2	B	Fri	9:00
Fred Waring Show	38–39	43t	9.4	N	Sat	8:30
Fred Waring Chesterfield Supper Club	39–40	62t	10.1	N	M–F	7:00
Fred Waring Chesterfield Supper Club	40–41	65t	9.2	N	M–F	7:00
Fred Waring Chesterfield Supper Club	41–42	64	9.3	N	M–F	7:00
Fred Waring Chesterfield Supper Club	42–43	52t	10.4	N	M–F	7:00
Fred Waring Chesterfield Supper Club	43–44	67t	9.4	N	M–F	7:00
Fred Waring Show	44–45	157t	3.8	B	Thu	10:00
Fred Waring Show	48–49	101	7.6	N	Thu	10:30
Freedom of Opportunity	43–44	181	2.2	M	Fri	8:30
Freedom of Opportunity	44–45	185	2.6	M	Fri	8:30
Freedom of Opportunity	45–46	191t	1.7	M	Sun	10:00
Fresh Up Show (Bert Wheeler)	44–45	173t	3.0	M	Wed	8:30
Fresh Up Show (Bert Lahr)	45–46	159t	3.8	M	Wed	8:30
Friday Night Boxing (Don Dunphy)	44–45	173t	3.0	M	Fri	10:00
Friday Night Boxing (Don Dunphy)	45–46	146	4.6	A	Fri	10:00
Friday Night Boxing (Don Dunphy)	46–47	131t	5.6	A	Fri	10:00
Friday Night Boxing (Don Dunphy)	47–48	70t	13.1	A	Fri	10:00
Friday Night Boxing (Don Dunphy)	48–49	109t	6.9	A	Fri	10:00
Friday Night Boxing (Don Dunphy)	49–50	98t	5.8	A	Fri	10:00
Friday Night Boxing (Don Dunphy)	50–51	76t	5.9	A	Fri	10:00
Friday Night Boxing (Don Dunphy)	51–52	70	4.9	A	Fri	10:00
Friday Night Boxing (Don Dunphy)	52–53	62t	4.2	A	Fri	10:00
Friday on Broadway (Frank Parker)	43–44	132	4.7	C	Fri	7:30
Friday on Broadway (Frank Parker)	44–45	136t	5.2	C	Fri	7:30
Friendship Town	32–33	86t	4.4	B	Tue	9:30
Fu Manchu Mysteries (John Daly)	32–33	31	14.5	C	Mon	8:30
Fulton Lewis Jr News & Comment	40–41	128	3.4	M	M–F	7:00
Fulton Lewis Jr News & Comment	41–42	129t	4.2	M	M–F	7:00
Fulton Lewis Jr News & Comment	42–43	121t	5.1	M	M–F	7:00
Fulton Lewis Jr News & Comment	43–44	122t	5.1	M	M–F	7:00
Fulton Lewis Jr News & Comment	44–45	127	6.0	M	M–F	7:00
Fulton Lewis Jr News & Comment	45–46	139t	5.1	M	M–F	7:00
Fulton Lewis Jr News & Comment	45–46	149t	4.4	M	Sun	6:45
Fulton Lewis Jr News & Comment	46–47	131t	5.6	M	M–F	7:00
Fulton Lewis Jr News & Comment	47–48	149	3.4	M	M–F	7:00
Fulton Lewis Jr News & Comment	48–49	133	3.7	M	M–F	7:00
Fulton Lewis Jr News & Comment	49–50	122	2.7	M	M–F	7:00
Fulton Lewis Jr News & Comment	50–51	110t	2.6	M	M–F	7:00
Fulton Lewis Jr News & Comment	51–52	91	2.9	M	M–F	7:00
Fulton Lewis Jr News & Comment	52–53	86	2.7	M	M–F	7:00
Fulton Oursler Commentary	43–44	158t	8.7	M	M–F	8:15
Gabby Hayes Show	51–52	84t	4.0	M	Sun	6:00
Gabriel Heatter News & Comment	40–41	92t	7.4	M	M,W,F	9:00
Gabriel Heatter News & Comment	41–42	72t	8.8	M	M–F	9:00
Gabriel Heatter News & Comment	41–42	81t	8.2	M	Sun	8:45
Gabriel Heatter News & Comment	42–43	73t	9.4	M	M–F	9:00
Gabriel Heatter News & Comment	42–43	93t	7.6	M	Sun	8:45
Gabriel Heatter News & Comment	43–44	73t	9.2	M	M–F	9:00
Gabriel Heatter News & Comment	43–44	84	8.4	M	Sun	8:45
Gabriel Heatter News & Comment	44–45	48t	11.4	M	M–F	9:00
Gabriel Heatter News & Comment	44–45	74t	9.8	M	Sun	8:45

6–11 P.M., Sept through June Programs
Rated 13 Weeks or More

Program	Season	Rank	Rtg	Net	Day	Time
Gabriel Heatter News & Comment	45–46	117t	6.2	M	M-F	9:00
Gabriel Heatter News & Comment	45–46	139t	5.1	M	Sun	8:45
Gabriel Heatter News & Comment	46–47	126t	5.9	M	M-F	9:00
Gabriel Heatter News & Comment	47–48	133	6.8	M	M-F	9:00
Gabriel Heatter News & Comment	48–49	123	4.8	M	M-F	9:00
Gabriel Heatter News & Comment	49–50	109	4.2	M	M-Th	7:30
Gabriel Heatter News & Comment	50–51	109	2.7	M	Sun	9:30
Gabriel Heatter News & Comment	50–51	93t	4.4	M	M-F	7:30
Gabriel Heatter News & Comment	51–52	83	4.1	M	M-F	7:30
Gabriel Heatter News & Comment	52–53	67t	4.0	M	M-F	7:30
Gabriel Heatter's Brighter Tomorrow	46–47	164	2.3	M	Sun	10:00
Gabriel Heatter's Brighter Tomorrow	47–48	130t	7.1	M	Sun	7:30
Gabriel Heatter's Behind the Front Page	47–48	132	7.0	M	Sun	7:30
Gabriel Heatter's Behind the Front Page	48–49	81	9.3	M	Sun	7:30
Gangbusters (Phillips H Lord)	35–36	37	9.3	C	Wed	10:00
Gangbusters (Phillips H Lord)	36–37	20	12.0	C	Wed	10:00
Gangbusters (Col H Norman Schwarzkopf)	37–38	16t	14.7	C	Wed	10:00
Gangbusters (Col H Norman Schwarzkopf)	38–39	25	12.8	C	Wed	8:00
Gangbusters (Col H Norman Schwarzkopf)	39–40	19	14.7	C	Sat	8:00
Gangbusters (Col H Norman Schwarzkopf)	40–41	35t	12.0	B	Fri	9:00
Gangbusters (Col H Norman Schwarzkopf)	41–42	48	10.6	B	Fri	9:00
Gangbusters (Col H Norman Schwarzkopf)	42–43	66t	9.6	B	Fri	9:00
Gangbusters (Col H Norman Schwarzkopf)	43–44	59t	10.0	B	Fri	9:00
Gangbusters (Col H Norman Schwarzkopf)	44–45	68t	10.1	B	Fri	9:00
Gangbusters (Lewis J Valentine)	45–46	85t	8.3	A	Sat	9:00
Gangbusters	46–47	46	11.2	A	Sat	9:00
Gangbusters	47–48	82t	11.9	A	Sat	9:00
Gangbusters	48–49	75t	9.6	C	Sat	9:00
Gangbusters	49–50	36	11.5	C	Sat	9:00
Gangbusters	50–51	25	10.1	C	Sat	9:00
Gangbusters	51–52	20	8.2	C	Sat	9:00
Gangbusters	52–53	9t	7.4	C	Sat	9:00
Gateway to Hollywood (Jesse Lasky)	39–40	54t	10.5	C	Sun	6:30
Gay Nineties Revue (Joe Howard)	40–41	33	12.7	C	Mon	8:30
Gay Nineties Revue (Joe Howard)	41–42	30	13.5	C	Mon	8:30
Gay Nineties Revue (Joe Howard)	42–43	37	12.8	C	Mon	8:30
Gay Nineties Revue (Joe Howard)	43–44	49	11.1	C	Mon	8:30
Gems of Melody	33–34	122	1.6	N	Sun	6:45
Gems of Melody	34–35	119	3.4	B	Thu	7:15
Gene & Glenn (Gene Carroll & Glenn Rowell)	33–34	77t	6.8	N	M-F	7:15
Gene Autry's Melody Ranch	39–40	68	9.6	C	Sun	6:30
Gene Autry's Melody Ranch	40–41	57t	9.5	C	Sun	6:30
Gene Autry's Melody Ranch	41–42	94	7.5	C	Sun	6:30
Sergeant Gene Autry	42–43	93t	7.6	C	Sun	6:30
Gene Autry's Melody Ranch	46–47	128t	5.7	C	Sun	7:00
Gene Autry's Melody Ranch	47–48	70t	13.1	C	Sun	7:00
Gene Autry's Melody Ranch	48–49	82t	9.1	C	Sat	8:00
Gene Autry's Melody Ranch	49–50	53t	9.4	C	Sat	8:00
Gene Autry's Melody Ranch	50–51	22t	10.2	C	Sat	8:00
Gene Autry's Melody Ranch	51–52	22t	7.9	C	Sat	8:00
Gene Autry's Melody Ranch	52–53	16t	6.6	C	Sat	8:00
General Electric Circle	32–33	101t	2.3	N	MWF	6:30
General Hugh Johnson Commentary	37–38	92	3.0	M	M-Th	10:00
General Motors Concert (Erno Rapee Orch)	34–35	68	10.5	B	Sun	8:00
General Motors Concert (Erno Rapee Orch)	35–36	23	11.4	N	Sun	10:00
General Motors Concert (Erno Rapee Orch)	36–37	38t	8.4	B	Sun	8:00
George M Cohan Gulf Headliners	33–34	21	19.5	B	Sun	9:00
George Jessel Show	39–40	52	10.6	N	Thu	8:00
George McCall Hollywood News	37–38	86t	4.2	C	Tu,Th	7:15
Gertrude Nielsen Ex Lax Big Show	33–34	57t	9.3	C	Mon	9:30
Gertrude Lawrence Show	43–44	141t	4.3	B	Thu	10:30
Get More Out of Life	49–50	126t	2.0	A	Sun	10:15
Gibson Family (Adele Ronson & Jack Clemens)	34–35	36	15.1	N	Sun	10:00
Gillette Community Sing (Milton Berle)	36–37	54t	6.8	C	Sun	10:00
Ginny Simms Show aka Johnny Presents	42–43	30	14.2	N	Tue	8:00
Ginny Simms Show aka Johnny Presents	43–44	35t	13.0	N	Tue	8:00
Ginny Simms Show aka Johnny Presents	44–45	47	11.5	N	Tue	8:00
Ginny Simms Show	45–46	78t	8.7	C	Fri	7:30
Ginny Simms Show	46–47	106t	7.4	C	Fri	9:00

6–11 P.M., Sept through June Programs
Rated 13 Weeks or More

	Season	Rank	Rtg	Net	Day	Time
Glen Gray Orch Camel Caravan	33–34	68	8.0	C	Tu,Th	10:00
Glen Gray Orch Camel Caravan	34–35	74t	9.4	C	Tu,Th	10&9
Glen Gray Orch Camel Caravan	35–36	70t	5.9	C	Tu,Th	9:00
Glen Gray Orch	36–37	67	6.0	C	Tue	9:30
Glenn Miller Orch	39–40	96	6.6	C	TWT	10:00
Glenn Miller Orch	40–41	101t	6.7	C	TWT	10:00
Glenn Miller Orch	41–42	97t	6.6	C	WThF	10:00
The Goldbergs (Gertrude Berg)	32–33	22t	17.2	N	M-F	7:45
The Goldbergs (Gertrude Berg)	33–34	38	13.6	N	M-F	7:45
The Goldbergs (Gertrude Berg)	49–50	94t	6.1	C	Fri	8:00
Good News of 1938 (Robert Taylor, Fanny Brice, Frank Morgan)	37–38	11	16.6	N	Thu	9:00
Good News of 1939 (Various Hosts, Fanny Brice, Frank Morgan)	38–39	6t	17.3	N	Thu	9:00
Good News of 1940 (Dick Powell, Fanny Brice)	39–40	12	16.9	N	Thu	9:00
Goodwill Hour (John J Anthony)	38–39	58	8.2	M	Sun	10:00
Goodwill Hour (John J Anthony)	39–40	76t	8.8	M	Sun	10:00
Goodwill Hour (John J Anthony)	40–41	79t	8.1	B	Sun	10:00
Goodwill Hour (John J Anthony)	41–42	88t	7.8	B	Sun	10:00
Goodwill Hour (John J Anthony)	42–43	92	7.8	B	Sun	10:00
Goodwill Hour (John J Anthony)	43–44	119t	5.2	M	Sun	10:15
Goodwill Hour (John J Anthony)	44–45	114t	6.9	M	Sun	10:15
Goodwill Hour (John J Anthony)	51–52	95t	2.5	M	Sun	9:30
Goodwill Hour (John J Anthony)	52–53	95t	2.3	M	Sun	9:30
Goose Creek Parson	36–37	107t	2.5	C	MWF	7:30
Gracie Fields Show	42–43	133	3.7	B	M-F	10:15
Gracie Fields Victory Show	43–44	122t	5.1	M	M-F	9:15
Gracie Fields Show	44–45	134t	5.3	B	Tue	9:00
Grand Central Station	37–38	64t	7.1	B	Fri	8:00
Grand Central Station	38–39	48t	9.1	C	Fri	10:00
Grand Central Station	39–40	37	11.9	C	Fri	10:00
Grand Central Station	40–41	60t	9.4	B	Tue	9:00
Grand Central Station	41–42	56	9.9	N	Fri	7:30
Grand Hotel (Don Ameche & Anne Seymour)	34–35	60	12.3	B	Sun	6:30
Grand Hotel (Jim Ameche & Betty Lou Gerson)	35–36	26	11.0	B	Mon	8:30
Grand Hotel (Jim Ameche & Betty Lou Gerson)	37–38	54t	8.3	B	Mon	8:30
Grand Marquee (Jim Ameche & Beryl Vaughn)	46–47	106t	7.4	N	Thu	7:30
Grand Ole Opry	41–42	53t	10.0	N	Sat	10:30
Grand Ole Opry	42–43	66t	9.6	N	Sat	10:30
Grand Ole Opry	43–44	42	11.8	N	Sat	10:30
Grand Ole Opry	44–45	52t	11.0	N	Sat	10:30
Grand Ole Opry	45–46	58t	10.3	N	Sat	10:30
Grand Ole Opry	46–47	68t	9.6	N	Sat	10:30
Grand Ole Opry	47–48	59t	14.0	N	Sat	10:30
Grand Ole Opry	48–49	61t	11.0	N	Sat	10:30
Grand Ole Opry	49–50	64t	8.5	N	Sat	10:30
Grand Ole Opry	50–51	53	8.0	N	Sat	10:30
Grand Ole Opry	51–52	60t	5.4	N	Sat	10:30
Grand Ole Opry	52–53	65t	4.1	N	Sat	9:30
Great Gildersleeve (Hal Peary)	41–42	50t	10.3	N	Sun	6:30
Great Gildersleeve (Hal Peary)	42–43	24t	15.1	N	Sun	6:30
Great Gildersleeve (Hal Peary)	43–44	21	16.3	N	Sun	6:30
Great Gildersleeve (Hal Peary)	44–45	25	13.9	N	Sun	6:30
Great Gildersleeve (Hal Peary)	45–46	18t	14.6	N	Sun	6:30
Great Gildersleeve (Hal Peary)	46–47	15t	15.2	N	Wed	8:30
Great Gildersleeve (Hal Peary)	47–48	19t	19.1	N	Wed	8:30
Great Gildersleeve (Hal Peary)	48–49	33	13.4	N	Wed	8:30
Great Gildersleeve (Hal Peary)	49–50	24t	12.5	N	Wed	8:30
Great Gildersleeve (Willard Waterman)	50–51	29t	9.7	N	Wed	8:30
Great Gildersleeve (Willard Waterman)	51–52	28	7.6	N	Wed	8:30
Great Gildersleeve (Willard Waterman)	52–53	14	7.0	N	Wed	8:30
Great Moments Great Plays	40–41	89t	7.6	C	Fri	9:00
Great Moments in History	32–33	74t	6.1	B	Sun	7:30
Great Moments in Music (George Sebastian Orch)	41–42	131t	4.1	C	Wed	10:15
Great Moments in Music (George Sebastian Orch)	42–43	125t	4.8	C	Wed	10:00
Great Moments in Music (George Sebastian Orch)	43–44	115t	5.4	C	Wed	10:00
Great Moments in Music (George Sebastian Orch)	44–45	124t	6.1	C	Wed	10:00
Great Moments in Music (George Sebastian Orch)	45–46	127t	5.7	C	Wed	10:00
Great Scenes from Great Plays	48–49	127t	4.3	M	Fri	8:00
Greatest Story Ever Told (Warren Parker)	46–47	148t	3.6	A	Sun	6:30
Greatest Story Ever Told (Warren Parker)	47–48	122	8.9	A	Sun	6:30

6–11 P.M., Sept through June Programs
Rated 13 Weeks or More

Program	Season	Rank	Rtg	Net	Day	Time
Greatest Story Ever Told (Warren Parker)	48–49	118	6.4	A	Sun	6:30
Green Hornet (Bob Hall)	47–48	86t	11.7	A	Tue	7:30
Greenfield Village Chapel Choir	43–44	176t	2.3	B	Sun	8:00
Greenfield Village Chapel Choir	44–45	192t	2.0	B	Sun	8:00
Grouch Club (Jack Lescoulie)	39–40	86t	7.6	N	Sun	6:30
Guy Lombardo Orch w/Burns & Allen	32–33	10	26.5	C	Wed	9:30
Guy Lombardo Orch w/Burns & Allen	33–34	6	28.2	C	Wed	9:30
Guy Lombardo Orch Pleasure Isle	34–35	20	20.1	N	Wed	10:00
Guy Lombardo Orch	35–36	45t	8.5	C	Mon	8:00
Guy Lombardo Orch	38–39	35t	10.4	C	Mon	10:00
Guy Lombardo Orch	38–39	55t	8.6	N	Fri	10:00
Guy Lombardo Orch	39–40	22t	13.6	C	Mon	10:00
Guy Lombardo Orch	40–41	22t	13.6	C	Mon	10:00
Guy Lombardo Orch	41–42	79t	8.4	C	Sat	8:00
Guy Lombardo Orch	43–44	161t	3.1	B	Sun	10:30
Guy Lombardo Orch	44–45	146t	4.6	B	Mon	10:00
Guy Lombardo Orch	45–46	124t	5.8	A	Tue	9:00
Hal Kemp Orch	34–35	107	5.0	B	Wed	8:00
Hal Kemp & Alice Faye	36–37	52t	6.9	C	Fri	8:30
Hall of Fame (Lily Pons)	33–34	39t	13.2	N	Sun	10:30
Hallmark Playhouse (James Hilton)	48–49	48	12.0	C	Thu	10:00
Hallmark Playhouse (James Hilton)	49–50	32t	11.9	C	Thu	10:00
Hallmark Playhouse (James Hilton)	50–51	29t	9.7	C	Thu	9:30
Hallmark Playhouse (James Hilton)	51–52	35t	6.7	C	Thu	8:30
Hallmark Playhouse/Hallmark Hall of Fame	52–53	37t	5.2	C	Sun	9:00
Halls of Ivy (Ronald Colman)	49–50	93	6.5	N	Fri	8:00
Halls of Ivy (Ronald Colman)	50–51	67t	6.6	N	Wed	8:00
Halls of Ivy (Ronald Colman)	51–52	35t	6.7	N	Wed	8:00
Hammerstein's Music Hall	35–36	85t	5.5	N	Mon	8:00
Hammerstein's Music Hall	36–37	62t	6.5	C	Tue	8:00
Hammerstein's Music Hall	37–38	67t	6.9	C	Fri	8:00
Happy Wonder Bakers	33–34	88t	5.2	C	MWF	8:00
Harriet Parsons Hollywood News	37–38	94	2.2	B	Wed	8:30
Harry James Orch	42–43	93t	7.6	C	T,W,T	7:15
Harry James Orch	43–44	95	7.6	C	T,W,T	7:15
Harry Richman Show	34–35	87t	7.6	B	Wed	10:30
Harv & Esther (Alan Reed aka Teddy Bergman & Audrey Marsh)	35–36	127t	1.9	C	Thu	8:00
Harvest of Stars (James Melton)	47–48	111	9.8	C	Wed	9:30
Harvest of Stars (James Melton)	48–49	105t	7.2	C	Wed	9:30
Hedda Hopper Hollywood News	39–40	101	5.7	C	MWF	6:15
Hedda Hopper Hollywood News	40–41	109t	6.3	C	MWF	6:15
Hedda Hopper Hollywood News	41–42	112t	5.8	C	MWF	6:15
Hedda Hopper Hollywood News	44–45	117	6.8	C	Mon	7:15
Hedda Hopper Hollywood News	45–46	162t	3.6	A	Mon	8:15
Hedda Hopper This Is Hollywood	46–47	117t	6.9	C	Sat	10:15
Helen Hayes Theater	35–36	27t	10.9	B	Tue	9:30
Helen Hayes Theater	36–37	49t	7.2	B	Tue	9:30
Helen Hayes Theater	40–41	35t	12.0	C	Sun	8:00
Helen Hayes Theater	41–42	47	10.9	C	Sun	8:00
Helen Hayes Theater	45–46	105	7.5	C	Sat	7:00
Helen Hayes Electric Theater	48–49	68	10.1	C	Sun	9:00
Henry Gladstone News & Comment	43–44	173t	2.6	M	M,Th	10:00
Henry Gladstone News & Comment	44–45	172	3.1	M	M,Th	10:00
Henry J Taylor Your Land & Mine News	45–46	193	1.6	M	M,Fr	7:30
Henry J Taylor Your Land & Mine News	46–47	157t	2.6	M	M,Fr	7:30
Henry J Taylor Your Land & Mine News	47–48	145	4.2	M	M,Fr	7:30
Henry J Taylor Your Land & Mine News	48–49	143	2.4	A	M	8:45
Henry J Taylor Your Land & Mine News	49–50	125	2.4	A	M	8:30
Henry J Taylor Your Land & Mine News	50–51	105t	3.1	A	M	8:30
Henry J Taylor Your Land & Mine News	51–52	92	2.7	A	M	8:00
Henry J Taylor Your Land & Mine News	52–53	89t	2.5	A	M	8:00
Henry Morgan Show	46–47	77t	9.1	A	Wed	10:30
Henry Morgan Show	47–48	114t	9.5	A	Thu	7:30
Here's to Romance (Dick Haymes)	43–44	111t	5.7	C	Thu	10:30
Here's to Romance (Martha Tilton)	44–45	142t	5.0	C	Thu	10:30
Hildegarde's Raleigh Room	44–45	14	16.6	N	Tue	10:30
Hildegarde's Raleigh Room	45–46	40t	12.0	N	Wed	8:30
Hildegarde's Campbell Room	46–47	126t	5.9	C	Sun	9:00

6–11 P.M., Sept through June Programs
Rated 13 Weeks or More

Program	Season	Rank	Rtg	Net	Day	Time
Hillman & Clapper News & Comment	41–42	142t	2.3	B	Thu	9:00
His Honor the Barber (Barry Fitzgerald)	45–46	70t	9.5	N	Tue	7:30
Hit the Jackpot (Bill Cullen)	48–49	61t	11.0	C	Tue	10:00
Hit the Jackpot (Bill Cullen)	49–50	85t	7.2	C	Tue	10:00
Hobby Lobby (Dave Elman)	37–38	81	5.0	C	Wed	7:15
Hobby Lobby (Dave Elman)	38–39	69	7.5	B	Wed	8:30
Hobby Lobby (Dave Elman)	41–42	62t	9.5	C	Sat	8:30
Hobby Lobby (Dave Elman)	42–43	83t	8.7	C	Sat	8:30
Hobby Lobby (Dave Elman)	45–46	117t	6.2	C	Thu	9:30
Holiday & Company (Abe Burrows)	45–46	122t	5.9	C	Fri	9:00
Holiday for Music (Curt Massey)	45–46	141	5.0	C	Wed	10:30
Hollywood Calling (George Murphy)	49–50	111t	3.9	N	Sun	7:00
Hollywood Hotel (Louella Parsons)	34–35	30	17.5	C	Fri	9:30
Hollywood Hotel (Louella Parsons)	35–36	10	16.4	C	Fri	9:00
Hollywood Hotel (Louella Parsons)	36–37	12t	14.9	C	Fri	9:00
Hollywood Hotel (Louella Parsons)	37–38	16t	14.7	C	Fri	9:00
Hollywood Hotel (William Powell)	38–39	21	13.7	C	Fri	9:00
Hollywood Mystery Time (Carleton Young & Gloria Blondell)	44–45	65t	10.2	B	Sun	9:15
Hollywood Mystery Time (Dennis O'Keefe & Constance Moore)	45–46	78t	8.7	A	Sun	9:15
Hollywood Players	46–47	88t	8.5	C	Tue	9:30
Hollywood Playhouse (Tyrone Power)	37–38	33t	10.7	B	Sun	9:00
Hollywood Playhouse (Tyrone Power, Charles Boyer)	38–39	26	12.7	B	Sun	9:00
Hollywood Playhouse (Jim Ameche, Charles Boyer)	39–40	44t	11.2	N	Wed	8:00
Hollywood Playhouse (Jim Ameche, Gale Page)	40–41	60t	9.4	N	Wed	8:00
Hollywood Premiere (Louella Parsons)	40–41	79t	8.1	C	Fri	10:00
Hollywood Premiere (Louella Parsons)	41–42	46	11.2	C	Fri	10:00
Hollywood Star Playhouse (Herbert Rawlinson)	50–51	20t	10.3	C	Mon	8:00
Hollywood Star Preview/Theater	47–48	93	11.4	N	Sun	6:00
Hollywood Star Theater	48–49	103t	7.4	N	Sat	8:00
Hollywood Star Theater	49–50	77t	7.6	N	Sat	8:00
Hollywood Stars on Stage	51–52	89	3.5	A	Sun	9:30
Hollywoood Star Time (Herbert Marshall)	46–47	109	7.3	C	Sat	8:00
Hopalong Cassidy (William Boyd)	50–51	26t	9.8	C	Sat	8:30
Hopalong Cassidy (William Boyd)	51–52	14t	8.7	C	Sat	8:30
Horace Heidt Brigadiers Orch	35–36	106t	3.3	C	Thu	10:00
Horace Heidt Brigadiers Orch	36–37	75t	5.2	C	Mon	8:00
Horace Heidt Brigadiers Orch	37–38	83t	4.6	B	Tue	9:00
Horace Heidt Brigadiers Orch	38–39	45t	9.3	N	Sun	10:00
Horace Heidt Time for Hires	43–44	156t	3.3	B	Mon	7:00
Horace Heidt Time for Hires	44–45	162	3.5	B	Mon	7:00
Horace Heidt Youth Opportunity Program	47–48	51	14.9	N	Sun	10:30
Horace Heidt Youth Opportunity Program	48–49	61t	11.0	N	Sun	10:30
Horace Heidt Youth Opportunity Program	49–50	28t	12.2	C	Sun	9:30
Horace Heidt Youth Opportunity Program	50–51	29t	9.7	C	Sun	9:30
Horace Heidt Youth Opportunity Program	51–52	13	8.8	C	Sun	8:30
Horace Heidt's the American Way	52–53	62t	4.2	C	Thu	10:00
Hot from Hollywood	32–33	95	3.1	C	TWT	7:45
Hour of Charm (Phil Spitalny All Girl Orch)	34–35	91t	7.2	C	Tue	9:30
Hour of Charm (Phil Spitalny All Girl Orch)	35–36	109t	3.1	C	Sun	6:00
Hour of Charm (Phil Spitalny All Girl Orch)	37–38	48t	8.8	N	Mon	9:00
Hour of Charm (Phil Spitalny All Girl Orch)	38–39	63	7.9	N	Mon	9:00
Hour of Charm (Phil Spitalny All Girl Orch)	39–40	65t	9.9	N	Sun	10:00
Hour of Charm (Phil Spitalny All Girl Orch)	40–41	75t	8.3	N	Sun	10:00
Hour of Charm (Phil Spitalny All Girl Orch)	41–42	79t	8.4	N	Sun	10:00
Hour of Charm (Phil Spitalny All Girl Orch)	42–43	66t	9.6	N	Sun	10:00
Hour of Charm (Phil Spitalny All Girl Orch)	43–44	73t	9.2	N	Sun	10:00
Hour of Charm (Phil Spitalny All Girl Orch)	44–45	79t	9.6	N	Sun	10:00
Hour of Charm (Phil Spitalny All Girl Orch)	45–46	67t	9.6	N	Sun	10:00
Hour of Charm (Phil Spitalny All Girl Orch)	46–47	##	6.2	N	Sun	4:00
House of Glass (Gertrude Berg)	34–35	45t	13.7	B	Wed	8:30
House of Glass (Gertrude Berg)	35–36	40	8.9	B	Wed	8:30
How Am I Doin'? (Bob Hawk)	41–42	65t	9.2	C	Fri	7:30
How Did You Meet?	40–41	106t	6.4	N	Wed	8:15
How to Play the Piano by Homecraft	51–52	103	1.8	A	Var	Var
Howard Thurston the Magician	32–33	83t	4.5	B	Th,Fr	8:45
Hudson Vocalians (Conrad Thibault)	33–34	95t	4.5	B	Tue	8:30
Husbands & Wives (Sedley Brown & Allie Lowe Miles)	36–37	71t	5.4	B	Tue	9:30
HV Kaltenborn News & Comment	40–41	38t	11.6	N	T,T,Sa	7:45
HV Kaltenborn News & Comment	41–42	22	15.2	N	T,T,Sa	7:45

6–11 P.M., Sept through June Programs
Rated 13 Weeks or More

	Season	Rank	Rtg	Net	Day	Time
HV Kaltenborn News & Comment	42–43	27t	14.8	N	M-F	7:45
HV Kaltenborn News & Comment	43–44	31	13.4	N	M-F	7:45
HV Kaltenborn News & Comment	44–45	21t	14.7	N	M-F	7:45
HV Kaltenborn News & Comment	45–46	58t	10.3	N	M-F	7:45
HV Kaltenborn News & Comment	46–47	83t	8.8	N	M-F	7:45
HV Kaltenborn News & Comment	47–48	153t	2.4	N	M-F	7:45
HV Kaltenborn/Richard Harkeness News	48–49	117	6.5	N	M-F	7:45
HV Kaltenborn/Richard Harkeness News	49–50	103t	5.4	N	M-F	7:45
I Deal in Crime (William Gargan)	46–47	100	8.0	A	Sat	8:30
I Love a Mystery (M Raffetto, W Patterson, B Yarborough)	39–40	52t	10.6	N	M-F	7:15
I Love a Mystery (M Raffetto, W Patterson, B Yarborough)	39–40	60t	10.3	N	Thu	8:30
I Love a Mystery (M Raffetto, W Patterson, B Yarborough)	40–41	70t	8.7	B	Mon	8:00
I Love a Mystery (Michael Raffetto, Barton Yarborough)	41–42	57t	9.8	B	Mon	8:00
I Love a Mystery (John McIntire, Barton Yarborough)	42–43	100	6.9	C	M-F	7:00
I Love a Mystery (Jay Novello, Barton Yarborough)	43–44	87t	8.0	C	M-F	7:00
I Love a Mystery (Michael Raffetto, Barton Yarborough)	44–45	114t	6.9	C	Wed	10:00
I Want a Divorce (Joan Blondell)	40–41	116t	5.7	M	Fri	9:30
Ice Box Follies (Wendell Niles & Don Prindle)	44–45	183t	2.7	B	Wed	10:00
Imperial Hawaiian Band	35–36	118t	2.6	C	Thu	6:45
Information Please (Clifton Fadiman)	38–39	66t	7.6	B	Tue	8:30
Information Please (Clifton Fadiman)	39–40	27t	13.1	B	Tue	8:30
Information Please (Clifton Fadiman)	40–41	28t	12.9	N	Fri	8:30
Information Please (Clifton Fadiman)	41–42	41t	12.2	N	Fri	8:30
Information Please (Clifton Fadiman)	42–43	38	12.6	N	Mon	10:30
Information Please (Clifton Fadiman)	43–44	45t	11.5	N	Mon	10:30
Information Please (Clifton Fadiman)	44–45	58t	10.7	N	Mon	9:30
Information Please (Clifton Fadiman)	45–46	62t	10.1	N	Mon	9:30
Information Please (Clifton Fadiman)	46–47	101	7.9	C	Wed	10:30
Information Please (Clifton Fadiman)	47–48	142	4.7	M	Fri	9:30
Inner Sanctum (Raymond Edward Johnson)	40–41	126	4.0	B	Sun	8:30
Inner Sanctum (Raymond Edward Johnson)	41–42	69t	8.9	B	Sun	8:30
Inner Sanctum (Raymond Edward Johnson)	42–43	62t	9.7	B	Sun	8:30
Inner Sanctum (Raymond Edward Johnson)	43–44	73t	9.2	C	Sat	8:30
Inner Sanctum (Raymond Edward Johnson)	44–45	71t	10.0	C	Tue	9:00
Inner Sanctum (Paul McGrath)	45–46	42	11.9	C	Tue	9:00
Inner Sanctum (Paul McGrath)	46–47	24t	13.3	C	Mon	8:00
Inner Sanctum (Paul McGrath)	47–48	22	18.6	C	Mon	8:00
Inner Sanctum (Paul McGrath)	48–49	20	15.0	C	Mon	8:00
Inner Sanctum (Paul McGrath)	49–50	19t	13.0	C	Mon	8:00
Inner Sanctum (Paul McGrath)	50–51	92	4.5	A	Mon	8:00
Inside of Sports (Sam Balter)	40–41	129	3.3	M	T,T,Sa	7:45
Inside of Sports (Sam Balter)	41–42	140t	2.6	M	T,T,Sa	7:45
Inside of Sports (Bill Brandt)	45–46	183t	2.5	M	M-F	7:45
Inside of Sports (Bill Brandt)	46–47	160t	2.5	M	M-F	7:45
Inside of Sports (Bill Brandt)	47–48	151	3.1	M	M-F	7:45
Inside of Sports (Joe Cummisky)	48–49	142	2.5	M	M-F	7:45
Inside Story (Edwin C Hill)	32–33	32	14.2	C	Fri	9:30
Inside Story (Fred Sullivan)	38–39	99	2.5	B	Tue	8:00
Interesting Neighbors (Jerry Belcher)	37–38	41	9.7	N	Sun	7:30
Ipana Troubadours	33–34	52	10.8	N	Wed	9:00
Irene Rich Dramas	33–34	112	2.9	B	Wed	7:45
Irene Rich Dramas	34–35	113t	4.2	B	Fri	8:00
Irene Rich Dramas	35–36	106t	3.3	B	Fri	8:00
Irene Rich Dramas	36–37	84t	4.4	B	Fri	8:00
Irene Rich Dramas	37–38	70	6.8	B	Sun	9:45
Irene Rich Dramas	38–39	57	8.5	B	Sun	9:45
Irene Rich Dramas	39–40	72t	9.1	B	Sun	9:30
Irene Rich Dramas	40–41	51t	9.9	B	Sun	9:30
Irene Rich Dramas	41–42	81t	8.2	B	Sun	9:30
Irene Rich Dramas	42–43	121t	5.1	C	Sun	6:15
Isham Jones Orch	34–35	87t	7.6	C	Tue	9:30
Island Venture (Jerry Walter)	45–46	149t	4.4	C	Thu	10:00
It Pays to Be Ignorant (Tom Howard)	43–44	91t	7.8	C	Fri	9:00
It Pays to Be Ignorant (Tom Howard)	44–45	68t	10.1	C	Fri	9:00
It Pays to Be Ignorant (Tom Howard)	45–46	88t	8.2	C	Fri	9:00
It Pays to Be Ignorant (Tom Howard)	46–47	60t	9.9	C	Fri	10:00
It Pays to Be Ignorant (Tom Howard)	47–48	56	14.3	C	Fri	10:00
It's Up to Youth	46–47	157t	2.6	M	Wed	8:00
Jack Benny Program	32–33	19	18.3	B,C,N	Var	Var

6–11 P.M., Sept through June Programs
Rated 13 Weeks or More

	Season	Rank	Rtg	Net	Day	Time
Jack Benny Program	33–34	16	21.9	N	Fri	9:30
Jack Benny Program	34–35	5	35.0	B	Sun	7:00
Jack Benny Program	35–36	2	25.8	B	Sun	7:00
Jack Benny Program	36–37	1	28.9	N	Sun	7:00
Jack Benny Program	37–38	2	29.5	N	Sun	7:00
Jack Benny Program	38–39	2	27.7	N	Sun	7:00
Jack Benny Program	39–40	1	30.9	N	Sun	7:00
Jack Benny Program	40–41	1	30.8	N	Sun	7:00
Jack Benny Program	41–42	5	27.2	N	Sun	7:00
Jack Benny Program	42–43	5	26.3	N	Sun	7:00
Jack Benny Program	43–44	5	23.7	N	Sun	7:00
Jack Benny Program	44–45	10	20.4	N	Sun	7:00
Jack Benny Program	45–46	7	21.3	N	Sun	7:00
Jack Benny Program	46–47	3	25.8	N	Sun	7:00
Jack Benny Program	47–48	10t	21.9	N	Sun	7:00
Jack Benny Program	48–49	3	22.9	C	Sun	7:00
Jack Benny Program	49–50	2	20.7	C	Sun	7:00
Jack Benny Program	50–51	2	15.6	C	Sun	7:00
Jack Benny Program	51–52	3	12.9	C	Sun	7:00
Jack Benny Program	52–53	1	11.0	C	Sun	7:00
Jack Carson Show	43–44	87t	8.0	C	Wed	9:30
Jack Carson Show	44–45	93t	8.4	C	Wed	8:00
Jack Carson Show	45–46	72	9.4	C	Wed	8:00
Jack Carson Show	46–47	68t	9.6	C	Wed	8:00
Jack Carson & Eve Arden Sealtest Village Store	47–48	56	14.5	N	Thu	9:30
Jack Carson Show	48–49	89t	8.7	C	Fri	8:00
Jack Denny Orch	33–34	56	9.7	B	Wed	10:30
Jack Frost's Melody Moments	32–33	62t	7.6	B	Mon	9:30
Jack Frost's Melody Moments	33–34	49t	10.9	B	Mon	9:30
Jack Haley Show	37–38	26t	12.4	N	Sat	8:30
Jack Haley Show	38–39	53	8.8	C	Fri	7:30
Jack Haley & Joan Davis Sealtest Village Store	43–44	10t	21.3	N	Thu	9:30
Jack Haley & Joan Davis Sealtest Village Store	44–45	7	21.5	N	Thu	9:30
Jack Haley & Eve Arden Sealtest Village Store	45–46	13	16.9	N	Thu	9:30
Jack Haley & Eve Arden Sealtest Village Store	46–47	36t	12.3	N	Thu	9:30
Jack Hylton Continental Revue	35–36	85t	5.5	B	Sun	9:00
Jack Kirkwood Show	44–45	130	5.6	C	M–F	7:00
Jack Kirkwood Show	45–46	122t	5.9	C	M–F	7:00
Jack Oakie's College	36–37	30	9.6	C	Tue	9:30
Jack Oakie Show	37–38	23	13.1	C	Tue	9:30
Jack Paar Show	47–48	100t	10.7	A	Wed	9:30
Jack Pearl as Baron Munchausen & Cliff Hall	32–33	3	39.4	N	Thu	10:00
Jack Pearl as Baron Munchausen & Cliff Hall	33–34	27	16.1	N	Wed	8:00
Jack Pearl as Peter Pfeiffer & Cliff Hall	34–35	52t	12.7	C	Wed	10:00
Jack Pearl & Cliff Hall	36–37	79	5.1	B	Fri	10:00
Jack Smith Show	45–46	101	7.8	C	M–F	7:15
Jack Smith Show	46–47	96t	8.1	C	M–F	7:15
Jack Smith Show	47–48	109t	9.9	C	M–F	7:15
Jack Smith Show	48–49	72t	9.8	C	M–F	7:15
Jack Smith Show	49–50	59	9.1	C	M–F	7:15
Jack Smith Show	50–51	55	7.8	C	M–F	7:15
Jack Smith Show	51–52	57t	5.5	C	M–F	7:15
Jack Smith Show	52–53	59t	4.3	C	M–F	7:15
James Melton Show	44–45	96t	8.3	C	Sun	9:30
James Melton Show	45–46	103t	7.6	C	Sun	9:30
Jan August Show	47–48	145	3.6	M	Thu	8:00
Jan Garber Yeast Foamers Orch	33–34	106t	3.3	B	Mon	8:00
Jan Garber Orch Supper Club	34–35	86	7.7	B	Mon	8:00
Jean Sablon Sings	46–47	125	6.0	C	Sat	7:15
Jerry Cooper Show	44–45	187t	2.4	M	Sun	9:45
Jerry Wayne Sings	44–45	168t	3.2	B	Mon	9:00
Jim Backus Show	47–48	136	6.3	M	Sun	9:30
Jimmie Fidler Hollywood News	34–35	122	3.1	B	Wed	10:00
Jimmie Fidler Hollywood News	35–36	109t	3.1	N	Tue	10:30
Jimmie Fidler Hollywood News	38–39	59t	8.1	N	Fri	7:15
Jimmie Fidler Hollywood News	38–39	64t	7.7	C	Tue	7:15
Jimmie Fidler Hollywood News	39–40	69	9.5	C	Tue	7:15
Jimmie Fidler Hollywood News	41–42	131t	4.1	B	Mon	7:00
Jimmie Fidler Hollywood News	42–43	90t	7.9	B	Sun	9:30

6–11 P.M., Sept through June Programs
  Rated 13 Weeks or More

	Season	Rank	Rtg	Net	Day	Time
Jimmie Fidler Hollywood News	43–44	89t	7.9	B	Sun	9:45
Jimmie Fidler Hollywood News	44–45	52t	11.0	B	Sun	9:45
Jimmie Fidler Hollywood News	45–46	108	7.2	A	Sun	9:45
Jimmie Fidler Hollywood News	46–47	90t	8.4	A	Sun	9:30
Jimmie Fidler Hollywood News	47–48	135	6.5	M	Sun	8:30
Jimmie Fidler Hollywood News	47–48	137	6.2	A	Sun	10:30
Jimmie Fidler Hollywood News	48–49	124t	4.4	M	Sun	9:30
Jimmie Fidler Hollywood News	48–49	120	6.1	A	Sun	10:30
Jimmie Fidler Hollywood News	49–50	100t	5.7	A	Sun	10:00
Jimmy Carroll Sings	44–45	163t	3.4	C	MWF	6:15
Jimmy Durante Jumbo Texaco Fire Chief Show	35–36	53t	7.5	N	Tue	9:30
Jimmy Durante & Garry Moore	42–43	31	14.1	N	Thu	10:00
Jimmy Durante & Garry Moore	43–44	41	12.1	C	Fri	10:00
Jimmy Durante & Garry Moore	44–45	45	11.7	C	Fri	10:00
Jimmy Durante & Garry Moore	45–46	51t	10.8	C	Fri	10:00
Jimmy Durante & Garry Moore	46–47	49t	10.9	C	Fri	9:30
Jimmy Durante Show	47–48	62t	13.9	N	Wed	10:30
Jimmy Durante Show	48–49	67	10.3	N	Fri	8:30
Jimmy Durante Show	49–50	47	9.9	N	Fri	9:30
Jo Stafford Show	48–49	136t	3.2	A	Thu	9:30
Joan Davis & Jack Haley Sealtest Village Store	43–44	10t	21.3	N	Thu	9:30
Joan Davis & Jack Haley Sealtest Village Store	44–45	7	21.5	N	Thu	9:30
Joan Davis Joanie's Tea Room	45–46	21	14.4	C	Mon	8:30
Joan Davis Joanie's Tea Room	46–47	20	13.9	C	Mon	8:30
Joan Davis Time	47–48	140	5.1	C	Sat	9:00
Joan Davis Leave It to Joan	49–50	62	8.8	C	Fri	9:00
Joe E Brown Show	38–39	48t	9.1	C	Thu	7:30
Joe Penner Bakers' Broadcast	33–34	11	24.9	B	Sun	7:30
Joe Penner Bakers' Broadcast	34–35	6	31.3	B	Sun	7:30
Joe Penner Show	38–39	30	11.7	C	Thu	7:30
Joe Penner Show	39–40	74	9.0	B	Thu	8:30
John B Hughes News & Comment	41–42	127t	4.4	M	Tu,W	10:00
John B Hughes News & Comment	42–43	103t	6.5	M	W,Sa	10:00
John B Hughes News & Comment	43–44	151t	3.6	M	W,Sa	10:00
John B Kennedy News	50–51	124t	1.2	A	M–Th	10:30
John Cameron Swayze News	52–53	87t	2.6	N	M–F	10:30
John Charles Thomas Sings	35–36	76t	5.7	B	Wed	10:00
John Daly News	52–53	105t	1.2	A	M–F	10:00
John Gunther News & Comment	43–44	143t	4.2	B	Fr,Sa	10:00
John McCormack Sings	33–34	29t	15.6	B	Wed	9:30
John McCormack Sings	34–35	54	12.6	B	Wed	9:30
John Nesbitt's Passing Parade	38–39	91	4.9	C	Sun	7:30
John Nesbitt's Passing Parade	43–44	122t	5.1	C	T,W,T	7:15
Johnny Hart in Hollywood	32–33	104	1.7	B	M–F	7:45
Johnny Presents (Ray Bloch Orch)	39–40	83t	8.3	N	Tue	8:00
Johnny Presents (Ray Bloch Orch)	40–41	60t	9.4	N	Tue	8:00
Johnny Presents (Ray Bloch & Una Merkel/Tallulah Bankhead)	41–42	50t	10.3	N	Tue	8:00
Johnny Presents (Barry Wood)	45–46	65	10.0	N	Tue	8:00
Jones & Hare (Billy Jones & Ernie Hare)	32–33	66t	7.1	N	MWF	7:30
Joseph C Harsch BF Goodrich News	44–45	131	5.5	C	M–F	6:55
Judy Canova Show	43–44	43	11.7	C	Tue	8:30
Judy Canova Show	44–45	32	13.2	N	Sat	10:00
Judy Canova Show	45–46	24	13.8	N	Sat	10:00
Judy Canova Show	46–47	22t	13.5	N	Sat	10:00
Judy Canova Show	47–48	28t	17.3	N	Sat	9:30
Judy Canova Show	48–49	27t	13.9	N	Sat	9:30
Judy Canova Show	49–50	30t	12.0	N	Sat	10:00
Judy Canova Show	50–51	35t	9.4	N	Sat	10:00
Judy Canova Show	52–53	51t	4.8	N	Thu	10:00
Junior Miss (Shirley Temple)	41–42	69t	8.9	C	Wed	9:00
Just Entertainment	37–38	91	3.1	C	M–F	7:00
Just Plain Bill (Arthur Hughes)	32–33	47	10.5	C	M–F	6:45
Just Plain Bill (Arthur Hughes)	33–34	71t	7.6	C	M–F	7:15
Just Plain Bill (Arthur Hughes)	34–35	84	7.9	C	M–F	7:15
Kate Smith LaPalina Show	32–33	37	12.9	C	TWT	8:00
Kate Smith New Star Revue	34–35	42	14.6	C	Mon	8:30
Kate Smith Coffee Time	35–36	59t	6.9	C	TWT	7:30
Kate Smith A&P Bandwagon	36–37	34t	8.8	C	Thu	8:00

6–11 P.M., Sept through June Programs
* Rated 13 Weeks or More*

Program	Season	Rank	Rtg	Net	Day	Time
Kate Smith Hour	37–38	50	8.7	C	Thu	8:00
Kate Smith Hour	38–39	16t	14.5	C	Thu	8:00
Kate Smith Hour	39–40	13	16.8	C	Fri	8:00
Kate Smith Hour	40–41	12	16.1	C	Fri	8:00
Kate Smith Hour	41–42	17t	15.7	C	Fri	8:00
Kate Smith Show	42–43	22	15.5	C	Fri	8:00
Kate Smith Hour	43–44	29t	14.1	C	Fri	8:00
Kate Smith Hour	44–45	93t	8.4	C	Sun	7:00
Kate Smith Sings	45–46	62t	10.1	C	Fri	8:30
Kate Smith Sings	46–47	62t	9.8	C	Sun	6:30
Kay Kyser Kollege of Musical Knowledge	37–38	31t	10.9	N	Wed	10:00
Kay Kyser Kollege of Musical Knowledge	38–39	9	16.9	N	Wed	10:00
Kay Kyser Kollege of Musical Knowledge	39–40	10t	18.0	N	Wed	10:00
Kay Kyser Kollege of Musical Knowledge	40–41	11	16.6	N	Wed	10:00
Kay Kyser Kollege of Musical Knowledge	41–42	11t	18.4	N	Wed	10:00
Kay Kyser Kollege of Musical Knowledge	42–43	11t	20.5	N	Wed	10:00
Kay Kyser Kollege of Musical Knowledge	43–44	16	19.1	N	Wed	10:00
Kay Kyser Kollege of Musical Knowledge	44–45	13	17.2	N	Wed	10:00
Kay Kyser Kollege of Musical Knowledge	45–46	26t	13.4	N	Wed	10:00
Kay Kyser Kollege of Musical Knowledge	46–47	65t	9.7	N	Wed	10:30
Kay Kyser Kollege of Musical Knowledge	47–48	41	15.9	N	Sat	10:00
Keep Up with the World	44–45	168t	3.2	B	Wed	9:00
Keep Working, Keep Singing, America (Walter Cassel)	42–43	128	4.5	C	MWF	6:30
Keep Working, Keep Singing, America (Jimmy Carroll)	45–46	164	3.5	C	MWF	6:15
Keepsakes (Dorothy Kirsten)	43–44	137t	4.5	B	Sun	8:30
Kellogg College Prom	34–35	111t	4.4	B	Fri	8:30
Kellogg College Prom	35–36	109t	3.1	B	Fri	8:30
Ken Murray Show	35–36	70t	5.9	C	Tue	8:30
Ken Murray Show	36–37	23	11.0	C	Tue	8:30
Ken Murray Show	39–40	30t	12.6	C	Wed	9:00
Kenny Baker Show	44–45	101	8.1	C	Sat	8:00
Knickerbocker Playhouse	40–41	47t	10.2	N	Sat	8:00
Knickerbocker Playhouse	41–42	87	8.0	N	Sat	8:00
Kraft Music Hall (Paul Whiteman & Al Jolson)	33–34	10	26.3	N	Thu	10:00
Kraft Music Hall (Paul Whiteman)	34–35	13	22.8	N	Thu	10:00
Kraft Music Hall (Paul Whiteman)	35–36	7	18.2	N	Thu	10:00
Kraft Music Hall (Bing Crosby)	35–36	8	16.9	N	Thu	10:00
Kraft Music Hall (Bing Crosby)	36–37	7	17.4	N	Thu	10:00
Kraft Music Hall (Bing Crosby)	37–38	4	22.7	N	Thu	10:00
Kraft Music Hall (Bing Crosby)	38–39	4	21.8	N	Thu	10:00
Kraft Music Hall (Bing Crosby)	39–40	6	21.1	N	Thu	10:00
Kraft Music Hall (Bing Crosby)	40–41	14	15.6	N	Thu	9:00
Kraft Music Hall (Bing Crosby)	41–42	13	17.4	N	Thu	9:00
Kraft Music Hall (Bing Crosby)	42–43	14	20.0	N	Thu	9:00
Kraft Music Hall (Bing Crosby)	43–44	14	19.6	N	Thu	9:00
Kraft Music Hall (Bing Crosby)	44–45	5	22.2	N	Thu	9:00
Kraft Music Hall (Bing Crosby)	45–46	6	21.5	N	Thu	9:00
Kraft Music Hall (Frank Morgan)	45–46	15	16.7	N	Thu	9:00
Kraft Music Hall (Edward Everett Horton & Eddie Foy)	46–47	42t	11.6	N	Thu	9:00
Kraft Music Hall (Al Jolson)	47–48	20t	18.9	N	Thu	9:00
Kraft Music Hall (Al Jolson)	48–49	38t	12.8	N	Thu	9:00
Laguardia Speaks for Liberty	45–46	114t	6.4	A	Sun	9:30
Lanny Ross' Log Cabin Orch	34–35	40	14.8	B	Wed	8:30
Lanny Ross Show	39–40	78t	8.6	C	M-F	7:15
Lanny Ross Show	40–41	44t	10.4	C	M-F	7:15
Lanny Ross Show	41–42	59t	9.7	C	M-F	7:15
Lanny Ross Show	45–46	132t	5.4	C	M-F	7:00
Larry Clinton Orch	39–40	103	4.6	N	Mon	7:30
Larry LeSueur News	50–51	108	2.8	C	Sat	7:25
Larry LeSueur News	50–51	112t	2.4	C	Thu	10:30
Larry LeSueur News	50–51	118t	1.9	C	Tue	10:25
Lavender & Old Lace (Frank Munn & Lucy Monroe)	34–35	90	7.4	C	Tue	8:00
Lavender & Old Lace (Frank Munn & Lucy Monroe)	35–36	85t	5.5	C	Tue	8:00
Lavender & Old Lace (Frank Munn & Lucy Monroe)	36–37	104	3.1	B	Wed	8:30
Lawrence Tibbett Sings	34–35	31	17.0	B	Tue	8:30
Lawrence Tibbett Sings	35–36	34t	9.9	C	Tue	8:30
Lawrence Welk Show	49–50	130t	1.6	A	Wed	10:00
Lawrence Welk's Highlife Revue	50–51	114t	2.3	A	Wed	10:00
Lazy Dan the Minstrel Man (Irving Kaufman)	35–36	76t	5.7	C	Tue	8:00

6–11 P.M., Sept through June Programs
** Rated 13 Weeks or More**

	Season	Rank	Rtg	Net	Day	Time
Leave It to the Girls (Paula Stone & Ted Malone)	48–49	129	4.2	M	Fri	8:30
Leland Stowe News	44–45	183t	2.7	B	Sat	7:15
Leo Reisman Orch	33–34	53	10.7	N	Sat	9:30
Leo Reisman Orch	33–34	90t	4.8	N	Tue	8:00
Leo Reisman Orch	34–35	93	7.1	N	Tue	8:00
Leo Reisman Orch	35–36	82t	5.6	N	Tue	8:00
Leo Reisman Orch	36–37	54t	6.8	N	Tue	8:00
Leon Henderson News	43–44	176t	2.3	B	Sat	6:45
Les Griffith News	50–51	104	3.3	A	Wed	8:55
Les Griffith News	50–51	105t	3.1	A	Thu	8:00
Les Griffith News	52–53	79	3.1	A	M-F	7:55
Leslie Howard Program	35–36	89t	5.3	C	Sun	8:30
Let Yourself Go (Milton Berle)	43–44	165t	3.0	B	Tue	7:00
Let Yourself Go (Milton Berle)	44–45	128	5.8	C	Wed	10:30
Let's Dance (Xavier Cugat, Benny Goodman, Al Goodman Orchs)	34–35	24	19.4	N	Sat	10:30
Let's Talk It Over (Quentin Reynolds)	45–46	188	2.3	M	Sun	6:45
Life Begins at 80 (Jack Barry)	52–53	99t	1.7	A	Wed	8:30
Life of Riley (William Bendix)	44–45	120t	6.5	B	Sun	10:00
Life of Riley (William Bendix)	45–46	28t	13.2	N	Sat	8:00
Life of Riley (William Bendix)	46–47	26t	13.2	N	Sat	8:00
Life of Riley (William Bendix)	47–48	14	20.1	N	Sat	8:00
Life of Riley (William Bendix)	48–49	27t	13.9	N	Fri	10:00
Life of Riley (William Bendix)	49–50	44	10.2	N	Fri	10:00
Life of Riley (William Bendix)	50–51	50t	8.1	N	Fri	10:00
Life with Luigi (J Carrol Naish)	49–50	32t	11.9	C	Tue	9:00
Life with Luigi (J Carrol Naish)	50–51	13t	11.1	C	Tue	9:00
Life with Luigi (J Carrol Naish)	51–52	10t	9.1	C	Tue	9:00
Life with Luigi (J Carrol Naish)	52–53	8	7.7	C	Tue	9:00
Lifetime Revue	32–33	86t	4.4	B	Sun	9:45
Light Up Time (Frank Sinatra & Dorothy Kirsten)	49–50	96t	5.9	N	M-F	7:00
Lights Out (Arch Oboler)	42–43	59t	10.0	C	Tue	8:00
Lilac Time (Arthur Murray & The Night Singer)	34–35	108t	4.7	C	Mon	10:30
Listen to a Love Song (Tony Martin)	45–46	114t	6.4	C	Sat	7:30
Little Herman (Bill Quinn)	48–49	131t	4.0	A	Tue	8:00
Little Italy	33–34	108t	3.2	C	Tu,Th	6:45
Little Jack Little Orch	33–34	105	3.4	C	Sat	10:15
Little Jackie Heller	34–35	120t	3.3	B	Mon	10:00
Little Known Facts (Dale Carnegie)	44–45	181t	2.8	M	Wed	10:00
Little Show	43–44	176t	2.3	M	Sun	6:45
Log Cabin News	52–53	59t	4.3	N	Thu	8:25
Log Cabin Revue Frank Crumit	35–36	67t	6.1	N	Wed	10:00
The Lone Ranger (Brace Beemer)	41–42	96	6.9	M	MWF	7:30
The Lone Ranger (Brace Beemer)	42–43	99	7.0	B	MWF	7:30
The Lone Ranger (Brace Beemer)	43–44	102	7.2	B	MWF	7:30
The Lone Ranger (Brace Beemer)	44–45	110	7.3	B	MWF	7:30
The Lone Ranger (Brace Beemer)	45–46	102	7.7	A	MWF	7:30
The Lone Ranger (Brace Beemer)	46–47	86t	8.6	A	MWF	7:30
The Lone Ranger (Brace Beemer)	47–48	35	16.4	A	MWF	7:30
The Lone Ranger (Brace Beemer)	48–49	52t	11.7	A	MWF	7:30
The Lone Ranger (Brace Beemer)	49–50	46	10.0	A	MWF	7:30
The Lone Ranger (Brace Beemer)	50–51	58	7.5	A	MWF	7:30
The Lone Ranger (Brace Beemer)	51–52	51t	5.8	A	MWF	7:30
The Lone Ranger (Brace Beemer)	52–53	57	4.6	A	MWF	7:30
Longine Choraliers	50–51	78t	5.7	C	Sun	10:30
Longine Choraliers	51–52	76t	4.4	C	Sun	10:30
Longine Choraliers	52–53	80t	3.0	C	Sun	10:05
Longine Symphonette	50–51	123	1.4	A	M-Th	10:35
Louella Parsons Hollywood News	45–46	70t	9.5	A	Sun	9:15
Louella Parsons Hollywood News	46–47	52t	10.7	A	Sun	9:15
Louella Parsons Hollywood News	47–48	75t	12.6	A	Sun	9:15
Louella Parsons Hollywood News	48–49	34t	13.3	A	Sun	9:15
Louella Parsons Hollywood News	49–50	45	10.1	A	Sun	9:15
Louella Parsons Hollywood News	50–51	64	6.8	A	Sun	9:15
Louella Parsons Hollywood News	51–52	74t	4.7	A	Sun	9:15
Louella Parsons Hollywood News	52–53	70	3.7	C	Tue	10:00
Louis Armstrong Orch	36–37	114	1.7	B	Fri	9:00
Lowell Thomas News	32–33	33	13.7	B	M-F	6:45
Lowell Thomas News	33–34	19	21.0	B	M-F	6:45
Lowell Thomas News	34–35	21	20.0	B	M-F	6:45

6–11 P.M., Sept through June Programs
Rated 13 Weeks or More

	Season	Rank	Rtg	Net	Day	Time
Lowell Thomas News	35–36	24	11.2	B	M-F	6:45
Lowell Thomas News	36–37	26	10.4	B	M-F	6:45
Lowell Thomas News	37–38	29	11.3	B	M-F	6:45
Lowell Thomas News	38–39	19t	14.0	B	M-F	6:45
Lowell Thomas News	39–40	20	14.5	B	M-F	6:45
Lowell Thomas News	40–41	21	14.2	B	M-F	6:45
Lowell Thomas News	41–42	19t	15.6	B	M-F	6:45
Lowell Thomas News	42–43	32	14.0	B	M-F	6:45
Lowell Thomas News	43–44	37t	12.7	N	M-F	6:45
Lowell Thomas News	44–45	27t	13.6	N	M-F	6:45
Lowell Thomas News	45–46	40t	12.0	N	M-F	6:45
Lowell Thomas News	46–47	45	11.3	N	M-F	6:45
Lowell Thomas News	47–48	126	8.2	C	M-F	6:45
Lowell Thomas News	48–49	94t	8.4	C	M-F	6:45
Lowell Thomas News	49–50	74t	7.7	C	M-F	6:45
Lowell Thomas News	50–51	62t	7.1	C	M-F	6:45
Lowell Thomas News	51–52	65t	5.3	C	M-F	6:45
Lowell Thomas News	52–53	62t	4.2	C	M-F	6:45
Lucky Strike Dance Bands (Walter O'Keefe)	32–33	9	27.5	N	Sat	10:00
Lucky Strike Hour (Walter O'Keefe)	32–33	4	33.8	N	Tue	10:00
Ludens Musical Revue	34–35	104	5.4	C	Sat	8:45
Lum & Abner (Chet Lauck & Norris Goff)	33–34	71t	7.6	N	M-Thu	7:30
Lum & Abner (Chet Lauck & Norris Goff)	34–35	103	5.5	M	M-F	6:15
Lum & Abner (Chet Lauck & Norris Goff)	35–36	69	6.0	B	M-F	7:30
Lum & Abner (Chet Lauck & Norris Goff)	36–37	34t	8.8	B	M-F	7:30
Lum & Abner (Chet Lauck & Norris Goff)	37–38	48t	8.8	B	MWF	7:30
Lum & Abner (Chet Lauck & Norris Goff)	38–39	73	7.2	C	MWF	7:15
Lum & Abner (Chet Lauck & Norris Goff)	39–40	57t	10.4	C	MWF	7:15
Lum & Abner (Chet Lauck & Norris Goff)	41–42	112t	5.8	B	M-F	6:30
Lum & Abner (Chet Lauck & Norris Goff)	42–43	124	4.9	B	M-Thu	8:15
Lum & Abner (Chet Lauck & Norris Goff)	43–44	131	4.8	B	M-Thu	8:15
Lum & Abner (Chet Lauck & Norris Goff)	44–45	142t	4.8	B	M-Thu	8:15
Lum & Abner (Chet Lauck & Norris Goff)	45–46	149t	4.4	A	M-Thu	8:00
Lum & Abner (Chet Lauck & Norris Goff)	46–47	143t	4.2	A	M-Thu	8:00
Lum & Abner (Chet Lauck & Norris Goff)	48–49	88	8.8	C	Sun	10:00
Lux Radio Theater (Cecil B DeMille)	35–36	15	14.6	C	Mon	9:00
Lux Radio Theater (Cecil B DeMille)	36–37	4	21.0	C	Mon	9:00
Lux Radio Theater (Cecil B DeMille)	37–38	3	23.4	C	Mon	9:00
Lux Radio Theater (Cecil B DeMille)	38–39	3	22.5	C	Mon	9:00
Lux Radio Theater (Cecil B DeMille)	39–40	4	23.7	C	Mon	9:00
Lux Radio Theater (Cecil B DeMille)	40–41	6	23.4	C	Mon	9:00
Lux Radio Theater (Cecil B DeMille)	41–42	8	25.1	C	Mon	9:00
Lux Radio Theater (Cecil B DeMille)	42–43	7	24.1	C	Mon	9:00
Lux Radio Theater (Cecil B DeMille)	43–44	6	23.3	C	Mon	9:00
Lux Radio Theater (Cecil B DeMille/Various Hosts)	44–45	3	23.0	C	Mon	9:00
Lux Radio Theater (William Keighley)	45–46	5	21.9	C	Mon	9:00
Lux Radio Theater (William Keighley)	46–47	8	21.9	C	Mon	9:00
Lux Radio Theater (William Keighley)	47–48	1	31.2	C	Mon	9:00
Lux Radio Theater (William Keighley)	48–49	1	25.5	C	Mon	9:00
Lux Radio Theater (William Keighley)	49–50	1	22.3	C	Mon	9:00
Lux Radio Theater (William Keighley)	50–51	1	17.9	C	Mon	9:00
Lux Radio Theater (William Keighley)	51–52	1	13.9	C	Mon	9:00
Lux Radio Theater (Irving Cummings)	52–53	4	10.4	C	Mon	9:00
Lyn Murray Show	43–44	176t	2.3	C	MWF	6:15
Lyn Murray Show	44–45	177t	2.9	C	MWF	6:15
Ma & Pa (Parker Fennelly & Margaret Burlen)	36–37	91t	4.1	C	M-Sat	7:15
Madame Sylvia Hollywood News	33–34	101t	3.7	N	Tu,Th	10:30
Madame Sylvia Hollywood News	34–35	132t	2.0	B	Wed	10:15
Magic Voice (Elsie Hitz & Nick Dawson)	32–33	38	12.5	C	Tu,Sa	8:15
Maisie (Ann Sothern)	45–46	83	8.5	C	Fri	10:30
Maisie (Ann Sothern)	46–47	68t	9.6	C	Fri	10:30
Major Bowes Original Amateur Hour	34–35	3	36.0	N	Sun	8:00
Major Bowes Original Amateur Hour	35–36	1	37.5	N	Sun	8:00
Major Bowes Original Amateur Hour	36–37	3	21.3	C	Thu	9:00
Major Bowes Original Amateur Hour	37–38	6t	19.4	C	Thu	9:00
Major Bowes Original Amateur Hour	38–39	10	16.6	C	Thu	9:00
Major Bowes Original Amateur Hour	39–40	9	18.4	C	Thu	9:00
Major Bowes Original Amateur Hour	40–41	8	18.2	C	Thu	9:00
Major Bowes Original Amateur Hour	41–42	21	15.3	C	Thu	9:00

6–11 P.M., Sept through June Programs
Rated 13 Weeks or More

	Season	Rank	Rtg	Net	Day	Time
Major Bowes Original Amateur Hour	42–43	39	12.4	C	Thu	9:00
Major Bowes Original Amateur Hour	43–44	71t	9.3	C	Thu	9:00
Major Bowes Original Amateur Hour	44–45	106	7.6	C	Thu	9:00
Man Behind the Gun	42–43	76t	9.2	C	Sun	10:30
Man Behind the Gun	43–44	127t	4.9	C	Sat	7:00
Man Called X (Herbert Marshall)	44–45	139t	5.0	B	Sat	10:30
Man Called X (Herbert Marshall)	47–48	49	15.2	C	Sun	8:30
Man Called X (Herbert Marshall)	50–51	76t	5.9	N	Sat	8:30
Manhattan at Midnight (Jeanette Nolan)	40–41	117t	5.7	B	Wed	8:30
Manhattan at Midnight (Jeanette Nolan)	41–42	105t	6.3	B	Wed	8:30
Manhattan at Midnight (Jeanette Nolan)	42–43	107t	6.2	B	Wed	8:30
Manhattan Merry Go Round (David Percy)	32–33	60	8.0	N	Sun	9:00
Manhattan Merry Go Round (David Percy)	33–34	49t	10.9	N	Sun	9:00
Manhattan Merry Go Round (Rachel Carlay)	34–35	56t	12.4	N	Sun	9:00
Manhattan Merry Go Round (Rachel Carlay)	35–36	22	12.0	N	Sun	9:00
Manhattan Merry Go Round (Abe Lyman Orch)	36–37	73t	5.3	N	Sun	9:00
Manhattan Merry Go Round (Victor Arden Orch)	37–38	38t	9.8	N	Sun	9:00
Manhattan Merry Go Round (Victor Arden Orch)	38–39	41	5.9	N	Sun	9:00
Manhattan Merry Go Round (Victor Arden Orch)	39–40	54t	10.5	N	Sun	9:00
Manhattan Merry Go Round (Victor Arden Orch)	40–41	87t	7.8	N	Sun	9:00
Manhattan Merry Go Round (Victor Arden Orch)	41–42	76t	8.5	N	Sun	9:00
Manhattan Merry Go Round (Victor Arden Orch)	42–43	46t	11.1	N	Sun	9:00
Manhattan Merry Go Round (Thomas L. Thomas)	43–44	78t	9.1	N	Sun	9:00
Manhattan Merry Go Round (Thomas L. Thomas)	44–45	79t	9.6	N	Sun	9:00
Manhattan Merry Go Round (Thomas L. Thomas)	45–46	43t	11.7	N	Sun	9:00
Manhattan Merry Go Round (Thomas L. Thomas)	46–47	38t	11.8	N	Sun	9:00
Manhattan Merry Go Round (Thomas L. Thomas)	47–48	31t	17.1	N	Sun	9:00
Manhattan Merry Go Round (Thomas L. Thomas)	48–49	42t	12.5	N	Sun	9:00
The March of Time	32–33	26	15.3	C	Fri	8:30
The March of Time	33–34	23	18.9	C	Fri	8:30
The March of Time	34–35	17	21.5	C	Fri	9:00
The March of Time	35–36	36	9.5	C	M-F	10:30
The March of Time	37–38	88	4.1	B	Thu	8:00
The March of Time	38–39	89t	5.2	B	Fri	9:30
The March of Time	41–42	119t	5.4	B	Fri	9:30
The March of Time	42–43	18	17.9	N	Thu	10:30
The March of Time	43–44	22	16.0	N	Thu	10:30
The March of Time	44–45	103t	7.7	B	Thu	10:30
Mardi Gras (Lanny Ross)	37–38	24	12.8	N	Tue	9:30
Mario Lanza Show	51–52	74t	4.7	N	Fri	9:00
Marion Talley Sings	35–36	101	4.3	N	Fri	10:30
Marriage Club (Haven MacQuarrie)	40–41	89t	7.6	C	Sat	8:00
Martin & Lewis Show	51–52	57t	5.5	N	Fri	8:30
Martin & Lewis Show	52–53	27	5.9	N	Tue	9:00
Marvelous Melodies	33–34	84	6.0	C	Fri	9:30
Marx Brothers' Flywheel, Shyster & Flywheel	32–33	17	18.9	B	Mon	7:30
Marx Brothers' the Marx of Time	33–34	59t	9.2	C	Sun	7:00
Mary & Bob (Elizabeth & Eddie Wragge)	38–39	95	3.6	B	Tue	9:00
Mary Pickford & Co	34–35	22t	19.8	N	Wed	8:00
Maud & Cousin Bill (Vivian Block & Andy Donnelly)	32–33	105t	1.0	B	M-W	6:00
Maudie's Diary (Mary Mason)	41–42	101t	6.5	C	Thu	7:30
Maxwell House Show Boat (Charles Winninger)	32–33	5	30.5	N	Thu	9:00
Maxwell House Show Boat (Charles Winninger)	33–34	2	44.6	N	Thu	9:00
Maxwell House Show Boat (Charles Winninger)	34–35	2	37.8	N	Thu	9:00
Maxwell House Show Boat (Frank McIntyre)	35–36	4	20.8	N	Thu	9:00
Maxwell House Show Boat (Frank McIntyre)	36–37	27t	10.1	N	Thu	9:00
Maxwell House Show Boat (Charles Winninger)	37–38	38t	9.8	N	Thu	9:00
Mayor of the Town (Lionel Barrymore)	42–43	62t	9.7	C	Wed	9:00
Mayor of the Town (Lionel Barrymore)	43–44	80t	9.0	C	Sat	7:00
Mayor of the Town (Lionel Barrymore)	44–45	74t	9.8	C	Sat	7:00
Mayor of the Town (Lionel Barrymore)	45–46	56t	10.5	C	Sat	8:30
Mayor of the Town (Lionel Barrymore)	46–47	79t	9.0	C	Sat	8:30
Mayor of the Town (Lionel Barrymore)	47–48	52	14.8	A	Wed	8:00
Mayor of the Town (Lionel Barrymore)	48–49	131t	4.0	M	Sun	7:30
McGarry & His Mouse (Wendell Corey)	46–47	145t	4.0	M	Mon	8:00
Me & Janie (George O'Hanlon)	49–50	103t	5.4	N	Tue	8:30
Meet Corliss Archer (Janet Waldo)	44–45	112	7.1	C	Thu	9:30
Meet Corliss Archer (Janet Waldo)	46–47	122t	6.4	C	Sun	9:00
Meet Corliss Archer (Janet Waldo)	47–48	44t	15.6	C	Sun	9:00

6–11 P.M., Sept through June Programs
Rated 13 Weeks or More

Program	Season	Rank	Rtg	Net	Day	Time
Meet Corliss Archer (Janet Waldo)	49–50	58	9.2	C	Sun	9:00
Meet Corliss Archer (Janet Waldo)	50–51	38t	9.3	C	Sun	9:00
Meet Corliss Archer (Janet Waldo)	51–52	45	6.3	C	Sun	9:00
Meet Corliss Archer (Janet Waldo)	52–53	65t	4.1	A	Fri	9:30
Meet Me at Parky's (Harry Einstein)	45–46	98t	7.9	N	Sun	10:30
Meet Me at Parky's (Harry Einstein)	46–47	110t	7.2	N	Sun	10:30
Meet Millie (Elena Verdugo)	52–53	40t	5.1	C	Thu	8:00
Meet Mr Meek (Frank Readick)	40–41	57t	9.5	C	Wed	7:30
Meet Mr Meek (Frank Readick)	41–42	38t	12.5	C	Wed	8:00
Meet the Boss (Guy Lombardo)	48–49	114t	6.7	M	Sat	9:30
Meet the Press (Lawrence Spivak)	49–50	135	1.1	M	Fri	9:30
Meet Your Navy	42–43	137t	3.4	B	Fri	8:30
Meet Your Navy	43–44	151t	3.6	B	Fri	8:30
Meet Your Navy	44–45	168t	3.2	B	Sat	7:30
Mel Allen Sports	48–49	122	5.3	M	Sat	7:45
Mel Blanc Show	46–47	106t	7.4	C	Tue	8:30
Melodiana (Vivienne Segal & Oliver Smith)	34–35	98t	6.5	C	Tue	8:30
Melodiana (Frank Munn)	36–37	99t	3.4	B	Mon	8:30
Melody Master	35–36	130	1.5	N	Sun	11:00
Melody Puzzles (Fred Uttal)	37–38	80	5.2	B	Mon	8:00
Meredith Willson Show	48–49	105t	7.2	A	Wed	10:30
Meredith Willson's Music Room	51–52	76t	4.4	N	Wed	10:30
Metropolitan Opera Auditions (Edward Johnson, Milton Cross)	42–43	136	3.5	B	Sun	6:30
Mexican Musical Tours	34–35	125t	2.4	B	Thu	9:30
MGM Musical Comedy Theater (Howard Dietz)	52–53	80t	3.0	M	Wed	8:00
Michael & Kitty (Elizabeth Reller)	41–42	134	3.8	B	Fri	9:30
Michael Shane Private Detective (Wally Maher)	46–47	128t	5.7	M	Tue	8:00
Million Dollar Band/Palmolive Party (Barry Wood)	43–44	52t	10.8	N	Sat	10:00
Mills Brothers Show	32–33	55	8.5	C	Mo,Th	9:15
Milton Berle Show	42–43	93t	7.6	C	Wed	9:30
Milton Berle Show	46–47	74t	9.3	N	Tue	8:00
Milton Berle Show	47–48	46	15.4	N	Tue	8:00
Milton Berle Show	48–49	75t	9.6	A	Wed	9:00
Mr & Mrs North (Joseph Curtin & Alice Frost)	42–43	34	13.7	N	Wed	8:00
Mr & Mrs North (Joseph Curtin & Alice Frost)	43–44	29t	14.1	N	Wed	8:00
Mr & Mrs North (Joseph Curtin & Alice Frost)	44–45	24	14.0	N	Wed	8:00
Mr & Mrs North (Joseph Curtin & Alice Frost)	45–46	39	12.1	N	Wed	8:00
Mr & Mrs North (Joseph Curtin & Alice Frost)	46–47	36t	12.3	N	Wed	8:00
Mr & Mrs North (Joseph Curtin & Alice Frost)	47–48	31t	17.1	C	Tue	8:30
Mr & Mrs North (Joseph Curtin & Alice Frost)	48–49	30t	13.7	C	Tue	8:30
Mr & Mrs North (Joseph Curtin & Alice Frost)	49–50	26t	12.3	C	Tue	8:30
Mr & Mrs North (Joseph Curtin & Alice Frost)	50–51	12	11.2	C	Tue	8:30
Mr & Mrs North (Richard Denning & Barbara Britton)	51–52	16t	8.6	C	Tue	8:30
Mr & Mrs North (Richard Denning & Barbara Britton)	52–53	16t	6.6	C	Tue	8:30
Mr Chameleon (Karl Swenson)	48–49	44	12.3	C	Wed	8:00
Mr Chameleon (Karl Swenson)	49–50	15	13.4	C	Wed	8:00
Mr Chameleon (Karl Swenson)	50–51	10	11.6	C	Wed	8:00
Mr Chameleon (Karl Swenson)	51–52	49t	5.9	C	Thu	9:00
Mr District Attorney (Raymond Edward Johnson/Dwight Weist)	39–40	72t	9.1	N	Thu	8:00
Mr District Attorney (Jay Jostyn)	40–41	18	14.7	N	Wed	9:30
Mr District Attorney (Jay Jostyn)	41–42	11t	18.4	N	Wed	9:30
Mr District Attorney (Jay Jostyn)	42–43	10	21.7	N	Wed	9:30
Mr District Attorney (Jay Jostyn)	43–44	8t	21.4	N	Wed	9:30
Mr District Attorney (Jay Jostyn)	44–45	8	21.3	N	Wed	9:30
Mr District Attorney (Jay Jostyn)	45–46	11	19.6	N	Wed	9:30
Mr District Attorney (Jay Jostyn)	46–47	11	18.5	N	Wed	9:30
Mr District Attorney (Jay Jostyn)	47–48	12	21.1	N	Wed	9:30
Mr District Attorney (Jay Jostyn)	48–49	12	16.6	N	Wed	9:30
Mr District Attorney (Jay Jostyn)	49–50	24t	12.5	N	Wed	9:30
Mr District Attorney (Jay Jostyn)	50–51	15t	10.7	N	Wed	9:30
Mr District Attorney (Jay Jostyn)	51–52	34	6.8	A	Fri	9:30
Mr Keen Tracer of Lost Persons (Bennett Kilpack)	37–38	72	6.5	B	TWT	7:15
Mr Keen Tracer of Lost Persons (Bennett Kilpack)	38–39	85	5.7	B	TWT	7:15
Mr Keen Tracer of Lost Persons (Bennett Kilpack)	39–40	98	6.2	B	TWT	7:15
Mr Keen Tracer of Lost Persons (Bennett Kilpack)	40–41	114	6.2	B	TWT	7:15
Mr Keen Tracer of Lost Persons (Bennett Kilpack)	41–42	123	4.8	B	TWT	7:15
Mr Keen Tracer of Lost Persons (Bennett Kilpack)	42–43	115	5.7	C	WThF	7:45
Mr Keen Tracer of Lost Persons (Bennett Kilpack)	43–44	108t	6.6	C	Thu	7:30
Mr Keen Tracer of Lost Persons (Bennett Kilpack)	44–45	96t	8.3	C	Thu	7:30

6–11 P.M., Sept through June Programs
  Rated 13 Weeks or More

	Season	Rank	Rtg	Net	Day	Time
Mr Keen Tracer of Lost Persons (Bennett Kilpack)	45–46	76	9.1	C	Thu	7:30
Mr Keen Tracer of Lost Persons (Bennett Kilpack)	46–47	51	10.8	C	Thu	7:30
Mr Keen Tracer of Lost Persons (Bennett Kilpack)	47–48	33t	16.7	C	Thu	8:30
Mr Keen Tracer of Lost Persons (Bennett Kilpack)	48–49	15	16.0	C	Thu	8:30
Mr Keen Tracer of Lost Persons (Bennett Kilpack)	49–50	12	13.9	C	Thu	8:30
Mr Keen Tracer of Lost Persons (Arthur Hughes)	50–51	15t	10.7	C	Thu	8:30
Mr Keen Tracer of Lost Persons (Arthur Hughes)	51–52	25t	7.8	N	Thu	8:30
Mr Keen Tracer of Lost Persons (Arthur Hughes)	52–53	40t	5.1	C	Fri	8:00
Mr Mercury (Staats Cotsworth)	51–52	79t	4.3	A	Tue	7:30
Model Minstrels (Pick Malone & Pat Padgett)	37–38	37t	10.3	C	Mon	8:30
Model Minstrels (Pick Malone & Pat Padgett)	38–39	35t	10.4	C	Mon	8:30
Model Minstrels (Pick Malone & Pat Padgett)	39–40	33t	12.2	C	Mon	8:30
Modern Adventures of Casanova (Errol Flynn)	51–52	99t	2.0	M	Thu	8:00
Modern Adventures of Casanova (Errol Flynn)	52–53	92t	2.4	M	Thu	8:00
Molle Dixie Dandies	34–35	125t	2.4	N	Thu	7:30
Molle Merry Minstrels	34–35	108t	4.7	N	Thu	7:30
Molle Mystery Theater (Bernard Lenrow)	43–44	65t	9.5	N	Tue	9:00
Molle Mystery Theater (Bernard Lenrow)	44–45	46	11.6	N	Tue	9:00
Molle Mystery Theater (Bernard Lenrow)	45–46	53t	10.6	N	Fri	10:00
Molle Mystery Theater (Bernard Lenrow)	46–47	52t	10.7	N	Fri	10:00
Molle Mystery Theater (Bernard Lenrow)	47–48	66	13.6	N	Fri	10:00
Molle Show (Shirley Howard)	33–34	123	1.4	N	MWTh	7:30
Mommie & The Men	45–46	134t	5.3	C	M-F	7:00
Monday Merry Go Round	41–42	136	3.4	B	Mon	10:00
Mortimer Gooch (Bob Bailey)	36–37	112t	1.8	C	Fri	7:00
Morton Downey Sings	32–33	54	8.9	B	Wed	9:30
Morton Downey Sings	34–35	101	5.9	B	Fri	8:15
Movie Quiz	52–53	97	2.2	M	Fri	8:00
Murder & Mr Malone (Frank Lovejoy)	46–47	90t	8.4	A	Sat	9:30
Murder & Mr Malone (Frank Lovejoy)	47–48	82t	11.9	A	Sat	9:30
Music America Loves Best	43–44	168t	2.9	B	Sat	7:30
Music at the Hadyn's	34–35	66	11.1	N	Mon	9:30
Music by Gershwin	33–34	93t	4.7	B	M,F	7:30
Music by Raymond Paige	44–45	189t	2.2	B	Fri	8:00
Music on the Air (Robert Armbruster Orch)	33–34	108t	3.2	C	MWF	7:30
Music That Satisfies (Various Artists)	32–33	44t	10.8	C	M-Sa	9:00
Music That Satisfies (Various Artists)	44–45	120t	6.5	C	T,W,T	7:15
Music with the Hormel Girls	49–50	120	2.9	A	Sun	6:30
Musical Americana (Deems Taylor)	39–40	108	3.2	B	Thu	8:00
Musical Cruise (Vincent Lopez Orch)	33–34	83	6.3	B	Wed	10:00
Musical Toast	35–36	115	2.9	C	Tu,Th	7:15
Mutual Fight of the Week	45–46	180t	2.7	M	Mon	10:15
My Best Girls (Roland Winters)	43–44	161t	3.1	B	Wed	8:30
My Best Girls (Roland Winters)	44–45	134t	5.3	B	Wed	8:30
My Favorite Husband (Lucille Ball & Richard Denning)	48–49	114t	6.7	C	Fri	8:30
My Favorite Husband (Lucille Ball & Richard Denning)	49–50	85t	7.2	C	Sun	6:00
My Favorite Husband (Lucille Ball & Richard Denning)	50–51	42t	8.8	C	Sat	9:30
My Friend Irma (Marie Wilson)	47–48	8	22.2	C	Mon	10:00
My Friend Irma (Marie Wilson)	48–49	8	19.5	C	Mon	10:00
My Friend Irma (Marie Wilson)	49–50	5	17.4	C	Mon	10:00
My Friend Irma (Marie Wilson)	50–51	6	13.3	C	Mon	10:00
My Friend Irma (Marie Wilson)	51–52	51t	5.8	C	Sun	6:00
My Friend Irma (Marie Wilson)	52–53	19	6.5	C	Tue	9:30
My Little Margie (Gale Storm)	52–53	9t	7.4	C	Sun	8:30
Myrt & Marge (Myrtle Vail & Donna Damerel)	32–33	12	23.5	C	M-F	7:00
Myrt & Marge (Myrtle Vail & Donna Damerel)	33–34	22	19.2	C	M-F	7:00
Myrt & Marge (Myrtle Vail & Donna Damerel)	34–35	28t	18.0	C	M-F	7:00
Myrt & Marge (Myrtle Vail & Donna Damerel)	35–36	55	7.4	C	M-F	7:00
Mysteries in Paris	32–33	41t	11.7	C	Mon	9:30
Mysterious Island	33–34	103t	3.5	N	TuFSa	6:00
Mystery of the Week (Harold Huber)	45–46	129t	5.6	C	M-F	7:00
Mystery of the Week (Harold Huber)	46–47	134	5.4	C	M-F	7:00
Mystery of the Week (Harold Huber)	47–48	138	6.0	C	M-F	7:00
Mystery Theater aka Hearthstone of the Death Squad (Alfred Shirley)	48–49	18t	15.2	C	Tue	8:00
Mystery Theater aka Hearthstone of the Death Squad (Alfred Shirley)	49–50	16t	13.3	C	Tue	8:00
Mystery Theater aka Hearthstone of the Death Squad (Alfred Shirley)	50–51	11	11.4	C	Tue	8:00

6–11 P.M., Sept through June Programs
Rated 13 Weeks or More

	Season	Rank	Rtg	Net	Day	Time
Mystery Theater aka Mark Sabre (Robert Carroll)	51–52	60t	5.4	A	Wed	8:00
Mystery Theater aka Mark Sabre (Robert Carroll)	52–53	69	3.9	A	Wed	8:00
Name the Movie (Clark Dennis)	49–50	121	2.8	A	Thu	9:45
National Amateur Night (Ray Perkins)	34–35	95	6.7	C	Sun	6:00
National Amateur Night (Ray Perkins)	35–36	64t	6.3	M	Sun	6:00
National Barn Dance (Joe Kelly)	33–34	64	8.5	B	Sat	10:30
National Barn Dance (Joe Kelly)	34–35	25	19.1	B	Sat	9:30
National Barn Dance (Joe Kelly)	35–36	29t	10.8	B	Sat	9:30
National Barn Dance (Joe Kelly)	36–37	57t	6.7	B	Sat	9:00
National Barn Dance (Joe Kelly)	37–38	46t	9.0	B	Sat	9:00
National Barn Dance (Joe Kelly)	38–39	43t	9.4	B	Sat	9:00
National Barn Dance (Joe Kelly)	39–40	71	9.3	B	Sat	9:00
National Barn Dance (Joe Kelly)	40–41	53t	9.7	N	Sat	9:00
National Barn Dance (Joe Kelly)	41–42	62t	9.5	N	Sat	9:00
National Barn Dance (Joe Kelly)	42–43	52t	10.4	N	Sat	9:00
National Barn Dance (Joe Kelly)	43–44	55t	10.7	N	Sat	9:00
National Barn Dance (Joe Kelly)	44–45	61t	10.5	N	Sat	9:00
National Barn Dance (Joe Kelly)	45–46	77	9.0	N	Sat	9:00
National Barn Dance (Joe Kelly)	48–49	135	3.5	A	Sat	10:00
National Barn Dance (Joe Kelly)	49–50	123	2.6	A	Sat	10:00
NBC Symphony (Fritz Reiner)	50–51	87	5.2	N	Mon	10:00
Ned Calmer Parker Pen News	44–45	63t	10.4	C	Sa,Su	8:55
Ned Calmer Parker Pen News	45–46	82	8.6	C	Sa,Su	8:55
Ned Calmer Parker Pen News	46–47	90t	8.4	C	Sa,Su	8:55
Ned Calmer News	47–48	105t	10.4	C	Sun	8:55
Neila Goodelle Sings	35–36	125t	2.0	B	Sun	9:45
Nelson Eddy Show	42–43	83t	8.7	C	Wed	8:00
Nelson Eddy Show	44–45	118t	6.6	C	Wed	10:30
Nero Wolfe (Santos Ortega)	43–44	146t	4.0	B	Fri	7:00
New Old Gold Show (Herbert Marshall & Lucille Ball)	41–42	121	5.2	B	Fri	8:00
News for the Americas	40–41	127	3.5	B	Sun	7:30
News of the World (John W Vandercook)	41–42	95	7.3	N	M-F	7:15
News of the World (John W Vandercook)	42–43	83t	8.7	N	M-F	7:15
News of the World (John W Vandercook)	43–44	96	7.5	N	M-F	7:15
News of the World (John W Vandercook)	44–45	96t	8.3	N	M-F	7:15
News of the World (John W Vandercook)	45–46	107	7.3	N	M-F	7:15
News of the World (Morgan Beatty)	46–47	113	7.1	N	M-F	7:15
News of the World (Morgan Beatty)	47–48	123t	8.5	N	M-F	7:15
News of the World (Morgan Beatty)	48–49	112t	6.8	N	M-F	7:15
News of the World (Morgan Beatty)	49–50	102	5.5	N	M-F	7:15
News of the World (Morgan Beatty)	50–51	75	6.0	N	M-F	7:15
News of the World (Morgan Beatty)	51–52	54	5.7	N	M-F	7:30
News of the World (Morgan Beatty)	52–53	47t	5.0	N	M-F	7:30
News of Tomorrow	50–51	124t	1.2	A	M-Th	10:30
News of Youth	35–36	129	1.6	C	T,T,Sa	6:15
Newscope (Wendell Noble)	47–48	141	4.9	M	Sa,Su	7:30
Newsroom of the Air (John W Vandercook)	40–41	118	5.6	N	M-F	7:15
Nick Carter Master Detective (Lon Clark)	46–47	114t	7.0	M	Sun	6:30
Nick Carter Master Detective (Lon Clark)	47–48	72t	13.0	M	Sun	6:30
Nick Carter Master Detective (Lon Clark)	48–49	84t	9.0	M	Sun	6:30
Nick Carter Master Detective (Lon Clark)	49–50	72t	7.8	M	Sun	6:30
Nick Carter Master Detective (Lon Clark)	50–51	65t	6.7	M	Sun	6:30
99 Men & a Girl (Hildegarde)	38–39	92	4.5	C	Wed	10:00
NTG & His Girls (Nils T Granlund)	35–36	91t	5.2	N	Tue	9:00
Official Detective (Craig McDonnell)	47–48	125	8.3	M	Tue	8:30
Official Detective (Craig McDonnell)	52–53	76t	3.2	M	Thu	8:00
The O'Flynn's	34–35	132t	2.0	C	Fri	10:30
Old Singing Master	32–33	71	6.7	B	Sun	9:15
Oldsmobile Show (Ethel Shutta & George Olsen Orch)	32–33	35t	13.0	N	Sat	9:30
Olsen & Johnson's Swift Revue (Ole Olsen & Chic Johnson)	33–34	47	11.1	C	Fri	10:00
Omar Khayam	32–33	83t	4.5	C	Thu	9:30
One Man's Family (J Anthony Smythe)	34–35	26	18.7	N	Wed	9:30
One Man's Family (J Anthony Smythe)	35–36	16	14.0	N	Wed	8:00
One Man's Family (J Anthony Smythe)	36–37	16	13.0	N	Wed	8:00
One Man's Family (J Anthony Smythe)	37–38	13	15.3	N	Wed	8:00
One Man's Family (J Anthony Smythe)	38–39	16t	14.5	N	Wed	8:00
One Man's Family (J Anthony Smythe)	39–40	7	20.3	N	Sun	8:30
One Man's Family (J Anthony Smythe)	40–41	10	16.9	N	Sun	8:30
One Man's Family (J Anthony Smythe)	41–42	16	16.5	N	Sun	8:30

6–11 P.M., Sept through June Programs Rated 13 Weeks or More

	Season	Rank	Rtg	Net	Day	Time
One Man's Family (J Anthony Smythe)	42–43	27t	14.8	N	Sun	8:30
One Man's Family (J Anthony Smythe)	43–44	34	13.1	N	Sun	8:30
One Man's Family (J Anthony Smythe)	44–45	83t	9.4	B	Tue	7:30
One Man's Family (J Anthony Smythe)	45–46	##	8.9	N	Sun	3:30
One Man's Family (J Anthony Smythe)	46–47	##	8.9	N	Sun	3:30
One Man's Family (J Anthony Smythe)	47–48	##	10.4	N	Sun	3:30
One Man's Family (J Anthony Smythe)	48–49	##	8.3	N	Sun	3:30
One Man's Family (J Anthony Smythe)	50–51	72	6.3	N	M–F	7:45
One Man's Family (J Anthony Smythe)	51–52	49t	5.9	N	M–F	7:45
One Man's Family (J Anthony Smythe)	52–53	34t	5.3	N	M–F	7:45
The O'Neill's (Kate McComb)	34–35	78	8.7	C	MWF	7:30
Ontario Show	41–42	140t	2.6	B	Fri	7:00
Original Amateur Hour (Ted Mack)	48–49	61t	11.0	A	Wed	8:00
Original Amateur Hour (Ted Mack)	49–50	79t	7.5	A	Thu	9:00
Original Amateur Hour (Ted Mack)	50–51	65t	6.7	A	Thu	9:00
Original Amateur Hour (Ted Mack)	51–52	68t	5.2	A	Thu	9:00
Orphans of Divorce (Margaret Anglin)	38–39	97	3.3	B	Mon	7:00
Orson Welles Dramas	41–42	15	16.8	C	Mon	10:00
Our Miss Brooks (Eve Arden)	48–49	56	11.6	C	Sun	9:30
Our Miss Brooks (Eve Arden)	49–50	40	11.0	C	Sun	6:30
Our Miss Brooks (Eve Arden)	50–51	26t	9.8	C	Sun	6:30
Our Miss Brooks (Eve Arden)	51–52	16t	8.6	C	Sun	6:30
Our Miss Brooks (Eve Arden)	52–53	6	8.4	C	Sun	6:30
Our Secret Weapon (Rex Stout)	42–43	116t	5.4	C	Fri	7:15
Outdoor Girl Beauty Parade	34–35	118	3.5	C	Sat	7:30
Ozzie Nelson Show	37–38	76	5.8	B	Sun	7:30
Palmer House Program	33–34	90t	4.8	B	Tue	10:00
Palmolive Party (Barry Wood)	44–45	50	11.2	N	Sat	10:00
Paris Night Life	35–36	94t	4.9	C	Fri	7:30
Parker Family (Leon Janney)	39–40	62t	10.1	B	Sun	9:15
Parker Family (Leon Janney)	40–41	26t	13.0	B	Sun	9:15
Parker Family (Leon Janney)	41–42	37	12.8	B	Sun	9:15
Parker Family (Leon Janney)	42–43	70t	9.5	B	Sun	9:15
Parker Family (Leon Janney)	43–44	143t	4.2	B	Fri	8:15
Parties at Pickfair (Mary Pickford)	35–36	45t	8.5	C	Tue	10:00
Paul Barnes Front Page News	45–46	180t	2.7	A	M–F	9:55
Paul Harvey News & Comment	50–51	114t	2.3	A	Sun	10:15
Paul Harvey News & Comment	51–52	97	2.3	A	Sun	10:00
Paul Harvey News & Comment	52–53	99t	1.7	A	Sun	10:00
Paul Sullivan News	40–41	83t	8.0	C	M–F	6:30
Paul Whiteman Buick Show	32–33	27t	15.2	N	Mon	9:30
Paul Whiteman Kraft Music Hall	33–34	10	26.3	N	Thu	10:00
Paul Whiteman Kraft Music Hall	34–35	13	22.8	N	Thu	10:00
Paul Whiteman Kraft Music Hall	35–36	7	18.2	N	Thu	10:00
Paul Whiteman Varieties	35–36	58	7.0	B	Sun	9:45
Paul Whiteman Show	37–38	45	9.1	C	Fri	8:30
Paul Whiteman Show	38–39	71t	7.3	C	Wed	8:30
Pause That Refreshes (Frank Parker)	34–35	62t	11.7	N	Fri	10:30
Pause That Refreshes (Andre Kostelanetz Orch)	47–48	99	10.8	C	Sun	6:30
Pause That Refreshes (Percy Faith Orch)	48–49	91t	8.6	C	Sun	6:30
Pennzoil Parade of Melodies	32–33	78	5.6	B	Fri	10:00
Penthouse Party (Ilka Chase)	41–42	139	2.7	B	Wed	9:30
People Are Funny (Art Baker)	42–43	40t	12.1	N	Fri	9:30
People Are Funny (Art Linkletter)	43–44	45t	11.5	N	Fri	9:30
People Are Funny (Art Linkletter)	44–45	31	13.4	N	Fri	9:30
People Are Funny (Art Linkletter)	45–46	28t	13.2	N	Fri	9:00
People Are Funny (Art Linkletter)	46–47	32	12.7	N	Fri	9:00
People Are Funny (Art Linkletter)	47–48	33t	16.7	N	Fri	9:00
People Are Funny (Art Linkletter)	48–49	9t	17.1	N	Tue	10:30
People Are Funny (Art Linkletter)	49–50	13	13.7	N	Tue	10:30
People Are Funny (Art Linkletter)	50–51	20t	10.3	N	Tue	10:30
People Are Funny (Art Linkletter)	50–51	100t	3.7	N	Sat	7:30
People Are Funny (Art Linkletter)	51–52	6t	9.6	C	Tue	8:00
People Are Funny (Art Linkletter)	52–53	5	8.7	C	Tue	8:00
Pet Milk Show (Vic Damone)	48–49	102	7.5	N	Sat	7:30
Pet Milk Show (Bob Crosby)	49–50	74t	7.7	N	Sun	10:30
Phil Baker the Armour Jester	32–33	24	16.1	B	Fri	9:30
Phil Baker the Armour Jester	33–34	13	23.9	B	Fri	9:30
Phil Baker the Armour Jester	34–35	22t	19.8	B	Fri	9:30

6–11 P.M., Sept through June Programs
Rated 13 Weeks or More

	Season	Rank	Rtg	Net	Day	Time
Phil Baker's Gulf Headliners	35–36	13t	14.9	C	Sun	7:30
Phil Baker's Gulf Headliners	36–37	9	15.8	C	Sun	7:30
Phil Baker's Gulf Headliners	37–38	12	16.4	C	Sun	7:30
Phil Baker's Honolulu Bound	38–39	66t	7.6	C	Sat	9:00
Phil Cook's Ingram Shavers	32–33	73	6.2	B	Mo,We	8:45
Phil Harris Orch	33–34	43	11.7	B	Fri	9:00
Phil Harris & Alice Faye Show	46–47	12	17.9	N	Sun	7:30
Phil Harris & Alice Faye Show	47–48	9	22.1	N	Sun	7:30
Phil Harris & Alice Faye Show	48–49	17	15.4	N	Sun	7:30
Phil Harris & Alice Faye Show	49–50	50t	9.6	N	Sun	7:30
Phil Harris & Alice Faye Show	51–52	40t	6.4	N	Sun	8:00
Phil Harris & Alice Faye Show	52–53	37t	5.2	N	Sun	8:00
Phil Spitalny Nestle Chocolateers Orch	32–33	96	2.9	B	Fri	8:00
Philadelphia Symphony	33–34	55	9.8	C	MWSa	9:00
Philadelphia Symphony	36–37	103	3.2	C	Fri	10:00
Philadelphia Symphony	37–38	93	2.7	B	Mon	9:00
Philip Morris Playhouse	41–42	45	11.3	C	Fri	9:00
Philip Morris Playhouse	42–43	45	11.2	C	Fri	9:00
Philip Morris Playhouse	43–44	50	11.0	C	Fri	9:00
Philip Morris Playhouse	48–49	84t	9.0	C	Fri	10:00
Philip Morris Playhouse	50–51	67t	6.6	C	Thu	10:00
Philip Morris Playhouse on Broadway	51–52	30	7.3	C	Sun	8:30
Philip Morris Playhouse on Broadway	52–53	22t	6.3	C	Wed	9:00
Pick & Pat Dill's Best (Pick Malone & Pat Padgett)	33–34	119	2.1	N	Sat	6:45
Pick & Pat (Pick Malone & Pat Padgett)	33–34	71t	7.6	N	Fri	9:30
Pick & Pat (Pick Malone & Pat Padgett)	34–35	69t	10.4	N	Fri	9:30
Pick & Pat (Pick Malone & Pat Padgett)	35–36	44	8.6	C	Mon	8:30
Pick & Pat (Pick Malone & Pat Padgett)	36–37	22	11.3	C	Mon	8:30
Pick & Pat's Model Minstrels (Pick Malone & Pat Padgett)	37–38	37t	10.3	C	Mon	8:30
Pick & Pat's Model Minstrels (Pick Malone & Pat Padgett)	38–39	35t	10.4	C	Mon	8:30
Pick & Pat's Model Minstrels (Pick Malone & Pat Padgett)	39–40	33t	12.2	C	Mon	8:30
Pick & Pat (Pick Malone & Pat Padgett)	43–44	161t	3.1	M	Tue	8:30
Pipe Smoking Time (Tom Howard & George Shelton)	39–40	47t	10.8	C	Mon	8:30
Pipe Smoking Time (Tom Howard & George Shelton)	40–41	43	10.5	C	Mon	8:30
Pittsburgh Symphony	35–36	112t	3.0	B	Thu	8:00
Plantation Echos (Mildred Bailey)	34–35	113t	4.2	B	MWF	7:15
Plantation Party (Whitey Ford & Red Foley)	38–39	93t	3.7	B	Fri	9:00
Plantation Party (Whitey Ford & Red Foley)	39–40	100	5.8	B	Fri	9:00
Plantation Party (Whitey Ford & Red Foley)	40–41	74	8.4	N	Wed	8:30
Plantation Party (Whitey Ford & Red Foley)	41–42	74	8.7	N	Fri	9:30
Plantation Party (Whitey Ford & Red Foley)	42–43	59t	10.0	N	Fri	9:30
Play Broadcast	40–41	125	4.7	M	Mon	8:00
Poetic Melodies	36–37	115	1.4	C	M-Th	7:00
Point Sublime (Cliff Arquette)	47–48	79t	12.1	A	Mon	8:00
Policewoman (Betty Garde)	46–47	120t	6.5	A	Sun	9:45
Pond's Players (Maude Adams)	33–34	77t	6.8	N	Fri	9:30
Ponds Variety Program	32–33	62t	7.6	N	Fri	9:30
Pontiac Program (Jane Froman)	34–35	91t	7.2	N	Sun	10:00
Popeye the Sailor (Detmar Poppen)	35–36	70t	5.9	N	T,T,Sa	7:15
Popeye the Sailor (Detmar Poppen)	36–37	57t	6.7	C	MWF	7:15
Portraits in Music (Percy Faith Orch)	41–42	97t	6.6	N	Mon	10:00
Pot O Gold (Ben Grauer & Horace Heidt Orch)	39–40	10t	18.0	N	Tue	8:30
Pot O Gold (Ben Grauer & Horace Heidt Orch)	40–41	53t	9.7	B	Thu	8:00
Pot O Gold (Happy Felton)	46–47	128t	5.7	A	Wed	9:30
Potash & Perlmutter	33–34	106t	3.3	B	MWF	7:30
Powder Box Theater	45–46	137	5.2	C	Thu	10:30
Princess Pat Players	34–35	79t	8.4	B	Mon	9:30
Princess Pat Tales of Today	35–36	105	3.7	B	Mon	9:30
Professor Quiz (Craig Earl)	36–37	44	7.7	C	Sat	8:00
Professor Quiz (Craig Earl)	37–38	26t	12.4	C	Sat	9:00
Professor Quiz (Craig Earl)	38–39	39	9.9	C	Sat	8:30
Professor Quiz (Craig Earl)	39–40	38	11.8	C	Fri	7:30
Professor Quiz (Craig Earl)	40–41	75t	8.3	C	Thu	10:15
Professor Quiz (Craig Earl)	45–46	175t	2.9	A	Thu	7:30
Professor Quiz (Craig Earl)	46–47	145t	4.0	A	Sat	10:00
Pursuit (Ben Wright)	51–52	35t	6.7	C	Tue	9:30
Quentin Reynolds News/Comment	45–46	189	2.3	M	Sun	6:45
Quick as a Flash (Ken Roberts)	44–45	142t	4.8	M	Sun	6:00
Quick as a Flash (Ken Roberts)	45–46	132t	5.4	M	Sun	6:00

6–11 P.M., Sept through June Programs
  Rated 13 Weeks or More

	Season	Rank	Rtg	Net	Day	Time
Quick as a Flash (Ken Roberts)	45–46	##	5.7	M	Sun	5:30
Quick as a Flash (Ken Roberts)	46–47	##	6.3	M	Sun	5:30
Quick as a Flash (Win Elliot)	49–50	110	4.0	M	Sat	7:30
Quicksilver (Ransom Sherman)	39–40	99	6.1	B	Wed	8:30
Quixie Doodle Contest (F Chase Taylor)	39–40	93t	6.8	M	Fri	8:00
Quiz Kids (Joe Kelly)	40–41	70t	8.7	B	Wed	8:00
Quiz Kids (Joe Kelly)	41–42	81t	8.2	B	Wed	8:00
Quiz Kids (Joe Kelly)	42–43	90t	7.9	B	Sun	7:30
Quiz Kids (Joe Kelly)	43–44	65t	9.5	B	Sun	7:30
Quiz Kids (Joe Kelly)	44–45	83t	9.4	B	Sun	7:30
Quiz Kids (Joe Kelly)	45–46	98t	7.9	A	Sun	7:30
Quiz Kids (Joe Kelly)	46–47	##	7.3	N	Sun	4:00
Radio Auction Show	45–46	175t	2.9	M	Mon	10:00
Radio City Party (John B Kennedy)	34–35	43	14.0	B	Sat	9:00
Radio Hall of Fame (Deems Taylor & Paul Whiteman)	43–44	111t	5.7	B	Sun	6:00
Radio Hall of Fame (Deems Taylor & Paul Whiteman)	44–45	113	7.0	B	Sun	6:00
Radio Hall of Fame (Deems Taylor & Paul Whiteman)	45–46	114t	6.4	A	Sun	6:00
Radio Readers Digest (Conrad Nagel)	42–43	79t	9.1	C	Sun	9:00
Radio Readers Digest (Conrad Nagel)	43–44	67t	9.4	C	Sun	9:00
Radio Readers Digest (Conrad Nagel)	44–45	91t	8.6	C	Sun	9:00
Radio Readers Digest (Richard Kollmar)	46–47	65t	9.7	C	Thu	10:00
Radio Readers Digest (Les Tremayne/George Murphy)	47–48	58t	14.0	C	Thu	10:00
Railroad Hour (Gordon MacRae)	48–49	91t	8.6	A	Mon	8:00
Railroad Hour (Gordon MacRae)	49–50	70t	7.9	N	Mon	8:00
Railroad Hour (Gordon MacRae)	50–51	48	8.3	N	Mon	8:00
Railroad Hour (Gordon MacRae)	51–52	31t	7.2	N	Mon	8:00
Railroad Hour (Gordon MacRae)	52–53	31	5.7	N	Mon	8:00
Ralph Flanagan Orch	50–51	118t	1.9	A	Mon	10:00
Ransom Sherman Show	41–42	93	7.6	C	Wed	9:30
Ransom Sherman Show	42–43	134t	3.6	C	Thu	8:00
Ray Noble Orch	34–35	65	11.3	N	Wed	10:30
Ray Perkins	32–33	81t	4.9	N	Tu,Th	7:30
Raymond Clapper News & Comment	42–43	132	3.9	M	Mo,Th	10:00
Raymond Clapper News & Comment	43–44	158t	3.2	M	Mo,Th	10:00
Raymond Gram Swing News & Comment	40–41	96	7.1	M	M-F	10:00
Raymond Gram Swing News & Comment	41–42	103t	6.4	M	M-Th	10:00
Raymond Gram Swing News & Comment	42–43	125t	4.8	B	M-Th	10:00
Raymond Gram Swing News & Comment	43–44	139t	4.4	B	M-Th	10:00
Raymond Gram Swing News & Comment	44–45	154t	4.1	B	M-F	7:15
Raymond Gram Swing News & Comment	45–46	180t	2.7	A	M-F	7:15
Raymond Gram Swing News & Comment	46–47	157t	2.6	A	WThF	7:15
Raymond Paige Orch	43–44	103t	7.1	N	Tue	7:30
Real Stories from Real Life	45–46	159t	3.8	M	M-F	9:15
Real Stories from Real Life	46–47	148t	3.6	M	M-F	9:15
Real Stories from Real Life	47–48	151	3.3	M	M-F	9:15
Red Davis (Burgess Meredith)	33–34	95t	4.5	B	MWF	8:45
Red Davis (Burgess Meredith)	34–35	48t	13.5	B	MWF	8:00
Red Grange Sports	36–37	82t	4.5	N	Sat	7:00
Red Skelton Show	41–42	4	27.7	N	Tue	10:30
Red Skelton Show	42–43	1t	32.3	N	Tue	10:30
Red Skelton Show	43–44	3	29.9	N	Tue	10:30
Red Skelton Show	45–46	3	23.1	N	Tue	10:30
Red Skelton Show	46–47	6	22.2	N	Tue	10:30
Red Skelton Show	47–48	13	20.4	N	Tue	10:30
Red Skelton Show	48–49	25	14.4	N	Fri	9:30
Red Skelton Show	49–50	14	13.5	C	Sun	8:30
Red Skelton Show	50–51	8	11.9	C	Sun	8:30
Red Skelton Show	51–52	86	3.9	C	Wed	9:00
Red Skelton Show	52–53	47t	5.0	N	Tue	8:30
Red Trails (Victor McLaglen)	34–35	105	5.3	B	Tue	9:00
Refreshment Time (Ray Noble Orch)	35–36	70t	5.9	C	Wed	9:30
Refreshment Time (Morton Downey)	50–51	89	4.8	C	Sat	10:30
Rendezvous	35–36	121t	2.3	B	Wed	8:00
Renfrew of the Mounted (House Jameson)	35–36	121t	2.3	C	M-F	6:45
Renfro Valley Folks (Whitey Ford & Red Foley)	40–41	94t	7.3	N	Mon	9:30
Report to the Nation (John Daly)	43–44	114	5.5	C	Tue	9:30
Report to the Nation (John Daly)	45–46	135t	5.3	C	Sat	10:30
Request Performance	45–46	96t	8.0	C	Sun	9:00
Rex Allen Show	49–50	126t	2.0	C	Fri	10:00

6–11 P.M., Sept through June Programs
Rated 13 Weeks or More

	Season	Rank	Rtg	Net	Day	Time
Rex Allen Show	50–51	110t	2.6	C	Fri	10:00
Rex Allen Show	51–52	94t	2.5	C	Fri	8:30
Richard Diamond, Private Detective (Dick Powell)	50–51	49	8.2	A	Fri	8:00
Richard Diamond, Private Detective (Dick Powell)	51–52	40t	6.4	A	Fri	8:00
Richard Himber Orch	34–35	96t	6.6	N	Mon	8:00
Richard Himber Orch	34–35	94	6.9	C	Fri	10:00
Richard Himber Orch	35–36	76t	5.7	C	Fri	10:00
Richard Himber Orch	36–37	95	3.7	N	Mon	10:30
Richfield Country Club	32–33	90	4.0	N	Fri	10:30
Rin Tin Tin Thriller (Don Ameche, Junior McLain)	32–33	83t	4.5	B	Thu	8:30
Rin Tin Tin Thriller (Don Ameche, Junior McLain)	33–34	120t	1.7	B	MWF	8:45
Rising Musical Stars (Richard Gordon)	37–38	73t	6.2	N	Sun	10:00
Robert Benchley Show	38–39	86t	5.5	C	Sun	10:00
Robert Montgomery Comments	49–50	111t	3.9	A	Thu	9:45
Robert Montgomery Comments	50–51	96	4.3	A	Thu	9:45
Robert Ripley Saturday Night Party	33–34	24	18.6	N	Sat	10:00
Robert Ripley Bakers' Broadcast	35–36	11	16.0	B	Sun	7:30
Robert Ripley Bakers' Broadcast	36–37	25	10.6	B	Sun	7:30
Robert Ripley Show	37–38	21t	13.3	N	Tue	10:00
Robert Ripley Believe It or Not	40–41	51t	9.9	C	Fri	10:00
Robert Ripley Believe It or Not	43–44	133t	4.6	M	M–F	9:15
Romance Rhythm & Robert Ripley	44–45	149t	4.5	C	Thu	10:30
Robert Trout News	45–46	165t	3.4	C	M–F	6:45
Robert Trout News	46–47	142	4.3	C	M–F	6:45
Rogues Gallery (Dick Powell)	45–46	149t	4.4	M	Thu	8:30
Romantic Bachelor Sings	32–33	81t	4.9	C	Wed	9:15
Ronald Colman Program	43–44	61t	9.9	N	Tue	7:30
Roxy & His Gang (Samuel "Roxy" Rothafel)	34–35	47	13.6	C	Sat	8:00
Roy Rogers Show	44–45	132t	5.4	M	Tue	8:30
Roy Rogers Show	46–47	76	9.2	N	Sat	9:00
Roy Rogers Show	48–49	78t	9.5	M	Sun	6:00
Roy Rogers Show	49–50	66t	8.2	M	Sun	6:00
Roy Rogers Show	50–51	50t	8.1	M	Sun	6:00
Roy Rogers Show	51–52	60t	5.4	N	Fri	8:00
Roy Rogers Show	52–53	40t	5.1	N	Thu	8:00
Royal Crown Review (Tim Ryan & Irene Noblette)	37–38	82	4.7	B	Fri	9:00
Royal Vagabonds (Ward Wilson)	32–33	91t	3.8	B	W,Fri	7:15
Rubinoff & His Violin	35–36	29t	10.8	C	Sat	9:00
Rudy Vallee Show	32–33	6	29.2	N	Thu	8:00
Rudy Vallee Show	33–34	3	39.8	N	Thu	8:00
Rudy Vallee Show	34–35	4	35.6	N	Thu	8:00
Rudy Vallee Show	35–36	3	22.4	N	Thu	8:00
Rudy Vallee Show	36–37	8	16.4	N	Thu	8:00
Rudy Vallee Show	37–38	9	18.6	N	Thu	8:00
Rudy Vallee Show	38–39	18	14.4	N	Thu	8:00
Rudy Vallee Show	39–40	24t	13.4	N	Thu	9:30
Rudy Vallee Show	40–41	19t	14.4	N	Thu	10:00
Rudy Vallee Show	41–42	14	16.9	N	Thu	10:00
Rudy Vallee Show	42–43	13	20.2	N	Thu	9:30
Rudy Vallee's Villa Vallee	44–45	38t	12.7	N	Thu	10:30
Rudy Vallee's Villa Vallee	45–46	46	11.4	N	Thu	10:30
Rudy Vallee Show	46–47	57	10.3	N	Tue	8:00
Ruggles, Astor & Auer (Charles Ruggles, Mary Astor, Mischa Auer)	43–44	122t	5.1	C	Thu	8:00
Russ Morgan Orch	36–37	38t	8.4	N	Tue	8:00
Russ Morgan Orch	36–37	61	6.6	C	Sat	8:30
Russ Morgan Orch	37–38	46t	9.0	N	Tue	8:00
Russ Morgan Orch	37–38	51t	8.4	C	Sa	8:30
Russ Morgan Orch	38–39	52	8.9	N	Tue	8:00
Russ Morgan Orch	38–39	54	8.7	C	Sat	8:00
Russ Morgan Orch	39–40	30t	12.6	C	Fri	9:00
Russ Morgan Orch	40–41	57t	9.5	C	Fri	9:00
The Saint (Edgar Barrier)	44–45	52t	11.0	N	Sat	7:30
Sammy Kaye Orch	39–40	86t	7.6	N	Mon	7:30
Sammy Kaye Orch	42–43	103t	6.5	C	Wed	8:00
Sammy Kaye Orch	43–44	89t	7.9	C	Wed	8:00
Sammy Kaye Orch	44–45	159t	3.7	B	Fri	10:00
Sanka News Roundup	51–52	84t	4.0	A	Fri	9:55
Sanka Salutes (Win Elliott)	51–52	65t	5.3	A	Sat	7:55

6–11 P.M., Sept through June Programs
  Rated 13 Weeks or More

	Season	Rank	Rtg	Net	Day	Time
Sanka Salutes (Win Elliott)	52–53	40t	5.1	C	Sat	9:25
Saturday Evening Party	36–37	65t	6.3	N	Sat	8:00
Saturday Night Dancing Party	32–33	22t	17.2	N	Sat	10:00
Saturday Night Serenade (Mary Eastman)	36–37	101t	3.3	C	Sat	9:30
Saturday Night Serenade (Mary Eastman)	37–38	71	6.6	C	Sat	9:30
Saturday Night Serenade (Mary Eastman)	38–39	74t	0.1	C	Sat	9:30
Saturday Night Serenade (Mary Eastman)	39–40	81	8.5	C	Sat	9:45
Saturday Night Serenade (Mary Eastman)	40–41	77t	8.2	C	Sat	9:45
Saturday Night Serenade (Jessica Dragonette)	41–42	75	8.6	C	Sat	9:45
Saturday Night Serenade (Jessica Dragonette)	42–43	75	15.1	C	Sat	9:45
Saturday Night Serenade (Jessica Dragonette)	43–44	67t	9.4	C	Sat	9:45
Saturday Night Serenade (Jessica Dragonette)	44–45	79t	9.6	C	Sat	9:45
Saturday Night Serenade (Jessica Dragonette)	45–46	73t	9.3	C	Sat	9:45
Saturday Night Serenade (Various Artists)	46–47	94t	8.3	C	Sat	9:45
Saturday Night Serenade (Various Artists)	47–48	123t	8.5	C	Sat	10:00
Scramby Amby (Perry Ward)	44–45	177t	2.9	B	Wed	10:30
Screen Directors' Playhouse	49–50	88t	7.1	N	Fri	9:00
Screen Directors' Playhouse	50–51	54	7.9	N	Thu	10:00
Screen Guild Theater	38–39	40	9.8	C	Sun	7:30
Screen Guild Theater	39–40	29	12.8	C	Sun	7:30
Screen Guild Theater	40–41	15t	15.3	C	Sun	7:30
Screen Guild Theater	41–42	33	13.1	C	Sun	7:30
Screen Guild Players	42–43	15	19.7	C	Mon	10:00
Screen Guild Players	43–44	12	20.5	C	Mon	10:00
Screen Guild Players	44–45	9	20.6	C	Mon	10:00
Screen Guild Players	45–46	10	19.7	C	Mon	10:00
Screen Guild Players	46–47	10	20.0	C	Mon	10:00
Screen Guild Players	47–48	20t	18.9	C	Mon	10:30
Screen Guild Players	48–49	59t	11.1	N	Thu	10:00
Screen Guild Players	49–50	60t	8.9	N	Thu	9:00
Screen Test	44–45	161	3.6	M	M-F	9:15
Sealed Power Program	32–33	103	2.2	B	Sun	6:00
Sealed Power Side Show	33–34	90t	4.8	B	Mon	8:00
Sealtest Village Store (Jack Haley & Joan Davis)	43–44	10t	21.3	N	Thu	9:30
Sealtest Village Store (Jack Haley & Joan Davis)	44–45	7	21.5	N	Thu	9:30
Sealtest Village Store (Jack Haley & Eve Arden)	45–46	13	16.9	N	Thu	9:30
Sealtest Village Store (Jack Haley & Eve Arden)	46–47	36t	12.3	N	Thu	9:30
Sealtest Village Store (Jack Carson & Eve Arden)	47–48	56	14.5	N	Thu	9:30
Sealtest Variety Show (Dorothy Lamour)	48–49	74	9.7	N	Thu	9:30
Second Husband (Helen Menken)	37–38	57	8.2	C	Tue	7:30
Second Husband (Helen Menken)	38–39	45t	9.3	C	Tue	7:30
Second Husband (Helen Menken)	39–40	44t	11.2	C	Tue	7:30
Second Husband (Helen Menken)	40–41	68	9.1	C	Tue	7:30
Second Husband (Helen Menken)	41–42	91t	7.7	C	Tue	7:30
Service to the Front	44–45	163t	3.4	C	Tue	10:00
Service with a Smile	41–42	142t	2.3	B	Thu	8:30
Seth Parker Show (Phillips H Lord)	38–39	59t	8.1	B	Sun	7:30
Seven Star Revue (Jane Froman)	33–34	79	6.7	C	Sun	9:00
The Shadow (Frank Readick)	32–33	40	11.8	N	Wed	8:30
The Shadow (Frank Readick)	34–35	98t	6.5	C	M,W	6:30
The Shadow (Bill Johnstone)	41–42	##	10.9	M	Sun	5:30
The Shadow (Bill Johnstone, Bret Morrison)	42–43	##	15.5	M	Sun	5:30
The Shadow (Bret Morrison)	43–44	##	13.2	M	Sun	5:30
The Shadow (John Archer)	44–45	##	9.5	M	Sun	5:30
The Shadow (Bret Morrison)	45–46	##	8.7	M	Sun	5:00
The Shadow (Bret Morrison)	46–47	##	9.9	M	Sun	5:00
The Shadow (Bret Morrison)	47–48	##	13.1	M	Sun	5:00
The Shadow (Bret Morrison)	48–49	##	10.4	M	Sun	5:00
The Shadow (Bret Morrison)	49–50	##	9.1	M	Sun	5:00
The Shadow (Bret Morrison)	50–51	##	7.9	M	Sun	5:00
The Shadow (Bret Morrison)	51–52	##	5.8	M	Sun	5:00
The Shadow (Bret Morrison)	52–53	##	4.1	M	Sun	5:00
Share the Weath (Bill Slater)	49–50	114	3.7	A	Mon	8:00
Shell Chateau (Al Jolson)	34–35	11	25.2	N	Sat	9:30
Shell Chateau (Al Jolson)	35–36	9	16.7	N	Sat	9:30
Shell Chateau (Wallace Beery)	35–36	34t	9.9	N	Sat	9:30
Shell Chateau (Joe Cook)	36–37	37	8.5	N	Sat	9:30
Shep Fields Orch	36–37	54t	6.8	B	Sun	9:00
The Sheriff (Robert Haag)	45–46	98t	7.9	A	Fri	9:30

6–11 P.M., Sept through June Programs Rated 13 Weeks or More	Season	Rank	Rtg	Net	Day	Time
The Sheriff (Robert Haag)	46–47	103t	7.6	A	Fri	9:30
The Sheriff (Robert Haag)	47–48	67t	13.4	A	Fri	9:30
The Sheriff (Robert Haag)	48–49	93	8.5	A	Fri	9:30
The Sheriff (Robert Haag)	49–50	82t	7.3	A	Fri	9:30
The Sheriff (Robert Haag)	50–51	74	6.1	A	Fri	9:30
Ship of Joy (Hugh Dobbs & Horace Heidt Orch)	33–34	33	14.9	N	Mon	9:30
Show of the Week	40–41	120t	5.2	M	Sun	6:30
Sigmund Romberg Revue	34–35	32	15.6	N	Sat	8:00
Silken Strings	32–33	69	6.9	B	Sun	8:00
Silken Strings	33–34	71t	7.6	B	Sun	8:00
Silken Strings	34–35	81t	8.2	B	Sun	9:00
Silver Dust Serenaders	33–34	103t	3.5	C	MWF	7:30
Silver Eagle (Jim Ameche)	51–52	81t	4.2	A	Tu,Th	7:30
Silver Eagle (Jim Ameche)	52–53	67t	4.0	A	Tu,Th	7:30
Silver Theater (Conrad Nagel & John Loder)	39–40	24t	13.4	C	Sun	6:00
Silver Theater (Conrad Nagel & John Loder)	40–41	47t	10.2	C	Sun	6:00
Silver Theater (Conrad Nagel & John Loder)	41–42	40	12.4	C	Sun	6:00
Silver Theater (Conrad Nagel & John Loder)	43–44	91t	7.8	C	Sun	6:00
Sinclair Minstrels (Gene Arnold)	32–33	13t	21.8	B	Mon	9:00
Sinclair Minstrels (Gene Arnold)	33–34	12	24.4	B	Mon	9:00
Sinclair Minstrels (Gene Arnold)	34–35	19	20.7	B	Mon	9:00
Sinclair Minstrels (Gene Arnold)	35–36	48	8.0	B	Mon	9:00
Sinclair Minstrels (Gene Arnold)	36–37	95t	3.7	B	Mon	9:00
Sing It Again (Dan Seymour)	49–50	66t	8.2	C	Sat	10:00
Sing It Again (Dan Seymour)	50–51	85	5.4	C	Sat	10:00
Singin Sam (Harry Frankel)	32–33	57t	8.2	C	MWF	8:15
Singin Sam (Harry Frankel)	35–36	76t	5.7	C	Mon	7:30
Singin Sam (Harry Frankel)	36–37	82t	4.5	B	Fri	8:15
Singin Sam (Harry Frankel)	42–43	137t	3.4	M	Tu,Th	8:00
64 Dollar Question aka Take It or Leave It (Jack Paar/Phil Baker)	50–51	56t	7.7	N	Sun	10:00
Sizing Up the News (Cal Tinney)	41–42	127t	4.4	M	MWF	8:00
Sizing Up the News (Cal Tinney)	42–43	115t	5.4	M	MWF	8:00
Sizing Up the News (Cal Tinney)	43–44	137t	4.5	M	MWF	8:00
Sizing Up the News (Cecil Brown)	44–45	122	6.4	M	MWF	8:00
Skippy Hollywood Theater (CP McGregor)	49–50	82t	7.3	C	Thu	10:30
Sky Blazers (Col Roscoe Turner)	39–40	85	7.9	C	Sat	7:30
Smilin' Ed McConell	33–34	117t	2.2	C	Sun	6:30
Smilin' Ed McConell	34–35	127t	2.3	C	Sun	6:30
Smilin' Ed McConell	35–36	112t	3.0	C	Sun	6:30
Smith Brothers Trade & Mark (Billy Hillpott & Scrappy Lambert)	32–33	100	2.4	NC	Su,Fr	Var
Smith Brothers Trade & Mark (Billy Hillpott & Scrappy Lambert)	33–34	120t	1.7	C	Fri	7:30
Snow Village Sketches (Arthur Allen & Parker Fennelly)	36–37	69	5.6	N	Sat	9:00
Solly Ward Show	32–33	53	9.0	C	Tue	10:00
Song Shop (Frank Crumit/Kitty Carlisle)	37–38	75	5.9	C	Fri	10:00
Songs by Morton Downey	47–48	156	1.5	N	TTSa	11:15
Songs by Morton Downey	48–49	127t	4.3	N	TTSa	11:15
Songs by Morton Downey	49–50	124	2.5	N	TTSa	11:15
Songs You Love to Hear	34–35	76	9.1	N	Sat	9:00
Sparkle Time (Meredith Willson)	46–47	103t	7.6	C	Fri	7:30
Special Investigator (Richard Keith)	46–47	155t	2.8	M	Sun	8:30
Spike Jones Spotlight Revue	47–48	90t	11.6	C	Fri	10:30
Spike Jones Spotlight Revue	48–49	87	8.9	C	Sat	7:00
Sports for All aka Fishing & Hunting Club	49–50	136	1.0	M	Thu	8:30
Spotlight Bands	41–42	133	4.0	M	Sat	9:30
Spotlight Bands	41–42	135	3.7	M	M-F	9:30
Spotlight Bands	42–43	139	3.4	B	M-Sa	9:30
Spotlight Bands	43–44	165t	3.0	B	M-Sa	9:30
Spotlight Bands Victory Parade	44–45	168t	3.2	B	M-Sa	9:30
Spotlight Bands	45–46	170t	3.2	M	MWF	9:30
Spotlight Bands	46–47	151t	3.2	M	MWF	9:30
Spotlight on America (George Putnam)	46–47	168	1.8	M	Fri	10:00
Stage Door Canteen (Bert Lytell)	42–43	73t	9.4	C	Thu	9:30
Stage Door Canteen (Bert Lytell)	43–44	44	11.6	C	Fri	10:30
Stage Door Canteen (Bert Lytell)	44–45	52t	11.0	C	Fri	10:30
Stainless Show	36–37	117	0.8	B	Fri	7:15
Star & the Story (Walter Pidgeon)	43–44	109t	6.6	C	Sun	8:00
Star for a Night (Paul Douglas)	43–44	168t	2.9	B	Wed	10:30
Starlight Serenade	44–45	181t	2.8	M	Thu	9:30
Starlight Serenade	45–46	172	3.1	M	Thu	9:30

6–11 P.M., Sept through June Programs
  Rated 13 Weeks or More

	Season	Rank	Rtg	Net	Day	Time
Stars of the Future	44–45	173t	3.0	B	Fri	8:00
Steel Horizons	44–45	189t	2.2	M	Sun	9:00
Stoopnagle & Budd Gulf Headliners	34–35	18	21.3	C	Sun	9:30
Stop Me If You Heard This One (Milton Berle)	39–40	42t	11.4	N	Sat	8:30
Stop or Go (Joe E Brown)	43–44	153t	3.5	B	Thu	10:30
Stop or Go (Joe E Brown)	44–45	123	6.2	B	Sun	8:30
Stop That Villain (Marvin Miller & Jack Bailey)	44–45	157t	3.8	M	Wed	8:30
Stop the Music (Bert Parks)	48–49	18t	15.2	A	Sun	8:00
Stop the Music (Bert Parks)	49–50	57	9.3	A	Sun	8:00
Stop the Music (Bert Parks)	50–51	73	6.2	A	Sun	8:00
Stop the Music (Bert Parks)	51–52	71t	4.8	A	Sun	8:00
Stories of the Black Chamber (Jack Arthur)	34–35	123	2.9	N	MWF	7:15
Stories That Should Be Told	33–34	117t	2.2	B	Fri	10:00
Story Teller (Marvin Miller)	44–45	173t	3.0	B	M-F	9:55
Strange as It Seems (Alois Havrilla)	39–40	62t	10.1	C	Thu	8:30
Strange as It Seems (Alois Havrilla)	40–41	87t	7.8	C	Thu	8:30
Strike It Rich (Todd Russell)	47–48	97t	10.9	C	Sun	10:30
Sumner Welles Commentary	44–45	163t	3.4	M	Wed	10:00
Sunday at Seth Parker's (Phillips H Lord)	32–33	20	17.7	N	Sun	10:45
Sunday Evening Party (Phil Davis)	45–46	155t	4.1	A	Sun	6:30
Sunday Evening Party (Phil Davis)	46–47	141	4.5	A	Sun	6:00
Sunset Dreams (The Morin Sisters)	35–36	116t	2.8	N	Sun	7:45
Sunset Dreams (The Morin Sisters)	36–37	95t	3.7	N	Sun	7:45
Suspense (Joseph Kearns & Ted Osborne)	43–44	86	8.3	C	Thu	8:00
Suspense (Joseph Kearns & Ted Osborne)	44–45	51	11.1	C	Thu	8:00
Suspense (Joseph Kearns & Ted Osborne)	45–46	36	12.5	C	Thu	8:00
Suspense (Joseph Kearns & Ted Osborne)	46–47	22t	13.5	C	Thu	8:00
Suspense (Joseph Kearns & Ted Osborne)	47–48	50	15.0	C	Thu	8:00
Suspense (Harlow Wilcox)	48–49	13t	16.4	C	Thu	9:00
Suspense (Harlow Wilcox)	49–50	16t	13.3	C	Thu	9:00
Suspense (Harlow Wilcox)	50–51	38t	9.3	C	Thu	9:00
Suspense (Harlow Wilcox)	51–52	12	9.0	C	Mon	8:00
Suspense (Harlow Wilcox)	52–53	9t	7.4	C	Mon	8:00
Sweetest Love Songs	36–37	107t	2.5	B	Mon	8:30
Swift Studio Party (Sigmund Romberg)	35–36	64t	6.3	N	Mon	9:30
Swing's the Thing	44–45	189t	2.2	M	Thu	10:30
Swing's the Thing	45–46	185t	2.4	M	Thu	10:30
Take a Number (Red Benson)	48–49	134	3.6	M	Sat	8:30
Take a Number (Happy Felton)	52–53	99t	1.7	M	Fri	8:00
Take It or Leave It (Bob Hawk)	40–41	28t	12.9	C	Sun	10:00
Take It or Leave It (Bob Hawk, Phil Baker)	41–42	23t	14.8	C	Sun	10:00
Take It or Leave It (Phil Baker)	42–43	17	18.1	C	Sun	10:00
Take It or Leave It (Phil Baker)	43–44	15	19.2	C	Sun	10:00
Take It or Leave It (Phil Baker)	44–45	15	16.4	C	Sun	10:00
Take It or Leave It (Phil Baker)	45–46	16	16.5	C	Sun	10:00
Take It or Leave It (Phil Baker)	46–47	18	14.5	C	Sun	10:00
Take It or Leave It (Garry Moore)	47–48	40	16.0	N	Sun	10:00
Take It or Leave It (Garry Moore)	48–49	51	11.8	N	Sun	10:00
Take It or Leave It (Eddie Cantor)	49–50	41	10.9	N	Sun	10:00
Take It or Leave It aka 64 Dollar Question (Jack Paar, Phil Baker)	50–51	56t	7.7	N	Sun	10:00
Tales of Fatima (Basil Rathbone)	48–49	121	6.0	C	Sat	9:30
Tales of Willie Piper (Dick Nelson/Elaine Rost)	47–48	120	9.3	A	Thu	9:00
Tarzan (James Pierce)	51–52	88	3.5	C	Sat	8:30
Tarzan (James Pierce)	52–53	34t	5.3	C	Sat	8:30
Tastyeast Original Jesters	36–37	101t	3.3	B	TWT	7:15
Tastyeast Theater	33–34	113t	2.6	B	Sun	9:45
Taylor Grant Headline Edition News	45–46	165t	3.4	A	M-F	7:00
Taylor Grant Headline Edition News	46–47	167	2.0	A	M-F	7:00
Taylor Grant News	52–53	71t	3.5	A	Sun	9:15
Ted Husing & the Charioteers	35–36	106t	3.3	C	Mon	7:15
Ted Husing Sports	36–37	75t	5.2	C	TTSa	7:15
Ted Malone News from Overseas	44–45	156	3.9	B	MWF	8:00
Telegram for You	52–53	99t	1.7	A	Sun	8:55
Telephone Hour (Donald Voorhees Orch & Soloists)	40–41	72t	8.5	N	Mon	8:00
Telephone Hour (Donald Voorhees Orch & Soloists)	41–42	84t	8.1	N	Mon	8:00
Telephone Hour (Donald Voorhees Orch & Soloists)	42–43	89	8.0	N	Mon	9:00
Telephone Hour (Donald Voorhees Orch & Soloists)	43–44	105	7.0	N	Mon	9:00
Telephone Hour (Donald Voorhees Orch & Soloists)	44–45	107	7.5	N	Mon	9:00
Telephone Hour (Donald Voorhees Orch & Soloists)	45–46	88t	8.2	N	Mon	9:00

6–11 P.M., Sept through June Programs
Rated 13 Weeks or More

	Season	Rank	Rtg	Net	Day	Time
Telephone Hour (Donald Voorhees Orch & Soloists)	46–47	90t	8.4	N	Mon	9:00
Telephone Hour (Donald Voorhees Orch & Soloists)	47–48	100t	10.7	N	Mon	9:00
Telephone Hour (Donald Voorhees Orch & Soloists)	48–49	97	8.1	N	Mon	9:00
Telephone Hour (Donald Voorhees Orch & Soloists)	49–50	88t	7.1	N	Mon	9:00
Telephone Hour (Donald Voorhees Orch & Soloists)	50–51	67t	6.6	N	Mon	9:00
Telephone Hour (Donald Voorhees Orch & Soloists)	51–52	51t	5.8	N	Mon	9:00
Telephone Hour (Donald Voorhees Orch & Soloists)	52–53	51t	4.8	N	Mon	9:00
Terraplane Travelcade	33–34	69	7.8	N	Sat	9:00
Terry & The Pirates (Owen Jordan)	42–43	129	4.4	B	M–F	6:00
Terry & The Pirates (Owen Jordan)	43–44	150	3.8	B	M–F	6:00
Texaco Fire Chief Show (Jane Pickens)	35–36	56t	7.2	N	Tue	9:30
Texaco Star Theater (Ken Murray)	38–39	38	10.0	C	Wed	9:00
Texaco Star Theater (James Melton)	43–44	86	8.2	C	Sun	9:30
Texaco Star Theater (Tony Martin)	47–48	75t	12.6	C	Sun	9:30
Texaco Star Theater (Tony Martin)	47–48	100t	10.7	A	Wed	10:30
Thanks to the Yanks (Bob Hawk)	42–43	83t	8.7	C	Sat	7:30
Thanks to the Yanks (Bob Hawk)	43–44	73t	9.2	C	Sat	7:30
Thanks to the Yanks (Bob Hawk)	44–45	41t	12.4	C	Mon	7:30
Thanks to Yanks & Bob Hawk Show	45–46	37	12.4	C	Mon	7:30
That Brewster Boy (Eddie Firestone)	41–42	97t	6.6	N	Mon	9:30
That Brewster Boy (Eddie Firestone)	42–43	46t	11.1	C	Fri	9:30
That Brewster Boy (Arnold Stang)	43–44	52t	10.8	C	Fri	9:30
That Brewster Boy (Dick York)	44–45	65t	10.2	C	Fri	9:30
That Hammer Guy aka Mickey Spillane Mysteries (Larry Haines)	52–53	74	3.4	M	Tue	8:00
That's a Good One (Hope Emerson & Ward Wilson)	43–44	173t	2.6	B	Sun	8:15
That's Finnegan (Frank McHugh)	46–47	133	5.5	C	Thu	10:30
Theater Guild on the Air	45–46	142t	4.9	A	Sun	10:00
Theater Guild on the Air	46–47	96t	8.1	A	Sun	10:00
Theater Guild on the Air	47–48	48	15.3	A	Sun	9:30
Theater Guild on the Air	48–49	46t	12.1	A	Sun	9:30
Theater Guild on the Air	49–50	48t	9.8	N	Sun	8:30
Theater Guild on the Air	50–51	50t	8.1	N	Sun	8:30
Theater Guild on the Air	51–52	25t	7.8	N	Sun	8:30
Theater Guild on the Air	52–53	20t	6.4	N	Sun	8:30
Theater of Romance aka Romance (Frank Gallop)	44–45	61t	10.5	C	Tue	8:30
Theater of Romance aka Romance (Frank Graham)	45–46	58t	10.3	C	Tue	8:30
Theater USA (Vinton Freedley)	48–49	139t	3.0	A	Thu	8:30
Then & Now	36–37	75t	5.2	C	Thu	10:00
This Amazing America (Bob Brown)	39–40	107	3.5	B	Fri	8:00
This Is Helen Hayes	44–45	194	1.4	M	Sun	10:15
This Is My Best (Orson Welles)	44–45	111	7.2	C	Tue	9:30
This Is My Best (Orson Welles)	45–46	90t	8.1	C	Tue	9:30
This Is Your FBI (Frank Lovejoy)	45–46	90t	8.1	A	Fri	8:30
This Is Your FBI (Dean Carlton)	46–47	58	10.2	A	Fri	8:30
This Is Your FBI (Dean Carlton)	47–48	25t	18.0	A	Fri	8:30
This Is Your FBI (William Woodson & Stacy Harris)	48–49	22t	14.6	A	Fri	8:30
This Is Your FBI (William Woodson & Stacy Harris)	49–50	35	11.8	A	Fri	8:30
This Is Your FBI (William Woodson & Stacy Harris)	50–51	42t	8.8	A	Fri	8:30
This Is Your FBI (William Woodson & Stacy Harris)	51–52	31t	7.2	A	Fri	8:30
This Is Your FBI (William Woodson & Stacy Harris)	52–53	40t	5.1	A	Fri	8:30
This Is Your Life (Ralph Edwards)	48–49	59t	11.1	N	Tue	8:00
This Is Your Life (Ralph Edwards)	49–50	63	8.7	N	Wed	8:00
Thornton Fisher Briggs Sports Report	34–35	124	2.5	N	Sat	6:45
Those We Love (Nan Grey)	37–38	89	3.7	B	Tue	8:00
Those We Love (Nan Grey)	38–39	76t	6.9	B	Mon	8:30
Those We Love (Nan Grey)	39–40	33t	12.2	N	Thu	8:30
Those We Love (Nan Grey)	40–41	38t	11.6	C	Mon	8:00
Those Websters (Willard Waterman)	44–45	103t	7.7	C	Fri	9:30
Those Websters (Willard Waterman)	45–46	117t	6.2	M	Sun	6:00
Those Websters (Willard Waterman)	46–47	135t	5.1	M	Sun	6:00
Those Websters (Willard Waterman)	47–48	79t	12.1	M	Sun	6:00
Threads of Happiness (Andre Kostelanetz Orch)	32–33	94	3.6	C	Tue	9:15
Threads of Happiness (Andre Kostelanetz Orch)	33–34	98	3.9	C	Fri	9:15
Three Ring Time (Milton Berle & Charles Laughton)	41–42	129t	4.2	B	Tue	8:30
Three Star Extra News	47–48	144	4.4	N	M–F	6:45
Three Star Extra News	48–49	124t	4.4	N	M–F	6:45
Three Star Extra News	49–50	113	3.8	N	M–F	6:45
Three Star Extra News	50–51	112t	2.4	N	M–F	6:45
Three Star Extra News	51–52	99t	2.0	N	M–F	6:45

6–11 P.M., Sept through June Programs

Rated 13 Weeks or More	Season	Rank	Rtg	Net	Day	Time
Three Star Extra News	52–53	103t	1.6	N	M-F	6:45
Time to Shine (Hal Kemp Orch)	37–38	60t	7.7	C	Tue	10:00
Time to Shine (Hal Kemp Orch)	38–39	82t	6.2	C	Tue	10:00
Titus Moody (Parker Fennely)	52–53	95t	2.3	M	Tu,Th	7:55
To the Ladies (Morton Downey)	32–33	64t	7.4	C	Fri	9:30
To Your Good Health	43–44	168t	2.9	C	MWF	6:15
Today at Duncan's (Frank Nelson & Mary Lansing)	42–43	134t	3.6	C	Fri	6:15
Tom Harmon Sports	45–46	175t	2.9	M	Sat	7:45
Tommy Dorsey Orch	37–38	66	7.0	N	Wed	8:30
Tommy Dorsey Orch	38–39	34	10.7	N	Wed	8:30
Tommy Dorsey Orch	42–43	58	10.1	N	Wed	8:30
Tommy Riggs & Betty Lou	38–39	32	11.3	N	Sat	8:00
Tommy Riggs & Betty Lou	39–40	36	12.0	N	Mon	8:00
Tommy Riggs & Betty Lou	42–43	44	11.6	N	Fri	7:30
Tony Martin Show	40–41	109t	6.3	N	Wed	8:00
Tony Martin Sings	46–47	120t	6.5	C	Sun	9:30
Top Guy (J Scott Smart)	51–52	71t	4.8	A	Wed	8:30
Top of the Evening	43–44	182	2.1	B	MWF	10:15
Treasure Hour of Song (Alfred Antonini Orch)	41–42	138	2.9	M	Sat	8:00
Treasure Hour of Song (Alfred Antonini Orch)	42–43	142	2.2	M	Thu	9:30
Treasure Hour of Song (Alfred Antonini Orch)	43–44	168t	2.9	M	Thu	9:30
Treasure Hour of Song (Alfred Antonini Orch)	44–45	163t	3.4	M	Thu	9:30
Treasure Hour of Song (Alfred Antonini Orch)	45–46	175t	2.9	M	Thu	9:30
Treasure Hour of Song (Alfred Antonini Orch)	46–47	150	3.3	M	Thu	9:30
Treasury Hour	41–42	109	6.1	B	Tue	8:00
True or False (Harry Hagen)	38–39	78	6.8	B	Mon	10:00
True or False (Harry Hagen)	39–40	75	8.9	B	Mon	8:30
True or False (Harry Hagen)	40–41	65t	9.2	B	Mon	8:30
True or False (Harry Hagen)	41–42	84t	8.1	B	Mon	8:30
True or False (Harry Hagen)	42–43	101t	6.6	B	Mon	8:30
Truth or Consequences (Ralph Edwards)	40–41	22t	13.6	N	Sat	8:30
Truth or Consequences (Ralph Edwards)	41–42	31	13.4	N	Sat	8:30
Truth or Consequences (Ralph Edwards)	42–43	23	15.4	N	Sat	8:30
Truth or Consequences (Ralph Edwards)	43–44	27	14.7	N	Sat	8:30
Truth or Consequences (Ralph Edwards)	44–45	23	14.5	N	Sat	8:30
Truth or Consequences (Ralph Edwards)	45–46	19t	14.6	N	Sat	8:30
Truth or Consequences (Ralph Edwards)	46–47	17	14.8	N	Sat	8:30
Truth or Consequences (Ralph Edwards)	47–48	6t	22.3	N	Sat	8:30
Truth or Consequences (Ralph Edwards)	48–49	30t	13.7	N	Sat	8:30
Truth or Consequences (Ralph Edwards)	49–50	37	11.4	N	Sat	8:30
Truth or Consequences (Ralph Edwards)	50–51	41	9.0	C	Tue	9:30
Truth or Consequences (Ralph Edwards)	52–53	28t	5.8	N	Thu	9:00
Tuesday Night Party (Walter O'Keefe)	39–40	60t	10.3	C	Tue	8:30
Tums Hollywood Theater	51–52	35t	6.7	N	Tue	8:30
Tums Treasure Chest (Horace Heidt)	40–41	53t	9.7	N	Tue	8:30
Tums Treasure Chest (Horace Heidt)	41–42	53t	10.0	N	Tue	8:30
Tums Treasure Chest (Horace Heidt)	42–43	55t	10.3	N	Tue	8:30
Tums Treasure Chest (Horace Heidt)	43–44	61t	9.9	N	Tue	8:30
Tune Up Time (Tony Martin & Andre Kostelanetz Orch)	39–40	76t	8.8	C	Mon	8:00
Twenty Questions (Bill Slater)	46–47	138t	4.9	M	Sat	8:00
Twenty Questions (Bill Slater)	47–48	130t	7.1	M	Sat	8:00
Twenty Questions (Bill Slater)	48–49	99	7.9	M	Sat	8:00
Twenty Questions (Bill Slater)	49–50	77t	7.6	M	Sat	8:00
Twenty Questions (Bill Slater)	50–51	82t	5.5	M	Sat	8:00
Twenty Questions (Bill Slater)	52–53	71t	3.5	M	Sat	8:00
Twin Stars Show (Victor Moore)	36–37	105	3.0	B	Fri	9:30
Two for the Money (Herb Shriner)	52–53	40t	5.1	N	Tue	10:00
Tydol Jubilee (Freddy Martin Orch)	32–33	105t	1.0	C	MWF	7:30
Uncle Ezra's Radio Station (Pat Barrett)	34–35	127t	2.3	N	MWF	7:45
Uncle Ezra's Radio Station (Pat Barrett)	35–36	61	6.8	N	MWF	7:15
Uncle Ezra's Radio Station (Pat Barrett)	36–37	32t	9.2	N	MWF	7:15
Uncle Ezra's Radio Station (Pat Barrett)	37–38	38t	9.8	N	MWF	7:15
Uncle Ezra's Radio Station (Pat Barrett)	40–41	53t	9.7	N	Sat	10:00
Uncle Jim's Question Bee (Jim McWilliams)	36–37	41	8.3	B	Sat	7:30
Uncle Jim's Question Bee (Jim McWilliams)	38–39	51	9.0	B	Sat	7:30
Uncle Jim's Question Bee (Bill Slater)	40–41	97	7.0	B	Tue	8:30
Uncle Walter's Doghouse (Tom Wallace)	41–42	65t	9.2	N	Wed	8:30
Universal Rhythm	36–37	110	2.2	B	Fri	9:00
Upton Close News News & Comment	42–43	141	2.7	M	Sat	8:30

6–11 P.M., Sept through June Programs
Rated 13 Weeks or More

	Season	Rank	Rtg	Net	Day	Time
Upton Close News News & Comment	42–43	125t	4.8	M	Sun	6:30
Upton Close News News & Comment	43–44	127t	4.9	M	Sun	6:30
Upton Close News News & Comment	44–45	146t	4.6	M	Sun	6:30
Upton Close News News & Comment	45–46	185t	2.4	M	Tue	10:15
Upton Close News News & Comment	46–47	151t	3.2	M	Tue	10:15
Vanished Voices	35–36	116t	2.8	C	Mo,We	6:35
Vaughn Monroe Show	46–47	96t	8.1	C	Sat	7:30
Vaughn Monroe Show	47–48	120t	9.1	C	Sat	9:30
Vaughn Monroe Show	48–49	65	10.6	C	Sat	7:30
Vaughn Monroe Show	49–50	53t	9.4	C	Sat	7:30
Vaughn Monroe Show	50–51	47	8.6	C	Sat	7:30
Vaughn Monroe Show	51–52	57t	5.5	N	Sat	10:00
Vaughn Monroe Show	52–53	32t	5.4	C	Sat	7:30
Vee Lawnhurst	36–37	111	2.1	C	Thu	7:30
Vera Brodsky & Harold Triggs	34–35	129t	2.2	B	Sun	10:15
Vic & Sade (Art Van Harvey & Benadine Flynn)	36–37	112t	1.8	B	Wed	10:00
Vic & Sade (Art Van Harvey & Benadine Flynn)	45–46	145	4.7	C	M–F	7:15
Vick's Open House (Grace Moore)	35–36	21	12.3	C	Sun	8:00
Vick's Open House (Nelson Eddy)	36–37	12t	14.9	C	Sun	8:00
Vick's Open House (Jeanette McDonald)	37–38	64t	7.1	C	Sun	7:00
Victor Borge & Benny Goodman	46–47	122t	6.4	N	Mon	9:30
Vocal Varieties	36–37	99t	3.4	N	Tu,Th	7:15
Vocal Varieties	37–38	67t	6.9	N	Tu,Th	7:15
Vocal Varieties	38–39	86t	5.5	N	Tu,Th	7:15
Voice of America	33–34	82	6.4	C	Thu	8:30
Voice of Broadway (Dorothy Kilgallen)	41–42	126	4.5	C	Tue	6:15
Voice of Experience (Marion Sayle Taylor)	33–34	84t	5.7	C	Tue	8:30
Voice of Experience (Marion Sayle Taylor)	34–35	120t	3.3	C	Sun	6:45
Voice of Experience (Marion Sayle Taylor)	35–36	104	3.8	C	Sun	6:45
Voice of Experience (Marion Sayle Taylor)	36–37	46t	7.4	N	Tu,Th	7:15
Voice of Firestone (William Daly Orch & Soloists)	32–33	13t	21.8	N	Mon	8:30
Voice of Firestone (William Daly Orch & Soloists)	33–34	25	17.9	N	Mon	8:30
Voice of Firestone (William Daly Orch & Soloists)	34–35	51	12.8	N	Mon	8:30
Voice of Firestone (William Daly Orch & Soloists)	35–36	31	10.7	N	Mon	8:30
Voice of Firestone (Alfred Wallenstein Orch & Soloists)	36–37	46t	7.4	N	Mon	8:30
Voice of Firestone (Alfred Wallenstein Orch & Soloists)	37–38	42	9.5	N	Mon	8:30
Voice of Firestone (Alfred Wallenstein Orch & Soloists)	38–39	37	10.1	N	Mon	8:30
Voice of Firestone (Alfred Wallenstein Orch & Soloists)	39–40	65t	9.9	N	Mon	8:30
Voice of Firestone (Alfred Wallenstein Orch & Soloists)	40–41	63t	9.3	N	Mon	8:30
Voice of Firestone (Alfred Wallenstein Orch & Soloists)	41–42	84t	8.1	N	Mon	8:30
Voice of Firestone (Alfred Wallenstein Orch & Soloists)	42–43	81	9.0	N	Mon	8:30
Voice of Firestone (Howard Barlow Orch & Soloists)	43–44	91t	7.8	N	Mon	8:30
Voice of Firestone (Howard Barlow Orch & Soloists)	44–45	108t	7.4	N	Mon	8:30
Voice of Firestone (Howard Barlow Orch & Soloists)	45–46	90t	8.1	N	Mon	8:30
Voice of Firestone (Howard Barlow Orch & Soloists)	46–47	77t	9.1	N	Mon	8:30
Voice of Firestone (Howard Barlow Orch & Soloists)	47–48	78	12.2	N	Mon	8:30
Voice of Firestone (Howard Barlow Orch & Soloists)	48–49	98	8.0	N	Mon	8:30
Voice of Firestone (Howard Barlow Orch & Soloists)	49–50	88t	7.1	N	Mon	8:30
Voice of Firestone (Howard Barlow Orch & Soloists)	50–51	60t	7.2	N	Mon	8:30
Voice of Firestone (Howard Barlow Orch & Soloists)	51–52	40t	6.4	N	Mon	8:30
Voice of Firestone (Howard Barlow Orch & Soloists)	52–53	50	4.9	N	Mon	8:30
Voice of Liberty	40–41	94t	7.3	M	Th,Sa	9:00
Vox Pop (Parks Johnson & Jerry Belcher)	35–36	82t	5.6	N	Tue	9:00
Vox Pop (Parks Johnson & Wally Butterworth)	36–37	29	9.7	N	Tue	9:00
Vox Pop (Parks Johnson & Wally Butterworth)	37–38	30	11.1	N	Tue	9:00
Vox Pop (Parks Johnson & Wally Butterworth)	38–39	62	8.9	N	Sat	9:00
Vox Pop (Parks Johnson & Wally Butterworth)	39–40	67	9.8	C	Thu	7:30
Vox Pop (Parks Johnson & Wally Butterworth)	40–41	40	11.3	C	Thu	7:30
Vox Pop (Parks Johnson & Wally Butterworth)	41–42	43	12.0	C	Mon	8:00
Vox Pop (Parks Johnson & Warren Hull)	42–43	35	13.6	C	Mon	8:00
Vox Pop (Parks Johnson & Warren Hull)	43–44	37t	12.7	C	Mon	8:00
Vox Pop (Parks Johnson & Warren Hull)	44–45	34t	13.0	C	Mon	8:00
Vox Pop (Parks Johnson & Warren Hull)	45–46	28t	13.2	C	Mon	8:00
Vox Pop (Parks Johnson & Warren Hull)	46–47	94t	8.3	C	Tue	9:00
Vox Pop (Parks Johnson & Warren Hull)	47–48	85	11.8	A	Wed	8:30
Wake Up America	40–41	132	2.7	M	Mon	9:15
Waldorf Astoria Orch	32–33	97t	2.8	N	Tu,Th	6:00
Walk a Mile (John Henry Faulk)	52–53	32t	5.4	N	Wed	8:00
Walter O'Keefe Nestle Show	33–34	59t	9.2	B	Fri	8:00

6–11 P.M., Sept through June Programs
Rated 13 Weeks or More

	Season	Rank	Rtg	Net	Day	Time
Walter Winchell's Jergens Journal	32–33	44	11.6	B	Sun	9:30
Walter Winchell's Jergens Journal	33–34	49t	10.9	B	Sun	9:30
Walter Winchell's Jergens Journal	34–35	45t	13.7	B	Sun	9:30
Walter Winchell's Jergens Journal	35–36	38t	9.2	B	Sun	9:30
Walter Winchell's Jergens Journal	36–37	15	13.1	B	Sun	9:30
Walter Winchell's Jergens Journal	37–38	18t	13.7	B	Sun	9:30
Walter Winchell's Jergens Journal	38–39	19t	14.0	B	Sun	9:30
Walter Winchell's Jergens Journal	39–40	8	19.3	B	Sun	9:00
Walter Winchell's Jergens Journal	40–41	5	24.1	B	Sun	9:00
Walter Winchell's Jergens Journal	41–42	7	26.0	B	Sun	9:00
Walter Winchell's Jergens Journal	42–43	9	22.9	B	Sun	9:00
Walter Winchell's Jergens Journal	43–44	8t	21.4	B	Sun	9:00
Walter Winchell's Jergens Journal	44–45	4	22.8	B	Sun	9:00
Walter Winchell's Jergens Journal	45–46	9	19.8	A	Sun	9:00
Walter Winchell's Jergens Journal	46–47	9	20.8	A	Sun	9:00
Walter Winchell's Jergens Journal	47–48	30	17.2	A	Sun	9:00
Walter Winchell's Journal	48–49	4	21.7	A	Sun	9:00
Walter Winchell's Journal	49–50	6	16.3	A	Sun	9:00
Walter Winchell's Journal	50–51	7	12.4	A	Sun	9:00
Walter Winchell's Journal	51–52	9	9.2	A	Sun	9:00
Walter Winchell's Journal	52–53	37t	5.2	A	Sun	9:00
Waltz Time (Frank Munn & Abe Lyman Orch)	33–34	54	10.2	N	Fri	8:00
Waltz Time (Frank Munn & Abe Lyman Orch)	34–35	73	10.1	N	Fri	9:00
Waltz Time (Frank Munn & Abe Lyman Orch)	35–36	94t	4.9	N	Fri	9:00
Waltz Time (Frank Munn & Abe Lyman Orch)	36–37	87t	4.2	N	Fri	9:00
Waltz Time (Frank Munn & Abe Lyman Orch)	37–38	67t	6.9	N	Fri	9:00
Waltz Time (Frank Munn & Abe Lyman Orch)	38–39	84	6.1	N	Fri	9:00
Waltz Time (Frank Munn & Abe Lyman Orch)	39–40	83t	8.3	N	Fri	9:00
Waltz Time (Frank Munn & Abe Lyman Orch)	40–41	69	8.8	N	Fri	9:00
Waltz Time (Frank Munn & Abe Lyman Orch)	41–42	76t	8.5	N	Fri	9:00
Waltz Time (Frank Munn & Abe Lyman Orch)	42–43	57	10.2	N	Fri	9:00
Waltz Time (Frank Munn & Abe Lyman Orch)	43–44	59t	10.0	N	Fri	9:00
Waltz Time (Frank Munn & Abe Lyman Orch)	44–45	58t	10.7	N	Fri	9:00
Waltz Time (Bob Hannon & Victor Arden Orch)	45–46	50	11.1	N	Fri	9:30
Waltz Time (Bob Hannon & Victor Arden Orch)	46–47	71t	9.5	N	Fri	9:30
Waltz Time (Bob Hannon & Victor Arden Orch)	47–48	36t	16.1	N	Fri	9:30
Want to Be an Actor?	36–37	36	8.6	N	Sun	8:00
Warden Lawes at Sing Sing	33–34	29t	15.6	B	Wed	9:00
Warden Lawes at Sing Sing	34–35	50	13.1	B	Wed	9:00
Warden Lawes at Sing Sing	35–36	53t	7.5	B	Wed	9:30
Warden Lawes at Sing Sing	36–37	65t	6.3	N	Mon	9:00
Warden Lawes at Sing Sing	37–38	77	5.6	B	Mon	10:00
Warden Lawes at Sing Sing	38–39	89t	5.2	B	Fri	8:00
Ward's Family Theater	33–34	99t	3.8	C	Sun	6:30
Wayne King Orch	32–33	68	7.0	N	Tu,Th	8:30
Wayne King Orch	33–34	36	14.4	N	Tu,W	8:30
Wayne King Orch	34–35	37	15.0	N	Tu,W	8:30
Wayne King Orch	34–35	72	10.2	C	Su,M	10:00
Wayne King Orch	35–36	42t	8.7	N	Tu,W	8:30
Wayne King Orch	35–36	51t	7.6	C	Sun	8:30
Wayne King Orch	36–37	27t	10.1	C	Mon	10:00
Wayne King Orch	36–37	46t	7.4	N	Tue	8:30
Wayne King Orch	36–37	49t	7.2	N	Wed	8:30
Wayne King Orch	37–38	43	9.4	C	Mon	10:00
Wayne King Orch	37–38	54t	8.3	N	Wed	8:30
Wayne King Orch	37–38	60t	7.7	N	Tue	8:30
Wayne King Orch	39–40	30t	12.6	C	Sat	8:30
Wayne King Orch	40–41	72t	8.5	C	Sat	7:30
Wayne King Orch	41–42	57t	9.8	C	Mon	10:00
We the People (Gabriel Heatter)	37–38	59	8.0	C	Thu	7:30
We the People (Gabriel Heatter)	38–39	24	13.0	C	Tue	9:00
We the People (Gabriel Heatter)	39–40	15	15.5	C	Tue	9:00
We the People (Gabriel Heatter)	40–41	15t	15.3	C	Tue	9:00
We the People (Gabriel Heatter)	41–42	38t	12.5	C	Tue	9:00
We the People at War (Gabriel Heatter, Milo Boulton)	42–43	61	9.9	C	Sun	7:30
We the People at War (Milo Boulton)	43–44	73t	9.2	C	Sun	7:30
We the People at War (Milo Boulton)	44–45	27t	13.6	C	Sun	10:30
We the People (Milo Boulton)	45–46	53t	10.6	C	Sun	10:30
We the People (Milo Boulton)	46–47	48	11.0	C	Sun	10:30

6–11 P.M., Sept through June Programs
Rated 13 Weeks or More

	Season	Rank	Rtg	Net	Day	Time
We the People (Dwight Weist)	47–48	94t	11.3	C	Tue	9:00
We the People (Dwight Weist)	48–49	70t	9.9	C	Tue	9:00
We the People (Dan Seymour)	49–50	98t	5.8	N	Fri	8:30
We the People (Dan Seymour)	50–51	97t	4.1	N	Thu	9:30
We Who Dream	43–44	156	3.4	C	Fri	7:15
Wendell Hall Sings	33–34	110	3.1	N	Sun	6:45
Wendell Hall Sings	34–35	116t	4.0	N	Sun	7:45
Wendell Hall Sings	35–36	120	2.4	B	Fri	8:15
What Would You Have Done? (Ben Grauer)	39–40	106	3.6	B	Fri	9:30
What's My Line? (John Daly)	52–53	40t	5.1	C	Wed	9:30
What's My Name? (Arlene Francis)	39–40	47t	10.8	N	Fri	9:30
What's My Name? (Arlene Francis)	41–42	105t	6.3	M	Tue	8:00
What's New? (Don Ameche)	43–44	139t	4.4	B	Sat	7:00
What's Your Idea?	40–41	122t	5.0	N	Sun	6:30
Wheatenaville Sketches (Ray Knight)	32–33	91t	3.8	N	Su-Th	7:15
Which Is Which? (Ken Murray)	44–45	89t	8.8	C	Wed	9:30
Whispering Jack Smith Sings	32–33	97t	2.8	C	M,W	7:15
Whispering Jack Smith Sings	34–35	129t	2.2	N	T,T,Sa	7:15
The Whistler (Bill Forman)	47–48	134	6.6	C	Wed	10:00
Whiz Quiz	48–49	109t	6.9	A	Sat	10:00
Who Knows?	40–41	130	3.2	M	Mon	10:15
Wild Bill Hickock (Guy Madison)	50–51	116t	2.2	M	Sun	7:00
Wild Bill Hickock (Guy Madison)	51–52	87	3.7	M	Sun	7:00
Will Rogers Gulf Headliners	33–34	4	37.0	B	Sun	9:00
Will Rogers Gulf Headliners	34–35	9t	23.9	C	Sun	8:30
William L Shirer News & Comment	43–44	141t	4.3	C	Sun	7:00
Wings of Destiny (Carlton KaDell)	40–41	83t	8.0	N	Fri	10:00
Wings of Destiny (John Hodiak)	41–42	76t	8.5	N	Fri	10:00
Woman of the Year	52–53	87t	2.6	M	Mon	8:00
Woody Herman Orch	45–46	168t	3.3	A	Fri	8:00
World Today News (Douglas Edwards)	39–40	93t	6.8	C	MWF	6:45
World Today News (Douglas Edwards)	41–42	115t	5.6	C	M-F	6:45
World Today News (Douglas Edwards)	43–44	133t	4.6	C	M-Sat	6:45
World Today News (Douglas Edwards)	44–45	138	5.1	C	M-F	6:45
World Today News (Douglas Edwards)	45–46	149t	4.4	C	M-F	6:45
Wythe Williams News	40–41	122t	5.0	M	Tu,Th	8:00
Xavier Cugat Orch	40–41	109t	6.3	N	Thu	7:30
Xavier Cugat Orch	41–42	110t	6.0	B	Tue	8:00
Xavier Cugat Orch	43–44	133t	4.6	M	Wed	8:30
You Bet Your Life (Groucho Marx)	47–48	72t	13.0	A	Wed	9:30
You Bet Your Life (Groucho Marx)	48–49	46t	12.1	A	Wed	9:30
You Bet Your Life (Groucho Marx)	49–50	11	14.9	C	Wed	9:00
You Bet Your Life (Groucho Marx)	50–51	9	11.8	N	Wed	9:00
You Bet Your Life (Groucho Marx)	51–52	6t	9.6	N	Wed	9:00
You Bet Your Life (Groucho Marx)	52–53	7	7.9	N	Wed	9:00
You Said It	37–38	78	5.4	C	Mon	8:00
Your All Time Hit Parade	42–43	76t	9.2	N	Fri	8:30
Your All Time Hit Parade	43–44	64	9.6	N	Fri	8:30
Your Happy Birthday (Jimmy Dorsey Orch)	40–41	124	4.9	B	Fri	9:30
Your Hit Parade (Gogo De Lys & Kay Thompson)	34–35	33	15.5	N	Sat	8:00
Your Hit Parade (Various)	35–36	19	13.0	N	Sat	8:00
Your Hit Parade (Buddy Clark)	36–37	17t	12.8	N	Wed	10:00
Your Hit Parade (Buddy Clark)	36–37	24	10.9	C	Sat	10:00
Your Hit Parade (Buddy Clark)	37–38	36	10.6	N	Wed	10:00
Your Hit Parade (Buddy Clark)	37–38	26t	12.4	C	Sat	10:00
Your Hit Parade (Buddy Clark/Lanny Ross)	38–39	22	13.6	C	Sat	10:00
Your Hit Parade (Lanny Ross/Barry Wood & Bea Wain/ Bonnie Baker)	39–40	22t	13.6	C	Sat	9:00
Your Hit Parade (Barry Wood & Bea Wain)	40–41	26t	13.0	C	Sat	9:00
Your Hit Parade (Barry Wood & Louise King/Joan Edwards)	41–42	25t	14.2	C	Sat	9:00
Your Hit Parade (Barry Wood/Frank Sinatra & Joan Edwards)	42–43	29	14.5	C	Sat	9:00
Your Hit Parade (Frank Sinatra & Bea Wain/Joan Edwards)	43–44	20	16.7	C	Sat	9:00
Your Hit Parade (Frank Sinatra/Lawrence Tibbett & Joan Edwards)	44–45	17	15.3	C	Sat	9:00
Your Hit Parade (Dick Todd & Joan Edwards)	45–46	32	13.0	C	Sat	9:00
Your Hit Parade (Andy Russell & Joan Edwards/Ginny Simms)	46–47	33	12.6	N	Sat	9:00
Your Hit Parade (Frank Sinatra & Beryl Davis)	47–48	15t	20.0	N	Sat	9:00
Your Hit Parade (Frank Sinatra & Beryl Davis//Eileen Wilson)	48–49	29	13.8	N	Sat	9:00
Your Hit Parade (Eileen Wilson & Bill Harrington/Jeff Clark)	49–50	42	10.4	N	Sat	9:00
Your Hit Parade (Eileen Wilson & Snooky Lanson)	50–51	56t	7.7	N	Sat	9:00

6–11 P.M., Sept through June Programs
Rated 13 Weeks or More

	Season	Rank	Rtg	Net	Day	Time
Your Hit Parade (Guy Lombardo Orch)	51–52	40t	6.4	N	Thu	10:00
Your Hit Parade (Guy Lombardo Orch)	52–53	51t	4.8	N	Fri	8:00
Your Song & Mine (Thomas L Thomas)	48–49	34t	13.3	C	Wed	9:00
Yours for a Song (Gordon MacRae)	48–49	148	1.6	M	Fri	8:30
Yours Truly Johnny Dollar (John Lund)	52–53	22t	6.3	C	Tue	9:00
Youth Vs Age (Cal Tinney & Paul Wing)	39–40	97	6.5	N	Sat	9:00
Zenith Radio Foundation	37–38	83t	4.6	C	Sun	10:00

Appendix C: Rated (Less Than 13 Weeks per Season) Prime-Time Programs, 1932–1953

Programs Rated Less Than 13 Weeks	Season	Rating	Net	Day	Time
Abbott & Costello Show (Bud Abbott & Lou Costello)	48–49	5.1	A	Thu	8:00
ABC's of Music (Robert Q Lewis)	49–50	7.0	C	Wed	9:30
ABC's of Music (Robert Q Lewis)	50–51	6.3	C	Wed	9:30
Accordiana	33–34	4.4	B	Tue	6:45
Adventures of Archie Andrews (Bob Hastings)	48–49	4.8	N	Wed	8:30
Adventures of Bulldog Drummond (George Coulouris)	40–41	6.4	M	Sun	6:30
Adventures of Bulldog Drummond (George Coulouris)	41–42	8.9	M	Sun	6:30
Adventures of Charlie Chan (Ed Begley)	44–45	8.4	N	Thur	7:30
Adventures of Ellery Queen (Hugh Marlowe)	39–40	9.5	C	Sun	7:30
Adventures of Ellery Queen (Hugh Marlowe)	40–41	8.6	C	Sun	7:30
Adventures of Ellery Queen (Lawrence Dobkin)	47–48	6.4	N	Sun	6:30
Adventures of Philip Marlow (Gerald Mohr)	49–50	4.7	C	Wed	10:00
Adventures of Philip Marlow (Gerald Mohr)	49–50	10.0	C	Sat	8:30
Adventures of Sam Spade (Howard Duff)	46–47	5.2	A	Fri	8:00
Adventures of Sam Spade (Steve Dunn)	50–51	8.5	N	Sun	8:00
Adventures of Sherlock Holmes (Basil Rathbone & Nigel Bruce)	42–43	4.3	M	Fri	8:30
Adventures of the Falcon (Les Tremayne)	47–48	9.8	M	Tue	8:30
Adventures of the Falcon (Les Tremayne)	49–50	5.5	N	Wed	8:30
Adventures of the Thin Man (Joseph Curtin & Claudia Morgan)	49–50	6.2	A	Fri	9:00
Adventures of Topper (Roland Young)	44–45	7.1	N	Thu	8:30
Alan Young Show	43–44	5.8	N	Wed	9:00
Aldrich Family (Bobby Ellis)	52–53	1.9	N	Sun	7:30
Alec Templeton Show	45–46	10.0	N	Sun	8:00
Alexander's Mediation Board	50–51	0.8	M	Sun	8:30
Allan Jones & Frankie Carle Orch	44–45	5.5	C	Wed	8:00
American Forum of the Air	47–48	3.3	M	Tue	10:00
An Evening with Romberg	46–47	10.0	N	Tue	10:30
Angelo Patri's Your Child	32–33	2.3	C	Wed	7:45
Armco Iron Master Brass Band (Frank Simon)	33–34	5.2	B	Fri	10:00
Armco Iron Master Brass Band (Frank Simon)	36–37	1.3	B	Tue	10:00
Ask Me Another (Happy Felton)	45–46	5.6	N	Sun	6:30
Ask Me Another (Happy Felton)	46–47	5.1	N	Sun	6:30
Atwater Kent Radio Hour	34–35	1.7	C	Mon	8:30
Auction Quiz (Chuck Acree)	41–42	2.9	B	Fri	8:00
Bakers' Theater of Stars	52–53	2.3	C	Sun	6:00
Benny Goodman Orch	46–47	6.0	N	Mon	9:30
Bert Lytell Show	38–39	2.1	B	Fri	7:00
Best of Groucho (Repeat Bdcsts)	52–53	5.1	N	Wed	9:00
Best Things in Life	46–47	2.8	A	Thu	9:30
Better Half (Tom Slater)	42–43	3.5	M	Mon	8:30
The Bickersons (Lew Parker & Frances Langford)	50–51	5.9	C	Tue	9:30
Big Game Hunt	38–39	12.4	N	Wed	9:00
Big Time	32–33	4.8	N	Wed	7:00
Birth of the Blues	41–42	4.9	M	Sat	9:00
Blatz Reporter News	50–51	0.4	A	M-F	10:45
Blatz Reporter News	50–51	0.9	A	Tu-F	10:00
Blondie (Ann Rutherford & Arthur Lake)	49–50	7.0	A	Thu	8:00
Blue Coal Musical Review	32–33	3.4	N	Sun	7:00
Bob Burns Show	38–39	22.2	N	Thu	10:00
Bob Crosby Orch	35–36	2.6	B	Fri	8:15
Bob Trout News	52–53	3.1	C	Thu	10:00
Bob Trout News	52–53	3.1	C	Sun	10:00
Boston Blackie (Chester Morris)	43–44	6.9	N	Fri	10:00
Boston Blackie (Chester Morris)	44–45	8.2	N	Fri	10:00

Programs Rated Less Than 13 Weeks	*Season*	*Rating*	*Net*	*Day*	*Time*
Boston Pops Orch	51–52	3.5	N	Mon	10:00
Break the Bank (Bert Parks)	50–51	10.3	N	Wed	9:00
Briggs Sports Review	35–36	2.1	N	Sat	7:45
Broadway Is My Beat (Larry Thor)	51–52	6.2	C	Mon	9:30
Broadway Vanities (Everett Marshall)	33–34	3.6	C	Wed	8:30
Bugler Showboat	39–40	4.9	B	Fri	9:00
Cafe Istanbul (Marlene Dietrich)	52–53	3.4	A	Sun	8:30
Call the Police (George Petrie)	49–50	5.0	C	Sun	7:30
Can You Top This? (Ward Wilson)	48–49	11.8	N	Sat	9:30
Can You Top This? (Ward Wilson)	49–50	3.4	M	Wed	8:00
Carborundum Band	32–33	4.1	C	Sat	9:30
Carborundum Band	33–34	6.4	C	Sat	9:30
Carborundum Band	34–35	5.5	C	Sat	9:00
Carborundum Band	37–38	5.1	C	Sat	7:30
Carmen Dragon Orch	50–51	4.9	N	Tue	8:30
Carson Robison Buckeroos	32–33	1.6	C	Fri	8:30
Casebook of Gregory Hood (Gale Gordon)	45–46	6.1	M	Mon	8:30
Casebook of Gregory Hood (Elliot Lewis)	51–52	4.2	A	Wed	8:30
Casey Crime Photographer (Staats Cotsworth)	50–51	10.0	C	Thu	9:30
Cecil Brown News/Comment	50–51	1.7	M	Sat	10:45
Cecil Brown News/Comment	51–52	2.7	M	Sat	7:50
Chamber Music Society of Lower Basin Street (Milton Cross)	40–41	2.0	B	Mon	9:30
Chamber Music Society of Lower Basin Street (Milton Cross)	44–45	6.8	B	Sun	9:15
Charlie Winninger Gulf Headliners	34–35	19.7	C	Sun	7:30
Charlotte Greenwood Show	44–45	10.2	N	Tue	10:00
Chase & Sanborn Hour (Bert Lahr)	32–33	29.5	N	Sun	8:00
Chase & Sanborn Hour (Georgie Price)	32–33	27.5	N	Sun	8:00
Cities Service Concert (Lucille Manners & Frank Black Orch)	44–45	6.8	N	Fri	8:00
"Clara, Lu & Em"	36–37	1.9	B	Fri	9:30
Club Romance	34–35	6.6	C	Sun	8:00
Coca-Cola Show	52–53	3.4	N	Fri	9:00
Coke Time (Eddie Fisher)	52–53	2.9	N	Tu,F	8:00
Colonel Howe Commentary	32–33	7.4	N	Sun	10:30
Colonel Howe Commentary	33–34	4.5	N	Sun	10:30
Colonel Stoopnagle & Budd (F Chase Taylor & Budd Hulick)	33–34	8.2	C	W,Sa	9:15
Colonel Stoopnagle & Budd (F Chase Taylor & Budd Hulick)	34–35	5.1	C	Fri	10:30
Conoco Tourist Adventures	33–34	8.3	N	Wed	10:30
Counterspy (Don MacLaughlin)	52–53	4.6	N	Thu	9:30
Crime Doctor (Everett Sloane)	47–48	16.2	C	Sun	8:30
Crime Fighters	49–50	4.5	M	Mon	9:30
Crumit & Sanderson	35–36	10.6	C	Sun	7:30
Cyrena Van Gordon Sings	33–34	1.8	B	Mon	8:30
Dale Carnegie	37–38	4.7	N	Sat	8:30
Danger Is My Business	40–41	2.5	M	Wed	10:15
Danger Is My Business	41–42	2.1	M	Wed	9:15
Dangerous Assignment (Brian Donlevy)	49–50	8.4	N	Wed	10:30
Dangerous Assignment (Brian Donlevy)	50–51	7.1	N	Wed	10:30
David Rose Orch	50–51	5.3	C	Sun	8:30
Defense Attorney (Mercedes McCambridge)	52–53	3.4	A	Thu	8:30
Dennis King	34–35	4.8	B	Wed	10:00
Detect & Collect (Fred Uttal & Wendie Barrie)	46–47	4.2	A	Sat	9:30
Detroit Symphony	45–46	3.3	M	Sat	8:30
Diane's Life Saver Musical Comedy	34–35	2.0	C	M,W	8:00
Dick Tracy	38–39	5.5	N	Sat	7:00
Dixie Circus	33–34	1.1	N	Mon	8:00
Doctors Talk It Over	47–48	3.1	A	Mon	10:00
Don Ameche Show	39–40	9.0	N	Fri	10:00
Don Carney's Dog Stories	33–34	1.4	B	Tue	7:45
Doris Day Show	51–52	4.4	C	Sun	7:30
Dorothy Thompson News/Comment	41–42	2.8	B	Thu	8:45
Dorris Lorraine Sings	33–34	2.5	C	Thu	10:30
Dr IQ Junior	40–41	4.0	N	Sun	6:30
Dr Rockwell	38–39	1.0	B	Tue	9:30
Dunninger the Mentalist	45–46	8.8	N	Fri	10:00
Easy Aces (Goodman & Jane Ace)	33–34	5.0	C	WThF	8:15
Ed Sullivan on Broadway	46–47	2.8	A	Mon	8:15
Eddie Dooley Sports	33–34	3.4	C	ThFSa	6:30
Eddie Rickenbacker	36–37	1.3	C	W,F	7:30
Eddy Duchin Orch	35–36	11.5	N	Tue	9:30
Edward Maher News	45–46	1.1	A	Mon	10:00

Programs Rated Less Than 13 Weeks	Season	Rating	Net	Day	Time
Edward R Murrow in London	41–42	6.0	C	Sun	6:00
Edwin C Hill News/Comment	32–33	9.8	C	MWF	10:30
Edwin C Hill News/Comment	49–50	1.5	A	Tu,Th	7:00
Eleanor Roosevelt Commentary	34–35	6.8	C	Fri	8:00
Elgin Adventurers' Club (Floyd Gibbons)	32–33	7.8	N	Fri	10:30
Encore Theater	45–46	6.7	C	Tue	9:30
Escape (William Conrad & Paul Frees)	49–50	10.6	C	Tue	9:30
Everything for the Boys (Dick Haymes & Helen Forrest)	45–46	6.0	N	Tue	7:30
Family Skeleton	52–53	2.0	C	M-F	7:15
The Fat Man (J Scott Smart)	51–52	2.1	A	Fri	8:00
Ferde Grofe Orch	32–33	2.9	N	M,W,Sa	7:45
Festival of American Music	46–47	2.7	A	Sun	8:00
Fibber McGee & Molly (Jim & Marian Jordan)	34–35	4.5	B	Tue	10:00
Fighting Senator	46–47	6.1	C	Mon	8:30
First Nighter (Barbara Luddy & Olan Soule)	44–45	4.1	M	Wed	9:30
First Nighter (Barbara Luddy & Olan Soule)	49–50	9.2	C	Thu	10:30
Fitch Bandwagon Mysteries	45–46	6.8	N	Sun	7:30
Five Star Theater	32–33	9.0	N	Thu	7:30
Five Star Theater	32–33	8.2	N	Fri	7:30
Floyd Gibbons News	32–33	5.9	B	Su,T,T	8:45
Flying Red Horse Tavern (Walter Wolff King)	36–37	5.4	C	Fri	8:00
Forever Ernest (Jackie Coogan)	45–46	5.0	C	Mon	8:00
Forty-Five Minutes in Hollywood	34–35	8.8	C	Thu	10:00
Frances Langford & Spike Jones	44–45	15.0	N	Sun	8:00
Frank Buck	34–35	7.8	N	M-F	7:45
Frank Fay Calling	35–36	8.0	N	Sat	9:00
Frank Morgan Show	45–46	7.6	N	Sun	7:00
Fred Stone Gulf Headliners	33–34	17.2	B	Sun	9:00
Fred Waring Show	45–46	10.5	N	Tue	9:30
Fred Waring Show	46–47	9.2	N	Tue	9:30
Fred Waring Show	49–50	4.5	N	Thu	10:30
Friday Night Boxing	41–42	6.4	B	Fri	10:00
Fulton Oursler	38–39	1.9	B	Tue	9:30
Fun in Print	39–40	5.7	C	Sun	6:00
G Men	35–36	17.1	N	Sat	9:00
Gateway to Hollywood (Jesse Lansky)	38–39	4.8	C	Sun	7:00
Gay Nineties Revue (Beatrice Kay)	44–45	7.8	C	Mon	8:30
Gem Highlights	32–33	8.7	C	Sun	9:00
Gene Autry's Melody Ranch	45–46	5.0	C	Sun	7:00
General Electric Concert	32–33	23.7	B	Sun	8:00
George McCall Hollywood News	38–39	4.5	C	Tu,Th	7:15
Get More Out of Life	50–51	0.7	C	Sun	9:45
Gladys Swarthout Sings	36–37	4.8	N	Sun	10:00
Gold Medal Musical Fast Freight	32–33	4.9	C	Tu,W	8:45
Golden Treasury of Song	41–42	4.8	C	MWF	6:30
Goodwill Court (AL Alexander)	36–37	17.0	N	Sun	8:00
Good Will Hour (John J Anthony)	35–36	3.8	M	Sun	10:30
Gracie Fields Show	43–44	11.4	N	Sun	8:00
Grantland Rice Sports	51–52	2.3	C	Fri	8:00
Great Moments of Great Plays	41–42	9.8	C	Fri	9:00
Green Hornet	46–47	4.5	A	Tue	7:30
Gunsmoke (William Conrad)	52–53	5.0	C	Fri	8:30
Guy Lombardo Orch	48–49	2.7	M	Sat	9:30
Guy Lombardo Orch	49–50	4.5	N	Sun	7:30
Guy Lombardo Orch	49–50	8.7	C	Sun	7:00
Guy Lombardo Orch	50–51	5.6	C	Sun	7:00
Guy Lombardo Orch	51–52	4.5	C	Sun	7:00
Guy Lombardo Orch	52–53	3.6	C	Sun	7:00
Hal MacIntyre Orch	44–45	3.1	B	Tue	10:30
Hal Peary Show	50–51	8.1	C	Wed	9:00
Harry James Orch	45–46	5.0	C	Fri	10:30
Harry Savoy Show	43–44	8.7	N	Thu	10:00
Harry Savoy Show	44–45	11.6	N	Thu	10:00
Harry Wismer Sports	45–46	5.8	A	M-F	9:55
Hawaii Calls (Webley Edwards)	49–50	3.5	M	Sat	7:00
Headline Edition News/ Taylor Grant	48–49	1.6	A	M-F	7:05
Hearthstone of the Death Squad (Alfred Shirley)	51–52	5.9	C	Thu	9:00
Hedda Hopper Hollywood News	42–43	4.7	C	MWF	6:15
Henry Morgan Show	49–50	9.5	N	Wed	9:00
Here's to Romance (Buddy Clark)	42–43	2.9	B	Sun	6:00

Programs Rated Less Than 13 Weeks	Season	Rating	Net	Day	Time
Hildegarde's Raleigh Room	43–44	14.7	N	Tue	10:30
Hobby Lobby (Dave Elman)	39–40	7.8	B	Wed	8:30
Hogan's Daughter	49–50	4.1	N	Wed	8:00
Holiday for Music	46–47	5.5	C	Wed	10:30
Hollywood Star Playhouse	49–50	9.6	C	Mon	8:00
Hour of Charm (Phil Spitalny All Girl Orch)	36–37	3.3	N	Mon	9:30
Hour of Charm (Phil Spitalny All Girl Orch)	46–47	4.2	N	Sun	10:00
Hour of Mystery	45–46	5.0	A	Sun	10:00
Hour of Mystery	46–47	5.9	A	Sun	10:00
Human Adventure	45–46	2.4	M	Sun	9:00
Husbands & Wives	35–36	11.7	B	Sun	7:30
Imperial Time	40–41	3.4	M	Mon	10:15
Inside of Sports (Joe Cummisky)	49–50	2.0	M	M-F	7:45
Irving Berlin Gulf Headliners	33–34	13.7	B	Sun	9:00
Irwin S Cobb Commentary	32–33	10.7	C	We,Fr	9:00
Irwin S Cobb Commentary	33–34	11.1	C	We,Fr	9:00
It Happens Every Day	52–53	0.8	A	Tu,Th	10:35
It Pays to Be Ignorant	50–51	9.5	C	Wed	9:00
It Pays to Be Ignorant	51–52	5.3	C	Wed	9:00
Jack Carson Show	42–43	5.0	C	Wed	9:30
Jack Dempsey's Gymnasium	32–33	2.9	C	T,T,Sa	6:30
Jack Pearl Show	50–51	3.9	N	Tue	9:30
Jack Pearl Show	51–52	5.0	N	Tue	9:30
James Melton Show	46–47	5.7	C	Sun	9:30
Jan Savitt Orch	45–46	4.5	N	Sun	10:30
Jan Savitt Orch	46–47	5.2	N	Sun	10:30
Jason & Golden Fleece	52–53	5.7	N	Wed	10:00
Jello Summer Show	35–36	19.0	B	Sun	7:00
Jerry Wayne Show	45–46	5.1	C	Fri	7:30
Jimmy Durante Show	34–35	28.5	N	Sun	8:00
Joe E Brown Show	39–40	8.0	C	Thu	7:30
John B Kennedy News/Comment	42–43	4.4	C	T,T	6:30
John B Kennedy News/Comment	49–50	5.1	M	Sat	7:55
John Charles Thomas Sings	34–35	11.2	N	Wed	10:00
John Nesbitt's Passing Parade	44–45	5.1	C	TWT	7:15
Johnnie & The Foursome	34–35	1.1	C	Wed	8:00
Johnnie & The Foursome	35–36	1.5	C	Wed	8:00
Johnny Desmond Show	49–50	3.5	A	Wed	9:25
Johnny Mercer Show	44–45	8.8	N	M-F	7:00
Junior Miss (Barbara Whiting)	52–53	4.7	C	Thu	8:30
Just Entertainment	45–46	4.9	C	Sat	7:30
Just Entertainment	45–46	4.9	C	Tue	10:00
Keepsakes (Dorothy Kirsten)	44–45	3.1	B	Sun	8:30
Keller, Sargent & Ross	32–33	0.7	C	Tu,Th	7:30
Ken Murray Royal Gelatin Show	32–33	6.5	N	Wed	8:00
King's Henchmen	33–34	6.3	C	Sat	7:30
King's Men Quartet	48–49	6.4	N	Tue	9:30
Kraft Music Hall Eddy Duchin Orch	45–46	12.3	N	Thu	9:00
Kraft Music Hall Ed Everett Horton	45–46	9.9	N	Thu	9:00
Kraft Music Hall Nelson Eddy	49–50	5.2	N	Thu	9:00
Kraft Music Hall Summer Show	44–45	12.8	N	Thu	9:00
Lanny Ross' State Fair	35–36	12.7	B	Sun	7:00
Law & You	51–52	1.3	A	Sun	9:30
Lawrence Welk Show	48–49	3.5	A	Wed	9:30
LeBlanc's Comedy & Musical Show	50–51	2.9	A	Sat	9:00
LeBlanc's Hollywood Party	50–51	3.3	M	Fri	9:00
A Life in Your Hands (Ned LeFevre)	48–49	7.2	N	Tue	10:30
A Life in Your Hands (Carleton KaDell)	49–50	8.1	N	Tue	10:30
A Life in Your Hands (Carleton KaDell)	50–51	7.3	N	Tue	10:30
A Life in Your Hands (Lee Bowman)	51–52	5.2	A	Fri	9:00
Life Is Worth Living	52–53	2.4	M	Thu	9:05
The Lineup (Bill Johnstone)	50–51	7.5	C	Thu	10:00
The Lineup (Bill Johnstone)	51–52	6.2	C	Tue	9:00
The Lineup (Bill Johnstone)	52–53	5.1	C	Wed	9:00
Literary Digest	33–34	1.5	B	Wed	6:15
Literary Digest Political Poll	36–37	4.6	B	MWF	7:15
Lives at Stake	32–33	10.1	N	Tue	10:00
Lives at Stake	33–34	9.6	N	Tue	10:00
The Lone Ranger (Earle Graser)	40–41	5.1	M	MWF	7:30
Longine Symphonette	50–51	3.3	C	Sun	10:30

Programs Rated Less Than 13 Weeks	Season	Rating	Net	Day	Time
Louella Parsons Hollywood News	51–52	3.7	C	Tue	9:30
Love Story Program	32–33	11.1	C	Thu	9:30
Love Story Program	33–34	5.6	B	Wed	9:30
Lucky Smith	34–35	7.5	N	Mon	10:30
Lum & Abner (Chet Lauck & Norris Goff)	49–50	6.8	C	Wed	10:30
Lux Summer Theater	52–53	7.1	C	Mon	9:00
Madame Schumann-Heink Sings	33–34	9.2	B	Sun	9:00
Magic Carpet Program	33–34	37.8	N	Sat	9:00
Magnificent Montague (Monty Woolley)	51–52	3.6	N	Sat	8:30
Man Called X (Herbert Marshall)	48–49	12.8	C	Sun	8:30
Man Called X (Herbert Marshall)	46–47	7.5	C	Thu	10:30
Man Called X (Herbert Marshall)	45–46	9.5	N	Tue	10:00
Man Called X (Herbert Marshall)	46–47	10.7	N	Tue	10:00
Maple City Four	33–34	1.6	B	MWF	7:30
Margaret Whiting Show	46–47	5.2	N	Tue	8:00
Mario Lanza Show	50–51	4.3	C	Sun	8:00
Matty Melnick Orch	38–39	3.6	C	Thu	7:15
Meet Corliss Archer (Janet Waldo)	45–46	5.5	C	Sun	9:00
Meet the Stars	48–49	2.8	A	Thu	8:55
Meet Your Navy	45–46	1.7	A	Mon	8:30
Melodiana	35–36	2.1	B	Mon	8:30
Melody & Madness	39–40	6.1	B	Tue	9:00
Memories in Melody	32–33	2.3	C	Sun	7:30
Mercury Summer Theater (Orson Welles)	45–46	5.5	C	Fri	10:00
Mercury Summer Theater (Orson Welles)	46–47	6.2	C	Fri	10:00
Meredith Willson Show	45–46	5.3	N	Thu	8:30
Meredith Willson Show	49–50	4.2	N	Thu	8:00
Meredith Willson's Music Room	52–53	3.1	N	Mon	10:00
MGM Musical Comedy Theater	51–52	2.4	M	Wed	8:00
Mindy Carson Sings	50–51	1.0	N	TTSa	11:15
Minneapolis Symphony	33–34	8.9	N	Sun	10:30
Monday Night Show	38–39	6.3	C	Mon	8:00
Mr Chameleon (Karl Swenson)	52–53	5.0	C	Fri	9:00
Mr District Attorney (Dwight Weist)	38–39	5.1	N	M-F	7:00
Music by Gershwin	34–35	2.4	C	Sun	6:00
Music by Morton Gould	44–45	4.0	C	Thu	9:00
Musical Americana (Deems Taylor)	40–41	5.5	B	Tue	9:00
Musical Merry Go Round	50–51	3.1	N	Sat	8:00
Musical Merry Go Round	51–52	3.8	N	Sat	9:00
Mystery in the Air	45–46	9.8	N	Thu	10:00
Mystery Is My Hobby	46–47	4.0	M	Sun	10:00
Name the Movie (Clark Dennis)	48–49	2.2	A	Thu	9:30
Nat Shilkret Orch	33–34	1.8	B	Sun	9:45
National Barn Dance (Joe Kelly)	46–47	6.3	N	Sat	9:00
NBC Symphony	48–49	3.4	N	Sun	8:30
NBC Symphony	50–51	4.2	N	Sun	8:30
NBC Symphony	51–52	4.5	N	Sun	8:30
NBC Symphony	50–51	5.6	N	Sat	6:30
NBC Symphony	49–50	4.6	N	Sun	8:30
Nelson Eddy Show	41–42	7.5	C	Wed	8:00
News of Tomorrow	51–52	1.1	A	M-Th	10:30
News of Tomorrow	52–53	1.3	A	M-Th	10:00
Nick Carter Master Detective (Lon Clark)	51–52	6.4	M	Sun	6:30
Nightbeat (Frank Lovejoy)	49–50	6.0	N	Mon	10:00
Nine to Five	35–36	1.4	B	Thu	7:15
Norman Brokenshire Show	52–53	0.2	A	Sun	6:15
Official Detective (Craig McDonnell)	49–50	6.3	M	Tue	8:30
Ohman & Arden	32–33	2.0	N	Sun	9:45
Old Gold Program	44–45	8.1	N	Sun	10:30
Old Gold Sports Page	35–36	3.8	N	Sat	7:00
One Man's Family (J Anthony Smythe)	49–50	3.9	N	M-F	7:00
Original Amateur Hour (Ted Mack)	52–53	3.3	A	Thu	9:00
Our Daily Food	32–33	0.7	B	Fri	6:00
Our Home on the Range	34–35	9.3	B	Wed	9:00
Parade of States	32–33	14.3	N	Mon	9:30
Parker Family (Leon Janney)	44–45	2.9	B	Fri	8:15
Pat Barnes	32–33	2.8	B	M-W	8:45
Paul Sullivan News/Comment	39–40	7.1	C	M-F	6:30
Paul Whiteman Rhythmic Concert	32–33	8.8	B	Sun	6:30
Paul Whiteman Show	39–40	10.2	C	Wed	8:30

Programs Rated Less Than 13 Weeks	Season	Rating	Net	Day	Time
Pause That Refreshes (Ginny Simms & Percy Faith Orch)	49–50	6.1	C	Sun	8:00
Pause That Refreshes (Jane Froman & Percy Faith Orch)	50–51	6.3	C	Sun	8:00
Peggy Lee Show	50–51	2.9	C	Sun	7:30
Penny Singleton Story	49–50	6.4	N	Tue	9:00
Penthouse Party (Mark Hellinger)	34–35	5.1	B	Wed	8:30
People Are Funny (Art Baker, Art Linkletter)	41–42	9.9	N	Fri	10:00
Pet Milk Show (Bob Crosby)	50–51	6.0	N	Sun	10:30
Peter Salem	49–50	5.2	M	Mon	8:30
Phil Baker Show	39–40	7.2	C	Wed	8:00
Phil Harris Orch	32–33	5.3	N	Fri	9:00
Phil Harris Orch	34–35	9.2	B	Fri	9:00
Phil Harris Show	44–45	12.8	N	Wed	10:00
Phil Harris Show	50–51	6.3	N	Sun	7:30
Phil Spitalney Ensemble	33–34	1.6	C	Wed	7:00
Philadelphia Symphony Orch	32–33	15.9	C	Sat	9:00
Philco Summer Hour	44–45	5.4	B	Sun	6:00
Philo Vance (Jose Ferrer)	45–46	8.2	N	Thu	7:30
Private Files of Rex Saunders (Rex Harrison)	50–51	5.7	N	Wed	10:30
Program of the Week	33–34	3.7	C	Fri	10:00
Radio Readers Digest	45–46	7.2	C	Sun	9:00
Ransom Sherman Show	44–45	4.2	B	Tue	8:30
Ray Noble by Request	44–45	5.0	C	Wed	9:00
Raymond Paige Orch	42–43	5.4	N	Tue	7:30
Rebuttal (John W Vandercook)	49–50	1.7	M	Sun	9:15
Red Barber's Clubhouse Sports	49–50	2.2	C	Sat	6:30
Red Grange Sports	34–35	9.2	N	ThFSa	6:30
Revere All Star Revue	48–49	3.6	M	Thu	9:30
Rhythm at Eight	34–35	4.3	C	Sun	8:00
Richard Diamond, Private Detective (Dick Powell)	49–50	8.6	N	Wed	10:30
Richard Diamond, Private Detective (Dick Powell)	52–53	4.1	C	Sun	7:30
Richard Himber Orch	33–34	4.4	N	Mon	8:00
Richfield Country Club	33–34	3.0	B	Mon	7:30
Road Ahead	44–45	2.9	B	Wed	9:00
Robert Benchley Buick Show	33–34	4.0	C	T,T	9:15
Robert Q's Waxworks (Robert Q Lewis)	52–53	0.6	C	Sun	10:00
Robert Ripley Believe It or Not	38–39	14.0	N	Mon	8:00
Rogues Gallery (Dick Powell)	46–47	7.4	N	Sun	7:30
Romance Rhythm & Robert Ripley	45–46	3.4	C	Thu	10:30
Romantic Melodies	33–34	2.4	B	Thu	7:30
The Sad Sack (Herb Vigran)	45–46	5.6	C	Wed	9:00
The Sad Sack (Herb Vigran)	46–47	7.7	C	Wed	9:00
The Saint (Vincent Price)	49–50	5.9	M	Sun	7:30
Sara's Private Caper (Sara Berner)	49–50	4.3	N	Thu	10:30
Satan's Waitin'	49–50	8.0	C	Tue	8:30
Saturday Night Serenade (Various Artists)	48–49	6.9	C	Sat	7:30
Screen Directors' Playhouse	51–52	5.1	N	Fri	8:30
The Sheriff (Robert Haag)	51–52	2.2	A	Fri	9:30
Shirley Temple Time	41–42	14.7	C	Fri	10:00
Sidney Walton News/Comment	51–52	2.6	A	Thu	9:45
Sidney Walton News/Comment	51–52	2.1	A	M,T	8:00
Silken Strings	35–36	9.0	B	Sun	9:00
Silver Dust Serenaders	34–35	2.2	C	MWF	7:30
Silver Theater (Conrad Nagel & John Loder)	44–45	7.0	C	Sun	6:00
Singin' Sam	33–34	6.2	C	Mon	10:30
$64 Question akaTake It or Leave It (Jack Paar)	51–52	4.9	N	Sun	10:00
Skippy Hollywood Theater	50–51	6.1	C	Thu	10:30
Soconyland Sketches	34–35	14.1	C	Sat	7:00
Songs for Sale (Steve Allen)	50–51	5.6	C	Fri	8:30
Songs for Sale (Steve Allen)	51–52	4.0	C	Sat	10:00
Songs My Mother Used to Sing	33–34	2.1	C	Sun	6:00
Speak Up America	40–41	3.3	B	Sun	7:30
Spin & Win	40–41	2.9	B	Wed	9:30
Spotlight	40–41	3.8	C	Thu	8:00
Stairway to Stars (Paul Whiteman)	45–46	4.3	A	Sun	6:00
Star Spangled Theater	40–41	1.8	B	Sun	8:00
Starlight Concert	49–50	5.2	N	Tue	8:30
Starlight Concert	50–51	5.9	N	Tue	8:30
Stebbins Boys	32–33	8.5	B	Tu–Fr	7:30
Steel Horizons	45–46	1.7	M	Sun	9:00
Steve Allen Show	49–50	6.6	C	Sun	6:30

Programs Rated Less Than 13 Weeks	Season	Rating	Net	Day	Time
Stop the Music (Bert Parks)	47–48	12.6	A	Sun	8:00
Story Teller (Marvin Miller)	45–46	2.0	A	M-F	9:55
Street Singer (Arthur Tracy)	32–33	7.3	C	MWF	8:15
Sunbrite Junior Nurse Corps	35–36	1.6	C	MWF	6:15
Sunday at Seth Parker's (Phillips H Lord)	33–34	18.5	N	Sun	10:45
Sunday Night Party	36–37	3.6	B	Sun	10:00
Swingo/Musical Game	39–40	6.5	C	Sun	8:30
Symphony of the Americas	44–45	1.9	M	Sat	8:30
Take It or Leave It (Bob Hawk)	39–40	7.8	C	Sun	10:00
Tales of Fatima (Basil Rathbone)	49–50	7.3	C	Sat	9:30
Tastyeast Theater	34–35	2.0	B	Sun	9:45
Telephone Hour	39–40	5.3	N	Mon	8:00
This Is Your FBI (Frank Lovejoy)	44–45	5.4	B	Fri	8:30
Thompkins Corners (George Frame Brown)	32–33	8.5	B	Thu	9:30
Three X Sisters	32–33	2.8	B	MWF	6:30
Tic Toc Revue	36–37	1.3	B	Mon	7:00
Time to Shine	39–40	6.3	C	Tue	10:00
To Arms for Peace	35–36	3.8	C	Thu	9:30
Tommy Dorsey Orch	39–40	10.2	N	Wed	8:30
Tommy Dorsey Orch	46–47	10.1	N	Sun	8:30
Tommy Riggs & Betty Lou	45–46	6.6	C	Fri	7:30
Tommy Riggs & Betty Lou	46–47	4.6	C	Fri	7:30
Tony & Gus (Mario Chamlee & George Frame Brown)	34–35	8.6	B	M-F	7:15
Tony & Gus (Mario Chamlee & George Frame Brown)	35–36	7.7	B	MWF	7:15
Tony Martin Sings	46–47	6.6	C	Sat	7:30
Top Guy (J Scott Smart)	52–53	4.6	A	Fri	8:00
Townsend Murder Mystery	32–33	4.8	B	T,T,Sa	7:15
Treasure Island	33–34	2.2	B	MWF	7:15
Truth or Consequences (Ralph Edwards)	51–52	4.0	C	Tue	9:30
Twenty Grand Club	41–42	3.2	M	Mon	9:15
Uncle Walter's Doghouse (Tom Wallace)	40–41	7.0	N	Fri	9:30
Unsung Champions	36–37	2.6	B	TWT	7:15
Vacation with Music	46–47	5.4	N	Fri	9:00
Vic & Sade (Art Van Harvey & Bernadine Flynn)	46–47	2.1	M	Thu	8:30
Vicks Open House (Warren Hull)	34–35	16.9	B	Tue	9:00
Victor Borge Show	45–46	11.7	N	Tue	9:30
Vince Program	33–34	11.4	B	Wed	9:30
Voice of Experience (Marion Sayle Taylor)	32–33	2.2	C	Wed	7:00
Voice of the People	35–36	11.2	B	Sun	7:30
Walk a Mile (John Henry Faulk)	51–52	5.0	C	Mon	10:00
Walter Damrosch Music Appreciation Hour	33–34	9.2	B	Fri	11:00
Warden Lawes at Sing Sing	32–33	6.9	B	Sun	9:00
Wayne King Orch	38–39	9.0	N	Fri	10:00
Wayne King Orch	38–39	10.7	C	Mon	10:00
Wayne King Orch	45–46	6.6	N	Sun	7:00
Wayne King Orch	46–47	5.5	C	Fri	9:30
We Who Dream	44–45	2.9	C	Fri	7:15
Wednesday with You	45–46	8.1	N	Wed	9:00
What's My Line? (John Daly)	51–52	5.2	N	Tue	10:00
The Whistler (Everett Clarke)	46–47	6.6	C	Wed	10:00
The Whistler (Bill Johnstone)	48–49	6.3	C	Wed	10:00
Whitman Sampler Program	32–33	4.4	N	Tu,W, Th	7:30
Will Rogers Gulf Headliners Show	32–33	34.1	B	Sun	9:00
William Hard GOP Political	36–37	3.5	C	M-F	7:00
Win Your Lady	38–39	9.3	B	Sun	9:00
Woman of the Year	51–52	2.2	M	Mon	8:00
World News Tonight	40–41	5.2	C	Sun	7:30
Your All Time Hit Parade (Jerry Wayne & Bea Wain)	44–45	7.5	N	Sun	7:00
Your Hit Parade on Parade	48–49	5.3	C	Sun	7:00
Your Hit Parade on Parade	49–50	4.0	C	Sun	7:00
"Yours Truly, Johnny Dollar"	49–50	6.5	C	Thu	10:00
Zoel Parenteau Orch	33–34	1.2	C	Fri	6:45

Bibliography

Allen, Fred. *Treadmill to Oblivion*. Boston: Atlantic Monthly Press, 1954.

Ansbro, George. *I Have a Lady in the Balcony*. Jefferson, NC: McFarland, 2006.

Archer, Gleason. *Big Business & Radio*. Washington, DC: American Historical Society, 1939.

_____. *The History of Radio to 1926*. Washington, DC: American Historical Society, 1938.

Auerbach, Arnold. *Funny Men Don't Laugh*. Garden City, NY: Doubleday, 1965

Balk, Alfred. *The Rise of Radio from Marconi Through the Golden Age*. Jefferson, NC: McFarland, 2006.

Bannister, Harry. *The Education of a Broadcaster*. New York: Simon & Schuster, 1965.

Barnouw, Erik. *A Tower in Babel — A History of Broadcasting in the United States to 1933*. New York: Oxford, 1966.

_____. *The Golden Web — A History of Broadcasting in the United States, 1933–1953*. New York: Oxford, 1968.

_____. *The Sponsor — Notes on a Modern Potentate*. New Brunswick, NJ: Transaction, 2004.

Benny, Jack, and Joan Benny. *Sunday Nights at Seven*. New York: Warner Books, 1990.

Benny, Mary Livingstone, and Hillard Marks. *Jack Benny*. Garden City, NY: Doubleday, 1978.

Bergen, Candice. *Knock Wood*. New York: Linden Press/ Simon & Schuster, 1984.

Bergreen, Laurence. *Look Now, Pay Later — The Rise of Network Broadcasting*. Garden City, NY: Doubleday, 1980.

Bilby, Kenneth. *The General. David Sarnoff & The Rise of the Communications Industry*. New York: Harper & Row, 1986.

Blanc, Mel, and Philip Bashe. *That's Not All Folks!* New York: Warner Books, 1988.

Broadcasting Publications. *Broadcasting Magazine — The 50th Anniversary Issue*. Washington, DC: 1981.

Burns, George. *Gracie — A Love Story*. New York: Putnam, 1988.

Campbell, Robert. *The Golden Years of Broadcasting — Celebrating the First 50 Years of NBC Radio and TV.* New York: Charles Scribner's Sons, 1976.

Cantor, Eddie. *As I Remember Them*. New York: Duell, Sloan & Pearce, 1963.

Columbia Broadcasting System. *The Sound of Your Life — A Record of Radio's First Generation*. New York: CBS, 1950.

Carroll, Carroll. *None of Your Business — Or My Life with J. Walter Thompson*. New York: Cowles, 1970.

Cox, Jim. *Frank & Anne Hummert's Radio Factory*. Jefferson, NC: McFarland, 2003.

_____. *The Great Radio Audience Participation Shows*. Jefferson, NC: McFarland, 2001.

DeLong, Thomas. *The Mighty Music Box — Golden Age of Musical Radio*. Los Angeles: Amber Crest, 1980

Douglas, Susan. *Inventing American Broadcasting*. Baltimore: Johns Hopkins University Press, 1987.

Dunning, John. *On the Air — The Encyclopedia of Old Time Radio*. New York: Oxford, 1998.

Fang, Irving. *Those Radio Commentators!* Ames: Iowa State University Press, 1977.

Firestone, Ross. *The Big Radio Comedy Program*. Chicago: Contemporary, 1978.

Fowler, Gene, and Bill Crawford. *Border Radio*. Austin: Texas Press, 2002.

Gabler, Neal. *An Empire of Their Own*. New York: Crown, 1988.

_____. *Winchell — Gossip, Power & The Culture of Celebrity*. New York: Alfred Knopf, 1994.

Garner, Joe. *We Interrupt This Broadcast*. Naperville, IL: Sourcebooks, 1998.

Gaver, Jack, and Dave Stanley. *There's Laughter in the Air*. New York: Greenberg, 1945.

Giddens, Gary. *A Pocketful of Dreams — Bing Crosby — The Early Years*. New York: Little, Brown, 2001.

Goldin, J. David. *The Golden Age of Radio*. Sandy Hook, CT: Radio Yesteryear, 1998.

Goldman, Herbert. *Banjo Eyes — Eddie Cantor — The Birth of Modern Stardom*. New York: Oxford, 1997.

Green, Abel, and Joe Laurie. *Show Biz from Vaude to Video*. New York: Henry Holt, 1951.

Gross, Ben. *I Looked and I Listened*. New York: Random House, 1954.

Harmon, Jim. *The Great Radio Comedians*. Garden City, NY: Doubleday, 1970.

_____. *The Great Radio Heroes*. Garden City, NY: Doubleday, 1967.

Havig, Alan. *Fred Allen's Radio Comedy*. Philadelphia: Temple University Press, 1990.

Higby, Mary Jane. *Tune in Tomorrow*. New York: Cowles, 1968.

Hilliard, Robert, and Michael Keith. *The Broadcast Century*. Burlington MA: Focal Press, 1997.

Hilmes, Michele. *Radio Voices — American Broadcasting, 1922–1952*. Minneapolis: University of Minnesota Press, 1997.

Hope, Bob, and Mel Shavelson. *Don't Shoot, it's Only Me*. New York: Putnam, 1990.

Jaker, Bill, Kanze, Peter, and Frank Sulek. *The Airwaves of New York*. Jefferson NC: McFarland, 1996.

Julian, Joseph. *This Was Radio*. New York: Viking Press, 1975.

Lackmann, Ron. *The Encyclopedia of American Radio*. New York: Checkmark Books, 2000.

Lazarfeld, Paul, and Harry Field. *The People Look at Radio*. Chapel Hill: University of North Carolina Press, 1946.

Lewis, Tom. *Empire of the Air*. New York: Harper Collins, 1991.

Linkletter, Art. *People Are Funny*. Garden City NY: Doubleday, 1947.

_____ and George Bishop. *I Didn't Do It Alone*. Ottawa IL: Caroline House, 1980.

MacDonald, J. Fred. *Don't Touch That Dial!* Chicago: Nelson-Hall, 1979.

Maltin, Leonard. *The Great American Broadcast.* New York: Penguin, 1997.

Marx, Arthur. *Red Skelton—An Unauthorized Biography.* New York: Dutton, 1979.

_____. *The Secret Life of Bob Hope.* New York: Barricade Books, 1993.

McCarthy, Albert. *The Dance Band Era, 1910–1950.* Radnor, PA: Chilton, 1971.

McMahon, Mogan. *A Flick of the Switch, 1930–1950.* Tempe AZ: Antique Electronic Supply, 1975.

Metz, Robert. *CBS—Reflections in a Bloodshot Eye.* Chicago: Playboy Press, 1975.

Mordden, Ethan. *The Hollywood Studios.* New York: Alfred Knopf, 1988.

Nye, Frank. *"Hoop" of Hooperatings: The Man & His Work.* Norwalk, CT: Self-published, 1958.

Osgood, Dick. *Wyxie Wonderland—An Unauthorized 50 Year Diary of WXYZ Detroit.* Bowling Green, KY: Bowling Green University Press, 1981.

Paley, William S. *As It Happened—A Memoir.* Garden City NY: Doubleday, 1979.

The Pulse, Inc. *The 100% Yardstick—New York Radio Station Audiences—Vol I, No 1.* 1941.

Quirk, Lawrence. *Bob Hope—The Road Well-Traveled.* Milwaukee, WI: Applause Books, 1998.

Radio Corporation of America. *The Radio Decade.* New York: RCA, 1930.

Reck, Franklin. *Radio from Start to Finish.* New York: Thomas Crowell, 1942.

Rhoads, B. Eric. *Blast from the Past—A Pictorial History of Radio's First 75 Years.* New York: Streamline, 1996.

Rhymer, Paul. *The Small House Halfway Up in the Next Block.* New York: McGraw-Hill, 1972.

Ritchie, Michael. *Please Stand By—A Prehistory of Television.* Woodstock NY: Overlook Press, 1995.

Schecter, Abel Alan, and Edward Anthony. *I Live On Air.* New York: Frederick Stokes, 1941.

Schatz, Thomas. *The Genius of the System.* New York: Pantheon, 1988.

Settel, Irving. *A Pictorial History of Radio.* New York: Citadel Press, 1960.

Slate, Sam, and Joe Cook. *It Sounds Impossible.* New York: Macmillan. 1963.

Slater, Robert. *This ... Is CBS—A Chronicle of 60 Years.* Englewood Cliffs, NJ: Prentice-Hall, 1988.

Slide, Anthony. *Great Radio Personalities in Historic Photographs.* Vestal, NY: Vestal Press, 1982.

Smulyan, Susan. *Selling Radio—The Commercialization of American Broadcasting, 1920–1934.* Washington, DC: Smithsonian Institution Press, 1994.

Stedman, William. *The Serials—Suspense & Drama By Installment.* Norman: University of Oklahoma Press, 1971.

Sperling, Cass Warner, and Cork Millner. *Hollywood Be Thy Name.* Rocklin, CA: Prima, 1994.

Sponsor Magazine. *Sponsor—The 40 Year Album of Pioneer Radio Stations.* New York: Sponsor Publications, 1962.

Sterling, Christopher, and John Kittross. *Stay Tuned—A Concise History of American Broadcasting.* Belmont, CA: Wadsworth, 1990.

Stewart, Travis. *No Applause, Just Throw Money.* London: Faber & Faber, 2005.

Stuart, Lyle. *The Secret Life of Walter Winchell.* Fort Lee, NJ: Barricade Books, 2003.

Stumpf, Charles, and Tom Price. *Heavenly Days! The Story of Fibber McGee & Molly.* Waynesville, NC: World of Yesterday, 1987.

Summers, Harrison. *A 30 Year History of National Network Radio Programs in the United States, 1926–1956.* Salem, NH: Ayer, 1986.

Swartz, Jon, and Robert Reinehr. *The Handbook of Old Time Radio.* Lanham, MD: Scarecrow Press, 1993.

Taylor, Robert. *Fred Allen—His Life & Wit.* New York: Little Brown, 1989.

Terrance, Vincent. *Radio's Golden Years.* San Diego, CA: A.S. Barnes, 1981.

Thomas, Lowell. *Good Evening, Everybody.* New York: William Morrow, 1976.

Tumbusch, Tom. The *Illustrated Radio Premium Catalog & Price Guide.* Dayton, OH: Tomart, 1983.

Vallee, Eleanor, and Jill Amadio. *My Vagabond Lover.* Dallas: Taylor , 1996.

Vallee, Rudy. *Let the Chips Fall...* Harrisburg, PA: Stackpole Books, 1975.

Wertheim, Arthur. *Radio Comedy.* New York, Oxford University Press, 1979.

Woodfin, Jane. *Of Mikes and Men.* New York: McGraw Hill, 1951.

Young, Morris, and John Stoltzfus. *Radio Music Live, 1920–1950.* Highland City, FL: Rainbow Books, 1999.

Index